Literature and Ourselves

A Thematic Introduction for Readers and Writers

FIFTH EDITION

Gloria Mason Henderson
Gordon College

Bill Day
Gordon College
Professor Emeritus

Sandra Stevenson Waller
Georgia Perimeter College
Associate Professor Emerita of Humanities

PEARSON
Longman

New York Boston San Francisco
London Toronto Sydney Tokyo Singapore Madrid
Mexico City Munich Paris Cape Town Hong Kong Montreal

Managing Editor: Erika Berg
Development Editor: Anne Brunell
Executive Marketing Manager: Ann Stypuloski
Senior Supplements Editor: Donna Campion
Production Manager: Ellen MacElree
Project Coordination, Text Design, and Electronic Page Makeup: Electronic Publishing Services Inc., NYC
Cover Designer/Manager: Nancy Danahy
Cover Image: © Getty Images, Inc./National Geographic Society
Photo Researcher: Vivette Porges
Manufacturing Manager: Mary Fisher
Printer and Binder: Courier Corporation
Cover Printer: Coral Graphic Services

For permission to use copyrighted material, grateful acknowledgment is made to the copyright holders on pp. 1461–1472, which are hereby made part of this copyright page.

Library of Congress Cataloging-in-Publication Data
Literature and ourselves : a thematic introduction for readers and writers / Gloria Mason Henderson, Bill Day, Sandra Stevenson Waller.— 5th ed.
    p. cm.
  Includes bibliographical references and index.
  ISBN 0-321-27713-9 (paperbound)
    1. Literature—Collections. I. Henderson, Gloria Mason, II. Day, William, III. Waller, Sandra Stevenson.
PN6014.L5562 2006
808.8—dc22

        2005003670

Please visit our website at http://www.ablongman.com

ISBN 0-321-27713-9

1 2 3 4 5 6 7 8 9 10—CRW—08 07 06 05

Contents

THEMATIC ANTHOLOGY

FAMILY   60

MEN AND WOMEN   262

Writing about Men and Women   264

Essays

Fiction

FEAR AND LOSS   548

Writing about Fear and Loss   550

Essays

Fiction

Poetry

Drama

Casebook on Amy Tan

FREEDOM AND RESPONSIBILITY   868

Essays

Fiction

Poetry

Drama

Casebook on Tim O'Brien
Writing about War 993

IMAGINATION AND REALITY   1054

Writing about Imagination and Reality   1056

QUEST   1210

Drama

Casebook on Flannery O'Connor

Alternate Contents
by Genre

Essays

Fiction

Poetry

Drama

Preface

*L*iterature and Ourselves: A Thematic Introduction for Readers and *Writers* was written to speak to students' experiences, hopes, and ideas through a variety of selections representing a panorama of authors and nationalities. Suitable for both freshman composition courses and introduction to literature courses, the new edition continues its dual emphasis on excellence and diversity.

Literature and Ourselves treats literature as a continually expanding commentary on people's infinitely varied lives, helping students make the connection between literature and their own unique life stories. The six themes—Family, Men and Women, Fear and Loss, Freedom and Responsibility, Imagination and Reality, and Quest—progress outward from the self. They also move from the concrete to the abstract, becoming progressively more challenging. These thematic sections are designed to form a coherent whole, as each selection constitutes a rich and varied commentary on its respective theme, further assisting students in building confidence in their study of literature. Each section begins with a brief introduction and a discussion on writing about a particular theme. Within thematic units selections are ordered by genre, and within genres selections are ordered chronologically. The "Alternate Contents by Genre" arranges the works according to genre for instructors who wish to cross-reference works that fit into more than one of the thematic units or to concentrate on one genre.

We have packed an extraordinary variety of works into a relatively small anthology. The traditional works allow instructors to assign what they are familiar with, and new works allow them to share with their students the joy of discovery. The selections also represent a variety of cultures, with works by authors from around the world. Questions for Discussion and Suggestions for Exploring, Writing, and Persuading follow virtually every work and are designed to promote critical thinking—not only about literature, but also about students' own experiences. Our approach, then, is inductive, encouraging students to learn and develop their own ideas as they read.

Unlike many literature anthologies that emphasize text over author and reader, *Literature and Ourselves* includes many author-oriented and reader-oriented questions as well as text-oriented ones. Students are encouraged to see the works as commentaries on their own lives and to bring their own experience to bear on what they read and write. They also are encouraged to analyze and evaluate their own experience based on what they read. As a result, students will develop a lifelong appreciation of literature and come to view it as intimately connected to their lives.

The Organization

The Introduction discusses text-, author-, and reader-oriented approaches to literature; explores the basic elements of the four genres; and provides expanded guidance on writing about literature and the research paper. It also includes a new section on writing literary arguments.

The expanded anthology, organized thematically, gives students a rich array of literature drawn from the finest writers of fiction, poetry, drama, and the essay. The themes have been chosen to engage students in exploring their own lives through literature. Each thematic unit includes literature from all four genres and balances classic with contemporary selections. Casebooks on individual authors provide a context for writing short research papers about literature and build toward full-length research papers for instructors who cover the research paper in their course. Additional writing suggestions for each section further emphasize the relationship between works of literature and film interpretations of those works of literature.

Appendix A, "Critical Approaches to Literature," briefly discusses some of the major approaches to literature. Appendix B, "Writing about Film: *The Matrix* and *The Lord of the Rings* as Case Studies," guides students in the techniques and terminology needed to enjoy, interpret, and write effective, perceptive essays about film and about the relationship of film to literary sources. Appendix C, "Documenting a Research Paper: MLA Style Sheet," includes MLA documentation guidelines. Finally, a glossary defines literary terms mentioned in the introductions and the questions.

New To This Edition

- **New Emphasis on Argument.** The most significant change is the focus on argument throughout the book. Critical thinking and writing are two of the most important skills students ought to possess because arguing persuasively allows students to see the complexity of the issues they write about. To this end, we have added an introductory section on argument, complete with a sample student essay. In addition, we have integrated argument-focused questions and suggestions for writing into the end-of-selection and end-of-unit apparati.

- **New Selections—Both Classic and Contemporary.** One major addition from the traditional canon is Sophocles's *Oedipus Rex*. Other changes in drama include the addition of Susan Glaspell's thought-provoking play *Trifles* and Tom Stoppard's *The Real Inspector Hound*. In addition to William Golding's "Thinking as a Hobby," we have also added delightful essays by such writers as Lorian Hemingway, David James Duncan, and Janisse Ray as well as three hilarious essays—John Gierach's "The Fishing Car," Garrison Keillor's "Attitude," and Ian Frazier's *Coyote v. Acme*—and a timely essay on terrorism by H. H. A. Cooper. New stories include a variety of contemporary voices such as Sherman Alexie's "Because My Father Always Said He Was the Only Indian Who Saw Jimi Hendrix Play the

Star Spangled Banner at Woodstock," Bharati Mukherjee's "The Management of Grief," Jhumpa Lahiri's "A Temporary Matter," and Isabel Allende's "And of Clay Are We Created."

- **New Casebook.** The end of each thematic unit features a casebook that encompasses original works by a noted author and critical analyses of these works. Each casebook gives students an opportunity to write documented literary-analysis essays before they progress to longer papers using library and Internet research. In this edition, we have added a new casebook on Sylvia Plath, including seven of her most famous poems and six critical essays.

- **Re-Titling of Thematic Units.** We have renamed the Grief and Loss unit Fear and Loss and have changed the focus and questions accordingly. We have also renamed the Imagination and Discovery unit Imagination and Reality, again with some slight changes in content and questions. These title changes give a more precise focus to the units and better define the selections included within them.

- **Increased Focus on Film.** A growing number of students are visually oriented and a growing number of instructors use film in their classrooms. Therefore, we have expanded our coverage of film, focusing on film adaptations of works of literature. Students learn to write essays that make connections between films they have seen and the literature they have read. In addition to our new part openers, featuring photo stills from films adapted from the selections in our text, we have added more questions about film following many of the works that have been either made into films or have influenced them. A section at the end of each theme, Writing about Film, asks students to apply the knowledge gained from studying literature to the study of films that feature the same theme. Appendix B, Writing about Film, provides a student-friendly guide to the terminology and interpretation of film using specific examples from two films that are part of recent trilogies: *The Matrix* and *The Fellowship of the Ring*. This appendix is followed by a student essay on *Under the Tuscan Sun*, the film based on the book by Frances Mayes from which the essay "*Bramare:* (Archaic) To Yearn For" in the Family unit is taken. These film-related features are designed to help instructors share their love of film and literature with their students and enable students to write stronger essays on both of these genres.

Resources for Students and Instructors

- **Instructor's Manual (0-321-27741-4).** An Instructor's Manual with detailed comments and suggestions for teaching each selection is available. Written by the authors, this important resource also contains references to critical articles and books that we have found helpful.

- **MyLiteratureLab (0-321-36777-4).** This online resource features the Longman Lectures. Richly illustrated and narrated by award-winning teachers and performance poets, these audiovisual lectures demonstrate various ways to read, interpret, and write about works of literature. Other features of this lab include diagnostic tests, a glossary of literary and critical terms, interactive readings, writing and research resources, and a tutor center. Access to this password-protected Web site is available for free with this text, or may be purchased separately. Please visit www.myliteraturelab.com.

- **MLA Documentation Style: A Concise Guide for Students (0-321-10337-8).** Replete with examples and clear explanations, this straightforward and accessible manual helps students understand and properly use the basic principles of MLA documentation. This brief guide includes information students need to properly cite works, avoid plagiarism, and format their papers. Available FREE when value-packed with *Literature and Ourselves.*

- **Responding to Literature: A Writer's Journal (0-321-09542-1).** This free journal provides students with their own personal space for writing. Helpful writing prompts for responding to fiction, poetry, and drama are also included. Available FREE when value-packed with *Literature and Ourselves.*

- **Evaluating a Performance (0-321-09541-3).** Perfect for the student assigned to review a local production, this free supplement offers students a convenient place to record their evaluation. Useful tips and suggestions of things to consider when evaluating a production are included. Available FREE when value-packed with *Literature and Ourselves.*

- **Merriam-Webster Collegiate Dictionary (0-87779-709-9).** This hardcover comprehensive dictionary is available at a significant discount when packaged with *Literature and Ourselves.*

- **Penguin Discount Novel Program.** In cooperation with Penguin Putnam, Inc., one of our sibling companies, Longman is proud to offer a variety of Penguin paperbacks at a significant discount when packaged with *Literature and Ourselves.* Excellent additions to any literature course, Penguin titles give students the opportunity to explore contemporary and classical fiction and drama. The available titles include works by authors as diverse as Toni Morrison, Julia Alvarez, Mary Shelley, and Shakespeare. To review the complete list of titles available, visit the Longman-Penguin-Putnam website: **http://www.ablongman.com/penguin**.

- **Video Program.** For qualified adopters, an impressive selection of videotapes is available to enrich students' experience of literature. Contact your Longman sales representative for details.

Acknowledgments

We are deeply indebted to many people for their assistance in the fifth edition of *Literature and Ourselves.* Our acquisitions editor, Erika Berg, has been invaluable. She has inspired us by sharing her enthusiasm for the book, by encouraging us to make the contents and questions even better, and by finding wonderful people for us to work with. Chief among these people is our development editor, Anne Brunell Ehrenworth, who has gone above and beyond in sharing her innovative ideas, in finding perceptive reviewers, in keeping us informed at each stage of our work, and in finding ways to save us time.

We are also deeply indebted to many colleagues at Gordon College and Georgia Perimeter College. We want to thank Dr. Richard Baskin, Chair of the Division of Humanities at Gordon College; Dr. Robert Vaughan, Vice President of Academics at Gordon; and Dr. Laurence V. Weill, President of Gordon College, for their encouragement and support. We are also deeply appreciative of our colleagues on the English faculty at Gordon College, who suggested works that added both diversity and excellence to the new edition. For example, Ed Whitelock suggested the new poem by W. S. Merwin and contributed an original poem. We are especially indebted to Drs. Caroline and Floyd Collins for their extensive and loving work on the new Sylvia Plath Casebook. The librarians at Gordon College, under the leadership of head librarian Nancy Anderson, were extremely helpful in ordering and locating materials for the text. Beth Pye, reference librarian at Gordon, has helped both with valuable suggestions and with locating information when we had become frustrated in our searches. Brett Cox, English professor at Norwich University, shared his love of science fiction and suggested the hilarious essay, "Coyote v. Acme." We also wish again to thank Dr. Michael Montgomery of Life College in Atlanta for suggesting works that we have added in each edition. A special thanks to Patrick McCord for revising the appendix on Writing about Film, making it more student-friendly and adding the section on *The Fellowship of the Ring*. We would also like to thank Ellen Barker, Tim Tarkington, Martha Bowles, and Mark Nunes from Georgia Perimeter College for their encouragement and support.

Finally, we would like to thank the instructors who reviewed our manuscript at various phases of the writing process and who provided invaluable feedback to us. We are certainly grateful for their assistance: Michael Anzelone, Nassau Community College; Jonathan Lee Campbell, Valdosta State University; F. Brett Cox, Norwich University; Thomas Deans, Haverford College; Lisa Dennis, Valencia Community College; Debra Deroian, Bristol Community College; Robert Dial, University of Akron; James Ford, University of Nebraska-Lincoln; Bryon Lee Grigsby, Centenary College; David Johnson, Volunteer State Community College; Jane M. Kinney, Valdosta State University; Rita Kumar, University of Cincinnati; Jennifer Lane, Glendale Community College; Shelby Lee, Broward Community College; Reginald Lockett, San Jose City College; Jody Malcolm, University of West Florida; Christopher McDermott, University of Georgia; Robin Mosher, Kansas State University; Pamela Stinson, Northern Oklahoma College.

Gloria Mason Henderson
Bill Day
Sandra Stevenson Waller

Introduction

Literature

Literature is an art form whose medium is language, oral and written. It differs from ordinary spoken or written language primarily in three ways: (1) it is concentrated and meaningful (even when it sometimes denies meaning); (2) its purpose is not simply to explain, argue, or make a point but rather to give a sense of pleasure in the discovery of a new experience; (3) it demands intense concentration from readers. Literature, as defined and included in this text, falls into four large classes or **genres:** essays, fiction, poetry, and drama.

Literature is not only about ideas but also about experiences. It communicates what it feels like to undergo an experience, whether physical or emotional. A psychiatrist, in writing a case study of a patient, concentrates strictly on the facts. Though the doctor may give readers an understanding of the patient, he or she does not attempt to make readers feel what it is like to be that patient. In fact, the psychiatrist must strive to remain strictly objective, as should the readers. Writers of essays, fiction, drama, and poetry, however, may try to put their readers inside the mind of such a character, making readers intimately share the patient's experience and feel what it is like to be the patient. In interpreting literature, readers may adopt one or more of three basic approaches: text-oriented approaches, author-oriented approaches, and reader-oriented approaches.

Text-Oriented Approaches

Adopting a text-oriented approach, a reader may analyze a work of literature as complete in itself without relating it to the outside world. This approach, which was fashionable from about 1920 to 1950, dominates many literature anthologies. It finds expression in the line "a poem should not mean but be" from Archibald MacLeish's poem "Ars Poetica." In its extreme form, this approach insists that the author's life and time as well as readers' responses to his or her work are not only unnecessary, but irrelevant. The kind of close analysis and attention to words and their contexts that this method requires can be very useful, both in illuminating a literary work and in teaching students to read carefully and critically. Consequently, this book emphasizes a text-oriented approach in the introductions to the four genres and in many of the questions for discussion and suggestions for exploration and writing that follow anthologized works.

Writing suggestions in *Literature and Ourselves* that require analysis of tone, theme, plot, or character are text-oriented. For example, one question about August Wilson's *Fences* asks, "What does Troy's story about wrestling with death reveal about his attitude toward death?" In asking about character, the question requires only an analysis of various passages in the story. A text-oriented question about Wilfred Owen's "Dulce et Decorum Est" requires the reader to contrast the patriotic last line to the first stanza. This question requires only a close examination of the poem itself.

Author-Oriented Approaches

Adopting an author-oriented approach, a reader may study an author's life, time, and culture to better understand the author's work. This approach requires research. A reader might, for example, in studying *Othello*, research the roles of women in Renaissance Venice and Elizabethan England in order to understand Othello's expectations of Desdemona. In addition to historical and biographical research, research on other literature, myths, rituals, and art forms can illuminate a work. Other works by the author being studied, including letters, statements of artistic purpose, and reviews, can also enhance a reader's understanding of a work. Many of the questions and suggestions in the casebooks require an author-oriented approach.

Reader-Oriented Approaches

Each reader brings a unique set of experiences and expectations to literature. In its extreme form, the reader-oriented approach argues that a work of literature is recreated each time it is read; that it is produced by the reading, perceiving, imagining mind of the reader; and that, consequently, any reading of a work is valid. Certainly a range of interpretation, some of it conditioned by the reader's particular expectations, is not only valid, but desirable. Men and women, for example, are likely to react differently to such works as Shakespeare's *Othello*, Tim O'Brien's "How to Tell a True War Story," and August Wilson's *Fences*. Similarly, atheists, Jews, evangelical Christians, and persons of other religious perspectives will react differently to the stories of Flannery O'Connor; the poems of Judith Ortiz Cofer, Gerard Manley Hopkins, and William Butler Yeats; and the plays of August Wilson and Terrence McNally. Quite fashionable today, reader-oriented interpretation is far from new. The writers of the New Testament, for example, read and reinterpreted Old Testament scripture in the light of Jesus' life and ministry.

Some of the questions for discussion and suggestions for exploration and writing in this text require a reader-oriented approach in conjunction with a text-oriented approach. For example, a text-oriented question on Ursula LeGuin's "The Ones Who Walk Away from Omelas," which asks about the details that make Omelas a Utopia, is immediately followed by the reader-oriented question "How does LeGuin involve the reader in making her description of Omelas believable?" The latter question requires readers to examine their own response, then return to the text to analyze the sources of that response.

Because one function of literature is to expose us to other people's experience, we should be open to others' interpretations as well as our own. This is not to say, however, that all interpretations are equal in value or even that all are valid. The most satisfying readings of literature may incorporate all three approaches, and all three apply equally to the four genres of literature included in this anthology.

Essays

The word **essay** as used in this text refers to a short, unified work of non-fiction prose. Included in this anthology are many kinds of essays, such as expository essays, argumentative essays, sermons, epistolary essays, biographical essays, critical essays, personal essays, and even essays excerpted from books. These categories are not mutually exclusive, and a single essay may fit more than one category. The most common are expository essays, argumentative essays, and personal essays. The primary purpose of an **expository essay** is to inform or explain; one example of such an essay is H.H.A. Cooper's "Terrorism: the Problem of Definition Revisited." In an **argumentative essay,** the writer tries to convince an audience to agree with his or her position on an issue; the Declaration of Independence and Martin Luther King Jr.'s "Letter from Birmingham City Jail" are argumentative essays. The vast majority of essays in this anthology are **personal essays,** which, as their name implies, reveal much about their authors. Examples of personal essays include Joan Didion's "On Going Home," Janisse Ray's "Native Genius," and David Osborne's "Beyond the Cult of Fatherhood."

Perhaps because they do not present fictional, imagined worlds but explore facts and ideas, essays are often neglected in literature textbooks. Unlike stories and plays, essays do not ordinarily develop characters or plots. They may contain well-developed portraits of actual human beings and may even tell stories, but these portraits and stories usually develop and are subordinate to an idea.

Theme

The reader of an essay must understand its **theme,** or main idea, and the various subpoints and examples that develop the theme. In expository and argumentative essays, the theme is usually quite clear. There is little question about the main idea of the Declaration of Independence or of King's "Letter from Birmingham City Jail." In personal essays like most of the ones in this anthology, the theme may be more subtly and obliquely stated, hence more difficult to comprehend. Often, a reader can find no **thesis,** no single sentence or group of sentences that fairly summarize the author's theme.

In addition to understanding an essayist's theme, a reader must under-stand how an essay is **unified,** how every part of the essay develops its theme. David Osborne's "Beyond the Cult of Fatherhood" focuses thought on the sheer difficulty of taking care of a very young child; while John Gierach's "The Fishing Car" focuses on the relationship between a boy and his uncle that develops as they take his uncle's old, beaten up car fishing. The comfortable shabbiness of the fishing car becomes a kind of unifying symbol of their friendship. In the Declaration of Independence, Thomas Jefferson lists the colonists' many grievances against the English king. This list has a purpose in Jefferson's argument: to demon-strate that the king has violated the unwritten contract between govern-ments and the people they govern. Thus, a good essay is unified; all its details and ideas develop its theme.

Tone

Tone may be defined as an author's attitude toward his or her subject. In some essays, the tone may be so personal that readers come to feel they know the author intimately. Among the essays on home and family included in this text, Frances Mayes's "*Bramare*" brims with enthusiasm over buying a new home, an eighteenth-century villa in Tuscany, whereas Didion's "On Going Home" is regretful over lost intimacy with her fam-ily. Even in Martin Luther King Jr.'s "Letter from Birmingham City Jail," the carefully measured, calmly reasoning tone becomes an integral part of the argument. In John Gierach's "The Fishing Car," on the other hand, the consistently informal, comic tone helps to define the comfortable, affirming relationship between the narrator and his Uncle Leonard.

In reading or writing about an essay, then, a reader must consider not only the author's main idea but also his or her distinctive tone. Is he or she gently humorous or bitingly satiric, nostalgic or regretful, angry or forgiving, calmly controlled or awestruck? Like theme, tone helps to unify an essay. A reader should see how particular details form a pattern, thereby developing the theme and creating a tone appropriate to it.

Imagery

Essayists frequently use **images,** combinations of words that create pic-tures. In his "My One Conversation with Collin Walcott," David James Duncan uses images of a spring and a bird to describe some of the music played by a jazz band in an outdoor amphitheater on the Oregon Coast. These images not only describe the music but relate it to the landscape.

Diction

A good essayist chooses words very carefully, paying particular attention to their **connotations,** their suggested or implied meanings, as opposed to their **denotations,** or explicit meanings. As the jazz band Oregon plays on a rock outcropping above the Pacific Ocean, David James Duncan describes the thunder from an approaching storm as a "perfectly pitched, perfectly played crescendo." Here the carefully chosen words "pitched" and "crescendo" reinforce Duncan's point that the thunder blends with the band's playing to produce music of extraordinary volume and grandeur.

An essayist's **level of diction,** his or her choice of words that are slangy or formal, unfamiliar or common, should also be appropriate to his or her theme and tone. The elevated diction of the Declaration of Independence and of Martin Luther King Jr.'s "Letter from Birmingham City Jail" reinforces the seriousness of those documents.

Syntax

Finally, **syntax,** the patterns of an author's sentences, may develop his or her theme and tone. An author's sentences may be predominantly short and simple, even abrupt; or they may be predominantly long, ornate, and complex. The long, complex sentences of the Declaration of Independence suggest the logical relationships between ideas in a serious and carefully reasoned document. The long opening sentence is an example:

> When in the course of human events, it becomes necessary for one people to dissolve the political bands which have connected them with another, and to assume among the powers of the earth, the separate and equal station to which the Laws of Nature and Nature's God entitle them, a decent respect to the opinions of mankind requires that they should declare the causes which impel them to the separation.

Here the many subordinate clauses and phrases, including the long opening clause beginning with *when,* precisely define the logical dependence of one idea on another. Every part of the very long sentence is logically related to every other part.

Tone, imagery, diction, and syntax, then, develop the theme of an essay. In the following passage from Martin Luther King Jr.'s "Letter from Birmingham City Jail," all four work together:

> I guess it is easy for those who have never felt the stinging darts of segregation to say "Wait." But when you have seen vicious mobs lynch your mothers and fathers at will and drown your sisters and brothers at whim; when you have seen hate-filled policemen curse, kick, brutalize and even kill your black brothers and sisters with impunity; when you see the vast majority of your twenty million Negro brothers smothering in an airtight cage of poverty in the midst of an affluent society; when you suddenly find your tongue twisted and your speech stammering as you seek to explain to your six-year-old daughter why she can't go to the public amusement park that has just been advertised on television, and see tears welling up in her little eyes when she is told that Funtown is closed to colored children, and see the depressing clouds of inferiority begin to form in her little mental sky . . . ; then you will know why we cannot wait.

Here the brutal images of oppression, the very formal diction, and the long parallel clauses all work together to create a tone of great weight, of intensely dignified seriousness.

REVIEW: READING AND ANALYZING ESSAYS

Theme

1. What is the author's theme? Is it simple enough to summarize in a sentence, or will it require several sentences?
2. How do the author's subpoints and examples develop his or her theme?

Tone

1. How would you describe the essay's tone?
2. How does the essay's tone help develop its theme?

Imagery

1. How does the writer's use of imagery contribute to the theme and tone of the essay?
2. What kinds of images does the essay contain? Are there images of animals? of violence? of religion?
3. How do the various images relate to one another?

Diction

1. What highly connotative words does the writer choose?
2. Is the essay's diction elevated, vulgar, simple, obscure?
3. How does the writer's diction contribute to the theme and tone of the essay?

Syntax

1. Is the writer's syntax complex and elaborate, simple, precise?
2. How does the writer's syntax contribute to the theme and tone of the essay?

Fiction

The short story is a relatively new form, although short fiction has long been a source of enjoyment and instruction in such forms as parables, fables, and anecdotes or jokes. **Fiction** is often thought of as the opposite of fact, but it may be based on facts and certainly can include factual material. A work described as fiction should be a **narrative;** that is, it should tell about a sequence of events. In addition, most works of fiction are unified, all their parts working together to create a coherent whole. Short stories differ from other forms of short fiction in purpose. **Parables** and **fables** teach a lesson or a moral; **anecdotes** generally illustrate a point; and **jokes** entertain through humor. Furthermore, anecdotes and jokes, and even parables and fables, usually lack the complicated plots or the structure of most short stories. The longest form of fiction, the **novel,** is not included in this text precisely because of its prohibitive length, but most novels are made up of the same elements as short stories. The primary difference is length. In fact, readers sometimes disagree about whether a piece of fiction is a long short story, a **novella** or **novelette** (both terms used for short novels), or a novel. Because of the brevity of the short story, the writer should make every word and every scene an integral part of the creation.

Reading short stories with real understanding and appreciation is demanding. This kind of appreciation often requires at least three readings: a first reading of the story to enjoy the plot; a second reading to analyze its individual elements; and a third reading to see how those elements work together to create a cohesive, integrated whole. These elements include point of view, setting, style, character, plot, and theme.

Point of View

Point of view, the focus from which the story is told, is a crucial element; for it determines what we know about the characters and the action. The **omniscient,** all-knowing, point of view allows the author, writing in third person, to tell readers what any or all of the characters think or do.

The **first-person** point of view allows readers to see the action through the eyes of one character and to know only that character's thoughts. That character may be the main character or a minor character. When the author uses first person point of view, readers must decide whether the narrator is reliable or unreliable, whether the reader can trust him or her to tell the truth or even to understand the truth. An unreliable narrator may be too young or too slow-witted to perceive the truth, or he or she may select or alter details in order to present a biased account. For example, by using a biased and unreliable narrator, an author may effectively create irony or humor, as in Tim O'Brien's "The Man I Killed." One very popular first-person point of view in modern literature is that of a child whose innocence and lack of knowledge allow readers to draw their own conclusions or that of an adult remembering his or her childhood experiences and drawing adult conclusions, as in Truman Capote's "A Christmas Memory."

In the **third-person-limited** point of view, the author tells readers the thoughts of only one character and follows that character throughout the action. Carson McCullers uses this point of view when she follows Martin throughout "A Domestic Dilemma," telling only his thoughts and his theories about the causes of Emily's behavior rather than letting readers into her mind. When using third-person-limited point of view, as in first person, authors select the character who can reveal the information they want told in the story but who will not know the information they want withheld from readers. Finally, the author may write from the **objective** point of view, simply describing observable events.

Setting

The **setting** of a story—the time, place, and culture in which the action occurs— may be extremely significant. Time, place, and culture are integral elements in James Baldwin's "Sonny's Blues," for neither the music nor the racial relationships would be the same in another setting. Kurt Vonnegut's "Harrison Bergeron" takes place in the United States in 2081, a setting that is essential because the story depicts the ultimate fulfillment of the constitutional guarantee of equality. Ursula LeGuin's "The Ones Who Walk Away from Omelas" gains universality by taking place in some unknown mythic time and place.

Style

Style—the selection of words (**diction**); sentence structure (**syntax**); figurative devices, such as simile and metaphor; and symbolism—sets the tone and reflects the individuality of each author. Some writers use fairly simple, straightforward sentences, especially if they are using a first-person narrator who is unsophisticated. In "A Christmas Memory," Capote's adult narrator, remembering his childhood friendship and writing in present tense as if he were still a child, uses simple sentences like "Imagine a morning in late November" and "Queenie [the dog] tries to eat an angel." However, he combines childhood delight with adult perception and style when he vividly describes shelling pecans: "A cheery crunch, scraps of miniature thunder sound as the shells collapse and the golden mound of sweet oily ivory meat mounts in the milk-glass bowl." Some writers, like William Faulkner, use styles that are extremely complex and often almost poetic. They employ many of the metaphorical devices and sometimes even the rhythmical effects that readers expect from poetry.

The author's selection of descriptive details or his or her inclusion of a scene in a story may seem casual but seldom is. For example, in "A Good Man Is Hard to Find," Flannery O'Connor's vivid description of the grandmother's apparel as the family leaves home subtly reveals character and foreshadows the end of the story. While the other members of the family dress comfortably, the grandmother wears a "navy blue straw sailor hat with a bunch of white violets on the brim and a navy blue dress with a small white dot in the print," believing that "anyone seeing her dead on the highway would know at once that she was a lady." Similarly, the scene at Red Sammy's Barbecue, which at first glance may seem unimportant, further reveals the grandmother's character as she describes the cheating Red Sammy as a "good man." The scene also prepares readers for her reaction to the Misfit in the conclusion.

Similes, metaphors, and **personification** are elements of style that can make description more vivid and aid in interpretation. In Philip Roth's "The Conversion of the Jews," to Ozzie, who is standing on the roof,

> it looked as though Rabbi Binder was trying to tug the fireman's head out of his body, like a cork from a bottle. He had to giggle at the picture they made: it was a family portrait—rabbi in black skullcap, fireman in red fire hat, and the little yellow hydrant squatting beside like a kid brother, bareheaded.

In O'Connor's "A Good Man Is Hard to Find," the simile describing the forest "like a dark open mouth" foreshadows the death of the family in the woods.

A **symbol** stands for both the thing it names and something else. Some symbols are almost universal: light is often used to symbolize a growth in knowledge, a realization, or enlightenment. Other elements are symbolic only in the particular context of the story and may be interpreted differently by different readers. For example, the tiny hand on Georgiana's cheek in Nathaniel Hawthorne's "The Birthmark" may symbolize her humanity or, as it does to Aylmer, her one imperfection.

All elements of style help the author create the tone of the story, the author's attitude toward the work, or the mood. The ominous and foreboding atmosphere of Charlotte Perkins Gilman's "The Yellow Wallpaper," for example, is emphasized by the unusual alliterative sounds with which the narrator describes her perceptions: "The color is repellent, almost revolting: a smouldering unclean yellow, strangely faded by the slow-turning sunlight. It is a dull yet lurid orange in some places, a sickly sulphur tint in others." The description seems to be hissing at the reader. Similarly, the short, choppy paragraphs reflect the narrator's thought patterns as she approaches insanity.

Character

Character refers to the people authors create to inhabit their stories. Characters should be believable and consistent. Being believable means not that all characters be like people we have known but that they be believable in the context of the story. Consistency requires not that the characters remain exactly the same, but that any changes in character be sufficiently motivated by what happens to them in the story. Authors may reveal characters in a variety of ways: by telling about them directly, by letting their actions and speech reveal their personalities, or by having other characters tell about them.

The major characters are usually **round characters;** that is, their personalities are well developed and believable. These characters frequently change as the story progresses; if they do, they are also described as **dynamic.** Minor characters often are **flat characters:** we see only one aspect of their personalities, presumably because the author does not need to reveal more about them for the purposes of the story. Flat characters are usually **static** characters; that is, they do not change. In Philip K. Dick's "Minority Report," the precogs are flat and static characters; Anderton is both round and dynamic.

Plot

The most apparent element of most short stories is the **plot,** the pattern of the action. A story has a beginning, a middle, and an end. The beginning of the story may not be the beginning of the action, for the story may begin at some high point in the action and use **flashback** or some other technique to fill in the information necessary for an understanding of the situation. If readers are to comprehend the plot of a story, the beginning must include **exposition,** information about the setting and the characters. The middle of the story presents a complication or conflict within the main character, between the character and some force in nature, or between characters. This conflict builds until the story reaches a **climax,** a peak of action or suspense. The end presents the **resolution,** a solution or unraveling of the conflict, sometimes called the **denouement.** In modern stories, the ending seldom resolves all of the problems faced by the characters; however, the ending should include a sense of completion and an increase in the characters' or at least the readers' knowledge. In James Baldwin's "Sonny's Blues," the exposition begins simultaneously with the complication when the narrator reads in a newspaper article that his brother Sonny has been arrested on a drug charge. This shock triggers a flashback: the narrator's memory of the first time Sonny tried heroin. The complication continues with Sonny's release and return to Harlem and with further flashbacks describing their mother's advice and her account of a parallel situation faced by their father and uncle. The death of the narrator's little girl marks a turning point in the narrator's understanding of human suffering. The climax and resolution occur at the nightclub when the narrator sees Sonny in his element and, for the first time, really listens to Sonny's music.

Theme

Perhaps surprisingly, theme may be the most difficult aspect of a short story to identify. The **theme** is the major idea of the story. Readers often disagree about a story's theme. One reader may believe the theme of Carson McCullers's "A Domestic Dilemma" is the ways in which the complexities of love can serve as traps; another reader may say that the theme is that modern mobility may cause insecurity; a third reader might say that the theme is the conflict between love for a spouse and love for one's children.

While we may disagree about themes, a story without a theme usually seems trivial. We expect the author of a short story to use style, plot, and character to offer us insight into human behavior, to leave us feeling as if we have learned something about our world and about ourselves. This new insight may be repugnant or inspirational, sad or delightful; it may make us aware of human bestiality or nobility, of the wonders of friendship, or of the complexities of love. Whatever it says to readers and however they respond, the theme is the heart of the short story, its reason for being.

The following questions provide a general guide to reading and writing about short stories. Specific guidance follows each short story in the anthology.

REVIEW: READING AND WRITING ABOUT SHORT STORIES

Point of View
1. What is the point of view in the story?
2. If it is first person or third person limited, through which character do readers see the story? Is the character a reliable or an unreliable narrator? How does his or her personality affect the perception of other characters and of the action?
3. Could the story be written just as effectively or more effectively from another point of view? If so, how and why? If not, why not?

Setting
1. Where and when does the story take place?
2. How does the author let readers know the time and place?
3. Could the story take place in any other time or place?

Style
1. What kind of sentence structure does the author seem to prefer in this story? Could the sentences be described as simple or complex? Are the language and sentence structure dictated by the point of view? By the subject? If so, how?
2. What kind of imagery does the author use? Does the language seem poetic? Examine any examples of similes, metaphors, or personification to see if they give clues about characters or foreshadow later actions or events.
3. Look for any symbols in the story, both symbols that are universally accepted and symbols that are particular to the story. What do they represent in the story, and how do they enrich its meaning?
4. What is the tone of the story? How is it reflected in the attitudes expressed or the connotations of words?

Character
1. Are the characters in the story believable? Why or why not?
2. How are the characters revealed: through what the author says about them, through what the other characters say about them, and/or through what they say and do?
3. Which characters are round characters?

4. Which characters are flat characters? Does their lack of development affect the success of the story? If so, in what way?
5. Do any of the characters develop or change in the story? Is this change one of the major points of the story?

Plot
1. What is the conflict in the story? When does the reader first realize there is a conflict?
2. List the steps in the development of the conflict. If possible, identify them as exposition, complication, crisis, climax, and resolution.
3. Where does the conflict reach a climax?
4. What is the resolution of the conflict?

Theme
1. What is the theme of the story? If possible, state it in one sentence.
2. How do the elements of the story work together to convey the theme?
3. Does the main character reach an epiphany or make a significant decision?
4. Did the theme provide an insight or understanding that is new to you? Does the theme relate to insights you have had?
5. Could the author have conveyed the same idea just as effectively in an essay? Why or why not?

Poetry

Unlike essays and short stories, poems are written in verse. Their primary units are lines and stanzas rather than sentences and paragraphs. Lyric poems, the main kind included in this anthology, differ from narrative poems, which tell a story, and epic poems, which are very long and heroic narrative poems. Usually short and often songlike in their rhythms, lyric poems lack plots. They focus not on a sequence of related events leading from conflict to climax but on a speaker's response to a single event, object, situation, or person.

Speaker and Situation

In most poems, the **speaker** is a character created by the author. For example, in T. S. Eliot's "The Love Song of J. Alfred Prufrock," Prufrock speaks; and in Robert Browning's "My Last Duchess," the Duke of Ferrara speaks. In Eliot's poem, Prufrock reveals himself to be a very timid man who has "measured out [his] life with coffee spoons" and who cannot generate enough assertiveness even to ask a question. Browning's Ferrara, on the other hand, shows himself to be a callous and egotistical murderer. Neither Prufrock nor Ferrara bears a clear resemblance to his creator.

Occasionally, if they have compelling reasons for doing so, readers may identify the speaker of a poem with the author. Sylvia Plath's "Daddy," for example, is clearly autobiographical. Like the speaker, Plath lost her father when she was quite young and had difficulty coping with his death. Also like her speaker, Plath had tried to kill herself. It is reasonable, then, to identify the speaker of "Daddy" with Plath.

Some poems, too, seem to arise out of a clearly defined **situation** in which the speaker is addressing a particular person for a particular purpose. In "My Last Duchess," for example, the Duke of Ferrara addresses the agent of a count in order to arrange a marriage to the count's daughter. Plath in "Daddy" clearly is addressing her dead father, hoping through the ritual of the poem to exorcise from her memory his oppressive presence. In Andrew Marvell's "To His Coy Mistress," the speaker addresses a woman he loves, trying to get her to realize their mortality and enjoy her youth and beauty while they can. Finally, in Dwight Okita's "In Response to Executive Order 9066," a teenage girl addresses the impersonal U.S. government that has consigned her to an internment camp. In each of these cases, understanding the speaker and the speaker's situation is essential to understanding the poem.

Theme

Though not all poems have a recognizable and paraphrasable **theme,** or major idea, many do. William Shakespeare's Sonnet 116, for example, clearly states that the beloved is "more lovely" than a beautiful day in summer and that the sonnet itself will ensure her immortality. Similarly, Mary TallMountain's "There Is No Word for Goodbye" clearly states the theme in its title, and Dylan Thomas's "Do Not Go Gentle into That Good Night" insistently repeats its theme that we should fight death with every ounce of will and energy we can muster. Other poems seem to have no readily paraphrasable theme, so subtle and complex is their meaning. For example, though we may understand them, it would be difficult to state the theme of T. S. Eliot's "The Love Song of J. Alfred Prufrock" or Sylvia Plath's "Daddy."

Tone

Whatever its apparent subject, the true subject of a lyric is a state of mind or attitude, known by the technical term **tone.** Tone may be defined as a complex of interrelated attitudes, those of the speaker, writer, and reader, toward the poem's situation. A lyric, then, communicates a tone or attitude, the essence of what it feels like to be in a particular situation. In describing the speaker's relationship to God, John Donne's "Holy Sonnet 14" evokes a complex range of emotions, including awe at the holiness of God, fear of but also exultation at His power, and deep contrition. No single word can adequately characterize this complex range of emotions.

The tone of a poem may be quite complex, expressing feeling that cannot even be suggested by such general words as *love, joy,* and *pain.* Anne

Sexton's apparently simple poem "Ringing the Bells," for example, not only communicates the mind-numbing boredom of therapy in a mental institution but simultaneously communicates the speaker's mounting hysteria:

> And this is the way they ring
> the bells in Bedlam
> and this is the bell-lady
> who comes each Tuesday morning
> to give us a music lesson
> and because the attendants make you go
> and because we mind by instinct
> like bees caught in the wrong hive,
> we are the circle of the crazy ladies
> who sit in the lounge of the mental house.

As a poem's situation changes, its tone may change as well. In Wilfred Owen's "Dulce et Decorum Est," the first stanza graphically communicates the pain and exhaustion of World War I soldiers moving from trenches on the front lines to a place of rest behind the lines:

> Men marched asleep. Many had lost their boots
> But limped on, bloodshod. All went lame; all blind.

In the second stanza, as gas bombs drop among the soldiers and one soldier, unable to don his gas mask in time, dies a gruesome death, the tone changes to panic and horror:

> Gas! Gas! Quick boys!—An ecstasy of fumbling,
> Fitting the clumsy helmets just in time;
> But someone still was yelling out and stumbling
> And flound'ring like a man in fire or lime. . .

Though "Dulce et Decorum Est" is charged with overwhelming emotion that the speaker seems unable to control, in many poems the emotion seems much more subdued. The speaker in Mary TallMountain's "There Is No Word for Goodbye," for example, adopts a very controlled, accepting, reassuring tone, reinforced by the lines' relaxed, conversational rhythm:

> We always think you're coming back,
>   But if you don't
> We'll see you someplace else.
>   You understand.
> There is no word for goodbye.

Similarly, the urbane speaker of Andrew Marvell's "To His Coy Mistress" declares his love in a carefully measured, precise, and witty compliment:

> Had we but world enough, and time,
>   This coyness, lady, were no crime.

We would sit down, and think which way
To walk, and pass our long love's day.

Various elements of a poem work together to create its tone. The main elements are diction, syntax, imagery, and sound.

Diction

In creating tone, a poet uses language that communicates emotion. Curses, groans, and common adjectives such as *beautiful, wonderful,* and *marvelous* express emotion, but they do not often communicate so that the listener shares the speaker's feeling. Successful poets use language not merely to express but also to communicate emotion precisely. Their choice of words is called **diction.**

The level of diction in a poem may range from the very polite, complex, and formal to the very simple, slangy, even vulgar or profane. In Anne Sexton's "Ringing the Bells," for example, the very simple, ordinary, flat diction suggests the boredom of the music therapy session in which the speaker is trapped. In Robert Browning's "My Last Duchess," the Duke of Ferrara is speaking to a count's agent about marrying the count's daughter. As the Duke subtly recalls how he had his first duchess murdered, his precise, formal diction reveals his extraordinary self-control and frightening callousness:

That's my last Duchess painted on the wall,
Looking as if she were alive. I call
That piece a wonder, now; Fra Pandolf's hands
Worked busily a day, and there she stands.

A poet may choose to use many verbs to emphasize action, as in the following lines from John Donne's "Holy Sonnet 14":

Batter my heart, three-person'd God; for, you
As yet but knocke, breathe, shine, and seeke to mend.

A poet's diction, his or her choice of words, may create paradox or verbal irony. A **paradox** is an apparent contradiction. For example, in "Batter My Heart," John Donne addresses God with the paradoxes:

Except You enthrall mee, never shall be free,
Nor ever chast, except you ravish mee.

Because *enthrall* literally means to enslave or imprison, *chaste* means sexually pure, and *ravish* means rape, the two statements appear contradictory. For Donne, however, the ultimate freedom is service to God, and being overpowered by God is the ultimate purity. **Verbal irony** is simply saying the opposite of what one means. Owen's title "Dulce et Decorum Est," meaning "It is sweet and proper," is bitterly ironic because the entire poem emphatically demonstrates that dying in war is neither sweet nor proper.

Syntax

A poem's **syntax**—the structure of its phrases, clauses, and sentences—
may also contribute to its tone. For example, though it is one very long sentence throughout most of its length, Sexton's "Ringing the Bells" is
syntactically simple. The long sentence is almost childlike in its compounding of clauses, not complex like most adult writing and speech. Coor-
dinating conjunctions like *and,* used frequently in Sexton's poem, merely
connect phrases and clauses without emphasizing one over the other:

> And this is the way they ring
> the bells in Bedlam
> and this is the bell-lady
> . . . .
> and this is the gray dress next to me
> . . . .
> and this is the small hunched squirrel-girl
> . . . .
> and this is how the bells really sound

Like the poem's very ordinary diction, the dull, repetitious compounding
of clauses contributes to the sense of stifling boredom in the mental institution.

On the other hand, in Browning's "My Last Duchess," the sentences
are long, formal, and complex, with many subordinate clauses. The
speaker uses perfect parallelism, similar forms in phrases and clauses
joined by *and.* This parallelism, followed by a brutally short, blunt, and
unemotional recounting of his command to have his wife murdered, contributes to a reader's sense of the Duke's self-control and monstrous callousness:

> Who'd stoop to blame
> This sort of trifling? Even had you skill
> In speech—(which I have not)—to make your will
> Quite clear to such a one, and say, "Just this
> Or that in you disgusts me; here you miss,
> Or there exceed the mark"—and if she let
> Herself be lessoned so, nor plainly set
> Her wits to yours, forsooth, and made excuse
> —E'en then would be some stooping; and I choose
> Never to stoop. Oh sir, she smiled, no doubt,
> Whene'er I passed her; but who passed without
> Much the same smile? This grew; I gave commands;
> Then all smiles stopped together. . . .

Who among us could speak so well in recalling a murder we had ordered?
The perfect and precise control of the long second sentence and the
short, matter-of-fact, almost smirking last sentence seem to reveal a mind
incapable of guilt.

Imagery

Probably a poet's most powerful tool for creating tone is **imagery.** An image is a word picture; the phrase "neatly trimmed lawn," for example, is an image. In analyzing images in a poem, readers should look for patterns, for the kinds of images that predominate. In stanza 3 of Owen's "Dulce et Decorum Est," images such as the following powerfully convey the horror of war:

> If in some smothering dreams you too could pace
> Behind the wagon that we flung him in,
> And watch the white eyes writhing in his face
> . . . .
> If you could hear, at every jolt, the blood
> Come gargling from the froth-corrupted lungs.

Similes, explicit comparisons between unlike things using such indicators of comparison as *like* and *as*, and **metaphors,** implicit comparisons between unlike things lacking such indicators, create images. In Sexton's "Ringing the Bells," there are several images of animals; the simile "like bees caught in the wrong hive" and the metaphor "the small hunched squirrel-girl" suggest that the institution in which the speaker finds herself reduces its inmates to a subhuman state.

A **symbol** is an image used in such a way that it comes to mean more than it ordinarily would. A symbol, however, must be distinguished from a sign. A sign is a word or image that exactly corresponds to a particular meaning beyond itself. The meaning of a symbol is far less definite. For example, a stop sign signifies a particular command universally agreed upon throughout our culture. On the other hand, a stop sign removed from its normal setting, mangled into a heap of barely recognizable metal, and placed in an art museum may symbolize far more: perhaps the brutality of our culture, perhaps the degree to which machines dominate and even destroy lives, perhaps our sheer wastefulness and carelessness. Similarly, the word *bell* signifies a kind of musical instrument. In Sexton's "Ringing the Bells," however, bells take on far more meaning: they symbolize the dull, mechanical lives of the women in the mental hospital.

Sound

Finally, in poetry, as in music, **sound** is important. Poems create patterns in sound as they do in diction, imagery, and syntax. **Onomatopoeia** is the use of words that imitate the sounds they stand for, such as the word *buzz*. Words need not be onomatopoeic, however, for their sounds to affect a poem. At the most basic level, the sounds of words themselves may have emotional overtones apart from the meanings of those words. Such nonsense syllables as *hey diddle diddle* and *heigh ho* suggest joy, while *ugh* suggests pain or disgust. In the first stanza of Wilfred Owen's "Dulce et Decorum Est," such words as *trudge, sludge,* and *hags* have harsh, unpleasant sounds appropriate to the tone of the stanza. The smooth vowels and soft consonants in Marvell's "To His Coy Mistress" are pleasantly mellifluous:

> Had we but world enough, and time,
> This coyness, lady, were no crime.
> We would sit down, and think which way
> To walk, and pass our long love's day.

The movement or flow of a poem's sound may be fast or slow, smooth or rough, steady or broken and disjointed. For example, in the lines quoted above from the first stanza of "To His Coy Mistress," the movement is very smooth, stately, and unhurried. The frequent commas slow the passage to the pace of pleasant conversation and prevent the lines from becoming monotonous. On the other hand, the first stanza of Owen's "Dulce et Decorum Est" moves slowly and unsteadily, with frequent stops and starts:

> Bent double, like old beggars under sacks,
> Knock-kneed, coughing like hags, we cursed through sludge.

Here the frequent commas and the difficulty of pronouncing hard consonants slow down the line so that it moves in fits and starts, seeming to imitate the movement of the soldiers as they stagger forward, hurting and exhausted.

Meter, an important element in a poem's sound, refers to the regular pattern of accented and unaccented syllables in a poetic line. There are five basic metrical patterns in English: iambic, trochaic, anapestic, dactylic, and spondaic. An **iambic foot,** or metrical unit, consists of an unaccented syllable followed by an accented one. In the following line from Marvell's "To His Coy Mistress," accented syllables have been marked by ´, unaccented ones by ˘, and metrical feet separated by /:

> Nŏr wóuld/Ĭ\ lóve/ăt lów/ĕr ráte.

A **trochaic foot** consists of an accented foot followed by an unaccented foot. An **anapestic foot,** consisting of three syllables, accents the third syllable, and a **dactylic foot,** also containing three syllables, accents the first. A **spondaic foot** consists of two consecutive accented syllables.

Trimeter, tetrameter, pentameter, and hexameter refer to the number of feet in a line. Thus, iambic **trimeter** refers to a poetic line of three iambic feet; trochaic **tetrameter** to a line of four trochaic feet; **pentameter** to a line of five feet; and **hexameter** to a line of six feet.

Iambic is by far the most natural and common metrical pattern in English. In fact, the rhythms of English prose are often iambic. Departures from the natural iambs of English often call attention to themselves. John Donne uses a strong trochaic foot to emphasize the word *batter* in the opening of "Holy Sonnet 14":

> Báttĕr/m̃y heárt,/thřee-pér/sŏñed Gód.

In the following lines from the second stanza of "To His Coy Mistress," the fourth line begins with a strong trochaic foot:

> Bŭt át/m̆y báck/Ĭ ál/wăys heár,
> Tímé's wíng/ĕd chár/Ĭŏt húr/ryĭng néar.
> Ăňd yónd/ĕr áll/bĕfóre/ŭs líe
> Dĕsĕrts/ŏf vást/ĕtér/nĭtý.

The inverted accent emphasizes the word *deserts*. This accent and the metaphor "deserts of vast eternity" increase the poem's urgency.

In spite of such departures from the basic meter, "To His Coy Mistress" is a very regular poem, using one of the most regular, tightly controlled verse forms in English poetry, the **couplet,** a pair of metrically regular, rhymed lines. This regularity of meter suggests that the speaker is very much in control of his emotion. Often, regularity suggests control, as it does in Marvell's poem. In Browning's "My Last Duchess," also written in couplets, the regularity suggests the wife-murdering Duke of Ferrara's inappropriate, even pathological control. Sometimes metrical regularity may be comic, as in nursery rhymes. Lack of regularity, on the other hand, may suggest a speaker's lack of emotional control, as in Sexton's "Ringing the Bells" and Owen's "Dulce et Decorum Est." Poetry is so rich and diverse, however, that it is dangerous to generalize.

Alliteration and **rhyme** repeat certain sounds, thereby emphasizing them and helping to unify the poem. Alliteration, the repetition of consonants at the beginning of words or syllables, may enhance the effect of the repeated sounds. In the following lines from John Donne's "Holy Sonnet 14," the hard, alliterative *b*'s reinforce the violence of the strong verbs:

> That I may rise, and stand, o'erthrow mee, and bend
> Your force, to breake, blowe, burn, and make me new.

When words rhyme, their final accented syllables sound alike, as in *bestow* and *below* or *career* and *fear*. Rhymes usually occur at the end of poetic lines and are designated by letters so that the first sound is designated *a* and each new sound gets the next letter in the alphabet. In the following example from John Donne's "A Valediction: Forbidding Mourning," the rhyme scheme is *abab:*

As virtuous men pass mildly away	*a*
And whisper to their souls to go	*b*
Whilst some of their sad friends do say	*a*
The breath goes now, and some say no	*b*

Common rhyme patterns in English poetry include *abab, abba, abcb,* and couplets, in which successive lines rhyme.

Together, meter and rhyme define the stanza patterns of poems. The most common patterns in English include the quatrain, the couplet, and the sonnet. The **quatrain,** a stanza of four lines using any one of various rhyme schemes and metrical patterns, is the most often used stanza in

English poetry. William Blake's "The Tyger" is written in quatrains. Quatrains are the loosest and most flexible of the three stanza forms defined here. A couplet is simply a pair of metrically regular, rhymed lines. Couplets are tightly controlled and challenging to write because of the difficulty of finding rhymes in English. A **sonnet** is a tightly controlled poem of fourteen lines written in iambic pentameter. The **Italian sonnet** consists of two parts, an eight-line octave rhyming *abbaabba* and a six-line sestet often rhyming *cdecde* or *cdcdcd*. The **English** or **Shakespearean sonnet** consists of three quatrains followed by a couplet. The most common rhyme scheme is *abab cdcd efef gg*. Because of its precise rhyme scheme and meter, the sonnet is a demanding form. William Shakespeare, John Donne, William Wordsworth, Edna St. Vincent Millay, and Gerard Manley Hopkins are among the writers of sonnets included in this text.

REVIEW: READING AND WRITING ABOUT POEMS

Speaker, Situation, and Theme

1. What kind of person is speaking in the poem?
2. Is there reason to equate the speaker with the poet?
3. To whom is the poem addressed?
4. What is the situation of the poem?
5. Does the poem have a paraphrasable theme? If so, what is it?
6. Do tone, diction, syntax, imagery, and sound develop the theme of the poem?

Tone

1. How would you describe the tone of the poem?
2. Does the tone change over the course of the poem?
3. Do diction, syntax, imagery, and sound develop the tone of the poem?

Diction

1. What is the level of the poem's diction? Is it formal, informal, colloquial? Is it simple, difficult, elegant, profane, coarse?
2. Does the poem use paradox or verbal irony?

Syntax

1. How difficult are the sentences? Are they short and simple, or are they long and complex?
2. Are there any departures from standard grammar or syntax such as fragmented elliptical passages (incomplete due to words left out)?
3. Does the syntax change over the course of the poem?

Imagery

1. What patterns does the imagery suggest?
2. What colors predominate?
3. To what senses does the imagery appeal?
4. What similes, metaphors, and symbols does the poet use?

5. Are there contrasting images?
6. Does the imagery change over the course of the poem?

Sound
1. What effects are created by the sounds and location of particular words?
2. Does the poem move quickly or slowly? Does it flow smoothly, or does it contain abrupt shifts, stops, and starts?
3. How regular is the meter of the poem? If the poem uses a regular metrical pattern, what is that pattern? What meter does it use?
4. Does the poem use rhyme or alliteration? If so, what effects are created?
5. Does the sound of the poem change?

Drama

When people first looked at the sunset or the mating games of animals and birds, they saw drama unfolding. Imitating nature became an inevitable step. Whereas nature's dramas are not orchestrated for human entertainment, on a stage actors can orchestrate nature's rituals and embellish scenes for human amusement and diversion. People can change the locales, shift words in the mouths of participants, add or subtract colorful costumes, and tell the story realistically, abstractly, surrealistically, or absurdly. The playwright can also combine creation's dramas with critical or sometimes solemn discussions of issues pertinent to his or her agenda; thus, the playwright blends the uncomplicated with the complicated.

Performance versus Reading: Stage Directions

A play is meant to be performed and to be watched; therefore, the substance of a play can best be conveyed before an audience. Spectators are able to notice the actor's body language, to inspect the set, and to scrutinize the interplay between the people on the stage. The playwright may give elaborate instructions, such as descriptions of the characters, staging, entrances, and exits, to the stage manager, the director, the actors, and all others involved in the production. These instructions are called **stage directions.**

Included in the stage directions are references to the set and props, which, along with the curtain, may be among the first items the audience sees. In some plays, the stage directions may be vague or unspecified, leaving the set, movement, and gestures entirely or partially dependent upon the director. In other plays, the stage directions may allow the actors and actresses to improvise. The opening and closing of a curtain and the dimming of lights in some productions indicate changes in dramatic time, while **props** and **set** help to define the **setting,** the cultural and physical environment as well as the time when the action takes place.

Another element of a play, technically known as blocking, is readily apparent only in performance. **Blocking** includes the gestures and body language of characters as well as their interactions and movements on stage. Again, many times the stage directions may be explicit; at other times they may be implied and, therefore, open to interpretation. Blocking enhances performance. Even Shakespeare's great play *Othello* would be dull if the actors simply stood on stage and mechanically recited their lines. Iago's facial expressions and movement can reveal much about him, and an actor portraying Iago has much room for interpretation. In his soliloquy in act I, scene 3, ll. 366–377, beginning "Thus do I ever make my fool my purse," one actor may portray Iago with a snarling smile; another may assume a dark and deadly serious facial expression.

Unfortunately, not everyone can see a particular play. The written words of the play then become the primary vehicle by which the playwright offers readers his or her version of truth. Nor does the playwright have the option, as does the fiction writer, of using narrative point of view to reveal necessary background information or a character's innermost thoughts. Rather, the playwright must rely almost exclusively on **dialogue,** the conversations the characters have with each other, to develop character and to handle **exposition,** background information necessary to the readers' understanding.

Setting

Setting encompasses both the physical location and the cultural environment, as well as the background and locale. For example, in Henrik Ibsen's *A Doll's House*, set in 1870s Norway, the Victorian attitude toward women is crucial to our understanding of the play. Similarly, the "gloomy" and disheveled kitchen in the New England farmhouse in Glaspell's *Trifles* is crucial to understanding Minnie Wright's situation in a house dominated by John Wright. This stage with its dirty pots and towel bar and the broken preserve jar enhances the audience's ability to imagine the unbearable conditions that might cause a rope to be tied around Wright's neck and pulled until he is dead. In *Andre's Mother*, the setting of Central Park in New York is also bare except for the balloons that are used as props to signify letting go of Andre. The cultural environment of the African American family struggling with racial problems clarifies family relationships and deepens the understanding of August Wilson's *Fences*.

Style

Style, the manner in which the playwright expresses himself or herself, also encompasses imagery, symbolism, diction, and sentence structure. When a playwright must reveal to the audience information about a character but wants to conceal the details from other characters, he or she relies on the **soliloquy,** a stylistic technique in which a character voices thoughts aloud to the audience. In Shakespeare's *Othello,* for example, Iago reveals to the audience through soliloquies motives he wants to conceal from other characters. Iago's deception is revealed in part by his variations in style. To those around him he appears the blunt, direct military man unable to embellish a compliment to women. But the complexity of imagery in his soliloquies and in some of his dialogues with Othello reveals a far more facile and manipulative command of language. His use of coarse sexual and animal imagery, too, helps to reveal his malignity.

Another stylistic device used to impart characters' thoughts is the **aside,** a passage or remark the characters speak to the audience or to themselves, giving the illusion that, while the audience hears them, other characters on stage do not. Tom Stoppard in *The Real Inspector Hound* uses the elements of the aside when Moon and Birdboot, the two theater critics and actors in the play, sit in front of the stage with microphones so that the "real" audience can hear every comment they make about their jobs, the play, and the actors, thus creating the illusion that the audience hears them while the actors do not. On the other hand, some playwrights embellish their plays with a blend of music, dialogue, and action or depend on a choreographer to incorporate dance. A chorus, such as the one used by the Greek dramatist Sophocles in *Oedipus Rex*, created for the ancient Greeks the illusion of the townspeople's commentaries, an integral part of the structure. Unlike the early playwrights, the modern playwrights do not use the chorus although an argument can be made that Mrs. Hale and Mrs. Peters act as a chorus of women to establish motivation for the murder of John Wright in *Trifles*.

Finally, playwrights may use their unique style to reveal much about a character's concealed attitudes and motivation by having him or her voice opposing opinions in different scenes with different characters present. As a simple hypothetical example, the playwright might imagine two consecutive scenes in a comedy: in the first, a woman laughingly rejects her would-be lover's advances; in the next, she tells her friend how much she loves that would-be lover. A series of scenes that effectively reveal concealed motives occur in the first act of *Othello*. In one scene, Iago promises loyalty to Roderigo in the latter's efforts to destroy Othello; then, in the next scene, Iago appears loyal to Othello. In one scene in *Trifles*, the women present opposing opinions after they realize the extent of Minnie Wright's isolation and misery yet appear to be concerned only with the trifles in her life when their husbands appear.

Character

The term **character** refers, of course, to the people created by the playwright and actors and imagined by the readers or spectators. The main character in a play is the **protagonist;** his or her opponent or opposing force is the **antagonist.** Minor characters can also play a role in establishing meaning in any given situation. Christine Linde does not appear on stage often in Ibsen's *A Doll's House*, yet she acts as a foil for Nora.

Another element of character is **motivation,** the driving force or incentive for an action or actions. Sometimes the motivation is determined by a character flaw or defect, called **hamartia** by the ancient Greek philosopher Aristotle. In classical Greek tragedy, this hamartia often leads to the downfall of the protagonist. Thus, in Sophocles's *Oedipus Rex*, readers and spectators are acutely aware of how Oedipus's quick temper and his rush to judgment, qualities he does not think he has because he had once saved the city from destruction by answering the riddle of the Sphinx, contribute to his devastating reversal of fortune at the end. In *Fences*, Troy Maxson, a responsible worker who gives his paycheck to his wife every Friday night, minus his "allowance" for the week, is driven to act irresponsibly by the fences that restrict his life and by his desire to escape the boundaries of his marriage. These acts seem contradictory in nature but reflect the complexity of reality.

Another element of characterization is the protagonist's or antagonist's **anagnorisis,** Aristotle's term for recognition or discovery of some important truth. This discovery leads to the protagonist's self-awareness, a very important part of character development. For example, anagnorisis or, to use a modern term, **epiphany,** a manifestation or revelation, occurs in *Oedipus Rex*. Oedipus, in discovering the truth about his father and mother, gains an understanding that arrogance and a desire for knowledge can lead to disaster. This epiphany is emphasized when his wife/mother commits suicide and he gouges out his eyes. In *A Doll's House*, Nora comes to realize that Torvald Helmer, her husband, has responded to the threat of exposure only as a father or authoritarian figure, demanding and controlling her life. This epiphany or anagnorisis leads to her bold decision at the end. In *Trifles*, although the women's epiphany occurs when attention is paid to details of "trifles," it is uncertain whether the men ever truly understand the magnitude of what has happened on the farm that eventful night or of the years which Mrs. Wright spent with the "good" Mr. Wright. Whether or not a character comprehends or discovers truth is a distinguishing trait in his or her temperament.

Dramatic characters may be classified as dynamic or static. If a character changes or grows during the course of the play, he or she is **dynamic.** If, on the other hand, the character is stereotyped and simplified and fails to change or grow, he or she is **static.** In Ibsen's *A Doll's House*, Nora is a dynamic character; a series of experiences causes her to change as she learns more about her own identity.

Plot

In his *Poetics*, Aristotle claims that the most important element of a play is its plot. Most dramatists rely on **plot** as a framework, using a pattern of exposition, conflict, complication, climax, and resolution. As in fiction, a playwright may also use the **flashback** technique to convey missing information; he or she breaks into the chronology of the play to return to a previous time. Sometimes flashbacks allow readers to connect past events with present situations in order to understand personalities, the playwright's purpose, and/or theme. As a plot approaches its **climax,** the high point of the action, **dramatic tension,** the audience's desire to see the conflict resolved, increases. In Sophocles's *Oedipus Rex*, for instance, attentive readers and spectators learn immediately that Oedipus and Creon are at odds. This tension builds when the chorus, Creon, and the blind Teiresias tell Oedipus that his arrogance may cause suffering. As Oedipus proceeds to ignore everyone in pursuit of the cause of the plague in Thebes, the dramatic tension builds until he realizes his obstinacy has caused damage to his own family; tension decreases as he comes to accept his lonely fate.

Dramatic irony, which may increase the dramatic tension of the plot, occurs when an important character, lacking information the audience knows, behaves in a way that is diametrically opposed to his or her own best interest or unknowingly says something that has a double meaning. *Oedipus Rex* is a famous example of dramatic irony. The audience knows that in *Oedipus* the tragic hero has killed his father, married his mother, and fathered four children by her. Accepting his fate of banishment and the subsequent curse on the family, Oedipus has left Thebes. However, the audience knows that the curse will follow the family in the battle between Creon and Antigone, two obstinate people whose growing arrogance and failure to listen to anyone will eventually lead to their doom.

Though most of the plays in this anthology follow traditional patterns of plot, some modern and contemporary playwrights have experimented with plot, sometimes eliminating one or more of its traditional parts, sometimes deliberately avoiding a chronological sequence, and sometimes obscuring altogether any sense that one event necessarily follows or causes another. **Theater of the absurd,** in which both the form and the content of the play reflect the playwright's view of the absurdity of the human condition, exemplifies this experimentation with plot.

Theme

Theme refers to the major ideas or moral precepts that the play embodies. Sometimes it is impossible for any two people to agree upon the wording of the theme or themes because moral positions and abstract principles are, naturally, more difficult to express than concrete facts. Even when theme is expressed, often the tendency is to simplify a sometimes complex idea. In many cases, themes can also be related to social problems. For instance, in *Andre's Mother*, when Cal confronts Andre's mother about her son's death from AIDS, his last speech about being "fugitives from our parents' scorn or heartbreak" and his quotation from *Hamlet* ("Good night, sweet prince, and flights of angels sing thee to thy rest!") help the audience to arrive at a statement of theme.

Though drama may elucidate problems, it seldom advocates solutions to them. Glaspell's *Trifles*, for example, raises questions about laws as well as the inflexibility of lawmakers who refuse to grant mercy with justice. Tragic as John Wright's death is, however, the play also affirms the dignity of suffering humanity. To understand the theme of the play, an audience or reader must consider all of these questions and ideas.

The following questions are intended as a general guide to reading and writing about a play. Specific guidance is provided by the questions following each of the plays in this anthology.

REVIEW: READING AND WRITING ABOUT PLAYS

Stage Directions

1. Have the stage directions helped you to envision the play? If so, how? Have the directions transmitted any of the author's meaning? If so, how?
2. What are some of the explicit descriptions of the set? How does the set help develop character, plot, theme, and setting?
3. What objects or props have contributed the most to the understanding of the story? How?

Setting

1. How does the playwright use the setting to convey character traits, theme, conflict, or irony?
2. How or why is the cultural or physical environment important to the readers' understanding of the play?
3. How important is the setting to the play as a whole?

Style

1. Are characters distinguished from each other by their speaking style—their use of imagery, diction, and sentence structure?
2. How does the playwright use language to develop characters or to convey information about them?
3. Does the playwright use structural devices to convey meaning? How?

Character

1. What types of characters are presented on the stage? Are they stereotypes or individuals?
2. Are the characters dynamic or static? If dynamic, how do they change or grow? How does the author reveal their depth and complexity?
3. How does the playwright develop character? What does the dialogue tell about characters? Does the playwright also use stage movements, gestures, or facial expressions to develop characters?
4. How does the playwright impart to the audience the thoughts, feelings, and ideas a character wants to conceal from other characters?
5. What motivates the protagonist, antagonist, and/or minor characters?
6. Does the protagonist experience anagnorisis? If so, precisely when does it occur and what does the character discover?

7. Does the protagonist have a tragic flaw (hamartia)? If so, how does this defect in character or mistake in deduction lead to his or her downfall?
8. What actions and/or words reveal qualities of character or personality?

Plot
1. Is the plot the traditional Aristotelian plot of beginning, middle, and end? If it is not traditional, what structure does the playwright use? How do the acts and/or scenes contribute to the overall understanding of the play?
2. What is the basic conflict in the play? Is it between two characters, within a character, or between a character and some large force such as fate, the environment, or an institution?
3. How does the author reveal the conflict? How does he or she create and sustain dramatic tension?
4. Is dramatic irony used to reinforce dramatic tension? If so, how does the playwright overcome the problem of revealing to the audience what he or she does not want a character to know?

Theme
1. What, in your opinion, is the main idea or theme in the play? Is there more than one theme?
2. What questions does the play raise or illuminate? Does it attempt to answer the questions or to solve a problem?
3. How do the plot, character, setting, style, and conflict develop the play's theme or central issue?

The Writing Process

Writing a paper is a process like building a house or baking bread; you should not try doing everything at once. A competent builder will not lay a foundation without blueprints or frame the walls before laying a foundation and floor. Similarly, in writing you should not try to plan, write, edit, and proofread all at the same time. Rather, you should write one step at a time.

Some papers may require more steps than others. A short, timed, in-class writing assignment may allow for only three steps: planning, writing, and proofreading. A simple plan for such an assignment need answer only two questions: "What am I going to say?" and "How am I going to develop my idea convincingly?" Suppose, for example, you have thirty minutes to answer the question, "Is the narrator of Bell's 'Customs of the Country' simply an evil person, or does she have redeeming qualities?" You might decide to answer "though she admits to having broken her son Davey's leg, the narrator of Bell's 'Customs of the Country' is an extraordinarily honest woman who cares deeply about her son." You might go on to develop this response by citing examples from the story.

A longer out-of-class paper allows for more time to plan and organize your material and write more than one draft. You may also consider ways of developing your response, such as description, exemplification, enumeration, analysis, classification, comparison-contrast, and cause-effect. This section addresses the different aspects and steps of the writing process and some of the different essay models you can use when developing your essay.

Developing Ideas

Even seasoned writers sometimes have difficulty getting started on their writing. Common problems you may face include focusing your ideas, not knowing where to begin, having too little to say, having too much to say, and not knowing where exactly you stand on an issue. Whatever your particular "writer's block" may be, there are development strategies that can help get you started. Brainstorming, freewriting, clustering, and journaling all help you through the development process. You may find that you prefer only one or a combination of methods to help get your creative juices flowing.

Brainstorming

Brainstorming is a way of generating observations and ideas. You simply list your ideas as they come to mind without paying attention to sentence structure, spelling, order, or even relevance. The purpose is to produce ideas, not to criticize or edit them. Brainstorming can be done alone or in class groups; your teacher may even have the entire class brainstorm together. You may devote as few as five or as many as thirty minutes to the brainstorming process. Try to keep listing ideas as they pop into your head. Don't worry about whether the ideas are good or bad. Even a "dumb" idea can trigger a brilliant one.

Jodi Deeter decided to write her paper on Ibsen's concern for women's rights as shown in Torvald's treatment of Nora in *A Doll's House*. Brainstorming for a few minutes, she produced the following list:

```
Ibsen—concern for women's rights

Analyze Torvald—"a man of his time," egotystical, worried

     about reputation, He's selfish, and imature.

               concerned w/society

          morals

     Nora trinket

Selfish Nora is there for him

     Treating her as a child (she'll never make it w/o him)
```

Notice that this list has no apparent order or consistent form and that it contains spelling and grammatical errors. Even such a random list of ideas can help you focus and organize your paper. You should brainstorm until you have a wealth of specific ideas about your topic.

Freewriting

Freewriting works much the same way as brainstorming does—on hunches, impressions, and quick reactions. The important thing to remember when freewriting is to keep writing without consciously thinking about what you are saying. Set aside about ten minutes and make yourself write without pausing for the whole ten minutes. As with brainstorming, don't worry about mistakes, grammar, or spelling. When you freewrite with a focus, write down the focus point at the top of your paper to help you stick with it as you write. This way you will have a visual reminder to keep you from straying too far away from the topic. Again, remember the rule of freewriting: *don't stop writing,* even if all you write is gibberish.

Clustering

Clustering, also called "mind mapping," "ballooning," or "grouping," is a visually presented variation of brainstorming popular in the corporate world. Clustering is best done with a large sheet of paper. In the middle of the page, write the main topic and draw a circle around it. Think of subtopics related to the main topic and write them down around the main topic circle. Then, draw a box around each of them (to differentiate them from the main idea) and then draw lines to connect the boxes back to the center circle. Try to express these subtopics in one or two key words. Repeat this process around the subcategories. This technique not only helps you to develop your ideas but also enables you to see the connections between them.

Keeping a Journal

Keeping a journal gives you a reservoir of ideas to draw from in developing essays. Most great writers, including Nathaniel Hawthorne, F. Scott Fitzgerald, and Virginia Woolf, kept idea journals. Journaling helps you store away ideas, review them for further consideration, and develop them more fully over time.

A reader-response journal records your reaction to works you have read. Such a journal works best if you write down your first impressions immediately after you finish reading. Jot down any questions, ideas, or thoughts you had concerning the work. Include any emotional reactions you had (anger, pity, joy) and your impressions of the characters, theme, and plot. Later, reread your initial impressions and develop them more fully in the journal.

In addition to helping you develop ideas, a journal allows you to improve your writing without the fear of correction. It involves you more deeply with the material you read in class. By writing about your initial impressions of a story or poem, you may find yourself developing ideas that would not have otherwise occurred to you—ideas from which you can later draw for future essay assignments.

Narrowing the Topic

Once you have a general concept of what your topic will be, you need to narrow it down to a manageable idea. Some writers have trouble narrowing their topic because they like several ideas developed during brainstorming and they are not sure which one to choose, or they are afraid of committing to only one concept. This step does involve an element of risk, but remember that you can always backtrack to another idea if you find that you simply can't get your first choice off the ground. If your essay involves outside research, you may wish to locate your sources before committing to the final topic. The sources that you find can help determine the focus of your essay. Once you have narrowed your topic, you need to focus your paper and to develop a thesis statement for it.

Developing a Thesis Statement

When developing your thesis statement, think about what you want to say about the topic. A thesis statement makes an assertion; it indicates exactly what the writer intends to say about a subject. You might think of your paper as a kind of contract in which you make a commitment to discuss an idea. The first paragraph of your paper should provide a brief statement of the main point. The rest of the paper develops this point. If it is properly organized, it will first create an expectation in its thesis, a brief statement of the main point contained in the introduction to the paper. It will then fulfill that expectation in the body that follows. A thesis like "Henrik Ibsen's *A Doll's House* is about men and women" or "Ibsen's *A Doll's House* shows ideas of Ibsen's time" creates no clear expectation. A better thesis might be "Torvald Helmer consistently treats his wife Nora as a piece of property to be used for his own selfish ends." This thesis constitutes an informal contract with the reader that what follows, the body of the paper, will discuss Ibsen's play, showing Torvald's selfish possessiveness. It is perfectly normal for the thesis statement to change as you write your paper, becoming clearer and more precise as the paper evolves.

As she talked to her teacher and to other students in the class, Jodi came to realize what she wanted to emphasize in her paper: that while he had many faults and often treated Nora abysmally, Torvald loved Nora deeply. She began to rework her plan to emphasize Torvald's love:

```
1. show he's egotistical—selfish

2. show his concern for his reputation—how he uses Nora

3. show shallowness when he explodes (disowns Nora)
```

4. show he is like most men of his day—both victims of

    society's expectations

5. show that he <u>loves</u> Nora

Focusing Your Paper

Taking the time to define your focus is especially helpful if you have many fragmented ideas. The key to focusing your paper effectively is to answer the question "What is my paper about?" and to proceed from there. This is also an excellent way to develop your thesis statement. Try to keep your answer to only one sentence. This forces you to identify the main idea of the paper. After you have identified exactly what your paper is about, you can then begin organizing the ideas that connect to the main point. This may involve answering another question, "How will I support my point?" which should prompt you to list the ways you intend to present and prove your idea. After you have provided the answers to this question, arrange your list in a logical order.

Defining the Purpose

The purpose of your paper is the reason you are writing it. Your objective may be to persuade your audience to your view or opinion, to inform them about new information or ideas, or to describe an experience or event so that they may understand it better. Your audience should be able to identify your paper's objective and then realize what you need to do to accomplish this objective.

When preparing a persuasive paper, you should organize your material by first determining what you are trying to prove. Then list the support you will provide to prove your idea. Review your supporting evidence list and figure out how you should order this support to present a convincing discussion. From this simple organization, you should be able to begin writing your paper. For a more detailed discussion of how to write a persuasive paper, see the section on argument that follows.

If your objective is to inform your readers, you first need to anticipate the questions your audience may have regarding the topic and how much background they will need to understand it. Once you have developed a list of questions about your topic that you will address in your paper, determine what order will best present the information.

A descriptive paper also involves answering several questions. First, you must identify what is important or relevant about the subject you intend to describe. To demonstrate its importance to your reader, you should determine what images, details, scenes, characters, and themes are vital to communicating this importance. List these elements and order them so that they present the reader with a clear view of the experience or topic that you are trying to present.

Researching

Once you have a strong thesis and a good list of supporting ideas, the next step is to research the topic. Research helps you to support the points you want to make in your paper. Research can involve a few or many steps, depending on the type and length of the paper you are writing. For lengthy critical papers that require outside sources, you will probably need to tap into library resources or even find information online.

Many students think that researching their paper means a trip to the library. While this is often the case, you should start by rereading the work about which you are writing, marking passages that relate to your ideas. You may find it helpful to copy onto three-by-five cards or to write in a file on your computer the passages from the stories that you want to quote in order to draft your paper without repeatedly referring to the textbook. As you read, write down any questions you have about the work. You may wish to discuss these questions with your teacher or peers. Discussion is an effective way to focus your ideas and find out how other people react to your topic.

Finding Sources

Researching a paper about a literary topic can be a daunting prospect. If you are unfamiliar with library research, the librarian should be the first person you speak to. Don't be afraid to ask librarians for assistance; they are there to help get you started. Most libraries now use computerized card catalogues. These systems allow you to look up books by author, title, and subject. Remember that books are dated—that is, they are usually at least a year old by the time they reach the shelves and may not contain the most up-to-date information. However, having the latest information is usually not an issue when writing about literature.

The library also contains many journals and periodicals on a wide variety of subjects. Literary journals can be a good source of information on your topic, allowing you to see what other people have written about the work. Frequently, English professors and graduate students write the contributions to these journals, so don't be discouraged if the articles seem very academic and even hard to understand. They can still be excellent resources to help support your ideas.

The Internet is a relatively new way to research your topic. Many college-level English classes have webpages, on which students post their work and interact with each other. You may even find a literary newsgroup discussing your story or poem online! Some of these newsgroups are open to enrolled students only, but you can still read the groups' postings.

You should surf the web with the careful eye of a critic. Remember that other users can post anything they wish on the Internet, and some online material may be inaccurate or undocumented. Whenever possible, verify what you find on the web with its paper source. A few of the reputable Internet resources for literary research include:

www.ipl.org/ref/litcrit/ The Internet Public Library's Online Literary
   Criticism Collection contains over 1000 critical and biographical

websites about authors and works that can be referenced by author, title, or literary period.

www.promo.net/pg/ Project Gutenberg provides a huge library of electronically stored books that can be downloaded for free and viewed offline.

humanitas.ucsb.edu/shuttle/english.html The University of California, Santa Barbara, maintains a website on general English literature resources, as well as categories for time period and genre.

www.poets.org/ The Academy of American Poets' website features an online poet database and critical essays about poetry.

Selecting Material

Once you have found a source that you think will be helpful, write it down immediately. The traditional way of doing this was to use a bibliography card; most teachers now prefer that students list their bibliography entries and notes on computer. List on your computer each source you plan to use (for guidance in using the correct form, see in this book Appendix C, "Documenting a Research Paper: MLA Style Sheet"). For example:

```
Melton, Quimby IV. "Greenleaf's Destructive Bull and
     the Paean to the Common Man." Literature and
     Ourselves: A Thematic Introduction for Readers
     and Writers. 5th ed. Ed. Gloria Mason Henderson,
     Bill Day, and Sandra Stevenson Waller. New
     York: Longman, 2006. 1472-76.
```

```
Richardson, William. "Over There: Remembering
     Flannery O'Conner." Southern Humanities Review
     36.1 (Winter 2002):1. [here put the date that
     you found the article, e.g., 6 Jan 2002]
     <http://www.poets.org/LIT/poet/ehirfst2.htm>.
```

If you write each bibliography entry carefully, being sure to use the correct MLA form, you will not have to waste time later hunting for details you forgot to copy. For more information on how to write bibliography entries on a computer, see the section of this introduction on argument (page 46).

You should also make notes on your computer, listing the author, page, and topic at the top and writing only one piece of information, either quoted or carefully paraphrased, on each note. For example:

```
Cochran 402
"Torvald insinuates throughout the play that he will
    be there to protect Nora; however, he fails
    miserably."
Torvald repeatedly tells Nora how he will keep her
    out of danger, but his actions are quite
    opposite of his words.
```

You may also find it helpful to copy into notes on your computer passages from the work or works that you want to quote in order to draft the paper without repeatedly referring to the book.

Documenting Sources

Remember that you use sources to support your ideas and emphasize your points. It is important to document these sources whether you quote or paraphrase the material. You must let your reader know where the information you borrowed came from. Documenting your sources gives credit to the person who did the work and helps your readers locate information for further reading.

Even if you rewrite information in your own words, you still must document the source. Failure to document original information is called plagiarism—presenting someone else's work as your own—and it is considered by academic institutions as a form of theft. While it is not necessary to document common knowledge, such as dates, facts, or ideas that are generally known, to be safe, you may want to document any information that is new to you. The following checklist should help you determine when to document your sources:

- Quoting someone's exact words
- Citing someone else's opinion
- Summarizing someone else's ideas, although not directly quoting them
- Using specific information from a study
- Citing statistical data
- Reporting the results of someone else's research
- Paraphrasing someone else's ideas, even if it is in your own words

See the appendix on MLA documentation for information on how to cite your sources properly both in the body of your paper and in the Works Cited section at the end of your paper.

Organizing

Many students think organizing their paper means writing a structured and detailed outline, complete with Roman numerals and indented sub-points. While this is an effective way to organize your paper, it is not the only way to plan your essay. Organizing includes defining your focus, planning how to make your paper flow smoothly from point to point, and determining the order of your material. Quite often, organizing involves answering for yourself a series of questions designed to help you identify and keep to the points you want to cover.

Blocking and Planning

Although your teacher may require an outline, you may find other, less formal methods of organization helpful. One such method is called blocking, the arranging and rearranging of ideas in groups or blocks. Blocking produces not a finished order but a series of starting points from which to work. You might begin simply by blocking information by characters, listing together ideas related to each. Then you might rearrange the blocks until you arrive at a pattern that seems promising.

Identifying Your Audience

Identifying your audience is essential. Anticipating what your audience needs to know will help you compose a convincing, effective paper. Start by answering a few simple questions:

- Who is my audience?
- How much does my audience already know about my topic?
- How might my audience feel about this topic?
- What questions might my audience have about my topic or my conclusions?
- What does my audience need to know to understand my points?
- What is the best order to present the necessary information?
- Why are people in my audience reading my paper?

After you answer these questions, you should be able to organize your material to satisfy the needs of your audience while presenting your points and achieving your objective—writing a thoughtful essay.

These informal organization techniques can be the last step before you write your paper. If you feel more comfortable with an extensive and detailed outline, you will find that applying the above techniques before you construct your formal outline will make your task much easier. Once you have organized your material and composed your writing plan, you are ready to begin writing the actual paper.

Drafting

In drafting a paper, you should not think of your draft as a finished product. At this stage, neither neatness nor correctness is important. Your primary goal in drafting should be to get your ideas down in a reasonable order. If you stop to concern yourself with spelling, sentence structure, grammar, and neatness, you may lose your train of thought. If you find that you cannot continue with one paragraph, begin another and return later to the difficult one. You may want to leave gaps or write marginal notes in your manuscript to indicate omissions or changes you want to make later. Note the mark-outs and inattention to spelling in Jodi's rough draft on *A Doll's House*:

1 maybe 2 par

Set in the late nineteen-century, Henrick Ibsen's <u>A Doll's House</u> is justly viewed as an obvious fight for women's rights. Although Ibsen denied ever being directly involved in the fight for women's rights, he publicly displayed his position by submitting two recommendations to the Scandinavian Club in Rome in the spring before he wrote <u>A Doll's House</u>. Both of his suggestion were benificial to women and Ibsen made a lengthy, outspoken commentary trying ~~to to get~~ persuade members to—let women—become librarians and allow them to vote in club meetings (Templeton 399). Contrary to Ibsen's denials, it is apparent he was very much in favor of support of the fight for women's rights. /Many women can relate to Ibsen's <u>A Doll's House</u>. The Confusion of a love-hate relationship with a man who refuses to let go of his (the) "I am the man and you are the women" attitude. ~~Torvald and Nora~~ Taking on individual roles set by society, Torvald and Nora spend eight years of marriage playing games with one another instead of growing together. However, Torvald's position concerning women is typical seemingly of men throughout the nineteenth-century (Cochran 401). Cochran also ~~see~~ understands the psychological implication so of a socieities views as a whole by sying "He (Torvald) is not intentionally abusing Nora but is acting as society dictates. He simply behaves like most men of his time." (Cochran 403). Torvald loves

Nora in the best way he knows how. ~~His age is large~~ Being

overly concerned with what society will think of him,

Torvald has a large ego ~~ego is quite large~~. He continually

makes reference to how beautiful Nora ~~looks~~ adding to his

~~own appeal~~ or outside appearance. ~~His~~ Torvald's moralistic

views are also questioned throughout the play.

As this example indicates, when you draft a paper, you are likely to begin one way, change your mind, and then begin another way. While Jodi's introduction is neither well organized nor economically written, it is a promising start. Sometimes half the battle is just getting something on paper that you can go back and revise.

Getting Started: Writing Your Introduction

Many students find that the most challenging and daunting part of writing an essay is writing the very first paragraph. Of course, many writers experience that age-old malady, "writer's block." In *Shoptalk*, his biography of humor writer James Thurber, Donald Murray quotes Thurber as saying "Don't get it right, get it written." What he means is simply to start writing, regardless of whether you think what you are writing is good or not. Some students fear that if their first paragraph is not perfect, the rest of their paper will go downhill from there. You may wish to use your thesis statement as a starting point. Remember, a good thesis statement is worth the time and effort because you can frame your paragraph around your thesis. After you have written the first paragraph, you can revise it immediately or continue writing and return to it later. For examples of effective introductions you might examine the introductions to the professional essays such as Swift's "A Modest Proposal" or Frances Mayes' "*Bramare*." If you prefer to look at student essays, you might read the introductions to Jim Fowler's "Baseball Metaphors in <u>Fences</u>" or Johna Childers' "Symbolism in 'Sonny's Blues.'"

Developing Paragraphs and Making Transitions

A paragraph is a group of sentences that support and develop a central idea. The central idea serves as the core point of the paragraph, and the surrounding sentences support it. There are three primary types of sentences in a paragraph: the topic sentence, supporting sentences, and transitional sentences.

The core point, or the topic sentence, usually appears as the first or second sentence in the paragraph. It is the controlling idea of the paragraph. Featuring the topic sentence first lets the reader know immediately what the paragraph is about. However, sometimes you may need to provide a transition sentence or some supporting material before stating the topic sentence, in which case it may appear as the second or third sentence in the paragraph. Think of the topic sentence as a mini thesis statement; it should connect logically to the topic sentences in the paragraphs before and after it.

Supporting sentences do just that: support the topic sentence. This support may be from outside sources in the form of quotes or paraphrased material, or it may be from your own ideas. Think of the support sentences as "proving" the validity of your topic sentence.

Transition sentences link paragraphs together, connecting the paper as a cohesive unit and promoting the essay's readability. Transition sentences usually appear as the first and last sentence of the paragraph. When they appear at the end of the paragraph, they foreshadow the topic that will come next. Words such as *in addition, yet, moreover, furthermore, meanwhile, likewise, also, since, before, hence, on the other hand, as well,* and *thus* are often used in transition sentences. Another natural and effective way to create transition is to repeat key words and phrases. All of these transition devices act as road signs for your readers, helping them to identify connections between your ideas and to know what to expect next.

Paragraphs have no required length. You should remember, however, that an essay composed of long, detailed paragraphs might prove tiresome and confusing to the reader. Likewise, short, choppy paragraphs may sacrifice clarity and leave the reader with unanswered questions. Remember that a paragraph presents a single unified idea. It should be just long enough to support its subject effectively. Begin a new paragraph when your subject changes.

Use this list to help keep your paragraphs organized and coherent:

- Organize material logically—present your core idea early in the paragraph.
- Include a topic sentence that expresses the core point of the paragraph.
- Support and explain the core point.
- Use transitional sentences and phrases to indicate where you are going and where you have been.

Concluding Well

Your **conclusion** should pull together the points made in your paper while also reiterating your final point. You may also use your conclusion as an opportunity to provoke a final thought you wish your audience to consider. Try to frame your conclusion to mirror your introduction—in other words, be consistent in your style. You may wish to repeat the point of the paper, revisit its key points, and then leave your reader with a final idea or thought on your topic.

Conclusions are your opportunity to explain to your reader how all your material fits together. Avoid the temptation simply to summarize your material; try to give your conclusions a little punch. However, it is equally important not to be overly dramatic. Rather, conclusions should sound confident and reflective. Almost all of the essays in this text provide examples of effective conclusions. You might examine the conclusions written by professional writers, for example, the conclusions in William Golding's "Thinking as a Hobby" or David Osbourne's "Beyond the Cult of Fatherhood." Excellent examples of conclusions in student essays include the last paragraphs of Nick Hembree's "Dreams of Truth, Reality, and War," Kimberly Prevett's "Escape from Reality," and Stephanie Minter's "Under the Tuscan Sun."

Revising and Editing

Once you have drafted a paper and, if possible, spent several hours or even a day away from it, you should begin revising and editing it. First, reread the essay to determine whether the organizational pattern you have selected is the best possible way to present your ideas. Rearranging or adding paragraphs or sections may create a clearer, more convincing essay; if you move or add sections, however, you may need to revise your thesis to reflect the new order.

To edit your paper, read it closely, marking the words, phrases, and sections you want to change. Have your grammar handbook nearby to check any grammar questions that may arise. Look for ideas that seem out of place or sound awkward, passages that lack adequate support and detail, and sentences that seem wordy or unclear. Many students find that reading the essay aloud helps them to recognize awkward sentences and ambiguous wording. This technique may also reveal missing words.

As you read, think about the voice and style you are using to present your material. Is your style smooth and confident? How much of yourself is in the essay, and is this level appropriate for the type of paper you are writing? Watch out for passive sentence construction. Employing the active voice in your sentences keeps the paper vibrant and engaging.

Using Active Voice

Although grammatically correct, passive voice can slow down the flow of a paper or distance the reader from your material. In active voice, you make your agent "actively" perform an action. Consider the following examples:

Passive: In "The Yellow Wallpaper," John's wife is locked away in a room to give her the "rest cure."

Active: In "The Yellow Wallpaper," John locks his wife away in a room to give her the "rest cure."

Passive: Torvald is baited by Nora.

Active: Nora baits Torvald.

Passive: In the poem "Daddy," Plath's perception of her

father and childhood is described.

Active: Plath describes her perception of her father and

childhood in her poem "Daddy."

The first example presents a very different impression of John from that in the second sentence, which makes clear that he imprisons his wife. In each case, the second sentences, using the active voice, are more concise and emphatic.

Grammar and Punctuation

You probably already have a grammar handbook; most first-year composition courses require students to purchase these invaluable books. If you don't have a grammar handbook, get one. You will use it throughout your college—and probably your professional—career. Grammar handbooks can help you identify problems with phrases and clauses, parallel structure, verb tense, agreement, and punctuation. Most have useful sections on common mistakes in diction, such as when to use "further" and "farther" and "effect" and "affect." While "grammar checkers" on word processors may be helpful in identifying agreement problems and even passive constructions, they are not infallible. Frequently, they highlight compound sentences as "too long" or claim that a sentence is incorrect when it is, in fact, correct. Remember that you are the best grammar checker for your writing.

Proofreading Effectively

The final step in preparing a paper is proofreading, the process of reading your paper to correct errors. You will probably be more successful if you wait until you are fresh to start: proofreading a paper at 3:00 am immediately after finishing it is not a good idea. With the use of word-processing programs, proofreading usually involves three steps: spellchecking, reading, and correcting.

If you are writing your paper using a word-processing system, you probably have been using the spellchecker throughout the composition process. Most word-processing systems highlight misspelled words as you type them into the computer. Remember to run the spellchecker every time you change or revise your paper. Many students make last-minute changes to their papers and neglect to run the spellchecker one last time before printing it, only to discover a misspelled word as they turn in their paper or when it is returned to them. Keep in mind that spellcheckers can fix only words that are misspelled—not words that are mistyped but are still real words. Common typing errors in which letters are transposed, such as "from" and "form" and "won" and "own," will not be caught by a spellchecker because all are real words. Other common errors not caught by spellcheckers include words incompletely typed, such as leaving off the "t" in "the" or the second "e" in "here." Reading your paper carefully will catch these errors.

To proofread effectively, you must read slowly and critically. Try to distance yourself from the material. One careful, slow, attentive proofreading is better than six careless reads. Look for and mark the following: errors in spelling and usage, sentence fragments and comma splices, inconsistencies in number between nouns and pronouns and between subjects and verbs, faulty parallelism, other grammar errors, unintentional repetitions, and omissions.

After you have proofread and identified the errors, go back and correct them. When you have finished, proofread the paper one last time to make sure you caught everything. If you wrote your paper by hand and your errors are few, you may be able to correct them directly on the paper. Correct the errors *even if doing so will detract from the neatness of your paper.* Most teachers prefer a *slightly* messy but correct paper to a neat, incorrect one.

After editing and revising her paper, Jodi produced a final paper whose introduction and first two paragraphs read as follows:

Many women can relate to the confusion of a love-hate relationship with a man who refuses to let go of his "I am the man, you are the woman" attitude. That is the relationship between Torvald and Nora in Henrik Ibsen's <u>A Doll's House</u>. Taking on individual roles set by society, Torvald and Nora spend the eight years of their marriage playing games with one another. Torvald's position concerning women is typical of men throughout the nineteenth century (Cochran 401). Cochran understands the psychological implications of a society's view when she says, "He [Torvald] is not intentionally abusing Nora but is acting as society dictates. He simply behaves like most men of his time" (Cochran 403). Overly concerned with what society will think, Torvald often uses Nora as a pawn to enhance his own appearance. Torvald's moralistic views are also in question throughout the play. In addition, Torvald shows excessive selfishness in dealing with Nora. However, Torvald has loved Nora in the best way he knew how, by providing her with a stable home, money, security, and companionship.

Despite the surface appearance of Torvald's actions toward Nora, we soon come to realize the love and depth of emotion that he actually feels for her. Torvald's initial reaction to Krogstad's letter emerges as a selfish concern for himself. Understanding exactly what Nora has done, Torvald shouts:

> this thing must be hushed up at any price. As regards our relationship—we must appear to be living together just as before. Only appear, of course. You will therefore continue to reside here. That is understood. But the children shall be taken out of your hands. I dare no longer entrust them to you. Oh, to have to say this to the woman I once loved so dearly—and who I still—! (Ibsen 383)

Listening to what is not said, we are able to hear a lot more than Torvald would like to reveal. In the very last part of his reprimand, Torvald clearly admits that he loves Nora. The first part of his reprimand is said out of anger and fear. When Nora feels the impact of Torvald's words, without listening to their meaning, she mistakenly feels that Torvald doesn't love her. In fact, Nora has never told Torvald how she felt about his treatment of her. She has simply played out the role just as Torvald has.

In all fairness to Torvald, he was completely ignorant of the cruelty of his behavior; that does not mean he did not truly love Nora. Unfortunately, he learns too late of the profound effect his behavior has caused his marriage. His demeanor completely changes from anger

to sadness realizing Nora's intent to leave. He says
calmly, "I see it, I see it. A gulf has indeed opened
between us. Oh, but Nora—couldn't it be bridged?" (Ibsen
398) In the last act we are able to see the true Torvald.
He shows his weaknesses, bares his soul, and literally
begs Nora not to leave. Torvald does need Nora, a fact
that she should have been able to pick up on when he said,
"Nora, Nora, not now! Wait till tomorrow!" (Ibsen 390) He
repeatedly asks Nora how to mend what is wrong. Nora says
that only the "miracle of miracles" can save their
marriage, and after she is gone Torvald says to himself:
"Nora! Nora! Empty! She's gone! (a hope strikes him) The
miracle of miracles?—" (Ibsen 391)

Ways to Write About Literature

The Literary Response Essay

Response essays allow you to make connections between the literary work and your impressions of it. Did the work remind you of something in your childhood? Did you find it uplifting and affirming, or tragic? Perhaps you see a similarity between a particular character and someone you know. How did the work affect you? The literary response essay conveys to the audience your feelings and impressions of the work.

The response essay often applies a type of literary theory known as reader response criticism. Reader response is based on the idea that each reader brings a different history, personal outlook, and set of values and experiences to the work. Therefore, readers respond to literary works differently based on these variations in background. This way of approaching literature assumes that there is no "correct" reading of a text but that meaning is created when the reader interacts with the text. Thus, reactions will vary depending on factors such as the gender, socioeconomic background, occupation, and age of the reader. Think of the literary response essay as an opportunity to express your particular point of view and reaction to the work.

For example, Darren found the story "The Ones Who Walk Away from Omelas" by Ursula LeGuin particularly disturbing. In his opinion, the child in the closet in the story represents children in third-world countries who work in squalid factories in wretched conditions manufacturing American products such as sneakers and designer clothing. Such children are "locked away" from American consciousness because their labor and suffering produces goods that make American life luxurious and comfortable. Darren chose to write about his impressions of the story and connect them to this real-life circumstance.

The Comparison/Contrast Essay

The comparison essay usually compares two literary works to each other. More than simply listing the similarities and differences of two works, comparison/contrast essays make connections and provide thoughtful literary analysis. Start by critically reading the works to be compared, noting any parallel themes or ideas. Themes can include love and hate, innocence and experience, life, death and rebirth, progress and tradition, gender, family issues, freedom and responsibility, human nature, searches for identity, etc.

You may find after reading two works that you notice certain themes or similarities that approach the same issue from different perspectives. Likewise, two works may address the same issue and come to the same conclusions but approach the subject differently. You may be asked to compare one type of literature, such as a play, to another type, such as a poem, or even to another art form, such as a painting or piece of music.

When given the assignment to compare how two poems approach the same subject, Rose decided to write about the theme of love. She chose William Shakespeare's Sonnet 116, "Let me not to the marriage of true minds," and Elizabeth Barrett Browning's Sonnet 43, "How do I love thee?" While the poems are similar in theme, partially because the authors are of different genders and time periods, they express different attitudes toward love.

The Critical Analysis Essay

When you write a critical analysis essay, you examine how a part or parts of a literary work connect to the whole work. In other words, you evaluate how a particular part of a work contributes to the understanding of the whole. Analyzing a piece of literature requires that you look carefully at its parts to see how these parts contribute to the meaning of the entire work. For example, you might examine how a particular character in a story influences the outcome of the tale, or you could evaluate how a play turns on a particularly critical scene. You could also address how the language of a poem contributes to its overall meaning or message.

Analysis often focuses on an element (or elements) of literature. It may center on structure, language, characters, sound, plot development, and even irony. It demonstrates how the particular elements analyzed contribute to the whole meaning of the work. Remember that an analysis is not a paraphrasing of the work (your impression in your own words) but an explanation on how the work communicates its idea—how its parts convey the meaning.

William decided to address the way the language in Robert Browning's poem "My Last Duchess" contributes to the overall message of the poem. His essay specifically addressed the Duke's use of language and how it reveals the Duke's true message to the court ambassador. To write his essay, William needed to read through the poem many times to extract all the subtleties of the Duke's language. He then highlighted each of these conversational distinctions and explained how they connected to the overall point of the poem.

The Evaluative Essay

When you evaluate a literary work, you identify the values and beliefs expressed in the work and assess the validity of these elements. You may opt to support the values and beliefs expressed in the work or to refute or question them. Evaluative essays judge a work based on criteria set by what you have learned, experienced, and observed. In an evaluative essay, you could address whether you agree with the set of values expressed in an essay. You could also prove why the conclusions in a literary work are faulty or why you feel a particular play is unrealistic.

Evaluative essays are more than simply your opinion of a work. You must support your perspective by drawing from both the work and the value and belief system you use to evaluate it. In her essay on *A Doll's House*, Jodi evaluated Ibsen's play by placing it in social and historical context. She came to the conclusion, after initially believing otherwise, that Torvald loved Nora the best way he knew how. In her essay, Jodi proved her thesis using examples from the work and historical analysis.

The Research Paper

Literary research papers allow you to explore in depth a particular aspect of a work, using resources such as books, journals, Internet sources, and interviews to support your ideas. Research papers may employ the techniques of any of the essay forms described earlier in this section or may address a specific question you have about the work.

Juan wondered if the poem "Daddy" by Sylvia Plath reflected the reality of the author's life. Had she really tried to kill herself? What relationship did she have with her father? He decided to find out about the life of the author first and, depending on what he discovered, write a research paper on how "Daddy" is or is not an autobiographical poem.

Juan began his research at the library, where he found several biographies on Plath. He also located some literary criticism on Plath's work and her personal connection to her writings. With the help of a biography, he discovered that Plath was the daughter of German immigrants, that her father had died when she was eight years old of a gangrenous leg, and that she had indeed attempted suicide as a teenager—all events she describes in the poem "Daddy."

Although his research did seem to connect the real Plath with the voice of "Daddy," Juan read something in a literary journal that made him pause. A critic named Elizabeth Hardwick wrote that Plath's internal self-constructed chaos contributed much to this particular poem and that Plath wrote it shortly before committing suicide. Juan decided that rather than portraying a real-life description of her father, Plath's poem relayed her psychological state of mind. Her father became representative of her internal struggles—her scapegoat. Thus, the father in "Daddy" was a generalized perception rather than an accurate description of a particular person in Plath's life.

Juan continued his research on the Internet, locating a website maintained by the University of Alberta in Canada devoted entirely to the work of Sylvia Plath. The site answered some remaining questions he had regarding the author and gave him different literary perspectives on her work. The site also provided him with some supporting material he could use in his research paper. Although his topic deviated from his original idea of proving Plath's poem to be strictly autobiographical, Juan felt he had a solid and interesting topic to research and develop.

Writing a Strong Argumentative Essay

Of all the ways to write about literature, perhaps the most valuable and important is argumentative writing. Writing argumentative essays about literature prepares you to use argument in a great variety of fields, including history, economics, political science, sociology, and psychology. It also teaches you to think critically—that is, clearly, rationally, and systematically—about issues that may impact your life. Such actions as voting intelligently, making informed decisions about purchases or credit, or trying to convince a friend to stop smoking or end a potentially abusive relationship all require critical thinking. A student who thinks he or she has been treated unfairly, whether by a teacher, the school administration, or the police, can use the skills learned in writing arguments to make his or her case.

Broadly defined, **argument** is writing or speech designed to persuade or convince. It is, therefore, intended to be read or heard by people who disagree with the writer or speaker. Other methods of persuasion include advertisement, propaganda, litigation, threats—even violence and torture. Unlike these methods, argument respects the intellect of the audience and tries to persuade using largely rational means. It might be said, then, that argument is more civilized than other means of persuasion. Argument is critical to a free, democratic society. Ideally, it is at the heart of political and economic debate whether between candidates for office, among legislators considering legislation, or in newspaper editorials or television commentary. Ideally, too, honesty, integrity, and genuine desire to get at the heart of truth are essential to effective argument. Clearly, though, much argument fails to achieve this ideal.

In its simplest form, argument might simply consist of a list of reasons for a proposal or action. The reasoning in such an argument, as in all arguments, may take two forms: deductive and inductive. **Deductive reasoning** uses widely accepted general principles to demonstrate the truth of a more specific statement. The Declaration of Independence uses deductive reasoning when it declares as "self-evident truth" that "all men are created equal and are endowed by their Creator with certain inalienable rights among which are life, liberty, and the pursuit of happiness." The Declaration goes on to assume another general principle: that governments exist to protect these "inalienable rights." Arguing further that when governments fail in this purpose, the governed have a right, even a responsibility, to overthrow the government, the document then goes on to demonstrate that the British government has failed to protect the "inalienable rights" of colonists. After a long list of those failures, the Declaration concludes that the colonists have every right to go to war to separate from the mother country. Dr. Martin Luther King Jr. in his "Letter from Birmingham City Jail" argues similarly from general principles of justice and equality to a specific conclusion that the Southern Christian Leadership Conference (SCLC) and the African American people of Birmingham were right to demonstrate in protest against their treatment. It is worth noting that both arguments support actions already taking place—in the case of the Declaration, armed rebellion, in King's case, nonviolent protest.

Inductive reasoning, on the other hand, uses specific observations, or **evidence,** to arrive at general conclusions. Such reasoning is essential to the scientific method. Had Jefferson chosen to rely more heavily on such reasoning in the Declaration of Independence, he might have developed in more detail the particular abuses of the British government to support the conclusion that the colonists should separate from England. King might have cited statistics and examples demonstrating that black people in Birmingham had been systematically excluded from restaurants, churches, theaters, spectator sports, and an extraordinary variety of other facilities and events and that, when they were not excluded, they were segregated into separate and often inferior facilities. He might have gone on to argue that a "nonviolent action campaign" was necessary to end such exclusions.

In our society today, deductive argument can be very difficult. Our culture is extraordinarily diverse and inclusive. As a result, it is hard to find general principles on which a writer and his or her audience agree. Difficult as it is, deductive argument is commonly used. Our judicial system relies on deductive reasoning: attorneys argue that cases in dispute do or do not violate a more general principle, a law. Of course, they also rely on inductive reasoning, citing specific precedent after precedent to support a particular interpretation of the law or sometimes even the Constitution. Because deductive reasoning may reinforce previously held prejudices or stereotypes while inductive reasoning requires inquiry and may lead you to discover new information that challenges such stereotypes and prejudices, concentration on inductive argument seems more valuable.

Inductive Argument

Inductive argument may take many forms. It may be as simple as a list of facts in support of a conclusion. It may be essentially anecdotal, listing several cases or examples. Or it may be elaborate and formal, first considering the other side, then refuting it. The structure of formal argument in this book is simply one of several possibilities. Whatever your topic, your thesis, technically referred to in argument as a **claim**, must be debatable; you must be able to conceive of a **counterclaim**, a claim made by those who disagree with you. Statements such as *last year Georgia suffered a serious drought* or *Western states are arguing over rights to water* or *airport security measures cause delays* are not arguable. Argumentative claims make judgments about what <u>must</u>, <u>should</u>, or <u>needs to</u> be done, about the inadequacy of current practices, or about debatable matters of interpretation. Such a judgment states or implies that something is right or wrong. Examples of such claims include the following:

1. *<u>Because Atlanta's traffic is nightmarish</u>, <u>because its streams and rivers are increasingly polluted</u>*, and *<u>because smog often reaches hazardous levels</u>*, the municipalities around Atlanta should limit development.
2. *<u>Because they are ineffective</u>, <u>because they cause serious delays</u>*, and *<u>because they threaten our economy</u>*, the government should end airport security checks.

Such statements are claims; they are argumentative because they are controversial. Each also reveals three warrants, or reasons for the author's position, which will connect the claim to the evidence or support for that claim. For our purposes, the warrants in each statement above have been underlined; obviously, you may want to use more than three warrants.

Warrants are assumptions or interpretive principles that an author shares with his or her audience and that provide the basis for interpreting the facts. The precedent laws or the Constitution to which an attorney refers in supporting his or her argument are referred to as warrants. These warrants show the connection between the thesis or claim and the facts that support it. For claim #1 in the preceding paragraph that development should be limited, the warrants are *because Atlanta's traffic is nightmarish, because its streams and rivers are increasingly polluted*, and *because smog often reaches hazardous levels*. For claim #2, that the government should end airport security checks, the warrants are *because they are ineffective, because they cause serious delays*, and *because they threaten our economy*.

Literary Argument

If you are required to write an argument about a work of literature, you must keep in mind that not all literary analysis is argumentative; such theses as *Flannery O'Connor's stories often use landscape to foreshadow disaster* or *Iago in Shakespeare's <u>Othello</u> is a master of manipulation* are not arguable claims because their truth is readily observable. On the other hand, because they are often interpretive in nature, hence controversial, articles and papers about works of literature are often argumentative. Whenever an essay deals with issues having more than one interpretation, it will be argumentative. One example of an argumentative essay on literature is Frederick Hoffman's "The Search for Redemption: Flannery O'Connor's Fiction," in the Quest section of this book. Hoffman claims, "Her [Flannery O'Connor's] major subjects are the struggle for redemption, the search for Jesus, and the meaning of 'prophecy'" (page 1377). Among Hoffman's warrants, or reasons for his position, is the statement, "The figure of Jesus haunts almost all of her characters" (page 1379).

Another example of literary argument is Quimby Melton IV's essay "Greenleaf's Destructive Bull and Paean to the Common Man," also in the Quest section. Melton claims that Flannery O'Connor's story "Greenleaf" is "a song of praise for the worker and the injustice he and his family face from the higher social strata" (page 1390). Melton's warrants include the following statement: "O'Connor praises the unity of the Greenleafs and uses the symbols of unity versus disunity to further separate the class of worker and owner/worker" (page 1392).

Evaluating and Using Sources

For your argument to be convincing, you must use reliable sources of evidence. In evaluating any source, print or electronic, you should first consider the credentials of the writer and the reputation of the publication. The most reliable sources are unbiased, authoritative primary sources. Primary sources are essentially eyewitnesses, people who have observed the facts they report. To be authoritative, a source must demonstrate by credentials (profession, degrees, scholarly publications, etc.) a wide range of knowledge about the subject. An unbiased source is one who is willing to consider both sides of the issue—or, at the very least, one who has nothing to gain from either side of the issue. For example, a spokesperson for the Southern Company, a huge utility company, would be a primary and authoritative source on power plant pollution. However, if she or he argues that stronger pollution controls on power plants are unnecessary, one might well be suspicious because this source clearly has an economic stake in that argument.

In practice, you are not likely to have the time to track down authoritative primary sources for all your evidence. More likely, you will have to rely at least to some degree on reputable secondary sources, sources who are not able to observe directly what they report on. In evaluating such sources we might first look at the reputation of their publishers. Though you should always be skeptical about editorial and opinion pages, reporting of large newspapers and newsmagazines is generally reliable. Internet sources, however, are often unreliable. Virtually anyone with access to a computer and minimal computer literacy can create a website on virtually any subject whether or not he or she knows anything about the subject. In general, you should not consider an Internet source reliable unless it is an online version of a reliable print source, unless it is written by a scholar in the field of your subject, or unless it has been produced by a reliable agency (such as a government agency). Advocacy websites such as the National Rifle Association, the American Civil Liberties Union, or Mothers Against Drunk Driving may be authoritative, but these sites have the potential to be biased; such sites should be consulted on a limited basis. For a literary essay on Flannery O'Connor, for example, you would want to rely on essays by established scholars, not on a student essay you come across while searching the Internet. This is not to say you should avoid every source whose reliability is unknown, but certainly you should use such sources very carefully and in conjunction with reliable sources.

For literary argument the primary source, the best and most important source, is the work itself. If your teacher requires that you use secondary sources, evaluate them carefully according to the criteria discussed in the paragraphs above. You can evaluate the secondary sources you use by the reliability of the sources they cite and by the weight of the evidence they present. Are the sources cited by your sources primary and authoritative? For example, in an article on a story by Flannery O'Connor, does the writer cite other works by O'Connor such as letters, journals, and essays? Are the sources unbiased? Do your sources present a wide range of evidence such as, in an analysis of an O'Connor story, quotations from a variety of characters or points in the story itself? Or does the evidence seem carefully selected to give a distorted impression, perhaps coming primarily or wholly from one minor character's dialogue? In order for your own argument to be convincing, you will need to cite an abundance of evidence.

Because the evidence you must cite is readily available to you and your instructor in the work you are analyzing, writing literary arguments allows an instructor to guide you effectively in constructing an argument. Literary argument may be primarily analytic in nature, arguing for a particular interpretation against other possible interpretations. Such would be the case with an argument that Connie's encounter with Arnold Friend in Oates's "Where Are You Going, Where Have You Been?" is a dream; other possible interpretations might be that the encounter is real and Arnold is a psychopath or that Arnold is the devil. Literary argument may also go beyond the work of literature to argue judgments on issues raised by that work. For example, you might choose to argue that the social workers in Bell's "Customs of the Country" are right to grant the custody of Davey to the Bakers; on the other hand, one might argue that the social workers should have granted custody to Davey's mother. Similarly, you might argue for or against Nora's decision to leave Torvald in *A Doll's House*. Or you might argue that Tim O'Brien's war stories demonstrate that war turns reasonably civilized young men into brutes. These propositions are not wholly about the stories themselves, but rather about a reader's response to the stories.

Suppose you have chosen to argue in a paper that the social service agency is right to award custody of Davey to his mother in Bell's "Customs of the Country." Certainly, many readers feel great sympathy for Davey's mother; but her personal situation, the willingness of the Bakers to adopt him, and his mother's temper, as well as her past as drug addict and abuser, make her an inappropriate candidate for custody. Your thesis, or claim, for this paper, then might look something like this: *The agency responsible is right not to award custody to this mother.*

Having decided on a topic and written a thesis, you should begin to plan the structure of your paper. Your main structural components or subtopics, whether paragraphs, groups of paragraphs, or chapters, will be reasons or warrants for your position. These should be stated so that they can be supported with facts, perhaps best defined as statements verifiable by observation; as you plan, your reasons may also be tentative, subject to change depending on the facts, or **evidence,** you find. Your tentative supporting points or warrants, then, might be the following: *the mother is in no position to take care of Davey; she does not seem consistently able to control her temper; the Bakers represent a loving and stable alternative.*

In order to convince an opposed or indifferent group of readers, an argument must respect the opposition. To demonstrate such respect, an argument should not only avoid name-calling and insults to its audience, but also should even concede that there is at least one strong point, or counterclaim, to be made on the other side. Of course, the argument should go on to refute that point or to show that evidence in support of the writer's position is more compelling. In classic argument the part devoted to the other side's position appears near the end. It is often more effective, however, to handle this so-called **concession** immediately after the introduction, leaving the rest of the paper to respond to the other side's argument. Your plan, then, might look something like this:

1. *Thesis or **claim**: The agency responsible is right not to award custody to this mother.*
2. **Counterclaim:** *It is clear throughout the story that Davey's mother loves her son.*
3. **Warrant:** *She is in no position to take care of Davey.*
4. **Warrant:** *She does not seem consistently able to control her temper.*
5. **Warrant:** *The Bakers represent a loving, stable alternative.*

The primary source for your paper on Bell's story is the story itself. The **evidence** to support your plan is in the story. While you could use secondary sources written by various critics, let us suppose here that you are not required to do so. If you use secondary sources, you must carefully cite each quotation or paraphrase, each piece of information you use from a source, with the author's last name and page in parentheses. Because you are not using secondary sources and will be citing only one source, you need not use the author's name each time you quote the story but must cite the page number. For models of literary papers using secondary sources, see the examples written by students in the casebooks at the end of each thematic unit of this book.

Having thus planned your essay, you should next reread the story, looking for at least three or four passages or examples to support each body paragraph of your paper. You should highlight each supporting passage, using a different color highlighter for each paragraph. Then, in a computer file, which you might name "Notes for Bell Paper," you should write for each passage the page number followed by the passage itself. Because you must cite the page number when you quote, it is important that you indicate page numbers in your notes; that will save you the work later of having to go back to the story to look up the pages. Keep in mind as you select the passages to support your points that, in a short paper, you should avoid using very long quotations. The notes for your paper on Bell might look something like this:

Notes for Bell Paper

It is clear throughout the story that the mother loves her son.

580

"Sometimes you don't get but one mistake if the one you pick is bad enough. . . . during those two years I taught myself to believe that this mistake of mine could be wiped out, that if I struggled hard enough with myself and the world I could make it like it never had been."

578

". . . I have had to think about it time and again, with never a break for a long, long time, because I needed to get to understand it at least well enough to believe it never would ever happen again."

573

"I wore my hands out scrubbing everything clean and then saw to it that it stayed that way. . . . I never cared about any of it. It was an act, and I wasn't putting it on for me or for Davey, but for all the people I expected to see it and judge it."

574

"all the while I would just be thinking about some other thing like what might be going on with Davey."

575

"We would just play like both of us were children."

Though clearly the mother loves Davey and is crushed by losing custody of him, she is in no position to take care of him.

574

"swing shift" that has her "getting back to [her] apartment around three in the morning."

574

"pretty sorry," include "small time criminals, dope dealers and thieves . . . one check forger . . . and a man who would break into the other apartments looking for whiskey."

573

the man next door to her beats his wife, "[slamming] her bang into [their] common wall."

577

"it was just warm enough so [she] couldn't see [her] breath."

Not only is her living situation inappropriate for raising a child, but she also has had trouble controlling her temper.

579

". . . before long I began screaming at him outright . . . And the next thing I knew I got myself in the kitchen someway and I was snatching him up off the floor. . . . But all I ever knew was one minute I was grabbing a hold of him and the next he was laying on the far side of the room with his right leg folded up funny where it was broke."

581

When, after she has lost custody of Davey, her boss gets angry and tells the customers at the truckstop to "'get out,'" calling them "'fat as hogs,'" Davey's mother comments: "It was the first time he ever blew up at the customers that way, it had always been me or Prissy or one of the cooks"

582

When she returns home after learning she has lost custody and hears her neighbor beating his wife, she picks up a frying pan, goes next door, and hits him in the face with the pan "as hard as [she knows] how"

The Bakers, Davey's foster parents, represent a loving, stable alternative.

575

They own a small farm of which Mr. Baker makes "a paying thing"

575

which includes a "pasture, a creek with a patch of woods, [and] a hay barn,"

575

"they were real sweet to Davey and he seemed to like being with them pretty well."

575

Davey has "made out better in the first grade than anybody would have thought."

575

"they were always pleasant to me."

576

"At first I worried that the Bakers might have been talking against me, but after I had seen a little more of them I knew they wouldn't have done anything like that, wouldn't have thought it right."

Once you have sufficient quotations to support your argument, you can begin to draft your paper. In your introduction you should provide the author and title of the story, briefly explain what the story is about, and state your thesis. In each body paragraph, begin with a topic sentence and support it with quotations and summarized examples from the story. You can copy and paste quotations from your notes into your final paper, thereby saving time and reducing errors. You should introduce each quotation, put it in quotation marks, and document it with the page number. In most cases, you should then analyze the quotation, showing how it develops your topic. Your conclusion should briefly summarize your argument. At the end of the paper you should attach a Work Cited page, listing the one source you have cited in the paper, Bell's "Customs of the Country." The final draft of your paper, arrived at after a rough draft, careful editing, and proofreading, might look something like this.

Seeking Custody

In Madison Smartt Bell's harrowing story "Customs of the Country," a mother who broke her son's leg while suffering withdrawal from drugs tells her story. While her son, Davey, is in foster care with a family who wants to adopt him, the mother, who remains nameless throughout the story, waits, hoping to regain custody. Her situation, however, is clearly hopeless; the agency responsible is right not to award custody to this mother.

It is clear throughout the story that the mother loves her son. She has been honest enough with herself to admit the gravity of what she did to Davey. She repeatedly recalls the day when she broke his leg: ". . . I have had to think about it time and again, with never a break for a

long, long time, because I needed to get to understand it
at least well enough to believe it never would ever happen
again" (578). Everything she does in an effort to clean and
polish her shabby apartment she does in the constantly
diminishing hope that she will regain custody. She says:

> I wore my hands out scrubbing everything clean
> and then saw to it that it stayed that way. . .
> . I never cared about any of it. It was an act,
> and I wasn't putting it on for me or for Davey,
> but for all the people I expected to see it and
> judge it. (573)

Nothing seems to matter to her but Davey. She says of
work, "all the while I would just be thinking about some
other thing like what might be going on with Davey" (574).
Clearly, Davey dominates her every thought. She visits him
at the Bakers as often as she dares, playing with him in
the creek and woods, clearly delighting in his company. She
says of these times, "We would just play like both of us
were children" (575). At the end of the story when she
loses custody, her despair is almost palpable:

> Sometimes you don't get but one mistake if the
> one you pick is bad enough. . . . during those
> two years I taught myself to believe that this
> mistake of mine could be wiped out, that if I
> struggled hard enough with myself and the world
> I could make it like it never had been. (580)

At this point it is clear that Davey is the absolute
center of his mother's life, the one source of purpose in
her otherwise meaningless existence.

Though clearly the mother loves Davey and is crushed
by losing custody of him, she is in no position to take
care of him. She works as a waitress at Truckstops of

America, where she sometimes works a "swing shift" that has her "getting back to [her] apartment around three in the morning" (574). Surely it would be nearly impossible to find someone to stay with Davey during such a shift. Her neighbors, whom she describes as "pretty sorry," include "small time criminals, dope dealers and thieves. . . one check forger. . . and a man who would break into the other apartments looking for whiskey" (574). In addition, the man next door to her beats his wife, "[slamming] her bang into [their] common wall" (573). Davey's mother cannot even afford to heat her apartment, keeping "it. . . just warm enough so [she] couldn't see [her] breath" (577). Clearly, this is no environment in which to bring up a child.

Not only is her living situation inappropriate for raising a child, but Davey's mother also has had trouble controlling her temper. Her abuse of Davey occurred as she was suffering withdrawal from Dilaudid, too miserable to pay attention to her son. She describes her reaction as he began banging on pots to get her attention:

> . . . before long I began screaming at him
> outright. . . And the next thing I knew I got
> myself in the kitchen someway and I was
> snatching him up off the floor. . . . But all I
> ever knew was one minute I was grabbing a hold
> of him and the next he was laying on the far
> side of the room with his right leg folded up
> funny where it was broke. (579)

Given her clear remorse, her obvious love for Davey, and her determination never to let such a thing happen again, one might forgive this episode. However, Davey's mother fails to control her anger on other occasions as well. When, after she has lost custody of Davey, her boss gets angry and tells the customers at the truck stop to "'get out,'" calling them "'fat as hogs,'" Davey's mother comments: "It was the first time he ever blew up at the customers that way, it had always been me or Prissy or one of the cooks" (581). It would appear from this passage that she has a history of angrily berating the customers she serves. When she returns home after learning she has lost custody and hears her neighbor beating his wife, she picks up a frying pan, goes next door, and hits him in the face with the pan "as hard as [she knows] how" (582), leaving his nose bloody and knocking out some of his teeth. Such a violent history casts doubt on her resolution never again to abuse Davey.

The Bakers, Davey's foster parents, stand in sharp contrast to his mother. They own a small farm which Mr. Baker makes "a paying thing" (575) and which includes a "pasture, a creek with a patch of woods, [and] a hay barn," a seemingly safe, pastoral environment for a child to play in. The mother herself admits that "they were real sweet to Davey and he seemed to like being with them pretty well" (575). Perhaps responding to the stable environment offered by the Bakers, Davey has "made out better in the first grade than anybody would have thought" (575). Not only that, they treat his mother with courtesy and respect, even kindness. She says, "they were always pleasant to me" (575), then adds, "At first I worried that the Bakers might have been talking against me, but after I had seen a little more of them I knew they wouldn't have done anything like that, wouldn't have thought it right" (576). Clearly, this kind, fair, stable couple on their farm represent a far better choice than his mother for custody of Davey.

Hence, though the mother clearly loves her son, though without him her life appears to be without direction or hope, in the end the Bakers receive custody of Davey. Heart wrenching and unforgiving as such a decision may seem, it is essential for Davey's well being. And in such cases, the well being of the child must be the paramount consideration.

[New page]   Work Cited

Bell, Madison Smartt. "Customs of the Country." <u>Barking Man and Other Stories</u>. N.p: Ticknor and Fields, 1990.

<u>Literature and Ourselves: A Thematic Introduction for Readers and Writers</u>. 5th ed. Ed. Gloria Mason Henderson, Bill Day, and Sandra Stevenson Waller. New York: Longman, 2006.

This literary argument goes beyond mere analysis to argue a controversial judgment based on the story. It includes a concession recognizing the rationality of those who might disagree with its position. In addition, it is based on substantial evidence from the story itself, consisting largely of quotations selected to support its thesis or claim. These quotations are introduced, enclosed in quotation marks or blocked as appropriate, documented, and analyzed.

In addition to leading you to a better understanding of the literature you are interpreting, such arguments as this one help train you to think critically. The skills you learn in literary argument may help you think through such personal decisions as whom to vote for or what causes to support. They may also prepare you to write arguments in other classes or to argue your case for a better work environment or against businesses or government agencies that have wronged you. Asked by your teacher to write on a current issue, you should be prepared to research and write an argument on any one of a virtually endless range of topics. In any of these cases, you can use the principles and methods discussed here to prepare an effective argument.

Family

A scene from *Under the Tuscan Sun*. Buena Vista/Photofest.

The earliest and usually the strongest influence on each of us is the family. Throughout history, people from every walk of life have accused or thanked, bemoaned or celebrated members of their own families. As a result, family relationships have provided the subject matter for a wide variety of literature. Some of the families may seem destructive while others are loving and supportive. As readers, we can sympathize with, perhaps even identify with, authors as they share their own family experiences and as they cope with problems involving parents, siblings, and other family members.

Through the characters in the stories or poems or the real people in the essays, we can vicariously experience family life in a variety of times, on different economic levels, and through diverse cultures. We can laugh at the narrator's experience with Mr. Haha in Capote's "A Christmas Memory" or recoil at the alcoholic mother in McCullers' "A Domestic Dilemma." We can also understand the joys and sorrows of a mother-daughter relationship as we read Didion, Ostriker, or Walker; with Tall-Mountain we can share the beauty and wisdom of the Athabaskan language. Further, we can gain insight into the dynamics of a father-son relationship by reading Luke, Whitelock, Salinas, and Li-Young Lee. Just as Yeats writes of a prayer for a daughter, Weaver wishes aloud for a son's security as he goes out into a hostile world. With the help of writers like Alexie, we can compare our experiences of growing up with those of children from other cultural backgrounds such as Native Americans. Writers as diverse as these share with us what it is like to be inside or outside their communities. By allowing us to participate in the hardships and confusion of modern dysfunctional families such as those portrayed by McCullers and Walker, literature helps us to understand that the "immense complexity of love" sometimes causes problems that have no easy solutions.

Authors teach us the value of learning to laugh at our problems within our families. They also share with us the realization that even the most disparate family members can work through problems to reach solutions and an even greater depth of love. August Wilson, in *Fences*, reveals a family in crisis. Li-Young Lee portrays two generations who will benefit from the father's "gift." Terrence McNally portrays a mother's and a partner's love.

Similarly, we can compare our experiences within the family unit with those of others. James Baldwin lets us share in the stories of two brothers and participate in their reconciliation. Truman Capote, drawing from his real-life experiences, tells us of the beautiful friendship between a little boy and an older woman in "A Christmas Memory." Langston Hughes reminds us of the tenderness between a mother who knows the hardships of the world and a child who does not. Most important, through the enjoyment of this literature—the tears, the curses, the prayers, and the laughter—we can deepen our own understanding of others and ourselves.

Writing About Family

The essays you write about the works in the Family unit will be diverse. As you plan your essays, you should refer to the questions at the end of each genre section on writing about literature as well as to the questions after individual works and at the end of the thematic unit. Then consider which genre you want to write about and which work or works you prefer. You might select an essay or a poem that is rich in metaphorical devices and focus your essay on the ways that the metaphors expand, clarify, or enrich the work. For example, you could examine the way in which Frances Mayes, in "Bramare," uses both metaphors and a variety of sound devices to create the feelings and sounds of a peaceful time that lives in the narrator's memory. You might also examine the colorful language that Janisse Ray uses in "Native Genius" to explain her father, her mother, and her native Georgia. If you wanted to write about a poem, you might write an essay explaining how W. B. Yeats uses the images of the horn of plenty and the laurel tree to convey the kind of life he wishes for his daughter. If you prefer to write about fiction, you might write about point of view in James Baldwin's "Sonny's Blues" or examine the symbolism in Truman Capote's "A Christmas Memory." An essay on one of the plays might combine a researched study of the setting—time, place, and culture—with illustrations of the effect of that setting on the actions and opinions of the characters or on the theme. If your teacher asks you to write a personal essay as a reaction to one of the works, you might reread Joan Didion's description of her return home and write an essay on your home, or you might use Alicia Ostriker's poem as a basis for a description of your empathy with your child.

Another very important essay for freshmen writers is the argumentative essay. In this essay you would strive to persuade your reader that your thesis is true, believable, or appropriate. For example, using Langston Hughes' "Mother to Son," you could argue that the poem is as relevant today as it was in 1922. Or you may choose to tackle a problem such as alcoholism in McCullers' "A Domestic Dilemma" and argue for your own solutions. Solutions to an alcohol problem could come from a different perspective if you choose Roethke's "My Papa's Waltz" or Alexie's "Because My Father Always Said He was the Only Indian Who Saw Jimi Hendrix Play 'The Star Spangled Banner.'" Another argumentative essay could evolve from Whitelock's "Future Connected By." Do parents have the right to steer their children away from certain careers, especially their own? Is it more manly to work with the hands or with the head? What are the causes of a generation gap? These and other argumentative or persuasive topics make appealing essays because of their ability to engage the writer and the reader in a meaningful and insightful discussion and/or debate.

Fences, the play by August Wilson included in the casebook, provides a variety of topics for a documented essay using critical essays as well as your own ideas. When he was assigned an essay using the casebook, Jim Fowler first carefully read the play. Then, in order to get an overall picture of the assignment, he read the articles about the author and about the play. Because of his personal interest in baseball and because baseball is so relevant to the main character, he chose for his subject the effect of baseball on Troy. Before deciding on a more specific subject and a thesis, Jim used his computer to list the many references to baseball and his interpretations of them in random order. He also listed any supporting references from the critical articles that he thought might be helpful. After examining the lists for ideas, Jim decided to cut and paste them into three categories: language, lifestyle, and character. His preliminary thesis statement was "The reader can easily conclude that Troy's baseball experience has a very significant effect upon his language, his lifestyle, and even his moral character." Jim was now ready to write his first draft, and he chose to write it by hand, using the ideas he had listed by category as the building blocks and tying them together coherently.

From this rough draft, Jim typed the essay into the computer so that he could easily make corrections and write revisions. At this point, he checked with his professor to see if he was on the right track with his essay. The professor made a few suggestions and corrections but felt that the essay really needed little work other than polishing, correcting, and documenting. For example, in a few places the essay included past tense when talking about the events in the play, and these were changed to present tense. Back on his computer, Jim made the necessary changes and added his documentation, double-checking his quotations and paraphrases to ensure that he had not plagiarized any material. He decided that the conclusion could also be improved; therefore, he rewrote the concluding paragraph. Finally, he selected a title for his essay. He was now ready to print the final copy of his essay, "Baseball Metaphors in *Fences*," which is included at the end of the casebook in this unit.

ESSAYS

Joan Didion (b. 1934)

Didion, an American novelist and journalist who grew up in California, writes both fiction and nonfiction. Her novel The Last Thing He Wanted *(1996) is a tightly plotted story about an American journalist who investigated the sale of arms in Central America. She has also collaborated with her husband, John Gregory Dunn, on screenplays. In elegant essays such as those collected in* Slouching Toward Bethlehem *(1967), from which "On Going Home" comes, she examines contemporary Americans' loss of communal values and direction.*

ON GOING HOME   (1967)

1   I am home for my daughter's first birthday. By "home" I do not mean the house in Los Angeles where my husband and I and the baby live, but the place where my family is, in the Central Valley of California. It is a vital although troublesome distinction. My husband likes my family but is uneasy in their house, because once there I fall into their ways, which are difficult, oblique, deliberately inarticulate, not my husband's ways. We live in dusty houses ("D-U-S-T," he once wrote with his finger on surfaces all over the house, but no one noticed it) filled with mementos quite without value to him (what could the Canton dessert plates mean to him? how could he have known about the assay scales, why should he care if he did know?), and we appear to talk exclusively about people we know who have been committed to mental hospitals, about people we know who have been booked on drunk-driving charges, and about property, particularly about property, land, price per acre and C-2 zoning and assessments and freeway access. My brother does not understand my husband's inability to perceive the advantage in the rather common real-estate transaction known as "sale-leaseback," and my husband in turn does not understand why so many of the people he hears about in my father's house have recently been committed to mental hospitals or booked on drunk-driving charges. Nor does he understand that when we talk about sale-leasebacks and right-of-way condemnations we are talking in code about things we like best, the yellow fields and the cotton-woods and the rivers rising and falling and the mountain roads closing when the heavy snow comes in. We miss each other's points, have another drink and regard the fire. My brother refers to my husband, in his presence, as "Joan's husband." Marriage is the classic betrayal.

2   Or perhaps it is not any more. Sometimes, I think that those of us who are now in our thirties were born into the last generation to carry the bur-

den of "home," to find in family life the source of all tension and drama. I had by all objective accounts a "normal" and a "happy" family situation, and yet I was almost thirty years old before I could talk to my family on the telephone without crying after I had hung up. We did not fight. Nothing was wrong. And yet some nameless anxiety colored the emotional charges between me and the place that I came from. The question of whether or not you could go home again was a very real part of the sentimental and largely literary baggage with which we left home in the fifties; I suspect that it is irrelevant to the children born of the fragmentation after World War II. A few weeks ago in a San Francisco bar I saw a pretty young girl on crystal take off her clothes and dance for the cash prize in an "amateur-topless" contest. There was no particular sense of moment about this, none of the effect of romantic degradation, of "dark journey," for which my generation strived so assiduously. What sense could that girl possibly make of, say, *Long Day's Journey into Night?* Who is beside the point?

3   That I am trapped in this particular irrelevancy is never more apparent to me than when I am home. Paralyzed by the neurotic lassitude engendered by meeting one's past at every turn, around every corner, inside every cupboard, I go aimlessly from room to room. I decide to meet it head-on and clear out a drawer, and I spread the contents on the bed. A bathing suit I wore the summer I was seventeen. A letter of rejection from *The Nation*, an aerial photograph of the site for a shopping center my father did not build in 1954. Three teacups hand-painted with cabbage roses and signed "E.M.," my grandmother's initials. There is no final solution for letters of rejection from *The Nation* and teacups handpainted in 1900. Nor is there any answer to snapshots of one's grandfather as a young man on skis, surveying around Donner Pass in the year 1910. I smooth out the snapshot and look into his face, and do and do not see my own. I close the drawer, and have another cup of coffee with my mother. We get along very well, veterans of a guerilla war we never understood.

4   Days pass. I see no one. I come to dread my husband's evening call, not only because he is full of news of what by now seems to me our remote life in Los Angeles, people he has seen, letters which require attention, but because he asks what I have been doing, suggests uneasily that I get out, drive to San Francisco or Berkeley. Instead I drive across the river to a family graveyard. It has been vandalized since my last visit and the monuments are broken, overturned in the dry grass. Because I once saw a rattlesnake in the grass I stay in the car and listen to a country-and-Western station. Later I drive with my father to a ranch he has in the foothills. The man who runs his cattle on it asks us to the round-up, a week from Sunday, and although I know that I will be in Los Angeles I say, in the oblique way my family talks, that I will come. Once home I mention the broken monuments in the graveyard. My mother shrugs.

5   I go to visit my great-aunts. A few of them think now that I am my cousin, or their daughter who died young. We recall an anecdote about a relative last seen in 1948, and they ask if I still like living in New York City.

I have lived in Los Angeles for three years, but I say that I do. The baby is offered a horehound drop, and I am slipped a dollar bill "to buy a treat." Questions trail off, answers are abandoned, the baby plays with the dust motes in a shaft of the afternoon sun.

6   It is time for the baby's birthday party: a white cake, strawberry-marshmallow ice cream, a bottle of champagne saved from another party. In the evening, after she has gone to sleep, I kneel beside the crib and touch her face, where it is pressed against the slats, with mine. She is an open and trusting child, unprepared for and unaccustomed to the ambushes of family life, and perhaps it is just as well that I can offer her little of that life. I would like to give her more. I would like to promise her that she will grow up with a sense of her cousins and of rivers and her great-grandmother's teacups, would like to pledge her a picnic on a river with fried chicken and her hair uncombed, would like to give her *home* for her birthday, but we live differently now and I can promise her nothing like that. I give her a xylophone and a sundress from Madeira, and promise to tell her a funny story.

Questions for Discussion

1. What does Didion mean when she says, "Marriage is the classic betrayal"? What is the source of tension between Didion's family and her husband? Why is the distinction between where she and her husband and daughter live and where her "family" lives "vital although troublesome"?

2. What does she mean by "the emotional charges between me and the place that I come from"?

3. What is Didion's definition of home? What does she mean when she says, "I would like to give her [her daughter] *home*,. . . but we live differently now"? How does the **symbolism** of the graveyard develop Didion's feeling of rootlessness?

4. Explain Didion's statement that she and her mother are "veterans of a guerilla war we never understood."

5. Why, in an essay about going home, does Didion begin and end with her daughter's first birthday?

Suggestions for Exploring, Writing, and Persuading

1. Discuss in detail how your relationship to your family has changed since you began college. How does your experience compare with Didion's?

2. In an essay, explain how you and other members of your family are "veterans of a guerilla war."

3. Nuclear families often develop private rituals, in-jokes, and special word usages that only they understand. Such rituals, jokes, and usages

are one source of conflict between the writer's family and her husband. Write an essay in which you examine the private rituals and language of your own family.

4. Write an essay agreeing with or disputing Didion's belief that today's generation is unlikely to know the kind of home she describes.

Faye Moskowitz

As a child of immigrants, Moskowitz grew up in Michigan, where she was a Jew in a predominantly Christian community. Her experiences are chronicled in her collections of essays and memoirs A Leak in the Heart: Personal Essays and Life Stories *(1985) and* And the Bridge Is Love *(1991) and in her collection of stories,* Whoever Finds This: I Love You *(1991).* Her Face in the Mirror *(1994), an anthology edited by Moskowitz, showcases Jewish women's writings. After attending Wayne State University, she attended and now teaches creative writing at George Washington University.*

JEWISH CHRISTMAS   (1991)

1   "Jewish Christmas"—that's what my gentile friends called Chanukah when I was growing up in Michigan in the thirties and forties. Anachronistic, yes, but they had a point. Observing the dietary laws of separating milk and meat dishes was far easier for the handful of Jewish families in our little town than getting through December without mixing the two holidays.

2   Christmas was a miserable time for Jewish children in those days, nothing short of quarantine could have kept us from catching the Christmas fever. My parents were no help. Immigrants who had fled pogroms in Russia and Poland, they were world-class outsiders. If tee shirts with mottos had been in fashion then, our shirts would surely have read Keep a Low Profile. My mother would never have considered going to my school to complain about the Christmas tree in the lobby or the creche in our principal's office or the three life-size wise men, complete with camels, that we cut out of construction paper in Art and hung on our classroom walls.

3   If I still wasn't convinced Christmas was coming after all those reminders, I had only to look at the advent calendar hanging behind my teacher's desk or walk downtown, where carols blared out over loudspeakers and built to a crescendo in front of the six-foot neon cross decorating our largest department store. And as for keeping a low profile, try it when yours is the only neighborhood house in work clothes while every other is dressed for a party.

4   By the time we moved to the Jewish section of Detroit, I was old enough to accept Christmas as a holiday other people celebrated. Chanukah was our winter holiday, not a substitute at all, but a minor-

league festival that paled before Passover, Rosh Hashanah, and Yom Kippur. All the cousins gathered at our grandparents' house where we lined up to get Chanukah gelt from the uncles: quarters and half dollars, and dollar bills, perhaps, for the older children. Mostly we ran around a lot, got very flushed, and ate latkes, plenty of them.

5   My own children were raised in a diverse neighborhood in Washington, D.C. The Ghost of Christmas Past clanked its chains for a while, and my husband and I learned to make a few concessions. Still, we never sunk to the Chanukah bush or an actual Christmas tree, though we knew Jews who did, we lit the menorah, bought presents for each of the eight nights, decorated our house with blue and white paper chains, and played with dreidels. In spite of that, our kids were pretty disgruntled for most of December, although even their non-Jewish friends had to concede we had something with those latkes.

6   For the past few years, with our children grown, my husband and I have cut off the Chanukah/Christmas debate entirely. We distribute the Chanukah gelt early and then leave the country. That's going to a lot of trouble to avoid office parties and the egg nog and pfeffernuss for which we never did develop a taste, but at least we don't have to get caught up in the general depression that afflicts not only the people who celebrate Christmas but all the rest who don't and wish they did.

7   Several years ago, we found ourselves in Venice during the holidays. In spite of all our rationalizations, we missed being home with our children, missed the ritual of lighting the menorah, the tacky paper chains, the dreidel game we play, gambling for raisins or nuts, and at that moment we would have traded any pasta dish, no matter how delectable, for potato latkes like the ones we ate at Chanukah as far back as we both could remember.

8   So maybe that's why, with the help of guidebooks and our faltering Italian, we threaded our way through the city's bewildering twists and turns until we suddenly emerged into a spacious square that marks the old Jewish ghetto of Venice. The clip-clop of our heels on cobblestones and the flutter of pigeons punctuated a silence that might have existed for centuries or only on that particular rest day, we didn't know. "There's an old synagogue at the other end of the square," my husband said. "Let's go see if maybe it's open for visitors." We pulled at the heavy brass-studded wooden door, and far down a long corridor I heard the sound of many voices chattering in Italian. "I'm probably hallucinating," I whispered to my husband, "but I swear I smell latkes."

9   In that musty, crumbling building, the memories flooded back as clear as the icicles we licked in those nose-numbing December days of my Michigan childhood. Bundled against the stunning cold, we walked hand in hand, my mother and father, my brothers and I, along darkened streets where orange candles in brass menorahs bravely illuminated each front window we passed.

10   In my grandparents' vestibule, we shed our snowy boots. The welcoming warmth of the coal furnace promised more coziness deep inside, there my aunts sucked in their bellies as they elbowed past one another in and out of Bobbe's tiny kitchen, from which they pulled a seemingly endless array of delicious dishes as if from a magician's opera hat: platters of bagels slathered with cream cheese, smoked fish with skins of iridescent gold, pickled herring, thick slices of Bermuda onion strong enough to prompt a double-dare, boiled potatoes with their red jackets on, wallowing in butter. Best of all were the crisp potato latkes, hot from Bobbe's frying pan, to eat swaddled in cool sour cream, the contrasting textures and temperatures indelibly printing themselves on our memory.

11   Though our mothers' cooking styles were virtually interchangeable, my husband and I used to quarrel every year about whose family made the better latkes. My mother's potato pancakes were thin and lacy, delicate enough to float in their hot cooking oil. His mother's latkes, I pointed out at every opportunity, utterly lacked refinement: colossal, digestion-defying pancakes the size of hockey pucks, they were each a meal in themselves. "Just the way I like them," my husband would tell me as he wolfed yet another one.

12   I never learned to make my mother's latkes. She died just before my husband and I were married, and when we came to Washington we brought my mother-in-law with us, so her potato latkes won by default and became part of our children's Chanukah tradition. Which is not to say I ever accepted them graciously, and as we moved into our middle years, and cholesterol moved into our lexicon, my husband, too, scorned the latkes of his childhood. "The Israeli secret weapon," he called them when his mother wasn't listening. "Eat two, and you're on sick call for at least a week."

13   But friends came each Chanukah and brought their children to celebrate with ours. We exchanged small gifts: boxes of crayons, pretty bars of soap, cellophane bags of sour candies for Grandma, who, of course, supplied the latkes. Early in the afternoon, she would begin grating potatoes on a vicious four-sided grater, the invention of some fiendish anti-Semite who must have seen the opportunity to maim half the Jewish population each December.

14   The trick was to finish grating just before the guests arrived so the potatoes would not blacken, as they have a discouraging tendency to do. Meanwhile, as she mixed in eggs, matzo meal, salt, and baking powder, Grandma heated a frying pan with enough oil to light the Chanukah lamps into the next century. The finished latkes were drained on supermarket paper bags that promptly turned translucent with fat. Still, we ate them: great, golden, greasy, dolloped-with-sour-cream latkes, and our complaints became part of our Chanukah tradition, too.

15   The Venetian latkes didn't taste very much like Grandma's, but there was enough resemblance to quell our homesickness. Well, that was a

while ago. Today, though November leaves, red and brown and gold, still hang on stubbornly, the Christmas drumming has already begun. My morning's *Washington Post* bursts with ads like a ripe pomegranate spewing seeds. Overnight, green wreaths have sprouted on our neighbors' doors, and the Salvation Army kettle, come out of storage, stands on its tripod in front of the Giant food store once again. I remember how little I cared for this time. For a moment, the buried stones of jealousy and of shame and not belonging work themselves to the surface with a speed that surprises me.

16   But this year something is different, suddenly, finally, *I* am the grandma who makes the latkes. Two little grandchildren, both named for my mother-in-law (may she rest in peace), will come to our house to watch us light the menorah. Baby Helen at two and a half can already say the Hebrew blessing over the candles, and if my joy in that could translate to Chanukah gelt, all the banks in America would be forced to close.

17   I close my eyes and think of Grandma tasting a bit of her childhood each Chanukah when she prepared the latkes as her mother had made them before her. My mother, my aunts, my own grandmothers float back to me, young and vibrant once more, making days holy in the sanctuaries of their kitchens, feeding me, cradling me, connecting me to the intricately plaited braid of their past, and even at this moment, looking down the corridor of what's to come, I see myself join them as they open their arms wide to enfold my children and grandchildren in their embrace.

Questions for Discussion

1. What made Christmas "a miserable time for Jewish children" in the 30s and 40s? Why would "Keep a Low Profile" be appropriate for them?

2. What is the significance of Chanukah? What does it celebrate? Why does Moskowitz refer to it as a "minor-league festival"?

3. Explain why Moskowitz and her husband might find it easier to leave the country at Christmas.

4. What particular traditions and rituals associated with Chanukah does the speaker remember fondly, even after seeking escape from them?

5. What effect do all the sales pitches associated with Christmas have on the speaker's celebration of Chanukah?

6. Define the following words: creche, advent, gelt, latke, menorah, and dreidels. What is the significance of the discussion of potato latkes?

7. List some characteristics of typical Jewish humor. How does Moskowitz's Jewish humor enrich her short memoir?

Suggestions for Exploring, Writing, and Persuading

1. If you are Jewish and living or working in a non-Jewish community, write an expository essay about your Christmas experiences and Chanukah.

2. Moskowitz says that her female ancestors through her memories "[connect her] to the intricately plaited braid of their past. . . . " Write an essay explaining how some of your memories have braided you to your past.

3. In an essay, argue that traditional religious festivals such as Christmas and Chanukah are or are not threatened by their commercialization and secularization.

4. Write a documented essay on the "pograms" in Europe and their effects on Jewish people during the first half of the twentieth century.

Frances Mayes (b. 1940)

A native of Fitzgerald, Georgia, Frances Mayes is a gourmet cook and the author of numerous articles on food and cooking as well as five books of poetry. Mayes became famous nationwide with the publication of Under the Tuscan Sun *(1996) which, along with the later volume,* Bella Tuscany *(1999), celebrates with passion and gusto not only the centuries-old villa Mayes bought near Cortona, Italy, but also the centuries-old traditions and culture of the surrounding Tuscan hill country. In 2003, a film version of* Under the Tuscan Sun *staring Diane Lane featured a fictionalized version of Mayes' book. Formerly chair of the creative writing program at San Francisco State University, Mayes recently retired to devote full time to writing. With her second husband, Ed Kleinschmidt, who adopted her name when they married, Mayes lives alternately in San Francisco and in her villa near Cortona.*

BRAMARE: (ARCHAIC) TO YEARN FOR   (1996)

1   I am about to buy a house in a foreign country. A house with the beautiful name of Bramasole. It is tall, square, and apricot-colored with faded green shutters, ancient tile roof, and an iron balcony on the second level, where ladies might have sat with their fans to watch some spectacle below. But below, overgrown briars, tangles of roses, and knee-high weeds run rampant. The balcony faces southeast, looking into a deep valley, then into the Tuscan Apennines. When it rains or when the light changes, the facade of the house turns gold, sienna, ocher; a previous scarlet paint job seeps through in rosy spots like a box of crayons left to melt in the sun. In places where the stucco has fallen away, rugged stone shows what the exterior once was. The house rises above a *strada bianca*, a road white with pebbles, on a terraced slab of hillside covered with fruit and olive trees. Bramasole: from *bramare*, to yearn for, and *sole*, sun: something that yearns for the sun, and yes, I do.

2   The family wisdom runs strongly against this decision. My mother has said "Ridiculous," with her certain and forceful stress on the second

syllable, "RiDICulous," and my sisters, although excited, fear I am eighteen, about to run off with a sailor in the family car. I quietly have my own doubts. The upright seats in the *notaio*'s outer office don't help. Through my thin white linen dress, spiky horsehairs pierce me every time I shift, which is often in the hundred-degree waiting room. I look over to see what Ed is writing on the back of a receipt: Parmesan, salami, coffee, bread. How can he? Finally, the signora opens her door and her torrential Italian flows over us.

3   The *notaio* is nothing like a notary; she's the legal person who conducts real-estate transactions in Italy. Ours, Signora Mantucci, is a small, fierce Sicilian woman with thick tinted glasses that enlarge her green eyes. She talks faster than any human I have ever heard. She reads long laws aloud. I thought all Italian was mellifluous; she makes it sound like rocks crashing down a chute. Ed looks at her raptly; I know he's in thrall to the sound of her voice. The owner, Dr. Carta, suddenly thinks he has asked too little; he *must* have, since we have agreed to buy it. We think his price is exorbitant. We *know* his price is exorbitant. The Sicilian doesn't pause; she will not be interrupted by anyone except by Giuseppe from the bar downstairs, who suddenly swings open the dark doors, tray aloft, and seems surprised to see his *Americani* customers sitting there almost cross-eyed in confusion. He brings the signora her midmorning thimble of espresso, which she downs in a gulp, hardly pausing. The owner expects to claim that the house cost one amount while it really cost much more. "That is just the way it's done," he insists. "No one is fool enough to declare the real value." He proposes we bring one check to the *notaio*'s office, then pass him ten smaller checks literally under the table.

4   Anselmo Martini, our agent, shrugs.

5   Ian, the English estate agent we hired to help with translation, shrugs also.

6   Dr. Carta concludes, "You Americans! You take things so seriously. And, *per favore*, date the checks at one-week intervals so the bank isn't alerted to large sums."

7   Was that the same bank I know, whose sloe-eyed teller languidly conducts a transaction every fifteen minutes, between smokes and telephone calls? The signora comes to an abrupt halt, scrambles the papers into a folder and stands up. We are to come back when the money and papers are ready.

8   A window in our hotel room opens onto an expansive view over the ancient roofs of Cortona, down to the dark expanse of the Val di Chiana. A hot and wild wind—the *scirocco*—is driving normal people a little crazy. For me, it seems to reflect my state of mind. I can't sleep. In the United States, I've bought and sold a few houses before—loaded up the car with my mother's Spode, the cat, and the ficus for the five- or five-thousand-mile drive to the next doorway where a new key would fit. You *have* to churn somewhat when the roof covering your head is at stake,

since to sell is to walk away from a cluster of memories and to buy is to choose where the future will take place. And the place, never neutral of course, will cast its influence. Beyond that, legal complications and contingencies must be worked out. But here, absolutely everything conspires to keep me staring into the dark.

9   Italy always has had a magnetic north pull on my psyche. Houses have been on my mind for four summers of renting farmhouses all over Tuscany. In the first place Ed and I rented with friends, we started calculating on the first night, trying to figure out if our four pooled savings would buy the tumbled stone farm we could see from the terrace. Ed immediately fell for farm life and roamed over our neighbors' land looking at the work in progress. The Antolinis grew tobacco, a beautiful if hated crop. We could hear workers shout *"Vipera!"* to warn the others of a poisonous snake. At evening, a violet blue haze rose from the dark leaves. The well-ordered farm looked peaceful from the vantage point of our terrace. Our friends never came back, but for the next three vacations, the circuitous search for a summer home became a quest for us—whether we ever found a place or not, we were happening on places that made pure green olive oil, discovering sweet country Romanesque churches in villages, meandering the back roads of vineyards, and stopping to taste the softest Brunello and the blackest Vino Nobile. Looking for a house gives an intense focus. We visited weekly markets not just with the purchase of picnic peaches in mind; we looked carefully at all the produce's quality and variety, mentally forecasting birthday dinners, new holidays, and breakfasts for weekend guests. We spent hours sitting in piazzas or sipping lemonade in local bars, secretly getting a sense of the place's ambiance. I soaked many a heel blister in a hotel bidet, rubbed bottles of lotion on my feet, which had covered miles of stony streets. We hauled histories and guides and wildflower books and novels in and out of rented houses and hotels. Always we asked local people where they liked to eat and headed to restaurants our many guidebooks never mentioned. We both have an insatiable curiosity about each jagged castle ruin on the hillsides. My idea of heaven still is to drive the gravel farm roads of Umbria and Tuscany, very pleasantly lost.

10   Cortona was the first town we ever stayed in and we always came back to it during the summers we rented near Volterra, Florence, Montisi, Rignano, Vicchio, Quercegrossa, all those fascinating, quirky houses. One had a kitchen two people could not pass in, but there was a slice of a view of the Arno. Another kitchen had no hot water and no knives, but the house was built into medieval ramparts overlooking vineyards. One had several sets of china for forty, countless glasses and silverware, but the refrigerator iced over every day and by four the door swung open, revealing a new igloo. When the weather was damp, I got a tingling shock if I touched anything in the kitchen. On the property, Cimabue, legend says, discovered the young Giotto drawing a sheep in the dirt. One house had beds with back-crunching dips in the middles. Bats flew down the

chimney and buzzed us, while worms in the beams sent down a steady sifting of sawdust onto the pillows. The fireplace was so big we could sit in it while grilling our veal chops and peppers.

11   We drove hundreds of dusty miles looking at houses that turned out to be in the flood plain of the Tiber or overlooking strip mines. The Siena agent blithely promised that the view would be wonderful again in twenty years; replanting stripped areas was a law. A glorious medieval village house was wildly expensive. The saw-toothed peasant we met in a bar tried to sell us his childhood home, a windowless stone chicken house joined to another house, with snarling dogs lunging at us from their ropes. We fell hard for a farm outside Montisi; the *contessa* who owned it led us on for days, then decided she needed a sign from God before she could sell it. We had to leave before the sign arrived.

12   As I think back over those places, they suddenly seem preposterously alien and Cortona does, too. Ed doesn't think so. He's in the piazza every afternoon, gazing at the young couple trying to wheel their new baby down the street. They're halted every few steps. Everyone circles the carriage. They're leaning into the baby's face, making noises, praising the baby. "In my next life," Ed tells me, "I want to come back as an Italian baby." He steeps in the piazza life: the sultry and buffed man pushing up his sleeve so his muscles show when he languidly props his chin in his hand; the pure flute notes of Vivaldi drifting from an upstairs window; the flower seller's fan of bright flowers against the stone shop; a man with no neck at all unloading lambs from his truck. He slings them like flour sacks over his shoulder and the lambs' eyeballs bulge out. Every few minutes, Ed looks up at the big clock that has kept time for so long over this piazza. Finally, he takes a stroll, memorizing the stones in the street.

13   Across the hotel courtyard a visiting Arab chants his prayers toward dawn, just when I finally can fall asleep. He sounds as though he is gargling with salt water. For hours, he rings the voice's changes over a small register, over and over. I want to lean out and shout, "Shut up!" Now and then I have to laugh. I look out, see him nodding in the window, a sweet smile on his face. He reminds me so much of tobacco auctioneers I heard in hot warehouses in the South as a child. I am seven thousand miles from home, plunking down my life savings on a whim. Is it a whim? It feels very close to falling in love and that's never really whimsical but comes from some deep source. Or does it?

14   Each time we step out of the cool, high rooms of the hotel and into the sharp-edged sun, we walk around town and like it more and more. The outdoor tables at Bar Sport face the Piazza Signorelli. A few farmers sell produce on the steps of the nineteenth-century *teatro* every morning. As we drink espresso, we watch them holding up rusty hand scales to weigh the tomatoes. The rest of the piazza is lined with perfectly intact medieval or Renaissance *palazzi*. Easily, someone might step out any second and break into *La Traviata*. Every day we visit each keystoned medieval gate

in the Etruscan walls, explore the Fiat-wide stone streets lined with Renaissance and older houses and the even narrower *vicoli*, mysterious pedestrian passageways, often steeply stepped. The bricked-up fourteenth-century "doors of the dead" are still visible. These ghosts of doors beside the main entrance were designed, some say, to take out the plague victims—bad luck for them to exit by the main entrance. I notice in the regular doors, people often leave their keys in the lock.

15   Guidebooks describe Cortona as "somber" and "austere." They misjudge. The hilltop position, the walls and upright, massive stone buildings give a distinctly vertical feel to the architecture. Walking across the piazza, I feel the abrupt, angular shadows fall with Euclidean purity. I want to stand up straight—the upright posture of the buildings seems to carry over to the inhabitants. They walk slowly, with very fine, I want to say, *carriage*. I keep saying, "Isn't she beautiful?" "Isn't he gorgeous?" "Look at *that* face—pure Raphael." By late afternoon, we're sitting again with our espressi, this time facing the other piazza. A woman of about sixty with her daughter and the teenage granddaughter pass by us, strolling, their arms linked, sun on their vibrant faces. We don't know why light has such a luminous quality. Perhaps the sunflower crops radiate gold from the surrounding fields. The three women look peaceful, proud, impressively pleased. There should be a gold coin with their faces on it.

16   Meanwhile, as we sip, the dollar is falling fast. We rouse ourselves from the piazza every morning to run around to all the banks, checking their posted exchange rates. When you're cashing traveler's checks for a last-minute spree at the leather market, the rate doesn't matter that much, but this is a house with five acres and every lira counts. A slight drop at those multiples makes the stomach drop also. Every hundred lire it falls, we calculate how much more expensive the house becomes. Irrationally, I also calculate how many pairs of shoes that could buy. Shoes, before, have been my major purchase in Italy, a secret sin. Sometimes I'd go home with nine new pairs: red snake-skin flats, sandals, navy suede boots, and several pairs of black pumps of varying heels.

17   Typically, the banks vary in how much commission they bite when they receive a large transfer from overseas. We want a break. It looks like a significant chunk of interest they'll collect, since clearing a check in Italy can take weeks.

18   Finally, we have a lesson in the way things work. Dr. Carta, anxious to close, calls his bank—the bank his father and his father-in-law use—in Arezzo, a half hour away. Then he calls us. "Go there," he says. "They won't take a commission for receiving the money at all, and they'll give you whatever the posted rate is when it arrives."

19   His savvy doesn't surprise me, though he has seemed spectacularly uninterested in money the entire time we have negotiated—just named his high price and stuck to it. He bought the property from the five old sisters of an landowning family in Perugia the year before, thinking, he said, to make it a summer place for his family. However, he and his wife

inherited property on the coast and decided to use that instead. Was that the case, or had he scooped up a bargain from ladies in their nineties and now is making a bundle, possibly buying coast property with our money? Not that I begrudge him. He's smart.

20   Dr. Carta, perhaps fearing we might back out, calls and asks to meet us at the house. He roars up in his Alfa 164, Armani from stem to stern. "There is something more," he says, as though continuing a conversation. "If you follow me, I will show you something." A few hundred feet down the road, he leads us up a stone path through fragrant yellow broom. Odd, the stone path continues up the hill, curving along a ridge. Soon we come to a two-hundred-degree view of the valley, with the cypress-lined road below us and a mellow landscape dotted with tended vineyards and olive groves. In the distance lies a blue daub, which is Lake Trasimeno; off to the right, we see the red-roofed silhouette of Cortona cleanly outlined against the sky, Dr. Carta turns to us triumphantly. The flat paving stones widen here. "The Romans—this road was built by the Romans—it goes straight into Cortona." The sun is broiling. He goes on and on about the large church at the top of the hill. He points out where the rest of the road might have run, right through Bramasole's property.

21   Back at the house he turns on an outside faucet and splashes his face. "You'll enjoy the finest water, truly your own abundant *acqua minerale*, excellent for the liver. *Eccellente!*" He manages to be at once enthusiastic and a little bored, friendly and slightly condescending. I am afraid we have spoken too bluntly about money. Or maybe he has interpreted our law-abiding American expectations about the transaction as incredibly naive. He lets the faucet run, cupping his hand under the water, somehow leaning over for a drink without dislodging the well-cut linen coat tossed over his shoulders. "Enough water for a swimming pool," he insists, "which would be perfect out on the point where you can see the lake, overlooking right where Hannibal defeated the Romans."

22   We're dazzled by the remains of a Roman road over the hill covered with wildflowers. We will follow the stone road into town for a coffee late in the afternoons. He shows us the old cistern. Water is precious in Tuscany and was collected drop by drop. By shining a flashlight into the opening, we've already noticed that the underground cistern has a stone archway, obviously some kind of passageway. Up the hill in the Medici fortress, we saw the same arch in the cistern there and the caretaker told us that a secret underground escape route goes downhill to the valley, then to Lake Trasimeno. Italians take such remains casually. That one is allowed to own such ancient things seems impossible to me.

23   When I first saw Bramasole, I immediately wanted to hang my summer clothes in an *armadio* and arrange my books under one of those windows looking out over the valley. We'd spent four days with Signor Martini, who had a dark little office on Via Sacco e Vanzetti down in the lower town. Above his desk hung a photo of him as a soldier, I assumed

for Mussolini. He listened to us as though we spoke perfect Italian. When we finished describing what we thought we wanted, he rose, put on his Borsolino, and said one word, *"Andiamo,"* let's go. Although he'd recently had a foot operation, he drove us over nonexistent roads and pushed through jungles of thorns to show us places only he knew about. Some were farmhouses with roofs collapsed onto the floor, miles from town and costing the earth. One had a tower built by the Crusaders, but the *contessa* who owned it cried and doubled the price on the spot when she saw that we really were interested. Another was attached to other farmhouses where chickens were truly free range—they ran in and out of the houses. The yard was full of rusted farm equipment and hogs. Several felt airless or sat hard by the road. One would have required putting in a road—it was hidden in blackberry brambles and we could only peer in one window because a coiled black snake refused to budge from the threshold.

24   We took Signor Martini flowers, thanked him and said goodbye. He seemed genuinely sorry to see us go.

25   The next morning we ran into him in the piazza after coffee. He said, "I just saw a doctor from Arezzo. He might be interested in selling a house. *Una bella villa,*" he added emphatically. The house was within walking distance of Cortona.

26   "How much?" we asked, although we knew by then he cringes at being asked that direct question.

27   "Let's just go take a look," was all he said. Out of Cortona, he took the road that climbs and winds to the other side of the hill. He turned onto the *strada bianca* and, after a couple of kilometers, pulled into a long, sloping driveway. I caught a glimpse of a shrine, then looked up at the three-story house with a curly iron fanlight above the front door and two tall, exotic palm trees on either side. On that fresh morning, the facade seemed radiant, glazed with layers of lemon, rouge, and terra-cotta. We both became silent as we got out of the car. After all the turns into unknown roads, the house seemed just to have been waiting all along.

28   "Perfect, we'll take it," I joked as we stepped through the weeds. Just as he had at other houses, Signor Martini made no sales pitch; he simply looked with us. We walked up to the house under a rusted pergola leaning under the weight of climbing roses. The double front door squawked like something alive when we pushed it open. The house's walls, thick as my arm is long, radiated coolness. The glass in the windows wavered. I scuffed through silty dust and saw below it smooth brick floors in perfect condition. In each room, Ed opened the inside window and pushed open the shutters to one glorious view after another of cypresses, rippling green hills, distant villas, a valley. There were even two bathrooms that functioned. They were not beautiful, but *bathrooms*, after all the houses we'd seen with no floors, much less plumbing. No one had lived there in thirty years and the grounds seemed like an enchanted garden, overgrown and tumbling with blackberries and vines. I could see Signor

Martini regarding the grounds with a countryman's practiced eye. Ivy twisted into the trees and ran over fallen terrace walls. *"Molto lavoro,"* much work, was all he said.

29   During several years of looking, sometimes casually, sometimes to the point of exhaustion, I never heard a house say *yes* so completely. However, we were leaving the next day, and when we learned the price, we sadly said no and went home.

30   During the next months, I mentioned Bramasole now and then. I stuck a photo on my mirror and often wandered the grounds or rooms in my mind. The house is a metaphor for the self, of course, but it also is totally real. And a *foreign* house exaggerates all the associations houses carry. Because I had ended a long marriage that was not supposed to end and was establishing a new relationship, this house quest felt tied to whatever new identity I would manage to forge. When the flying fur from the divorce settled, I had found myself with a grown daughter, a full-time university job (after years of part-time teaching), a modest securities portfolio, and an entire future to invent. Although divorce was harder than a death, still I felt oddly returned to myself after many years in a close family. I had the urge to examine my life in another culture and move beyond what I knew. I wanted something of a *physical* dimension that would occupy the mental volume the years of my former life had. Ed shares my passion for Italy completely and also shares the boon of three-month summer breaks from university teaching. There we would have long days for exploring and for our writing and research projects. When he is at the wheel, he'll *always* take the turn down the intriguing little road. The language, history, art, places in Italy are endless—two lifetimes wouldn't be enough. And, ah, the foreign self. The new life might shape itself to the contours of the house, which already is at home in the landscape, and to the rhythms around it.

31   In the spring, I called a California woman who was starting a real-estate development business in Tuscany. I asked her to check on Bramasole; perhaps if it had not sold, the price had come down. A week later, she called from a bar after meeting with the owner. "Yes, it's still for sale, but with that particular brand of Italian logic, the price has been raised. The dollar," she reminded me, "has fallen. And that house needs a lot of work."

32   Now we've returned. By this time, with equally peculiar logic, I've become fixed on buying Bramasole. After all, the only thing wrong is the expense. We both love the setting, the town, the house and land. If only one little thing is wrong, I tell myself, go ahead.

33   Still, this costs a *sacco di soldi*. It will be an enormous hassle to recover the house and land from neglect. Leaks, mold, tumbling stone terraces, crumbling plaster, one funky bathroom, another with an adorable metal hip bathtub and a cracked toilet.

34   Why does the prospect seem fun, when I found remodeling my kitchen in San Francisco a deep shock to my equilibrium? At home, we can't even

hang a picture without knocking out a fistful of plaster. When we plunge the stopped-up sink, forgetting once again that the disposal doesn't like artichoke petals, sludge seems to rise from San Francisco Bay.

35   On the other hand, a dignified house near a Roman road, an Etruscan (Etruscan!) wall looming at the top of the hillside, a Medici fortress in sight, a view toward Monte Amiata, a passageway underground, one hundred and seventeen olive trees, twenty plums, and still uncounted apricot, almond, apple, and pear trees. Several figs seem to thrive near the well. Beside the front steps there's a large hazelnut. Then, proximity to one of the most superb towns I've ever seen. Wouldn't we be crazy not to buy this lovely house called Bramasole?

36   What if one of us is hit by a potato chip truck and can't work? I run through a litany of diseases we could get. An aunt died of a heart attack at forty-two, my grandmother went blind, all the ugly illnesses. . . . What if an earthquake shakes down the universities where we teach? The Humanities Building is on a list of state structures most likely to fall in a moderately severe quake. What if the stock market spirals down?

37   I leap out of bed at three A.M. and step in the shower, letting my whole face take the cold water. Coming back to bed in the dark, feeling my way, I jam my toe on the iron bed frame. Pain jags all the way up my backbone. "Ed, wake up. I think I've broken my toe. How can you sleep?"

38   He sits up. "I was just dreaming of cutting herbs in the garden. Sage and lemon balm. Sage is *salvia* in Italian." He has never wavered from his belief that this is a brilliant idea, that this is heaven on earth. He clicks on the bedside lamp. He's smiling.

39   My half-on toenail is hanging half off, ugly purple spreading underneath. I can't bear to leave it or to pull it off. "I want to go home," I say.

40   He puts a Band-Aid around my toe. "You mean Bramasole, don't you?" he asks.

41   This sack of money in question has been wired from California but has not arrived. How can that be, I ask at the bank, money is wired, it arrives instantaneously. More shrugs. Perhaps the main bank in Florence is holding it. Days pass. I call Steve, my broker in California, from a bar. I'm shouting over the noise of a soccer match on the TV. "You'll have to check from that end;" he shouts back, "it's long gone from here and did you know the government there has changed forty-seven times since World War II? This money was well invested in tax-free bonds and the best growth funds. Those Australian bonds of yours earned seventeen percent. Oh well, *la dolce vita*."

42   The mosquitoes (*zanzare* they're called, just like they sound) invade the hotel with the desert wind. I spin in the sheets until my skin burns. I get up in the middle of the night and lean out the shuttered window, imagining all the sleeping guests, blisters on their feet from the stony streets, their guidebooks still in their hands. We could still back out. Just throw our bags in the rented Fiat and say *arrivederci*. Go hang out on the

Amalfi coast for a month and head home, tanned and relaxed. Buy lots of sandals. I can hear my grandfather when I was twenty: "Be realistic. Come down out of the clouds." He was furious that I was studying poetry and Latin etymology, something utterly useless. Now, what am I thinking of? Buying an abandoned house in a place where I hardly can speak the language. He probably has worn out his shroud turning over in his grave. We don't have a mountain of reserves to bale us out in case that mysterious something goes wrong.

43   What is this thrall for houses? I come from a long line of women who open their handbags and take out swatches of upholstery material, colored squares of bathroom tile, seven shades of yellow paint samples, and strips of flowered wallpaper. We love the concept of four walls. "What is her house like?" my sister asks, and we both know she means what is *she* like. I pick up the free real-estate guide outside the grocery store when I go somewhere for the weekend, even if it's close to home. One June, two friends and I rented a house on Majorca; another summer I stayed in a little *casa* in San Miguel de Allende in which I developed a serious love for fountained courtyards and bedrooms with bougainvillea cascading down the balcony, the austere Sierra Madre. One summer in Santa Fe, I started looking at adobes there, imagining I would become a Southwesterner, cook with chilies, wear squash blossom turquoise jewelry—a different life, the chance to be extant in another version. At the end of a month I left and never have wanted to return.

44   I love the islands off the Georgia coast, where I spent summers when I was growing up. Why not a weathered gray house there, made of wood that looks as though it washed up on the beach? Cotton rugs, peach iced tea, a watermelon cooling in the creek, sleeping with waves churning and rolling outside the window. A place where my sisters, friends, and their families could visit easily. But I keep remembering that anytime I've stepped in my own footprints again, I haven't felt renewed. Though I'm susceptible to the pull to the known, I'm just slightly more susceptible to surprise. Italy seems endlessly alluring to me—why not, at this point, consider the opening of *The Divine Comedy:* What must one do in order to grow? Better to remember my father, the son of my very literal-minded, penny-pinching grandfather. "The family motto," he'd say, "is 'Packing and Unpacking.'" And also, "If you can't go first class, don't go at all."

45   Lying awake, I feel the familiar sense of The Answer arriving. Like answers on the bottom of the black fortune-telling eight ball that I loved when I was ten, often I can feel an idea or the solution to a dilemma floating up through murky liquid, then it is as if I see the suddenly clear white writing. I like the charged zone of waiting, a mental and physical sensation of the bends as something mysterious zigzags to the surface of consciousness.

46   What if you did *not* feel uncertainty, the white writing says. Are you exempt from doubt? Why not rename it excitement? I lean over the wide

sill just as the first gilded mauve light of sunrise begins. The Arab is still sleeping. The undulant landscape looks serene in every direction. Honey-colored farmhouses, gently placed in hollows, rise like thick loaves of bread set out to cool. I know some Jurassic upheaval violently tossed up the hills, but they appear rounded as though by a big hand. As the sun brightens, the land spreads out a soft spectrum: the green of a dollar bill gone through the wash, old cream, blue sky like a blind person's eye. The Renaissance painters had it just right. I never thought of Perugino, Giotto, Signorelli, et al., as realists, but their background views are still here, as most tourists discover, with dark cypress trees brushed in to emphasize each composition the eye falls on. Now I see why the red boot on a gold and blond angel in the Cortona museum has such a glow, why the Madonna's cobalt dress looks intense and deep. Against this landscape and light, everything takes on a primary outline. Even a red towel drying on a line below becomes totally saturated with its own redness.

47   Think: What if the sky doesn't fall? What if it's glorious? What if the house is transformed in three years? There will be by then hand-printed labels for the house's olive oil, thin linen curtains pulled across the shutters for siesta, jars of plum jam on the shelves, a long table for feasts under the linden trees, baskets piled by the door for picking tomatoes, arugula, wild fennel, roses, and rosemary. And who are we in that strange new life?

48   Finally the money arrives, the account is open. However, they have no checks. This enormous bank, the seat of dozens of branches in the gold center of Italy, has no checks to give us. "Maybe next week," Signora Raguzzi explains. "Right now, nothing." We sputter. Two days later, she calls. "I have ten checks for you." What is the big deal with checks? I get boxes of them at home. Signora Raguzzi parcels them out to us. Signora Raguzzi in tight skirt, tight T-shirt, has lips that are perpetually wet and pouting. Her skin glistens. She is astonishingly gorgeous. She wears a magnificent square gold necklace and bracelets on both wrists that jangle as she stamps our account number on each check.

47   "What great jewelry. I love those bracelets," I say.

50   "All we have here is gold," she replies glumly. She is bored with Arezzo's tombs and piazzas. California sounds good to her. She brightens every time she sees us. "Ah, California," she says as greeting. The bank begins to seem surreal. We're in the back room. A man wheels in a cart stacked with gold ingots—actual small bricks of gold. No one seems to be on guard. Another man loads two into dingy manila folders. He's plainly dressed, like a workman. He walks out into the street, taking the ingots somewhere. So much for Brinks delivery—but what a clever plain-clothes disguise. We turn back to the checks. There will be no insignia of boats or palm trees or pony express riders, there will be no name, address, driver's license, Social Security number. Only these pale green checks that look as though they were printed in the twenties. We're enormously pleased. That's close to citizenship—a bank account.

51   Finally we are gathered in the *notaio*'s office for the final reckoning. It's quick. Everyone talks at once and no one listens. The baroque legal terms leave us way behind. A jackhammer outside drills into my brain cells. There's something about two oxen and two days. Ian, who's translating, stops to explain this archaic spiral of language as an eighteenth-century legal description of the amount of land, measured by how long it would take two oxen to plow it. We have, it seems, two plowing days worth of property.

52   I write checks, my fingers cramping over all the times I write *milione*. I think of all the nice dependable bonds and utility stocks and blue chips from the years of my marriage magically turning into a terraced hillside and a big empty house. The glass house in California where I lived for a decade, surrounded by kumquat, lemon, mock orange, and guava, its bright pool and covered patio with wicker and flowered cushions—all seem to recede, as though seen through the long focus in binoculars. *Million* is such a big word in English it's hard to treat it casually. Ed carefully monitors the zeros, not wanting me to unwittingly write *miliardo*, billion, instead. He pays Signor Martini in cash. He never has mentioned a fee; we have found out the normal percentage from the owner. Signor Martini seems pleased, as though we've given him a gift. For me this is a confusing but delightful way to conduct business. Handshakes all around. Is that a little cat smile on the mouth of the owner's wife? We're expecting a parchment deed, lettered in ancient script, but no, the *notaio* is going on vacation and she'll try to get to the paperwork before she leaves. *"Normale,"* Signor Martini says. I've noticed all along that someone's word is still taken for that. Endless contracts and stipulations and contingencies simply have not come up. We walk out into the brutally hot afternoon with nothing but two heavy iron keys longer than my hand, one to a rusted iron gate, the other to the front door. They look nothing like the keys to anything I've ever owned. There is no hope for spare copies.

53   Giuseppe waves from the door of the bar and we tell him we have bought a house. "Where is it?" he wants to know.

54   "Bramasole," Ed begins, about to say where it is.

55   "Ah, Bramasole, *una bella villa!*" He has picked cherries there as a boy. Although it is only afternoon, he pulls us in and pours a *grappa* for us. "Mama!" he shouts. His mother and her sister come in from the back and everyone toasts us. They're all talking at once, speaking of us as the *stranieri*, foreigners. The *grappa* is blindingly strong. We drink ours as fast as Signora Mantucci nips her espresso and wander out in the sun. The car is as hot as a pizza oven. We sit there with the doors open, suddenly laughing and laughing.

56   We'd arranged for two women to clean and for a bed to be delivered while we signed the final papers. In town we picked up a bottle of cold

prosecco, then stopped at the *rosticceria* for marinated zucchini, olives, roast chicken, and potatoes.

57   We arrive at the house dazed by the events and the *grappa*. Anna and Lucia have washed the windows and exorcised layers of dust, as well as many spiders' webs. The second-floor bedroom that opens onto a brick terrace gleams. They've made the bed with the new blue sheets and left the terrace door open to the sound of cuckoos and wild canaries in the linden trees. We pick the last of the pink roses on the front terrace and fill two old Chianti bottles with them. The shuttered room with its white-washed walls, just-waxed floors, pristine bed with new sheets, and sweet roses on the windowsill, all lit with a dangling forty-watt bulb, seems as pure as a Franciscan cell. As soon as I walk in, I think it is the most perfect room in the world.

58   We shower and dress in fresh clothes. In the quiet twilight, we sit on the stone wall of the terrace and toast each other and the house with tumblers of the spicy *prosecco*, which seems like a liquid form of the air. We toast the cypress trees along the road and the white horse in the neighbor's field, the villa in the distance that was built for the visit of a pope. The olive pits we toss over the wall, hoping they will spring from the ground next year. Dinner is delicious. As the darkness comes, a barn owl flies over so close that we hear the whir of wings and, when it settles in the black locust, a strange cry that we take for a greeting. The Big Dipper hangs over the house, about to pour on the roof. The constellations pop out, clear as a star chart. When it finally is dark, we see that the Milky Way sweeps right over the house. I forget the stars, living in the ambient light of a city. Here they are, all along, spangling and dense, falling and pulsating. We stare up until our necks ache. The Milky Way looks like a flung bolt of lace unfurling. Ed, because he likes to whisper, leans to my ear. "Still want to go home," he asks, "or can this be home?"

Questions for Discussion

1. What attracts Mayes to the home in Italy? What is her family's opinion of her choice?

2. Mayes says of moving, "to sell is to walk away from a cluster of memories and to buy is to choose where the future will take place." What are your impressions of moving? To what extent is her move affected by her divorce?

3. Explain Mayes's comment that "anytime I've stepped in my own footprints again, I haven't felt renewed."

4. Mayes says, "[T]he circuitous search for a summer house became a quest for us." In what ways is the search for a place to live a kind of quest? What are the goals of such a quest?

5. Although Mayes says little about Ed, their shared interests are apparent. What adjectives would you use to describe their relationship?

6. What difficulties do Mayes and Ed encounter in purchasing and renovating Bramasole? What do these difficulties suggest about methods of conducting business in Italy?

7. Why, in spite of the difficulties and the alien culture, do Mayes and Ed buy Bramasole?

8. How does the author build to the climax of buying Bramasole? What other stylistic techniques does she use throughout the essay?

9. At what point does Mayes decide that Bramasole is "home"?

Suggestions for Exploring, Writing, and Persuading

1. In an essay, apply to yourself Mayes' statement: "The house is a metaphor for the self."

2. Using your own family's various emotions associated with moves made while you were growing up, persuade your audience that multiple moves do or do not necessarily cause stress within families.

3. Discuss in detail the reasons for Mayes' fascination with houses in general and Bramasole in particular, or discuss your own fascination with houses or with one particular house. What part might "an insatiable curiosity" play in her search or your search?

4. Using this essay and Frost's definitions of *home* in "The Death of the Hired Man" in the next unit as a basis for your discussion, define what home means to you.

5. Research the Tuscan area of Italy and write an essay arguing that Mayes' description does or does not portray it accurately.

6. Examine the techniques Mayes uses to make her description vivid and moving. Then write an essay using similar techniques to describe your home environment.

7. After watching the 2003 film *Under the Tuscan Sun*, write an essay comparing one aspect of Mayes' factual account with the fictionalized film version OR argue that the film version does or does not retain the mood and obvious love of this Italian home.

Janisse Ray (b. 1962)

Growing up in a junkyard in Baxley, Georgia, Janisse Ray was reared by fundamentalist parents who, with the family of five, attended an all-black Pentecostal church. After leaving to attend college, she returned several years later to live on a farm with her son. Ray has published several essays in nature magazines, and on Georgia Public Radio, she is a nature commentator. During the 2003–2004 acad-

emic year, she was the John and Renee Grisham Writer in Residence at the University of Mississippi's department of English. Ray published Wild Card Quilt: Taking a Chance on Home *in 2003. Her environment has made her a naturalist who laments the vanishing longleaf pine ecosystem and the rural life that supported this system in middle Georgia. Both of these ideas are colorfully portrayed in* Ecology of a Cracker Childhood (1999), *from which the following chapter is taken.*

NATIVE GENIUS   (1999)

1   Daddy's was an amazing triad of traits—frugality, creativity, and mechanical ingenuity—so that as I grew, our estate grew. Junk bred junk.

2   I know now my father's occupation has an actual title; he is a *bricoleur*, a term given by French anthropologist Claude Levi-Strauss to folk recyclers, people of creativity, vision, and skill who use castaways for purposes other than those originally intended, sometimes for art. Theirs is a native genius—as Joe Graham explains in his paper about *milusos*, meaning thousand uses, of Mexico—that goes beyond simply making do with what one has. Native geniuses are "able to take the materials and technology at hand and solve complex problems."

3   "Let me show you how I get corn off the cob," my father says, inviting me outside. He shows me a sharpened length of metal pipe six inches long, through which he slides the plump ears, their kernels falling into a pail. I'm impressed.

4   "That beats cutting with a knife, looks like," I say.

5   "You bet."

6   Daddy made an arbor for the grapevine behind the shop by welding together truck driveshafts, hollow metal rods that connect engines to tires, like iron logs. He formed a skeletal box out of them, with the grapevine growing inside center, and strung fence wire across the driveshafts for tendrils to catch on, like a net ceiling. From beneath, the arbor was a secret and green room, ranks of leaves so thick only fragments of sunlight passed between their jagged margins, cliffs of vines like walls hanging almost to the ground.

7   We could stand underneath and pick dangling grapes, but our favorite thing to do was hoist off an old car parked nearby, chin up on a driveshaft, and crawl into the leafy joy of wire and vine. There was no falling through. From on top, the arbor was like heaven, high and surrounded by all the ripe grapes you could eat. The grapes were scuppernongs—a domesticated kind of muscadine whose Indian name means "place of the magnolia"—and they'd be all around us, champagne balls about the size of radio knobs hidden among a mass of green vines and leaves. Eating them, sweet rushed against the mouth over and over. Mostly we swallowed juice and pulp, seeds and all, and threw the tough, empty rind at the nearest sibling.

8   Underneath the grapevine the ground was scattered with old leather boots and shoes, warped and twisted with rain and hard sun. That was Grandpa Charlie's idea. Grapevines need a slow fertilizer because they quit bearing if heavily nitrogenized. Shoes, being leather, were rich in nitrogen and since they decomposed gradually according to his theory, the fertilizer would slowly enter the ground beneath the arbor, enriching the vine without overwhelming it. It looked like a shoe dump.

9   When he built guns, Daddy manufactured firing pins out of old Chevrolet push rods and flat gun springs from Ford door-handle springs. The swing set we played on he welded of pipe. He cut glass with nothing more than a table or other flat surface, a bottle of alcohol, and a glass cutter. He fit a Buick piston in a John Deere tractor.

10   "Did it work?" I asked him.

11   "Couldn't sell the tractor without it," he said.

12   He built a pair of indestructible firedogs out of lengths of driveshafts, packed with sand, welded to connecting rods from an old engine. He used flat leaf springs for prising up tile and engineered a nut-removing tool for Uncle Percy out of a lawnmower blade and two or three pieces of flat-iron. When six-lug, fifteen-inch tires were hard to come by and in high demand by farmers, needed on trailers that hauled heavy loads of corn to market, he welded the six-lug centers of common sixteen-inch tires into five-lug fifteens. He could make anything, fix anything.

13   "Genius, sometimes inspired by necessity and encouraged by opportunity, is not satisfied with merely the status quo," writes Graham. "What is clear is that genius, whether it is represented by a Thomas Edison or an Albert Einstein or an Alberto Ramirez, leaves the world a better place."

14   The day my father was taken sick he had gone to a gun show on Jacksonville Beach with an older man he had not known long, a Mr. Paschol, a white-collar regional manager of Goodyear Tires who had befriended Daddy, daily stopping at the junkyard to talk about their common passion for guns. Paschol owned a sackful of old and beautiful pistols. He was in charge of franchises in three states, but his south Georgia business was so lucrative he even took a room in Baxley. One Saturday he invited Daddy to ride to the Jacksonville Beach Gun Show with him— Daddy thought to do a little trading.

15   They parted in the parking arena, leaving their lunches in the car and arranging to rendezvous at the noon hour to eat. Daddy said that after lunch he began to feel unusual sensations. He felt shaky, his insides turning to gelatin, then shakier, as if he operated a noiseless and invisible jackhammer. He couldn't calm down. His heart sped up, beating like a crazed vulture inside his chest. By the time Paschol delivered him to his door, he no longer controlled much of his body, the mind chopped from it the way you'd chop a chicken's neck, leaving the carcass to go dancing off in its manic convolutions of nerve endings. He had begun to hallucinate.

16   The suspicion, of course, is that the episode was caused by drugs, since this occurred in the flowering of the late sixties. The other suspi-

cion raiser is that Paschol, who had visited daily, was never seen or heard from again. Even the sheriff agreed that it was odd. Genetic predisposition was undeniable, but a hit of LSD could've been all that was needed to send Daddy over the edge of a three-year cliff.

17   I don't know how many weeks Mama bore Daddy's sickness, hoping he'd turn back to us as surely as he'd turned away, but in the end she had to give up. I think it was the day he locked Mama and us four children in the back bedroom, which my sister and I shared with a six-foot chest freezer. That day, he wanted us to be quiet, and we were. We sat where he told us to sit. Each of us obeyed him perfectly and immediately, watching wide-eyed as Daddy ranted in what I now know to be mania.

18   I have not wanted to ask my mother how long we were there, all those years ago, but I know it was hours. We began to be hungry and to beg for food, but my father would not allow anyone to leave the room. No matter how rationally my mother spoke, how gently, as if she crooned to a sick lamb, my father said *no*. If we cried, he scared us to a hush. The telephone rang and rang between the empty chairs in the living room.

19   It was as if Daddy knew that he was losing what was most precious to him and wanted to hold on to it. He wanted to gather up this family he loved and lock us away with him, in this mind-gone place he'd been taken. He was no longer in control, but he didn't want to be in that place without this beloved wife and these children he would gladly lay down his life for. Toward evening he permitted Mama to reach into the freezer with her eyes closed and choose one thing for us to eat.

20   "Honey, you know we can't eat raw food out of that freezer. Let me go cook us some supper," she protested.

21   "One thing," he said, "No more no less. I'll hold the lid for you. You have to close your eyes. That's the way God says to feed the children. One thing." Everything Daddy said was a rant, a poem, a list of possibilities, a monologue with the nether world. He was out of his mind.

22   Like my mother, I knew what was in the freezer: hamburger patties she shaped from ground beef and froze, quart bags of blanched field peas, sliced okra, a chicken or two, bags of turnips, stewed tomatoes from Grandmama Beulah's garden. Raw and solid cold.

23   In summer, when peaches are plentiful in Georgia, my mother puts them away for winter. She'll spend all day peeling a bushel, cutting the coral-colored flesh into slices, tossing aside the pits. When she fills a dishpan, she stops and transfers the slices to freezer bags, upright on the counter. She mixes sugar water and pours it over the fresh fruit, making peach-colored bladders, twist-tied. Then she carries them gently to the freezer.

24   When the lid was raised a few inches the day Daddy locked us in the back room, my mother stuck her arm inside. I can still feel on my face the cold vapor that billowed from the white crack. Our eyes watched her as she withdrew a package, brushed away a skift of frost. It was peaches.

25   Looking back, I wonder if Mama had remembered where she'd piled the fruit or if her blind fingers had roamed desperately among the icy

piles, feeling the awful sameness of the bags. Was it utter luck? Later I tried to do what she did, sticking my arm into the freezer, the heavy lid pinching my shoulder, feeling in the burning cold until my fingers stung. When I'd open my eyes, I'd be holding chicken necks or turnip roots.

26   My grandmother, knowing something was awfully wrong, rescued us by calling the sheriff who sent deputies for Daddy. Kay says she remembers them putting a white sheet over his body, even over his face. He stayed overnight at the county jail, and the next day was transported to the state hospital at Milledgeville. Mama was at the jail when he left.

27   She told us that he cried when they left with him. The last thing he said was, "Take care of the children."

28   On the way to Milledgeville, Daddy slipped into a coma from which he did not wake for four days. When he came to, he sat up on a bed in a white room, rubbed color back into his face, and combed his fingers through his wire-grass hair. He was weak, his stomach concave. He lifted weakly to his feet and went slowly to the doorway. A man was sweeping the long corridor. The gentleman paused his push broom.

29   "Sir," Daddy asked, "Can you tell me where I am?"

30   "I sure can," the man replied. "You in Milledgeville."

31   "Milledgeville?"

32   "That's right. The very same."

33   "Does my wife know I'm here?"

34   "I don't know about that, man."

35   An orderly came bustling down the hall in a white coat.

36   "You awake," he declared unnecessarily.

37   "I guess so," Daddy replied.

38   "Good," the man said. "We was wondering when you'd wake."

39   "How long have I been sleeping?"

40   "Four days now. We didn't know if you'd ever wake up."

41   "What day is it?" Daddy asked.

42   "This is Wednesday."

43   By then, the bottom had dropped out of the world. Daddy did not wake up healed but stayed gone. His absence was a steep-sided quarry, filled with marbling water, and there was no climbing out of it.

44   Mama waited, her husband three hours and a thousand light-years away. She found the money to visit Daddy, packing us children into the car along with enough food for the day, hoping the Mustang would not break down and leave us completely at the mercy of strangers. At the state hospital the doctors told her that her husband might never be well, might never be released, and not to expect him ever to return to the family.

45   What faith she had. She was so strong a ship could have been hewn from her body. If it weren't for us children and her powerful mothering instincts, she would have broken, I think. Instead, she kept a vigil of prayer—praying as every pan of biscuits rose in the hot hot oven, praying as she mended a sweater, praying that the chair at the head of the table would again be filled with the man she loved. Every sweep of the

worn broom was a prayer. During our visits, Daddy was his old self for minutes at a time and, as the weeks passed, these minutes expanded until they came together, like warm currents of water in the river, until all of it is summer. And then he was able to come home.

46   Although my grandfather took to wilderness for solace to ease his wracked mind, my father turned to machines, and somewhere, between the two of them, the thread of nature was lost. Fierceness took different forms in them, one savage, one inventive. What was balm for one was terror for the other. Not long ago I asked Daddy why he never fishes or hunts.

47   "Didn't Grandpa ever take you with him?" I queried.

48   "One time," he said, "and that was enough for me never to want to go again."

49   "How old were you?" I asked.

50   "Oh, four, five, six." He lifted his hand and held it for a moment in midair, dropped it.

51   "What happened?"

52   "He took us coon hunting one night," my father told me. "We followed him for hours in the dark. We got tired and hungry and wanted to go home. He made out like we were lost and something might attack and kill us, all such as that. He had us all crying."

53   "He meant to do it?" I asked.

54   "Oh, he got a kick out of it," Daddy said. "He liked to play tricks."

55   And that was that. So much for tradition. So much for a long line of outdoorspeople. So much for the woods. What my grandfather planted in my father was a crazy fear and mistrust of being lost in a wilderness alone. If there ever was a wilderness misunderstood, insanity is it.

56   I think of my own life, how it embraces a great quest to know every cog of nature—the names of oaks and ferns, the secret lives of birds, the taste of venison and Ogeechee lime, wax myrtle's smell and rattlesnake's, the contour of bobcat tracks, the number of barred owl cackles, the feel of Okefenokee Swamp water on my skin under a blistering sun.

57   I search for vital knowledge of the land that my father could not teach me, as he was not taught, and guidance to know and honor it, as he was not guided, as if this will shield me from the errancies of the mind, or bring me back from that dark territory should I happen to wander there. I search as if there were a peace to be found.

Questions for Discussion

1. Explain the double meanings of "Junk bred junk."
2. What is the purpose of Grandpa Charlie's "shoe dump"? How would you describe the relationships among Ray, her mother, her father, and her grandfather?

3. What does Ray mean when she refers to her father as a "native genius"? Explain her reference from Graham: "'. . . genius. . . leaves the world a better place.'"

4. Explain her daddy's fall "over the edge of a three-year cliff" into "a steep-sided quarry, filled with marbling water [where] there was no climbing out of it." Analyze the analogy of the wilderness and insanity as related to Daddy and Grandpa Charlie.

5. What is the relationship between Ray's father's illness, his love of junk, and his skill in using it creatively and Ray's own love of wilderness?

6. Ray concludes her essay by stating, "I search for vital knowledge of the land that my father could not teach me, as he was not taught, and guidance to know and honor it, as he was not guided, as if this will shield me from the errancies of the mind, or bring me back from the dark territory should I happen to wander there. I search as if there were a peace to be found." Explain the implications of her ending.

Suggestions for Exploring, Writing, and Persuading

1. In an essay analyze someone you know who is a "native genius," able to put common "junk" to uncommon uses as Ray's father does. Or analyze someone who can be defined by "'Genius sometimes inspired by necessity and encouraged by opportunity.'"

2. Argue in an essay for or against the notion that common concepts of art or of genius are too narrow and stereotyped.

3. Ray uses colorful language including figures of speech. Make a list of some of her phrases or sentences, and explain how they add to the overall effect of this essay.

FICTION

Luke

Although few facts about the life of Luke are positively known, scholars believe that Luke, "the beloved physician," wrote the New Testament books Luke and Acts. They believe that Luke was a Gentile from Antioch in Syria and that he was a close companion of Paul. Although the exact date is unknown, the book of Luke was probably written between 59 and 80 A.D. The following is from the King James version.

The Parable of the Prodigal Son
Luke 15:11-32

11 And he said, A certain man had two sons:

12 And the younger of them said to *his* father, Father, give me the portion of goods that falleth to *me*. And he divided unto them *his* living.

13 And not many days after the younger son gathered all together, and took his journey into a far country, and there wasted his substance with riotous living.

14 And when he had spent all, there arose a mighty famine in that land; and he began to be in want.

15 And he went and joined himself to a citizen of that country; and he sent him into his fields to feed swine.

16 And he would fain have filled his belly with the husks that the swine did eat: and no man gave unto him.

17 And when he came to himself, he said, How many hired servants of my father's have bread enough and to spare, and I perish with hunger!

18 I will arise and go to my father, and will say unto him, Father, I have sinned against heaven, and before thee.

19 And am no more worthy to be called thy son: make me as one of thy hired servants.

20 And he arose, and came to his father. But when he was yet a great way off, his father saw him, and had compassion, and ran, and fell on his neck, and kissed him.

21 And the son said unto him, Father, I have sinned against heaven, and in thy sight, and am no more worthy to be called thy son.

22 But the father said to his servants, Bring forth the best robe, and put *it* on him; and put a ring on his hand, and shoes on *his* feet:

23 And bring hither the fatted calf, and kill *it;* and let us eat, and be merry:

24 For this my son was dead, and is alive again; he was lost, and is found. And they began to be merry.

25 Now his elder son was in the field: and as he came and drew nigh to the house, he heard musick and dancing.

26 And he called one of the servants, and asked what these things meant.

27 And he said unto him, Thy brother is come; and thy father hath killed the fatted calf, because he hath received him safe and sound.

28 And he was angry, and would not go in: therefore came his father out, and intreated him.

29 And he answering said to *his* father, Lo, these many years do I serve thee, neither transgressed I at any time thy commandment: and yet thou never gavest me a kid, that I might make merry with my friends:

30 But as soon as this thy son was come, which hath devoured thy living with harlots, thou hast killed for him the fatted calf.

31 And he said unto him, Son, thou art ever with me, and all that I have is thine.

32 It was meet that we should make merry, and be glad: for this thy brother was dead, and is alive again; and was lost, and is found.

Questions for Discussion

1. What is a parable? How does this form differ from the form of the modern short story?

2. Why would the son choose to give up the security of home and family for "riotous living" in a "far country"? Is it realistic for him to do so?

3. The father, upon seeing his son's return, prepares a rich feast and gives the returning son the "best robe" and a ring. Is such behavior fair or just? Why does the father greet the wasteful son so warmly? Why is the oldest son so angry? Is his reaction an expected one? Explain.

4. What does the father mean by the following words to the oldest son: "Son, thou art ever with me, and all that I have is thine"?

Suggestions for Exploring, Writing, and Persuading

1. Write an essay examining an act of unconditional love from several points of view.

2. Write an essay discussing a modern-day conflict between two siblings and discuss ways in which they might solve this conflict. For example, one brother might have fought in a war while the other marched for peace, or one sister might support abortion while the other opposes it.

3. Using the format of Luke, write a modern-day parable.

Carson McCullers (1917–1967)

Born in Columbus, Georgia, Carson Smith McCullers is famous for her portrayal of lonely and insecure people. Some of her short stories and novels are described as modern Gothic. Her most famous novels include The Heart Is a Lonely Hunter *(1940),* The Ballad of the Sad Cafe *(1951), and* The Member of the Wedding *(1946), which was made into an award-winning play and into a movie starring Julie Harris and Ethel Waters. McCullers learned about suffering firsthand: her health began to deteriorate because of a misdiagnosis of rheumatic fever while she was still in high school, and her marriage to Reeves McCullers was marked by many separations.*

A Domestic Dilemma   (1951)

1   On Thursday Martin Meadows left the office early enough to make the first express bus home. It was the hour when the evening lilac glow was fading in the slushy streets, but by the time the bus had left the Mid-town terminal the bright city night had come. On Thursdays the maid had a

half-day off and Martin liked to get home as soon as possible, since for the past year his wife had not been—well. This Thursday he was very tired and, hoping that no regular commuter would single him out for conversation, he fastened his attention to the newspaper until the bus had crossed the George Washington Bridge. Once on 9-W Highway Martin always felt that the trip was halfway done, he breathed deeply, even in cold weather when only ribbons of draught cut through the smoky air of the bus, confident that he was breathing country air. It used to be that at this point he would relax and begin to think with pleasure of his home. But in this last year nearness brought only a sense of tension and he did not anticipate the journey's end. This evening Martin kept his face close to the window and watched the barren fields and lonely lights of passing townships. There was a moon, pale on the dark earth and areas of late, porous snow; to Martin the countryside seemed vast and somehow desolate that evening. He took his hat from the rack and put his folded newspaper in the pocket of his overcoat a few minutes before time to pull the cord.

2   The cottage was a block from the bus stop, near the river but not directly on the shore; from the living-room window you could look across the street and opposite yard and see the Hudson. The cottage was modern, almost too white and new on the narrow plot of yard. In summer the grass was soft and bright and Martin carefully tended a flower border and a rose trellis. But during the cold, fallow months the yard was bleak and the cottage seemed naked. Lights were on that evening in all the rooms in the little house and Martin hurried up the front walk. Before the steps he stopped to move a wagon out of the way.

3   The children were in the living room, so intent on play that the opening of the front door was at first unnoticed. Martin stood looking at his safe, lovely children. They had opened the bottom drawer of the secretary and taken out the Christmas decorations. Andy had managed to plug in the Christmas tree lights and the green and red bulbs glowed with out-of-season festivity on the rug of the living room. At the moment he was trying to trail the bright cord over Marianne's rocking horse. Marianne sat on the floor pulling off an angel's wings. The children wailed a startling welcome. Martin swung the fat little baby girl up to his shoulder and Andy threw himself against his father's legs.

4   "Daddy, Daddy, Daddy!"

5   Martin set down the little girl carefully and swung Andy a few times like a pendulum. Then he picked up the Christmas tree cord.

6   "What's all this stuff doing out? Help me put it back in the drawer. You're not to fool with the light socket. Remember I told you that before. I mean it, Andy."

7   The six-year-old child nodded and shut the secretary drawer. Martin stroked his fair soft hair and his hand lingered tenderly on the nape of the child's frail neck.

8   "Had supper yet, Bumpkin?"

9   "It hurt. The toast was hot."

10   The baby girl stumbled on the rug and, after the first surprise of the fall, began to cry; Martin picked her up and carried her in his arms back to the kitchen.

11   "See, Daddy," said Andy. "The toast—"

12   Emily had laid the children's supper on the uncovered porcelain table. There were two plates with the remains of cream-of-wheat and eggs and silver mugs that had held milk. There was also a platter of cinnamon toast, untouched except for one tooth-marked bite. Martin sniffed the bitten piece and nibbled gingerly. Then he put the toast into the garbage pail.

13   "Hoo—phui—What on earth!"

14   Emily had mistaken the tin of cayenne for the cinnamon.

15   "I like to have burnt up," Andy said. "Drank water and ran outdoors and opened my mouth. Marianne didn't eat none."

16   "Any," corrected Martin. He stood helpless, looking around the walls of the kitchen. "Well, that's that, I guess," he said finally. "Where is your mother now?"

17   "She's up in you alls' room."

18   Martin left the children in the kitchen and went up to his wife. Outside the door he waited for a moment to still his anger. He did not knock and once inside the room he closed the door behind him.

19   Emily sat in the rocking chair by the window of the pleasant room. She had been drinking something from a tumbler and as he entered she put the glass hurriedly on the floor behind the chair. In her attitude there was confusion and guilt which she tried to hide by a show of spurious vivacity.

20   "Oh, Marty! You home already? The time slipped up on me. I was just going down—" She lurched to him and her kiss was strong with sherry. When he stood unresponsive she stepped back a pace and giggled nervously.

21   "What's the matter with you? Standing there like a barber pole. Is anything wrong with you?"

22   "Wrong with me?" Martin bent over the rocking chair and picked up the tumbler from the floor. "If you could only realize how sick I am—how bad it is for all of us."

23   Emily spoke in a false, airy voice that had become too familiar to him. Often at such times she affected a slight English accent, copying perhaps some actress she admired. "I haven't the vaguest idea what you mean. Unless you are referring to the glass I used for a spot of sherry. I had a finger of sherry—maybe two. But what is the crime in that, pray tell me? I'm quite all right. Quite all right."

24   "So anyone can see."

25   As she went into the bathroom Emily walked with careful gravity. She turned on the cold water and dashed some on her face with her cupped hands, then patted herself dry with the corner of a bath towel. Her face was delicately featured and young, unblemished.

26   "I was just going down to make dinner." She tottered and balanced herself by holding to the door frame.

27   "I'll take care of dinner. You stay up here. I'll bring it up."

28   "I'll do nothing of the sort. Why, whoever heard of such a thing?"

29   "Please," Martin said.

30   "Leave me alone. I'm quite all right. I was just on the way down—"

31   "Mind what I say."

32   "Mind your grandmother."

33   She lurched toward the door, but Martin caught her by the arm. "I don't want the children to see you in this condition. Be reasonable."

34   "Condition!" Emily jerked her arm. Her voice rose angrily. "Why, because I drink a couple of sherries in the afternoon you're trying to make me out a drunkard. Condition! Why, I don't even touch whiskey. As well you know. I don't swill liquor at bars. And that's more than you can say. I don't even have a cocktail at dinnertime. I only sometimes have a glass of sherry. What, I ask you, is the disgrace of that? Condition!"

35   Martin sought words to calm his wife. "We'll have a quiet supper by ourselves up here. That's a good girl." Emily sat on the side of the bed and he opened the door for a quick departure.

36   "I'll be back in a jiffy."

37   As he busied himself with the dinner downstairs he was lost in the familiar question as to how this problem had come upon his home. He himself had always enjoyed a good drink. When they were still in Alabama they had served long drinks or cocktails as a matter of course. For years they had drunk one or two—possibly three drinks before dinner, and at bedtime a long nightcap. Evenings before holidays they might get a buzz on, might even become a little tight. But alcohol had never seemed a problem to him, only a bothersome expense that with the increase in the family they could scarcely afford. It was only after his company had transferred him to New York that Martin was aware that certainly his wife was drinking too much. She was tippling, he noticed, during the day.

38   The problem acknowledged, he tried to analyze the source. The change from Alabama to New York had somehow disturbed her; accustomed to the idle warmth of a small Southern town, the matrix of the family and cousinship and childhood friends, she had failed to accommodate herself to the stricter, lonelier mores of the North. The duties of motherhood and housekeeping were onerous to her. Homesick for Paris City, she had made no friends in the suburban town. She read only magazines and murder books. Her interior life was insufficient without the artifice of alcohol.

39   The revelations of incontinence insidiously undermined his previous conceptions of his wife. There were times of unexplainable malevolence, times when the alcoholic fuse caused an explosion of unseemly anger. He encountered a latent coarseness in Emily, inconsistent with her natural simplicity. She lied about drinking and deceived him with unsuspected stratagems.

40   Then there was an accident. Coming home from work one evening about a year ago, he was greeted with screams from the children's room. He found Emily holding the baby, wet and naked from her bath. The baby had been dropped, her frail, frail skull striking the table edge, so that a thread of blood was soaking into the gossamer hair. Emily was sobbing and intoxicated. As Martin cradled the hurt child, so infinitely precious at that moment, he had an affrighted vision of the future.

41   The next day Marianne was all right. Emily vowed that never again would she touch liquor, and for a few weeks she was sober, cold and downcast. Then gradually she began—not whiskey or gin—but quantities of beer, or sherry, or outlandish liqueurs; once he had come across a hatbox of empty crème de menthe bottles. Martin found a dependable maid who managed the household competently. Virgie was also from Alabama and Martin had never dared tell Emily the wage scale customary in New York. Emily's drinking was entirely secret now, done before he reached the house. Usually the effects were almost imperceptible—a looseness of movement or the heavy-lidded eyes. The times of irresponsibilities, such as the cayenne-pepper toast were rare, and Martin could dismiss his worries when Virgie was at the house. But, nevertheless, anxiety was always latent, a threat of undefined disaster that underlaid his days.

42   "Marianne!" Martin called, for even the recollection of that time brought the need for reassurance. The baby girl, no longer hurt, but no less precious to her father, came into the kitchen with her brother. Martin went on with the preparations for the meal. He opened a can of soup and put two chops in the frying pan. Then he sat down by the table and took his Marianne on his knees for a pony ride. Andy watched them, his fingers wobbling the tooth that had been loose all that week.

43   "Andy-the-candyman!" Martin said. "Is that old critter still in your mouth? Come closer, let Daddy have a look."

44   "I got a string to pull it with." The child brought from his pocket a tangled thread. "Virgie said to tie it to the tooth and tie the other end to the doorknob and shut the door real suddenly."

45   Martin took out a clean handkerchief and felt the loose tooth carefully. "That tooth is coming out of my Andy's mouth tonight. Otherwise I'm awfully afraid we'll have a tooth tree in the family."

46   "A what?"

47   "A tooth tree," Martin said. "You'll bite into something and swallow that tooth. And the tooth will take root in poor Andy's stomach and grow into a tooth tree with sharp little teeth instead of leaves."

48   "Shoo, Daddy," Andy said. But he held the tooth firmly between his grimy little thumb and forefinger. "There ain't any tree like that. I never seen one."

49   "There isn't any tree like that and I never saw one."

50   Martin tensed suddenly. Emily was coming down the stairs. He listened to her fumbling footsteps, his arm embracing the little boy with dread. When Emily came into the room he saw from her movements and

her sullen face that she had again been at the sherry bottle. She began to yank open drawers and set the table.

51   "Condition!" she said in a furry voice. "You talk to me like that. Don't think I'll forget. I remember every dirty lie you say to me. Don't you think for a minute that I forget."

52   "Emily!" he begged. "The children—"

53   "The children—yes! Don't think I don't see through your dirty plots and schemes. Down here trying to turn my own children against me. Don't think I don't see and understand."

54   "Emily! I beg you—please go upstairs."

55   "So you can turn my children—my very own children—" Two large tears coursed rapidly down her cheeks. "Trying to turn my little boy, my Andy, against his own mother."

56   With drunken impulsiveness Emily knelt on the floor before the startled child. Her hands on his shoulders balanced her. "Listen, my Andy—you wouldn't listen to any lies your father tells you? You wouldn't believe what he says? Listen, Andy, what was your father telling you before I came downstairs?" Uncertain, the child sought his father's face. "Tell me. Mama wants to know."

57   "About the tooth tree."

58   "What?"

59   The child repeated the words and she echoed them with unbelieving terror. "The tooth tree!" She swayed and renewed her grasp on the child's shoulder. "I don't know what you're talking about. But listen, Andy, Mama is all right, isn't she?" The tears were spilling down her face and Andy drew back from her, for he was afraid. Grasping the table edge, Emily stood up.

60   "See! You have turned my child against me."

61   Marianne began to cry, and Martin took her in his arms.

62   "That's all right, you can take your child. You have always shown partiality from the very first. I don't mind, but at least you can leave me my little boy."

63   Andy edged close to his father and touched his leg. "Daddy," he wailed.

64   Martin took the children to the foot of the stairs. "Andy, you take up Marianne and Daddy will follow you in a minute."

65   "But Mama?" the child asked, whispering.

66   "Mama will be all right. Don't worry."

67   Emily was sobbing at the kitchen table, her face buried in the crook of her arm. Martin poured a cup of soup and set it before her. Her rasping sobs unnerved him; the vehemence of her emotion, irrespective of the source, touched in him a strain of tenderness. Unwillingly he laid his hand on her dark hair. "Sit up and drink the soup." Her face as she looked up at him was chastened and imploring. The boy's withdrawal or the touch of Martin's hand had turned the tenor of her mood.

68   "Ma-Martin," she sobbed. "I'm so ashamed."

69   "Drink the soup."

70   Obeying him, she drank between gasping breaths. After a second cup she allowed him to lead her up to their room. She was docile now and more restrained. He laid her nightgown on the bed and was about to leave when a fresh round of grief, the alcoholic tumult, came again.

71   "He turned away. My Andy looked at me and turned away."

72   Impatience and fatigue hardened his voice, but he spoke warily. "You forget that Andy is still a little child—he can't comprehend the meaning of such scenes."

73   "Did I make a scene? Oh, Martin, did I make a scene before the children?"

74   Her horrified face touched and amused him against his will. "Forget it. Put on your nightgown and go to sleep."

75   "My child turned away from me. Andy looked at his mother and turned away. The children—"

76   She was caught in the rhythmic sorrow of alcohol. Martin withdrew from the room saying: "For God's sake go to sleep. The children will forget by tomorrow."

77   As he said this he wondered if it was true. Would the scene glide so easily from memory—or would it root in the unconscious to fester in the after-years? Martin did not know, and the last alternative sickened him. He thought of Emily, foresaw the morning-after humiliation: the shards of memory, the lucidities that glared from the obliterating darkness of shame. She would call the New York office twice—possibly three or four times. Martin anticipated his own embarrassment, wondering if the others at the office could possibly suspect. He felt that his secretary had divined the trouble long ago and that she pitied him. He suffered a moment of rebellion against his fate; he hated his wife.

78   Once in the children's room he closed the door and felt secure for the first time that evening. Marianne fell down on the floor, picked herself up and calling: "Daddy, watch me," fell again, got up, and continued the falling-calling routine. Andy sat in the child's low chair, wobbling the tooth. Martin ran the water in the tub, washed his own hands in the lavatory, and called the boy into the bathroom.

79   "Let's have another look at that tooth." Martin sat on the toilet, holding Andy between his knees. The child's mouth gaped and Martin grasped the tooth. A wobble, a quick twist and the nacreous milk tooth was free. Andy's face was for the first moment split between terror, astonishment, and delight. He mouthed a swallow of water and spat into the lavatory.

80   "Look, Daddy! It's blood. Marianne!"

81   Martin loved to bathe his children, loved inexpressibly the tender, naked bodies as they stood in the water so exposed. It was not fair of Emily to say that he showed partiality. As Martin soaped the delicate boy-body of his son he felt that further love would be impossible. Yet he admitted the difference in the quality of his emotions for the two children. His love for his daughter was graver, touched with a strain of melancholy, a gentleness that was akin to pain. His pet names for the little boy

were the absurdities of daily inspiration—he called the little girl always
Marianne, and his voice as he spoke it was a caress. Martin patted dry
the fat baby stomach and the sweet little genital fold. The washed child
faces were radiant as flower petals, equally loved.

82   "I'm putting the tooth under my pillow. I'm supposed to get a quarter."

83   "What for?"

84   "You know, Daddy. Johnny got a quarter for his tooth."

85   "Who puts the quarter there?" asked Martin. "I used to think the fairies
left it in the night. It was a dime in my day, though."

86   "That's what they say in kindergarden."

87   "Who does put it there?"

88   "Your parents," Andy said. "You!"

89   Martin was pinning the cover on Marianne's bed. His daughter was
already asleep. Scarcely breathing, Martin bent over and kissed her forehead, kissed again the tiny hand that lay palm-upward, flung in slumber
beside her head.

90   "Good night, Andy-man."

91   The answer was only a drowsy murmur. After a minute Martin took
out his change and slid a quarter underneath the pillow. He left a night
light in the room.

92   As Martin prowled about the kitchen making a late meal, it occurred
to him that the children had not once mentioned their mother or the
scene that must have seemed to them incomprehensible. Absorbed in the
instant—the tooth, the bath, the quarter—the fluid passage of child-time
had borne these weightless episodes like leaves in the swift current of a
shallow stream while the adult enigma was beached and forgotten on the
shore. Martin thanked the Lord for that.

93   But his own anger, repressed and lurking, arose again. His youth was
being frittered by a drunkard's waste, his very manhood subtly undermined. And the children, once the immunity of incomprehension
passed—what would it be like in a year or so? With his elbows on the
table he ate his food brutishly, untasting. There was no hiding the truth—
soon there would be gossip in the office and in the town; his wife was a
dissolute woman. Dissolute. And he and his children were bound to a
future of degradation and slow ruin.

94   Martin pushed away from the table and stalked into the living room.
He followed the lines of a book with his eyes but his mind conjured miserable images: he saw his children drowned in the river, his wife a disgrace on the public street. By bedtime the dull, hard anger was like a
weight upon his chest and his feet dragged as he climbed the stairs.

95   The room was dark except for the shafting light from the half-opened
bathroom door. Martin undressed quietly. Little by little, mysteriously,
there came in him a change. His wife was asleep, her peaceful respira-
tion sounding gently in the room. Her high-heeled shoes with the carelessly dropped stockings made to him a mute appeal. Her underclothes
were flung in disorder on the chair. Martin picked up the girdle and the

soft, silk brassière and stood for a moment with them in his hands. For the first time that evening he looked at his wife. His eyes rested on the sweet forehead, the arch of the fine brow. The brow had descended to Marianne, and the tilt at the end of the delicate nose. In his son he could trace the high cheekbones and pointed chin. Her body was full-bosomed, slender and undulant. As Martin watched the tranquil slumber of his wife the ghost of the old anger vanished. All thoughts of blame or blemish were distant from him now. Martin put out the bathroom light and raised the window. Careful not to awaken Emily he slid into the bed. By moonlight he watched his wife for the last time. His hand sought the adjacent flesh and sorrow paralleled desire in the immense complexity of love.

Questions for Discussion

1. What clues does McCullers give early in the story that foreshadow the problem in this family?

2. If you were in Martin's position, how would you react to the scene that greets him when he returns home?

3. What particular scenes and actions affect your judgment of Martin as a father? How does he show feelings toward his children?

4. Martin feels anger at Emily's drunkenness and fear for the children under her care. Yet only a few minutes later, Martin feels tenderness and love for Emily. How can his feelings change so drastically in a few minutes? How is the theme of the story summed up in the phrase "the immense complexity of love"?

5. Explain what you think Martin should do in this situation. Justify your position.

Suggestions for Exploring, Writing, and Persuading

1. Examine a disturbing problem in your life that you refused to confront. Why did you fail to confront the problem? What were the consequences of this failure?

2. Families today must often cope with the stress of moving. Write either a personal narrative about a relocation of your family or a cause-and-effect essay about moving and its effect on family members.

3. Write a character sketch of either Martin or Emily.

4. Write a persuasive essay in which you argue your theories about what the situation in this family will be ten years in the future.

5. Research the effect of an alcoholic parent or parents on children. Then write a documented essay on these effects.

6. In an essay, describe the actions you believe Martin should take. Then persuade your readers that your suggested course of action is the best solution.

James Baldwin (1924–1987)

James Baldwin knew firsthand the rigors of poverty in Harlem, for he grew up there along with eight half-brothers and -sisters. His mother worked as a domestic; his stepfather, a laborer and part-time preacher, seemed to resent his small, unattractive stepson. Thus Baldwin learned early the importance of family and the need for love, themes that appear in "Sonny's Blues" and in his other works. Baldwin's novels, essays, and stories reveal both his talent as a writer and his intolerance of bigotry. To escape American racial prejudice, he spent much of his life in France. His most famous novels are Go Tell It on the Mountain *(1953) and* Giovanni's Room *(1956). Baldwin's essays, collected in* Notes of a Native Son *(1955),* Nobody Knows My Name *(1961), and* The Fire Next Time *(1963), strongly influenced his contemporaries.*

SONNY'S BLUES   (1957)

1   I heard about it in the paper, in the subway, on my way to work. I read it, and I couldn't believe it, and I read it again. Then perhaps I just stared at it, at the newsprint spelling out his name, spelling out the story. I stared at it in the swinging lights of the subway car, and in the faces and bodies of the people, and in my own face, trapped in the darkness which roared outside.

2   It was not to be believed and I kept telling myself that, as I walked from the subway station to the high school. And at the same time I couldn't doubt it. I was scared, scared for Sonny. He became real to me again. A great block of ice got settled in my belly and kept melting there slowly all day long, while I taught my classes algebra. It was a special kind of ice. It kept melting, sending trickles of ice water all up and down my veins, but it never got less. Sometimes it hardened and seemed to expand until I felt my guts were going to come spilling out or that I was going to choke or scream. This would always be at a moment when I was remembering some specific thing Sonny had once said or done.

3   When he was about as old as the boys in my classes his face had been bright and open, there was a lot of copper in it; and he'd had wonderfully direct brown eyes, and great gentleness and privacy. I wondered what he looked like now. He had been picked up, the evening before, in a raid on an apartment downtown, for peddling and using heroin.

4   I couldn't believe it: but what I mean by that is that I couldn't find any room for it anywhere inside me. I had kept it outside me for a long time. I hadn't wanted to know. I had had suspicions, but I didn't name them, I kept putting them away. I told myself that Sonny was wild, but he wasn't crazy. And he'd always been a good boy, he hadn't ever turned hard or evil or disrespectful, the way kids can, so quick, so quick, especially in Harlem, I didn't want to believe that I'd ever see my brother going down,

coming to nothing, all that light in his face gone out, in the condition I'd already seen so many others. Yet it had happened and here I was, talking about algebra to a lot of boys who might, every one of them for all I knew, be popping off needles every time they went to the head. Maybe it did more for them than algebra could.

5   I was sure that the first time Sonny had ever had horse, he couldn't have been much older than these boys were now. These boys, now, were living as we'd been living then, they were growing up with a rush and their heads bumped abruptly against the low ceiling of their actual possibilities. They were filled with rage. All they really knew were two darknesses, the darkness of their lives, which was now closing in on them and the darkness of the movies, which had blinded them to that other darkness, and in which they now, vindictively, dreamed, at once more together than they were at any other time, and more alone.

6   When the last bell rang, the class ended, I let out my breath. It seemed I'd been holding it for all that time. My clothes were wet—I may have looked as though I'd been sitting in a steam bath, all dressed up, all afternoon. I sat alone in the classroom a long time. I listened to the boys outside, downstairs, shouting and cursing and laughing. Their laughter struck me for perhaps the first time. It was not the joyous laughter which—God knows why—one associates with children. It was mocking and insular, its intent was to denigrate. It was disenchanted, and in this, also, lay the authority of their curses. Perhaps I was listening to them because I was thinking about my brother and in them I heard my brother. And myself.

7   One boy was whistling a tune, at once very complicated and very simple, it seemed to be pouring out of him as though he were a bird, and it sounded very cool and moving through all that harsh, bright air, only just holding its own through all those other sounds.

8   I stood up and walked over to the window and looked down into the courtyard. It was the beginning of the spring and the sap was rising in the boys. A teacher passed through them every now and again, quickly, as though he or she couldn't wait to get out of that courtyard, to get those boys out of their sight and off their minds. I started collecting my stuff. I thought I'd better get home and talk to Isabel.

9   The courtyard was almost deserted by the time I got downstairs. I saw this boy standing in the shadow of a doorway, looking just like Sonny. I almost called his name. Then I saw that it wasn't Sonny, but somebody we used to know, a boy from around our block. He'd been Sonny's friend. He'd never been mine, having been too young for me, and anyway, I'd never liked him. And now, even though he was a grown-up man, he still hung around that block, still spent hours on the street corners, was always high and raggy. I used to run into him from time to time and he'd often work around to asking me for a quarter or fifty cents. He always had some real good excuse, too, and I always gave it to him. I don't know why.

10   But now, abruptly, I hated him. I couldn't stand the way he looked at me, partly like a dog, partly like a cunning child. I wanted to ask him what the hell he was doing in the school courtyard.

11   He sort of shuffled over to me, and he said, "I see you got the papers. So you already know about it."

12   "You mean about Sonny? Yes, I already know about it. How come they didn't get you?"

13   He grinned. It made him repulsive and it also brought to mind what he'd looked like as a kid. "I wasn't there. I stay away from them people."

14   "Good for you." I offered him a cigarette and I watched him through the smoke. "You come all the way down here just to tell me about Sonny?"

15   "That's right." He was sort of shaking his head and his eyes looked strange, as though they were about to cross. The bright sun deadened his damp dark brown skin and it made his eyes look yellow and showed up the dirt in his kinked hair. He smelled funky. I moved a little away from him and I said, "Well, thanks. But I already know about it and I got to get home."

16   "I'll walk you a little ways," he said. We started walking. There were a couple of kids still loitering in the courtyard and one of them said goodnight to me and looked strangely at the boy beside me.

17   "What're you going to do?" he asked me. "I mean, about Sonny?"

18   "Look. I haven't seen Sonny for over a year, I'm not sure I'm going to do anything. Anyway, what the hell *can* I do?"

19   "That's right," he said quickly, "ain't nothing you can do. Can't much help old Sonny no more, I guess."

20   It was what I was thinking and so it seemed to me he had no right to say it.

21   "I'm surprised at Sonny, though," he went on—he had a funny way of talking, he looked straight ahead as though he were talking to himself— "I thought Sonny was a smart boy, I thought he was too smart to get hung."

22   "I guess he thought so too," I said sharply, "and that's how he got hung. And how about you? You're pretty goddamn smart, I bet."

23   Then he looked directly at me, just for a minute. "I ain't smart," he said. "If I was smart, I'd have reached for a pistol a long time ago."

24   "Look. Don't tell *me* your sad story, if it was up to me, I'd give you one." Then I felt guilty—guilty, probably, for never having supposed that the poor bastard *had* a story of his own, much less a sad one, and I asked, quickly, "What's going to happen to him now?"

25   He didn't answer this. He was off by himself some place. "Funny thing," he said, and from his tone we might have been discussing the quickest way to get to Brooklyn, "when I saw the papers this morning, the first thing I asked myself was if I had anything to do with it. I felt sort of responsible."

26   I began to listen more carefully. The subway station was on the corner, just before us, and I stopped. He stopped, too. We were in front of a bar and he ducked slightly, peering in, but whoever he was looking for didn't seem to be there. The juke box was blasting away with something black and bouncy and I half watched the barmaid as she danced her way from the juke box to her place behind the bar. And I watched her face as she laughingly responded to something someone said to her, still keeping time to the music. When she smiled one saw the little girl, one sensed the doomed, still-struggling woman beneath the battered face of the semiwhore.

27   "I never *give* Sonny nothing," the boy said finally, "but a long time ago I come to school high and Sonny asked me how it felt." He paused, I couldn't bear to watch him, I watched the barmaid, and I listened to the music which seemed to be causing the pavement to shake. "I told him it felt great." The music stopped, the barmaid paused and watched the juke box until the music began again. "It did."

28   All this was carrying me some place I didn't want to go. I certainly didn't want to know how it felt. It filled everything, the people, the houses, the music, the dark, quicksilver barmaid, with menace; and this menace was their reality.

29   "What's going to happen to him now?" I asked again.

30   "They'll send him away some place and they'll try to cure him." He shook his head. "Maybe he'll even think he's kicked the habit. Then they'll let him loose"—he gestured, throwing his cigarette into the gutter. "That's all."

31   "What do you mean, that's *all?*"

32   But I knew what he meant.

33   "I *mean*, that's *all*." He turned his head and looked at me, pulling down the corners of his mouth. "Don't you know what I mean?" he asked, softly.

34   "How the hell *would* I know what you mean?" I almost whispered it, I don't know why.

35   "That's right," he said to the air, "how would *he* know what I mean?" He turned toward me again, patient and calm, and yet I somehow felt him shaking, shaking as though he were going to fall apart. I felt that ice in my guts again, the dread I'd felt all afternoon; and again I watched the barmaid, moving about the bar, washing glasses, and singing. "Listen. They'll let him out and then it'll just start all over again. That's what I mean."

36   "You mean—they'll let him out. And then he'll just start working his way back in again. You mean he'll never kick the habit. Is that what you mean?"

37   "That's right," he said, cheerfully. "*You* see what I mean."

38   "Tell me," I said at last, "why does he want to die? He must want to die, he's killing himself, why does he want to die?"

39   He looked at me in surprise. He licked his lips. "He don't want to die. He wants to live. Don't nobody want to die, ever."

40   Then I wanted to ask him—too many things. He could not have answered, or if he had, I could not have borne the answers. I started walking. "Well, I guess it's none of my business."

41   "It's going to be rough on old Sonny," he said. We reached the subway station. "This is your station?" he asked. I nodded. I took one step down. "Damn!" he said, suddenly. I looked up at him. He grinned again. "Damn it if I didn't leave all my money home. You ain't got a dollar on you, have you? Just for a couple of days, is all."

42   All at once something inside gave and threatened to come pouring out of me. I didn't hate him any more. I felt that in another moment I'd start crying like a child.

43   "Sure," I said, "Don't sweat." I looked in my wallet and didn't have a dollar, I only had a five. "Here," I said. "That hold you?"

44   He didn't look at it—he didn't want to look at it. A terrible, closed look come over his face, as though he were keeping the number on the bill a secret from him and me. "Thanks," he said, and now he was dying to see me go. "Don't worry about Sonny. Maybe I'll write him or something."

45   "Sure," I said. "You do that. So long."

46   "Be seeing you," he said. I went on down the steps.

47   And I didn't write Sonny or send him anything for a long time. When I finally did, it was just after my little girl died, he wrote me back a letter which made me feel like a bastard.

48   Here's what he said:

49   Dear brother,

50   You don't know how much I needed to hear from you. I wanted to write you many a time but I dug how much I must have hurt you and so I didn't write. But now I feel like a man who's been trying to climb up out of some deep, real deep and funky hole and just saw the sun up there, outside. I got to get outside.

51   I can't tell you much about how I got here. I mean I don't know how to tell you. I guess I was afraid of something or I was trying to escape from something and you know I have never been very strong in the head (smile). I'm glad Mama and Daddy are dead and can't see what's happened to their son and I swear if I'd known what I was doing I would never have hurt you so, you and a lot of other fine people who were nice to me and who believed in me.

52   I don't want you to think it had anything to do with me being a musician. It's more than that. Or maybe less than that. I can't get anything straight in my head down here and I try not to think about what's going to happen to me when I get outside again. Sometime I think I'm going to flip and *never* get outside and sometime I think I'll come straight back. I tell you one thing, though, I'd rather blow my brains out than go through this again. But that's what they all say, so they tell me. If I tell you when I'm coming to New York and if you could meet me, I sure would appreciate it. Give my love to Isabel and the kids and I was sure sorry to hear about little Gracie. I wish I could be like Mama and say the Lord's will be done, but

I don't know it seems to me that trouble is the one thing that never does get stopped and I don't know what good it does to blame it on the Lord. But maybe it does some good if you believe it.

53   Your brother,
54   Sonny

55   Then I kept in constant touch with him and I sent him whatever I could and I went to meet him when he came back to New York. When I saw him many things I thought I had forgotten came flooding back to me. This was because I had begun, finally, to wonder about Sonny, about the life that Sonny lived inside. This life, whatever it was, had made him older and thinner and it had deepened the distant stillness in which he had always moved. He looked very unlike my baby brother. Yet, when he smiled, when we shook hands, the baby brother I'd never known looked out from the depths of his private life, like an animal waiting to be coaxed into the light.

56   "How you been keeping?" he asked me.

57   "All right. And you?"

58   "Just fine." He was smiling all over his face. "It's good to see you again."

59   "It's good to see you."

60   The seven years' difference in our ages lay between us like a chasm: I wondered if these years would ever operate between us as a bridge. I was remembering, and it made it hard to catch my breath, that I had been there when he was born; and I had heard the first words he had ever spoken. When he started to walk, he walked from our mother straight to me. I caught him just before he fell when he took the first steps he ever took in this world.

61   "How's Isabel?"

62   "Just fine. She's dying to see you."

63   "And the boys?"

64   "They're fine, too. They're anxious to see their uncle."

65   "Oh, come on. You know they don't remember me."

66   "Are you kidding? Of course they remember you."

67   He grinned again. We got into a taxi. We had a lot to say to each other, far too much to know how to begin.

68   As the taxi began to move, I asked, "You still want to go to India?"

69   He laughed. "You still remember that. Hell, no. This place is Indian enough to me."

70   "It used to belong to them," I said.

71   And he laughed again. "They damn sure knew what they were doing when they got rid of it."

72   Years ago, when he was around fourteen, he'd been all hipped up on the idea of going to India. He read books about people sitting on rocks, naked, in all kinds of weather, but mostly bad, naturally, and walking barefoot through hot coals and arriving at wisdom. I used to say that it sounded to me as though they were getting away from wisdom as fast as they could. I think he sort of looked down on me for that.

73   "Do you mind," he asked "if we have the driver drive alongside the park? On the west side—I haven't seen the city in so long."

74   "Of course not," I said. I was afraid that I might sound as though I were humoring him, but I hoped he wouldn't take it that way.

75   So we drove along, between the green of the park and the stony, lifeless elegance of hotels and apartment buildings, toward the vivid, killing streets of our childhood. These streets hadn't changed, though housing projects jutted up out of them now like rocks in the middle of a boiling sea. Most of the houses in which we had grown up had vanished, as had the stores from which we had stolen, the basements in which we had first tried sex, the rooftops from which we had hurled tin cans and bricks. But houses exactly like the houses of our past yet dominated the landscape, boys exactly like the boys we once had been found themselves smothering in these houses, came down into the streets for light and air and found themselves encircled by disaster. Some escaped the trap, most didn't. Those who got out always left something of themselves behind, as some animals amputate a leg and leave it in the trap. It might be said, perhaps, that I had escaped, after all, I was a school teacher; or that Sonny had, he hadn't lived in Harlem for years. Yet, as the cab moved uptown through streets which seemed, with a rush, to darken with dark people, and as I covertly studied Sonny's face, it came to me that what we both were seeking through our separate cab windows was that part of ourselves which had been left behind. It's always at the hour of trouble and confrontation that the missing member aches.

76   We hit 110th Street and started rolling up Lenox Avenue. And I'd known this avenue all my life, but it seemed to me again, as it had seemed on the day I'd first heard about Sonny's trouble, filled with a hidden menace which was its very breath of life.

77   "We almost there," said Sonny..

78   "Almost." We were both too nervous to say anything more.

79   We live in a housing project. It hasn't been up long. A few days after it was up it seemed uninhabitably new, now, of course, it's already rundown. It looks like a parody of the good, clean, faceless life—God knows the people who live in it do their best to make it a parody. The beat-looking grass lying around isn't enough to make their lives green, the hedges will never hold out the streets, and they know it. The big windows fool no one, they aren't big enough to make space out of no space. They don't bother with the windows, they watch the TV screen instead. The playground is most popular with the children who don't play at jacks, or skip rope, or roller skate, or swing, and they can be found in it after dark. We moved in partly because it's not too far from where I teach, and partly for the kids; but it's really just like the houses in which Sonny and I grew up. The same things happen, they'll have the same things to remember. The moment Sonny and I started into the house I had the feeling that I was simply bringing him back into the danger he had almost died trying to escape.

80   Sonny has never been talkative. So I don't know why I was sure he'd be dying to talk to me when supper was over the first night. Everything went fine, the oldest boy remembered him, and the youngest boy liked him, and Sonny had remembered to bring something for each of them; and Isabel, who is really much nicer than I am, more open and giving, had gone to a lot of trouble about dinner and was genuinely glad to see him. And she's always been able to tease Sonny in a way that I haven't. It was nice to see her face so vivid again and to hear her laugh and watch her make Sonny laugh. She wasn't, or, anyway, she didn't seem to be, at all uneasy or embarrassed. She chatted as though there were no subject which had to be avoided and she got Sonny past his first, faint stiffness. And thank God she was there, for I was filled with that icy dread again. Everything I did seemed awkward to me, and everything I said sounded freighted with hidden meaning. I was trying to remember everything I'd heard about dope addiction and I couldn't help watching Sonny for signs. I wasn't doing it out of malice. I was trying to find out something about my brother. I was dying to hear him tell me he was safe.

81   "Safe!" my father grunted, whenever Mama suggested trying to move to a neighborhood which might be safer for children. "Safe, hell! Ain't no place safe for kids, nor nobody."

82   He always went on like this, but he wasn't, ever, really as bad as he sounded, not even on weekends, when he got drunk. As a matter of fact, he was always on the lookout for "something a little better," but he died before he found it. He died suddenly, during a drunken weekend in the middle of the war, when Sonny was fifteen. He and Sonny hadn't ever got on too well. And this was partly because Sonny was the apple of his father's eye. It was because he loved Sonny so much and was frightened for him, that he was always fighting with him. It doesn't do any good to fight with Sonny. Sonny just moves back, inside himself, where he can't be reached. But the principal reason that they never hit it off is that they were so much alike. Daddy was big and rough and loud-talking, just the opposite of Sonny, but they both had—that same privacy.

83   Mama tried to tell me something about this, just after Daddy died. I was home on leave from the army.

84   This was the last time I ever saw my mother alive. Just the same, this picture gets all mixed up in my mind with pictures I had of her when she was younger. The way I always see her is the way she used to be on Sunday afternoon, say, when the old folks were talking after the big Sunday dinner. I always see her wearing pale blue. She'd be sitting on the sofa. And my father would be sitting in the easy chair, not far from her. And the living room would be full of church folks and relatives. There they sit, on chairs all around the living room, and the night is creeping up outside, but nobody knows it yet. You can see the darkness growing against the windowpanes and you hear the street noises every now and again, or maybe the jangling beat of a tambourine from one of the churches close by, but it's real quiet in the room. For a moment nobody's talking, but every face looks darken-

ing, like the sky outside. And my mother rocks a little from the waist, and my father's eyes are closed. Everyone is looking at something a child can't see. For a minute they've forgotten the children. Maybe a kid is lying on the rug, half asleep. Maybe somebody's got a kid in his lap and is absent-mindedly stroking the kid's head. Maybe there's a kid, quiet and big-eyed, curled up in a big chair in the corner. The silence, the darkness coming, and the darkness in the faces frightens the child obscurely. He hopes that the hand which strokes his forehead will never stop—will never die. He hopes that there will never come a time when the old folks won't be sitting around the living room, talking about where they've come from, and what they've seen, and what's happened to them and their kinfolk.

85   But something deep and watchful in the child knows that this is bound to end, is already ending. In a moment someone will get up and turn on the light. Then the old folks will remember the children and they won't talk any more that day. And when light fills the room, the child is filled with darkness. He knows that every time this happens he's moved just a little closer to that darkness outside. The darkness outside is what the old folks have been talking about. It's what they've come from. It's what they endure. The child knows that they won't talk any more because if he knows too much about what's happened to *them*, he'll know too much too soon, about what's going to happen to *him*.

86   The last time I talked to my mother, I remember I was restless. I wanted to get out and see Isabel. We weren't married then and we had a lot to straighten out between us.

87   There Mama sat, in black, by the window. She was humming an old church song, *Lord, you brought me from a long ways off.* Sonny was out somewhere. Mama kept watching the streets.

88   "I don't know," she said, "if I'll ever see you again, after you go off from here. But I hope you'll remember the things I tried to teach you."

89   "Don't talk like that," I said, and smiled. "You'll be here a long time yet."

90   She smiled, too, but she said nothing. She was quiet for a long time. And I said, "Mama, don't you worry about nothing. I'll be writing all the time, and you be getting the checks. . . . "

91   "I want to talk to you about your brother," she said, suddenly. "If anything happens to me he ain't going to have nobody to look out for him."

92   "Mama," I said, "ain't nothing going to happen to you *or* Sonny. Sonny's all right. He's a good boy and he's got good sense."

93   "It ain't a question of his being a good boy," Mama said, "nor of his having good sense. It ain't only the bad ones, nor yet the dumb ones that gets sucked under." She stopped, looking at me. "Your Daddy once had a brother," she said, and she smiled, in a way that made me feel she was in pain. "You didn't never know that, did you?"

94   "No," I said, "I never knew that," and I watched her face.

95   "Oh, yes," she said, "your Daddy had a brother." She looked out of the window again. "I know you never saw your Daddy cry. But I did—many a time, through all these years."

96   I asked her, "What happened to his brother? How come nobody's ever talked about him?"

97   This was the first time I ever saw my mother look old.

98   "His brother got killed," she said, "when he was just a little younger than you are now. I knew him. He was a fine boy. He was maybe a little full of the devil, but he didn't mean nobody no harm."

99   Then she stopped and the room was silent, exactly as it had sometimes been on those Sunday afternoons. Mama kept looking out into the streets.

100   "He used to have a job in the mill," she said, "and, like all young folks, he just liked to perform on Saturday nights. Saturday nights, him and your father would drift around to different places, go to dances and things like that, or just sit around with people they knew, and your father's brother would sing, he had a fine voice, and play along with himself on his guitar. Well, this particular Saturday night him and your father was coming home from some place, and they were both a little drunk and there was a moon that night, it was bright like day. Your father's brother was feeling kind of good, and he was whistling to himself, and he had his guitar slung over his shoulder. They was coming down a hill and beneath them was a road that turned off from the highway. Well, your father's brother, being always kind of frisky, decided to run down this hill, and he did, with that guitar banging and clanging behind him, and he ran across the road, and he was making water behind a tree. And your father was sort of amused at him and he was still coming down the hill, kind of slow. Then he heard a car motor and that same minute his brother stepped from behind the tree, into the road, in the moonlight. And he started to cross the road. And your father started to run down the hill, he says he don't know why. This car was full of white men. They was all drunk, and when they seen your father's brother they let out a great whoop and holler and they aimed the car straight at him. They was having fun, they just wanted to scare him, the way they do sometimes, you know. But they was drunk. And I guess the boy, being drunk, too, and scared, kind of lost his head. By the time he jumped it was too late. Your father says he heard his brother scream when the car rolled over him, and he heard the wood of that guitar when it give, and he heard them strings go flying, and he heard them white men shouting and the car kept on a-going and it ain't stopped till this day. And, time your father got down the hill, his brother weren't nothing but blood and pulp."

101   Tears were gleaming on my mother's face. There wasn't anything I could say.

102   "He never mentioned it," she said, "because I never let him mention it before you children. Your Daddy was like a crazy man that night and for many a night thereafter. He says he never in his life seen anything as dark as that road after the lights of that car had gone away. Weren't nothing, weren't nobody on that road, just your Daddy and his brother and that busted guitar. Oh, yes. Your Daddy never did really get right again. Till the day he died he weren't sure but that every white man he saw was the man that killed his brother."

103   She stopped and took out her handkerchief and dried her eyes and looked at me.

104   "I ain't telling you all this," she said, "to make you scared or bitter or to make you hate nobody. I'm telling you this because you got a brother. And the world ain't changed."

105   I guess I didn't want to believe this. I guess she saw this in my face. She turned away from me, toward the window again, searching those streets.

106   "But I praise my Redeemer," she said at last, "that He called your Daddy home before me. I ain't saying it to throw no flowers at myself, but, I declare, it keeps me from feeling too cast down to know I helped your father get safely through this world. Your father always acted like he was the roughest, strongest man on earth. And everybody took him to be like that. But if he hadn't had *me* there—to see his tears!"

107   She was crying again. Still I couldn't move. I said, "Lord, Lord, Mama, I didn't know it was like that."

108   "Oh, honey," she said, "there's a lot that you don't know. But you are going to find it out." She stood up from the window and came over to me. "You got to hold on to your brother," she said, "and don't let him fall, no matter what it looks like is happening to him and no matter how evil you gets with him. You going to be evil with him many a time. But don't you forget what I told you, you hear?"

109   "I won't forget," I said. "Don't you worry, I won't forget. I won't let nothing happen to Sonny."

110   My mother smiled as though she were amused at something she saw in my face. Then, "You may not be able to stop nothing from happening. But you got to let him know you's *there*."

111   Two days later I was married, and then I was gone. And I had a lot of things on my mind and I pretty well forgot my promise to Mama until I got shipped home on a special furlough for her funeral.

112   And, after the funeral, with just Sonny and me alone in the empty kitchen, I tried to find out something about him.

113   "What do you want to do?" I asked him.

114   "I'm going to be a musician," he said.

115   For he had graduated, in the time I had been away, from dancing to the juke box to finding out who was playing what, and what they were doing with it, and he had bought himself a set of drums.

116   "You mean, you want to be a drummer?" I somehow had the feeling that being a drummer might be all right for other people but not for my brother Sonny.

117   "I don't think," he said, looking at me very gravely, "that I'll ever be a good drummer. But I think I can play a piano."

118   I frowned. I'd never played the role of the older brother quite so seriously before, had scarcely ever, in fact, *asked* Sonny a damn thing. I sensed myself in the presence of something I didn't really know how to handle, didn't understand. So I made my frown a little deeper as I asked: "What kind of musician do you want to be?"

119   He grinned. "How many kinds do you think there are?"

120   "Be *serious*," I said.

121   He laughed, throwing his head back, and then looked at me. "I *am* serious."

122   "Well, then, for Christ's sake, stop kidding around and answer a serious question. I mean, do you want to be a concert pianist, you want to play classical music and all that, or—or what?" Long before I finished he was laughing again. "For Christ's *sake*, Sonny!"

123   He sobered, but with difficulty. "I'm sorry. But you sound so—*scared!*" and he was off again.

124   "Well, you may think it's funny now, baby, but it's not going to be so funny when you have to make your living at it, let me tell you *that*." I was furious because I knew he was laughing at me and I didn't know why.

125   "No," he said, very sober now, and afraid, perhaps, that he'd hurt me, "I don't want to be a classical pianist. That isn't what interests me. I mean"—he paused, looking hard at me, as though his eyes would help me to understand, and then gestured helplessly, as though perhaps his hand would help—"I mean, I'll have a lot of studying to do, and I'll have to study *everything*, but, I mean, I want to play *with*—jazz musicians." He stopped. "I want to play jazz," he said.

126   Well, the word had never before sounded as heavy, as real, as it sounded that afternoon in Sonny's mouth. I just looked at him and I was probably frowning a real frown by this time. I simply couldn't see why on earth he'd want to spend his time hanging around nightclubs, clowning around on bandstands, while people pushed each other around a dance floor. It seemed—beneath him, somehow. I had never thought about it before, had never been forced to, but I suppose I had always put jazz musicians in a class with what Daddy called "good-time people."

127   "Are you *serious*?"

128   "Hell, *yes*, I'm serious."

129   He looked more helpless than ever, and annoyed, and deeply hurt.

130   I suggested, helpfully: "You mean—like Louis Armstrong?"

131   His face closed as though I'd struck him. "No. I'm not talking about none of that old-time, down home crap."

132   "Well, look, Sonny, I'm sorry, don't get mad. I just don't altogether get it, that's all. Name somebody—you know a jazz musician you admire."

133   "Bird."

134   "Who?"

135   "Bird! Charlie Parker! Don't they teach you nothing in the goddamn army?"

136   I lit a cigarette. I was surprised and then a little amused to discover that I was trembling. "I've been out of touch," I said. "You'll have to be patient with me. Now. Who's this Parker character?"

137   "He's just one of the greatest jazz musicians alive," said Sonny, sullenly, his hands in his pockets, his back to me. "Maybe *the* greatest," he added, bitterly, "that's probably why *you* never heard of him."

138   "All right," I said, "I'm ignorant. I'm sorry. I'll go out and buy all the cat's records right away, all right?"

139   "It don't" said Sonny, with dignity, "make any difference to me. I don't care what you listen to. Don't do me no favors."

140   I was beginning to realize that I'd never seen him so upset before. With another part of my mind I was thinking that this would probably turn out to be one of those things kids go through and that I shouldn't make it seem important by pushing it too hard. Still, I didn't think it would do any harm to ask: "Doesn't all this take a lot of time? Can you make a living at it?"

141   He turned back to me and half leaned, half sat, on the kitchen table. "Everything takes time," he said, "and—well, yes, sure, I can make a living at it. But what I don't seem to be able to make you understand is that it's the only thing I want to do."

142   "Well, Sonny," I said, gently, "you know people can't always do exactly what they *want* to do—"

143   "*No*, I don't know that," said Sonny, surprising me. "I think people *ought* to do what they want to do, what else are they alive for?"

144   "You getting to be a big boy," I said desperately, "it's time you started thinking about your future."

145   "I'm thinking about my future," said Sonny, grimly. "I think about it all the time."

146   I gave up. I decided, if he didn't change his mind, that we could always talk about it later. "In the meantime," I said, "you got to finish school." We had already decided that he'd have to move in with Isabel and her folks. I knew this wasn't the ideal arrangement because Isabel's folks are inclined to be dicty and they hadn't especially wanted Isabel to marry me. But I didn't know what else to do. "And we have to get you fixed up at Isabel's."

147   There was a long silence. He moved from the kitchen table to the window. "That's a terrible idea. You know it yourself."

148   "Do you have a *better* idea?"

149   He just walked up and down the kitchen for a minute. He was as tall as I was. He had started to shave. I suddenly had the feeling that I didn't know him at all.

150   He stopped at the kitchen table and picked up my cigarettes. Looking at me with a kind of mocking, amused defiance, he put one between his lips. "You mind?"

151   "You smoking already?"

152   He lit the cigarette and nodded, watching me through the smoke. "I just wanted to see if I'd have the courage to smoke in front of you." He grinned and blew a great cloud of smoke to the ceiling. "It was easy." He looked at my face. "Come on, now. I bet you was smoking at my age, tell the truth."

153   I didn't say anything but the truth was on my face, and he laughed. But now there was something very strained in his laugh. "Sure. And I bet that ain't all you was doing."

154   He was frightening me a little. "Cut the crap," I said. "We already decided that you was going to go and live at Isabel's. Now what's got into you all of a sudden?"

155   "*You* decided it," he pointed out. "*I* didn't decide nothing." He stopped in front of me, leaning against the stove, arms loosely folded. "Look, brother. I don't want to stay in Harlem no more, I really don't." He was very earnest. He looked at me, then over toward the kitchen window. There was something in his eyes I'd never seen before, some thoughtfulness, some worry all his own. He rubbed the muscle of one arm. "It's time I was getting out of here."

156   "Where do you want to go, Sonny?"

157   "I want to join the army. Or the navy, I don't care. If I say I'm old enough, they'll believe me."

158   Then I got mad. It was because I was so scared. "You must be crazy. You goddamn fool, what the hell do you want to go and join the *army* for?"

159   "I just told you. To get out of Harlem."

160   "Sonny, you haven't even finished *school.* And if you really want to be a musician, how do you expect to study if you're in the *army?*"

161   He looked at me, trapped, and in anguish. "There's ways. I might be able to work out some kind of deal. Anyway, I'll have the G.I. Bill when I come out."

162   "*If* you come out." We stared at each other. "Sonny, please. Be reasonable. I know the setup is far from perfect. But we got to do the best we can."

163   "I ain't learning nothing in school," he said. "Even when I go." He turned away from me and opened the window and threw his cigarette out into the narrow alley. I watched his back. "At least, I ain't learning nothing you'd want me to learn." He slammed the window so hard I thought the glass would fly out, and turned back to me. "And I'm sick of the stink of these garbage cans!"

164   "Sonny," I said, "I know how you feel. But if you don't finish school now, you're going to be sorry later that you didn't." I grabbed him by the shoulders. "And you only got another year. It ain't so bad. And I'll come back and I swear I'll help you do *whatever* you want to do. Just try to put up with it till I come back. Will you please do that? For me?"

165   He didn't answer and he wouldn't look at me.

166   "Sonny. You hear me?"

167   He pulled away. "I hear you. But you never hear anything I say."

168   I didn't know what to say to that. He looked out of the window and then back at me. "OK," he said, and sighed. "I'll try."

169   Then I said, trying to cheer him up a little, "They got a piano at Isabel's. You can practice on it."

170   And as a matter of fact, it did cheer him up for a minute. "That's right," he said to himself. "I forgot that." His face relaxed a little. But the worry, the thoughtfulness, played on it still, the way shadows play on a face which is staring into the fire.

171   But I thought I'd never hear the end of that piano. At first, Isabel would write me, saying how nice it was that Sonny was so serious about his music and how, as soon as he came in from school, or wherever he had been when he was supposed to be at school, he went straight to that piano and stayed there until suppertime. And, after supper, he went back to that piano and stayed there until everybody went to bed. He was at the piano all day Saturday and all day Sunday. Then he bought a record player and started playing records. He'd play one record over and over again, all day long sometimes, and he'd improvise along with it on the piano. Or he'd play one section of the record, one chord, one change, one progression, then he'd do it on the piano. Then back to the record. Then back to the piano.

172   Well, I really don't know how they stood it. Isabel finally confessed that it wasn't like living with a person at all, it was like living with sound. And the sound didn't make any sense to her, didn't make any sense to any of them—naturally. They began, in a way, to be afflicted by this presence that was living in their home. It was as though Sonny were some sort of god, or monster. He moved in an atmosphere which wasn't like theirs at all. They fed him and he ate, he washed himself, he walked in and out of their door; he certainly wasn't nasty or unpleasant or rude, Sonny isn't any of those things; but it was as though he were all wrapped up in some cloud, some fire, some vision all his own; and there wasn't any way to reach him.

173   At the same time, he wasn't really a man yet, he was still a child, and they had to watch out for him in all kinds of ways. They certainly couldn't throw him out. Neither did they dare to make a great scene about that piano because even they dimly sensed, as I sensed, from so many thousands of miles away, that Sonny was at that piano playing for his life.

174   But he hadn't been going to school. One day a letter came from the school board and Isabel's mother got it—there had apparently, been other letters but Sonny had torn them up. This day, when Sonny came in, Isabel's mother showed him the letter and asked where he'd been spending his time. And she finally got it out of him that he'd been down in Greenwich Village, with musicians and other characters, in a white girl's apartment. And this scared her and she started to scream at him and what came up, once she began—though she denies it to this day—was what sacrifices they were making to give Sonny a decent home and how little he appreciated it.

175   Sonny didn't play the piano that day. By evening, Isabel's mother had calmed down but then there was the old man to deal with, and Isabel herself. Isabel says she did her best to be calm but she broke down and started crying. She says she just watched Sonny's face. She could tell, by watching him, what was happening with him. And what was happening was that they penetrated his cloud, they had reached him. Even if their fingers had been a thousand times more gentle than human fingers ever are, he could hardly help feeling that they had stripped him naked and

were spitting on that nakedness. For he also had to see that his presence, that music, which was life or death to him, had been torture for them, and that they had endured it, not at all for his sake, but only for mine. And Sonny couldn't take that. He can take it a little better today than he could then but he's still not very good at it and, frankly, I don't know anybody who is.

176   The silence of the next few days must have been louder than the sound of all the music ever played since time began. One morning, before she went to work, Isabel was in his room for something and she suddenly realized that all of his records were gone. And she knew for certain that he was gone. And he was. He went as far as the navy would carry him. He finally sent me a postcard from some place in Greece and that was the first I knew that Sonny was still alive. I didn't see him any more until we were both back in New York and the war had long been over.

177   He was a man by then, of course, but I wasn't willing to see it. He came by the house from time to time, but we fought almost every time we met. I didn't like the way he carried himself, loose and dreamlike all the time, and I didn't like his friends, and his music seemed to be merely an excuse for the life he led. It sounded just that weird and disordered.

178   Then we had a fight, a pretty awful fight, and I didn't see him for months. By and by I looked him up, where he was living, in a furnished room in the Village, and I tried to make it up. But there were lots of other people in the room and Sonny just lay on his bed, and he wouldn't come downstairs with me, and he treated these other people as though they were his family and I weren't. So I got mad and then he got mad, and then I told him that he might just as well be dead as live the way he was living. Then he stood up and he told me not to worry about him any more in life, that he *was* dead as far as I was concerned. Then he pushed me to the door and the other people looked on as though nothing were happening, and he slammed the door behind me. I stood in the hallway, staring at the door. I heard somebody laugh in the room and then the tears came to my eyes. I started down the steps, whistling to keep from crying, I kept whistling to myself, *You going to need me, baby, one of these cold, rainy days.*

179   I read about Sonny's trouble in the spring. Little Grace died in the fall. She was a beautiful little girl. But she only lived a little over two years. She died of polio and she suffered. She had a slight fever for a couple of days, but it didn't seem like anything and we just kept her in bed. And we would certainly have called the doctor, but the fever dropped, she seemed to be all right. So we thought it had just been a cold. Then, one day, she was up, playing, Isabel was in the kitchen fixing lunch for the two boys when they'd come in from school, and she heard Grace fall down in the living room. When you have a lot of children you don't always start running when one of them falls, unless they start screaming or something. And, this time, Grace was quiet. Yet, Isabel says that when she heard that *thump* and then that silence, something happened in her

to make her afraid. And she ran to the living room and there was little Grace on the floor, all twisted up, and the reason she hadn't screamed was that she couldn't get her breath. And when she did scream, it was the worst sound, Isabel says, that she'd ever heard in all her life, and she still hears it sometimes in her dreams. Isabel will sometimes wake me up with a low, moaning, strangled sound and I have to be quick to awaken her and hold her to me and where Isabel is weeping against me seems a mortal wound.

180   I think I may have written Sonny the very day that little Grace was buried. I was sitting in the living room in the dark, by myself, and I suddenly thought of Sonny. My trouble made his real.

181   One Saturday afternoon, when Sonny had been living with us, or, anyway, been in our house, for nearly two weeks, I found myself wandering aimlessly about the living room, drinking from a can of beer, and trying to work up the courage to search Sonny's room. He was out, he was usually out whenever I was home, and Isabel had taken the children to see their grandparents. Suddenly I was standing still in front of the living room window, watching Seventh Avenue. The idea of searching Sonny's room made me still. I scarcely dared to admit to myself what I'd be searching for. I didn't know what I'd do if I found it. Or if I didn't.

182   On the sidewalk across from me, near the entrance to a barbecue joint, some people were holding an old-fashioned revival meeting. The barbecue cook, wearing a dirty white apron, his conked hair reddish and metallic in the pale sun, and a cigarette between his lips, stood in the doorway, watching them. Kids and older people paused in their errands and stood there, along with some older men and a couple of very tough-looking women who watched everything that happened on the avenue, as though they owned it, or were maybe owned by it. Well, they were watching this, too. The revival was being carried on by three sisters in black, and a brother. All they had were their voices and their Bibles and a tambourine. The brother was testifying and while he testified two of the sisters stood together, seeming to say, amen, and the third sister walked around with the tambourine outstretched and a couple of people dropped coins into it. Then the brother's testimony ended and the sister who had been taking up the collection dumped the coins into her palm and transferred them to the pocket of her long black robe. Then she raised both hands, striking the tambourine against the air, and then against one hand, and she started to sing. And the two other sisters and the brother joined in.

183   It was strange, suddenly, to watch, though I had been seeing these street meetings all my life. So, of course, had everybody else down there. Yet, they paused and watched and listened and I stood still at the window. *"Tis the old ship of Zion,"* they sang and the sister with the tambourine kept a steady, jangling beat, *"it has rescued many a thousand!"* Not a soul under the sound of their voices was hearing this song for the first time, not one of them had been rescued. Nor had they seen much in the way of rescue work being done around them. Neither did they especially believe

in the holiness of the three sisters and the brother, they knew too much about them, knew where they lived, and how. The woman with the tambourine, whose voice dominated the air, whose face was bright with joy, was divided by very little from the woman who stood watching her, a cigarette between her heavy, chapped lips, her hair a cuckoo's nest, her face scarred and swollen from many beatings, and her black eyes glittering like coal. Perhaps they both knew this, which was why, when, as rarely, they addressed each other, they addressed each other as Sister. As the singing filled the air the watching, listening faces underwent a change, the eyes focusing on something within; the music seemed to soothe a poison out of them; and time seemed, nearly, to fall away from the sullen, belligerent, battered faces, as though they were fleeing back to their first condition, while dreaming of their last. The barbecue cook half shook his head and smiled, and dropped his cigarette and disappeared into his joint. A man fumbled in his pockets for change and stood holding it in his hand impatiently, as though he had just remembered a pressing appointment further up the avenue. He looked furious. Then I saw Sonny, standing on the edge of the crowd. He was carrying a wide, flat notebook with a green cover, and it made him look, from where I was standing, almost like a school-boy. The coppery sun brought out the copper in his skin, he was very faintly smiling, standing very still. Then the singing stopped, the tambourine turned into a collection plate again. The furious man dropped in his coins and vanished, so did a couple of the women, and Sonny dropped some change in the plate, looking directly at the woman with a little smile. He started across the avenue, toward the house. He has a slow, loping walk, something like the way Harlem hipsters walk, only he's imposed on this his own half-beat. I had never really noticed it before.

184   I stayed at the window, both relieved and apprehensive. As Sonny disappeared from my sight, they began singing again. And they were still singing when his key turned in the lock.

185   "Hey," he said.

186   "Hey, yourself. You want some beer?"

187   "No. Well, maybe." But he came up to the window and stood beside me, looking out. "What a warm voice," he said.

188   They were singing *If I could only hear my mother pray again!*

189   "Yes," I said, "and she can sure beat that tambourine."

190   "But what a terrible song," he said, and laughed. He dropped his notebook on the sofa and disappeared into the kitchen. "Where's Isabel and the kids?"

191   "I think they went to see their grandparents. You hungry?"

192   "No." He came back into the living room with his can of beer. "You want to come some place with me tonight?"

193   I sensed, I don't know how, that I couldn't possibly say no. "Sure. Where?"

194   He sat down on the sofa and picked up his notebook and started leafing through it. "I'm going to sit in with some fellows in a joint in the Village."

195   "You mean, you're going to play, tonight?"

196   "That's right." He took a swallow of his beer and moved back to the window. He gave me a sidelong look. "If you can stand it."

197   "I'll try," I said.

198   He smiled to himself and we both watched as the meeting across the way broke up. The three sisters and their brother, heads bowed, were singing *God be with you till we meet again.* The faces around them were very quiet. Then the song ended. The small crowd dispersed. We watched the three women and the lone man walk slowly up the avenue.

199   "When she was singing before," said Sonny, abruptly, "her voice reminded me for a minute of what heroin feels like sometimes—when it's in your veins. It makes you feel sort of warm and cool at the same time. And distant. And—and sure." He sipped his beer, very deliberately not looking at me. I watched his face. "It makes you feel—in control. Sometimes you've got to have that feeling."

200   "Do you?" I sat down slowly in the easy chair.

201   "Sometimes." He went to the sofa and picked up his notebook again. "Some people do."

202   "In order," I asked, "to play?" And my voice was very ugly, full of contempt and anger.

203   "Well"—he looked at me with great, troubled eyes, as though, in fact, he hoped his eyes would tell me things he could never otherwise say— "they *think* so. And *if* they think so—!"

204   "And what do *you* think?" I asked.

205   He sat on the sofa and put his can of beer on the floor. "I don't know," he said, and I couldn't be sure if he was answering my question or pursuing his thoughts. His face didn't tell me. "It's not so much to *play.* It's to *stand* it, to be able to make it at all. On any level." He frowned and smiled: "In order to keep from shaking to pieces."

206   "But these friends of yours," I said, "they seem to shake themselves to pieces pretty goddamn fast."

207   "Maybe." He played with the notebook. And something told me that I should curb my tongue, that Sonny was doing his best to talk, that I should listen. "But of course you only know the ones that've gone to pieces. Some don't—or at least they haven't *yet* and that's just about all any of us can say." He paused. "And then there are some who just live, really, in hell, and they know it and they see what's happening and they go right on. I don't know." He sighed, dropped the notebook, folded his arms. "Some guys, you can tell from the way they play, they on something *all* the time. And you can see that, well, it makes something real for them. But of course," he picked up his beer from the floor and sipped it and put the can down again, "they *want* to, too, you've got to see that. Even some of them that say they don't—*some*, not all."

208   "And what about you?" I asked—I couldn't help it. "What about you? Do *you* want to?"

209   He stood up and walked to the window and remained silent for a long time. Then he sighed. "Me," he said. Then: "While I was downstairs before, on my way here, listening to that woman sing, it struck me all of a sudden how much suffering she must have had to go through—to sing like that. It's *repulsive* to think you have to suffer that much."

210   I said: "But there's no way not to suffer—is there, Sonny?"

211   "I believe not," he said and smiled, "but that's never stopped anyone from trying." He looked at me. "Has it?" I realized, with this mocking look, that there stood between us, forever, beyond the power of time or forgiveness, the fact that I had held silence—so long!—when he needed human speech to help him. He turned back to the window. "No, there's no way not to suffer. But you try all kinds of ways to keep from drowning in it, to keep on top of it, and to make it seem—well, like *you*. Like you did something, all right, and now you're suffering for it. You know?" I said nothing. "Well you know," he said, impatiently, "why *do* people suffer? Maybe it's better to do something to give it a reason, *any* reason."

212   "But we just agreed," I said, "that there's no way not to suffer. Isn't it better, then, just to—take it?"

213   "But nobody just takes it," Sonny cried, "that's what I'm telling you! *Everybody* tries not to. You're just hung up on the *way* some people try—it's not *your* way!"

214   The hair on my face began to itch, my face felt wet. "That's not true," I said, "that's not true. I don't give a damn what other people do, I don't even care how they suffer. I just care how *you* suffer." And he looked at me. "Please believe me," I said, "I don't want to see you—die—trying not to suffer."

215   "I won't," he said, flatly, "die trying not to suffer. At least, not any faster than anybody else."

216   "But there's no need," I said, trying to laugh, "is there? in killing yourself."

217   I wanted to say more, but I couldn't. I wanted to talk about will power and how life could be—well, beautiful. I wanted to say that it was all within; but was it? or, rather, wasn't that exactly the trouble? And I wanted to promise that I would never fail him again. But it would all have sounded—empty words and lies.

218   So I made the promise to myself and prayed that I would keep it.

219   "It's terrible sometimes, inside," he said, "that's what's the trouble. You walk these streets, black and funky and cold, and there's not really a living ass to talk to, and there's nothing shaking, and there's no way of getting it out—that storm inside. You can't talk it and you can't make love with it, and when you finally try to get with it and play it, you realize *nobody's* listening. So *you've* got to listen. You got to find a way to listen."

220   And then he walked away from the window and sat on the sofa again, as though all the wind had suddenly been knocked out of him. "Some-

times you'll do *anything* to play, even cut your mother's throat." He laughed and looked at me. "Or your brother's." Then he sobered. "Or your own." Then: "Don't worry. I'm all right now and I think I'll *be* all right. But I can't forget—where I've been. I don't mean just the physical place I've been, I mean where I've *been*. And *what* I've been."

221   "What have you been, Sonny?" I asked.

222   He smiled—but sat sideways on the sofa, his elbow resting on the back, his fingers playing with his mouth and chin, not looking at me. "I've been something I didn't recognize, didn't know I could be. Didn't know anybody could be." He stopped, looking inward, looking helplessly young, looking old. "I'm not talking about it now because I feel *guilty* or anything like that—maybe it would be better if I did, I don't know. Anyway, I can't really talk about it. Not to you, not to anybody," and now he turned and faced me. "Sometimes, you know, and it was actually when I was most *out* of the world, I felt that I was in it, that I was *with* it, really, and I could play or I didn't really have to *play*, it just came out of me, it was there. And I don't know how I played, thinking about it now, but I know I did awful things, those times, sometimes, to people. Or it wasn't that I *did* anything to them—it was that they weren't real." He picked up the beer can; it was empty; he rolled it between his palms: "And other times—well, I needed a fix, I needed to find a place to lean, I needed to clear a space to *listen*— and I couldn't find it, and I—went crazy, I did terrible things to *me*, I was terrible *for* me." He began pressing the beer can between his hands, I watched the metal begin to give. It glittered, as he played with it, like a knife, and I was afraid he would cut himself, but I said nothing. "Oh well. I can never tell you. I was all by myself at the bottom of something, stink-ing and sweating and crying and shaking, and I smelled it, you know? *my* stink, and I thought I'd die if I couldn't get away from it and yet, all the same, I knew that everything I was doing was just locking me in with it. And I didn't know," he paused, still flattening the beer can, "I didn't know, I still *don't* know, something kept telling me that maybe it was good to smell your own stink, but I didn't think that *that* was what I'd been trying to do—and—who can stand it?" and he abruptly dropped the ruined beer can, looking at me with a small, still smile, and then rose, walking to the window as though it were the lodestone rock. I watched his face, he watched the avenue. "I couldn't tell you when Mama died—but the rea-son I wanted to leave Harlem so bad was to get away from drugs. And then, when I ran away, that's what I was running from—really. When I came back, nothing had changed, I hadn't changed, I was just—older." And he stopped, drumming with his fingers on the windowpane. The sun had vanished, soon darkness would fall. I watched his face. "It can come again," he said, almost as though speaking to himself. Then he turned to me. "It can come again," he repeated. "I just want you to know that."

223   "All right," I said, at last. "So it can come again. All right."

224   He smiled, but the smile was sorrowful. "I had to try to tell you," he said.

225   "Yes," I said. "I understand that."

226   "You're my brother," he said, looking straight at me, and not smiling at all.

227   "Yes," I repeated, "yes. I understand that."

228   He turned back to the window, looking out. "All that hatred down there," he said, "all that hatred and misery and love. It's a wonder it doesn't blow the avenue apart."

229   We went to the only nightclub on a short, dark street, downtown. We squeezed through the narrow, chattering, jam-packed bar to the entrance of the big room, where the bandstand was. And we stood there for a moment, for the lights were very dim in this room and we couldn't see. Then, "Hello, boy," said a voice and an enormous black man, much older than Sonny or myself, erupted out of all that atmospheric lighting and put an arm around Sonny's shoulder. "I been sitting right here," he said, "waiting for you."

230   He had a big voice, too, and heads in the darkness turned toward us.

231   Sonny grinned and pulled a little away, and said, "Creole, this is my brother. I told you about him."

232   Creole shook my hand. "I'm glad to meet you, son," he said, and it was clear that he was glad to meet me *there*, for Sonny's sake. And he smiled, "You got a real musician in *your* family," and he took his arm from Sonny's shoulder and slapped him, lightly, affectionately, with the back of his hand.

233   "Well. Now I've heard it all," said a voice behind us. This was another musician, a friend of Sonny's, a coal-black, cheerful-looking man, built close to the ground. He immediately began confiding to me, at the top of his lungs, the most terrible things about Sonny, his teeth gleaming like a lighthouse and his laugh coming up out of him like the beginning of an earthquake. And it turned out that everyone at the bar knew Sonny, or almost everyone; some were musicians, working there, or nearby, or not working, some were simply hangers-on, and some were there to hear Sonny play. I was introduced to all of them and they were all very polite to me. Yet, it was clear that, for them, I was only Sonny's brother. Here, I was in Sonny's world. Or, rather: his kingdom. Here, it was not even a question that his veins bore royal blood.

234   They were going to play soon and Creole installed me, by myself, at a table in a dark corner. Then I watched them, Creole, and the little black man, and Sonny, and the others, while they horsed around, standing just below the bandstand. The light from the bandstand spilled just a little short of them and, watching them laughing and gesturing and moving about, I had the feeling that they, nevertheless, were being most careful not to step into that circle of light too suddenly: that if they moved into the light too suddenly, without thinking, they would perish in flame. Then, while I watched, one of them, the small, black man, moved into the light and crossed the bandstand and started fooling around with his drums. Then—being funny and being, also, extremely ceremonious—Creole took Sonny by the arm and led him to the piano. A woman's voice called

Sonny's name and a few hands started clapping. And Sonny, also being funny and being ceremonious, and so touched, I think, that he could have cried, but neither hiding it nor showing it, riding it like a man, grinned, and put both hands to his heart and bowed from the waist.

235   Creole then went to the bass fiddle and a lean, very bright-skinned brown man jumped up on the bandstand and picked up his horn. So there they were, and the atmosphere on the bandstand and in the room began to change and tighten. Someone stepped up to the microphone and announced them. Then there were all kinds of murmurs. Some people at the bar shushed others. The waitress ran around, frantically getting in the last orders, guys and chicks got closer to each other, and the lights on the bandstand, on the quartet, turned to a kind of indigo. Then they all looked different there. Creole looked about him for the last time, as though he were making certain that all his chickens were in the coop, and then he— jumped and struck the fiddle. And there they were.

236   All I know about music is that not many people ever really hear it. And even then, on the rare occasions when something opens within, and the music enters, what we mainly hear, or hear corroborated, are personal, private, vanishing evocations. But the man who creates the music is hearing something else, is dealing with the roar rising from the void and imposing order on it as it hits the air. What is evoked in him, then, is of another order, more terrible because it has no words, and triumphant, too, for that same reason. And his triumph, when he triumphs, is ours. I just watched Sonny's face. His face was troubled, he was working hard, but he wasn't with it. And I had the feeling that, in a way, everyone on the bandstand was waiting for him, both waiting for him and pushing him along. But as I began to watch Creole, I realized that it was Creole who held them all back. He had them on a short rein. Up there, keeping the beat with his whole body, wailing on the fiddle, with his eyes half closed, he was listening to everything, but he was listening to Sonny. He was having a dialogue with Sonny. He wanted Sonny to leave the shoreline and strike out for the deep water. He was Sonny's witness that deep water and drowning were not the same thing—he had been there, and he knew. And he wanted Sonny to know. He was waiting for Sonny to do the thing on the keys which would let Creole know that Sonny was in the water.

237   And, while Creole listened, Sonny moved, deep within, exactly like someone in torment. I had never before thought of how awful the relationship must be between the musician and his instrument. He has to fill it, this instrument, with the breath of life, his own. He has to make it do what he wants it to do. And a piano is just a piano. It's made out of so much wood and wires and little hammers and big ones, and ivory. While there's only so much you can do with it, the only way to find this out is to try; to try and make it do everything.

238   And Sonny hadn't been near a piano for over a year. And he wasn't on much better terms with his life, not the life that stretched before him now.

He and the piano stammered, started one way, got scared, stopped; started another way, panicked, marked time, started again; then seemed to have found a direction, panicked again, got stuck. And the face I saw on Sonny I'd never seen before. Everything had been burned out of it, and, at the same time, things usually hidden were being burned in, by the fire and fury of the battle which was occurring in him up there.

239   Yet, watching Creole's face as they neared the end of the first set, I had the feeling that something had happened, something I hadn't heard. Then they finished, there was scattered applause, and then, without an instant's warning, Creole started into something else, it was almost sardonic, it was *Am I Blue*. And, as though he commanded, Sonny began to play. Something began to happen. And Creole let out the reins. The dry, low, black man said something awful on the drums, Creole answered, and the drums talked back. Then the horn insisted, sweet and high, slightly detached perhaps, and Creole listened, commenting now and then, dry, and driving, beautiful and calm and old. Then they all came together again, and Sonny was part of the family again. I could tell this from his face. He seemed to have found, right there beneath his fingers, a damn brand-new piano. It seemed that he couldn't get over it. Then, for awhile, just being happy with Sonny, they seemed to be agreeing with him that brand-new pianos certainly were a gas.

240   Then Creole stepped forward to remind them that what they were playing was the blues. He hit something in all of them, he hit something in me, myself, and the music tightened and deepened, apprehension began to beat the air. Creole began to tell us what the blues were all about. They were not about anything very new. He and his boys up there were keeping it new, at the risk of ruin, destruction, madness, and death, in order to find new ways to make us listen. For, while the tale of how we suffer, and how we are delighted, and how we may triumph is never new, it always must be heard. There isn't any other tale to tell, it's the only light we've got in all this darkness.

241   And this tale, according to that face, that body, those strong hands on those strings, has another aspect in every country, and a new depth in every generation. Listen, Creole seemed to be saying listen. Now these are Sonny's blues. He made the little black man on the drums know it, and the bright, brown man on the horn. Creole wasn't trying any longer to get Sonny in the water. He was wishing him Godspeed. Then he stepped back, very slowly, filling the air with the immense suggestion that Sonny speak for himself.

242   Then they all gathered around Sonny and Sonny played. Every now and again one of them seemed to say, amen. Sonny's fingers filled the air with life, his life. But that life contained so many others. And Sonny went all the way back, he really began with the spare, flat statement of the opening phrase of the song. Then he began to make it his. It was very beautiful because it wasn't hurried and it was no longer a lament. I seemed to hear with what burning he had made it his, with what burning we had yet

to make it ours, how we could cease lamenting. Freedom lurked around us and I understood, at last, that he could help us to be free if we would listen, that he would never be free until we did. Yet, there was no battle in his face now. I heard what he had gone through, and would continue to go through until he came to rest in earth. He had made it his: that long line, of which we knew only Mama and Daddy. And he was giving it back, as everything must be given back, so that, passing through death, it can live forever. I saw my mother's face again, and felt, for the first time, how the stones of the road she had walked on must have bruised her feet. I saw the moonlit road where my father's brother died. And it brought something else back to me, and carried me past it, I saw my little girl again and felt Isabel's tears again, and I felt my own tears begin to rise. And I was yet aware that this was only a moment, that the world waited outside, as hungry as a tiger, and that trouble stretched above us, longer than the sky.

243   Then it was over. Creole and Sonny let out their breath, both soaking wet, and grinning. There was a lot of applause and some of it was real. In the dark, the girl came by and I asked her to take drinks to the bandstand. There was a long pause, while they talked up there in the indigo light and after awhile I saw the girl put a Scotch and milk on top of the piano for Sonny. He didn't seem to notice it, but just before they started playing again, he sipped from it and looked toward me, and nodded. Then he put it back on top of the piano. For me, then, as they began to play again, it glowed and shook above my brother's head like the very cup of trembling.

Questions for Discussion

1. Explain why the narrator has ignored Sonny for years. Why do you think the narrator, after his daughter dies, chooses to write to Sonny?

2. Why does Sonny's letter make the narrator feel guilty?

3. Explain why Isabel and her family disapprove of Sonny. Does the narrator share this attitude? What is Sonny willing to sacrifice for music and why?

4. What does the narrator mean when he says of his students, "All they really knew were two darknesses, the darkness of their lives. . . and the darkness of the movies"? What is suggested by these and other references to darkness?

5. "Sonny's Blues" contains a story within a story, the mother's tale of the narrator's father and his brother. What is the significance of this story?

6. In the last scene, the narrator enters Sonny's world for the first time. Explain the symbolism of the location, the jazz, and the drink.

Suggestions for Exploring, Writing, and Persuading

1. A key to an understanding of this story is an understanding of the character of the narrator, since we see Sonny only through his eyes. How

does the narrator perceive himself? How does this perception affect his opinion of Sonny?

2. Write an essay illustrating the ways in which the narrator changes in the story and the causes for these changes.

3. Compare and contrast the story of the father and his brother with the story of Sonny and the narrator. Explain what the story within the story adds to the understanding of both the narrator and the reader.

4. Baldwin's symbolism enriches "Sonny's Blues." Write an essay exploring the use of one or more of these symbols: light and darkness, windows, music.

5. What special claims does this story make for music as an art form? How can the blues played on instruments in a nightclub bring to mind for the narrator not only his own past but that of his whole family?

6. In an essay, describe the Harlem neighborhood where the brothers grew up, and explain the influence of Harlem on them.

7. One of the major themes in literature is that we learn wisdom through suffering. Discuss the wisdom that the brothers learn through suffering.

Truman Capote (1924–1984)

Truman Capote, born Truman Streckfus Persons in New Orleans, spent much of his childhood in Alabama, the background for "A Christmas Memory." He took the surname of his stepfather and during his adolescence lived in Greenwich, Connecticut, and New York City. Capote began to write as a copy boy for The New Yorker. *His first short story, "Miriam," was published in 1946;* Other Voices, Other Rooms, *a novel, was published in 1948. From that point he became what he called a media presence; moving to Hollywood, he wrote the script for* Breakfast at Tiffany's. *The publication of* In Cold Blood: A True Account of a Multiple Murder and Its Consequences *in 1965 marked the beginning of a new genre called the nonfiction novel. A collection of short essays,* Music for Chameleon, *was published in 1980. His unfinished novel,* Answered Prayers, *was published after his death.*

A Christmas Memory   (1956)

1   Imagine a morning in late November. A coming of winter morning more than twenty years ago. Consider the kitchen of a spreading old house in a country town. A great black stove is its main feature; but there is also a big round table and a fireplace with two rocking chairs placed in front of it. Just today the fireplace commenced its seasonal roar.

2   A woman with shorn white hair is standing at the kitchen window. She is wearing tennis shoes and a shapeless gray sweater over a summery cal-

ico dress. She is small and sprightly, like a bantam hen; but, due to a long youthful illness, her shoulders are pitifully hunched. Her face is remarkable—not unlike Lincoln's, craggy like that, and tinted by sun and wind; but it is delicate too, finely boned, and her eyes are sherry-colored and timid. "Oh my," she exclaims, her breath smoking the windowpane, "it's fruitcake weather!"

3   The person to whom she is speaking is myself. I am seven; she is sixty-something. We are cousins, very distant ones, and we have lived together—well, as long as I can remember. Other people inhabit the house, relatives; and though they have power over us, and frequently make us cry, we are not, on the whole, too much aware of them. We are each other's best friend. She calls me Buddy, in memory of a boy who was formerly her best friend. The other Buddy died in the 1880's, when she was still a child. She is still a child.

4   "I knew it before I got out of bed," she says, turning away from the window with a purposeful excitement in her eyes. "The courthouse bell sounded so cold and clear. And there were no birds singing; they've gone to warmer country, yes indeed. Oh, Buddy, stop stuffing biscuit and fetch our buggy. Help me find my hat. We've thirty cakes to bake."

5   It's always the same: a morning arrives in November, and my friend, as though officially inaugurating the Christmas time of year that exhilarates her imagination and fuels the blaze of her heart, announces: "It's fruitcake weather! Fetch our buggy. Help me find my hat."

6   The hat is found, a straw cartwheel corsaged with velvet roses out-of-doors has faded: it once belonged to a more fashionable relative. Together, we guide our buggy, a dilapidated baby carriage, out to the garden and into a grove of pecan trees. The buggy is mine; that is, it was bought for me when I was born. It is made of wicker, rather unraveled, and the wheels wobble like a drunkard's legs. But it is a faithful object; spring-times, we take it to the woods and fill it with flowers, herbs, wild fern for our porch pots; in the summer we pile it with picnic paraphernalia and sugar-cane fishing poles and roll it down to the edge of a creek; it has its winter uses, too: as a truck for hauling firewood from the yard to the kitchen, as a warm bed for Queenie, our tough little orange and white rat terrier who has survived distemper and two rattlesnake bites. Queenie is trotting beside it now.

7   Three hours later we are back in the kitchen hulling a heaping buggy-load of windfall pecans. Our backs hurt from gathering them: how hard they were to find (the main crop having been shaken off the trees and sold by the orchard's owners, who are not us) among the concealing leaves, the frosted, deceiving grass. Caarackle! A cheery crunch, scraps of miniature thunder sound as the shells collapse and the golden mound of sweet oily ivory meat mounts in the milk-glass bowl. Queenie begs to taste, and now and again my friend sneaks her a mite, though insisting we deprive ourselves. "We mustn't, Buddy. If we start, we won't stop. And there's scarcely enough as there is. For thirty cakes." The kitchen is growing dark.

Dusk turns the window into a mirror: our reflections mingle with the rising moon as we work by the fireside in the firelight. At last, when the moon is quite high, we toss the final hull into the fire and, with joined sighs, watch it catch flame. The buggy is empty, the bowl is brimful.

8   We eat our supper (cold biscuits, bacon, blackberry jam) and discuss tomorrow. Tomorrow the kind of work I like best begins: buying. Cherries and citron, ginger and vanilla and canned Hawaiian pineapple, rinds and raisins and walnuts and whiskey and oh, so much flour, butter, so many eggs, spices, flavorings: why, we'll need a pony to pull the buggy home.

9   But before these purchases can be made, there is the question of money. Neither of us has any. Except for skinflint sums persons in the house occasionally provide (a dime is considered very big money); or what we earn ourselves from various activities: holding rummage sales, selling buckets of hand-picked blackberries, jars of homemade jam and apple jelly and peach preserves, rounding up flowers for funerals and weddings. Once we won seventy-ninth prize, five dollars, in a national football contest. Not that we know a fool thing about football. It's just that we enter any contest we hear about: at the moment our hopes are centered on the fifty-thousand-dollar Grand Prize being offered to name a new brand of coffee (we suggested "A.M."; and, after some hesitation, for my friend thought it perhaps sacrilegious, the slogan "A.M.! Amen!"). To tell the truth, our only really profitable enterprise was the Fun and Freak Museum we conducted in a back-yard woodshed two summers ago. The Fun was a stereopticon with slide views of Washington and New York lent us by a relative who had been to those places (she was furious when she discovered why we'd borrowed it); the Freak was a three-legged biddy chicken hatched by one of our own hens. Everybody hereabouts wanted to see that biddy: we charged grownups a nickel, kids two cents. And took in a good twenty dollars before the museum shut down due to the decease of the main attraction.

10   But one way and another we do each year accumulate Christmas savings, a Fruitcake Fund. These moneys we keep hidden in an ancient bead purse under a loose board under the floor under a chamber pot under my friend's bed. The purse is seldom removed from this safe location except to make a deposit, or, as happens every Saturday, a withdrawal; for on Saturdays I am allowed ten cents to go to the picture show. My friend has never been to a picture show, nor does she intend to: "I'd rather hear you tell the story, Buddy. That way I can imagine it more. Besides, a person my age shouldn't squander their eyes. When the Lord comes, let me see Him clear." In addition to never having seen a movie, she has never: eaten in a restaurant, traveled more than five miles from home, received or sent a telegram, read anything except funny papers and the Bible, worn cosmetics, cursed, wished someone harm, told a lie on purpose, let a hungry dog go hungry. Here are the few things she has done, does do: killed with a hoe the biggest rattlesnake ever seen in this county (sixteen rattles), dip snuff (secretly), tame hummingbirds (just try it) till they bal-

ance on her finger, tell ghost stories (we both believe in ghosts) so tingling they chill you in July, talk to herself, take walks in the rain, grow the prettiest japonicas in town, know the recipe for every sort of old-time Indian cure, including a magical wart-remover.

11   Now, with supper finished, we retire to the room in a faraway part of the house where my friend sleeps in a scrap-quilt-covered iron bed painted rose pink, her favorite color. Silently, wallowing in the pleasures of conspiracy, we take the bead purse from its secret place and spill its contents on the scrap quilt. Dollar bills, tightly rolled and green as May buds. Somber fifty-cent pieces, heavy enough to weight a dead man's eyes. Lovely dimes, the liveliest coin, the one that really jingles. Nickels and quarters, worn smooth as creek pebbles. But mostly a hateful heap of bitter-odored pennies. Last summer others in the house contracted to pay us a penny for every twenty-five flies we killed. Oh, the carnage of August: the flies that flew to heaven! Yet it was not work in which we took pride. And, as we sit counting pennies, it is as though we were back tabulating dead flies. Neither of us has a head for figures; we count slowly, lose track, start again. According to her calculations, we have $12.73. According to mine, exactly $13. "I do hope you're wrong, Buddy. We can't mess around with thirteen. The cakes will fall. Or put somebody in the cemetery. Why, I wouldn't dream of getting out of bed on the thirteenth." This is true: she always spends thirteenths in bed. So, to be on the safe side, we subtract a penny and toss it out the window.

12   Of the ingredients that go into our fruitcakes, whiskey is the most expensive, as well as the hardest to obtain: State laws forbid its sale. But everybody knows you can buy a bottle from Mr. Haha Jones. And the next day, having completed our more prosaic shopping, we set out for Mr. Haha's business address, a "sinful" (to quote public opinion) fish-fry and dancing café down by the river. We've been there before, and on the same errand; but in previous years our dealings have been with Haha's wife, an iodine-dark Indian woman with brassy peroxided hair and a dead-tired disposition. Actually, we've never laid eyes on her husband, though we've heard that he's an Indian too. A giant with razor scars across his cheeks. They call him Haha because he's so gloomy, a man who never laughs. As we approach his café (a large log cabin festooned inside and out with chains of garish-gay naked light bulbs and standing by the river's muddy edge under the shade of river trees where moss drifts through the branches like gray mist) our steps slow down. Even Queenie stops prancing and sticks close by. People have been murdered in Haha's café. Cut to pieces. Hit on the head. There's a case coming up in court next month. Naturally these goings-on happen at night when the colored lights cast crazy patterns and the victrola wails. In the daytime Haha's is shabby and deserted. I knock at the door, Queenie barks, my friend calls: "Mrs. Haha, ma'am? Anyone to home?"

13   Footsteps. The door opens. Our hearts overturn. It's Mr. Haha Jones himself! And he is a giant; he does have scars; he doesn't smile. No, he

glowers at us through Satan-tilted eyes and demands to know: "What you want with Haha?"

14   For a moment we are too paralyzed to tell. Presently my friend half-finds her voice, a whispery voice at best: "If you please, Mr. Haha, we'd like a quart of your finest whiskey."

15   His eyes tilt more. Would you believe it? Haha is smiling! Laughing, too. "Which one of you is a drinkin' man?"

16   "It's for making fruitcakes, Mr. Haha. Cooking."

17   This sobers him. He frowns. "That's no way to waste good whiskey." Nevertheless, he retreats into the shadowed café and seconds later appears carrying a bottle of daisy-yellow unlabeled liquor. He demonstrates its sparkle in the sunlight and says: "Two dollars."

18   We pay him with nickels and dimes and pennies. Suddenly, as he jangles the coins in his hand like a fistful of dice, his face softens. "Tell you what," he proposed, pouring the money back into our bead purse, "just send me one of them fruitcakes instead."

19   "Well," my friend remarks on our way home, "there's a lovely man. We'll put an extra cup of raisins in his cake."

20   The black stove, stoked with coal and firewood, glows like a lighted pumpkin. Eggbeaters whirl, spoons spin round in bowls of butter and sugar, vanilla sweetens the air, ginger spices it; melting, nose-tingling odors saturate the kitchen, suffuse the house, drift out to the world on puffs of chimney smoke. In four days our work is done. Thirty-one cakes, dampened with whiskey, bask on window sills and shelves.

21   Who are they for?

22   Friends. Not necessarily neighbor friends: indeed, the larger share is intended for persons we've met maybe once, perhaps not at all. People who've struck our fancy. Like President Roosevelt. Like the Reverend and Mrs. J. C. Lucey, Baptist missionaries to Borneo who lectured here last winter. Or the little knife grinder who comes through town twice a year. Or Abner Packer, the driver of the six o'clock bus from Mobile, who exchanges waves with us every day as he passes in a dust-cloud whoosh. Or the young Wistons, a California couple whose car one afternoon broke down outside the house and who spent a pleasant hour chatting with us on the porch (young Mr. Wiston snapped our picture, the only one we've ever had taken). Is it because my friend is shy with everyone except strangers that these strangers, and merest acquaintances, seem to us our truest friends? I think yes. Also the scrapbooks we keep of thank-you's on White House stationery, time-to-time communications from California and Borneo, the knife grinder's penny post cards, make us feel connected to eventful worlds beyond the kitchen with its view of a sky that stops.

23   Now a nude December fig branch grates against the window. The kitchen is empty, the cakes are gone; yesterday we carted the last of them to the post office, where the cost of stamps turned our purse inside out. We're broke. That rather depresses me, but my friend insists on cele-

brating—with two inches of whiskey left in Haha's bottle. Queenie has a spoonful in a bowl of coffee (she likes her coffee chicory-flavored and strong). The rest we divide between a pair of jelly glasses. We're both quite awed at the prospect of drinking straight whiskey; the taste of it brings screwed-up expressions and sour shudders. But by and by we begin to sing, the two of us singing different songs simultaneously. I don't know the words to mine, just: Come on along, come on along, to the dark-town strutters' ball. But I can dance: that's what I mean to be, a tap-dancer in the movies. My dancing shadow rollicks on the walls; our voices rock the chinaware; we giggle: as if unseen hands were tickling us. Queenie rolls on her back, her paws plow the air, something like a grin stretches her black lips. Inside myself, I feel warm and sparky as those crumbling logs, carefree as the wind in the chimney. My friend waltzes round the stove, the hem of her poor calico skirt pinched between her fingers as though it were a party dress: Show me the way to go home, she sings, her tennis shoes squeaking on the floor. Show me the way to go home.

24   Enter: two relatives. Very angry. Potent with eyes that scold, tongues that scald. Listen to what they have to say, the words tumbling together into a wrathful tune: "A child of seven! whiskey on his breath! are you out of your mind? feeding a child of seven! must be loony! road to ruination! remember Cousin Kate? Uncle Charlie? Uncle Charlie's brother-in-law? shame! scandal! humiliation! kneel, pray, beg the Lord!"

25   Queenie sneaks under the stove. My friend gazes at her shoes, her chin quivers, she lifts her skirt and blows her nose and runs to her room. Long after the town has gone to sleep and the house is silent except for the chimings of clocks and the sputter of fading fires, she is weeping into a pillow already as wet as a widow's handkerchief.

26   "Don't cry," I say, sitting at the bottom of her bed and shivering despite my flannel nightgown that smells of last winter's cough syrup, "don't cry," I beg, teasing her toes, tickling her feet, "you're too old for that."

27   "It's because," she hiccups, "I am too old. Old and funny."

28   "Not funny. Fun. More fun than anybody. Listen. If you don't stop crying you'll be so tired tomorrow we can't go cut a tree."

29   She straightens up. Queenie jumps on the bed (where Queenie is not allowed) to lick her cheeks. "I know where we'll find real pretty trees, Buddy. And holly, too. With berries big as your eyes. It's way off in the woods. Farther than we've ever been. Papa used to bring us Christmas trees from there: carry them on his shoulder. That's fifty years ago. Well, now: I can't wait for morning."

30   Morning. Frozen rime lusters the grass; the sun, round as an orange and orange as hot-weather moons, balances on the horizon, burnishes the silvered winter woods. A wild turkey calls. A renegade hog grunts in the undergrowth. Soon, by the edge of knee-deep, rapid-running water we have to abandon the buggy. Queenie wades the stream first, paddles across barking complaints at the swiftness of the current, the pneumonia-making

coldness of it. We follow, holding our shoes and equipment (a hatchet, a burlap sack) above our heads. A mile more: of chastising thorns, burs and briers that catch at our clothes; of rusty pine needles brilliant with gaudy fungus and molted feathers. Here, there, a flash, a flutter, an ecstasy of shrillings remind us that not all the birds have flown south. Always, the path unwinds through lemony sun pools and pitch-black vine tunnels. Another creek to cross: a disturbed armada of speckled trout froths the water round us, and frogs the size of plates practice belly flops; beaver workmen are building a dam. On the farther shore, Queenie shakes herself and trembles. My friend shivers, too: not with cold but enthusiasm. One of her hat's ragged roses sheds a petal as she lifts her head and inhales the pine-heavy air. "We're almost there; can you smell it, Buddy?" she says, as though we were approaching an ocean.

31   And, indeed, it is a kind of ocean. Scented acres of holiday trees, prickly-leafed holly. Red berries shiny as Chinese bells: black crows swoop upon them screaming. Having stuffed our burlap sacks with enough greenery and crimson to garland a dozen windows, we set about choosing a tree. "It should be," muses my friend, "twice as tall as a boy. So a boy can't steal the star." The one we pick is twice as tall as me. A brave handsome brute that survives thirty hatchet strokes before it keels with a creaking rending cry. Lugging it like a kill, we commence the long trek out. Every few yards we abandon the struggle, sit down and pant. But we have the strength of triumphant huntsmen; that and the tree's virile, icy perfume revive us, goad us on. Many compliments accompany our sunset return along the red clay road to town; but my friend is sly and noncommittal when passersby praise the treasure perched in our buggy: what a fine tree and where did it come from? "Yonderways," she murmurs vaguely. Once a car stops and the rich mill owner's lazy wife leans out and whines: "Giveya two-bits cash for that ol tree." Ordinarily my friend is afraid of saying no; but on this occasion she promptly shakes her head: "We wouldn't take a dollar." The mill owner's wife persists. "A dollar, my foot! Fifty cents. That's my last offer. Goodness, woman, you can get another one." In answer, my friend gently reflects: "I doubt it. There's never two of anything."

32   Home: Queenie slumps by the fire and sleeps till tomorrow, snoring loud as a human.

33   A trunk in the attic contains: a shoebox of ermine tails (off the opera cape of a curious lady who once rented a room in the house), coils of frazzled tinsel gone gold with age, one silver star, a brief rope of dilapidated, undoubtedly dangerous candy-like light bulbs. Excellent decorations, as far as they go, which isn't far enough: my friend wants our tree to blaze "like a Baptist window," droop with weighty snows of ornament. But we can't afford the made-in-Japan splendors at the five-and-dime. So we do what we've always done: sit for days at the kitchen table with scissors and crayons and stacks of colored paper. I make sketches and my friend cuts them out: lots of cats, fish too (because they're easy to draw), some

apples, some watermelons, a few winged angels devised from saved-up sheets of Hershey-bar tin foil. We use safety pins to attach these creations to the tree; as a final touch, we sprinkle the branches with shredded cotton (picked in August for this purpose). My friend, surveying the effect, clasps her hands together. "Now honest, Buddy. Doesn't it look good enough to eat?" Queenie tries to eat an angel.

34   After weaving and ribboning holly wreaths for all the front windows, our next project is the fashioning of family gifts. Tie-dye scarves for the ladies, for the men a home-brewed lemon and licorice and aspirin syrup to be taken "at the first Symptoms of a Cold and after Hunting." But when it comes time for making each other's gift, my friend and I separate to work secretly. I would like to buy her a pearl-handled knife, a radio, a whole pound of chocolate-covered cherries (we tasted some once, and she always swears: "I could live on them, Buddy, Lord yes I could—and that's not taking His name in vain"). Instead, I am building her a kite. She would like to give me a bicycle (she's said so on several million occasions: "If only I could, Buddy. It's bad enough in life to do without something you want; but confound it, what gets my goat is not being able to give somebody something you want them to have. Only one of these days I will, Buddy. Locate you a bike. Don't ask how. Steal it, maybe"). Instead, I'm fairly certain that she is building me a kite—the same as last year, and the year before: the year before that we exchanged slingshots. All of which is fine by me. For we are champion kite-fliers who study the wind like sailors; my friend, more accomplished than I, can get a kite aloft when there isn't enough breeze to carry clouds.

35   Christmas Eve afternoon we scrape together a nickel and go to the butcher's to buy Queenie's traditional gift, a good gnawable beef bone. The bone, wrapped in funny paper, is placed high in the tree near the silver star. Queenie knows it's there. She squats at the foot of the tree staring up in a trance of greed: when bedtime arrives she refuses to budge. Her excitement is equaled by my own. I kick the covers and turn my pillow as though it were a scorching summer's night. Somewhere a rooster crows: falsely, for the sun is still on the other side of the world.

36   "Buddy, are you awake?" It is my friend, calling from her room, which is next to mine; and an instant later she is sitting on my bed holding a candle. "Well, I can't sleep a hoot," she declares. "My mind's jumping like a jack rabbit. Buddy, do you think Mrs. Roosevelt will serve our cake at dinner?" We huddle in the bed, and she squeezes my hand I-love-you. "Seems like your hand used to be so much smaller, I guess I hate to see you grow up. When you're grown up, will we still be friends?" I say always. "But I feel so bad, Buddy. I wanted so bad to give you a bike. I tried to sell my cameo Papa gave me. Buddy"—she hesitates, as though embarrassed—"I made you another kite." Then I confess that I made her one, too; and we laugh. The candle burns too short to hold. Out it goes, exposing the starlight, the stars spinning at the window like a visible caroling that slowly, slowly daybreak silences. Possibly we doze; but the

beginnings of dawn splash us like cold water: we're up, wide-eyed and wandering while we wait for others to waken. Quite deliberately my friend drops a kettle on the kitchen floor. I tap-dance in front of closed doors. One by one the household emerges, looking as though they'd like to kill us both; but it's Christmas so they can't. First, a gorgeous break-fast: just everything you can imagine—from flapjacks and fried squirrel to hominy grits and honey-in-the-comb. Which puts everyone in a good humor except my friend and me. Frankly, we're so impatient to get at the presents we can't eat a mouthful.

37   Well, I'm disappointed. Who wouldn't be? With socks, a Sunday school shirt, some handkerchiefs, a hand-me-down sweater and a year's sub-scription to a religious magazine for children. The Little Shepherd. It makes me boil. It really does.

38   My friend has a better haul. A sack of Satsumas, that's her best pre-sent. She is proudest, however, of a white wool shawl knitted by her mar-ried sister. But she says her favorite gift is the kite I built her. And it is very beautiful; though not as beautiful as the one she made me, which is blue and scattered with gold and green Good Conduct stars; moreover, my name is painted on it, "Buddy."

39   "Buddy, the wind is blowing."

40   The wind is blowing, and nothing will do till we've run to a pasture below the house where Queenie has scooted to bury her bone (and where, a winter hence, Queenie will be buried, too). There, plunging through the healthy waist-high grass we unreel our kites, feel them twitching at the string like sky fish as they swim into the wind. Satisfied, sun-warmed, we sprawl in the grass and peel Satsumas and watch our kites cavort. Soon I forget the socks and hand-me-down sweater. I'm as happy as if we'd already won the fifty-thousand-dollar Grand Prize in the coffee-naming contest.

41   "My, how foolish I am!" my friend cries, suddenly alert, like a woman remembering too late she has biscuits in the oven. "You know what I've always thought?" she asks in a tone of discovery, and not smiling at me but a point beyond. "I've always thought a body would have to be sick and dying before they saw the Lord. And I imagined that when He came it would be like looking at the Baptist window: pretty as colored glass with the sun pouring through, such a shine you don't know it's getting dark. And it's been a comfort: to think of that shine taking away all the spooky feel-ing. But I'll wager it never happens. I'll wager at the very end a body real-izes the Lord has already shown Himself. That things as they are"—her hand circles in a gesture that gathers clouds and kites and grass and Quee-nie pawing earth over her bone—"just what they've always seen, was see-ing Him. As for me, I could leave the world with today in my eyes."

42   This is our last Christmas together.

43   Life separates us. Those who Know Best decide that I belong in a mil-itary school. And so follows a miserable succession of bugle-blowing pris-ons, grim reveille-ridden summer camps. I have a new home too. But it doesn't count. Home is where my friend is, and there I never go.

44   And there she remains, puttering around the kitchen. Alone with Queeie. Then alone. ("Buddy dear," she writes in her wild hard-to-read script, "yesterday Jim Macy's horse kicked Queenie bad. Be thankful she didn't feel much. I wrapped her in a Fine Linen sheet and rode her in the buggy down to Simpson's pasture where she can be with all her Bones. . . "). For a few Novembers she continues to bake her fruitcakes single-handed; not as many, but some: and, of course, she always sends me "the best of the batch." Also, in every letter she encloses a dime wadded in toilet paper: "See a picture show and write me the story." But gradually in her letters she tends to confuse me with her other friend, the Buddy who died in the 1880's; more and more thirteenths are not the only days she stays in bed: a morning arrives in November, a leafless birdless coming of winter morning, when she cannot rouse herself to exclaim: "Oh my, it's fruitcake weather!"

45   And when that happens, I know it. A message saying so merely confirms a piece of news some secret vein had already received, severing from me an irreplaceable part of myself, letting loose like a kite on a broken string. That is why, walking across a school campus on this particular December morning, I keep searching the sky. As if I expected to see, rather like hearts, a lost pair of kites hurrying toward heaven.

Questions for Discussion

1. In this story of an unusual friendship, the boy says of his friend, "She is still a child." Does he mean this statement as a compliment or an insult? What are her childlike qualities? In what ways are the boy and the woman alike?

2. What does "she" mean by "'As for me, I could leave the world with today in my eyes'"?

3. How would you describe the rest of the family's relationship to Buddy and his friend?

4. Why do the two friends go to the great trouble and expense of making and mailing fruitcakes every Christmas?

5. What is the point of view in this story? Why is this point of view essential to the creation of the story? Why is it written in present tense? How would this story differ in style and diction if the narrator were still a child?

6. Explain the symbolism of the kites.

Suggestions for Exploring, Writing, and Persuading

1. Write an essay describing your most memorable holiday.

2. One of the strengths of the story is the vivid sensory detail given in the descriptions. Discuss Capote's use of such details, concentrating on at least three senses.

3. Write an essay explaining the relationship Buddy and his friend have with other people, both nearby and far away.

4. In an age of dysfunctional families, persuade the reader that this short story exemplifies a truly functional family.

5. The narrator writes that "Home is where my friend is, and there I never go." In an essay, argue that home is a place as in Mayes' "Bramere" or that home is people.

Alice Walker (b. 1944)

Alice Walker, writer of novels, short stories, poems, and essays, is perhaps best known for her popular novel The Color Purple *(1982), which was made into a movie. Many of her earlier works, including* The Color Purple *and the story included here, draw on her rural Southern upbringing and celebrate the complex, rich art of rural Southern African American women. However,* Possessing the Secret of Joy *(1992) is set in Africa. Her 1998 novel,* By the Light of My Father's Smile, *uses multiple narrators to examine father-daughter relationships. In 2003, she published two books,* Meridian *and* Absolute Trust in the Goodness of the Earth, *a collection of poems; in 2004, she also published two books,* Now is the Time to Open Your Heart *and* You Can't Keep a Good Woman Down, *a collection of short stories. Her recent works frequently blend autobiography with fiction.*

EVERYDAY USE (1973)

FOR YOUR GRANDMAMA

1 I will wait for her in the yard that Maggie and I made so clean and wavy yesterday afternoon. A yard like this is more comfortable than most people know. It is not just a yard. It is like an extended living room. When the hard clay is swept clean as a floor and the fine sand around the edges lined with tiny, irregular grooves, anyone can come and sit and look up into the elm tree and wait for the breezes that never come inside the house.

2 Maggie will be nervous until after her sister goes: she will stand hopelessly in corners, homely and ashamed of the burn scars down her arms and legs, eying her sister with a mixture of envy and awe. She thinks her sister has held life always in the palm of one hand, that "no" is a word the world never learned to say to her.

3 You've no doubt seen those TV shows where the child who has "made it" is confronted, as a surprise, by her own mother and father, tottering in weakly from backstage. (A pleasant surprise, of course: What would

they do if parent and child came on the show only to curse out and insult each other?) On TV mother and child embrace and smile into each other's faces. Sometimes the mother and father weep, the child wraps them in her arms and leans across the table to tell how she would not have made it without their help. I have seen these programs.

4   Sometimes I dream a dream in which Dee and I are suddenly brought together on a TV program of this sort. Out of a dark and soft-seated limousine I am ushered into a bright room filled with many people. There I meet a smiling, gray, sporty man like Johnny Carson who shakes my hand and tells me what a fine girl I have. Then we are on the stage and Dee is embracing me with tears in her eyes. She pins on my dress a large orchid, even though she has told me once that she thinks orchids are tacky flowers.

5   In real life I am a large, big-boned woman with rough, man-working hands. In the winter I wear flannel nightgowns to bed and overalls during the day. I can kill and clean a hog as mercilessly as a man. My fat keeps me hot in zero weather. I can work outside all day, breaking ice to get water for washing; I can eat pork liver cooked over the open fire minutes after it comes steaming from the hog. One winter I knocked a bull calf straight in the brain between the eyes with a sledge hammer and had the meat hung up to chill before nightfall. But of course all this does not show on television. I am the way my daughter would want me to be: a hundred pounds lighter, my skin like an uncooked barley pancake. My hair glistens in the hot bright lights. Johnny Carson has much to do to keep up with my quick and witty tongue.

6   But that is a mistake. I know even before I wake up. Who ever knew a Johnson with a quick tongue? Who can even imagine me looking a strange white man in the eye? It seems to me I have talked to them always with one foot raised in flight, with my head turned in whichever way is farthest from them. Dee, though. She would always look anyone in the eye. Hesitation was no part of her nature.

7   "How do I look, Mama?" Maggie says, showing just enough of her thin body enveloped in pink skirt and red blouse for me to know she's there, almost hidden by the door.

8   "Come out into the yard," I say.

9   Have you ever seen a lame animal, perhaps a dog run over by some careless person rich enough to own a car, sidle up to someone who is ignorant enough to be kind to him? That is the way my Maggie walks. She has been like this, chin on chest, eyes on ground, feet in shuffle, ever since the fire that burned the other house to the ground.

10   Dee is lighter than Maggie, with nicer hair and a fuller figure. She's a woman now, though sometimes I forget. How long ago was it that the other house burned? Ten, twelve years? Sometimes I can still hear the flame and feel Maggie's arms sticking to me, her hair smoking and her dress falling off her in little black papery flakes. Her eyes seemed

stretched open, blazed open by the flames reflected in them. And Dee. I see her standing off under the sweet gum tree she used to dig gum out of; a look of concentration on her face as she watched the last dingy gray board of the house fall in toward the red-hot brick chimney. Why don't you do a dance around the ashes? I'd wanted to ask her. She had hated the house that much.

11   I used to think she hated Maggie, too. But that was before we raised the money, the church and me, to send her to Augusta to school. She used to read to us without pity; forcing words, lies, other folks' habits, whole lives upon us two, sitting trapped and ignorant underneath her voice. She washed us in a river of make-believe, burned us with a lot of knowledge we didn't necessarily need to know. Pressed us to her with the serious way she read, to shove us away at just the moment, like dimwits, we seemed about to understand.

12   Dee wanted nice things. A yellow organdy dress to wear to her graduation from high school; black pumps to match a green suit she'd made from an old suit somebody gave me. She was determined to stare down any disaster in her efforts. Her eyelids would not flicker for minutes at a time. Often I fought off the temptation to shake her. At sixteen she had a style of her own: and knew what style was.

13   I never had an education myself. After second grade the school was closed down. Don't ask me why: in 1927 colored asked fewer questions than they do now. Sometimes Maggie reads to me. She stumbles along good-naturedly but can't see well. She knows she is not bright. Like good looks and money, quickness passed her by. She will marry John Thomas (who has mossy teeth in an earnest face) and then I'll be free to sit here and I guess just sing church songs to myself. Although I never was a good singer. Never could carry a tune. I was always better at a man's job. I used to love to milk till I was hooked in the side in '49. Cows are soothing and slow and don't bother you, unless you try to milk them the wrong way.

14   I have deliberately turned my back on the house. It is three rooms, just like the one that burned, except the roof is tin; they don't make shingle roofs any more. There are no real windows, just some holes cut in the sides, like the portholes in a ship, but not round and not square, with rawhide holding the shutters up on the outside. This house is in a pasture too, like the other one. No doubt when Dee sees it she will want to tear it down. She wrote me once that no matter where we "choose" to live, she will manage to come see us. But she will never bring her friends. Maggie and I thought about this and Maggie asked me, "Mama, when did Dee ever *have* any friends?"

15   She had a few. Furtive boys in pink shirts hanging about on washday after school. Nervous girls who never laughed. Impressed with her they worshiped the well-turned phrase, the cute shape, the scalding humor that erupted like bubbles in lye. She read to them.

16   When she was courting Jimmy T she didn't have much time to pay to us, but turned all her faultfinding power on him. He *flew* to marry a cheap city girl from a family of ignorant flashy people. She hardly had time to recompose herself.

17   When she comes I will meet—but there they are!

18   Maggie attempts to make a dash for the house, in her shuffling way, but I stay her with my hand. "Come back here," I say. And she stops and tries to dig a well in the sand with her toe.

19   It is hard to see them clearly through the strong sun. But even the first glimpse of leg out of the car tells me it is Dee. Her feet were always neat-looking, as if God himself had shaped them with a certain style. From the other side of the car comes a short, stocky man. Hair is all over his head a foot long and hanging from his chin like a kinky mule tail. I hear Maggie suck in her breath. "Uhnnnh," is what it sounds like. Like when you see the wriggling end of a snake just in front of your foot on the road. "Uhnnnh."

20   Dee next. A dress down to the ground, in this hot weather. A dress so loud it hurts my eyes. There are yellows and oranges enough to throw back the light of the sun. I feel my whole face warming from the heat waves it throws out. Earrings gold, too, and hanging down to her shoulders. Bracelets dangling and making noises when she moves her arm up to shake the folds of the dress out of her armpits. The dress is loose and flows, and as she walks closer, I like it. I hear Maggie go "Uhnnnh" again. It is her sister's hair. It stands straight up like the wool on a sheep. It is black as night and around the edges are two long pigtails that rope about like small lizards disappearing behind her ears.

21   "Wa-su-zo-Tean-o!" she says, coming on in that gliding way the dress makes her move. The short stocky fellow with the hair to his navel is all grinning and he follows up with "Asalamalakim, my mother and sister!" He moves to hug Maggie but she falls back, right up against the back of my chair. I feel her trembling there and when I look up I see the perspiration falling off her chin.

22   "Don't get up," says Dee. Since I am stout it takes something of a push. You can see me trying to move a second or two before I make it. She turns, showing white heels through her sandals, and goes back to the car. Out she peeks next with a Polaroid. She stoops down quickly and lines up picture after picture of me sitting there in front of the house with Maggie cowering behind me. She never takes a shot without making sure the house is included. When a cow comes nibbling around the edge of the yard she snaps it and me and Maggie *and* the house. Then she puts the Polaroid in the back seat of the car, and comes up and kisses me on the forehead.

23   Meanwhile Asalamalakim is going through motions with Maggie's hand. Maggie's hand is as limp as a fish, and probably as cold, despite the sweat, and she keeps trying to pull it back. It looks like Asalamalakim

wants to shake hands but wants to do it fancy. Or maybe he don't know how people shake hands. Anyhow, he soon gives up on Maggie.

24   "Well," I say. "Dee."

25   "No, Mama," she says. "Not 'Dee,' Wangero Leewanika Kemanjo!"

26   "What happened to 'Dee'?" I wanted to know.

27   "She's dead," Wangero said. "I couldn't bear it any longer, being named after the people who oppress me."

28   "You know as well as me you was named after your aunt Dicie," I said. Dicie is my sister. She named Dee. We called her "Big Dee" after Dee was born.

29   "But who was she named after?" asked Wangero.

30   "I guess after Grandma Dee," I said.

31   "And who was she named after?" asked Wangero.

32   "Her mother," I said, and saw Wangero was getting tired. "That's about as far back as I can trace it," I said. Though, in fact, I probably could have carried it back beyond the Civil War through the branches.

33   "Well," said Asalamalakim, "there you are."

34   "Uhnnnh," I heard Maggie say.

35   "There I was not," I said, "before 'Dicie' cropped up in our family, so why should I try to trace it that far back?"

36   He just stood there grinning, looking down on me like somebody inspecting a Model A car. Every once in a while he and Wangero sent eye signals over my head.

37   "How do you pronounce this name?" I asked.

38   "You don't have to call me by it if you don't want to," said Wangero.

39   "Why shouldn't I?" I asked. "If that's what you want us to call you, we'll call you."

40   "I know it might sound awkward at first," said Wangero.

41   "I'll get used to it," I said. "Ream it out again."

42   Well, soon we got the name out of the way. Asalamalakim had a name twice as long and three times as hard. After I tripped over it two or three times he told me to just call him Hakim-a-barber. I wanted to ask him was he a barber, but I didn't really think he was, so I didn't ask.

43   "You must belong to those beef-cattle peoples down the road," I said. They said "Asalamalakim" when they met you, too, but they didn't shake hands. Always too busy: feeding the cattle, fixing the fences, putting up salt-lick shelters, throwing down hay. When the white folks poisoned some of the herd the men stayed up all night with rifles in their hands. I walked a mile and a half just to see the sight.

44   Hakim-a-barber said, "I accept some of their doctrines, but farming and raising cattle is not my style." (They didn't tell me, and I didn't ask, whether Wangero (Dee) had really gone and married him.)

45   We sat down to eat and right away he said he didn't eat collards and pork was unclean. Wangero, though, went on through the chitlins and corn bread, the greens and everything else. She talked a blue streak over the sweet potatoes. Everything delighted her. Even the fact that we still

used the benches her daddy made for the table when we couldn't afford to buy chairs.

46   "Oh, Mama!" she cried. Then turned to Hakim-a-barber. "I never knew how lovely these benches are. You can feel the rump prints," she said, running her hands underneath her and along the bench. Then she gave a sigh and her hand closed over Grandma Dee's butter dish. "That's it!" she said. "I knew there was something I wanted to ask you if I could have." She jumped up from the table and went over in the corner where the churn stood, the milk in it clabber by now. She looked at the churn and looked at it.

47   "This churn top is what I need," she said. "Didn't Uncle Buddy whittle it out of a tree you all used to have?"

48   "Yes," I said.

49   "Uh huh," she said happily. "And I want the dasher, too."

50   "Uncle Buddy whittle that, too?" asked the barber.

51   Dee (Wangero) looked up at me.

52   "Aunt Dee's first husband whittled the dash," said Maggie so low you almost couldn't hear her. "His name was Henry, but they called him Stash."

53   "Maggie's brain is like an elephant's," Wangero said, laughing. "I can use the churn top as a centerpiece for the alcove table," she said, sliding a plate over the churn, "and I'll think of something artistic to do with the dasher."

54   When she finished wrapping the dasher the handle stuck out. I took it for a moment in my hands. You didn't even have to look close to see where hands pushing the dasher up and down to make butter had left a kind of sink in the wood. In fact, there were a lot of small sinks; you could see where thumbs and fingers had sunk into the wood. It was a beautiful light yellow wood, from a tree that grew in the yard where Big Dee and Stash had lived.

55   After dinner Dee (Wangero) went to the trunk at the foot of my bed and started rifling through it. Maggie hung back in the kitchen over the dishpan. Out came Wangero with two quilts. They had been pieced by Grandma Dee and then Big Dee and me had hung them on the quilt frames on the front porch and quilted them. One was in the Lone Star pattern. The other was Walk Around the Mountain. In both of them were scraps of dresses Grandma Dee had worn fifty and more years ago. Bits and pieces of Grandpa Jarrell's Paisley shirts. And one teeny faded blue piece, about the size of a penny matchbox, that was from Great Grandpa Ezra's uniform that he wore in the Civil War.

56   "Mama," Wangero said sweet as a bird. "Can I have these old quilts?"

57   I heard something fall in the kitchen, and a minute later the kitchen door slammed.

58   "Why don't you take one or two of the others?" I asked. "These old things was just done by me and Big Dee from some tops your grandma pieced before she died."

59   "No," said Wangero. "I don't want those. They are stitched around the borders by machine."

60   "That'll make them last better," I said.

61   "That's not the point," said Wangero. "These are all pieces of dresses Grandma used to wear. She did all this stitching by hand. Imagine!" She held the quilts securely in her arms, stroking them.

62   "Some of the pieces, like those lavender ones, come from old clothes her mother handed down to her," I said, moving up to touch the quilts. Dee (Wangero) moved back just enough so that I couldn't reach the quilts. They already belonged to her.

63   "Imagine!" she breathed again, clutching them closely to her bosom.

64   "The truth is," I said, "I promised to give them quilts to Maggie, for when she marries John Thomas."

65   She gasped like a bee had stung her.

66   "Maggie can't appreciate these quilts!" she said. "She'd probably be backward enough to put them to everyday use."

67   "I reckon she would," I said. "God knows I been saving 'em for long enough with nobody using 'em. I hope she will!" I didn't want to bring up how I had offered Dee (Wangero) a quilt when she went away to college. Then she had told me they were old-fashioned, out of style.

68   "But they're *priceless!*" she was saying now, furiously; for she has a temper. "Maggie would put them on the bed and in five years they'd be in rags. Less than that!"

69   "She can always make some more," I said. "Maggie knows how to quilt."

70   Dee (Wangero) looked at me with hatred. "You just will not understand. The point is these quilts, *these* quilts!"

71   "Well," I said, stumped. "What would *you* do with them?"

72   "Hang them," she said. As if that was the only thing you *could* do with quilts.

73   Maggie by now was standing in the door. I could almost hear the sound her feet made as they scraped over each other.

74   "She can have them, Mama," she said, like somebody used to never winning anything, or having anything reserved for her. "I can 'member Grandma Dee without the quilts."

75   I looked at her hard. She had filled her bottom lip with checkerberry snuff and it gave her face a kind of dopey, hangdog look. It was Grandma Dee and Big Dee who taught her how to quilt herself. She stood there with her scarred hands hidden in the folds of her skirt. She looked at her sister with something like fear but she wasn't mad at her. This was Maggie's portion. This was the way she knew God to work.

76   When I looked at her like that something hit me in the top of my head and ran down to the soles of my feet. Just like when I'm in church and the spirit of God touches me and I get happy and shout. I did something I never had done before: hugged Maggie to me, then dragged her on into the room, snatched the quilts out of Miss Wangero's hands and

dumped them into Maggie's lap. Maggie just sat there on my bed with her mouth open.

77   "Take one or two of the others," I said to Dee.

78   But she turned without a word and went out to Hakim-a-barber.

79   "You just don't understand," she said, as Maggie and I came out to the car.

80   "What don't I understand?" I wanted to know.

81   "Your heritage," she said. And then she turned to Maggie, kissed her, and said, "You ought to try to make something of yourself, too, Maggie. It's really a new day for us. But from the way you and Mama still live you'd never know it."

82   She put on some sunglasses that hid everything above the tip of her nose and her chin.

83   Maggie smiled; maybe at the sunglasses. But a real smile, not scared. After we watched the car dust settle I asked Maggie to bring me a dip of snuff. And then the two of us sat there just enjoying, until it was time to go in the house and go to bed.

Questions for Discussion

1. What does the narrating mother's opening description of the yard tell you about her and Maggie? What do the mother's recurring dream and her response to it reveal about her relationship to Dee?

2. The narrator says of Dee, "She used to read to us without pity: forcing words, lies, other folks' habits, whole lives upon us two, sitting trapped and ignorant underneath her voice." Why does the narrator feel trapped by, rather than appreciative of, Dee's reading? Is the narrator merely ignorant and insensitive? Why does she regard what she hears as lies?

3. Why do Dee and her male friend use a strange language, and why has Dee changed her name?

4. Note that after the arrival of Dee, the narrator's style changes, becoming less formal and more colloquial. Why might Walker have chosen to change the style here?

5. What is the distinction between the mother's use of the churn and Dee's proposed use of it?

6. What is the significance of Maggie's saying, "'I can 'member Grandma Dee without the quilts'"?

Suggestions for Exploring, Writing, and Persuading

1. In a documented essay, contrast the distinctively different lifestyles of the intruders, Dee and her companion, with those of their hosts, Mama and Maggie, and explain how these lifestyles affect the intruders' attitudes toward art.

2. Walker is adept at using gestures to reveal her characters. In an essay on "Everyday Use," analyze Walker's use of such gestures to create her characters.

3. Using the contrasting conceptions of "heritage" exemplified by Dee and by Maggie, explain in a persuasive essay whether a heritage is best preserved by protecting it or by living it.

Sherman Alexie (b. 1966)

*Sherman Alexie was born on the Spokane Indian Reservation in Wellpinit, Washington. His mother is a Spokane Indian and his father a Coeur d'Alene Indian. When he was a child, his chances for survival were precarious, but by the age of three, he was already proving to be a child prodigy. After attending Gonzaga University, Alexie transferred to Washington State University, where he received a degree in American Studies. While at Washington State, Alexie discovered a lifelong love of poetry. His first two books of poetry—*The Business of Fancydancing *(1991) and* I Would Steal Horses *(1993)—were published while he was still in his early twenties, and his remarkable first collection of short stories,* The Lone Ranger and Tonto Fistfight in Heaven *(1993), from which the following story is taken, received a PEN/Hemingway Award for Best First Book of Fiction and a Lila Wallace-Reader's Digest Writers' Award. One story from this collection—"This Is What It Means to Say Phoenix, Arizona"—was the basis for the award-winning film* Smoke Signals *(1998). A prolific writer, Alexie has continued to publish poetry, short stories, and novels. His unique style and his sense of humor have made him popular with both scholars and general readers.*

BECAUSE MY FATHER ALWAYS SAID HE WAS THE ONLY INDIAN WHO SAW JIMI HENDRIX PLAY "THE STAR-SPANGLED BANNER" AT WOODSTOCK   (1993)

1   During the sixties, my father was the perfect hippie, since all the hippies were trying to be Indians. Because of that, how could anyone recognize that my father was trying to make a social statement?

2   But there is evidence, a photograph of my father demonstrating in Spokane, Washington, during the Vietnam war. The photograph made it onto the wire service and was reprinted in newspapers throughout the country. In fact, it was on the cover of *Time*.

3   In the photograph, my father is dressed in bell-bottoms and flowered shirt, his hair in braids, with red peace symbols splashed across his face like war paint. In his hands my father holds a rifle above his head, captured in that moment just before he proceeded to beat the shit out of the

National Guard private lying prone on the ground. A fellow demonstrator holds a sign that is just barely visible over my father's left shoulder. It reads MAKE LOVE NOT WAR.

4   The photographer won a Pulitzer Prize, and editors across the country had a lot of fun creating captions and headlines. I've read many of them collected in my father's scrapbook, and my favorite was run in the *Seattle Times*. The caption under the photograph read DEMONSTRATOR GOES TO WAR FOR PEACE. The editors capitalized on my father's Native American identity with other headlines like ONE WARRIOR AGAINST WAR and PEACEFUL GATHERING TURNS INTO NATIVE UPRISING.

5   Anyway, my father was arrested, charged with attempted murder, which was reduced to assault with a deadly weapon. It was a high-profile case so my father was used as an example. Convicted and sentenced quickly, he spent two years in Walla Walla State Penitentiary. Although his prison sentence effectively kept him out of the war, my father went through a different kind of war behind bars.

6   "There was Indian gangs and white gangs and black gangs and Mexican gangs," he told me once. "And there was somebody new killed every day. We'd hear about somebody getting it in the shower or wherever and the word would go down the line. Just one word. Just the color of his skin. Red, white, black, or brown. Then we'd chalk it up on the mental scoreboard and wait for the next broadcast."

7   My father made it through all that, never got into any serious trouble, somehow avoided rape, and got out of prison just in time to hitchhike to Woodstock to watch Jimi Hendrix play "The Star-Spangled Banner."

8   "After all the shit I'd been through," my father said, "I figured Jimi must have known I was there in the crowd to play something like that. It was exactly how I felt."

9   Twenty years later, my father played his Jimi Hendrix tape until it wore down. Over and over, the house filled with the rockets' red glare and the bombs bursting in air. He'd sit by the stereo with a cooler of beer beside him and cry, laugh, call me over and hold me tight in his arms, his bad breath and body odor covering me like a blanket.

10   Jimi Hendrix and my father became drinking buddies. Jimi Hendrix waited for my father to come home after a long night of drinking. Here's how the ceremony worked:
1. I would lie awake all night and listen for the sounds of my father's pickup.
2. When I heard my father's pickup, I would run upstairs and throw Jimi's tape into the stereo.
3. Jimi would bend his guitar into the first note of "The Star-Spangled Banner" just as my father walked inside.
4. My father would weep, attempt to hum along with Jimi, and then pass out with his head on the kitchen table.
5. I would fall asleep under the table with my head near my father's feet.
6. We'd dream together until the sun came up.

11   The days after, my father would feel so guilty that he would tell me stories as a means of apology.

12   "I met your mother at a party in Spokane," my father told me once. "We were the only two Indians at the party. Maybe the only two Indians in the whole town. I thought she was so beautiful. I figured she was the kind of woman who could make buffalo walk on up to her and give up their lives. She wouldn't have needed to hunt. Every time we went walking, birds would follow us around. Hell, tumbleweeds would follow us around."

13   Somehow my father's memories of my mother grew more beautiful as their relationship became more hostile. By the time the divorce was final, my mother was quite possibly the most beautiful woman who ever lived.

14   "Your father was always half crazy," my mother told me more than once. "And the other half was on medication."

15   But she loved him, too, with a ferocity that eventually forced her to leave him. They fought each other with the kind of graceful anger that only love can create. Still, their love was passionate, unpredictable, and selfish. My mother and father would get drunk and leave parties abruptly to go home and make love.

16   "Don't tell your father I told you this," my mother said. "But there must have been a hundred times he passed out on top of me. We'd be right in the middle of it, he'd say *I love you*, his eyes would roll backwards, and then out went his lights. It sounds strange, I know, but those were good times."

17   I was conceived during one of those drunken nights, half of me formed by my father's whiskey sperm, the other half formed by my mother's vodka egg. I was born a goofy reservation mixed drink, and my father needed me just as much as he needed every other kind of drink.

18   One night my father and I were driving home in a near-blizzard after a basketball game, listening to the radio. We didn't talk much. One, because my father didn't talk much when he was sober, and two, because Indians don't need to talk to communicate.

19   "Hello out there, folks, this is Big Bill Baggins, with the late-night classics show on KROC, 97.2 on your FM dial. We have a request from Betty in Tekoa. She wants to hear Jimi Hendrix's version of 'The Star-Spangled Banner' recorded live at Woodstock."

20   My father smiled, turned the volume up, and we rode down the highway while Jimi led the way like a snowplow. Until that night, I'd always been neutral about Jimi Hendrix. But, in that near-blizzard with my father at the wheel, with the nervous silence caused by the dangerous roads and Jimi's guitar, there seemed to be more to all that music. The reverberation came to mean something, took form and function.

21   That song made me want to learn to play guitar, not because I wanted to be Jimi Hendrix and not because I thought I'd ever play for anyone. I just wanted to touch the strings, to hold the guitar tight against my body, invent a chord, and come closer to what Jimi knew, to what my father knew.

22   "You know," I said to my father after the song was over, "my generation of Indian boys ain't ever had no real war to fight. The first Indians had Custer to fight. My great-grandfather had World War I, my grandfather had World War II, you had Vietnam. All I have is video games."

23   My father laughed for a long time, nearly drove off the road into the snowy fields.

24   "Shit," he said. "I don't know why you're feeling sorry for yourself because you ain't had to fight a war. You're lucky. Shit, all you had was that damn Desert Storm. Should have called it Dessert Storm because it just made the fat cats get fatter. It was all sugar and whipped cream with a cherry on top. And besides that, you didn't even have to fight it. All you lost during that war was sleep because you stayed up all night watching CNN."

25   We kept driving through the snow, talked about war and peace.

26   "That's all there is," my father said. "War and peace with nothing in between. It's always one or the other."

27   "You sound like a book," I said.

28   "Yeah, well, that's how it is. Just because it's in a book doesn't make it not true. And besides, why the hell would you want to fight a war for this country? It's been trying to kill Indians since the very beginning. Indians are pretty much born soldiers anyway. Don't need a uniform to prove it."

29   Those were the kinds of conversations that Jimi Hendrix forced us to have. I guess every song has a special meaning for someone somewhere. Elvis Presley is still showing up in 7–11 stores across the country, even though he's been dead for years, so I figure music just might be the most important thing there is. Music turned my father into a reservation philosopher. Music had powerful medicine.

30   "I remember the first time your mother and I danced," my father told me once. "We were in this cowboy bar. We were the only real cowboys there despite the fact that we're Indians. We danced to a Hank Williams song. Danced to that real sad one, you know. 'I'm So Lonesome I Could Cry.' Except your mother and I weren't lonesome or crying. We just shuffled along and fell right goddamn down into love."

31   "Hank Williams and Jimi Hendrix don't have much in common," I said.

32   "Hell, yes, they do. They knew all about broken hearts," my father said.

33   "You sound like a bad movie."

34   "Yeah, well, that's how it is. You kids today don't know shit about romance. Don't know shit about music either. Especially you Indian kids. You all have been spoiled by those drums. Been hearing them beat so long, you think that's all you need. Hell, son, even an Indian needs a piano or guitar or saxophone now and again."

35   My father played in a band in high school. He was the drummer. I guess he'd burned out on those. Now, he was like the universal defender of the guitar.

36   "I remember when your father would haul that old guitar out and play me songs," my mother said. "He couldn't play all that well but he tried. You could see him thinking about what chord he was going to play next.

His eyes got all squeezed up and his face turned all red. He kind of looked that way when he kissed me, too. But don't tell him I said that."

37   Some nights I lay awake and listened to my parents' lovemaking. I know white people keep it quiet, pretend they don't ever make love. My white friends tell me they can't even imagine their own parents getting it on. I know exactly what it sounds like when my parents are touching each other. It makes up for knowing exactly what they sound like when they're fighting. Plus and minus. Add and subtract. It comes out just about even.

38   Some nights I would fall asleep to the sounds of my parents' lovemaking. I would dream Jimi Hendrix. I could see my father standing in the front row in the dark at Woodstock as Jimi Hendrix played "The Star-Spangled Banner." My mother was at home with me, both of us waiting for my father to find his way back home to the reservation. It's amazing to realize I was alive, breathing and wetting my bed, when Jimi was alive and breaking guitars.

39   I dreamed my father dancing with all these skinny hippie women, smoking a few joints, dropping acid, laughing when the rain fell. And it did rain there. I've seen actual news footage. I've seen the documentaries. It rained. People had to share food. People got sick. People got married. People cried all kinds of tears.

40   But as much as I dream about it, I don't have any clue about what it meant for my father to be the only Indian who saw Jimi Hendrix play at Woodstock. And maybe he wasn't the only Indian there. Most likely there were hundreds but my father thought he was the only one. He told me that a million times when he was drunk and a couple hundred times when he was sober.

41   "I was there," he said. "You got to remember this was near the end and there weren't as many people as before. Not nearly as many. But I waited it out. I waited for Jimi."

42   A few years back, my father packed up the family and the three of us drove to Seattle to visit Jimi Hendrix's grave. We had our photograph taken lying down next to the grave. There isn't a gravestone there. Just one of those flat markers.

43   Jimi was twenty-eight when he died. That's younger than Jesus Christ when he died. Younger than my father as we stood over the grave.

44   "Only the good die young," my father said.

45   "No," my mother said. "Only the crazy people choke to death on their own vomit."

46   "Why you talking about my hero that way?" my father asked.

47   "Shit," my mother said. "Old Jesse WildShoe choked to death on his own vomit and he ain't anybody's hero."

48   I stood back and watched my parents argue. I was used to these battles. When an Indian marriage starts to fall apart, it's even more destructive and painful than usual. A hundred years ago, an Indian marriage was broken easily. The woman or man just packed up all their possessions

and left the tipi. There were no arguments, no discussions. Now, Indians fight their way to the end, holding onto the last good thing, because our whole lives have to do with survival.

49   After a while, after too much fighting and too many angry words had been exchanged, my father went out and bought a motorcycle. A big bike. He left the house often to ride that thing for hours, sometimes for days. He even strapped an old cassette player to the gas tank so he could listen to music. With that bike, he learned something new about running away. He stopped talking as much, stopped drinking as much. He didn't do much of anything except ride that bike and listen to music.

50   Then one night my father wrecked his bike on Devil's Gap Road and ended up in the hospital for two months. He broke both his legs, cracked his ribs, and punctured a lung. He also lacerated his kidney. The doctors said he could have died easily. In fact, they were surprised he made it through surgery, let alone survived those first few hours when he lay on the road, bleeding. But I wasn't surprised. That's how my father was.

51   And even though my mother didn't want to be married to him anymore and his wreck didn't change her mind about that, she still came to see him every day. She sang Indian tunes under her breath, in time with the hum of the machines hooked into my father. Although my father could barely move, he tapped his finger in rhythm.

52   When he had the strength to finally sit up and talk, hold conversations, and tell stories, he called for me.

53   "Victor," he said. "Stick with four wheels."

54   After he began to recover, my mother stopped visiting as often. She helped him through the worst, though. When he didn't need her anymore, she went back to the life she had created. She traveled to powwows, started to dance again. She was a champion traditional dancer when she was younger.

55   "I remember your mother when she was the best traditional dancer in the world," my father said. "Everyone wanted to call her sweetheart. But she only danced for me. That's how it was. She told me that every other step was just for me."

56   "But that's only half of the dance," I said.

57   "Yeah," my father said. "She was keeping the rest for herself. Nobody can give everything away. It ain't healthy."

58   "You know," I said, "sometimes you sound like you ain't even real."

59   "What's real? I ain't interested in what's real. I'm interested in how things should be."

60   My father's mind always worked that way. If you don't like the things you remember, then all you have to do is change the memories. Instead of remembering the bad things, remember what happened immediately before. That's what I learned from my father. For me, I remember how good the first drink of that Diet Pepsi tasted instead of how my mouth felt when I swallowed a wasp with the second drink.

61   Because of all that, my father always remembered the second before my mother left him for good and took me with her. No. I remembered the second before my father left my mother and me. No. My mother remembered the second before my father left her to finish raising me all by herself.

62   But however memory actually worked, it was my father who climbed on his motorcycle, waved to me as I stood in the window, and rode away. He lived in Seattle, San Francisco, Los Angeles, before he finally ended up in Phoenix. For a while, I got postcards nearly every week. Then it was once a month. Then it was on Christmas and my birthday.

63   On a reservation, Indian men who abandon their children are treated worse than white fathers who do the same thing. It's because white men have been doing that forever and Indian men have just learned how. That's how assimilation can work.

64   My mother did her best to explain it all to me, although I understood most of what happened.

65   "Was it because of Jimi Hendrix?" I asked her.

66   "Part of it, yeah," she said. "This might be the only marriage broken up by a dead guitar player."

67   "There's a first time for everything, enit?"

68   "I guess. Your father just likes being alone more than he likes being with other people. Even me and you."

69   Sometimes I caught my mother digging through old photo albums or staring at the wall or out the window. She'd get that look on her face that I knew meant she missed my father. Not enough to want him back. She missed him just enough for it to hurt.

70   On those nights I missed him most I listened to music. Not always Jimi Hendrix. Usually I listened to the blues. Robert Johnson mostly. The first time I heard Robert Johnson sing I knew he understood what it meant to be Indian on the edge of the twenty-first century, even if he was black at the beginning of the twentieth. That must have been how my father felt when he heard Jimi Hendrix. When he stood there in the rain at Woodstock.

71   Then on the night I missed my father most, when I lay in bed and cried, with that photograph of him beating that National Guard private in my hands, I imagined his motorcycle pulling up outside. I knew I was dreaming it all but I let it be real for a moment.

72   "Victor," my father yelled. "Let's go for a ride."

73   "I'll be right down. I need to get my coat on."

74   I rushed around the house, pulled my shoes and socks on, struggled into my coat, and ran outside to find an empty driveway. It was so quiet, a reservation kind of quiet, where you can hear somebody drinking whiskey on the rocks three miles away. I stood on the porch and waited until my mother came outside.

75   "Come on back inside," she said. "It's cold."

76   "No," I said. "I know he's coming back tonight."

77   My mother didn't say anything. She just wrapped me in her favorite quilt and went back to sleep. I stood on the porch all night long and imagined I heard motorcycles and guitars, until the sun rose so bright that I knew it was time to go back inside to my mother. She made breakfast for both of us and we ate until we were full.

Questions for Discussion

1. Explain the statement that "Music turned my father into a reservation philosopher." How does the narrator feel about his father? Why does Jimi Hendrix's version of "The Star-Spangled Banner" appeal to the narrator and his father?
2. What does the father mean when he says, "War and peace with nothing in between. It's always one or the other"?
3. Explain Alexie's claim that he is "a goofy reservation mixed drink"?
4. Explain the relationship between his parents. Why do they separate even though they apparently love each other? Contrast this break-up with the typical Indian marriage break-up.

Suggestions for Exploring, Writing, and Persuading

1. Write a definition essay on what it meant to be a hippie.
2. Research Jimi Hendrix and his music. Then write a critique of both.
3. In an argumentative essay, agree or disagree with the boy's statement that "music just might be the most important thing there is. . . . Music had powerful medicine."
4. After researching conditions on a reservation, argue for or against a Native American's choosing to live on a reservation.

P O E T R Y

William Butler Yeats (1865–1939)

An Irish poet and playwright, William Butler Yeats is regarded by many as one of the greatest twentieth-century poets. Yeats's first poems were published in 1885. Active in the Irish National Theatre, he became a leader in the Irish literary revival. His Collected Poems *(1933), spanning fifty years, shows his extraordinary range and his growth as a poet. Much of Yeats's poetry is powerfully and elaborately symbolic, referring to his vision of a spiritual world and his cyclical theory of history.*

A PRAYER FOR MY DAUGHTER   (1924)

Once more the storm is howling, and half hid
Under this cradle-hood and coverlid
My child sleeps on. There is no obstacle
But Gregory's wood and one bare hill
5   Whereby the haystack- and roof-levelling wind,
Bred on the Atlantic, can be stayed;
And for an hour I have walked and prayed
Because of the great gloom that is in my mind.
I have walked and prayed for this young child an hour
10   And heard the sea-wind scream upon the tower,
And under the arches of the bridge, and scream
In the elms above the flooded stream;
Imagining in excited reverie
That the future years had come,
15   Dancing to a frenzied drum,
Out of the murderous innocence of the sea.
May she be granted beauty and yet not
Beauty to make a stranger's eye distraught,
Or hers before a looking-glass, for such,
20   Being made beautiful overmuch,
Consider beauty a sufficient end,
Lose natural kindness and maybe
The heart-revealing intimacy
That chooses right, and never find a friend.
25   Helen being chosen found life flat and dull
And later had much trouble from a fool,
While that great Queen, that rose out of the spray,
Being fatherless could have her way
Yet chose a bandy-legg`ed smith for man.
30   It's certain that fine women eat
A crazy salad with their meat
Whereby the Horn of Plenty is undone.
In courtesy I'd have her chiefly learned;
Hearts are not had as a gift but hearts are earned
35   By those that are not entirely beautiful;
Yet many, that have played the fool
For beauty's very self, has charm made wise,
And many a poor man that has roved,
Loved and thought himself beloved,
40   From a glad kindness cannot take his eyes.
May she become a flourishing hidden tree

That all her thoughts may like the linnet be,
And have no business but dispensing round
Their magnanimities of sound,
45 Nor but in merriment begin a chase,
Nor but in merriment a quarrel.
O may she live like some green laurel
Rooted in one dear perpetual place.
My mind, because the minds that I have loved,
50 The sort of beauty that I have approved,
Prosper but little, has dried up of late,
Yet knows that to be choked with hate
May well be of all evil chances chief.
If there's no hatred in a mind
55 Assault and battery of the wind
Can never tear the linnet from the leaf.
An intellectual hatred is the worst,
So let her think opinions are accursed.
Have I not seen the loveliest woman born
60 Out of the mouth of Plenty's horn,
Because of her opinionated mind
Barter that horn and every good
By quiet natures understood
For an old bellows full of angry wind?
65 Considering that, all hatred driven hence,
The soul recovers radical innocence
And learns at last that it is self-delighting,
Self-appeasing, self-affrighting,
And that its own sweet will is Heaven's will;
70 She can, though every face should scowl
And every windy quarter howl
Or every bellows burst, be happy still.
And may her bridegroom bring her to a house
Where all's accustomed, ceremonious;
75 For arrogance and hatred are the wares
Peddled in the thoroughfares.
How but in custom and in ceremony
Are innocence and beauty born?
Ceremony's a name for the rich horn,
80 And custom for the spreading laurel tree.

Questions for Discussion

1. The speaker of the poem has been praying silently for an entire hour. What is he so concerned about that he prays at such length? Why does he pray that his daughter not be "beautiful overmuch"?

2. Why does Yeats declare "opinions accursed"?

3. In light of the women's movement, do you think any of Yeats's comments are sexist? If so, which ones and why?

Suggestions for Exploring, Writing, and Persuading

1. If you have children, explain how you combine control with loving encouragement in raising them.

2. Yeats does not pray for control of his daughter; rather he prays that she may grow into a resilient, joyous woman who can protect herself psychologically from the perils of a hostile world. To what degree have your parents tried to control you and to what degree have they encouraged you to grow?

3. Throughout the poem Yeats uses the images of the Horn of Plenty and "a flourishing hidden" laurel tree, and he returns to these in the last two lines of the poem. What do these images suggest that the narrator wants for his daughter as a result of his own experiences?

4. Choosing one of Yeats's abstract words such as *innocence, kindness,* or *beauty,* write an essay arguing that this quality is or is not vitally important.

5. Yeats clearly regards custom and ceremony as important elements in a family's life. In an essay, discuss the importance of custom and ceremony in your own family or in two or more works in this section.

Langston Hughes (1902–1967)

Born in Joplin, Missouri, James Langston Hughes was a novelist, poet, and playwright who often wrote in dialect to reflect what he considered to be the language of the ordinary "Negro." He graduated from Lincoln University in 1929 after attending Columbia University and after working with some of the most famous black writers of the Harlem Renaissance. Hughes founded theaters, produced plays, and traveled to such locales as Haiti, the Soviet Union, and Spain, where he covered the Spanish Civil War. His many works include the Semple tales, the novels Not Without Laughter *(1930) and* Ask Your Mama *(1961), and the gospel musical* Tambourines to Glory *(1959). Hughes's poetry reflects several recurring themes: the racial tension that the black man experiences, the glorification of the common man or woman, and the importance of music, especially jazz and the blues. The following poem represents these themes.*

MOTHER TO SON   (1922)

Well, son, I'll tell you:
Life for me ain't been no crystal stair.

It's had tacks in it,
And splinters,
5 And boards torn up,
And places with no carpet on the floor—
Bare.
But all the time
I'se been a-climbin' on,
10 And reachin' landin's,
And turnin' corners,
And sometimes goin' in the dark
Where there ain't been no light.
So boy, don't you turn back.
15 Don't you set down on the steps
'Cause you finds it's kinder hard.
Don't you fall now—
For I'se still goin', honey,
I'se still climbin',

20 And life for me ain't been no crystal stair.

Questions for Discussion

1. What is the significance of the stair as a metaphor? Explain the meaning of each part of the metaphor.

2. Explain who is the best example for the son of what a strong black man should be.

3. Instead of telling her son what life *has* been, the mother tells him what life *has not* been. Why? What is the significance of the mother's telling the son she is "still climbing"?

Suggestions for Exploring, Writing, and Persuading

1. Write an essay in which you discuss what life has not been for you.

2. Reread the poem and discuss in an essay what you think have been the "tacks," "splinters," "boards torn up," and bare floors in the woman's life. What are they likely to be in the son's life as a man?

Theodore Roethke (1908–1963)

Theodore Roethke was both an acclaimed poet and an exuberant and popular professor of poetry. Partly because he threw himself wholeheartedly into both professions, he often suffered from exhaustion and mental breakdowns. Roethke's relationship with his own father, a German-American who combined authoritarianism with sensitivity, seems to have been ambivalent. His father died when Roethke was fourteen.

Roethke received many awards during his long literary career, including two Guggenheim Fellowships, two Ford Foundation Grants, and a Pulitzer Prize in poetry in 1954 for The Waking: Poems *1933–53.*

MY PAPA'S WALTZ   (1942)

The whiskey on your breath
Could make a small boy dizzy;
But I hung on like death:
Such waltzing was not easy.

5   We romped until the pans
Slid from the kitchen shelf;
My mother's countenance
Could not unfrown itself.

The hand that held my wrist
10 Was battered on one knuckle;
At every step you missed
My right ear scraped a buckle.

You beat time on my head
With a palm caked hard by dirt,
15 Then waltzed me off to bed
Still clinging to your shirt.

Questions for Discussion

1. What evidence in the poem indicates that there is a deep love within the family? What details might be interpreted differently?

2. To what does the word *waltz* in the title refer? As he is "waltzed" to bed, the boy is "still clinging" to his father. What does this reaction indicate about the boy's feelings for his father?

3. What details does Roethke use to describe the father? What do these details indicate?

4. Roethke uses the three-beat line, which reflects the three beats of the waltz. Does the total effect of the poem reflect the smooth gliding motion of the dance? Why or why not?

5. What does the mother's behavior reveal about her?

Suggestions for Exploring, Writing, and Persuading

1. Use specific details from this poem to argue that this family is functional or dysfunctional.

2. Write an essay, using this poem and Giovanni's "Nikki-Rosa," to analyze why memories that may be negative to some adults are not so to children.

Gwendolyn Brooks (1917–2001)

Born in Topeka, Kansas, Gwendolyn Brooks began writing while still a teenager. In high school, she met Langston Hughes, who encouraged her to write and follow her literary ambitions. Brooks is the author of more than twenty books of poetry, including A Street in Bronzeville (1945); The Bean Eaters (1960); *and* Children Coming Home (1991). *She also wrote other works such as the novel* Maud Martha (1953) *and a book of essays,* Young Poet's Primer (1981). *In 1950, Brooks became the first African American to win the Pulitzer Prize in literature, for* Annie Allen. *In 1968, she became the poet laureate for the state of Illinois, and from 1985 to 1986 she was Consultant in Poetry for the Library of Congress.*

THE MOTHER (1945)

Abortions will not let you forget.
You remember the children you got that you did not get,
The damp small pulps with a little or with no hair,
The singers and workers that never handled the air.
5 You will never neglect or beat
Them, or silence or buy with a sweet.
You will never wind up the sucking-thumb
Or scuttle off ghosts that come.
You will never leave them, controlling your luscious sigh,
10 Return for a snack of them, with gobbling mother-eye.

I have heard in the voices of the wind the voices of my dim killed
    children.
I have contracted. I have eased
My dim dears at the breasts they could never suck.
15 I have said, Sweets, if I sinned, if I seized
Your luck
And your lives from your unfinished reach,
If I stole your births and your names,
Your straight baby tears and your games,
20 Your stilted or lovely loves, your tumults, your marriages, aches,
    and your deaths,
If I poisoned the beginnings of your breaths,
Believe that even in my deliberateness I was not deliberate.
Though why should I whine,

25 Whine that the crime was other than mine?—
    Since anyhow you are dead.
    Or rather, or instead,
    You were never made.
    But that too, I am afraid,
30 Is faulty: oh, what shall I say, how is the truth to be said?
    You were born, you had body, you died.
    It is just that you never giggled or planned or cried.

    Believe me, I loved you all.
    Believe me, I knew you, though faintly, and I loved, I loved you
35 All.

Questions for Discussion

1. What are some of the things that the narrator says aborted children will never have, feel, or want?

2. Why does she call them "killed children"? Do you think she called them that before she aborted them? Why or why not? What is the impact of using negative words such as "stole," "poisoned," "crime," and "dead"?

3. Explain what she means by "faulty."

Suggestions for Exploring, Writing, and Persuading

1. Research the psychological effects of abortions on some women. Then write a documented essay on these effects.

2. Write a letter to this woman either denouncing her actions or encouraging her to forget the past and get on with her life.

3. If she loved the children, why did she abort them? Explain your answer in an essay.

Mary TallMountain (1918–1994)

Mary TallMountain, a native Alaskan, was born along the Yukon River to a Koyukon/Athabaskan mother, but after her mother's death, she was adopted by a non-native couple and moved to California. During most of her adult life, she lived in the Tenderloin district of San Francisco, where she was poet-in-residence at the Tenderloin Reflection and Education Center (TREC), a community-based program for writers and artists. TREC established the TallMountain Circle, which distributes and promotes the works of Mary TallMountain and selects the recipients of the TallMountain Award to be given to Tenderloin district or Native American writers. TallMountain reclaims her ancestry and homeland in her stories and poems. Among her books of poems are Nine Poems *(1979) and* There Is No Word for Goodbye

*(1981). She celebrates in this poem a unique feature of her
Native American language and culture.*

THERE IS NO WORD FOR GOODBYE   (1981)

Sokoya, I said, looking through
   the net of wrinkles into
   wise black pools
   of her eyes.
5   What do you say in Athabaskan
   when you leave each other?
   What is the word
   for goodbye?
10   A shade of feeling rippled
   the wind-tanned skin.
   Ah, nothing, she said,
   watching the river flash.
She looked at me close.
   We just say, Tlaa. That means,
15   See you.
   We never leave each other.
   When does your mouth
   say goodbye to your heart?
She touched me light
20   as a bluebell.
   You forget when you leave us;
   you're so small then.
   We don't use that word.
We always think you're coming back,
25   but if you don't,
   we'll see you someplace else.
   You understand.
   There is no word for goodbye.

Questions for Discussion

1. The speaker's *sokoya*, or aunt, is described with natural images, particularly water. What do these images suggest about her character?
What do they say about the sources of her wisdom?

2. Why is there no Athabaskan word for goodbye? What does the
absence of such a word suggest about Athabaskans?

3. Explain the meaning of the question "When does your mouth / say
goodbye to your heart?" What does this question reveal about the relationship between the speaker and her aunt?

4. The speaker says, "we'll see you someplace else." What clues does the
imagery give about where they might see each other?

Suggestions for Exploring, Writing, and Persuading

1. Write an essay about a word you think should not exist in your native
   language or about words you would like added to your language.

2. Some theorists claim that we cannot think about concepts for which
   we have no words. Using this poem as a starting point, argue that this
   claim is or is not true.

Maxine Kumin (b. 1925)

*Pulitzer Prize–winning writer Maxine Kumin is an
extremely versatile writer who has won awards for her
poetry, essays, and fiction. Her works include four novels,
a short story collection, many children's books, three books
of essays, and eleven books of poetry. Kumin often
expresses in her poetry a fascination with nature—with
its rhythms and its survival in the face of brutal human
manipulation.*

NURTURE   (1987)

From a documentary on marsupials I learn
that a pillowcase makes a fine
substitute pouch for an orphaned kangaroo.
I am drawn to such dramas of animal rescue.
5   They are warm in the throat. I suffer, the critic proclaims,
from an overabundance of maternal genes.
Bring me your fallen fledgling, your bummer lamb,
lead the abused, the starvelings, into my barn.
Advise the hunted deer to leap into my corn.
10 And had there been a wild child—
filthy and fierce as a ferret, he is called
in one nineteenth-century account—
a wild child to love, it is safe to assume,
given my fireside inked with paw prints,
15 there would have been room.
Think of the language we two, same, and not-same,
might have constructed from sign,
scratch, grimace, grunt, vowel:
Laughter our first noun, and our long verb, howl.

Questions for Discussion

1. How does the opening reference to "a documentary on marsupials"
   relate to the speaker's "maternal genes"?

2. In what ways do the speaker and the "wild child" she imagines taking
   in constitute a family?

3. What does the "fireside inked with paw prints" reveal about the speaker?

4. Why might the speaker and the "wild child" she imagines construct a language from gestures and inarticulate sounds? How does the speaker feel about creating such a language? What does she mean by "Laughter our first noun, and our long verb, howl"?

Suggestions for Exploring, Writing, and Persuading

1. Write an essay discussing how your pet or pets are a part of your family. How do they communicate with you and the rest of the family? How do you communicate with them?

2. Develop a lexicon of noises, idioms, and signs that the narrator and her wild child might use to communicate.

3. Reread the third verse. Then write an essay arguing why people such as the narrator might be attracted to the wounded.

Alicia Ostriker (b. 1937)

Alicia Ostriker is a contemporary American poet who is especially noted for her ability to portray the wide range of emotions shared by women of all ages. A professor of English at Rutgers University, mother of two daughters and a son, and wife of an astrophysicist, she lives in Princeton, New Jersey. She is the author of eight books of poetry, most recently The Little Space: Poems Selected and New, *which was a finalist for the 1998 National Book Awards. In 1999 she published* Dancing at the Devil's Party: Essays on Poetry, Politics, and the Erotic. *As a critic, Ostriker is the author of books on poetry and on the Bible.*

First Love   (1989)

When the child begins to suffer, the mother
Finds in her mouth those burning coals
You can neither spit out nor swallow—
It tells you about this in Zen, you know
5   You're illuminated when
The coals dissolve and your mouth is cool—
The child's lost boyfriend permeates the home
Like hyacinth perfume,
Nothing can escape it, it is too much,
10   It is maddening, like the insane yellow
Of the first blooming forsythia, like a missing
Limb that goes on hurting the survivor.
Whatever doesn't suffer isn't alive,

You know your daughter's pain is perfectly normal.
15   Nevertheless you imagine
Rinsing all grief from the child's tender face
The way a sculptor might peel the damp dropcloths

Off the clay figure she's been working on
So she can add fresh clay, play
20   With some details, pat it, bring it closer
To completion, and so people can see
How good and beautiful it already is.

Questions for Discussion

1. What is the meaning of the burning coals? Why does the speaker use the Zen image of burning coals in her mouth?
2. Why is a fragrance appropriate to describe the way "the child's lost boyfriend permeates the home"?
3. Explain the double meaning of the poem's title.
4. In describing her empathy for her daughter, the mother uses a series of similes and metaphors. Identify each of these devices. Why do you think the mother uses metaphors rather than direct statements? What is particularly appropriate about the simile of the sculpture to describe the child?

Suggestions for Exploring, Writing, and Persuading

1. Write an essay about a first in your family: perhaps the first to graduate from high school or to go to college, the first grandchild, the first date, or the first born.
2. Using two of the following works, explain how the mother or father conveys a daughter's specialness: Yeats, "A Prayer for My Daughter"; McCullers, "A Domestic Dilemma"; Ostriker, "First Love."
3. Write an essay in which you support or deny the speaker's statement that "Whatever doesn't suffer isn't alive."

Luis Omar Salinas (b. 1938)

Salinas, born in Robstown, Texas, later moved to Monterrey, Mexico. After his mother's death the family moved back to Robstown, where his mother's brother adopted him. They lived in several towns in California, where Salinas's exposure to the majority white culture and the lack of overt racism such as he had experienced in Texas influenced his feelings of loneliness and alienation, themes often examined in his poems. Salinas has written several volumes of poetry

*and won the General Electric Foundation Award for Young
Writers in 1985. He has suffered several nervous breakdowns and was institutionalized numerous times during
the 1960s. Salinas is known for his portrayal of characters
and his sensitivity toward people and the conditions that
affect them.*

MY FATHER IS A SIMPLE MAN   (1987)

I walk to town with my father
to buy a newspaper. He walks slower
than I do so I must slow up.
The street is filled with children.
5 We argue about the price
of pomegranates, I convince
him it is the fruit of scholars.
He has taken me on this journey
and it's been lifelong.
10 He's sure I'll be healthy
so long as I eat more oranges,
and tells me the orange
has seeds and so is perpetual;
and we too will come back
15 like the orange trees.
I ask him what he thinks
about death and he says
he will gladly face it when
it comes but won't jump
20 out in front of a car.
I'd gladly give my life
for this man with a sixth
grade education, whose kindness
and patience are true. . .
25 The truth of it is, he's the scholar,
and when the bitter-hard reality
comes at me like a punishing
evil stranger, I can always
remember that here was a man
30 who was a worker and provider,
who learned the simple facts
in life and lived by them,

who held no pretense.
And when he leaves without
35 benefit of fanfare or applause
I shall have learned what little
there is about greatness.

Questions for Discussion

1. What does the argument over pomegranates versus oranges tell about the character of the father and son?
2. What is the lifelong journey on which the father has taken the narrator? What is its destination?
3. How is the father's sense of humor shown?
4. List the father's character traits as shown in this short poem.

Suggestions for Exploring, Writing, and Persuading

1. Write an essay or a poem about your relationship with either your father or your mother.
2. Write an essay in which you show the character of a parent or a guardian as revealed through a simple act such as walking to the store for a newspaper.
3. Using quotations from the poem, write an essay describing the relationship between the narrator and his father.
4. Write an essay in which you compare Salinas's father with Whitelock's father or with Li-Young Lee's father.

Nikki Giovanni (b. 1943)

Yolande Cornelia Giovanni Jr. was born in Knoxville, Tennessee. She received her BA from Fisk University in 1967 and attended both the University of Pennsylvania and Columbia University. Since 1987 Giovanni has been a professor of English at Virginia Tech. Giovanni has published many poems and articles, notably Black Feeling Black Talk *(1968);* Spin a Soft Black Song: Poems for Children *(1971);* My House: Poems *(1972), a collection of poems about being black in America; and* Grand Mothers: A Multicultural Anthology of Poems, Reminiscences, and Short Stories about the Keepers of Our Traditions. *In 1996 she published both* Selected Poems of Nikki Giovanni *and* The Genie in the Jar. James Baldwin and Nikki Giovanni: A Dialogue *was published in 1973 and* Cotton Candy on a Rainy Day *in 1980. Known as a militant African American poet, Giovanni also writes very personal poetry.*

NIKKI-ROSA   (1968)

childhood remembrances are always a drag
if you're Black
you always remember things like living in Woodlawn

with no inside toilet
5   and if you become famous or something
they never talk about how happy you were to have your mother
all to yourself and
how good the water felt when you got your bath from one of those
big tubs that folk in chicago barbecue in
10   and somehow when you talk about home
it never gets across how much you
understood their feelings
as the whole family attended meetings about Hollydale
and even though you remember
15   your biographers never understand
your father's pain as he sells his stock
and another dream goes
and though you're poor it isn't poverty that
concerns you
20   and though they fought a lot
it isn't your father's drinking that makes any difference
but only that everybody is together and you
and your sister have happy birthdays and very good christmasses
and I really hope no white person ever has cause to write about me
25   because they never understand Black love is Black wealth and they'll
probably talk about my hard childhood and never understand that
all the while I was quite happy

Questions for Discussion

1. What stereotype does Giovanni attack in this poem? Why does Giovanni not want a white biographer?

2. What attitude does this poem take toward poverty? Using specific examples from the poem, show how the speaker's attitude is reflected in the tone. What matters most to Giovanni about her childhood?

3. What does Giovanni mean by "Black love is Black wealth"? What are the qualities of "Black love" that Giovanni speaks of?

4. Why, in the opening line, does Giovanni say that "childhood remembrances"—not childhood—"are always a drag"?

Suggestions for Exploring, Writing, and Persuading

1. Discuss ways in which outsiders may misunderstand events, relationships, or traditions that occur within your family.

2. Discuss some differences between private, ordinary families and public, famous families.

Marilyn Nelson (b. 1946)

Marilyn Nelson has published six books of poems, two of which, The Homeplace *in 1991 and* The Fields of Praise *in 1997, were finalists for the National Book Award in poetry. With Pamela Espeland, she has also published two collections of verse for children:* The Cat Walked through the Casserole and Other Poems for Children *(1984) and* Halfdan Rasmussen's Hundreds of Hens and Other Poems for Children *(1982), translated from Danish. Nelson has a Ph.D. from the University of Minnesota and has served on the faculty of the University of Connecticut since 1978.*

THE HOUSE ON MOSCOW STREET   (1990)

It's the ragged source of memory,
a tarpaper-shingled bungalow
whose floors tilt toward the porch,
whose back yard ends abruptly
5   in a weedy ravine. Nothing special:
a chain of three bedrooms
and a long side porch turned parlor
where my great-grandfather, Pomp, smoked
every evening over the news,
10 a long sunny kitchen
where Annie, his wife,
measured cornmeal
dreaming through the window
across the ravine and up to Shelby Hill
15 where she had borne their spirited,
high-yellow brood.
In the middle bedroom's hard,
high antique double bed

the ghost of Aunt Jane,
20 the laundress
who bought the house in 1872,
though I call with all my voices,
does not appear.
Nor does Pomp's ghost,
25 with whom one of my cousins believes
she once had a long and intimate
unspoken midnight talk.
He told her, though they'd never met,
that he loved her; promised
30 her raw widowhood would heal
without leaving a scar.
The conveniences in an enclosed corner
of the slant-floored back side porch

were the first indoor plumbing in town.
35   Aunt Jane put them in,
incurring the wrath of the woman
who lived in the big house next door.
Aunt Jane left the house
to Annie, whose mother she had known

40   as a slave on the plantation,
so Annie and Pomp could move their children
into town, down off Shelby Hill.
My grandmother, her brother, and five sisters
watched their faces change slowly

45   in the oval mirror on the wall outside the door
into teachers' faces, golden with respect.
Here Geneva, the randy sister,
damned their colleges,
daubing her quicksilver breasts

50   with gifts of perfume.
As much as love,
as much as a visit
to the grave of a known ancestor,
the homeplace moves me not to silence

55   but to righteous, praise Jesus song:
Oh, catfish and turnip greens,
hot-water cornbread and grits.
Oh, musty, much-underlined Bibles;
generations lost to be found,

60   to be found.

Questions for Discussion

1. What gives this rather ramshackle, ordinary house its special significance?

2. Explain Nelson's use of the term "ragged" to refer to memory.

3. What kind of ghosts are said to inhabit this house? What does the narrator mean by "the ghost of Aunt Jane,. . . though I call with all my voices, / does not appear"?

4. How and why did Aunt Jane anger "the woman / who lived in the big house"?

5. Explain how the narrator's family acquired the house and the phrase "generations lost to be found."

Suggestions for Exploring, Writing, and Persuading

1. Write an essay about a place or heirloom that has been very important in your family's history. Describe in detail the place or heirloom and examine in detail the history that gives it special significance.

2. Nelson says, "the homeplace moves me not to silence / but to right-eous, praise Jesus song." What kind of songs does your homeplace elicit from you?

3. Write an essay persuading your reader that memories are indeed "ragged."

4. In an essay, compare the narrator's memories of this house with Nikki Giovanni's memories of her home in "Nikki-Rosa."

5. Compare or contrast the return home of Didion and Nelson.

Afaa M. Weaver (b. 1951)

Born in Baltimore, Maryland, Weaver, formerly known as Michael S. Weaver, received fellowships from the Pennsylvania Council of the Arts and the National Endowment of the Arts. He has written several volumes of poetry, including Water Song *(1985),* My Father's Geography *(1992),* Timber and Prayer *(1995),* Talisman *(1998),* The Lights of God *(1999), and* Multitudes: Poems Selected and New *(2000). In addition, Weaver is a freelance journalist, a play-wright, and a novelist. Currently he is Alumni Professor of English at Simmons College in Boston.*

IMPROVISATION FOR PIANO   (1985)
AFTER *MOOD INDIGO*

Freshly lit cigarette in his mouth,
his collar turned up in the cold,
his face turned wry, and the question,
the awful question hidden beneath.
5   It is so difficult to see the baby
I sent scooting over to my mother,
laughing out, "He can walk, see."
It is difficult to look in my arms and
remember how he once fit there, how
10   I could keep the world away from him
if it threatened to hurt him, to rob him.
When I admit that he has been hurt,
that he has been robbed and that I was helpless,
I wonder what register there is for pain.
15   He is leaving home, and I am sending
another black man into life's teeth and jaws.
All that I know about being black
is some kind of totem knotted with the prints

of my fists beating out a syncopated pain.
20   I can't begin to tell him how to carve.
I can cry. I can counsel other black men,
but love is its own resistance in

the eye a father shares with his son.
The storm window glass sticks to me
25 with its cold, and I watch him go under
the big tree up the street and away.
The night is some slow rendition of
Mood Indigo, and the blues takes me
away to some place and frightens the shit
30 out of me, as I think of how my son will live.
What life will he have without proper
attire, I wonder. I think to run after him,
catch him, and say, "Here, another sweater."
And I know the other sweater is the first time
35 I saw "nigger" in a white man's eyes.
I know he needs gloves, too, for his hands,
when they stiffen, as he wonders how
blackness colors his life. I close the door.
There is a silence like dead flesh
40 in the bedroom. My son has left home,
a big, black manchild. I pull my cold feet
under the comforter and swallow sleep medicine.
I slip away hoping there are angels.

Questions for Discussion

1. What is "the awful question hidden beneath"?
2. What are the fears of the father for his son? How are his fears intensified by his race?
3. Why does the father, who counsels others, feel unable to counsel his
son?
4. What does "the proper attire" mean to the father? What does he wish
it could do?
5. Explain what the father means by "love is its own resistance in / the
eye a father shares with his son."
6. Explain the simile "silence like dead flesh."
7. What is the tone of the poem, and what does this tone reveal about the
narrator?
8. Explain the last line: "I slip away hoping there are angels."

Suggestions for Exploring, Writing, and Persuading

1. Write an essay comparing what your parents want for you in your
future and what you want for yourself.
2. Write an essay contrasting the father's mental image of his son with
the way the son probably sees himself.

3. Write a letter home from the son explaining why he left home and how he coped with the world as a black man out in "life's teeth and jaws."

4. Compare the hopes, fears, and prayers of the father for his son in this poem with the hopes, fears, and prayers of the father for his daughter in Yeats's "A Prayer for My Daughter."

Li-Young Lee (b. 1957)

Born of Chinese parents in Jakarta, Indonesia, Lee has written three highly regarded books of poems, including Rose *(1986), which contains "The Gift," and* City in Which I Love You, *which won the Lamont Poetry Award of the Academy of American Poets for 1990. In 1995, Lee published a memoir,* The Winged Seed: A Remembrance; *and* Book of My Nights *was published in 2001. Lee has been strongly influenced by his father, a physician, philosopher, writer, and minister who spent a year as a political prisoner in an Indonesian prison.*

THE GIFT   (1986)

To pull the metal splinter from my palm
my father recited a story in a low voice.
I watched his lovely face and not the blade.
Before the story ended he'd removed
5   the iron sliver I thought I'd die from.
I can't remember the tale
but hear his voice still, a well
of dark water, a prayer.
And I recall his hands,
10   two measures of tenderness
he laid against my face,
the flames of discipline
he raised above my head.
Had you entered that afternoon

15   you would have thought you saw a man
planting something in a boy's palm,
a silver tear, a tiny flame.
Had you followed that boy
you would have arrived here,
20   where I bend over my wife's right hand.
Look how I shave her thumbnail down
so carefully she feels no pain.
Watch as I lift the splinter out.
I was seven when my father

25 took my hand like this,
and I did not hold that shard
between my fingers and think,
Metal that will bury me,
christen it Little Assassin,
30 Ore Going Deep for My Heart.
And I did not lift up my wound and cry,
Death visited here!
I did what a child does
when he's given something to keep.
35 I kissed my father.

Questions for Discussion

1. Explain the gift that the poet receives and gives to his family.
2. What is meant by *"Metal that will bury me,"* "Little Assassin," and *"Death visited here!"?* Why does the speaker use these words in this gentle poem?
3. Explain Lee's meaning in these lines:
   two measures of tenderness
   he laid against my face,
   the flames of discipline
   he raised above my head.

Suggestions for Exploring, Writing, and Persuading

1. Using one incident from your childhood, show how one of your parents, a grandparent, or some other relative gave you a lifelong "gift."
2. Using specific examples from the poem, write an essay describing the relationship between the narrator and his father.
3. Write an essay classifying and interpreting the metaphors in this poem.

Ed Whitelock (b. 1966)

A poet, essayist, and professor, Ed Whitelock received his B.A. and M.A. degrees from Millersville University of Pennsylvania and his Ph.D. from Indiana University of Pennsylvania. He taught at Indiana University of Pennsylvania and Mt. Aloysius before moving to Gordon College in 1998. Whitelock's poems, mainly about the working class, have been published in Exquisite Corpse, Welcome Home, *and* Shifts of Vision. *In this autobiographical poem, "Future Connected By," Whitelock contrasts the son's pride in his father's work with the father's desire for a different profession for his son.*

FUTURE CONNECTED BY   (2002)

"A good handshake makes a good impression."
All of a Sunday afternoon.
My dad and a work buddy,
supposed to be fixing the basement toilet.
5   Drinking beer. Smoking cigarettes.
    "Make sure it's strong, certain."
Benny or Red or Smitty. Whoever he was.
He squeezed my hand til my knuckles rattled.
    "You don't want anyone to get the wrong impression."
10 These were *men*.
Every day balanced on girders a hundred feet up.
Eating lunch, feet dangling over the Delaware River.
    "You lose your grip, last thing you'll lose."
    "Yup, your butt becomes a suction cup."
15 Eleven hour days. Dinner. A couple beers with tv.
    But weekends were for hanging around.

    Another time.
A snow day home from school day.
My father came home early.
20 No blood in his face.
Late morning, opened a beer in his chair.
    "They sent me home.
    I slipped off a girder, but I caught myself."
    Feet dangling over the Delaware River.
25 "It's okay."
We watched cartoons all day. Ate dinner.
He went to bed early.
And back the next day.

I was an every weekend tagalong,
30 under foot and into everything.
Once, when one of his buddies asked,
    "So, what're you gonna be when you grow up?"
I had been waiting for the question,
and looked longingly up to my father.
35   "I'm going to be a welder, just like my dad."
I waited for the proud pat on the head,
but got instead that first, finalizing denial.
    "No yer not. Yer too smart for that.
    Yer gonna go'ta college and getta good job.
40   Gonna make it with your head, not your back."
The words spilled like stone from a gravel truck,
the raw materials of a wall I knew would be too high to see over.
Dad's buddy nodded his approval, so I just said "Okay."
I'd be the good son. I'd leave him behind.

Questions for Discussion

1. What is the economic situation of the described family? What details suggest that in spite of some deprivation, the family is happy?

2. Why is there so much camaraderie among the workers? What ties bind them? Explain the narrator's comment "These were *men.*"

3. What does the narrator mean by the simile, "The words spilled like stone from a gravel truck, / the raw materials of a wall I knew would be too high to see over"? What is the wall?

4. Why had the boy been waiting for the question of what he wanted to be when he grew up? What doesn't he understand about his father and his father's buddies and his father's job? Explain why he says that he will be "the good son" and "leave [his father] behind" for a "good job."

5. How do the structure of the poem and the diction help to contrast the father's and the son's lives?

6. What does the title ask or imply?

7. What, in your opinion, would the father think about his son's poem?

Suggestions for Exploring, Writing, and Persuading

1. Analyze a job that you definitely would not want your son, daughter, or another relative to take because it takes work with "your back" instead of with "your head." Give detailed reasons.

2. Write an essay analyzing the relationship between the father and son in this poem and explaining why the son wants to be "'just like [his] dad.'"

3. Using the poem as the basis for an argumentative essay, persuade your audience that the son is right to admire his father and want to enter his profession or that his father is right to want more for his son.

DRAMA

Terrence McNally (b. 1939)

Terrence McNally was born in Florida but grew up in Texas. His talents in the theater are many and varied: he has been stage manager and film critic as well as author of a wide variety of plays, musicals, and television scripts. His awards include three Tony Awards—one for the book for the musical adaptation of Kiss of the Spider Woman—*and an Emmy Award for the television script of* Andre's Mother.

ANDRE'S MOTHER   (1988)

List of Characters

CAL: a young man
ARTHUR: his father
PENNY: his sister
ANDRE'S MOTHER

Time: Now

Place: New York City, Central Park

(*Four people—Cal, Arthur, Penny, and Andre's Mother—enter. They are nicely dressed and each carries a white helium-filled balloon on a string.*)

CAL: You know what's really terrible? I can't think of anything terrific to say. Goodbye. I love you. I'll miss you. And I'm supposed to be so great with words!

PENNY: What's that over there?

ARTHUR: Ask your brother.

CAL: It's a theatre. An outdoor theatre. They do plays there in the summer. Shakespeare's plays. (*To Andre's Mother.*) God, how much he wanted to play Hamlet again. He would have gone to Timbuktu to have another go at that part. The summer he did it in Boston, he was
10   so happy!

PENNY: Cal. I don't think she. . . ! It's not the time. Later.

ARTHUR: Your son was a. . . the Jews have a word for it. . .

PENNY (*quietly appalled*): Oh my God!

ARTHUR: Mensch, I believe it is, and I think I'm using it right. It means warm, solid, the real thing. Correct me if I'm wrong.

PENNY: Fine, Dad, fine. Just quit while you're ahead.

ARTHUR: I won't say he was like a son to me. Even my son isn't always like a son to me. I mean. . . ! In my clumsy way, I'm trying to say how much I liked Andre. And how much he helped me to know my own
20   boy. Cal was always two handsful but Andre and I could talk about anything under the sun. My wife was very fond of him, too.

PENNY: Cal, I don't understand about the balloons.

CAL: They represent the soul. When you let go, it means you're letting his soul ascend to Heaven. That you're willing to let go. Breaking the last earthly ties.

PENNY: Does the Pope know about this?

ARTHUR: Penny!

PENNY: Andre loved my sense of humor. Listen, you can hear him laughing. (*She lets go of her white balloon.*) So long, you glorious, won-
30   derful, I-know-what-Cal-means-about-words. . . *man!* God forgive
me for wishing you were straight every time I laid eyes on you. But if
any man was going to have you, I'm glad it was my brother! Look
how fast it went up. I bet that means something. Something terrific.
ARTHUR (*lets his balloon go*): Goodbye. God speed.
PENNY: Cal?
CAL: I'm not ready yet.
PENNY: Okay. We'll be over there. Come on, Pop, you can buy your little
girl a Good Humor.
ARTHUR: They still make Good Humor?
40   PENNY: Only now they're called Dove Bars and they cost twelve dollars.

*(Penny takes Arthur off. Cal and Andre's Mother stand with their
balloons.)*

CAL: I wish I knew what you were thinking. I think it would help me.
You know almost nothing about me and I only know what Andre
told me about you. I'd always had it in my mind that one day we
would be friends, you and me. But if you didn't know about Andre
and me. . . If this hadn't happened. I wonder if he would have ever
told you. When he was sick, if I asked him once I asked him a thousand times, tell her. She's your mother. She won't mind. But he was
so afraid of hurting you and of your disapproval. I don't know which
was worse. (*No response. He sighs.*) God, how many of us live in
50   this city because we don't want to hurt our mothers and live in mortal terror of their disapproval. We lose ourselves here. Our lives
aren't furtive, just our feelings toward people like you are! A city of
fugitives from our parents' scorn or heartbreak. Sometimes he'd
seem a little down and I'd say, "What's the matter, babe?" and this
funny sweet, sad smile would cross his face and he'd say, "Just a little homesick, Cal, just a little bit." I always accused him of being a
country boy just playing at being a hotshot, sophisticated New
York. (*He sighs.*)
    It's bullshit. It's all bullshit. (*Still no response.*)
60   Do you remember the comic strip *Little Lulu?* Her mother had
no name, she was so remote, so formidable to all the children.
She was just Lulu's mother. "Hello, Lulu's Mother," Lulu's friends
would say. She was almost anonymous in her remoteness. You
remind me of her. Andre's mother. Let me answer the questions
you can't ask and then I'll leave you alone and you won't ever
have to see me again. Andre died of AIDS. I don't know how he
got it. I tested negative. He died bravely. You would have been
proud of him. The only thing that frightened him was you. I'll
have everything that was his sent to you. I'll pay for it. There isn't

70 much. You should have come up the summer he played Hamlet. He was magnificent. Yes, I'm bitter. I'm bitter I've lost him. I'm bitter what's happening. I'm bitter even now, after all this, I can't reach you. I'm beginning to feel your disapproval and it's making me ill. (*He looks at his balloon.*) Sorry, old friend. I blew it. (*He lets go of the balloon.*)

Good night, sweet prince, and flights of angels sing thee to thy rest! (*Beat.*)

Goodbye, Andre's mother.

(*He goes. Andre's Mother stands alone holding her white balloon. Her lips tremble. She looks on the verge of breaking down. She is about to let go of the balloon when she pulls it down to her. She looks at it awhile before she gently kisses it. She lets go of the balloon. She follows it with her eyes as it rises and rises. The lights are beginning to fade. Andre's Mother's eyes are still on the balloon. The lights fade.*)

Questions for Discussion

1. Cal's family has never before met Andre's mother. Why, then, do they assume that they understand her? How might their assumptions make her feel?
2. Why is it appropriate for this situation that Good Humor bars have been renamed Dove Bars?
3. What do the balloons symbolize?
4. Does Cal make things better or worse for the mother by what he tells her? Explain.
5. Explain the appropriateness of the quotation from Hamlet with which Cal says goodbye to his balloon.
6. Why did Andre fail to tell his mother the truth about his life and his death? What did his failure to do so deprive her of?
7. Why is Andre's mother silent?
8. Explain the significance of Andre's mother's releasing the balloon at the end. Why does she alone of all the characters keep watching it?

Suggestions for Exploring, Writing, and Persuading

1. What do the other characters' comments reveal about Andre?
2. Analyze what the release of the balloons reveals about each of the characters.

3. Discuss in an essay the following quotation from McNally's play: "God, how many of us live in this city because we don't want to hurt our mothers and live in mortal terror of their disapproval."

4. Discuss in an essay the causes and/or effects of one person's silence on another person who cares about him or her.

5. In an essay, discuss the failure of parents and children to communicate clearly.

6. Write an essay showing that each character's concept of Andre differs from every other character's concept.

Casebook
on August Wilson

WRITING ABOUT RELATIONSHIPS

This casebook on August Wilson's play *Fences* provides a glimpse into the joys and sorrows of a complex family at a time in United States history when opportunities for black people were limited. After you have carefully read the play and formed your own ideas about elements such as the themes, characters, and symbols, you can use the essays about *Fences* to expand your knowledge of the writer and the play. The essays included here also allow you to write a brief documented essay using the play as your primary source and the essays as secondary sources.

August Wilson (b. 1945)

August Wilson grew up in a Pittsburgh, Pennsylvania, ghetto probably much like the one in which Fences *is set. Able to read by age four, Wilson dropped out of high school at age fifteen, bought a typewriter, and began writing poetry. Still searching for his distinctive voice as poet and dramatist, Wilson in 1967 founded the Black Horizons Theater Company. Besides his Pulitzer Prize–winning* Fences, *first produced by the Yale Repertory Theater in 1985, Wilson's plays include* Ma Rainey's Black Bottom *(1984);* Joe Turner's Come and Gone *(1986), which was voted Broadway play of the 1987–1988 season by the New York Drama Critics' Circle;* The Piano Lesson *(1986), which in 1990 won*

Wilson a second Pulitzer Prize; Two Trains Running *(1990);* Seven Guitars *(1995); and* King Hedley II *(2001).*

FENCES (1985)

List of Characters

TROY MAXSON	
JIM BONO:	Troy's friend
ROSE:	Troy's wife
LYONS:	Troy's oldest son by previous marriage
GABRIEL:	Troy's brother
CORY:	Troy and Rose's son
RAYNELL:	Troy's daughter

SETTING

The setting is the yard which fronts the only entrance to the Maxson household, an ancient two-story brick house set back off a small alley in a big-city neighborhood. The entrance to the house is gained by two or three steps leading to a wooden porch badly in need of paint.

A relatively recent addition to the house and running its full width, the porch lacks congruence. It is a sturdy porch with a flat roof. One or two chairs of dubious value sit at one end where the kitchen window opens onto the porch. An old-fashioned icebox stands silent guard at the opposite end.

The yard is a small dirt yard, partially fenced, except for the last scene, with a wooden sawhorse, a pile of lumber, and other fencebuilding equipment set off to the side. Opposite is a tree from which hangs a ball made of rags.

A baseball bat leans against the tree. Two oil drums serve as garbage receptacles and sit near the house at right to complete the setting.

THE PLAY

Near the turn of the century, the destitute of Europe sprang on the city with tenacious claws and an honest and solid dream. The city devoured them. They swelled its belly until it burst into a thousand furnaces and sewing machines, a thousand butcher shops and bakers' ovens, a thousand churches and hospitals and funeral parlors and moneylenders. The city grew. It nourished itself and offered each man a partnership limited only by his talent, his guile, and his willingness and capacity for hard work. For the immigrants of Europe, a dream dared and won true.

*The descendants of African slaves were offered no such welcome
or participation. They came from places called the Carolinas and
the Virginias, Georgia, Alabama, Mississippi, and Tennessee.
They came strong, eager, searching. The city rejected them and
they fled and settled along the riverbanks and under bridges in
shallow, ramshackle houses made of sticks and tarpaper. They collected rags and wood. They sold the use of their muscles and their
bodies. They cleaned houses and washed clothes, they shined shoes,
and in quiet desperation and vengeful pride, they stole, and lived
in pursuit of their own dream so that they could breathe free,
finally, and stand to meet life with the force of dignity and whatever eloquence the heart could call upon.*

*By 1957, the hard-won victories of the European immigrants
had solidified the industrial might of America. War had been confronted and won with new energies that used loyalty and patriotism as its fuel. Life was rich, full, and flourishing. The
Milwaukee Braves won the World Series, and the hot winds of
change that would make the sixties a turbulent, racing, dangerous,
and provocative decade had not yet begun to blow full.*

ACT 1
SCENE 1

*It is 1957. Troy and Bono enter the yard, engaged in conversation.
Troy is fifty-three years old, a large man with thick, heavy hands; it
is this largeness that he strives to fill out and make an accommodation with. Together with his blackness, his largeness informs his
sensibilities and the choices he has made in his life.*

*Of the two men, Bono is obviously the follower. His commitment
to their friendship of thirty-odd years is rooted in his admiration
of Troy's honesty, capacity for hard work, and his strength, which
Bono seeks to emulate.*

*It is Friday night, payday, and the one night of the week the two
men engage in a ritual of talk and drink. Troy is usually the most
talkative and at times he can be crude and almost vulgar, though he
is capable of rising to profound heights of expression. The men carry
lunch buckets and wear or carry burlap aprons and are dressed in
clothes suitable to their jobs as garbage collectors.*

BONO: Troy, you ought to stop that lying!
TROY: I ain't lying! The nigger had a watermelon this big. *(He indicates
with his hands.)* Talking about. . . "What watermelon, Mr. Rand?" I
liked to fell out! "What watermelon, Mr. Rand?". . . And it sitting
there big as life.
BONO: What did Mr. Rand say?
TROY: Ain't said nothing. Figure if the nigger too dumb to know he carrying a watermelon, he wasn't gonna get much sense out of him. Try-

ing to hide that great big old watermelon under his coat. Afraid to let
10   the white man see him carry it home.

BONO: I'm like you. . . I ain't got no time for them kind of people.

TROY: Now what he look like getting mad cause he see the man from
the union talking to Mr. Rand?

BONO: He come to me talking about. . . "Maxson gonna get us fired."
I told him to get away from me with that. He walked away from me
calling you a trouble maker. What Mr. Rand say?

TROY: Ain't said nothing. He told me to go down the Commissioner's
office next Friday. They called me down there to see them.

BONO: Well, as long as you got your complaint filed, they can't fire you.
20   That's what one of them white fellows tell me.

TROY: I ain't worried about them firing me. They gonna fire me cause I
asked a question? That's all I did. I went to Mr. Rand and asked him,
"Why? Why you got the white mens driving and the colored lifting?"
Told him, "what's the matter, don't I count? You think only white fellows got sense enough to drive a truck. That ain't no paper job! Hell,
anybody can drive a truck. How come you got all white driving and
the colored lifting?" He told me "take it to the union." Well, hell
that's what I done! Now they wanna come up with this pack of lies.

BONO: I told Brownie if the man come and ask him any questions. . .
30   just tell the truth! It ain't nothing but something they done trumped
up on you cause you filed a complaint on them.

TROY: Brownie don't understand nothing. All I want them to do is
change the job description. Give everybody a chance to drive the
truck. Brownie can't see that. He ain't got that much sense.

BONO: How you figure he be making out with that gal be up at Taylors'
all the time. . . that Alberta gal?

TROY: Same as you and me. Getting just as much as we is. Which is to
say nothing.

BONO: It is, huh? I figure you doing a little better than me. . . and I ain't
40   saying what I'm doing.

TROY: Aw, nigger, look here. . . I know you. If you had got anywhere
near that gal, twenty minutes later you be looking to tell somebody.
And the first one you gonna tell. . . that you gonna want to brag
to. . . is gonna be me.

BONO: I ain't saying that. I see where you be eyeing her.

TROY: I eye all the women. I don't miss nothing. Don't never let nobody
tell you Troy Maxson don't eye the women.

BONO: You been doing more than eyeing her. You done bought her a
drink or two.

50   TROY: Hell yeah, I bought her a drink! What that mean? I bought you one,
too. What that mean cause I buy her a drink? I'm just being polite.

BONO: It's all right to buy her one drink. That's what you call being
polite. But when you wanna be buying two or three. . . that's what
you call eyeing her.

TROY: Look here, as long as you known me. . . you ever known me to chase after women?

BONO: Hell yeah! Long as I done known you. You forgetting I knew you when.

TROY: Naw, I'm talking about since I been married to Rose?

60 BONO: Oh, not since you been married to Rose. Now, that's the truth, there. I can say that.

TROY: All right then! Case closed.

BONO: I see you be walking up around Alberta's house. You supposed to be at Taylors' and you be walking up around there.

TROY: What you watching where I'm walking for? I ain't watching after you.

BONO: I seen you walking around there more than once.

Troy: Hell, you liable to see me walking anywhere! That don't mean nothing cause you see me walking around there.

70 BONO: Where she come from anyway? She just kinda showed up one day.

TROY: Tallahassee. You can look at her and tell she one of them Florida gals. They got some big healthy women down there. Grow them right up out the ground. Got a little bit of Indian in her. Most of them niggers down in Florida got some Indian in them.

BONO: I don't know about that Indian part. But she damn sure big and healthy. Woman wear some big stockings. Got them great big old legs and hips as wide as the Mississippi River.

TROY: Legs don't mean nothing. You don't do nothing but push them out
80   of the way. But them hips cushion the ride!

BONO: Troy, you ain't got no sense.

TROY: It's the truth! Like you riding on Goodyears!

(*Rose enters from the house. She is ten years younger than Troy, her devotion to him stems from her recognition of the possibilities of her life without him: a succession of abusive men and their babies, a life of partying and running the streets, the Church, or aloneness with its attendant pain and frustration. She recognizes Troy's spirit as a fine and illuminating one and she either ignores or forgives his faults, only some of which she recognizes. Though she doesn't drink, her presence is an integral part of the Friday night rituals. She alternates between the porch and the kitchen, where supper preparations are under way.*)

ROSE: What you all out here getting into?

TROY: What you worried about what we getting into for? This is men talk, woman.

ROSE: What I care what you all talking about? Bono, you gonna stay for supper?

BONO: No, I thank you, Rose. But Lucille say she cooking up a pot of pigfeet.

90 TROY: Pigfeet! Hell, I'm going home with you! Might even stay the night if you got some pigfeet. You got something in there to top them pigfeet, Rose?

ROSE: I'm cooking up some chicken. I got some chicken and collard greens.

TROY: Well, go on back in the house and let me and Bono finish what we was talking about. This is men talk. I got some talk for you later. You know what kind of talk I mean. You go on and powder it up.

ROSE: Troy Maxson, don't you start that now!

TROY *(puts his arm around her):* Aw, woman. . . come here. Look here,
100 Bono. . . when I met this woman. . . I got out that place, say, "Hitch up my pony, saddle up my mare. . . there's a woman out there for me somewhere. I looked here. Looked there. Saw Rose and latched on to her." I latched on to her and told her—I'm gonna tell you the truth—I told her, "Baby, I don't wanna marry, I just wanna be your man." Rose told me. . . tell him what you told me, Rose.

ROSE: I told him if he wasn't the marrying kind, then move out the way so the marrying kind could find me.

TROY: That's what she told me. "Nigger, you in my way. You blocking the view! Move out the way so I can find me a husband." I thought it
110 over two or three days. Come back—

ROSE: Ain't no two or three days nothing. You was back the same night.

TROY: Come back, told her. . . "Okay, baby. . . but I'm gonna buy me a banty rooster and put him out there in the backyard. . . and when he sees a stranger come, he'll flap his wings and crow. . . " Look here, Bono, I could watch the front door by myself. . . it was that back door I was worried about.

ROSE: Troy, you ought not talk like that. Troy ain't doing nothing but telling a lie.

TROY: Only thing is. . . when we first got married. . . forget the rooster. . .
120 we ain't had no yard!

BONO: I hear you tell it. Me and Lucille was staying down there on Logan Street. Had two rooms with the outhouse in the back. I ain't mind the outhouse none. But when the goddamn wind blow through there in the winter. . . that's what I'm talking about! To this day I wonder why in the hell I ever stayed down there for six long years. But see, I didn't know I could do no better. I thought only white folks had inside toilets and things.

ROSE: There's a lot of people don't know they can do no better than they doing now. That's just something you got to learn. A lot of folks
130 still shop at Bella's.

TROY: Ain't nothing wrong with shopping at Bella's. She got fresh food.

ROSE: I ain't said nothing about if she got fresh food. I'm talking about what she charge. She charge ten cents more than the A&P.

TROY: The A&P ain't never done nothing for me. I spends my money where I'm treated right. I go down to Bella, say, "I need a loaf of bread, I'll pay you Friday." She give it to me. What sense that make when I got money to go and spend it somewhere else and ignore the person who done right by me? That ain't in the Bible.

ROSE: We ain't talking about what's in the Bible. What sense it make to
140   shop there when she overcharge?

TROY: You shop where you want to. I'll do my shopping where the people been good to me.

ROSE: Well, I don't think it's right for her to overcharge. That's all I was saying.

BONO: Look here. . . I got to get on. Lucille going be raising all kind of hell.

TROY: Where you going, nigger? We ain't finished this pint. Come here, finish this pint.

BONO: Well, hell, I am. . . if you ever turn the bottle loose.

TROY (hands him the bottle): The only thing I say about the A&P is I'm
150   glad Cory got that job down there. Help him take care of his school clothes and things. Gabe done moved out and things getting tight around here. He got that job. . . . He can start to look out for himself.

ROSE: Cory done went and got recruited by a college football team.

TROY: I told that boy about that football stuff. The white man ain't gonna let him get nowhere with that football. I told him when he first come to me with it. Now you come telling me he done went and got more tied up in it. He ought to go and get recruited in how to fix cars or something where he can make a living.

ROSE: He ain't talking about making no living playing football. It's just
160   something the boys in school do. They gonna send a recruiter by to talk to you. He'll tell you he ain't talking about making no living playing football. It's a honor to be recruited.

TROY: It ain't gonna get him nowhere. Bono'll tell you that.

BONO: If he be like you in the sports. . . he's gonna be all right. Ain't but two men ever played baseball as good as you. That's Babe Ruth and Josh Gibson. Them's the only two men ever hit more home runs than you.

TROY: What it ever get me? Ain't got a pot to piss in or a window to throw it out of.

ROSE: Times have changed since you was playing baseball, Troy. That
170   was before the war. Times have changed a lot since then.

TROY: How in hell they done changed?

ROSE: They got lots of colored boys playing ball now. Baseball and football.

BONO: You right about that, Rose. Times have changed, Troy. You just come along too early.

TROY: There ought not never have been no time called too early! Now you take that fellow. . . what's that fellow they had playing right field for the Yankees back then? You know who I'm talking about Bono. Used to play right field for the Yankees.

ROSE: Selkirk?

180   TROY: Selkirk! That's it! Man batting .269, understand? .269. What kind of sense that make? I was hitting .432 with thirty-seven home runs! Man batting .269 and playing right field for the Yankees! I saw Josh

Gibson's daughter yesterday. She walking around with raggedy shoes on her feet. Now I bet you Selkirk's daughter ain't walking around with raggedy shoes on her feet! I bet you that!

ROSE: They got a lot of colored baseball players now. Jackie Robinson was the first. Folks had to wait for Jackie Robinson.

TROY: I done seen a hundred niggers play baseball better than Jackie Robinson. Hell, I know some teams Jackie Robinson couldn't even make! What you talking about Jackie Robinson. Jackie Robinson wasn't nobody. I'm talking about if you could play ball then they ought to have let you play. Don't care what color you were. Come telling me I come along too early. If you could play. . . then they ought to have let you play.

(Troy takes a long drink from the bottle.)

ROSE: You gonna drink yourself to death. You don't need to be drinking like that.

TROY: Death ain't nothing. I done seen him. Done wrassled with him. You can't tell me nothing about death. Death ain't nothing but a fastball on the outside corner. And you know what I'll do to that! Lookee here, Bono. . . am I lying? You get one of them fastballs, about waist high, over the outside corner of the plate where you can get the meat of the bat on it. . . and good god! You can kiss it goodbye. Now, am I lying?

BONO: Naw, you telling the truth there. I seen you do it.

TROY: If I'm lying. . . that 450 feet worth of lying! *(Pause.)* That's all death is to me. A fastball on the outside corner.

ROSE: I don't know why you want to get on talking about death.

TROY: Ain't nothing wrong with talking about death. That's part of life. Everybody gonna die. You gonna die, I'm gonna die. Bono's gonna die. Hell, we all gonna die.

ROSE: But you ain't got to talk about it. I don't like to talk about it.

TROY: You the one brought it up. Me and Bono was talking about baseball. . . you tell me I'm gonna drink myself to death. Ain't that right, Bono? You know I don't drink this but one night out of the week. That's Friday night. I'm gonna drink just enough to where I can handle it. Then I cuts it loose. I leave it alone. So don't you worry about me drinking myself to death. 'Cause I ain't worried about Death. I done seen him. I done wrestled with him.

Look here, Bono. . . I looked up one day and Death was marching straight at me. Like Soldiers on Parade! The Army of Death was marching straight at me. The middle of July, 1941. It got real cold just like it be winter. It seem like Death himself reached out and touched me on the shoulder. He touch me just like I touch you. I got cold as ice and Death standing there grinning at me.

ROSE: Troy, why don't you hush that talk.

TROY: I say. . . What you want, Mr. Death? You be wanting me? You done brought your army to be getting me? I looked him dead in the eye.

I wasn't fearing nothing. I was ready to tangle. Just like I'm ready to tangle now. The Bible say be ever vigilant. That's why I don't get but so drunk. I got to keep watch.

230

ROSE: Troy was right down there in Mercy Hospital. You remember he had pneumonia? Laying there with a fever talking plumb out of his head.

TROY: Death standing there staring at me. . . carrying that sickle in his hand. Finally he say, "You want bound over for another year?" See, just like that. . . "You want bound over for another year?" I told him, "Bound over hell! Let's settle this now!"

It seem like he kinda fell back when I said that, and all the cold went out of me. I reached down and grabbed that sickle and threw it just as far as I could throw it. . . and me and him commenced to wrestling.

240

We wrestled for three days and three nights. I can't say where I found the strength from. Every time it seemed like he was gonna get the best of me, I'd reach way down deep inside myself and find the strength to do him one better.

ROSE: Every time Troy tell the story he find different ways to tell it. Different things to make up about it.

TROY: I ain't making up nothing. I'm telling you the facts of what happened. I wrestled with Death for three days and three nights and I'm standing here to tell you about it. *(Pause.)* All right. At the end of the third night we done weakened each other to where we can't hardly move. Death stood up, throwed on his robe. . . had him a white robe with a hood on it. He threwed on that robe and went off to look for his sickle. Say, "I'll be back." Just like that. "I'll be back." I told him, say, "Yeah, but. . . you gonna have to find me!" I wasn't no fool. I wasn't going looking for him. Death ain't nothing to play with. And I know he's gonna get me. I know I got to join his army. . . his camp followers. But as long as I keep my strength and see him coming. . . as long as I keep up my vigilance. . . he's gonna have to fight to get me. I ain't going easy.

250

260

BONO: Well, look here, since you got to keep up your vigilance. . . let me have the bottle.

TROY: Aw hell, I shouldn't have told you that part. I should have left out that part.

ROSE: Troy be talking that stuff and half the time don't even know what he be talking about.

TROY: Bono know me better than that.

BONO: That's right, I know you. I know you got some Uncle Remus in your blood. You got more stories than the devil got sinners.

270

TROY: Aw hell, I done seen him too! Done talked with the devil.

ROSE: Troy, don't nobody wanna be hearing all that stuff.

(Lyons enters the yard from the street. Thirty-four years old, Troy's son by a previous marriage, he sports a neatly trimmed goatee, sport

coat, white shirt, tieless and buttoned at the collar. Though he fancies himself a musician, he is more caught up in the rituals and "idea" of being a musician than in the actual practice of the music. He has come to borrow money from Troy, and while he knows he will be successful, he is uncertain as to what extent his lifestyle will be held up to scrutiny and ridicule.)

LYONS: Hey, Pop.

TROY: What you come "Hey, Popping" me for?

LYONS: How you doing, Rose? *(He kisses her.)* Mr. Bono. How you doing?

BONO: Hey, Lyons. . . how you been?

TROY: He must have been doing all right. I ain't seen him around here last week.

ROSE: Troy, leave your boy alone. He come by to see you and you
280   wanna start all that nonsense.

TROY: I ain't bothering Lyons. *(Offers him the bottle.)* Here. . . get you a drink. We got an understanding. I know why he come by to see me and he know I know.

LYONS: Come on, Pop. . . I just stopped by to say hi. . . see how you was doing.

TROY: You ain't stopped by yesterday.

ROSE: You gonna stay for supper, Lyons? I got some chicken cooking in the oven.

LYONS: No, Rose. . . thanks. I was just in the neighborhood and thought
290   I'd stop by for a minute.

TROY: You was in the neighborhood alright, nigger. You telling the truth there. You was in the neighborhood cause it's my payday.

LYONS: Well, hell, since you mentioned it. . . let me have ten dollars.

TROY: I'll be damned! I'll die and go to hell and play blackjack with the devil before I give you ten dollars.

BONO: That's what I wanna know about. . . that devil you done seen.

LYONS: What. . . Pop done seen the devil? You too much, Pops.

TROY: Yeah, I done seen him. Talked to him too!

ROSE: You ain't seen no devil. I done told you that man ain't had nothing
300   to do with the devil. Anything you can't understand, you want to call it the devil.

TROY: Look here, Bono. . . I went down to see Hertzberger about some furniture. Got three rooms for two-ninety-eight. That what it say on the radio. "Three rooms. . . two-ninety-eight." Even made up a little song about it. Go down there. . . man tell me I can't get no credit. I'm working every day and can't get no credit. What to do? I got an empty house with some raggedy furniture in it. Cory ain't got no bed. He's sleeping on a pile of rags on the floor. Working every day and can't get no credit. Come back here—Rose'll tell you—madder than
310   hell. Sit down. . . try to figure what I'm gonna do. Come a knock on

the door. Ain't been living here but three days. Who know I'm here? Open the door. . . devil standing there bigger than life. White fellow. . . got on good clothes and everything. Standing there with a clipboard in his hand. I ain't had to say nothing. First words come out of his mouth was. . . "I understand you need some furniture and can't get no credit." I liked to fell over. He say, "I'll give you all the credit you want, but you got to pay the interest on it." I told him, "Give me three rooms worth and charge whatever you want." Next day a truck pulled up here and two men unloaded them three rooms. Man what drove the truck give me a book. Say send ten dollars, first of every month to the address in the book and everything will be alright. Say if I miss a payment the devil was coming back and it'll be hell to pay. That was fifteen years ago. To this day. . . the first of the month I send my ten dollars, Rose'll tell you.

ROSE: Troy lying.

TROY: I ain't never seen that man since. Now you tell me who else that could have been but the devil? I ain't sold my soul or nothing like that, you understand. Naw, I wouldn't have truck with the devil about nothing like that. I got my furniture and pays my ten dollars the first of the month just like clockwork.

BONO: How long you say you been paying this ten dollars a month?

TROY: Fifteen years!

BONO: Hell, ain't you finished paying for it yet? How much the man done charged you.

TROY: Aw hell, I done paid for it. I done paid for it ten times over! The fact is I'm scared to stop paying it.

ROSE: Troy lying. He got that furniture from Mr. Glickman. He ain't paying no ten dollars a month to nobody.

TROY: Aw hell, woman. Bono know I ain't that big a fool.

LYONS: I was just getting ready to say. . . I know where there's a bridge for sale.

TROY: Look here, I'll tell you this. . . it don't matter to me if he was the devil. It don't matter if the devil give credit. Somebody had got to give it.

ROSE: It ought to matter. You going around talking about having truck with the devil. . . God's the one you gonna have to answer to. He's the one gonna be at the Judgment.

LYONS: Yeah, well, look here, Pop. . . let me have that ten dollars. I'll give it back to you. Bonnie got a job working at the hospital.

TROY: What I tell you, Bono? The only time I see this nigger is when he wants something. That's the only time I see him.

LYONS: Come on, Pop, Mr. Bono don't want to hear all that. Let me have the ten dollars. I told you Bonnie working.

TROY: What that mean to me? "Bonnie working." I don't care if she working. Go ask her for the ten dollars if she working. Talking about "Bonnie working." Why ain't you working?

LYONS: Aw, Pop, you know I can't find no decent job. Where am I gonna get a job at? You know I can't get no job.

TROY: I told you I know some people down there. I can get you on the rubbish if you want to work. I told you that the last time you came by here asking me for something.

360 LYONS: Naw, Pop. . . thanks. That ain't for me. I don't wanna be carrying nobody's rubbish. I don't wanna be punching nobody's time clock.

TROY: What's the matter, you too good to carry people's rubbish? Where you think that ten dollars you talking about come from? I'm just supposed to haul people's rubbish and give my money to you cause you too lazy to work. You too lazy to work and wanna know why you ain't got what I got.

ROSE: What hospital Bonnie working at? Mercy?

LYONS: She's down at Passavant working in the laundry.

TROY: I ain't got nothing as it is. I give you that ten dollars and I got to eat
370 beans the rest of the week. Naw. . . you ain't getting no ten dollars here.

LYONS: You ain't got to be eating no beans. I don't know why you wanna say that.

TROY: I ain't got no extra money. Gabe done moved over to Miss Pearl's paying her the rent and things done got tight around here. I can't afford to be giving you every payday.

LYONS: I ain't asked you to give me nothing. I asked you to loan me ten dollars. I know you got ten dollars.

TROY: Yeah. I got it. You know why I got it? Cause I don't throw my money away out there in the streets. You living the fast life. . . wanna
380 be a musician. . . running around in them clubs and things. . . then, you learn to take care of yourself. You ain't gonna find me going and asking nobody for nothing. I done spent too many years without.

LYONS: You and me is two different people, Pop.

TROY: I done learned my mistake and learned to do what's right by it. You still trying to get something for nothing. Life don't owe you nothing. You owe it to yourself. Ask Bono. He'll tell you I'm right.

LYONS: You got your way of dealing with the world. . . I got mine. The only thing that matters to me is the music.

TROY: Yeah, I can see that! It don't matter how you gonna eat. . . where
390 your next dollar is coming from. You telling the truth there.

LYONS: I know I got to eat. But I got to live too. I need something that gonna help me to get out of the bed in the morning. Make me feel like I belong in the world. I don't bother nobody. Just stay with my music cause that's the only way I can find to live in the world. Otherwise there ain't no telling what I might do. Now I don't come criticizing you and how you live. I just come by to ask you for ten dollars. I don't wanna hear all that about how I live.

TROY: Boy, your mama did a hell of a job raising you.

LYONS: You can't change me, Pop. I'm thirty-four years old. If you
400 wanted to change me, you should have been there when I was growing up. I come by to see you. . . ask for ten dollars and you want to talk about how I was raised. You don't know nothing about how I was raised.

ROSE: Let the boy have ten dollars, Troy.

TROY *(to Lyons):* What the hell you looking at me for? I ain't got no ten dollars. You know what I do with my money. *(To Rose)* Give him ten dollars if you want him to have it.

ROSE: I will. Just as soon as you turn it loose.

TROY *(handing Rose the money):* There it is. Seventy-six dollars and forty-two cents. You see this, Bono? Now, I ain't gonna get but six of
410   that back.

ROSE: You ought to stop telling that lie. Here, Lyons. *(She hands him the money.)*

LYONS: Thanks, Rose. Look. . . I got to run. . . I'll see you later.

TROY: Wait a minute. You gonna say, "thanks, Rose" and ain't gonna look to see where she got that ten dollars from? See how they do me, Bono?

LYONS: I know she got it from you, Pop. Thanks. I'll give it back to you.

TROY: There he go telling another lie. Time I see that ten dollars. . . he'll be owing me thirty more.

420   LYONS: See you, Mr. Bono.

BONO: Take care, Lyons!

LYONS: Thanks, Pop. I'll see you again.

(Lyons exits the yard.)

TROY: I don't know why he don't go and get him a decent job and take care of that woman he got.

BONO: He'll be alright, Troy. The boy is still young.

TROY: The *boy* is thirty-four years old.

ROSE: Let's not get off into all that.

BONO: Look here. . . I got to be going. I got to be getting on. Lucille gonna be waiting.

430   TROY *(puts his arm round Rose):* See this woman, Bono? I love this woman. I love this woman so much it hurts. I love her so much. . . I done run out of ways of loving her. So I got to go back to basics. Don't you come by my house Monday morning talking about time to go to work. . . 'cause I'm still gonna be stroking!

ROSE: Troy! Stop it now!

BONO: I ain't paying him no mind. Rose. That ain't nothing but gin-talk. Go on, Troy. I'll see you Monday.

TROY: Don't you come by my house, nigger! I done told you what I'm gonna be doing.

(The lights go down to black.)

SCENE 2

The lights come up on Rose hanging up clothes. She hums and sings softly to herself. It is the following morning.

440 ROSE (*sings*):Jesus, be a fence all around me every day
Jesus, I want you to protect me as I travel on my way
Jesus, be a fence all around me every day.

(*Troy enters from the house.*)

ROSE (*continues*):
Jesus, I want you to protect me
As I travel on my way.
(*To Troy*) 'Morning. You ready for breakfast? I can fix it soon as I finish hanging up these clothes.

TROY: I got the coffee on. That'll be all right. I'll just drink some of that this morning.

450 ROSE: That *651* hit yesterday. That's the second time this month. Miss Pearl hit for a dollar. . . seem like those that need the least always get lucky. Poor folks can't get nothing.

TROY: Them numbers don't know nobody. I don't know why you fool with them. You and Lyons both.

ROSE: It's something to do.

TROY: You ain't doing nothing but throwing your money away.

ROSE: Troy, you know I don't play foolishly. I just play a nickel here and a nickel there.

TROY: That's two nickels you done thrown away.

460 ROSE: Now I hit sometimes. . . that makes up for it. It always comes in handy when I do hit. I don't hear you complaining then.

TROY: I ain't complaining now. I just say it's foolish. Trying to guess out of six hundred ways which way the number gonna come. If I had all the money niggers, these Negroes, throw away on numbers for one week—just one week—I'd be a rich man.

ROSE: Well, you wishing and calling it foolish ain't gonna stop folks from playing numbers. That's one thing for sure. Besides. . . some good things come from playing numbers. Look where Pope done bought him that restaurant off of numbers.

470 TROY: I can't stand niggers like that. Man ain't had two dimes to rub together. He walking around with his shoes all run over bumming money for cigarettes. All right. Got lucky there and hit the numbers. . .

ROSE: Troy, I know all about it.

TROY: Had good sense, I'll say that for him. He ain't throwed his money away. I seen niggers hit the numbers and go through two thousand dollars in four days. Man bought him that restaurant down there. . . fixed it up real nice. . . and then didn't want nobody to come in it! A Negro go in there and can't get no kind of service. I seen a white fellow come in there and order a bowl of stew. Pope picked all the
480 meat out the pot for him. Man ain't had nothing but a bowl of meat! Negro come behind him and ain't got nothing but the potatoes and carrots. Talking about what numbers do for people, you picked a

wrong example. Ain't done nothing but make a worser fool out of
him than he was before.

ROSE: Troy, you ought to stop worrying about what happened at work
yesterday.

TROY: I ain't worried. Just told me to be down there at the Commissioner's office on Friday. Everybody think they gonna fire me. I ain't
worried about them firing me. You ain't got to worry about that.
490 *(Pause.)* Where's Cory? Cory in the house? *(Calls)* Cory?

ROSE: He gone out.

TROY: Out, huh? He gone out cause he know I want him to help me with
this fence. I know how he is. That boy scared of work.

*(Gabriel enters. He comes halfway down the alley and, hearing
Troy's voice, stops.)*

TROY *(continues):* He ain't done a lick of work in his life.

ROSE: He had to go to football practice. Coach wanted them to get in a
little extra practice before the season start.
500 TROY: I got his practice. . . running out of here before he get his chores
done.

ROSE: Troy, what is wrong with you this morning? Don't nothing set
right with you. Go on back in there and go to bed. . . get up on the
other side.

TROY: Why something got to be wrong with me? I ain't said nothing
wrong with me.

ROSE: You got something to say about everything. First it's the numbers. . . then it's the way the man runs his restaurant. . . then you
done got on Cory. What's it gonna be next? Take a look up there and
510 see if the weather suits you. . . or is it gonna be how you gonna put
up the fence with the clothes hanging in the yard.

TROY: You hit the nail on the head then.

ROSE: I know you like I know the back of my hand. Go on in there and
get you some coffee. . . see if that straighten you up. 'Cause you ain't
right this morning.

*(Troy starts into the house and sees Gabriel. Gabriel starts singing.
Troy's brother, he is seven years younger than Troy. Injured in World
War II, he has a metal plate in his head. He carries an old trumpet
tied around his waist and believes with every fiber of his being that
he is the Archangel Gabriel. He carries a chipped basket with an
assortment of discarded fruits and vegetables he has picked up in
the strip district and which he attempts to sell.)*

GABRIEL *(singing):*
Yes, ma'am, I got plums.
You ask me how I sell them
Oh ten cents apiece
520   Three for a quarter

Come and buy now
'Cause I'm here today
And tomorrow I'll be gone

(Gabriel enters.)

Hey, Rose!
ROSE: How you doing, Gabe?
GABRIEL: There's Troy. . . Hey, Troy!
TROY: Hey, Gabe. *(Exits into kitchen.)*
ROSE *(to Gabriel):* What you got there?
GABRIEL: You know what I got, Rose. I got fruits and vegetables.
530   ROSE *(looking in basket):* Where's all these plums you talking about?
GABRIEL: I ain't got no plums today, Rose. I was just singing that. Have
        some tomorrow. Put me in a big order for plums. Have enough
        plums tomorrow for St. Peter and everybody.

(Troy re-enters from kitchen, crosses to steps.)

(To Rose) Troy's mad at me.
TROY: I ain't mad at you. What I got to be mad at you about? You ain't
        done nothing to me.
GABRIEL: I just moved over to Miss Pearl's to keep out from in your way.
540   I ain't mean no harm by it.
TROY: Who said anything about that? I ain't said anything about that.
GABRIEL: You ain't mad at me, is you?
TROY: Naw. . . I ain't mad at you, Gabe. If I was mad at you I'd tell you
        about it.
GABRIEL: Got me two rooms. In the basement. Got my own door, too.
        Wanna see my key? *(He holds up a key.)* That's my own key! Ain't
        nobody else got a key like that. That's my key! My two rooms!
TROY: Well, that's good, Gabe. You got your own key. . . that's good.
ROSE: You hungry, Gabe? I was just fixing to cook Troy his breakfast.
550   GABRIEL: I'll take some biscuits. You got some biscuits? Did you know
        when I was in heaven. . . every morning me and St. Peter would sit
        down by the gate and eat some big fat biscuits? Oh, yeah! We had us
        a good time. We'd sit there and eat us them biscuits and then St.
        Peter would go off to sleep and tell me to wake him up when it's
        time to open the gates for the judgment.
ROSE: Well, come on. . . I'll make up a batch of biscuits.

(Rose exits into the house.)

GABRIEL: Troy. . . St. Peter got your name in the book. I seen it. It say. . .
        Troy Maxson. I say. . . I know him! He got the same name like what I
        got. That's my brother!
560   TROY: How many times you gonna tell me that, Gabe?
GABRIEL: Ain't got my name in the book. Don't have to have my name.
        I done died and went to heaven. He got your name though. One

morning St. Peter was looking at his book. . . marking it up for the judgment. . . and he let me see your name. Got it in there under M. Got Rose's name. . . I ain't seen it like I seen yours. . . but I know it's in there. He got a great big book. Got everybody's name what was ever been born. That's what he told me. But I seen your name. Seen it with my own eyes.

TROY: Go on in the house there. Rose going to fix you something to eat.

570 GABRIEL: Oh, I ain't hungry. I done had breakfast with Aunt Jemimah. She come by and cooked me up a whole mess of flapjacks. Remember how we used to eat them flapjacks?

TROY: Go on in the house and get you something to eat now.

GABRIEL: I got to sell my plums. I done sold some tomatoes. Got me two quarters. Wanna see? *(He shows Troy his quarters.)* I'm gonna save them and buy me a new horn so St. Peter can hear me when it's time to open the gates. *(Gabriel stops suddenly. Listens.)* Hear that? That's the hellhounds. I got to chase them out of here. . . Go on get out of here! Get out! *(Gabriel exits singing.)*

580 Better get ready for the judgment
Better get ready for the judgment
My Lord is coming down

(Rose enters from the house.)

TROY: He gone off somewhere.

GABRIEL *(offstage):* Better get ready for the judgment
Better get ready for the judgment morning
Better get ready for the judgment
My God is coming down

ROSE: He ain't eating right. Miss Pearl say she can't get him to eat nothing.

590 TROY: What you want me to do about it, Rose? I done did everything I can for the man. I can't make him get well. Man got half his head blown away. . . what you expect?

ROSE: Seem like something ought to be done to help him.

TROY: Man don't bother nobody. He just mixed up from that metal plate he got in his head. Ain't no sense for him to go back into the hospital.

ROSE: Least he be eating right. They can help him take care of himself.

TROY: Don't nobody wanna be locked up, Rose. What you wanna lock him up for? Man go over there and fight the war. . . messin' around with them Japs. . . get half his head blown off. . . and they give him a

600 lousy three thousand dollars. And I had to swoop down on that.

ROSE: Is you fixing to go into that again?

TROY: That's the only way I got a roof over my head. . . cause of that metal plate.

ROSE: Ain't no sense you blaming yourself for nothing. Gabe wasn't in no condition to manage that money. You done what was right by him. Can't nobody say you ain't done what was right by him. Look how long you took care of him. . . till he wanted to have his own place and moved over there with Miss Pearl.

TROY: That ain't what I'm saying, woman! I'm just stating the facts. If

610   my brother didn't have that metal plate in his head. . . I wouldn't have a pot to piss in or a window to throw it out of. And I'm fifty-three years old. Now see if you can understand that!

(Troy gets up from the porch and starts to exit the yard.)

ROSE: Where you going off to? You been running out of here every Saturday for weeks. I thought you was gonna work on this fence?

TROY: I'm gonna walk down to Taylors'. Listen to the ball game. I'll be back in a bit. I'll work on it when I get back.

(He exits the yard. The lights go to black.)

SCENE 3

The lights come up on the yard. It is four hours later. Rose is taking down the clothes from the line. Cory enters carrying his football equipment.

ROSE: Your daddy like to had a fit with you running out of here without doing your chores.

620 CORY: I told you I had to go to practice.

ROSE: He say you were supposed to help him with this fence.

CORY: He been saying that the last four or five Saturdays, and then he don't never do nothing, but go down to Taylors'. Did you tell him about the recruiter?

ROSE: Yeah, I told him.

CORY: What he say?

ROSE: He ain't said nothing too much. You get in there and get started on your chores before he gets back. Go on and scrub down them steps before he gets back here hollering and carrying on.

630 CORY: I'm hungry. What you got to eat, Mama?

ROSE: Go on and get started on your chores. I got some meat loaf in there. Go on and make you a sandwich. . . and don't leave no mess in there. *(Cory exits into the house. Rose continues to take down the clothes. Troy enters the yard and sneaks up and grabs her from behind.)* Troy! Go on, now. You liked to scared me to death. What was the score of the game? Lucille had me on the phone and I couldn't keep up with it.

TROY: What I care about the game? Come here, woman. *(He tries to kiss her.)*

640 ROSE: I thought you went down Taylors' to listen to the game. Go on, Troy! You supposed to be putting up this fence.

TROY *(attempting to kiss her again):* I'll put it up when I finish with what is at hand.

ROSE: Go on, Troy. I ain't studying you.

TROY *(chasing after her):* I'm studying you. . . fixing to do my home-
work!

ROSE: Troy, you better leave me alone.

TROY: Where's Cory? That boy brought his butt home yet?

ROSE: He's in the house doing his chores.

650   TROY *(calling):* Cory! Get your butt out here, boy!

*(Rose exits into the house with the laundry. Troy goes over to the pile
of wood, picks up a board, and starts sawing. Cory enters from the
house.)*

TROY: You just now coming in here from leaving this morning?

CORY: Yeah, I had to go to football practice.

TROY: Yeah, what?

CORY: Yessir.

TROY: I ain't but two seconds off you noway. The garbage sitting in
there overflowing. . . you ain't done none of your chores. . . and you
come in here talking about "Yeah."

CORY: I was just getting ready to do my chores now, Pop. . .

TROY: Your first chore is to help me with this fence on Saturday. Every-
660   thing else come after that. Now get that saw and cut them boards.

*(Cory takes the saw and begins cutting the boards. Troy continues
working. There is a long pause.)*

CORY: Hey, Pop. . . why don't you buy a TV?

TROY: What I want with a TV? What I want one of them for?

CORY: Everybody got one. Earl, Ba Bra. . . Jesse!

TROY: I ain't asked you who had one. I say what I want with one?

CORY: So you can watch it. They got lots of things on TV. Baseball
games and everything. We could watch the World Series.

TROY: Yeah. . . and how much this TV cost?

CORY: I don't know. They got them on sale for around two hundred dollars.

670   TROY: Two hundred dollars, huh?

CORY: That ain't that much, Pop.

TROY: Naw, it's just two hundred dollars. See that roof you got over
your head at night? Let me tell you something about that roof. It's
been over ten years since that roof was last tarred. See now. . . the
snow come this winter and sit up there on that roof like it is. . . and
it's gonna seep inside. It's just gonna be a little bit. . . ain't gonna
hardly notice it. Then the next thing you know, it's gonna be leaking
all over the house. Then the wood rot from all that water and you
gonna need a whole new roof. Now, how much you think it cost to
680   get that roof tarred?

CORY: I don't know.

TROY: Two hundred and sixty-four dollars. . . cash money. While you
thinking about a TV, I got to be thinking about the roof. . . and

whatever else go wrong around here. Now if you had two hundred dollars, what would you do. . . fix the roof or buy a TV?

CORY: I'd buy a TV. Then when the roof started to leak. . . when it needed fixing. . . I'd fix it.

TROY: Where you gonna get the money from? You done spent it for a TV. You gonna sit up and watch the water run all over your brand new TV.

690   CORY: Aw, Pop. You got money. I know you do.

TROY: Where I got it at, huh?

CORY: You got it in the bank.

TROY: You wanna see my bankbook? You wanna see that seventy-three dollars and twenty-two cents I got sitting up in there?

CORY: You ain't got to pay for it all at one time. You can put a down payment on it and carry it on home with you.

TROY: Not me. I ain't gonna owe nobody nothing if I can help it. Miss a payment and they come and snatch it right out of your house. Then what you got? Now, soon as I get two hundred dollars clear, then I'll

700   buy a TV. Right now, as soon as I get two hundred and sixty-four dollars, I'm gonna have this roof tarred.

CORY: Aw. . . Pop!

TROY: You go on and get your two hundred dollars and buy one if ya want it. I got better things to do with my money.

CORY: I can't get no two hundred dollars. I ain't never seen two hundred dollars.

TROY: I'll tell you what. . . you get a hundred dollars and I'll put the other hundred with it.

CORY: All right, I'm gonna show you.

710   TROY: You gonna show me how you can cut them boards right now.

(Cory begins to cut the boards. There is a long pause.)

CORY: The Pirates won today. That make five in a row.

TROY: I ain't thinking about the Pirates. Got an all-white team. Got that boy. . . that Puerto Rican boy. . . Clemente. Don't even half-play him. That boy could be something if they give him a chance. Play him one day and sit him on the bench the next.

CORY: He gets a lot of chances to play.

TROY: I'm talking about playing regular. Playing every day so you can get your timing. That's what I'm talking about.

CORY: They got some white guys on the team that don't play everyday.

720   You can't play everybody at the same time.

TROY: If they got a white fellow sitting on the bench. . . you can bet your last dollar he can't play! The colored guy got to be twice as good before he get on the team. That's why I don't want you to get all tied up in them sports. Man on the team and what it get him? They got colored on the team and don't use them. Same as not having them. All them teams the same.

CORY: The Braves got Hank Aaron and Wes Covington. Hank Aaron hit two home runs today. That makes forty-three.

TROY: Hank Aaron ain't nobody. That's what you supposed to do. That's
730   how you supposed to play the game. Ain't nothing to it. It's just a
        matter of timing. . . getting the right follow-through. Hell, I can hit
        forty-three home runs right now!

CORY: Not off no major-league pitching, you couldn't.

TROY: We had better pitching in the Negro leagues. I hit seven home
        runs off of Satchel Paige. You can't get no better than that!

CORY: Sandy Koufax. He's leading the league in strike-outs.

TROY: I ain't thinking of no Sandy Koufax.

CORY: You got Warren Spahn and Lew Burdette. I bet you couldn't hit
        no home runs off of Warren Spahn.

740   TROY: I'm through with it now. You go on and cut them boards. *(Pause.)*
        Your mama tell me you done got recruited by a college football
        team? Is that right?

CORY: Yeah. Coach Zellman say the recruiter gonna be coming by to
        talk to you. Get you to sign the permission papers.

TROY: I thought you supposed to be working down there at the A&P.
        Ain't you suppose to be working down there after school?

CORY: Mr. Stawicki say he gonna hold my job for me until after the foot-
        ball season. Say starting next week I can work weekends.

TROY: I thought we had an understanding about this football stuff? You
750   suppose to keep up with your chores and hold that job down at the
        A&P. Ain't been around here all day on a Saturday. Ain't none of your
        chores done. . . and now you telling me you done quit your job.

CORY: I'm gonna be working weekends.

TROY: You damn right you are! And ain't no need for nobody coming
        around here to talk to me about signing nothing.

CORY: Hey, Pop. . . you can't do that. He's coming all the way from
        North Carolina.

TROY: I don't care where he coming from. The white man ain't gonna let
        you get nowhere with that football noway. You go on and get your
760   book-learning so you can work yourself up in that A&P or learn how
        to fix cars or build houses or something, get you a trade. That way
        you have something can't nobody take away from you. You go on
        and learn how to put your hands to some good use. Besides hauling
        people's garbage.

CORY: I get good grades, Pop. That's why the recruiter wants to talk
        with you. You got to keep up your grades to get recruited. This way
        I'll be going to college. I'll get a chance. . .

TROY: First you gonna get your butt down there to the A&P and get
        your job back.

770   CORY: Mr. Stawicki done already hired somebody else cause I told him I
        was playing football.

TROY: You a bigger fool than I thought. . . to let somebody take away
        your job so you can play some football. Where you gonna get your
        money to take out your girlfriend and whatnot? What kind of fool-
        ishness is that to let somebody take away your job?

CORY: I'm still gonna be working weekends.

TROY: Naw. . . naw. You getting your butt out of here and finding you another job.

CORY: Come on, Pop! I got to practice. I can't work after school and play
780   football, too. The team needs me. That's what Coach Zellman say. . .

TROY: I don't care what nobody else say. I'm the boss. . . you understand? I'm the boss around here. I do the only saying what counts.

CORY: Come on, Pop!

TROY: I asked you. . . did you understand?

CORY: Yeah. . .

TROY: What?!

CORY: Yessir.

TROY: You go on down there to that A&P and see if you can get your job back. If you can't do both. . . then you quit the football team. You've
790   got to take the crookeds with the straights.

CORY: Yessir. *(Pause.)* Can I ask you a question?

TROY: What the hell you wanna ask me? Mr. Stawicki the one you got the questions for.

CORY: How come you ain't never liked me?

TROY: Liked you? Who the hell say I got to like you? What law is there say I got to like you? Wanna stand up in my face and ask a damn foolass question like that. Talking about liking somebody. Come here, boy, when I talk to you.

(Cory comes over to where Troy is working. He stands slouched over and Troy shoves him on his shoulder.)

Straighten up, goddammit! I asked you a question. . . what law is
800   there say I got to like you?

CORY: None.

TROY: Well, all right then! Don't you eat every day? *(Pause.)* Answer me when I talk to you! Don't you eat every day?

CORY: Yeah.

TROY: Nigger, as long as you in my house, you put that sir on the end of it when you talk to me!

CORY: Yes. . . sir.

TROY: You eat every day.

CORY: Yessir!

810   TROY: Got a roof over your head.

CORY: Yessir!

TROY: Got clothes on your back.

CORY: Yessir.

TROY: Why you think that is?

CORY: Cause of you.

TROY: Aw, hell I know it's cause of me. . . but why do you think that is?

CORY *(hesitant):* Cause you like me.

TROY: Like you? I go out of here every morning. . . bust my butt. . .
putting up with them crackers every day. . . cause I like you? You

820 about the biggest fool I ever saw. *(Pause.)* It's my job. It's my responsibility! You understand that? A man got to take care of his family. You live in my house. . . sleep you behind on my bedclothes. . . fill you belly up with my food. . . cause you my son. You my flesh and blood. Not cause I like you! Cause it's my duty to take care of you. I owe a responsibility to you!

Let's get this straight right here. . . before it go along any further. . . I ain't got to like you. Mr. Rand don't give me money come payday cause he likes me. He gives me cause he owe me. I done give you everything I had to give you. I gave you your life! Me and your mama
830 worked that out between us. And liking your black ass wasn't part of the bargain. Don't you try and go through life worrying about if somebody like you or not. You best be making sure they doing right by you. You understand what I'm saying, boy?

CORY: Yessir.

TROY: Then get the hell out of my face, and get on down to that A&P.

(Rose has been standing behind the screen door for much of the scene. She enters as Cory exits.)

ROSE: Why don't you let the boy go ahead and play football, Troy? Ain't no harm in that. He's just trying to be like you with the sports.

TROY: I don't want him to be like me! I want him to move as far away from my life as he can get. You the only decent thing that ever hap-
840 pened to me. I wish him that. But I don't wish him a thing else from my life. I decided seventeen years ago that boy wasn't getting involved in no sports. Not after what they did to me in the sports.

ROSE: Troy, why don't you admit you was too old to play in the major leagues? For once. . . why don't you admit that?

TROY: What do you mean too old? Don't come telling me I was too old. I just wasn't the right color. Hell, I'm fifty-three years old and can do better then Selkirk's .269 right now!

ROSE: How's was you gonna play ball when you were over forty? Some-times I can't get no sense out of you.

850 TROY: I got good sense, woman. I got sense enough not to let my boy get hurt over playing no sports. You been mothering that boy too much. Worried about if people like him.

ROSE: Everything that boy do. . . he do for you. He wants you to say "Good job, son." That's all.

TROY: Rose, I ain't got time for that. He's alive. He's healthy. He's got to make his own way. I made mine. Ain't nobody gonna hold his hand when he get out there in that world.

ROSE: Times have changed from when you was young, Troy. People change. The world's changing around you and you can't even see it.

860 TROY *(slow, methodical)*: Woman. . . I do the best I can do. I come in here every Friday. I carry a sack of potatoes and a bucket of lard. You all line up at the door with your hand out. I give you the lint

from my pockets. I give you my sweat and my blood. I ain't got no
tears. I done spent them. We go upstairs in that room at night. . . and
I fall down on you and try to blast a hole into forever. I get up Mon-
day morning. . . find my lunch on the table. I go out. Make my way.
Find my strength to carry me through to the next Friday. *(Pause.)*
That's all I got, Rose. That's all I got to give. I can't give nothing else.

(Troy exits into the house. The lights go down to black.)

SCENE 4

*It is Friday. Two weeks later. Cory starts out of the house with his
football equipment. The phone rings.*

CORY *(calling):* I got it!

(He answers the phone and stands in the screen door talking.)

870   Hello? Hey, Jesse. Naw. . . I was just getting ready to leave now.
ROSE *(calling):* Cory!
CORY: I told you, man, them spikes is all tore up. You can use them if
you want, but they ain't no good. Earl got some spikes.
ROSE *(calling):* Cory!
CORY *(calling to Rose):* Mam? I'm talking to Jesse. *(Into phone)* When
she say that? *(Pause.)* Aw, you lying, man. I'm gonna tell her you
said that.
ROSE *(calling):* Cory, don't you go nowhere!
CORY: I got to go to the game, Ma! *(Into the phone)* Yeah, hey, look, I'll
880   talk to you later. Yeah, I'll meet you over Earl's house. Later. Bye, Ma.

(Cory exits the house and starts out the yard.)

ROSE: Cory, where you going off to? You got that stuff all pulled out and
thrown all over your room.
CORY *(in the yard):* I was looking for my spikes. Jesse wanted to borrow my spikes.
ROSE: Get up there and get that cleaned up before your daddy get back
in here.
CORY: I got to go to the game! I'll clean it up when I get back.

(Cory exits.)

ROSE: That's all he need to do is see that room all messed up.

*(Rose exits into the house. Troy and Bono enter the yard. Troy is
dressed in clothes other than his work clothes.)*

890 BONO: He told him the same thing he told you. Take it to the union.
TROY: Brownie ain't got that much sense. Man wasn't thinking about
nothing. He wait until I confront them on it. . . then he wanna come
crying seniority. *(Calls)* Hey Rose!

BONO: I wish I could have seen Mr. Rand's face when he told you.

TROY: He couldn't get it out of his mouth! Liked to bit his tongue! When they called me down there to the Commissioner's office. . . he thought they was gonna fire me. Like everybody else.

BONO: I didn't think they was gonna fire you. I thought they was gonna put you on the warning paper.

900 TROY: Hey, Rose! *(To Bono)* Yeah, Mr. Rand like to bit his tongue.

(Troy breaks the seal on the bottle, takes a drink, and hands it to Bono.)

BONO: I see you run right down to Taylors' and told that Alberta gal.

TROY *(calling):* Hey Rose! *(To Bono)* I told everybody. Hey, Rose! I went down there to cash my check.

ROSE *(entering from the house):* Hush all that hollering, man! I know you out here. What they say down there at the Commissioner's office?

TROY: You supposed to come when I call you, woman. Bono'll tell you that. *(To Bono)* Don't Lucille come when you call her?

ROSE: Man, hush your mouth. I ain't no dog. . . talk about "come when

910 you call me."

TROY *(puts his arm around Rose):* You hear this Bono? I had me an old dog used to get uppity like that. You say, "C'mere, Blue!". . . and he just lay there and look at you. End up getting a stick and chasing him away trying to make him come.

ROSE: I ain't studying you and your dog. I remember you used to sing that old song.

TROY *(he sings):*
Hear it ring! Hear it ring!
I had a dog and his name was Blue.

920 ROSE: Don't nobody wanna hear you sing that old song.

TROY *(sings):* You know Blue was mighty true.

ROSE: Used to have Cory running around here singing that song.

BONO: Hell, I remember that song myself.

TROY *(sings):*
You know Blue was a good old dog
Blue treed a possum in a hollow log.
That was my daddy's song. My daddy made up that song.

ROSE: I don't care who made it up. Don't nobody wanna hear you sing it.

TROY *(makes a sound like calling a dog):* Come here, woman.

930 ROSE: You come in here carrying on, I reckon they ain't fired you. What they say down there at the Commissioner's office?

TROY: Look here, Rose. . . Mr. Rand called me into his office today when I got back from talking to them people down there. . . it come from up top. . . he called me in and told me they was making me a driver.

ROSE: Troy, you kidding!

TROY: No I ain't. Ask Bono.

ROSE: Well, that's great, Troy. Now you don't have to hassle them people no more.

(Lyons enters from the street.)

940 TROY: Aw hell, I wasn't looking to see you today. I thought you was in jail. Got it all over the front page of the *Courier* about them raiding Sefus' place. . . where you be hanging out with all them thugs.

LYONS: Hey, Pop. . . that ain't got nothing to do with me. I don't go down there gambling. I go down there to sit in with the band. I ain't got nothing to do with the gambling part. They got some good music down there.

TROY: They got some rogues. . . is what they got.

LYONS: How you been, Mr. Bono? Hi, Rose.

BONO: I see where you playing down at the Crawford Grill tonight.

ROSE: How come you ain't brought Bonnie like I told you. You should have
950 brought Bonnie with you, she ain't been over in a month of Sundays.

LYONS: I was just in the neighborhood. . . thought I'd stop by.

TROY: Here he come. . .

BONO: Your daddy got a promotion on the rubbish. He's gonna be the first colored driver. Ain't got to do nothing but sit up there and read the paper like them white fellows.

LYONS: Hey, Pop. . . if you knew how to read you'd be all right.

BONO: Naw. . . naw. . . you mean if the nigger knew how to drive he'd be all right. Been fighting with them people about driving and ain't even got a license. Mr. Rand know you ain't got no driver's license?

960 TROY: Driving ain't nothing. All you do is point the truck where you want it to go. Driving ain't nothing.

BONO: Do Mr. Rand know you ain't got no driver's license? That's what I'm talking about. I ain't asked if driving was easy. I asked if Mr. Rand know you ain't got no driver's license.

TROY: He ain't got to know. The man ain't got to know my business. Time he find out, I have two or three driver's licenses.

LYONS *(going into his pocket):* Say look here, Pop. . .

TROY: I knew it was coming. Didn't I tell you, Bono? I know what kind of "Look here, Pop" that was. The nigger fixing to ask me for some
970 money. It's Friday night. It's my payday. All them rogues down there on the avenue. . . the ones that ain't in jail. . . and Lyons is hopping in his shoes to get down there with them.

LYONS: See, Pop. . . if you give somebody else a chance to talk sometime, you'd see that I was fixing to pay you back your ten dollars like I told you. Here. . . I told you I'd pay you when Bonnie got paid.

TROY: Naw. . . you go ahead and keep that ten dollars. Put it in the bank. The next time you feel like you wanna come by here and ask me for something. . . you go on down there and get that.

LYONS: Here's your ten dollars, Pop. I told you I don't want you to give
980 me nothing. I just wanted to borrow ten dollars.

TROY: Naw. . . you go on and keep that for the next time you want to ask me.

LYONS: Come on, Pop. . . here go your ten dollars.

ROSE: Why don't you go on and let the boy pay you back, Troy?

LYONS: Here you go, Rose. If you don't take it I'm gonna have to hear about it for the next six months. *(He hands her the money.)*

ROSE: You can hand yours over here too, Troy.

TROY: You see this, Bono. You see how they do me.

BONO: Yeah, Lucille do me the same way.

(Gabriel is heard singing offstage. He enters.)

990 GABRIEL: Better get ready for the Judgment! Better get ready for. . . Hey!. . . Hey!. . . There's Troy's boy!

LYONS: How you doing, Uncle Gabe?

GABRIEL: Lyons. . . The King of the Jungle! Rose. . . hey, Rose. Got a flower for you. *(He takes a rose from his pocket.)* Picked it myself. That's the same rose like you is!

ROSE: That's right nice of you, Gabe.

LYONS: What you been doing, Uncle Gabe?

GABRIEL: Oh, I been chasing hellhounds and waiting on the time to tell St. Peter to open the gates.

1000 LYONS: You been chasing hellhounds, huh? Well. . . you doing the right thing, Uncle Gabe. Somebody got to chase them.

GABRIEL: Oh, yeah. . . I know it. The devil's strong. The devil ain't no pushover. Hellhounds snipping at everybody's heels. But I got my trumpet waiting on the judgment time.

LYONS: Waiting on the Battle of Armageddon, huh?

GABRIEL: Ain't gonna be too much of a battle when God get to waving that Judgment sword. But the people's gonna have a hell of a time trying to get into heaven if them gates ain't open.

LYONS *(putting his arm around Gabriel):* You hear this, Pop. Uncle

1010 Gabe, you all right!

GABRIEL *(laughing with Lyons):* Lyons! King of the Jungle.

ROSE: You gonna stay for supper, Gabe. Want me to fix you a plate?

GABRIEL: I'll take a sandwich, Rose. Don't want no plate. Just wanna eat with my hands. I'll take a sandwich.

ROSE: How about you, Lyons? You staying? Got some short ribs cooking.

LYONS: Naw, I won't eat nothing till after we finished playing. *(Pause.)* You ought to come down and listen to me play, Pop.

TROY: I don't like that Chinese music. All that noise.

1020 ROSE: Go on in the house and wash up, Gabe. . . I'll fix you a sandwich.

GABRIEL *(to Lyons, as he exits):* Troy's mad at me.

LYONS: What you mad at Uncle Gabe for, Pop?

ROSE: He thinks Troy's mad at him cause he moved over to Miss Pearl's.

TROY: I ain't mad at the man. He can live where he want to live at.

LYONS: What he move over there for? Miss Pearl don't like nobody.

ROSE: She don't mind him none. She treats him real nice. She just don't allow all that singing.

TROY: She don't mind that rent he be paying. . . that's what she don't mind.

1020 ROSE: Troy, I ain't going through that with you no more. He's over there cause he want to have his own place. He can come and go as he please.

TROY: Hell, he could come and go as he please here. I wasn't stopping him. I ain't put no rules on him.

ROSE: It ain't the same thing, Troy. And you know it. *(Gabriel comes to the door.)* Now that's the last I wanna hear about that. I don't wanna hear nothing else about Gabe and Miss Pearl. And next week. . .

GABRIEL: I'm ready for my sandwich, Rose.

ROSE: And next week when that recruiter come from that school. . . I want you to sign that paper and go on and let Cory play football.

1030 Then that'll be the last I have to hear about that.

TROY *(to Rose as she exits into the house):* I ain't thinking about Cory nothing.

LYONS: What. . . Cory got recruited? What school he going to?

TROY: That boy walking around here smelling his piss. . . thinking he's grown. Thinking he's gonna do what he want, irrespective of what I say. Look here, Bono. . . I left the Commissioner's office and went down to the A&P. . . that boy ain't working down there. He lying to me. Telling me he got his job back. . . telling me he working week-ends. . . telling me he working after school. . . Mr. Stawicki tell me he

1040 ain't working down there at all!

LYONS: Cory just growing up. He's just busting at the seams trying to fill out your shoes.

TROY: I don't care what he's doing. When he get to the point where he wanna disobey me. . . then it's time for him to move on. Bono'll tell you that. I bet he ain't never disobeyed his daddy without paying the consequences.

BONO: I ain't never had a chance. My daddy came on through. . . but I ain't never knew him to see him. . . or what he had on his mind or where he went. Just moving on through. Searching out the New

1050 Land. That's what the old folks used to call it. See a fellow moving around from place to place. . . woman to woman. . . called it search-ing out the New Land. I can't say if he ever found it. I come along, didn't want no kids. Didn't know if I was gonna be in one place long enough to fix on them right as their daddy. I figured I was going searching, too. As it turned out I been hooked up with Lucille near about as long as your daddy been with Rose. Going on sixteen years.

TROY: Sometimes I wish I hadn't known my daddy. He ain't cared noth-ing about no kids. A kid to him wasn't nothing. All he wanted was for you to learn how to walk so he could start you to working. When

1060 it come time for eating. . . he ate first. If there was anything left over, that's what you got. Man would sit down and eat two chickens and give you the wing.

LYONS: You ought to stop that, Pop. Everybody feed their kids. No matter how hard times is. . . everybody care about their kids. Make sure they have something to eat.

TROY: The only thing my daddy cared about was getting them bales of cotton in to Mr. Lubin. That's the only thing that mattered to him. Sometimes I used to wonder why he was living. Wonder why the devil hadn't come and got him "Get them bales of cotton in to Mr.
1070   Lubin" and find out he owe him money. . .

LYONS: He should have just went on and left when he saw he couldn't get nowhere. That's what I would have done.

TROY: How he gonna leave with eleven kids? And where he gonna go? He ain't knew how to do nothing but farm. No, he was trapped and I think he knew it. But I'll say this for him. . . he felt a responsibility toward us. Maybe he ain't treated us the way I felt he should have. . . but without that responsibility he could have walked off and left us. . . made his own way.

BONO: A lot of them did. Back in those days what you talking about. . .
1080   they walk out their front door and just take on down one road or another and keep on walking.

LYONS: There you go! That's what I'm talking about.

BONO: Just keep on walking till you come to something else. Ain't you never heard of nobody having the walking blues? Well, that's what you call it when you just take off like that.

TROY: My daddy ain't had them walking blues! What you talking about? He stayed right there with his family. But he was just as evil as he could be. My mama couldn't stand him. Couldn't stand that evilness. She run off when I was about eight. She sneaked off one night after
1090   he had gone to sleep. Told me she was coming back for me. I ain't never seen her no more. All his women run off and left him. He wasn't good for nobody.

When my turn come to head out, I was fourteen and got to sniffing around Joe Canewell's daughter. Had us an old mule we called Greyboy. My daddy sent me out to do some plowing and I tied Greyboy and went to fooling around with Joe Canewell's daughter. We done found us a nice little spot, got real cozy with each other. She about thirteen and we done figured we was grown anyway. . . so we down there enjoying ourselves. . . ain't thinking about nothing. We didn't know
1100   Greyboy had got loose and wandered back to the house and my daddy was looking for me. We down there by the creek enjoying ourselves when my daddy come up on us. Surprised us. He had them leather straps off the mule and commenced to whupping me like there was no tomorrow. I jumped up, mad and embarrassed. I was scared of my daddy. When he commenced to whupping on me. . . quite naturally I run to get out of the way. (Pause.)

Now I thought he was mad cause I ain't done my work. But I see where he was chasing me off so he could have the gal for himself.

1120 When I see what the matter of it was, I lost all fear of my daddy. Right there is where I become a man. . . at fourteen years of age. *(Pause.)*

Now it was my turn to run him off. I picked up them same reins that he had used on me. I picked up them reins and commenced to whupping on him. The gal jumped up and run off. . . and when my daddy turned to face me, I could see why the devil had never come to get him. . . cause he was the devil himself. I don't know what happened. When I woke up, I was laying right there by the creek, and Blue. . . this old dog we had. . . was licking my face. I thought I was blind. I couldn't see nothing. Both my eyes were swollen shut. I layed there and cried. I didn't know what I was gonna do. The only

1130 thing I knew was the time had come for me to leave my daddy's house. And right there the world suddenly got big. And it was a long time before I could cut it down to where I could handle it.

Part of that cutting down was when I got to the place where I could feel him kicking in my blood and knew that the only thing that separated us was the matter of a few years.

(Gabriel enters from the house with a sandwich.)

LYONS: What you got there, Uncle Gabe?

GABRIEL: Got me a ham sandwich. Rose gave me a ham sandwich.

TROY: I don't know what happened to him. I done lost touch with everybody except Gabriel. But I hope he's dead. I hope he found some

1140 peace.

LYONS: That's a heavy story, Pop. I didn't know you left home when you was fourteen.

TROY: And didn't know nothing. The only part of the world I knew was the forty-two acres of Mr. Lubin's land. That's all I knew about life.

LYONS: Fourteen's kinda young to be out on your own. *(Phone rings.)* I don't even think I was ready to be out on my own at fourteen. I don't know what I would have done.

TROY: I got up from the creek and walked on down to Mobile. I was through with farming. Figured I could do better in the city. So I

1150 walked the two hundred miles to Mobile.

LYONS: Wait a minute. . . you ain't walked no two hundred miles, Pop. Ain't nobody gonna walk no two hundred miles. You talking about some walking there.

BONO: That's the only way you got anywhere back in them days.

LYONS: Shhh. Damn if I wouldn't have hitched a ride with somebody!

TROY: Who you gonna hitch it with? They ain't had no cars and things like they got now. We talking about 1918.

ROSE *(entering):* What you all out here getting into?

TROY *(to Rose):* I'm telling Lyons how good he got it. He don't know

1160 nothing about this I'm talking.

ROSE: Lyons, that was Bonnie on the phone. She say you supposed to pick her up.

LYONS: Yeah, okay, Rose.

TROY: I walked on down to Mobile and hitched up with some of them fellows that was heading this way. Got up here and found out. . . not only couldn't you get a job. . . you couldn't find no place to live. I thought I was in freedom. Shhh. Colored folks living down there on the riverbanks in whatever kind of shelter they could find for themselves. Right down there under the Brady Street Bridge. Living in
1170   shacks made of sticks and tarpaper. Messed around there and went from bad to worse. Started stealing. First it was food. Then I figure, hell, if I steal money I can buy me some food. Buy me some shoes, too! One thing led to another. Met your mama and had you. What I do that for? Now I got to worry about feeding you and her. Got to steal three times as much. Went out one day looking for somebody to rob. . . that's what I was, a robber. I'll tell you the truth. I'm ashamed of it today. But it's the truth. Went to rob this fellow. . . pulled out my knife. . . and he pulled out a gun. Shot me in the chest. It felt just like somebody had taken a hot branding iron and laid it on
1180   me. When he shot me I jumped at him with my knife. They told me I killed him and they put me in the penitentiary and locked me up for fifteen years. That's where I met Bono. That's where I learned how to play baseball. Got out that place and your mama had taken you and went on to make life without me. Fifteen years was a long time for her to wait. But that fifteen years cured me of that robbing stuff. Rose'll tell you. She asked me when I met her if I had gotten all that foolishness out of my system. And I told her "Baby, it's you and baseball all what count with me." You hear me, Bono? I meant it, too. She say, "Which one comes first?" I told her, "Baby, ain't no doubt it's
1190   baseball. . . but you stick and get old with me and we'll both outlive this baseball." Am I right, Rose? And it's true.

ROSE: Man, hush your mouth. You ain't said no such thing. Talking about "Baby, you know you'll always be number one with me." That's what you was talking.

TROY: You hear that, Bono. That's why I love her.

BONO: Rose'll keep you straight. You get off the track, she'll straighten you up.

ROSE: Lyons, you better get on up and get Bonnie. She waiting on you.

LYONS (gets up to go): Hey, Pop, why don't you come on down to the
1200   Grill and hear me play?

TROY: I ain't going down there. I'm too old to be sitting around in them clubs.

BONO: You got to be good to play down at the Grill.

LYONS: Come on, Pop. . .

TROY: I got to get up in the morning.

LYONS: You ain't got to stay long.

TROY: Naw, I'm gonna get my supper and go on to bed.

LYONS: Well, I got to go. I'll see you again.

TROY: Don't you come around my house on my payday.

1210 ROSE: Pick up the phone and let somebody know you coming. And bring Bonnie with you. You know I'm always glad to see her.

LYONS: Yeah, I'll do that, Rose. You take care now. See you, Pop. See you, Mr. Bono. See you, Uncle Gabe.

GABRIEL: Lyons! King of the Jungle!

(Lyons exits.)

TROY: Is supper ready, woman? Me and you got some business to take care of. I'm gonna tear it up, too.

ROSE: Troy, I done told you now!

TROY *(puts his arm around Bono):* Aw hell, woman. . . this is Bono. Bono like family. I done known this nigger since. . . how long I done
1220 know you?

BONO: It's been a long time.

TROY: I done known this nigger since Skippy was a pup. Me and him done been through some times.

BONO: You sure right about that.

TROY: Hell, I done know him longer than I known you. And we still standing shoulder to shoulder. Hey, look here, Bono. . . a man can't ask for no more than that. *(Drinks to him.)* I love you, nigger.

BONO: Hell, I love you too. . . but I got to get home see my woman. You got yours in hand. I got to go get mine.

(Bono starts to exit as Cory enters the yard, dressed in his football uniform. He gives Troy a hard, uncompromising look.)

1230 CORY: What you do that for, Pop? *(He throws his helmet down in the direction of Troy.)*

ROSE: What's the matter? Cory. . . what's the matter?

CORY: Pa done went up to the school and told Coach Zellman I can't play football no more. Wouldn't even let me play the game. Told him to tell the recruiter not to come.

ROSE: Troy. . .

TROY: What you Troying me for. Yeah, I did it. And the boy know why I did it.

CORY: Why you wanna do that to me? That was the one chance I had.

1240 ROSE: Ain't nothing wrong with Cory playing football, Troy.

TROY: The boy lied to me. I told the nigger if he wanna play football. . . to keep up his chores and hold down that job at the A&P. That was the conditions. Stopped down there to see Mr. Stawicki. . .

CORY: I can't work after school during the football season, Pop! I tried to tell you that Mr. Stawicki's holding my job for me. You don't never want to listen to nobody. And then you wanna go and do this to me!

TROY: I ain't done nothing to you. You done it to yourself.

CORY: Just cause you didn't have a chance! You just scared I'm gonna be better than you, that's all.

1250   TROY: Come here.
    ROSE: Troy. . .

(Cory reluctantly crosses over to Troy.)

TROY: All right! See. You done made a mistake.
CORY: I didn't even do nothing!
TROY: I'm gonna tell you what your mistake was. See. . . you swung at
    the ball and didn't hit it. That's strike one. See, you in the batter's
    box now. You swung and you missed. That's strike one. Don't you
    strike out!

(Lights fade to black.)

ACT 2
SCENE 1

*The following morning. Cory is at the tree hitting the ball with the
bat. He tries to mimic Troy, but his swing is awkward, less sure.
Rose enters from the house.*

1260   ROSE: Cory, I want you to help me with this cupboard.
    CORY: I ain't quitting the team. I don't care what Poppa say.
    ROSE: I'll talk to him when he gets back. He had to go see about your
    Uncle Gabe. The police done arrested him. Say he was disturbing
    the peace. He'll be back directly. Come on in here and help me clean
    out the top of this cupboard.

*(Cory exits into the house. Rose sees Troy and Bono coming down
the alley.)*

Troy. . . what they say down there?
TROY: Ain't said nothing. I give them fifty dollars and they let him go. I'll
    talk to you about it. Where's Cory?
ROSE: He's in there helping me clean out these cupboards.
1270   TROY: Tell him to get his butt out here.

*(Troy and Bono go over to the pile of wood. Bono picks up the saw
and begins sawing.)*

TROY *(to Bono):* All they want is the money. That makes six or seven
    times I done went down there and got him. See me coming they
    stick out their *hands.*
BONO: Yeah. I know what you mean. That's all they care about. . . that
    money. They don't care about what's right. *(Pause.)* Nigger, why you
    got to go and get some hard wood? You ain't doing nothing but build-
    ing a little old fence. Get you some soft pine wood. That's all you need.
TROY: I know what I'm doing. This is outside wood. You put pine wood
    inside the house. Pine wood is inside wood. This here is outside
1280   wood. Now you tell me where the fence is gonna be?

BONO: You don't need this wood. You can put it up with pine wood and it'll stand as long as you gonna be here looking at it.

TROY: How you know how long I'm gonna be here, nigger? Hell, I might just live forever. Live longer than old man Horsely.

BONO: That's what Magee used to say.

TROY: Magee's a damn fool. Now you tell me who you ever heard of gonna pull their own teeth with a pair of rusty pliers.

BONO: The old folks. . . my granddaddy used to pull his teeth with pliers. They ain't had no dentists for the colored folks back then.

1270 TROY: Get clean pliers! You understand? Clean, pliers! Sterilize them! Besides we ain't living back then. All Magee had to do was walk over to Doc Goldblum's.

BONO: I see where you and that Tallahassee gal. . . that Alberta. . . I see where you all done got tight.

TROY: What do you mean "got tight?"

BONO: I see where you be laughing and joking with her all the time.

TROY: I laughs and jokes with all of them, Bono. You know me.

BONO: That ain't the kind of laughing and joking I'm talking about.

(Cory enters from the house.)

CORY: How you doing, Mr. Bono?

1280 TROY: Cory? Get that saw from Bono and cut some wood. He talking about the wood's too hard to cut. Stand back there, Jim, and let that young boy show you how it's done.

BONO: He's sure welcome to it.

(Cory takes the saw and begins to cut the wood.)

Whew-e-e! Look at that. Big old strong boy. Look like Joe Louis. Hell, must be getting old the way I'm watching that boy whip through that wood.

CORY: I don't see why Mama want a fence around the yard noways.

TROY: Damn if I know either. What the hell she keeping out with it? She ain't got nothing nobody want.

1280 BONO: Some people build fences to keep people out. . . and other people build fences to keep people in. Rose wants to hold on to you all. She loves you.

TROY: Hell, nigger, I don't need nobody to tell me my wife loves me. Cory. . . go on in the house and see if you can find that other saw.

CORY: Where's it at?

TROY: I said find it! Look for it till you find it!

(Cory exits into the house.)

What's that supposed to mean? Wanna keep us in?

BONO: Troy. . . I done known you seem like damn near my whole life. You and Rose both. I done know both of you all for a long time. I

1290 remember when you met Rose. When you was hitting them baseball

out the park. A lot of them old gals was after you then. You had the
pick of the litter. When you picked Rose, I was happy for you. That
was the first time I knew you had any sense. I said. . . My man Troy
knows what he's doing. . . I'm gonna follow this nigger. . . he might
take me somewhere. I been following you, too. I done learned a
whole heap of things about life watching you. I done learned how to
tell where the shit lies. How to tell it from the alfalfa. You done
learned me a lot of things. You showed me how to not make the
same mistakes. . . to take life as it comes along and keep putting one
1300   foot in front of the other. *(Pause.)* Rose a good woman, Troy.
TROY: Hell, nigger, I know she a good woman. I been married to her for
eighteen years. What you got on your mind, Bono?
BONO: I just say she a good woman. Just like I say anything. I ain't got
to have nothing on my mind.
TROY: You just gonna say she a good woman and leave it hanging out
there like that? Why you telling me she a good woman?
BONO: She loves you, Troy. Rose loves you.
TROY: You saying I don't measure up. That's what you trying to say. I
don't measure up cause I'm seeing this other gal. I know what you
1310   trying to say.
BONO: I know what Rose means to you, Troy. I'm just trying to say I
don't want to see you mess up.
TROY: Yeah, I appreciate that, Bono. If you was messing around on
Lucille I'd be telling you the same thing.
BONO: Well that's all I got to say. I just say that because I love you both.
TROY: Hell, you know me. . . I wasn't out there looking for nothing. You
can't find a better woman than Rose. I know that. But seems like
this woman just stuck onto me where I can't shake her loose. I done
wrestled with it, tried to throw her off me. . . but she just stuck on
1320   tighter. Now she's stuck on for good.
BONO: You's in control. . . that's what you tell me all the time. You
responsible for what you do.
TROY: I ain't ducking the responsibility of it. As long as it sets right in
my heart. . . then I'm okay. Cause that's all I listen to. It'll tell me
right from wrong every time. And I ain't talking about doing Rose no
bad turn. I love Rose. She done carried me a long ways and I love
and respect her for that.
BONO: I know you do. That's why I don't want to see you hurt her. But
what you gonna do when she find out? What you got then? If you try
1290   to juggle both of them. . . sooner or later you gonna drop one of
them. That's common sense.
TROY: Yeah, I hear what you saying, Bono. I been trying to figure a way
to work it out.
BONO: Work it out right, Troy. I don't want to be getting all up between
you and Rose's business. . . but work it so it come out right.
TROY: Aw hell, I get all up between you and Lucille's business. When
you gonna get that woman that refrigerator she been wanting? Don't

tell me you ain't got no money now. I know who your banker is. Mellon don't need that money bad as Lucille want that refrigerator. I'll

1300   tell you that.

BONO: Tell you what I'll do. . . when you finish building this fence for Rose. . . I'll buy Lucille that refrigerator.

TROY: You done stuck your foot in your mouth now! (*Troy grabs up a board and begins to saw. Bono starts to walk out the yard.*) Hey, nigger. . . where you going?

BONO: I'm going home. I know you don't expect me to help you now. I'm protecting my money. I wanna see you put that fence up by yourself. That's what I want to see. You'll be here another six months without me.

1310   TROY: Nigger, you ain't right.

BONO: When it comes to my money. . . I'm right as fireworks on the Fourth of July.

TROY: All right, we gonna see now. You better get out your bankbook.

(*Bono exits, and Troy continues to work. Rose enters from the house.*)

ROSE: What they say down there? What's happening with Gabe?

TROY: I went down there and got him out. Cost me fifty dollars. Say he was disturbing the peace. Judge set up a hearing for him in three weeks. Say to show cause why he shouldn't be recommitted.

ROSE: What was he doing that cause them to arrest him?

TROY: Some kids was teasing him and he run them off home. Say he

1320   was howling and carrying on. Some folks seen him and called the police. That's all it was.

ROSE: Well, what's you say? What'd you tell the Judge?

TROY: Told him I'd look after him. It didn't make no sense to recommit the man. He stuck out his big greasy palm and told me to give him fifty dollars and take him on home.

ROSE: Where's he at now? Where'd he go off to?

TROY: He's gone on about his business. He don't need nobody to hold his hand.

ROSE: Well, I don't know. Seem like that would be the best place for

1330   him if they did put him into the hospital. I know what you're gonna say. But that's what I think would be best.

TROY: The man done had his life ruined fighting for what? And they wanna take and lock him up. Let him be free. He don't bother nobody.

ROSE: Well, everybody got their own way of looking at it I guess. Come on and get your lunch. I got a bowl of lima beans and some cornbread in the oven. Come on get something to eat. Ain't no sense you fretting over Gabe.

(*Rose turns to go into the house.*)

TROY: Rose. . . got something to tell you.

1340   ROSE: Well, come on. . . wait till I get this food on the table.

TROY: Rose! *(She stops and turns around.)* I don't know how to say this. *(Pause.)* I can't explain it none. It just sort of grows on you till it gets out of hand. It starts out like a little bush. . . and the next thing you know it's a whole forest.

ROSE: Troy. . . what is you talking about?

TROY: I'm talking, woman, let me talk. I'm trying to find a way to tell you. . . I'm gonna be a daddy. I'm gonna be somebody's daddy.

ROSE: Troy. . . you're not telling me this? You're gonna be. . . what?

TROY: Rose. . . now. . . see. . .

1350   ROSE: You telling me you gonna be somebody's daddy? You telling your *wife* this?

(Gabriel enters from the street. He carries a rose in his hand.)

GABRIEL: Hey, Troy! Hey, Rose!

ROSE: I have to wait eighteen years to hear something like this.

GABRIEL: Hey, Rose. . . I got a flower for you. *(He hands it to her.)* That's a rose. Same rose like you is.

ROSE: Thanks, Gabe.

GABRIEL: Troy, you ain't mad at me is you? Them bad mens come and put me away. You ain't mad at me is you?

TROY: Naw, Gabe, I ain't mad at you.

1360   ROSE: Eighteen years and you wanna come with this.

GABRIEL *(takes a quarter out of his pocket):* See what I got? Got a brand new quarter.

TROY: Rose. . . it's just. . .

ROSE: Ain't nothing you can say, Troy. Ain't no way of explaining that.

GABRIEL: Fellow that give me this quarter had a whole mess of them. I'm gonna keep this quarter till it stop shining.

ROSE: Gabe, go on in the house there. I got some watermelon in the frigidaire. Go on and get you a piece.

GABRIEL: Say, Rose. . . you know I was chasing hellhounds and them
1370   bad mens come and get me and take me away. Troy helped me. He come down there and told them they better let me go before he beat them up. Yeah, he did!

ROSE: You go on and get you a piece of watermelon, Gabe. Them bad mens is gone now.

GABRIEL: Okay, Rose. . . gonna get me some watermelon. The kind with the stripes on it.

(Gabriel exits into the house.)

ROSE: Why, Troy? Why? After all these years to come dragging this in to me now. It don't make no sense at your age. I could have expected this ten or fifteen years ago, but not now.

1380   TROY: Age ain't got nothing to do with it, Rose.

ROSE: I done tried to be everything a wife should be. Everything a wife could be. Been married eighteen years and I got to live to see the

day you tell me you been seeing another woman and done fathered a
child by her. And you know I ain't never wanted no half nothing in
my family. My whole family is half. Everybody got different fathers
and mothers... my two sisters and my brother. Can't hardly tell
who's who. Can't never sit down and talk about Papa and Mama. It's
your papa and your mama and my papa and my mama...

TROY: Rose... stop it now.

1390   ROSE: I ain't never wanted that for none of my children. And now you
wanna drag your behind in here and tell me something like this.

TROY: You ought to know. It's time for you to know.

ROSE: Well, I don't want to know, goddamn it!

TROY: I can't just make it go away. It's done now. I can't wish the circumstance of the thing away.

ROSE: And you don't want to either. Maybe you want to wish me and
my boy away. Maybe that's what you want? Well, you can't wish us
away. I've got eighteen years of my life invested in you. You ought to
have stayed upstairs in my bed where you belong.

1400   TROY: Rose... now listen to me... we can get a handle on this thing. We
can talk this out... come to an understanding.

ROSE: All of a sudden it's "we." Where was "we" at when you was down
there rolling around with some god-forsaken woman? "We" should
have come to an understanding before you started making a damn
fool of yourself. You're a day late and a dollar short when it comes
to an understanding with me.

TROY: It's just... She gives me a different idea... a different understanding about myself. I can step out of this house and get away
from the pressures and problems... be a different man. I ain't got to

1410   wonder how I'm gonna pay the bills or get the roof fixed. I can just
be a part of myself that ain't never been.

ROSE: What I want to know... is do you plan to continue seeing her.
That's all you can say to me.

TROY: I can sit up in her house and laugh. Do you understand what I'm
saying. I can laugh out loud... and it feels good. It reaches all the
way down to the bottom of my shoes. *(Pause.)* Rose, I can't give
that up.

ROSE: Maybe you ought to go on and stay down there with her... if she
a better woman than me.

1420   TROY: It ain't about nobody being a better woman or nothing. Rose, you
ain't the blame. A man couldn't ask for no woman to be a better wife
than you've been. I'm responsible for it. I done locked myself into a
pattern trying to take care of you all that I forget about myself.

ROSE: What the hell was I there for? That was my job, not somebody
else's.

TROY: Rose, I done tried all my life to live decent... to live a clean...
hard... useful life. I tried to be a good husband to you. In every way I
knew how. Maybe I come into the world backwards, I don't know.
But... you born with two strikes on you before you come to the

1430   plate. You got to guard it closely. . . always looking for the curve-ball on the inside corner. You can't afford to let none get past you. You can't afford a call strike. If you going down. . . you going down swinging. Everything lined up against you. What you gonna do. I fooled them, Rose. I bunted. When I found you and Cory and a halfway decent job. . . I was safe. Couldn't nothing touch me. I wasn't gonna strike out no more. I wasn't going back to the penitentiary. I wasn't gonna lay in the streets with a bottle of wine. I was safe. I had me a family. A job. I wasn't gonna get that last strike. I was on first looking for one of them boys to knock me in. To get me home.

1440   ROSE: You should have stayed in my bed, Troy.

TROY: Then when I saw that gal. . . she firmed up my backbone. And I got to thinking that if I tried. . . I just might be able to steal second. Do you understand after eighteen years I wanted to steal second.

ROSE: You should have held me tight. You should have grabbed me and held on.

TROY: I stood on first base for eighteen years and I thought. . . well, goddamn it. . . go on for it!

ROSE: We're not talking about baseball! We're talking about you going off to lay in bed with another woman. . . and then bring it home to
1450   me. That's what we're talking about. We ain't talking about no baseball.

TROY: Rose, you're not listening to me. I'm trying the best I can to explain it to you. It's not easy for me to admit that I been standing in the same place for eighteen years.

ROSE: I been standing with you! I been right here with you, Troy. I got a life too. I gave eighteen years of my life to stand in the same spot with you. Don't you think I ever wanted other things? Don't you think I had dreams and hopes? What about my life? What about me? Don't you think it ever crossed my mind to want to know other
1460   men? That I wanted to lay up somewhere and forget about my responsibilities? That I wanted someone to make me laugh so I could feel good? You not the only one who's got wants and needs. But I held on to you, Troy. I took all my feelings, my wants and needs, my dreams. . . and I buried them inside you. I planted a seed and watched and prayed over it. I planted myself inside you and waited to bloom. And it didn't take me no eighteen years to find out the soil was hard and rocky and it wasn't never gonna bloom.

But I held on to you, Troy. I held on tighter. You was my husband. I owed you everything I had. Every part of me I could find to give
1470   you. And upstairs in that room. . . with the darkness falling in on me. . . I gave everything I had to try and erase the doubt that you wasn't the finest man in the world. And wherever you was going. . . I wanted to be there with you. Cause you was my husband. Cause that's the only way I was gonna survive as your wife. You always talking about what you give. . . and what you don't have to give. But you take, too. You take. . . and don't even know nobody's giving!

(Rose turns to exit into the house; Troy grabs her arm.)

TROY: You say I take and don't give!

ROSE: Troy! You're hurting me!

TROY: You say I take and don't give.

1480   ROSE: Troy. . . you're hurting my arm! Let go!

TROY: I done give you everything I got. Don't you tell that lie on me.

ROSE: Troy!

TROY: Don't you tell that lie on me!

(Cory enters from the house.)

CORY: Mama!

ROSE: Troy. You're hurting me.

TROY: Don't you tell me about no taking and giving.

(Cory comes up behind Troy and grabs him. Troy, surprised, is thrown off balance just as Cory throws a glancing blow that catches him on the chest and knocks him down. Troy is stunned, as is Cory.)

ROSE: Troy. Troy. No!

(Troy gets to his feet and starts at Cory.)

Troy. . . no. Please! Troy!

(Rose pulls on Troy to hold him back. Troy stops himself.)

TROY: *(to Cory):* All right. That's strike two. You stay away from around

1490   me, boy. Don't you strike out. You living with a full count. Don't you strike out.

(Troy exits out the yard as the lights go down.)

SCENE 2

It is six months later, early afternoon. Troy enters from the house and starts to exit the yard. Rose enters from the house.

ROSE: Troy, I want to talk to you.

TROY: All of a sudden, after all this time, you want to talk to me, huh? You ain't wanted to talk to me for months. You ain't wanted to talk to me last night. You ain't wanted no part of me then. What you wanna talk to me about now?

ROSE: Tomorrow's Friday.

TROY: I know what day tomorrow is. You think I don't know tomorrow's Friday? My whole life I ain't done nothing but look to see Friday

1500   coming and you got to tell me it's Friday.

ROSE: I want to know if you're coming home.

TROY: I always come home, Rose. You know that. There ain't never been a night I ain't come home.

ROSE: That ain't what I mean. . . and you know it. I want to know if you're coming straight home after work.

TROY: I figure I'd cash my check. . . hang out at Taylors' with the
boys. . . maybe play a game of checkers. . .

ROSE: Troy, I can't live like this. I won't live like this. You livin' on borrowed time with me. It's been going on six months now you ain't
been coming home.

TROY: I be here every night. Every night of the year. That's 365 days.

ROSE: I want you to come home tomorrow after work.

TROY: Rose. . . I don't mess up my pay. You know that now. I take my
pay and I give it to you. I don't have no money but what you give me
back. I just want to have a little time to myself. . . a little time to
enjoy life.

ROSE: What about me? When's my time to enjoy life?

TROY: I don't know what to tell you, Rose. I'm doing the best I can.

ROSE: You ain't been home from work but time enough to change your
clothes and run out. . . and you wanna call that the best you can do?

TROY: I'm going over to the hospital to see Alberta. She went into the
hospital this afternoon. Look like she might have the baby early. I
won't be gone long.

ROSE: Well, you ought to know. They went over to Miss Pearl's and got
Gabe today. She said you told them to go ahead and lock him up.

TROY: I ain't said no such thing. Whoever told you that is telling a lie.
Pearl ain't doing nothing but telling a big fat lie.

ROSE: She ain't had to tell me. I read it on the papers.

TROY: I ain't told them nothing of the kind.

ROSE: I saw it right there on the papers.

TROY: What it say, huh?

ROSE: It said you told them to take him.

TROY: Then they screwed that up, just the way they screw up everything. I ain't worried about what they got on the paper.

ROSE: Say the government send part of his check to the hospital and
the other part to you.

TROY: I ain't got nothing to do with that if that's the way it works. I ain't
made up the rules about how it work.

ROSE: You did Gabe just like you did Cory. You wouldn't sign the paper
for Cory. . . but you signed for Gabe. You signed that paper.

(The telephone is heard ringing inside the house.)

TROY: I told you I ain't signed nothing, woman! The only thing I signed
was the release form. Hell, I can't read, I don't know what they had
on that paper! I ain't signed nothing about sending Gabe away.

ROSE: I said send him to the hospital. . . you said let him be free. . . now
you done went down there and signed him to the hospital for half
his money. You went back on yourself, Troy. You gonna have to
answer for that.

TROY: See now. . . you been over there talking to Miss Pearl. She done
got mad cause she ain't getting Gabe's rent money. That's all it is.
She's liable to say anything.

ROSE: Troy, I seen where you signed the paper.

TROY: You ain't seen nothing I signed. What she doing got papers on my brother anyway? Miss Pearl telling a big fat lie. And I'm gonna tell her about it too! You ain't seen nothing I signed. Say. . . you ain't seen nothing I signed.

(Rose exits into the house to answer the telephone. Presently she returns.)

ROSE: Troy. . . that was the hospital. Alberta had the baby.

TROY: What she have? What is it?

ROSE: It's a girl.

TROY: I better get on down to the hospital to see her.

1560   ROSE: Troy.

TROY: Rose. . . I got to see her now. That's only right. . . what's the matter. . . the baby's all right, ain't it?

ROSE: Alberta died having the baby.

TROY: Died. . . you say she's dead? Alberta's dead?

ROSE: They said they done all they could. They couldn't do nothing for her.

TROY: The baby? How's the baby?

ROSE: They say it's healthy. I wonder who's gonna bury her.

TROY: She had family, Rose. She wasn't living in the world by herself.

1570   ROSE: I know she wasn't living in the world by herself.

TROY: Next thing you gonna want to know if she had any insurance.

ROSE: Troy, you ain't got to talk like that.

TROY: That's the first thing that jumped out your mouth. "Who's gonna bury her?" Like I'm fixing to take on that task for myself.

ROSE: I am your wife. Don't push me away.

TROY: I ain't pushing nobody away. Just give me some space. That's all. Just give me some room to breathe.

(Rose exits into the house. Troy walks about the yard.)

TROY: *(with a quiet rage that threatens to consume him):* All right. . . Mr. Death. See now. . . I'm gonna tell you what I'm gonna do. I'm gonna take
1580   and build me a fence around this yard. See? I'm gonna build me a fence around what belongs to me. And then I want you to stay on the other side. See? You stay over there until you're ready for me. Then you come on. Bring your army. Bring your sickle. Bring your wrestling clothes. I ain't gonna fall down on my vigilance this time. You ain't gonna sneak up on me no more. When you ready for me. . . when the top of your list say Troy Maxson. . . that's when you come around here. You come up and knock on the front door. Ain't nobody else got nothing to do with this. This is between you and me. Man to man. You stay on the other side of that fence until you ready for me. Then you come up and knock
1590   on the front door. Anytime you want. I'll be ready for you.

(The lights go down to black.)

SCENE 3

The lights come up on the porch. It is late evening three days later. Rose sits listening to the ball game waiting for Troy. The final out of the game is made and Rose switches off the radio. Troy enters the yard carrying an infant wrapped in blankets. He stands back from the house and calls.

Rose enters and stands on the porch. There is a long, awkward silence, the weight of which grows heavier with each passing second.

TROY: Rose. . . I'm standing here with my daughter in my arms. She ain't but a wee bittie little old thing. She don't know nothing about grownups' business. She innocent. . . and she ain't got no mama.

ROSE: What you telling me for, Troy?

(She turns and exits into the house.)

TROY: Well. . . I guess we'll just sit out here on the porch.

(He sits down on the porch. There is an awkward indelicateness about the way he handles the baby. His largeness engulfs and seems to swallow it. He speaks loud enough for Rose to hear.)

A man's got to do what's right for him. I ain't sorry for nothing I done. It felt right in my heart. *(To the baby):* What you smiling at? Your daddy's a big man. Got these great big old hands. But sometimes he's scared. And right now your daddy's scared cause we sitting out here and ain't got no home. Oh, I been homeless before. I ain't had no little baby with me. But I been homeless. You just be out on the road by your lonesome and you see one of them trains coming and you just kinda go like this. . . *(He sings as a lullaby):*
Please, Mr. Engineer let a man ride the line
Please, Mr. Engineer let a man ride the line
I ain't got no ticket please let me ride the blinds

(Rose enters from the house. Troy, hearing her steps behind him, stands and faces her.)

She's my daughter, Rose. My own flesh and blood. I can't deny her no more than I can deny them boys. *(Pause.)* You and them boys is my family. You and them and this child is all I got in the world. So I guess what I'm saying is. . . I'd appreciate it if you'd help me take care of her.

ROSE: Okay, Troy. . . you're right. I'll take care of your baby for you. . . cause. . . like you say. . . she's innocent. . . and you can't visit the sins of the father upon the child. A motherless child has got a hard time. *(She takes the baby from him.)* From right now. . . this child got a mother. But you a womanless man.

(Rose turns and exits into the house with the baby. Lights go down to black.)

SCENE 4

> *It is two months later. Lyons enters from the street. He knocks on the door and calls.*

LYONS: Hey, Rose! *(Pause.)* Rose!

ROSE *(from inside the house):* Stop that yelling. You gonna wake up Raynell. I just got her to sleep.

1620 LYONS: I just stopped by to pay Papa this twenty dollars I owe him. Where's Papa at?

ROSE: He should be here in a minute. I'm getting ready to go down to the church. Sit down and wait on him.

LYONS: I got to go pick up Bonnie over her mother's house.

ROSE: Well, sit it down there on the table. He'll get it.

LYONS *(enters the house and sets the money on the table):* Tell Papa I said thanks. I'll see you again.

ROSE: All right, Lyons. We'll see you.

> *(Lyons starts to exit as Cory enters.)*

CORY: Hey, Lyons.

1630 LYONS: What's happening, Cory. Say man, I'm sorry I missed your graduation. You know I had a gig and couldn't get away. Otherwise, I would have been there, man. So what you doing?

CORY: I'm trying to find a job.

LYONS: Yeah I know how that go, man. It's rough out here. Jobs are scarce.

CORY: Yeah, I know.

LYONS: Look here, I got to run. Talk to Papa. . . he know some people. He'll be able to help get you a job. Talk to him. . . see what he say.

CORY: Yeah. . . all right, Lyons.

1640 LYONS: You take care. I'll talk to you soon. We'll find some time to talk.

> *(Lyons exits the yard. Cory wanders over to the tree, picks up the bat and assumes a batting stance. He studies an imaginary pitcher and swings. Dissatisfied with the result, he tries again. Troy enters. They eye each other for a beat. Cory puts the bat down and exits the yard. Troy starts into the house as Rose exits with Raynell. She is carrying a cake.)*

TROY: I'm coming in and everybody's going out.

ROSE: I'm taking this cake down to the church for the bake sale. Lyons was by to see you. He stopped by to pay you your twenty dollars. It's laying in there on the table.

TROY *(going into his pocket):* Well. . . here go this money.

ROSE: Put it in there on the table, Troy. I'll get it.

TROY: What time you coming back?

ROSE: Ain't no use you studying me. It don't matter what time I come back.

TROY: I just asked you a question, woman. What's the matter. . . can't I

1650 ask you a question?

ROSE: Troy, I don't want to go into it. Your dinner's in there on the
stove. All you got to do is heat it up. And don't you be eating the rest
of them cakes in there. I'm coming back for them. We having a bake
sale at the church tomorrow.

*(Rose exits the yard. Troy sits down on the steps, takes a pint bottle
from his pocket, opens it and drinks. He begins to sing.)*

TROY:
Hear it ring! Hear it ring!
Had an old dog his name was Blue
You know Blue was mighty true
You know Blue was a good old dog
1660   Blue treed a possum in a hollow log
You know from that he was a good old dog

(Bono enters the yard.)

BONO: Hey, Troy.
TROY: Hey, what's happening, Bono?
BONO: I just thought I'd stop by to see you.
TROY: What you stop by and see me for? You ain't stopped by in a
month of Sundays. Hell, I must owe you money or something.
BONO: Since you got your promotion I can't keep up with you. Used to
see you every day. Now I don't even know what route you working.
TROY: They keep switching me around. Got me out in Greentree
now. . . hauling white folks' garbage.
1670   BONO: Greentree, huh? You lucky, at least you ain't got to be lifting
them barrels. Damn if they ain't getting heavier. I'm gonna put in my
two years and call it quits.
TROY: I'm thinking about retiring myself.
BONO: You got it easy. You can *drive* for another five years.
TROY: It ain't the same, Bono. It ain't like working the back of the truck.
Ain't got nobody to talk to. . . feel like you working by yourself. Naw,
I'm thinking about retiring. How's Lucille?
BONO: She all right. Her arthritis get to acting up on her sometime. Saw
Rose on my way in. She going down to the church, huh?
1680   TROY: Yeah, she took up going down there. All them preachers looking
for somebody to fatten their pockets. *(Pause.)* Got some gin here.
BONO: Naw, thanks. I just stopped by to say hello.
TROY: Hell, nigger. . . you can take a drink. I ain't never known you to
say no to a drink. You ain't got to work tomorrow.
BONO: I just stopped by. I'm fixing to go over to Skinner's. We got us a
domino game going over his house every Friday.
TROY: Nigger, you can't play no dominoes. I used to whup you four
games out of five.
BONO: Well, that learned me. I'm getting better.
1690   TROY: Yeah? Well, that's all right.
BONO: Look here. . . I got to be getting on. Stop by sometime, huh?

TROY: Yeah, I'll do that, Bono. Lucille told Rose you bought her a new refrigerator.

BONO: Yeah, Rose told Lucille you had finally built your fence. . . so I figured we'd call it even.

TROY: I knew you would.

BONO: Yeah. . . okay. I'll be talking to you.

TROY: Yeah, take care, Bono. Good to see you. I'm gonna stop over.

BONO: Yeah. Okay, Troy.

(Bono exits. Troy drinks from the bottle.)

1700   TROY:

> Old Blue died and I dig his grave
> Let him down with a golden chain
> Every night when I hear old Blue bark
> I know Blue treed a possum in Noah's Ark.
> Hear it ring! Hear it ring!

(Cory enters the yard. They eye each other for a beat. Troy is sitting in the middle of the steps. Cory walks over.)

CORY: I got to get by.

TROY: Say what? What's you say?

CORY: You in my way. I got to get by.

TROY: You got to get by where? This is my house. Bought and paid for.
1710   Took me fifteen years. And if you wanna go in my house and I'm sitting on the steps. . . you say excuse me. Like your mama taught you.

CORY: Come on, Pop. . . I got to get by.

(Cory starts to maneuver his way past Troy. Troy grabs his leg and shoves him back.)

TROY: You just gonna walk over top of me?

CORY: I live here, too!

TROY *(advancing toward him):* You just gonna walk over top of me in my own house?

CORY: I ain't scared of you.

TROY: I ain't asked if you was scared of me. I asked you if you was fixing to walk over top of me in my own house? That's the question.
1720   You ain't gonna say excuse me? You just gonna walk over top of me?

CORY: If you wanna put it like that.

TROY: How else am I gonna put it?

CORY: I was walking by you to go into the house cause you sitting on the steps drunk, singing to yourself. You can put it like that.

TROY: Without saying excuse me???

(Cory doesn't respond.)

I asked you a question. Without saying excuse me???

CORY: I ain't got to say excuse me to you. You don't count around here
1730   no more.

TROY: Oh, I see. . . I don't count around here no more. You ain't got to say excuse me to your daddy. All of a sudden you done got so grown that your daddy don't count around here no more. . . Around here in his own house and yard that he done paid for with the sweat of his brow. You done got so grown to where you gonna take over. You gonna take over my house. Is that right? You gonna wear my pants. You gonna go in there and stretch out on my bed. You ain't got to say excuse me cause I don't count around here no more. Is that right?

CORY: That's right. You always talking this dumb stuff. Now, why don't
1740   you just get out my way.

TROY: I guess you got someplace to sleep and something to put in your belly. You got that, huh? You got that? That's what you need. You got that, huh?

CORY: You don't know what I got. You ain't got to worry about what I got.

TROY: You right! You one hundred percent right! I done spent the last seventeen years worrying about what you got. Now it's your turn, see? I'll tell you what to do. You grown. . . we done established that. You a man. Now, let's see you act like one. Turn your behind around
1750   and walk out this yard. And when you get out there in the alley. . . you can forget about this house. See? Cause this is my house. You go on and be a man and get your own house. You can forget about this. Cause this is mine. You go on and get yours cause I'm through with doing for you.

CORY: You talking about what you did for me. . . what'd you ever give me?

TROY: Them feet and bones! That pumping heart, nigger! I give you more than anybody else is ever gonna give you.

CORY: You ain't never gave me nothing! You ain't never done nothing
1760   but hold me back. Afraid I was gonna be better than you. All you ever did was try and make me scared of you. I used to tremble every time you called my name. Every time I heard your footsteps in the house. Wondering all the time. . . what's Papa gonna say if I do this?. . . What's he gonna say if I do that?. . . What's Papa gonna say if I turn on the radio? And Mama, too. . . she tries. . . but she's scared of you.

TROY: You leave your mama out of this. She ain't got nothing to do with this.

CORY: I don't know how she stands you. . . after what you did to her.
1770   TROY: I told you to leave your mama out of this!

(He advances toward Cory.)

CORY: What you gonna do. . . give me a whupping? You can't whup me no more. You're too old. You just an old man.

TROY *(shoves him on his shoulder):* Nigger! That's what you are. You just another nigger on the street to me!

CORY: You crazy! You know that?

TROY: Go on now! You got the devil in you. Get on away from me!

CORY: You just a crazy old man. . . talking about I got the devil in me.

TROY: Yeah, I'm crazy! If you don't get on the other side of that yard. . . I'm gonna show you how crazy I am! Go on. . . get the hell out of my yard.

1780   CORY: It ain't your yard. You took Uncle Gabe's money he got from the army to buy this house and then you put him out.

TROY (*advances on Cory*): Get your black ass out of my yard!

(Troy's advance backs Cory up against the tree. Cory grabs up the bat.)

CORY: I ain't going nowhere! Come on. . . put me out! I ain't scared of you.

TROY: That's my bat!

CORY: Come on!

TROY: Put my bat down!

CORY: Come on, put me out.

(Cory swings at Troy, who backs across the yard.)

What's the matter? You so bad. . . put me out!

(Troy advances toward Cory.)

1790   CORY (*backing up*): Come on! Come on!

TROY: You're gonna have to use it! You wanna draw that bat back on me. . . you're gonna have to use it.

CORY: Come on!. . . Come on!

(Cory swings the bat at Troy a second time. He misses. Troy continues to advance toward him.)

TROY: You're gonna have to kill me! You wanna draw that bat back on me. You're gonna have to kill me.

(Cory, backed up against the tree, can go no farther. Troy taunts him. He sticks out his head and offers him a target.)

Come on! Come on!

(Cory is unable to swing the bat. Troy grabs it.)

TROY: Then I'll show you.

(Cory and Troy struggle over the bat. The struggle is fierce and fully engaged. Troy ultimately is the stronger, and takes the bat from Cory and stands over him ready to swing. He stops himself.)

Go on and get away from around my house.

(Cory, stung by his defeat, picks himself up, walks slowly out of the yard and up the alley.)

CORY: Tell Mama I'll be back for my things.

1800   TROY: They'll be on the other side of that fence.

(Cory exits.)

TROY: I can't taste nothing. Helluljah! I can't taste nothing no more.

(Troy assumes a batting posture and begins to taunt Death, the fast-ball in the outside corner.) Come on! It's between you and me now! Come on! Anytime you want! Come on! I be ready for you. . . but I ain't gonna be easy..

(The lights go down on the scene.)

SCENE 5

The time is 1965. The lights come up in the yard. It is the morning of Troy's funeral. A funeral plaque with a light hangs beside the door. There is a small garden plot off to the side. There is noise and activity in the house as Rose, Lyons, and Bono have gathered. The door opens and Raynell, seven years old, enters dressed in a flannel night-gown. She crosses to the garden and pokes around with a stick. Rose calls from the house.

ROSE: Raynell!

RAYNELL: Mam?

ROSE: What you doing out there?

RAYNELL: Nothing.

(Rose comes to the door.)

ROSE: Girl, get in here and get dressed. What you doing?

RAYNELL: Seeing if my garden growed.

ROSE: I told you it ain't gonna grow overnight. You got to wait.

1810   RAYNELL: It don't look like it never gonna grow. Dag!

ROSE: I told you a watched pot never boils. Get in here and get dressed.

RAYNELL: This ain't even no pot, Mama.

ROSE: You just have to give it a chance. It'll grow. Now you come on and do what I told you. We got to be getting ready. This ain't no morning to be playing around. You hear me?

RAYNELL: Yes, Mam.

(Rose exits into the house. Raynell continues to poke at her garden with a stick. Cory enters. He is dressed in a Marine corporal's uni-form, and carries a duffel bag. His posture is that of a military man, and his speech has a clipped sternness.)

CORY *(to Raynell)*: Hi. *(Pause.)* I bet your name is Raynell.

RAYNELL: Uh huh.

CORY: Is your mama home?

(Raynell runs up on the porch and calls through the screen door.)

RAYNELL: Mama. . . there's some man out here. Mama?

(Rose comes to the door.)

1820   ROSE: Cory? Lord have mercy! Look here, you all!

(Rose and Cory embrace in a tearful reunion as Bono and Lyons enter from the house dressed in funeral clothes.)

BONO: Aw, looka here. . .

ROSE: Done got all grown up!

CORY: Don't cry, Mama. What you crying about?

ROSE: I'm just so glad you made it.

CORY: Hey, Lyons. How you doing, Mr. Bono.
    (Lyons goes to embrace Cory.)

LYONS: Look at you, man. Look at you. Don't he look good, Rose? Got
    them Corporal stripes.

ROSE: What took you so long?

CORY: You know how the Marines are, Mama. They got to get all their
1830   paperwork straight before they let you do anything.

ROSE: Well, I'm sure glad you made it. They let Lyons come. Your Uncle
    Gabe's still in the hospital. They don't know if they gonna let him out
    or not. I just talked to them a little while ago.

LYONS: A Corporal in the United States Marines.

BONO: Your daddy knew you had it in you. He used to tell me all the
    time.

LYONS: Don't he look good, Mr. Bono?

BONO: Yeah, he remind me of Troy when I first met him. *(Pause.)* Say,
    Rose, Lucille's down at the church with the choir. I'm gonna go
1840   down and get the pallbearers lined up. I'll be back to get you all.

ROSE: Thanks, Jim.

CORY: See you, Mr. Bono.

LYONS *(with his arm around Raynell)*: Cory. . . look at Raynell. Ain't
    she precious? She gonna break a whole lot of hearts.

ROSE: Raynell, come and say hello to your brother. This is your brother,
    Cory. You remember Cory.

RAYNELL: No, Mam.

CORY: She don't remember me, Mama.

ROSE: Well, we talk about you. She heard us talk about you. *(To*
1850   *Raynell):* This is your brother, Cory. Come on and say hello.

RAYNELL: Hi.

CORY: Hi. So you're Raynell. Mama told me a lot about you.

ROSE: You all come on into the house and let me fix you some break-
    fast. Keep up your strength.

CORY: I ain't hungry, Mama.

LYONS: You can fix me something, Rose. I'll be in there in a minute.

ROSE: Cory, you sure you don't want nothing? I know they ain't feeding you right.

CORY: No, Mama. . . thanks. I don't feel like eating. I'll get something later.

ROSE: Raynell. . . get on upstairs and get that dress on like I told you.

(Rose and Raynell exit into the house.)

LYONS: So. . . I hear you thinking about getting married.

CORY: Yeah, I done found the right one, Lyons. It's about time.

LYONS: Me and Bonnie been split up about four years now. About the time Papa retired. I guess she just got tired of all them changes I was putting her through. *(Pause.)* I always knew you was gonna make something out yourself. Your head was always in the right direction. So. . . you gonna stay in. . . make it a career. . . put in your twenty years?

CORY: I don't know. I got six already. I think that's enough.

LYONS: Stick with Uncle Sam and retire early. Ain't nothing out here. I guess Rose told you what happened with me. They got me down the workhouse. I thought I was being slick cashing other people's checks.

CORY: How much time you doing?

LYONS: They give me three years. I got that beat now. I ain't got but nine more months. It ain't so bad. You learn to deal with it like anything else. You got to take the crookeds with the straights. That's what Papa used to say. He used to say that when he struck out. I seen him strike out three times in a row. . . and the next time up he hit the ball over the grandstand. Right out there in Homestead Field. He wasn't satisfied hitting in the seats. . . he want to hit it over everything! After the game he had two hundred people standing around waiting to shake his hand. You got to take the crookeds with the straights. Yeah, Papa was something else.

CORY: You still playing?

LYONS: Cory. . . you know I'm gonna do that. There's some fellows down there we got us a band. . . we gonna try and stay together when we get out. . . but yeah, I'm still playing. It still helps me to get out of bed in the morning. As long as it do that I'm gonna be right there playing and trying to make some sense out of it.

ROSE *(calling):* Lyons, I got these eggs in the pan.

LYONS: Let me go on and get these eggs, man. Get ready to go bury Papa. *(Pause.)* How you doing? You doing all right?

(Cory nods. Lyons touches him on the shoulder and they share a moment of silent grief. Lyons exits into the house. Cory wanders about the yard. Raynell enters.)

RAYNELL: Hi.

CORY: Hi.

RAYNELL: Did you used to sleep in my room?

CORY: Yeah. . . that used to be my room.

RAYNELL: That's what Papa call it. "Cory's room." It got your football in
the closet.

(Rose comes to the door.)

ROSE: Raynell, get in there and get them good shoes on.

RAYNELL: Mama, can't I wear these? Them other one hurt my feet.

ROSE: Well, they just gonna have to hurt your feet for a while. You ain't
said they hurt your feet when you went down to the store and got
them.

RAYNELL: They didn't hurt then. My feet done got bigger.

ROSE: Don't you give me no backtalk now. You get in there and get
them shoes on. *(Raynell exits into the house.)* Ain't too much
changed. He still got that piece of rag tied to that tree. He was out
here swinging that bat. I was just ready to go back in the house. He
swung that bat and then he just fell over. Seem like he swung it and
stood there with this grin on his face. . . and then he just fell over.
They carried him on down to the hospital, but I knew there wasn't
no need. . . why don't you come on in the house?

CORY: Mama. . . I got something to tell you. I don't know how to tell you
this. . . but I've got to tell you. . . I'm not going to Papa's funeral.

ROSE: Boy, hush your mouth. That's your daddy you talking about. I
don't want hear that kind of talk this morning. I done raised you to
come to this? You standing there all healthy and grown talking about
you ain't going to your daddy's funeral?

CORY: Mama. . . listen. . .

ROSE: I don't want to hear it, Cory. You just get that thought out of your
head.

CORY: I can't drag Papa with me everywhere I go. I've got to say no to
him. One time in my life I've got to say no.

ROSE: Don't nobody have to listen to nothing like that. I know you and
your daddy ain't seen eye to eye, but I ain't got to listen to that kind
of talk this morning. Whatever was between you and your daddy. . .
the time has come to put it aside. Just take it and set it over there on
the shelf and forget about it. Disrespecting your daddy ain't gonna
make you a man, Cory. You got to find a way to come to that on your
own. Not going to your daddy's funeral ain't gonna make you a man.

CORY: The whole time I was growing up. . . living in his house. . . Papa
was like a shadow that followed you everywhere. It weighed on you
and sunk into your flesh. It would wrap around you and lay there
until you couldn't tell which one was you anymore. That shadow digging in your flesh. Trying to crawl in. Trying to live through you.
Everywhere I looked, Troy Maxson was staring back at me. . . hiding
under the bed. . . in the closet. I'm just saying I've got to find a way
to get rid of that shadow, Mama.

ROSE: You just like him. You got him in you good.

CORY: Don't tell me that, Mama.

ROSE: You Troy Maxson all over again.

CORY: I don't want to be Troy Maxson. I want to be me.

ROSE: You can't be nobody but who you are, Cory. That shadow wasn't nothing but you growing into yourself. You either got to grow into it or cut it down to fit you. But that's all you got to make life with. That's all you got to measure yourself against that world out there. Your daddy wanted you to be everything he wasn't. . . and at the same time he tried to make you into everything he was. I don't know if he was right or wrong. . . but I do know he meant to do more good than he meant to do harm. He wasn't always right. Sometimes when he touched he bruised. And sometimes when he took me in his arms he cut.

When I first met your daddy I thought. . . Here is a man I can lay down with and make a baby. That's the first thing I thought when I seen him. I was thirty years old and had done seen my share of men. But when he walked up to me and said, "I can dance a waltz that'll make you dizzy," I thought, Rose Lee, here is a man that you can open yourself up to and be filled to bursting. Here is a man that can fill all them empty spaces you been tipping around the edges of. One of them empty spaces was being somebody's mother.

I married your daddy and settled down to cooking his supper and keeping clean sheets on the bed. When your daddy walked through the house he was so big he filled it up. That was my first mistake. Not to make him leave some room for me. For my part in the matter. But at that time I wanted that. I wanted a house that I could sing in. And that's what your daddy gave me. I didn't know to keep up his strength I had to give up little pieces of mine. I did that. I took on his life as mine and mixed up the pieces so that you couldn't hardly tell which was which anymore. It was my choice. It was my life and I didn't have to live it like that. But that's what life offered me in the way of being a woman and I took it. I grabbed hold of it with both hands.

By the time Raynell came into the house, me and your daddy had done lost touch with one another. I didn't want to make my blessing off of nobody's misfortune. . . but I took on to Raynell like she was all them babies I had wanted and never had. *(The phone rings.)* Like I'd been blessed to relive a part of my life. And if the Lord see fit to keep up my strength. . . I'm gonna do her just like your daddy did you. . . I'm gonna give her the best of what's in me.

RAYNELL *(entering, still with her old shoes):* Mama. . . Reverend Tollivier on the phone.

(Rose exits into the house.)

RAYNELL: Hi.

CORY: Hi.

RAYNELL: You in the Army or the Marines?

CORY: Marines.

RAYNELL: Papa said it was the Army. Did you know Blue?

CORY: Blue? Who's Blue?

1990 RAYNELL: Papa's dog what he sing about all the time.

CORY *(singing):*

    Hear it ring! Hear it ring!

    I had a dog his name was Blue

    You know Blue was mighty true

    You know Blue was a good old dog

    Blue treed a possum in a hollow log

    You know from that he was a good old dog.

    Hear it ring! Hear it ring!

(Raynell joins in singing.)

CORY AND RAYNELL:

2000   Blue treed a possum out on a limb

    Blue looked at me and I looked at him

    Grabbed that possum and put him in a sack

    Blue stayed there till I came back

    Old Blue's feets was big and round

    Never allowed a possum to touch the ground.

    Old Blue died and I dug his grave

    I dug his grave with a silver spade

    Let him down with a golden chain

    And every night I call his name

2010   Go on Blue, you good dog you

    Go on Blue, you good dog you.

RAYNELL:

    Blue laid down and died like a man

    Blue laid down and died. . .

BOTH: Blue laid down and died like a man

    Now he's treeing possums in the Promised Land

    I'm gonna tell you this to let you know

    Blue's gone where the good dogs go

    When I hear old Blue bark

2020   When I hear old Blue bark

    Blue treed a possum in Noah's Ark

    Blue treed a possum in Noah's Ark.

(Rose comes to the screen door.)

ROSE: Cory, we gonna be ready to go in a minute.

CORY *(to Raynell):* You go on in the house and change them shoes like Mama told you so we can go to Papa's funeral.

RAYNELL: Okay, I'll be back.

(Raynell exits into the house. Cory gets up and crosses over to the tree. Rose stands in the screen door watching him. Gabriel enters from the alley.)

GABRIEL *(calling):* Hey, Rose!
ROSE: Gabe?
GABRIEL: I'm here, Rose. Hey Rose, I'm here!

(Rose enters from the house.)

2030   ROSE: Lord. . . Look here, Lyons!
LYONS: See, I told you, Rose. . . I told you they'd let him come.
CORY: How you doing, Uncle Gabe?
LYONS: How you doing, Uncle Gabe?
GABRIEL: Hey, Rose. It's time. It's time to tell St. Peter to open the gates. Troy, you ready? You ready, Troy. I'm gonna tell St. Peter to open the gates. You get ready now.

(Gabriel, with great fanfare, braces himself to blow. The trumpet is without a mouthpiece. He puts the end of it into his mouth and blows with great force, like a man who has been waiting some twenty-odd years for this single moment. No sound comes out of the trumpet. He braces himself and blows again with the same result. A third time he blows. There is a weight of impossible description that falls away and leaves him bare and exposed to a frightful realization. It is a trauma that a sane and normal mind would be unable to withstand. He begins to dance. A slow, strange dance, eerie and life-giving. A dance of atavistic signature and ritual. Lyons attempts to embrace him. Gabriel pushes Lyons away. He begins to howl in what is an attempt at song, or perhaps a song turning back into itself in an attempt at speech. He finishes his dance and the gates of heaven stand open as wide as God's closet.)

That's the way that go!

Blackout

Questions for Discussion

Act I

Scene 1

1. In the introduction, Wilson describes Troy as "a large man with thick, heavy hands" and says it is "this largeness that he strives to fill out and make an accommodation with. Together with his blackness, his largeness informs his sensibilities and the choices he has made in his life." After you have read the play, interpret this description.

2. Why does Rose shop at the A&P and Troy at Bella's? Why are the prices at Bella's higher?

3. Rose tells Troy, "Times have changed since you was playing baseball." Why is he not comforted by this fact?

4. Troy says, "Death ain't nothing but a fastball on the outside corner." Explain what he means by this baseball imagery.

5. What does Troy's story about wrestling with death reveal about his attitude toward life?

6. Why does Troy call the man who gave him credit to buy furniture the devil? Explain similar financial practices that exist today.

7. Lyons says that he cannot find a job. What would be a more accurate statement about his situation? Why does Troy hassle him before giving him money?

8. Explain Lyons's statement to Troy: "You and me is two different people."

Scene 2

1. Compare Rose's and Troy's attitudes toward gambling.

2. Explain Troy's treatment of Gabriel.

Scene 3

1. What does Cory view as his two primary jobs? What does Troy believe Cory's responsibilities should be?

2. Troy asks Cory, "What law is there I got to like you?" What does this question reveal about Troy's concept of fatherhood?

3. Explain Troy's statement to Rose at the end of scene 3.

Scene 4

1. Why does Troy, who cannot read and has no driver's license, want to drive the garbage truck?

2. Gabriel's severance money, which he received as a result of his injury while fighting for his country, pays for the house Troy lives in. Why, then, does Gabriel want to live at Miss Pearl's, where he has to pay rent?

3. Both Rose and Lyons tell Troy that Cory is trying to live up to Troy's example. Why does this assertion not please Troy?

4. Describe Troy's father's behavior. In what ways has his experience with his father influenced Troy's behavior toward Lyons and Cory?

5. What does Lyons's comment that Troy's father "should have just went on and left when he saw he couldn't get nowhere" reveal about Lyons's attitude toward responsibility?

6. Why does Troy sabotage Cory's chances to play football?

7. Explain Troy's comment to Cory at the end of Act 1.

Act 2

Scene 1

1. How and why do Troy's and Rose's opinions about Gabriel's being institutionalized differ?

2. In what way does Troy's statement that the situation with Alberta "starts out like a little bush. . . and the next thing you know it's a whole forest" contradict his other statements about personal responsibility?

3. Explain Troy's statement that at Alberta's "I can. . . get away from the pressures and problems. . . and be a different man. . . . I can just be a part of myself that ain't never been."

4. Interpret the baseball analogy with which Troy tries to explain why he has been unfaithful to Rose.

5. Explain Rose's analogy about the seed.

Scene 2

1. Explain Rose's statement to Troy that "You did Gabe just like you did Cory. You wouldn't sign the paper for Cory. . . but you signed for Gabe." Why did Troy sign Gabriel's commitment papers?

2. Why, after Alberta's death, does Troy tell death that he is going to finish the fence?

Scene 3

1. Explain Rose's statement at the end of this scene: "From right now. . . this child got a mother. But you a womanless man."

Scene 4

1. Why does Cory threaten Troy with a baseball bat? Why does Troy drive his own son away from home?

Scene 5

1. Discuss the contrasting attitudes of Lyons and Cory about responsibility and their consequent adult roles.

2. Support or argue against Cory's statement that his father was "trying to live through" him when Cory was growing up and Rose's answer that "Your daddy wanted you to be everything he wasn't. . . and at the same time he tried to make you into everything he was."

3. Analyze Rose's explanation of her marriage to Troy.

4. Troy sings a favorite song, "Old Blue," when he is drinking, and Raynell and Cory sing "Old Blue" at the end of the play. What is the significance of this song?

THE DRAMATIC VISION OF AUGUST WILSON[1]

SANDRA SHANNON

According to Wilson, he began *Fences* "with the image of a man standing in his yard with a baby in his arms" (DeVries 25). From the play's inception, he was aware of the amount of dramatic leverage provided by this visually

[1]Sandra G. Shannon, *The Dramatic Vision of August Wilson* (Washington, DC: Howard UP, 1995), 103–17. Parenthetical references to play are pages from the New American Library edition.

powerful image, born of his desire to prove that, contrary to myth, black men are responsible: "We have been told so many times how irresponsible we are as black males that I try and present positive images of responsibility" (25). But Troy appears not to pose much of a challenge to this myth. Although he heroically acknowledges the infant as his own—"She's my daughter, Rose. My own flesh and blood" (*F* 79)—his idea of responsibility is seen in his decision to hand over the child to someone who apparently is more responsible than he. Indeed, Wilson's perspective on responsibility might appear dubious to those unfamiliar with his decidedly male ethos, which he links to the history of black male-female relations in America. In an interview with Mark Rocha, Wilson states:

> You've got to understand the sociology of it. The transition from slavery to freedom was a cultural shock for blacks. All of a sudden black men had to ask themselves things like, "What is money?" "What is marriage?" Black women, for all their own struggles, were relatively stable. Economically, they had control of the house. But what were black men supposed to do to make a living? (Rocha 38).

Still, for Wilson or any member of an audience to view Troy's actions as "responsible" depends on focusing not on the responsibility of the distraught middle-aged garbageman for the entire situation but on his responsibility in honoring his daughter and ultimately facing the evils of his own making. That he does not simply flee apparently saves him from the total damnation heaped upon so many black men caught in similar dilemmas.

Troy's entertaining anecdotes and searing monologues only seem incongruous with his station in life: in fact, language has become his most effective defense against victimization. That his own father was essentially a failure and a victim of the ruthless tenant farming system rests heavily upon Troy, for, as a young boy, he witnessed firsthand his father's destruction: "Sometimes I use to wonder why he was living. . . . He ain't knew how to do nothing but farm. No, he was trapped and I think he knew it" (*F* 51). Unfortunately, Troy's predicament is not very far removed from the bleak conditions that doomed his father—a dead-end job and no chance for a better life. Still, Troy's words portray him as the ultimate warrior, even though circumstances suggest otherwise. Expansive rhetoric justifies his wrongdoing, appeases his family, and apparently soothes his conscience.

Troy's fondness for talk is grounded in the African American oral tradition not yet affected by the cultural shock that followed the invention of the television and the spread of modern audiovisual devices. In fact, the Maxsons do not own a television set, and, as Troy explains to Cory, patching their leaky roof will most certainly take precedence over purchasing an electronic gadget. In the absence of such diversions, verbal communication becomes an art form for Troy. Rarely does he spare words when he has an opportunity to dominate center stage. When Rose cautions him against consuming too much liquor, he launches into a speech on death based upon a series of metaphors that provide a window to his character. By invoking the rules of baseball, he familiarizes death's power: "Death ain't nothing but a fastball on an outside corner" (10). By borrowing images from the military, he acknowledges and, to some extent, admires death's persistence: "I looked up one day and Death was marching straight at me. The middle of July, 1941" (11). And by alluding to wrestling, he suggests that he, as if heeding the speaker of Dylan Thomas's poem, will not "go gentle into that good night": "We wrestled for three days and three nights. I can't say where I found the strength from. Every time it seemed like he was gonna get the best of me, I'd reach way down deep inside myself and find the strength to do him one better" (12).

In addition to being a master at metaphors, Troy is skilled at using language to deflect attention from his faults. One of the most dramatically poignant moments in *Fences* occurs when Troy scrambles to find suitable words to explain to his wife of eighteen years that he has fathered a child with another woman: "I'm trying to find a way to tell you. . . I'm gonna be a daddy. I'm gonna be somebody's daddy" (66). He is moving as he justifies his relationship with Alberta, the "other woman": "I can sit up in her house and laugh. Do you understand what I'm saying. I can laugh . . . and it feels good. It reaches all the way down to the bottom of my shoes" (69). He even succeeds at presenting a convincing plea to Rose to take in and raise his orphaned daughter as her own. Apparently language creates a larger-than-life reality for Troy. In each of these situations, Troy's words redirect any feelings of guilt away from himself. He seems free from remorse and actually appears heroic against all charges while a less eloquent man might appear villainous.

Like all of Wilson's plays to date, *Fences* is very much a black man's story. Black women do have appreciable roles in his dramas; however, they seldom are as developed as the men, who freely commune with other black men, whether in a dingy bandroom, on a back porch stoop, at a kitchen table, or in a one-room cafe. Wilson's sharply drawn male characters are, no doubt, also the result of his early devotion to listening to their conversations in the barrooms and tobacco houses of Pittsburgh. As a young, inexperienced poet who admitted that his verse suffered because he knew nothing of the world, he unconsciously absorbed the larger-than-life narratives of these storytellers. Also, deep within the psyche of young Wilson was (and still is) an urge to search for and create the image of a father he never had, one who would fill his son's head with his wisdom and guide him toward a responsible adulthood. As evidenced by Troy, Wilson assembles from the variety of black men that he has encountered a paternal image—by no means angelic, but an image of a father nonetheless.

Regardless of the process behind Wilson's depictions of his characters, the women's realities are decidedly different from those of the men around them and are limited to those possibilities sustained and promoted by Western culture. Critic and novelist Marilyn French sees a general dualism in the portrayal of women: "This split in principle of nature, the feminine principle, still exists in our perception of actual women; there is the mother madonna, and the whore; the nourisher and the castrator. This split in the feminine principle I call inlaw and outlaw aspects of it" (23). According to French, the outlaw is described in terms of "darkness, chaos, flesh, the sinister, magic and above all, sexuality," while the inlaw suggests completely different values: "nutritiveness, compassion, mercy, and the ability to create felicity" (24).

These two categories can be usefully applied to the women in *Fences*. Consider Troy's mistress Alberta as an "outlaw": she disrupts the Maxson family circle, sundering relationships between husband and wife and father and son as well as the deeply fraternal bond between Troy and Bono. She represents everything that sticks its tongue out at the responsibility that Troy faces as a family man and as head of the household. She demands nothing of him—not his loyalty, not his money, not even his time. She provides a haven from the chronic concerns of survival weighing down upon the frustrated garbage collector and would-be Major Leaguer, a place where he can simply laugh out loud. Nevertheless, Alberta is not blamed as the "whore," though she is the key to the disintegration of the Maxson family and ultimately to Troy's tragic demise. When Rose finally does learn about Troy's affair, her fury is directed solely at her husband as a willing party, not at Alberta as his temptress. Never physically appearing in the play, known only through conversations about her, Alberta becomes merely a manifestation of Troy's own flawed character.

While the outlaw Alberta appeals to Troy's hedonistic nature, the "inlaw" Rose reminds him of responsibility. She manages the home, wrestles with daily worries over money, and single-handedly tries to keep the Maxson family together. She does all of this while willfully neglecting to establish time and space for her own growth. As her name suggests, Rose thrives amid adversity and stands out from the moral squalor around her. While few might be expected to withstand the amount of humiliation she endures, Rose seems to thrive upon it; she is able to transform a motherless infant into a stable young girl and pull the loose threads of her family together at the play's end.

Rose Maxson lingers half in the shadows during the entire first act of *Fences*, speaking largely in reaction to her husband's exaggerated stories about himself. However, when she finally discovers her voice, she is convincing even as her character transforms. Though before she was the predictable image of temperance, she suddenly becomes a woman who stands eye-to-eye with her egoistic husband: "I been standing with you! I been right here with you, Troy. I got a life too. I gave eighteen years of my life to stand in the same spot with you. Don't you think I ever wanted other things? Don't you think I had dreams and hopes?" (70–71). In one impassioned scene, Rose's entire history rushes forward out of nearly two decades of dormancy. Yet this moment of revelation does not lessen Rose Maxson's extreme altruism. She is so thoroughly and persistently moral that her character becomes more obviously symbolic than realistic. She is her husband's conscience, quite literally his better half. Like Alberta, she is basically an extension of Troy's ego, not one whose own story requires a full hearing. Her eighteen-year suppression of self and allegiance to family perfectly match the mold of the inlaw, for as French describes it, the inlaw prototype "requires volitional subordination[;]. . . it values above all the good of the whole. . . and finds pleasure in that good rather than in assertion of self" (24).

❧

Wilson's symbolic depictions of black women such as Rose have their basis in his capabilities as a poet. Also a by-product of his grounding in poetry is a conscious tendency to incorporate powerful metaphors to communicate his plays' larger thematic concerns. He believes this to be an important part of his strength as a dramatist: "The idea of metaphor. . . is a very large idea in my plays and something that I find lacking in most other contemporary plays. . . . I think I write the kinds of plays that I do because I have twenty-six years of writing poetry underneath all that" (interview).

The title image of *Fences*, the third play in Wilson's black history chronicle, very appropriately conveys a number of realities for the black family of late '50s America. It raises issues ranging from economic and professional deprivation to emotional and moral isolation. The fence, which may either inhibit or protect, is both a positive and negative image to various members of the Maxson family. To Rose, who nags Troy about completing this wooden border, the fence promises to keep in those whom she loves, preventing them from leaving the fortress she so lovingly sustains for them. To Cory, however, the fence becomes a tangible symbol of all that stands in the way of his independence. His work on it is merely an exercise in obedience and a reminder that he is not yet a man—at least not to Troy. To Troy, the fence represents added restrictions placed upon him. Thus he half-heartedly erects one section of the fence at a time and completes the job only after accepting a challenge from Bono, who agrees to buy his wife, Lucille, a refrigerator as soon as Troy completes the fence. It takes Bono to explain to him the importance of the fence:

CORY: I don't know why Mama want a fence around the yard noways.
TROY: Damn if I know either. What the hell she keeping out with it? She ain't
    got nothing nobody want.
BONO: Some people build fences to keep people out. . . and other people
    build fences to keep people in. Rose wants to hold on to you all. She
    loves you. (F 61)

On a deeper level, Troy sees the fence's completion as a reminder of his own mortality; he senses that he is erecting his own monument. His anxiety about death's inevitability emerges when his longtime friend questions Troy's choice of wood:

> BONO: You don't need this wood [hard wood]. You can put it up with pine wood and it'll stand as long as you gonna be here looking at it.
>
> TROY: How you know how long I'm gonna be here, nigger? Hell, I might just live forever. Live longer than old man Horsely. (60)

Troy's reluctance to complete the fence seems ominous, for shortly after finishing it for Rose, he dies. The fence, then, becomes a gauge for his life, during which he experiences both literal and figurative incarceration. He is fenced off from society during a lengthy prison term; he is fenced out of the Major Leagues because of racial segregation; and after he initiates the breakup of his family, he is fenced out of his home as well as out of the hearts of Rose and Cory.

Other metaphors that the poet-turned-playwright effectively weaves throughout *Fences* adopt their imagery from the game of baseball. Images of the game loom large in the consciousness of the onetime Negro Leaguer, Troy, who often borrows the behavioral codes of this game to suit various situations in his life. Part of the tragedy of *Fences* is Troy's belief that he would have surpassed current black players and the white Major League players of his youth had he been allowed to play among them. His ego and professional potential have been devastated because he has been cheated out of at least a chance to play Major League ball. As an outward manifestation of the blues he surely feels because of this loss, Troy adopts the language of the game in order to explain the "deprivation of possibility" (Reed 93) that has hurt him so deeply.

For Troy, life is a baseball game riddled with fast balls, curve balls, sacrifice flies, and an occasional strikeout, but too few homeruns. Although the conflict of the ball game lasts for only nine innings, Troy sees himself as being constantly at bat. From keeping death at bay to announcing a "full count" against his defiant son Cory, Troy flavors his conversation with baseball metaphors at every chance he gets. The various rules of the game become his basis for interpreting his actions and another avenue for expressing his blues. His preoccupation with images associated with the traditionally masculine, extremely competitive sport robs him of the candor necessary to handle the delicate relationships in his life. In one of the most intense moments of the play, Troy struggles to explain to his wife that he has not only been unfaithful to her but has also fathered a child outside of their marriage bed: "I fooled them, Rose. I bunted. When I found you and Cory and a halfway decent job. . . I was safe. Couldn't nothing touch me. I wasn't gonna strike out no more. . . . I stood on first base for eighteen years and I thought. . . well, goddamn it. . . go on for it!" (*F* 70). In using this second language, Troy comes to live it. He completely alienates both his son and his wife by forcing upon them his very selfish view of life. Consequently, he cannot see past immediate self-gratification; he cannot compromise, nor can he ask for forgiveness.

Wilson's use of metaphor in *Fences* extends to include Gabriel, Troy's disabled brother. Gabriel's war injury, a severe head wound, required that a metal plate be surgically implanted in his head. The brain-damaged Gabriel fantasizes that he is Archangel Gabriel, whose tasks are to open Heaven's pearly gates and to chase away hellhounds. When Troy is certain of Gabriel's irreversible condition, he claims the $3,000 compensation awarded his brother and uses it to purchase the home where he, Rose, Cory, and Gabriel live.

Gabriel is what Wilson refers to as a "spectacle character" (interview) whose role, as its label suggests, is to command attention and to force both acknowledgment and understanding of issues that are sooner ignored. Here, he serves as a glaring reminder of the crippling injustices black men endure at the hands of their own country. Wilson notes, "This black man had suffered this wound fighting for a country in which his brother could not play baseball." America cannot hide the shame of thousands of black veterans like Gabriel, who sacrificed dearly in the service of their country yet possibly faced homelessness, prison, or the insane asylum upon their return. Gabriel's payment of $3,000 is ludicrously low for an injury that has maimed him for life.

Although Gabriel is not crucial to the central conflict of *Fences*, his presence gives Troy another dimension. In addition to being an embarrassing emblem of America's darker side, Gabriel is also a manifestation of the worst in Troy. He exposes a man who has become immune to the emotions of self-pity and remorse; a man who, after capitalizing on his brother's misfortune, has him committed to a mental institution. Troy has become so devastated by his own deferred dreams that nothing, save pleasing himself, matters to him. He can sign papers to prevent his son from receiving free tuition as a football recruit; he can sign papers to put his brother away indefinitely. To Wilson, Gabriel has a significant function in *Fences*, and he is bothered by critics who dismiss this wounded man as a halfwit:

> They [critics] make me mad when I read the reviews and they would refer to Gabriel as an idiot. . . . Gabriel is one of those self-sufficient characters. He gets up and goes to work every day. He goes out and collects those discarded fruit and vegetables, but he's taking care of himself. He doesn't want Troy to take care of him. He moves out of Troy's house and lives down there and pays his rent to the extent that he is able. (interview)

Wilson plays upon the dramatic tension inherent in the spectacle of Gabriel's character, but he also relies upon this highly sensitive man to introduce an identifiable element of African American culture: belief in a spiritual world. Although Gabriel's perceptions of Christianity and images associated with the afterlife are apparently the results of his dementia, he articulates several myths that have their origins in traditional religious beliefs among African Americans. For example, he revives the myth of Saint Peter, so-called keeper of the pearly gates, and keeps alive the fear of Judgment Day: "Ain't gonna be too much of a battle when God get to waving that Judgment sword. But the people's gonna have a hell of a time trying to get into heaven if them gates ain't open" (*F* 47–48).

Gabriel also confirms the existence of a great Judgment Book in which Saint Peter records "everybody's name what was ever been born" (26). Gabriel, who believes he has already died and gone to Heaven, is a privileged soul, for, according to him, Saint Peter has allowed him to see both Troy and Rose's names recorded in the ledger. And, again, according to Gabriel, he sometimes relieves Saint Peter from the eternal task of guarding the pearly gates: "Did you know when I was in heaven. . . every morning me and St. Peter would sit down by the gate and eat some big fat biscuits? Oh, yeah! We had us a good time. We'd sit there and eat us them biscuits and then St. Peter would go off to sleep and tell me to wake him up when it's time to open the gates for the judgment" (26).

Each encounter with Gabriel convinces one to look beyond his surface disability and concentrate instead upon the spiritual and mythical worlds he creates and the realms of possibility that these worlds offer. Gabriel's ability to look beyond the literal is his own means of negotiating an indifferent world, yet it also exemplifies a long-standing Christian belief among African Americans to look toward things-not-seen for salvation. He has adopted both a frame of mind and a vision that get him through the daily drudgery of his condition. This special vision is most evident in the final scene of *Fences*, when the Maxson family prepares to bury Troy. At this time Gabriel experiences "a trauma that a sane and normal mind would be unable to withstand. He begins to dance. A slow, strange dance, eerie and life-giving. A dance of atavistic signature and ritual. . . . He finishes his dance and the gates of heaven stand open as wide as God's closet" (101). As a spectacle character, Gabriel's significance is in providing a flawed icon of African Americans' cultural past. He is a cultural paradox—not taken seriously by those around him yet conveying in his distorted sensibilities the cultural bedrock of generations past and to come.

Works Cited

De Vries, Hillary. "A Song in Search of Itself." *American Theater* January 1987, 22–25.

Reed, Ishmael. "In Search of August Wilson." *Connoisseur* 217 (March 1987): 92–97.

Rocha, Mark. "A Conversation with August Wilson." *Diversity: A Journal of Multicultural Issues* 1 (Spring 1993): 24–42.

Wilson, August. *Fences*. New York: New American Library, 1987.

BOUNDARIES, LOGISTICS, AND IDENTITY: THE PROPERTY OF METAPHOR IN *FENCES* AND *JOE TURNER'S COME AND GONE*[1]

ALAN NADEL

In *Fences*, August Wilson . . . describes Troy Maxson's struggle to build a fence around his property. . . . A fifty-three-year-old garbageman who owns a small house in a run-down section of Pittsburgh, in 1957, Troy during the course of the play works at building a small fence around his meager back yard. At the same time, he works constantly to delineate his rights and responsibilities, as husband, brother, worker, friend, and father. His name, Maxson, suggests a shortened "Mason-Dixon,"[2] a personalized version of the national division over the properties of blackness. His character similarly embodies the personal divisions that come from living in a world where the Mason-Dixon line exists as the ubiquitous circumscription of black American claims to human rights.

Troy lives in a house with Rose, his wife of eighteen years, and their seventeen-year-old son, Cory. The down payment for the house came from the $3,000 his brother Gabriel received in compensation for a World War II head wound that left him a virtual half-wit, harboring the belief "with every fiber of his being that he is the Archangel Gabriel" (23). Troy takes pride at having housed and cared for Gabriel since the injury, and at the same time expresses shame at having had to rely on Gabriel's misfortune to provide the down payment he could never have acquired through years of honest labor. Having run away from a cruel and abusive father when he was a teenager, he found his way to the city, where he married and supported his family through theft until he was convicted of assault and armed robbery and sent to jail for fifteen years. There he learned to play baseball and give up robbery. By the time he was released, his wife having left him, he met Rose, remarried, and after playing baseball in the Negro Leagues, became a garbageman.

The central conflicts in the play arise from his refusal to let his son play football or accept a football scholarship to college, and from his having fathered a daughter through an extramarital affair. But these are framed by conflicts with the father he fled, the major leagues that wouldn't let him play baseball, and Death himself, with whom Troy had once wrestled. Whatever else he loses, he vigilantly maintains his property and his property rights, demanding his authority within its confines, eventually building a fence around his yard and guarding the entrance

---

[1]Alan Nadel, "Boundaries, Logistics, and Identity: The Property of Metaphor in *Fences* and *Joe Turner's Come and Gone," May All Your Fences Have Gates: Essays on the Drama of August Wilson*, ed. Alan Nadel (Iowa City: U of Iowa P, 1994), 86–95. Parenthetical page references are to the New American Library edition of *Fences*.

[2]In *Ma Rainey's Black Bottom*, in fact, Levee refers to it as the "Maxon-Dixon line" (82).

with all of his human power against the force of Death, whose representation in human form is generally perceived to be metaphoric.

It is on these grounds—and on his home ground—that Troy chooses to be sized up. For in all other locales he is a large man who has been underestimated. As a baseball player and even as a garbageman, the world has not taken his measure. To "take the measure of a man" is to make a metaphor derived from a set of primary physical traits. "To measure up" means to fulfill a role in the same way one fills out a suit of clothes; "to take measure of oneself" means to assess one's ability to fill a specific role in the same way that one selects that suit of clothes. Implicit in all these metaphors is a set of objective physical standards— what Locke called primary characteristics—against which such intangibles as character, courage, loyalty, skill, or talent can be determined.

In the logistics of *Fences*, however, these standards form the variables measured against the standard of Troy Maxson's largeness. From the outset of the play, his size is a given: "Troy is fifty-three years old, a large man with thick heavy hands; it is this largeness that he strives to fill out and make an accommodation with. Together with his blackness, his largeness informs his sensibilities and the choices he has made in life" (1). And after his death, as Rose explains to Cory, "When I first met your daddy,. . . I thought here is a man you can open yourself up to and be filled to bursting. Here is a man that can fill all them empty spaces you been tipping around the edges of. . . . When your daddy walked through the house, he filled it up" (93). Cory perceived Troy as "a shadow that followed you everywhere. It weighed on you and sunk in your flesh. It would wrap around you and lay there until you couldn't tell which one was you any more" (93), but Rose argues that Cory is just like his father:

> That shadow wasn't nothing but you growing into yourself. You either got
> to grow into it or cut it down to fit you. But that's all you got to make life
> with. That's all you got to measure yourself against that world out there.
> Your daddy wanted you to be everything he wasn't. . . and at the same time
> he tried to make you into everything he was. (93)

In addition to establishing Troy's size as the standard, both negative and positive, Rose is setting that standard against the standards asserted by the dominant white culture. Cory, in other words, is being urged not to measure himself against Troy but to use Troy's size as a defense against the other, implicitly figurative, norms of "that world out there."

In so doing, Rose is asking him, in fact, to continue his father's quest. For the problem of the play can be seen as Troy's attempt to take measure of himself in a world that has denied him the external referents. His struggle is to act in the literal world in such a way as to become not just the literal but the figurative father, brother, husband, man he desires to be. The role of father is the most complex because he is the father of three children from three different women. The children, precisely seventeen years apart, represent Troy's paternal responsibilities to three successive generations of black children. As each of these children makes demands on him, he must measure up to his responsibilities, and for each generation he measures up differently.

When his older son, Lyons, a would-be musician, for example, regularly borrows money from him, Troy puts Lyons through a ritual of humiliation constructed out of the process of differentiating Lyons from himself: "I done learned my mistake and learned to do what's right by it. You still trying to get something for nothing. Life don't owe you nothing. You owe it to yourself." At issue here is not only Troy's sense of himself as role model but also his sense of himself as negative example. He is both the father to emulate and the father not to emulate: Lyons should be like Troy by not making Troy's mistake. This lesson has a double edge, though, because the earlier, error-ridden life that Troy has learned to reject included not only his criminal acts but also his marriage to Lyons's mother and his fathering of Lyons. At that point in his life, we later learn, he felt he was not ready to be a father or to accept the responsibilities of fatherhood. For Lyons to recognize Troy's mistakes, then, is for him to acknowledge the inappropriateness of his own existence.

Troy deals with his younger son, Cory, in the same way. Like Troy, Cory is a talented athlete. A superstar in the Negro baseball leagues, Troy was never given an opportunity to play in the white leagues. Believing that white America would never allow a black to be successful in professional sports, he refuses to allow his son to go to college on a football scholarship. Once again, he becomes what he sees as a positive example for his son by virtue of his ability to reject himself. In a completely self-contained economy, he becomes both the model of error and the model of correction.

In regard to sports, particularly, he does this by constructing a division between personal history and American history. An extraordinary baseball player whose talents are compared with those of Babe Ruth and Josh Gibson, Troy was unfortunately over forty years old when professional baseball was first integrated. Within the time frame of American history, as his friend Bono says, "Troy just come along too early" (9). Troy rejects Bono's opinion with a triple negative: "There ought not never have been no time called too early" (9). "I'm talking about," he explains, "if you could play ball then they ought to have let you play. Don't care what color you were. Come telling me I come along too early. If you could play, then they ought to have let you play" (9).

After the death in childbirth of his girlfriend. . . Troy issues his challenge to Death in terms of the wall he is constructing between himself and it:

> I'm gonna build me a fence around what belongs to me. And I want you to stay on the other side. See? You stay over there until you're ready for me. Then you come on. Bring your army. Bring your sickle. Bring your wrestling

clothes. I ain't gonna fall down on my vigilance this time. You ain't gonna sneak up on me no more. When you ready for me. . . that's when you come around here. . . . Then we gonna find out what manner of man you are. . . . You stay on the other side of that fence until you ready for me.

This is the metaphoric fence constructed to complement the literal fence Rose had been requesting from the outset. When Death accepts Troy's challenge, he confirms Troy's mastery over the literal, his power to turn his property into the visible recognition of his human properties, such that his responsibilities to his family, his athletic prowess, and his physical presence confirm his ability to confront Death—and hence to construct his life—on his own terms. In his terms, as he stated earlier in the play, "Death ain't nothing but a fastball on the outside corner" (10). Rose's description of Troy's death confirms that terminology: "He was out there swinging that bat and then he just fell over. Seem like he swung it and stood there with this grin on his face. . . and then he just fell over" (91). The inference is not only that he had protected his family by striking a final blow at Death but, more significantly, that he was able to do so because Troy made Death come to him on Troy's terms. Although Troy's challenge may be seen as figurative, Death's accepting it makes it literal, and thus the man-to-man battle between Troy and Death becomes a literal fight and simultaneously affirms Troy's power to create a site—however small—in which the figurative becomes literal. The conversion not only reduces Death to a man but also affirms Troy's status as one.

Within the context of the play, moreover, Wilson affirms the literal status of that conversion by having Gabriel perform a similar feat. Released from the mental hospital in order to attend Troy's funeral, Gabriel arrives carrying his trumpet. Although it has no mouthpiece, he uses it to "tell St. Peter to open the gates" (99). After three attempts, with no sound coming from the trumpet, "he begins to dance. A slow, strange dance, eerie and life-giving. A dance of atavistic signature and ritual. He begins to howl in what is an attempt at song, or perhaps a song turning back into itself in an attempt at speech. He finishes his song and the gates of heaven stand open as wide as God's closet" (100).

Gabriel's ability to invert the literal and the figurative thus confirms our understanding of Troy's death, at the same time that it revises our understanding of Gabriel's marginality or "madness." For we can read his wound as a function of attributing literal power to such figurative institutions as nation and warfare. As a soldier in World War II, he invested his primary literal claim to human rights—his human life—in support of a figurative structure—the United States—that on the very site of his investment, the segregated armed forces, denied the status of that life as human. One can only assume that the part of his brain blown away in the war contained the beliefs and conceptions that allowed him to accept the figurative status of his own humanity. Lacking that part of his brain, he is not functional within the dominant white culture, as is evidenced by his numerous arrests as well as his institutionalizations.

The Mason-Dixon line, marking off the site where he may consider himself literally human, has become for Gabriel the walls of the mental institution. By the end of the play—providing a virtual survey of the institutionalized power critiqued by Michel Foucault—all the Maxsons are disciplined within figurative Mason-Dixon lines. With Gabriel in the mental hospital, Cory in the armed services, Lyons in prison (we could conceivably even add Rose's recent involvement with the church), they find only this moment of relief within the boundary of the fence that Troy built. In the play's final pronouncement, with Gabriel speaking now as prophet and miracle worker rather than as marginalized madman, he asserts and demonstrates that the order of things—the relationship of figurative to literal—should be reversed: "And that's the way that go!" (100).

This is a tactical victory, a method of subverting and resisting the strategic power of the dominant culture. For that culture has urged the black American man to flight with the implication that his humanity was the function of logistics; confined by sites that denied literal confirmation of that humanity, the culture has offered the promise of an elsewhere, a site where the literal and figurative reconfigure. To pursue that promise, to seek that site, often meant sacrificing familial responsibilities. Instead of pursuing that site at the expense of his family, Troy created it in order to protect them. As Rose, referring to the fence, noted to Cory: "Oh, that's been up there ever since Raynell wasn't but a wee little bitty old thing. Your daddy finally got around to putting that up to keep her in the yard" (91).

In this way, Troy fought not only Death, but also history. For the normative discourse of white American history, in 1957, was one of progress and assimilation. Textbooks promoted the idea of the melting pot and of upward mobility; historical films and dramas reinscribed the myth of the nuclear family; and despite the continued presence of Jim Crow laws, segregated schools and facilities, rampant denial of voter rights, and extensive discrimination in housing and employment, American history and, more important, its popularizations represented the United States as a land of equal opportunity, with liberty and justice for all. Those whose personal narratives failed to confirm this hegemonic discourse became invisible; as Ralph Ellison so dramatically illustrated in *Invisible Man*, they fell outside of history. Despairing of the possibility of altering dominant historical discourse, Troy devotes himself to reconfiguring the paternal patterns that compose his personal history.

In thus making himself both the positive and the negative model for his sons, he also makes his father a positive and a negative model. For unlike many men of his generation—Bono's father, for example—Troy's father refused to leave the family, however much he detested it. As Troy points out, "He felt a responsibility toward us. May be he ain't treated us the way I felt he should have, but without that responsibility he could have walked off and left us, made his own way" (49). In contrast, as Bono points out, "Back in those days what you talking about, niggers used to travel all over.

They get up one day and see where the day ain't sitting right with them and they walk out their front door and just take on down one road or another and keep on walking. . . . Just walk on till you come to something else. Ain't you never heard of nobody having the walking blues?" (50–51).

Works Cited

Wilson, August. *Fences*. New York: New American Library, Plume, 1986.

———. *Ma Rainey's Black Bottom*. New York: New American Library, Plume, 1985.

FILLING THE TIME: READING HISTORY IN THE DRAMA OF AUGUST WILSON[1]

JOHN TIMPANE

In the prefatorial piece "The Play," Wilson locates *Fences* in a "big-city neighborhood" of an eastern industrial town—probably Pittsburgh—in 1957. In 1957, "the Milwaukee Braves won the World Series, and the hot winds of change that would make the sixties a turbulent, racing, dangerous, and provocative decade had not yet begun to blow full."[2] The year 1957, as Wilson does not mean us to forget, was the year of Little Rock, when Eisenhower reluctantly ordered regular army paratroops to prevent interference with court-ordered racial integration at Little Rock Central High School. That was the year of H.R. 6127, the Civil Rights Act of 1957, passed after virulent debate and filibuster in the Senate. Texas, Tennessee, Delaware, Maryland, and other states were in the throes of court-ordered desegregation; Little Rock stood out because of the prospect that state and federal troops might face each other. The winds of change blew both hot and cold. The possibility of new positivities coexisted with the fact of ancient recalcitrance. Only three weeks before Little Rock, Ku Klux Klan members had castrated a black man outside of Zion, Alabama. And Louis "Satchmo" Armstrong, in a public gesture that attracted both widespread praise and widespread blame, canceled a much-publicized tour of the USSR, saying that "the way they are treating my people in the South, the government can go to hell. . . . It's getting almost so bad, a colored man hasn't got any country."

In *Fences*, baseball operates metonymically, as a metaphoric stand-in for the troubled changes of 1957. Much of the action takes place just before the Milwaukee Braves' victory over the New York Yankees in the

[1]John Timpane, "Filling the Time: Reading History in the Drama of August Wilson," *May All Your Fences Have Gates: Essays on the Drama of August Wilson*, ed. Alan Nadel (Iowa City: U of Iowa P, 1994), 69–74. Parenthetical page numbers are from the Plume edition of *Fences*.

[2]Richards, Introduction, pp. vii, xviii.

1957 World Series. That victory signified a year of many changes in base-ball, changes that reflected the social upheavals of 1957. One change, very much in progress, was the emergence of the black ballplayer. Black players had played prominent roles in previous World Series—Willie Mays in the 1954 series and Jackie Robinson in the Brooklyn Dodgers' victory over the Yankees in 1955. Milwaukee was the first non–New York team led by a black star to win a World Series. Hank Aaron, the most powerful hitter in baseball history, played alongside Eddie Mathews, white and a great slugger, and alongside three excellent white pitchers: Warren Spahn, Bob Buhl, and Lew Burdette. Because of the quick rise to prominence of Mays, Aaron, Roberto Clemente, and Frank Robinson, the question was no longer whether blacks would play but whether they could become leaders. As the success of the Braves portended, the answer was yes: Aaron led the league in power statistics, hit a home run on the last day of the season to give the Braves the pennant, rampaged through Yankee pitching to give his team the World Series, and won the National League Most Valuable Player Award for 1957.

Yet the Braves were far from being a truly integrated team, and inte-gration was far from complete in baseball. Though blacks had been play-ing in the major leagues since 1947, it would take until 1959 for each major league team to have at least one black player. Behind the grudging, piece-meal process of integration in sports lies a Foucaultian "disjunction"—World War II—and a resultant "redistribution": the postwar move west. Hard times in postwar Boston meant dwindling patronage for the Boston Braves, so the team moved west to Milwaukee in 1953. In 1957, the Dodgers left Brooklyn for Los Angeles, and the New York Giants left for San Fran-cisco. In so doing, these teams mirrored an accelerating westward shift in the center of population. Further, the war probably created new social potential (to this day not completely realized) for women and blacks. For baseball, all this meant new teams, new audiences, and new pressures to tap at last the large pool of talented black players. The National League led in this regard. Indeed, it was not until Frank Robinson was traded from the Cincinnati Reds to the Baltimore Orioles and won the Triple Crown in 1966 that a black player dominated American League pitching the way Mays, Clemente, and Aaron had done in the National League.

Changes in baseball and changes in American life complicate the abil-ity of anyone who, like Troy, bases his assumptions about reality on the facts of a prewar world. In the first scene of *Fences*, Troy pits his read-ing of things against those of Bono, Rose, and Lyons. Troy intersperses lies with truths, claiming he has seen and contended with Death and the devil. Rose challenges the way Troy presents these tales: "Anything you can't understand, you want to call it the devil" (14). Rose and Bono are a chorus parenthesizing Troy's insistence on his reading:

ROSE: Times have changed since you was playing baseball, Troy. That was
    before the war. Times have changed a lot since then.
TROY: How in hell they done changed?

ROSE: They got lots of colored boys playing ball now. Baseball and football.
BONO: You right about that, Rose. Times have changed, Troy. You done come
along too early.
TROY: There ought not never have been no time called too early! (9)

James calls the present "a saddle-back. . . from which we look in two
directions into time."[3] Throughout *Fences*, Troy Maxson straddles this
saddleback, constantly constructing a present selectively out of memory
(the past) and desire (the future).

Desire figures most clearly in his conflict with his son, Cory. Troy is
affronted by Cory's desire to try out before a college football recruiter
from North Carolina. Troy's own sport, and the source of his personal language of metaphors, is baseball; Cory's choice of football galls him. American popular culture has forgotten that integration had come to major
league football long before Jackie Robinson signed a baseball contract.
Fritz Pollard had played with the Akron Indians beginning in 1919, and
black players played professional football until 1933, when the disruption
of the Depression made football a whites-only sport for thirteen years.

As with baseball, this redistribution was tied to the postwar westward
push. The National Football League (NFL) had originally centered in the
Midwest, gradually adding franchises in eastern industrial centers. Long-
standing interest in starting a franchise on the West Coast was realized
when the Cleveland Rams moved to Los Angeles after the war. A rival
league, the All-American Football Conference (AAFC), started up in 1946.
Though the two leagues would soon merge, the AAFC forced some innovative moves, including the initiation of western franchises (the Los
Angeles Dons and the San Francisco 49ers) and the signing of black players. That same year, the Los Angeles Rams signed Kenny Washington and
Woody Strode, and the Cleveland Browns signed Bill Willis and Marion
Motley. Motley became a record-breaking rusher, beginning a strong tradition of black running backs that included Joe Perry, who, while playing for the San Francisco 49ers and Baltimore Colts, broke all rushing
records through the 1950s. (His heir-apparent was Jim Brown.) By 1953,
a black collegiate running back, J. C. Caroline of the University of Illinois,
had broken the hallowed records of "Red" Grange, a white runner of the
1920s and 1930s. By the late 1950s, black athletes had established a
prominence in football that at least equaled the standing of Mays, Aaron,
and the Robinsons in baseball.[4]

With the stronger tradition of integration, football was on the verge of
becoming a truly national sport in 1957. Cory believes, as Troy does not,
that a talented black athlete can get a chance. This disagreement emerges
when they discuss Roberto Clemente, now in his third year with the local
baseball club, the Pittsburgh Pirates.

[3]James, *Principles of Psychology*, p. 574.
[4]For a more detailed discussion about the vexed issue of integration in professional
football, see Ocania Chalk, *Pioneers of Black Sport* (New York: Dodd, Mead, 1975).

> TROY: I ain't thinking about the Pirates. Got an all-white team. Got that
>   boy. . . that Puerto Rican boy. . . Clemente. Don't even half-play him. That
>   boy could be something if they give him a chance. Play him one
>   day and sit him on the bench the next.
> CORY: He gets a lot of chances to play.
> TROY: I'm talking about playing regular. Playing every day so you can get
>   your timing. That's what I'm talking about.
> CORY: They got some white guys on the team that don't play every day. You
>   can't play everybody at the same time.
> TROY: If they got a white fellow sitting on the bench. . . you can bet your last
>   dollar he can't play! The colored guy got to be twice as good before he get
>   on the team. That's why I don't want you to get all tied up in them sports.
>   Man on the team and what it get him? They got colored on the team and
>   don't use them. Same as not having them. All them teams the same.
> CORY: The Braves got Hank Aaron and Wes Covington. Hank Aaron hit two
>   home runs today. That makes forty-three.
> TROY: Hank Aaron ain't nobody. (33–34)

Far beyond baseball, the ulterior difference here is over whether a change has occurred in American society. Generational differences indicate a difference in reading. All Cory knows are the achievements of Aaron (who would hit forty-four home runs in 1957), Covington, and Clemente; these seem incontrovertible evidence that his dreams have a foundation.

What Troy knows is his own frustration as a great player in the Negro Leagues. His success was also his self-sacrifice: The Negro Leagues began to die as soon as black players began to be accepted in numbers into professional baseball. What killed Troy's career was, ironically, the *advent* of integrated baseball. Although he is clearly aware of these facts, and clearly damaged by them, Troy insists that history is continuous, that what was once true is still true. Cory assumes that what is true is new— that there is now a new form of positivity, a sudden redistribution—and this assumption on Cory's part outrages his father. For one the gap signifies the death he constantly pits himself against, and for the other it signifies a life in the future, liberated from his father's limitations. Granted, Troy's knowing dictum that "the colored guy got to be twice as good before he get on the team" was quite true in 1957 and is still a widely shared perception today. But Cory is not arguing that his chance is likely; he is arguing that it is possible.

Troy gives many names to his resistance. Compassion is one. As he says to Rose, "I got sense enough not to let my boy get hurt over playing no sports" (39). Jealousy is another. Cory is getting a chance while he is still young, whereas even in 1947 Troy was "too old to play in the major leagues" (39). Both these "reasons" are versions of his resistance to reading the change that is making Clemente and Aaron into national heroes. Both Troy's compassion for his son and his jealousy of him are ways to deny his own death.

Here, we may remember one of Foucault's more disturbing claims: that the traditional view of history as a seamless continuity really disguised the quest to construct the self as authoritative, continuous, integrated, and eternal. In *Archaeology of Knowledge* he pictures the outraged author crying, "Must I suppose that in my discourse I can have no survival? And that in speaking I am not banishing my death, but actually establishing it?"[5] For Troy, to acknowledge the possibility of Cory's success is to acknowledge that his own time has passed. Thus his repression of a fact that would have been available to any avid baseball fan in Pittsburgh—that Roberto Clemente really is getting a chance to play. Clemente had 543 at-bats in 1956 and 451 in 1957.[6] Thus his claim that Aaron is "nobody." Note the extreme care with which Wilson has placed the action of the third act: quite late in September 1957, seemingly to show that reality takes no heed of Troy's judgments. Aaron would win the home-run and runs-batted-in titles, earning him the Most Valuable Player Award. Clemente would go on to 3,000 hits and the Hall of Fame.

Works Cited

Foucault, Michel. *Archaeology of Knowledge*. Trans. by A. M. Sheridan Smith. New York: Pantheon, 1972.

James, William. *Principles of Psychology*. Ed. by Frederick H. Burkhardt. Vol. 1. Cambridge: Harvard University Press, 1981.

Neft, David S., and Richard M. Cohen. *The Sports Encyclopedia: Baseball*. New York: St. Martin's Press, 1989.

Richards, Lloyd. Introduction to *Fences*, by August Wilson, vii–viii. New York: New American Library, Plume, 1986.

Wilson, August. *Fences*. New York: New American Library, Plume, 1986.

[5]Foucault, *Archaeology of Knowledge*, p. 210.
[6]Neft and Cohen, *Sports Encyclopedia*, pp. 309, 312.

AUGUST WILSON'S WOMEN[1]

HARRY ELAM JR.

The idea of a woman "needing a man" is. . . implicit in the action of *Fences*. It underlines Rose Maxson's reasons for marrying her husband, Troy, and remaining married to him despite his infidelity. Rose Maxson in *Fences* reflects strong traditional values associated with black women and yet asserts a strong feminist voice. Unlike the other women discussed, she is both wife and mother. In these roles she sacrifices self, supports her family, and holds it together. Barbara Christian notes that in African American communities, "the idea that mothers should lead lives of sacrifice has become the norm."[2] Rose embodies this norm. Christian observes that the literature of black males has often perpetuated this

[1]Harry Elam Jr. "August Wilson's Women," *May All Your Fences Have Gates: Essays on the Drama of August Wilson*, ed. Alan Nadel (Iowa City: U of Iowa P, 1994), 178–80. Parenthetical documentation is to Wilson's *Three Plays*.
[2]Christian, *Black Feminist Criticism*, p. 234.

image.[3] Yet with Rose, Wilson expands on the stereotype while exploring this question of need as well as consistent truths of black female experience as wife and mother.

Rose exudes both love and strength. Each Friday her husband, Troy, hands over his paycheck to Rose. He relinquishes this element of economic authority, and she controls the household budget. From a position of "outsider-within" she observes the weekly payday rituals of the men. When necessary and from a distance, she participates, playfully teasing Troy, always bolstering his authority and publicly demonstrating her support for her man. As mother she nurtures her son, Cory. Aggressively, she defends Cory against the stubborn will of his father.

Rose understands that she has consigned herself to the limits imposed upon her by marriage and social expectations. Unlike Risa or Berniece, Rose articulates her perspective and the motivation for her actions. When Troy rationalizes his infidelity to her, she reaffirms her commitment to the relationship and castigates him for not doing the same.

> But I held onto you, Troy. I took all my feelings, my wants and needs, my dreams and I buried them inside you. I planted a seed and watched and prayed over it. I planted myself inside you and waited to bloom. And it didn't take me no eighteen years to find out the soil was hard and rocky and it wasn't never gonna bloom. But I held onto you, Troy. I held tighter. You was my husband. I owed you everything I had. Every part of me I could find to give you. And upstairs in that room, with the darkness falling in on me, I gave everything I had to try and erase the doubt that you wasn't the finest man in the world. And wherever you was going I wanted to be there with you. 'Cause you was my husband,' cause that's the only way I was gonna survive as your wife. (165)

Rose's verbal assault on Troy earns the audience's sympathy. Faced with the realities and imperfections of marriage, she is determined to make their marriage work. Still, Rose clearly accepts her own material oppression. "I *owed* you everything I had," she says. Troy's adultery provides that catalyst that propels her to reassess her position, to gain a greater self-awareness and to change.

Quite powerfully, Rose, hurt and betrayed, asserts her independence. When Troy presents her with his illegitimate, motherless daughter, Rose informs him, "Okay Troy. You're right. I'll take care of your baby for you 'cause, like you say, she's innocent and you can't visit the sins of the father upon the child. A motherless child has got a hard time. From right now. . . this child has a mother. But you a womanless man" (173). In the Broadway production, when Mary Alice as Rose accented this line by taking the baby and then slamming the back door in Troy's face, the audience, particularly black female spectators, erupted with cheers and applause. For at that moment Rose stands as a champion of black women, of any woman who has suffered under the constraints of a restrictive and inequitable marriage.

[3]Ibid., p. 236.

The avenues into which Rose channels her new freedom, neverthe-less, affirm rather than assault traditional gender limitations and hege-monic legitimacy. She finds solace in the church and the mothering of her adopted daughter, Raynell. While Rose spiritually distances herself from Troy, she does not leave the marriage. The church becomes a surrogate. Collins argues that institutions such as the church can be "contradictory locations," where black women not only learn independence but also "learn to subordinate our interests as women to the allegedly greater good of the larger African American community."[4] Thus Rose, despite her spiritual independence, continues to conform to the traditional expecta-tions and limitations placed on women. Black feminist scholar bell hooks criticizes the play and Rose for their conformity:

Fences poignantly portrays complex and negative contradictions within black masculinity in a white supremacist context. However, patri-archy is not critiqued, and even though tragic expressions of conven-tional masculinity are evoked, sexist values are re-inscribed via the black woman's redemption message as the play ends.[5]

Rose's words at the end of the play, however, both critique and con-firm the patriarchy. She tells Cory, who has returned for his father's funeral:

That was my first mistake. Not to make him leave some room for me, for my part in the matter. But at that time I wanted that. I wanted a house that I could sing in. And that's what your daddy gave me. I didn't know to keep his strength I had to give up little pieces of mine. I did that. I took his life as mine and mixed up the pieces so that I couldn't hardly tell which was which anymore. It was my choice. It was my life and I didn't have to live it like that. But that's what life offered me in the way of being a woman, and I took it. (189–90)

As a black woman in 1957, Rose had extremely restricted options. Mar-riage required compromise and, quite often for women, a loss of self. The traditional nature of their marriage allowed Troy to dominate, while Rose suppressed her will and desires. Rose reflects on this reality, on a historic truth experienced by many black women. Thus her words call attention to the limitations of gender roles and critique the patriarchal system that created these limitations. Yet Rose also professes her own complicity. Rose's acceptance of the blame, her internalization of external conditions of oppression, prevent her from challenging the status quo. She chooses to accept her subservient position in her marriage; this she believes is what "life offers her as a woman."

Works Cited

Christian, Barbara. *Black Feminist Criticism*. New York: Pergamon Press, 1985.

---

[4]Collins, *Black Feminist Thought*, p. 86.
[5]hooks, *Yearning*, p. 18.

Collins, Patricia Hill. *Black Feminist Thought*. Boston: Unwin Hyman, 1990.

hooks, bell. *Yearning: Race, Gender, and Cultural Politics*. Boston: South End Press, 1990.

Wilson, August. *Three Plays: "Ma Rainey's Black Bottom," "Fences," "Joe Turner's Come and Gone."* Pittsburgh: University of Pittsburgh Press, 1991.

AN INTERVIEW WITH AUGUST WILSON[1]
BONNIE LYONS

This interview took place in February 1997 in Merchants Cafe in Pioneer Square in downtown Seattle, near August Wilson's office. Dressed in a white dress shirt and tie coupled with a casual jacket and a cap, Wilson was soft-spoken and somewhat restrained at first. He became more and more animated as he spoke about his passion for black life in America and for his plays. Wilson is well aware that he created his characters, but he spoke of them with such knowledge and affection that I was reminded of the famous story of Balzac calling for his characters on his deathbed.

Q. Elsewhere you've talked about writing as a way of effecting social change and said that all your plays are political, but that you try not to make them didactic or polemical. Can you talk a little about how plays can effect social change without being polemical or didactic?

A. I don't write primarily to effect social change. I believe writing can do that, but that's not why I write. I work as an artist. However, all art is political in the sense that it serves the politics of someone. Here in America whites have a particular view of blacks, and I think my plays offer them a different and new way to look at black Americans. For instance, in *Fences* they see a garbageman, a person they really don't look at, although they may see a garbageman every day. By looking at Troy's life, white people find out that the content of this black garbageman's life is very similar to their own, that he is affected by the same things—love, honor, beauty, betrayal, duty. Recognizing that these things are as much a part of his life as of theirs can be revolutionary and can affect how they think about and deal with black people in their lives.

Q. How would that same play, *Fences*, affect a black audience?

A. Blacks see the content of their lives being elevated into art. They don't always know that is possible, and it's important to know that.

Q. You've talked about how important black music was for your development. Was there any black literature that showed you that black lives can be the subject of great art?

[1]Bonnie Lyons, "An Interview with August Wilson," *Contemporary Literature* 40.1 (Spring 1999): 1–21.

A. *Invisible Man.* When I was fourteen I discovered the Negro section
    of the library. I read *Invisible Man,* Langston Hughes, and all the
    thirty or forty books in the section, including the sociology. I remem-
    ber reading a book that talked about the "Negro's power of hard
    work" and how much that phrase affected me. . . . Forty years ago we
    had few black writers compared to today. There have been forty years
    of education and many more college graduates. And it's important to
    remember that blacks don't have a long history of writing. We come
    from an oral tradition. At one point in America it was a crime to teach
    blacks to read and write. So it's only in the past 150 years that we've
    been writing in this country.

Q. You're self-educated. How do you feel about schools and self-educa-
    tion?
A. The schools are horrible and don't teach anybody anything. From
    about the fifth grade on, I was always butting heads with my teach-
    ers. I would ask them questions and they would say, "Shut up. Sit
    down," because they didn't know the answers. So I'd go to the
    library to find out. When I quit school at fourteen, I didn't want my
    mother to know, so I'd get up and go to the library and stay there
    until three o'clock. My mother taught me to read when I was four
    years old, and in the library for the first time in my life I felt free. I
    could read whole books on subjects that interested me. I'd read
    about the Civil War or theology. By the time I left the library, I
    thought, "Okay, I'm ready. I know a lot of stuff." It always amazed
    me that libraries were free.

Q. When you look at your work as a whole, what patterns do you see?
A. *Fences* is the odd man out because it's about one individual and
    everything focuses around him. The others are ensemble plays. I think
    I need to write another one like *Fences* to balance it out.

Q. How were things better in the forties?
A. We used to have our own black baseball league, for example. Every-
    thing was black-owned. On a Sunday black families would go over to
    the field, and some would sell peanuts or chicken sandwiches and so
    on. We were more self-sufficient. When blacks were finally allowed
    to play in the white leagues, the loss for the black community was
    great. Similarly in the forties black women were not allowed to go
    downtown and try on dresses in the department stores. So we had our
    own dress stores in the neighborhood and the doctors and dentists
    and teachers and business owners all lived in the same neighborhood
    and we had a thriving community. Then the doctors and dentists

started moving out, and the whole community began to fall down. So now we're in a situation in which the basketball league is 99 percent black, but it's owned by whites. If all the money made from black sports and black music were in black hands, if it were spent in our neighborhoods, things would be very different.

Q. Elsewhere you've said you want your audience to see your characters as Africans, not just black folks in America. Can you talk about that?

A. I'm talking about black Americans having uniquely African ways of participating in the world, of doing things, different ways of socializing. I have no fascination with Africa itself. I've never been to Africa and have no desire to go.

Q. You've said that you try not to create characters who are victims. Yet aren't all these scars a sign that they have been victimized? Is the issue how they deal with their victimization, how they respond to it?

A. We're all victims of white America's paranoia. My characters don't respond as victims. No matter what society does to them, they are engaged with life, wrestling with it, trying to make sense out of it. Nobody is sitting around saying, "Woe is me."

Baseball Metaphors in Fences

Jim Fowler

1   Many factors related to life experience work together to influence an individual's thought and character. In August Wilson's play Fences, the character Troy Maxson is an excellent portrayal of how numerous factors influence the complex personality of a black man in the 1950's. One very influential factor which is highlighted throughout the play involves Troy's experience as a former Negro league baseball player. Troy's baseball experience has a significant effect upon his language, his lifestyle, and even his character.

2   Troy Maxson uses the language of baseball to express many of his thoughts and emotions. As Sandra Shannon states, "Troy flavors his conversation with baseball metaphors at every chance he gets" (239). Troy deals with many issues in his personal life by using baseball terms and experiences to reflect how he feels.

One illustration of how baseball affects his emotional expression occurs when he and his son Cory are fighting. Troy angrily informs Cory that he already has two strikes, and he cautions his son, "Don't you strike out" (210). On another occasion, Troy uses baseball lingo to reveal the thrill and excitement he experiences when he engages in an extramarital affair. Troy attempts to explain his infidelity by stating to his wife, "Do you understand after eighteen years I wanted to steal second" (216). When he refers to his more serious emotions involving the duties and responsibility of wife and family, he uses the analogy of bunting his way on base and states, "I was safe. I had me a family. A job. I wasn't gonna get that last strike" (216).

3   Troy's lifestyle is certainly affected in significant ways by his prior baseball experience. Playing the sport of baseball has probably contributed to Troy's self-centered and egotistical behavior. His friend tells Troy, "When you was hitting them baseballs out the park. A lot of them old gals was after you then" (211–12). Troy seems to miss the excitement and fun of baseball, and at times he resents the demanding responsibilities of work and his family. Baseball also influenced Troy's lifestyle by affecting his parenting. Because of the injustice Troy experienced when he played in the Negro league before the integration of baseball, he robs his son Cory of a chance to enjoy and possibly make something of himself in sports. In response to his own personal experience, Troy states, "I got sense enough not to let my boy get hurt over playing no sports" (200). Troy's decision not to allow his son to make his own choices and decisions causes anger and resentment in their relationship.

4   His experiences with baseball also affect Troy's character in significant ways. Troy describes his perception of the black person's experience when he states, "you born with two strikes

on you before you come to the plate" (215-16). Facing the obstacles of life as a black man in a hostile society makes Troy very strong-willed and independent. Because of his experiences in baseball, Troy believes that black athletes will always be treated unfairly. Unlike his son, Troy cannot believe that "a change has occurred in American society" (Timpane 250). He somewhat pessimistically accepts the unfairness of his life and tries to deal with his difficulties in his own manner. The way in which Troy views his life also strongly impacts his attitude toward death. Troy refers to death as a "fastball on the outside corner" (185). This analogy indicates that Troy believes that although he cannot hold power over death, he can try his best to fight it off. When he receives a fastball on the outside corner, he may not hit a home run, but he has a very good chance of defending the plate. Troy is able "to confront Death—and hence to construct his life—on his own terms" (Nadel 245).

5   In the play <u>Fences</u>, August Wilson reveals how environmental factors contribute to the character formation of Troy Maxson. Troy Maxson's life is strongly affected by his experience of playing baseball in the Negro league prior to World War II. At this time in the history of the sport, Troy realized that having the athletic ability to play baseball did not guarantee African American players equal opportunities with white players. Troy's bitter disappointment over this experience of injustice has a great impact on shaping his perception of the world and his lifestyle choices. The baseball metaphors and images in the play provide excellent insight into the character of Troy Maxson.

[New page]   Works Cited

Henderson, Gloria Mason, Bill Day, and Sandra Stevenson
    Waller, eds. <u>Literature and Ourselves: A Thematic</u>

Introduction for Readers and Writers. 5th ed. New York:

Longman, 2006.

Nadel, Alan. "Boundaries, Logistics, and Identity: The Property

of Metaphor in Fences and Joe Turner's Come and Gone." May

All Your Fences Have Gates: Essays on the Drama of August

Wilson. Ed. Alan Nadel. Iowa City: U of Iowa P, 1994.

Henderson, Day, and Waller. 242-47.

Shannon, Sandra G. The Dramatic Vision of August Wilson.

Washington, DC: Howard UP, 1995. 103-17. Henderson, Day,

and Waller. 234-41.

Timpane, John. "Filling the Time: Reading History in the

Drama of August Wilson." May All Your Fences Have Gates:

Essays on the Drama of August Wilson. Ed. Alan Nadel. Iowa

City: U of Iowa P, 1994. Henderson, Day, and Waller. 247-51.

Wilson, August. Fences. N.p.: New American Library, 1986.

Henderson, Day, and Waller. 179-232.

Suggestions for Exploring, Writing, and Persuading

1. Troy says to Rose, "Woman. . . . I do the best I can do. I come in here every Friday. I carry a sack of potatoes and a bucket of lard. You all line up at the door with your hands out. I give you the lint from my pockets. I give you my sweat and my blood." What is Troy's conception of a husband's responsibilities? What does he lack as a husband? Why?

2. Using the sources contained in this casebook, explain the symbolism of fences in the play. Why is Troy building a fence? Why does it take him so long to finish it?

3. Discuss in detail how baseball has affected Troy's lifestyle, his language, and his character. Use the primary and secondary sources that you find in this casebook.

4. Analyze the means by which Troy uses language to justify himself and his behavior and thereby to protect his self-esteem.

5. Write an essay comparing Troy's sons.

6. Troy tells Rose that in Alberta's house he can "laugh out loud." Beginning with this idea, contrast Troy's relationship with Rose to his relationship with Alberta.

7. Analyze the relationship between Rose and Troy, comparing their marriage before and after Troy tells Rose about Alberta.

8. Using research on the treatment and condition of African Americans in northeastern industrial cities on the eve of the civil rights movement, analyze the effect of white oppression on Troy and / or other characters in the play.

9. After researching the "Negro Leagues" and the integration of baseball, use that research and the secondary sources in this casebook to discuss the impact that playing in the "Negro Leagues" and failing to make the major leagues has had on Troy.

10. Analyze the role of Gabriel in the play. How does he retain dignity and independence in spite of brain damage and mistreatment by the government and by Troy? What are the implications of his part in the final scene?

11. List examples of the **foreshadowing** of Troy's death, and write an essay on Wilson's use of foreshadowing in *Fences*.

12. Why, living and working in the midst of so many people, is Troy almost always lonely?

13. Write an essay using the primary and secondary sources to support one of the following statements:
    Troy uses his own past to justify his unfair treatment of Cory and Rose.
    Troy tries to make the best decisions for his family.

Family: Suggestions for Writing

1. We often tend to think of families as consisting of a mother, a father, and one or more children who relate to each other in various conventional ways. Many of the families in this section are unconventional. Discuss any two unconventional families in this unit.

2. Write an essay comparing the mothers, fathers, or situations in any of the works in this unit. Or compare any two mothers.

3. Use at least two of the poems in this unit as a basis for an essay about a parent's feelings for a child or about a child's perception of a parent.

4. Discuss problems faced by members of dysfunctional families, using two of the short stories in this unit.

5. Write an essay exploring the ways in which family problems vary in different cultures, or discuss similarities of family situations between two cultures.

6. Write an essay on two families depicted in this unit, explaining how they deal successfully with crises. Or argue that one is successful and the other is not.

7. Use at least two of the works in this unit to write an essay arguing that an abundance of wealth is not a necessary ingredient for a happy family.

8. Write an essay describing the ways in which your family has shaped your identity.

9. In several essays in this unit, the authors return to the past: a particular time or place, such as their childhood or their home. Using one of the essays as a guide, write an essay that describes a particular time in your past.

Family: Writing About Film

1. View a contemporary film in which the theme of family is central (*American Beauty, Boyz N' the Hood. American Dream, My Big Fat Greek Wedding, Bend It Like Beckham, Mi Familia, Cheaper By the Dozen, Mystic River, My Life As a House, Thirteen, Raising Helen, What's Eating Gilbert Grape?* to name just a few). Do any of the poems and stories in this unit deal with similar events or characters? Select an event or character from a poem or story and compare it to an event or character in the film. What makes them similar? Don't worry too much about superficial characteristics; think in terms of relationships and problems. What is your response to each, and how has the author, director, or actor created that effect?

2. From *The Simpsons* to *Everybody Loves Raymond* to *Still Standing* to *Two and a Half Men*, families that put the "fun" in dysfunctional are a favorite setting for American situation comedies. Select one television show or film that is especially appealing to you. What is it about your own family experience that makes you like this show? Consider your family as characters and how they might compare to two or three of the main characters on the show.

3. Imagine you've been hired to write a screenplay of one of the short stories or dramas in this unit. Your producer wants you to shoot an opening montage sequence—a three-minute series of shots to be shown with a musical soundtrack as background for the opening credits. You know that screen time is very valuable, so you want to design this montage to set the tone, introduce main characters and relationships, give a sense of setting, and foreshadow events or themes. Describe two or three shots in detail and decide on the music (pop, jazz, classical, hip hop, or rock) that will accompany them; then explain why these shots and this music will work well to prepare for the rest of the story. Try to make every shot work with three specific purposes (tone, setting, character, relationship, event, or theme).

4. Select a recent film that is advertised as family fare (G or PG-13) and write an essay arguing that the film does or does not deserve that rating.

Men and Women

A scene from *North by Northwest*. MGM/The Kobal Collection.

Through the ages, men and women have treated each other respectfully and disrespectfully, honestly and dishonestly. They have loved and hated each other, fought and made up, understood and misunderstood each other. In literature, we can examine these complex relationships with an objectivity often impossible in real-life relationships. The attitudes of men and women toward each other portrayed in this anthology range from humorous to serious and from lightly sarcastic to bitter.

We can also examine the parameters of being a woman or of being a man. For example, Gloria Naylor's "Mama Day" uses the double point of view to show how a man and a woman react to the same situation just as Rita Dove's "Courtship" and "Courtship, Diligence" reflect how two people see the same courtship: Thomas thinks he has made a lasting, positive impression; Beulah is unimpressed. Both David Osborne and Rose Del Castillo Guilbault in their essays discuss male stereotypes, he from personal experience and she from a linguistic and cultural perspective. In *A Doll's House* and in "The Yellow Wallpaper," the authors explore the problems faced by women in the past—problems similar to those some women confront today.

Another part of learning to be a man or woman is learning to live in the generation to which we belong and to deal effectively with members of other generations. Janice Mirikitani in "Breaking Tradition" explores three generations of women and applauds their differences.

The tone of each selection also suggests attitudes toward gender. While Maya Angelou celebrates her phenomenal womanhood, Marge Piercy takes issue with the destructive outcome of a female's attempts to be attractive to others in society. Edna St. Vincent Millay shows the sometimes transitory nature of love in "What lips my lips have kissed, and where, and why." In contrast, Shakespeare's "Sonnet 116" lauds the permanence of love. Similarly, Elizabeth Barrett Browning in "Sonnet 43" celebrates how two people love unselfishly as she answers the question "How do I love thee?"

Literary treatment of relationships is not always humorous or light. The disasters that result from the failure of a man and a woman to understand each another are vividly portrayed by Ernest Hemingway in "Hills Like White Elephants," by Charlotte Perkins Gilman in "The Yellow Wallpaper," and by Robert Browning in "Porphyria's Lover" and "My Last Duchess."

In literature as in life, the roles of men and women are not always precisely defined. Perhaps the lesson most clearly revealed is that men and women are individuals who face insecurities, share romance, and struggle to understand themselves as well as members of the opposite sex.

Writing About Men and Women

The works in this unit offer many gender issues that would be good subjects for essays. For help in selecting a suitable topic, reread the questions at the end of this unit. For example, several of the selections could lead to an analysis of women. If you select a short story such as Zora Neale Hurston's "The Gilded Six-Bits" and an essay such as Max Shulman's "Love is a Fallacy," you might begin with two lists: one could be about the concerns of the central character or the author; the other would list the resolutions for these concerns. Then you could review the works to look for similarities or differences and write a rough outline for a comparison/contrast essay. You might choose to rewrite the ending of Jhumpa Lahiri's "A Temporary Matter" to show a different way the couple might cope with their loss.

Many argumentative essays should come from this unit since many references to men and women are controversial. You might write about the stereotypes that men or women have to live by. Using "Barbie Doll" by Marge Piercy, "Beyond the Cult of Fatherhood" by David Osborne, or "Americanization Is Tough on 'Macho'" by Rose Del Castillo Guilbault, you might plan an argumentative essay in which you defend your position on these stereotypes. Another argument might come from Kate Chopin's "Désirée's Baby." Does Armand know before he drives Désirée away that he is responsible for the baby's mixed blood or does he find out only after she is gone? Many women are thought to be concerned only with physical beauty; however, you might argue that men are also obsessed with physical beauty by citing Nathaniel Hawthorne's "The Birth-Mark" and Edgar Allan Poe's "To Helen," although the authors tackle the subject in different ways.

Many of the poems in this section deal with love: imperfect love, perfect love, and love gone wrong. After reading Shakespeare's "Sonnet 138" and Elizabeth Barrett Browning's "Sonnet 43," you could write an essay about true love. If you prefer to write about disastrous love, you might use Robert Browning's "My Last Duchess" or "Porphyria's Lover." If your instructor asks for a personal essay, you might write an epistolary essay, one that explains your love ideal in the form of a letter.

This unit is also rich in showing relations between men and women. For an expository essay, you might list in separate columns the negative and positive characteristics of the relationships in "The Yellow Wallpaper" by Charlotte Perkins Gilman or "Hills Like White Elephants" by Ernest Hemingway. Using one or more of the works from this list, you could write an essay that examines relationships between men and women.

Because she had been told that Plath's poetry and her novel, *The Bell Jar*, included many autobiographical references, Natasha Harden, in preparation for writing an essay about Sylvia Plath, first read some biographical information about Plath. Next she watched *Sylvia*, the 2003 film starring Gwyneth Paltrow. Finally Natasha read the Plath poems from which she could choose for her assigned essay. Because she wanted to discuss Plath's ideas about death, she chose "Daddy" and "Lady Lazarus."

Natasha read and reread the poems many times in order to clarify her ideas about her subject and to select appropriate quotations. Next she examined the critical essays included in the casebook. At this point she made a rough outline of her essay and began the first draft. In order to concentrate on her subject, Natasha wrote the first draft with only marginal documentation. Then she went for her first conference with her professor, who approved her overall plan and made a few suggestions about additions. In her first revision, Natasha added the documentation and improved her thesis statement. After another brief conference with her professor, Natasha submitted her final essay, which is included at the end of the Plath Casebook.

ESSAYS

Virginia Woolf (1882–1941)

*Though plagued throughout her lifetime by nervous break-
downs, Virginia Stephen Woolf became a major influence on
English literature. Today she is considered one of the most
significant writers in the field of women's literature. Woolf
was a member of the famous Bloomsbury circle, a group that
stressed culture and opposed many restrictive Victorian
standards. She excelled as a novelist with such works as* Mrs.
Dalloway *(1925) and* To the Lighthouse *(1927); as a critic;
and as an essayist with* A Room of One's Own *(1929) and*
Three Guineas *(1938). This speech was presented to the
Women's Service League, a group of career women, in 1936.*

PROFESSIONS FOR WOMEN   (1936)

1   When your secretary invited me to come here, she told me that your
Society is concerned with the employment of women and she suggested
that I might tell you something about my own professional experiences.
It is true I am a woman; it is true I am employed; but what professional
experiences have I had? It is difficult to say. My profession is literature;
and in that profession there are fewer experiences for women than in any
other, with the exception of the stage—fewer, I mean, that are peculiar
to women. For the road was cut many years ago—by Fanny Burney, by
Aphra Behn, by Harriet Martineau, by Jane Austen, by George Eliot—
many famous women, and many more unknown and forgotten, have been
before me, making the path smooth, and regulating my steps. Thus, when
I came to write, there were very few material obstacles in my way. Writing was a reputable and harmless occupation. The family peace was not
broken by the scratching of a pen. No demand was made upon the family purse. For ten and sixpence one can buy paper enough to write all the
plays of Shakespeare—if one has a mind that way. Pianos and models,
Paris, Vienna and Berlin, masters and mistresses, are not needed by a
writer. The cheapness of writing paper is, of course, the reason why
women have succeeded as writers before they have succeeded in the
other professions.

2   But to tell you my story—it is a simple one. You have only got to figure to yourselves a girl in a bedroom with a pen in her hand. She had
only to move that pen from left to right—from ten o'clock to one. Then
it occurred to her to do what is simple and cheap enough after all—to
slip a few of those pages into an envelope, fix a penny stamp in the cor-

ner, and drop the envelope in the red box at the corner. It was thus that I became a journalist; and my effort was rewarded on the first day of the following month—a very glorious day it was for me—by a letter from an editor containing a cheque for one pound ten shillings and six-pence. But to show you how little I deserve to be called a professional woman, how little I know of the struggles and difficulties of such lives, I have to admit that instead of spending that sum upon bread and but-ter, rent, shoes and stockings, or butcher's bills, I went out and bought a cat—a beautiful cat, a Persian cat, which very soon involved me in bitter disputes with my neighbours.

3   What could be easier than to write articles and to buy Persian cats with the profits? But wait a moment. Articles have to be about something. Mine, I seem to remember, was about a novel by a famous man. And while I was writing this review, I discovered that if I were going to review books I should need to do battle with a certain phantom. And the phan-tom was a woman, and when I came to know her better I called her after the heroine of a famous poem, The Angel in the House. It was she who used to come between me and my paper when I was writing reviews. It was she who bothered me and wasted my time and so tormented me that at last I killed her. You who come of a younger and happier generation may not have heard of her—you may not know what I mean by the Angel in the House. I will describe her as shortly as I can. She was intensely sympathetic. She was immensely charming. She was utterly unselfish. She excelled in the difficult arts of family life. She sacrificed herself daily. If there was chicken, she took the leg; if there was a draught she sat in it—in short she was so constituted that she never had a mind or a wish of her own, but preferred to sympathize always with the minds and wishes of others. Above all—I need not say it—she was pure. Her purity was supposed to be her chief beauty—her blushes, her great grace. In those days—the last of Queen Victoria—every house had its Angel. And when I came to write I encountered her with the very first words. The shadow of her wings fell on my page; I heard the rustling of her skirts in the room. Directly, that is to say, I took my pen in hand to review that novel by a famous man, she slipped behind me and whispered: "My dear, you are a young woman. You are writing about a book that has been writ-ten by a man. Be sympathetic; be tender; flatter; deceive; use all the arts and wiles of our sex. Never let anybody guess that you have a mind of your own. Above all, be pure." And she made as if to guide my pen. I now record the one act for which I take some credit to myself, though the credit rightly belongs to some excellent ancestors of mine who left me a certain sum of money—shall we say five hundred pounds a year?—so that it was not necessary for me to depend solely on charm for my living. I turned upon her and caught her by the throat. I did my best to kill her. My excuse, if I were to be had up in a court of law, would be that I acted in self-defence. Had I not killed her she would have killed me. She would have plucked the heart out of my writing. For, as I found, directly I put

pen to paper, you cannot review even a novel without having a mind of
your own, without expressing what you think to be the truth about human
relations, morality, sex. And all these questions, according to the Angel in
the House, cannot be dealt with freely and openly by women; they must
charm, they must conciliate, they must—to put it bluntly—tell lies if they
are to succeed. Thus, whenever I felt the shadow of her wing or the radiance of her halo upon my page, I took up the inkpot and flung it at her. She
died hard. Her fictitious nature was of great assistance to her. It is far
harder to kill a phantom than a reality. She was always creeping back when
I thought I had despatched her. Though I flatter myself that I killed her in
the end, the struggle was severe; it took much time that had better have
been spent upon learning Greek grammar; or in roaming the world in
search of adventures. But it was a real experience; it was an experience
that was bound to befall all women writers at that time. Killing the Angel
in the House was part of the occupation of a woman writer.

4   But to continue my story. The Angel was dead; what then remained? You
may say that what remained was a simple and common object—a young
woman in a bedroom with an inkpot. In other words, now that she had rid
herself of falsehood, that young woman had only to be herself. Ah, but
what is "herself"? I mean, what is a woman? I assure you, I do not know. I
do not believe that you know. I do not believe that anybody can know until
she has expressed herself in all the arts and professions open to human
skill. That indeed is one of the reasons why I have come here—out of
respect for you, who are in process of showing us by your experiments
what a woman is, who are in process of providing us, by your failures and
successes, with that extremely important piece of information.

5   But to continue the story of my professional experiences. I made one
pound ten and six by my first review; and I bought a Persian cat with the
proceeds. Then I grew ambitious. A Persian cat is all very well, I said; but
a Persian cat is not enough. I must have a motor car. And it was thus that
I became a novelist—for it is a very strange thing that people will give
you a motor car if you will tell them a story. It is a still stranger thing that
there is nothing so delightful in the world as telling stories. It is far pleas-
anter than writing reviews of famous novels. And yet, if I am to obey your
secretary and tell you my professional experiences as a novelist, I must
tell you about a very strange experience that befell me as a novelist. And
to understand it you must try first to imagine a novelist's state of mind. I
hope I am not giving away professional secrets if I say that a novelist's
chief desire is to be as unconscious as possible. He has to induce in himself a state of perpetual lethargy. He wants life to proceed with the utmost
quiet and regularity. He wants to see the same faces, to read the same
books, to do the same things day after day, month after month, while he
is writing, so that nothing may break the illusion in which he is living—
so that nothing may disturb or disquiet the mysterious nosings about,
feelings round, darts, dashes and sudden discoveries of that very shy and
illusive spirit, the imagination. I suspect that this state is the same both

for men and women. Be that as it may, I want you to imagine me writing a novel in a state of trance. I want you to figure to yourselves a girl sitting with a pen in her hand, which for minutes, and indeed for hours, she never dips into the inkpot. The image that comes to my mind when I think of this girl is the image of a fisherman lying sunk in dreams on the verge of a deep lake with a rod held out over the water. She was letting her imagination sweep unchecked round every rock and cranny of the world that lies submerged in the depths of our unconscious being. Now came the experience, the experience that I believe to be far commoner with women writers than with men. The line raced through the girl's fingers. Her imagination had rushed away. It had sought the pools, the depths, the dark places where the largest fish slumber. And then there was a smash. There was an explosion. There was foam and confusion. The imagination had dashed itself against something hard. The girl was roused from her dream. She was indeed in a state of the most acute and difficult distress. To speak without figure she had thought of something, something about the body, about the passions which it was unfitting for her as a woman to say. Men, her reason told her, would be shocked. The consciousness of what men will say of a woman who speaks the truth about her passions had roused her from her artist's state of unconsciousness. She could write no more. The trance was over. Her imagination could work no longer. This I believe to be a very common experience with women writers—they are impeded by the extreme conventionality of the other sex. For though men sensibly allow themselves great freedom in these respects, I doubt that they realize or can control the extreme severity with which they condemn such freedom in women.

6   These then were two very genuine experiences of my own. These were two of the adventures of my professional life. The first—killing the Angel in the House—I think I solved. She died. But the second, telling the truth about my own experiences as a body, I do not think I solved. I doubt that any woman has solved it yet. The obstacles against her are still immensely powerful—and yet they are very difficult to define. Outwardly, what is simpler than to write books? Outwardly, what obstacles are there for a woman rather than for a man? Inwardly, I think, the case is very different; she has still many ghosts to fight, many prejudices to overcome. Indeed it will be a long time still, I think, before a woman can sit down to write a book without finding a phantom to be slain, a rock to be dashed against. And if this is so in literature, the freest of all professions for women, how is it in the new professions which you are now for the first time entering?

7   Those are the questions that I should like, had I time, to ask you. And indeed, if I have laid stress upon these professional experiences of mine, it is because I believe that they are, though in different forms, yours also. Even when the path is nominally open—when there is nothing to prevent a woman from being a doctor, a lawyer, a civil servant—there are many phantoms and obstacles, as I believe, looming in her way. To discuss and

define them is I think of great value and importance; for thus only can the labour be shared, the difficulties be solved. But besides this, it is necessary also to discuss the ends and the aims for which we are fighting, for which we are doing battle with these formidable obstacles. Those aims cannot be taken for granted; they must be perpetually questioned and examined. The whole position, as I see it—here in this hall surrounded by women practicing for the first time in history I know not how many different professions—is one of extraordinary interest and importance. You have won rooms of your own in the house hitherto exclusively owned by men. You are able, though not without great labour and effort, to pay the rent. You are earning your five hundred pounds a year. But this freedom is only a beginning; the room is your own, but it is still bare. It has to be furnished; it has to be decorated; it has to be shared. How are you going to furnish it, how are you going to decorate it? With whom are you going to share it, and upon what terms? These, I think are questions of the utmost importance and interest. For the first time in history you are able to ask them; for the first time you are able to decide for yourselves what the answers should be. Willingly would I stay and discuss those questions and answers—but not tonight. My time is up; and I must cease.

Questions for Discussion

1. According to Woolf, why have women "succeeded as writers before they have succeeded in the other professions"?
2. Who is the "Angel in the House," and what did she have to do with Woolf's writing? Why did the author have to kill the "Angel"?
3. What obstacle other than the "Angel in the House" did Woolf face? Why has she not overcome the obstacle?
4. What does Woolf mean when, after killing the "Angel," she asks herself, "What is a woman?" and reports that she does not know?
5. What, according to Woolf, can a man talk about or write about that a woman cannot? What limits on free expression do women today face?
6. Explain Woolf's analogy between women pioneering in professions and an unfurnished room.

Suggestions for Exploring, Writing, and Persuading

1. In an essay, discuss the degree to which the "Angel in the House" haunts women you know.
2. Argue for or against the following statement from Woolf's essay: "Even when the path is nominally open—when there is nothing to prevent a woman from being a doctor, a lawyer, a civil servant—there are many phantoms and obstacles, as I believe, looming in her way."

3. Beginning with number 2 under **Questions for Discussion**, discuss other angels that a person might have to kill off, such as the Angel at Work, the Angel in School, the Angel in the Family, or the Angel of Friendship.

4. Write an essay arguing for or against the statement that though women have made great strides in the workplace, statistics indicate that a glass ceiling still exists in the business world.

Max Shulman (1919–1988)

American humorist Max Shulman wrote short stories, novels, plays, and screenplays. He adapted many of his works for film or television, often serving as composer and lyricist as well. His collection titled The Many Loves of Dobie Gillis, *from which the following essay is taken, was made into the 1953 movie called* The Affairs of Dobie Gillis, *starring Debbie Reynolds, and into a 1959 television series starring Dwayne Hickman as Dobie and Bob Denver as his friend Maynard G. Krebs. His 1955 play* The Tender Trap *was rewritten as a movie for Debbie Reynolds and Frank Sinatra, and the movie made from the 1958 novel* Rally Round the Flag, Boys! *starred Paul Newman and Joanne Woodward.*

Love is a Fallacy   (1951)

1   Cool was I and logical. Keen, calculating, perspicacious, acute and astute—I was all of these. My brain was as powerful as a dynamo, as precise as a chemist's scales, as penetrating as a scalpel. And—think of it!— I was only eighteen.

2   It is not often that one so young has such a giant intellect. Take, for example, Petey Burch, my roommate at the University of Minnesota. Same age, same background, but dumb as an ox. A nice enough fellow, you understand, but nothing upstairs. Emotional type. Unstable. Impressionable. Worst of all, a faddist. Fads, I submit, are the very negation of reason. To be swept up in every new craze that comes along, to surrender yourself to idiocy just because everybody else is doing it—this, to me, is the acme of mindlessness. Not, however, to Petey.

3   One afternoon I found Petey lying on his bed with an expression of such distress on his face that I immediately diagnosed appendicitis. "Don't move," I said. "Don't take a laxative. I'll get a doctor."

4   "Raccoon," he mumbled thickly.

5   "Raccoon?" I said, pausing in my flight.

6   "I want a raccoon coat," he wailed.

7   I perceived that his trouble was not physical, but mental. "Why do you want a raccoon coat?"

8   "I should have known it," he cried, pounding his temples. "I should have known they'd come back when the Charleston came back. Like a fool I spent all my money for textbooks, and now I can't get a raccoon coat."

9   "Can you mean," I said incredulously, "that people are actually wearing raccoon coats again?"

10   "All the Big Men on Campus are wearing them. Where've you been?"

11   "In the library," I said, naming a place not frequented by Big Men on Campus.

12   He leaped from the bed and paced the room. "I've got to have a raccoon coat," he said passionately. "I've got to!"

13   "Petey, why? Look at it rationally. Raccoon coats are unsanitary. They shed. They smell bad. They weigh too much. They're unsightly."

14   You don't understand," he interrupted impatiently. "It's the thing to do. Don't you want to be in the swim?"

15   "No," I said truthfully.

16   "Well, I do," he declared. "I'd give anything for a raccoon coat. Anything!"

17   My brain, that precision instrument, slipped into high gear. "Anything?" I asked, looking at him narrowly.

18   "Anything," he affirmed in ringing tones.

19   I stroked my chin thoughtfully. It so happened that I knew where to get my hands on a raccoon coat. My father had had one in his undergraduate days; it lay now in a trunk in the attic back home. It also happened that Petey had something I wanted. He didn't *have* it exactly, but at least he had first rights on it. I refer to his girl, Polly Espy.

20   I had long coveted Polly Espy. Let me emphasize that my desire for this young woman was not emotional in nature. She was, to be sure, a girl who excited the emotions, but I was not one to let my heart rule my head. I wanted Polly for a shrewdly calculated, entirely cerebral reason.

21   I was a freshman in law school. In a few years I would be out in practice. I was well aware of the importance of the right kind of wife in furthering a lawyer's career. The successful lawyers I had observed were, almost without exception, married to beautiful, gracious, intelligent women. With one omission, Polly fitted these specifications perfectly.

22   Beautiful she was. She was not yet of pin-up proportions, but I felt sure that time would supply the lack. She already had the makings.

23   Gracious she was. By gracious I mean full of graces. She had an erectness of carriage, an ease of bearing, a poise that clearly indicated the best of breeding. At table her manners were exquisite. I had seen her at the Kozy Kampus Korner eating the specialty of the house—a sandwich that contained scraps of pot roast, gravy, chopped nuts, and a dipper of sauerkraut—without even getting her fingers moist.

24   Intelligent she was not. In fact, she veered in the opposite direction. But I believed that under my guidance she would smarten up. At any rate, it was worth a try. It is, after all, easier to make a beautiful dumb girl smart than to make an ugly smart girl beautiful.

25   "Petey," I said, "are you in love with Polly Espy?"

26   "I think she's a keen kid," he replied, "but I don't know if you'd call it love. Why?"

27   "Do you," I asked, "have any kind of formal arrangement with her? I mean are you going steady or anything like that?"

28   "No. We see each other quite a bit, but we both have other dates."

29   "Is there," I asked, "any other man for whom she has a particular fondness?"

30   "Not that I know of. Why?"

31   I nodded with satisfaction. "In other words, if you were out of the picture, the field would be open. Is that right?"

32   "I guess so. What are you getting at?"

33   "Nothing, nothing," I said innocently, and took my suitcase out of the closet.

34   "Where are you going?" asked Petey.

35   "Home for the weekend." I threw a few things into the bag.

36   "Listen," he said, clutching my arm eagerly, "while you're home, you couldn't get some money from your old man, could you, and lend it to me so I can buy a raccoon coat?"

37   "I may do better than that," I said with a mysterious wink and closed my bag and left.

38   "Look," I said to Petey when I got back Monday morning. I threw open the suitcase and revealed the huge, hairy, gamy object that my father had worn in his Stutz Bearcat in 1925.

39   "Holy Toledo!" said Petey reverently. He plunged his hands into the raccoon coat and then his face. "Holy Toledo!" he repeated fifteen or twenty times.

40   "Would you like it?" I asked.

41   "Oh yes!" he cried, clutching the greasy pelt to him. Then a canny look came into his eyes. "What do you want for it?"

42   "Your girl," I said, mincing no words.

43   "Polly?" he said in a horrified whisper. "You want Polly?"

44   "That's right."

45   He flung the coat from him. "Never," he said stoutly.

46   I shrugged. "Okay. If you don't want to be in the swim, I guess it's your business."

47   I sat down in a chair and pretended to read a book, but out of the corner of my eye I kept watching Petey. He was a torn man. First he looked at the coat with the expression of a waif at a bakery window. Then he turned away and set his jaw resolutely. Then he looked back at the coat, with even more longing in his face. Then he turned away, but with not so much resolution this time. Back and forth his head swiveled, desire waxing, resolution waning. Finally he didn't turn away at all; he just stood and stared with mad lust at the coat.

48   "It isn't as though I was in love with Polly," he said thickly. "Or going steady or anything like that."

49   "That's right," I murmured.

50   "What's Polly to me, or me to Polly?"

51   "Not a thing," said I.

52   "It's just been a casual kick—just a few laughs, that's all."

53   "Try on the coat," said I.

54   He complied. The coat bunched high over his ears and dropped all the way down to his shoe tops. He looked like a mound of dead raccoons. "Fits fine," he said happily.

55   I rose from my chair. "Is it a deal?" I asked, extending my hand.

56   He swallowed. "It's a deal," he said and shook my hand.

57   I had my first date with Polly the following evening. This was in the nature of a survey; I wanted to find out just how much work I had to do to get her mind up to the standard I required. I took her first to dinner. "Gee, that was a delish dinner," she said as we left the restaurant. Then I took her to a movie. "Gee, that was a marvy movie," she said as we left the theater. And then I took her home. "Gee, I had a sensaysh time," she said as she bade me good night.

58   I went back to my room with a heavy heart. I had gravely under-estimated the size of my task. This girl's lack of information was terrify-ing. Nor would it be enough merely to supply her with information. First she had to be taught to *think*. This loomed as a project of no small dimen-sions, and at first I was tempted to give her back to Petey. But then I got to thinking about her abundant physical charms and about the way she entered a room and the way she handled a knife and fork, and I decided to make an effort.

59   I went about it, as in all things, systematically. I gave her a course in logic. It happened that I, as a law student, was taking a course in logic myself, so I had all the facts at my finger tips. "Polly," I said to her when I picked her up on our next date, "tonight we are going over to the Knoll and talk."

60   "Oo, terrif," she replied. One thing I will say for this girl: you would go far to find another so agreeable.

61   We went to the Knoll, the campus trysting place, and we sat down under an old oak, and she looked at me expectantly. "What are we going to talk about?" she asked.

62   "Logic."

63   She thought this over for a minute and decided she liked it. "Magnif," she said.

64   "Logic," I said, clearing my throat, "is the science of thinking. Before we can think correctly, we must first learn to recognize the common fal-lacies of logic. These we will take up tonight."

65   "Wow-dow!" she cried, clapping her hands delightedly.

66   I winced, but went bravely on. "First let us examine the fallacy called Dicto Simpliciter."

67   "By all means," she urged, batting her lashes eagerly.

68   "Dicto Simpliciter means an argument based on an unqualified generalization. For example: Exercise is good. Therefore everybody should exercise."

69   "I agree," said Polly earnestly. "I mean exercise is wonderful. I mean it builds the body and everything."

70   "Polly," I said gently, "the argument is a fallacy. *Exercise is good* is an unqualified generalization. For instance, if you have heart disease, exercise is bad, not good. Many people are ordered by their doctors *not* to exercise. You must *qualify* the generalization. You must say exercise is *usually* good, or exercise is good *for most people*. Otherwise you have committed a Dicto Simpliciter. Do you see?"

71   "No," she confessed. "But this is marvy. Do more! Do more!"

72   "It will be better if you stop tugging at my sleeve," I told her, and when she desisted, I continued. "Next we take up a fallacy called Hasty Generalization. Listen carefully: You can't speak French. I can't speak French. Petey Burch can't speak French. I must therefore conclude that nobody at the University of Minnesota can speak French."

73   "Really?" said Polly, amazed. "*Nobody?*"

74   I hid my exasperation. "Polly, it's a fallacy. The generalization is reached too hastily. There are too few instances to support such a conclusion."

75   "Know any more fallacies?" she asked breathlessly. "This is more fun than dancing even."

76   I fought off a wave of despair. I was getting nowhere with this girl, absolutely nowhere. Still, I am nothing if not persistent. I continued. "Next comes Post Hoc. Listen to this: Let's not take Bill on our picnic. Every time we take him out with us, it rains."

77   "I know somebody just like that," she exclaimed. "A girl back home— Eula Becker, her name is. It never fails. Every single time we take her on a picnic—"

78   "Polly," I said sharply, "it's a fallacy. Eula Becker doesn't *cause* the rain. She has no connection with the rain. You are guilty of Post Hoc if you blame Eula Becker."

79   "I'll never do it again," she promised contritely. "Are you mad at me?"

80   I sighed deeply. "No, Polly, I'm not mad."

81   "Then tell me some more fallacies."

82   "All right. Let's try Contradictory Premises."

83   "Yes, let's," she chirped, blinking her eyes happily.

84   I frowned, but plunged ahead. "Here's an example of Contradictory Premises: If God can do anything, can He make a stone so heavy that He won't be able to lift it?"

85   "Of course," she replied promptly.

86   "But if He can do anything, He can lift the stone," I pointed out.

87   "Yeah," she said thoughtfully. "Well, then I guess He can't make the stone."

88   "But He can do anything," I reminded her.

89   She scratched her pretty, empty head. "I'm all confused," she admitted.

90   "Of course you are. Because when the premises of an argument contradict each other, there can be no argument. If there is an irresistible force, there can be no immovable object. If there is an immovable object, there can be no irresistible force. Get it?"

91   "Tell me some more of this keen stuff," she said eagerly.

92   I consulted my watch. "I think we'd better call it a night. I'll take you home now, and you go over all the things you've learned. We'll have another session tomorrow night."

93   I deposited her at the girls' dormitory, where she assured me that she had had a perfectly terrif evening, and I went glumly home to my room. Petey lay snoring in his bed, the raccoon coat huddled like a great hairy beast at his feet. For a moment I considered waking him and telling him that he could have his girl back. It seemed clear that my project was doomed to failure. The girl simply had a logic-proof head.

94   But then I reconsidered. I had wasted one evening; I might as well waste another. Who knew? Maybe somewhere in the extinct crater of her mind, a few embers still smoldered. Maybe somehow I could fan them into flame. Admittedly it was not a prospect fraught with hope, but I decided to give it one more try.

95   Seated under the oak the next evening I said, "Our first fallacy tonight is called Ad Misericordiam."

96   She quivered with delight.

97   "Listen closely," I said. "A man applies for a job. When the boss asks him what his qualifications are, he replies that he has a wife and six children at home, the wife is a helpless cripple, the children have nothing to eat, no clothes to wear, no shoes on their feet, there are no beds in the house, no coal in the cellar, and winter is coming."

98   A tear rolled down each of Polly's pink cheeks. "Oh, this is awful, awful," she sobbed.

99   "Yes, it's awful," I agreed, "but it's no argument. The man never answered the boss's question about his qualifications. Instead he appealed to the boss's sympathy. He committed the fallacy of Ad Misericordiam. Do you understand?"

100   "Have you got a handkerchief?" she blubbered.

101   I handed her a handkerchief and tried to keep from screaming while she wiped her eyes. "Next," I said in a carefully controlled tone, "we will discuss False Analogy. Here is an example: Students should be allowed to look at their textbooks during examinations. After all, surgeons have X-rays to guide them during an operation, lawyers have briefs to guide them during a trial, carpenters have blueprints to guide them when they are building a house. Why, then, shouldn't students be allowed to look at their textbooks during an examination?"

102   "There now," she said enthusiastically, "is the most marvy idea I've heard in years."

103   "Polly," I said testily, "the argument is all wrong. Doctors, lawyers, and carpenters aren't taking a test to see how much they have learned, but students are. The situations are altogether different, and you can't make an analogy between them."

104   "I still think it's a good idea," said Polly.

105   "Nuts," I muttered. Doggedly I pressed on. "Next we'll try Hypothesis Contrary to Fact."

106   "Sounds yummy," was Polly's reaction.

107   "Listen: If Madame Curie had not happened to leave a photographic plate in a drawer with a chunk of pitchblende, the world today would not know about radium."

108   "True, true," said Polly, nodding her head. "Did you see the movie? Oh, it just knocked me out. That Walter Pidgeon is so dreamy. I mean he fractures me."

109   "If you can forget Mr. Pidgeon for a moment," I said coldly, "I would like to point out that the statement is a fallacy. Maybe Madame Curie would have discovered radium at some later date. Maybe somebody else would have discovered it. Maybe any number of things would have happened. You can't start with a hypothesis that is not true and then draw any supportable conclusions from it."

110   "They ought to put Walter Pidgeon in more pictures," said Polly. "I hardly ever see him any more."

111   One more chance, I decided. But just one more. There is a limit to what flesh and blood can bear. "The next fallacy is called Poisoning the Well."

112   "How cute!" she gurgled.

113   "Two men are having a debate. The first one gets up and says, 'My opponent is a notorious liar. You can't believe a word that he is going to say.'. . . Now, Polly, think. Think hard. What's wrong?"

114   I watched her closely as she knit her creamy brow in concentration. Suddenly a glimmer of intelligence—the first I had seen—came into her eyes. "It's not fair," she said with indignation. "It's not a bit fair. What chance has the second man got if the first man calls him a liar before he even begins talking?"

115   "Right!" I cried exultantly. "One hundred percent right. It's not fair. The first man has *poisoned the well* before anybody could drink from it. He has hamstrung his opponent before he could even start....Polly, I'm proud of you."

116   "Pshaw," she murmured, blushing with pleasure.

117   "You see, my dear, these things aren't so hard. All you have to do is concentrate. Think—examine—evaluate. Come now, let's review everything we have learned."

118   "Fire away," she said with an airy wave of her hand.

119   Heartened by the knowledge that Polly was not altogether a cretin, I began a long, patient review of all I had told her. Over and over and over again I cited instances, pointed out flaws, kept hammering away without let-up. It was like digging a tunnel. At first everything was work, sweat,

and darkness. I had no idea when I would reach the light, or even *if* I would. But I persisted. I pounded and clawed and scraped, and finally I was rewarded. I saw a chink of light. And then the chink got bigger and the sun came pouring in and all was bright.

120   Five grueling nights this took, but it was worth it. I had made a logician out of Polly; I had taught her to think. My job was done. She was worthy of me at last. She was a fit wife for me, a proper hostess for my many mansions, a suitable mother for my well-heeled children.

121   It must not be thought that I was without love for this girl. Quite the contrary. Just as Pygmalion loved the perfect woman he had fashioned, so I loved mine. I determined to acquaint her with my feelings at our very next meeting. The time had come to change our relationship from academic to romantic.

122   "Polly," I said when next we sat beneath our oak, "tonight we will not discuss fallacies."

123   "Aw, gee," she said, disappointed.

124   "My dear," I said, favoring her with a smile, "we have now spent five evenings together. We have gotten along splendidly. It is clear that we are well matched."

125   "Hasty Generalization," said Polly brightly.

126   "I beg your pardon," said I.

127   "Hasty Generalization," she repeated. "How can you say that we are well matched on the basis of only five dates?"

128   I chuckled with amusement. The dear child had learned her lessons well. "My dear," I said, patting her hand in a tolerant manner, "five dates is plenty. After all, you don't have to eat a whole cake to know that it's good."

129   "False Analogy," said Polly promptly. "I'm not a cake. I'm a girl."

130   I chuckled with somewhat less amusement. The dear child had learned her lessons perhaps too well. I decided to change tactics. Obviously the best approach was a simple, strong, direct declaration of love. I paused for a moment while my massive brain chose the proper words. Then I began:

131   "Polly, I love you. You are the whole world to me, and the moon and the stars and the constellations of outer space. Please, my darling, say that you will go steady with me, for if you will not, life will be meaningless. I will languish. I will refuse my meals. I will wander the face of the earth, a shambling, hollow-eyed hulk."

132   There, I thought, folding my arms, that ought to do it.

133   "Ad Misericordiam," said Polly.

134   I ground my teeth. I was not Pygmalion; I was Frankenstein, and my monster had me by the throat. Frantically I fought back the tide of panic surging through me. At all costs I had to keep cool.

135   "Well, Polly," I said, forcing a smile, "you certainly have learned your fallacies."

136   "You're darn right," she said with a vigorous nod.

137   "And who taught them to you, Polly?"

138   "You did."

139   "That's right. So you do owe me something, don't you, my dear? If I hadn't come along you never would have learned about fallacies."

140   "Hypothesis Contrary to Fact," she said instantly.

141   I dashed perspiration from my brow. "Polly," I croaked, "you mustn't take all these things so literally. I mean this is just classroom stuff. You know that the things you learn in school don't have anything to do with life."

142   "Dicto Simpliciter," she said, wagging her finger at me playfully.

143   That did it. I leaped to my feet, bellowing like a bull. "Will you or will you not go steady with me?"

144   "I will not," she replied.

145   "Why not?" I demanded.

146   "Because this afternoon I promised Petey Burch that I would go steady with him."

147   I reeled back, overcome with the infamy of it. After he promised, after he made a deal, after he shook my hand! "The rat!" I shrieked, kicking up great chunks of turf. "You can't go with him, Polly. He's a liar. He's a cheat. He's a rat."

148   "Poisoning the Well," said Polly, "and stop shouting. I think shouting must be a fallacy too."

149   With an immense effort of will, I modulated my voice. "All right," I said. "You're a logician. Let's look at this thing logically. How could you choose Petey Burch over me? Look at me—a brilliant student, a tremendous intellectual, a man with an assured future. Look at Petey—a knothead, a jitterbug, a guy who'll never know where his next meal is coming from. Can you give me one logical reason why you should go steady with Petey Burch?"

150   "I certainly can," declared Polly. "He's got a raccoon coat."

Questions for Discussion

1. Why does the narrator want to make Polly smarter? How would you describe the narrator's attitude toward Polly? Evaluate the narrator's condescending opinion of Petey and Polly and his opinion of himself.

2. Why does Petey so desire the coat? What are your generation's equivalents? Do you know people who have similar longings for items of clothing or other materialistic things?

3. Explain the literary allusions to Pygmalion and Frankenstein. How does their inclusion add to the humor of the story?

4. How does the narrator's final date illustrate the limits of logic?

5. What is the point of view? How is this point of view necessary in order to create the humor in the story? What would the story be like if it were written from Polly's point of view?

6. Give examples of Shulman's use of inverted sentence structure and explain the effect of his inversion.

Suggestions for Exploring, Writing, and Persuading

1. Write an essay on present day attraction to the superficial—clothes, cars, and other possessions.
2. To what degree do you think that men or women choose partners on the basis of beauty, grace, and intelligence? Write an essay supporting your premise.
3. Write a character sketch of the narrator, presumably Dobie Gillis.
4. Trace the ways in which Polly's speech patterns differ before and after she learns about fallacies.
5. List and define the fallacies that the narrator teaches Polly. Then find examples of each in other sources such as advertisements or talk shows.
6. Write an essay agreeing or disagreeing with Shulman's assertion that "It is, after all, easier to make a beautiful dumb girl smart than to make an ugly smart girl beautiful."

Paul Theroux (b. 1941)

Travel writer and novelist Paul Theroux was born in Medford, Massachusetts. He published his first novel, Waldo, *in 1967. Later novels include* Mosquito Coast *(1986), which was made into a popular movie and which was an American Book Award nominee, and* My Secret History *(1989). Theroux wrote many travel books that earned him accolades as an excellent travel writer. These include* Riding the Iron Rooster: By Train Through China *(1989),* Happy Isles of Oceania: Paddling the Pacific *(1993),* Great Railway Bazaar: By Train Through Asia *(1995),* Sir Vidia's Shadow: A Friendship Across Five Continents *(2003), and* Dark Star Safari: Overland from Cairo to Cape Town *(2004). Theroux is a part-time professional beekeeper and lives in Cape Cod.*

HERE'S TO YOU MRS. ROBINSON   (2002)

1   My younger self often fantasized about older women, though seldom acted upon those fantasies; my younger self seldom acted upon anything. The habit of yearning probably turned me into a writer. People who live rich lives full of opportunity tend not to become writers, while fantasists do, which, oddly, makes us seem worldly when in reality we are anxious geeks, pining after someone confident, glamorous, and truly worldly.

2   My fantasizing has never been the boring defloration mania, nor the connoisseurship of the paedomorphic face and figure, the Hollywood star-

let, the pop-music object of desire that looks like a seal pup in a tank top labeled BOY CANDY. That kittenish teenybopper with soulful eyes and skinny legs is the undoing of many drooling geezers, which is just what they deserve. I don't think I could describe my ideal woman, but my fantasies have often circled around someone resembling Mrs. Robinson. How else to explain myself as a 16-year-old boy in a movie theater looking at Ava Gardner in *The Barefoot Contessa* and having trouble breathing?

3   The subject of the younger man having an affair with an older woman still interests me greatly, because time passes, and "younger" and "older" mean different things to me. Thirty is old to a young man of 20. I don't spend much time with 30-somethings. I am now older than Mrs. Robinson, and yet sex is not theoretical; it is actual, always a possibility. I still stare at women all the time thinking, Are you beautiful? and, like all men, flunk some, pass others, and give a few of them high marks. This is what most men do all their waking hours.

4   I have grown older, but this question of age difference and desire is all the more fascinating to me now. Age is the central point in *The Graduate*: the affair between the young man and the older woman is what we remember most clearly: and the same drama is central to a great many masterpieces. The subject is invariably an older man and a young object of desire, usually a girl, sometimes a boy. *Death in Venice* is obsessional on the subject of the desirability, the perfection of youth, Tadzio's beauty and von Aschenbach's helpless adoration of the unattainable boy. *Lolita* is the self-conscious, classic study of a middle-aged man infatuated with a teenager. She is a nightmare, we know, and hardly virginal, but that does not deter Humbert from his pursuit. It's the source of the novel's comedy, for we see him as he sees himself, a much mocked but willing victim.

5   Almost 25 years ago I wrote an essay, "Homage to Mrs. Robinson," in which I tried to imagine what it might be like to be involved with an older woman. I imagined her self-possessed, confident, and intensely sexual, somewhat domineering, and most of all knowing the score. Her most attractive quality, it seemed to me, was the one we usually assign to the young, the ability to live in the moment. But younger people tend not to do that. They worry about the future; they don't want to waste time; they think: Is this good for my resumé? They fear casual sex might erode their self-esteem. They tend to look for Miss Right, not Mrs. Robinson.

6   I said all those years ago that the older woman is not husband-hunting. She knows what she wants, and if you measure up, you are hers for the taking. She knows the essential things about concealment and has a heightened awareness of time. As a boy sees maturity in a sexual encounter—proof of his manhood, another statistic to relish—the older woman has been granted a reprieve and in the encounter has outwitted her age. For her it is a private, mutual compliment. The classic situation is nothing long-term; indeed she might not particularly want to see you afterward. The preliminaries, the half-truths, the confidences, the wooing—all these are dispensed with. There isn't time; she comes straight to

the point and then goes back to her life. She is doing to you what older men do to younger women.

7   And, unlike many of her younger counterparts, she does not want to be entrapped. She doesn't need witnesses. For someone younger, sex is not an end in itself but a means to another end: job, money, marriage, power, family, position. And so, if they never know an older woman and deal only with the 20-year-old and her tough twinkle, most men grow up believing in sex as a favor they've been granted—sex as strategy or currency or power. Therefore, the act itself is full of threat. The older woman typically is indifferent to being dominated or getting something in return. Her age has liberated her from those deceptions. She is not interested in power but in pleasure.

8   At the time I was writing on this subject I was a theoretician in my presumptuous 30s. I said, "A woman between the ages of 30 and 50, sexually, is alight—her manner might be cool but her body blazes." Now that I am older and know more of hormones, I would raise the bar: Women of 60 can be intensely sexual, too. And if they have been the least bit active, they know every trick in the book. I am not speaking of love but of desire. Many are still beautiful.

9   In general, literature is no help in understanding this mismatch. Robert Louis Stevenson was married to a much older woman, and so was Raymond Chandler. Their wives were extremely attractive if a bit neurotic. Neither of the men wrote fiction on the subject. Turgenev was involved with an older married woman, but his most memorable tale of sexuality is about a man who has an affair with his son's girlfriend. Henry James adored the company of older women but tended to limit his hugs and endearments to younger men. Madame de Vionnet in *The Ambassadors* is his Mrs. Robinson, and Byron offers up one or two in Don Juan. Of the other greats, Dickens, Melville, Conrad, Dreiser, Fitzgerald, there are no Robinsonian affairs. The older woman has not been well served by fiction writers.

10   Movies and plays have succeeded where literature has failed to deliver the goods. The films that come to mind are *Sunset Boulevard, Bergman's Torment, This Sporting Life, Nothing but the Best, Sweet Bird of Youth, The Roman Spring of Mrs. Stone* (also a novel but better as a film), *A Cold Wind in August, The Last Picture Show, Room at the Top*, and the brilliant Fassbinder film *Fear Eats the Soul.* Deborah Kerr in *The Gypsy Moths* is the older woman to perfection.

11   And, of course, Mrs. Robinson in *The Graduate.* The director, Mike Nichols, created a powerful reality in the scenes between the young man and the older woman. The most telling episode was not in the bedroom but in a bar when the young man was out of his depth, leaving Mrs. Robinson to take charge. Taking charge is the essence of sexual vitality. Mrs. Robinson is resourceful, responsive, independent, and a knockout. Was there anyone who saw that movie and did not regret that the hero went off with the daughter and not the mother?

12   It is nonsense to relate such desire to the Oedipus complex, which is about infants anyway. I think much more often of myself at 10 or 11, when my mother's old school friend visited and left behind an odor of perfume and cigarette smoke and the aphrodisiacal smudge of lipstick on her gin glass. I think of the first schoolteacher I wanted to possess—Miss Murphy at the Washington School, probably no more than 22—though I did not know how it was done. The first woman who knew more about sex than I did was older than me, more experienced, and perhaps for the first time in my life I felt I was in capable hands.

13   Twenty-five years ago, I wrote, "The older woman gives us something that is very nearly incomparable, the chance to complete in adulthood what was impossible to complete as a child, a blameless gift of lechery that combines the best of youth, a maturity, romance, and realism in equal parts."

14   I still think so. Sex is only sometimes procreation, and the rest of the time it is pure lust, from the imagery imprinted in childhood. The fulfillment in adulthood of childhood fantasies is the very definition of happiness.

Questions for Discussion

1. What kind of woman does Theroux describe as the typical object of male fantasies? How do Theroux's fantasies differ? What do his preferences suggest about him?

2. What does Theroux believe are the advantages of a relationship with an older woman?

3. How have his thoughts about older women changed as he has aged?

4. When Theroux says that men spend most of "their waking hours" staring at and evaluating women, what is he implying is important to men? What does his implication suggest about male values? Explain why you do or do not agree with his assessment of males.

5. If you have seen *The Graduate*, explain why you do or do not agree with Theroux's suggestion that most people who view the film regret that "the hero went off with the daughter and not the mother."

6. Look carefully at the diction that Theroux uses. What does his choice of words imply about him?

Suggestions for Exploring, Writing, and Persuading

1. Theroux says, "The older woman has not been well served by fiction writers." Use one or more works of fiction to support or deny his claim.

2. Select one of the films Theroux mentions as an example of an older man's obsession with a younger woman and write an essay about the effects of such an obsession.

3. One of the obvious premises behind Theroux's essay is that physical intimacy without emotional commitment is both appealing and desirable. Write an essay supporting or contradicting his premise.

4. Many of the films Theroux lists as examples of relationships with older women are considered classics. After carefully watching one of them, analyze one aspect such as theme, camera techniques, or score. Or explain how the film supports or contradicts Theroux's premise.

5. Agree, disagree or modify one of the following assertions by Theroux:

"She [the older woman] is doing to you what older men do to younger women."
"She [the older woman] is not interested in power but in pleasure."
"Taking charge is the essence of sexual vitality."
"The older woman gives us something that is very nearly incomparable, the chance to complete in adulthood what was impossible to complete as a child, a blameless gift of lechery that combines the best of youth, a maturity, romance, and realism in equal parts."

John Gierach (1946)

John Gierach is an avid fly fisherman and a journalist who writes primarily for outdoor magazines. A regular columnist for Sports Afield *and* Fly Rod and Reel, *he has also written articles for* Field and Stream *and* Fly Fisherman *in addition to occasional outdoor columns for newspapers. He has published thirteen books of non-fiction including* The View from Rat Lake *(1988)*, Sex, Death, and Fly Fishing *(1990)*, Even Brook Trout Get the Blues *(1993)*, Dances with Trout *(1995)*, Standing in a River Holding a Stick *(2000)*, and Death, Taxes, and Leaky Waders *(2000)*, a collection of essays selected from his earlier books. As some of the titles suggest, his essays display a wry humor and strong sense of irony. Ostensibly about fly fishing, Gierach's essays are often also about writing, male friendships, and the search for meaning in an exquisitely beautiful but incomprehensibly chaotic world. Gierach lives near a trout stream in Lyons, Colorado.*

THE FISHING CAR   (1988)

1   When I was a young feller, I thought my Uncle Leonard had invented the concept of the fishing car; the elderly but still serviceable vehicle that was reserved for angling and angling-related activities to the extent that it was kept loaded, like the shotgun behind the kitchen door. But then I thought Leonard had invented a lot of things, some of which have since turned out to be among the oldest jokes in the world. It's understandable, I guess. In matters pertaining to fishing—not to mention farming, guitar

playing, and a number of other things—he had the authority that comes from experience; and I was also into a bit of adolescent hero worship.

2   The idea of the fishing car spoke to me of a way of life. It was the thought that you could be a sportsman in the same way you could be a Baptist or a farmer or a blond; that being a fisherman could be as much a part of your identity as your fingerprints. And I was at the age where I had just started to puzzle over my identity.

3   The fishing car in those days was the "ambler." It had actually once said "Rambler" in chrome letters on the hood, but a minor run-in with a fence post had resulted in the abbreviated version. Of course, there was no thought of having it fixed.

4   It was a black station wagon with many thousands of miles on it that somehow always ran—after a little prodding—and that was always stocked with axes, minnow buckets, tackle boxes, rods, etc. The upholstery was ragged, the windshield was pitted, the dashboard was dusty, the tires were fair, and it had an aroma about it of beer, Coke, cleaned fish, wet wool, and a few other things that were hard to place. The exact opposite of that new car smell.

5   I don't know what ever happened to it, but, by all rights, it should have been bronzed and placed on a pedestal on the banks of a good bass pond somewhere in Indiana.

6   I spent as much time as I could with Leonard while I was growing up, and much of it passed in the front seat of the ambler following lazy, circuitous routes to one bass pond or another. We drove the dirt roads most of the time. Some were so little used that by midsummer the tall grass growing between the wheel ruts would slap the front bumper. The roads in those rural counties were laid out more or less on grids, and we got to where we were going by starting at a known point and then angling in what seemed like the right direction.

7   In the course of things we discovered several little towns that were doubtless unknown to the outside world; towns so slowly paced that a dog could safely sleep on the warm pavement of Main Street in the late afternoon, because everyone knew that Butch might be taking a nap in the road in front of the hardware store. Butch himself, a fair-to-middling hunting dog in his younger years, could live to the ripe age of eighteen or twenty, and when he finally passed away—quietly, in his sleep—the whole town would feel bad about it for a day or two.

8   Sometimes we'd stop and ask directions, which could be a laborious process. Everyone knew where everything was, but what was County Road 23 to us was usually the Road Out to the Jones Place to everyone else. I never saw Leonard use a store-bought map, but we followed several that were scratched on paper napkins or matchbook covers.

9   Leonard was a master at navigating in farm country, but we did occasionally get lost. This was known as "taking the scenic route." There were rare times when we never quite got to where we were going, but we always got *somewhere*.

10   Leonard made a point of appearing confident and in charge, so it was difficult to tell when he knew where he was and when he didn't. There were times when I'd have sworn we were hopelessly lost, but then we'd pull up to an unlocked gate that looked exactly like the last twenty unlocked gates we'd passed, and he would describe the pond that was still out of sight down a two-wheel dirt track: its size, its shape, the muddy bank, the cattails along the east side, everything. Of course, he did have the reputation of knowing where every bass and most of the panfish in three counties lived.

11   He also knew half the people in the same area, and if he *didn't* know them, he soon would. He was deeply in touch with the interlocking networks of relations, work, church, and grange that tied the farming community together, and all he needed to make a connection was a name off a mailbox.

12   It was something to see. Leonard would bounce the ambler up a perfectly strange driveway, negotiate through the dogs, find the owner (who was invariably poking at some broken piece of machinery), and deftly establish himself as a neighbor, if not an out-and-out friend of the family. There would then follow an interminable period of fence leaning, gravel kicking, sky squinting, and a rambling philosophical discussion that included everything from the hound dog at your feet to the President of the United States. Of the two, the dog was the more competent.

13   It took time, but sooner or later we'd end up catching large bass from an obscure pond that hadn't been fished five times in as many years. The farmer always got some cleaned fish out of it, and then we'd pile into the ambler and drive off, waving at a man who was now our friend or who, at the very least, was too polite to say no to a couple of nice enough guys. Driving home at night it would occur to me that, although life would surely provide some interruptions, there'd be nothing wrong with doing this all the time.

14   Of all the trips Leonard and I took in that car, the one I remember most clearly was our longest and last. My family had moved to Minnesota, and I hadn't seen Leonard in a while. I was a teenager then, having attained some height and a considerable dose of that quality that was once known as strong-headedness. My mother smiles about those years now, but Dad didn't live quite long enough to see all the humor in it. Maybe strong-headed is too mild a term.

15   Dad and I did hunt and fish together, though, and that was our one stable point of agreement through some years that could easily have ended in a complete severing of diplomatic relations.

16   It was Dad who gave me my first view of fly-fishing. I'd read about it in the outdoor magazines and had even once seen a man using what was known back then in the Midwest as a "trout rod." Dad said he didn't know much about it, but that the people who practiced it were the true artists of the sport. Leonard gave me my second view. "Fly-fishermen are a bunch of conceited pricks," he said.

17   It took me a number of years to realize that both men were right.

18   You see, Dad was what you'd have to call a gentleman sportsman type. He would never have considered poaching or doing anything out of season; he loved fine tackle and thought it was vastly superior to catch a fish on a lure rather than bait, because this actually involved fooling the game with your skill and cunning. Leonard, on the other hand, fished to catch fish, which he then killed and ate. He respected private property, but he also believed that God had put fish on the earth for all the people, and these two ideas constantly battled for his soul. His gear was wired, glued, and duct-taped together, and he fished with whatever it took, stopping short only of explosives, and then only because they'd have been too loud.

19   If I'd actually set out to get a perfectly balanced education as a fisherman, I couldn't have chosen two better teachers.

20   Where was I? Right. The longest and last trip in the ambler.

21   It so happened that my sister decided to get married one summer not long after we'd moved to Minnesota, a state that was full of lakes which were, in turn, lousy with fish. Weeks before the actual festivities, the family began to gather. By the time Leonard and Aunt Dora arrived, the house was filled with grannies and aunts and mobs of cousins on the way.

22   Leonard and I got together out in the backyard, where it was quiet, and decided the best thing for us to do was go wet a line somewhere, just to get out from underfoot, you understand. We packed quickly, left quietly, and drove north in the ambler.

23   We drove for some eighteen or twenty hours, watching the landscape go from fields to scattered groves to coniferous forests and feeling the hot closeness of the summer air become cool and sharply scented with pine. Somewhere along the line we turned off the main highway onto a dirt county road.

24   Up there the roads were fewer and farther between than in rural Indiana and anything but straight. They didn't seem to go much of anywhere, but all roads go somewhere, and we finally pulled up to a medium-sized lake with tree-lined banks and water lilies as if it had been our destination from the start. We rented a small, rickety cabin that came with an equally small and rickety rowboat. Both leaked, but were thoughtfully equipped with the appropriate tin cans.

25   In the days that followed, we caught fish.

26   There were foot-long perch in the little bay right outside the cabin door that came into the boat with the kind of regularity you somehow only remember from long ago. On the first night we sat down to baked beans from a can and a platter of breaded and fried perch fillets from a lake that neither of us had seen or even heard of before. Definitely the way to begin a fishing trip.

27   We took smallmouth bass from around the rocky points on small floating lures and spoons. They were an olivish-bronze color and jumped the way I would later learn that rainbow trout do.

28   The northern pike came from deeper water to big, heavy Johnson's Weedless Spoons trailing strips of pickled pork rind. They were my favorites, being large, prehistorically ugly, and—by stretching the imagination some—even a little dangerous. Leonard said the real fight with a big pike began when you got him in the boat. In any case, there were some minor injuries, complete with blood, and I loved it.

29   During the middle of some days, we drove around the back roads to look at other lakes and talk to sellers of bait and renters of boats, all of whom were getting their share of fish that week. "Getting our share" is one of those wonderful fishing euphemisms that sound promising, but that can mean damn near anything.

30   As I said, Leonard was a great raconteur of the fence-leaning or one-foot-up-on-the-dock-piling school, and he enjoyed talking and joking with fishermen as much as he liked fishing itself. He was good at it, too. He knew that few fishermen, himself included, would tell a stranger what he needed to know straight out, so he assembled information not so much by the facts as by evaluating the empty space around them. He taught me, for example, not to pay attention to the lures that were well stocked, regardless of how pretty they were or how hard the sales pitch was, but to always ask what had once hung on the empty pegs. The ones that were sold out were the ones that caught fish.

31   I guess it took me a long time to come to appreciate the charms and real advantages of just *talking* about fishing, looking at water, leaning on things, reading between lines. At the time I was a little impatient. You remember, it was childhood; the days of wooden rowboats when men who didn't know each other could stand and chew the fat for hours. But I knew I'd be doing it myself someday, so I paid attention and mostly kept my mouth shut in the borrowed style of the strong, silent type. The compliment I was being paid was that of being left to myself—of not having to be watched and kept amused. Back home I felt like a man who was being treated like a boy. Out fishing with Leonard, it was the other way around.

32   Then, as now, these conversations tended to dissolve around late afternoon when the first boils could be seen out along the weed beds. There was a slow, satisfying logic about it all.

33   I drove the ambler on many of those back roads, not because I was allowed to, as I'd been in the past, but because a fishing partner shares the driving chores. Never mind that I was too young to have a license.

34   It wasn't until a few hours before the wedding—not quite the last possible moment—that we strolled in the back door sublimely unconcerned, wearing clothes we'd fished in for a week and carrying armloads of fillets. The house was in a uniform state of hysteria: the women were all at a dead run or off in a corner weeping, while the men were looking mounted in suits that had last been worn at funerals. I've since come to recognize the pained, furtive look they wore as symptomatic of the powerful need for a drink.

35   "It's about time," someone said, and we were grabbed by the ears and forcibly washed. The story is told that our clothes had to be burned, but that may be an exaggeration. I've never felt less welcome arriving at an event I was supposed to attend.

36   I remember coming downstairs to the kitchen all clean and dressed up and running into Dad. He'd been stuffed into a tuxedo and was fondling a big glass of bourbon with a single, lonely ice cube floating in it. We were alone, but the sound of chattering washed in from the front room.

37   "Caught some fish," Dad said (not a question).

38   "Yup," I answered, all puffed up with teenage conceit and vanity.

39   He raised his glass slightly in a toast and flashed me an evil little grin, something between envy, pride, and resignation. Now that I think about it, maybe he *did* see the humor in it now and then, or if not the humor, then something. Dad always tried to be strict and straight-laced with me, but word around the family was he'd had his moments as a young man. I remember wanting to tell him I'd driven the car for hundreds of miles, and then thinking I'd best not push my luck.

40   I've traveled in a number of fishing cars since then, from a Volkswagen that must have been a contemporary of the ambler to a gas-guzzling road slug that blotted out the sun as it passed by. Each has had a certain romance about it, based not so much on its looks or performance as on what it was, where it had been, and where it might be going next.

41   Koke has a station wagon now that will be just fine after a little breaking in, but he used to own one of the most famous fishing cars in the Rocky Mountain West. I remember it as a Ford, while A.K. swears it was a Dodge. Odd. Whatever make it was, it was big and white with a combination boat-and-rod rack on the roof and the biggest trunk I've ever seen.

42   Somewhere in this trunk you could find anything any three people would need on a month-long fishing trip, except that you couldn't find anything if you weren't Koke. The stuff was there in layers, like at an archeological dig, and if you were asked to get something ("It's right on top, you can't miss it."), it could take an hour, during which time you'd come across a dozen articles of tackle that had gone out of production twenty years ago. It became a simile, as in, "What have you been doing? This place looks like Koke's trunk."

43   A.K. himself has a good one now, a vintage Chevrolet pickup with a 400-some cubic inch V-8 and a camper shell. One of the first custom features he installed was an electric lantern hung just inside the back hatch for de-rigging in the dark, something we end up doing on three out of four trips.

44   On one of our recent expeditions, A.K.'s tent blew down in a wind that was not quite bad enough to make us get our belly boats off the water (which, I think, speaks volumes of ill about the tent), and we ended up sleeping in the truck. It was a pain at the time because all the float tubes, spare waders, fly tying travel kits, spare rods, camp kitchen, and such had to be unloaded in the dark and stowed under tarps, because it was

raining as well as blowing. But in the end I think it was fitting. A car that hasn't been slept in on an emergency basis isn't quite broken in.

45   Then there's my own succession of fishing cars. There was a white International Scout and then a blue and white Scout that had once been a U.S. Mail truck and had the steering wheel on the wrong side. It was a conversation piece, but that's about the best I can say for it. Both cars were tinny, didn't have enough room in the back, and the four-cylinder engines were too weak. Great for delivering mail, but not too hot for fishing.

46   Why two of them? I'd just given up on the first one as being not enough truck when a guy who owed me $400—and who was not about to get the cash and who was also about to leave town suddenly for some reason— gave me the second one to clear the debt. "Thanks a lot," I said.

47   People assumed that I loved Scouts because I had a pair of them.

48   Those were followed by the longest running fishing car to date, a 1966 red Ford three-quarter-ton pickup with a long bed, a big engine, and four-wheel drive. It was a ten-mile-to-the-gallon monster that was, if anything, too much truck rather than too little. Still, I had great luck with it, partly because it was a solid vehicle with lots of spirit and partly because I had aged some by then, learning some lessons in the process. One lesson was that four-wheel drive doesn't mean you can go anywhere, it just means you can get stuck in worse places.

49   In his formative months, my late bird dog (and I use the term lightly) was left in the cab and, with nothing better to do, ate the seat on the driver's side. "Why didn't you chew up *your* side?" I asked, but he just wagged his tail and smiled, happy to see me. That dog lived for almost sixteen years, but he never got any more considerate.

50   Once, while hauling a load of firewood out of the National Forest on a muddy road, I skidded sideways against a ponderosa pine tree and bashed in the left door, closing and locking it permanently, but otherwise doing little damage. I didn't really mind having to get in on the wrong side and slide across, although I did tear the back pockets off more than one pair of jeans on the exposed springs. And it wasn't all that pretty when I got it, either, having once been a yard truck at a lumber mill.

51   You get the picture.

52   I got so attached to that truck that I honestly cried when it went the way of all flesh, having de-evolved from a powerful, soulful V-8 into a pitiful, wheezing V-6. I kept the gearshift knob as a souvenir, because even that had a heavy, well-built feel to it. I haven't seen it in a while, though. One of my ex-cats used to like to play with it, so it's probably under the couch now. The cat, Maggie, also had soul. She died a few years ago in a valiant, if misguided, attempt to eat a rattlesnake. The cat got a decent burial, but I don't own enough land, nor the right equipment, to inter a pickup truck.

53   You may have noticed I have a thing for big American trucks. Some of that is pure genetic patriotism, but there are also some practical considerations.

54   I buy inexpensive vehicles, for reasons that will become obvious if you ever drop by the place here, and big old American trucks are cheap. They're also well built, heavy, and they're powerful if the rings are still okay. They do burn a lot of gas, but you have to look at that closely. You can buy a $12,000 pickup that gets twenty-three miles to the gallon of no-lead, or you can buy a $1,000 gunboat that gets eight miles to a gallon of regular. Work it out yourself. How many miles do you have to drive to save $11,000 in gas money?

55   Your big old pickup will also carry a lot of gear and will sleep two comfortably under the basic camper shell. If you ever break down (it's a fair bet you will), you'll open the hood of your venerable machine to find an engine block, valve covers, starter motor, fuel pump, distributor, carburetor...you know, the usual parts. If you're a fair-to-middling roadside mechanic with a wrench, screw-driver, a pair of pliers, and maybe a hammer, it will all make a certain sense. The motors in new trucks look like time machines and, anyway, the problem could be a computer malfunction.

56   If your old truck looks seedy enough, it's also the last one in the parking lot anyone would think of breaking into, which can be a real advantage. On a normal outing, the gear in my truck is worth more than the vehicle itself.

57   Along those same lines, I was once told by a retired police officer to remove the decals on my back window, you know, the ones that tell the world what organizations I belong to. "All they do is tell the bad guys what kind of merchandise is probably inside," he said.

58   Something to think about.

59   The worst is the one that says, "This Vehicle Insured by Smith & Wesson." It doesn't scare anyone, but it tells them there's probably a valuable handgun under the seat.

60   You get attached to an old heap, but you don't worry about it like you would a shiny new one. I once left the Ford in a bus stop parking lot for three days while I was off fishing the Frying Pan and Roaring Fork rivers with Koke. When I got back the truck was as I'd left it, except that most of the gas had been siphoned from the tank and the gas cap was missing. On the plus side, it hadn't been broken into or vandalized. I can almost picture the bum standing there thinking, "Well, there's probably nothing in it, and as for smashing it up for kicks, it looks like someone has beat me to it."

61   I had enough fuel left to get to a town and buy some more, and, since I'd been happily catching trout for three days (during which time I never once stopped to worry about the truck), I decided to feel charitable. It is, after all, easy enough to construct a scenario where some destitute fellow human being is trying to get from point A to point B without enough money for gas, possibly on a very important errand. A job, maybe, or a death in the family or a girlfriend. Something crucial.

62   And the gas cap? Well, maybe he just dropped it. It was dark and I was tired. I didn't even look.

63   As an interim measure, I stuck one of those red mechanics' rags where the cap should have gone. It worked fine, and I didn't get a real store-bought gas cap until someone asked me if I'd decided to turn the truck into a Molotov cocktail and go on a suicide mission.

64   There's just something *about* the older American pickups. They're like model 94 Winchester rifles or Granger fly rods: ordinary and workman-like, but still classy and dripping with romance. To drive one is to make a statement about enduring values. It's a way of identifying yourself, in this big, sprawling culture of ours, as a guy who occasionally has to haul stuff.

65   Of course, it's a personal matter, and there is another side to all this. Last winter I jokingly said to a friend of mine—the owner of a new Oriental recreational vehicle—that a real man drives an American pickup. In an impressively level way, he replied that a real man drives whatever he, by God, pleases.

66   Okay.

67   The old blue Chevy pickup I have now—referred to in some circles as The Blue Streak and in others as Old Blue—is a serviceable truck, though it has not quite become the cosmic fishing car. These things take time, not to mention the proper accumulation of adventures and mishaps.

68   It has some streamer flies and a bass bug stuck in the dashboard, which is a nice, homey touch, and is chugging away on its second used engine. It took me through Wyoming, Idaho, and Montana last summer with only one small electrical problem that was easily fixed, though not so easily diagnosed. It's never let me down seriously except for the time it caught fire at the corner of Canyon Boulevard and 28th Street in Boulder, Colorado. During rush hour. I had no idea so many people carried fire extinguishers in their cars.

69   Still, it's seventeen years old, and to fix everything that is wrong, or about to *go* wrong, would cost too much. So it's on its way out. I'll always fondly remember tying flies on its tailgate, but I can't trust it far from home anymore.

70   Buying a new (old) pickup is like fishing a new pond that you know nothing about. It could be full of big fish; it could also be full of alkali—not only fishless, but poisoned. Over the years I have learned the following things:

71   It will be hard to find, but you want one with a bunged up body that's still in working order. Most people are embarrassingly superficial in this regard and will pay more for a smooth body and a good paint job than for a truck that actually runs. Don't even look under the hood, just take it somewhere and have the compression checked. Then tell the guy who's selling it that it looks like hell.

72   The shape the bed is in will tell you more about a pickup than any other single thing. If the bed is all dented and scratched up, it was a work truck and was probably used hard. Is the tailgate bunged up on the top edge? It means a lot of heavy stuff was loaded and unloaded. Is the tailgate *missing*? Bad sign. So much stuff was loaded that it got in the way and they took it off.

73   Well, not always. A missing tailgate combined with a clean, almost pristine bed probably means that a camper sat there until very recently.

74   What you want is a ten- or twelve-year-old pickup that was used recreationally a few times a year by a seventy-five-year-old fisherman who doesn't kick ass like he used to and who does his running around town in his wife's sedan.

75   With even some of the used trucks now being too tinny and having too many moving parts to be reasonable, I'm beginning to think the answer is to get hold of a good, solid, well-seasoned pickup and commit to whatever it takes to keep it running for the rest of my life. This would solve a number of problems and would also be a big step toward firmly establishing me as an old fart, something I believe to be the secret, lifelong ambition of every serious fisherman.

76   I'm fully aware that somewhere down the road I'll run head-on into the fact that nothing can or does last forever. That's one of the reasons why I've never tried to find that lake and that cabin up in Minnesota again. You and I both know what has surely happened there by now. It would be like coming on the ambler rotting away in a field somewhere with the windows shot out.

77   I guess my sister got married okay that summer, although I can't say I actually remember the ceremony. All the fish got eaten, and Leonard and I were eventually forgiven, though I've never been quite sure what for.

78   When it was all over, I walked Leonard and Aunt Dora out to the fishing car. They were headed back to Indiana, and the ambler didn't look right with suitcases and garment bags in it. Leonard and I ran down some brief, vague plans for future fishing trips, and then, with nothing left to say, they drove off. As it turned out, I would never see the ambler again, and Leonard and I would never fish together again, either, although I didn't know that at the time. You never know those things at the time.

79   The last time I saw it, the car was still dusty from the trip to the lake. Aunt Dora had wanted to have it washed, but there just wasn't time.

Questions for Discussion

1. What characteristic of his Uncle Leonard appeals to the young narrator? Why? In what sense is Leonard a hero or role model for a young boy who is "just [starting] to puzzle over [his] identity"?

2. What does their regarding getting lost as "'taking the scenic route'" reveal about the narrator and his uncle?

3. The narrator says of his uncle's and his father's diametrically opposed attitudes toward fly-fishing that they are both "right." How is that possible? How do their different methods of fishing reveal the deep character differences between the narrator's father and Leonard? How do they both serve as role models for the boy?

4. For the narrator what is the relative importance of the two facts that Minnesota is "full of lakes" that are full of fish and "It so happened that [his] sister decided to get married"?

5. Why do the narrator and Uncle Leonard decide to go fishing on the narrator's sister's wedding day?

6. What does the narrator mean by "Back home I felt like a man who was being treated like a boy. Out fishing with Leonard, it was the other way around"?

7. The narrator says about his sister's wedding, "Leonard and I were eventually forgiven though I've never been quite sure what for." What does this statement reveal about the narrator's character?

8. At the end of the essay, the narrator says, "Aunt Dora had wanted to have [the fishing car] washed, but there just wasn't time." Why "wasn't" there "time"?

Suggestions for Exploring, Writing, and Persuading

1. Write an essay contrasting the narrator's father and Uncle Leonard as male role models.

2. In an essay discuss the importance of male role models in a young boy's life.

3. Argue for or against going fishing on your sister's wedding day.

David Osborne (b. 1951)

David Osborne, a political journalist and a consultant to the Clinton presidential campaign in 1992, has published articles in many prestigious magazines. His book Reinventing Government *(1992), coauthored with Ted Gaebler, presents guidelines and suggestions for changes in government;* Banishing Bureaucracy *(1997) suggests strategies for implementing these changes. Osborne and his wife, Rose, an obstetrician and gynecologist, and their four children live in Dedham, Massachusetts.*

BEYOND THE CULT OF FATHERHOOD   (1985)

1   If I ever finish this article, it will be a miracle. Nicholas woke up this morning with an earache and a temperature, and I spent half the day at the doctor's office and pharmacy. Another ear infection.

2   Nicholas is my son. Twenty months old, a stout little bundle of energy and affection.

3   I will never forget the moment when I realized how completely Nick would change my life. My wife is a resident in obstetrics and gynecology, which means, among other things, that she works 100 hours a week,

leaves the house every day by six and works all night several times a week, and often all weekend too. I'm not a househusband; I take Nick to day care five days a week. But I come about as close to house-husbandry as I care to. I am what you might call a "nontraditional" father.

4   Nick was three weeks old when I learned what that actually meant. Rose had just gone back to work, and Nick and I were learning about bottles. I don't remember if it was Rose's first night back or her second, but she wasn't home.

5   I stayed up too late; I had not yet learned that, with a baby in the house, you grab sleep whenever you can—even if it means going to bed at nine. Just as I drifted off, about 11:30, Nick woke up. I fed him and rocked him and put him back to sleep. About 2 a.m. he woke again, crying, and I rocked him for 45 minutes before he quieted down.

6   When he started screaming at four, I was in the kitchen by the time I woke up. As every parent knows, the sound of an infant—your infant—screaming sends lightning bolts up the spine. Bells ring in the head; nerves jangle. Racing against my son's hunger, I boiled water, poured it into the little plastic sack, slipped the sack into the plastic bottle, put on the top, and plunged the bottle into a bowl of cold water to cool it. I had not yet learned that in Connecticut, where I live, the water need not be sterilized. (Fathers are the last to know.)

7   It takes a long time to boil water and cool it back to body temperature, and I was dead on my feet even before the screams rearranged my vertebrae. By the time the water had cooled, I was half-crazed, my motions rapid and jerky. I mixed in the powdered formula and slipped the nipple back on. I ran toward Nick's room, shaking the bottle as hard as I could to make sure it was thoroughly mixed. As I reached his crib, the top flew off—and the contents sprayed all over the room.

8   At that point, I lost it. I swore at the top of my lungs, I stomped around the room, I slammed the changing table, and I swore some more. That was when I realized what I had gotten myself into—and how much I had to learn.

9   With baby boomers well ensconced in the nation's newsrooms, fatherhood is sweeping American journalism. You can pick up the *New York Times Magazine*, or *Esquire*, or Bob Greene's best-seller, *Good Morning, Merry Sunshine: A Father's Journal of His Child's First Year* (Penguin), and read all about the wonders of being a father.

10   By all accounts, today's fathers are more involved and more sensitive than their own fathers were. But as warm and tender as their writing may be, it rings false. Rosalie Ziomek, a mother in Evanston, Illinois, said it perfectly in a letter to the *New Republic*, after it printed a scathing review of Bob Greene's book. "I was enraged by Greene's book," Ziomek wrote. "Anyone taking care of a newborn infant doesn't have time to write about it. Greene was cashing in on the experiences that most women have quietly and painfully lived without the glorification of fame and money. Meanwhile, because of the structure of his work/social life, which he is

unwilling to alter, he avoids the thing that is the hardest part of new motherhood: the moment-to-moment dependency of a tiny, helpless, and demanding human being. I have more to say on the subject, but I have three children to take care of and writing is a luxury I can't afford right now."

11   Ziomek is right. I've been trying to keep a journal as Greene did, and it's impossible. There's no time. And how do you capture the essence of an exhausting, never-ending 24-hour day in a few paragraphs? Snapshots work if you spend an hour or two with a child, but if you spend days, everything dissolves in a blur.

12   My experience is different from that of the fathers I read about. Certainly I am not fulfilling the role of a traditional mother, and certainly no child could ask for a more loving mother than Nick has. But I do fix most of the meals and do most of the laundry and change a lot of the diapers and get Nick up and dressed in the morning and shuttle him back and forth to day care and cart him to the grocery store and sing him to sleep and clean up his toys and wipe his nose and deal with his tantrums and cuddle with him and tickle him and all the other wonderful and exhausting things mothers do. If you ask me what it all means, I can't say. After 20 months, I'm still dizzy, still desperate for a free hour or two, and still hopelessly in love with my little boy. All I have to offer are fragments; profound thoughts are for people who have more time. But if you want to go beyond the cult of fatherhood, I think I've been there.

13   My day starts about 6:30 or 7 a.m., when Nick stands up in his crib and calls out for me. I stumble into his room, pick him up, give him a kiss and a "Good morning, Pumpkin," and carry him back to bed. I lay him down on his mother's empty pillow, lie down beside him, and sometimes I drowse again before it's really time to get up. But most mornings Nick is ready to start his day, and he gradually drags me up toward consciousness. He smiles at me, climbs up on me, and rests his head against my cheek—even kisses me if I'm really lucky, or sits on my bladder and bounces, if I'm not. I tickle him, and he laughs and squirms and shrieks for more.

14   Sometimes he lies there for a few minutes, thinking his little boy thoughts, before sliding himself backward off the bed and going in search of something to do. Often he arrives back with a toy or two and asks to be picked "Up! Up!" Then he plays for a few minutes, making sure to keep an eye on my progress toward wakefulness. When he has waited long enough, he hands me my glasses, takes my hand, and pulls me out of bed.

15   While I shower, Nick plays in the bathroom, sitting on the floor with his toys. By the time I'm dressed, the kettle is whistling, and he's ready for breakfast. We always eat together, he has hot cereal, I have cold cereal, and often we share a bagel. I wish you could hear him say "cream cheese."

16   The rough times come on weekends. After 24 hours, I'm ready to be hung out on the line to dry. After 48 hours, I'm ready to pin medals on women who stay home every day with their kids. For single mothers, I'm ready to build monuments.

17   Don't let anyone tell you otherwise: traditional mothers work harder than anyone else can even imagine. They are on duty 24 hours a day, 365 days a year. I remember wondering, as a youth, why my own mother always rushed around with such urgency when she was cooking or cleaning. To me, she was like a woman possessed. Now I do the same thing. When you have a young child (or two, or three), you have very little time to get the dishes done, or cook dinner, or vacuum, or do the laundry so when you get a moment, you proceed with all possible haste. If your children are asleep, they might wake up. If they're playing, they might get bored and demand your attention.

18   Friends who visit me nowadays probably think I'm crazy, the way I rush compulsively to get dinner ready or mow the lawn or finish the laundry. I do feel somewhat self-conscious about it. But the fact is, if I'm cooking, Nick is going to start demanding his meal soon, and if it's not ready, he's going to get very cranky. And with all the chores that pile up on a weekend—the lawn, the laundry, the groceries, and so on—I have to seize every possible instant. If he naps, that may give me an hour and a half. If he wakes up before I'm done, whatever I'm doing will never get finished.

19   In any case, it is on weekends alone with Nick that I feel the full brunt of child-rearing. Consider a typical weekend: Nick wakes at 7:00, and we lie in bed and play for half an hour before getting up. But this morning he feels feverish, so I take his temperature. It is 101.6—not high for a young child, but a fever nonetheless.

20   The first thing I do is call Maureen, who takes care of him during the week. Both of her kids have a bug, and I want to find out what the symptoms are, to see if Nick has the same thing. From what we can tell, he does. On that basis, I decide to give him Tylenol for the fever, rather than taking him in to the pediatrician to see if he's got an ear infection. Besides, he wants to lie down for a nap at 10:00, before I have decided, and doesn't wake until 1:00. By then the office is closed.

21   After lunch he feels much better—cool, happy, and bubbling. We play with his lock-blocks for a while, then watch a basketball game. He's very cuddly, because he's not feeling well. After the game it's off to the bank and grocery store. He falls asleep on the way home, at 5:45. It's an awkward time for a nap, but he only sleeps until 6:30. He wakes up crying, with a high fever, feeling miserable.

22   To get him to swallow more Tylenol, which he hates, I promise him ice cream. I give him half an ice-cream sandwich while I rush around the kitchen cooking dinner, and when he finishes it, he cries for the other half. I tell him he can have it after he eats his dinner. But when dinner is ready, he won't eat; he just sits there pointing at the freezer, where the ice cream is, and wailing. This is a major tantrum—hot tears, red face. I can't help but sympathize, though, because it's born of feeling absolutely wretched. How should I respond? I don't want to give in and teach him he can get his way by screaming. I try to comfort him by holding him in my lap, but he just sobs. Finally I take him into his room and rock him,

holding him close. Gradually the sobs subside, and after 10 minutes I take him back into the kitchen, hold him on my lap, and feed him myself. He doesn't eat much, but enough to deserve his ice cream.

23   Though Nick gets over the incident in no time, I am traumatized. The fever is frightening—it has hit 102 by dinnertime, and it only drops to 101.4 by 8 p.m. Should I have taken him to the doctor? Will he spike a really high fever tonight? Am I being too relaxed? And what will Rose say? I cannot stop worrying; I feel heartsick as I read him his bedtime stories, though he cools down as he drifts to sleep in my arms. Would a mother feel so uncertain, I wonder? Do mothers feel adequate at moments like this? Or am I in a father's territory here?

24   Sunday morning Nick wakes at 6:30 and devours his breakfast, but pretty soon his temperature begins to rise. I call our pediatrician, who reassures me that it doesn't sound like an ear infection, and that I'm doing the right thing. Still, Nick isn't feeling well, and it makes him more demanding. He wants to be held; he wants me with him constantly; he insists that I do what he wants me to do and cries if I balk. It is a wearing day. He naps late, and when I wake him at seven, he is again miserable—temperature at 102.4, crying, refusing to let me change his diaper. But after more Tylenol and a good dinner he feels better.

25   I haven't heard from Rose all weekend, so I decide to call her at the hospital. She is furious that I haven't taken Nick to the doctor. A child who gets ear infections as often as he does has to be checked, she yells at me. He could blow out an eardrum! And why haven't I called her— she's his mother, for God's sake! I'm exhausted, I've been busting my hump all weekend, alone, doing the best I can, and now I'm being abused. I don't like it. My first impulse is to hang up on her, but instead I hand the phone to Nicholas, who has a long talk with her. He says "Mommy!" she says "Nicholas!" and he laughs and laughs.

26   Rose may be right, I know, but that doesn't help my anger. We part tersely, and I promise to take him to the pediatrician the next morning before I leave for California on an article assignment. After that's out of the way, Nick and I have a good evening. We read books, and several times he leads me into his room to get another handful. A short bath, more books, then off to bed. He wants to take two of his trucks to bed with him—a new wrinkle—but I finally convince him to say "night-night" to his trucks and turn out the lights.

27   I have several hours of work to do before I leave, so I don't get to bed until after midnight. I'm absolutely shot. When the alarm rings at 6:00, I haul myself out of bed, shower, get dressed, and get Nick up and fed and dressed. We speed down to the library to return several books, then to the doctor's office. No ear infection; it's just a bug, says the doc, and he should be over it by nightfall. I drop Nick off at Maureen's by 9:30, race home, and spend the next hour packing, vacuuming, cleaning up the dishes and defrosting something for Rose and Nick's dinner. When I get to the airport, I realize I've misread my ticket and I'm half an hour early. I'm exhausted, and the trip has yet to begin.

28   Two nights later I call Rose. When I ask how she is, she bursts into tears. Nicholas has fallen at Maureen's and cut his forehead on a metal toy. Rose was caught in an ice storm between the hospital and home, so Maureen had to take her own kids to a neighbor's and rush Nick to the pediatrician's office for stitches. They gave him a local anesthetic, but he screamed the whole time.

29   "I feel so awful," Rose sobs, over and over. "I should have been there. I just feel awful." Guilt floods in, but it is nothing to match Rose's guilt. This is one of the differences I have discovered between mothers and fathers.

30   Rose has felt guilty since the day she went back to work—the hardest single thing I've ever watched her do. Deep inside her psyche lies a powerful message that she belongs at home, that if she is not with her child she is terribly irresponsible.

31   I feel guilty only occasionally. When I dropped Nick off at day care the first day after returning from California, and he sobbed because he thought I was leaving him again, the guilt just about killed me. I turned into a classic mother: as soon as I got home, I called to see if he was still crying. (He was.) Two guilt-ridden hours later I called again, desperate to hear that everything was fine. (It was.)

32   Deep within my psyche, however, the most powerful message is that I belong at work, that if I am not out making my mark on the world I am worth nothing.

33   The contradiction between family and career is nothing new; it is perhaps the central unresolved conflict in the lives of American women today. What I did not expect was the force with which that conflict would erupt in my life.

34   Like an addict, I now find myself squeezing in every last minute of work that I can. I wait until the last possible instant before rushing out the door to pick Nick up in the afternoon. I dart out to my study while he naps on weekends, using a portable intercom to listen for his cries. At night I compulsively page through old newspapers that pile up because I can no longer read them over breakfast, afraid I've missed something important. As I hit deadline time, I pray that Nicholas doesn't get sick. I have even tried writing on a Saturday afternoon, with Nick playing in my studio. That experiment lasted half an hour, at which point he hit the reset button on the back of my computer and my prose was lost to the ages.

35   This frantic effort to keep up is clearly not good for me, but I cannot seem to abandon it. I constantly feel as if I live in a pressure cooker. I long for a free day, even a free hour. But my career has taken off just as my responsibilities as a father have hit their peak, and I cannot seem to scale down my commitment to either.

36   When Nick was four months old, I took him to a Christmas party, one Saturday when Rose was working. After an hour or so he got cranky, so I took him upstairs with a bottle. A little girl followed, and soon her brother and sister—equally bored by the goings-on downstairs—had joined us. It wasn't long before Dad came looking for them.

37   We introduced ourselves and talked for a bit. His wife, it turned out, was also a doctor. The curious part came when I asked what he did. First he told me all the things he had done in the past: carpentry, business, you name it. Then he said he'd done enough—he was about 40—and felt no need to prove himself any more. Finally he told me he stayed at home with the kids. And frankly, he pulled it off with far more dignity and less stammering than I would have, had our places been reversed.

38   I don't think I could do what he does. If I were to stay home full-time with Nick, I would quickly lose my self-esteem, and within months I would be deep into an identity crisis. Part of the reason I love my role as a father is that I am secure in my role as a writer. Without that, I would not feel good enough about myself to be the kind of father I am.

39   This is not simply a problem inside male heads. How many women would be content with men who stayed home with the kids? Not many, I'll wager. And not my wife, I know. From my experience, modern women want a man who will share the responsibilities at home but still be John Wayne in the outside world. They don't want any wimps wearing aprons. And men know it.

40   We are in a Burger King, in Fall River, Massachusetts. We are not having a good day. We drove two hours to shop in the factory outlets here, and all but a handful are closed because it's Sunday.

41   Nick likes Burger King, but he's not having a great day either. He has recently learned about tantrums, and as we get ready to leave, he decides to throw one. He doesn't want to leave; he doesn't want to put on his coat; he just doesn't want to be hauled around any more. So he stands up and wails.

42   Rose is mortified; she takes any misbehavior in public as an advertisement of her failings as a mother. It triggers all her guilt about working. This time, the timing couldn't be worse, because she is already on edge.

43   Our tantrum strategy is generally to let him yell, to ignore him, and thus to teach him that it does no good. But in a public restaurant, I don't have the stamina to ignore him, so I cross the room to pick him up.

44   Rose orders me away from him, in no uncertain terms. There are no negotiations, no consultations. We are going to do this her way or no way.

45   That lights my fuse, of course, and after simmering for 10 minutes, I bring it up. "Let it go," she tells me, almost in tears over Nicholas. "It's not important."

46   It's not important.

47   Ah, the double bind. You're in charge one day, playing mother and father all wrapped into one, depended upon to feed him and clothe him and change him and bathe him and rock him and meet his every need. And the next day you're a third wheel, because Mom is around. You are expected to put in the long hours, but to pretend in public that you don't, for fear of undercutting your wife's sense of self-worth as a mother. How could she be doing her job, her psyche seems to whisper, if she's letting someone else make half the decisions and give half the

care? There are many double binds in modern relationships, and this is the one I like the least.

48   I didn't let it drop that day, of course. At home, when Rose asserts the traditional mother's prerogative to make decisions and handle problems alone, on her terms, I often let it go. But when it happens in public, or in front of family, it is too much. It is as if my entire contribution to raising Nicholas is being denied, as if the world is being told that I am nothing more than a spectator. Luckily, as Nick grows older, and it becomes clear to Rose that she will always be number one in his heart, she has begun to relax her public vigilance, and this problem seems to have abated.

49   This is the first time I've ever been part of a woman's world. I'm not really a part of it, of course; the chasm between the sexes is too wide to step across so lightly. But when it comes to children, I have instant rapport with most mothers. We talk about the same things, think about the same things, joke about the same things. With men, it is almost never that way, even when the men are fathers and the subject is kids. We can share enthusiasms, but the sense of being there, on the inside—the unspoken understanding that comes out of shared experience—that is missing.

50   In fact, most men don't have the slightest idea what my life with Nick is like. When I tell colleagues—even those with children—that I have no time to read, or to watch television, I get blank stares. (I never tell mothers that; they already know. Who has time to read?) One friend, also a writer, stopped in the middle of a recent conversation and said, "You have Nick at home while you're working, don't you? What do you do with him?" No such thought could pass a mother's lips.

51   None of this would have been possible had I not been forced into taking care of Nick on my own much of the time. In fact, my entire relationship with Nick would have been different had I not been forced off the sidelines. I am convinced that in our society, when Mom is home with the kids, it is almost impossible for Dad to be an equal partner in their upbringing, even if he wants to be.

52   I believe this because for three weeks, while Rose was home after Nick's birth, it felt impossible to me. Rose had carried Nick for nine months; Rose had been through labor; and Rose was nursing him. For nine months he had listened to her heartbeat, felt her pulse, been a part of her being. Now he hunted her scent and drank from her body, and the bond between them was awesome. I was like some voyeur, peeking through the window at an ancient and sacred rite.

53   Then Rose went back to work, and I had no choice but to get off the sidelines. I *had* to get Nick dressed in the morning. I *had* to feed him. I *had* to burp him and rock him and change him and get up with him in the night. He may have wanted his mother, but she wasn't there.

54   Gradually, it all began to come naturally. I learned to carry him on my (nonexistent) hip and do anything—or any combination of things—with one hand. I learned to whip up a bottle in no time, to change a diaper and treat diaper rash and calm his tears.

55   Even on vacation, it is remarkably easy to slip back into a traditional role—for both Rose and me. But the day Rose goes back to work, I am always yanked back to reality. I complain a lot, but in truth, this is my great good fortune.

56   Last night Nick asked to go to the beach—"Go? Beach? Go? Beach?" I walked him the two blocks down, one of his hands firmly in mine, the other proudly holding the leash for Sam, our dog. We played on the swings for a long time, then strolled along the beach while Sam went swimming. It was that very still hour before dark, when the world slows to a hush, and little boys and girls slowly wind down. It was almost dark when we returned. Nick asked his daddy to give him his bath, then his mommy to put him to bed.

57   This morning when I woke he was lying beside me, on his mother's empty pillow. I looked over and he gave me a big smile, his eyes shining with that special, undiluted joy one sees only in children. Then he propped himself up on his elbows, leaned over and kissed me. If there are any better moments in life, I've never found them.

Questions for Discussion

1. To what does the title of Osborne's essay refer?

2. Osborne's staying home with his son defies traditional family roles. What difficulties does this defiance create?

3. Certainly, Osborne's role as father differs from that of other, traditional fathers. As he says, however, it also differs from that of traditional mothers. How?

4. Osborne quotes a letter by Rosalie Ziomek to the *New Republic* as describing "'the hardest part of new motherhood: the moment-to-moment dependency of a tiny, helpless, and demanding human being.'" Precisely what does that dependency entail for the mother? How does Osborne's essay convincingly develop the consequences of that dependency?

5. Osborne spends much more time with Nicholas than does his wife, yet Rose feels greater guilt than Osborne when Nicholas is hurt or sick, or when he throws a tantrum. What do these different reactions reveal about their perceptions of their roles?

Suggestions for Exploring, Writing, and Persuading

1. In an essay, persuade your audience that men can or cannot be just as effective staying at home and rearing the children as women can.

2. Write an essay for or against the following proposition: the parent who stays at home with the children has both a greater share of the work and a greater privilege in shaping who the children become.

3. Osborne declares that he could not stay at home full time: "Part of the reason I love my role as a father is that I am secure in my role as a writer. Without that, I would not feel good enough about myself to be the kind of father I am." Why must he prove himself in ways other than fatherhood? Do men share the "unresolved conflict" Osborne attributes to women?

4. Osborne calls the "contradiction between family and career . . . The central unresolved conflict in the lives of American women today." In an essay drawn from your experience or observation, develop this assertion.

Rose Del Castillo Guilbault (b. 1952)

Born in Sonora, Mexico, Rose Del Castillo Guilbault has directed in television and published in magazines. This essay is taken from her column in the San Francisco Chronicle.

AMERICANIZATION IS TOUGH ON "MACHO"   (1989)

1   What is *macho?* That depends which side of the border you come from.

2   Although it's not unusual for words and expressions to lose their subtlety in translation, the negative connotations of *macho* in this country are troublesome to Hispanics.

3   Take the newspaper descriptions of alleged mass murderer Ramon Salcido. That an insensitive, insanely jealous, hard-drinking, violent Latin male is referred to as *macho* makes Hispanics cringe.

4   *"Es muy macho,"* the women in my family nod approvingly, describing a man they respect. But in the United States, when women say, "He's so macho," it's with disdain.

5   The Hispanic *macho* is manly, responsible, hardworking, a man in charge, a patriarch. A man who expresses strength through silence. What the Yiddish language would call a *mensch.*

6   The American *macho* is a chauvinist, a brute, uncouth, selfish, loud, abrasive, capable of inflicting pain, and sexually promiscuous.

7   Quintessential *macho* models in this country are Sylvester Stallone, Arnold Schwarzenegger and Charles Bronson. In their movies, they exude toughness, independence, masculinity. But a closer look reveals their machismo is really violence masquerading as courage, sullenness disguised as silence and irresponsibility camouflaged as independence.

8   If the Hispanic ideal of *macho* were translated to American screen roles, they might be Jimmy Stewart, Sean Connery and Laurence Olivier.

9   In Spanish, *macho* ennobles Latin males. In English it devalues them. This pattern seems consistent with the conflicts ethnic minority males experience in this country. Typically the cultural traits other societies value don't translate as desirable characteristics in America.

10   I watched my own father struggle with these cultural ambiguities. He worked on a farm for twenty years. He laid down miles of irrigation pipe, carefully plowed long, neat rows in fields, hacked away at recalcitrant weeds and drove tractors through whirlpools of dust. He stoically worked twenty-hour days during harvest season, accepting the long hours as part of agricultural work. When the boss complained or upbraided him for minor mistakes, he kept quiet, even when it was obvious the boss had erred.

11   He handled the most menial tasks with pride. At home he was a good provider, helped out my mother's family in Mexico without complaint, and was indulgent with me. Arguments between my mother and him generally had to do with money, or with his stubborn reluctance to share his troubles. He tried to work them out in his own silence. He didn't want to trouble my mother—a course that backfired, because the imagined is always worse than the reality.

12   Americans regarded my father as decidedly un-*macho*. His character was interpreted as nonassertive, his loyalty non-ambition, and his quietness, ignorance. I once overheard the boss's son blame him for plowing crooked rows in a field. My father merely smiled at the lie, knowing the boy had done it, but didn't refute it, confident his good work was well known. But the boss instead ridiculed him for being "stupid" and letting a kid get away with a lie. Seeing my embarrassment, my father dismissed the incident, saying "They're the dumb ones. Imagine, me fighting with a kid."

13   I tried not to look at him with American eyes because sometimes the reflection hurt.

14   Listening to my aunts' clucks of approval, my vision focused on the qualities America overlooked. "He's such a hard worker. So serious, so responsible." My aunts would secretly compliment my mother. The unspoken comparison was that he was not like some of their husbands, who drank and womanized. My uncles represented the darker side of *macho*.

15   In a patriarchal society, few challenge their roles. If men drink, it's because it's the manly thing to do. If they gamble, it's because it's how men relax. And if they fool around, well, it's because a man simply can't hold back so much man! My aunts didn't exactly meekly sit back, but they put up with these transgressions because Mexican society dictated this was their lot in life.

16   In the United States, I believe it was the feminist movement of the early '70s that changed *macho*'s meaning. Perhaps my generation of Latin women was in part responsible. I recall Chicanas complaining about the chauvinistic nature of Latin men and the notion they wanted their women barefoot, pregnant and in the kitchen. The generalization that Latin men embodied chauvinistic traits led to this interesting twist of semantics. Suddenly a word that represented something positive in one culture became a negative prototype in another.

17   The problem with the use of *macho* today is that it's become an accepted stereotype of the Latin male. And like all stereotypes, it distorts truth.

18   The impact of language in our society is undeniable. And the misuse of *macho* hints at a deeper cultural misunderstanding that extends beyond mere word definitions.

Questions for Discussion

1. The author gives two contrasting meanings of the word *macho*. What does she believe are the origins of these meanings?

2. What is the tone of the essay? How does diction contribute to this tone?

3. List other words that we use in stereotyping males or females. In what ways can these words be misleading or dangerous?

4. If you speak a language other than American English, explain a word that has different meanings in these two languages.

Suggestions for Exploring, Writing, and Persuading

1. Write an essay persuading your audience what qualities you believe a "real man" or a "real woman" should have.

2. In an essay, discuss the qualities that men and women have in common.

3. Write an essay in which you support or refute Guilbault's claim that "the misuse of *macho* hints at a deeper cultural misunderstanding that extends beyond mere word definitions."

FICTION

Geoffrey Chaucer (1343–1400)

The son of a London merchant, Geoffrey Chaucer became the greatest of medieval English poets. He served the court of King Edward III on numerous diplomatic missions, particularly to France and to such Italian city-states as Genoa and Florence. An urbane and learned court poet, Chaucer is best known for such long poems as The Book of the Duchess, The House of Fame, Troilus and Criseyde, *and, preeminently,* Canterbury Tales. *The latter, of which "The Wife of Bath's Tale" is a part, consists of a series of stories told*

by a strikingly diverse group of pilgrims traveling from
London to Thomas à Becket's shrine at Canterbury. The
Wife of Bath, who has outlived five husbands, appears to
have joined the pilgrimage to find husband number six.

THE WIFE OF BATH'S TALE (1386-1400)

TRANSLATED BY THEODORE MORRISON

1   In the old days when King Arthur ruled the nation,
Whom Welshmen speak of with such veneration,
This realm we live in was a fairy land.
The fairy queen danced with her jolly band
On the green meadows where they held dominion.
This was, as I have read, the old opinion;
I speak of many hundred years ago.
But no one sees an elf now, as you know,
For in our time the charity and prayers
And all the begging of these holy friars
Who swarm through every nook and every stream
Thicker than motes of dust in a sunbeam,
Blessing our chambers, kitchens, halls, and bowers,
Our cities, towns, and castles, our high towers,
Our villages, our stables, barns, and dairies,
They keep us all from seeing any fairies,
For where you might have come upon an elf
There now you find the holy friar himself
Working his district on industrious legs
And saying his devotions while he begs.
Women are safe now under every tree.
No incubus is there unless it's he,
And all they have to fear from him is shame.

2   It chanced that Arthur had a knight who came
Lustily riding home one day from hawking,
And in his path he saw a maiden walking
Before him, stark alone, right in his course.
This young knight took her maidenhead by force,
A crime at which the outcry was so keen
It would have cost his neck, but that the queen,
With other ladies, begged the king so long
That Arthur spared his life, for right or wrong,
And gave him to the queen, at her own will,
According to her choice, to save or kill.

3   She thanked the king, and later told this knight,
Choosing her time, "You are still in such a plight
Your very life has no security.
I grant your life, if you can answer me

This question: what is the thing that most of all
Women desire? Think, or your neck will fall
Under the ax! If you cannot let me know
Immediately, I give you leave to go
A twelvemonth and a day, no more, in quest
Of such an answer as will meet the test.
But you must pledge your honor to return
And yield your body, whatever you may learn."

4   The knight sighed; he was rueful beyond measure.
But what! He could not follow his own pleasure.
He chose at last upon his way to ride
And with such answer as God might provide
To come back when the year was at the close.
And so he takes his leave, and off he goes.

5   He seeks out every house and every place
Where he has any hope, by luck or grace,
Of learning what thing women covet most.
But it seemed he could not light on any coast
Where on this point two people would agree,
For some said wealth and some said jollity,
Some said position, some said sport in bed
And often to be widowed, often wed.
Some said that to a woman's heart what mattered
Above all else was to be pleased and flattered.
That shaft, to tell the truth, was a close hit.
Men win us best by flattery, I admit,
And by attention. Some say our greatest ease
Is to be free and do just as we please,
And not to have our faults thrown in our eyes,
But always to be praised for being wise.
And true enough, there's not one of us all
Who will not kick if you rub us on a gall.
Whatever vices we may have within,
We won't be taxed with any fault or sin.

6   Some say that women are delighted well
If it is thought that they will never tell
A secret they are trusted with, or scandal.
But that tale isn't worth an old rake handle!
We women, for a fact, can never hold
A secret. Will you hear a story told?
Then witness Midas! For it can be read
In Ovid that he had upon his head
Two ass's ears that he kept out of sight
Beneath his long hair with such skill and sleight
That no one else besides his wife could guess.
He loved her well, and trusted her no less.

He begged her not to make his blemish known,
But keep her knowledge to herself alone.
She swore that never, though to save her skin,
Would she be guilty of so mean a sin,
And yet it seemed to her she nearly died
Keeping a secret locked so long inside.
It swelled about her heart so hard and deep
She was afraid some word was bound to leap
Out of her mouth, and since there was no man
She dared to tell, down to a swamp she ran—
Her heart, until she got there, all agog—
And like a bittern booming in the bog
She put her mouth close to the watery ground:
"Water, do not betray me with your sound!
I speak to you, and you alone," she said.
"Two ass's ears grow on my husband's head!
And now my heart is whole, now it is out.
I'd burst if I held it longer, past all doubt."
Safely, you see, awhile you may confide
In us, but it will out; we cannot hide
A secret. Look in Ovid if you care
To learn what followed; the whole tale is there.

7   This knight, when he perceived he could not find
What women covet most, was low in mind;
But the day had come when homeward he must ride,
And as he crossed a wooded countryside
Some four and twenty ladies there by chance
He saw, all circling in a woodland dance,
And toward this dance he eagerly drew near
In hope of any counsel he might hear.
But the truth was, he had not reached the place
When dance and all, they vanished into space.
No living soul remained there to be seen
Save an old woman sitting on the green,
As ugly a witch as fancy could devise.
As he approached her she began to rise
And said, "Sir knight, here runs no thoroughfare.
What are you seeking with such anxious air?
Tell me! The better may your fortune be.
We old folk know a lot of things," said she.

8   "Good mother," said the knight, "my life's to pay,
That's all too certain, if I cannot say
What women covet most. If you could tell
That secret to me, I'd requite you well."

9   "Give me your hand," she answered. "Swear me true
That whatsoever I next ask of you,

You'll do it if it lies within your might
And I'll enlighten you before the night."

10   "Granted, upon my honor," he replied.

11   "Then I dare boast, and with no empty pride,
Your life is safe," she told him. "Let me die
If the queen herself won't say the same as I.
Let's learn if the haughtiest of all who wear
A net or coverchief upon their hair
Will be so forward as to answer 'no'
To what I'll teach you. No more; let us go."
With that she whispered something in his ear,
And told him to be glad and have no fear.

12   When they had reached the court, the knight declared
That he had kept his day, and was prepared
To give his answer, standing for his life.
Many the wise widow, many the wife,
Many the maid who rallied to the scene,
And at the head as justice sat the queen.
Then silence was enjoined; the knight was told
In open court to say what women hold
Precious above all else. He did not stand
Dumb like a beast, but spoke up at command
And plainly offered them his answering word
In manly voice, so that the whole court heard.

13   "My liege and lady, most of all," said he,
"Women desire to have the sovereignty
And sit in rule and government above
Their husbands, and to have their way in love.
That is what most you want. Spare me or kill
As you may like; I stand here by your will."

14   No widow, wife, or maid gave any token
Of contradicting what the knight had spoken.
He should not die; he should be spared instead;
He was worthy of his life, the whole court said.

15   The old woman whom the knight met on the green
Sprang up at this. "My sovereign lady queen,
Before your court has risen, do me right!
It was I who taught this answer to the knight,
For which he pledged his honor in my hand,
Solemnly, that the first thing I demand,
He would do it, if it lay within his might.
Before the court I ask you, then, sir knight,
To take me," said the woman, "as your wife,
For well you know that I have saved your life.
Deny me, on your honor, if you can."

16   "Alas," replied this miserable man,

"That was my promise, it must be confessed.
For the love of God, though, choose a new request!
Take all my wealth, and let my body be."

17   "If that's your tune, then curse both you and me,"
She said. "Though I am ugly, old, and poor,
I'll have, for all the metal and the ore
That under earth is hidden or lies above,
Nothing, except to be your wife and love."

18   "My love? No, my damnation, if you can!
Alas," he said, "that any of my clan
Should be so miserably misallied!"

19   All to no good; force overruled his pride,
And in the end he is constrained to wed,
And marries his old wife and goes to bed.

20   Now some will charge me with an oversight
In failing to describe the day's delight,
The merriment, the food, the dress at least.
But I reply, there was no joy nor feast;
There was only sorrow and sharp misery.
He married her in private, secretly,
And all day after, such was his distress,
Hid like an owl from his wife's ugliness.

21   Great was the woe this knight had in his head
When in due time they both were brought to bed.
He shuddered, tossed, and turned, and all the while
His old wife lay and waited with a smile.
"Is every knight so backward with a spouse?
Is it," she said, "a law in Arthur's house?
I am your love, your own, your wedded wife,
I am the woman who has saved your life.
I have never done you anything but right.
Why do you treat me this way the first night?
You must be mad, the way that you behave!
Tell me my fault, and as God's love can save,
I will amend it, truly, if I can."

22   "Amend it?" answered this unhappy man.
"It can never be amended, truth to tell.
You are so loathsome and so old as well,
And your low birth besides is such a cross
It is no wonder that I turn and toss.
God take my woeful spirit from my breast!"

23   "Is this," she said, "the cause of your unrest?"

24   "No wonder!" said the knight. "It truly is."

25   "Now sir," she said, "I could amend all this
Within three days, if it should please me to,
And if you deal with me as you should do.

26   "But since you speak of that nobility
      That comes from ancient wealth and pedigree,
      As if *that* constituted gentlemen,
      I hold such arrogance not worth a hen!
      The man whose virtue is pre-eminent,
      In public and alone, always intent
      On doing every generous act he can,
      Take him—he is the greatest gentleman!
      Christ wills that we should claim nobility
      From him, not from old wealth or family.
      Our elders left us all that they were worth
      And through their wealth and blood we claim high birth,
      But never, since it was beyond their giving,
      Could they bequeath to us their virtuous living;
      Although it first conferred on them the name
      Of gentlemen, they could not leave that claim!

27   "Dante the Florentine on this was wise:
      'Frail is the branch on which man's virtues rise'—
      Thus runs his rhyme—'God's goodness wills that we
      Should claim from him alone nobility.'
      Thus from our elders we can only claim
      Such temporal things as men may hurt and maim.

28   "It is clear enough that true nobility
      Is not bequeathed along with property,
      For many a lord's son does a deed of shame
      And yet, God knows, enjoys his noble name.
      But though descended from a noble house
      And elders who were wise and virtuous,
      If he will not follow his elders, who are dead,
      But leads, himself, a shameful life instead,
      He is not noble, be he duke or earl.
      It is the churlish deed that makes the churl.
      And therefore, my dear husband, I conclude
      That though my ancestors were rough and rude,
      Yet may Almighty God confer on me
      The grace to live, as I hope, virtuously.
      Call me of noble blood when I begin
      To live in virtue and to cast out sin.

29   "As for my poverty, at which you grieve,
      Almighty God in whom we all believe
      In willful poverty chose to lead his life,
      And surely every man and maid and wife
      Can understand that Jesus, heaven's king,
      Would never choose a low or vicious thing.
      A poor and cheerful life is nobly led;
      So Seneca and others have well said.

The man so poor he doesn't have a stitch,
If he thinks himself repaid, I count him rich.
He that is covetous, he is the poor man,
Pining to have the things he never can.
It is of cheerful mind, true poverty.
Juvenal says about it happily:
'The poor man as he goes along his way
And passes thieves is free to sing and play.'
Poverty is a good we loathe, a great
Reliever of our busy worldly state,
A great amender also of our minds
As he that patiently will bear it finds.
And poverty, for all it seems distressed,
Is a possession no one will contest.
Poverty, too, by bringing a man low,
Helps him the better both God and self to know.
Poverty is a glass where we can see
Which are our true friends, as it seems to me.
So, sir, I do not wrong you on this score;
Reproach me with my poverty no more.

30   "Now, sir, you tax me with my age; but, sir,
You gentlemen of breeding all aver
That men should not despise old age, but rather
Grant an old man respect, and call him 'father.'

31   "If I am old and ugly, as you have said,
You have less fear of being cuckolded,
For ugliness and age, as all agree,
Are notable guardians of chastity.
But since I know in what you take delight,
I'll gratify your worldly appetite.

32   "Choose now, which of two courses you will try:
To have me old and ugly till I die
But evermore your true and humble wife,
Never displeasing you in all my life,
Or will you have me rather young and fair
And take your chances on who may repair
Either to your house on account of me
Or to some other place, it well may be.
Now make your choice, whichever you prefer."

33   The knight took thought, and sighed, and said to her
At last, "My love and lady, my dear wife,
In your wise government I put my life.
Choose for yourself which course will best agree
With pleasure and honor, both for you and me.
I do not care, choose either of the two;
I am content, whatever pleases you."

34   "Then have I won from you the sovereignty,
Since I may choose and rule at will?" said she.

35   He answered, "That is best, I think, dear wife."

36   "Kiss me," she said. "Now we are done with strife,
For on my word, I will be both to you,
That is to say, fair, yes, and faithful too.
May I die mad unless I am as true
As ever wife was since the world was new.
Unless I am as lovely to be seen
By morning as an empress or a queen
Or any lady between east and west,
Do with my life or death as you think best.
Lift up the curtain, see what you may see."

37   And when the knight saw what had come to be
And knew her as she was, so young, so fair,
His joy was such that it was past compare.
He took her in his arms and gave her kisses
A thousand times on end; he bathed in blisses.
And she obeyed him also in full measure
In everything that tended to his pleasure.

38   And so they lived in full joy to the end.
And now to all us women may Christ send
Submissive husbands, full of youth in bed,
And grace to outlive all the men we wed.
And I pray Jesus to cut short the lives
Of those who won't be governed by their wives;
And old, ill-tempered niggards who hate expense,
God promptly bring them down with pestilence!

Questions for Discussion

1. Why does King Arthur leave the knight's fate to be decided by the queen? In what ways is his doing so appropriate?

2. What, according to the old woman, do women most desire? Explain why you agree or do not agree with her assessment.

3. Defend your point of view as to why the knight's correct answer should or should not save him from the penalty of death for committing rape.

4. What attitude does the knight display in answering the old woman's demand that he marry her? What is the old woman's answer to his complaint that she is old, ugly, poor, and common?

5. In the end, the knight allows his wife to decide whether she will be beautiful or faithful. In what ways is this decision appropriate? What does it suggest that the knight has learned?

Suggestions for Exploring, Writing, and Persuading

1. In what ways is the knight's search for what women most want a quest? In what ways does this quest gently mock the traditional knightly quest?

2. What does this tale reveal about its teller, the Wife of Bath?

3. Write an essay arguing that the old woman's statement about what women want most is or is not accurate and suggesting other possible answers.

Nathaniel Hawthorne (1804–1864)

One of America's greatest fiction writers, Nathaniel Hawthorne was born in Salem, Massachusetts, and was strongly influenced by his Puritan heritage. The Scarlet Letter *(1850) is considered an American classic.* The House of Seven Gables *(1851) and* The Blithedale Romance *(1852) continued his stories about New England, but in his last novel,* The Marble Faun *(1860), Hawthorne chose Italy as his setting. In his short story collections—*Twice-Told Tales *(1837),* Mosses from an Old Manse *(1846), and* The Snow-Image, and Other Twice-Told Tales *(1851)—Hawthorne gave American literature some of its most memorable short fiction. Many of these stories, like "The Birth-Mark," portray men who overestimate their own intelligence and power over science and consequently lose touch with the heart of humanity. Though Hawthorne seldom portrayed successful marriages in his fiction, his own marriage was a loving and lasting one.*

THE BIRTH-MARK   (1843)

1   In the latter part of the last century, there lived a man of science—an eminent proficient in every branch of natural philosophy—who, not long before our story opens, had made experience of a spiritual affinity, more attractive than any chemical one. He had left his laboratory to the care of an assistant, cleared his fine countenance from the furnace-smoke, washed the stain of acids from his fingers, and persuaded a beautiful woman to become his wife. In those days, when the comparatively recent discovery of electricity, and other kindred mysteries of nature, seemed to open paths into the region of miracle, it was not unusual for the love of science to rival the love of woman, in its depth and absorbing energy. The higher intellect, the imagination, the spirit, and even the heart, might all find their congenial aliment in pursuits which, as some of their ardent votaries believed, would ascend from one step of powerful intelligence to another, until the philosopher should lay his hand on the secret of creative force, and perhaps make new worlds for himself. We know not

whether Aylmer possessed this degree of faith in man's ultimate control over nature. He had devoted himself, however, too unreservedly to scientific studies, ever to be weaned from them by any second passion. His love for his young wife might prove the stronger of the two; but it could only be by intertwining itself with his love of science, and uniting the strength of the latter to its own.

2   Such a union accordingly took place, and was attended with truly remarkable consequences, and a deeply impressive moral. One day, very soon after their marriage, Aylmer sat gazing at his wife, with a trouble in his countenance that grew stronger, until he spoke.

3   "Georgiana," said he, "has it never occurred to you that the mark upon your cheek might be removed?"

4   "No, indeed," said she, smiling; but perceiving the seriousness of his manner, she blushed deeply. "To tell you the truth, it has been so often called a charm, that I was simple enough to imagine it might be so."

5   "Ah, upon another face, perhaps it might," replied her husband. "But never on yours! No, dearest Georgiana, you came so nearly perfect from the hand of Nature, that this slightest possible defect—which we hesitate whether to term a defect or a beauty—shocks me, as being the visible mark of earthly imperfection."

6   "Shocks you, my husband!" cried Georgiana, deeply hurt; at first reddening with momentary anger, but then bursting into tears. "Then why did you take me from my mother's side? You cannot love what shocks you!"

7   To explain this conversation, it must be mentioned, that, in the centre of Georgiana's left cheek, there was a singular mark, deeply interwoven, as it were, with the texture and substance of her face. In the usual state of her complexion,—a healthy, though delicate bloom,—the mark wore a tint of deeper crimson, which imperfectly defined its shape amid the surrounding rosiness. When she blushed, it gradually became more indistinct, and finally vanished amid the triumphant rush of blood, that bathed the whole check with its brilliant glow. But, if any shifting emotion caused her to turn pale, there was the mark again, a crimson stain upon the snow, in what Aylmer sometimes deemed an almost fearful distinctness. Its shape bore not a little similarity to the human hand, though of the smallest pigmy size. Georgiana's lovers were wont to say, that some fairy, at her birth-hour, had laid her tiny hand upon the infant's cheek, and left this impress there, in token of the magic endowments that were to give her such sway over all hearts. Many a desperate swain would have risked life for the privilege of pressing his lips to the mysterious hand. It must not be concealed, however, that the impression wrought by this fairy sign-manual varied exceedingly, according to the difference of temperament in the beholders. Some fastidious persons—but they were exclusively of her own sex—affirmed that the Bloody Hand, as they chose to call it, quite destroyed the effect of Georgiana's beauty, and rendered her countenance even hideous. But it would be as reasonable to

say that one of those small blue stains, which sometimes occur in the purest statuary marble, would convert the Eve of Powers to a monster. Masculine observers, if the birth-mark did not heighten their admiration, contented themselves with wishing it away, that the world might possess one living specimen of ideal loveliness, without the semblance of a flaw. After his marriage—for he thought little or nothing of the matter before—Aylmer discovered that this was the case with himself.

8   Had she been less beautiful—if Envy's self could have found aught else to sneer at—he might have felt his affection heightened by the prettiness of this mimic hand, now vaguely portrayed, now lost, now stealing forth again and glimmering to-and-fro with every pulse of emotion that throbbed within her heart. But, seeing her otherwise so perfect, he found this one defect grow more and more intolerable, with every moment of their united lives. It was the fatal flaw of humanity, which Nature, in one shape or another, stamps ineffaceably on all her productions, either to imply that they are temporary and finite, or that their perfection must be wrought by toil and pain. The Crimson Hand expressed the ineludible gripe, in which mortality clutches the highest and purest of earthly mould, degrading them into kindred with the lowest, and even with the very brutes, like whom their visible frames return to dust. In this manner, selecting it as the symbol of his wife's liability to sin, sorrow, decay, and death, Alymer's sombre imagination was not long in rendering the birth-mark a frightful object, causing him more trouble and horror than ever Georgiana's beauty, whether of soul or sense, had given him delight.

9   At all the seasons which should have been their happiest, he invariable and without intending it—nay, in spite of a purpose to the contrary—reverted to this one disastrous topic. Trifling as it at first appeared, it so connected itself with innumerable trains of thought, and modes of feeling, that it became the central point of all. With the morning twilight, Aylmer opened his eyes upon his wife's face, and recognized the symbol of imperfection; and when they sat together at the evening hearth, his eyes wandered stealthily to her cheek, and beheld, flickering with the blaze of the wood fire, the spectral Hand that wrote mortality, where he would fain have worshipped. Georgiana soon learned to shudder at his gaze. It needed but a glance, with the peculiar expression that his face often wore, to change the roses of her cheek into a deathlike paleness, amid which the Crimson Hand was brought strongly out, like a bas-relief of ruby on the whitest marble.

10   Late, one night, when the lights were growing dim, so as hardly to betray the stain on the poor wife's cheek, she herself, for the first time, voluntarily took up the subject.

11   "Do you remember, my dear Aylmer," said she, with a feeble attempt at a smile—"have you any recollection of a dream, last night, about this odious Hand?"

12   "None!—none whatever!" replied Aylmer, starting; but then he added in a dry, cold tone, affected for the sake of concealing the real depth of

his emotion:—"I might well dream of it; for before I fell asleep, it had taken a pretty firm hold of my fancy."

13   "And you did dream of it," continued Georgiana, hastily; for she dreaded lest a gush of tears should interrupt what she had to say—"A terrible dream! I wonder that you can forget it. Is it possible to forget this one expression?—'It is in her heart now—we must have it out'—Reflect, my husband; for by all means I would have you recall that dream."

14   The mind is in a sad note, when Sleep, the all-involving, cannot confine her spectres within the dim region of her sway, but suffers them to break forth, affrighting this actual life with secrets that perchance belong to a deeper one. Aylmer now remembered his dream. He had fancied himself, with his servant Aminadab, attempting an operation for the removal of the birth-mark. But the deeper went the knife, the deeper sank the Hand, until at length its tiny grasp appeared to have caught hold of Georgiana's heart; whence, however, her husband was inexorably resolved to cut or wrench it away.

15   When the dream had shaped itself perfectly in his memory, Aylmer sat in his wife's presence with a guilty feeling. Truth often finds its way to the mind close-muffled in robes of sleep, and then speaks with uncompromising directness of matters in regard to which we practise an unconscious self-deception, during our waking moments. Until now, he had not been aware of the tyrannizing influence acquired by one idea over his mind, and of the lengths which he might find in his heart to go, for the sake of giving himself peace.

16   "Aylmer," resumed Georgiana, solemnly, "I know not what may be the cost to both of us, to rid me of this fatal birth-mark. Perhaps its removal may cause cureless deformity. Or, it may be, the stain goes as deep as life itself. Again, do we know that there is a possibility, on any terms, of unclasping the firm gripe of this little Hand, which was laid upon me before I came into the world?"

17   "Dearest Georgiana, I have spent much thought upon the subject," hastily interrupted Aylmer—"I am convinced of the perfect practicability of its removal."

18   "If there be the remotest possibility of it," continued Georgiana, "let the attempt be made, at whatever risk. Danger is nothing to me; for life—while this hateful mark makes me the object of your horror and disgust—life is a burthen which I would fling down with joy. Either remove this dreadful Hand, or take my wretched life! You have deep science! All the world bears witness of it. You have achieved great wonders! Cannot you remove this little little mark, which I cover with the tips of two small fingers? Is this beyond your power, for the sake of your own peace, and to save your poor wife from madness?"

19   "Noblest—dearest—tenderest wife!" cried Aylmer, rapturously. "Doubt not my power. I have already given this matter the deepest thought—thought which might almost have enlightened me to create a being less perfect than yourself. Georgiana, you have led me deeper than ever into

the heart of science. I feel myself fully competent to render this dear cheek as faultless as its fellow; and then, most beloved, what will be my triumph, when I shall have corrected what Nature left imperfect, in her fairest work! Even Pygmalion, when his sculptured woman assumed life, felt not greater ecstasy than mine will be."

20   "It is resolved, then," said Georgiana, faintly smiling,—"And, Aylmer, spare me not, though you should find the birth-mark take refuge in my heart at last."

21   Her husband tenderly kissed her cheek—her right cheek—not that which bore the impress of the Crimson Hand.

22   The next day, Aylmer apprized his wife of a plan that he had formed, whereby he might have opportunity for the intense thought and constant watchfulness, which the proposed operation would require; while Georgiana, likewise, would enjoy the perfect repose essential to its success. They were to seclude themselves in the extensive apartments occupied by Aylmer as a laboratory, and where, during his toilsome youth, he had made discoveries in the elemental powers of nature, that had roused the admiration of all the learned societies in Europe. Seated calmly in this laboratory, the pale philosopher had investigated the secrets of the highest cloud-region, and of the profoundest mines; he had satisfied himself of the causes that kindled and kept alive the fires of the volcano; and had explained the mystery of fountains, and how it is that they gush forth, some so bright and pure, and others with such rich medicinal virtues, from the dark bosom of the earth. Here, too, at an earlier period, he had studied the wonders of the human frame, and attempted to fathom the very process by which Nature assimilates all her precious influences from earth and air, and from the spiritual world to create and foster Man, her masterpiece. The latter pursuit, however Aylmer had long laid aside, in unwilling recognition of the truth, against which all seekers sooner or later stumble, that our great creative Mother while she amuses us with apparently working in the broadest sunshine, is yet severely careful to keep her own secrets, and, in spite of her pretended openness, shows us nothing but results. She permits us indeed, to mar, but seldom to mend, and, like a jealous patentee, on no account to make. Now, however, Aylmer resumed these half-forgotten investigations; not, of course, with such hopes or wishes as first suggested them; but because they involved much physiological truth, and lay in the path of his proposed scheme for the treatment of Georgiana.

23   As he led her over the threshold of the laboratory, Georgiana was cold and tremulous. Aylmer looked cheerfully into her face, with intent to reassure her, but was so startled with the intense glow of the birth-mark upon the whiteness of her cheek, that he could not restrain a strong convulsive shudder. His wife fainted.

24   "Aminadab! Aminadab!" shouted Aylmer, stamping violently on the floor.

25   Forthwith, there issued from an inner apartment a man of low stature, but bulky frame, with shaggy hair hanging about his visage, which was

grimed with the vapors of the furnace. This personage had been Aylmer's underworker during his whole scientific career, and was admirably fitted for that office by his great mechanical readiness, and the skill with which, while incapable of comprehending a single principle, he executed all the practical details of his master's experiments. With his vast strength, his shaggy hair, his smoky aspect, and the indescribable earthiness that incrusted him, he seemed to represent man's physical nature; while Aylmer's slender figure, and pale, intellectual face, were no less apt a type of the spiritual element.

26   "Throw open the door of the boudoir, Aminadab," said Aylmer, "and burn a pastille."

27   "Yes, master," answered Aminadab, looking intently at the lifeless form of Georgiana; and then he muttered to himself:-"If she were my wife, I'd never part with that birth-mark."

28   When Georgiana recovered consciousness, she found herself breathing an atmosphere of penetrating fragrance, the gentle potency of which had recalled her from her deathlike faintness. The scene around her looked like enchantment. Aylmer had converted those smoky, dingy, sombre rooms, where he had spent his brightest years in recondite pursuits, into a series of beautiful apartments, not unfit to be the secluded abode of a lovely woman. The walls were hung with gorgeous curtains, which imparted the combination of grandeur and grace, that no other species of adornment can achieve; and as they fell from the ceiling to the floor, their rich and ponderous folds, concealing all angles and straight lines, appeared to shut in the scene from infinite space. For aught Georgiana knew, it might be a pavilion among the clouds. And Aylmer, excluding the sunshine, which would have interfered with his chemical processes, had supplied its place with perfumed lamps, emitting flames of various hue, but all uniting in a soft, empurpled radiance. He now knelt by his wife's side, watching her earnestly, but without alarm; for he was confident in his science, and felt that he could draw a magic circle round her, within which no evil might intrude.

29   "Where am I?—Ah, I remember!" said Georgiana, faintly; and she placed her hand over her cheek, to hide the terrible mark from her husband's eyes.

30   "Fear not, dearest!" exclaimed he. "Do not shrink from me! Believe me, Georgiana, I even rejoice in this single imperfection, since it will be such rapture to remove it."

31   "Oh, spare me!" sadly replied his wife—"Pray do not look at it again. I never can forget that convulsive shudder."

32   In order to soothe Georgiana, and, as it were, to release her mind from the burthen of actual things, Aylmer now put in practice some of the light and playful secrets, which science had taught him among its profounder lore. Airy figures, absolutely bodiless ideas, and forms of unsubstantial beauty came and danced before her, imprinting their momentary footsteps on beams of light. Though she had some indistinct idea of the

method of these optical phenomena, still the illusion was almost perfect enough to warrant the belief that her husband possessed sway over the spiritual world. Then again, when she felt a wish to look forth from her seclusion, immediately, as if her thoughts were answered, the procession of external existence flitted across a screen. The scenery and the figures of actual life were perfectly represented, but with that bewitching, yet indescribable difference, which always makes a picture, an image, or a shadow, so much more attractive than the original. When wearied of this, Aylmer bade her cast her eyes upon a vessel, containing a quantity of earth. She did so, with little interest at first, but was soon startled, to perceive the germ of a plant, shooting upward from the soil. Then came the slender stalk—the leaves gradually unfolded themselves—and amid them was a perfect and lovely flower.

33   "It is magical!" cried Georgiana, "I dare not touch it."

34   "Nay, pluck it," answered Aylmer, "pluck it, and inhale its brief perfume while you may. The flower will wither in a few moments, and leave nothing save its brown seed-vessels—but thence may be perpetuated a race as ephemeral as itself."

35   But Georgiana had no sooner touched the flower than the whole plant suffered a blight, its leaves turning coal-black, as if by the agency of fire.

36   "There was too powerful a stimulus," said Aylmer thoughtfully.

37   To make up for this abortive experiment, he proposed to take her portrait by a scientific process of his own invention. It was to be effected by rays of light striking upon a polished plate of metal. Georgiana assented-but, on looking at the result, was affrighted to find the features of the portrait blurred and indefinable; while the minute figure of a hand appeared where the cheek should have been. Aylmer snatched the metallic plate and threw it into a jar of corrosive acid.

38   Soon, however, he forgot these mortifying failures. In the intervals of study and chemical experiment, he came to her, flushed and exhausted, but seemed invigorated by her presence, and spoke in glowing language of the resources of his art. He gave a history of the long dynasty of the Alchemists, who spent so many ages in quest of the universal solvent, by which the Golden Principle might be elicited from all things vile and base. Aylmer appeared to believe that, by the plainest scientific logic, it was altogether within the limits of possibility to discover this long-sought medium; but, he added, a philosopher who should go deep enough to acquire the power would attain too lofty a wisdom to stoop to the exercise of it. Not less singular were his opinions in regard to the Elixir Vitae. He more than intimated that it was his option to concoct a liquid that should prolong life for years—perhaps interminably—but that it would produce a discord in nature, which all the world, and chiefly the quaffer of the immortal nostrum, would find cause to curse.

39   "Aylmer, are you in earnest?" asked Georgiana, looking at him with amazement and fear; "it is terrible to possess such power, or even to dream of possessing it!"

40   "Oh, do not tremble, my love!" said her husband, "I would not wrong either you or myself by working such inharmonious effects upon our lives. But I would have you consider how trifling, in comparison, is the skill requisite to remove this little Hand."

41   At the mention of the birth-mark, Georgiana, as usual, shrank, as if a red-hot iron had touched her cheek.

42   Again, Aylmer applied himself to his labors. She could hear his voice in the distant furnace-room, giving directions to Aminadab, whose harsh, uncouth, misshapen tones were audible in response, more like the grunt or growl of a brute than human speech. After hours of absence, Aylmer reappeared, and proposed that she should now examine his cabinet of chemical products and natural treasures of the earth. Among the former he showed her a small vial, in which, he remarked, was contained a gentle yet most powerful fragrance, capable of impregnating all the breezes that blow across a kingdom. They were of inestimable value, the contents of that little vial; and, as he said so, he threw some of the perfume into the air, and filled the room with piercing and invigorating delight.

43   "And what is this?" asked Georgiana, pointing to a small crystal globe, containing a gold-colored liquid. "It is so beautiful to the eye, that I could imagine it the Elixir of Life."

44   "In one sense it is," replied Aylmer, "or rather the Elixir of Immortality. It is the most precious poison that ever was concocted in this world. By its aid, I could apportion the lifetime of any mortal at whom you might point your finger. The strength of the dose would determine whether he were to linger out years, or drop dead in the midst of a breath. No king, on his guarded throne, could keep his life, if I, in my private station, should deem that the welfare of millions justified me in depriving him of it."

45   "Why do you keep such a terrific drug?" inquired Georgiana in horror.

46   "Do not mistrust me, dearest!" said her husband, smiling; "its virtuous potency is yet greater than its harmful one. But, see! here is a powerful cosmetic. With a few drops of this, in a vase of water, freckles may be washed away as easily as the hands are cleansed. A stronger infusion would take the blood out of the cheek, and leave the rosiest beauty a pale ghost."

47   "Is it with this lotion that you intend to bathe my cheek?" asked Georgiana anxiously.

48   "Oh, no!" hastily replied her husband—"this is merely superficial. Your case demands a remedy that shall go deeper."

49   In his interviews with Georgiana, Aylmer generally made minute inquiries as to her sensations, and whether the confinement of the rooms, and the temperature of the atmosphere, agreed with her. These questions had such a particular drift that Georgiana began to conjecture that she was already subjected to certain physical influences, either breathed in with the fragrant air, or taken with her food. She fancied likewise—but it might be altogether fancy—that there was a stirring up of her system,— a strange indefinite sensation creeping through her veins, and tingling,

half painfully, half pleasurably, at her heart. Still, whenever she dared to look into the mirror, there she beheld herself, pale as a white rose, and with the crimson birth-mark stamped upon her cheek. Not even Aylmer now hated it so much as she.

50   To dispel the tedium of the hours which her husband found it necessary to devote to the processes of combination and analysis, Georgiana turned over the volumes of his scientific library. In many dark old tomes, she met with chapters full of romance and poetry. They were the works of the philosophers of the middle ages, such as Albertus Magnus, Cornelius Agrippa, Paracelsus, and the famous friar who created the prophetic Brazen Head. All these antique naturalists stood in advance of their centuries, yet were imbued with some of their credulity, and therefore were believed, and perhaps imagined themselves, to have acquired from the investigation of nature a power above nature, and from physics a sway over the spiritual world. Hardly less curious and imaginative were the early volumes of the Transactions of the Royal Society, in which the members, knowing little of the limits of natural possibility, were continually recording wonders, or proposing methods whereby wonders might be wrought.

51   But, to Georgiana, the most engrossing volume was a large folio from her husband's own hand, in which he had recorded every experiment of his scientific career, with its original aim, the methods adopted for its development, and its final success or failure, with the circumstances to which either event was attributable. The book, in truth, was both the history and emblem of his ardent, ambitious, imaginative, yet practical and laborious life. He handled physical details, as if there were nothing beyond them; yet spiritualized them all, and redeemed himself from materialism, by his strong and eager aspiration towards the infinite. In his grasp, the veriest clod of earth assumed a soul. Georgiana, as she read, reverenced Aylmer, and loved him more profoundly than ever, but with a less entire dependence on his judgment than heretofore. Much as he had accomplished, she could not but observe that his most splendid successes were almost invariably failures, if compared with the ideal at which he aimed. His brightest diamonds were the merest pebbles, and felt to be so by himself, in comparison with the inestimable gems which lay hidden beyond his reach. The volume, rich with achievements that had won renown for its author, was yet as melancholy a record as ever mortal hand had penned. It was the sad confession, and continual exemplification, of the short-comings of the composite man—the spirit burthened with clay and working in matter—and of the despair that assails the higher nature at finding itself so miserably thwarted by the earthly part. Perhaps every man of genius, in whatever sphere, might recognize the image of his own experience in Aylmer's journal.

52   So deeply did these reflections affect Georgiana that she laid her face upon the open volume and burst into tears. In this situation she was found by her husband.

53   "It is dangerous to read in a sorcerer's books," said he, with a smile, though his countenance was uneasy and displeased. "Georgiana, there are pages in that volume, which I can scarcely glance over and keep my senses. Take heed lest it prove as detrimental to you!"

54   "It has made me worship you more than ever," said she.

55   "Ah! wait for this one success," rejoined he, "then worship me if you will. I shall deem myself hardly unworthy of it. But, come! I have sought you for the luxury of your voice. Sing to me, dearest!"

56   So she poured out the liquid music of her voice to quench the thirst of his spirit. He then took his leave, with a boyish exuberance of gaiety, assuring her that her seclusion would endure but a little longer, and that the result was already certain. Scarcely had he departed, when Georgiana felt irresistibly impelled to follow him. She had forgotten to inform Aylmer of a symptom, which, for two or three hours past, had begun to excite her attention. It was a sensation in the fatal birth-mark, not painful, but which induced a restlessness throughout her system. Hastening after her husband, she intruded, for the first time, into the laboratory.

57   The first thing that struck her eye was the furnace, that hot and fever-ish worker, with the intense glow of its fire, which, by the quantities of soot clustered above it, seemed to have been burning for ages. There was a distilling apparatus in full operation. Around the room were retorts, tubes, cylinders, crucibles, and other apparatus of chemical research. An electrical machine stood ready for immediate use. The atmosphere felt oppressively close, and was tainted with gaseous odors, which had been tormented forth by the processes of science. The severe and homely sim-plicity of the apartment, with its naked walls and brick pavement, looked strange, accustomed as Georgiana had become to the fantastic elegance of her boudoir. But what chiefly, indeed almost solely, drew her attention, was the aspect of Aylmer himself.

58   He was pale as death, anxious, and absorbed, and hung over the fur-nace as if it depended upon his utmost watchfulness whether the liquid, which it was distilling, should be the draught of immortal happiness or misery. How different from the sanguine and joyous mien that he had assumed for Georgiana's encouragement!

59   "Carefully now, Aminadab! Carefully, thou human machine! Carefully, thou man of clay!" muttered Aylmer, more to himself than his assistant. "Now, if there be a thought too much or too little, it is all over!"

60   "Ho! ho!" mumbled Aminadab—"look, master, look!"

61   Aylmer raised his eyes hastily, and at first reddened, then grew paler than ever, on beholding Georgiana. He rushed towards her, and seized her arm with a gripe that left the print of his fingers upon it.

62   "Why do you come hither? Have you no trust in your husband?" cried he impetuously. "Would you throw the blight of that fatal birth-mark over my labors? It is not well done. Go, prying woman, go!"

63   "Nay, Aylmer," said Georgiana, with the firmness of which she pos-sessed no stinted endowment, "it is not you that have a right to complain.

You mistrust your wife! You have concealed the anxiety with which you watch the development of this experiment. Think not so unworthily of me, my husband! Tell me all the risk we run; and fear not that I shall shrink, for my share in it is far less than your own!"

64   "No, no, Georgiana!" said Aylmer impatiently, "it must not be."

65   "I submit," replied she calmly. "And, Aylmer, I shall quaff whatever draught you bring me; but it will be on the same principle that would induce me to take a dose of poison, if offered by your hand."

66   "My noble wife," said Aylmer, deeply moved, "I knew not the height and depth of your nature, until now. Nothing shall be concealed. Know, then, that this Crimson Hand, superficial as it seems, has clutched its grasp into your being, with a strength of which I had no previous conception. I have already administered agents powerful enough to do aught except to change your entire physical system. Only one thing remains to be tried. If that fail us, we are ruined!"

67   "Why did you hesitate to tell me this?" asked she.

68   "Because, Georgiana," said Aylmer, in a low voice, "there is danger!"

69   "Danger? There is but one danger—that this horrible stigma shall be left upon my cheek!" cried Georgiana. "Remove it! remove it!—whatever be the cost—or we shall both go mad!"

70   "Heaven knows, your words are too true," said Aylmer, sadly. "And now, dearest, return to your boudoir. In a little while, all will be tested."

71   He conducted her back, and took leave of her with a solemn tenderness, which spoke far more than his words how much was now at stake. After his departure, Georgiana became wrapt in musings. She considered the character of Aylmer, and did it completer justice than at any previous moment. Her heart exulted, while it trembled, at his honorable love, so pure and lofty that it would accept nothing less than perfection, nor miserably make itself contented with an earthlier nature than he had dreamed of. She felt how much more precious was such a sentiment, than that meaner kind which would have borne with the imperfection for her sake, and have been guilty of treason to holy love, by degrading its perfect idea to the level of the actual. And, with her whole spirit, she prayed, that, for a single moment, she might satisfy his highest and deepest conception. Longer than one moment, she well knew, it could not be; for his spirit was ever on the march—ever ascending—and each instant required something that was beyond the scope of the instant before.

72   The sound of her husband's footsteps aroused her. He bore a crystal goblet, containing a liquor colorless as water, but bright enough to be the draught of immortality. Aylmer was pale; but it seemed rather the consequence of a highly wrought state of mind, and tension of spirit, than of fear or doubt.

73   "The concoction of the draught has been perfect," said he, in answer to Georgiana's look. "Unless all my science have deceived me, it cannot fail."

74   "Save on your account, my dearest Aylmer," observed his wife, "I might wish to put off this birth-mark of mortality by relinquishing mortality itself, in preference to any other mode. Life is but a sad possession to those who have attained precisely the degree of moral advancement at which I stand. Were I weaker and blinder, it might be happiness. Were I stronger, it might be endured hopefully. But, being what I find myself, methinks I am of all mortals the most fit to die."

75   "You are fit for heaven without tasting death!" replied her husband. "But why do we speak of dying? The draught cannot fail. Behold its effect upon this plant!"

76   On the window-seat there stood a geranium, diseased with yellow blotches which had overspread all its leaves. Aylmer poured a small quantity of the liquid upon the soil in which it grew. In a little time, when the roots of the plant had taken up the moisture, the unsightly blotches began to be extinguished in a living verdure.

77   "There needed no proof," said Georgiana, quietly. "Give me the goblet. I joyfully stake all upon your word."

78   "Drink, then, thou lofty creature!" exclaimed Aylmer, with fervid admiration. "There is no taint of imperfection on thy spirit. Thy sensible frame, too, shall be all perfect!"

79   She quaffed the liquid, and returned the goblet to his hand.

80   "It is grateful," said she, with a placid smile. "Methinks it is like water from a heavenly fountain; for it contains I know not what of unobtrusive fragrance and deliciousness. It allays a feverish thirst that had parched me for many days. Now, dearest, let me sleep. My earthly senses are closing over my spirit like the leaves round the heart of a rose at sunset."

81   She spoke the last words with a gentle reluctance, as if it required almost more energy than she could command to pronounce the faint and lingering syllables. Scarcely had they loitered through her lips, ere she was lost in slumber. Aylmer sat by her side, watching her aspect with the emotions proper to a man, the whole value of whose existence was involved in the process now to be tested. Mingled with this mood, however, was the philosophic investigation, characteristic of the man of science. Not the minutest symptom escaped him. A heightened flush of the cheek—a slight irregularity of breath—a quiver of the eyelid—a hardly perceptible tremor through the frame—such were the details which, as the moments passed, he wrote down in his folio volume. Intense thought had set its stamp upon every previous page of that volume; but the thoughts of years were all concentrated upon the last.

82   While thus employed, he failed not to gaze often at the fatal Hand, and not without a shudder. Yet once, by a strange and unaccountable impulse, he pressed it with his lips. His spirit recoiled, however, in the very act, and Georgiana, out of the midst of her deep sleep, moved uneasily and murmured as if in remonstrance. Again, Aylmer resumed his watch. Nor was it without avail. The Crimson Hand, which at first had been strongly visible upon the marble paleness of Georgiana's

cheek now grew more faintly outlined. She remained not less pale than ever; but the birth-mark, with every breath that came and went, lost somewhat of its former distinctness. Its presence had been awful; its departure was more awful still. Watch the stain of the rainbow fading out of the sky; and you will know how that mysterious symbol passed away.

83   "By Heaven, it is well nigh gone!" said Aylmer to himself, in almost irrepressible ecstasy. "I can scarcely trace it now. Success! Success! And now it is like the faintest rose-color. The slightest flush of blood across her cheek would overcome it. But she is so pale!"

84   He drew aside the window-curtain and suffered the light of natural day to fall into the room and rest upon her cheek. At the same time, he heard a gross, hoarse chuckle, which he had long known as his servant Aminadab's expression of delight.

85   "Ah, clod! Ah, earthly mass!" cried Aylmer, laughing in a sort of frenzy. "You have served me well! Matter and Spirit—Earth and Heaven—have both done their part in this! Laugh, thing of senses! You have earned the right to laugh."

86   These exclamations broke Georgiana's sleep. She slowly unclosed her eyes and gazed into the mirror, which her husband had arranged for that purpose. A faint smile flitted over her lips, when she recognized how barely perceptible was now that Crimson Hand, which had once blazed forth with such disastrous brilliancy as to scare away all their happiness. But then her eyes sought Aylmer's face, with a trouble and anxiety that he could by no means account for.

87   "My poor Aylmer!" murmured she.

88   "Poor? Nay, richest! Happiest! Most favored!" exclaimed he. "My peerless bride, it is successful! You are perfect!"

89   "My poor Aylmer!" she repeated, with a more than human tenderness. "You have aimed loftily!—you have done nobly! Do not repent, that, with so high and pure a feeling, you have rejected the best that earth could offer. Aylmer—dearest Aylmer—I am dying!"

90   Alas, it was too true! The fatal Hand had grappled with the mystery of life, and was the bond by which an angelic spirit kept itself in union with a mortal frame. As the last crimson tint of the birth-mark—that sole token of human imperfection—faded from her cheek, the parting breath of the now perfect woman passed into the atmosphere, and her soul, lingering a moment near her husband, took its heavenward flight. Then a hoarse, chuckling laugh was heard again! Thus ever does the gross Fatality of Earth exult in its invariable triumph over the immortal essence, which, in this dim sphere of half-development, demands the completeness of a higher state. Yet, had Aylmer reached a profounder wisdom, he need not thus have flung away the happiness, which would have woven his mortal life of the self-same texture with the celestial. The momentary circumstance was strong for him; he failed to look beyond the shadowy scope of Time, and living once for all in Eternity, to find the perfect Future in the present.

Questions for Discussion

1. Describe the elevated view of science that, according to Hawthorne, existed for some people at the end of the eighteenth century.

2. Explain why or how "the love of science" might "rival the love of woman." Why would the two be opposing forces? How does Aylmer try to blend the two?

3. Why did the birthmark not bother Aylmer when he courted Georgiana yet bother him after marriage? What does it represent to him? Why?

4. How do Aylmer's dream and the pattern of the results in Aylmer's experiments foreshadow the end of the story?

5. How and why do the views of women and men about the birthmark differ?

6. Why does Georgiana agree to submit to Aylmer's treatments? What does the wilting of the flower when Georgiana touches it suggest about these treatments?

7. Why is Aylmer upset when his wife enters his laboratory?

8. If Aylmer represents science, what does Aminadab represent?

9. Explain Georgiana's statement to Aylmer: "[Y]ou have aimed loftily; you have done nobly. Do not repent that with so high and pure a feeling, you have rejected the best the earth could offer."

10. How does the last sentence sum up one of Hawthorne's major points?

Suggestions for Exploring, Writing, and Persuading

1. Apply Hawthorne's statement, "She [Mother Nature] permits us indeed, to mar, but seldom to mend, and, like a jealous patentee, on no account to make," to one aspect of modern science, such as cloning.

2. The story is full of symbolic meaning from the birthmark itself to nature. In an essay, explain one or more of the symbols.

3. In an essay, explain and illustrate what you think the theme of Hawthorne's story is.

4. After analyzing the character of Aylmer and examining his motivation, argue that he is or is not guilty of hubris which costs Georgiana her life.

5. Contrast Georgiana's situation with that of the girl child in "Barbie Doll."

Kate Chopin (1850–1904)

Katherine O'Flaherty was born in St. Louis, Missouri, but moved to Louisiana when she married Oscar Chopin in 1870. New Orleans and the Grande Isle are the setting for most of her stories and for her novel The Awakening *(1899), which shocked readers because of her treatment of adultery*

*and suicide. Chopin's stories deal with marriages that are
failing, women in the process of achieving independence, or
subjects such as miscegenation and integration. "Désirée's
Baby" deals honestly with women's emotions.*

DÉSIRÉE'S BABY   (1894)

1   As the day was pleasant, Madame Valmondé drove over to L'Abri to
see Désirée and the baby.

2   It made her laugh to think of Désirée with a baby. Why, it seemed but
yesterday that Désirée was little more than a baby herself; when Monsieur in riding through the gateway of Valmondé had found her lying
asleep in the shadow of the big stone pillar.

3   The little one awoke in his arms and began to cry for "Dada." That was
as much as she could do or say. Some people thought she might have
strayed there of her own accord, for she was of the toddling age. The pre-
vailing belief was that she had been purposely left by a party of Texans,
whose canvas-covered wagon, late in the day, had crossed the ferry that
Coton Maïs kept, just below the plantation. In time Madame Valmondé
abandoned every speculation but the one that Désirée had been sent to
her by a beneficent Providence to be the child of her affection, seeing
that she was without child of the flesh. For the girl grew to be beautiful
and gentle, affectionate and sincere—the idol of Valmondé.

4   It was no wonder, when she stood one day against the stone pillar in
whose shadow she had lain asleep, eighteen years before, that Armand
Aubigny riding by and seeing her there, had fallen in love with her. That
was the way all the Aubignys fell in love, as if struck by a pistol shot. The
wonder was that he had not loved her before; for he had known her since
his father brought him home from Paris, a boy of eight, after his mother
died there. The passion that awoke in him that day, when he saw her at
the gate, swept along like an avalanche, or like a prairie fire, or like anything that drives headlong over all obstacles.

5   Monsieur Valmondé grew practical and wanted things well considered:
that is, the girl's obscure origin. Armand looked into her eyes and did not
care. He was reminded that she was nameless. What did it matter about
a name when he could give her one of the oldest and proudest in
Louisiana? He ordered the *corbeille* from Paris, and contained himself
with what patience he could until it arrived; then they were married.

6   Madame Valmondé had not seen Désirée and the baby for four weeks.
When she reached L'Abri she shuddered at the first sight of it, as she always
did. It was a sad looking place, which for many years had not known the
gentle presence of a mistress, old Monsieur Aubigny having married and
buried his wife in France, and she having loved her own land too well ever
to leave it. The roof came down steep and black like a cowl, reaching out
beyond the wide galleries that encircled the yellow stuccoed house. Big,
solemn oaks grew close to it, and their thick-leaved, far-reaching

branches shadowed it like a pall. Young Aubigny's rule was a strict one, too, and under it his negroes had forgotten how to be gay, as they had been during the old master's easy-going and indulgent lifetime.

7   The young mother was recovering slowly, and lay full length, in her soft white muslins and laces, upon a couch. The baby was beside her, upon her arm, where he had fallen asleep, at her breast. The yellow nurse woman sat beside a window fanning herself.

8   Madame Valmondé bent her portly figure over Désirée and kissed her, holding her an instant tenderly in her arms. Then she turned to the child.

9   "This is not the baby!" she exclaimed, in startled tones. French was the language spoken at Valmondé in those days.

10   "I knew you would be astonished," laughed Désirée, "at the way he has grown. The little *cochon de lait!* Look at his legs, mamma, and his hands and fingernails,—real finger-nails. Zandrine had to cut them this morning. Isn't it true, Zandrine?"

11   The woman bowed her turbaned head majestically, "Mais si, Madame."

12   "And the way he cries," went on Désirée, "is deafening. Armand heard him the other day as far away as La Blanche's cabin."

13   Madame Valmondé had never removed her eyes from the child. She lifted it and walked with it over to the window that was lightest. She scanned the baby narrowly, then looked as searchingly at Zandrine, whose face was turned to gaze across the fields.

14   "Yes, the child has grown, has changed," said Madame Valmondé, slowly, as she replaced it beside its mother. "What does Armand say?"

15   Désirée's face became suffused with a glow that was happiness itself.

16   "Oh, Armand is the proudest father in the parish, I believe, chiefly because it is a boy, to bear his name; though he says not,—that he would have loved a girl as well. But I know it isn't true. I know he says that to please me. And mamma," she added, drawing Madame Valmondé's head down to her, and speaking in a whisper, "he hasn't punished one of them— not one of them—since baby is born. Even Négrillon, who pretended to have burnt his leg that he might rest from work—he only laughed, and said Négrillon was a great scamp. Oh, mamma, I'm so happy; it frightens me."

17   What Désirée said was true. Marriage, and later the birth of his son, had softened Armand Aubigny's imperious and exacting nature greatly. This was what made the gentle Désirée so happy, for she loved him desperately. When he frowned she trembled, but loved him. When he smiled, she asked no greater blessing of God. But Armand's dark, handsome face had not often been disfigured by frowns since the day he fell in love with her.

18   When the baby was about three months old, Désirée awoke one day to the conviction that there was something in the air menacing her peace. It was at first too subtle to grasp. It had only been a disquieting suggestion; an air of mystery among the blacks; unexpected visits from far-off neighbors who could hardly account for their coming. Then a strange, an awful change in her husband's manner, which she dared not ask him to explain. When he spoke to her, it was with averted eyes, from which the

old love-light seemed to have gone out. He absented himself from home; and when there, avoided her presence and that of her child, without excuse. And the very spirit of Satan seemed suddenly to take hold of him in his dealings with the slaves. Désirée was miserable enough to die.

19   She sat in her room, one hot afternoon, in her *peignoir*, listlessly drawing through her fingers the strands of her long, silky brown hair that hung about her shoulders. The baby, half naked, lay asleep upon her own great mahogany bed, that was like a sumptuous throne, with its satin lined half-canopy. One of La Blanche's little quadroon boys—half naked too—stood fanning the child slowly with a fan of peacock feathers. Désirée's eyes had been fixed absently and sadly upon the baby, while she was striving to penetrate the threatening mist that she felt closing about her. She looked from her child to the boy who stood beside him, and back again; over and over. "Ah!" It was a cry that she could not help, which she was not conscious of having uttered. The blood turned like ice in her veins, and a clammy moisture gathered upon her face.

20   She tried to speak to the little quadroon boy; but no sound would come, at first. When he heard his name uttered, he looked up, and his mistress was pointing to the door. He laid aside the great, soft fan, and obediently stole away, over the polished floor, on his bare tiptoes.

21   She stayed motionless, with gaze riveted upon her child, and her face the picture of fright.

22   Presently her husband entered the room, and without noticing her, went to a table and began to search among some papers which covered it.

23   "Armand," she called to him, in a voice which must have stabbed him, if he was human. But he did not notice. "Armand," she said again. Then she rose and tottered toward him. "Armand," she panted once more, clutching his arm, "look at our child. What does it mean? Tell me."

24   He coldly but gently loosened her fingers from about his arm and thrust the hand away from him. "Tell me what it means!" she cried despairingly.

25   "It means," he answered lightly, "that the child is not white; it means that you are not white."

26   A quick conception of all that this accusation meant for her nerved her with unwonted courage to deny it. "It is a lie; it is not true, I am white! Look at my hair, it is brown; and my eyes are gray, Armand, you know they are gray. And my skin is fair," seizing his wrist. "Look at my hand; whiter than yours, Armand," she laughed hysterically.

27   "As white as La Blanche's," he returned cruelly; and went away leaving her alone with their child.

28   When she could hold a pen in her hand, she sent a despairing letter to Madame Valmondé.

29   "My mother, they tell me I am not white. Armand has told me I am not white. For God's sake tell them it is not true. You must know it is not true. I shall die. I must die. I cannot be so unhappy, and live."

30   The answer that came was as brief:

31   "My own Désirée: Come home to Valmondé; back to your mother who loves you. Come with your child."

32   When the letter reached Désirée she went with it to her husband's study, and laid it open upon the desk before which he sat. She was like a stone image: silent, white, motionless after she placed it there.

33   In silence he ran his cold eyes over the written words. He said nothing. "Shall I go, Armand?" she asked in tones sharp with agonized suspense.

34   "Yes, go."

35   "Do you want me to go?"

36   "Yes, I want you to go."

37   He thought Almighty God had dealt cruelly and unjustly with him; and felt, somehow, that he was paying Him back in kind when he stabbed thus into his wife's soul. Moreover he no longer loved her, because of the unconscious injury she had brought upon his home and his name.

38   She turned away like one stunned by a blow, and walked slowly towards the door, hoping he would call her back.

39   "Good-by, Armand," she moaned.

40   He did not answer her. That was his last blow at fate.

41   Désirée went in search of her child. Zandrine was pacing the sombre gallery with it. She took the little one from the nurse's arms with no word of explanation, and descending the steps, walked away, under the live-oak branches.

42   It was an October afternoon; the sun was just sinking. Out in the still fields the negroes were picking cotton.

43   Désirée had not changed the thin white garment nor the slippers which she wore. Her hair was uncovered and the sun's rays brought a golden gleam from its brown meshes. She did not take the broad, beaten road which led to the far-off plantation of Valmondé. She walked across a deserted field, where the stubble bruised her tender feet, so delicately shod, and tore her thin gown to shreds.

44   She disappeared among the reeds and willows that grew thick along the banks of the deep, sluggish bayou; and she did not come back again.

45   Some weeks later there was a curious scene enacted at L'Abri. In the centre of the smoothly swept back yard was a great bonfire. Armand Aubigny sat in the wide hallway that commanded a view of the specta-cle; and it was he who dealt out to a half dozen negroes the material which kept this fire ablaze.

46   A graceful cradle of willow, with all its dainty furbishings, was laid upon the pyre, which had already been fed with the richness of a price-less *layette*. Then there were silk gowns, and velvet and satin ones added to these; laces, too, and embroideries; bonnets and gloves; for the *corbeille* had been of rare quality.

47   The last thing to go was a tiny bundle of letters; innocent little scrib-blings that Désirée had sent to him during the days of their espousal. There was the remnant of one back in the drawer from which he took them. But it was not Désirée's; it was part of an old letter from his mother

to his father. He read it. She was thanking God for the blessing of her husband's love:-

48   "But, above all," she wrote, "night and day, I thank the good God for having so arranged our lives that our dear Armand will never know that his mother, who adores him, belongs to the race that is cursed with the brand of slavery."

Questions for Discussion

1. Define *white* and *quadroon*.
2. Describe the tone used in the phrase "cursed with the brand of slavery." What is the effect of this tone on the meaning of this story? In what ways is the phrase an ironic reversal?
3. Why does Armand choose a foundling for a wife? How does he take advantage of her sweetness and naivety? How does the social structure of this time and place encourage Armand's treatment of Désirée and the slaves?
4. What does Chopin gradually reveal about Armand's character as the story builds? What details reveal this? How consistent is Désirée as a character?
5. Examine Madame Valmondé's motivation. Did she think that Désirée had mixed blood when she found her? Why does she tell Désirée to come home "back to your mother who loves you. Come with your child" instead of answering Désirée's plea to tell Armand that she is white.
6. This story has a surprise ending. For such an ending to be artistically effective, the author should give readers clues that such an eventuality is possible. Explain whether you are sufficiently prepared for the end of the story.

Suggestions for Exploring, Writing, and Persuading

1. Write an essay either on the social acceptability of interracial marriages or on your personal feelings toward them.
2. Go beyond the story to speculate on what happens to Désirée and her baby.
3. Consider the effect of having one's basic identity challenged. Désirée's identity is threatened due to one element of background over which she has no control. Her value as a person in the eyes of her society and in her own eyes is redefined and reduced. Explain the ramifications of loss of or redefinition of identity.
4. Argue that Armand, once he sees that the baby progressively darkens, makes Désirée the scapegoat for his own feelings of culpability.

Charlotte Perkins Gilman (1860–1935)

Charlotte Perkins Gilman was best known during her life-time as a lecturer and author of books on the rights of women and on socialism. Yet today she is most famous for what is generally acknowledged as her best short story, "The Yellow Wallpaper." According to Gilman, the story was written after she had suffered a nervous breakdown. A specialist in nervous diseases, consulted as a result of Gilman's depression, advised her first husband to allow her to participate only in domestic life and to terminate her painting and writing. After three months of this treatment, she was near a mental breakdown. Unlike the narrator of "The Yellow Wallpaper," Gilman went on to a successful second marriage and a career. She continued to suffer from depression at times and committed suicide in 1935 as a result of severe pain caused by cancer.

THE YELLOW WALLPAPER (1899)

1   It is very seldom that mere ordinary people like John and myself secure ancestral halls for the summer.

2   A colonial mansion, a hereditary estate, I would say a haunted house and reach the height of romantic felicity—but that would be asking too much of fate!

3   Still I will proudly declare that there is something queer about it.

4   Else, why should it be let so cheaply? And why have stood so long untenanted?

5   John laughs at me, of course, but one expects that.

6   John is practical in the extreme. He has no patience with faith, an intense horror of superstition, and he scoffs openly at any talk of things not to be felt and seen and put down in figures.

7   John is a physician, and *perhaps*—(I would not say it to a living soul, of course, but this is dead paper and a great relief to my mind)—*perhaps* that is one reason I do not get well faster.

8   You see, he does not believe I am sick! And what can one do?

9   If a physician of high standing, and one's own husband, assures friends and relatives that there is really nothing the matter with one but temporary nervous depression—a slight hysterical tendency—what is one to do?

10   My brother is also a physician, and also of high standing, and he says the same thing.

11   So I take phosphates or phosphites—whichever it is—and tonics, and air and exercise, and journeys, and am absolutely forbidden to "work" until I am well again.

12   Personally, I disagree with their ideas.

13   Personally, I believe that congenial work, with excitement and change, would do me good.

14   But what is one to do?

15   I did write for a while in spite of them; but it *does* exhaust me a good deal—having to be so sly about it, or else meet with heavy opposition.

16   I sometimes fancy that in my condition, if I had less opposition and more society and stimulus—but John says the very worst thing I can do is to think about my condition, and I confess it always makes me feel bad.

17   So I will let it alone and talk about the house.

18   The most beautiful place! It is quite alone, standing well back from the road, quite three miles from the village. It makes me think of English places that you read about, for there are hedges and walls and gates that lock, and lots of separate little houses for the gardeners and people.

19   There is a *delicious* garden! I never saw such a garden—large and shady, full of box-bordered paths, and lined with long grape-covered arbors with seats under them.

20   There were greenhouses, but they are all broken now.

21   There was some legal trouble, I believe, something about the heirs and co-heirs; anyhow, the place has been empty for years.

22   That spoils my ghostliness, I am afraid, but I don't care—there is something strange about the house—I can feel it.

23   I even said so to John one moonlight evening, but he said what I felt was a draught, and shut the window.

24   I get unreasonably angry with John sometimes. I'm sure I never used to be so sensitive. I think it is due to this nervous condition.

25   But John says if I feel so I shall neglect proper self-control; so I take pains to control myself—before him, at least, and that makes me very tired.

26   I don't like our room a bit. I wanted one downstairs that opened onto the piazza and had roses all over the window, and such pretty old-fashioned chintz hangings! But John would not hear of it.

27   He said there was only one window and not room for two beds, and no near room for him if he took another.

28   He is very careful and loving, and hardly lets me stir without special direction.

29   I have a schedule prescription for each hour in the day; he takes all care from me, and so I feel basely ungrateful not to value it more.

30   He said he came here solely on my account, that I was to have perfect rest and all the air I could get. "Your exercise depends on your strength, my dear," said he, "and your food somewhat on your appetite; but air you can absorb all the time." So we took the nursery at the top of the house.

31   It is a big, airy room, the whole floor nearly, with windows that look all ways, and air and sunshine galore. It was nursery first, and then playroom and gymnasium, I should judge, for the windows are barred for little children, and there are rings and things in the walls.

32   The paint and paper look as if a boys' school had used it. It is stripped off—the paper—in great patches all around the head of my bed, about as far as I can reach, and in a great place on the other side of the room low down. I never saw a worse paper in my life. One of those sprawling, flamboyant patterns committing every artistic sin.

33   It is dull enough to confuse the eye in following, pronounced enough constantly to irritate and provoke study, and when you follow the lame uncertain curves for a little distance they suddenly commit suicide—plunge off at outrageous angles, destroy themselves in unheard-of contradictions.

34   The color is repellent, almost revolting: a smouldering unclean yellow, strangely faded by the slow-turning sunlight. It is a dull yet lurid orange in some places, a sickly sulphur tint in others.

35   No wonder the children hated it! I should hate it myself if I had to live in this room long.

36   There comes John, and I must put this away—he hates to have me write a word.

37   We have been here two weeks, and I haven't felt like writing before, since that first day.

38   I am sitting by the window now, up in this atrocious nursery, and there is nothing to hinder my writing as much as I please, save lack of strength.

39   John is away all day, and even some nights when his cases are serious.

40   I am glad my case is not serious!

41   But these nervous troubles are dreadfully depressing.

42   John does not know how much I really suffer. He knows there is no reason to suffer, and that satisfies him.

43   Of course it is only nervousness. It does weigh on me so not to do my duty in any way!

44   I meant to be such a help to John, such a real rest and comfort, and here I am a comparative burden already!

45   Nobody would believe what an effort it is to do what little I am able— to dress and entertain, and order things.

46   It is fortunate Mary is so good with the baby. Such a dear baby!

47   And yet I *cannot* be with him, it makes me so nervous.

48   I suppose John never was nervous in his life. He laughs at me so about this wallpaper!

49   At first he meant to repaper the room, but afterward he said that I was letting it get the better of me, and that nothing was worse for a nervous patient than to give way to such fancies.

50   He said that after the wallpaper was changed it would be the heavy bedstead, and then the barred windows, and then the gate at the head of the stairs, and so on.

51   "You know the place is doing you good," he said, "and really, dear, I don't care to renovate the house just for a three months' rental."

52   "Then do let us go downstairs," I said. "There are such pretty rooms there."

53   Then he took me in his arms and called me a blessed little goose, and said he would go down cellar, if I wished, and have it whitewashed into the bargain.

54   But he is right enough about the beds and windows and things.

55   It is as airy and comfortable a room as anyone need wish, and, of course, I would not be so silly as to make him uncomfortable just for a whim.

56   I'm really getting quite fond of the big room, all but that horrid paper.

57   Out of one window I can see the garden—those mysterious deep-shaded arbors, the riotous old-fashioned flowers, and bushes and gnarly trees.

58   Out of another I get a lovely view of the bay and a little private wharf belonging to the estate. There is a beautiful shaded lane that runs down there from the house. I always fancy I see people walking in these numerous paths and arbors, but John has cautioned me not to give way to fancy in the least. He says that with my imaginative power and habit of story-making, a nervous weakness like mine is sure to lead to all manner of excited fancies, and that I ought to use my will and good sense to check the tendency. So I try.

59   I think sometimes that if I were only well enough to write a little it would relieve the press of ideas and rest me.

60   But I find I get pretty tired when I try.

61   It is so discouraging not to have any advice and companionship about my work. When I get really well, John says we will ask Cousin Henry and Julia down for a long visit; but he says he would as soon put fireworks in my pillow-case as to let me have those stimulating people about now.

62   I wish I could get well faster.

63   But I must not think about that. This paper looks to me as if it *knew* what a vicious influence it had!

64   There is a recurrent spot where the pattern lolls like a broken neck and two bulbous eyes stare at you upside down.

65   I get positively angry with the impertinence of it and the everlastingness. Up and down and sideways they crawl, and those absurd unblinking eyes are everywhere. There is one place where two breadths didn't match, and the eyes go all up and down the line, one a little higher than the other.

66   I never saw so much expression in an inanimate thing before, and we all know how much expression they have! I used to lie awake as a child and get more entertainment and terror out of blank walls and plain furniture than most children could find in a toy-store.

67   I remember what a kindly wink the knobs of our big old bureau used to have, and there was one chair that always seemed like a strong friend.

68   I used to feel that if any of the other things looked too fierce I could always hop into that chair and be safe.

69   The furniture in this room is no worse than inharmonious, however, for we had to bring it all from downstairs. I suppose when this was used as a playroom they had to take the nursery things out, and no wonder! I never saw such ravages as the children have made here.

70   The wallpaper, as I said before, is torn off in spots, and it sticketh closer than a brother—they must have had perseverance as well as hatred.

71   Then the floor is scratched and gouged and splintered, the plaster itself is dug out here and there, and this great heavy bed, which is all we found in the room, looks as if it had been through the wars.

72   But I don't mind it a bit—only the paper.

73   There comes John's sister. Such a dear girl as she is, and so careful of me! I must not let her find me writing.

74   She is a perfect and enthusiastic housekeeper, and hopes for no better profession. I verily believe she thinks it is the writing which made me sick!

75   But I can write when she is out, and see her a long way off from these windows.

76   There is one that commands the road, a lovely shaded winding road, and one that just looks off over the country. A lovely country, too, full of great elms and velvet meadows.

77   This wallpaper has a kind of sub-pattern in a different shade, a particularly irritating one, for you can only see it in certain lights, and not clearly then.

78   But in the places where it isn't faded and where the sun is just so—I can see a strange, provoking, formless sort of figure that seems to skulk about behind that silly and conspicuous front design.

79   There's sister on the stairs!

80   Well, the Fourth of July is over! The people are all gone, and I am tired out. John thought it might do me good to see a little company, so we just had Mother and Nellie and the children down for a week.

81   Of course I didn't do a thing. Jennie sees to everything now.

82   But it tired me all the same.

83   John says if I don't pick up faster he shall send me to Weir Mitchell in the fall.

84   But I don't want to go there at all. I had a friend who was in his hands once, and she says he is just like John and my brother, only more so!

85   Besides, it is such an undertaking to go so far.

86   I don't feel as if it was worthwhile to turn my hand over for anything, and I'm getting dreadfully fretful and querulous.

87   I cry at nothing, and cry most of the time.

88   Of course I don't when John is here, or anybody else, but when I am alone.

89   And I am alone a good deal just now. John is kept in town very often by serious cases, and Jennie is good and lets me alone when I want her to.

90   So I walk a little in the garden or down that lovely lane, sit on the porch under the roses, and lie down up here a good deal.

91   I'm getting really fond of the room in spite of the wallpaper. Perhaps *because* of the wallpaper.

92   It dwells in my mind so!

93   I lie here on this great immovable bed—it is nailed down, I believe—and follow that pattern about by the hour. It is as good as gymnastics, I assure you. I start, we'll say, at the bottom, down in the corner over there where it has not been touched, and I determine for the thousandth time that I *will* follow that pointless pattern to some sort of a conclusion.

94   I know a little of the principle of design, and I know this thing was not arranged on any laws of radiation, or alternation, or repetition, or symmetry, or anything else that I ever heard of.

95 It is repeated, of course, by the breadths, but not otherwise.

96 Looked at in one way, each breadth stands alone; the bloated curves and flourishes—a kind of "debased Romanesque" with delirium tremens—go waddling up and down in isolated columns of fatuity.

97 But, on the other hand, they connect diagonally, and the sprawling outlines run off in great slanting waves of optic horror, like a lot of wallowing sea-weeds in full chase.

98 The whole thing goes horizontally, too, at least it seems so, and I exhaust myself trying to distinguish the order of its going in that direction.

99 They have used a horizontal breadth for a frieze, and that adds wonderfully to the confusion.

100 There is one end of the room where it is almost intact, and there, when the crosslights fade and the low sun shines directly upon it, I can almost fancy radiation after all—the interminable grotesque seems to form around a common center and rush off in headlong plunges of equal distraction.

101 It makes me tired to follow it. I will take a nap, I guess.

102 I don't know why I should write this.

103 I don't want to.

104 I don't feel able.

105 And I know John would think it absurd. But I *must* say what I feel and think in some way—it is such a relief!

106 But the effort is getting to be greater than the relief.

107 Half the time now I am awfully lazy, and lie down ever so much. John says I mustn't lose my strength, and has me take cod liver oil and lots of tonics and things, to say nothing of ale and wine and rare meat.

108 Dear John! He loves me very dearly, and hates to have me sick. I tried to have a real earnest reasonable talk with him the other day, and tell him how I wish he would let me go and make a visit to Cousin Henry and Julia.

109 But he said I wasn't able to go, nor able to stand it after I got there; and I did not make out a very good case for myself, for I was crying before I had finished.

110 It is getting to be a great effort for me to think straight. Just this nervous weakness, I suppose.

111 And dear John gathered me up in his arms, and just carried me upstairs and laid me on the bed, and sat by me and read to me till it tired my head.

112 He said I was his darling and his comfort and all he had, and that I must take care of myself for his sake, and keep well.

113 He says no one but myself can help me out of it, that I must use my will and self-control and not let any silly fancies run away with me.

114 There's one comfort—the baby is well and happy, and does not have to occupy this nursery with the horrid wallpaper.

115 If we had not used it, that blessed child would have! What a fortunate escape! Why, I wouldn't have a child of mine, an impressionable little thing, live in such a room for worlds.

116 I never thought of it before, but it is lucky that John kept me here after all; I can stand it so much easier than a baby, you see.

117   Of course I never mention it to them any more—I am too wise—but I keep watch for it all the same.

118   There are things in that wallpaper that nobody knows about but me, or ever will.

119   Behind that outside pattern the dim shapes get clearer every day.

120   It is always the same shape, only very numerous.

121   And it is like a woman stooping down and creeping about behind that pattern. I don't like it a bit. I wonder—I begin to think—I wish John would take me away from here!

122   It is so hard to talk with John about my case, because he is so wise, and because he loves me so.

123   But I tried it last night.

124   It was moonlight. The moon shines in all around just as the sun does.

125   I hate to see it sometimes, it creeps so slowly, and always comes in by one window or another.

126   John was asleep and I hated to waken him, so I kept still and watched the moonlight on that undulating wallpaper till I felt creepy.

127   The faint figure behind seemed to shake the pattern, just as if she wanted to get out.

128   I got up softly and went to feel and see if the paper *did* move, and when I came back John was awake.

129   "What is it, little girl?" he said. "Don't go walking about like that— you'll get cold."

130   I thought it was a good time to talk, so I told him that I really was not gaining here, and that I wished he would take me away.

131   "Why, darling!" said he. "Our lease will be up in three weeks, and I can't see how to leave before."

132   "The repairs aren't done at home, and I cannot possibly leave town just now. Of course, if you were in any danger, I could and would, but you really are better, dear, whether you can see it or not. I am a doctor, dear, and I know. You are gaining flesh and color, your appetite is better, I feel really much easier about you."

133   "I don't weigh a bit more," said I, "not as much; and my appetite may be better in the evening when you are here but it is worse in the morning when you are away!"

134   "Bless her little heart!" said he with a big hug. "She shall be as sick as she pleases! But now let's improve the shining hours by going to sleep, and talk about it in the morning!"

135   "And you won't go away?" I asked gloomily.

136   "Why, how can I, dear? It is only three weeks more and then we will take a nice little trip of a few days while Jennie is getting the house ready. Really, dear, you are better!"

137   "Better in body perhaps—" I began, and stopped short, for he sat up straight and looked at me with such a stern, reproachful look that I could not say another word.

138   "My darling," said he, "I beg of you, for my sake and for our child's sake, as well as for your own, that you will never for one instant let that idea enter your mind! There is nothing so dangerous, so fascinating, to a temperament like yours. It is a false and foolish fancy. Can you not trust me as a physician when I tell you so?"

139   So of course I said no more on that score, and we went to sleep before long. He thought I was asleep first, but I wasn't, and lay there for hours trying to decide whether that front pattern and the back pattern really did move together or separately.

140   On a pattern like this, by daylight, there is a lack of sequence, a defiance of law, that is a constant irritant to a normal mind.

141   The color is hideous enough, and unreliable enough, and infuriating enough, but the pattern is torturing.

142   You think you have mastered it, but just as you get well under way in following, it turns a back-somersault and there you are. It slaps you in the face, knocks you down, and tramples upon you. It is like a bad dream.

143   The outside pattern is a florid arabesque, reminding one of a fungus. If you can imagine a toadstool in joints, an interminable string of toadstools, budding and sprouting in endless convolutions—why, that is something like it.

144   That is, sometimes!

145   There is one marked peculiarity about this paper, a thing nobody seems to notice but myself, and that is that it changes as the light changes.

146   When the sun shoots in through the east window—I always watch for that first long, straight ray—it changes so quickly that I never can quite believe it.

147   That is why I watch it always

148   By moonlight—the moon shines in all night when there is a moon—I wouldn't know it was the same paper.

149   At night in any kind of light, in twilight, candlelight, lamplight, and worst of all by moonlight, it becomes bars! The outside pattern, I mean, and the woman behind it is as plain as can be.

150   I didn't realize for a long time what the thing was that showed behind, that dim sub-pattern, but now I am quite sure it is a woman.

151   By daylight she is subdued, quiet. I fancy it is the pattern that keeps her so still. It is so puzzling. It keeps me quiet by the hour.

152   I lie down ever so much now. John says it is good for me, and to sleep all I can.

153   Indeed he started the habit by making me lie down for an hour after each meal.

154   It is a very bad habit, I am convinced, for you see, I don't sleep.

155   And that cultivates deceit, for I don't tell them I'm awake—oh, no!

156   The fact is I am getting a little afraid of John.

157   He seems very queer sometimes, and even Jennie has an inexplicable look.

158   It strikes me occasionally, just as a scientific hypothesis, that perhaps it is the paper!

159   I have watched John when he did not know I was looking, and come into the room suddenly on the most innocent excuses, and I've caught him several times *looking at the paper!* And Jennie too. I caught Jennie with her hand on it once.

160   She didn't know I was in the room, and when I asked her in a quiet, a very quiet voice, with the most restrained manner possible, what she was doing with the paper, she turned around as if she had been caught stealing, and looked quite angry—asked me why I should frighten her so!

161   Then she said that the paper stained everything it touched, that she had found yellow smooches on all my clothes and John's and she wished we would be more careful!

162   Did not that sound innocent? But I know she was studying that pattern, and I am determined that nobody shall find it out but myself!

163   Life is very much more exciting now than it used to be. You see, I have something more to expect, to look forward to, to watch. I really do eat better, and am more quiet than I was.

164   John is so pleased to see me improve! He laughed a little the other day, and said I seemed to be flourishing in spite of my wallpaper.

165   I turned it off with a laugh. I had no intention of telling him it was *because* of the wallpaper—he would make fun of me. He might even want to take me away.

166   I don't want to leave now until I have found it out. There is a week more, and I think that will be enough.

167   I'm feeling so much better!

168   I don't sleep much at night, for it is so interesting to watch developments; but I sleep a good deal during the daytime.

169   In the daytime it is tiresome and perplexing.

170   There are always new shoots on the fungus, and new shades of yellow all over it. I cannot keep count of them, though I have tried conscientiously.

171   It is the strangest yellow, the wallpaper! It makes me think of all the yellow things I ever saw—not beautiful ones like buttercups, but old, foul, bad yellow things.

172   But there is something else about that paper—the smell! I noticed it the moment we came into the room, but with so much air and sun it was not bad. Now we have had a week of fog and rain, and whether the windows are open or not, the smell is here.

173   It creeps all over the house.

174   I find it hovering in the dining-room, skulking in the parlor, hiding in the hall, lying in wait for me on the stairs.

175   It gets into my hair.

176   Even when I go to ride, if I turn my head suddenly and surprise it—there is that smell!

177   Such a peculiar odor, too! I have spent hours in trying to analyze it, to find what it smelled like.

178   It is not bad—at first—and very gentle, but quite the subtlest, most enduring odor I ever met.

179   In this damp weather it is awful. I wake up in the night and find it hanging over me.

180   It used to disturb me at first. I thought seriously of burning the house—to reach the smell.

181   But now I am used to it. The only thing I can think of that it is like is the *color* of the paper! A yellow smell.

182   There is a very funny mark on this wall, low down, near the mopboard. A streak that runs round the room. It goes behind every piece of furniture, except the bed, a long, straight, even *smooch*, as if it had been rubbed over and over.

183   I wonder how it was done and who did it, and what they did it for. Round and round and round—round and round and round—it makes me dizzy!

184   I really have discovered something at last.

185   Through watching so much at night, when it changes so, I have finally found out.

186   The front pattern *does* move—and no wonder! The woman behind shakes it!

187   Sometimes I think there are a great many women behind, and sometimes only one, and she crawls around fast, and her crawling shakes it all over.

188   Then in the very bright spots she keeps still, and in the very shady spots she just takes hold of the bars and shakes them hard.

189   And she is all the time trying to climb through. But nobody could climb through that pattern—it strangles so; I think that is why it has so many heads.

190   They get through and then the pattern strangles them off and turns them upside down, and makes their eyes white!

191   If those heads were covered or taken off it would not be half so bad.

192   I think that woman gets out in the daytime!

193   And I'll tell you why—privately—I've seen her!

194   I can see her out of every one of my windows!

195   It is the same woman, I know, for she is always creeping, and most women do not creep by daylight.

196   I see her in that long shaded lane, creeping up and down. I see her in those dark grape arbors, creeping all around the garden.

197   I see her on that long road under the trees, creeping along, and when a carriage comes she hides under the blackberry vines.

198   I don't blame her a bit. It must be very humiliating to be caught creeping by daylight!

199   I always lock the door when I creep by daylight. I can't do it at night, for I know John would suspect something at once.

200   And John is so queer now that I don't want to irritate him. I wish he would take another room! Besides, I don't want anybody to get that woman out at night but myself.

201   I often wonder if I could see her out of all the windows at once.

202   But, turn as fast as I can, I can only see out of one at one time.

203   And though I always see her, she *may* be able to creep faster than I can turn! I have watched her sometimes away off in the open country, creeping as fast as a cloud shadow in a wind.

204   If only that top pattern could be gotten off from the under one! I mean to try it, little by little.

205   I have found out another funny thing, but I shan't tell it this time! It does not do to trust people too much.

206   There are only two more days to get this paper off, and I believe John is beginning to notice. I don't like the look in his eyes.

207   And I heard him ask Jennie a lot of professional questions about me. She had a very good report to give.

208   She said I slept a good deal in the daytime.

209   John knows I don't sleep very well at night, for all I'm so quiet!

210   He asked me all sorts of questions, too, and pretended to be very loving and kind.

211   As if I couldn't see through him!

212   Still, I don't wonder he acts so, sleeping under this paper for three months.

213   It only interests me, but I feel sure John and Jennie are affected by it.

214   Hurrah! This is the last day, but it is enough. John is to stay in town over night, and won't be out until this evening.

215   Jennie wanted to sleep with me—the sly thing; but I told her I should undoubtedly rest better for a night all alone.

216   That was clever, for really I wasn't alone a bit! As soon as it was moonlight and that poor thing began to crawl and shake the pattern, I got up and ran to help her.

217   I pulled and she shook. I shook and she pulled, and before morning we had peeled off yards of that paper.

218   A strip about as high as my head and half around the room.

219   And then when the sun came and that awful pattern began to laugh at me, I declared I would finish it today!

220   We go away tomorrow, and they are moving all my furniture down again to leave things as they were before.

221   Jennie looked at the wall in amazement, but I told her merrily that I did it out of pure spite at the vicious thing.

222   She laughed and said she wouldn't mind doing it herself, but I must not get tired.

223   How she betrayed herself that time!

224   But I am here, and no person touches this paper but Me—not *alive!*

225   She tried to get me out of the room—it was too patent! But I said it was so quiet and empty and clean now that I believed I would lie down again and sleep all I could, and not to wake me even for dinner—I would call when I woke.

226   So now she is gone, and the servants are gone, and the things are gone, and there is nothing left but that great bedstead nailed down, with the canvas mattress we found on it.

227   We shall sleep downstairs tonight, and take the boat home tomorrow.

228   I quite enjoy the room, now it is bare again.

229   How those children did tear about here!

230   This bedstead is fairly gnawed!

231   But I must get to work.

232   I have locked the door and thrown the key down into the front path.

233   I don't want to go out, and I don't want to have anybody come in, till John comes.

234   I want to astonish him.

235   I've got a rope up here that even Jennie did not find. If that woman does get out, and tries to get away, I can tie her!

236   But I forgot I could not reach far without anything to stand on!

237   This bed will *not* move!

238   I tried to lift and push it until I was lame, and then I got so angry I bit off a little piece at one corner—but it hurt my teeth.

239   Then I peeled off all the paper I could reach standing on the floor. It sticks horribly and the pattern just enjoys it! All those strangled heads and bulbous eyes and waddling fungus growths just shriek with derision!

240   I am getting angry enough to do something desperate. To jump out of the window would be admirable exercise, but the bars are too strong even to try.

241   Besides I wouldn't do it. Of course not. I know well enough that a step like that is improper and might be misconstrued.

242   I don't like to *look* out of the windows even—there are so many of those creeping women and they creep so fast.

243   I wonder if they all come out of that wallpaper as I did?

244   But I am securely fastened now by my well-hidden rope—you don't get *me* out in the road there!

245   I suppose I shall have to get back behind the pattern when it comes night, and that is hard!

246   It is so pleasant to be out in this great room and creep around as I please!

247   I don't want to go outside. I won't, even if Jennie asks me to.

248   For outside you have to creep on the ground, and everything is green instead of yellow.

249   But here I can creep smoothly on the floor, and my shoulder just fits in that long smooch around the wall, so I cannot lose my way.

250   Why, there's John at the door!

251   It is no use, young man, you can't open it!

252   How he does call and pound!

253   Now he's crying to Jennie for an axe.

254   It would be a shame to break down that beautiful door!

255   "John, dear!" said I in the gentlest voice. "The key is down by the front steps, under a plantain leaf!"

256   That silenced him for a few moments.

257   Then he said, very quietly indeed, "Open the door, my darling!"

258   "I can't," said I. "The key is down by the front door under a plantain leaf!" And then I said it again, several times, very gently and slowly, and said it so often that he had to go and see, and he got it of course, and came in. He stopped short by the door.

259   "What is the matter?" he cried. "For God's sake, what are you doing!"

260   I kept on creeping just the same, but I looked at him over my shoulder.

261   "I've got out at last," said I, "in spite of you and Jane. And I've pulled off most of the paper, so you can't put me back!"

262   Now why should that man have fainted? But he did, and right across my path by the wall, so that I had to creep over him every time!

Questions for Discussion

1. Why is John's profession important? What does his choice of profession reveal about him? How does his profession affect his relationship with his wife? How does he treat her? List the times that the narrator, after having given her opinion, adds "but John says" or a similar phrase.

2. What is the point of view of this story? Why is it crucial to the effectiveness of the story? How does the point of view create an ironic tone?

3. What is the role of John's sister in the story?

4. What is the significance of the narrator's not being allowed to see her baby?

5. Explain the significance of the wallpaper's appeal to four of the five senses (touch, smell, sound, and sight).

6. Why is the narrator unnamed for much of the story while John and Jennie have names? What is the significance of the name Jane?

Suggestions for Exploring, Writing, and Persuading

1. Describe the ideal husband of the nineteenth century. In what ways is John's attitude toward his wife typical of the attitudes of men toward women in the late nineteenth and early twentieth centuries in the United States? Does John love his wife? Support your answer.

2. Gilman's narrator says she feels "basely ungrateful" for not appreciating John's regulation of her days by the hour or his choice of their bedroom. Compare her feelings with those expressed by Missie May in "The Gilded Six-Bits."

3. Why does the wallpaper have an "everlastingness" about it? How does the narrator's changing attitude toward the wallpaper depict the state of her mind? Trace the evidence in the story.

4. In an essay, trace the changes in the narrator's attitudes toward John.

5. Agree or disagree with this statement: In comparing the narrator with Woolf's metaphor, the narrator is an example of a failed "Angel in the House."

Zora Neale Hurston (1891–1960)

Born in Alabama, Hurston moved with her family to Eatonville, Florida, the first "Negro" community to be incorporated; from there she moved to Jacksonville, Baltimore, and then New York. In New York she received good reviews for "Spunk" in 1925 and became part of the Harlem Renaissance. Hurston published four novels, two volumes of poetry, and an autobiography. One of her novels, Their Eyes Were Watching God *(1937), has been praised by modern critics. Hurston spent five years traveling the rural South, collecting some of the folklore and music of her people, information she assimilated into her stories. Much of her writing uses as a setting the general store porch because she felt that that part of the community was the most interesting place in town, even though women were excluded from it.*

THE GILDED SIX-BITS   (1933)

1   It was a Negro yard around a Negro house in a Negro settlement that looked to the payroll of the G. and G. Fertilizer works for its support.

2   But there was something happy about the place. The front yard was parted in the middle by a sidewalk from gate to doorstep, a sidewalk edged on either side by quart bottles driven neck down into the ground on a slant. A mess of homey flowers planted without a plan but blooming cheerily from their helter-skelter places. The fence and house were white-washed. The porch and steps scrubbed white.

3   The front door stood open to the sunshine so that the floor of the front room could finish drying after its weekly scouring. It was Saturday. Everything clean from the front gate to the privy house. Yard raked so that the strokes of the rake would make a pattern. Fresh newspaper cut in fancy edge on the kitchen shelves.

4   Missie May was bathing herself in the galvanized washtub in the bedroom. Her dark-brown skin glistened under the soapsuds that skittered down from her washrag. Her stiff young breasts thrust forward aggressively, like broad-based cones with the tips lacquered in black.

5   She heard men's voices in the distance and glanced at the dollar clock on the dresser.

6   "Humph! Ah'm way behind time t'day! Joe gointer be heah 'fore Ah git mah clothes on if Ah don't make haste."

7   She grabbed the clean mealsack at hand and dried herself hurriedly and began to dress. But before she could tie her slippers, there came the ring of singing metal on wood. Nine times.

8   Missie May grinned with delight. She had not seen the big tall man come stealing in the gate and creep up the walk grinning happily at the joyful mischief he was about to commit. But she knew that it was her husband throwing silver dollars in the door for her to pick up and pile beside her plate at dinner. It was this way every Saturday afternoon. The nine dollars hurled into the open door, he scurried to a hiding place behind the Cape jasmine bush and waited.

9   Missie May promptly appeared at the door in mock alarm.

10   "Who dat chunkin' money in mah do'way?" she demanded. No answer from the yard. She leaped off the porch and began to search the shrubbery. She peeped under the porch and hung over the gate to look up and down the road. While she did this, the man behind the jasmine darted to the chinaberry tree. She spied him and gave chase.

11   "Nobody ain't gointer be chunkin' money at me and Ah not do 'em nothin'," she shouted in mock anger. He ran around the house with Missie May at his heels. She overtook him at the kitchen door. He ran inside but could not close it after him before she crowded in and locked with him in a rough-and-tumble. For several minutes the two were a furious mass of male and female energy. Shouting, laughing, twisting, turning, tussling, tickling each other in the ribs; Missie May clutching onto Joe and Joe trying, but not too hard, to get away.

12   "Missie May, take yo' hand out mah pocket!" Joe shouted out between laughs.

13   "Ah ain't, Joe, not lessen you gwine gimme whateve' it is good you got in yo' pocket. Turn it go, Joe, do. Ah'll tear yo' clothes."

14   "Go on tear 'em. You de one dat pushes de needles round heah. Move yo' hand, Missie May."

15   "Lemme git dat paper sak out yo' pocket. Ah bet it's candy kisses."

16   "Tain't. Move yo' hand. Woman ain't got no business in a man's clothes nohow. Go way."

17   Missie May gouged way down and gave an upward jerk and triumphed.

18   "Unhhunh! Ah got it! It 'tis so candy kisses. Ah knowed you had somethin' for me in yo' clothes. Now Ah got to see whut's in every pocket you got."

19   Joe smiled indulgently and let his wife go through all of his pockets and take out the things that he had hidden there for her to find. She bore off the chewing gum, the cake of sweet soap, the pocket handkerchief as if she had wrested them from him, as if they had not been bought for the sake of this friendly battle.

20   "Whew! dat play-fight done got me all warmed up!" Joe exclaimed. "Got me some water in de kittle?"

21   "Yo' water is on de fire and yo' clean things is cross de bed. Hurry up and wash yo'self and get changed so we kin eat. Ah'm hongry." As Missie said this, she bore the steaming kettle into the bedroom.

22   "You ain't hongry, sugar," Joe contradicted her. "Youse jus' a little empty. Ah'm de one what's hongry. Ah could eat up camp meetin', back off 'ssociation, and drink Jurdan dry. Have it on de table when Ah get out de tub."

23   "Don't you mess wid mah business, man. You get in yo' clothes. Ah'm a real wife, not no dress and breath. Ah might not look lak one, but if you burn me, you won't git a thing but wife ashes."

24   Joe splashed in the bedroom and Missie May fanned around in the kitchen. A fresh red-and-white checked cloth on the table. Big pitcher of buttermilk beaded with pale drops of butter from the churn. Hot fried mullet, crackling bread, ham hock atop a mound of string beans and new potatoes, and perched on the windowsill a pone of spicy potato pudding.

25   Very little talk during the meal but that little consisted of banter that pretended to deny affection but in reality flaunted it. Like when Missie May reached for a second helping of the tater pone. Joe snatched it out of her reach.

26   After Missie May had made two or three unsuccessful grabs at the pan, she begged, "Aw, Joe, gimme some mo' dat tater pone."

27   "Nope, sweetenin' is for us menfolks. Y'all pritty li'l frail eels don't need nothin' lak dis. You too sweet already."

28   "Please, Joe."

29   "Naw, naw. Ah don't want you to git no sweeter than whut you is already. We goin' down de road a lil piece t'night so you go put on yo' Sunday-go-to-meetin' things."

30   Missie May looked at her husband to see if he was playing some prank. "Sho nuff, Joe?"

31   "Yeah. We goin' to de ice cream parlor."

32   "Where de ice cream parlor at, Joe?"

33   "A new man done come heah from Chicago and he done got a place and took and opened it up for a ice cream parlor, and bein' as it's real swell, Ah wants you to be one de first ladies to walk in dere and have some set down."

34   "Do Jesus, Ah ain't knowed nothin' bout it. Who de man done it?"

35   "Mister Otis D. Slemmons, of spots and places—Memphis, Chicago, Jacksonville, Philadelphia and so on."

36   "Dat heavyset man wid his mouth full of gold teeths?"

37   "Yeah. Where did you see 'im at?"

38   "Ah went down to de sto' tuh git a box of lye and Ah seen 'im standin' on de corner talkin' to some of de mens, and Ah come on back and went to scrubbin' de floor, and he passed and tipped his hat whilst Ah was scourin' de steps. Ah thought 'Ah never seen *him* befo'."

39   Joe smiled pleasantly. "Yeah, he's up-to-date. He got de finest clothes Ah ever seen on a colored man's back."

40   "Aw, he don't look no better in his clothes than you do in yourn. He got a puzzlegut on 'im and he so chuckleheaded he got a pone behind his neck."

41   Joe looked down at his own abdomen and said wistfully: "Wisht Ah had a build on me lak he got. He ain't puzzlegutted, honey. He jes' got a corperation. Dat make 'm look lak a rich white man. All rich mens is got some belly on 'em."

42   "Ah seen de pitchers of Henry Ford and he's a spare-built man and Rockefeller look lak he ain't got but one gut. But Ford and Rockefeller and dis Slemmons and all de rest kin be as many-gutted as dey please, Ah'm satisfied wid you jes' lak you is, baby. God took pattern after a pine tree and built you noble. Youse a pritty still man, and if Ah knowed any way to make you mo' pritty Ah'd take and do it."

43   Joe reached over gently and toyed with Missie May's ear. "You jes' say dat cause you love me, but Ah know Ah can't hold no light to Otis D. Slemmons. Ah ain't never been nowhere and Ah ain't got nothin' but you."

44   Missie May got on his lap and kissed him and he kissed back in kind. Then he went on. "All de womens is crazy 'bout 'im everywhere he go."

45   "How you know dat, Joe?"

46   "He tole us so hisself."

47   "Dat don't make it so. His mouf is cut crossways, ain't it? Well, he kin lie jes' lak anybody else."

48   "Good Lawd, Missie! You womens sho is hard to sense into things. He's got a five-dollar gold piece for a stickpin and he got a ten-dollar gold piece on his watch chain and his mouf is jes' crammed full of gold teeths. Sho wisht it wuz mine. And what make it so cool, he got money 'cumulated. And womens give it all to 'im."

49   "Ah don't see whut de womens see on 'im. Ah wouldn't give 'im a wink if de sheriff wuz after 'im."

50   "Well, he tole us how de white womens in Chicago give 'im all dat gold money. So he don't 'low nobody to touch it at all. Not even put dey finger on it. Dey told 'im not to. You kin make 'miration at it, but don't tetch it."

51   "Whyn't he stay up dere where dey so crazy 'bout 'im?"

52   "Ah reckon dey done made 'im vast-rich and he wants to travel some. He says dey wouldn't leave 'im hit a lick of work. He got mo' lady people crazy 'bout him than he kin shake a stick at."

53   "Joe, Ah hates to see you so dumb. Dat stray nigger jes' tell y'all any-thing and y'all b'lieve it."

54   "Go 'head on now, honey, and put on yo' clothes. He talkin' 'bout his pritty womens—Ah wan 'im to see *mine*."

55   Missie May went off to dress and Joe spent the time trying to make his stomach punch out like Slemmons's middle. He tried the rolling swagger of the stranger, but found that his tall bone-and-muscle stride fitted ill with it. He just had time to drop back into his seat before Missie May came in dressed to go.

56   On the way home that night Joe was exultant. "Didn't Ah say ole Otis was swell? Can't he talk Chicago talk? Wuzn't dat funny whut he said when great big fat ole Ida Armstrong come in? He asted me, 'Who is dat broad wid de forty shake?' Dat's a new word. Us always thought forty was a set of figgers but he showed us where it means a whole heap of things. Sometimes he don't say forty, he jes' say thirty-eight and two and dat mean de same thing. Know whut he told me when Ah wuz payin' for our ice cream? He say, "Ah have to hand it to you, Joe. Dat wife of yours is jes' thirty-eight and two. Yessuh, she's forty!' Ain't he killin'?"

57   "He'll do in case of a rush. But he sho is got uh heap uh gold on 'im. Dat's de first time Ah ever seed gold money. It lookted good on him sho nuff, but it'd look a whole heap better on you."

58   "Who, me? Missie May, youse crazy! Where would a po' man lak me git gold money from?"

59   Missie May was silent for a minute, then she said, "Us might find some goin' long de road some time. Us could."

60   "Who would be losin' gold money round heah? We ain't even seen none dese white folks wearin' no gold money on dey watch chain. You must be figgerin' Mister Packard or Mister Cadillac goin' pass through heah."

61   "You don't know whut been lost 'round heah. Maybe somebody way back in memorial times lost they gold money and went on off and it ain't never been found. And then if we wuz to find it, you could wear some 'thout havin' no gang of womens lak dat Slemmons say he got."

62   Joe laughed and hugged her. "Don't be so wishful 'bout me. Ah'm satisfied de way Ah is. So long as Ah be yo' husband. Ah don't keer 'bout nothin' else. Ah'd ruther all de other womens in de world to be dead than for you to have de toothache. Less we go to bed and get our night rest."

63   It was Saturday night once more before Joe could parade his wife in Slemmons's ice cream parlor again. He worked the night shift and Saturday was his only night off. Every other evening around six o'clock he left home, and dying dawn saw him hustling home around the lake, where the challenging sun flung a flaming sword from east to west across the trembling water.

64   That was the best part of life—going home to Missie May. Their whitewashed house, the mock battle on Saturday, the dinner and ice cream parlor afterwards, church on Sunday nights when Missie outdressed any woman in town—all, everything, was right.

65   One night around eleven the acid ran out at the G. and G. The foreman knocked off the crew and let the steam die down. As Joe rounded the lake on his way home, a lean moon rode the lake in a silver boat. If anybody had asked Joe about the moon on the lake, he would have said he hadn't paid it any attention. But he saw it with his feelings. It made him yearn painfully for Missie. Creation obsessed him. He thought about children. They had been married more than a year now. They had money put away. They ought to be making little feet for shoes. A little boy child would be about right.

66   He saw a dim light in the bedroom and decided to come in through the kitchen door. He could wash the fertilizer dust off himself before presenting himself to Missie May. It would be nice for her not to know that he was there until he slipped into his place in bed and hugged her back. She always liked that.

67   He eased the kitchen door open slowly and silently, but when he went to set his dinner bucket on the table he bumped it into a pile of dishes, and something crashed to the floor. He heard his wife gasp in fright and hurried to reassure her.

68   "Iss me, honey. Don't git skeered."

69   There was a quick, large movement in the bedroom. A rustle, a thud, and a stealthy silence. The light went out.

70   What? Robbers? Murderers? Some varmint attacking his helpless wife, perhaps. He struck a match, threw himself on guard and stepped over the doorsill into the bedroom.

71   The great belt on the wheel of Time slipped and eternity stood still. By the match light he could see the man's legs fighting with his breeches in his frantic desire to get them on. He had both chance and time to kill the intruder in his helpless condition—half in and half out of his pants—but he was too weak to take action. The shapeless enemies of humanity that live in the hours of Time had waylaid Joe. He was assaulted in his weakness. Like Samson awakening after his haircut. So he just opened his mouth and laughed.

72   The match went out and he struck another and lit the lamp. A howling wind raced across his heart, but underneath its fury he heard his wife sobbing and Slemmons pleading for his life. Offering to buy it with all that he had. "Please, suh, don't kill me. Sixty-two dollars at de sto'. Gold money."

73   Joe just stood. Slemmons looked at the window, but it was screened. Joe stood out like a rough-backed mountain between him and the door. Barring him from escape, from sunrise, from life.

74   He considered a surprise attack upon the big clown that stood there laughing like a chessy cat. But before his fist could travel an inch, Joe's own rushed out to crush him like a battering ram. Then Joe stood over him.

75   "Git into yo' damn rags, Slemmons, and dat quick."

76   Slemmons scrambled to his feet and into his vest and coat. As he grabbed his hat, Joe's fury overrode his intentions and he grabbed at Slemmons with his left hand and struck at him with his right. The right landed. The left grazed the front of his vest. Slemmons was knocked a somersault into the kitchen and fled through the open door. Joe found himself alone with Missie May, with the golden watch charm clutched in his left fist. A short bit of broken chain dangled between his fingers.

77   Missie May was sobbing. Wails of weeping without words. Joe stood, and after a while he found out that he had something in his hand. And then he stood and felt without thinking and without seeing with his natural eyes. Missie May kept on crying and Joe kept on feeling so much, and not knowing what to do with all his feelings, he put Slemmons's watch charm in his pants pocket and took a good laugh and went to bed.

78   "Missie May, whut you cryin' for?"

79   "Cause Ah love you so hard and Ah know you don't love *me* no mo'."

80   Joe sank his face into the pillow for a spell, then he said huskily, "You don't know de feelings of dat yet, Missie May."

81   "Oh Joe, honey, he said he wuz gointer give me dat gold money and he jes' kept on after me—"

82   Joe was very still and silent for a long time. Then he said, "Well, don't cry no mo', Missie May. Ah got yo' gold piece for you."

83   The hours went past on their rusty ankles. Joe still and quiet on one bed rail and Missie May wrung dry of sobs on the other. Finally the sun's tide crept upon the shore of night and drowned all its hours. Missie May with her face stiff and streaked towards the window saw the dawn come into her yard. It was day. Nothing more. Joe wouldn't be coming home as usual. No need to fling open the front door and sweep off the porch, making it nice for Joe. Never no more breakfast to cook; no more washing and starching of Joe's jumper-jackets and pants. No more nothing. So why get up?

84   With this strange man in her bed, she felt embarrassed to get up and dress. She decided to wait till he had dressed and gone. Then she would get up, dress quickly and be gone forever beyond reach of Joe's looks and laughs. But he never moved. Red light turned to yellow, then white.

85   From beyond the no-man's land between them came a voice. A strange voice that yesterday had been Joe's.

86   "Missie May, ain't you gonna fix me no breakfus'?"

87   She sprang out of bed. "Yeah, Joe. Ah didn't reckon you wuz hongry."

88   No need to die today. Joe needed her for a few more minutes anyhow.

89   Soon there was a roaring fire in the cookstove. Water bucket full and two chickens killed. Joe loved fried chicken and rice. She didn't deserve a thing and good Joe was letting her cook him some breakfast. She rushed hot biscuits to the table as Joe took his seat.

90   He ate with his eyes in his plate. No laughter, no banter.

91   "Missie May, you ain't eatin' yo' breakfus'."

92   "Ah don't choose none, Ah thank yuh."

93   His coffee cup was empty. She sprang to refill it. When she turned from the stove and bent to set the cup beside Joe's plate, she saw the yellow coin on the table between them.

94   She slumped into her seat and wept into her arms.

95   Presently Joe said calmly, "Missie May, you cry too much. Don't look back lak Lot's wife and turn to salt."

96   The sun, the hero of every day, the impersonal old man that beams as brightly on death as on birth, came up every morning and raced across the blue dome and dipped into the sea of fire every morning. Water ran downhill and birds nested.

97   Missie knew why she didn't leave Joe. She couldn't. She loved him too much, but she could not understand why Joe didn't leave her. He was polite, even kind at times, but aloof.

98   There were no more Saturday romps. No ringing silver dollars to stack beside her plate. No pockets to rifle. In fact, the yellow coin in his trousers was like a monster hiding in the cave of his pockets to destroy her.

99   She often wondered if he still had it, but nothing could have induced her to ask nor yet to explore his pockets to see for herself. Its shadow was in the house whether or no.

100   One night Joe came home around midnight and complained of pains in the back. He asked Missie to rub him down with liniment. It had been three months since Missie had touched his body and it all seemed strange. But she rubbed him. Grateful for the chance. Before morning youth triumphed and Missie exulted. But the next day, as she joyfully made up their bed, beneath her pillow she found the piece of money with the bit of chain attached.

101   Alone to herself, she looked at the thing with loathing, but look she must. She took it into her hands with trembling and saw first thing that it was no gold piece. It was a gilded half dollar. Then she knew why Slemmons had forbidden anyone to touch his gold. He trusted village eyes at a distance not to recognize his stickpin as a gilded quarter, and his watch charm as a four-bit piece.

102   They were man and wife again. Then another thought came clawing at her. He had come home to buy from her as if she were any woman in the longhouse. Fifty cents for her love. As if to say that he could pay as well as Slemmons. She slid the coin into his Sunday pants pocket and dressed herself and left his house.

103   Halfway between her house and the quarters she met her husband's mother, and after a short talk she turned and went back home. Never would she admit defeat to that woman who prayed for it nightly. If she had not the substance of marriage she had the outside show. Joe must leave *her*. She let him see she didn't want his old gold four-bits, too.

104   She saw no more of the coin for some time though she knew that Joe could not help finding it in his pocket. But his health kept poor, and he came home at least every ten days to be rubbed.

105   The sun swept around the horizon, trailing its robes of weeks and days. One morning as Joe came in from work, he found Missie May chopping wood. Without a word he took the ax and chopped a huge pile before he stopped.

106   "You ain't got no business choppin' wood, and you know it."

107   "How come? Ah been choppin' it for the last longest."

108   "Ah ain't blind. You makin' feet for shoes."

109   "Won't you be glad to have a lil baby chile, Joe?"

110   "You know dat 'thout astin' me."

111   "Iss gointer be a boy chile and de very spit of you."

112   "You reckon, Missie May?"

113   "Who else could it look lak?"

114   Joe said nothing, but he thrust his hand deep into his pocket and fingered something there.

115   It was almost six months later Missie May took to bed and Joe went and got his mother to come wait on the house.

116   Missie May was delivered of a fine boy. Her travail was over when Joe came in from work one morning. His mother and the old woman were drinking great bowls of coffee around the fire in the kitchen.

117   The minute Joe came into the room his mother called him aside.

118   "How did Missie May make out?" he asked quickly.

119   "Who, dat gal? She strong as a ox. She gointer have plenty mo'. We done fixed her wid de sugar and lard to sweeten her for de nex' one."

120   Joe stood silent awhile.

121   "You ain't ask 'bout de baby, Joe. You oughter be mighty proud cause he sho is de spittin' image of yuh, son. Dat's yourn all right, if you never git another one, dat un is yourn. And you know Ah'm mighty proud too, son, cause Ah never thought well of you marryin' Missie May cause her ma used tuh fan her foot round right smart and Ah been mighty skeered dat Missie May wuz gointer git misput on her road."

122   Joe said nothing. He fooled around the house till late in the day, then, just before he went to work, he went and stood at the foot of the bed and asked his wife how she felt. He did this every day during the week.

123   On Saturday he went to Orlando to make his market. It had been a long time since he had done that.

124   Meat and lard, meal and flour, soap and starch. Cans of corn and toma-toes. All the staples. He fooled around town for a while and bought bananas and apples. Way after while he went around to the candy store.

125   "Hellow, Joe," the clerk greeted him. "Ain't seen you in a long time."

126   "Nope, Ah ain't been heah. Been round in spots and places."

127   "Want some of them molasses kisses you always buy?"

128   "Yessuh." He threw the gilded half dollar on the counter. "Will dat spend?"

129   "What is it, Joe? Well, I'll be doggone! A gold-plated four-bit piece. Where'd you git it, Joe?"

130   "Offen a stray nigger dat come through Eatonville. He had it on his watch chain for a charm—goin' round making out iss gold money. Ha ha! He had a quarter on his tiepin and it wuz all golded up too. Tryin' to fool people. Makin' out he so rich and everything. Ha! Ha! Tryin' to tole off folkses wives from home."

131   "How did you git it, Joe? Did he fool you, too?"

132   "Who, me? Naw suh! He ain't fooled me none. Know what Ah done? He come round me wid his smart talk. Ah hauled off and knocked 'im down and took his old four-bits away from 'im. Gointer buy my wife some good ole lasses kisses wid it. Gimme fifty cents worth of dem candy kisses."

133   "Fifty cents buys a mighty lot of candy kisses, Joe. Why don't you split it up and take some chocolate bars, too? They eat good, too."

134   "Yessuh, dey do, but Ah wants all dat is kisses. Ah got a lil boy chile home now. Tain't a week old yet, but he kin suck a sugar tit and maybe eat one them kisses hisself."

135   Joe got his candy and left the store. The clerk turned to the next customer. "Wisht I could be like these darkies. Laughin' all the time. Nothin' worries 'em."

136   Back in Eatonville, Joe reached his own front door. There was the ring of singing metal on wood. Fifteen times. Missie May couldn't run to the door, but she crept there as quickly as she could.

137   "Joe Banks, Ah hear you chunkin' money in mah do'way. You wait till Ah got mah strength back and Ah'm gointer fix you for dat."

Questions for Discussion

1. How does the first sentence set the stage for the story?

2. What does Missie May mean when she tells Joe, "'Ah'm a real wife, not no dress and breath.'" What evidence in her behavior suggests that she is a "real wife"?

3. Why does Joe feel inferior to Otis D. Slemmons and try to imitate him?

4. When Joe arrives home unexpectedly, he laughs at the scene before him. Why? Later, why does he act with exaggerated politeness?

5. What is the significance of the "gold piece" under the pillow? Why is the title of the story appropriate?

6. At the end, the white clerk in the store remarks that the "darkies" are always laughing without a care in the world. Explain the irony of this statement.

7. Why does Joe forgive Missie May? Does he act responsibly?

Suggestions for Exploring, Writing, and Persuading

1. In an essay, discuss the strengths and weaknesses in this marriage.

2. How does the happy Saturday ritual reveal the relationship between Missie May and Joe?

3. In a researched essay, show how Hurston reveals the complexity of characters who appear to the outside world to be simple and happy.

4. In an essay argue that infidelity or adultery should or should not be grounds for divorce.

5. This story involves a conflict in which one character's pursuit of unlimited freedom infringes on the dignity of a more responsible character. Discuss how the story explores and defines the limits of freedom.

6. In an essay, argue that Joe should or should not have divorced Missie May.

Ernest Hemingway (1899–1961)

Hemingway began his literary career as a cub reporter for the Kansas City Star. There he learned a style of writing that many critics believe had a lasting influence on his fiction: his frequent use of short, simple or compound sentences. Hemingway continued his newspaper writing as a foreign correspondent throughout much of his life. As his works became famous, Hemingway also became a celebrity, often living the kind of adventures he wrote about: he fought in World War I, supported the Spanish Civil War, hunted in Africa, and married four times. His most famous novels include The Sun Also Rises *(1926),* A Farewell to Arms *(1929),* For Whom the Bell Tolls *(1940), and* The Old Man and the Sea *(1952). In 1954, Hemingway was awarded the Nobel Prize for Literature.*

HILLS LIKE WHITE ELEPHANTS (1927)

1   The hills across the valley of the Ebro were long and white. On this side there was no shade and no trees and the station was between two lines of rails in the sun. Close against the side of the station there was the warm shadow of the building and a curtain, made of strings of bamboo beads, hung across the open door into the bar, to keep out flies. The American and the girl with him sat at a table in the shade, outside the building. It was very hot and the express from Barcelona would come in forty minutes. It stopped at this junction for two minutes and went on to Madrid.

2   "What should we drink?" the girl asked. She had taken off her hat and put it on the table.

3   "It's pretty hot," the man said.

4   "Let's drink beer."

5   "Dos cervezas," the man said into the curtain.

6   "Big ones?" a woman asked from the doorway.

7   "Yes. Two big ones."

8   The woman brought two glasses of beer and two felt pads. She put the felt pads and the beer glasses on the table and looked at the man and the girl. The girl was looking off at the line of hills. They were white in the sun and the country was brown and dry.

9   "They look like white elephants," she said.

10   "I've never seen one," the man drank his beer.

11   "No, you wouldn't have."

12   "I might have," the man said. "Just because you say I wouldn't have doesn't prove anything."

13   The girl looked at the bead curtain. "They've painted something on it," she said. "What does it say?"

14   "Anis del Toro. It's a drink."

15   "Could we try it?"

16   The man called "Listen" through the curtain. The woman came out from the bar.

17   "Four reales."

18   "We want two Anis del Toro."

19   "With water?"

20   "Do you want it with water?"

21   "I don't know," the girl said. "Is it good with water?"

22   "It's all right."

23   "You want them with water?" asked the woman.

24   "Yes, with water."

25   "It tastes like licorice," the girl said and put the glass down.

26   "That's the way with everything."

27   "Yes," said the girl. "Everything tastes of licorice. Especially all the things you've waited so long for, like absinthe."

28   "Oh, cut it out."

29   "You started it," the girl said. "I was being amused. I was having a fine time."

30   "Well, let's try and have a fine time."

31   "All right. I was trying. I said the mountains looked like white elephants. Wasn't that bright?"

32   "That was bright."

33   "I wanted to try this new drink. That's all we do, isn't it—look at things and try new drinks?"

34   "I guess so."

35   The girl looked across at the hills.

36   "They're lovely hills," she said. "They don't really look like white elephants. I just meant the coloring of their skin through the trees."

37   "Should we have another drink?"

38   "All right."

39   The warm wind blew the bead curtain against the table.

40   "The beer's nice and cool," the man said.

41   "It's lovely," the girl said.

42   "It's really an awfully simple operation, Jig," the man said. "It's not really an operation at all."

43   The girl looked at the ground the table legs rested on.

44   "I know you wouldn't mind it, Jig. It's really not anything. It's just to let the air in."

45   The girl did not say anything.

46   "I'll go with you and I'll stay with you all the time. They just let the air in and then it's all perfectly natural."

47   "Then what will we do afterward?"

48   "We'll be fine afterward. Just like we were before."

49   "What makes you think so?"

50   "That's the only thing that bothers us. It's the only thing that's made us unhappy."

51   The girl looked at the bead curtain, put her hand out and took hold of two of the strings of beads.

52   "And you think then we'll be all right and be happy."

53   "I know we will. You don't have to be afraid. I've known lots of people that have done it."

54   "So have I," said the girl. "And afterward they were all so happy."

55   "Well," the man said, "if you don't want to you don't have to. I wouldn't have you do it if you didn't want to. But I know it's perfectly simple."

56   "And you really want to?"

57   "I think it's the best thing to do. But I don't want you to do it if you don't really want to."

58   "And if I do it you'll be happy and things will be like they were and you'll love me?"

59   "I love you now. You know I love you."

60   "I know. But if I do it, then it will be nice again if I say things are like white elephants, and you'll like it?"

61   "I'll love it. I love it now but I just can't think about it. You know how I get when I worry."

62   "If I do it you won't ever worry?"

63   "I won't worry about that because it's perfectly simple."

64   "Then I'll do it. Because I don't care about me."

65   "What do you mean?"

66   "I don't care about me."

67   "Well, I care about you."

68   "Oh, yes. But I don't care about me. And I'll do it and then everything will be fine."

69   "I don't want you to do it if you feel that way."

70   The girl stood up and walked to the end of the station. Across, on the other side, were fields of grain and trees along the banks of the Ebro. Far away, beyond the river, were mountains. The shadow of a cloud moved across the field of grain and she saw the river through the trees.

71   "And we could have all this," she said. "And we could have everything and every day we make it more impossible."

72   "What did you say?"

73   "I said we could have everything."

74   "We can have everything."

75   "No, we can't."

76   "We can have the whole world."

77   "No, we can't."

78   "We can go everywhere."

79   "No, we can't. It isn't ours any more."

80   "It's ours."

81   "No, it isn't. And once they take it away, you never get it back."

82   "But they haven't taken it away."

83   "We'll wait and see."

84   "Come on back in the shade," he said. "You mustn't feel that way."

85   "I don't feel any way," the girl said. "I just know things."

86   "I don't want you to do anything that you don't want to do—"

87   "Nor that isn't good for me," she said. "I know. Could we have another beer?"

88   "All right. But you've got to realize—"

89   "I realize," the girl said. "Can't we maybe stop talking?"

90   They sat down at the table and the girl looked across at the hills on the dry side of the valley and the man looked at her and at the table.

91   "You've got to realize," he said, "that I don't want you to do it if you don't want to. I'm perfectly willing to go through with it if it means anything to you."

92   "Doesn't it mean anything to you? We could get along."

93   "Of course it does. But I don't want anybody but you. I don't want any one else. And I know it's perfectly simple."

94   "Yes, you know it's perfectly simple."

95   "It's all right for you to say that, but I do know it."

96   "Would you do something for me now?"

97   "I'd do anything for you."

98   "Would you please please please please please please please stop talking?"

99   He did not say anything but looked at the bags against the wall of the station. There were labels on them from all the hotels where they had spent nights.

100   "But I don't want you to," he said, "I don't care anything about it."

101   "I'll scream," the girl said.

102   The woman came out through the curtains with two glasses of beer and put them down on the damp felt pads. "The train comes in five minutes," she said.

103   "What did she say?" asked the girl.

104   "That the train is coming in five minutes."

105   The girl smiled brightly at the woman, to thank her.

106   "I'd better take the bags over to the other side of the station," the man said. She smiled at him.

107   "All right. Then come back and we'll finish the beer."

108   He picked up the two heavy bags and carried them around the station to the other tracks. He looked up the tracks but could not see the train. Coming back, he walked through the barroom, where people waiting for the train were drinking. He drank an Anis at the bar and looked at the people. They were all waiting reasonably for the train. He went out through the bead curtain. She was sitting at the table and smiled at him.

109   "Do you feel better?" he asked.

110   "I feel fine," she said. "There's nothing wrong with me. I feel fine."

Questions for Discussion

1. What is the couple's relationship like at the beginning of the story? How has that relationship recently changed? Explain how the story reveals the relationship.

2. How does the man attempt to manipulate the woman into having a "simple operation"? How responsible does he seem? What does he mean by "'We'll be fine afterward. Just like we were before'"?

3. How would you describe the woman's tone in talking about a "simple operation"?

4. How do the landscapes on either side of the river differ? What might these contrasting landscapes suggest about the woman's state of mind?

5. Considering the symbolism of the landscapes, the man's references to the "simple operation," the recent changes in the couple's relationship, and the expected effect of the "operation" on the couple's relationship, what kind of operation do you think the couple are talking about? Why do they never openly name the operation?

6. At what point in the conversation does the relationship between the two seem to change?

7. How do you interpret the woman's final words?

Suggestions for Exploring, Writing, and Persuading

1. Clearly, in this story the man tries to manipulate the woman into doing what he wants done without himself taking any responsibility for her action. In an essay, discuss how a family member, friend, or acquaintance has similarly attempted to manipulate you.

2. In an essay, discuss how the relationship between the man and woman changes through the course of this very short story.

3. Defend, refute, or modify this statement: Because of the man's attempt to manipulate the woman, the relationship will never be the same.

4. Write an essay in which you argue that 1) the man is using persuasive techniques to convince the woman to do something she does not want to do or 2) the woman does or does not make the right decision.

Gloria Naylor (b. 1950)

Gloria Naylor was born in New York but had her roots in Mississippi. In 1968, Naylor followed her parents, who became Jehovah's Witnesses. Becoming a Jehovah's Witness brought Naylor out of her shell and made her aware of the power of the written word. Eventually she left this religion, received a B.A. in English from Brooklyn College, and attended graduate school at Yale in 1981. She published her first novel, The Women of Brewster Place, *in 1982. This novel won critical acclaim and was later produced by Oprah Winfrey as a television movie. Naylor's other books include* Linden Hills *(1985),* Mama Day *(1988), and* Bailey's Café *(1992). Currently, she is working on her fifth novel,* Saphhira

Wade, *and hoping to produce movies through her production
company, One Way Productions. All of Naylor's writings
reflect her spiritual and moral sensitivities and positive
images of the African American communities.*

MAMA DAY   (1988)

1   You were picking your teeth with a plastic straw—I know, I know, it
wasn't really a straw, it was a coffee stirrer. But, George, let's be fair, there
are two little openings in those things that you could possibly suck liquid through if you were desperate enough, so I think I'm justified in calling it a straw since dumps like that Third Avenue coffee shop had no
shame in calling it a coffee stirrer, when the stuff they poured into your
cup certainly didn't qualify as coffee. Everything about those types of
places was a little more or less than they should have been. I was always
thrown off balance: the stainless steel display cases were too clean, and
did you ever notice that the cakes and pies inside of them never made
crumbs when they were cut, and no juice ever dripped from the can-
taloupes and honeydews? The Formica tabletops were a bit too slippery
for your elbows, and the smell of those red vinyl seats—always red
vinyl—seeped into the taste of your food, which came warm if it was a
hot dish and warm if it was a cold dish. I swear to you, once I got warm
pistachio ice cream and it was solid as a rock. Those places in New York
were designed for assembly-line nutrition, and it worked—there was
nothing in there to encourage you to linger. Especially when the bill came
glued to the bottom of your dessert plate—who would want to ask for a
second cup of coffee and have to sit there watching a big greasy
thumbprint spread slowly over the "Thank You" printed on the back?

2   I suppose you had picked up the stirrer for your coffee because you'd
already used the teaspoon for your soup. I saw the waitress bring you the
Wednesday special, and that meant pea soup, which had to be attacked
quickly before it lumped up. So not risking another twenty-minute wait
for a soup spoon, you used your teaspoon, which left you without anything to use in your coffee when it came with the bill. And obviously you
knew that our pleasant waitress's "Catch ya in a men-it, babe," doomed
you to either your finger, a plastic stirrer, or coffee straight up. And you
used plenty of sugar and milk. That guy knows the art of dining successfully on Third Avenue, I thought. When the lunch menu has nothing
priced above six dollars, it's make do if you're gonna make it back to
work without ulcers.

3   And there wasn't a doubt in my mind that you were going back to some
office or somewhere definite after that meal. It wasn't just the short-
sleeved blue shirt and tie; you ate with a certain ease and decisiveness
that spelled *employed* with each forkful of their stringy roast beef. Six
months of looking for a job had made me an expert at picking out the
people who, like me, were hurrying up to wait—in somebody's outer anything for a chance to make it through their inner doors to prove that you

could type two words a minute, or not drool on your blouse while answering difficult questions about your middle initial and date of birth.

4   By that August I had it down to a science, although the folks here would say that I was gifted with a bit of Mama Day's second sight. Second sight had nothing to do with it: in March of that year coats started coming off, and it was the kind of April that already had you dodging spit from the air conditioners along the side streets, so by midsummer I saw it all hanging out—those crisp butterflies along the avenues, their dresses still holding the sharp edges of cloth that had been under cool air all morning in some temperature-controlled box. Or the briefcases that hung near some guy's thigh with a balance that said there was more in them than empty partitions and his gym shorts. And I guess being a woman, I could always tell hair: heads are held differently when they've been pampered every week, the necks massaged to relax tense muscles "so the layers will fall right, dear." The blonds in their Dutch-boy cuts, my counterparts in Jerri curls, those Asian women who had to do practically nothing to be gorgeous with theirs so they frizzed it or chopped it off, because then everybody knew they had the thirty-five dollars a week to keep it looking that way. Yeah, that group all had jobs. And it was definitely first sight on any evening rush-hour train: all those open-neck cotton shirts—always plaid or colored—with the dried sweat marks under the arms of riders who had the privilege of a seat before the northbound IRT hit midtown because those men had done their stint in the factories, warehouses, and loading docks farther down on Delancey or in East New York or Brooklyn.

5   But it took a little extra attention for the in-betweens: figuring out which briefcases that swung with the right weight held only pounds of résumés, or which Gucci appointment books had the classifieds neatly clipped out and taped onto the pages so you'd think she was expected wherever she was heading instead of just expected to wait. I have to admit, the appointment-book scam took a bit of originality and class. That type knew that a newspaper folded to the last section was a dead giveaway. And I don't know who the others were trying to fool by pretending to scan the headlines and editorial page before going to the classifieds and there finally creasing the paper and shifting it an inch or two closer to their faces. When all else failed, I was left with watching the way they walked—either too determined or too hesitantly through some revolving door on Sixth Avenue. Misery loves company, and that's exactly what I was searching for on the streets during that crushing August in New York. I out-and-out resented the phonies, and when I could pick one out I felt a little better about myself. At least I was being real: I didn't have a job, and I wanted one—badly. When your unemployment checks have a remaining life span that's shorter than a tsetse fly's, and you know that temp agencies are barely going to pay your rent, and all the doorways around Times Square are already taken by very determined-looking ladies, masquerades go right out the window. It's begging your friends for a new lead every other day, a newspaper folded straight to the classifieds,

and a cup of herb tea and the house salad anywhere the bill will come in under two bucks with a table near the air conditioner.

6   While you finished your lunch and were trying to discreetly get the roast beef from between your teeth, I had twenty minutes before the next cattle call. I was to be in the herd slotted between one and three at the Andrews & Stein Engineering Company. And if my feet hadn't swollen because I'd slipped off my high heels under the table, I might have gone over and offered you one of the mint-flavored toothpicks I always carried around with me. I'd met quite a few guys in restaurants with my box of toothpicks: it was a foolproof way to start up a conversation once I'd checked out what they ordered and how they ate it. The way a man chews can tell you loads about the kind of lover he'll turn out to be. Don't laugh—meat is meat. And you had given those three slabs of roast beef a consideration they didn't deserve, so I actually played with the idea that you might be worth the pain of forcing on my shoes. You had nice teeth and strong, blunt fingers, and your nails were clean but, thank God, not manicured. I had been trying to figure out what you did for a living. The combination of a short-sleeved colored shirt and knit tie could mean anything from security guard to eccentric V.P. Regardless, anyone who preferred a plastic stirrer over that open saucer of toothpicks near the cash register, collecting flecks of ear wax and grease from a hundred rummaging fingernails, at least had common sense if not a high regard for the finer points of etiquette.

7   But when you walked past me, I let you and the idea go. My toothpicks had already gotten me two dates in the last month: one whole creep and a half creep. I could have gambled that my luck was getting progressively better and you'd only be a quarter creep. But even so, meeting a quarter creep in a Third Avenue coffee shop usually meant he'd figure that I would consider a free lecture on the mating habits of African violets at the Botanical Gardens and dinner at a Greek restaurant—red vinyl *booths*—a step up. That much this Southern girl had learned: there was a definite relationship between where you met some guy in New York and where he asked you out. Now, getting picked up in one of those booths at a Greek restaurant meant dinner at a mid-drawer ethnic: Mexican, Chinese, southern Italian, with real table-cloths but under glass shields, and probably Off-Broadway tickets. And if you hooked into someone at one of *those* restaurants, then it was out to top-drawer ethnic: northern Italian, French, Russian, or Continental, with waiters, not waitresses, and balcony seats on Broadway. East Side restaurants, Village jazz clubs, and orchestra seats at Lincoln Center were nights out with the pool you found available at Maxwell's Plum or any singles bar *above* Fifty-ninth Street on the East Side, and *below* Ninety-sixth on the West.

8   I'd never graduated to the bar scene because I didn't drink and refused to pay three-fifty for a club soda until the evening bore returns. Some of my friends said that you could run up an eighteen-dollar tab in no time that way, only to luck out with a pink quarter creep who figured that

because you were a black woman it was down to mid-drawer ethnic for dinner the next week. And if he was a brown quarter creep, he had waited just before closing time to pick up the tab for your last drink. And if you didn't show the proper amount of gratitude for a hand on your thigh and an invitation to his third-floor walk-up into paradise, you got told in so many words that your bad attitude was the exact reason why he had come there looking for white girls in the first place.

9   I sound awful, don't I? Well, those were awful times for a single woman in that city of yours. There was something so desperate and sad about it all—especially for my friends. You know, Selma kept going to those fancy singles bars, insisting that was the only way to meet "certain" black men. And she did meet them, those who certainly weren't looking for her. Then it was in Central Park, of all places, that she snagged this doctor. Not just any doctor, a Park Avenue neurosurgeon. After only three months he was hinting marriage, and she was shouting to us about a future of douching with Chanel No. 5, using laminated dollar bills for shower curtains—the whole bit. And the sad thing wasn't really how it turned out—I mean, as weird as it was when he finally told her that he was going to have a sex-change operation, but he was waiting for the right woman who was also willing to get one along with him, because he'd never dream of sleeping with another man—even after the operation; weirder—and much sadder—than all of that, George, was the fact that she debated seriously about following him to Denmark and doing it. So let me tell you, my toothpicks, as small a gesture as they were, helped me to stay on top of all that madness.

10   I finally left the coffee shop and felt whatever life that might have been revived in my linen suit and hair wilting away. How could it get so hot along Third Avenue when the buildings blocked out the sunlight? When I had come to New York seven years before that, I wondered about the need for such huge buildings. No one ever seemed to be in them for very long; everyone was out on the sidewalks, moving, moving, moving—and to where? My first month I was determined to find out. I followed a woman once: she had a beehive hairdo with rhinestone bobby pins along the side of her head that matched the rhinestones on her tinted cat-eyed glasses. Her thumbnails were the only ones polished, in a glossy lacquer on both hands, and they were so long they had curled under like hooks. I figured that she was so strange no one would ever notice me trailing her. We began on Fifty-third Street and Sixth Avenue near the Sheraton, moved west to Eighth Avenue before turning right, where she stopped at a Korean fruit stand, bought a kiwi, and walked along peeling the skin with her thumbnails. I lost her at Columbus Circle; she threw the peeled fruit uneaten into a trash can and took the escalator down into the sub-way. As she was going down, another woman was coming up the escala-tor with two bulging plastic bags. This one took me along Broadway up to where it meets Columbus Avenue at Sixty-third, and she sat down on one of those benches in the traffic median with her bags between her knees. She kept beating her heels against the sides and it sounded as if

she had loose pots and pans in them. A really distinguished looking guy with a tweed jacket and gray sideburns got up from the bench the moment she sat down, went into a flower shop across Columbus Avenue, came out empty-handed, and I followed him back downtown toward the Circle until we got to the entrance to Central Park. He slowed up, turned around, looked me straight in the face, and smiled. That's when I noticed that he had diaper pins holding his fly front together—you know, the kind they used to have with pink rabbit heads on them. I never thought anyone could beat my Central Park story until Selma met her neurosurgeon there. After that guy I gave up—I was exhausted by that time anyway. I hated to walk, almost as much as I hated the subways. There's something hypocritical about a city that keeps half of its population underground half of the time; you can start believing that there's much more space than there really is—to live, to work. And I had trouble doing both in spite of those endless classifieds in the Sunday *Times*. You know, there are more pages in just their Help Wanted section than in the telephone book here in Willow Springs. But it took me a while to figure out that New York racism moved underground like most of the people did.

11   Mama Day and Grandma had told me that there was a time when the want ads and housing listings in newspapers—even up north—were clearly marked colored or white. It must have been wonderfully easy to go job hunting then. You were spared a lot of legwork and headwork. And how I longed for those times, when I was busting my butt up and down the streets. I said as much at one of those parties Selma was always giving for her certain people. You would've thought I had announced that they were really drinking domestic wine, the place got that quiet. One of her certain people was so upset his voice shook. "You mean, you want to bring back segregation?" I looked at him like he was a fool—Where had it gone? I just wanted to bring the clarity about it back—it would save me a whole lot of subway tokens. What I was left to deal with were the ads labeled *Equal Opportunity Employer*, or nothing—which might as well have been labeled *Colored apply* or *Take your chances*. And if I wanted to limit myself to the sure bets, then it was an equal opportunity to be what, or earn what? That's where the headwork came in.

12   It's like the ad I was running down that afternoon: a one-incher in Monday's paper for an office manager. A long job description so there wasn't enough room to print Equal Opportunity Employer even if they were. They hadn't advertised Sunday, because I'd double-checked. They didn't want to get lost among the full and half columns the agencies ran. Obviously, a small operation. *Andrews & Stein Engineering Company*: it was half Jewish at least, so that said liberal—maybe. Or maybe they only wanted their own. I had never seen any Jewish people except on television until I arrived in New York. I had heard that they were clannish, and coming from Willow Springs I could identify with that. *Salary competitive*: that could mean anything, depending upon whether they were competing with Burger King or IBM. *Position begins September 1st*: that was

the clincher, with all the other questions hanging in the balance. If I got the job, I could still go home for mid-August. Even if I didn't get it, I was going home. Mama Day and Grandma could forgive me for leaving Willow Springs, but not for staying away.

13   I got to the address and found exactly what I had feared. A six-floor office building—low-rent district, if you could call anything low in New York. Andrews & Stein was suite 511. The elevator, like the ancient marble foyer and maroon print carpeting on the fifth floor, was worn but carefully maintained. Dimly lit hallways to save on overhead, and painted walls that looked just a month short of needing a fresh coat. I could see that the whole building was being held together by some dedicated janitor who was probably near retirement. Oh, no, if these folks were going to hire me, it would be for peanuts. Operations renting space in a place like this shelled out decent salaries only for Mr. Stein's brainless niece, or Mr. Andrews's current lay. Well, you're here, Cocoa, I thought, go through the motions.

14   The cherry vanilla who buzzed me in the door was predictable, but there might still be reason for hope. When small, liberal establishments put a fudge cream behind their glass reception cages, there were rarely any more back in the offices. Sticking you out front let them sleep pretty good at night, thinking they'd put the ghost of Martin Luther King to rest. There were three other women there ahead of me, and one very very gay Oriental. God, those were rare—at least in my circles. The four of them already had clipboards and were filling out one-page applications— mimeographed. Cherry Vanilla was pleasant enough. She apologized for there being no more seats, and told me I had to wait until one of the clipboards was free unless I had something to write on. A small, small operation. But she wasn't pouring out that oily politeness that's normally used to slide you quietly out of any chance of getting the job. One of the women sitting there filling out an application was actually licorice. Her hair was in deep body waves with the sheen of patent leather, and close as I was, I couldn't tell where her hair ended and her skin began. And she had the body and courage to wear a Danskin top as tight as it was red. I guess that lady said, You're going to see me coming from a mile away, like it or not. I bet a lot of men did like it. If they were replacing Mr. Andrews's bimbo, she'd get the job. And the way she looked me up and down—dismissing my washed-out complexion and wilted linen suit—made me want to push out my pathetic chest, but that meant bringing in my nonexistent hips. Forget it, I thought, you're standing here with no tits, no ass, and no color. So console yourself with the fantasy that she's mixed up her addresses and is applying for the wrong job. Why else come to an interview in an outfit that would look better the wetter it got, unless you wanted to be a lifeguard? I could dismiss the other two women right away—milk shakes. One had her résumés typed on different shades of pasted paper and she was shifting through them, I guess trying to figure out which one matched the decor of the office. The other had forgotten

her social security card and wanted to know if she should call home for the number. To be stupid enough not to memorize it was one thing, but not to know enough to sit there and shut up about it was beyond witless. I didn't care if Andrews & Stein was a front for the American Nazi party, she didn't have a chance. So the only serious contenders in that bunch were me, Patent Leather Hair, and the kumquat.

15   I inherited the clipboard from the one who'd forgotten her social security card, and she was in and out still babbling about that damn number before I had gotten down to Educational Background. Beyond high school there was just two years in business school in Atlanta—but I'd graduated at the top of my class. It was work experience that really counted for a job like this. This wasn't the type of place where you'd worry about moving up—all of those boxes and file cabinets crowded behind the receptionist's shoulder—it was simply a matter of moving around.

16   One job in seven years looked very good—with a fifty percent increase in salary. Duties: diverse, and more complex as I went along. The insurance company simply folded, that's all. If I'd stayed, I probably would have gone on to be an underwriter—but I was truly managing that office. Twelve secretaries, thirty-five salesmen, six adjusters, and one greedy president who didn't have the sense to avoid insuring half of the buildings in the South Bronx—even at triple premiums for fire and water damage. Those crooked landlords made a bundle, and every time I saw someone with a cigarette lighter, I cringed. I was down to Hobbies—which always annoyed me; what does your free time have to do with them?—when Patent Leather Hair was called in. She stood up the way women do knowing they look better when all of them is at last in view. I wondered what she had put down for extra-curricular activities. I sighed and crossed my legs. It was going to be a long wait. After twenty minutes Kumquat smiled over at me sympathetically—at least we both knew that he didn't have a possible ace in the hole anymore.

17   The intercom button on the receptionist's phone lit up, and when she got off she beckoned to the Oriental guy.

18   "Mr. Andrews is still interviewing, so Mr. Stein will have to see you. Just take your application to the second door on the left, Mr. Weisman."

19   He grinned at me again as I felt my linen suit losing its final bit of crispness under the low-voltage air conditioner. God, I wanted to go home—and I meant, home home. With all of Willow Springs's problems, you knew when you saw a catfish, you called it a catfish.

20   Well, Weisman was in and out pretty fast. I told myself for the thousandth time, Nothing about New York is ever going to surprise me anymore. Stein was probably anti-Semitic. It was another ten minutes and I was still sitting there and really starting to get ticked off. Couldn't Mr. Stein see me as well? No, she'd just put through a long-distance call from a client, but Mr. Andrews would be ready for me soon. I seriously doubted it. He was in there trying to convince Patent Leather that even though she thought she was applying for a position as a lifeguard, they

could find room for someone with her potential. I didn't give her the satisfaction of my half-hour wait when she came flaming out—I was busily reading the wrapper on my pack of Trident, having ditched my newspaper before I came in. The thing was irreversibly creased at the classifieds, my bag was too small to hide it, and you never wanted to look that desperate at an interview. And there weren't even any old issues of *Popular Mechanics* or something in the waiting area—bottom drawer all the way.

21   I was finally buzzed into the inner sanctum, and without a shred of hope walked past the clutter of file cabinets through another door that opened into a deceptively large network of smaller offices. I entered the third on the left as I'd been instructed and there you were: blue shirt, knitted tie, nice teeth, and all. Feeling the box of mint toothpicks press against my thigh through the mesh bag as I sat down and crossed my legs, I smiled sincerely for the first time that day.

22   Until you walked into my office that afternoon, I would have never called myself a superstitious man. Far from it. To believe in fate or predestination means you have to believe there's a future, and I grew up without one. It was either that or not grow up at all. Our guardians at the Wallace P. Andrews Shelter for Boys were adamant about the fact that we learned to invest in ourselves alone. "Keep it in the now, fellas," Chip would say, chewing on his bottom right jaw and spitting as if he still had the plug of tobacco in there Mrs. Jackson refused to let him use in front of us. And I knew I'd hear her until the day I died. "Only the present has potential, *sir*." I could see her even then, the way she'd jerk up the face, gripping the chin of some kid who was crying because his last foster home hadn't worked out, or because he was teased at school about not having a mother. She'd even reach up and clamp on to some muscled teenager who was trying to excuse a bad report card. I could still feel the ache in my bottom lip from the relentless grip of her thumb and forefinger pressed into the bone of my chin—"Only the present has potential, *sir*."

23   They may not have been loving people, she and Chip—or when you think about it, even lovable. But they were devoted to their jobs if not to us individually. And Mrs. Jackson saw part of her job as making sure that that scraggly bunch of misfits—misfitted into somebody's game plan so we were thrown away—would at least hear themselves addressed with respect. There were so many boys and the faces kept changing, she was getting old and never remembered our individual names and didn't try to hide it. All of us were beneath poor, most of us were black or Puerto Rican, so it was very likely that this would be the first and last time in our lives anyone would call us "sir." And if talking to you and pinching the skin off your chin didn't work, she was not beneath enforcing those same words with a brown leather strap—a man's belt with the buckle removed. We always wondered where she'd gotten a man's belt. You could look at Mrs. Jackson and tell she'd never been a Mrs., the older boys would say. Or if she had snagged some poor slob a thousand years ago, he never could have

gotten it up over her to need to undo his pants. But that was said only well out of her earshot after she had lashed one of them across the back or arms. She'd bring that belt down with a cold precision that was more frightening than the pain she was causing, and she'd bring it down for exactly ten strokes—one for each syllable: "Only the present has potential, *sir*."

24   No boy was touched above the neck or below his waist in front. And she never, ever hit the ones—regardless of their behavior—who had come to Wallace P. Andrews with fractured arms or cigarette burns on their groins. For those she'd take away dinner plus breakfast the next morning, and even lunch if she felt they warranted it. Bernie Sinclair passed out that way once, and when he woke up in the infirmary she was standing over him explaining that he had remained unconscious past the dinner he *still* would have been deprived of if he hadn't fainted.

25   Cruel? No, I would call it controlled. Bernie had spit in her face. And she never altered her expression, either when it happened during hygiene check or when she stood over him in the infirmary. Bernie had come to us with half of his teeth busted out, and he hated brushing the other half. She was going down the usual morning lineup for the boys under twelve, checking fingernails, behind ears, calling for the morning stretch (hands above head, legs spread, knees bent, and bounce) to detect unwashed armpits and crotches. Bernie wouldn't open his mouth for her and was getting his daily list of facts (she never lectured, she called it listing simple facts): if the remainder of his teeth rotted out from lack of personal care, then the dentist would have to fit him for a full plate instead of a partial plate. And it would take her twice as long to requisition twice the money that would then be needed from the state. That would lead to him spending twice as long being teased at school and restricted to a soft diet in the cafeteria. She said this like she did everything—slowly, clearly, and without emotion. For the second time she bent over and told him to open his mouth. He did, and sent a wad of spit against her right cheek. Even Joey Santiago cringed—all six feet and almost two hundred pounds of him. But Mrs. Jackson never blinked. She took out the embroidered handkerchief she kept in her rolled-up blouse sleeve and wiped her face as she listed another set of facts: she had asked him twice, she never asked any child to do anything more than twice—those were the rules at Wallace P. Andrews. No lunch, no dinner, and he still had his full share of duties. I guess that's why he passed out, no food under the hot sun and weeding our garden—that and fear of what she was really going to do to him for spitting on her. He was still new and didn't understand that she was going to do nothing at all.

26   Our rage didn't matter to her, our hurts or disappointments over what life had done to us. None of that was going to matter a damn in the outside world, so we might as well start learning it at Wallace P. Andrews. There were only rules and facts. Mrs. Jackson's world out there on Staten Island had rules that you could argue might not be fair, but they were consistent. And when they were broken we were guaranteed that, however

she had to do it, we would be made to *feel* responsibility for our present actions—and our actions alone. And oddly enough, we understood that those punishments were an improvement upon our situations: before coming there, we had been beaten and starved just for being born.

27   And she was the only person on the staff allowed to touch us. Even Chip, who had the role of "good cop" to her "bad cop"—you needed a shoulder to cry on sometimes—could only recommend discipline. It must have been difficult with sixty boys, and I'd seen some kids really provoke a dorm director or workshop leader, and the guy would never lay a hand on them. They all knew her rules, and it was clear those men were afraid of her. And I could never figure it out, even with the rumor that was going around, which Joey Santiago swore by. Joey was a notorious liar, but he was the oldest guy there when I was growing up. And he said that some years back there was a dorm director who used to sneak into the rooms where we had the "rubber sheet jockeys"—kids under eight—and take them into the bathroom. After he was finished with them, they'd fall asleep on the toilet, where he'd make them sit until their rectums stopped bleeding. Mrs. Jackson and Chip came over one night, caught him at it, and she told the boys she was going to call the police. They took him back to the old stucco house she lived in on the grounds. The police car never came, but her basement lights stayed on. And Joey swore you could hear that man screaming throughout the entire night, although all of her windows were bolted down. It was loud enough to even wake up the older ones in the other dorms. That man was never seen again, and they knew better than to question Mrs. Jackson when she came over to pack up his things herself. And Chip had absolutely nothing to say about what had happened but "Keep it in the now, fellas" as he dug Mrs. Jackson a new rose garden the following morning. Every staff member and boy who came to Wallace P. Andrews heard that rumor and one way or another, went over to see those roses in the corner of her garden. I can only tell you this, they were incredibly large and beautiful. And in the summer, when the evening breeze came from the east, their fragrance was strong enough to blanket your sleep.

28   Some thought that I was her favorite. I was one of the few who had grown up there through the nursery, and she couldn't punish me the way she did them, because I had a congenital heart condition. So she took away my books, knowing that I'd rather give up food or even have her use her strap. And once pleaded with her to do so, because I said I'd die if I had to wait a full week to find out how the Count of Monte Cristo escaped from prison. She said that was a fitting death for little boys who were caught cheating on their math exams. But fractions are hard, and I wanted a good grade at the end of the term. Ah, so I was worried about the *end* of the term? Well, she would now keep my books for two weeks. "Only the present has potential, *sir*."

29   And the discipline she tailor-made for all of us said, like it or not, the present is *you*. And what else did we have but ourselves? We had a more than forgettable past and no future that was guaranteed. And she never

let us pretend that anything else was the case as she'd often listed the facts of life: I am not your mother. I am paid to run this place. You have no mothers or fathers. This is not your home. And it is not a prison—it is a state shelter for boys. And it is not a dumping ground for delinquents, rejects, or somebody's garbage, because you are not delinquents, rejects, or garbage—you are boys. It is not a place to be tortured, exploited, or raped. It is a state shelter for boys. Here you have a clean room, decent food, and clothing for each season because it is a shelter. There is a library in which you study for three hours after school—and you *will* go to school, because you are boys. When you are eighteen, the state says you are men. And when you are men you leave here to go where and do what you want. But you stay here until you are men.

30   Yes, those were the facts of life at Wallace P. Andrews. And those were her methods. And if any of the boys complained to the state inspectors about being punished, nothing was ever done. I guess at the bottom line, she saved them money. We grew and canned a lot of our own food, painted our own dorms, made most of the furniture, and even sewed curtains and bedspreads. And the ones she turned out weren't a burden on the state, either. I don't know of anyone who became a drug addict, petty thief, or a derelict. I guess it's because you grew up with absolutely no illusions about yourself or the world. Most of us went from there either to college or into a trade. No, it wasn't the kind of place that turned out many poets or artists—those who could draw became draftsmen, and the musicians were taught to tune pianos. If she erred in directing our careers, she erred on the side of caution. Sure, the arts were waiting for poor black kids who were encouraged to dream big, and so was death row.

31   Looking back, I can see how easy it would have been for her to let us just sit there and reach the right age to get out. It only takes time for a man to grow older, but how many of them grow up? And I couldn't have grown up if I had wasted my time crying about a family I wasn't given or believing in a future that I didn't have. When I left Wallace P. Andrews I had what I could see: my head and my two hands, and I had each day to do something with them. Each day, that's how I took it—each moment, sometimes, when the going got really rough. I may have knocked my head against the walls, figuring out how to buy food, supplies, and books, but I never knocked on wood. No rabbit's foot, no crucifixes—not even a lottery ticket. I couldn't afford the dollar or the dreams while I was working my way through Columbia. So until you walked into my office, everything I was—all the odds I had beat—was owed to my living fully in the now. How was I to reconcile the *fact* of seeing you the second time that day with the *feeling* I had had the first time? Not the feeling I told myself I had, but the one I really had.

32   You see, there was no way for me to deny that you were there in front of me and I couldn't deny any longer that I knew it would happen—you would be in my future. What had been captured—and dismissed—in a space too quickly for recorded time was now like a bizarre photograph

that was developing in front of my face. I am passing you in the coffee shop, your head is bent over your folded newspaper, and small strands of your reddish-brown hair have come undone from the bobby pins and lie against the curve of your neck. The feeling is so strong it almost physically stops me: *I will see that neck again.* Not her, not the woman but the skin that's tinted from amber to cream as it stretches over the lean bone underneath. That is the feeling I actually had, while the feeling I quickly exchanged it with was: *I've seen this woman before.* That can be recorded; it took a split second. But a glance at the side of your high cheekbones, pointed chin, slender profile, and I knew I was mistaken. I hadn't even seen you sitting those three tables away during lunch. But I remembered your waitress well. The dark-brown arms, full breasts threatening to tear open the front of her uniform, the crease of her apron strings around a nonexistent waist that swung against a hip line that could only be called a promise of heaven on earth—her I had seen. And you had to have been there when she took your order and brought you whatever you were eating, and the fact is I never saw you. Not when I stood up, reached into my pocket for change, passed the two tables between us, and didn't see you then—until the neck bent over the newspaper. And it all could have been such a wonderful coincidence when you first walked into my office, a natural icebreaker for the interview, which I always hated, being forced to judge someone else. I could have brought up the final image of the weary slump, the open classifieds, and the shoes pulled off beneath the table. A woman looking for a job; we were looking for an office manager five blocks away. Afternoon interviews began at one o'clock, and it was twelve-forty-five. *And just imagine, Miss Day, when I passed you I said to myself, Wouldn't it be funny if I saw her again?* Except that it was terrifying when you sat down, and then ran your hand up the curve of your neck in a nervous mannerism, pushing up a few loose hairs and pushing me smack into a confrontation with fate. When you unconsciously did that, I must have looked as if someone had stuck a knife into my gut, because that's the way it felt.

33   You said, Call me George. And I thought, Oh God, this is going to be one of those let's-get-chummy-fast masquerades. Nine times out of ten, some clown giving you his first name is a sure bet he's not giving you the job. And they can comfort themselves because, after all, they went out of their way to be "nice." And in this case, you were stealing my thunder when the moment came for pulling out my toothpicks and reminding *Mr. Andrews* where I'd seen him before. But if we were George and Ophelia—chat, chat, chat—my mint toothpicks would just be added fuel to the fire that was sending this job up in smoke. These fudge-on-fudge interviews were always tricky anyway. You have the power freaks who wanted you to grovel at their importance. They figure if they don't get it from the other bonbons, it's sure not coming from anywhere else. Or there were the disciples of a free market with a Christ complex: they went to the Cross and

rose without affirmative action, so you can, too. But our interview wasn't anything I could put my finger on. You just seemed downright scared of me and anxious to get me out of that office. And I knew the fastest way was this call-me-George business. I decided to fight fire with fire.

34 "And I'm used to answering to Cocoa. I guess we might as well start now because if I get the position and anyone here calls me Ophelia, I'll be so busy concentrating on my work, it won't register. I truly doubt I could have moved up as fast as I did at my last job—with a fifty percent increase in salary—if those twelve secretaries, thirty-five salesmen, and six adjusters in the office I was managing almost single-handedly had called me Ophelia. The way I see it, over half of the overtime I put in would have been spent trying to figure out who they were talking to."

35 There, I stuck that one to you. And you knew it, too, because you were finally smiling. And this time you took a real good look at my application.

36 "So you picked up this nickname at your last job—Omega Home Insurance?"

37 "No, I've had it from a child—in the South it's called a pet name. My grandmother and great-aunt gave it to me, the same women who put me through business school in Atlanta where I ended up graduating at the top of my class—A's in statistics, typing, bookkeeping. B plusses in—"

38 "That's fascinating. How do they decide on the pet name?"

39 "They just try to figure out what fits."

40 "So a child with skin the color of buttered cream gets called Cocoa. I can see how that fits."

41 I wanted to slap that smirk off your face. "It does if you understood my family and where I come from."

42 "Willow Springs, is it? That's in Georgia?"

43 "No, it's actually in no state. But that's a long story. And not to be rude, Mr. Andrews, but I really would like to talk about my credentials for working here. Where I was born and what name I was given were both beyond my control. But what *I* could do about my life, I've done well. And I'd like to spend the few minutes I have left of your time being judged on that."

44 Something happened to your face then. I had hit a raw nerve somewhere, and I cursed myself because I was sure I had succeeded in destroying the whole thing. It was little consolation knowing that I was going to be on your mind long after you kicked me out of your office.

45 "That's the only way I'd ever dream of judging anyone, Miss Day. And I meant it when I said call me George."

46 Great, I'd been demoted *up* to Miss Day. This man was really angry, and that George business again just clinched it, I guess. But then he did say *I meant it*, which means he knows about the whole charade and he's trying to reassure me that he's not angry about what I said. Ah, who can figure this shit out.

47 "And you can call me..." I was suddenly very tired—of you, of the whole game. "Just call me when you decide. I do need this job, and if you check out my references, you'll find that I'll be more than able to perform well."

48 "Fine. And this is the number where you can be reached?"

49 "Yes, but I'll be away for the next two weeks. If you don't mind, you could drop me a card, or I'll call when I get back since the job doesn't start until the first."

50 You frowned, but it came out the way it came out. Sure, he's thinking, how badly does someone need a job who's taking a vacation?

51 "But we'll be making our final decision after tomorrow. The person starts Monday."

52 "Your ad said the first."

53 "It did, but our current office manager told us this morning that she has to leave earlier than she had planned. And she'll have to break in her successor. This is a deceptively busy place and to have someone come in here cold—well, it wouldn't be fair to the new employee or to us. And we thought whoever got the position would probably appreciate starting work before September. I know how tight things are out there right now—most people have been looking for a long time."

54 Jesus, all we needed was the organ music and a slow fade to my receding back as the swirling sand of the rocky coastline began to spell out The End. Oh, yeah, if you aren't ready to start yesterday, there are a dozen who will be.

55 "I understand, and I wouldn't have wasted your time if I knew it was necessary to begin right away. I have to go home every August. It's never been a problem before because I had the same job for seven years. You see, my grandmother is eighty-three, and since we lost my cousin and her family last year, I'm the only grandchild left."

56 If you thought it was a cheap shot, sorry. At that point I was beyond caring.

57 "The whole family? That's really terrible—what happened?"

58 "Did you read about the fire in Linden Hills this past Christmas? Well, that was my cousin Willa and her husband and son. It upset us all a lot."

59 "I did read about it. It was an awful, awful thing—and on Christmas of all days."

60 My God, the look in your eyes. You actually meant that. This would go down in Guinness as the strangest interview I'd ever been on.

61 "So you understand why I'm going back to Willow Springs."

62 "Of course I do. And you must understand why any qualified applicant would need to start Monday."

63 "Yes, I do."

64 We had sure become one understanding pair of folks by the time the lights in the theater came up and they pulled the curtain across the screen. We got up out of our seats and shook hands. Was it my imagination—did his fingers linger just a bit? Was it possible that since I was more than qualified, no one else would come along and they'd save...My heart sank when I got back to the reception area. I had to wade through a whole Baskin-Robbins on my way to the outside hall.

65   You had spunk, Ophelia, and that's what I admired in a woman. You were justified to come right out and tell me I was prying, and I hated myself all the while I was doing it. I had always valued my own privacy, and just because you were in a position where you had to answer questions that bordered on an invasion on yours made what I did all the more unfair. If it's any consolation, I didn't enjoy the sour aftertaste of abused power. But I was searching for some connection, some rational explanation. The only way I could sit through that interview was by lying to myself about what had really happened in that coffee shop: when I passed your bent neck, I stopped because I had seen you somewhere before, and I couldn't remember—that's all.

66   I had definitely seen your type before, and had even slept with some of them—those too bright, too jaded colored girls. There were a few at Columbia, but many more would come across the street from Barnard. They made no bones about their plans to hook into a man who—what was the expression then?—who was going somewhere. Well, after classes I went to work as a room-service waiter in the Hilton. It wasn't as glamorous as the work-study jobs in the library or dean's office, but it paid a lot better when you counted tips. During the slack periods my boss let me read, and I had Sundays off. But you see, that wasn't the right day. All the guys who were going somewhere had been able to take girls to the fraternity dances on Friday and Saturday nights where they could show off their brand-name clothes. They only needed a pair of jeans to go to the park with me, or to sit in my room and study. I was too serious, too dull. George doesn't know how to have fun, they'd say, he's so quiet. I suppose I was, but what could I honestly talk to them about? They would have thought I was crazy if I had told them that seeing them flow around me like dark jewels on campus was one of the most beautiful sights on earth.

67   Yes, I was one of the quiet ones who thought them beautiful, even with the polished iron webbing around their hearts. I understood exactly what they were protecting themselves against, and I was willing to help them shine that armor all the more, to be the shoulder they could cry on when it got too heavy—if they had only let me in. But they didn't want me then. And I was to meet them years later, at parties and dinners, when the iron had served them a bit too well. They were successful and they were alone: those guys who were going somewhere had by either inclination or lack of numbers left a good deal of them behind. They had stopped being frivolous, but they were hurt and suspicious. And maturity made me much more hesitant to take a chance on finding an opening into hearts like those. Often I had wanted to go over and shake some silk-clad shoulder who thought she was righteously justified in spreading the tired old gospel about not being able to meet good black men. She had met *me*. But I would have been too proud to remind her where.

68   Yeah, I knew your type well. And you sat there with your mind racing, trying to double-think me, so sure you had me and the game down pat. Give him what he wants. I fooled you, didn't I. All I wanted was for you to

be yourself. And I wondered if it was too late, if seven years in New York had been just enough for you to lose that, like you were trying to lose your Southern accent. It amused me the way your tongue and lips were determined to clip along, and then your accent would find you in the spaces between two words—"talking about," "graduating at." In spite of yourself, the music would squeeze through at the ending of those verbs to tilt the following vowels up just half a key. That's why I wanted you to call me George. There isn't a Southerner alive who could bring that name in under two syllables. And for those brief seconds it allowed me to imagine you as you must have been: softer, slower—open. It conjured up images of jasmine-scented nights, warm biscuits and honey being brought to me on flowered china plates as you sat at my feet and rubbed your cheek against my knee. Go ahead and laugh, you have a perfect right. I had never been South, and you couldn't count the times I had spent in Miami at the Super Bowl—that city was a humid and pastel New York. So I had the same myths about Southern women that you did about Northern men. But it was a fact that when you said my name, you became yourself.

69   And it was also a fact that there was no way I was going to give you that job. And your firm plans about returning to Willow Springs helped to alleviate my guilt about that. We were going to turn other qualified people down—and it's never a matter of the most qualified, there's no such animal. It's either do they or don't they "fit." And where could I possibly place you? My life was already made at thirty-one. My engineering degree, the accelerating success of Andrews & Stein, proved beyond a shadow of a doubt that you got nothing from believing in crossed fingers, broken mirrors, spilled salt—a twist in your gut in the middle of a Third Avenue coffee shop. You either do or you don't. And you, Ophelia, were the don't. Don't get near a woman who has the power to turn your existence upside-down by simply running a hand up the back of her neck.

Questions for Discussion

1. What is the effect of alternating narrators in the story? What does the use of the double point of view reveal about the ability or inability of one person accurately to estimate what another person is thinking?

2. How does the tone of the story change when the speaker changes? Explain what you consider each tone to be.

3. What stereotypes, particularly of men, does Cocoa express in her narrative? On what does she base her opinions?

4. In George's narrative, why does Mrs. Jackson insist so strongly that "'only the present has potential'"? What, according to George, have been the advantages and disadvantages of this insistence?

5. Why does Mrs. Jackson discipline the boys so harshly? Explain whether her methods are effective.

6. How accurate is George's reading of Cocoa's character? How accurate is Cocoa's reading of George's character?

7. On what does George base his conclusion on whether to hire Cocoa? Explain why you think this is or is not a valid reason not to hire her.

Suggestions for Exploring, Writing, and Persuading

1. In an essay, classify at least five of your friends or acquaintances according to their flavors as Cocoa does.

2. Write a character sketch of either of the narrators.

3. Argue in an essay for or against hiring Cocoa.

4. In an essay argue that Cocoa and George would or would not be likely to have a lasting relationship.

Jhumpa Lahiri (b. 1967)

Born in London to parents who were born and reared in India, Jhumpa Lahiri grew up in Rhode Island and was educated at Barnard College, where she earned a B.A. in English, and at Boston College, where she received M.A.'s in English, Creative Writing, and Comparative Literature and the Arts, and a Ph.D. in Renaissance Studies. The New Yorker published three of her stories in 1998, and her 1999 short story collection Interpreter of Maladies, *from which this story is taken, received the 2000 Pulitzer Prize for Fiction. Lahiri's 2003 novel,* The Namesake, *like her stories, has been praised for its quiet language and realistic and compassionate portrayal of South Asians living in the United States.*

A TEMPORARY MATTER   (1999)

1   The notice informed them that it was a temporary matter: for five days their electricity would be cut off for one hour, beginning at eight P.M. A line had gone down in the last snowstorm, and the repairmen were going to take advantage of the milder evenings to set it right. The work would affect only the houses on the quiet tree-lined street, within walking distance of a row of brick-faced stores and a trolley stop, where Shoba and Shukumar had lived for three years.

2   "It's good of them to warn us," Shoba conceded after reading the notice aloud, more for her own benefit than Shukumar's. She let the strap of her leather satchel, plump with files, slip from her shoulders, and left it in the hallway as she walked into the kitchen. She wore a navy blue poplin raincoat over gray sweatpants and white sneakers, looking, at thirty-three, like the type of woman she'd once claimed she would never resemble.

3   She'd come from the gym. Her cranberry lipstick was visible only on the outer reaches of her mouth, and her eyeliner had left charcoal patches beneath her lower lashes. She used to look this way sometimes, Shukumar thought, on mornings after a party or a night at a bar, when she'd been too lazy to wash her face, too eager to collapse into his arms. She dropped a sheaf of mail on the table without a glance. Her eyes were still fixed on the notice in her other hand. "But they should do this sort of thing during the day."

4   "When I'm here, you mean," Shukumar said. He put a glass lid on a pot of lamb, adjusting it so only the slightest bit of steam could escape. Since January he'd been working at home, trying to complete the final chapters of his dissertation on agrarian revolts in India. "When do the repairs start?"

5   "It says March nineteenth. Is today the nineteenth?" Shoba walked over to the framed corkboard that hung on the wall by the fridge, bare except for a calendar of William Morris wallpaper patterns. She looked at it as if for the first time, studying the wallpaper pattern carefully on the top half before allowing her eyes to fall to the numbered grid on the bottom. A friend had sent the calendar in the mail as a Christmas gift, even though Shoba and Shukumar hadn't celebrated Christmas that year.

6   "Today then," Shoba announced. "You have a dentist appointment next Friday, by the way."

7   He ran his tongue over the tops of his teeth; he'd forgotten to brush them that morning. It wasn't the first time. He hadn't left the house at all that day, or the day before. The more Shoba stayed out, the more she began putting in extra hours at work and taking on additional projects, the more he wanted to stay in, not even leaving to get the mail, or to buy fruit or wine at the stores by the trolley stop.

8   Six months ago, in September, Shukumar was at an academic conference in Baltimore when Shoba went into labor, three weeks before her due date. He hadn't wanted to go to the conference, but she had insisted; it was important to make contacts, and he would be entering the job market next year. She told him that she had his number at the hotel, and a copy of his schedule and flight numbers, and she had arranged with her friend Gillian for a ride to the hospital in the event of an emergency. When the cab pulled away that morning for the airport, Shoba stood waving good-bye in her robe, with one arm resting on the mound of her belly as if it were a perfectly natural part of her body.

9   Each time he thought of that moment, the last moment he saw Shoba pregnant, it was the cab he remembered most, a station wagon, painted red with blue lettering. It was cavernous compared to their own car. Although Shukumar was six feet tall, with hands too big ever to rest comfortably in the pockets of his jeans, he felt dwarfed in the back seat. As the cab sped down Beacon Street, he imagined a day when he and Shoba might need to buy a station wagon of their own, to cart their children back and forth from music lessons and dentist appointments. He imagined himself gripping the wheel, as Shoba turned around to hand the children juice boxes. Once, these images of parenthood had troubled

Shukumar, adding to his anxiety that he was still a student at thirty-five. But that early autumn morning, the trees still heavy with bronze leaves, he welcomed the image for the first time.

10   A member of the staff had found him somehow among the identical convention rooms and handed him a stiff square of stationery. It was only a telephone number, but Shukumar knew it was the hospital. When he returned to Boston it was over. The baby had been born dead. Shoba was lying on a bed, asleep, in a private room so small there was barely enough space to stand beside her, in a wing of the hospital they hadn't been to on the tour for expectant parents. Her placenta had weakened and she'd had a cesarean, though not quickly enough. The doctor explained that these things happen. He smiled in the kindest way it was possible to smile at people known only professionally. Shoba would be back on her feet in a few weeks. There was nothing to indicate that she would not be able to have children in the future.

11   These days Shoba was always gone by the time Shukumar woke up. He would open his eyes and see the long black hairs she shed on her pillow and think of her, dressed, sipping her third cup of coffee already, in her office downtown, where she searched for typographical errors in textbooks and marked them, in a code she had once explained to him, with an assortment of colored pencils. She would do the same for his dissertation, she promised, when it was ready. He envied her the specificity of her task, so unlike the elusive nature of his. He was a mediocre student who had a facility for absorbing details without curiosity. Until September he had been diligent if not dedicated, summarizing chapters, outlining arguments on pads of yellow lined paper. But now he would lie in their bed until he grew bored, gazing at his side of the closet which Shoba always left partly open, at the row of the tweed jackets and corduroy trousers he would not have to choose from to teach his classes that semester. After the baby died it was too late to withdraw from his teaching duties. But his adviser had arranged things so that he had the spring semester to himself. Shukumar was in his sixth year of graduate school. "That and the summer should give you a good push," his adviser had said. "You should be able to wrap things up by next September."

12   But nothing was pushing Shukumar. Instead he thought of how he and Shoba had become experts at avoiding each other in their three-bedroom house, spending as much time on separate floors as possible. He thought of how he no longer looked forward to weekends, when she sat for hours on the sofa with her colored pencils and her files, so that he feared that putting on a record in his own house might be rude. He thought of how long it had been since she looked into his eyes and smiled, or whispered his name on those rare occasions they still reached for each other's bodies before sleeping.

13   In the beginning he had believed that it would pass, that he and Shoba would get through it all somehow. She was only thirty-three. She was strong, on her feet again. But it wasn't a consolation. It was often nearly lunchtime when Shukumar would finally pull himself out of bed and head

downstairs to the coffeepot, pouring out the extra bit Shoba left for him, along with an empty mug, on the countertop.

14   Shukumar gathered onion skins in his hands and let them drop into the garbage pail, on top of the ribbons of fat he'd trimmed from the lamb. He ran the water in the sink, soaking the knife and the cutting board, and rubbed a lemon half along his fingertips to get rid of the garlic smell, a trick he'd learned from Shoba. It was seven-thirty. Through the window he saw the sky, like soft black pitch. Uneven banks of snow still lined the sidewalks, though it was warm enough for people to walk about without hats or gloves. Nearly three feet had fallen in the last storm, so that for a week people had to walk single file, in narrow trenches. For a week that was Shukumar's excuse for not leaving the house. But now the trenches were widening, and water drained steadily into grates in the pavement.

15   "The lamb won't be done by eight," Shukumar said. "We may have to eat in the dark."

16   "We can light candles," Shoba suggested. She unclipped her hair, coiled neatly at her nape during the days, and pried the sneakers from her feet without untying them. "I'm going to shower before the lights go," she said, heading for the staircase. "I'll be down."

17   Shukumar moved her satchel and her sneakers to the side of the fridge. She wasn't this way before. She used to put her coat on a hanger, her sneakers in the closet, and she paid bills as soon as they came. But now she treated the house as if it were a hotel. The fact that the yellow chintz armchair in the living room clashed with the blue-and-maroon Turkish carpet no longer bothered her. On the enclosed porch at the back of the house, a crisp white bag still sat on the wicker chaise, filled with lace she had once planned to turn into curtains.

18   While Shoba showered, Shukumar went into the downstairs bathroom and found a new toothbrush in its box beneath the sink. The cheap, stiff bristles hurt his gums, and he spit some blood into the basin. The spare brush was one of many stored in a metal basket. Shoba had bought them once when they were on sale, in the event that a visitor decided, at the last minute, to spend the night.

19   It was typical of her. She was the type to prepare for surprises, good and bad. If she found a skirt or a purse she liked she bought two. She kept the bonuses from her job in a separate bank account in her name. It hadn't bothered him. His own mother had fallen to pieces when his father died, abandoning the house he grew up in and moving back to Calcutta, leaving Shukumar to settle it all. He liked that Shoba was different. It astonished him, her capacity to think ahead. When she used to do the shopping, the pantry was always stocked with extra bottles of olive and corn oil, depending on whether they were cooking Italian or Indian. There were endless boxes of pasta in all shapes and colors, zippered sacks of basmati rice, whole sides of lambs and goats from the Muslim butchers at Haymarket, chopped up and frozen in endless plastic bags. Every other Saturday they wound through the maze of stalls Shukumar

eventually knew by heart. He watched in disbelief as she bought more food, trailing behind her with canvas bags as she pushed through the crowd, arguing under the morning sun with boys too young to shave but already missing teeth, who twisted up brown paper bags of artichokes, plums, gingerroot, and yams, and dropped them on their scales, and tossed them to Shoba one by one. She didn't mind being jostled, even when she was pregnant. She was tall, and broad-shouldered, with hips that her obstetrician assured her were made for childbearing. During the drive back home, as the car curved along the Charles, they invariably marveled at how much food they'd bought.

20   It never went to waste. When friends dropped by, Shoba would throw together meals that appeared to have taken half a day to prepare, from things she had frozen and bottled, not cheap things in tins but peppers she had marinated herself with rosemary, and chutneys that she cooked on Sundays, stirring boiling pots of tomatoes and prunes. Her labeled mason jars lined the shelves of the kitchen, in endless sealed pyramids, enough, they'd agreed, to last for their grandchildren to taste. They'd eaten it all by now. Shukumar had been going through their supplies steadily, preparing meals for the two of them, measuring out cupfuls of rice, defrosting bags of meat day after day. He combed through her cookbooks every afternoon, following her penciled instructions to use two teaspoons of ground corian-der seeds instead of one, or red lentils instead of yellow. Each of the recipes was dated, telling the first time they had eaten the dish together. April 2, cauliflower with fennel. January 14, chicken with almonds and sul-tanas. He had no memory of eating those meals, and yet there they were, recorded in her neat proofreader's hand. Shukumar enjoyed cooking now. It was the one thing that made him feel productive. If it weren't for him, he knew, Shoba would eat a bowl of cereal for her dinner.

21   Tonight, with no lights, they would have to eat together. For months now they'd served themselves from the stove, and he'd taken his plate into his study, letting the meal grow cold on his desk before shoving it into his mouth without pause, while Shoba took her plate to the living room and watched game shows, or proofread files with her arsenal of colored pencils at hand.

22   At some point in the evening she visited him. When he heard her approach he would put away his novel and begin typing sentences. She would rest her hands on his shoulders and stare with him into the blue glow of the computer screen. "Don't work too hard," she would say after a minute or two, and head off to bed. It was the one time in the day she sought him out, and yet he'd come to dread it. He knew it was something she forced herself to do. She would look around the walls of the room, which they had decorated together last summer with a border or march-ing ducks and rabbits playing trumpets and drums. By the end of August there was a cherry crib under the window, a white changing table with mint-green knobs, and a rocking chair with checkered cushions. Shuku-mar had disassembled it all before bringing Shoba back from the hospi-tal, scraping off the rabbits and ducks with a spatula. For some reason

the room did not haunt him the way it haunted Shoba. In January, when he stopped working at his carrel in the library, he set up his desk there deliberately, partly because the room soothed him, and partly because it was a place Shoba avoided.

23   Shukumar returned to the kitchen and began to open drawers. He tried to locate a candle among the scissors, the eggbeaters and whisks, the mortar and pestle she'd bought in a bazaar in Calcutta, and used to pound garlic cloves and cardamom pods, back when she used to cook. He found a flashlight, but no batteries, and a half-empty box of birthday candles. Shoba had thrown him a surprise birthday party last May. One hundred and twenty people had crammed into the house—all the friends and the friends of friends they now systematically avoided. Bottles of vinho verde had nested in a bed of ice in the bathtub. Shoba was in her fifth month, drinking ginger ale from a martini glass. She had made a vanilla cream cake with custard and spun sugar. All night she kept Shukumar's long fingers linked with hers as they walked among the guests at the party.

24   Since September their only guest had been Shoba's mother. She came from Arizona and stayed with them for two months after Shoba returned from the hospital. She cooked dinner every night, drove herself to the supermarket, washed their clothes, put them away. She was a religious woman. She set up a small shrine, a framed picture of a lavender-faced goddess and a plate of marigold petals, on the bedside table in the guest room, and prayed twice a day for healthy grandchildren in the future. She was polite to Shukumar without being friendly. She folded his sweaters with an expertise she had learned from her job in a department store. She replaced a missing button on his winter coat and knit him a beige and brown scarf, presenting it to him without the least bit of ceremony, as if he had only dropped it and hadn't noticed. She never talked to him about Shoba; once, when he mentioned the baby's death, she looked up from her knitting, and said, "But you weren't even there."

25   It struck him as odd that there were no real candles in the house. That Shoba hadn't prepared for such an ordinary emergency. He looked now for something to put the birthday candles in and settled on the soil of a potted ivy that normally sat on the windowsill over the sink. Even though the plant was inches from the tap, the soil was so dry that he had to water it first before the candles would stand straight. He pushed aside the things on the kitchen table, the piles of mail, the unread library books. He remembered their first meals there, when they were so thrilled to be married, to be living together in the same house at last, that they would just reach for each other foolishly, more eager to make love than to eat. He put down two embroidered place mats, a wedding gift from an uncle in Lucknow, and set out the plates and wineglasses they usually saved for guests. He put the ivy in the middle, the white-edged, star-shaped leaves girded by ten little candles. He switched on the digital clock radio and tuned it to a jazz station.

26   "What's all this?" Shoba said when she came downstairs. Her hair was wrapped in a thick white towel. She undid the towel and draped it over a chair, allowing her hair, damp and dark, to fall across her back. As she walked absently toward the stove she took out a few tangles with her fingers. She wore a clean pair of sweatpants, a T-shirt, an old flannel robe. Her stomach was flat again, her waist narrow before the flare of her hips, the belt of the robe tied in a floppy knot.

27   It was nearly eight. Shukumar put the rice on the table and the lentils from the night before into the microwave oven, punching the numbers on the timer.

28   "You made *rogan josh*," Shoba observed, looking through the glass lid at the bright paprika stew.

29   Shukumar took out a piece of lamb, pinching it quickly between his fingers so as not to scald himself. He prodded a larger piece with a serving spoon to make sure the meat slipped easily from the bone. "It's ready," he announced.

30   The microwave had just beeped when the lights went out, and the music disappeared.

31   "Perfect timing," Shoba said.

32   "All I could find were birthday candles." He lit up the ivy, keeping the rest of the candles and a book of matches by his plate.

33   "It doesn't matter," she said, running a finger along the stem of her wineglass. "It looks lovely."

34   In the dimness, he knew how she sat, a bit forward in her chair, ankles crossed against the lowest rung, left elbow on the table. During his search for the candles, Shukumar had found a bottle of wine in a crate he had thought was empty. He clamped the bottle between his knees while he turned in the corkscrew. He worried about spilling, and so he picked up the glasses and held them close to his lap while he filled them. They served themselves, stirring the rice with their forks, squinting as they extracted bay leaves and cloves from the stew. Every few minutes Shukumar lit a few more birthday candles and drove them into the soil of the pot.

35   "It's like India," Shoba said, watching him tend his makeshift candelabra. "Sometimes the current disappears for hours at a stretch. I once had to attend an entire rice ceremony in the dark. The baby just cried and cried. It must have been so hot."

36   Their baby had never cried, Shukumar considered. Their baby would never have a rice ceremony, even though Shoba had already made the guest list, and decided on which of her three brothers she was going to ask to feed the child its first taste of solid food, at six months if it was a boy, seven if it was a girl.

37   "Are you hot?" he asked her. He pushed the blazing ivy pot to the other end of the table, closer to the piles of books and mail, making it even more difficult for them to see each other. He was suddenly irritated that he couldn't go upstairs and sit in front of the computer.

38   "No. It's delicious," she said, tapping her plate with her fork. "It really is."

39   He refilled the wine in her glass. She thanked him.

40   They weren't like this before. Now he had to struggle to say something that interested her, something that made her look up from her plate, or from her proofreading files. Eventually he gave up trying to amuse her. He learned not to mind the silences.

41   "I remember during power failures at my grandmother's house, we all had to say something," Shoba continued. He could barely see her face, but from her tone he knew her eyes were narrowed, as if trying to focus on a distant object. It was a habit of hers.

42   "Like what?"

43   "I don't know. A little poem. A joke. A fact about the world. For some reason my relatives always wanted me to tell them the names of my friends in America. I don't know why the information was so interesting to them. The last time I saw my aunt she asked after four girls I went to elementary school with in Tucson. I barely remember them now."

44   Shukumar hadn't spent as much time in India as Shoba had. His parents, who settled in New Hampshire, used to go back without him. The first time he'd gone as an infant he'd nearly died of amoebic dysentery. His father, a nervous type, was afraid to take him again, in case something were to happen, and left him with his aunt and uncle in Concord. As a teenager he preferred sailing camp or scooping ice cream during the summers to going to Calcutta. It wasn't until after his father died, in his last year of college, that the country began to interest him, and he studied its history from course books as if it were any other subject. He wished now that he had his own childhood story of India.

45   "Let's do that," she said suddenly.

46   "Do what?"

47   "Say something to each other in the dark."

48   "Like what? I don't know any jokes."

49   "No, no jokes." She thought for a minute. "How about telling each other something we've never told before."

50   "I used to play this game in high school," Shukumar recalled. "When I got drunk."

51   "You're thinking of truth or dare. This is different. Okay, I'll start." She took a sip of wine. "The first time I was alone in your apartment, I looked in your address book to see if you'd written me in. I think we'd known each other two weeks."

52   "Where was I?"

53   "You went to answer the telephone in the other room. It was your mother, and I figured it would be a long call. I wanted to know if you'd promoted me from the margins of your newspaper."

54   "Had I?"

55   "No. But I didn't give up on you. Now it's your turn."

56   He couldn't think of anything, but Shoba was waiting for him to speak. She hadn't appeared so determined in months. What was there left to say to her? He thought back to their first meeting, four years earlier at a lec-

ture hall in Cambridge, where a group of Bengali poets were giving a recital. They'd ended up side by side, on folding wooden chairs. Shuku-mar was soon bored; he was unable to decipher the literary diction, and couldn't join the rest of the audience as they sighed and nodded solemnly after certain phrases. Peering at the newspaper folded in his lap, he stud-ied the temperatures of cities around the world. Ninety-one degrees in Singapore yesterday, fifty-one in Stockholm. When he turned his head to the left, he saw a woman next to him making a grocery list on the back of a folder, and was startled to find that she was beautiful.

57   "Okay," he said, remembering. "The first time we went out to dinner, to the Portuguese place, I forgot to tip the waiter. I went back the next morning, found out his name, left money with the manager."

58   "You went all the way back to Somerville just to tip a waiter?"

59   "I took a cab."

60   "Why did you forget to tip the waiter?"

61   The birthday candles had burned out, but he pictured her face clearly in the dark, the wide tilting eyes, the full grape-toned lips, the fall at age two from her high chair still visible as a comma on her chin. Each day, Shukumar noticed, her beauty, which had once overwhelmed him, seemed to fade. The cosmetics that had seemed superfluous were nec-essary now, not to improve her but to define her somehow.

62   "By the end of the meal I had a funny feeling that I might marry you," he said, admitting it to himself as well as to her for the first time. "It must have distracted me."

63   The next night Shoba came home earlier than usual. There was lamb left over from the evening before, and Shukumar heated it up so that they were able to eat by seven. He'd gone out that day, through the melting snow, and bought a packet of taper candles from the corner store, and batteries to fit the flashlight. He had the candles ready on the counter-top, standing in brass holders shaped like lotuses, but they ate under the glow of the copper-shaded ceiling lamp that hung over the table.

64   When they had finished eating, Shukumar was surprised to see that Shoba was stacking her plate on top of his, and then carrying them over to the sink. He had assumed she would retreat to the living room, behind her barricade of files.

65   "Don't worry about the dishes," he said, taking them from her hands.

66   "It seems silly not to," she replied, pouring a drop of detergent onto a sponge. "It's nearly eight o'clock."

67   His heart quickened. All day Shukumar had looked forward to the lights going out. He thought about what Shoba had said the night before, about looking in his address book. It felt good to remember her as she was then, how bold yet nervous she'd been when they first met, how hopeful. They stood side by side at the sink, their reflections fitting together in the frame of the window. It made him shy, the way he felt the first time they stood together in a mirror. He couldn't recall the last time they'd been photographed. They had stopped attending parties, went

nowhere together. The film in his camera still contained pictures of Shoba, in the yard, when she was pregnant.

68   After finishing the dishes, they leaned against the counter, drying their hands on either end of a towel. At eight o'clock the house went black. Shukumar lit the wicks of the candles, impressed by their long, steady flames.

69   "Let's sit outside," Shoba said. "I think it's warm still."

70   They each took a candle and sat down on the steps. It seemed strange to be sitting outside with patches of snow still on the ground. But everyone was out of their houses tonight, the air fresh enough to make people restless. Screen doors opened and closed. A small parade of neighbors passed by with flashlights.

71   "We're going to the bookstore to browse," a silver-haired man called out. He was walking with his wife, a thin woman in a windbreaker, and holding a dog on a leash. They were the Bradfords, and they had tucked a sympathy card into Shoba and Shukumar's mailbox back in September. "I hear they've got their power."

72   "They'd better," Shukumar said. "Or you'll be browsing in the dark."

73   The woman laughed, slipping her arm through the crook of her husband's elbow. "Want to join us?"

74   "No thanks," Shoba and Shukumar called out together. It surprised Shukumar that his words matched hers.

75   He wondered what Shoba would tell him in the dark. The worst possibilities had already run through his head. That she'd had an affair. That she didn't respect him for being thirty-five and still a student. That she blamed him for being in Baltimore the way her mother did. But he knew those things weren't true. She'd been faithful, as had he. She believed in him. It was she who had insisted he go to Baltimore. What didn't they know about each other? He knew she curled her fingers tightly when she slept, that her body twitched during bad dreams. He knew it was honeydew she favored over cantaloupe. He knew that when they returned from the hospital the first thing she did when she walked into the house was pick out objects of theirs and toss them into a pile in the hallway: books from the shelves, plants from the windowsills, paintings from walls, photos from tables, pots and pans that hung from the hooks over the stove. Shukumar had stepped out of her way, watching as she moved methodically from room to room. When she was satisfied, she stood there staring at the pile she'd made, her lips drawn back in such distaste that Shukumar had thought she would spit. Then she'd started to cry.

76   He began to feel cold as he sat there on the steps. He felt that he needed her to talk first, in order to reciprocate.

77   "That time when your mother came to visit us," she said finally. "When I said one night that I had to stay late at work, I went out with Gillian and had a martini."

78   He looked at her profile, the slender nose, the slightly masculine set of her jaw. He remembered that night well; eating with his mother, tired

from teaching two classes back to back, wishing Shoba were there to say more of the right things because he came up with only the wrong ones. It had been twelve years since his father had died, and his mother had come to spend two weeks with him and Shoba, so they could honor his father's memory together. Each night his mother cooked something his father had liked, but she was too upset to eat the dishes herself, and her eyes would well up as Shoba stroked her hand. "It's so touching," Shoba had said to him at the time. Now he pictured Shoba with Gillian, in a bar with striped velvet sofas, the one they used to go to after the movies, making sure she got her extra olive, asking Gillian for a cigarette. He imagined her complaining, and Gillian sympathizing about visits from in-laws. It was Gillian who had driven Shoba to the hospital.

79   "Your turn," she said, stopping his thoughts.

80   At the end of their street Shukumar heard sounds of a drill and the electricians shouting over it. He looked at the darkened facades of the houses lining the street. Candles glowed in the windows of one. In spite of the warmth, smoke rose from the chimney.

81   "I cheated on my Oriental Civilization exam in college," he said. "It was my last semester, my last set of exams. My father had died a few months before. I could see the blue book of the guy next to me. He was an American guy, a maniac. He knew Urdu and Sanskrit. I couldn't remember if the verse we had to identify was an example of a *ghazal* or not. I looked at his answer and copied it down."

82   It had happened over fifteen years ago. He felt relief now, having told her.

83   She turned to him, looking not at his face, but at his shoes—old moccasins he wore as if they were slippers, the leather at the back permanently flattened. He wondered if it bothered her, what he'd said. She took his hand and pressed it. "You didn't have to tell me why you did it," she said, moving closer to him.

84   They sat together until nine o'clock, when the lights came on. They heard some people across the street clapping from their porch, and televisions being turned on. The Bradfords walked back down the street, eating ice-cream cones and waving. Shoba and Shukumar waved back. Then they stood up, his hand still in hers, and went inside.

85   Somehow, without saying anything, it had turned into this. Into an exchange of confessions—the little ways they'd hurt or disappointed each other, and themselves. The following day Shukumar thought for hours about what to say to her. He was torn between admitting that he once ripped out a photo of a woman in one of the fashion magazines she used to subscribe to and carried it in his books for a week, or saying that he really hadn't lost the sweater-vest she bought him for their third wedding anniversary but had exchanged it for cash at Filene's, and that he had gotten drunk alone in the middle of the day at a hotel bar. For their first anniversary, Shoba had cooked a ten-course dinner just for him. The

vest depressed him. "My wife gave me a sweater-vest for our anniversary," he complained to the bartender, his head heavy with cognac. "What
do you expect?" the bartender had replied. "You're married."

86   As for the picture of the woman, he didn't know why he'd ripped it out.
She wasn't as pretty as Shoba. She wore a white sequined dress, and had
a sullen face and lean, mannish legs. Her bare arms were raised, her fists
around her head, as if she were about to punch herself in the ears. It was
an advertisement for stockings. Shoba had been pregnant at the time, her
stomach suddenly immense, to the point where Shukumar no longer
wanted to touch her. The first time he saw the picture he was lying in bed
next to her, watching her as she read. When he noticed the magazine in
the recycling pile he found the woman and tore out the page as carefully
as he could. For about a week he allowed himself a glimpse each day. He
felt an intense desire for the woman, but it was a desire that turned to
disgust after a minute or two. It was the closest he'd come to infidelity.

87   He told Shoba about the sweater on the third night, the picture on the
fourth. She said nothing as he spoke, expressed no protest or reproach. She
simply listened, and then she took his hand, pressing it as she had before.
On the third night, she told him that once after a lecture they'd attended,
she let him speak to the chairman of his department without telling him that
he had a dab of pâté on his chin. She'd been irritated with him for some reason, and so she'd let him go on and on, about securing his fellowship for the
following semester, without putting a finger to her own chin as a signal. The
fourth night, she said that she never liked the one poem he'd ever published
in his life, in a literary magazine in Utah. He'd written the poem after meeting Shoba. She added that she found the poem sentimental.

88   Something happened when the house was dark. They were able to talk
to each other again. The third night after supper they'd sat together on
the sofa, and once it was dark he began kissing her awkwardly on her
forehead and her face, and though it was dark he closed his eyes, and
knew that she did, too. The fourth night they walked carefully upstairs,
to bed, feeling together for the final step with their feet before the landing, and making love with a desperation they had forgotten. She wept
without sound, and whispered his name, and traced his eyebrows with
her finger in the dark. As he made love to her he wondered what he
would say to her the next night, and what she would say, the thought of
it exciting him. "Hold me," he said, "hold me in your arms." By the time
the lights came back on downstairs, they'd fallen asleep.

89   The morning of the fifth night Shukumar found another notice from
the electric company in the mailbox. The line had been repaired ahead
of schedule, it said. He was disappointed. He had planned on making
shrimp *malai* for Shoba, but when he arrived at the store he didn't feel
like cooking anymore. It wasn't the same, he thought, knowing that the
lights wouldn't go out. In the store the shrimp looked gray and thin. The
coconut milk tin was dusty and overpriced. Still, he bought them, along
with a beeswax candle and two bottles of wine.

90   She came home at seven-thirty. "I suppose this is the end of our game," he said when he saw her reading the notice.

91   She looked at him. "You can still light candles if you want." She hadn't been to the gym tonight. She wore a suit beneath the raincoat. Her makeup had been retouched recently.

92   When she went upstairs to change, Shukumar poured himself some wine and put on a record, a Thelonius Monk album he knew she liked.

93   When she came downstairs they ate together. She didn't thank him or compliment him. They simply ate in a darkened room, in the glow of a beeswax candle. They had survived a difficult time. They finished off the shrimp. They finished off the first bottle of wine and moved on to the second. They sat together until the candle had nearly burned away. She shifted in her chair, and Shukumar thought that she was about to say something. But instead she blew out the candle, stood up, turned on the light switch, and sat down again.

94   "Shouldn't we keep the lights off?" Shukumar asked.

95   She set her plate aside and clasped her hands on the table. "I want you to see my face when I tell you this," she said gently.

96   His heart began to pound. The day she told him she was pregnant, she had used the very same words, saying them in the same gentle way, turning off the basketball game he'd been watching on television. He hadn't been prepared then. Now he was.

97   Only he didn't want her to be pregnant again. He didn't want to have to pretend to be happy.

98   "I've been looking for an apartment and I've found one," she said, narrowing her eyes on something, it seemed, behind his left shoulder. It was nobody's fault, she continued. They'd been through enough. She needed some time alone. She had money saved up for a security deposit. The apartment was on Beacon Hill, so she could walk to work. She had signed the lease that night before coming home.

99   She wouldn't look at him, but he stared at her. It was obvious that she'd rehearsed the lines. All this time she'd been looking for an apartment, testing the water pressure, asking a Realtor if heat and hot water were included in the rent. It sickened Shukumar, knowing that she had spent these past evenings preparing for a life without him. He was relieved and yet he was sickened. This was what she'd been trying to tell him for the past four evenings. This was the point of her game.

100   Now it was his turn to speak. There was something he'd sworn he would never tell her, and for six months he had done his best to block it from his mind. Before the ultrasound she had asked the doctor not to tell her the sex of their child, and Shukumar had agreed. She had wanted it to be a surprise.

101   Later, those few times they talked about what had happened, she said at least they'd been spared that knowledge. In a way she almost took pride in her decision, for it enabled her to seek refuge in a mystery. He knew that she assumed it was a mystery for him, too. He'd arrived too late from Baltimore—when it was all over and she was lying on the hospital bed.

But he hadn't. He'd arrived early enough to see their baby, and to hold him before they cremated him. At first he had recoiled at the suggestion, but the doctor said holding the baby might help him with the process of grieving. Shoba was asleep. The baby had been cleaned off, his bulbous lids shut tight to the world.

102   "Our baby was a boy," he said. "His skin was more red than brown. He had black hair on his head. He weighed almost five pounds. His fingers were curled shut, just like yours in the night."

103   Shoba looked at him now, her face contorted with sorrow. He had cheated on a college exam, ripped a picture of a woman out of a magazine. He had returned a sweater and got drunk in the middle of the day instead. These were the things he had told her. He had held his son, who had known life only within her, against his chest in a darkened room in an unknown wing of the hospital. He had held him until a nurse knocked and took him away, and he promised himself that day that he would never tell Shoba, because he still loved her then, and it was the one thing in her life that she had wanted to be a surprise.

104   Shukumar stood up and stacked his plate on top of hers. He carried the plates to the sink, but instead of running the tap he looked out the window. Outside the evening was still warm, and the Bradfords were walking arm in arm. As he watched the couple the room went dark, and he spun around. Shoba had turned the lights off. She came back to the table and sat down, and after a moment Shukumar joined her. They wept together, for the things they now knew.

Questions for Discussion

1. What event precipitated the alienation between Shoba and Shukumar? How and why has it affected each of them?

2. When Shoba decides that they each should tell the other something they've not told before, Shukumar wonders, "What was there left to say to her?" Why would he have nothing new to say? What does that reveal about his relationship to Shoba? How common is such a feeling of having nothing new to say in long-term relationships?

3. Why does Shukumar look forward to the lights' going out? Why are the revelations they make during the blackouts so meaningful and important to him? What, according to Shukumar, was "the point of this game"?

4. In what ways have the ceremonies and foods of the couple's Indian background influenced their life in the United States?

5. What is the point of view? How would the story differ if told from the point of view of the other spouse?

6. Why, when Shoba tells Shukumar that she has found an apartment, does he feel both sickened and relieved?

7. What does the last line, "They wept together for the things they now knew" mean for their relationship?

Suggestions for Exploring, Writing, and Persuading

1. Write an essay exploring the importance of communication in a relationship important to you.

2. Argue why, in your opinion, this marriage will or will not survive.

3. In an essay, compare this couple's reaction to the death of their son to the reaction of Amy and her husband in Frost's "Home Burial."

POETRY

William Shakespeare (1564–1616)

The biography of William Shakespeare precedes Othello *in the Grief and Loss Unit.*

SONNET 116 (1609)

Let me not to the marriage of true minds
Admit impediments. Love is not love
Which alters when it alteration finds,
Or bends with the remover to remove:
5 O, no! it is an ever-fixed mark,
That looks on tempests and is never shaken;
It is the star to every wandering bark,
Whose worth's unknown, although his height be taken.
Love's not Time's fool, though rosy lips and cheeks
10 Within his bending sickle's compass come;
Love alters not with his brief hours and weeks,
But bears it out even to the edge of doom.
    If this be error, and upon me prov'd,
    I never writ, nor no man ever lov'd.

SONNET 130 (1609)

My mistress' eyes are nothing like the sun;
Coral is far more red than her lips' red:
If snow be white, why then her breasts are dun;
If hairs be wires, black wires grow on her head.
5 I have seen roses damask'd, red and white,
But no such roses see I in her cheeks;
And in some perfumes is there more delight
Than in the breath that from my mistress reeks.

I love to hear her speak, yet well I know

10 That music hath a far more pleasing sound:

I grant I never saw a goddess go;

My mistress, when she walks, treads on the ground:

 And yet, by heaven, I think my love as rare

 As any she belied with false compare.

SONNET 138   (1609)

When my love swears that she is made of truth,

I do believe her, though I know she lies,

That she might think me some untutor'd youth,

Unlearned in the world's false subtleties.

5 Thus vainly thinking that she thinks me young,

Although she knows my days are past the best,

Simply I credit her false-speaking tongue:

On both sides thus is simple truth supprest.

But wherefore says she not she is unjust?

10 And wherefore say not I that I am old?

O, love's best habit is in seeming trust,

And age in love loves not to have years told:

 Therefore I lie with her, and she with me,

 And in our faults by lies we flatter'd be.

Questions for Discussion

1. In Sonnet 116, what claims does the speaker make for love? What cannot change love? What can?

2. Sonnet 130 differs from most love poetry of Shakespeare's day in its unflattering description of the loved woman's appearance. What does the speaker claim for his love?

3. Why do the speaker and his beloved lie to each other in Sonnet 138? What do you think of their behavior?

Suggestions for Exploring, Writing, and Persuading

1. Write a descriptive essay—either serious or humorous—about your love.

2. Explain the qualities, other than physical appearance, that attract members of the opposite sex to each other.

3. Examine one or more pairs of lovers in this section in light of Shakespeare's definition of love in Sonnet 116.

4. Discuss some of the pressures that are put on a man and/or a woman in a seemingly "good" marriage or in "true love."

5. Explain why you agree or disagree that the "marriage of true minds" is unaffected by change or time. Explain why marriage is or is not an "ever-fixed mark."

John Donne (1572–1631)

John Donne, an Anglican priest highly regarded for his sermons, wrote conversational, sometimes tortuous, but carefully controlled poetry. His works include cynical court poetry such as the Satires, *strikingly sensual love poems in* Songs and Sonnets, *and powerful, often anguished religious poems such as the* Holy Sonnets. *Foremost among those poets later called metaphysical by Samuel Johnson, Donne often joins quite disparate concepts in elaborate images or conceits. The speaker's comparison of himself and his beloved to a compass in "A Valediction: Forbidding Mourning" is among the most famous of Donne's conceits.*

A VALEDICTION: FORBIDDING MOURNING   (1611)

As virtuous men passe mildly away,
    And whisper to their soules, to goe,
Whilst some of their sad friends doe say,
    The breath goes now, and some say, no:

5   So let us melt, and make no noise,
    No teare-floods, nor sigh-tempests move,
'Twere prophanation of our joyes
    To tell the layetie our love.

Moving of th'earth brings harmes and feares,
10   Men reckon what it did and meant,
But trepidation of the spheares,
    Though greater farre, is innocent.

Dull sublunary lovers love
    (Whose soule is sense) cannot admit
15   Absence, because it doth remove
    Those things which elemented it.

But we by a love, so much refin'd,
    That our selves know not what it is,
Inter-assured of the mind,
20   Care lesse, eyes, lips, and hands to misse.
Our two soules therefore, which are one,
    Though I must goe, endure not yet
A breach, but an expansion,
    Like gold to airy thinnesse beate.

25   If they be two, they are two so
    As stiffe twin compasses are two,
Thy soule the fixt foot, makes no show
    To move, but doth, if th' other doe.

And though it in the center sit,
30   Yet when the other far doth rome,

It leanes, and hearkens after it,
    And growes erect, as it comes home.

Such wilt thou be to mee, who must
    Like th'other foot, obliquely runne;
35 Thy firmnes makes my circle just,
    And makes me end, where I begunne.

Questions for Discussion

1. What is the occasion for the poem?
2. How does the woman whom the speaker is addressing seem to feel about his impending departure? What, then, is the purpose of the poem?
3. How do the various images that define the couple's love help to fulfill the poem's purpose?
4. According to the speaker, how does this couple's love differ from that of other couples?

Suggestion for Exploring, Writing, and Persuading

1. Carefully analyze Donne's poem, showing how diction, imagery, sound, and syntax all contribute to the soothing, reassuring tone of the poem.

Andrew Marvell (1621–1678)

Andrew Marvell was a Puritan, a vocal advocate of personal freedom, and a member of the British Parliament. He, like John Donne, was one of the poets whom Samuel Johnson later called metaphysical. Marvell is known today for the exquisite craftsmanship of such poems as "The Garden," "To His Coy Mistress," and "An Horatian Ode upon Cromwell's Return from Ireland."

To His Coy Mistress   (1681)

Had we but world enough, and time,
This coyness, Lady, were no crime.
We would sit down, and think which way
To walk, and pass our long love's day.
5   Thou by the Indian Ganges' side
Shouldst rubies find: I by the tide
Of Humber would complain. I would
Love you ten years before the flood:
And you should, if you please, refuse
10 Till the conversion of the Jews.
My vegetable love should grow
Vaster than empires, and more slow.

An hundred years should go to praise
Thine eyes, and on thy forehead gaze.
15   Two hundred to adore each breast:
But thirty thousand to the rest.
An age at least to every part,
And the last age should show your heart:
For, Lady, you deserve this state;
20   Nor would I love at lower rate.
    But at my back I always hear
Time's wingèd chariot hurrying near:
And yonder all before us lie
Deserts of vast eternity.
25   Thy beauty shall no more be found;
Nor, in thy marble vault, shall sound
My echoing song: then worms shall try
That long-preserved virginity:
And your quaint honour turn to dust;
30   And into ashes all my lust.
The grave's a fine and private place,
But none, I think, do there embrace.
    Now, therefore, while the youthful hew
Sits on thy skin like morning dew,
35   And while thy willing soul transpires
At every pore with instant fires,
Now let us sport us while we may;
And now, like amorous birds of prey,
Rather at once our time devour,
40   Than languish in his slow-chapped power.
Let us roll all our strength, and all
Our sweetness, up into one ball:
And tear our pleasures with rough strife,
Thorough the iron gates of life.
45   Thus, though we cannot make our sun
Stand still, yet we will make him run.

Questions for Discussion

1. How does the tone of the poem change from the first stanza to the second to the last?

2. Do you think the speaker genuinely loves his listener, or is he just feeding her a line? Defend your answer.

Suggestions for Exploring, Writing, and Persuading

1. Define *carpe diem,* and explain how Marvell's narrator uses this concept to further his seduction.

2. This poem is obviously intended to persuade. Analyze the persuasive techniques that the speaker uses.

3. Analyze some techniques that men or women use to be coy or to play hard to get.

Elizabeth Barrett Browning (1806–1861)

Elizabeth Barrett was famous as a well-educated and pre-cocious poet. By the time Robert Browning fell in love with her, she had become a semi-invalid forbidden by her tyran-nical father to marry. After Elizabeth and Robert eloped to Italy, her health improved. The depth of her love for her hus-band is beautifully illustrated by the Sonnets from the Por-tuguese *(1850), forty-four verses tracing the progress of her love for Robert, who called her his little Portuguese. "How Do I Love Thee?" is the most famous of these sonnets.*

Sonnet 43   (1850)

How do I love thee? Let me count the ways.
I love thee to the depth and breadth and height
My soul can reach, when feeling out of sight
For the ends of Being and ideal Grace.
5   I love thee to the level of everyday's
Most quiet need, by sun and candlelight.
I love thee freely, as men strive for Right;
I love thee purely, as they turn from Praise.
I love thee with the passion put to use
10 In my old griefs, and with my childhood's faith.
I love thee with a love I seemed to lose
With my lost saints—I love thee with the breath,
Smiles, tears, of all my life!—and, if God choose,
I shall but love thee better after death.

Questions for Discussion

1. How and why does Browning use this tightly controlled form to express boundless love?

2. According to this sonnet, what are the different types of love neces-sary for a marriage to last?

Suggestions for Exploring, Writing, and Persuading

1. Browning uses a series of metaphorical devices—personification, metonymy, and synecdoche—to describe her love. These are combined with poetic sound devices such as anaphora, alliteration, assonance,

and caesura. Write an essay explaining how these devices, as well as the sonnet form, enable Browning to express great depths of feeling in the confined space of a sonnet.

2. Compare and contrast the depth of love described in this sonnet with the depth of love in one of Shakespeare's sonnets.

Edgar Allan Poe (1809–1849)

Best known for his brilliantly macabre stories, Poe was one of the earliest masters of the modern short story and has been credited with inventing the detective story. Raised in the home of his godfather, John Allan, after both his parents died, Poe struggled in his personal life with alcoholism, serious gambling debts, and the loss of one promising job after another. Poe's stories create a world that is surreal, mysterious, and highly symbolic. Poe was also highly regarded as a literary critic and a poet. In its richness of music and imagery, "To Helen" is typical of his poems.

TO HELEN   (1831)

Helen, thy beauty is to me
   Like those Nicéan barks of yore,
That gently, o'er a perfumed sea,
   The weary, way-worn wanderer bore
5   To his own native shore.

On desperate seas long wont to roam,
   Thy hyacinth hair, thy classic face,
Thy Naiad airs have brought me home
   To the glory that was Greece,
10 And the grandeur that was Rome.

Lo! in yon brilliant window-niche
   How statue-like I see thee stand,
The agate lamp within thy hand!
Ah, Psyche, from the regions which
15   Are Holy-Land!

Questions for Discussion

1. What does the speaker appear most to appreciate about Helen's beauty?

2. To what does the speaker compare Helen? What qualities in her do these comparisons suggest?

3. What extravagant claim does the speaker make for Helen's beauty in the last stanza? Is she to him simply a lovely woman or is she something more?

Suggestions for Exploring, Writing, and Persuading

1. Discuss in an essay Poe's highly musical and suggestive use of sound in this poem. How does sound help convey the poem's tone of adoration and develop its meaning? Consider the effects of alliteration, assonance, and rhyme as well as the smooth vowels and liquids.

2. Research the poem's classical allusions and show how they contribute to the poem's meaning.

3. If you have seen one or more of the recent films on Helen of Troy, compare Poe's portrayal with one or more of the film's portrayals.

Robert Browning (1812–1889)

The English poet Robert Browning is famous for his perfection of the dramatic monologue, for the depth and breadth of knowledge displayed in his poetry, for his ideas, and for his role in one of the most famous love stories of the nineteenth century. His wife, Elizabeth Barrett Browning, immortalized their love in her Sonnets from the Portuguese. *Robert Browning's most admired books,* Men and Women *(1855) and* Dramatis Personae *(1864), contain many of his frequently read poems. His book-length poem* The Ring and the Book *(1868), an account of a murder trial in seventeenth-century Rome, experiments with multiple* points of view *and is a precursor of the* nonfiction novel.

PORPHYRIA'S LOVER   (1836)

The rain set early in tonight,
   The sullen wind was soon awake,
It tore the elm-tops down for spite,
   And did its worst to vex the lake:
5   I listened with heart fit to break.
When glided in Porphyria; straight
   She shut the cold out and the storm,
And kneeled and made the cheerless grate
   Blaze up, and all the cottage warm;
10   Which done, she rose, and from her form
Withdrew the dripping cloak and shawl,
   And laid her soiled gloves by, untied
Her hat and let the damp hair fall,
   And, last, she sat down by my side
15   And called me. When no voice replied,
She put my arm about her waist,
   And made her smooth white shoulder bare,
And all her yellow hair displaced,
   And, stooping, made my cheek lie there,
20   And spread, o'er all, her yellow hair,

Murmuring how she loved me—she
  Too weak, for all her heart's endeavor,
To set its struggling passion free
  From pride, and vainer ties dissever,
25   And give herself to me forever.
But passion sometimes would prevail,
  Nor could tonight's gay feast restrain
A sudden thought of one so pale
  For love of her, and all in vain:
30   So, she was come through wind and rain.
Be sure I looked up at her eyes
  Happy and proud; at last I knew
Porphyria worshiped me: surprise
  Made my heart swell, and still it grew
35   While I debated what to do.
That moment she was mine, mine, fair,
  Perfectly pure and good: I found
A thing to do, and all her hair
  In one long yellow string I wound
40   Three times her little throat around,
And strangled her. No pain felt she;
  I am quite sure she felt no pain.
As a shut bud that holds a bee,
  I warily oped her lids: again
45   Laughed the blue eyes without a stain.
And I untightened next the tress
  About her neck; her cheek once more
Blushed bright beneath my burning kiss:
  I propped her head up as before,
50   Only, this time my shoulder bore
Her head, which droops upon it still:
  The smiling rosy little head,
So glad it has its utmost will,
  That all it scorned at once is fled,
55   And I, its love, am gained instead!
Porphyria's love: she guessed not how
  Her darling one wish would be heard.
And thus we sit together now,
  And all night long we have not stirred,
60   And yet God has not said a word!

Questions for Discussion

1. To whom is the narrator speaking? In what tone of voice? What does
   the tone reveal about the speaker?

2. What, according to the narrator, is Porphyria's "darling one wish"?
   How has the narrator granted it? Why?

Suggestions for Exploring, Writing, and Persuading

1. Contrast Porphyria with the Duchess in the following poem.
2. Argue one of the following:
   The narrator is insane
   Porphyria deserves to get her wish

My Last Duchess   (1842)

Ferrara

That's my last Duchess painted on the wall,
Looking as if she were alive. I call
That piece a wonder, now: Frà Pandolf's hands
Worked busily a day, and there she stands.
5 Will't please you sit and look at her? I said
"Frà Pandolf" by design, for never read
Strangers like you that pictured countenance,
The depth and passion of its earnest glance,
But to myself they turned (since none puts by
10 The curtain I have drawn for you, but I)
And seemed as they would ask me, if they durst,
How such a glance came there; so, not the first
Are you to turn and ask thus. Sir, 'twas not
Her husband's presence only, called that spot
15 Of joy into the Duchess' cheek: perhaps
Frà Pandolf chanced to say "Her mantle laps
Over my lady's wrist too much," or "Paint
Must never hope to reproduce the faint
Half-flush that dies along her throat": such stuff
20 Was courtesy, she thought, and cause enough
For calling up that spot of joy. She had
A heart—how shall I say?—too soon made glad,
Too easily impressed; she liked whate'er
She looked on, and her looks went everywhere.
25 Sir, 'twas all one! My favor at her breast,
The dropping of the daylight in the West,
The bough of cherries some officious fool
Broke in the orchard for her, the white mule
She rode with round the terrace—all and each
30 Would draw from her alike the approving speech,
Or blush, at least. She thanked men—good! but thanked
Somehow—I know not how—as if she ranked
My gift of a nine-hundred-years-old name
With anybody's gift. Who'd stoop to blame

35   This sort of trifling? Even had you skill
      In speech—(which I have not)—to make your will
      Quite clear to such an one, and say, "Just this
      Or that in you disgusts me; here you miss,
      Or there exceed the mark"—and if she let
40   Herself be lessoned so, nor plainly set
      Her wits to yours, forsooth, and made excuse
      —E'en then would be some stooping; and I choose
      Never to stoop. Oh sir, she smiled, no doubt,
      Whene'er I passed her; but who passed without
45   Much the same smile? This grew; I gave commands;
      Then all smiles stopped together. There she stands
      As if alive. Will't please you rise? We'll meet
      The company below, then. I repeat,
      The Count your master's known munificence
50   Is ample warrant that no just pretense
      Of mine for dowry will be disallowed;
      Though his fair daughter's self, as I avowed
      At starting, is my object. Nay, we'll go
      Together down, sir. Notice Neptune, though,
55   Taming a sea horse, thought a rarity,
      Which Claus of Innsbruck cast in bronze for me!

Questions for Discussion

1. What qualities of the deceased Duchess annoyed the Duke?

2. Why does the Duke want to make plain to this particular listener what he disliked about his deceased wife?

3. How do Ferrara's diction and sentence structure suggest his calloused egotism?

Suggestions for Exploring, Writing, and Persuading

1. This dramatic monologue in which the Duke describes his deceased wife reveals more about him than about her. Write a character sketch of the Duke. Or in an argumentative essay, debate what really happened between the Duke and his "Last Duchess."

2. In a researched essay, explain how a relationship can be hurt or enhanced by the different kinds of love: obsessive, clinical or analytical, romantic, or platonic.

3. Write an essay in which you argue that this negative, domineering kind of relationship can or cannot happen today.

Emily Dickinson (1830–1886)

Although very sociable as a girl and young woman, Emily Dickinson slowly became reclusive. In fact, she and her younger sister Lavinia lived their whole lives in their father's house, with their only other sibling, Austin, living only a stone's throw away. Despite her later tendency to "dwell" only in her house and the grounds surrounding it, Dickinson maintained close friendships with her sister-in-law, Susan Gilbert Dickinson, and with people with whom she corresponded but whom she seldom or never saw. The reasons for the poet's seclusion are nowhere stated clearly, though literary critics and lovers of her poetry are fascinated by the possibilities: was she agoraphobic; was she suffering from a broken heart; or was she choosing to avoid a patriarchal world that little valued women's writing? Few people in Amherst, Massachusetts, where Emily Dickinson spent most of her life, would have dreamed that within the confines of her yard a revolution in American poetry was taking place. Her poetry was far ahead of her time in form and content. The great bulk of her work—close to two thousand poems—was discovered only after her death. In little packets sewn together with thread and on scraps of paper, Dickinson had enclosed an extraordinary outpouring of creativity. Her brief poems, rich in metaphor and punctuated primarily by dashes, present a wealth of startling images and an intensity of thought that make her one of America's most loved and studied poets.

199

(1890)

I'm "wife"—I've finished that—
That other state—
I'm Czar—I'm "Woman" now—
It's safer so—

5   How odd the Girl's life looks
Behind this soft Eclipse—
I think that Earth feels so—
To folks in Heaven—now—

10   This being comfort—then
That other kind—was pain—
But why compare?
I'm "Wife"! Stop there!

Questions for Discussion

1. What two states does the poem speak about? How is each depicted? Does one seem to be drawn in a more positive way than the other?

2. What is "this soft Eclipse"? In what ways do the different meanings of "Eclipse" add richness to the poem's meaning?

3. The words "wife" and "Woman" are in quotation marks. How does this punctuation affect your interpretation of the poem?

Suggestions for Exploring, Writing, and Persuading

1. In an essay, discuss Dickinson's portrayal of men.

2. Argue, in an essay, that a woman gives up her sense of identity in a marriage. Or analyze the degree to which a man or a woman does so.

3. Write an essay comparing the woman's premarital state with her married state.

339   (1929)

I tend my flowers for thee—
Bright Absentee!
My Fuchsia's Coral Seams
Rip—while the Sower—dreams—

5   Geraniums—tint—and spot—
Low Daisies—dot—
My Cactus—splits her Beard
To show her throat—

Carnations—tip their spice—
10 And Bees—pick up—
A Hyacinth—I hid—
Puts out a Ruffled Head—
And odors fall
From flasks—so small—
15 You marvel how they held—

Globe Roses—break their satin flake—
Upon my Garden floor—
Yet—thou—not there—
I had as lief they bore
20 No Crimson—more—

Thy flower—be gay—
Her Lord—away!
It ill becometh me—
I'll dwell in Calyx—Gray—
How modestly—alway—
Thy Daisy—
Draped for thee!

Questions for Discussion

1. In this poem, the speaker, calling herself "Daisy," addresses a "Bright Absentee." Explain the metaphors she uses to speak to the absent one.
2. Stanzas 1 through 4 primarily describe; stanza 5 articulates the point the speaker wants to make about the earlier descriptions. What is the message?

Suggestions for Exploring, Writing, and Persuading

1. In an essay, discuss Dickinson's use of primary and secondary definitions and the effect of this poetic strategy on her poetry.
2. Write an essay that explicates Dickinson's use of metaphor in this poem.

Robert Frost (1874–1963)

Robert Frost's life, like many of his poems, was filled with ironies. Known as a New England poet, Frost was born in San Francisco and named after Robert E. Lee. When his poetry was not recognized in the United States, he moved to England and there published his first books of poetry, A Boy's Will *(1913) and* North of Boston *(1914). When he returned to the United States, his fame as a poet was already established. Early criticism identified Frost with the kindly New England speaker of many of his poems, and even now his most famous poems are those about nature, which often emphasize rising above life's problems.*

Frost had more than his share of family tragedies, however, and was always aware of the darker side of life. Even his famous definition of poetry as a "momentary stay against confusion" in "The Figure a Poem Makes" emphasizes the complexities of life and the necessity of finding ways to manage life's ambiguities. For Frost, precise form in poetry is one of those ways; as a master craftsman, he uses traditional poetic form so skillfully that he seems to recreate the natural speech patterns of the New England characters in his dialogues and monologues, and he adds to the meaning of his poems by using such tight forms as the sonnet and terza rima.

HOME BURIAL   (1914)

He saw her from the bottom of the stairs
Before she saw him. She was starting down,
Looking back over her shoulder at some fear.
She took a doubtful step and then undid it
5   To raise herself and look again. He spoke
Advancing toward her: "What is it you see

From up there always?—for I want to know."
She turned and sank upon her skirts at that,
And her face changed from terrified to dull.
He said to gain time: "What is it you see?"
Mounting until she cowered under him.
"I will find out now—you must tell me, dear."
She, in her place, refused him any help,
With the least stiffening of her neck and silence.
She let him look, sure that he wouldn't see,
Blind creature; and awhile he didn't see.
But at last he murmured, "Oh," and again, "Oh."

"What is it—what?" she said.

                    "Just that I see."

"You don't," she challenged. "Tell me what it is."

"The wonder is I didn't see at once.
I never noticed it from here before.
I must be wonted to it—that's the reason.
The little graveyard where my people are!
So small the window frames the whole of it.
Not so much larger than a bedroom, is it?
There are three stones of slate and one of marble,
Broad-shouldered little slabs there in the sunlight
On the sidehill. We haven't to mind *those*.
But I understand: it is not the stones,
But the child's mound—"

                    "Don't, don't, don't,
        don't," she cried.

She withdrew, shrinking from beneath his arm
That rested on the banister, and slid downstairs;
And turned on him with such a daunting look,
He said twice over before he knew himself:
"Can't a man speak of his own child he's lost?"

"Not you!—Oh, where's my hat? Oh, I don't need it!
I must get out of here. I must get air.—
I don't know rightly whether any man can."

"Amy! Don't go to someone else this time.
Listen to me. I won't come down the stairs."
He sat and fixed his chin between his fists.
"There's something I should like to ask you, dear."

"You don't know how to ask it."

                    "Help me, then."

Her fingers moved the latch for all reply.

10
15
20
25
30
35
40
45

"My words are nearly always an offense.
I don't know how to speak of anything
So as to please you. But I might be taught,
I should suppose. I can't say I see how.
A man must partly give up being a man
With womenfolk. We could have some arrangement
By which I'd bind myself to keep hands off
Anything special you're a-mind to name.
Though I don't like such things 'twixt those that love.
Two that don't love can't live together without them.
But two that do can't live together with them."
She moved the latch a little. "Don't—don't go.
Don't carry it to someone else this time.
Tell me about it if it's something human.
Let me into your grief. I'm not so much
Unlike other folks as your standing there
Apart would make me out. Give me my chance.
I do think, though, you overdo it a little.
What was it brought you up to think it the thing
To take your mother-loss of a first child
So inconsolably—in the face of love.
You'd think his memory might be satisfied—"

"There you go sneering now!"

"I'm not, I'm not!

You make me angry. I'll come down to you.
God, what a woman! And it's come to this,
A man can't speak of his own child that's dead."

"You can't because you don't know how to speak.
If you had any feelings, you that dug
With your own hand—how could you?—his little grave;
I saw you from that very window there,
Making the gravel leap and leap in air,
Leap up, like that, like that, and land so lightly
And roll back down the mound beside the hole.
I thought, Who is that man? I didn't know you.
And I crept down the stairs and up the stairs
To look again, and still your spade kept lifting.
Then you came in. I heard your rumbling voice
Out in the kitchen and I don't know why,
But I went near to see with my own eyes,
You could sit there with the stains on your shoes
Of the fresh earth from your own baby's grave
And talk about your everyday concerns.
You had stood the spade up against the wall

Outside there in the entry, for I saw it."

"I shall laugh the worst laugh I ever laughed.
95   I'm cursed. God, if I don't believe I'm cursed."

"I can repeat the very words you were saying:
'Three foggy mornings and one rainy day
Will rot the best birch fence a man can build.'
Think of it, talk like that at such a time!
100   What had how long it takes a birch to rot
To do with what was in the darkened parlor?
You *couldn't* care! The nearest friends can go
With anyone to death, comes so far short
They might as well not try to go at all.
105   No, from the time when one is sick to death,
One is alone, and he dies more alone.
Friends make pretense of following to the grave,
But before one is in it, their minds are turned
And making the best of their way back to life
110   And living people, and things they understand.
But the world's evil. I won't have grief so
If I can change it. Oh, I won't, I won't!"

"There, you have said it all and you feel better.
You won't go now. You're crying. Close the door.
115   The heart's gone out of it: why keep it up?
Amy! There's someone coming down the road!"

"*You*—oh, you think the talk is all. I must go—
Somewhere out of this house. How can I make you—"

"If—you—do!" She was opening the door wider.

120   "Where do you mean to go? First tell me that.
I'll follow and bring you back by force. I *will!*—"

Questions for Discussion

1. The husband says, "A man must partly give up being a man / With womenfolk." Explain these lines and agree or disagree with the husband's claim.

2. Explain the significance of Amy's statement about the rotting birch. Why does the husband's statement about the birch offend Amy? With whom do you agree? Why?

3. In lines 105–06, Amy says, "No, from the time when one is sick to death, / One is alone, and he dies more alone." Agree or disagree with this statement.

4. Has Amy grieved too long and blamed her husband unfairly? Explain.

5. Explain the double meaning of the title.

Suggestions for Exploring, Writing, and Persuading

1. Agree or disagree with this statement: It is a stereotype that men and women show distinctive differences in reaction to a tragedy.
2. Contrast Amy's view about death with the husband's view of death.

THE DEATH OF THE HIRED MAN   (1914)

Mary sat musing on the lamp-flame at the table,
Waiting for Warren. When she heard his step,
She ran on tiptoe down the darkened passage
To meet him in the doorway with the news
5   And put him on his guard. "Silas is back."
She pushed him outward with her through the door
And shut it after her. "Be kind," she said.
She took the market things from Warren's arms
And set them on the porch, then drew him down
10 To sit beside her on the wooden steps.

"When was I ever anything but kind to him?
But I'll not have the fellow back," he said.
"I told him so last haying, didn't I?
If he left then, I said, that ended it.
15 What good is he? Who else will harbor him
At his age for the little he can do?
What help he is there's no depending on.
Off he goes always when I need him most.
He thinks he ought to earn a little pay,
20 Enough at least to buy tobacco with,
So he won't have to beg and be beholden.
'All right,' I say, 'I can't afford to pay
Any fixed wages, though I wish I could.'
'Someone else can.' 'Then someone else will have to.'
25 I shouldn't mind his bettering himself
If that was what it was. You can be certain,
When he begins like that, there's someone at him
Trying to coax him off with pocket money—
In haying time, when any help is scarce.
30 In winter he comes back to us. I'm done."

"Sh! not so loud: he'll hear you," Mary said.

"I want him to: he'll have to soon or late."
"He's worn out. He's asleep beside the stove.
When I came up from Rowe's I found him here,
35 Huddled against the barn door fast asleep,
A miserable sight, and frightening, too—
You needn't smile—I didn't recognize him—

I wasn't looking for him—and he's changed.
Wait till you see."

"Where did you say he'd been?"
"He didn't say. I dragged him to the house,
And gave him tea and tried to make him smoke.
I tried to make him talk about his travels.
Nothing would do: he just kept nodding off."

45   "What did he say? Did he say anything?"

"But little."

"Anything? Mary confess
He said he'd come to ditch the meadow for me."

"Warren!"

50   "But did he? I just want to know."

"Of course he did. What would you have him say?
Surely you wouldn't grudge the poor old man
Some humble way to save his self-respect.
55   He added, if you really care to know,
He meant to clear the upper pasture, too.
That sounds like something you have heard before?
Warren, I wish you could have heard the way
He jumbled everything. I stopped to look
Two or three times—he made me feel so queer—
60   To see if he was talking in his sleep.
He ran on Harold Wilson—you remember—
The boy you had in haying four years since.
He's finished school, and teaching in his college.
Silas declares you'll have to get him back.
65   He says they two will make a team for work:
Between them they will lay this farm as smooth!
The way he mixed that in with other things.
He thinks young Wilson a likely lad, though daft
On education—you know how they fought
70   All through July under the blazing sun,
Silas up on the cart to build the load,
Harold along beside to pitch it on."

"Yes, I took care to keep well out of earshot."

"Well, those days trouble Silas like a dream.
75   You wouldn't think they would. How some things linger!
Harold's young college-boy's assurance piqued him.
After so many years he still keeps finding
Good arguments he sees he might have used.
I sympathize. I know just how it feels

80 To think of the right thing to say too late.
Harold's associated in his mind with Latin.
He asked me what I thought of Harold's saying
He studied Latin, like the violin,
Because he liked it—that an argument!
85 He said he couldn't make the boy believe
He could find water with a hazel prong—
Which showed how much good school had ever done him.
He wanted to go over that. But most of all
He thinks if he could have another chance
90 To teach him how to build a load of hay—"

"I know, that's Silas' one accomplishment.
He bundles every forkful in its place,
And tags and numbers it for future reference,
So he can find and easily dislodge it
95 In the unloading. Silas does that well.
He takes it out in bunches like big birds' nests.
You never see him standing on the hay
He's trying to lift, straining to lift himself."

"He thinks if he could teach him that, he'd be
100 Some good perhaps to someone in the world.
He hates to see a boy the fool of books.
Poor Silas, so concerned for other folk,
And nothing to look backward to with pride,
And nothing to look forward to with hope,
105 So now and never any different."

Part of a moon was falling down the west,
Dragging the whole sky with it to the hills.
Its light poured softly in her lap. She saw it
And spread her apron to it. She put out her hand
110 Among the harplike morning-glory strings,
Taut with the dew from garden bed to eaves,
As if she played unheard some tenderness
That wrought on him beside her in the night.
"Warren," she said, "he has come home to die:
115 You needn't be afraid he'll leave you this time."

"Home," he mocked gently.

    "Yes, what else but home?
It all depends on what you mean by home.
Of course he's nothing to us, any more
120 Than was the hound that came a stranger to us
Out of the woods, worn out upon the trail."

"Home is the place where, when you have to go there,

They have to take you in."

                 "I should have called it

125   Something you somehow haven't to deserve."

Warren leaned out and took a step or two,
Picked up a little stick, and brought it back
And broke it in his hand and tossed it by.
"Silas has better claim on us you think

130   Than on his brother? Thirteen little miles
As the road winds would bring him to his door.
Silas has walked that far no doubt today.
Why doesn't he go there? His brother's rich,
a somebody—director in the bank."

He never told us that."

                 "We know it, though."

"I think his brother ought to help, of course.
I'll see to that if there is need. He ought of right
To take him in, and might be willing to—

140   He may be better than appearances.
But have some pity on Silas. Do you think
If he had any pride in claiming kin
Or anything he looked for from his brother,
He'd keep so still about him all this time?"

145   "I wonder what's between them."

                 "I can tell you.
Silas is what he is—we wouldn't mind him—
But just the kind that kinsfolk can't abide.
He never did a thing so very bad.

150   He don't know why he isn't quite as good
As anybody. Worthless though he is,
He won't be made ashamed to please his brother."

"*I* can't think Si ever hurt anyone."

No, but he hurt my heart the way he lay

155   And rolled his old head on that sharp-edged chair-back.
He wouldn't let me put him on the lounge.
You must go in and see what you can do.
I made the bed up for him there tonight.
You'll be surprised at him—how much he's broken.

160   His working days are done; I'm sure of it."

"I'd not be in a hurry to say that."

"I haven't been. Go, look, see for yourself.

But, Warren, please remember how it is:
He's come to help you ditch the meadow.
165   He has a plan. You mustn't laugh at him.
He may not speak of it, and then he may.
I'll sit and see if that small sailing cloud
Will hit or miss the moon."

It hit the moon.
170   Then there were three there, making a dim row,
The moon, the little silver cloud, and she.
Warren returned—too soon, it seemed to her—
Slipped to her side, caught up her hand and waited.

"Warren?" she questioned.

175   "Dead," was all he answered.

Questions for Discussion

1. Examine the passages describing the cloud, the moon, and the stick, and explain their significance or symbolism.

2. Support or attack Mary's statement that Silas had "nothing to look backward to with pride, / And nothing to look forward to with hope."

Suggestions for Exploring, Writing, and Persuading

1. Silas thinks that Harold's studying "Latin, like the violin, / Because he liked it" is ridiculous. Write an essay supporting or opposing Harold's point of view.

2. Mary says, "I know just how it feels / To think of the right thing to say too late." Write an essay about an incident in which you thought of "the right thing to say too late."

3. Write an essay comparing the marriage in "The Death of the Hired Man" with that in "Home Burial."

4. Warren and Mary handle the same situation differently. Discuss in an essay how these differences define their personalities.

5. The two dialogue poems by Frost, "Home Burial" and "The Death of the Hired Man," depicting the conversation between a husband and wife, are written in blank verse. Write an essay on one or both of these poems illustrating Frost's skill in writing poetry that successfully imitates conversation.

H[ilda] D[oolittle] (1886-1961)

H. D. is considered one of the finest of the Imagist poets.
Born in Bethlehem, Pennsylvania, H.D. moved to England

in 1911 and in 1913 married British novelist Richard Ald-
ington. Her friendship with other Imagist poets, such as
Marianne Moore, Ezra Pound, and Amy Lowell, influenced
her poetry and furthered the publication of her work. Her
poetry appeared in many of the influential magazines of the
day, including the English Review, *the* Transatlantic Review,
and The Egoist. *H.D. had a lifelong fascination with any-*
thing Greek, and many of her poems, like the one included
here, reflect this interest.

HELEN   (1924)

All Greece hates
the still eyes in the white face,
the lustre as of olives
where she stands,
5   and the white hands.

All Greece reviles
the wan face when she smiles,
hating it deeper still
when it grows wan and white,
10   remembering past enchantments
and past ills.

Greece sees unmoved,
God's daughter, born of love,
the beauty of cool feet
15   and slenderest knees,
could love indeed the maid,
only if she were laid,
white ash amid funereal cypresses.

Questions for Discussion

1. Why would the Greeks hate Helen?

2. Why does the author describe Helen's physical attributes while revealing the Greeks' hatred for her?

3. Explain the references to Helen's conception in the third verse.

4. Under what conditions would the Greeks be willing to love Helen?

Suggestions for Exploring, Writing, and Persuading

1. Choose a modern Helen (male or female) and explain why this person, whom many admire, would be hated by others. Use H.D.'s technique of giving one side's opinions about admirable qualities and
   contrasting these with the other side's reasons for hatred.

2. After researching the myths about Helen, write an essay comparing Poe's poem praising Helen's beauty with H.D.'s poem describing the hatred of the Greeks for her.

Edna St. Vincent Millay (1892–1950)

Edna St. Vincent Millay, winner of the 1923 Pulitzer Prize for Poetry, was talented as an actress, a musician, and a poet. After graduation from Vassar College, she moved to Greenwich Village, where she lived a bohemian life. Her poetry reflects this life and her later devotion to her husband, her zest for life, her sense of humor, her capability for great depths of feeling, and her love of beauty.

SONNET 42   (1923)

What lips my lips have kissed, and where, and why,
I have forgotten, and what arms have lain
Under my head till morning; but the rain
Is full of ghosts tonight, that tap and sigh
5   Upon the glass and listen for reply,
And in my heart there stirs a quiet pain
For unremembered lads that not again
Will turn to me at midnight with a cry.
Thus in the winter stands the lonely tree,
10   Nor knows what birds have vanished one by one,
Yet knows its boughs more silent than before:
I cannot say what loves have come and gone,
I only know that summer sang in me
A little while, that in me sings no more.

Questions for Discussion

1. In the octave, the poet describes her feelings. What is her mood?
2. In the sestet, rather than give an answer to her problem, as is traditional in the Italian sonnet, Millay uses a metaphor to repeat the same mood. What is the metaphor, and how does it apply to her?
3. What is the tone of the poem? What does the speaker regret the most about those lost "summers"?

Suggestions for Exploring, Writing, and Persuading

1. Write about a relationship that failed and explain the reasons for its failure.
2. Explain why remembered friendships or relationships sometimes seem so much sweeter than real, present ones.

3. Write an essay on the way the sonnet form, onomatapoeia, alliteration, and metaphors add to the meaning and create the mood of the poem.

Muriel Rukeyser (1913–1980)

Poet, biographer, playwright, and activist Muriel Rukeyser was born in New York City. She attended both Vassar College and Columbia University. Theory of Flight (1935), her first book of poems, was selected for publication in the Yale Younger Poets Series. Poetry and political commitment were the primary moving forces in Rukeyser's life. She covered the Scottsboro case in Alabama, was in Spain when the Spanish Civil War broke out, and went to Gauley Bridge, West Virginia, to investigate the cases of silicosis among miners. Her research on this situation resulted in her powerful poem sequence The Book of the Dead, published in U.S. 1 (1938). Among her other books of poetry are A Turning Wind (1939), Beast in View (1944), The Green Wave (1948), Elegies (1949), Body of Waking (1958), The Speed of Darkness (1968), Breaking Open (1973), and The Gates (1976). As a political activist as well as an artist, Rukeyser encouraged other writers, including Alice Walker and Anne Sexton.

Myth   (1973)

Long afterward, Oedipus, old and blinded, walked the
roads.   He smelled a familiar smell.   It was
the Sphinx.   Oedipus said, "I want to ask one question.
Why didn't I recognize my mother?"   "You gave the
5   wrong answer," said the Sphinx.   "But that was what
made everything possible," said Oedipus.   "No," she said
"When I asked, What walks on four legs in the morning,
two at noon, and three in the evening, you answered,
Man.   You didn't say anything about woman."
10   "When you say Man," said Oedipus, "you include women too.
Everyone knows that."   She said, "That's what you think."

Questions for Discussion

1. Why is Oedipus blind?

2. What did Oedipus get as a result of answering the Sphinx's question? What is the irony in this result?

3. Why does the word *man* not always include woman? What new twist does Rukeyser add to the myth?

Suggestions for Exploring, Writing, and Persuading

1. Define irony. Then write an interpretation of this poem, explaining the double use of irony.

2. Select another myth or popular story and rewrite it to make it conform to modern standards of sensitivity to individuals or groups.

Rosario Castellanos (1925–1974)

Mexican poet, fiction writer, and dramatist Rosario Castellanos studied aesthetics in Europe and the United States before returning to Chiapas, where she worked with Native American theater groups and studied the cultural traditions of Mexico. Her acute consciousness of women's lack of power and her own loneliness resulted in her frequent use of solitude as theme. Her works, like the poem included here, often combine vivid imagery with provocative metaphors.

CHESS

TRANSLATED BY MAUREEN AHERN

Because we were friends and sometimes loved each other,
perhaps to add one more tie
to the many that already bound us,
we decided to play games of the mind.

5   We set up a board between us;
equally divided into pieces, values,
and possible moves.
We learned the rules, we swore to respect them,
and the match began.

10   We've been sitting here for centuries, meditating
ferociously
how to deal the one last blow that will finally
annihilate the other one forever.

Questions for Discussion

1. To whom is the narrator speaking in this poem?

2. How can the speaker and his/her addressee have been "sitting here for centuries"?

3. Why would the friends or lovers want to "annihilate the other one forever"?

4. What is the game of chess a metaphor for in this poem?

5. How does the nature of the poem, hence the tone of the poem, change in the last sentence?

6. How does the last stanza change the perspective of the poem and suggest different interpretations?

Suggestions for Exploring, Writing, and Persuading

1. In an essay, explain the metaphorical implication of life or of relationships as being like a game of chess.
2. Select a game as a metaphor for your life or for a particular relationship and write an essay describing the parallels.

W. S. Merwin (b. 1927)

W. S. Merwin's literary career has been long, illustrious, and extraordinarily productive. He is a poet, a translator, and an essayist. The son of a Presbyterian minister, he began writing hymns before he was even school age. At Princeton, he studied writing and Romance languages, developing a love for language that led to his excelling as a translator. During his travels in Europe, he tutored Robert Graves' son and became fascinated by mythology, a love that is apparent in many of his poems. His first book of poetry, A Mask for Janus *(1952), was published in the* Yale Younger Poets *series.* The Carrier of Ladders *received the Pulitzer Prize in 1970. While his style has evolved in later books of poetry, becoming less formal, the beautiful and moving images continue. Merwin's translations include Dante's* Purgatorio *and* Sir Gawain and the Green Knight. *In 2004, he published* The Ends of the Earth, *a collection of essays about nature and exploration. If you are not already familiar with the Greek myth of the judgment of Paris, you might want to read it before studying the poem.*

THE JUDGMENT OF PARIS   (1970)

Long afterwards
the intelligent could deduce what had been offered
and not recognized
and they suggest that bitterness should be confined
5   to the fact that the gods chose for their arbiter
a mind and character so ordinary
albeit a prince

and brought up as a shepherd
a calling he must have liked
10   for he had returned to it

when they stood before him
the three

naked feminine deathless
and he realized that he was clothed
15   in nothing but mortality
the strap of his quiver of arrows crossing
between his nipples
making it seem stranger

and he knew he must choose
20   and on that day

the one with the gray eyes spoke first
and whatever she said he kept
thinking he remembered
but remembered it woven with confusion and fear
25   the two faces that he called father
the first sight of the palace
where the brothers were strangers
and the dogs watched him and refused to know him
she made everything clear she was dazzling she
30   offered it to him
to have for his own but what he saw
was the scorn above her eyes
and her words of which he understood few
all said to him *Take wisdom*
35   *take power*
you will forget anyway
the one with the dark eyes spoke
and everything she said
he imagined he had once wished for
40   but in confusion and cowardice
the crown
of his father the crowns the crowns bowing to him
his name everywhere like grass
only he and the sea
45   triumphant
she made everything sound possible she was
dazzling she offered it to him
to hold high but what he saw
was the cruelty around her mouth
50   and her words of which he understood more
all said to him *Take pride*
take glory
you will suffer anyway

the third one the color of whose eyes
55   later he could not remember
spoke last and slowly and
of desire and it was his

though up until then he had been
happy with his river nymph
60   here was his mind
filled utterly with one girl gathering
yellow flowers
and no one like her
the words
65   made everything seem present
almost present
present
they said to him *Take*
her
70   *you will lose her anyway*

it was only when he reached out to the voice
as though he could take the speaker
herself
that his hand filled with
75   something to give
but to give to only one of the three
an apple as it is told
discord itself in a single fruit its skin
already carved
80   *To the fairest*

then a mason working above the gates of Troy
in the sunlight thought he felt the stone
shiver

in the quiver on Paris's back the head
85   of the arrow for Achilles' heel
smiled in its sleep

and Helen stepped from the palace to gather
as she would do every day in that season
from the grove the yellow ray flowers tall
90   as herself

whose roots are said to dispel pain

Questions for Discussion

1. What is "so ordinary" about Paris' "mind and character"? How does
   Merwin emphasize the vulnerability of Paris in the opening stanzas?

2. Identify each of the three goddesses and explain what she offers Paris
   as a bribe. Explain the last line of each goddess' offer.

3. What does the goddess whose bribe Paris accepts get? What does
   Paris get? What are the consequences?

4. Explain why Paris cannot remember the color of Aphrodite's eyes.
5. According to this poem, what ultimately determines Paris's choice? What do the last four stanzas reveal about the importance of Paris's casual decision?
6. What are the implications of the last line? Is it ironic? Consolatory?

Suggestions for Exploring, Writing, and Persuading

1. If you were offered the same choices that Paris hears, which would you pick? Why?
2. In an essay describe a simple, casual decision by an ordinary person that changed the lives of people around him or her.
3. Watch one or more of the recent films about Troy. Then compare Paris as he is depicted in one of the films—by Orlando Bloom in *Troy*, for example—with Merwin's portrayal of Paris.
4. In a researched essay, support your point of view about what really caused the Trojan War.

Maya Angelou (b. 1929)

Marguerita Johnson, who later changed her name to Maya Angelou, was born in St. Louis but spent her childhood in Stamps, Arkansas, and in California. Before she became famous as a writer, she tried a wide variety of occupations, from streetcar conductor to cook to dancer and singer. Angelou has written five autobiographical books, the first, I Know Why the Caged Bird Sings *(1969), being the most popular. In addition, she excels in many areas: writing essays, novels, and short fiction; acting and directing; and participating in civil-rights activities. Maya Angelou is a colorful and popular speaker. At Bill Clinton's presidential inauguration in January 1993, Angelou read her poem "On the Pulse of Morning," written for the occasion. Two of her recent books of essays are* Wouldn't Take Nothing for My Journey Now *(1993) and* Even the Stars Look Lonesome *(1997).*

PHENOMENAL WOMAN   (1978)

Pretty women wonder where my secret lies.
I'm not cute or built to suit a fashion model's size
But when I start to tell them,
They think I'm telling lies.
5 I say,
It's in the reach of my arms,
The span of my hips,
The stride of my step,

The curl of my lips.
10   I'm a woman
Phenomenally.
Phenomenal woman,
That's me.

I walk into a room
15   Just as cool as you please,
And to a man,
The fellows stand or
Fall down on their knees.
Then they swarm around me,
20   A hive of honey bees.
I say,
It's the fire in my eyes,
And the flash of my teeth,
The swing in my waist,
25   And the joy in my feet.
I'm a woman
Phenomenally.
Phenomenal woman,
That's me.

30   Men themselves have wondered
What they see in me.
They try so much
But they can't touch
My inner mystery.
35   When I try to show them,
They say they still can't see.
I say,
It's in the arch of my back,
The sun of my smile,
40   The ride of my breasts,
The grace of my style.
I'm a woman
Phenomenally,
Phenomenal woman,
45   That's me.

Now you understand
Just why my head's not bowed.
I don't shout or jump about
Or have to talk real loud.
50   When you see me passing,
It ought to make you proud.
I say,
It's in the click of my heels,

The bend of my hair,
55   the palm of my hand,
The need for my care.
'Cause I'm a woman
Phenomenally.
Phenomenal woman,
60   That's me.

Questions for Discussion

1. What is the significance of the contrast between pretty women and the speaker? Why don't the women or the men understand her attractiveness?
2. What do others say is her attraction? In one or two words, give your opinion of what the attraction is. Can these words explain the truth about her attraction?
3. What does she believe is her secret?

Suggestions for Exploring, Writing, and Persuading

1. Write an essay in which you explain your own womanliness or manliness.
2. Get the words to Helen Reddy's song "I Am Woman" or Christina Aguillera's "Beautiful" and compare or contrast these words with Angelou's words.
3. In an essay, discuss the qualities that make women phenomenal, that enable them simultaneously to be wife, mother, homemaker, family social secretary, chauffeur, and sometimes breadwinner.
4. After examining tone, diction, and syntax, write an essay or poem titled "Phenomenal Man."

Ted Hughes (1930–1999)

Edward James Hughes, Poet Laureate of England from 1984 to 1999, was born in Yorkshire, and his experiences on the moors of England greatly influenced the mythic framework for his literary world. He graduated from Pembroke College, having switched from English as a major field to archeology and anthropology. Hughes was a prolific writer, and his works cover a wide variety of forms. His first collection of poems, The Hawk in the Rain, *from which the following poem is taken, appeared in 1957. Probably his most famous poetry collections are* Crow: From the Life and the Songs of the Crow *(1971) and* Birthday Letters *(1998), a controversial book about his relationship with Sylvia Plath, his wife. In addition to poems, Hughes wrote plays, stories, and poems for children, translated and edited classical literature, and edited his wife's poems and prose.*

INCOMPATIBILITIES

(1957)

Desire's a vicious separator in spite
    Of its twisting women round men:
Cold-chisels two selfs single as it welds hot
    Iron of their separates to one.

5   Old Eden commonplace: something magnets
    And furnaces and with fierce
Hammer-blows the one body on the other knits
    Till the division disappears.

But desire outstrips those hands that a nothing fills,
10   It dives into the opposite eyes,
Plummets through blackouts of impassables
    For the star that lights the face,

Each body still straining to follow down
    The maelstrom dark of the other, their limbs flail
15   Flesh and beat upon
    The inane everywhere of its obstacle,

Each, each second, lonelier and further
    Falling alone through the endless
Without-world of the other, through both here
20   Twist so close they choke their cries.

Questions for Discussion

1. According to Hughes, how does physical attraction (desire) separate two people? Explain.

2. Desire means several things in this poem. Explain at least two of them.

3. Analyze the images that suggest incompatibilities.

Suggestions for Exploring, Writing, and Persuading

1. In an essay, explain the last line as it relates to incompatibility of two people.

2. Analyze the tone in this poem, examining in particular the ways in which Hughes blends the ideas of love with a feeling of violence.

3. Select one of the poems by Sylvia Plath, Ted Hughes' wife; write an essay comparing their use of imagery.

Marge Piercy (b. 1936)

*Piercy was born in Detroit of a Jewish mother and a Pres-
byterian father. Leaving home at seventeen, she struggled
through such jobs as secretary, switchboard operator, artist's
model, and salesclerk while trying unsuccessfully to get her
novels published. She and her second husband were active
in the civil rights movement and the movement against the
Vietnam War. She has recently become involved in the Jewish renewal movement. Seriously involved in political
causes all her life, Piercy considers herself a political writer.
She has published more than thirty books, including novels,
poetry, essays, and a play. Her most recent works are* The
Art of Blessing the Day: Poems with a Jewish Theme *(1999)
and the novel* Three Women *(1999).*

BARBIE DOLL   (1970)

This girlchild was born as usual

and presented dolls that did pee-pee
and miniature GE stoves and irons
and wee lipsticks the color of cherry candy.
5   Then in the magic of puberty, a classmate said:
You have a great big nose and fat legs.

She was healthy, tested intelligent,
possessed strong arms and back,
abundant sexual drive and manual dexterity.
10   She went to and fro apologizing.
Everyone saw a fat nose on thick legs.

She was advised to play coy,
exhorted to come on hearty,
exercise, diet, smile and wheedle.
15   Her good nature wore out
like a fan belt.
So she cut off her nose and her legs
and offered them up.

In the casket displayed on satin she lay
20   with the undertaker's cosmetics painted on,
a turned-up putty nose,
dressed in a pink and white nightie.
Doesn't she look pretty? everyone said.
Consummation at last.
25   To every woman a happy ending.

Questions for Discussion

1. What is significant about the gifts "this girlchild" received?

2. Why is she not named but rather referred to generically as "this girl-child"?

3. The "girlchild" seems to be crushed by what her classmate says to her "in the magic of puberty." In what ways is puberty magic? In what ways is it a time of vulnerability?

4. Why does she allow others' perceptions of her few "unattractive" qualities to outweigh her strengths?

5. Explain the statement "her good nature wore out / like a fan belt."

6. In what ways is the contradictory advice she is given in the third verse typical of the advice teenage girls are given? What similar advice do teenage boys hear?

7. Explain the irony of the last verse. At what stereotypes is Piercy's satire directed?

Suggestions for Exploring, Writing, and Persuading

1. What does this poem say about society? Explain in an essay.

2. In an essay, contrast the girlchild in "Barbie Doll" with the speaker in "Phenomenal Woman."

3. Write an essay in which you show how physical attributes can have positive as well as negative influences on a person.

4. Determine what you consider to be the best solutions to dealing with the pressures of stereotyping an adolescent, and write an essay convincing a teenage girl or boy to adopt your solutions.

Janice Mirikitani (b. 1942)

Janice Mirikitani, a third-generation Japanese American who was interned during World War II, is president of the Glide Foundation, where she directs thirty-five programs that serve the poor and homeless of San Francisco. As a founding member of Third World Communications, Mirikitani has edited many works of struggling Japanese American writers. Her works, which express her outrage against racism, sexism, and oppression of any kind, include volumes of poetry: Awake in the River (1978), Shedding Silence (1987), and We the Dangerous (1995). Much of her work shows a dichotomy between traditional Japanese customs and beliefs and a newer Japanese American or American identity.

BREAKING TRADITION   (1987)

for my Daughter

My daughter denies she is like me,
Her secretive eyes avoid mine.

She reveals the hatreds of womanhood
already veiled behind music and smoke and telephones.
5   I want to tell her about the empty room
    of myself.
    This room we lock ourselves in
    where whispers live like fungus,
    giggles about small breasts and cellulite,
10   where we confine ourselves to jealousies,
    bedridden by menstruation.
    This waiting room where we feel our hands
    are useless, dead speechless clamps
    that need hospitals and forceps and kitchens
15   and plugs and ironing boards to make them useful.
I deny I am like my mother. I remember why:
    She kept her room neat with silence,
    defiance smothered in requirements to be otonashii,
    passion and loudness wrapped in an obi,
20   her steps confined to ceremony,
    the weight of her sacrifice she carried like
    a foetus. Guilt passed on in our bones.
I want to break tradition—unlock this room
    where women dress in the dark.
25   Discover the lies my mother told me.
    The lies that we are small and powerless.
    that our possibilities must be compressed
    to the size of pearls, displayed only as
    passive chokers, charms around our neck.
30 Break Tradition.
    I want to tell my daughter of this room
    of myself
    filled with tears of violins,
    the light in my hands,
35   poems about madness,
    the music of yellow guitars—
    sounds shaken from barbed wire and
    goodbyes and miracles of survival.
    This room of open window where daring ones escape.
40 My daughter denies she is like me
    her secretive eyes are walls of smoke
    and music and telephones,
    her pouting ruby lips, her skirts
    swaying to salsa, teena marie and the stones,
45   her thighs displayed in carnivals of color.
    I do not know the contents of her room.
She mirrors my aging.
She is breaking tradition.

Questions for Discussion

1. To what is the speaker referring by "this room we lock ourselves in," and "she kept her room neat with silence"? Why does she want to "unlock this room/where women dress in the dark"?
2. What are "the hatreds of womanhood" that the daughter expresses? What is the poem about other than the generation gap?
3. What does the speaker mean by "she mirrors my aging"?
4. What is the speaker's tone? Explain your answer.
5. Mirikitani addresses the poem "for my daughter." How does she also use addresses to her daughter to structure the poem?

Suggestions for Exploring, Writing, and Persuading

1. Discuss ways in which sons and daughters break tradition—for example, in music, career choices, lifestyles, or education.
2. Three generations are pictured in the poem. Discuss why each daughter denies being like her mother.
3. Write an essay discussing what details used to describe each generation reveal about changing standards and styles.
4. In some families, the parents are such high achievers that the children find it difficult to live up to their parents' standards. In other families, as in Whitelock's "Future Connected By," the child is encouraged not to emulate his parent. Select one or more works from Family or Men and Women to show the importance of family role models for sons or daughters, or discuss the need for sons or daughters to be distinct individuals.
5. After carefully watching *The Joy Luck Club*, the film based on Amy Tan's novel, discuss the similar generational problems and complications added by cultural differences.

Judith Ortiz Cofer (b. 1952)

Born in Puerto Rico, Judith Cofer spent part of her childhood in Paterson, New Jersey, where the library became an oasis to her literary yearnings. In 1987, she published two books of poetry, Terms of Survival *and* Reaching for the Mainland, *and in 1990 she published personal essays and poems in* Silent Dancing: A Partial Remembrance of a Puerto Rican Childhood *and a novel,* The Line of the Sun. *Her 1993 book,* The Latin Deli, *vividly reveals the dichotomy of a woman who is pulled between two cultures. Her 1995 book,* An Island Like You: Stories of the Barrio, *was a Best Book of the Year selection of the American Library Association. Cofer is presently a professor of English and Creative Writing at the University of Georgia. Her most recent works include* Year of Our Revolution *(1998),* Women in Front of the Sun: On Becoming a Writer *(2000), and* The Meaning of Consuelo *(2003).*

ANNIVERSARY   (1993)

Lying in bed late, you will sometimes read to me
about a past war that obsesses you;
about young men, like our brothers once,
who each year become more like our sons
5   because they died the year we met,
or the year we got married
or the year our child was born.

You read to me
about how they dragged their feet through a green maze
10   where they fell, again and again, victims
to an enemy wily enough to be the critter hero
of some nightmare folktale, with his booby traps
in the shape of human children, and his cities
under the earth; and how, even when they survived,
15   these boys left something behind
in the thick brush or muddy swamp where no one
can get it back—caught like a baseball cap
on a low-hanging tree branch.

And I think about you and me,
20   nineteen, angry, and in love, in that same year
when America broke out in violence
like a late-blooming adolescent, deep in a turmoil
it could neither understand nor control;
how we marched in the rough parade
25   decorated with the insignias of our rebellion:
peace symbols and scenes of Eden
embroidered on our torn and faded jeans,
necks heavy with beads we did not count on
for patience, singing *Revolution*—
30   a song we misconstrued for years.

Death was a slogan
to shout about with raised fists or hang on banners.
But here we are,
listening more closely than ever to the old songs,
35   sung for new reasons by new voices. We are survivors
of an undeclared war someone might decide to remake
like a popular tune. Sometimes, in the dark, alarmed
by too deep a silence, I will lay my hand on your chest,
for the familiar, steady beat to which I have attuned
40   my breathing for so many years.

Questions for Discussion

1. What war does the narrator describe? What clues identify the time and
   the war?

2. Explain why "young men, like our brothers once/...each year become more like our sons."

3. Explain the irony of "Death was a slogan / to shout about with raised fists or hang on banners."

4. What did the survivors of this war leave behind?

5. Explain the statement "We are survivors / of an undeclared war someone might decide to remake / like a popular tune."

6. What kind of marriage do this husband and wife celebrate? What clues in the poem reveal the relationship they have?

7. This poem celebrates several anniversaries. List them in the order of importance. Defend the order of your list.

Suggestions for Exploring, Writing, and Persuading

1. Write an essay about one of your anniversaries that brings back significant memories.

2. Shakespeare in Sonnet 116 describes love as "an ever-fixed mark." Explain in an essay how this marriage fits his description.

3. In an essay argue that many of the details in this poem could also apply to any "undeclared war."

Rita Dove (b. 1952)

Rita Dove has the distinction of being both the first African American and the youngest poet laureate of the United States. Born in Akron, Ohio, Dove graduated summa cum laude with a B.A. from Miami University in 1973. In 1977 she received an M.F.A. from the University of Iowa. Her works include books of poetry, The Yellow House on the Corner *(1980),* Museum *(1983), and* Grace Notes *(1989); a collection of short stories-*Fifth Sunday *(1985); and a novel,* Through the Ivory Gate *(1992). Dove won the Pulitzer Prize in poetry in 1987 for her biographical poems about her maternal grandparents,* Thomas and Beulah *(1986). Her other honors include a Guggenheim Fellowship, a Fulbright, and grants from the National Endowment for the Arts and the National Endowment for the Humanities. Her most recent book of poetry is* American Smooth *(2004). Currently she is Commonwealth Professor of English at the University of Virginia.*

COURTSHIP   (1986)

FROM *BEULAH AND THOMAS*

1.

Fine evening may I have
the pleasure...
up and down the block

waiting—for what? A
5 magnolia breeze, someone
to trot out the stars?

But she won't set a foot
in his turtledove Nash,
it wasn't proper.
10 Her pleated skirt fans
softly, a circlet of arrows.

King of the Crawfish
in his yellow scarf,
mandolin belly pressed tight
15 to his hounds-tooth vest—
his wrist flicks for the pleats
all in a row, sighing...

2.

...so he wraps the yellow silk
still warm from his throat
20 around her shoulders. (He made
good money; he could buy another.)
A gnat flies
in his eye and she thinks
he's crying.

25 Then the parlor festooned
like a ship and Thomas
twirling his hat in his hands
wondering how did I get here.
China pugs guarding a fringed settee
30 where a father, half-Cherokee,
smokes and frowns.
I'll give her a good life—
what was he doing,
selling all for a song?
35 His heart fluttering shut
then slowly opening.

Questions for Discussion

1. Describe the events on this night or several nights of courtship from Thomas's viewpoint. What are some of the courting conventions employed by both Thomas and Beulah?

2. How is this courtship similar to or different from a courtship today?

3. To Thomas, what is the importance of wrapping his yellow silk scarf around Beulah's shoulders? What is the significance of the gnat in his eye and her misconception about what he was doing?

4. The fifth verse changes the tone and location. What has taken place between the fourth and the fifth verse? Why does Thomas wonder how he got there?

5. Thomas says to Beulah's father, "*I'll give her a good life—.*" This sentence has become almost a cliché now. What are the connotations of this line, and why does he say these words?

6. Explain the meaning of the last two lines.

Suggestions for Exploring, Writing, and Persuading

1. Write a personal essay describing your first date. Then write another essay from the point of view of your date.

2. Write an essay comparing courtship past and present.

COURTSHIP, DILIGENCE   (1986)

A yellow scarf runs through his fingers
as if it were melting.
Thomas dabbing his brow.

And now his mandolin in a hurry
5 though the night, as they say,
is young,
though she is *getting on.*

Hush, the strings tinkle. *Pretty gal.*

Cigar-box music!
10 She'd much prefer a pianola
and scent in a sky-colored flask

Not that scarf, bright as butter.
Not his hands, cool as dimes.

Questions for Discussion

1. What is the significance of the yellow scarf and the mandolin?

2. Why is Beulah said to be "*getting on.*" What does this statement reveal about the different attitudes of men and women toward marriage?

3. Identify lines in the poem that reveal that both Thomas and Beulah have misgivings about one another or about their marriage.

Suggestion for Exploring, Writing, and Persuading

1. In an essay, contrast the first and last verses in this poem with the fourth verse in "Courtship."

DRAMA

Henrik Ibsen (1828–1906)

Norwegian playwright Henrik Ibsen is often called the father of modern drama. His early Romantic plays were written in verse. In his plays, Ibsen established the tradition of realism in drama, of plays that attempt to imitate life faithfully. His most famous realistic plays, A Doll's House *(1879),* Ghosts *(1881), and* Hedda Gabler *(1890), are also described as theater of ideas or* problem plays, *those that deal with social issues or depict social problems.*

A Doll's House caused immediate controversy when it was first produced, for it was performed before audiences accustomed to viewing a wife as virtually the property of her husband. When A Doll's House *was followed by* Ghosts, *a play about inherited venereal disease, Ibsen was forced to leave Norway. Later, when praised by leaders of the Women's Rights League for defending women's rights, Ibsen pointed out that he was describing all humanity in his plays. One reason for the continued popularity of* A Doll's House *is that it raises questions about the rights of women and about the multiple roles played by women—roles that sometimes pull women in different directions.*

A DOLL'S HOUSE

(1879)

TRANS. MICHAEL MEYER

List of Characters

TORVALD HELMER:	a lawyer
NORA:	his wife
DR. RANK	
MRS. LINDE	
NILS KROGSTAD:	also a lawyer
THE HELMERS' THREE SMALL CHILDREN	
ANNE-MARIE:	their nurse
HELEN:	the maid
A PORTER	

SCENE

The action takes place in the Helmers' apartment.

ACT I

A comfortably and tastefully but not expensively furnished room. Back-
stage right, a door leads out to the hall; backstage left, another door to
Helmer's study. Between these two doors stands a piano. In the mid-
dle of the left-hand wall is a door, with a window downstage of it. Near
the window, a round table with armchairs and a small sofa. In the
right-hand wall, slightly upstage, is a door; downstage of this, against
the same wall, a stove lined with porcelain tiles, with a couple of arm-
chairs and a rocking-chair in front of it. Between the stove and the side
door is a small table. Engravings on the wall. A what-not with china
and other bric-a-brac; a small bookcase with leather-bound books. A
carpet on the floor; a fire in the stove. A winter day.

A bell rings in the hall outside. After a moment, we hear the front
door being opened. Nora enters the room, humming contentedly to her-
self. She is wearing outdoor clothes and carrying a lot of parcels,
which she puts down on the table right. She leaves the door to the hall
open; through it, we can see a Porter carrying a Christmas tree and
a basket. He gives these to the Maid, who had opened the door for them.

NORA: Hide that Christmas tree away, Helen. The children mustn't see it
before I've decorated it this evening. *(To the Porter, taking out her*
purse.) How much—?
PORTER: A shilling.
NORA: Here's half a crown. No, keep it.

(The Porter touches his cap and goes. Nora closes the door. She con-
tinues to laugh happily to herself as she removes her coat, etc. She
takes from her pocket a bag containing macaroons and eats a cou-
ple. Then she tiptoes across and listens at her husband's door.)

NORA: Yes, he's here. *(Starts humming again as she goes over to the*
table, right.)
HELMER *(from his room)*: Is that my skylark twittering out there?
NORA *(opening some of the parcels)*: It is!
10   HELMER: Is that my squirrel rustling?
NORA: Yes!
HELMER: When did my squirrel come home?
NORA: Just now. *(Pops the bag of macaroons in her pocket and wipes*
her mouth.) Come out here, Torvald, and see what I've bought.
HELMER: You mustn't disturb me! *(Short pause; then he opens the door*
and looks in, his pen in his hand.) Bought, did you say? All that?
Has my little squanderbird been overspending again?
NORA: Oh, Torvald, surely we can let ourselves go a little this year! It's
the first Christmas we don't have to scrape.
20   HELMER: Well, you know, we can't afford to be extravagant.
NORA: Oh yes, Torvald, we can be a little extravagant now. Can't we?
Just a tiny bit? You've got a big salary now, and you're going to make
lots and lots of money.

HELMER: Next year, yes. But my new salary doesn't start till April.

NORA: Pooh; we can borrow till then.

HELMER: Nora! *(Goes over to her and takes her playfully by the ear.)* What a little spendthrift you are! Suppose I were to borrow fifty pounds today, and you spent it all over Christmas, and then on New Year's Eve a tile fell off a roof on to my head—

10   NORA *(puts her hand over his mouth):* Oh, Torvald! Don't say such dreadful things!

HELMER: Yes, but suppose something like that did happen? What then?

NORA: If anything as frightful as that happened, it wouldn't make much difference whether I was in debt or not.

HELMER: But what about the people I'd borrowed from?

NORA: Them? Who cares about them? They're strangers.

HELMER: Oh, Nora, Nora, how like a woman! No, but seriously, Nora, you know how I feel about this. No debts! Never borrow! A home that is founded on debts can never be a place of freedom and beauty.

20   We two have stuck it out bravely up to now; and we shall continue to do so for the short time we still have to.

NORA *(goes over towards the stove):* Very well, Torvald. As you say.

HELMER *(follows her):* Now, now! My little songbird mustn't droop her wings. What's this? Is little squirrel sulking? *(Takes out his purse.)* Nora; guess what I've got here!

NORA *(turns quickly):* Money!

HELMER: Look. *(Hands her some banknotes.)* I know how these small expenses crop up at Christmas.

NORA *(counts them):* One—two—three—four. Oh, thank you, Torvald,
30   thank you! I should be able to manage with this.

HELMER: You'll have to.

NORA: Yes, yes of course I will. But come over here, I want to show you everything I've bought. And so cheaply! Look, here are new clothes for Ivar—and a sword. And a horse and a trumpet for Bob. And a doll and a cradle for Emmy—they're nothing much, but she'll pull them apart in a few days. And some bits of material and handker-chiefs for the maids. Old Anne-Marie ought to have had something better, really.

HELMER: And what's in that parcel?

40   NORA *(cries):* No, Torvald, you mustn't see that before this evening!

HELMER: Very well. But now, tell me, you little spendthrift, what do you want for Christmas?

NORA: Me? Oh, pooh, I don't want anything.

HELMER: Oh, yes, you do. Now tell me, what, within reason, would you most like?

NORA: No, I really don't know. Oh, yes—Torvald—!

HELMER: Well?

NORA *(plays with his coat-buttons; not looking at him):* If you really want to give me something, you could—you could—

50   HELMER: Come on, out with it.

NORA *(quickly):* You could give me money, Torvald. Only as much as you feel you can afford; then later I'll buy something with it.

HELMER: But, Nora—

NORA: Oh yes, Torvald dear, please! Please! Then I'll wrap up the notes in pretty gold paper and hang them on the Christmas tree. Wouldn't that be fun!

HELMER: What's the name of that little bird that can never keep any money?

NORA: Yes, yes, squanderbird; I know. But let's do as I say, Torvald; then I'll
60   have time to think about what I need most. Isn't that the best way? Mm?

HELMER *(smiles):* To be sure it would be, if you could keep what I give you and really buy yourself something with it. But you'll spend it on all sorts of useless things for the house, and then I'll have to put my hand in my pocket again.

NORA: Oh, but Torvald—

HELMER: You can't deny it, Nora dear. *(Puts his arm round her waist.)* The squanderbird's a pretty little creature, but she gets through an awful lot of money. It's incredible what an expensive pet she is for a man to keep.

70   NORA: For shame! How can you say such a thing? I save every penny I can.

HELMER *(laughs):* That's quite true. Every penny you can. But you can't.

NORA *(hums and smiles, quietly gleeful):* Hm. If you only knew how many expenses we larks and squirrels have, Torvald.

HELMER: You're a funny little creature. Just like your father used to be. Always on the look-out for some way to get money, but as soon as you have any it just runs through your fingers, and you never know where it's gone. Well, I suppose I must take you as you are. It's in your blood. Yes, yes, yes, these things are hereditary, Nora.

NORA: Oh, I wish I'd inherited more of Papa's qualities.

80   HELMER: And I wouldn't wish my darling little songbird to be any different from what she is. By the way, that reminds me. You look awfully—how shall I put it?—awfully guilty today.

NORA: Do I?

HELMER: Yes, you do. Look me in the eyes.

NORA *(looks at him):* Well?

HELMER *(wags his finger):* Has my little sweet-tooth been indulging herself in town today, by any chance?

NORA: No, how can you think such a thing?

HELMER: Not a tiny little digression into a pastry shop?

90   NORA: No, Torvald, I promise—

HELMER: Not just a wee jam tart?

NORA: Certainly not.

HELMER: Not a little nibble at a macaroon?

NORA: No, Torvald—I promise you, honestly—

HELMER: There, there. I was only joking.

NORA (*goes over to the table, right*): You know I could never act against your wishes.

HELMER: Of course not. And you've given me your word— *(Goes over to her.)* Well, my beloved Nora, you keep your little Christmas secrets
100   to yourself. They'll be revealed this evening, I've no doubt, once the Christmas tree has been lit.

NORA: Have you remembered to invite Dr. Rank?

HELMER: No. But there's no need; he knows he'll be dining with us. Anyway, I'll ask him when he comes this morning. I've ordered some good wine. Oh, Nora, you can't imagine how I'm looking forward to this evening.

NORA: So am I. And, Torvald, how the children will love it!

HELMER: Yes, it's a wonderful thing to know that one's position is assured and that one has an ample income. Don't you agree? It's good to know that, isn't it?
120   NORA: Yes, it's almost like a miracle.

HELMER: Do you remember last Christmas? For three whole weeks you shut yourself away every evening to make flowers for the Christmas tree, and all those other things you were going to surprise us with. Ugh, it was the most boring time I've ever had in my life.

NORA: I didn't find it boring.

HELMER (*smiles*): But it all came to nothing in the end, didn't it?

NORA: Oh, are you going to bring that up again? How could I help the cat getting in and tearing everything to bits?

HELMER: No, my poor little Nora, of course you couldn't. You simply
130   wanted to make us happy, and that's all that matters. But it's good that those hard times are past.

NORA: Yes, it's wonderful.

HELMER: I don't have to sit by myself and be bored. And you don't have to tire your pretty eyes and your delicate little hands—

NORA (*claps her hands*): No, Torvald, that's true, isn't it—I don't have to any longer? Oh, it's really all just like a miracle. *(Takes his arm.)* Now, I'm going to tell you what I thought we might do, Torvald. As soon as Christmas is over—*(A bell rings in the hall.)* Oh, there's the doorbell. *(Tidies up one or two things in the room.)* Someone's
140   coming. What a bore.

HELMER: I'm not at home to any visitors. Remember!

MAID (*in the doorway*): A lady's called, madam. A stranger.

NORA: Well, ask her to come in.

MAID: And the doctor's here too, sir.

HELMER: Has he gone to my room?

MAID: Yes, sir.

(Helmer goes into his room. The Maid shows in Mrs. Linde, who is dressed in traveling clothes, and closes the door.)

MRS. LINDE (*shyly and a little hesitantly*): Good evening, Nora.

NORA (*uncertainly*): Good evening—

MRS. LINDE: I don't suppose you recognize me.

150 NORA: No, I'm afraid I—Yes, wait a minute—surely—*(Exclaims.)* Why, Christine! Is it really you?

MRS. LINDE: Yes, it's me.

NORA: Christine! And I didn't recognize you! But how could I—? *(More quietly.)* How you've changed, Christine!

MRS. LINDE: Yes, I know. It's been nine years—nearly ten—

NORA: Is it so long? Yes, it must be. Oh, these last eight years have been such a happy time for me! So you've come to town? All that way in winter! How brave of you!

MRS. LINDE: I arrived by the steamer this morning.

160 NORA: Yes, of course—to enjoy yourself over Christmas. Oh, how splendid! We'll have to celebrate! But take off your coat. You're not cold, are you? *(Helps her off with it.)* There! Now let's sit down here by the stove and be comfortable. No, you take the armchair. I'll sit here in the rocking chair. *(Clasps Mrs. Linde's hands.)* Yes, now you look like your old self. It was just at first that—you've got a little paler, though, Christine. And perhaps a bit thinner.

MRS. LINDE: And older, Nora. Much, much older.

NORA: Yes, perhaps a little older. Just a tiny bit. Not much. *(Checks herself suddenly and says earnestly.)* Oh, but how thoughtless of me to sit here

170 and chatter away like this! Dear, sweet Christine, can you forgive me?

MRS. LINDE: What do you mean, Nora?

NORA *(quietly):* Poor Christine, you've become a widow.

MRS. LINDE: Yes. Three years ago.

NORA: I know, I know—I read it in the papers. Oh, Christine, I meant to write to you so often, honestly. But I always put it off, and something else always cropped up.

MRS. LINDE: I understand, Nora dear.

NORA: No, Christine, it was beastly of me. Oh, my poor darling, what you've gone through! And he didn't leave you anything?

180 MRS. LINDE: No.

NORA: No children, either?

MRS. LINDE: No.

NORA: Nothing at all, then?

MRS.LINDE: Not even a feeling of loss or sorrow.

NORA *(looks incredulously at her):* But, Christine, how is that possible?

MRS. LINDE *(smiles sadly and strokes Nora's hair):* Oh, these things happen, Nora.

NORA: All alone. How dreadful that must be for you. I've three lovely children. I'm afraid you can't see them now, because they're out with

190 nanny. But you must tell me everything—

MRS.LINDE: No, no, no. I want to hear about you.

NORA: No, you start. I'm not going to be selfish today, I'm just going to think about you. Oh, but there's one thing I *must* tell you. Have you heard of the wonderful luck we've just had?

MRS. LINDE: No. What?

NORA: Would you believe it—my husband's just been made manager of the bank!

MRS. LINDE: Your husband? Oh, how lucky—!

NORA: Yes, isn't it? Being a lawyer is so uncertain, you know, especially
200   if one isn't prepared to touch any case that isn't—well—quite nice. And of course Torvald's been very firm about that—and I'm absolutely with him. Oh, you can imagine how happy we are! He's joining the bank in the New Year, and he'll be getting a big salary, and lots of percentages too. From now on we'll be able to live quite differently—we'll be able to do whatever we want. Oh, Christine, it's such a relief! I feel so happy! Well, I mean, it's lovely to have heaps of money and not to have to worry about anything. Don't you think?

MRS. LINDE: It must be lovely to have enough to cover one's needs, anyway.

210   NORA: Not just our needs! We're going to have heaps and heaps of money!

MRS. LINDE (*smiles*): Nora, Nora, haven't you grown up yet? When we were at school you were a terrible little spendthrift.

NORA (*laughs quietly*): Yes, Torvald still says that. (*Wags her finger.*) But "Nora, Nora" isn't as silly as you think. Oh, we've been in no position for me to waste money. We've both had to work.

MRS. LINDE: You too?

NORA: Yes, little things—fancy work, crocheting, embroidery and so forth. (*Casually.*) And other things too. I suppose you know Torvald
220   left the Ministry when we got married? There were no prospects of promotion in his department, and of course he needed more money. But the first year he overworked himself quite dreadfully. He had to take on all sorts of extra jobs, and worked day and night. But it was too much for him, and he became frightfully ill. The doctors said he'd have to go to a warmer climate.

MRS. LINDE: Yes, you spent a whole year in Italy, didn't you?

NORA: Yes. It wasn't easy for me to get away, you know. I'd just had Ivar. But of course we had to do it. Oh, it was a marvelous trip! And it saved Torvald's life. But it cost an awful lot of money, Christine.

230   MRS. LINDE: I can imagine.

NORA: Two hundred and fifty pounds. That's a lot of money, you know.

MRS. LINDE: How lucky you had it.

NORA: Well, actually, we got it from my father.

MRS. LINDE: Oh, I see. Didn't he die just about that time?

NORA: Yes, Christine, just about then. Wasn't it dreadful, I couldn't go and look after him. I was expecting little Ivar any day. And then I had my poor Torvald to care for—we really didn't think he'd live. Dear, kind Papa! I never saw him again, Christine. Oh, it's the saddest thing that's happened to me since I got married.

240   MRS. LINDE: I know you were very fond of him. But you went to Italy—?

NORA: Yes. Well, we had the money, you see, and the doctors said we mustn't delay. So we went the month after Papa died.

MRS. LINDE: And your husband came back completely cured?

NORA: Fit as a fiddle!

MRS. LINDE: But—the doctor?

NORA: How do you mean?

MRS. LINDE: I thought the maid said that the gentleman who arrived with me was the doctor.

NORA: Oh yes, that's Doctor Rank, but he doesn't come because any-
250   one's ill. He's our best friend, and he looks us up at least once every day. No, Torvald hasn't had a moment's illness since we went away. And the children are fit and healthy and so am I. *(Jumps up and claps her hands.)* Oh God, oh God, Christine, isn't it a wonderful thing to be alive and happy! Oh, but how beastly of me! I'm only talk-ing about myself. *(Sits on a footstool and rests her arms on Mrs. Linde's knee.)* Oh, please don't be angry with me! Tell me, is it really true you didn't love your husband? Why did you marry him, then?

MRS. LINDE: Well, my mother was still alive; and she was helpless and bedridden. And I had my two little brothers to take care of. I didn't
260   feel I could say no.

NORA: Yes, well, perhaps you're right. He was rich then, was he?

MRS. LINDE: Quite comfortably off, I believe. But his business was unsound, you see, Nora. When he died it went bankrupt, and there was nothing left.

NORA: What did you do?

MRS. LINDE: Well, I had to try to make ends meet somehow, so I started a little shop, and a little school, and anything else I could turn my hand to. These last three years have been just one endless slog for me, without a moment's rest. But now it's over, Nora. My poor dear
270   mother doesn't need me any more; she's passed away. And the boys don't need me either; they've got jobs now and can look after them-selves.

NORA: How relieved you must feel—

MRS. LINDE: No, Nora. Just unspeakably empty. No one to live for any-more. *(Gets up restlessly.)* That's why I couldn't bear to stay out there any longer, cut off from the world. I thought it'd be easier to find some work here that will exercise and occupy my mind. If only I could get a regular job—office work of some kind—

NORA: Oh, but, Christine, that's dreadfully exhausting; and you look
280   practically finished already. It'd be much better for you if you could go away somewhere.

MRS. LINDE *(goes over to the window):* I have no Papa to pay for my hol-idays, Nora.

NORA *(gets up):* Oh, please don't be angry with me.

MRS. LINDE: My dear Nora, it's I who should ask you not to be angry. That's the worst thing about this kind of situation—it makes one so

bitter. One has no one to work for; and yet one has to be continually sponging for jobs. One has to live; and so one becomes completely egocentric. When you told me about this luck you've just had with
290   Torvald's new job—can you imagine?—I was happy not so much on your account, as on my own.

NORA: How do you mean? Oh, I understand. You mean Torvald might be able to do something for you?

MRS. LINDE: Yes, I was thinking that.

NORA: He will too, Christine. Just you leave it to me. I'll lead up to it so delicately, so delicately; I'll get him in the right mood. Oh, Christine, I do so want to help you.

MRS. LINDE: It's sweet of you to bother so much about me, Nora. Especially since you know so little of the worries and hardships of life.

300   NORA: I? You say *I* know little of—?

MRS. LINDE *(smiles)*: Well, good heavens—those bits of fancy work of yours—well, really—! You're a child, Nora.

NORA *(tosses her head and walks across the room)*: You shouldn't say that so patronizingly.

MRS. LINDE: Oh?

NORA: You're like the rest. You all think I'm incapable of getting down to anything serious—

MRS. LINDE: My dear—

NORA: You think I've never had any worries like the rest of you.

310   MRS. LINDE: Nora dear, you've just told me about all your difficulties—

NORA: Pooh—that! *(Quietly.)* I haven't told you about the big thing.

MRS. LINDE: What big thing? What do you mean?

NORA: You patronize me, Christine; but you shouldn't. You're proud that you've worked so long and so hard for your mother.

MRS. LINDE: I don't patronize anyone, Nora. But you're right—I am both proud and happy that I was able to make my mother's last months on earth comparatively easy.

NORA: And you're also proud of what you've done for your brothers.

MRS. LINDE: I think I have a right to be.

320   NORA: I think so too. But let me tell you something, Christine. I too have done something to be proud and happy about.

MRS. LINDE: I don't doubt it. But—how do you mean?

NORA: Speak quietly! Suppose Torvald should hear! He mustn't, at any price—no one must know, Christine—no one but you.

MRS. LINDE: But what is this?

NORA: Come over here. *(Pulls her down on to the sofa beside her.)* Yes, Christine—I too have done something to be happy and proud about. It was I who saved Torvald's life.

MRS. LINDE: Saved his—? How did you save it?

330   NORA: I told you about our trip to Italy. Torvald couldn't have lived if he hadn't managed to get down there—

MRS. LINDE: Yes, well—your father provided the money—

NORA (*smiles*): So Torvald and everyone else thinks. But—

MRS. LINDE: Yes?

NORA: Papa didn't give us a penny. It was I who found the money.

MRS. LINDE: You? All of it?

NORA: Two hundred and fifty pounds. What do you say to that?

MRS. LINDE: But Nora, how could you? Did you win a lottery or something?

NORA (*scornfully*): Lottery? (Sniffs.) What would there be to be proud
340   of in that?

MRS. LINDE: But where did you get it from, then?

NORA (*hums and smiles secretively*): Hm; tra-la-la-la!

MRS. LINDE: You couldn't have borrowed it.

NORA: Oh? Why not?

MRS. LINDE: Well, a wife can't borrow money without her husband's consent.

NORA (*tosses her head*): Ah, but when a wife has a little business sense,
and knows how to be clever—

MRS. LINDE: But Nora, I simply don't understand—

350 NORA: You don't have to. No one has said I borrowed the money. I could
have got it in some other way. (*Throws herself back on the sofa.*) I
could have got it from an admirer. When a girl's as pretty as I am—

MRS. LINDE: Nora, you're crazy!

NORA: You're dying of curiosity now, aren't you, Christine?

MRS. LINDE: Nora dear, you haven't done anything foolish?

NORA (*sits up again*): Is it foolish to save one's husband's life?

MRS. LINDE: I think it's foolish if without his knowledge you—

NORA: But the whole point was that he mustn't know! Great heavens,
don't you see? He hadn't to know how dangerously ill he was. I was
360 the one they told that his life was in danger and that only going to a
warm climate could save him. Do you suppose I didn't try to think of
other ways of getting him down there? I told him how wonderful it
would be for me to go abroad like other young wives; I cried and
prayed; I asked him to remember my condition, and said he ought to
be nice and tender to me; and then I suggested he might quite easily
borrow the money. But then he got almost angry with me, Christine.
He said I was frivolous, and that it was his duty as a husband not to
pander to my moods and caprices—I think that's what he called
them. Well, well, I thought, you've got to be saved somehow. And
370 then I thought of a way—

MRS. LINDE: But didn't your husband find out from your father that the
money hadn't come from him?

NORA: No, never. Papa died just then. I'd thought of letting him into the
plot and asking him not to tell. But since he was so ill—! And as
things turned out, it didn't become necessary.

MRS. LINDE: And you've never told your husband about this?

NORA: For heaven's sake, no! What an idea! He's frightfully strict about
such matters. And besides—he's so proud of being a *man*—it'd be so

painful and humiliating for him to know that he owed anything to
380   me. It'd completely wreck our relationship. This life we have built
together would no longer exist.

MRS. LINDE: Will you never tell him?

NORA (*thoughtfully, half-smiling*)*:* Yes—some time, perhaps. Years
from now, when I'm no longer pretty. You mustn't laugh! I mean of
course,when Torvald no longer loves me as he does now; when it no
longer amuses him to see me dance and dress up and play the fool
for him. Then it might be useful to have something up my sleeve.
(*Breaks off.*) Stupid, stupid, stupid! That time will never come. Well,
what do you think of my big secret, Christine? I'm not completely
390   useless, am I? Mind you, all this has caused me a frightful lot of
worry. It hasn't been easy for me to meet my obligations punctually.
In case you don't know, in the world of business there are things
called quarterly installments and interest, and they're a terrible problem to cope with. So I've had to scrape a little here and save a little
there as best I can. I haven't been able to save much on the housekeeping money, because Torvald likes to live well; and I couldn't let
the children go short of clothes—I couldn't take anything out of
what he gives me for them. The poor little angels!

MRS. LINDE: So you've had to stint yourself, my poor Nora?

400   NORA: Of course. Well, after all, it was my problem. Whenever Torvald
gave me money to buy myself new clothes, I never used more than
half of it; and I always bought what was cheapest and plainest.
Thank heaven anything suits me, so that Torvald's never noticed. But
it made me a bit sad sometimes, because it's lovely to wear pretty
clothes. Don't you think?

MRS. LINDE: Indeed it is.

NORA: And then I've found one or two other sources of income. Last
winter I managed to get a lot of copying to do. So I shut myself away
and wrote every evening, late into the night. Oh, I often got so tired,
410   so tired. But it was great fun, though, sitting there working and earning money. It was almost like being a man.

MRS. LINDE: But how much have you managed to pay off like this?

NORA: Well, I can't say exactly. It's awfully difficult to keep an exact
check on these kinds of transactions. I only know I've paid everything I've managed to scrape together. Sometimes I really didn't
know where to turn. (*Smiles.*) Then I'd sit here and imagine some
rich old gentleman had fallen in love with me—

MRS. LINDE: What! What gentleman?

NORA: Silly! And that now he'd died and when they opened his will it
420   said in big letters: "Everything I possess is to be paid forthwith to my
beloved Mrs. Nora Helmer in cash."

MRS. LINDE: But, Nora dear, who was this gentleman?

NORA: Great heavens, don't you understand? There wasn't any old gentleman; he was just something I used to dream up as I sat here

evening after evening wondering how on earth I could raise some money. But what does it matter? The old bore can stay imaginary as far as I'm concerned, because now I don't have to worry any longer! *(Jumps up.)* Oh, Christine, isn't it wonderful? I don't have to worry any more! No more troubles! I can play all day with the children, I
430   can fill the house with pretty things, just the way Torvald likes. And, Christine, it'll soon be spring, and the air'll be fresh and the skies blue,—and then perhaps we'll be able to take a little trip some-where. I shall be able to see the sea again. Oh, yes, yes, it's a wonder-ful thing to be alive and happy!

(The bell rings in the hall.)

MRS. LINDE *(gets up):* You've a visitor. Perhaps I'd better go.

NORA: No, stay. It won't be for me. It's someone for Torvald—

MAID *(in the door):* Excuse me, madam, a gentleman's called who says he wants to speak to the master. But I didn't know—seeing as the doctor's with him—
440   NORA: Who is this gentleman?

KROGSTAD *(in the doorway):* It's me, Mrs. Helmer.

(Mrs. Linde starts, composes herself, and turns away to the window.)

NORA *(takes a step toward him and whispers tensely):* You? What is it? What do you want to talk to my husband about?

KROGSTAD: Business—you might call it. I hold a minor post in the bank, and I hear your husband is to become our new chief—

NORA: Oh—then it isn't—?

KROGSTAD: Pure business, Mrs. Helmer. Nothing more.

NORA: Well, you'll find him in his study.

(Nods indifferently as she closes the hall door behind him. Then she walks across the room and sees to the stove.)

MRS. LINDE: Nora, who was that man?
450   NORA: A lawyer called Krogstad.

MRS. LINDE: It was him, then.

NORA: Do you know that man?

MRS. LINDE: I used to know him—some years ago. He was a solicitor's clerk in our town, for a while.

NORA: Yes, of course, so he was.

MRS. LINDE: How he's changed!

NORA: He was very unhappily married, I believe.

MRS. LINDE: Is he a widower now?

NORA: Yes, with a lot of children. Ah, now it's alight.

(She closes the door of the stove and moves the rocking-chair a little to one side.)

460   MRS. LINDE: He does—various things now, I hear?

NORA: Does he? It's quite possible—I really don't know. But don't let's talk about business. It's so boring.

(Dr. Rank enters from Helmer's study.)

RANK: *(still in the doorway)* No, no, my dear chap, don't see me out. I'll go and have a word with your wife. *(Closes the door and notices Mrs. Linde.)* Oh, I beg your pardon. I seem to be *de trop* here too.

NORA: Not in the least. *(Introduces them.)* Dr. Rank. Mrs. Linde.

RANK: Ah! A name I have often heard in this house. I believe I passed you on the stairs as I came up.

MRS. LINDE: Yes. Stairs tire me; I have to take them slowly.

470   RANK: Oh, have you hurt yourself?

MRS. LINDE: No, I'm just a little run down.

RANK: Ah, is that all? Then I take it you've come to town to cure yourself by a round of parties?

MRS. LINDE: I have come here to find work.

RANK: Is that an approved remedy for being run down?

MRS. LINDE: One has to live, Doctor.

RANK: Yes, people do seem to regard it as a necessity.

NORA: Oh, really, Dr. Rank. I bet you want to stay alive.

RANK: You bet I do. However miserable I sometimes feel, I still want to
480   go on being tortured for as long as possible. It's the same with all my patients; and with people who are morally sick, too. There's a moral cripple in with Helmer at this very moment—

MRS. LINDE *(softly):* Oh!

NORA: Whom do you mean?

RANK: Oh, a lawyer fellow called Krogstad—you wouldn't know him. He's crippled all right; morally twisted. But even he started off by announcing, as though it were a matter of enormous importance, that he had to live.

NORA: Oh? What did he want to talk to Torvald about?

490   RANK: I haven't the faintest idea. All I heard was something about the bank.

NORA: I didn't know that Krog—that this man Krogstad had any connection with the bank.

RANK: Yes, he's got some kind of job down there. *(To Mrs. Linde.)* I wonder if in your part of the world you too have a species of human being that spends its time fussing around trying to smell out moral corruption? And when they find a case they give him some nice, comfortable position so that they can keep a good watch on him. The healthy ones just have to lump it.

500   MRS. LINDE: But surely it's the sick who need care most?

RANK *(shrugs his shoulders):* Well, there we have it. It's that attitude that's turning human society into a hospital.

(Nora, lost in her own thoughts, laughs half to herself and claps her hands.)

RANK: Why are you laughing? Do you really know what society is?

NORA: What do I care about society? I think it's a bore. I was laughing at something else—something frightfully funny. Tell me, Dr. Rank—will everyone who works at the bank come under Torvald now?

RANK: Do you find that particularly funny?

NORA (*smiles and hums*): Never you mind! Never you mind! (*Walks around the room.*) Yes, I find it very amusing to think that we—I mean, Torvald—has obtained so much influence over so many people. (*Takes the paper bag from her pocket.*) Dr. Rank, would you like a small macaroon?

RANK: Macaroons! I say! I thought they were forbidden here.

NORA: Yes, well, these are some Christine gave me.

MRS. LINDE: What? I—?

NORA: All right, all right, don't get frightened. You weren't to know Torvald had forbidden them. He's afraid they'll ruin my teeth. But, dash it—for once—! Don't you agree, Dr. Rank? Here! (*Pops a macaroon into his mouth.*) You too, Christine. And I'll have one too. Just a little one. Two at the most. (*Begins to walk around again.*) Yes, now I feel really, really happy. Now there's just one thing in the world I'd really love to do.

RANK: Oh? And what is that?

NORA: Just something I'd love to say to Torvald.

RANK: Well, why don't you say it?

NORA: No, I daren't. It's too dreadful.

MRS. LINDE: Dreadful?

RANK: Well, then, you'd better not. But you can say it to us. What is it you'd so love to say to Torvald?

NORA: I've the most extraordinary longing to say: "Bloody hell!"

RANK: Are you mad?

MRS. LINDE: My dear Nora—!

RANK: Say it. Here he is.

NORA (*hiding the bag of macaroons*): Ssh! Ssh!

(*Helmer, with his overcoat on his arm and his hat in his hand, enters from his study.*)

NORA (*goes to meet him*): Well, Torvald dear, did you get rid of him?

HELMER: Yes, he's just gone.

NORA: May I introduce you—? This is Christine. She's just arrived in town.

HELMER: Christine—? Forgive me, but I don't think—

NORA: Mrs. Linde, Torvald dear. Christine Linde.

HELMER: Ah. A childhood friend of my wife's, I presume.

MRS. LINDE: Yes, we knew each other in earlier days.

NORA: And imagine, now she's traveled all this way to talk to you.

HELMER: Oh?

MRS. LINDE: Well, I didn't really—

NORA: You see, Christine's frightfully good at office work, and she's mad to come under some really clever man who can teach her even more than she knows already—

HELMER: Very sensible, madam.

550 NORA: So when she heard you'd become head of the bank—it was in her local paper—she came here as quickly as she could and—Torvald, you will, won't you? Do a little something to help Christine? For my sake?

HELMER: Well, that shouldn't be impossible. You are a widow, I take it, Mrs. Linde?

MRS. LINDE: Yes.

HELMER: And you have experience of office work?

MRS. LINDE: Yes, quite a bit.

HELMER: Well then, it's quite likely I may be able to find some job for
560   you—

NORA (*claps her hands):* You see, you see!

HELMER: You've come at a lucky moment, Mrs. Linde.

MRS. LINDE: Oh, how can I ever thank you—?

HELMER: There's absolutely no need. *(Puts on his overcoat.)* But now I'm afraid I must ask you to excuse me—

RANK: Wait. I'll come with you.

(He gets his fur coat from the hall and warms it at the stove.)

NORA: Don't be long, Torvald dear.

HELMER: I'll only be an hour.

NORA: Are you going too, Christine?

570 MRS. LINDE (*puts on her outdoor clothes):* Yes, I must start to look round for a room.

HELMER: Then perhaps we can walk part of the way together.

NORA (*helps her):* It's such a nuisance we're so cramped here—I'm afraid we can't offer to—

MRS. LINDE: Oh, I wouldn't dream of it. Goodbye, Nora dear, and thanks for everything.

NORA: *Au revoir.* You'll be coming back this evening, of course. And you too, Dr. Rank. What? If you're well enough? Of course you'll be well enough. Wrap up warmly, though.

(They go out, talking, into the hall. Children's voices are heard from the stairs.)

580 NORA: Here they are! Here they are!

(She runs out and opens the door. Anne-Marie, the nurse, enters with the children.)

NORA: Come in, come in! *(Stoops down and kisses them.)* Oh, my sweet darlings—! Look at them, Christine! Aren't they beautiful?

RANK: Don't stand here chattering in this draught!

HELMER: Come, Mrs. Linde. This is for mothers only.

(Dr. Rank, Helmer, and Mrs. Linde go down the stairs. The nurse brings the children into the room. Nora follows, and closes the door to the hall.)

NORA: How well you look! What red cheeks you've got! Like apples and roses! *(The children answer her inaudibly as she talks to them.)* Have you had fun? That's splendid. You gave Emmy and Bob a ride on the sledge? What, both together? I say! What a clever boy you are, Ivar! Oh, let me hold her for a moment, Anne-Marie! My sweet little
590   baby doll! *(Takes the smallest child from the nurse and dances with her.)* Yes, yes, Mummy will dance with Bob too. What? Have you been throwing snowballs? Oh, I wish I'd been there! No, don't— I'll undress them myself, Anne-Marie. No, please let me; it's such fun. Go inside and warm yourself; you look frozen. There's some hot coffee on the stove. *(The nurse goes into the room on the left. Nora takes off the children's outdoor clothes and throws them anywhere while they all chatter simultaneously.)* What? A big dog ran after you? But he didn't bite you? No, dogs don't bite lovely little baby dolls. Leave those parcels alone, Ivar. What's in them? Ah, wouldn't
600   you like to know! No, no; it's nothing nice. Come on, let's play a game. What shall we play? Hide and seek. Yes, let's play hide and seek. Bob shall hide first. You want me to? All right, let me hide first.

(Nora and the children play around the room, and in the adjacent room to the left, laughing and shouting. At length Nora hides under the table. The children rush in, look, but cannot find her. Then they hear her half-stifled laughter, run to the table, lift up the cloth, and see her. Great excitement. She crawls out as though to frighten them. Further excitement. Meanwhile, there has been a knock on the door leading from the hall, but no one has noticed it. Now the door is half-opened and Krogstad enters. He waits for a moment; the game continues.)

KROGSTAD: Excuse me, Mrs. Helmer—
NORA *(turns with a stifled cry and half jumps up):* Oh! What do you want?
KROGSTAD: I beg your pardon; the front door was ajar. Someone must have forgotten to close it.
NORA *(gets up):* My husband is not at home, Mr. Krogstad.
KROGSTAD: I know.
NORA: Well, what do you want here, then?
610   KROGSTAD: A word with you.
NORA: With—? *(To the children, quietly.)* Go inside to Anne-Marie. What? No, the strange gentleman won't do anything to hurt Mummy. When he's gone we'll start playing again.

(She takes the children into the room on the left and closes the door behind them.)

NORA *(uneasy, tense):* You want to speak to me?

KROGSTAD: Yes.

NORA: Today? But it's not the first of the month yet.

KROGSTAD: No, it is Christmas Eve. Whether or not you have a merry Christmas depends on you.

NORA: What do you want? I can't give you anything today—

KROGSTAD: We won't talk about that for the present. There's something else. You have a moment to spare?

620   NORA: Oh, yes. Yes, I suppose so; though—

KROGSTAD: Good. I was sitting in the café down below and I saw your husband cross the street—

NORA: Yes.

KROGSTAD: With a lady.

NORA: Well?

KROGSTAD: Might I be so bold as to ask: was not that lady a Mrs. Linde?

NORA: Yes.

KROGSTAD: Recently arrived in town?

NORA: Yes, today.

630   KROGSTAD: She is a good friend of yours, is she not?

NORA: Yes, she is. But I don't see—

KROGSTAD: I used to know her too once.

NORA: I know.

KROGSTAD: Oh? You've discovered that. Yes, I thought you would. Well then, may I ask you a straight question: is Mrs. Linde to be employed at the bank?

NORA: How dare you presume to cross-examine me, Mr. Krogstad? You, one of my husband's employees? But since you ask, you shall have an answer. Yes, Mrs. Linde is to be employed by the bank. And I

640   arranged it, Mr. Krogstad. Now you know.

KROGSTAD: I guessed right, then.

NORA (*walks up and down the room*): Oh, one has a little influence, you know. Just because one's a woman it doesn't necessarily mean that—When one is in a humble position, Mr. Krogstad, one should think twice before offending someone who—hm—

KROGSTAD: —who has influence?

NORA: Precisely.

KROGSTAD (*changes his tone*): Mrs. Helmer, will you have the kindness to use your influence on my behalf?

650   NORA: What? What do you mean?

KROGSTAD: Will you be so good as to see that I keep my humble position at the bank?

NORA: What do you mean? Who is thinking of removing you from your position?

KROGSTAD: Oh, you don't need to play innocent with me. I realize it can't be very pleasant for your friend to risk bumping into me; and now I also realize whom I have to thank for being hounded out like this.

NORA: But I assure you—

KROGSTAD: Look, let's not beat about the bush. There's still time, and I'd
660   advise you to use your influence to stop it.

NORA: But, Mr. Krogstad, I have no influence!

KROGSTAD: Oh? I thought you just said—

NORA: But I didn't mean it like that! I? How on earth could you imagine
that I would have any influence over my husband?

KROGSTAD: Oh, I've known your husband since we were students
together. I imagine he has his weaknesses like other married men.

NORA: If you speak impertinently of my husband, I shall show you the door.

KROGSTAD: You're a bold woman, Mrs. Helmer.

NORA: I'm not afraid of you any longer. Once the New Year is in, I'll
670   soon be rid of you.

KROGSTAD (more controlled): Now listen to me, Mrs. Helmer. If I'm
forced to, I shall fight for my little job at the bank as I would fight
for my life.

NORA: So it sounds.

KROGSTAD: It isn't just the money; that's the last thing I care about.
There's something else—well, you might as well know. It's like this,
you see. You know of course, as everyone else does, that some years
ago I committed an indiscretion.

NORA: I think I did hear something—

680   KROGSTAD: It never came into court; but from that day, every opening
was barred to me. So I turned my hand to the kind of business you
know about. I had to do something; and I don't think I was one of
the worst. But now I want to give up all that. My sons are growing
up; for their sake, I must try to regain what respectability I can. This
job in the bank was the first step on the ladder. And now your husband wants to kick me off that ladder back into the dirt.

NORA: But my dear Mr. Krogstad, it simply isn't in my power to help you.

KROGSTAD: You say that because you don't want to help me. But I have
the means to make you.

690   NORA: You don't mean you'd tell my husband that I owe you money?

KROGSTAD: And if I did?

NORA: That'd be a filthy trick! (Almost in tears.) This secret that is my
pride and my joy—that he should hear about it in such a filthy,
beastly way—hear about it from you! It'd involve me in the most
dreadful unpleasantness—

KROGSTAD: Only—unpleasantness?

NORA (vehemently): All right, do it! You'll be the one who'll suffer. It'll
show my husband the kind of man you are, and then you'll never
keep your job.

700   KROGSTAD: I asked you whether it was merely domestic unpleasantness
you were afraid of.

NORA: If my husband hears about it, he will of course immediately pay
you whatever is owing. And then we shall have nothing more to do
with you.

KROGSTAD (*takes a step closer*): Listen, Mrs. Helmer. Either you've a bad memory or else you know very little about financial transactions. I had better enlighten you.

NORA: What do you mean?

KROGSTAD: When your husband was ill, you came to me to borrow two
710   hundred and fifty pounds.

NORA: I didn't know anyone else.

KROGSTAD: I promised to find that sum for you—

NORA: And you did find it.

KROGSTAD: I promised to find that sum for you on certain conditions. You were so worried about your husband's illness and so keen to get the money to take him abroad that I don't think you bothered much about the details. So it won't be out of place if I refresh your memory. Well—I promised to get you the money in exchange for an I.O.U., which I drew up.

720   NORA: Yes, and which I signed.

KROGSTAD: Exactly. But then I added a few lines naming your father as security for the debt. This paragraph was to be signed by your father.

NORA: Was to be? He did sign it.

KROGSTAD: I left the date blank for your father to fill in when he signed this paper. You remember, Mrs. Helmer?

NORA: Yes, I think so—

KROGSTAD: Then I gave you back this I.O.U. for you to post to your father. Is that not correct?

NORA: Yes.

730   KROGSTAD: And of course you posted it at once; for within five or six days you brought it along to me with your father's signature on it. Whereupon I handed you the money.

NORA: Yes, well. Haven't I repaid the installments as agreed?

KROGSTAD: Mm—yes, more or less. But to return to what we were speaking about—that was a difficult time for you just then, wasn't it, Mrs. Helmer?

NORA: Yes, it was.

KROGSTAD: And your father was very ill, if I am not mistaken.

NORA: He was dying.

740   KROGSTAD: He did in fact die shortly afterwards?

NORA: Yes.

KROGSTAD: Tell me, Mrs. Helmer, do you by any chance remember the date of your father's death? The day of the month, I mean.

NORA: Papa died on the twenty-ninth of September.

KROGSTAD: Quite correct; I took the trouble to confirm it. And that leaves me with a curious little problem—(*Takes out a paper.*)— which I simply cannot solve.

NORA: Problem? I don't see—

KROGSTAD: The problem, Mrs. Helmer, is that your father signed this
750   paper three days after his death.

NORA: What? I don't understand—

KROGSTAD: Your father died on the twenty-ninth of September. But look at this. Here your father has dated his signature the second of October. Isn't that a curious little problem, Mrs. Helmer? *(Nora is silent.)* Can you suggest any explanation? *(She remains silent.)* And there's another curious thing. The words "second of October" and the year are written in a hand which is not your father's, but which I seem to know. Well, there's a simple explanation to that. Your father could have forgotten to write in the date when he signed, and someone else could have added it before the news came of his death. There's nothing criminal about that. It's the signature itself I'm wondering about. It *is* genuine, I suppose, Mrs. Helmer? It was your father who wrote this name here?

NORA *(after a short silence, throws back her head and looks defiantly at him):* No, it was not. It was I who wrote Papa's name there.

KROGSTAD: Look, Mrs. Helmer, do you realize this is a dangerous admission?

NORA: Why? You'll get your money.

KROGSTAD: May I ask you a question? Why didn't you send this paper to your father?

NORA: I couldn't. Papa was very ill. If I'd asked him to sign this, I'd have had to tell him what the money was for. But I couldn't have told him in his condition that my husband's life was in danger. I couldn't have done that!

KROGSTAD: Then you would have been wiser to have given up your idea of a holiday.

NORA: But I couldn't! It was to save my husband's life. I couldn't put it off.

KROGSTAD: But didn't it occur to you that you were being dishonest towards me?

NORA: I couldn't bother about that. I didn't care about you. I hated you because of all the beastly difficulties you'd put in my way when you knew how dangerously ill my husband was.

KROGSTAD: Mrs. Helmer, you evidently don't appreciate exactly what you have done. But I can assure you that it is no bigger nor worse a crime than the one I once committed, and thereby ruined my whole social position.

NORA: You? Do you expect me to believe that you would have taken a risk like that to save your wife's life?

KROGSTAD: The law does not concern itself with motives.

NORA: Then the law must be very stupid.

KROGSTAD: Stupid or not, if I show this paper to the police, you will be judged according to it.

NORA: I don't believe that. Hasn't a daughter the right to shield her father from worry and anxiety when he's old and dying? Hasn't a wife the right to save her husband's life? I don't know much about the law, but there must be something somewhere that says that such things are allowed. You ought to know about that, you're meant to be a lawyer, aren't you? You can't be a very good lawyer, Mr. Krogstad.

KROGSTAD: Possibly not. But business, the kind of business we two have been transacting—I think you'll admit I understand something about that? Good. Do as you please. But I tell you this. If I get thrown into the gutter for a second time, I shall take you with me.

(He bows and goes out through the hall.)

NORA *(stands for a moment in thought, then tosses her head):* What nonsense! He's trying to frighten me! I'm not that stupid. *(Busies herself gathering together the children's clothes; then she suddenly stops.)* But—? No, it's impossible. I did it for love, didn't I?

CHILDREN *(in the doorway, left):* Mummy, the strange gentleman's gone out into the street.

NORA: Yes, yes, I know. But don't talk to anyone about the strange gentleman. You hear? Not even to Daddy.

CHILDREN: No, Mummy. Will you play with us again now?

NORA: No, no. Not now.

CHILDREN: Oh but, Mummy, you promised!

NORA: I know, but I can't just now. Go back to the nursery. I've a lot to do. Go away, my darlings, go away. *(She pushes them gently into the other room, and closes the door behind them. She sits on the sofa, takes up her embroidery, stitches for a few moments, but soon stops.)* No! *(Throws the embroidery aside, gets up, goes to the door leading to the hall, and calls.)* Helen! Bring in the Christmas tree! *(She goes to the table on the left and opens the drawer in it; then pauses again.)* No, but it's utterly impossible!

MAID *(enters with tree):* Where shall I put it, madam?

NORA: There, in the middle of the room.

MAID: Will you be wanting anything else?

NORA: No, thank you, I have everything I need.

(The maid puts down the tree and goes out.)

NORA *(busy decorating the tree):* Now—candles here—and flowers here. That loathsome man! Nonsense, nonsense, there's nothing to be frightened about. The Christmas tree must be beautiful. I'll do everything that you like, Torvald. I'll sing for you, dance for you—

(Helmer, with a bundle of papers under his arm, enters.)

NORA: Oh—are you back already?

HELMER: Yes. Has anyone been here?

NORA: Here? No.

HELMER: That's strange. I saw Krogstad come out of the front door.

NORA: Did you? Oh yes, that's quite right—Krogstad was here for a few minutes.

HELMER: Nora, I can tell from your face, he's been here and asked you
to put in a good word for him.

NORA: Yes.

HELMER: And you were to pretend you were doing it of your own
840   accord? You weren't going to tell me he'd been here? He asked you
to do that too, didn't he?

NORA: Yes, Torvald. But—

HELMER: Nora, Nora! And you were ready to enter into such a conspiracy? Talking to a man like that, and making him promises—and
then, on top of it all, to tell me an untruth!

NORA: An untruth?

HELMER: Didn't you say no one had been here? *(Wags his finger.)* My
little songbird must never do that again. A songbird must have a
clean beak to sing with; otherwise she'll start twittering out of tune.
850   *(Puts his arm round her waist.)* Isn't that the way we want things?
Yes, of course it is. *(Lets go of her.)* So let's hear no more about that.
(Sits down in front of the stove.) Ah, how cozy and peaceful it is
here. *(Glances for a few moments at his papers.)*

NORA *(busy with the tree; after a short silence):* Torvald.

HELMER: Yes.

NORA: I'm terribly looking forward to that fancy dress ball at the Sten-
borgs on Boxing Day.

HELMER: And I'm terribly curious to see what you're going to surprise
me with.

850   NORA: Oh, it's so maddening.

HELMER: What is?

NORA: I can't think of anything to wear. It all seems so stupid and meaningless.

HELMER: So my little Nora's come to that conclusion, has she?

NORA *(behind his chair, resting her arms on its back):* Are you very
busy, Torvald?

HELMER: Oh—

NORA: What are those papers?

HELMER: Just something to do with the bank.

860   NORA: Already?

HELMER: I persuaded the trustees to give me authority to make certain
immediate changes in the staff and organization. I want to have
everything straight by the New Year.

NORA: Then that's why this poor man Krogstad—

HELMER: Hm.

NORA *(still leaning over his chair, slowly strokes the back of his head):*
If you hadn't been so busy, I was going to ask you an enormous
favour, Torvald.

HELMER: Well, tell me. What was it to be?

870   NORA: You know I trust your taste more than anyone's. I'm so anxious
to look really beautiful at the fancy dress ball. Torvald, couldn't you

help me to decide what I shall go as, and what kind of costume I ought to wear?

HELMER: Aha! So little Miss Independent's in trouble and needs a man to rescue her, does she?

NORA: Yes, Torvald. I can't get anywhere without your help.

HELMER: Well, well, I'll give the matter thought. We'll find something.

NORA: Oh, how kind of you! *(Goes back to the tree. Pause.)* How pretty these red flowers look! But, tell me, is it so dreadful, this thing that
880   Krogstad's done?

HELMER: He forged someone else's name. Have you any idea what that means?

NORA: Mightn't he have been forced to do it by some emergency?

HELMER: He probably just didn't think—that's what usually happens. I'm not so heartless as to condemn a man for an isolated action.

NORA: No, Torvald, of course not!

HELMER: Men often succeed in reestablishing themselves if they admit their crime and take their punishment.

NORA: Punishment?

890   HELMER: But Krogstad didn't do that. He chose to try and trick his way out of it; and that's what has morally destroyed him.

NORA: You think that would—?

HELMER: Just think how a man with that load on his conscience must always be lying and cheating and dissembling; how he must wear a mask even in the presence of those who are dearest to him, even his own wife and children! Yes, the children. That's the worst danger, Nora.

NORA: Why?

HELMER: Because an atmosphere of lies contaminates and poisons
900   every corner of the home. Every breath that the children draw in such a house contains the germs of evil.

NORA *(comes closer behind him):* Do you really believe that?

HELMER: Oh, my dear, I've come across it so often in my work at the bar. Nearly all young criminals are the children of mothers who are con- stitutional liars.

NORA: Why do you say mothers?

HELMER: It's usually the mother; though of course the father can have the same influence. Every lawyer knows that only too well. And yet this fellow Krogstad has been sitting at home all these years poison-
910   ing his children with his lies and pretenses. That's why I say that, morally speaking, he is dead. *(Stretches out his hands toward her.)* So my pretty little Nora must promise me not to plead his case. Your hand on it. Come, come, what's this? Give me your hand. There. That's settled, now. I assure you it'd be quite impossible for me to work in the same building as him. I literally feel physically ill in the presence of a man like that.

NORA *(draws her hand from his and goes over to the other side of the Christmas tree):* How hot it is in here! And I've so much to do.

HELMER *(gets up and gathers his papers):* Yes, and I must try to get some of this read before dinner. I'll think about your costume too. And I may even have something up my sleeve to hang in gold paper on the Christmas tree. *(Lays his hand on her head.)* My precious little songbird!

(He goes into his study and closes the door.)

NORA *(softly, after a pause):* It's nonsense. It must be. It's impossible. It must be impossible!

NURSE *(in the doorway, left):* The children are asking if they can come in to Mummy.

NORA: No, no, no; don't let them in! You stay with them, Anne-Marie.

NURSE: Very good, madam. *(Closes the door.)*

NORA *(pale with fear):* Corrupt my little children—! Poison my home! *(Short pause. She throws back her head.)* It isn't true! It *couldn't* be true!

ACT 2

The same room. In the corner by the piano the Christmas tree stands, stripped and disheveled, its candles burned to their sockets. Nora's outdoor clothes lie on the sofa. She is alone in the room, walking restlessly to and fro. At length she stops by the sofa and picks up her coat.

NORA *(drops the coat again):* There's someone coming! *(Goes to the door and listens.)* No, it's no one. Of course—no one'll come today, it's Christmas Day. Nor tomorrow. But perhaps—! *(Opens the door and looks out.)* No. Nothing in the letter-box. Quite empty. *(Walks across the room.)* Silly, silly. Of course he won't do anything. It couldn't happen. It isn't possible. Why, I've three small children.

(The Nurse, carrying a large cardboard box, enters from the room on the left.)

NURSE: I found those fancy dress clothes at last, madam.

NORA: Thank you. Put them on the table.

NURSE *(does so):* They're all rumpled up.

NORA: Oh, I wish I could tear them into a million pieces!

NURSE: Why, madam! They'll be all right. Just a little patience.

NORA: Yes, of course. I'll go and get Mrs. Linde to help me.

NURSE: What, out again? In this dreadful weather? You'll catch a chill, madam.

NORA: Well, that wouldn't be the worst. How are the children?

NURSE: Playing with their Christmas presents, poor little dears. But—

NORA: Are they still asking to see me?

NURSE: They're so used to having their Mummy with them.

950   NORA: Yes, but, Anne-Marie, from now on I shan't be able to spend so
　　　　much time with them.

NURSE: Well, children get used to anything in time.

NORA: Do you think so? Do you think they'd forget their mother if she
　　　　went away from them—for ever?

NURSE: Mercy's sake, madam! For ever!

NORA: Tell me, Anne-Marie—I've so often wondered. How could you
　　　　bear to give your child away—to strangers?

NURSE: But I had to when I came to nurse my little Miss Nora.

NORA: Do you mean you wanted to?

960   NURSE: When I had the chance of such a good job? A poor girl what's
　　　　got into trouble can't afford to pick and choose. That good-for-noth-
　　　　ing didn't lift a finger.

NORA: But your daughter must have completely forgotten you.

NURSE: Oh no, indeed she hasn't. She's written to me twice, once when
　　　　she got confirmed and then again when she got married.

NORA (*hugs her):* Dear old Anne-Marie, you were a good mother to me.

NURSE: Poor little Miss Nora, you never had any mother but me.

NORA: And if my little ones had no one else, I know you would—no,
　　　　silly, silly, silly! *(Opens the cardboard box.)* Go back to them, Anne-
970   Marie. Now I must—Tomorrow you'll see how pretty I shall look.

NURSE: Why, there'll be no one at the ball as beautiful as my Miss Nora.

(She goes into the room, left.)

NORA (*begins to unpack the clothes from the box, but soon throws
them down again):* Oh, if only I dared to go out! If I could be sure
no one would come, and nothing would happen while I was away!
Stupid, stupid! No one will come. I just mustn't think about it. Brush
this muff. Pretty gloves, pretty gloves! Don't think about it, don't
think about it! One, two, three, four, five, six—*(Cries.)* Ah—they're
coming—!

*(She begins to run toward the door, but stops uncertainly. Mrs. Linde
enters from the hall where she has been taking off her outdoor clothes.)*

NORA: Oh, it's you, Christine. There's no one else out there, is there? Oh,
　　　　I'm so glad you've come.

980   MRS. LINDE: I hear you were at my room asking for me.

NORA: Yes, I just happened to be passing. I want to ask you to help me
　　　　with something. Let's sit down here on the sofa. Look at this. There's
　　　　going to be a fancy dress ball tomorrow night upstairs at Consul
　　　　Stenborg's, and Torvald wants me to go as a Neapolitan fisher-girl
　　　　and dance the tarantella. I learned it on Capri.

MRS. LINDE: I say, are you going to give a performance?

NORA: Yes, Torvald says I should. Look, here's the dress. Torvald had it
　　　　made for me in Italy; but now it's all so torn, I don't know—

MRS. LINDE: Oh, we'll soon put that right; the stitching's just come away.
990   Needle and thread? Ah, here we are.

NORA: You're being awfully sweet.

MRS. LINDE *(sews):* So you're going to dress up tomorrow, Nora? I must pop over for a moment to see how you look. Oh, but I've completely forgotten to thank you for that nice evening yesterday.

NORA *(gets up and walks across the room):* Oh, I didn't think it was as nice as usual. You ought to have come to town a little earlier, Christine....Yes, Torvald understands how to make a home look attractive.

MRS. LINDE: I'm sure you do, too. You're not your father's daughter for nothing. But, tell me. Is Dr. Rank always in such low spirits as he was yesterday?

NORA: No, last night it was very noticeable. But he's got a terrible disease; he's got spinal tuberculosis, poor man. His father was a frightful creature who kept mistresses and so on. As a result Dr. Rank has been sickly ever since he was a child—you understand—

MRS. LINDE *(puts down her sewing):* But, my dear Nora, how on earth did you get to know about such things?

NORA *(walks about the room):* Oh, don't be silly, Christine—when one has three children, one comes into contact with women who—well, who know about medical matters, and they tell one a thing or two.

MRS. LINDE *(sews again; a short silence):* Does Dr. Rank visit you every day?

NORA: Yes, every day. He's Torvald's oldest friend, and a good friend to me too. Dr. Rank's almost one of the family.

MRS. LINDE: But, tell me—is he quite sincere? I mean doesn't he rather say the sort of thing he thinks people want to hear?

NORA: No, quite the contrary. What gave you that idea?

MRS. LINDE: When you introduced me to him yesterday, he said he'd often heard my name mentioned here. But later I noticed your husband had no idea who I was. So how could Dr. Rank—?

NORA: Yes, that's quite right, Christine. You see, Torvald's so hopelessly in love with me that he wants to have me all to himself—those were his very words. When we were first married, he got quite jealous if I as much as mentioned any of my old friends back home. So naturally, I stopped talking about them. But I often chat with Dr. Rank about that kind of thing. He enjoys it, you see.

MRS. LINDE: Now listen, Nora. In many ways you're still a child; I'm a bit older than you and have a little more experience of the world. There's something I want to say to you. You ought to give up this business with Dr. Rank.

NORA: What business?

MRS. LINDE: Well, everything. Last night you were speaking about this rich admirer of yours who was going to give you money—

NORA: Yes, and who doesn't exist—unfortunately. But what's that got to do with—?

MRS. LINDE: Is Dr. Rank rich?

NORA: Yes.

MRS. LINDE: And he has no dependents?

NORA: No, no one. But—

MRS. LINDE: And he comes here to see you every day?

NORA: Yes, I've told you.

1040   MRS. LINDE: But how dare a man of his education be so forward?

NORA: What on earth are you talking about?

MRS. LINDE: Oh, stop pretending, Nora. Do you think I haven't guessed who it was who lent you that two hundred pounds?

NORA: Are you out of your mind? How could you imagine such a thing? A friend, someone who comes here every day! Why, that'd be an impossible situation!

MRS. LINDE: Then it really wasn't him?

NORA: No, of course not. I've never for a moment dreamed of—anyway, he hadn't any money to lend then. He didn't come into that till later.

1050   MRS. LINDE: Well, I think that was a lucky thing for you, Nora dear.

NORA: No, I could never have dreamed of asking Dr. Rank—Though I'm sure that if I ever did ask him—

MRS. LINDE: But of course you won't.

NORA: Of course not. I can't imagine that it should ever become necessary. But I'm perfectly sure that if I did speak to Dr. Rank—

MRS. LINDE: Behind your husband's back?

NORA: I've got to get out of this other business; and *that's* been going on behind his back. I've *got* to get out of it.

MRS. LINDE: Yes, well, that's what I told you yesterday. But—

1060   NORA (*walking up and down*): It's much easier for a man to arrange these things than a woman—

MRS. LINDE: One's own husband, yes.

NORA: Oh, bosh. *(Stops walking.)* When you've completely repaid a debt, you get your I.O.U. back, don't you?

MRS. LINDE: Yes, of course.

NORA: And you can tear it into a thousand pieces and burn the filthy, beastly thing!

MRS. LINDE (*looks hard at her, puts down her sewing, and gets up slowly*): Nora, you're hiding something from me.

1070   NORA: Can you see that?

MRS. LINDE: Something has happened since yesterday morning. Nora, what is it?

NORA (*goes toward her*): Christine! *(Listens.)* Ssh! There's Torvald. Would you mind going into the nursery for a few minutes? Torvald can't bear to see sewing around. Anne-Marie'll help you.

MRS. LINDE (*gathers some of her things together*): Very well. But I shan't leave this house until we've talked this matter out.

(She goes into the nursery, left. As she does so, Helmer enters from the hall.)

NORA (*runs to meet him*): Oh, Torvald dear, I've been so longing for you to come back!

1080   HELMER: Was that the dressmaker?

NORA: No, it was Christine. She's helping me mend my costume. I'm going to look rather splendid in that.

HELMER: Yes, that was quite a bright idea of mine, wasn't it?

NORA: Wonderful! But wasn't it nice of me to give in to you?

HELMER (*takes her chin in his hand*): Nice—to give in to your husband? All right, little silly, I know you didn't mean it like that. But I won't disturb you. I expect you'll be wanting to try it on.

NORA: Are you going to work now?

1090 HELMER: Yes. (*Shows her a bundle of papers.*) Look at these. I've been down to the bank—(*Turns to go into his study.*)

NORA: Torvald.

HELMER (*stops*): Yes.

NORA: If little squirrel asked you really prettily to grant her a wish—

HELMER: Well?

NORA: Would you grant it to her?

HELMER: First I should naturally have to know what it was.

NORA: Squirrel would do lots of pretty tricks for you if you granted her wish.

HELMER: Out with it, then.

1100 NORA: Your little skylark would sing in every room—

HELMER: My little skylark does that already.

NORA: I'd turn myself into a little fairy and dance for you in the moonlight, Torvald.

HELMER: Nora, it isn't that business you were talking about this morning?

NORA (*comes closer*): Yes, Torvald—oh, please! I beg of you!

HELMER: Have you really the nerve to bring that up again?

NORA: Yes, Torvald, yes, you must do as I ask! You must let Krogstad keep his place at the bank!

HELMER: My dear Nora, his is the job I'm giving to Mrs. Linde.

1110 NORA: Yes, that's terribly sweet of you. But you can get rid of one of the other clerks instead of Krogstad.

HELMER: Really, you're being incredibly obstinate. Just because you thoughtlessly promised to put in a word for him, you expect me to—

NORA: No, it isn't that, Helmer. It's for your own sake. The man writes for the most beastly newspapers—you said so yourself. He could do you tremendous harm. I'm so dreadfully frightened of him—

HELMER: Oh, I understand. Memories of the past. That's what's frightening you.

NORA: What do you mean?

1120 HELMER: You're thinking of your father, aren't you?

NORA: Yes, yes. Of course. Just think what those dreadful men wrote in the papers about Papa! The most frightful slanders. I really believe it would have lost him his job if the Ministry hadn't sent you down to investigate, and you hadn't been so kind and helpful to him.

HELMER: But my dear little Nora, there's a considerable difference between your father and me. Your father was not a man of unassailable reputation. But I am; and I hope to remain so all my life.

NORA: But no one knows what spiteful people may not dig up. We could be so peaceful and happy now, Torvald—we could be free from
1130   every worry—you and I and the children. Oh, please, Torvald, please—!

HELMER: The very fact of your pleading his cause makes it impossible for me to keep him. Everyone at the bank already knows that I intend to dismiss Krogstad. If the rumor got about that the new manager had allowed his wife to persuade him to change his mind—

NORA: Well, what then?

HELMER: Oh, nothing, nothing. As long as my little Miss Obstinate gets her way—Do you expect me to make a laughing-stock of myself before my entire staff—give people the idea that I am open to out-
1140   side influence? Believe me, I'd soon feel the consequences! Besides—there's something else that makes it impossible for Krogstad to remain in the bank while I am its manager.

NORA: What is that?

HELMER: I might conceivably have allowed myself to ignore his moral obloquies—

NORA: Yes, Torvald, surely?

HELMER: And I hear he's quite efficient at his job. But we—well, we were schoolfriends. It was one of those friendships that one enters into over-hastily and so often comes to regret late in life. I might as
1150   well confess the truth. We—well, we're on Christian name terms. And the tactless idiot makes no attempt to conceal it when other people are present. On the contrary, he thinks it gives him the right to be familiar with me. He shows off the whole time, with "Torvald this," and "Torvald that." I can tell you, I find it damned annoying. If he stayed, he'd make my position intolerable.

NORA: Torvald, you can't mean this seriously.

HELMER: Oh? And why not?

NORA: But it's so petty.

HELMER: What did you say? Petty? You think I am petty?

1160   NORA: No, Torvald dear, of course you're not. That's just why—

HELMER: Don't quibble! You call my motives petty. Then I must be petty too. Petty! I see. Well, I've had enough of this. *(Goes to the door and calls into the hall.)* Helen!

NORA: What are you going to do?

HELMER *(searching among his papers):* I'm going to settle this matter once and for all. *(The Maid enters.)* Take this letter downstairs at once. Find a messenger and see that he delivers it. Immediately! The address is on the envelope. Here's the money.

MAID: Very good, sir. *(Goes out with the letter.)*

1170   HELMER *(putting his papers in order):* There now, little Miss Obstinate.

NORA *(tensely):* Torvald—what was in that letter?

HELMER: Krogstad's dismissal.

NORA: Call her back, Torvald! There's still time. Oh, Torvald, call her back! Do it for my sake—for your own sake—for the children! Do you hear me, Torvald? Please do it! You don't realize what this may do to us all!

HELMER: Too late.

NORA: Yes. Too late.

HELMER: My dear Nora, I forgive you this anxiety. Though it is a bit of an
1180   insult to me. Oh, but it is! Isn't it an insult to imply that I should be
frightened by the vindictiveness of a depraved hack journalist? But I
forgive you, because it so charmingly testifies to the love you bear
me. *(Takes her in his arms.)* Which is as it should be, my own dearest Nora. Let what will happen, happen. When the real crisis comes,
you will not find me lacking in strength or courage. I am man
enough to bear the burden for us both.

NORA *(fearfully):* What do you mean?

HELMER: The whole burden, I say—

NORA *(calmly):* I shall never let you do that.

1190   HELMER: Very well. We shall share it, Nora—as man and wife. And that
is as it should be. *(Caresses her.)* Are you happy now? There, there,
there; don't look at me with those frightened little eyes. You're simply imagining things. You go ahead now and do your tarantella, and
get some practice on that tambourine. I'll sit in my study and close
the door. Then I won't hear anything, and you can make all the noise
you want. *(Turns in the doorway.)* When Dr. Rank comes, tell him
where to find me. *(He nods to her, goes into his room with his
papers, and closes the door.)*

NORA *(desperate with anxiety, stands as though transfixed, and whis-
1200   pers):* He said he'd do it. He will do it. He will do it, and nothing'll
stop him. No, never that. I'd rather anything. There must be some
escape—Some way out—! *(The bell rings in the hall.)* Dr. Rank—!
Anything but that! Anything, I don't care—!

*(She passes her hand across her face, composes herself, walks across,
and opens the door to the hall. Dr. Rank is standing there, hanging
up his fur coat. During the following scene, it begins to grow dark.)*

NORA: Good evening, Dr. Rank. I recognized your ring. But you mustn't
go to Torvald yet. I think he's busy.

RANK: And—you?

NORA *(as he enters the room and she closes the door behind him):* Oh,
you know very well I've always time to talk to you.

RANK: Thank you. I shall avail myself of that privilege as long as I can.

1210   NORA: What do you mean by that? As long as you *can?*

RANK: Yes. Does that frighten you?

NORA: Well, it's rather a curious expression. Is something going to happen?

RANK: Something I've been expecting to happen for a long time. But I
didn't think it would happen quite so soon.

NORA *(seizes his arm):* What is it? Dr. Rank, you must tell me!

RANK: *(sits down by the stove):* I'm on the way out. And there's nothing
to be done about it.

NORA (*sighs with relief*): Oh, it's you—?

RANK: Who else? No, it's no good lying to oneself. I am the most wretched of all my patients, Mrs. Helmer. These last few days I've been going through the books of this poor body of mine, and I find I am bankrupt. Within a month I may be rotting up there in the churchyard.

NORA: Ugh, what a nasty way to talk!

RANK: The facts aren't exactly nice. But the worst is that there's so much else that's nasty to come first. I've only one more test to make. When that's done I'll have a pretty accurate idea of when the final disintegration is likely to begin. I want to ask you a favour. Helmer's a sensitive chap, and I know how he hates anything ugly. I don't want him to visit me when I'm in hospital—

NORA: Oh but, Dr. Rank—

RANK: I don't want him there. On any pretext. I shan't have him allowed in. As soon as I know the worst, I'll send you my visiting card with a black cross on it, and then you'll know that the final filthy process has begun.

NORA: Really, you're being quite impossible this evening. And I did hope you'd be in a good mood.

RANK: With death on my hands? And all this to atone for someone else's sin? Is there justice in that? And in every single family, in one way or another, the same merciless law of retribution is at work—

NORA (*holds her hands to her ears*): Nonsense! Cheer up! Laugh!

RANK: Yes, you're right. Laughter's all the damned thing's fit for. My poor innocent spine must pay for the fun my father had as a gay young lieutenant.

NORA (*at the table, left*): You mean he was too fond of asparagus and *foie gras?*

RANK: Yes, and truffles too.

NORA: Yes, of course, truffles, yes. And oysters too, I suppose?

RANK: Yes, oysters, oysters. Of course.

NORA: And all that port and champagne to wash them down. It's too sad that all those lovely things should affect one's spine.

RANK: Especially a poor spine that never got any pleasure out of them.

NORA: Oh yes, that's the saddest thing of all.

RANK (*looks searchingly at her*): Hm—

NORA (*after a moment*): Why did you smile?

RANK: No, it was you who laughed.

NORA: No, it was you who smiled, Dr. Rank!

RANK (*gets up*): You're a worse little rogue than I thought.

NORA: Oh, I'm full of stupid tricks today.

RANK: So it seems.

NORA (*puts both her hands on his shoulders*): Dear, dear. Dr. Rank, you mustn't die and leave Torvald and me.

RANK: Oh, you'll soon get over it. Once one is gone, one is soon forgotten.

NORA *(looks at him anxiously):* Do you believe that?

RANK: One finds replacements, and then—

NORA: Who will find a replacement?

RANK: You and Helmer both will, when I am gone. You seem to have made a start already, haven't you? What was this Mrs. Linde doing here yesterday evening?

1270   NORA: Aha! But surely you can't be jealous of poor Christine?

RANK: Indeed I am. She will be my successor in this house. When I have moved on, this lady will—

NORA: Ssh—don't speak so loud! She's in there!

RANK: Today again? You see!

NORA: She's only come to mend my dress. Good heavens, how unreasonable you are! *(Sits on the sofa.)* Be nice now, Dr. Rank. Tomorrow you'll see how beautifully I shall dance; and you must imagine that I'm doing it just for you. And for Torvald of course; obviously. *(Takes some things out of the box.)* Dr. Rank, sit down here and I'll

1280   show you something.

RANK *(sits):* What's this?

NORA: Look here! Look!

RANK: Silk stockings!

NORA: Flesh-colored. Aren't they beautiful? It's very dark in here now, of course, but tomorrow—No, no, no; only the soles. Oh well, I suppose you can look a bit higher if you want to.

RANK: Hm—

NORA: Why are you looking so critical? Don't you think they'll fit me?

RANK: I can't really give you a qualified opinion on that.

1290   NORA *(looks at him for a moment):* Shame on you! *(Flicks him on the ear with the stockings.)* Take that. *(Puts them back in the box.)*

RANK: What other wonders are to be revealed to me?

NORA: I shan't show you anything else. You're being naughty.

(She hums a little and looks among the things in the box.)

RANK *(after a short silence):* When I sit here like this being so intimate with you, I can't think—I cannot imagine what would have become of me if I had never entered this house.

NORA *(smiles):* Yes, I think you enjoy being with us, don't you?

RANK *(more quietly, looking into the middle distance):* And now to

1300   have to leave it all—

NORA: Nonsense. You're not leaving us.

RANK *(as before):* And not to be able to leave even the most wretched token of gratitude behind; hardly even a passing sense of loss; only an empty place, to be filled by the next comer.

NORA: Suppose I were to ask you to—? No—

RANK: To do what?

NORA: To give me proof of your friendship—

RANK: Yes, yes?

1310 NORA: No, I mean—to do me a very great service—

RANK: Would you really for once grant me that happiness?

NORA: But you've no idea what it is.

RANK: Very well, tell me, then.

NORA: No, but, Dr. Rank, I can't. It's far too much—I want your help and advice, and I want you to do something for me.

RANK: The more the better. I've no idea what it can be. But tell me. You do trust me, don't you?

NORA: Oh, yes, more than anyone. You're my best and truest friend. Otherwise I couldn't tell you. Well then, Dr. Rank—there's something
1320   you must help me to prevent. You know how much Torvald loves me—he'd never hesitate for an instant to lay down his life for me—

RANK (*leans over toward her*): Nora—do you think he is the only one—?

NORA (*with a slight start*): What do you mean?

RANK: Who would gladly lay down his life for you?

NORA (*sadly*): Oh, I see.

RANK: I swore to myself I would let you know that before I go, I shall never have a better opportunity....Well, Nora, now you know that. And now you also know that you can trust me as you can trust nobody else.

1330 NORA (*rises; calmly and quietly*): Let me pass, please.

RANK (*makes room for her but remains seated*): Nora—

NORA (*in the doorway to the hall*): Helen, bring the lamp. (*Goes over to the stove.*) Oh, dear Dr. Rank, this was really horrid of you.

RANK (*gets up*): That I have loved you as deeply as anyone else has? Was that horrid of me?

NORA: No—but that you should go and tell me. That was quite unnecessary—

RANK: What do you mean? Did you know, then—?

(The Maid enters with the lamp, puts it on the table, and goes out.)

RANK: Nora—Mrs. Helmer—I am asking you, did you know this?

1340 NORA: Oh, what do I know, what did I know, what didn't I know—I really can't say. How could you be so stupid, Dr. Rank? Everything was so nice.

RANK: Well, at any rate now you know that I am ready to serve you, body and soul. So—please continue.

NORA (*looks at him*): After this?

RANK: Please tell me what it is.

NORA: I can't possibly tell you now.

RANK: Yes, yes! You mustn't punish me like this. Let me be allowed to do what I can for you.

1350 NORA: You can't do anything for me now. Anyway, I don't need any help. It was only my imagination—you'll see. Yes, really. Honestly. (*Sits in the rocking chair, looks at him, and smiles.)* Well, upon my word you *are* a fine gentleman, Dr. Rank. Aren't you ashamed of yourself, now that the lamp's been lit?

RANK: Frankly, no. But perhaps I ought to say—*adieu?*

NORA: Of course not. You will naturally continue to visit us as before. You know quite well how Torvald depends on your company.

RANK: Yes, but you?

NORA: Oh, I always think it's enormous fun having you here.

1360   RANK: That was what misled me. You're a riddle to me, you know. I'd often felt you'd just as soon be with me as with Helmer.

NORA: Well, you see, there are some people whom one loves, and others whom it's almost more fun to be with.

RANK: Oh yes, there's some truth in that.

NORA: When I was at home, of course I loved Papa best. But I always used to think it was terribly amusing to go down and talk to the servants; because they never told me what I ought to do; and they were such fun to listen to.

RANK: I see. So I've taken their place?

1370   NORA *(jumps up and runs over to him):* Oh, dear, sweet Dr. Rank, I didn't mean that at all. But I'm sure you understand—I feel the same about Torvald as I did about Papa.

MAID *(enters from the hall):* Excuse me, madam. *(Whispers to her and hands her a visiting card.)*

NORA *(glances at the card):* Oh! *(Puts it quickly in her pocket.)*

RANK: Anything wrong?

NORA: No, no, nothing at all. It's just something that—it's my new dress.

RANK: What? But your costume is lying over there.

NORA: Oh—that, yes—but there's another—I ordered it specially—

1380   Torvald mustn't know—

RANK: Ah, so that's your big secret?

NORA: Yes, yes. Go in and talk to him—he's in his study—keep him talking for a bit—

RANK: Don't worry. He won't get away from me. *(Goes into Helmer's study.)*

NORA *(to the Maid):* Is he waiting in the kitchen?

MAID: Yes, madam, he came up the back way—

NORA: But didn't you tell him I had a visitor?

MAID: Yes, but he wouldn't go.

1390   NORA: Wouldn't go?

MAID: No, madam, not until he'd spoken with you.

NORA: Very well, show him in; but quietly. Helen, you mustn't tell anyone about this. It's a surprise for my husband.

MAID: Very good, madam. I understand. *(Goes.)*

NORA: It's happening. It's happening after all. No, no, no, it can't happen, it mustn't happen.

(She walks across and bolts the door of Helmer's study. The Maid opens the door in the hall to admit Krogstad, and closes it behind him. He is wearing an overcoat, heavy boots, and a fur cap.)

NORA *(goes towards him):* Speak quietly. My husband's at home.

KROGSTAD: Let him hear.

NORA: What do you want from me?

1400   KROGSTAD: Information.

NORA: Hurry up, then. What is it?

KROGSTAD: I suppose you know I've been given the sack.

NORA: I couldn't stop it, Mr. Krogstad. I did my best for you, but it didn't help.

KROGSTAD: Does your husband love you so little? He knows what I can do to you, and yet he dares to—

NORA: Surely you don't imagine I told him?

KROGSTAD: No. I didn't really think you had. It wouldn't have been like my old friend Torvald Helmer to show that much courage—

1410   NORA: Mr. Krogstad, I'll trouble you to speak respectfully of my husband.

KROGSTAD: Don't worry, I'll show him all the respect he deserves. But since you're so anxious to keep this matter hushed up, I presume you're better informed than you were yesterday of the gravity of what you've done?

NORA: I've learned more than you could ever teach me.

KROGSTAD: Yes, a bad lawyer like me—

NORA: What do you want from me?

KROGSTAD: I just wanted to see how things were with you, Mrs. Helmer. I've been thinking about you all day. Even duns and hack journalists

1420   have hearts, you know.

NORA: Show some heart, then. Think of my little children.

KROGSTAD: Have you and your husband thought of mine? Well, let's forget that. I just wanted to tell you, you don't need to take this business too seriously. I'm not going to take any action, for the present.

NORA: Oh, no—you won't, will you? I knew it.

KROGSTAD: It can all be settled quite amicably. There's no need for it to become public, We'll keep it among the three of us.

NORA: My husband must never know about this.

KROGSTAD: How can you stop him? Can you pay the balance of what you

1430   owe me?

NORA: Not immediately.

KROGSTAD: Have you any means of raising the money during the next few days?

NORA: None that I would care to use.

KROGSTAD: Well, it wouldn't have helped anyway. However much money you offered me now I wouldn't give you back that paper.

NORA: What are you going to do with it?

KROGSTAD: Just keep it. No one else need ever hear about it. So in case you were thinking of doing anything desperate—

1440   NORA: I am.

KROGSTAD: Such as running away—

NORA: I am.

KROGSTAD: Or anything more desperate—

NORA: How did you know?

KROGSTAD: —just give up the idea.

NORA: How did you know?

KROGSTAD: Most of us think of that at first. I did. But I hadn't the courage—

NORA (*dully*): Neither have I.

KROGSTAD (*relieved*): It's true, isn't it? You haven't the courage either?

1450   NORA: No. I haven't. I haven't.

KROGSTAD: It'd be a stupid thing to do anyway. Once the first little
    domestic explosion is over....I've got a letter in my pocket here
    addressed to your husband—

NORA: Telling him everything?

KROGSTAD: As delicately as possible.

NORA (*quickly*): He must never see that letter. Tear it up. I'll find the
    money somehow—

KROGSTAD: I'm sorry, Mrs. Helmer, I thought I'd explained—

NORA: Oh, I don't mean the money I owe you. Let me know how much

1460   you want from my husband, and I'll find it for you.

KROGSTAD: I'm not asking your husband for money.

NORA: What do you want, then?

KROGSTAD: I'll tell you. I want to get on my feet again, Mrs. Helmer. I
    want to get to the top. And your husband's going to help me. For
    eighteen months now my record's been clean. I've been in hard
    straits all that time; I was content to fight my way back inch by inch.
    Now I've been chucked back into the mud, and I'm not going to be
    satisfied with just getting back my job. I'm going to get to the top, I
    tell you. I'm going to get back into the bank, and it's going to be

1470   higher up. Your husband's going to create a new job for me—

NORA: He'll never do that!

KROGSTAD: Oh, yes he will. I know him. He won't dare to risk a scandal.
    And once I'm in there with him, you'll see! Within a year I'll be his
    right-hand man. It'll be Nils Krogstad who'll be running that bank,
    not Torvald Helmer!

NORA: That will never happen.

KROGSTAD: Are you thinking of—?

NORA: Now I *have* the courage.

KROGSTAD: Oh, you can't frighten me. A pampered little pretty like you—

1480   NORA: You'll see! You'll see!

KROGSTAD: Under the ice? Down in the cold, black water? And then, in
    the spring, to float up again, ugly, unrecognizable, hairless—?

NORA: You can't frighten me.

KROGSTAD: And you can't frighten me. People don't do such things, Mrs.
    Helmer. And anyway, what'd be the use? I've got him in my pocket.

NORA: But afterwards? When I'm no longer—?

KROGSTAD: Have you forgotten that then your reputation will be in my hands? *(She looks at him speechlessly.)* Well, I've warned you. Don't do anything silly. When Helmer's read my letter, he'll get in touch with me. And remember, it's your husband who's forced me to act like this. And for that I'll never forgive him. Goodbye, Mrs. Helmer. *(He goes out through the hall.)*

NORA *(runs to the hall door, opens it a few inches, and listens):* He's going. He's not going to give him the letter. Oh, no, no, it couldn't possibly happen. *(Opens the door a little wider.)* What's he doing? Standing outside the front door. He's not going downstairs. Is he changing his mind? Yes, he—!

(A letter falls into the letter-box. Krogstad's footsteps die away down the stairs.)

NORA *(with a stifled cry, runs across the room towards the table by the sofa. A pause):* In the letter-box. *(Steals timidly over towards the hall door.)* There it is! Oh, Torvald, Torvald! Now we're lost!

MRS. LINDE *(enters from the nursery with Nora's costume):* Well, I've done the best I can. Shall we see how it looks—?

NORA *(whispers hoarsely):* Christine, come here.

MRS. LINDE *(throws the dress on the sofa):* What's wrong with you? You look as though you'd seen a ghost!

NORA: Come here. Do you see that letter? There—look—through the glass of the letter-box.

MRS. LINDE: Yes, yes, I see it.

NORA: That letter's from Krogstad—

MRS. LINDE: Nora! It was Krogstad who lent you the money!

NORA: Yes. And now Torvald's going to discover everything.

MRS. LINDE: Oh, believe me, Nora, it'll be best for you both.

NORA: You don't know what's happened. I've committed a forgery—

MRS. LINDE: But, for heaven's sake—!

NORA: Christine, all I want is for you to be my witness.

MRS. LINDE: What do you mean? Witness what?

NORA: If I should go out of my mind—and it might easily happen—

MRS. LINDE: Nora!

NORA: Or if anything else should happen to me—so that I wasn't here any longer—

MRS. LINDE: Nora, Nora, you don't know what you're saying!

NORA: If anyone should try to take the blame, and say it was all his fault—you understand—?

MRS. LINDE: Yes, yes—but how can you think—?

NORA: Then you must testify that it isn't true, Christine. I'm not mad— I know exactly what I'm saying—and I'm telling you, no one else knows anything about this. I did it entirely on my own. Remember that.

MRS. LINDE: All right. But I simply don't understand—

NORA: Oh, how could you understand? A—miracle—is about to happen.

1530   MRS. LINDE: Miracle?

NORA: Yes. A miracle. But it's so frightening, Christine. It *mustn't* happen, not for anything in the world.

MRS. LINDE: I'll go over and talk to Krogstad.

NORA: Don't go near him. He'll only do something to hurt you.

MRS. LINDE: Once upon a time he'd have done anything for my sake.

NORA: He?

MRS. LINDE: Where does he live?

NORA: Oh, how should I know—? Oh, yes, wait a moment—*(Feels in her pocket.)* Here's his card. But the letter, the letter—!

1540   HELMER *(in his study, knocks on the door):* Nora!

NORA *(cries in alarm):* What is it?

HELMER: Now, now, don't get alarmed. We're not coming in; you've closed the door. Are you trying on your costume?

NORA: Yes, yes—I'm trying on my costume. I'm going to look so pretty for you, Torvald.

MRS. LINDE *(who has been reading the card):* Why, he lives just around the corner.

NORA: Yes; but it's no use. There's nothing to be done now. The letter's lying there in the box.

1550   MRS. LINDE: And your husband has the key?

NORA: Yes, he always keeps it.

MRS. LINDE: Krogstad must ask him to send the letter back unread. He must find some excuse—

NORA: But Torvald always opens the box at just about this time—

MRS. LINDE: You must stop him. Go in and keep him talking. I'll be back as quickly as I can.

(She hurries out through the hall.)

NORA *(goes over to Helmer's door, opens it and peeps in):* Torvald!

HELMER *(offstage):* Well, may a man enter his own drawing room again? Come on, Rank, now we'll see what—*(In the doorway.)* But what's

1560   this?

NORA: What, Torvald dear?

HELMER: Rank's been preparing me for some great transformation scene.

RANK *(in the doorway):* So I understood. But I seem to have been mistaken.

NORA: Yes, no one's to be allowed to see me before tomorrow night.

HELMER: But, my dear Nora, you look quite worn out. Have you been practicing too hard?

NORA: No, I haven't practiced at all yet.

1570   HELMER: Well, you must.

NORA: Yes, Torvald, I must, I know. But I can't get anywhere without your help. I've completely forgotten everything.

HELMER: Oh, we'll soon put that to rights.

NORA: Yes, help me, Torvald. Promise me you will? Oh, I'm so nervous. All those people—! You must forget everything except me this evening. You mustn't think of business—I won't even let you touch a pen. Promise me, Torvald?

HELMER: I promise. This evening I shall think of nothing but you—my poor, helpless little darling. Oh, there's just one thing I must see to—

1580   *(Goes toward the hall door.)*

NORA: What do you want out there?

HELMER: I'm only going to see if any letters have come.

NORA: No, Torvald, no!

HELMER: Why, what's the matter?

NORA: Torvald, I beg you. There's nothing there.

HELMER: Well, I'll just make sure.

(He moves towards the door. Nora runs to the piano and plays the first bar of the tarantella.)

HELMER *(at the door, turns):* Aha!

NORA: I can't dance tomorrow if I don't practice with you now.

HELMER *(goes over to her):* Are you really so frightened, Nora dear?

1590   NORA: Yes, terribly frightened. Let me start practicing now, at once— we've still time before dinner. Oh, do sit down and play for me, Torvald dear. Correct me, lead me, the way you always do.

HELMER: Very well, my dear, if you wish it.

(He sits down at the piano. Nora seizes the tambourine and a long multicolored shawl from the cardboard box, wraps the latter hastily around her, then takes a quick leap into the center of the room.)

NORA: Play for me! I want to dance!

(Helmer plays and Nora dances. Dr. Rank stands behind Helmer at the piano and watches her.)

HELMER: Slower, slower!

NORA: I can't!

HELMER: Not so violently, Nora.

NORA: I must!

HELMER *(stops playing):* No, no, this won't do at all.

1600   NORA *(laughs and swings her tambourine):* Isn't that what I told you?

RANK: Let me play for her.

HELMER *(gets up):* Yes, would you? Then it'll be easier for me to show her.

(Rank sits down at the piano and plays. Nora dances more and more wildly. Helmer has stationed himself by the stove and tries repeatedly to correct her but she seems not to hear him. Her hair works loose and falls over her shoulders; she ignores it and continues to dance. Mrs. Linde enters.)

MRS. LINDE *(stands in the doorway as though tongue-tied):* Ah—!

NORA (*as she dances*): Oh, Christine, we're having such fun!

HELMER: But, Nora darling, you're dancing as if your life depended on it.

NORA: It does.

HELMER: Rank, stop it! This is sheer lunacy. Stop it, I say!

(*Rank ceases playing. Nora suddenly stops dancing.*)

HELMER (*goes over to her*): I'd never have believed it. You've forgotten everything I taught you.

1610 NORA (*throws away the tambourine*): You see!

HELMER: I'll have to show you every step.

NORA: You see how much I need you! You must show me every step of the way. Right to the end of the dance. Promise me you will, Torvald?

HELMER: Never fear. I will.

NORA: You mustn't think about anything but me—today or tomorrow. Don't open any letters—don't even open the letter-box—

HELMER: Aha, you're still worried about that fellow—

NORA: Oh, yes, yes, him too.

1620 HELMER: Nora, I can tell from the way you're behaving, there's a letter from him already lying there.

NORA: I don't know. I think so. But you mustn't read it now. I don't want anything ugly to come between us till it's all over.

RANK (*quietly, to Helmer*): Better give her her way.

HELMER (*puts his arm round her*): My child shall have her way. But tomorrow night, when your dance is over—

NORA: Then you will be free.

MAID (*appears in the doorway, right*): Dinner is served, madam.

NORA: Put out some champagne, Helen.

1630 MAID: Very good, madam. (*Goes.*)

HELMER: I say! What's this, a banquet?

NORA: We'll drink champagne until dawn! (*Calls.*) And, Helen! Put out some macaroons! Lots of macaroons—for once!

HELMER (*takes her hands in his*): Now, now, now. Don't get so excited. Where's my little songbird, the one I know?

NORA: All right. Go and sit down—and you too, Dr. Rank. I'll be with you in a minute. Christine, you must help me put my hair up.

RANK (*quietly, as they go*): There's nothing wrong, is there? I mean, she isn't—er—expecting—?

1640 HELMER: Good heavens no, my dear chap. She just gets scared like a child sometimes—I told you before—

(*They go out right.*)

NORA: Well?

MRS. LINDE: He's left town.

NORA: I saw it from your face.

MRS. LINDE: He'll be back tomorrow evening. I left a note for him.

NORA: You needn't have bothered. You can't stop anything now. Anyway, it's wonderful really, in a way—sitting here and waiting for the miracle to happen.

1650 MRS. LINDE: Waiting for what?

NORA: Oh, you wouldn't understand. Go in and join them. I'll be with you in a moment.

(Mrs. Linde goes into the dining-room.)

NORA *(stands for a moment as though collecting herself. Then she looks at her watch):* Five o'clock. Seven hours till midnight. Then another twenty-four hours till midnight tomorrow. And then the tarantella will be finished. Twenty-four and seven? Thirty-one hours to live.

HELMER *(appears in the doorway, right):* What's happened to my little songbird?

1660 NORA *(runs to him with her arms wide):* Your songbird is here!

Act 3

The same room. The table which was formerly by the sofa has been moved into the center of the room; the chairs surround it as before. The door to the hall stands open. Dance music can be heard from the floor above. Mrs. Linde is seated at the table, absent-mindedly glancing through a book. She is trying to read, but seems unable to keep her mind on it. More than once she turns and listens anxiously towards the front door.

MRS. LINDE *(looks at her watch):* Not here yet. There's not much time left. Please God he hasn't—! *(Listens again.)* Ah, here he is. *(Goes out into the hall and cautiously opens the front door. Footsteps can be heard softly ascending the stairs. She whispers.)* Come in. There's no one here.

KROGSTAD *(in the doorway):* I found a note from you at my lodgings. What does this mean?

MRS. LINDE: I must speak with you.

KROGSTAD: Oh? And must our conversation take place in this house?

1670 MRS. LINDE: We couldn't meet at my place; my room has no separate entrance. Come in. We're quite alone. The maid's asleep, and the Helmers are at the dance upstairs.

KROGSTAD *(comes into the room):* Well, well! So the Helmers are dancing this evening? Are they indeed?

MRS. LINDE: Yes. Why not?

KROGSTAD: True enough. Why not?

MRS. LINDE: Well, Krogstad. You and I must have a talk together.

KROGSTAD: Have we two anything further to discuss?

MRS. LINDE: We have a great deal to discuss.

1680 KROGSTAD: I wasn't aware of it.

MRS. LINDE: That's because you've never really understood me.

KROGSTAD: Was there anything to understand? It's the old story, isn't it—
a woman chucking a man because something better turns up?

MRS. LINDE: Do you really think I'm so utterly heartless? You think it
was easy for me to give you up?

KROGSTAD: Wasn't it?

MRS. LINDE: Oh, Nils, did you really believe that?

KROGSTAD: Then why did you write to me the way you did?

MRS. LINDE: I had to. Since I had to break with you, I thought it my duty
1690   to destroy all the feelings you had for me.

KROGSTAD (*clenches his fists*): So that was it. And you did this for
money!

MRS. LINDE: You mustn't forget I had a helpless mother to take care of,
and two little brothers. We couldn't wait for you, Nils. It would have
been so long before you'd had enough to support us.

KROGSTAD: Maybe. But you had no right to cast me off for someone else.

MRS. LINDE: Perhaps not. I've often asked myself that.

KROGSTAD (*more quietly*): When I lost you, it was just as though all
solid ground had been swept from under my feet. Look at me. Now I
1700   am a shipwrecked man clinging to a spar.

MRS. LINDE: Help may be near at hand.

KROGSTAD: It was near. But then you came, and stood between it and
me.

MRS. LINDE: I didn't know, Nils. No one told me till today that this job I'd
found was yours.

KROGSTAD: I believe you, since you say so. But now you know, won't
you give it up?

MRS. LINDE: No—because it wouldn't help you even if I did.

KROGSTAD: Wouldn't it? I'd do it all the same.

1710   MRS. LINDE: I've learned to look at things practically. Life and poverty
have taught me that.

KROGSTAD: And life has taught me to distrust fine words.

MRS. LINDE: Then it's taught you a useful lesson. But surely you still
believe in actions?

KROGSTAD: What do you mean?

MRS. LINDE: You said you were like a shipwrecked man clinging to a spar.

KROGSTAD: I have good reason to say it.

MRS. LINDE: I'm in the same position as you. No one to care about, no
one to care for.

1720   KROGSTAD: You made your own choice.

MRS. LINDE: I had no choice—then.

KROGSTAD: Well?

MRS. LINDE: Nils, suppose we two shipwrecked souls could join hands?

KROGSTAD: What are you saying?

MRS. LINDE: Castaways have a better chance of survival together than on
their own.

KROGSTAD: Christine!

MRS. LINDE: Why do you suppose I came to this town?

KROGSTAD: You mean—you came because of me?

1780 MRS. LINDE: I must work if I'm to find life worth living. I've always worked, for as long as I can remember; it's been the greatest joy of my life—my only joy. But now I'm alone in the world, and I feel so dreadfully lost and empty. There's no joy in working just for oneself. Oh, Nils, give me something—someone—to work for.

KROGSTAD: I don't believe all that. You're just being hysterical and romantic. You want to find an excuse for self-sacrifice.

MRS. LINDE: Have you ever known me to be hysterical?

KROGSTAD: You mean you really—? Is it possible? Tell me—you know all about my past?

1790 MRS. LINDE: Yes.

KROGSTAD: And you know what people think of me here?

MRS. LINDE: You said just now that with me you might have become a different person.

KROGSTAD: I know I could have.

MRS. LINDE: Couldn't it still happen?

KROGSTAD: Christine—do you really mean this? Yes—you do—I see it in your face. Have you really the courage—?

MRS. LINDE: I need someone to be a mother to; and your children need a mother. And you and I need each other. I believe in you, Nils. I am 1800 afraid of nothing—with you.

KROGSTAD (*clasps her hands*): Thank you, Christine—thank you! Now I shall make the world believe in me as you do! Oh— but I'd forgotten—

MRS. LINDE (*listens*): Ssh! The tarantella! Go quickly, go!

KROGSTAD: Why? What is it?

MRS. LINDE: You hear that dance? As soon as it's finished, they'll be coming down.

KROGSTAD: All right, I'll go. It's no good, Christine. I'd forgotten—you don't know what I've just done to the Helmers.

1810 MRS. LINDE: Yes, Nils. I know.

KROGSTAD: And yet you'd still have the courage to—?

MRS. LINDE: I know what despair can drive a man like you to.

KROGSTAD: Oh, if only I could undo this!

MRS. LINDE: You can. Your letter is still lying in the box.

KROGSTAD: Are you sure?

MRS. LINDE: Quite sure. But—

KROGSTAD (*looks searchingly at her*): Is that why you're doing this? You want to save your friend at any price? Tell me the truth. Is that the reason?

1820 MRS. LINDE: Nils, a woman who has sold herself once for the sake of others doesn't make the same mistake again.

KROGSTAD: I shall demand my letter back.

MRS. LINDE: No, no.

KROGSTAD: Of course I shall. I shall stay here till Helmer comes down. I'll tell him he must give me back my letter—I'll say it was only to do with my dismissal, and that I don't want him to read it—

MRS. LINDE: No, Nils, you mustn't ask for that letter back.

KROGSTAD: But—tell me—wasn't that the real reason you asked me to come here?

1830 MRS. LINDE: Yes—at first, when I was frightened. But a day has passed since then, and in that time I've seen incredible things happen in this house. Helmer must know the truth. This unhappy secret of Nora's must be revealed. They must come to a full understanding; there must be an end of all these shiftings and evasions.

KROGSTAD: Very well. If you're prepared to risk it. But one thing I can do—and at once—

MRS. LINDE (*listens*): Hurry! Go, go! The dance is over. We aren't safe here another moment.

KROGSTAD: I'll wait for you downstairs.

1840 MRS. LINDE: Yes, do. You can see me home.

KROGSTAD: I've never been so happy in my life before!

(*He goes out through the front door. The door leading from the room into the hall remains open.*)

MRS. LINDE (*tidies the room a little and gets her hat and coat):* What a change! Oh, what a change! Someone to work for—to live for! A home to bring joy into! I won't let this chance of happiness slip through my fingers. Oh, why don't they come? (*Listens.*) Ah, here they are. I must get my coat on.

(*She takes her hat and coat. Helmer's and Nora's voices become audible outside. A key is turned in the lock and Helmer leads Nora almost forcibly into the hall. She is dressed in an Italian costume with a large black shawl. He is in evening dress, with a black cloak.*)

NORA (*still in the doorway, resisting him):* No, no, no—not in here! I want to go back upstairs. I don't want to leave so early.

HELMER: But my dearest Nora—

1850 NORA: Oh, please, Torvald, please! Just another hour!

HELMER: Not another minute, Nora, my sweet. You know what we agreed. Come along, now. Into the drawing-room. You'll catch cold if you stay out here.

(*He leads her, despite her efforts to resist him, gently into the room.*)

MRS. LINDE: Good evening.

NORA: Christine!

HELMER: Oh, hullo, Mrs. Linde. You still here?

MRS. LINDE: Please forgive me. I did so want to see Nora in her costume.

NORA: Have you been sitting here waiting for me?

MRS. LINDE: Yes. I got here too late, I'm afraid. You'd already gone up.

1860 And I felt I really couldn't go back home without seeing you.

HELMER *(takes off Nora's shawl):* Well, take a good look at her. She's
  worth looking at, don't you think? Isn't she beautiful, Mrs. Linde?

MRS. LINDE: Oh, yes, indeed—

HELMER: Isn't she unbelievably beautiful? Everyone at the party said so.
  But dreadfully stubborn she is, bless her pretty little heart. What's to
  be done about that? Would you believe it, I practically had to use
  force to get her away!

NORA: Oh, Torvald, you're going to regret not letting me stay—just half
  an hour longer.

1870 HELMER: Hear that, Mrs. Linde? She dances her tarantella—makes a
  roaring success—and very well deserved—though possibly a trifle
  too realistic—more so than was aesthetically necessary, strictly
  speaking. But never mind that. Main thing is—she had a success—
  roaring success. Was I going to let her stay on after that and spoil
  the impression? No, thank you. I took my beautiful little Capri signo-
  rina—my capricious little Capricienne, what?—under my arm—a
  swift round of the ballroom, a curtsey to the company, and, as they
  say in novels, the beautiful apparition disappeared! An exit should
  always be dramatic, Mrs. Linde. But unfortunately that's just what I
1880 can't get Nora to realize. I say, it's hot in here. *(Throws his cloak on
  a chair and opens the door to his study.)* What's this? It's dark in
  here. Ah, yes, of course—excuse me. *(Goes in and lights a couple of
  candles.)*

NORA *(whispers swiftly, breathlessly):* Well?

MRS. LINDE *(quietly):* I've spoken to him.

NORA: Yes?

MRS. LINDE: Nora—you must tell your husband everything.

NORA *(dully):* I knew it.

MRS. LINDE: You've nothing to fear from Krogstad. But you must tell
1890 him.

NORA: I shan't tell him anything.

MRS. LINDE: Then the letter will.

NORA: Thank you, Christine. Now I know what I must do. Ssh!

HELMER *(returns):* Well, Mrs. Linde, finished admiring her?

MRS. LINDE: Yes. Now I must say goodnight.

HELMER: Oh, already? Does this knitting belong to you?

MRS. LINDE *(takes it):* Thank you, yes. I nearly forgot it.

HELMER: You knit, then?

MRS. LINDE: Why, yes.

1900 HELMER: Know what? You ought to take up embroidery.

MRS. LINDE: Oh? Why?

HELMER: It's much prettier. Watch me, now. You hold the embroidery in
  your left hand, like this, and then you take the needle in your right
  hand and go in and out in a slow, steady movement—like this. I am
  right, aren't I?

MRS. LINDE: Yes, I'm sure—

HELMER: But knitting, now—that's an ugly business—can't help it.
Look—arms all huddled up—great clumsy needles going up and
down—make you look like a damned Chinaman. I say, that really
1910   was a magnificent champagne they served us.

MRS. LINDE: Well, good night, Nora. And stop being stubborn. Remember!

HELMER: Quite right, Mrs. Linde!

MRS. LINDE: Good night, Mr. Helmer.

HELMER (accompanies her to the door): Good night, good night! I hope
you'll manage to get home all right? I'd gladly—but you haven't far
to go, have you? Good night, good night. (She goes. He closes the
door behind her and returns.) Well, we've got rid of her at last.
Dreadful bore that woman is!

1920   NORA: Aren't you very tired, Torvald?

HELMER: No, not in the least.

NORA: Aren't you sleepy?

HELMER: Not a bit. On the contrary, I feel extraordinarily exhilarated.
But what about you? Yes, you look very sleepy and tired.

NORA: Yes, I am very tired. Soon I shall sleep.

HELMER: You see, you see! How right I was not to let you stay longer!

NORA: Oh, you're always right, whatever you do.

HELMER (kisses her on the forehead): Now my little songbird's talking
just like a real big human being. I say, did you notice how cheerful
1930   Rank was this evening?

NORA: Oh? Was he? I didn't have a chance to speak with him.

HELMER: I hardly did. But I haven't seen him in such a jolly mood for
ages. (Looks at her for a moment, then comes closer.) I say, it's nice
to get back to one's home again, and be all alone with you. Upon my
word, you're a distractingly beautiful young woman.

NORA: Don't look at me like that, Torvald!

HELMER: What, not look at my most treasured possession? At all this
wonderful beauty that's mine, mine alone, all mine.

NORA (goes round to the other side of the table): You mustn't talk to me
1940   like that tonight.

HELMER (follows her): You've still the tarantella in your blood, I see.
And that makes you even more desirable. Listen! Now the other
guests are beginning to go. (More quietly.) Nora—soon the whole
house will be absolutely quiet.

NORA: Yes, I hope so.

HELMER: Yes, my beloved Nora, of course you do! Do you know—when
I'm out with you among other people like we were tonight, do you
know why I say so little to you, why I keep so aloof from you, and
just throw you an occasional glance? Do you know why I do that?
1950   It's because I pretend to myself that you're my secret mistress, my
clandestine little sweetheart, and that nobody knows there's anything at all between us.

NORA: Oh, yes, yes, yes—I know you never think of anything but me.

HELMER: And then when we're about to go, and I wrap the shawl round your lovely young shoulders, over this wonderful curve of your neck—then I pretend to myself that you are my young bride, that we've just come from the wedding, that I'm taking you to my house for the first time—that, for the first time, I am alone with you—quite alone with you, as you stand there young and trembling and beautiful. All evening I've had no eyes for anyone but you. When I saw you dance the tarantella, like a huntress, a temptress, my blood grew hot, I couldn't stand it any longer! That was why I seized you and dragged you down here with me—

NORA: Leave me, Torvald! Get away from me! I don't want all this.

HELMER: What? Now, Nora, you're joking with me. Don't want, don't want—? Aren't I your husband—?

(There is a knock on the front door.)

NORA *(starts):* What was that?

HELMER *(goes toward the hall):* Who is it?

RANK *(outside):* It's me. May I come in for a moment?

HELMER *(quietly, annoyed):* Oh, what does he want now? *(Calls.)* Wait a moment. *(Walks over and opens the door.)* Well! Nice of you not to go by without looking in.

RANK: I thought I heard your voice, so I felt I had to say goodbye. *(His eyes travel swiftly around the room.)* Ah, yes—these dear rooms, how well I know them. What a happy, peaceful home you two have.

HELMER: You seemed to be having a pretty happy time yourself upstairs.

RANK: Indeed I did. Why not? Why shouldn't one make the most of this world? As much as one can, and for as long as one can. The wine was excellent—

HELMER: Especially the champagne.

RANK: You noticed that too? It's almost incredible how much I managed to get down.

NORA: Torvald drank a lot of champagne too, this evening.

RANK: Oh?

NORA: Yes. It always makes him merry afterwards.

RANK: Well, why shouldn't a man have a merry evening after a well-spent day?

HELMER: Well-spent? Oh, I don't know that I can claim that.

RANK *(slaps him across the back):* I can, though, my dear fellow!

NORA: Yes, of course, Dr. Rank—you've been carrying out a scientific experiment today, haven't you?

RANK: Exactly.

HELMER: Scientific experiment! Those are big words for my little Nora to use!

NORA: And may I congratulate you on the finding?

RANK: You may indeed.

NORA: It was good, then?

RANK: The best possible finding—both for the doctor and the patient. Certainty.

2000 NORA *(quickly):* Certainty?

RANK: Absolute certainty. So aren't I entitled to have a merry evening after that?

NORA: Yes, Dr. Rank. You were quite right to.

HELMER: I agree. Provided you don't have to regret it tomorrow.

RANK: Well, you never get anything in this life without paying for it.

NORA: Dr. Rank—you like masquerades, don't you?

RANK: Yes, if the disguises are sufficiently amusing.

NORA: Tell me. What shall we two wear at the next masquerade?

HELMER: You little gadabout! Are you thinking about the next one already?

2010 RANK: We two? Yes, I'll tell you. You must go as the Spirit of Happiness—

HELMER: You try to think of a costume that'll convey that.

RANK: Your wife need only appear as her normal, everyday self—

HELMER: Quite right! Well said! But what are you going to be? Have you decided that?

RANK: Yes, my dear friend. I have decided that.

HELMER: Well?

RANK: At the next masquerade, I shall be invisible.

HELMER: Well, that's a funny idea.

RANK: There's a big, black hat—haven't you heard of the invisible hat?

2020 Once it's over your head, no one can see you any more.

HELMER *(represses a smile):* Ah yes, of course.

RANK: But I'm forgetting what I came for. Helmer, give me a cigar. One of your black Havanas.

HELMER: With the greatest pleasure. *(Offers him the box.)*

RANK *(takes one and cuts off the tip):* Thank you.

NORA *(strikes a match):* Let me give you a light.

RANK: Thank you. *(She holds out the match for him. He lights his cigar.)* And now—goodbye.

HELMER: Goodbye, my dear chap, goodbye.

2030 NORA: Sleep well, Dr. Rank.

RANK: Thank you for that kind wish.

NORA: Wish me the same.

RANK: You? Very well—since you ask. Sleep well. And thank you for the light. *(He nods to them both and goes.)*

HELMER *(quietly):* He's been drinking too much.

NORA *(abstractedly):* Perhaps.

(Helmer takes his bunch of keys from his pocket and goes out into the hall.)

NORA: Torvald, what do you want out there?

HELMER: I must empty the letter-box. It's absolutely full. There'll be no room for the newspapers in the morning.

2040 NORA: Are you going to work tonight?

HELMER: You know very well I'm not. Hullo, what's this? Someone's been at the lock.

NORA: At the lock—?

HELMER: Yes, I'm sure of it. Who on earth—? Surely not one of the maids? Here's a broken hairpin. Nora, it's yours—

NORA *(quickly):* Then it must have been the children.

HELMER: Well, you'll have to break them of that habit. Hm, hm. Ah, that's done it. *(Takes out the contents of the box and calls into the kitchen.)* Helen! Put out the light on the staircase. *(Comes back into*
2050 *the drawing-room with the letters in his hand and closes the door to the hall.)* Look at this! You see how they've piled up? *(Glances through them.)* What on earth's this?

NORA *(at the window):* The letter! Oh, no, Torvald no!

HELMER: Two visiting cards—from Rank.

NORA: From Dr. Rank?

HELMER *(looks at them):* Peter Rank, M.D. They were on top. He must have dropped them in as he left.

NORA: Has he written anything on them?

HELMER: There's a black cross above his name. Look. Rather gruesome,
2060 isn't it? It looks just as though he was announcing his death.

NORA: He is.

HELMER: What? Do you know something? Has he told you anything?

NORA: Yes. When these cards come, it means he's said goodbye to us. He wants to shut himself up in his house and die.

HELMER: Ah, poor fellow. I knew I wouldn't be seeing him for much longer. But so soon—! And now he's going to slink away and hide like a wounded beast.

NORA: When the time comes, it's best to go silently. Don't you think so, Torvald?

2070 HELMER *(walks up and down):* He was so much a part of our life. I can't realize that he's gone. His suffering and loneliness seemed to provide a dark background to the happy sunlight of our marriage. Well, perhaps it's best this way. For him, anyway. *(Stops walking.)* And perhaps for us too, Nora. Now we have only each other. *(Embraces her.)* Oh, my beloved wife—I feel as though I could never hold you close enough. Do you know, Nora, often I wish some terrible danger might threaten you, so that I could offer my life and my blood, everything, for your sake.

NORA *(tears herself loose and says in a clear, firm voice):* Read your letters now, Torvald.

2080 HELMER: No, no. Not tonight. Tonight I want to be with you, my darling wife—

NORA: When your friend is about to die—?

HELMER: You're right. This news has upset us both. An ugliness has come between us; thoughts of death and dissolution. We must try to forget them. Until then—you go to your room; I shall go to mine.

NORA (*throws her arms round his neck*): Good night, Torvald! Good night!

HELMER (*kisses her on the forehead*): Good night, my darling little song-bird. Sleep well, Nora. I'll go and read my letters.

(*He goes into the study with the letters in his hand, and closes the door.*)

NORA (*wild-eyed, fumbles around, seizes Helmer's cloak, throws it round herself and whispers quickly, hoarsely*): Never see him again. Never. Never. Never. (*Throws the shawl over her head.*) Never see the children again. Them too. Never. Never. Oh—the icy black water! Oh—that bottomless—that—! Oh, if only it were all over! Now he's got it—he's reading it. Oh, no, no! Not yet! Goodbye, Torvald! Goodbye, my darlings!

(*She turns to run into the hall. As she does so, Helmer throws open his door and stands there with an open letter in his hand.*)

HELMER: Nora!

NORA (*shrieks*): Ah—!

HELMER: What is this? Do you know what is in this letter?

NORA: Yes, I know. Let me go! Let me go!

HELMER (*holds her back*): Go? Where?

NORA (*tries to tear herself loose*): You mustn't try to save me, Torvald!

HELMER (*staggers back*): Is it true? Is it true, what he writes? Oh, my God! No, no—it's impossible, it can't be true!

NORA: It *is* true. I've loved you more than anything else in the world.

HELMER: Oh, don't try to make silly excuses.

NORA (*takes a step toward him*): Torvald—

HELMER: Wretched woman! What have you done?

NORA: Let me go! You're not going to suffer for my sake. I won't let you!

HELMER: Stop being theatrical. (*Locks the front door.*) You're going to stay here and explain yourself. Do you understand what you've done? Answer me! Do you understand?

NORA (*looks unflinchingly at him and, her expression growing colder, says*): Yes. Now I am beginning to understand.

HELMER (*walking around the room*): Oh, what a dreadful awakening! For eight whole years—she who was my joy and my pride—a hypocrite, a liar—worse, worse—a criminal! Oh, the hideousness of it! Shame on you, shame!

(*Nora is silent and stares unblinkingly at him.*)

HELMER (*stops in front of her*): I ought to have guessed that something of this sort would happen. I should have foreseen it. All your father's recklessness and instability—be quiet!—I repeat, all your father's recklessness and instability he had handed on to you. No religion, no morals, no sense of duty! Oh, how I have been punished for closing my eyes to his faults! I did it for your sake. And now you reward me like this.

NORA: Yes. Like this.

HELMER: Now you have destroyed all my happiness. You have ruined my whole future. Oh, it's too dreadful to contemplate! I am in the power of a man who is completely without scruples. He can do what he likes with me, demand what he pleases, order me to do anything—I dare not disobey him. I am condemned to humiliation and ruin simply for the weakness of a woman.

NORA: When I am gone from this world, you will be free.

HELMER: Oh, don't be melodramatic. Your father was always ready with that kind of remark. How would it help me if you were "gone from this world," as you put it? It wouldn't assist me in the slightest. He can still make all the facts public; and if he does, I may quite easily be suspected of having been an accomplice in your crime. People may think that I was behind it—that it was I who encouraged you! And for all this I have to thank you, you whom I have carried on my hands through all the years of our marriage! Now do you realize what you've done to me?

NORA *(coldly calm):* Yes.

HELMER: It's so unbelievable I can hardly credit it. But we must try to find some way out. Take off that shawl. Take it off, I say! I must try to buy him off somehow. This thing must be hushed up at any price. As regards our relationship—we must appear to be living together just as before. Only *appear,* of course. You will therefore continue to reside here. That is understood. But the children shall be taken out of your hands. I dare no longer entrust them to you. Oh, to have to say this to the woman I once loved so dearly—and whom I still—! Well, all that must be finished. Henceforth there can be no question of happiness; we must merely strive to save what shreds and tatters—*(The front bell rings. Helmer starts.)* What can that be? At this hour? Surely not—? He wouldn't—? Hide yourself, Nora. Say you're ill.

(Nora does not move. Helmer goes to the door of the room and opens it. The maid is standing half-dressed in the hall.)

MAID: A letter for madam.

HELMER: Give it to me. *(Seizes the letter and shuts the door.)* Yes, it's from him. You're not having it. I'll read this myself.

NORA: Read it.

HELMER *(by the lamp):* I hardly dare to. This may mean the end for us both. No, I must know. *(Tears open the letter hastily; reads a few lines; looks at a piece of paper which is enclosed with it; utters a cry of joy.)* Nora! *(She looks at him questioningly.)* Nora! No—I must read it once more. Yes, yes, it's true! I am saved! Nora, I am saved!

NORA: What about me?

HELMER: You too, of course. We're both saved, you and I. Look! He's returning your I.O.U. He writes that he is sorry for what has hap-

pened—a happy accident has changed his life—oh, what does it
matter what he writes? We are saved, Nora! No one can harm you
now. Oh, Nora, Nora—no, first let me destroy this filthy thing. Let
me see—! *(Glances at the I.O.U.)* No, I don't want to look at it. I
shall merely regard the whole business as a dream. *(He tears the
I.O.U. and both letters into pieces, throws them into the stove, and
watches them burn.)* There. Now they're destroyed. He wrote that
ever since Christmas Eve you've been—oh, these must have been
three dreadful days for you, Nora.

NORA: Yes. It's been a hard fight.

HELMER: It must have been terrible—seeing no way out except—no,
we'll forget the whole sordid business. We'll just be happy and go on
telling ourselves over and over again: "It's over! It's over!" Listen to
me, Nora. You don't seem to realize. It's over! Why are you looking
so pale? Ah, my poor little Nora, I understand. You can't believe that
I have forgiven you. But I have, Nora. I swear it to you. I have forgiven you everything. I know that what you did you did for your love
of me.

NORA: That is true.

HELMER: You have loved me as a wife should love her husband. It was
simply that in your inexperience you chose the wrong means. But do
you think I love you any the less because you don't know how to act
on your own initiative? No, no. Just lean on me. I shall counsel you. I
shall guide you. I would not be a true man if your feminine helplessness did not make you doubly attractive in my eyes. You mustn't
mind the hard words I said to you in those first dreadful moments
when my whole world seemed to be tumbling about my ears. I have
forgiven you, Nora. I swear it to you; I have forgiven you.

NORA: Thank you for your forgiveness.

(She goes out through the door, right.)

HELMER: No, don't go—*(Looks in.)* What are you doing there?

NORA *(offstage)*: Taking off my fancy dress.

HELMER *(by the open door)*: Yes, do that. Try to calm yourself and get
your balance again, my frightened little songbird. Don't be afraid. I
have broad wings to shield you. *(Begins to walk around near the
door.)* How lovely and peaceful this little home of ours is, Nora. You
are safe here; I shall watch over you like a hunted dove which I have
snatched unharmed from the claws of the falcon. Your wildly beating little heart shall find peace with me. It will happen, Nora; it will
take time, but it will happen, believe me. Tomorrow all this will
seem quite different. Soon everything will be as it was before. I shall
no longer need to remind you that I have forgiven you; your own
heart will tell you that it is true. Do you really think I could ever
bring myself to disown you, or even to reproach you? Ah, Nora, you
don't understand what goes on in a husband's heart. There is some-

thing indescribably wonderful and satisfying for a husband in knowing that he has forgiven his wife— forgiven her unreservedly, from
the bottom of his heart. It means that she has become his property
in a double sense; he has, as it were, brought her into the world
anew; she is now not only his wife but also his child. From now on
that is what you shall be to me, my poor, helpless, bewildered little
creature. Never be frightened of anything again, Nora. Just open
2220   your heart to me. I shall be both your will and your conscience.
What's this? Not in bed? Have you changed?

NORA (*in her everyday dress*): Yes, Torvald. I've changed.

HELMER: But why now—so late—?

NORA: I shall not sleep tonight.

HELMER: But, my dear Nora—

NORA (*looks at her watch*): It isn't that late. Sit down here, Torvald. You
and I have a lot to talk about.

(She sits down on one side of the table.)

HELMER: Nora, what does this mean? You look quite drawn—

NORA: Sit down. It's going to take a long time. I've a lot to say to you.

2230   HELMER (*sits down on the other side of the table*): You alarm me, Nora.
I don't understand you.

NORA: No, that's just it. You don't understand me. And I've never understood you—until this evening. No, don't interrupt me. Just listen to
what I have to say. You and I have got to face facts, Torvald.

HELMER: What do you mean by that?

NORA (*after a short silence*): Doesn't anything strike you about the way
we're sitting here?

HELMER: What?

NORA: We've been married for eight years. Does it occur to you that this
2240   is the first time that we two, you and I, man and wife, have ever had
a serious talk together?

HELMER: Serious? What do you mean, serious?

NORA: In eight whole years—no, longer—ever since we first met—we
have never exchanged a serious word on a serious subject.

HELMER: Did you expect me to drag you into all my worries—worries
you couldn't possibly have helped me with?

NORA: I'm not talking about worries. I'm simply saying that we have
never sat down seriously to try to get to the bottom of anything.

HELMER: But, my dear Nora, what on earth has that got to do with you?

2250   NORA: That's just the point. You have never understood me. A great
wrong has been done to me, Torvald. First by Papa, and then by you.

HELMER: What? But we two have loved you more than anyone in the
world!

NORA (*shakes her head*): You have never loved me. You just thought it
was fun to be in love with me.

HELMER: Nora, what kind of a way is this to talk?

NORA: It's the truth, Torvald. When I lived with Papa, he used to tell me what he thought about everything, so that I never had any opinions but his. And if I did have any of my own, I kept them quiet, because he wouldn't have liked them. He called me his little doll, and he played with me just the way I played with my dolls. Then I came here to live in your house.

HELMER: What kind of a way is that to describe our marriage?

NORA (*undisturbed*): I mean, then I passed from Papa's hands into yours. You arranged everything the way you wanted it, so that I simply took over your taste in everything—or pretended I did—I don't really know—I think it was a little of both—first one and then the other. Now I look back on it, it's as if I've been living here like a pauper, from hand to mouth. I performed tricks for you, and you gave me food and drink. But that was how you wanted it. You and Papa have done me a great wrong. It's your fault that I have done nothing with my life.

HELMER: Nora, how can you be so unreasonable and ungrateful? Haven't you been happy here?

NORA: No; never. I used to think I was; but I haven't ever been happy.

HELMER: Not—not happy?

NORA: No. I've just had fun. You've always been very kind to me. But our home has never been anything but a playroom. I've been your doll-wife, just as I used to be Papa's doll-child. And the children have been my dolls. I used to think it was fun when you came in and played with me, just as they think it's fun when I go in and play games with them. That's all our marriage has been, Torvald.

HELMER: There may be a little truth in what you say, though you exaggerate and romanticize. But from now on it'll be different. Playtime is over. Now the time has come for education.

NORA: Whose education? Mine or the children's?

HELMER: Both yours and the children's, my dearest Nora.

NORA: Oh, Torvald, you're not the man to educate me into being the right wife for you.

HELMER: How can you say that?

NORA: And what about me? Am I fit to educate the children?

HELMER: Nora!

NORA: Didn't you say yourself a few minutes ago that you dare not leave them in my charge?

HELMER: In a moment of excitement. Surely you don't think I meant it seriously?

NORA: Yes. You were perfectly right. I'm not fitted to educate them. There's something else I must do first. I must educate myself. And you can't help me with that. It's something I must do by myself. That's why I'm leaving you.

HELMER (*jumps up*): What did you say?

NORA: I must stand on my own feet if I am to find out the truth about myself and about life. So I can't go on living here with you any longer.

HELMER: Nora, Nora!

NORA: I'm leaving you now, at once. Christine will put me up for tonight—

HELMER: You're out of your mind! You can't do this! I forbid you!

NORA: It's no use your trying to forbid me any more. I shall take with me nothing but what is mine. I don't want anything from you, now or ever.

HELMER: What kind of madness is this?

2310   NORA: Tomorrow I shall go home—I mean, to where I was born. It'll be easiest for me to find some kind of job there.

HELMER: But you're blind! You've no experience of the world—

NORA: I must try to get some, Torvald.

HELMER: But to leave your home, your husband, your children! Have you thought what people will say?

NORA: I can't help that. I only know that I must do this.

HELMER: But this is monstrous! Can you neglect your most sacred duties?

NORA: What do you call my most sacred duties?

2320   HELMER: Do I have to tell you? Your duties towards your husband, and your children.

NORA: I have another duty which is equally sacred.

HELMER: You have not. What on earth could that be?

NORA: My duty towards myself.

HELMER: First and foremost you are a wife and a mother.

NORA: I don't believe that any longer. I believe that I am first and foremost a human being, like you—or anyway, that I must try to become one. I know most people think as you do, Torvald, and I know there's something of the sort to be found in books. But I'm no longer

2330   prepared to accept what people say and what's written in books. I must think things out for myself, and try to find my own answer.

HELMER: Do you need to ask where your duty lies in your own home? Haven't you an infallible guide in such matters—your religion?

NORA: Oh, Torvald, I don't really know what religion means.

HELMER: What are you saying?

NORA: I only know what Pastor Hansen told me when I went to confirmation. He explained that religion meant this and that. When I get away from all this and can think things out on my own, that's one of the questions I want to look into. I want to find out whether what

2340   Pastor Hansen said was right—or anyway, whether it is right for me.

HELMER: But it's unheard of for so young a woman to behave like this! If religion cannot guide you, let me at least appeal to your conscience. I presume you have some moral feelings left? Or—perhaps you haven't? Well, answer me.

NORA: Oh, Torvald, that isn't an easy question to answer. I simply don't know. I don't know where I am in these matters. I only know that these things mean something quite different to me from what they do to you. I've learned now that certain laws are different from what

I'd imagined them to be; but I can't accept that such laws can be
2350   right. Has a woman really not the right to spare her dying father
pain, or save her husband's life? I can't believe that.

HELMER: You're talking like a child. You don't understand how society
works.

NORA: No, I don't. But now I intend to learn. I must try to satisfy myself
which is right, society or I.

HELMER: Nora, you're ill; you're feverish. I almost believe you're out of
your mind.

NORA: I've never felt so sane and sure in my life.

HELMER: You feel sure that it is right to leave your husband and your
2360   children?

NORA: Yes. I do.

HELMER: Then there is only one possible explanation.

NORA: What?

HELMER: That you don't love me any longer.

NORA: No, that's exactly it.

HELMER: Nora! How can you say this to me?

NORA: Oh, Torvald, it hurts me terribly to have to say it, because you've
always been so kind to me. But I can't help it. I don't love you any
longer.

2370   HELMER (*controlling his emotions with difficulty*): And you feel quite
sure about this too?

NORA: Yes, absolutely sure. That's why I can't go on living here any
longer.

HELMER: Can you also explain why I have lost your love?

NORA: Yes, I can. It happened this evening, when the miracle failed to
happen. It was then that I realized you weren't the man I'd thought
you to be.

HELMER: Explain more clearly. I don't understand you.

NORA: I've waited so patiently, for eight whole years—well, good heav-
2380   ens, I'm not such a fool as to suppose that miracles occur everyday.
Then this dreadful thing happened to me, and then I *knew:* "Now the
miracle will take place!" When Krogstad's letter was lying out there,
it never occurred to me for a moment that you would let that man
trample over you. I *knew* that you would say to him: "Publish
the facts to the world." And when he had done this—

HELMER: Yes, what then? When I'd exposed my wife's name to shame
and scandal—

NORA: Then I was certain that you would step forward and take all the
blame on yourself, and say: "I am the one who is guilty!"

2390   HELMER: Nora!

NORA: You're thinking I wouldn't have accepted such a sacrifice from
you? No, of course I wouldn't! But what would my word have counted
for against yours? That was the miracle I was hoping for, and dread-
ing. And it was to prevent it happening that I wanted to end my life.

HELMER: Nora, I would gladly work for you night and day, and endure sorrow and hardship for your sake. But no man can be expected to sacrifice his honor, even for the person he loves.

NORA: Millions of women have done it.

HELMER: Oh, you think and talk like a stupid child.

2400 NORA: That may be. But you neither think nor talk like the man I could share my life with. Once you'd got over your fright—and you weren't frightened of what might threaten me, but only of what threatened you—once the danger was past, then as far as you were concerned it was exactly as though nothing had happened. I was your little song-bird just as before—your doll whom henceforth you would take particular care to protect from the world because she was so weak and fragile. *(Gets up.)* Torvald, in that moment I realized that for eight years I had been living here with a complete stranger, and had borne him three children—! Oh, I can't bear to think of it! I could tear
2410 myself to pieces!

HELMER *(sadly):* I see it, I see it. A gulf has indeed opened between us. Oh, but Nora—couldn't it be bridged?

NORA: As I am now, I am no wife for you.

HELMER: I have the strength to change.

NORA: Perhaps—if your doll is taken from you.

HELMER: But to be parted—to be parted from you! No, no, Nora, I can't conceive of it happening!

NORA *(goes into the room, right):* All the more necessary that it should happen.

(She comes back with her outdoor things and a small traveling bag, which she puts down on a chair by the table.)

2420 HELMER: Nora, Nora, not now! Wait till tomorrow!

NORA *(puts on her coat):* I can't spend the night in a strange man's house.

HELMER: But can't we live here as brother and sister, then—?

NORA *(fastens her hat):* You know quite well it wouldn't last. *(Puts on her shawl.)* Goodbye, Torvald. I don't want to see the children. I know they're in better hands than mine. As I am now, I can be nothing to them.

HELMER: But some time, Nora—some time—?

NORA: How can I tell? I've no idea what will happen to me.

2430 HELMER: But you are my wife, both as you are and as you will be.

NORA: Listen, Torvald. When a wife leaves her husband's house, as I'm doing now, I'm told that according to the law he is freed of any obligations towards her. In any case, I release you from any such obligations. You mustn't feel bound to me in any way, however small, just as I shall not feel bound to you. We must both be quite free. Here is your ring back. Give me mine.

HELMER: That too?

NORA: That too.

HELMER: Here it is.

2440 NORA: Good. Well, now it's over. I'll leave the keys here. The servants know about everything to do with the house—much better than I do. Tomorrow, when I have left town, Christine will come to pack the things I brought here from home. I'll have them sent on after me.

HELMER: This is the end then! Nora, will you never think of me any more?

NORA: Yes, of course. I shall often think of you and the children and this house.

HELMER: May I write to you, Nora?

NORA: No. Never. You mustn't do that.

2450 HELMER: But at least you must let me send you—

NORA: Nothing. Nothing.

HELMER: But if you should need help?—

NORA: I tell you, no. I don't accept things from strangers.

HELMER: Nora—can I never be anything but a stranger to you?

NORA *(picks up her bag):* Oh, Torvald! Then the miracle of miracles would have to happen.

HELMER: The miracle of miracles?

NORA: You and I would both have to change so much that—oh, Torvald, I don't believe in miracles any longer.

2460 HELMER: But I want to believe in them. Tell me. We should have to change so much that—?

NORA: That life together between us two could become a marriage. Goodbye.

(She goes out through the hall.)

HELMER *(sinks down on a chair by the door and buries his face in his hands):* Nora! Nora! *(Looks round and gets up.)* Empty! She's gone! *(A hope strikes him.)* The miracle of miracles—?

(The street door is slammed shut downstairs.)

Questions for Discussion

Act 1

1. Why does Nora want money for her Christmas gift?

2. When Torvald says, "I wouldn't wish my darling little songbird to be any different from what she is," what are the qualities he admires in Nora?

3. In what ways is Christine Linde a dramatic foil for Nora?

4. Why has Torvald not made a lot of money as a lawyer? In what ways does the knowledge of his attitude toward clients foreshadow his reaction to Nora's revelation?

5. Nora says of Torvald, "he's so proud of being a *man*—it'd be so painful and humiliating for him to know that he owed anything to me." What attitudes does Nora here reveal about male-female relationships?

6. Examine Torvald's statements about Krogstad near the end of Act 1. How do these opinions foreshadow Torvald's reaction to Nora's revelation in Act 3?

Act 2

1. Explain the irony of Torvald's statement, "When the real crisis comes, you will not find me lacking in strength or courage. I am man enough to bear the burden for us both."

2. Why does Dr. Rank refuse to let Torvald visit him in the hospital?

3. Explain Nora's statement to Dr. Rank that "there are some people whom one loves, and others whom it's almost more fun to be with."

4. List the pet names that Torvald calls Nora and explain the implications of each.

Act 3

1. Why does Christine tell Krogstad *not* to take his letter back?

2. From the opening scene of the play until the beginning of the last scene, Nora lies to Torvald. Why?

3. Explain Nora's statement to Torvald, "You don't understand me. And I've never understood you—until this evening."

4. Why would Nora's statement that she has a duty toward herself be so astonishing to a nineteenth-century audience? What would be the probable reaction of an audience today?

5. In what ways is Nora's situation at the end of the play more difficult than it would be for a woman today?

6. Compare Nora's behavior at the beginning of the play with her statements at the end and analyze the causes of the change.

7. What does Nora think Torvald will do when he learns the truth? How does her expectation make the reality even worse?

8. Explain the significance of the play's title.

Suggestions for Exploring, Writing, and Persuading

1. Write an essay explaining how you, as a modern wife or husband, would deal with a situation such as that faced by Nora or Torvald, or explain how you would conduct your life in such a way as to avoid facing such a situation.

2. Contrast Nora's behavior at the beginning of the play with her behavior at the end of Act 3 and explain the reasons for the change.

3. In an essay, explain the ironic contrast between Torvald's statements to Nora about protecting her and his actual behavior toward her.

4. In a cause-and-effect essay, explain why Nora has been, as Torvald says, for eight years "a hypocrite, [and] a liar."

5. Write an essay explaining why Nora leaves her children, even though she loves them.

6. In what ways does Nora misjudge the males in her life? Explain.

7. In a documented paper, discuss the roles of Krogstad and Christine in Ibsen's play.

8. Write an argumentative essay on one of the following:

   Nora does or does not make the correct decision at the end of the play.

   Torvald is just as trapped by the role dictated by society of his time for husbands as Nora is as a wife.

Casebook
on Sylvia Plath

WRITING ABOUT MEN AND WOMEN

Sylvia Plath (1932–1963)

Born in 1932 in Boston, Massachusetts, Sylvia Plath showed an aptitude for writing and a tremendous drive to excel even in childhood—qualities that were both evident throughout her short life. In 1956, while spending time in England on a Fulbright scholarship, she married English poet Ted Hughes. They had two children. Plath's poetry demonstrates a passionate engagement with language and a rare gift for image and metaphor; it also displays an impressive array of subjects, voices, and tones. Although her poems about death are her most frequently anthologized works, she also wrote books for children and splendid poems about motherhood. Though much of her poetry is written in free verse, she also handles rhyme and verse forms adeptly. As her poems "Daddy" and "Lady Lazarus" show, death is indeed a recurring theme in her writing: a number of her poems address her relationship with her father, Otto Plath, who died when she was eight years old. In her poetry, she often draws on history and myth to explore her obsessive love for her father and her unresolved feelings about his early death. Plath's poems about her emotional struggles possess a unique self-awareness and a wry sense of humor that keeps them from lapsing into sheer pathos. Whatever her subject, her poems are invariably well-crafted, marked by a playful, wide-ranging imagination and a tireless love of language. In the last months before her death, as she struggled with separation and impending divorce, depression, and single parenthood, she became increasingly prolific, writing the poems that would eventually go into Ariel *(1966). In her previous two collections,* The Colossus *(1962) and* Crossing the Water *(eventually published in 1971), she was still developing her own distinctive poetic style. In* Ariel, *she found her own voice and finally earned some measure of recognition for her accomplished poetry. Sadly, however, most of the recognition she received for her writing came after her death. Her autobiographical novel,* The Bell Jar, *was published shortly before her death, but* Ariel *did not appear until well after Plath had killed herself in 1963. Occasionally overshadowed by her struggles with depression, her troubled marriage, and her tragic death, Plath's poetry has stood the test of time. Today students of poetry value her work not only for the original images and literary allusions but also for the provocative themes, and contemporary poets admire her imagination and sense of craft. Approximately twenty years after her death, her* Collected Poems *(1981), compiled and edited by Ted Hughes, was awarded the Pulitzer Prize.*

DADDY

(1963)

You do not do, you do not do
Any more, black shoe
In which I have lived like a foot
For thirty years, poor and white,
5   Barely daring to breathe or Achoo.

Daddy, I have had to kill you.
You died before I had time—
Marble-heavy, a bag full of God,
Ghastly statue with one grey toe
10   Big as a Frisco seal

And a head in the freakish Atlantic
Where it pours bean green over blue
In the waters off beautiful Nauset.
I used to pray to recover you.
15   Ach, du.

In the German tongue, in the Polish town
Scraped flat by the roller

Of wars, wars, wars.
But the name of the town is common.
20   My Polack friend

Says there are a dozen or two.
So I never could tell where you
Put your foot, your root,
I never could talk to you.
25   The tongue stuck in my jaw.

It stuck in a barb wire snare.
Ich, ich, ich, ich,
I could hardly speak.
I thought every German was you.
30   And the language obscene

An engine, an engine
Chuffing me off like a Jew.
A Jew to Dachau, Auschwitz, Belsen.
I began to talk like a Jew.
35   I think I may well be a Jew.

The snows of the Tyrol, the clear beer of Vienna
Are not very pure or true.
With my gypsy ancestress and my weird luck
And my Taroc pack and my Taroc pack
40   I may be a bit of a Jew.

I have always been scared of *you*,
With your Luftwaffe, your gobbledygoo.
And your neat moustache
And your Aryan eye, bright blue
45   Panzer-man, panzer-man, O You—

Not God but a swastika
So black no sky could squeak through.
Every woman adores a Fascist,
The boot in the face, the brute
50   Brute heart of a brute like you.

You stand at the blackboard, daddy,
In the picture I have of you,
A cleft in your chin instead of your foot
But no less a devil for that, no not
55   Any less the black man who

Bit my pretty red heart in two.
I was ten when they buried you.
At twenty I tried to die
And get back, back, back to you.
60   I thought even the bones would do.

But they pulled me out of the sack.
And they stuck me together with glue.
And then I knew what to do.
I made a model of you,
65   A man in black with a Meinkampf look

And a love of the rack and the screw.
And I said I do, I do.
So daddy, I'm finally through.
The black telephone's off at the root,
70   The voices just can't worm through.

If I've killed one man, I've killed two—
The vampire who said he was you
And drank my blood for a year,
Seven years, if you want to know.
75   Daddy, you can lie back now.

There's a stake in your fat black heart
And the villagers never liked you.
They are dancing and stamping on you.
They always *knew* it was you.
80   Daddy, daddy, you bastard, I'm through.

Questions for Discussion

1. What role do rhyme and assonance play in the overall meaning of the poem?

2. What is the nature of the speaker's relationship to her father? What suggests that the relationship is a complex one?

3. What did the father do to break the speaker's heart? Why is the image of the heart significant in the poem?

4. In "Daddy" and "Lady Lazarus," both speakers describe their own suffering in terms of the Jews' suffering during the Holocaust. Other poets, some of them Plath's contemporaries, have objected to this comparison, for a variety of reasons. What valid objections might they have?

ALL THE DEAD DEARS   (1957)

In the Archaeological Museum in Cambridge is a stone coffin of the fourth century A.D. containing the skeletons of a woman, a mouse and a shrew. The ankle-bone of the woman has been slightly gnawn.

Rigged poker-stiff on her back
With a granite grin
This antique museum-cased lady
Lies, companioned by the gimcrack

5   Relics of a mouse and a shrew
     That battened for a day on her ankle-bone.

     These three, unmasked now, bear
     Dry witness
     To the gross eating game
10   We'd wink at if we didn't hear
     Stars grinding, crumb by crumb,
     Our own grist down to its bony face.

     How they grip us through thin and thick,
     These barnacle dead!
15   This lady here's no kin
     Of mine, yet kin she is: she'll suck
     Blood and whistle my marrow clean
     To prove it. As I think now of her head,

     From the mercury-backed glass
20   Mother, grandmother, greatgrandmother
     Reach hag hands to haul me in,
     And an image looms under the fishpond surface
     Where the daft father went down
     With orange duck-feet winnowing his hair—

25   All the long gone darlings: they
     Get back, though, soon,
     Soon: be it by wakes, weddings,
     Childbirths or a family barbecue:
     Any touch, taste, tang's
30   Fit for those outlaws to ride home on,

     And to sanctuary: usurping the armchair
     Between tick
     And tack of the clock, until we go,
     Each skulled-and-crossboned Gulliver
35   Riddled with ghosts, to lie
     Deadlocked with them, taking root as cradles rock.

Questions for Discussion

1. What appears to be the speaker's attitude toward the dead woman she encounters in the museum?
2. How do the alliteration, rhythm, internal rhyme, and near rhyme affect the tone of the poem?
3. What kind of "kinship" is the speaker discussing here? What is her relationship to the people she describes and mentions here?
4. What is the speaker's attitude toward death? How is it revealed?

THE COLOSSUS

(1960)

I shall never get you put together entirely,
Pieced, glued, and properly jointed.
Mule-bray, pig-grunt and bawdy cackles
Proceed from your great lips.
5   It's worse than a barnyard.

Perhaps you consider yourself an oracle,
Mouthpiece of the dead, or of some god or other.
Thirty years now I have labored
To dredge the silt from your throat.
10   I am none the wiser.

Scaling little ladders with gluepots and pails of Lysol
I crawl like an ant in mourning
Over the weedy acres of your brow
To mend the immense skull-plates and clear
15   The bald, white tumuli of your eyes.

A blue sky out of the Oresteia
Arches above us. O father, all by yourself
You are pithy and historical as the Roman Forum.
I open my lunch on a hill of black cypress.
20   Your fluted bones and acanthine hair are littered

In their old anarchy to the horizon-line.
It would take more than a lightning-stroke
To create such a ruin.
Nights, I squat in the cornucopia
25   Of your left ear, out of the wind,

Counting the red stars and those of plum-color.
The sun rises under the pillar of your tongue.
My hours are married to shadow.
No longer do I listen for the scrape of a keel
30   On the blank stones of the landing.

Questions for Discussion

1. What is the central metaphor of the poem?

2. What is the poem's tone? Does the tone change throughout the poem? How does that change affect the overall meaning of the poem?

3. What is the definition of "colossus"? Why is this an apt image for her subject matter?

4. What is the significance of the *Oresteia*? What is the significance of the poem's last two lines?

5. What connections exist, at a thematic level, between "The Colossus" and "Daddy"? How are the poems similar? How are they different?

BY CANDLELIGHT   (1963)

This is winter, this is night, small love—
A sort of black horsehair,
A rough, dumb country stuff
Steeled with the sheen
5   Of what green stars can make it to our gate.
I hold you on my arm.
It is very late.
The dull bells tongue the hour.
The mirror floats us at one candle power.

10   This is the fluid in which we meet each other,
This haloey radiance that seems to breathe
And lets our shadows wither
Only to blow
Them huge again, violent giants on the wall.
15   One match scratch makes you real.
At first the candle will not bloom at all—
It snuffs its bud
To almost nothing, to a dull blue dud.

I hold my breath until you creak to life,
20   Balled hedgehog,
Small and cross. The yellow knife
Grows tall. You clutch your bars.
My singing makes you roar.
I rock you like a boat
25   Across the Indian carpet, the cold floor,
While the brass man
Kneels, back bent, as best he can

Hefting his white pillar with the light
That keeps the sky at bay,
30   The sack of black! It is everywhere, tight, tight!
He is yours, the little brassy Atlas—
Poor heirloom, all you have,
At his heels a pile of five brass cannonballs,
No child, no wife.
35   Five balls! Five bright brass balls!
To juggle with, my love, when the sky falls.

Questions for Discussion

1. Who is addressing whom in this poem?

2. What images does the speaker use to describe her child? How do those contribute to the tone of the poem? What do the images of light and shadow in the first two stanzas suggest about the speaker's state of mind? What do the repeated images of the black sky suggest? What tone do they create?

3. How does the use of end rhyme and near rhyme contribute to the tone of the poem?

4. What details make it apparent that the speaker is a woman? What does she want or fear for her child?

5. What role does the mythological figure of Atlas play in the overall meaning of the poem? What is its symbolic significance?

6. What does the last line mean? What does it suggest about the speaker's mood?

MIRROR

(1962)

I am silver and exact. I have no preconceptions.
Whatever I see I swallow immediately
Just as it is, unmisted by love or dislike.
I am not cruel, only truthful—
5   The eye of a little god, four-cornered.
Most of the time I meditate on the opposite wall.
It is pink, with speckles. I have looked at it so long
I think it is a part of my heart. But it flickers.
Faces and darkness separate us over and over.
10   Now I am a lake. A woman bends over me,
Searching my reaches for what she really is.
Then she turns to those liars, the candles or the moon.
I see her back, and reflect it faithfully.
She rewards me with tears and an agitation of hands.
15   I am important to her. She comes and goes.
Each morning it is her face that replaces the darkness.
In me she has drowned a young girl, and in me an old woman
Rises toward her day after day, like a terrible fish.

Questions for Discussion

1. Who is speaking here? Why would the author use such a speaker?

2. What images does the author use to describe this speaker? Why?

3. What is the speaker's attitude toward its surroundings?

4. What do the poem's closing lines suggest about the changes in the reflection?

METAPHORS   (1960)

I'm a riddle in nine syllables,
An elephant, a ponderous house,
A melon strolling on two tendrils.
O red fruit, ivory, fine timbers!
5 This loaf's big with its yeasty rising.
Money's new-minted in this fat purse.
I'm a means, a stage, a cow in calf.
I've eaten a bag of green apples,
Boarded the train there's no getting off.

Questions for Discussion

1. What is the tone of the poem? How can you tell?

2. Look at each image carefully. What does each one suggest? Look carefully at the possibilities of each.

3. What do the images have in common? How do they work together? (What does money being minted "in a fat purse" have to do with an elephant, for example?)

4. What is the answer to the poem's riddle? In what way does the form of the poem help reveal the answer?

LADY LAZARUS   (1963)

I have done it again.
One year in every ten
I manage it—

A sort of walking miracle, my skin
5 Bright as a Nazi lampshade,
My right foot

A paperweight,
My face a featureless, fine
Jew linen.

10 Peel off the napkin
O my enemy.
Do I terrify?—

The nose, the eye pits, the full set of teeth?
The sour breath
15 Will vanish in a day.

Soon, soon the flesh
The grave cave ate will be
At home on me

And I a smiling woman.
20 I am only thirty.
And like the cat I have nine times to die.

This is Number Three.
What a trash
To annihilate each decade.

25 What a million filaments.
The peanut-crunching crowd
Shoves in to see

Them unwrap me hand and foot—
The big strip tease.
30 Gentlemen, ladies

These are my hands
My knees.
I may be skin and bone,

Nevertheless, I am the same, identical woman.
35 The first time it happened I was ten.
It was an accident.

The second time I meant
To last it out and not come back at all.
I rocked shut

40 As a seashell.
They had to call and call
And pick the worms off me like sticky pearls.

Dying
Is an art, like everything else.
45 I do it exceptionally well.

I do it so it feels like hell.
I do it so it feels real.
I guess you could say I've a call.

It's easy enough to do it in a cell.
50 It's easy enough to do it and stay put.
It's the theatrical

Comeback in broad day
To the same place, the same face, the same brute
Amused shout:

55 'A miracle!'
That knocks me out.
There is a charge

For the eyeing of my scars, there is a charge
For the hearing of my heart—
60   It really goes.

And there is a charge, a very large charge
For a word or a touch
Or a bit of blood

Or a piece of my hair or my clothes.
65   So, so, Herr Doktor.
So, Herr Enemy.

I am your opus,
I am your valuable,
The pure gold baby

70   That melts to a shriek.
I turn and burn.
Do not think I underestimate your great concern.

Ash, ash—
You poke and stir.
75   Flesh, bone, there is nothing there—

A cake of soap,
A wedding ring,
A gold filling.

Herr God, Herr Lucifer
80   Beware
Beware.

Out of the ash
I rise with my red hair
And I eat men like air.

Questions for Discussion

1. What is the significance of the title?
2. How would you describe the tone of the poem? How and why does it change throughout the poem?
3. What is the speaker describing in the first fifteen lines? Why?
4. Who are "the peanut-crunching crowd"? How does the speaker feel about them?
5. What does the narrator claim has happened to her three times? In what sense is this experience literal and in what sense is it metaphorical?
6. What role does the use of rhyme and near rhyme play in the overall meaning of the poem?

7. Which lines show a sense of humor on the part of the poem's speaker (even if it's a dark sense of humor)? Where does she almost seem to be laughing at herself?

8. Whom does the narrator appear to be addressing, particularly in the latter half of the poem?

9. How do the elements of history and myth contribute to the imagery, tone, and overall meaning of the poem?

ON WRITING FROM *THE JOURNALS OF SYLVIA PLATH*[1]   (1982)

Writing is a religious act: it is an ordering, a reforming, a relearning and reloving of people and the world as they are and as they might be. A shaping which does not pass away like a day of typing or a day of teaching. The writing lasts: it goes about on its own in the world. People read it: react to it as to a person, a philosophy, a religion, a flower: they like it, or do not. It helps them, or it does not. It feels to intensify living: you give more, probe, ask, look, learn, and shape this: you get more: monsters, answers, color and form, knowledge. You do it for itself first. If it brings in money, how nice. You do not do it first for money. Money isn't why you sit down at the typewriter. Not that you don't want it. It is only too lovely when a profession pays for your bread and butter. With writing, it is maybe, maybe-not. How to live with such insecurity? With what is worst, the occasional lack or loss of faith in the writing itself? How to live with these things?

The worst thing, worse than all of them, would be to live with not writing. So how to live with the lesser devils and keep them lesser?

Miscellanea: "Does Ted want you to get better?" Yes. He does. He wants me to see Dr. B. and is excited about my upswing in emotion and joy. He wants me to fight my devils with the best weapons I can muster and to win.

R. B. says: *There is a difference between dissatisfaction with yourself and anger, depression.* You can be dissatisfied and do something about it: if you don't know German, you can learn it. If you haven't worked at writing, you can work at it. If you are angry at someone else, and repress it, you get depressed. *Who am I angry at?* Myself. No, not yourself. Who is it? It is [omission]...all the mothers I have known who have wanted me to be what I have not felt like really being from my heart and at the society which seems to want us to be what we do not want to be from our hearts: I am angry at these people and images.

[1]Sylvia Plath, *The Journals of Sylvia Plath*, ed. Ted Hughes (New York: Dial P, 1982).

I wonder about the poems I am doing. They seem moving, interesting, but I wonder how deep they are. The absence of a tightly reasoned and rhythmed logic bothers me. Yet frees me....

Feel unlike writing anything today. A horror that I am really at bottom uninterested in people: the reason I don't write stories. Only a few psychological fantasias. Know very little about lives of others. Polly's ghost. The old superintendent standing at the foot of his bed in full moonlight holding a baby. She later finding a picture of him in same posture, holding a lamb.[2]

Get out big botany book at home. What an inertia has overcome me: a sense of fatality: the difficulty of learning out of school.

Ted's dreams about killing animals: bears, donkeys, kittens. Me or the baby? Starting to type his play. Ill-advised, said yesterday wished it were realistic. Of course, I want a Broadway hit in my cheap surface mind, an easy street. He has revised and really improved the children's book *Meet My Folks!* I feel we must find a publisher here, yet the macabre is so outside our tradition. There again, the real world must give the wonder. My *Bed Book* will probably fail because of no human, or child, interest—no plot....

Wednesday, November 4. Paralysis again. How I waste my days. I feel a terrific blocking and chilling go through me like anesthesia. I wonder, will I ever be rid of Johnny Panic? Ten years from my successful *Seventeen* [publication], and a cold voice says: What have you done, what have you done? When I take an equally cold look, I see that I have studied, thought, and somehow not done anything more than teach a year: my mind lies fallow. I don't look forward to a life of reading, and rereading, with no mentor or pupil but myself. I have written one or two unpleasant psychological stories: "Johnny Panic" and "The Mummy," which might well justify printing, a light tour de force about the tattooist, and that is all since Sunday at the Mintons' seven years ago. Where is that fine, free arrogant careless rapture? A cold mizzle of despair settles down on me when I try to think even of a story.

Miraculously I wrote seven poems in my Poem for a Birthday sequence, and the two little ones before it, "The Manor Garden" and "The Colossus," I find colorful and amusing. But my manuscript of my book seems dead to me. So far off, so far gone. It has almost no chance of finding a publisher: just sent it out to the seventh, and unless Dudley Fitts relents this year and gives me the Yale award, which I just missed last year, there is nothing for it but to try to publish it in England and forget prizes, which might well be a good thing. I think I should try the Yales, therefore hope I won't get it accepted as an entry to the Lamont, which I have even less chance of winning—that would cancel both. Comparing

[2]Babies and lambs were part of Plath's own system of correspondences. At this stage of her pregnancy, she had morning sickness.

it to [Philip] Booth's book, [Ned] O'Gorman's book, etc., and Starbuck's, I do feel I am not without merit.

I shall perish if I can write about no one but myself. Where is my old bawdy vigor and interest in the world around me? I am not meant for this monastery living. Find always traces of passive dependence: on Ted, on people around me. A desire even while I write poems about it, to have someone decide my life, tell me what to do, praise me for doing it. I know this is absurd. Yet what do I do about it?

If I can't build up pleasures in myself: seeing and learning about painting, old civilizations, birds, trees, flowers, French, German—what shall I do? My wanting to write books annihilates the original root impulse that would have me bravely and blunderingly working on them. When Johnny Panic sits on my heart, I can't be witty, or original, or creative.

...Writing is my health; if I could once break through my cold self-consciousness and enjoy things for their own sake, not for what presents and acclaim I may receive. Dr. B. was right: I avoid doing things, because if I do not do them, I can't be said to fail at them. A coward's custard....

Pleasant dream of return to London: renting a room with the bed in a garden of daffodils, waking to soil smells and bright yellow flowers.

November 7, 1959, Saturday. Despair. Impasse. I had a vision last night of our swimming in the Salt Lake: a solid beautiful thing. I thought: this light, this sensation is part of no story. It is a thing in itself and worthy of being worked out in words. If I could do that, get back the old joy, it would not matter what became of it. The problem is not my success, but my joy. A dead thing.

My Mummy story came back from *New World Writing* with a mimeographed rejection. It is a very bitter, often melodramatic story, simply an account. I have built up my old brother-rivalry praise-seeking impulses to something amounting to a great stone god-block. Ten years after my first talent-burst on the world, when everything flowed supplely to my touch. I could create the Mintons[3] seven years ago because I forgot myself in them.

Dangerous to be so close to Ted day in day out. I have no life separate from his, am likely to become a mere accessory. Important to take German lessons, go out on my own, think, work on my own. Lead separate lives. I must have a life that supports me inside. This place a kind of terrible nunnery for me. I hate our room: the sterile white of it, the beds filling the whole place. Loved the little crowded Boston apartment, even though J. Panic visited me there.

What horrifies me most is the idea of being useless: well-educated, brilliantly promising, and fading out into an indifferent middle-age. Instead of working at writing, I freeze in dreams, unable to take disillusion of

[3]Plath's early prize-winning story.

rejections. Absurd. I am inclined to go passive, and let Ted be my social self. Simply because we are never apart. Now, for example: the several things I can do apart from him: study German, write, read, walk alone in the woods or go to town. How many couples could stand to be so together? The minute we get to London I must strike out on my own. I'd be better off teaching than writing a couple of mediocre poems a year, a few mad, self-centered stories. Reading, studying, "making your own mind" all by oneself is just not my best way. I need the reality of other people, work, to fulfill myself. Must never become a mere mother and housewife. Challenge of baby when I am so unformed and unproductive as a writer. A fear for the meaning and purpose of my life. I will hate a child that substitutes itself for my own purpose: so I must make my own. Ted is weary of my talk of astrology and tarot and wanting to learn, and then not bothering to work on my own. I'm tired of it too. And tired of the terrific drifting uncertainty of our lives. Which, I suppose, from his point of view, is not at all uncertain, for his vocation of writing is so much stronger than mine.

My poems pall. A jay swallows my crumbs on the wet porch. My head is a batallion of fixes. I don't even dare open Yeats, Eliot-the old fresh joys—for the pain I have remembering my first bright encounters. Less able to lose myself. And myself is the more suited for quick losing.

Independent, self-possessed M. S. Ageless. Bird-watching before breakfast. What does she find for herself? Chess games. My old admiration for the strong, if lesbian, woman. The relief of limitation as a price for balance and surety....

November 11, Wednesday. I only write here when I am at wits end, in a cul-de-sac. Never when I am happy. As I am today....

Felt warm in my tweeds, pleasantly fat-stomached. The baby is a pleasure to dream on. My panics are seldom. If only I can get a doctor I trust, firm, capable and kind, and a hospital where I will know what is going on, I shall be all right. It can't last much more than 24 hours. And if the baby is sound and healthy....

SINCERITY KILLS[1]

HUGH KENNER

Very well, the obligatory note of the theatrical. Let's get on with it. Mr. Butscher can help us oblige: "In the new house, off the kitchen, was a windowless room, fairly large, which disturbed Sylvia....Too dark and airless....She felt uneasy when near that room, and her awareness of its

---

[1]Hugh Kenner, "Sincerity Kills." *Sylvia Plath: New View on the Poetry*, edited by Gary Lane (n.p.: Johns Hopkins University Press, 1979). Rpt. in *Sylvia Plath: Modern Critical Views*, edited by Harold Bloom (New York: Chelsea House, 1989), pp. 67–78.

existence plagued her sleep....She would later tell her new-found friend, Elizabeth Compton, that she had 'a very eerie feeling that there was another room behind it' and that the room was always there waiting for her."

Elizabeth Compton, you see, remembered that. Sylvia Plath had a life-long knack for saying things people would remember. It entailed sizing up the person, the occasion, as readily as she sized up the consumer of the magazine fiction she also had a knack for. "I just sat there with the whole summer turning sour in my mouth": that's how readers of *Seventeen* like stories to end, as Sylvia very well knew when she was nineteen and fitted "The Perfect Set-Up" with that ending. "I must study the magazines the way I did *Seventeen*," she wrote her mother not long afterward, disclosing plans to "hit *The New Yorker* in poetry and the *Ladies' Home Journal* in stories," and *Letters Home*, where we find that letter, demonstrates, end to end, her thorough mastery of the kind of letter her mother would find gratifying. "Dearest Mother, I am being very naughty and self-pitying in writing you a letter which is very private and which will have no point but the very immediate one of making me feel a little better. Every now and then I feel like being 'babied.'" She had studied *Seventeen*, we may want to reflect, the way she did her mother, for whom she was astute enough to get in there first with jargon like "self-pity," thus becoming the brave funny girl who's sorry for herself and knows it and wants her head patted. Esther and her mother in *The Bell Jar* seem another two people entirely.

If, looking back and forth between Sivvy and Esther, we are so unwise as to wish to choose the "real" Sylvia Plath, Freud seems to guide us toward Esther, as though on the principle that hatred of a parent is more apt to be the authentic emotion. Hatred of "Daddy," too; and hatred of self. But then Sylvia Plath knew quite well what it was that Freud had denominated authentic, and even claimed, with remarkable cool, that in "Daddy" she had merely created a little Freudian monologue. "The poem is spoken by a girl with an Electra complex. Her father died while she thought he was God. Her case is complicated by the fact that her father was also a Nazi and her mother very possibly part Jewish. In the daughter the two strains marry and paralyze each other—she has to act out the awful little allegory once over before she is free of it." Just a fictional exercise, in short; by the same token one might call *Letters Home* an epistolary novel. There's no bottom to this.

Like Aurelia Plath reading Sivvy's letters home, we are continually outflanked by someone who knows what we'll approve and how we'll categorize, and is herself ready with the taxonomic words before we can get them out.

> Daddy, I have had to kill you.
> You died before I had time—

Parlor psychiatry is forestalled; she sketches the complex herself. Lady Lazarus is a bitch? It's not news to *her*; "I eat men like air." (I'm also the only candid person here.) Our fantasies of anarchic candor stir into life and help animate *Ariel*. She persuades us that she's daring to say what we wouldn't, and if we succumb to the spell we're apt to end up believing that *this* is what we've always wished we could say. That experience isn't good for anybody, something else she knows. Fans send up a "brute/Amused shout: / 'A miracle!' That knocks me out"; and fans need reminding that voyeurism exacts costs:

> There is a charge
>
> For the eyeing of my scars, there is a charge
> For the hearing of my heart—
> It really goes.
>
> And there is a charge, a very large charge,
> For a word or a touch
> Or a bit of blood
>
> Or a piece of my hair or my clothes.

—As who should say, "The price of absorption in pornography is an incremental deadening of the spirit, an attenuation of an already frail belief in the sanctity of personhood. I shall now show you a pornographic film." All her life, a reader had been someone to manipulate.

To facilitate its understanding with its reader, poetry since Homer's time has had formal ceremonies. It is in this connection that Sylvia Plath herself speaks of manipulation:

> I think my poems come immediately out of the sensuous and emotional experiences I have, but I must say I cannot sympathise with these cries from the heart that are informed by nothing except a needle or a knife or whatever it is. I believe that one should be able to control and manipulate experiences, even the most terrifying—like madness, being tortured, this kind of experience—and one should be able to manipulate these experiences with an informed and intelligent mind. I think that personal experience shouldn't be a kind of shut box and mirror-looking narcissistic experience. I believe it should be generally relevant, to such things as Hiroshima and Dachau, and so on.

These unpremeditated words into a microphone will not be confined to a wholly coherent meaning—how a needle or a knife might inform is unclear, nor whether it's to anyone's advantage if the manipulating intellect connects its own fevers with the Hiroshima fireball—but what she started to say is surely that cries from the heart are not poems until subjected to a discipline like that of her own stanzaic and metrical structures. "Study *The Colossus*," said John Frederick Nims in 1970 [in *The Art of Sylvia Plath*, ed. Charles Newman]. "Notice all the stanza-forms, all the uses of rhythm and rhyme; notice how the images are chosen and related; how deliberately sound is used. It is no accident, for instance, that there are seven identical drab *a*'s in '...salt flats,/Gas tanks, factory stacks—that landscape....' Remember that *The Bell Jar* tells us that she 'wrote page after page of villanelles and sonnets,' and this in one semester of one class.

Perhaps for writers this is the gist of the Plath case: without the drudgery of *The Colossus*, the triumph of *Ariel* is unthinkable." So let's notice.

Notice the poem about the lady in the stone coffin, sixteen hundred years dead ("All the Dead Dears"). To abridge the discussion, I'll remark that its six stanzas rhyme *abcacb*, one "*b*" line shorter than the norm, the other longer.

> Rigged poker-stiff on her back
> With a granite grin
> This antique museum-cased lady
> Lies, companioned by the gimcrack
> Relics of a mouse and a shrew
> That battened for a day on her ankle-bone.

Stanza 1, and a single audible rhyme: back/gimcrack. It seems an accident in a rhymeless stanza. Stanza 2:

> These three, unmasked now, bear
> Dry witness
> To the gross eating game
> We'd wink at if we didn't hear
> Stars grinding, crumb by crumb,
> Our own grist down to its bony face.

Bear/hear, in the same place, *ala*, but again as if accidental; it would have been called an eye-rhyme once. Marianne Moore can unsettle in this way, but when Marianne Moore's rhymes fall askew they do so amid a rigorous syllable count. This poem isn't counting syllables. Counting stresses? Perhaps. You can fit the stresses into a 3-2-3-3-3-4 pattern, though with little confidence; "That battened for a day on her ankle-bone" can be read as iambic pentameter, though its partner, "Our own grist down to its bony face," has at most nine syllables, and perhaps five stresses but more likely four. Next stanza:

> How they grip us through thin and thick,
> These barnacle dead!
> This lady here's no kin
> Of mine, yet kin she is: she'll suck
> Blood and whistle my marrow clean
> To prove it. As I think now of her head,

At last an unequivocal rhyme, dead/head, *b/b*; and *a/a* is further off key than before, thick/suck. Which leaves kin/clean; are they *c/c*? In previous stanzas the corresponding words were lady/shrew and game/crumb. The "*c*" rhyme is not proven. And never will be; subsequent stanzas yield in/down, weddings/tang's, go/lie. "C" seems a position for—what may we call it?—assonant dissonance.

And in the last stanzas the "*a*" and "*b*" rhymes behave similarly, drifting off into dissonance. In stanza 5 the "*a*" rhymes are as far apart as "they" and "barbecue"; in stanza 4 the "*b*" rhymes are "greatgrandmother" and "hair."

None of which is to assert that poems "ought to" rhyme smartly: simply to notice that between a wholly unfamiliar pattern and a skewing of exemplification, "All the Dead Dears" nearly persuades us that it wasn't rhyming at all, merely striking similar sounds at random. Its mind seems intent on sharp newsmagazine phrases: "Rigged poker-stiff on her back"; "antique museum-cased lady"; "the gross eating game": a smart assurance of diction, O-so-American (she wrote the poem in England; the lady lies "in the Archaeological Museum in Cambridge," where Sylvia Plath was at the time an undergraduate). Stanza 1 and stanza 2 articulate with patness one sentence each.

But the sentence in stanza 3 stops three words into the final line, and when we set out to quote the sentence that offers to fill out the line we find ourselves copying out all the rest of the poem, stanzas 4, 5, 6, unrhymes and all:

> As I think now of her head,
>
>
> From the mercury-backed glass
> Mother, grandmother, greatgrandmother
> Reach hag hands to haul me in,
> And an image looms under the fishpond surface
> Where the daft father went down
> With orange duck-feet winnowing his hair-
>
> All the long-gone darlings: they
> Get back, though, soon,
> Soon: be it by wakes, weddings,
> Childbirths or a family barbecue:
> Any touch, taste, tang's
> Fit for those outlaws to ride home on,
>
> And to sanctuary: usurping the armchair
> Between tick
> And tack of the clock, until we go,
> Each skulled-and-crossboned Gulliver
> Riddled with ghosts, to lie
> Deadlocked with them, taking root as cradles rock.

—as though the poem had suddenly escaped from a sassy phrase-maker's control and commenced spewing out family secrets. Decorum is jettisoned; the daft father's hair, in a zany glimpse, is winnowed by duck-feet. "Darlings" reaches for the throttle; "they/Get back, though, soon,/Soon" asserts cool sarcasm; American diction is given brief rein as outlaws ride home; the final stanza has sweat on its brow. The armchair is a desperate maneuver, so is "skulled-and-crossboned," so is "Gulliver." The whole thing, once it got loose, has just barely been curbed.

That's what the forms in *The Colossus* are often for, to barely assert themselves and get disrupted. They are not like Yeatsian forms, assurances of "traditional sanctity and loveliness"; nor like Marianne Moore forms, assertions that clickety rigor rides what might be impudence; nor like, say, late-Roethke forms, strumming assurances that the balladeer has all this turbulence under control (sort of).

> The Kitty-Cat Bird, he moped and he cried
> Then a real cat came with a Mouth so Wide,
> That the Kitty-Cat Bird just hopped inside;
> "At last I'm myself!"—and he up and he died
> —Did the Kitty—the Kitty-Cat Bird.

That's pretty dreadful, come to think of it, but the verse won't let you think of it right away. Roethke was cunning in effecting such displacements, and Sylvia Plath was fascinated by his craft but never tried to emulate his confident Dada. She's closer, most of the time, to Robert Lowell, who contrived in his earlier work great rickety pseudo-Pindaric formalisms, the point of which is that they are akin only in geometry to seventeenth-century assurances, and later (e.g., "Skunk Hour") approximated as if casually to formalisms whose teasing near presence serves as gauge for nausea. Ted Hughes calls just one poem—"Point Shirley"—a direct Lowell imitation (she wrote it in 1959, while attending Lowell's Boston University seminar), but the similarities pervade her mature work.

Having said that, I'll talk only about Plath, on the understanding that much adjustment of nuance would be entailed in fitting my statements accurately to Lowell. The formalisms of *The Colossus*—assonance, rhyme, stanzaic pattern—serve a number of interdependent offices, one of which is to reassure the genteel reader (and notably the one who counts, the one who edits an upper-middlebrow magazine). This reader wants to see the candles lit and the silver laid out (and so do we, so do we), and will half-accept, half-overlook an intrusion of the mortuary, the morbid, or the demonic provided that table-manners are not disrupted. That first level of sheer calculation should not be discounted; it helps explain how *The New Yorker* came to accept four poems—"Hardcastle Crags," "Man in Black," "Mussel Hunter at Rock Harbor," "Watercolor of Grantchester Meadows"—that scan a scene and come to rest on some deathly emblem capable of disrupting with panic that magazine's normally trite sophistication. "Hardcastle Crags" is especially nightmarish, a journey on foot into fear that keeps inviting us to attend to its compact elegances of phrasing—

> the incessant seethe of grasses
> Riding in the full
>
> Of the moon, manes to the wind,
> Tireless, tied, as a moon-bound sea
> Moves on its root

—so that although clues abound, we barely notice the whole world growing steadily more inimical, stark, unassimilable, with one's death the only appropriate resolution:

Enough to snuff the quick
Of her small heat out.

Did any editor notice that the poem's walk was into a cosmic graveyard?

but before the weight
Of stones and hills of stones could break
Her down to mere quartz grit in that stony light
She turned back.

The wilfully patterned stanzas, the *ababa* off rhymes, effect attention's
displacement from perversity to craft.

Perversity? I call it that because, in displacing her own attention too,
she indulges herself in reconstructing that walk with lurid specificity,
forcing a stated unmeaning into its landscape, transforming a mood into
something like an article of belief.

All the night gave her, in return
For the paltry gift of her bulk and the beat
Of her heart was the humped indifferent iron
Of its hills, and its pastures bordered by black stone set
On black stone.

Living with the poem, working out its nine stanzas, fifty-four lines,
retouching its ingenious assonances (*struck*/ street/ *black*/ ignite/ *shake*)
and the riding of its sentences over stanza breaks (these coincide only
once, at the end of stanza 5), she could, telling herself she was solving
technical puzzles, pencil taboo combinations into its grid, almost as the
rhyme of a limerick gives one license to utter a scatology, and rise from
her work perhaps incrementally more convinced than before that Sivvy
and the huge physical world were incompatible.

I don't want to melodramatize this; but it's been contrived that the
manner of her death cannot but haunt any discussion of her work, and
read in that knowledge the poems of *The Colossus* offer us the spectacle
of someone accustoming herself to the necessity of a speedy death: the
more so the longer, clearly, they took to write (thesaurus on lap, Ted
Hughes tells us, for all the world as though nothing of more moment were
going forward than the completion of the day's crossword puzzle). Here
off-rhymes are especially betraying. Since they won't serve as finding
devices for one another the way "bright" prompts "light," they entail a
search and trial that must linger and brood; that can choose, as if unco-
erced, to call the hills "humped indifferent iron," yet justify "iron" by the
need of an assonance for "return." So, poem by poem, the universe was
fitted with a bleak vocabulary, freely chosen yet seemingly necessary.

By the time her poetic had gone into free fall—Ted Hughes dates this
from "The Stones," the last poem in the Knopf *Colossus*—that vocabulary came at call: stones, iron, bleak light, all solid things inimical, all gen-

tle locutions used bitterly ("My swaddled legs and arms smell sweet as rubber" and "There is nothing to do./ I shall be good as new.").

> There is nothing to do.
> I shall be good as new.

That's not an off-rhyme nor a dissonant assonance. It's a vibration on target, shrieking its mocking echo of psychiatric reassurance. It's also the rhyme sound of "Daddy."

Here and there, in *The Colossus*, we can detect her working back toward interdicted material: as when "All the Dead Dears" sidles from the innocuous Baedeker note about something you can see in the Archaeological Museum in Cambridge (nothing wrong, is there, with staring at an educational exhibit?) past two stanzas of brisk description to a sudden unmasking of family skeletons: "Mother, grandmother, great-grandmother / Reach hag hands to haul me in" and "daft father" looms "under the fishpond surface" beneath which he has long ago been drawn; and they won't stay dead, and they claim us, keep us "deadlocked." "The Stones," the first free-fall poem, need not sidle; it installs itself at a bound in the madhouse of six years before:

> This is the city where men are mended.
> I lie on a great anvil.

and

> The grafters are cheerful,
>
> Heating the pincers, hoisting the delicate hammers.
> A current agitates the wires
> Volt upon volt. Catgut stitches my fissures.

The unpardonable insult, electroshock therapy. Borrowing a melodramatic image from her, we can say that she has opened the eerie waiting room she told Elizabeth Compton about and stepped into a lurid past. Or we can say that when furies lurk just beyond the rim of consciousness there is paramount danger in improvising. All the formal defenses are down.

For that had been a final use of the intricate formalisms: they detained her mind upon the plane of craft, and so long as it was detained there it did not slip toward what beckoned it. Working on the plane of craft, it made some very good poems indeed, which the vertigo of *Ariel* has since persuaded readers to call contrived, frigid, academic. That seems a doubly erroneous judgment. If we think of *The Colossus* not as the frigid precursor to *Ariel* but as the work of a very intelligent girl in her mid twenties, it is an amazingly good collection. There is no guessing how far in ten more years she might have developed that way of working. It is a plausible guess that the arc of her development might have easily exceeded Lowell's. That rich resourcefulness of diction, that command of craft, that intentness—it is hard to think of a first collection that promises so much.

And the other error that adheres in our easy preference for *Ariel* is its overlooking of the fact that as long as she worked in the manner of *The Colossus* she kept safely alive. One prefers one's poets kept alive.

But no, *Ariel* has been made to seem a new and final sincerity. Ted Hughes gives conventional opinion its cue: until "The Stones," at Yaddo, he writes [in *The Art of Sylvia Plath*, ed. Charles Newman], "she had never in her life improvised. The powers that compelled her to write so slowly had always been stronger than she was. But quite suddenly she found herself free to let herself drop, rather than inch over bridges of concepts." Note the loaded terms: with "The Stones," which I would call her first sick poem, she had overcome the compulsion of inhibiting powers. She is "free" (to drop). And she inches no longer. Inching is an ignoble mode of progress, is it not? Never mind that Milton inched. Hughes goes on: in her final phase she "was able to turn to her advantage all the forces of a highly-disciplined, highly intellectual style of education which had, up to this point, worked mainly against her, but without which she could hardly have gone so coolly into the regions she now entered." What she did now was write "at top speed, as one might write an urgent letter. From then on, all her poems were written in this way."

What had, in Ted Hughes's phrase, "worked mainly against her" was a set of habits that, if I read aright, had kept her producing and alive. I would not blame those habits for the frigidities and immaturities of *The Colossus:* I would guess that she was late to mature, and frigid. The strident insincerities of even the later *Letters Home* may help us gauge how much of her mind was still taken up with role playing; will power and ambition incited, habits of craftsmanship released, extraordinary poems from the part of her talent that could be mobilized nonetheless.

> From Water-Tower Hill to the brick prison
> The shingle booms, bickering under
> The sea's collapse.
> Snowcakes break and welter.
>   ("Point Shirley")

Poets have imitated the sea's sound since Homer, never more authoritatively than in such a detail as this. Alert fidelity to the actual produced the *clou*-word, "bickering," with its aural reminiscence of "brick" and its fine antithetical play against "booms," before "sea's collapse" terminates the wave in a hiss of sibilants. She used less of her talent in better-known lines:

> Dying
> Is an art, like everything else.
> I do it exceptionally well.

> I do it so it feels like hell.
> I do it so it feels real.
> I guess you could say I've a call.

I find nothing to alter in the way I described [in "Ariel—Pop Sincerity"] the more lurid parts of *Ariel* the year it was published:

> Sparse rhymes come and go nearly at random, and the number of syllables in a line swings with the vertigo of her thought. Still, these are shaped poems, all but two of them measured out in stanzas, by preference with an odd number of lines (5 or 3). Not that they resemble in the least Villon's ceremonious ballades.
>
> Perhaps some of them only play the desperate game of repeating again and again the stanza the opening fell into; there's more of compulsion neurosis than mathematics in those forms; the breaks between stanzas are like cracks in the sidewalk, on which she is careful never to step.
>
> The resulting control, sometimes *look* of control, is a rhetoric, as cunning in its power over our nerves as the stream of repulsions. It in fact enacts its own inability to govern. Naked negation spilling down the sides of improvised vessels, that is the formal drama of poem after poem. Being formal, it saves them from shrillness.
>
> The negation, liquid, labile, repudiates with the gleeful craft of a mad child other persons, the poet's own body, the entire created universe....

> Only let down the veil, the veil, the veil.
> If it were death
>
> I would admire the deep gravity of it, its timeless eyes.
> I would know you were serious.
>
> There would be a nobility then, there would be a birthday.
> And the knife not carve, but enter
>
> Pure and clean as the cry of a baby,
> And the universe slide from my side.

> This is insidious nausea; Robert Lowell writes in his Foreword of the serpent he hears whispering from her lines, "Come, if you only had the courage, you too could have my rightness, audacity and ease of inspiration." But most of us, he adds, will turn back: "These poems are playing Russian roulette with six cartridges in the cylinder."

Poems like "A Birthday Present," from which that last quotation comes, have a Guignol fascination, like executions. She was somewhere on the far side of sanity, teasing herself with the thrill of courting extinction, as though on a high window ledge. Such spectacles gather crowds and win plaudits for "honesty" from critics who should know better. In those terrible months the habits of craft lasted, a feel for shaping and phrasing gone into her bones. Rhyme, though, was no longer a diffraction grating but a wild heuristic, prompting, encouraging—

You do not do, you do not do
Any more, black shoe.

She could have done without that voodoo encouragement. It's too much to say the poems killed her, but one can't see that they did anything to keep her alive. The death poems—say a third of *Ariel*—are bad for anyone's soul. They give a look of literary respectability to voyeurist passions: no gain for poetry, nor for her.

True Plath fans will detest all of the foregoing. True Plath fans, when articulate, are busy making points about purity and sincerity: in quest (I find I wrote eleven years ago) "of spiritual shortcuts to spiritual virtues, but preferring to see someone else try them out." The true self into which Sylvia Plath's soul merged when her careful habits of composition failed her—the habits Ted Hughes stigmatizes as having "worked mainly against her"—made a virtue of a Manichaean lack of patience with the world's slow turning. The world, its obduracy, respect for the waves and stones of which had once summoned all her craft, came to mean only minatory forms, the yew tree whose message "is blackness—blackness and silence," and the body's "aguey tendon, the sin, the sin." In fever, pulsating at a distance from the world,

I

Am a pure acetylene
Virgin
Attended by roses.

This is bogus spirituality, and it has its admirers, who even seem pleased that Sylvia Plath did not survive it.

FUELING THE PHOENIX FIRE:
THE MANUSCRIPTS OF SYLVIA PLATH'S "LADY LAZARUS"[1]

SUSAN VAN DYNE

Sylvia Plath turned thirty on October 27, 1962. During that week she composed eleven poems. The monumental "Lady Lazarus" was alone among them in being revised over a period of six days. "Lady Lazarus" looms large among the major poems from the last five months of Plath's life which we now regard as her poetic coming of age. These poems are almost obsessively concerned with the making of a literary alter ego—how to realize through language a new vision of the self. In "Lady Lazarus" the poet worried not only about how she would define the self but how she would defend it.

One of the poems conceived around her birthday, "Lady Lazarus" marks the poet's taking stock of her history. Her urge to reorder her past retrospectively and to utter a compelling prophesy about her future prompt this poem's terrifying self-dramatization. A poet who compulsively measured her achievements against others, Plath may well have dreaded her thirtieth birthday. She and her husband had separated dur-

[1]Susan Van Dyne, "Fueling the Phoenix Fire: The manuscripts of Sylvia Plath's 'Lady Lazarus.'" *The Massachusetts Review* 24.2 (Summer 1983). Rpt. in *Sylvia Plath: Modern Critical Views*, edited by Harold Bloom (New York: Chelsea House, 1989), pp. 133–47.

ing the summer, and she had remained with her two young children in Devon while he returned to London. In July, August, and September she'd written only six poems. For a time, her life seemed to dominate her art and paralyze the forces necessary to create poetry. Yet in the October poems Plath began to reconstruct a persona that was often volatile, violent, and sometimes overbearing in its egotism. She recognized in the aftermath of her marriage that she'd gained access to molten strata of unknown poetic power. She wrote, feverishly, to her mother on October 16 to claim she was ready "to make a new life. I am a writer....I am a genius of a writer; I have it in me. I am writing the best poems of my life; They will make my name" [quoted from *Letters Home*].

Now that scholars have access to the manuscripts from this period through the Sylvia Plath Collection at Smith College, we need to re-examine the nature of the relationship between Plath's biography and the poems that made her name. As critics we have created an overly neat, and probably false, dichotomy between Plath's early work in *The Colossus* period, which seems laboriously crafted and intellectually derived from literary models, and her later poems from the *Ariel* period, which appear to be, by contrast, an unmediated transcription of life. What the manuscripts for the *Ariel* poems reveal is unequivocal proof that although the events of Plath's life may have prompted the need for these poems, her characters and narratives were realized through a series of self-conscious, calculated artistic choices. While we are able to note, at many places in the drafts, correspondences between the emerging poem and its underlying personal history, the rearrangements, condensations, and distortions of persons and events in the dream work of the poem hold much more significance. In the manuscripts for the *Ariel* poems we begin to see as well that Plath's relationship to her personal history was no more vexed than her relationship to her literary past. We recognize a woman writer who struggles to conceive of her life outside of the conventional inherited stories that pretend to describe it. Because Plath's late poems are uniformly more daring in the narratives she borrows and subverts in order to make her inward life visible, they enable us to appreciate their resemblance to the fantastic reorderings of Anne Sexton, the Brontës, and Emily Dickinson. In addition, they should cause us to revalue her intentional divergence from the more literal confessions of Robert Lowell.

"Lady Lazarus" is one of the most Gothic of the lot. The poem means to give offense; it makes outrageous claims. One of these is the female persona's appropriation of the suffering of concentration camp inmates as a suitable analogy for the domestic tragedy of a failed marriage. This poem shows us Plath testing her authority, her myth-making capability, exercising a bold new voice that affronts and astonishes. Yet one of Lady Lazarus's strengths is her self-irony; she is as much aware of her excesses as her creator is in this description for a planned BBC broadcast: "The speaker is a woman who has the great and terrible gift of being reborn. The only trouble is she has to die first. She is the phoenix, the libertarian spirit, what you will. She is also just a good, plain, very resourceful woman" [quoted by M. L. Rosenthal in *The Art of Sylvia Plath*, ed. Charles Newman]. In her final months the resourceful woman poet pushed her literary self-conception steadily toward mythic representations that would transfigure or redeem her suffering in extraordinary ways.

Her journals suggest that Plath had always expected her life to be a fabulous story. As a young writer she was determined to master the formulaic fictions of women's magazines. Her fixation with imitating these stories successfully seems at times to govern the paradigms through which she perceived her own experience. Her ambition to be recognized as an artist and her expectation of womanly fulfillment reflect the conventions of popular art like an incongruous cartoon. Anticipating her birthday three years earlier, Plath records in her journal a dream in which "Marilyn Monroe appeared to me...as a kind of fairy godmother....She gave me an expert manicure....She invited me to visit her during the Christmas holidays, promising a new, flowering life."

But when she faced the end of her marriage in the summer of 1962, her lifescript threatened to turn into soap opera. Plath refused to play the pitiful roles of betrayed wife or abandoned mother. "What the person out of Belsen—physical or psychological—wants," she wrote her mother just before beginning "Lady Lazarus," "is nobody saying the birdies still go tweet-tweet, but the full knowledge that somebody else has been there and knows the *worst*, just what it is like. It is much more help for me, for example, to know that people are divorced and go through hell, than to hear about happy marriages. Let the *Ladies Home Journal* blither about *those*" (*Letters*, October 21, 1962). The old fictions had failed her. In "Lady Lazarus" she borrowed the miracle of Lazarus, the myth of the phoenix, the hype of the circus, and the horror of the holocaust to prophesy for herself a blazing triumph over her feelings of tawdriness and victimization.

What emerges strikingly when we examine her drafts are the persona's oscillations between feelings of control and powerlessness. We recover, too, a fuller awareness that Plath's reconstructed identity borrows from other stories she'd told about herself—as Esther Greenwood in *The Bell Jar*, as the emerging female alter ego in other poems written in October, most particularly "Stings" and "Ariel," and, in the less obviously fictionalized accounts, as daughter writing letters home to Aurelia Plath and as the self-conscious poet writing and rereading her journals. Her purpose in reshaping these autobiographical sources, as much as her literary sources, was to make available to herself a history she could live with. The history of artistic choices told by these documents individually is impressive enough, but what is most astonishing is that the stories are told in concert, often quite literally superimposed on each other. The Plath Collection, which is housed in Smith's rare book room, contains approximately 4,000 pages of her manuscripts and typescripts, including more than 200 poems in successive drafts, 850 pages of unpublished journals, and 150 annotated volumes from the poet's library.

"Lady Lazarus," like many of the poems from this period, is drafted on used paper. Plath's habit of reusing earlier manuscript material shows a marvellously conserving psychic economy or a reluctance to dispose of good bond paper, or most likely both. During the incredibly productive last two years of her life, she composed on the backs of the final printer's typescript of *The Colossus*, on the reverse of an edited typescript of *The Bell Jar*, used mostly in consecutive order from back to front during October and November, and on scraps of Ted Hughes's poems and plays, which she had originally typed for him. A handwritten six-page draft and the first two typescripts of "Lady Lazarus" all appear on pages from *The Bell Jar*; these are mostly used in sequence, starting with the opening of chapter 3 and running backward through almost all of chapter 2. *The Bell Jar* itself was typed on pink memo paper that Plath acquired when she taught at Smith.

When Plath felt she had a serviceable draft (usually within a single day) she moved to fresh paper for a clean typed version, almost inevitably with a carbon copy. While these typescripts often underwent further editing, Plath usually inscribed them in the upper right corner with her name and address, an encouraging signal to herself that the poems were ready to be mailed to her favorite journals. Often the carbon of the earliest typescript is dated; when revisions occurred over a period of time, she may note dates on the first handwritten draft and subsequent revisions, offering a day-by-day account of their evolution. Fair copies of a completed poem might subsequently be used as scrap when she began composing another poem several months later. Late in January Plath borrowed the back of the first typed copy of "Lady Lazarus" that was on clean bond and had been identified with her name and Devon address to begin composing "Totem" and "Bald Madonnas" (eventually "The Munich Mannequins").

What caused this endless turnover in the poet's paper supply? From her own dated lists, we know that she sent batches of poems out weekly from just after the composition of the sequence of bee poems during early October until a week before her death in early February. Because many of the same poems were recirculated to several different magazines, Plath was certain to have multiple fair copies of the final version on hand ready to go out or being returned in the mail. Yet Plath's habits were clearly prompted by more than convenience. The palimpsestic accretion of the poet's reinscribed manuscripts gives unexpected clues to the evolution of her personal symbol system. In all likelihood, Plath reused a particular page of manuscript because she had been rereading it, either to wonder why a group of poems had been returned or, in the case of the safely published *Colossus* and *Bell Jar*, to reassure herself of earlier productivity. That Plath returned to rework "Lady Lazarus" over a period of six days is significant. In only a few poems from these weeks in October, such as the powerful pivotal poem "Stings" in the bee sequence, did Plath make substantive revisions of a stanza or more after the initial draft or two. I think Plath's hesitation about being done with these poems marks her conviction that they were major works. Even more, I believe her prolonged attention to them and the nature of her revisions indicate the materials and areas of feeling she longed to order and control. Reseeing the manuscript evidence in the Collection as literal palimpsests, through which each document testifies twice or more, complicates our sense of their chronological sequence. We begin to know what images freed her genius or what material demanded to be rehearsed in order to free her.

It is entirely clear in the finished poem that one of the poet's primary needs is to believe in her own will as the agency of her resurrection. The persona of the final version is searingly self-confident—a taunting, bitchy phoenix who appears to loathe her earlier incarnations almost as much as she does her present audience. Although the published version of the poem brags that the voracious, terrifying self is unencumbered by her past, the manuscripts reveal the strain of reconstructing a self that could break free of the dependent, derivative definitions linked to the strong male figures in her life. Certain preoccupations that will ultimately find other shapes or be excised altogether in the finished poem appear in the drafts. What is evident throughout the drafts is her fixation on a male figure as the primary audience for her strenuous self-proclamation. Even more clearly than in the published version, the speaker's performance demands and depends on her audience to validate it. As she moves toward the finished version of her protagonist, Plath chooses to shape her as an active, even manipulative, agent who supersedes earlier images of the self as passive, tortured victim. The imaginative reconstruction of her identity is accomplished through an extended, often oblique, process of negative definition. What the speaker wishes to accomplish by sheer force of will is precisely the inversion of what she fears. Rather than be consumed by the fires of sexual jealousy and helpless rage that appear repeatedly in the imagery of the drafts, the speaker wants to separate herself from her fused identity with Hughes, eliminate the threat of his superior position, and finally appropriate his male powers to herself in a consuming gesture of her own fierce territoriality.

Throughout the manuscripts, Plath knows and names her antagonists more clearly than she can conceive of herself as independent of their claims on her: lover, enemy, professor, executioner, priest, torturer, doctor, God, Lucifer. In order to believe in her ability to reconstitute herself imaginatively as a "smiling woman" of thirty, she must dismiss the social constructions of the self which earlier sustained her. Like the Godiva figure in "Ariel," she must slough off the identities provided by the roles she had assumed as student, wife, mother, patient, even attempted suicide, as so much "trash / to annihilate each decade." Such faith didn't come easily to the poet. The hyperbole in the drafts is even more extreme than in the completed poem. In them the repetitiveness of the speaker's assertions of her power to survive each deconstruction of the self speaks more of fear than of easy self-assurance. As Plath works to hone her anger and turn it outward, to tighten the defense of her macabre self-irony in revisions, a consistent pattern emerges. Initially the persona's love is fused with death; ultimately, Lady Lazarus's new life is fueled by hate. The violent fantasy of the poem is informed by the wish to incorporate the forces that threaten to destroy her.

These are the figures that dominate the worksheets. In using Plath's original manuscripts in the Collection, we are constantly aware that these motifs are inscribed over the narrative of *The Bell Jar* that appears on the reverse. Although it is difficult to determine the origins of specific images in a symbolic system as densely interconnected as Plath's, eerie associative links exist between poem and novel in these double-faced documents. In both narratives, the heroine stresses her feelings of entitlement, expressed in a greedy orality. This defensive response seems prompted, more obliquely in the novel than in the poem, by a sense of deprivation caused by the defection of a significant male figure. Also central to both narratives is a necessary purification through which the persona attempts to free herself from old relational bonds.

In the poem, the first and last of the persona's "deaths" recall her abandonment by her father and by her husband twenty years later. Embedded in the chapter from the novel is Plath's remembrance of her grandfather, who served as surrogate when her father died, and his implied promise that this early loss would be repaired by marriage. The pages from chapter 3 of *The Bell Jar* that serve as scrap for the handwritten draft of the poem present the sumptuous *Ladies' Day* luncheon that will later make the heroine Esther Greenwood deathly ill. Eating caviar and avocados reminds her of the "stolen" treats provided by her grandfather when she was nine. The childhood luxury of caviar is not only an implied compensation for the loss of her father, but further, as Esther self-consciously elaborates, "at my wedding my grandfather would see I had all the caviar I could eat. It was a joke because I never intended to get married." Plath tended to lump male disappointments together; here she found reminders of several readily available for reworking in the poem. Even more striking is Esther's sense of her audience at lunch as alien, critical, and competitive. She gorges on the extra caviar to fortify her own feelings of entitlement against the other guests who might demand that she share. In the poem, Lady Lazarus must protect herself from the greedy encroachments of the "peanut-crunching crowd." Finally, the end of the first handwritten draft appears on the reverse of pages from chapter 2 in which Esther enacts a ritual bath purifying herself of all entangling relationships. As troubling men and rival females dissolve away in the bath, Esther proclaims, "I don't know them, I have never known them. [I am a virgin,] and I am very pure." To cleanse her heroine after another decade, Plath would need to subject Lady Lazarus to fire before she can "rise a [bloody] [blooming] [sweet white] virgin." (Note: brackets [] in these quotations enclose material deleted by the poet during her revision of a particular draft.)

What is remarkable about Plath's worksheets is the progressive purification the poem undergoes. Her deletions are almost always her most significant choices. Passages which take repeated tinkering often drop away altogether; yet the material worried over in such passages often prompts a key image or word choice that governs a later stage in the poem. I want to focus on two of the most reworked areas in the worksheets to demonstrate how a woman artist reshaped cultural stories in order to transmute personal autobiography into more public poetic myth. In order to re-imagine her heroine, Plath first had to probe the nature of her dependence on the male figures through whom she had previously defined herself. With the defection of Hughes and the end of their marriage, several of Plath's most elaborately maintained stories about her identity as woman and poet were threatened at once. In her letters and journals she often proposes the analogy that her poetry represented an excess of her natural fertility. She believed her poems would confirm and extend her procreative powers as child-bearer. Although she was widely published in magazines before she ever bore children, she rejoiced that the birth of her daughter Frieda marked the spring and the publication of her first book *The Colossus* marked the fall of the same year. She was convinced that her poetic fruitfulness would be rooted in her experience of motherhood.

Significantly, the Lazarus story was linked in Plath's associations with barrenness. In April of 1956, in the flush of Hughes' courtship, she boasted to her mother of the perfect integration of her life with Ted and her work as a poet: "My voice is taking shape, coming strong. Ted says he never read poems by a woman like mine; they are strong and full and rich...they are working, sweating, heaving poems born out of the way words should be said." She compared her full devotion to Ted with total self-knowledge and fulfillment: "Although I am using every fiber of my being to love him, even so, I am true to the essence of myself, and I know who that self is...I know this with a sure strong knowing to the tips of my toes, and having been on the other side of life like Lazarus, I know that my whole being shall be one song of affirmation and love all my life long" (*Letters*, April 29, 1956). Clearly, to be Lazarus was to doubt such integration and affirmation. Three years later in Boston, Plath connected Lazarus to an idea for a short story. She felt her life was stalled. Working part-time at Massachusetts General Hospital writing up mental patients' case histories, she despaired of her ability to produce poems or to generate characters or plots substantial enough for a novel. In the same period she berated herself for her inability to become pregnant, believing she was infertile and therefore fatally flawed as a woman. The seed for a story called "Lazarus My Love" was noted in her journals as a startling "Comeback from the dead. Kicking off thermometers" erupting in the "violent ward" of the mental hospital.

In fall of 1962 Plath needed to manage her own comeback after suffering the death of her chosen self-image as the perfect intellectual and biological partner for Hughes. In the drafts for "Lady Lazarus" the strains of separating her identity from his are everywhere apparent. With intense ambivalence, the speaker regards a male figure whom she must identify, within the same breath, as her greatest love and her greatest enemy. In the third stanza, she struggles to claim her separate reality in the face of this confounding fusion. The encounter is one of the most heavily reworked passages in the poem:

Peel off the napkin

[My] [Great] Love, [my] [great] enemy.

[It is certainly I] Do I terrify?

Yes [yes] Yes Herr Professor

[It is I] I is I

Can [You] you [cannot] deny

The nose, the eye pits, the full set of teeth?

Her sense of herself seems to depend here on gaining recognition from the other. Her anxious assertions demand confirmation, but she seems to expect only denial. She presents herself as Hughes's bad ghost, the walking corpse he can't walk out on.

In this scenario, who does he become? Throughout the handwritten draft the antagonism between them is intimate and pervasive. Whenever the poet invokes his presence in this fused image of lover/enemy, she releases a rush of affect that temporarily takes over the poem and that she chooses consistently later to delete. She imagines the speaker locked into a hellish cycle of aggression and recrimination with a male antagonist. She smoulders in the fires of sexual jealousy and thwarted rage, vowing that she'll emerge from the forge renewed and even more dangerous to her torturer:

[so love], [so] enemy

I burn & turn

So, Herr Enemy

You age, & I am new.

I am the baby/on/your/anvil./I eat fire

. . . .

You say I am dangerous

I burn & turn & have no need for you.

Well yes, I guess

I am very dangerous [when it comes to you!]

Very, very dangerous, when it comes to you!

These fires resemble the feverish purgation of sexual passion and rejection of her lover in "Fever 103°" written less than a week earlier. The evidence of these passages suggests that even to name the male figure as "love" proved too dangerous artistically for Plath. In order to see herself safely separate from him, the poet had to find cooler terms.

In her revisions, Plath substitutes epithets that would seem to entitle him to enviable positions of power and dominance: "Herr Professor," "Herr Doktor," "Herr Enemy," "Herr God," "Herr Lucifer." Yet naming these attributes or roles served to clarify for the poet what her developing heroine lacked, and what Lady Lazarus would need to claim as her own in order to survive. In the process of negative definition which organizes the poem, the association of the male figure with cruelty and authority yields a composite projection of what the speaker both fears and desires. Once appropriately named, these monolithic male figures apparently freed the poet to stage for Lady Lazarus a kind of guerilla theatre with her imagined audience in which their expected roles are systematically reversed. The speaker assaults her audience with her terrifying self-disclosures. In exhibiting her corpse, she will teach her former tutor a lesson in brutality; in annihilating the trash of her earlier selves, she'll prove to the doctor that she can cure herself; in performing her suicidal act "so it feels like hell," she'll rival Lucifer in her ability to suffer; and in arranging her own resurrection, she demonstrates she can do without God's intervention. In reworking the image of the male figure, the worksheets show a movement from a highly conflicted fusion with an intimate antagonist toward a defiant separation from stylized, archetypal representations of male authority. In working out these changes, Plath is able to eliminate the wordiness of threats such as "we are not done with each other" and "I am very dangerous when it comes to you" in favor of more overt intimidation and manipulation of her audience.

In reconstructing Lady Lazarus as a survivor rather than a compulsive suicide, Plath needed to try out several alternative visions of the heroine in the worksheets. In defining her character, probably the most important decision was choosing her voice. Except perhaps for the daughter in "Daddy," none of Plath's speakers is more determinedly unpleasant, more deserving of the predictable female pejorative, shrill. Her analogies are intentionally presumptuous, her flippant colloquialisms are knowingly in poor taste. Plath's control of voice is Lady Lazarus's chief defense for keeping the peanutcrunching crowd at bay. But this abrasive self-presentation is not uniformly present in the worksheets. In fact we can chart the evolution of Plath's new heroine in the passages whose tone is noticeably unlike the final poem. Given the brittle self-irony that distinguishes Lady Lazarus as carnival barker and suicidal stuntwoman, it's surprising to discover in the drafts several passages in which she speaks with unguarded vulnerability. The first is an extended image of the recovered suicide as a martyred saint:

I am supple, I breathe gently

And shall sit [here] a[while] little, [uncommon] [on
                    this green common]

Loving the death that killed me like a lover.

Now it is over

[And] I am involved & still, a wax madonna

The wax madonna's suffering is passive, even erotically willing; her tone is elegiac rather than acerbic. In her self-involvement she looks toward the grave rather than toward the crowd. This section, which was completely dropped after the first draft, most closely resembles the tranquility of the second suicide attempt which follows a few stanzas later. Describing that womb-like retreat, Plath adds and deletes the word "peaceful" four separate times within the space of two lines.

Just after recalling this event, Plath's speaker in the draft confesses her concern for her children. They are both identified as girls; Plath's apparent formal motive was to rhyme "girls" with "pearls" in the preceding line. Yet what follows this evocation is a touching brief rehearsal of the fairy tale of female fulfillment that had just failed the poet herself so miserably:

Now I have two girls.

I want to see them rich & married well
                    [comfortable]

They are already beautiful

And are They [are] proud

Of their mum's profession? Yes!

Dying//is an art like everything else.

I do it exceptionally well.

Implicit in this passage is one of the central brooding questions Plath tried to answer in the poems she wrote in October. What is her profession? She jokes, here, that she's had most success as an attempted suicide. Yet what does this vocation suggest about her other chosen role as mother? Furthermore, how has her experience of these two professions altered her definition of the poet as resurrected Lazarus, whose "whole being," she imagined in 1956, would be "one song of affirmation and love all my life long"?

In revising, Plath chose to excise both of these comparatively selfless portraits as uncharacteristic of the Lady Lazarus she now needed to imagine. The next stage in the reconstruction of the heroine is marked by passages whose tone is defensive rather than defenseless. Throughout the handwritten draft are complaints of victimization. These are alike in acknowledging the speaker's ambivalence about whether she chose her deaths or merely submitted to them. In two separate sections, she insists an executioner is a constant presence in these scenes. In an extended passage on the third page of the handwritten draft, the unequal forces arrayed against her include not only the executioner, but "a priest & a torturer," and a hostile "mob." This section is crucial for its evidence of the female persona's lingering feelings of paranoia and powerlessness that are subsequently deleted:

And there's always [a mob &] an executioner

And a priest & a torturer

And a couple of horses & a wheel to give the crowd

[to give the crowd that] [an extra] its thrill.

The extra kicks [they] it pays for.

Moreover, certain key terms here, "thrill" and "kicks" used to describe the mob's voyeuristic appetite, seem to suggest, several stanzas later, the pivotal term for the last stage in the heroine's transformation.

"Charge" comes to stand for the high-premium, high-voltage exchange between the final incarnation of Lady Lazarus and her audience. Between the deleted passage and what becomes stanza 19 of the finished poem, the balance of power is shifted dramatically from the crowd to the speaker: "There is a charge/For fingering my scars, There is a charge." She sets the price they must pay to see her suffer. But the word itself is charged, I think, with more than this meaning. The former tortured victim clearly intends to demand compensation for her pain; she will even affect a sadistic pleasure in exhibiting it and controlling their response. But, like the crowd, she also seems to get a thrill from the performance. While apparently disdaining their gullibility and voyeurism, the speaker's reactions demonstrate that she feels powerfully the reciprocal charge that flows between actor and observer:

the same brute

Amused shout:

'A miracle!'

That really knocks me out.

Finally, in the draft for this section, Plath returns to the intimate nexus of her intended role reversal. In the initial version, the speaker's orchestration of events for which her audience must pay is graphically physical and increasingly personal, from "fingering" her scars, to "stethoscoping" her heart, to the final veiled threat: "And there is a charge, a very large charge / For a [night in my bed]." Recovering this variant causes us to hear again the bitter ironies in the earlier lines "Are they proud/Of their mum's profession?" It also suggests the high cost to the poet of constructing such a callous persona in Lady Lazarus: the versatile stuntwoman who will pose as a saint and barter like a prostitute.

I've suggested the pattern and possible motives I see emerging from the poet's choices to delete and revise her worksheets. From the evidence of the initial handwritten draft, what I have described as stages in the reconstruction of the heroine, and her separation from the male antagonist, were choices made largely within a single day. Plath's instincts were certain and swift during this period of composition. She almost never doubted the beginning impulse for a poem; her dramatic first lines emerge at once and remain untouched. Yet she typically reworked a large section of the final movement of a poem in three or four successive efforts even within the initial draft. The last two-and-a-half pages of this six-page handwritten draft focus on recasting the ending.

Throughout these versions, the struggle to resurrect an image of a powerful, autonomous heroine exists in uneasy tension with the desire to reduce to ashes any remnant of a self derivatively defined by her relationship to Hughes. From what we can recover in the worksheets, the ritual of deconstructing that self resonates against a group of emotionally laden images from the recent and distant past. In "Burning the Letters," a poem written the previous August, Plath tries to purge herself of the accumulated burden of Hughes's correspondence and manuscripts, the record of what she now feels has been a past based on deception. The gestures of this ceremony resemble the imagined cremation of "Lady Lazarus":

So I poke at the carbon birds in my housedress.

. . . .

With the butt of a rake

I flake up papers that breathe like people
               ("Burning the Papers," August 13)

Out of that ash

You poked//till it lay in a hush/Without cough
                         or stir

I rise, [to eat the air] with my red hair.
               (draft for "Lady Lazarus," October 23)

In the second poem, however, the roles are significantly reversed. The effort to purge the past fails in "Burning the Letters" because the name of Ted's lover rises from the ashes to assault the stricken speaker anew. In "Lazarus," it's the male figure who fails in the attempt to incinerate the protean female force and who must witness her fiery ascension.

How her heroine would actually rise from the ashes was not entirely clear to Plath during the poem's gestation. Although her final vision is allied with the mythic phoenix, the worksheets reveal that the conception of this figure is more intimately related to similar images of the reborn self created in Plath's other October poems. In the poet's first effort to bring Lady Lazarus back from the dead, on the second page of the handwritten draft, she is virginal yet unequivocally mortal as well: "Each time I rise, I rise a [bloody] [blooming] [sweet white] virgin." During the same week that Plath was revising this poem, she also composed two others, "Poppies in October" and "Nick and the Candlestick," in which fresh blood "blooms" to remind her of the vitality of love and life. Later, Plath would drop this first image of the rising Lazarus as premature.

Her dramatic resurrection clearly belonged to the final movement of the poem; but even here Plath vacillated between having her come back as a newborn or as a fully-fledged creature. Twice she tries out a set of lines that picture Lazarus as an unkillable infant: "You age, and I am new. / I am the baby / on your anvil, / I eat fire." More appealing, finally, to Plath was the image of her as an avenging female who was both erotically tempting and fearsomely destructive. The fire that threatened to destroy her is reignited in her red hair: "I rise with my red [hair] [terrible, feathery hair] hair / My incendiary feathers, and I eat men like air."

Here the adjective "terrible" echoes the speaker's rhetorical question "Do I terrify?" in stanza three. Equally significant, "terrible" is a key term in the description of the recovered self in "Stings" in which the queen bee rises from apparent death "More terrible than she ever was, red / Scar in the sky, red comet." Interestingly, one of the most memorable images of the speaker in "Stings" is her "dense hair." Plath's composite image of the risen Lady Lazarus seems as much siren as phoenix. What's truly astonishing about the evolution of the heroine is her consistently voracious appetite. She rises "to eat the air." Unscathed by torture, she boasts, "I eat fire." Finally she threatens, "I eat men like air."

The heroine's last gesture underscores the wish driving the entire poem, the wish to appropriate the powers that threaten to destroy her. In moving away from the agonizing fusion with the male antagonist evident in the early stages of the poem, the speaker achieves separation by distancing herself from simplified authoritarian male roles. Through her verbal gestures, however, the speaker attempts to reverse the dominance she identifies with these male figures. By manipulating her audience's responses through her hyperbolic, aggressive self-disclosures, the speaker claims her ability to control the situation, to make good her opening bravado and "manage it." The poet's revenge is to turn the tables on the husband and fellow-poet who, she fears, objectified her as his "opus," his "valuable," his "pure gold baby." Her power is language, the power to name. She invokes as her final witnesses "Herr God" and "Herr Lucifer." She magnifies her opponents in order to make her victory more significant; finally, however, she trivializes them to make it more secure.

The ascension of Lady Lazarus marks one of several attempts to imagine a terrifying new integrity for the poet. Throughout most of the final version of the poem, the persona experiences herself as split. She reports her actions from the dual perspective of actor and observer at once, as in these lines:

Soon, soon the flesh

The grave cave ate will be

At home on me, and I a smiling woman

or

They had to call & call

And pick the worms off me like sticky pearls.

She is hyper-conscious not only of her own feelings, but of her image in others' eyes. Yet perceiving herself as split, as both subject and object, self and other, may be the last vestige of the alienating male perspective she longs to escape from.

In her last utterance, the speaker claims to have moved outside the orbit of male dominance altogether. But has she? Her efforts to heal the split, to articulate a radical integrity, are noticeably different from the closing visions of other October poems that predict the rebirth of a heroine. In "Ariel" the self-absorbed drive of the speaker is undeniably ecstatic even though it may spell the extinction of the individual self. In "Stings" the rising queen is autonomous; she is liberated from the "stingless dead men" who appear in the drafts but who are unmentioned in the final poem. The close of "Lady Lazarus" is more frightening in its explicit urge for revenge and more fearful in its need for it. In Plath's incandescent image, the phoenix rises in rage. The men that she eats like air fuel that final fire.

PLATH'S MIRROR[1]

DONNA RICHARDSON

Sylvia Plath's "Mirror" can be more fully understood if the reader visualizes the spatial relations in two key visual elements. In the simpler of the two, a careful reader will be struck by the peculiarities in the literal description of the mirror (never mind that it also talks!). In stanza one, it reflects a wall and therefore is vertical. But in stanza two, it is figuratively a "lake" over which the woman bends—and is therefore presumably now horizontal. This apparent discrepancy can be solved by contemplating what kind of mirror could be both. A plausible answer would be the old-fashioned kind of adjustable mirror that was either freestanding or built into a dresser. Aside from fitting Plath's literal description, this kind of

[1]Donna Richardson, "Plath's Mirror," *Explicator* 49.3 (Spring 1991): 193–95.

mirror suits one of her larger thematic implications—that a mirror adjusts to the viewer and becomes what she makes of it.

The issue of the mirror's objectivity as a "little god" is a central problem in interpreting the poem, and it is one that can be addressed by visualizing the two terms of a metaphor, the climactic comparison of what the woman sees in her mirror with a "terrible fish." The poem is often incompletely analyzed as being simply about the unavoidable horrors of growing old. This interpretation implies that the narrator is a spokesperson for the author—an odd idea, since the narrator is a mirror, whose point of view is not only emotionless but also extremely limited physically as well as morally. One should not be inclined, like the woman in the poem, to concede truth and godhood to an emotionless object, which sees nothing but what is placed in front of it by others and reflects nothing but two-dimensional surfaces. The tendency of audiences to split between trusters and doubters of the mirror-narrator suggests that the narrator is, in fact, ironically a "mirror" of the audience's values as well. The reader can make the mirror the god it says it is, giving it depths that it does not possess (just as it only becomes a lake in the second stanza, when the woman searches its "reaches for what she really is"), or the reader can reject its claim that its superficial truth accurately reflects human worth. Unfortunately, many women (as well as men) have traditionally done the former, especially in the 1950s when Plath wrote the poem and when the epitome of femininity was Marilyn Monroe.

The final image of the poem reinforces the dehumanizing effect of committing one's identity to the shallow truth of physical appearance. The mirror claims that the woman has "drowned a young girl" in it, and that "in me an old woman / Rises toward her day after day, like a terrible fish." Many readers plausibly connect the scaly skin of a fish with the unappealing appearance of aged human skin. But a large number of them less-plausibly envision the fish as a dead fish floating to the surface, representing the death of the woman's youth (the drowned girl) and the literal death that the woman eventually will encounter. More probably, the appearance of the fish should reflect what the woman literally sees in the mirror: her own face, head-on (it is difficult to see oneself otherwise in a mirror!). It is more appropriate to envision the fish as a live fish, swimming up out of the depths toward her, facing her directly and more clearly visible with each passing day.

Such an image conveys considerably more than the picture of a dead fish lying on its side. If it is the woman's own face, the fish is not "terrible" in the sense of fanged and ferocious. It is less an external reality come to get her than a reflection of horrors within her. A fish-face is not only representative of physical ugliness in the woman's appearance. The staring eyes and open mouth natural to a fish's face convey, as a reflection of a human face, the woman's moral state. Like a fish, the woman cannot close her eyes to what she is becoming; also like a fish, she cannot change her expression. This expression is one of terrible, fixed recognition, a self-awareness that includes no understanding or catharsis, only unavoidable doom. But this is more likely a suppressed recognition than a realistic facing of the truth about aging, inasmuch as the bug-eyes, pursed mouth, and other characteristics of a fish-face most literally suggest the facial grimaces of a person concealing the physical truth by putting on makeup.

If this is a picture of what a human being "really is," then Plath's vision is dark indeed. But the very fact that the simile does not refer to a human face, and is not the only expression possible to the human visage, may well imply that one only becomes this fixed and dehumanized if one chooses to take the two-dimensional reality of physical appearance as the only truth. The woman has not just helplessly watched her youth drown and float to the surface as an intimation that ugly mortality is the only truth. By fishing for the truth in a superficial place, in a mirror that has "reaches" but no depths, she has actively performed a sea-change upon her humanity and made herself into a very live "terrible fish," creating an image that literally would not be there if she stopped looking for it there. She is facing neither what she really could be, nor what she must be, but what she has allowed an inhuman version of truth to make her.

PLATH'S METAPHORS[1]

KAREN ALKALAY-GUT

Metaphors

I'm a riddle in nine syllables,
An elephant, a ponderous house,
A melon strolling on two tendrils.
O red fruit, ivory, fine timbers!
This loaf's big with its yeasty rising.
Money's new-minted in this fat purse.
I'm a means, a stage, a cow in calf.
I've eaten a bag of green apples,
Boarded the train there's no getting off. (*Poems*, 116).[2]

The relief with which seekers of a "normal" Sylvia Plath turn to the poem "Metaphors" is well known. Frequently anthologized, and referred to as an almost lighthearted exercise in determining the metaphors for pregnancy, "Metaphors" is usually considered at its most profound, as an attempt to find a "feminine" subject for poetry. For the otherwise critical Anne Stevenson, "Metaphors" is "the delightful little pregnancy poem" (153). Helen Vendler, however, sees in it an artificiality, an unconsciously ambivalent attempt to deal in an acceptably "healthy" fashion with a topic whose complexity is unacknowledged.

[1]Karen Alkalay-Gut, "Plath's Metaphors," *Explicator* 50.3 (Spring 1992): 189-92.

[2]"Metaphors" from the book *The Collected Poems of Sylvia Plath*, edited by Ted Hughes. Copyright © 1960, 1965, 1971, 1981 by the estate of Sylvia Plath. Reprinted by permission of HarperCollins Publishers.

Only the last line is grim enough to wake a reader's response. The rest is pure silliness. Still, in sympathy one wants to say that the aridity of the intellect in dealing with life, and its pure insufficiency to metabolic processes, is enough to send anyone round the bend in this particular fashion, to turn a woman into a talking melon. (Vendler 273)

While neither of these observations is in error, a closer look at the intricacies of "Metaphors" reveals the concentrated application of Plath's sophisticated linguistic, figurative and psychological analysis, which exceeds even her best-known poems in its condensed emotion.

Upon a second or third reading the introductory statement, "I'm a riddle," is answered laughingly by the reader with the dismissal, pregnancy. But to begin a poem with that line is to introduce the question of identity that may characterize the state of pregnancy. The speaker's altering body and her situation have the inevitable result of altering her concept of self, and indeed the nine lines, corresponding to the nine-months of gestation, shift the concept of self in each. A line-by-line reading of the poem reveals the development of carefully chosen and arranged metaphors and leads to an evaluation of the whole concept of self and metaphor. Corresponding to the first month, the "riddle" of the first line refers not only to the uncertainty about identity, but also the uncertainty of diagnosis in early pregnancy and the uncertainty of outcome, the external body revealing nothing of its inevitable changes. The nine syllables of the fine also correspond to the foreknowledge of the stages of pregnancy.

The second line, like the second month, does not manifest itself in extreme physical alterations, however great the preoccupation with these changes. The heaviness—figured in the simple, tired metaphor of the elephant—is given another dimension with the adjective of the second figure, for a "ponderous house" is not only heavy (with suggestion of something inside) but "ponderous" is also mentally weighty. The image of the ponderous house also suggests a re-evaluation of the elephant image, which may now also be identified as the animal that never forgets. More significantly, the self-identification with the standard Freudian symbol for woman also associates the pregnant self with a "container," a housing for some other being of more significance than itself.

By the third month, these metaphors of weight take on further implication. The melon on tendrils is not only fat (with the characteristically comic, disproportionately thin and unstable legs), but the word "tendrils" adds connotations to the image: too thin to bear the weight of this new situation, they threaten to collapse despite the disarming air of the stroller. Tendrils also recall the clinging of weighty fruit to a more solid and stable vine.

This weakness is forgotten in the fourth month, when the actual fetus becomes apparent, and the self-sacrifices become secondary to the joy of its existence. "Red fruit....ivory," and "fine timbers," metaphors for the infant, seem to be greeted with joyful anticipation. But the exclamation point may be misleading. For these metaphors of the infant necessitate "deconstruction" of the previous metaphors, metaphors for the mother.

To obtain ivory, the elephant must be killed. Fruit is plucked from the vine, and timbers precede or succeed the building of a house. The exclamation point, then, can be perceived as an acknowledgment of dissolution of the body or the individual psyche.

If she is "big" by the fifth month, then, it is not with any substance of her own but because of the baby's incorporation of her substance. The expansion of yeast in bread allows for no distinction between the internal and the external. This confusion is developed in the next three fines. The speaker becomes the container, the purse for what is valuable, in the sixth line, and in the seventh she perceives herself as "a means" (having lost her sense of identity), "a stage" (both the stage upon which the actor acts and a phase of the baby's life), and "a cow in calf" (in which case she is valuable only for what she produces, milk and calves). The "degeneration" of the metaphors parallels the degeneration of her self-image. By the end of this list she is not human, either to herself or to others.

In the eighth line the baby disappears, only present indirectly as a bag of unripe apples that cause illness. The emphasis is upon the speaker's own illness and unreadiness—the Fall from Eden—and all joy has gone.

Boarding a train for an uncontrollable voyage, the final metaphor for pregnancy, is also the most apt one, particularly for the moments preceding birth. The desire to escape from the body's inevitability is often strong at this point, especially in labor. But it is also an exceedingly ominous metaphor for pregnancy. Not only does it indicate a loss of control, but there is no sense of a living child. The poem concludes with sheer helplessness.

The point of the technical exercise becomes clear here, if it had not been so before. In writing a poem of nine, nine-syllable lines, the poet is contained, entirely identified, by the "nine-ness" of pregnancy. The nine-syllable fines and the nine lines of the poem contribute significantly to that feeling of "confinement," another metaphor for pregnancy.

But if Plath's form, as well as her subject, is confinement, the title becomes questionable. Why entitle a poem "Metaphors" and draw attention to the figurative language rather than the subject? It is not only that she uses metaphors, and is playing a cute game about being pregnant, nor that the poem is a metaphor for pregnancy. Because of the concept of identity of mother and child, the mother—as with the word metaphor, which contains within it the word mother—becomes linked with another as in a metaphor. "Am I tenor or am I vehicle?" the speaker seems to be asking. Do I contain these metaphors, do they help to define what I am, or am I contained in, defined by, them?

This conflict can be considered biographically, and indeed there is sufficient evidence to suggest Plath's strong ambivalence about becoming a mother. Months before "Metaphors," Plath voiced a significant terror of the loss of self and idyllic unity that having a child would bring:

> I have never in my life, except that deadly summer of 1953 and fall gone through such a black lethal two weeks. I couldn't write a word about it, although I did in my head. The horror, day by day more sure, of being preg-

nant. Remembering my growing casualness about contraception, as if it couldn't happen to me then: clang, clang, one door after another banged shut with the overhanging terror which, I know now, would end me, probably Ted, and our writing and our possible impregnable togetherness. (*Journals* 171, my emphasis)

But the couple decided to have a baby, and on the day "Metaphors" was written, Plath discovered that her recent attempts to become pregnant had not succeeded.

Friday, March 20, Yesterday a nadir of sorts. Woke up to cat's early mewling around six. Cramps Pregnant I thought Not, such luck. After a long 40 day period of hope, the old blood cramps and spilt fertility. I had lulled myself into a fattening calm and this was a blow... I'd like four in a row. Then dopey, and then cramps all day. (*Journals* 272)

This desire to conceive—increased, her biographers note, by her jealousy of her friend, Marcia Brown, who had recently given birth to twins (Butscher 265), and modified by her awareness that Anne Sexton had suffered her first breakdown following the birth of her daughter (Wagner 159)—is often considered a compromise, a means of fulfilling her identity in her prefeminist times. In "Metaphors," however, it is clear that Plath realized the dangers of identity inherent in maternity and used the techniques and language of poetry to contain them.

Works Cited

Butscher, Edward. *Sylvia Plath, Method and Madness*. New York: Pocket Books, 1977.

Ostriker, Alicia. *Stealing the Language: The Emergence of Women's Poetry in America*. Boston: Beacon, 1986.

Plath, Sylvia. *The Collected Poems*. Ed. Ted Hughes. New York: Harper, 1981.

———. *The Journals of Sylvia Plath*. Ed. Ted Hughes. New York: Dial, 1982.

Stevenson, Anne. *Bitter Fame: A Life of Sylvia Plath*. New York: Houghton Mifflin, 1989.

Vendler, Helen. "Sylvia Plath." *Part of Nature, Part of Us*. Cambridge: Harvard U P, 1980.

Wagner-Martin, Linda. *Sylvia Plath: A Biography*. New York: Simon and Schuster, 1987.

"Daddy": Sylvia Plath's Debt to Anne Sexton[1]

Heather Cam

"Daddy" is one of Sylvia Plath's most anthologised poems, and, some might say, one of her most quintessential; yet this seemingly original and

[1]Heather Cam, "'Daddy': Sylvia Plath's Debt to Anne Sexton," *American Literature* 59.3 (Oct. 1987): 429–32.

idiosyncratic work is deeply indebted to an early, virtually unknown, confessional poem by Anne Sexton:

"My Friend, My Friend"

For M. W. K. who hesitates each time she sees a young girl wearing The Cross.

Who will forgive me for the things I do?
With no special legend or God to refer to,
With my calm white pedigree, my yankee kin,
I think it would be better to be a Jew.

I forgive you for what you did not do,
I am impossibly guilty. Unlike you,
My friend, I can not blame my origin
With no special legend or God to refer to.

They wear The Crucifix as they are meant to do.
Why do their little crosses trouble you?
The effigies that I have made are genuine,
(I think it would be better to be a Jew).

Watching my mother slowly die I knew
My first release. I wish some ancient bugaboo
Followed me. But my sin is always my sin.
With no special legend or God to refer to.

Who will forgive me for the things I do?
To have your reasonable hurt to belong to
Might ease my trouble like liquor or aspirin.
I think it would be better to be a Jew.

And if I lie, I lie because I love you,
Because I am bothered by the things I do,
Because your hurt invades my calm white skin:
With no special legend or God to refer to,
I think it would be better to be a Jew[2]

"My Friend, My Friend," appeared in the *Antioch Review* during the summer of 1959. However Plath may have seen the poem some months earlier, late in 1958 or early in 1959, during one of Robert Lowell's workshops at Boston University, or after one of his classes when Plath, Sexton, and George Starbuck customarily retired to the Ritz Bar to continue their discussion of poetry informally over martinis.[3]

During this time Sexton was assembling her first book of poems, *To Bedlam and Part Way Back* (1960). She set Plath an example by tackling

[2]Anne Sexton, "My Friend, My Friend," *Antioch Review*, 19 (1959), 150. Copyright © 1959 by Anne Sexton. Reprinted by permission of the Sterling Lord Agency, Inc.
[3]See Anne Sexton, "The Barfly Ought to Sing," *The Art of Sylvia Plath: A Symposium*, edited by Charles Newman (London: Faber & Faber, 1970), pp. 174–81.

536 Men and Women

private and deeply personal material in an outspoken and colloquial fashion in the first person. Plath later acknowledged the liberating influence that Sexton and Lowell had on her poetic development:

> I've been very excited by what I feel is the new breakthrough that came with, say, Robert Lowell's *Life Studies* [1959], this intense breakthrough into very serious, very personal, emotional experience which I feel has been partly taboo....I think particularly...Ann Saxton [sic]...is an extremely emotional and feeling young woman and her poems are wonderfully craftsman-like poems and yet they have a kind of emotional and psychological depth which I think is something perhaps quite new, quite exciting.[4]

Both this statement, made in the course of a BBC interview on 30 October 1962, and "Daddy," written on the twelfth of that month, date from the most intensely creative period of Plath's brief life. During October and November 1962 she wrote over half of *Winter Trees* (1971) and *Ariel* (1965). It is for the poems of this period that she is best remembered, and perhaps for none better than "Daddy," the work that draws so extensively upon "My Friend, My Friend."

Sexton's poem is dedicated to M. W. K., making it plausible to say that it is addressed to Sexton's friend, Maxine Winokur Kumin. This is reinforced by the fact that, similar to Kumin, the friend in the poem is Jewish. The speaker claims to be without religion, "With no special legend or God to refer to," yet she is burdened by her sense of guilt. It pervades her life, coming to its fullest expression in her account of her mother's death, and crucially in the speaker's attendant feelings of liberation and "release." It is the awareness of her inescapable guilt that creates the poem's focus and accounts for the speaker's deep need to forgive and in turn to be forgiven.

"Daddy" is also addressed in the first person to someone close to the speaker. Undoubtedly Otto Plath and Ted Hughes inspired "Daddy," but they are no more a Nazi Daddy nor "a man in black with a Meinkampf look" than Plath is a gypsy Tarot mistress who feels herself to be Jewish. Plath used and distorted autobiographical facts to portray a sado-masochistic and, ultimately, mutually destructive relationship. In so doing, she found Sexton's model useful.

For its own purposes "Daddy" borrows and slightly alters rhythms, rhymes, words, and lines from the early Sexton poem. "My Friend, My Friend" has an AABA rhyme-scheme throughout its six stanzas, with the exception of the last stanza which adds a line with an A-rhyme to the basic quatrain. These A-rhymes repeat and echo in "Daddy." Plath borrows Sexton's "do," "you," and "Jew," adding ingenious variants of her own: "shoe," "Achoo," "blue," "du," "true," "through," "who," and "glue." Of particular note is Plath's "gobbledygoo" to Sexton's "bugaboo."

Sexton's quatrains end in alternate refrains, the second and fourth lines of the opening stanza: "With no special legend or God to refer to"

[4]Sylvia Plath, *The Poet Speaks*, edited by Peter Orr (London: Routledge & Kegan Paul, 1966), pp. 167–68.

and "I think it would be better to be a Jew." The second of these refrains is twice reworked by Plath, becoming in "Daddy": "I think I may well be a Jew" and "I may be a bit of a Jew." Furthermore, "With my calm white pedigree, my yankee kin, / I think it would be better to be a Jew," from the first quatrain of "My Friend, My Friend," clearly serves as the model for the lines leading into Plath's second variation on the "Jewish" refrain:

> With my gypsy ancestress and my weird luck
> And my Taroc pack and my Taroc pack
> I may be a bit of a Jew.

Here Plath's alterations are exotic and expansive, allowing the speaker to chant about her dark arts.

Another similarity is the concern with the death of, and subsequent release from, a parent. In "Daddy" however it takes twenty years of suffocating suffering and finally an exorcism and an elaborate ritual—the stake in the heart of vampire-like Daddy—to make him lie still enough, the persona hopes, to allow her to get "through" to personal freedom. Daddy's death is far more drawn out, dramatic, tortuous, and sinister than that of the mother in Sexton's poem. The death brings Plath's poem to its close, as the persona gasps her valediction, "Daddy, daddy, you bastard, I'm through," and collapses, exhausted by her efforts, into a world without Daddy. On this disturbing threshold the poem ends, leaving the reader teetering and searching for a foothold on the final and troubling word "through." In contrast, Sexton's poem turns back on itself, taking the reader back through the poem's closed circuit of guilt. This process is nicely captured in the closing couplet, which brings together the poem's alternating refrains.

It is in such differences in treatment that Plath reveals her true artistry. Clearly she drew upon her former classmate's poem as she wrote "Daddy," and her debt to Sexton is considerable. Acknowledging the debt, however, is not to detract from Plath's achievement. Whereas "My Friend, My Friend" is an unexceptional, early example of Sexton's confessional poetry, "Daddy" is a brilliant act of exorcism from Plath's glittering late period. Despite Plath's use of a source in the composition of "Daddy," the poem remains distinctly and uniquely hers.

COLOSSAL INFLUENCES ON SYLVIA PLATH[1]

THOMAS DILWORTH

A recurring image in Sylvia Plath's poetry, the statue first attains colossal proportions in her 1959 poem "Colossus," where it symbolizes her father. A similar gigantic statue appears in her most famous poem, "Daddy" (1962), in which her father is a toppled: "Ghastly statue with one

[1]Thomas Dilworth, "Colossal Influences on Sylvia Plath," *English Language Notes* 40.4 (June 2006): 77–78.

grey toe/Big as a Frisco seal/And a head in the freakish Atlantic" (lines 9–11).[2] And the motif of the colossus reappears in the gigantic supine figure in her late poem "Gulliver." Beginning in "Colossus," the image of the colossal statue seems influenced by Dylan Thomas and inspired primarily by Alfred Hitchcock.

Addressing the gigantic statue of her father in the first stanza of "The Colossus," Plath writes, "Mulebray, pig-grunt and bawdy cackles / Proceed from your great lips" (lines 3–4).[3] The first of these animal sounds echoes the opening of Dylan Thomas's "After the Funeral," a poem memorializing his aunt, which begins, "After the funeral, mule praises, brays." In his poem, Thomas imagines his aunt as a gigantic "skyward statue / With the wild breast and blessed and giant skull" (lines 27–28).[4] Plath's general and obvious early debt to Dylan Thomas makes this poem a likely influence on "The Colossus." But Plath would have known Dylan Thomas's poem for years, and so it probably did not provide the imaginative impetus for the image of the gigantic statue in "The Colossus."

In a sense, Plath had been moving toward "The Colossus" since her father died in 1940, when she was eight years old. But the poem first became the object of conscious deliberation in the spring of 1959. She had visited her father's grave on March 8, and records in her notebook her "temptation to dig him up. To prove he existed and really was dead. How far gone would he be?"[5] And on April 23, she records her intention, "Must do justice to my father's grave."[6] She wrote "The Colossus" in mid October 1959, implying its existence for the first time in her journal on October 19 of that year, where she contemplates entitling a new book "THE COLOSSUS and other poems."[7] It is likely that the experience which made it possible to "do justice" to her father's grave in "The Colossus" was a viewing of Alfred Hitchcock's now famous film *North by Northwest*, which premiered on July 1, 1959, a few months before Plath wrote the poem.[8]

She liked going to movies. In her journals and letters, Plath makes no mention of having seen *North by Northwest*, but, like most of us, she saw many films that she did not record having seen.[9] According to her journal entry for March 30, 1956, on that day in the company of friends visit-

[2]Sylvia Plath, *The Collected Poems*, edited by Ted Hughes (London: Faber and Faber, 1981): 222.

[3]Plath, *The Collected Poems*, 129.

[4]Dylan Thomas, *The Collected Poems* (New York: New Directions, 1971): 96.

[5]Sylvia Plath, *The Unabridged Journals*, edited by Karen V. Kukil (New York: Anchor Books, 2000): 473.

[6]*The Unabridged Journals*, 477.

[7]According to the November 4 entry in her journal, she wrote "The Colossus" immediately before writing her sequence "Poem for a Birthday," which she had not yet written on October 22, according to her journal entry for that day. *The Unabridged Journals*, 518, 523, 532.

[8]On the day of the premier, *Variety* reviewed the film.

[9]For information on the journals and unpublished letters of Plath and the unpublished letters of Ted Hughes, I am grateful to Karen Kukil at Smith College; Rebecca Cape at the Lilly Library, University of Indiana; and Sarah Stanton, Emory University Library.

ing Paris, she went to see "Grace Kelly in Hitchcock's fine technicolor film/'To Catch a Thief.'"[10] In July or August 1959, while she and Hughes were touring the United States and Canada, she could easily have seen *North by Northwest*, which was then playing in all cities and many small towns. Since they were travelling by themselves without the company of friends and the distraction and entertainment friends provide, it seems most likely that she saw Hitchcock's new film then. She may also have seen it in September or early October while at Yaddo, in Saratoga Springs. She does record on November 1, 1959, driving with friends nineteen miles from Yaddo to Scotia to see Bergman's *The Magician* and, in that journal entry, recalls having previously seen Bergman's *The Seventh Seal*.[11] She could have seen *North by Northwest* there or at nearby Schenectady or, for that matter, in Saratoga Springs. Absence in her journals of mention of seeing it is no indication that she did not see it, since the journals are far from being a complete diary. She makes no journal entries during the three months of her tour with Hughes—from July 1 to September 25—and only nineteen entries during the fifty-one days of their stay at Yaddo, from September 25 to November 15.

Aspects of "The Colossus" that resonate with *North by Northwest* include colossal statuary and what Freud calls the Electra complex. In "Colossus" the poet lives on the fallen, broken statue of her father:

> Scaling little ladders with gluepots and pails of Lysol
> I crawl like an ant in mourning
> Over the weedy acres of your brow
> To mend the immense skull-plates and clear
> The bald, white tumuli of your eyes,
> . . .
> Nights, I squat in the cornucopia
> Of your left ear, out of the wind...(lines 11–15, 24–25)[12]

Between these two references to the immense statue, Plath acknowledges her Electra complex by writing, "A blue sky out of the Oresteia / Arches above us" (lines 20–21). In the second play of Aeschylus's Oresteia, Electra visits her father's grave (as Plath had in February) and joins her brother, Orestes, in determining to kill their mother to avenge their murdered father. In her spoken introduction to "Daddy" for a BBC reading, Plath says, "Here is a poem spoken by a girl with an Electra complex. Her father died while she thought he was a God."[13] "The Colossus" was first collected in her book titled *Colossus and Other Poems* (New York: Knopf, 1957), which was type-set, as the concluding "Note on the Type" indicates, using the font named Electra.[14]

[10]*The Unabridged Journals*, 563.
[11]*The Unabridged Journals*, 522.
[12]Plath, *The Collected Poems*, 129, 130.
[13]Plath, *The Collected Poems*, 293 n. 183.
[14]For pointing out that the type is Electra, my thanks to Eric Hewett, a fourth-year English major at the University of Windsor.

Plath would have seen in Hitchcock's film aspects relating to her own life. As a major in English at Smith College and a reader of English Literature at Cambridge, she would have recognized the title of the film as an allusion to Hamlet telling Guildenstern, "I am but mad north-north-west" (*Hamlet* II, ii, 378). It is a title likely to intrigue a woman with a history of mental illness. Most readers will remember that, in the film, Eve Kendall, played by Eva-Marie Saint, dressed in elegant business suits, as had Sylvia Plath during her summer as guest editor for *Mademoiselle* fashion magazine. She was photographed wearing just such a suit while interviewing Elizabeth Bowen for *Mademoiselle* on May 26, 1953.[15] In the film, Eve is a light-haired blonde, like Plath when she dyed her hair in the years before her marriage and, after that, when her hair was bleached by the summer sun. Plath would have seen in Eve's then cinematically unconventional sexual aggressiveness a reflection of her own uninhibited behaviour. Eve's primary sexual relationship is with an older man, the foreign spy Phillip Vandamm, played by James Mason. (Saint was then thirty-five but could pass for thirty. Mason was fifty but seems older, in his mid fifties. Plath's father died at age fifty-five.) As an older man and an authority figure—the wealthy head of a spy ring—Vandamm seems, in relationship to Eve, a father figure. Their relationship corresponds to Plath's emotionally incestuous relationship with her foreign-born father, who, in "Daddy," would become a Nazi. In mid-movie, Eve falls in love with Roger Thornhill, played by Cary Grant. He was then fifty-five but appears forty. As "the other man," tall, handsome, younger, British-born (Grant, not Thornhill), he corresponds to Ted Hughes. Eve is actually an operative of the CIA and, as such, has in her life a second dominant older male, one who is certainly a father-figure. This is the elderly CIA master agent played by Leo G. Carroll, who was then sixty-seven. He is referred to simply and repeatedly as "the Professor"—a title that would have identified him, for Plath, with her father, who had been a professor of biology at Boston College.

These striking affinities with her own life and psychopathology—of which, after years of therapy, she was fully aware may have given her a more than superficial interest in the film, but what most appears to have influenced her poetry is the film's famous finale on Mount Rushmore, where Eve and Roger flee foreign agents by climbing down the colossal faces of the American presidents. Most prominent of these faces which is twice shown in profile and once full-face—is that of Washington, "the father of his country." Eve and Roger are shown climbing down the left side of his face while an enemy agent descends on the right side. Just below Washington's face, an enemy agent pushes Eve over a cliff, and Roger reaches out and grasps her hand, saving her from falling to her death. In what is literally a cliff-hanger—he grips the dangling Eve with one hand and the cliff's edge with the other—Vandamm's henchman, Leonard (played by Martin Landau), begins grinding with his foot the hand with which Roger grips the cliff edge. When all seems lost, the benign

[15]*The Unabridged Journals*, photo insert between 212 and 213.

father-figure, the Professor, comes to the rescue, arriving in the nick of time with a policeman whom he orders to shoot the henchman. The Professor's arrival is an instance of father-figure ex machina—Daddy to the rescue—precisely what Plath in "The Colossus" has longed for until, at the end of the poem, she loses hope in his arrival by ship: "No longer do I listen for the scrape of a keel / On the blank stones of the landing" (lines 29–30).[16] Apparently this daughter is an incestuous Penelope, the evocation of The Odyssey matching her earlier allusion to The Oresteia.

The prominence in the film of father-figures and the colossal face of Washington, the father of his and Plath's country, and the saving arrival of the benign fatherly Professor would have been powerfully suggestive for Plath. What seems in the film to be a duality between helpful and hurtful father-figures would also have been suggestive for Plath, whose attitude towards her father was ambiguous, especially in "Daddy," which is, at once, a love poem and a hate poem.

[16]Plath, *The Collected Poems*, 130.

Sylvia Plath---Madwoman or Genius?

Natasha Harden

1   Sylvia Plath was a remarkable twentieth century American poet. Plath's attempts to exorcise the oppressive male figures that haunted her life served as one of the fundamental themes in her poetry. Her poetry is a good example of how suffering can be transformed within traditional poetic contexts. She dealt with her problems though expressing her feelings through poetry, though what was expressed in her poems also foretold her fate in suicide. Perhaps most people do not see dying as an art, but to Sylvia Plath, it was an aspect of art that she intended to master, and master it she did. Sylvia Plath's life, like that of a person suffering from manic depression, constantly jumped between heaven and hell. Her seemingly perfect exterior hid a confused and deeply troubled spirit. Yet as she transformed her feelings into art, her sense of humor, though often dark humor, kept her works from becoming exercises in self pity. Two of her poems, "Daddy" and "Lady

Lazarus," both of which contain autobiographical elements, vividly portray her views of death.

2   A closer look at Plath's childhood and personal experiences removes some element of mystery from her writings. One central character to Sylvia Plath's poems is her father, Professor Otto Emile Plath. According to Butscher, Otto Plath was diabetic and refused to stay away from foods restricted by his doctor (12). This arrogance eventually caused an infection in his toe, which led to the amputation of his toe and finally his leg. In 1940, Otto Plath died. The knowledge that her father could have postponed his death left Sylvia Plath with a feeling that his demise was a "'deliberate' act of betrayal" (Butscher 13). Instead of reaching out to other people for comfort, she isolated herself with writing as her only expressive outlet. Remarkably, Plath published her first poem when she was only eight in the *Boston Sunday Herald*. As a result of her father's death, Sylvia was flooded with feelings of depression and scorn and thoughts of suicide, which generated her fixation on death (Butscher 14). In "Daddy," she writes:

> You stand at the blackboard, daddy,
>
> In the picture I have of you,
>
> A cleft in your chin instead of your foot
>
> But no less a devil for that, no not
>
> Any less the black man who
>
> Bit my pretty red heart in two
>
> I was ten when they buried you
>
> At twenty I tried to die
>
> And get back, back, back to you.

I thought even the bones would do.

(51-60)

3   This poem is a figurative drama about mourning, about
the human impulse to keep a dead loved one alive in the
emotions. At the time of her father's death, Sylvia saw him
as a "God" (Kenner 507). Not ready to be without a father,
Plath was unable to let go of his memory. In order to get
back to him, she felt as though she had to resurrect him
and then kill him a second time (Cam 537). In real life,
she first attempted suicide at the age of twenty-one to
reach him and then married a man, Ted Hughes, who resembled
him, all to no avail. The death of her father thus provoked
Sylvia's obsession with death, and the poem "Daddy" plainly
reflects that fact (Cam 536).

4   One of Plath's most famous poems, "Lady Lazarus,"
published in 1962, further demonstrates her preoccupation
with death: "I have done it again / One year in every
ten / I manage it" (1-3). Here, Plath, like her narrator,
seems to be boasting about her previous encounters with
death. The first death was her father's that occurred
when she was eight; the second encounter with death was
her suicide attempt at age twenty-one; finally, she
successfully killed herself at the age of thirty-one.
Later in the poem, she revels in her suicide attempts
(and possibly in anticipation of her actual suicide),
saying:

Dying

Is an art, like everything else.

I do it exceptionally well.

I do it so it feels like hell

```
I do it so it feels real.

I guess you could say I've had a call.

(43-48)
```

According to Van Dyne, throughout these lines, Plath
develops her madwoman "persona." Extremely successful
throughout her life, Sylvia, like her narrator, seems to
believe that she can also die exceptionally well. She means
not that she has literally died, of course, but rather that
she has already killed herself in a figurative sense. The
narrator arranges "her own resurrection," and "demonstrates
she can do without God's intervention" (524). According to
Van Dyne, this was Plath's attempt "to free herself from
old relational bonds" (521).

"Daddy" and "Lady Lazarus" strongly reflect Sylvia's
attitude towards death. Plath writes about suicide in much
the same tone that she used for any dangerous activity that
pushes the normal limits: a tone that is urgent, even fierce,
yet altogether without self-pity. She seemed to view death as
a physical challenge that she needed to overcome (Van Dyne
528). She spoke of suicide with a wry "detachment," and
without any mention of the suffering or drama inherent in the
act (Butscher 336). Toward the end of her life, Sylvia began
to write more and more insistently, as if she knew the end
was drawing near. Illness, loneliness, depression, despair
over the unfaithfulness of her husband and the demands of two
small children were too much for her. Sylvia Plath went down
to her kitchen, sealed the doorways and windows as best she
could with towels, opened the oven, laid her head in it, and
turned on the gas (Butscher 363). Plath's suicide established
her place in the world of poetry.

7   Though she was a brilliant, attractive woman, Sylvia Plath led a tragic life. For many years, Plath was filled with feelings of solitude and depression. Sylvia Plath's childhood--which was scarred from the demise of her father, her feelings of isolation, and her obsession with death--is reflected in her work. These personal influences, complicated by the problems in her marriage, helped shape her writing. Yet her wonderful facility with words, her vivid metaphors, and her shocking allusions have made her one of America's fascinating authors. Would one consider Sylvia Plath a genius or a madwoman? Well, that depends on the reader. Her writing has touched and continues to touch a great number of people, so does it really matter?

[New page]   Works Cited

Butscher, Edward. <u>Sylvia Plath: Method and Madness</u>. New York: Seabury Press, 1976.

Cam, Heather. "'Daddy': Sylvia Plath's Debt to Anne Sexton." <u>American Literature</u> 59.3 (Oct. 1987): 429-32. Henderson, Day, and Waller. 534-37.

Henderson, Gloria Mason, Bill Day, and Sandra Stevenson Waller, eds. <u>Literature and Ourselves: A Thematic Introduction for Readers and Writers</u>. 5th ed. New York: Longman, 2006.

Kenner, Hugh. "Sincerity Kills." <u>Sylvia Plath: New Views on the Poetry</u>. Ed. Gary Lane. N. p.: Johns Hopkins UP, 1979. Rpt. in <u>Sylvia Plath: Modern Critical Views</u>. Ed. Harold Bloom. New York: Chelsea House, 1989. 67-78. Henderson, Day, and Waller. 506-16.

Plath, Sylvia. "Daddy." <u>The Collected Poems</u>. Ed. Ted Hughes. New York: Harper & Row, 1981.

---. "Lady Lazarus." <u>The Collected Poems</u>. Ed. Ted Hughes. New

York: Harper & Row, 1981.

---. <u>The Journals of Sylvia Plath</u>. The Dial Press, New York:

1982.

Van Dyne, Susan. "Fueling the Phoenix Fire: The Manuscripts

of Sylvia Plath's 'Lady Lazarus.' <u>The Massachusetts</u>

<u>Review</u> 24.2 (Sum. 1983). Rpt. in <u>Sylvia Plath: Modern</u>

<u>Critical Views</u>. Ed. Harold Bloom. New York: Chelsea

House, 1989. 133-47. Henderson, Day, and Waller. 516-29.

Suggestions for Exploring, Writing, and Persuading

1. Research the allusions to either mythology or history in two or more of the poems, and write an essay showing how these allusions add to the depth of meaning and universality of the poems. Use one or more of the secondary sources in the casebook.
2. Contrast Plath's response to loss in "Daddy" with that revealed in Lahiri's "A Temporary Matter" or Mukherjee's "The Management of Grief."
3. Write an essay about a person you know who, after personal disaster, made himself or herself a completely different person as if reborn.
4. Select two poems and carefully examine the images that describe reflections—such as mirrors or lakes—or the images for light and dark. Then, using one or more of the critical essays in the casebook, write an essay describing the effect of these images on the **tone** of the poem or giving your interpretation of their meaning.
5. Review the movie *North By Northwest*, read the essay "Colossal Influences on Sylvia Plath," and use both to argue that Plath was or was not influenced by the movie.
6. Use one or more of Plath's poems and at least one of the critical essays to write a literary analysis of one of the following topics:
     Plath's ambivalent feelings about her father or Plath's feelings about men
     Plath's feelings about death—either her own death or another's
     Plath's unusual sense of humor and its effect on her portrayal of herself or of her female narrators
     Plath's vivid use of images to create tone
     Plath's use of surprising or shocking allusions and their effect on tone and meaning

Men and Women: Suggestions for Writing

1. Choose a character in one of the works in this unit and explain how this character dominates his or her spouse.

2. Several of the poems in this section deal with courtship. Use two or more of these poems to write an essay about the rituals of courtship.

3. Compare and/or contrast the problems faced by women and their methods of dealing with the problems in *A Doll's House* or "The Gilded Six-Bits."

4. Several of the poets use humor in their depiction of the male-female relationship. After rereading the poems and reviewing your own knowledge and experience about such relationships, write a humorous poem, story, or essay describing the complexities of such relationships.

5. Define irony. Using at least two selections from this unit, show how the authors use irony to enrich the meaning of their works.

6. Select two or three of the love poems in this unit and write an essay explaining what attributes of the loved one have caused the love to last and deepen.

Men and Women: Writing About Film

1. The essayists in this unit all have distinct ideas about the nature of male-female relationships. Select two essayists and consider what they might say about the man/woman relationships in your favorite film.

2. A romantic relationship is often at the center of popular Hollywood films. Compare and contrast the roles of men and women in the romantic relationship in two films from very different genres (for instance: action/adventure compared to romantic comedy; thriller compared to family drama; detective movie compared to animated feature). What do these movies teach us about romantic love? Consider issues of who is choosing whom and why, what kinds of communications the characters have, how well they seem to know each other, or whether there is any indication of how the future relationship will work.

3. Romantic comedies (*Sleepless in Seattle, Along Came Polly, Alex and Emma, Deliver Us From Eva, Bridget Jones' Diary, Sideways*) are staples of the popular film market, but why do we like them so much? What do they offer us that real life does not? If you have ever been in a serious relationship, what do the films add to or leave out of the actual dynamics of relationship? Compare and contrast your experiences or observations with the fictional world of a specific film.

4. Watch one of the recent films about a real man or woman, such as *A Beautiful Mind* (John Nash), *A Stroke of Genius* (Bobby Jones), *Sylvia* (Sylvia Plath), *Auto Focus* (Bob Crane), *Confessions of a Dangerous Mind* (Chuck Barris), *Frida* (Frida Kahlo), or *Ray* (Ray Charles), and examine the ways in which the creators of the film select details of the person's life to present in order to make an artistic presentation.

5. Select at least two of the film or stage interpretations of Nora or of Torvald, and in an essay, discuss the ways in which the performances of different actresses or actors help to mold the audiences' perception of these characters.

Fear and Loss

A scene from *The Joy Luck Club*. Buena Vista/Photofest.

When thousands of people died as the twin towers of the World Trade Center collapsed after a terrorist attack on September 11, 2001, our entire nation stood still, watching in outraged grief. However much we may have known in our hearts that we are always and everywhere vulnerable, the terrorist attacks on September 11 came as a shock. Mere quivering, soft, easily crushed masses that we are, how are we to live with the knowledge of such frightening vulnerability? Such questions have haunted writers since time immemorial, puzzling the ever-patient Job, the great tragedians of ancient Athens, and religious thinkers of quite diverse cultures and times. And they have haunted us as we have sought to respond to the tragedy of September 11th. The President and Congress along with vast numbers of lesser officials worked feverishly to build a security apparatus that might protect us from future attack. People now willingly wait in long lines for security checks at airports, hoping that such measures will protect them.

However, no matter how we try to protect ourselves with security systems, storm warnings, airbags, and quake-resistant structures, violence constantly threatens us. We are all vulnerable, fearing and suffering pain and heartbreak, the loss of loved ones, the loss of memory or physical ability as we age, the constant threat of accidental death or violent assault. The threat may come from outside in the ghastly devastation of war as in Wilfred Owen's poem *"Dulce et Decorum Est."* Perhaps more frighteningly, it may threaten us from within ourselves as well as from without, as it does the narrator in Madison Smartt Bell's "Customs of the Country," who reveals and must ultimately face the violence within that has led her to abuse her son and to assault the wife-abuser next door. Othello, in Shakespeare's tragedy, twisted and manipulated by the evil Iago, struggles with jealousy so violent that it leads him to kill his innocent wife, Desdemona. Like Othello, we may live in an illusion of security until the seductive face of evil draws us into its violent maw.

How we face fear and loss, our common vulnerability, defines us as people. As the narrator in Bharati Mukherjee's eloquent story "The Management of Grief" says, "we must all grieve in our own way"; even so, we must all handle fear in our own ways whether with the extraordinary courage in the face of doom of a Todd Beamer (leader in forcing al Quaeda terrorists to ditch UA flight 93 in Pennsylvania, on September 11, 2001), with the crazed rage of Othello, or with the insistence that our presumed tormenters suffer punishment as in "Coyote v. Acme." Confronted by the terrible brutality of Auschwitz, Pinhas, a rabbi in Elie Wiesel's essay "Yom Kippur: The Day without Forgiveness," doubts whether God knows what He is doing.

Others, like Dylan Thomas's speaker in "Do Not Go Gentle into That Good Night," may fight death with every ounce of will and courage they can muster. Still others, like Shakespeare's Othello or like the couple in Arna Bontemps "A Summer Tragedy," may choose self-inflicted death over a life consumed with humiliation or poverty or guilt. Yet others may face loss with stoic grace as did the Reagan family as the nation mourned with them in dignified ceremony the loss of their father and the former president.

However it may confront them, great literature does not ignore the horrors of evil in the world. Great literature reflects the extraordinary variety of our responses to them.

Writing About Fear and Loss

As you prepare your essay on one or more of the works in this section, you should consider that just as each genre allows you to take different approaches to the work, so too does each kind of essay. You might, for example, write an expository essay examining the language of fear. You might examine one or more of the different kinds of discrimination portrayed in the works in this unit: for example, religious discrimination in Wiesel's "Yom Kippur," racial discrimination in "On the Subway," or class discrimination against the homeless in Hughes's "Drama for Winter Nights." You might prefer a comparison-contrast essay on the attitudes toward death expressed in Thomas's "Do Not Go Gentle into That Good Night." Because so much excellent scholarship on *Othello* is available, you might write a researched expository essay on the evil of Iago or a cause-and-effect essay on the changes in Othello's language and personality.

Another possibility would be a persuasive essay. Many of the essays in this unit lend themselves to argumentation in answer to some of the following questions. Should there be limits to such frivolous lawsuits as that in "Coyote v. Acme"? Perhaps you might argue after reading Cooper's essay "Terrorism: The Problem of Definition Revisited" what your definition of terrorism is. How effective are personal acts of defiance or suicide on those who are left behind as in Wiesel's "Yom Kippur: The Day Without Forgiveness" or Bontemps' "A Summer Tragedy"? From the fiction unit, you could argue that the narrator in Bell's "Customs of the Country" does or does not deserve custody of her son. Or the question of culpability would make a good argumentative essay. Is the town culpable in any way for the murder of Homer in "A Rose for Emily" or Willis for the death of Rafa in "The Runt"? Does everyone wear a mask to disguise his or her true feelings as suggested by Dunbar's "We Wear the Mask"? Each section could provide lively argumentative essays that provoke interesting reading and reporting.

When Gael Fowler was asked to write a documented essay using the casebook on Amy Tan, she began by reading both stories and all of the critical essays. At first she considered writing on both of the stories, but as she tried several thesis statements, she could not decide on one that included both. She finally chose to write on the types of death in "Heart."

Gael wrote her first rough draft on paper but soon discarded that copy. She actually started several essays but in the end went back to her original idea. She wrote a partially completed draft of the essay on the computer and sent it to her professor by e-mail to see if she was following the directions of the assignment. The professor suggested adding a few different aspects to the paper. She also said that Gael needed to make it clear that the stories told by Precious Auntie were a retelling of things that happened in the past. At this point, Gael added to the introduction a part about what had happened to the main character of the story. The new version, because it focused more on the main character, made a better essay. Gael felt that this change caused the paper as a whole to flow more smoothly. This revision also solved a problem she had faced about the verb tenses because the whole paper now was written in present tense, except for the quotations. Next she polished the essay to make it read more smoothly. Her original conclusion had to be rearranged and reworded, but the content remained essentially the same. Gael chose her title after she wrote the first draft. Her final essay is included at the end of the casebook.

ESSAYS

H. H. A. Cooper (b.1928)

*H. H. A. Cooper has studied and written about counterter-
rorism and methods of survival for more than five decades.
He directed the National Advisory Committee Task Force on
Disorders and Terrorism from 1974 to 1977 and served as
the Director of the Criminal Law Education and Research
Center and Deputy Director of the Center of Forensic Psychiatry of New York University. President of Nuevevidas
International, Inc., a Texas consulting company, he also
teaches at the University of Texas at Dallas.*

TERRORISM: THE PROBLEM OF DEFINITION REVISITED (2001)

1   With the advent of the new millennium, whatever one's preference for the
mathematics of the event, a certain nostalgia for the past is inevitable.
Although it is still difficult for many of us to adjust to no longer living in
the 20th century, it seems even harder for others to let go of even the most
recent of bygone memories. As the century raced to its anticlimactic close,
a wave of recall swept through the media worldwide, made possible by
new technologies that have given potent meaning to the yet ill-defined term
globalization. Amid this feverish search for the most memorable this and
the most renowned that, the sensitive observer might discern a hankering
for earlier times, a kind of golden age in which everything was simpler,
much easier to understand and, to use appropriate *fin de siecle* terminology, less stressful. No examination of these impressions in general is
essayed here. Yet, it is of some importance to notice them in relation to the
present topic if for no other reason than to offer a pertinent rejoinder. It
can be stated with absolute certainty that there has never been, since the
topic began to command serious attention, some golden age in which terrorism was easy to define or, for that matter, to comprehend. And, as we
plunge gaily into the brave new world of the 21st century, there is not the
slightest reason to suppose that the problem of definition, or as it was once
described, the problem of the problem of definition (Cooper, 1978), will
come any closer to sensible resolution. With that solemn caveat in place,
let us proceed to consider how, variously, we may come to define terrorism or at least know it when we see it in the coming decades.

Definition Is Truly an Art

2   Parenthetically, we must deal here with what is implied in the process of
definition itself. Definition is truly an art. The artist seeks to represent,

in concrete or abstract terms, something he or she has conceptualized or observed so as to give it some meaning of a distinctive character. The resultant work is a vehicle of communication for the thought or revelation that the artist seeks to convey to others. The central problem in the process is that no two human beings ever see the same thing, however simple, in exactly the same light or from the same standpoint. There is rarely, if ever, an exact correspondence of interpretation, and the introduction of but the slightest complexity can alter the meaning intended by the artist. Most ordinary, social communication is imprecise by nature. It simply is not necessary that we define our terms with exactitude; it suffices that we are generally understood. Of course, misunderstandings abound, especially between the genders and persons of differing status, culture, occupation, education, and the like. This is sometimes a source of irritation and occasionally cause for amusement, but it is not often of great consequence. Yet, in serious discourse, especially on matters involving a potential for substantial disagreement or those bearing controversial or emotional overtones, the closest correspondence of understanding as to the meaning of the language employed is imperative. If we are discussing fruit, and I believe you are talking about apples when in fact you are trying to convey to me that you are referring to oranges, we are not going to get very far without timely clarification. With respect to terrorism, there is among the many participants to the discussion no agreement on the basic nature of the fruit under consideration. For some, it will always, unalterably be apples; for others, with equal rigor, it will remain oranges. No amount of sophistry or the introduction of other varietals will be helpful in resolving the issue of meaning. One person's terrorist will ever remain another's freedom fighter. The process of definition is wholly frustrated by the presence of irreconcilable antagonisms.

A Definition of Terrorism

3   Hope springs eternal in the human breast, and perhaps for this reason alone, so many conferences and writings on the subject of terrorism begin with the obligatory, almost ritualistic recitation by the presenter of some preferred definition of terrorism. This is not wholly an exercise in futility; whatever the discrepancies detected by others, the definitions at least provide starting points for debate. The search has always been for one all-embracing statement that could stand at least a chance of gaining a high degree of acceptance by others as well as covering a majority of the bases. It can be reasonably confidently asserted that this procedure will continue unaltered as we transit the 21st century. In a similar spirit, then, the following definition of terrorism is offered here so that we may have a basis for reflection on the problems of terrorism and how it is likely to present itself in the new millennium.

4   Terrorism is the intentional generation of massive fear by human beings for the purpose of securing or maintaining control over other human beings.

5   This definition evolved over some 25 years of teaching about the topic
of terrorism in a university setting, and during that time, it has undergone
a number of small refinements as experience has suggested. Other definitions have similarly been subject to modification as those who pro-
pounded them sought to meet criticisms extended by others and to
perfect the concepts enshrined in the words employed. In a very real
sense, all the earlier definitions had to be subject to this process of refinement if they were to survive at all. Even the most assiduous wordsmiths
were humbled by the task of encapsulating such powerful, at their simplest, contradictory ideas in one all-embracing sentence. It is no surprise,
then, to encounter definitions that run for paragraphs, even pages, in
frantic attempts to capture the elusive meaning embodied in the word
terrorism. This is dialectic rather than definition, but it is an inescapable
part of the process whether it is reduced to writing or articulated only in
discussion. The above definition, in the form it is presented here, owes
much to classroom discussion and the acuity of the students to whom it
was offered as a starting point for an exploration of the subject. Before
examining its components in detail, it seems helpful to explain the underlying philosophy orienting its construction. Although it is always dangerous to generalize, it may be observed that university students tend to
be an unforgiving bunch. They are quick to seize on any errors or inconsistencies they detect in the formula. And, if they have cause to doubt as
a result, their overall confidence in the instruction and the instructor is
shaken. In particular, in the matter of defining terrorism, the product
offered had necessarily to address succinctly the thorny issue of "one
person's terrorist is another's freedom fighter"; hence the formulation
offered here.

6   Again, a further thought has to be inserted at this juncture. However
much you may buy into the freedom fighter argument, you are forced, if
you are intellectually honest, to the conclusion that whatever label it
might bear, terrorism is a bad thing. All you can sensibly say in its defense
is that sometimes it may be necessary to do bad things to other people,
most usually with the apologetic justification that it is done to prevent or
deter them from doing bad or worse things to you. If it is conceded that
there is no "good" terrorism, that such an import would be a contradiction in terms, any definition must unambiguously take this into account,
for it goes to the fundamental nature of the concept. In practice, the definition of terrorism has been consistently plagued by an ever-increasing
need to justify the reprehensible. This has proved the biggest obstacle to
the production of anything approaching a widely acceptable definition,
especially in the international arena. It must be stressed that there is a
basic antinomy here: What I do, however unpleasant is not terrorism;
what you do is terrorism. From the point of view of definition, this is not
a question of degrees such as dogs, for example, the term high crimes
and misdemeanors in the impeachment realm (see Posner, 1999, pp.
98–105). What is asserted is a difference in kind; I don't commit terror-

ism, you do. You can no more have a little bit of terrorism than you can be a little bit pregnant. From a definitional perspective, it ought not to matter who does what to whom. Terrorism should be defined solely by the nature and quality of what is done. Difficult as this is, definition should strive for impartiality in this field, or the exercise must fail in its purposes.

Is Terrorism a Freestanding Concept?

7   Is terrorism, then, a freestanding concept? In terms of penal policy or normative configuration, is it something autonomous or simply a constituent element of certain kinds of criminal behavior that are already defined? What is offered above certainly has to be carefully considered in that light. An examination of any coherent legal system will reveal many crimes where the creation of great fear in the victim (e.g., rape) is a central, defining feature. Many would agree that rape is a terroristic act, especially when it is employed in warfare as an instrument of subjugation or humiliation. In any unbiased analysis, it might reasonably be put forward as terrorism par excellence. Yet, it is not the crime of rape that comes readily or immediately to mind in any discussion of the meaning of terrorism. This is not to deny the terroristic content within what is understood about the crime of rape, at least in its violent manifestation, but rather an unexpressed preference for seeing terrorism as something separate, distinct, and having an existence all its own. For those taking such a position, and no objection is taken to it here, terrorism seems to inhabit a different universe from the ordinary, from even the most heinous of otherwise criminal behavior. That it can or should do so comes as no surprise to the legal positivist. Although norms cannot be simply conjured up out of thin air, the power to create new crimes in response to altered circumstances is an inherent faculty of any legal system. At this point, it must be made clear that what has been offered above as a conceptualization of terrorism is in no way to be regarded as an inchoate norm awaiting the interposition of the legal system's authority to give it independent being. And, herein lies the central dilemma, which cannot be readily overcome by recourse to any legal artifice. It is only possible to construct a freestanding penal figure denominated terrorism out of elements borrowed from preexisting crimes already defined as such in their own right. Thus, rape can in this view be seen as a constituent element of an autonomous crime of terrorism, just as terrorism can be seen as a necessary ingredient in a violent rape. Although this does little to advance the process of definition per se, it does serve to expose a critical problem that cannot be evaded.

8   Even the most cursory examination of the many definitions of terrorism on offer should quickly persuade the critic how many of these rely for any sort of precision on the adjectives employed in their elaboration. These definitions tend to focus on purpose, and that, in each of them, is primarily political. Reduced to its simplest terms, terrorism is seen as extreme political coercion. This, truth to tell, is the *raison d'etre* of vir-

tually all these definitional exercises. For it is only in the realm of the political that these definitions have any useful employment; hence their adversarial nature. Yet, assuredly, the abused child knows exactly what terrorism is, even though he or she might be quite unable to enunciate the word. More is revealed in this of the purposes of the definers, or refiners, than of the nature of terrorism itself. All who seek to find a meaning in the term terrorism would have to agree on the centrality of the massive fear, or terror, it inspires in those on whom it is inflicted, as well as its coercive nature. What is in dispute is whether there is anything in the nature of a right to inflict such misery on others and, if so, in whom it inheres. Here, we come to another dilemma that cannot escape the notice of anyone seeking to define terrorism. In its nature, terrorism, by reason of its coercive aspects, has a marked similarity to the corrective and deterrent functions vested by common understanding and political theory in the state-and the responsible parent. The distinction is in degree rather than anything else. Consider, for example, the ultimate sanction permitted the nation-state seeking to exercise its authority internally to control crime, namely the death penalty. Those who subscribe to a belief in its efficacy, whether by way of deterrence or social hygiene, can only rely on its intimidatory effect; if it does not frighten others by way of example, its value is very limited. The state's power to wage war to maintain its integrity against external foes can be viewed in much the same way. Clearly, effectiveness turns on the ability to secure the desired result through intimidation. Here lies the road to Dresden, Hiroshima, and Nagasaki, but we accord the nation-state considerable latitude in these matters. But, there comes a point when the line is crossed and we would say that the state has begun to rule by terror. There are issues of proportionality involved of a most delicate kind, but they are the ones that perturb the definitional process in most awkward ways. Terrorism becomes, for those in power, an affront to established authority. Power, when stretched to its limits is, to many, no more than a reign of terror. Any definition that ignores this is open to attack as pure cant. The point here is that the way in which these things are done has always assumed lesser importance from the point of view of their characterization as terrorism than who does them and to whom!

9   It should be observed that there is a kind of parallel in this regard with what have come to be known in recent times as "hate crimes." Those who oppose the promulgation, altogether, of such a category argue simply that it is otiose; murder is murder is murder. What can be done to increase the gravity with which certain matters seem to clamor for attention? Is any greater protection afforded potential victims by this increment? Nothing is added, for example, to the crime of murder that might serve as a special deterrent to those who would commit it against some class supposedly in need of particular protection. Many behaviorists and mental health professionals would argue, with considerable force on their side, that an individual who kills any victim in a singularly vicious way is exhibiting a hatred

of that person regardless of the class to which that person belongs; in fact, so personalized may be the hatred that no issue of a class character enters into the matter (see Gourevich, 2000). None of this would satisfy those who argue for special hate crime legislation. Once more, the focus is plainly on who does what to whom and why. Hatred is an emotion and one that in civilized society is regarded as reprehensible, unhealthy, and socially harmful. It is the "why" of the matter that is troubling to those who see themselves as likely to be victimized by those who bear and exhibit these ugly emotions. The problem resides herein: The feelings we characterize as hatred cannot be punished unless they are exhibited in a way that is criminal in itself or in association with conduct that is already criminalized. If the device of making the element of hate is a way of making this latter punishable in a more severe fashion than would otherwise be the case, the position has something to commend it, but in the case of the most serious crimes, such as murder, they are already punishable to the limit; the rest is merely posturing. As with terrorism, we should define by reference to what is done rather than by shifting our focus to those who are victimized and the reasons they are targeted.

Good News/Bad News

10   Viewed in the formulation set down here, terrorism is a game of fixed quantities. It is cold comfort, but comfort nevertheless, that as we enter the new millennium, no new terrorism is possible. How can this be? Creating massive fear in human beings is based on the same principles that have always informed the process: You can kill them, you can mutilate them or otherwise damage their physical or mental integrity, you can deprive them of their liberty, you can damage or destroy their relationships with people and things, you can adversely alter the quality of their lives by affecting their environment or their economic prospects or by imposing onerous burdens on them, or you can achieve your ends by credibly threatening to do all or any of these things. It is not possible to conceive of anything else that might accomplish the goal of creating the massive fear, or terror, that is at the heart of terrorism. That is the good news. The bad news-and it is very, very bad-is that with each passing moment ever newer and more horrible ways of undertaking these things are being imagined and made possible by the implacable, onward sweep of technology. That is the awful prospect that looms before us as we proceed into the new millennium. The 19th-century terrorist, if he or she were lucky, might have anticipated a body count in the hundreds, although none attained that target. It was probably easier for the terrorist, especially the anarchist, to concentrate on trying to effect change through coercion against selected individual targets, for example, the assassination of key members of the ruling classes. The 20th-century terrorist never truly reached his or her potential, for which we should be devoutly grateful. The ingredients were there, but somehow, the deadly brew was never administered to its deadliest effect. With regard to the

concept and the resources available to it, the attack by Aum Shinrikyu on the Tokyo subway, judged on its results, was puny in the extreme; a 19th-century anarchist operating alone with black powder might have accomplished much more. The World Trade Center bombing in New York, similarly from the terrorists' point of view, produced a pathetically small death toll and nothing like the property damage that was possible. Although the horrific attack on the Murrah Building in Oklahoma City stands above them all in terms of execution, magnitude, and a lasting impression on the psyche of the American people, it is not difficult to imagine how much worse it might have been. This is the frightening face of the future, but in the matter of definition, it is no different from what we have struggled with in the past. This is the fact that is urged here on those who will have to cope with the practical implications of terrorism in the new millennium.

Comprehending Terrorism

11   We seek to define terrorism so as to be better able to cope with it. We cannot begin to counter effectively that which we are unable to fully comprehend or agree on as to its nature. Some 50-odd years have been wasted in trying to disentangle the topic of terrorism from the much grander subject of wars of national liberation. A great deal of time and effort has been expended in trying to make the truly reprehensible politically respectable. As the awesome possibilities of the new millennium are translated into ever more frightening realities, we can no longer afford the fiction that one person's terrorist may yet be another's freedom fighter. Fighting for freedom may well be his or her purpose, but if the mission is undertaken through the employment of terroristic means, a terrorist he or she must remain; we ought not to confuse the sophistry of refinement for the process of definition. This assumes considerable importance as the older forms of terrorism give way, as they must, before the newer and more horrible ways of going about this grim business. For the advances of technology have not all aided the terrorist's purposes. As in so many other departments of modern life, the audience has become increasingly difficult to shock. Indeed, the terrorist nowadays has to struggle mightily against a kind of ennui affecting those he or she would seek to impress. The audience, with the ever-present assistance of television reporting of the contemporaneous, has become sated on a diet of death and destruction. The misery of others is fast losing its ability to horrify or, at least, to horrify for very long. Terroristic violence on the screen, whether fact or fiction, has become commonplace; much of the mystery has faded. This has made the terrorist's task increasingly difficult: How do you recapture and refocus the jaded attention of such an audience? The possibilities are really quite limited. You can strive to increase the toll in terms of the body count; compared to conventional warfare, deaths resulting from acts of terrorism have been numerically insignificant. To measure the true potential of terrorism, one would have to look to, say, Rwanda. Alternatively,

the terrorist has to imagine novel, strikingly horrible means for doing the traditional things; and, significantly, the execution must match the imaginings. Clearly, whichever course is chosen, some of the mystery has to be reintroduced. Fear feeds off the unknown. We must be careful not to allow this development to warp the process of definition.

From Weapons of Mass Destruction to Cyberterrorism

12   The expression "weapons of mass destruction" has now entered firmly into common currency. The expression conjures up visions of lots and lots of casualties and people dying in horrid ways as a result of the employment of such weapons. Because of its awesome, proved potential, nuclear weaponry is perhaps the first type to come to mind when the expression is used. Credible fears of the terrorist nuclear bomb go back at least to the 1970s; much fiction has been written around the theme of the "basement nuclear bomb." The concept has dominated futuristic theorizing about the direction terroristic escalation might take. Nuclear terrorism has, thankfully, remained in the realm of fiction. But, as we stand on the threshold of the new millennium, we would be most unwise to conclude that it will be ever thus. Indeed, it is little short of a miracle that we have not had to face the realities of nuclear terrorism to date. The knowledge and the materials have long been available to those who might have been tempted to engage in some feat of superterrorism (see Schweitzer, 1998). The point here is that if and when this awful eventuality materializes, it will not require any redefinition of terrorism; it will simply sharpen the terms with which it is drawn. We might remind ourselves at this juncture that it matters little to the instant victims whether they are done to death with a hatpin or consigned to perish in a nuclear conflagration. But, viewed in prospect, which is the more fearful, which the more likely to produce social nightmares? Even serially, you cannot account for a great many victims with hatpins. A simple nuclear device in the possession of a competent terrorist would demolish much property, alter the landscape, and kill and horribly maim a great many human beings. Its employment would alter forever the face of terrorism, and the way we have come to think about it. It would not, however, require us to alter the way we define it.

13   Until the late 1980s, many tended to think of terrorism in almost climatological terms, as though it were blown by a cold wind out of the East. It was, for the most part, an indelibly Cold War phenomenon; terrorism was often referred to as a form of surrogate warfare. Unpleasant it undoubtedly was, especially for the instant victims, but there did exist a useful measure of control applied by the patron states. The euphoria of the early 1990s blinded us to the dangers inherent in the collapse of the control factor. Whether or not one subscribed to the mutually assured destruction theory, it was very unlikely that the principal antagonists would encourage their surrogates to use weapons of mass destruction that they would be unwilling themselves to employ. The disintegration of

the "evil empire" had another unpleasant consequence for terrorism: It unleashed deadly material and put a lot of disengaged experts on the "free" market. Now, we have to face the real possibility of a revitalized Cold War with old Cold Warriors such as Vladimir Putin in the driver's seat. What is uncertain is whether the old controls will be reimposed, or even whether they can. Although none of this is likely to unleash fresh fears of small-group nuclear terrorism in the West, it is likely to have an impact in other areas of perhaps greater concern. The fearful instruments of chemical and biological warfare, largely eschewed by a majority of civilized nations, have acquired the soubriquet of "the poor man's nuclear bomb." Certainly, as death-dealing implements, the term is well applied. There is a kind of inevitability about the employment of these weapons by terrorists. The amount of publicity they have received over the past decade or so alone would have assured that outcome. It is worthy of note, yet again, that these possibilities encouraged by technological advances and political shifts have no definitional significance. The alterations have been simply adjectival. But, they will change the way we think about terrorism as well as about those whose job it is to undertake countermeasures. Sooner maybe than later, one of those packets or envelopes is going to contain anthrax spores, the real thing, rather than the miscellaneous hoax powders that have turned up so far. There is a kind of fearfulness about handling this stuff that, as much as anything else, has probably protected society until now. The fears are not misplaced. Considering the number of terrorists who have blown themselves up with their own bombs, the very unfamiliarity with the handling of some of these substances, especially the nerve gases, suggests perils of an entirely different order from those previously experienced. The first successful employment of chemical and biological agents by terrorists will doubtlessly overcome any lingering inhibitions.

14   Now, yet another term has to be employed by those seeking to give precision to their particular definitions of terrorism. Not long after heaving a sigh of relief and congratulating ourselves at having avoided the catastrophes of Y2K predicted by the doomsayers, we have been hit with a wave of what is being called "cyberterrorism." Modern society is becoming more and more computer dependent. Everything from electronic commerce to the supply of energy is vulnerable, and although this may not be the immediate objective of the perpetrators, the potential for the associated loss of human life is not inconsiderable. This cyberterrorism is still very much in its infancy; the methods are primitive and unsophisticated but effective. This is not "virtual" terrorism or Game Boy stuff. Cyberspace is a real place; real operations and real functions take place there, and real interests are at risk. The methods are new, but the principles behind their application are as old as terrorism itself. The technology employed has enabled the terrorists to reintroduce a useful, from their point of view, element of mystery into the process. They can, for a little while at least, operate from a considerable distance, concealing

their identities and their purposes. The authorities, for the moment, can only confess to a sense of bafflement and try to reassure the affected public that everything possible is being done to protect the systems at risk and to apprehend the culprits. All this is going to generate a new lexicon, and already familiar terms such as hackers, computer viruses, trap doors, and the like will gain greater currency. Yet, we could as easily say these cybersystems were being "kidnapped," "hijacked," or "taken hostage," and when demands are presented to desist, the term extortion will come into play. Of greatest interest, perhaps, for the present purposes, a participant in an online discussion opined, "Hackers are freedom fighters for cyberspace" (Weise, 2000, p. 2A). Those who do not learn the lexical lessons of history are obliged to repeat the semester!

15   Terrorism, by its nature, seeks out and exploits its opponents' weaknesses. Again, a well-known aphorism has it that "terrorism is the weapon of the weak." This was a definitional device intended to characterize those tarnished with the terrorist label as being those who challenged rightful authority rather than those who abused it through practices that smacked of vicious cruelty. The nation-state has always been ultrasensitive to accusations that it is guilty of terrorism, whether against its own lawful residents or others (see, e.g., Herman & O'Sullivan, 1989). Where these cruelties are egregious, as in the case of Nazi Germany, few would cavil at defining what is done as terrorism. Yet, even that awful regime would claim its actions were in the nature of self-defense, a deterrent to behavior that threatened its cohesiveness and purposes! Unhappily, such state terrorism is very far from being a thing of the past. As we proceed into the new millennium, we shall be confronted more and more with terrorism that proceeds from the mighty rather than the weak. A practical consequence of this delicacy in the matter of labeling can be seen by studying in any particular year the nations that find themselves on the U.S. State Department's list of "terrorist states," and those that do not. There is a kind of hypocrisy about this process that no definitional sophistry can hide; it simply highlights the perennial difficulty of describing forthrightly what terrorism is, for fear of upsetting those we might find it inconvenient to criticize. This is unfortunate on much more than a linguistic level. Definition is dictated under such circumstances by the harsh realities of power: None dare call it by its rightful name. This is surely the road to Tiananmen Square, and the consequences of ignoring the route are much more than merely academic.

16   Terrorism is a naked struggle for power, who shall wield it, and to what ends. The coercive character of what is done is plain enough to require little beyond description. Where the process does not produce the requisite submission, escalation is inevitable; action begets reaction. This is the real challenge to the high-minded. It is here that the state finds it especially needful to characterize what its opponents do as terrorism while seeking to distinguish its own counteraction as something quite different, lacking in reprehensible qualities. While looking at the conduct of

those whose political philosophies we do not share, we ought not to disregard too cavalierly the mote in our own eye. No nation-state can relinquish its sovereign authority to an adversary, attempting to seize it by force, and retain its own integrity. Retaliation is an imperative in such cases, but one of the objectives of the adversary is to produce an overreaction. Brutal repression serves the adversary's purposes, so as to give rise to the charge, "See, you are as bad, or worse, than we are. Who is the terrorist now?" The audience is the community of nation-states, which has become increasingly censorious in judging the responses of others, especially when the judges are not directly confronted, for the moment, with terrorism problems of their own. In an ideal world, responses would be measured by much the same criteria as those against which an individual's rights of self-defense at law are evaluated, namely that the response should be necessary, reasonable, and proportionate to the harm suffered or apprehended (Cooper, 1998). We are forced to recognize that the real world in which modern-day terrorism takes place is very far from ideal. It is, rather, a Hobbesian universe in which all life is to be regarded as "nastie, brutish and short"-and cheap in the bargain. Terrorism thus becomes a battle for the moral high ground, with those in legitimate power trying to preserve their positions against opponents bent on dragging them into the gutter. The outcome is yet another phenomenological element in the process of defining terrorism that is likely to be of increasing importance in coming decades.

The Problem of Definition Remains Unaltered Throughout

17 Thus, at the start of the new millennium, we can say with a high degree of certainty that the definition of terrorism is as needful and as illusory as ever. The fine minds that have engaged in the task over the past three decades or so have provided much fuel for the crucible and a great deal of raw material for the process, but a truly pure ingot has eluded all. Once again, the focus here has been on the problem of definition, which remains unaltered throughout. It is realism rather than pessimism that prompts the observation that this is really a problem without a solution, for none can voluntarily yield the high ground to the others. Terrorism is not a struggle for the hearts and minds of the victims nor for their immortal souls. Rather, it is, as Humpty Dumpty would have said, about who is to be master, that is all. Yet, withal, no one who has experienced terrorism in the flesh has the slightest doubt about what it is or the sensations that it engenders. Ask any concentration camp survivor. Ask those fortunate enough to have returned from the gulag. Ask those who have experienced the more recent examples of ethnic cleansing in the former Yugoslavia or in East Timor. They may not be able to encapsulate the horrors of their respective experiences in a finely turned phrase or two, but what they have undergone is to them and countless others not in the slightest doubt, for it is indelibly engraved on their psyches. Although this

cannot suffice for the purposes of the polemic, it does help to focus the debate. As with obscenity, we know terrorism well enough when we see it. For the minds and bodies affected by it, this suffices; definition for these is otiose. This will not and cannot change in the years to come, strive as we may to give precision to the concept. It is diffidently opined here that we would be better employed in refocusing our efforts on what is done, the terrible acts themselves, whether by way of original initiative or retaliation. It might be more admirable to call a spade a spade, in the hands of whoever might be wielding it. These pathetic attempts at making the contemptible respectable will seem as ridiculous to those approaching the end of the present millennium as efforts to rehabilitate Attila the Hun or Genghis Khan would appear in our own times. So we are left, as we began, with our own imperfect formulas and the ever insistent need to explain and expound. As the incomparable Ludwig Wittgenstein (1921/1961) instructed us, "There are, indeed, things that cannot be put into words. They make themselves manifest. They are what is mystical" (p. 151). Terrorism is one of those things.

Works Cited

Alexander, Y., ed. *International Terrorism: National, Regional, and Global Perspectives.* New York: Praeger, 1976.

Cohen, R. *Culture and Conflict in Egyptian-Israeli Relations: A Dialogue of the Deaf.* Bloomington: Indiana University Press, 1990.

Cooper, H.H.A. "Terrorism: The problem of the problem of the problem of definition." *Chitty's Law Journal* 26.3 (1978): 105-08.

———. "Self-defense." In *Encyclopedia Americana* 25, pp. 532. Danbury, CT: Grolier, 1998.

Chomsky, N. "International Terrorism: Image and Reality. " In *Western State Terrorism*, ed. A. George, pp. 12-38. New York: Routledge: 1991.

Gourevich, P. "A Cold Case." *The New Yorker*, 2000, February 14: 42–60.

Hacker, F J. *Crusaders, Criminals, Crazies: Terror and Terrorism in Our Time.* New York: Norton, 1976.

Herman, E., and G. O'Sullivan. "The Western Model and Semantics of Terrorism." In *The Terrorism Industry: The Experts and Institutions that Shape Our View of Terror.* New York: Pantheon, 1989.

Livingston, M. H. (with L. B. Kress and M. G. Wanek), eds. *International Terrorism in the Contemporary World.* Westport, CT: Greenwood, 1978.

Office of the Chief Counsel for the Prosecution of Axis Criminality. *Nazi Conspiracy and Aggression.* Washington, D.C.: Government Printing Office, 1946.

Posner, R. A. *An Affair of State: The Investigation, Impeachment, and Trial of President Clinton.* Cambridge, MA: Harvard University Press, 1999.

Schweitzer, G. E. (with C. C. Dorsch). *Superterrorism: Assassins, Mobsters, and Weapons of Mass Destruction.* New York: Plenum, 1998.

Tannen, D. *You Just Don't Understand: Women and Men in Conversation.* New York: Ballantine, 1990.

Weise, E. "Online Talk Is of Conspiracy, Crime and Punishment." *USA Today,* 2000, February 10: p. 2A.

Wittgenstein, L. *Tractatus Logico-Philosophicus.* 1921. London: Routledge Kegan Paul, 1961.

Questions for Discussion

1. What, according to Cooper, are the problems in reaching any definition of terrorism? How does Cooper define terrorism? How was his definition formulated?

2. Explain Cooper's statement that "One person's terrorist will ever remain another's freedom fighter."

3. Why do we need to define terrorism?

4. What are the things Cooper lists as the only types of terrorism?

5. What is the frightening truth about terrorism in the twenty-first century?

6. How has television complicated the terrorists' task?

7. What events in the late twentieth century made terrorism more possible and more potentially destructive? How have events since the publication of this article proved Cooper's prediction for the new millennium?

Suggestions for Exploring, Writing, and Persuading

1. Cooper states, "Power, when stretched to its limits, is, to many, no more than a reign of terror." Apply his assertion to either the beheading of foreign workers by Al Qaeda or the abuse of prisoners at Abu Ghraib by American soldiers. What are the limits of power?

2. Select one of the following statements and write an essay giving examples to support or deny its validity:

    "[T]he definition of terrorism has been consistently plagued by an ever increasing need to justify the reprehensible."

    "[T]errorism seems to inhabit a different universe from the ordinary, from even the most heinous of otherwise criminal behavior."

    " [. . . T]he way in which these things are done has always assumed lesser importance from the point of view of their characterization as terrorism than who does them and to whom!"

    "[N]o new terrorism is possible."

    "[T]he perennial difficulty of describing forthrightly what terrorism is, for fear of upsetting those who might find it inconvenient to criticism," reveals our hypocrisy.

"[N]o one who has experienced terrorism in the flesh has the slightest doubt about what it is or the sensations that it engenders."

"[W]e would be better employed in refocusing our efforts on what is done, the terrible acts themselves, whether by way of original initiative or retaliation. It might be more admirable to call a spade a spade, in the hands of whoever might be wielding it."

Elie Wiesel (b. 1928)

Elie Wiesel was born in the village of Sighet in a part of Romania often claimed by Hungary. In 1944, the Nazis sent Wiesel and his family, along with all the other Jews of their village and region, to Auschwitz, where Wiesel's mother and younger sister were killed. Moved to Buchenwald, Wiesel and his father worked as slaves under horrendous conditions, which ultimately killed his father. Wiesel survived to become the foremost chronicler of the horrors of the Holocaust. Naturalized as a U.S. citizen in 1963, Wiesel has served as a faculty member in humanities at Boston University since 1976 and in 1978 was named chair of the U.S. Holocaust Museum. In 1985, he was awarded the National Medal of Freedom and, in 1986, the Nobel Peace Prize. Among his books, all of which focus on the Holocaust, are And the World Has Remained Silent *(1956), a powerful novel of life in Auschwitz from the point of view of a young boy, later translated and abridged as* Night: The Town Beyond the Wall *(1962);* A Beggar in Jerusalem *(1968);* Souls on Fire *(1972);* The Forgotten *(1989); and* All Rivers Run to the Sea: A Memoir *(1995).*

YOM KIPPUR: THE DAY WITHOUT FORGIVENESS   (1968)

1   With a lifeless look, a painful smile on his face, while digging a hole in the ground, Pinhas moved his lips in silence. He appeared to be arguing with someone within himself and, judging from his expression, seemed close to admitting defeat.

2   I had never seen him so downhearted. I knew that his body would not hold out much longer. His strength was already abandoning him, his movements were becoming more heavy, more chaotic. No doubt he knew it too. But death figured only rarely in our conversations. We preferred to deny its presence, to reduce it, as in the past, to a simple allusion, something abstract, inoffensive, a word like any other.

3   "What are you thinking about? What's wrong?"

4   Pinhas lowered his head, as if to conceal his embarrassment, or his sadness, or both, and let a long time go by before he answered, in a voice scarcely audible: "Tomorrow is Yom Kippur."

5   Then I too felt depressed. My first Yom Kippur in the camp. Perhaps my last. The day of judgment, of atonement. Tomorrow the heavenly tribunal

would sit and pass sentence: "And like unto a flock, the creatures of this world shall pass before thee." Once upon a time—last year—the approach of this day of tears, of penitence and fear, had made me tremble. Tomorrow, we would present ourselves before God, who sees everything and who knows everything, and we would say: "Father, have pity on your children." Would I be capable of praying with fervor again? Pinhas shook himself abruptly. His glance plunged into mine.

6   "Tomorrow is the Day of Atonement and I have just made a decision: I am not going to fast. Do you hear? I am not going to fast."

7   I asked for no explanation. I knew he was going to die and suddenly I was afraid that by way of justification he might declare: "It is simple, I have decided not to comply with the law anymore and not to fast because in the eyes of man and of God I am already dead, and the dead can disobey the commandments of the Torah." I lowered my head and made believe I was not thinking about anything but the earth I was digging up under a sky more dark than the earth itself.

8   We belonged to the same Kommando. We always managed to work side by side. Our age difference did not stop him from treating me like a friend. He must have been past forty. I was fifteen. Before the war, he had been *Rosh-Yeshiva*, director of a rabbinical school somewhere in Galicia. Often, to outwit our hunger or to forget our reasons for despair, we would study a page of the Talmud from memory. I relived my childhood by forcing myself not to think about those who were gone. If one of my arguments pleased Pinhas, if I quoted a commentary without distorting its meaning, he would smile at me and say: "I should have liked to have you among my disciples."

9   And I would answer: "But I am your disciple, where we are matters little."

10   That was false, the place was of capital importance. According to the law of the camp I was his equal; I used the familiar form when I addressed him. Any other form of address was inconceivable.

11   "Do you hear?" Pinhas shouted defiantly. "I will not fast."

12   "I understand. You are right. One must not fast. Not at Auschwitz. Here we live outside time, outside sin. Yom Kippur does not apply to Auschwitz."

13   Ever since Rosh Hashana, the New Year, the question had been bitterly debated all over camp. Fasting meant a quicker death. Here everybody fasted all year round. Every day was Yom Kippur. And the book of life and death was no longer in God's hands, but in the hands of the executioner. The words *mi yichye umi yamut*, "who shall live and who shall die," had a terrible real meaning here, an immediate bearing. And all the prayers in the world could not alter the *Gzar-din*, the inexorable movement of fate. Here, in order to live, one had to eat, not pray.

14   "You are right, Pinhas," I said, forcing myself to withstand his gaze. "You *must* eat tomorrow. You've been here longer than I have, longer than many of us. You need your strength. You have to save your strength, watch over it, protect it. You should not go beyond your limits. Or tempt misfortune. That would be a sin."

15   Me, his disciple? I gave him lessons, I gave him advice, as if I were his elder, his guide.

16   "That is not it," said Pinhas, getting irritated. "I could hold out for one day without food. It would not be the first time."

17   "Then what is it?"

18   "A decision. Until now, I've accepted everything. Without bitterness, without reservation. I have told myself: 'God knows what he is doing.' I have submitted to his will. Now I have had enough, I have reached my limit. If he knows what he is doing, then it is serious; and it is not any less serious if he does not. Therefore, I have decided to tell him: 'It is enough.'"

19   I said nothing. How could I argue with him? I was going through the same crisis. Every day I was moving a little further away from the God of my childhood. He had become a stranger to me; sometimes, I even thought he was my enemy.

20   The appearance of Edek put an end to our conversation. He was our master, our king. The Kapo. This young Pole with rosy cheeks, with the movements of a wild animal, enjoyed catching his slaves by surprise and making them shout with fear. Still an adolescent, he enjoyed possessing such power over so many adults. We dreaded his changeable moods, his sudden fits of anger: without unclenching his teeth, his eyes half-closed, he would beat his victims long after they had lost consciousness and had ceased to moan.

21   "Well?" he said, planting himself in front of us, his arms folded. "Taking a little nap? Talking over old times? You think you are at a resort? Or in the synagogue?"

22   A cruel flame lit his blue eyes, but it went out just as quickly. An aborted rage. We began to shovel furiously, not thinking about anything but the ground which opened up menacingly before us. Edek insulted us a few more times and then walked off.

23   Pinhas did not feel like talking anymore, neither did I. For him the die had been cast. The break with God appeared complete.

24   Meanwhile, the pit under our legs was becoming wider and deeper. Soon our heads would hardly be visible above the ground. I had the weird sensation that I was digging a grave. For whom? For Pinhas? For myself? Perhaps for our memories.

25   On my return to camp, I found it plunged in feverish anticipation: they were preparing to welcome the holiest and longest day of the year. My barracks neighbors, a father and son, were talking in low voices. One was saying: "Let us hope the roll-call does not last too long." The other added: "Let us hope that the soup is distributed before the sun sets, otherwise we will not have the right to touch it."

26   Their prayers were answered. The roll-call unfolded without incident, without delay, without public hanging. The section-chief hurriedly distributed the soup; I hurriedly gulped it down. I ran to wash, to purify myself. By the time the day was drawing to a close, I was ready.

27   Some days before, on the eve of Rosh Hashana, all the Jews in camp— Kapos included—had congregated at the square where roll was taken,

and we had implored the God of Abraham, Isaac, and Jacob to end our humiliation, to change sides, to break his pact with the enemy. In unison we had said *Kaddish* for the dead and for the living as well. Officers and soldiers, machine guns in hand, had stood by, amused spectators, on the other side of the barbed wire.

28   Now, we did not go back there for *Kol Nidre*. We were afraid of a selection: in preceding years, the Day of Atonement had been turned into a day of mourning. Yom Kippur had become *Tisha b'Av*, the day the Temple was destroyed.

29   Thus, each barracks housed its own synagogue. It was more prudent. I was sorry, because Pinhas was in another block.

30   A Hungarian rabbi officiated as our cantor. His voice stirred my memories and evoked that legend according to which, on the night of Yom Kippur, the dead rise from their graves and come to pray with the living. I thought: "Then it is true; that is what really happens. The legend is confirmed at Auschwitz."

31   For weeks, several learned Jews had gathered every night in our block to transcribe from memory—by hand, on toilet paper—the prayers for the High Holy Days. Each cantor received a copy. Ours read in a loud voice and we repeated each verse after him. The *Kol Nidre*, which releases us from all vows made under constraint, now seemed to me anachronistic, absurd, even though it had been composed in similar circumstances, in Spain, right near the Inquisition stakes. Once a year the converts would assemble and cry out to God: "Know this, all that we have said is unsaid, all that we have done is undone." *Kol Nidre?* A sad joke. Here and now we no longer had any secret vows to make or to deny: everything was clear, irrevocable.

32   Then came the *Vidui*, the great confession. There again, everything rang false, none of it concerned us anymore. *Ashamnu*, we have sinned. *Bagadnu*, we have betrayed. *Gazalnu*, we have stolen. What? Us? *We* have sinned? Against whom? By doing what? *We* have betrayed? Whom? Undoubtedly this was the first time since God judged his creation that victims beat their breasts accusing themselves of the crimes of their executioners.

33   Why did we take responsibility for sins and offenses which not one of us could ever have had the desire or the possibility of committing? Perhaps we felt guilty despite everything. Things were simpler that way. It was better to believe our punishments had meaning, that we had deserved them; to believe in a cruel but just God was better than not to believe at all. It was in order not to provoke an open war between God and his people that we had chosen to spare him, and we cried out: "You are our God, blessed be your name. You smite us without pity, you shed our blood, we give thanks to you for it, O Eternal One, for you are determined to show us that you are just and that your name is justice!"

34   I admit having joined my voice to the others and implored the heavens to grant me mercy and forgiveness. At variance with everything my

lips were saying, I indicted myself only to turn everything into derision, into farce. At any moment I expected the Master of the universe to strike me dumb and to say: "That is enough—you have gone too far." And I like to think I would have replied: "You, also, blessed be your name, you also."

35   Our services were dispersed by the camp bell. The section-chiefs began to yell: "Okay, go to sleep! If God hasn't heard you, it's because he is incapable of hearing."

36   The next day, at work, Pinhas joined another group. I thought: "He wants to eat without being embarrassed by my presence." A day later, he returned. His face even more pale, even more gaunt than before. Death was gnawing at him. I caught myself thinking: "He will die because he did not observe Yom Kippur."

37   We dug for several hours without looking at each other. From far off, the shouting of the Kapo reached us. He walked around hitting people relentlessly.

38   Toward the end of the afternoon, Pinhas spoke to me: "I have a confession to make."

39   I shuddered, but went on digging. A strange, almost child-like smile appeared on his lips when he spoke again: "You know, I fasted."

40   I remained motionless. My stupor amused him.

41   "Yes, I fasted. Like the others. But not for the same reasons. Not out of obedience, but out of defiance. Before the war, you see, some Jews rebelled against the divine will by going to restaurants on the Day of Atonement; here, it is by observing the fast that we can make our indignation heard. Yes, my disciple and teacher, know that I fasted. Not for love of God, but against God."

42   He left me a few weeks later, victim of the first selection.

43   He shook my hand: "I would have liked to die some other way and elsewhere. I had always hoped to make of my death, as of my life, an act of faith. It is a pity. God prevents me from realizing my dream. He no longer likes dreams."

44   Nonetheless, he asked me to say *Kaddish* for him after his death, which, according to his calculations, would take place three days after his departure from camp.

45   "But why?" I asked, "since you are no longer a believer?"

46   He took the tone he always used when he explained a passage in the Talmud to me: "You do not see the heart of the matter. Here and now, the only way to accuse him is by praising him."

47   And he went, laughing, to his death.

Questions for Discussion

1. What is Wiesel's relationship to Pinhas in the essay? What is Wiesel's age?

2. Yom Kippur is the one opportunity for divine forgiveness Pinhas will have during the year. He is unlikely to live until the next Day of

Atonement. Why, then, does he tell the narrator that he will not fast and will thereby willfully disobey God?

3. The narrator says, "Once upon a time—last year—the approach of this day of tears, of penitence and fear, had made me tremble." Why does he refer to a time as recently as "last year" as "once upon a time"? Why did he tremble? How and why has his attitude toward Yom Kippur changed?

4. Why would the inhabitants of Auschwitz want to reduce death to "a simple allusion, something abstract, inoffensive, a word like any other"?

5. Discuss Pinhas's statement "The only way to accuse him is by praising him."

6. Why does Pinhas die laughing?

Suggestions for Exploring, Writing, and Persuading

1. Write a character analysis of Edek, the "master of the camp."

2. Explain why both Pinhas and the narrator have such a hard time accepting God. Why might Pinhas doubt that God knows what He is doing? What are the implications of God's not knowing "what He is doing"? What are the implications of His knowing but nevertheless allowing a horror like the Holocaust to continue?

3. If you were asked to explain God's role (or lack of a role) in the treatment of Jews in Nazi concentration camps, what would your answer be? Defend your answer in an essay.

4. Research the treatment of prisoners at Auschwitz and write an essay explaining the accuracy of Wiesel's account.

5. Research the Jewish traditions referred to in Wiesel's essay. To what degree do the two characters in the tale remain faithful to those traditions?

6. Compare Pinhas's story to Job's. See especially Job 1, 2 (note particularly 1:22 and 2:10), 6, and 10.

7. What terrible contemporary events might lead one to doubt as Pinhas does? Why?

V. S. Naipaul (b. 1932)

Born in Trinidad to parents of Indian descent, V. S. Naipaul was educated at University College, Oxford, and began his long and distinguished writing career in 1954 in London. His ten novels, which have won numerous awards, include The Mystic Masseur *(1957);* Miguel Street *(1959);* A House for Mr. Biswas *(1961);* In a Free State *(1971), which won the Booker Award;* Guerrillas *(1975);* A Bend in the River *(1979); and* A Way in the World *(1971). He has also written*

*ten books of nonfiction about the extensive traveling he has
done since 1960. Two of his travel books,* Among the Believers: An Islamic Journey *(1981) and* Beyond Belief: Islamic
Excursions among the Converted Believers *(1998), from
which the essay "Loss" included here is taken, record his
travels among followers of Islam in Iran, Pakistan, Indonesia, and Malaysia.*

Loss   (1998)

1   For most of the Muslims of the subcontinent[1] the partition of 1947[2] had
been like a great victory, "like God," as a man had said to me in Lahore in
1979. Now every day in the newspapers there were stories of the killings
in the great port city of Karachi. That was where many of the Muslim
migrants from India, townspeople, middle-class or lower middle-class, had
gone after partition. Nearly half a century later the descendants of these
people, feeling themselves strangers still, unrepresented, cheated, without
power, had taken up arms against the state, in a merciless guerrilla war.

2   In Iqbal's[3] convert's scheme Islam should have been identity enough
for everybody. But the people of Sindh (the province where Karachi was)
didn't like seeing their land, half empty and half desert though it was,
overrun by better educated and more ambitious strangers. The land of
Sindh was ancient, and always slightly apart. The people had their own
history and language and feudal reverences. They had set up political barriers, some overt, some hidden, against the strangers from India, the
mohajirs. And in Pakistan the *mohajirs* had nowhere else to go.

3   Partition, once a cause for joy, had become like a wound for some of
these mohajirs. For some the memories of those days still lived.

4   Salman, a journalist, was born in 1952. He was tormented by, and endlessly sought to reconstruct, the events of four days in 1947 in the town
of Jalandhar, now in Indian Punjab. At some point in those four days,
between the fourteenth and eighteenth of August, 1947, the absolute
beginning of independence for both India and Pakistan, his grandmother
was murdered in her house in Jalandhar, with others of the family. On the
fourteenth she was alive, protected by Hindu neighbors. On the eighteenth Salman's mother's father, who had been hiding somewhere else,
went to the house, a middle-class Indian courtyard house, and found it
empty, with blood spattered on the walls but with no corpses.

[1]subcontinent: the Indian subcontinent, including India, Pakistan, and Bangladesh.
[2]partition of 1947: In 1947, Britain, by the Indian Independence Act, granted independence to India. Simultaneously, in response to pressure by the Muslim League, the Act
established a separate nation, Pakistan, in majority-Muslim parts of northern India. At
the time of this partition, there was much violence between Hindus and Muslims. Partition also created a serious refugee crisis, as millions of Hindus left Pakistan for predominantly Hindu India and millions of Muslims left India for predominantly Muslim Pakistan.
[3] Iqbal: Mohammed Iqbal, an Islamic poet living in pre-partition India, who in 1930
gave an impassioned address to the Muslim League advocating a separate all-Muslim
state on the Indian subcontinent.

5   Salman's grandfather ran away. He must have been about fifty at that time. He managed to get on a train going to what had become Pakistan— just a short run away, along lines that until four days before had been open and busy. The train was attacked on the way. He arrived in Lahore buried under dead bodies. He was one of the few survivors.

6   Salman got to know the story when he was fifteen. Until that time he had lived with the idea of the Hindu and the Sikh as the ultimate evil. But when he heard this story he felt no anger. The story was too terrible for anger. It didn't matter then who had done the killing.

7   The blood on the walls of a house he didn't know (Salman had not been to Jalandhar or India) and could only imagine, the absence of bodies: the details, or the blankness of detail, from a time before he was born, worked on Salman, became the background to his life in Pakistan. He could spend minutes wondering, when the story came back to him, how the people in the house had actually met death. Had they been cut to pieces? Had they—dreadful thought—been abused?

8   There were other stories of that time which he got from an uncle: of the uncle (and no doubt others) hiding behind oil drums and taunting the Hindu and Sikh rioters, who didn't want India to be broken up:

> But kay rahé ga Hindustan!
> Bun kay rahé ga Pakistan!
> Divided Hindustan will be!
> Pakistan will be founded!

In the 1960s these stories, of death and riot, began to rankle with Salman. "I would think we had lost so much for this country, and this is what we are doing to it now."

9   But there had been a long serene period in the new country. The family had lost everything in Jalandhar, but Salman's father, a civil engineer, was working for the government—he was in Baluchistan at the time of the riots in Jalandhar—and so there was money every month. In 1952, the year of Salman's birth, his father left the government to set up on his own. For ten years and more his practice flourished. He brought up his family in a religious way. All the rituals were honored, and there were Koranic recitations. Salman as a child knew many prayers by heart. Religion was part of the serenity of his childhood.

10   In 1965, when he was thirteen, Salman became aware of another kind of Islam. This was at the time of the short, inconclusive war with India. "There were songs exhorting mujahids to go to war and promising them paradise, heaven. Mobs of people from the city of Lahore, armed only with clubs, set out to fight the holy war against the infidel Hindu. They had to be turned back. They had been charged up by the mullah. The interesting thing was that the mullah was not leading those people. He was sitting safe in his mosque."

11   In this way Salman was introduced to the idea of *jihad*, holy war. It was a special Muslim idea. He explained it like this: "In Christianity Christ died for all Christians. He can ensure heaven for them. In Islam Mohammed can only make a submission in your favor for being a follower of his. It is only Allah who makes the final decision on the merit won by good deeds. Nothing is greater, so far as goodness goes, than jihad in the name of Allah." Jihad was not meant metaphorically. "The word of the Koran is taken very literally. It is blasphemous even to think of it as an allegory. The Koran lays great store by jihad. It is one of the sayings of Mohammed—not in the Koran, it's one of the traditions—'If you see an un-Islamic practice you stop it by force. If you do not possess the power to stop it, you condemn it verbally. If not that also, then you condemn it in your heart.' As far back as I remember I have known this. I think this tradition gives the Muslim license to act violently."

12   In 1965 he saw for the first time the idea given a public, mob expression. And though he saw people then doing "silly things," he understood both their need to win merit as followers of Mohammed, and also their fear of hell.

13   "Endless whipping with fiery flames, and fire beyond imagination. Having to drink pus. It's very graphic in the traditions. In the Koran there's just mention of the fires and the endlessness of punishment."

14   In 1968, when he was sixteen, and in his first year at Government Science College, Lahore, Salman found himself part of just such a mob. There was a review in *Time* or *Newsweek* of a book called *The Warrior Prophet*. Two or three copies of the magazine with the review had somehow got to the college and were passed around. No one had seen the book, but the boys decided to take out a procession to protest about it. It was during a break; the boys were sitting outside. There was no particular leader. The boys were all as religiously well trained as Salman. The idea of the public protest simply came to them, and they became a mob. Salman went along with them, though he remembered very clearly, all the way through, that he hadn't found anything obnoxious about Islam or the Prophet in the review. The weather was good. It was winter, the best season in Lahore, and they shouted slogans against the United States and broke up a couple of minibuses.

15   The mullah who in 1965 had charged up his congregation, and sent them off to the front to fight with sticks, had stayed behind quite safe in his mosque. It wasn't his business to fight. His business was to charge people up, to remind them as graphically and passionately as he could of the rewards of jihad and the horrors of hell.

16   He was like the mullah I heard about (from someone else) who had been drafted in, with other mullahs, to campaign against Mr. Bhutto in 1977. This mullah was short and fat, in no way personable, and known to be unreliable. But that didn't matter; he was a wonderful preacher, with a powerful voice. There was a curfew at the time, but it was relaxed (as it had to be) for the Friday prayers. The people who went to the mullah's mosque found themselves listening to more than prayers. They heard stories, from Islamic

history, of heroism and martyrdom, in the mullah's famous voice and wonderful declamatory style. He asked them to be worthy of the famous voice and wonderful declamatory style. He asked them to be worthy of the past, to take up jihad, and not to ignore the forces of evil around them. "Say to the enemy, 'You test your arrows on us, and we shall test our breast against your arrows.'" It sounded like poetry, and authoritative for that reason, though no one could place it. The actual words didn't mean anything, but they drove people wild; and at the end of those Friday prayers poor Mr. Bhutto's curfew had been rendered harmless. The congregation went away full of religious hate, determined to earn a little more merit in heaven by sending Mr. Bhutto to hell.

17   That the mullah was unreliable, and not a moral man in any recognizable way, was not important. He was not offering himself as a guide. It was his business as a mullah to keep the converted people on their toes, and when there was need to charge them up, to fix their minds on hell and heaven, and to tell them that when the time came only Allah would be their judge. This was an aspect of the religious state—the state created for converts alone, where religion was not a matter of private conscience—that the poet Iqbal had never considered: that such a state could always be manipulated, easy to undermine, full of simple roguery.

18   There was something else that Iqbal had never considered: that in the new state the nature of history would alter, and with that altering of the historical sense, the intellectual life of the country would inevitably be diminished. The mullahs would always hold the ring, would limit inquiry. All the history of the ancient land would cease to matter. In the school history books, or the school "civics" books, the history of Pakistan would become only an aspect of the history of Islam. The Muslim invaders, and especially the Arabs, would become the heroes of the Pakistan story. The local people would be hardly there, in their own land, or would be there only as ciphers swept aside by the agents of the faith.

19   It is a dreadful mangling of history. It is a convert's view; that is all that can be said for it. History has become a kind of neurosis. Too much has to be ignored or angled; there is too much fantasy. This fantasy isn't in the books alone; it affects people's lives.

20   Salman, talking of this neurosis, said, "Islam doesn't show on my face. We have nearly all, subcontinental Muslims, invented Arab ancestors for ourselves. Most of us are sayeds, descendants of Mohammed through his daughter Fatima and cousin and son-in-law Ali. There are others—like my family—who have invented a man called Salim al-Rai. And yet others who have invented a man called Qutub Shah. Everybody has got an ancestor who came from Arabia or Central Asia. I am convinced my ancestors would have been medium to low-caste Hindus, and despite their conversion they would not have been in the mainstream of Muslims. If you read Ibn Battuta and earlier travelers you can sense the condescending attitude of the Arab travelers to the

converts. They would give the Arab name of someone, and then say, 'But he's an Indian.'

21   "This invention of Arab ancestry soon became complete. It had been adopted by all families. If you hear people talking you would believe that this great and wonderful land was nothing but wild jungle, that no human beings lived here. All of this was magnified at the time of partition, this sense of not belonging to the land, but belonging to the religion. Only one people in Pakistan have reverence for their land, and that's the Sindhis."

22   This was what lay all around Salman's serene childhood. These fantasies and illusions, which to some extent were also his when he was a child, were to become his subject when he became a writer. They took time to discover; they needed the adult eye; they required him to stand a little outside himself.

23   But even while he was still an adolescent Salman began to have intimations of being somewhat apart. Just a few months after he had gone along with that schoolboy demonstration about *The Warrior Prophet* (feeling all the time that it was unjustified), and in that little afternoon jihad had helped to break up a couple of minibuses, something happened that unsettled him.

24   It was Ramadan, the fasting month. He had been told, and he believed, that if he stayed up praying on one particular night during the last ten days of Ramadan, he would be cleansed of all his sins; he would become a new man. They told him he would feel lighter; that was impressed on him. That year the big night was the night of the twenty-seventh. He and his brother and his sister and the rest of the family stayed up praying. In the morning he didn't feel any different. He had been looking forward to a great feeling of lightness. He was disappointed. But he didn't have the courage to tell anyone in the family.

25   His disappointment, and the worry about it, might have been greater at this particular time because, after a decade and a half of success, his father's civil engineering business had begun to fail. The actual work was holding up, but Salman's father had begun to make a series of misjudgments about people. Salman was still at school; his father's business troubles would have worried him.

26   Two or three years later—Salman's father's business going down all the time—there was another incident, this time at the end of Ramadan. Id is the great festival at the end of Ramadan, and the Id prayers are always in a congregation. Salman's father had taken the car to go to the mosque he always went to, and Salman and his brother were going on foot to look for a mosque in the neighborhood. Salman said to his brother, "What a waste of time."

27   The brother said, "Especially when you don't even believe in it."

28   Salman said, "What? You too?"

29   The brother said, "Our elder sister doesn't believe either. Don't you know?"

30   Salman had a high regard for his brother's intellect. The worry he had felt about losing his faith dropped away. He didn't feel he was letting down the people who had died in the riots in Jalandhar in 1947.

31   All three children of the family had lost religion. But, as his business had gone down, Salman's father had grown more devout and more intolerant. One of the festivals the family had celebrated when Salman was a child was the Basant, or Spring Festival. Now Salman's father banned it as un-Islamic, something from the Hindu and pagan past. There were great quarrels with his daughter when she came from Karachi, where she lived. She was not as quiet as Salman and his brother. She spoke her mind, and the arguments could become quite heated. One day, when Salman's father's brother was also present, Salman's father said, "Let her be. She's an apostate. Don't get into these arguments with her." And he walked away in anger. The house would have been full of strains.

32   Salman's father wanted Salman to be an engineer. But Salman's mathematics were bad, and just before his twentieth birthday he joined the army. He had developed an interest in guns. He had no religious faith now, but he was the complete Pakistani soldier. He was passionate about going to war with India, though there had been the Bangladesh defeat just the year before.

33   "It was in my mind that we—or I, personally—had to get even for the murder of my grandparents and my two aunts. It must have been with me always, but this was a very cold feeling. Like a seasoned murderer going in for his hundredth kill. I wasn't excited or emotional about it. It was just something I had to do. I didn't talk about my grandparents, but I was very vocal about going back to war with India. This was with my army companions. Not at home."

34   After two or three years this feeling left him. He also fell out of love with the army. He couldn't find people to talk to, and he was rebuked for talking about books and trying to impress. Three years later he was able to leave the army. He joined a multinational company in Karachi. The job came through an army friend whose uncle was the number two in the company.

35   So Salman went to Karachi, the mohajir city. Life was not easy. He lived in the beginning as a paying guest in a family; after that there was a shabby little rented room with a kitchen. He moved up the ladder slowly. He had a friend in the company. One day when they were talking Salman mentioned the *Reader's Digest*. The friend laughed. Salman said he wanted to learn. The friend was pleased; he began to guide Salman, and Salman looked back on this as the start of his education.

36   After five years he married, and then, like his father, he gave up the security of his job and became self-employed. He did so at a bad time. Karachi had grown and grown since independence; it had received immigrants from India and from all parts of Pakistan; and now the Sindhi-Punjabi-mohajir tensions were about to turn nasty.

37   In January 1987, less than four years after he had married, Salman and his wife lost all their money. A friend had told them that at their stage in life they should be thinking of the future and making some investments.

They had put their money in different investment companies; they had been careful, as they thought, to spread the risks; but one day all the companies just vanished. The friend had persuaded them to invest in a company run by missionary mullahs. These mullahs were not militant; they wanted only to make Muslims good, to bring strayers back into the fold, and to win fresh converts. The friend said to Salman and his wife, "You may not have faith, but this is the only company that's truly reliable." That was where most of Salman's money and his wife's money went.

38   This tragedy was matched by the tragedy of the streets. "Things were getting bad in Karachi and Sindh during this time. Between 1987 and 1989 this terrible thing began to happen in Karachi. A solitary pedestrian at night would be approached from behind by a motorcyclist and stabbed in the back. There must have been fifty or a hundred-odd cases. They would happen once every week or so. Just an isolated incident somewhere. I do not recall reading anywhere that any one stabber had been apprehended. I was getting more and more upset about it.

39   "In July 1987 this incident happened. I had to drive my wife to the airport at two in the morning. On the way back I ran out of petrol. I knew there wasn't enough when I started, but I thought I would buy at one of the many points. This was a city that never really slept. But every single petrol station was closed for fear of armed robberies. I took my wife to the airport. My petrol was now very low. On the way back, about two kilometers from home, the car stopped. It would have been just after two in the morning. So I parked the car and started walking.

40   "I have never felt such a raging fear—it was surging inside me. I still very distinctly remember looking at the walls at the side of the road to see which one was easier to jump over, and escape, in case I was attacked. And then I heard this motorcyclist coming up from far behind. *Put-put-put.* I was utterly and completely terrified. And in this scramble of thoughts the only thing I remember was this desire to escape, to go over a wall. I don't know what kept me there. And the *put-put-put* came nearer. I looked back. He was a lone rider. The attackers were always two. So I knew he wasn't one. But still the fear was real. I stopped walking. And he came *put-put-put.* He said, 'What are you doing on the street at this time? Don't you know it's dangerous?' I told him. He asked where I was going. When I told him he said, 'Get on, I will drive you home.' He was an Urdu-speaking man. I laughed and asked him, 'You said it's dangerous. What are you doing on the street?' He said, 'I'm on the way to the Indian consulate, to be first in line for the visa.' Just after two in the morning. That is what people had to do. He must have had relations in India. He was going visiting. He wasn't getting away from the danger."

41   Salman and his wife had been playing with the idea of leaving Karachi and going back to Lahore. This experience decided him. Later that morning he telephoned his wife and said, "We really have to get away."

42   "It wasn't really fear. Fear for my own life. It was the sorrow of living in an unjust, cruel society. Everything was collapsing. It's as though those

poor people who died in Jalandhar died in vain. Why should my aunts and grandparents have to pay with their lives—for nothing? There was no bitterness. Just a sense of the unfairness in it all."

43   About six months after the motorcycle incident, people who were suffering in Karachi, like Salman, organized a peace rally. There were about five hundred at the rally. They were people who had lost hope. It was wintertime, very lovely and pleasant in Karachi. The people in the rally smiled and nodded at one another. Many had tears in their eyes.

44   "There was an immense feeling of brotherhood, of belonging. No slogans. It was just a walk for peace in Karachi. And all along I had this lump in my throat and I thought I would break out crying. Everybody knew that we were all partners in this grief, for whatever was happening to that city. Everybody used to have this feeling for that city. It never went to sleep. And people used to say—the Punjabis and the Pathans—that it was a kindhearted city, especially good to its poorer inhabitants."

45   That year, in the first week of September, there was a massacre of some three hundred people in the city of Hyderabad, the second city of Sindh. Unidentified gunmen opened up, and in ten or fifteen minutes killed those three hundred. It was part of the mohajir war. Sometimes the mohajirs did the killing, sometimes the army. Salman met some friends that day. They said to him, "You look sick. Has someone died?" He said, "No, no. No one's died."

46   On that day Salman and his wife decided to leave Karachi. It took them three months to wind up their affairs.

47   It wasn't easy for Salman to make a living. The restricted intellectual needs of the country offered him few openings as a writer, didn't encourage him to grow. He was poorly rewarded for what he did.

48   He had become a kind of wanderer. He found solace now in wilderness. The country at least offered him that; there were great tracts of desert and mountain where a man might feel no one had been before.

49   He carried the old torment with him: the first four days of independence in 1947, from the fourteenth of August to the eighteenth, and the empty courtyard house in Jalandhar with blood on the walls.

50   He had not been to India, and he was beginning to think he should go there. There was a journey he wished to make. He wanted the journey to start on the eleventh of August, and he wanted it to start in the Himalayan hill station of Solan. From Solan on the eleventh of August, 1947, his aunt (who was to be murdered within a week) had written to her husband that it was getting very dangerous in Solan; he was to come at once and take her back to Jalandhar. He went and brought her down in the train. He said later (he was one of the survivors) that the hatred and tension in the railway coach was something they could feel. But they got without trouble to the house in Jalandhar on the fourteenth of August.

51   That was the journey Salman wanted to do again one year, within those dates, if he could get an Indian visa. "To mark the beginning of this thing."

Questions for Discussion

1. What explanation does Salman give for *jihad*, or Islamic holy war? How, according to Salman, do some Muslims justify violence?
2. Where did Salman and the people of his country get their names? Why?
3. What, according to Salman, has happened to the culture of Pakistan?
4. What leads to Salman's loss of faith?
5. Who is to blame for the violence in Sindhi and Jalandhar? Can blame be easily attributed to any single group?

Suggestions for Exploring, Writing, and Persuading

1. According to Salman, *jihad* refers to literal violence. Write a paper based on the Islamic concept of *jihad*, considering all of its meanings. Consider using a translation of the Koran as one of your sources, but be aware that few Muslims consider their holy book translatable from the Arabic.
2. Pakistan was established as a religious state. Discuss the reasons for its failure to achieve the ideal harmony its founders envisioned.
3. Discuss in detail the failure of another community based on an ideal—perhaps a church or a club.

Ian Frazier (b. 1951)

Ian Frazier was born in New Jersey and grew up in Ohio. At Harvard University, he wrote for The Lampoon *before graduating in 1977. Subsequently he became a staff writer for the* New Yorker. *His humorous essays, many previously published in the* New Yorker, *are collected in books such as* Coyote v. Acme *(1996) and his most recent,* Dating Your Mom *(2003). He presently lives in Miles City, Montana.*

COYOTE V. ACME   (1996)

1   In the United States District Court,
Southwestern District,
Tempe, Arizona Case No. B19294,
Judge Joan Kujava, Presiding

WILE E. COYOTE, Plaintiff
—v.—
ACME COMPANY, Defendant

2   Opening Statement of Mr. Harold Schoff, attorney for Mr. Coyote: My client, Mr. Wile E. Coyote, a resident of Arizona and contiguous states,

does hereby bring suit for damages against the Acme Company, manufacturer and retail distributor of assorted merchandise, incorporated in Delaware and doing business in every state, district, and territory. Mr. Coyote seeks compensation for personal injuries, loss of business income, and mental suffering caused as a direct result of the actions and/or gross negligence of said company, under Title 15 of the United States Code, Chapter 47, section 2072, subsection (a), relating to product liability.

3   Mr. Coyote states that on eighty-five separate occasions he has purchased of the Acme Company (hereinafter, "Defendant"), through that company's mail-order department, certain products which did cause him bodily injury due to defects in manufacture or improper cautionary labelling. Sales slips made out to Mr. Coyote as proof of purchase are at present in the possession of the Court, marked Exhibit A. Such injuries sustained by Mr. Coyote have temporarily restricted his ability to make a living in his profession of predator. Mr. Coyote is self-employed and thus not eligible for Workmen's Compensation.

4   Mr. Coyote states that on December 13th he received of Defendant via parcel post one Acme Rocket Sled. The intention of Mr. Coyote was to use the Rocket Sled to aid him in pursuit of his prey. Upon receipt of the Rocket Sled Mr. Coyote removed it from its wooden shipping crate and, sighting his prey in the distance, activated the ignition. As Mr. Coyote gripped the handlebars, the Rocket Sled accelerated with such sudden and precipitate force as to stretch Mr. Coyote's forelimbs to a length of fifty feet. Subsequently, the rest of Mr. Coyote's body shot forward with a violent jolt, causing severe strain to his back and neck and placing him unexpectedly astride the Rocket Sled. Disappearing over the horizon at such speed as to leave a diminishing jet trail along its path, the Rocket Sled soon brought Mr. Coyote abreast of his prey. At that moment the animal he was pursuing veered sharply to the right. Mr. Coyote vigorously attempted to follow this maneuver but was unable to, due to poorly designed steering on the Rocket Sled and a faulty or nonexistent braking system. Shortly thereafter, the unchecked progress of the Rocket Sled brought it and Mr. Coyote into collision with the side of a mesa.

5   Paragraph One of the Report of Attending Physician (Exhibit B), prepared by Dr. Ernest Grosscup, M.D., D.O., details the multiple fractures, contusions, and tissue damage suffered by Mr. Coyote as a result of this collision. Repair of the injuries required a full bandage around the head (excluding the ears), a neck brace, and full or partial casts on all four legs.

6   Hampered by these injuries, Mr. Coyote was nevertheless obliged to support himself. With this in mind, he purchased of Defendant as an aid to mobility one pair of Acme Rocket Skates. When he attempted to use this product, however, he became involved in an accident remarkably similar to that which occurred with the Rocket Sled. Again, Defendant sold over the counter, without caveat, a product which attached power-

ful jet engines (in this case, two) to inadequate vehicles, with little or no provision for passenger safety. Encumbered by his heavy casts, Mr. Coyote lost control of the Rocket Skates soon after strapping them on, and collided with a roadside billboard so violently as to leave a hole in the shape of his full silhouette.

7   Mr. Coyote states that on occasions too numerous to list in this document he has suffered mishaps with explosives purchased of Defendant: the Acme "Little Giant" Firecracker, the Acme Self-Guided Aerial Bomb, etc. (For a full listing, see the Acme Mail Order Explosives Catalogue and attached deposition, entered in evidence as Exhibit C.) Indeed, it is safe to say that not once has an explosive purchased of Defendant by Mr. Coyote performed in an expected manner. To cite just one example: At the expense of much time and personal effort, Mr. Coyote constructed around the outer rim of a butte a wooden trough beginning at the top of the butte and spiralling downward around it to some few feet above a black X painted on the desert floor. The trough was designed in such a way that a spherical explosive of the type sold by Defendant would roll easily and swiftly down to the point of detonation indicated by the X. Mr. Coyote placed a generous pile of birdseed directly on the X, and then, carrying the spherical Acme Bomb (Catalogue #78-832), climbed to the top of the butte. Mr. Coyote's prey, seeing the birdseed, approached, and Mr. Coyote proceeded to light the fuse. In an instant, the fuse burned down to the stem, causing the bomb to detonate.

8   In addition to reducing all Mr. Coyote's careful preparations to naught, the premature detonation of Defendant's product resulted in the following disfigurements to Mr. Coyote:

1. Severe singeing of the hair on the head, neck, and muzzle.
2. Sooty discoloration.
3. Fracture of the left ear at the stem, causing the ear to dangle in the aftershock with a creaking noise.
4. Full or partial combustion of whiskers, producing kinking, frazzling, and ashy disintegration.
5. Radical widening of the eyes, due to brow and lid charring.

9   We come now to the Acme Spring-Powered Shoes. The remains of a pair of these purchased by Mr. Coyote on June 23rd are Plaintiff's Exhibit D. Selected fragments have been shipped to the metallurgical laboratories of the University of California at Santa Barbara for analysis, but to date no explanation has been found for this product's sudden and extreme malfunction. As advertised by Defendant, this product is simplicity itself: two wood-and-metal sandals, each attached to milled-steel springs of high tensile strength and compressed in a tightly coiled position by a cocking device with a lanyard release. Mr. Coyote believed that this product would enable him to pounce upon his prey in the initial moments of the chase, when swift reflexes are at a premium.

10   To increase the shoes' thrusting power still further, Mr. Coyote affixed them by their bottoms to the side of a large boulder. Adjacent to the boulder was a path which Mr. Coyote's prey was known to frequent. Mr. Coyote put his hind feet in the wood-and-metal sandals and crouched in readiness, his right forepaw holding firmly to the lanyard release. Within a short time Mr. Coyote's prey did indeed appear on the path coming toward him. Unsuspecting, the prey stopped near Mr. Coyote, well within range of the springs at full extension. Mr. Coyote gauged the distance with care and proceeded to pull the lanyard release.

11   At this point, Defendant's product should have thrust Mr. Coyote forward and away from the boulder. Instead, for reasons yet unknown, the Acme Spring-Powered Shoes thrust the boulder away from Mr. Coyote. As the intended prey looked on unharmed, Mr. Coyote hung suspended in air. Then the twin springs recoiled, bringing Mr. Coyote to a violent feet-first collision with the boulder, the full weight of his head and forequarters falling upon his lower extremities.

12   The force of this impact then caused the springs to rebound, whereupon Mr. Coyote was thrust skyward. A second recoil and collision followed. The boulder, meanwhile, which was roughly ovoid in shape, had begun to bounce down a hillside, the coiling and recoiling of the springs adding to its velocity. At each bounce, Mr. Coyote came into contact with the boulder, or the boulder came into contact with Mr. Coyote, or both came into contact with the ground. As the grade was a long one, this process continued for some time.

13   The sequence of collisions resulted in systemic physical damage to Mr. Coyote, viz., flattening of the cranium, sideways displacement of the tongue, reduction of length of legs and upper body, and compression of vertebrae from base of tail to head. Repetition of blows along a vertical axis produced a series of regular horizontal folds in Mr. Coyote's body tissues-a rare and painful condition which caused Mr. Coyote to expand upward and contract downward alternately as he walked, and to emit an off-key accordionlike wheezing with every step. The distracting and embarrassing nature of this symptom has been a major impediment to Mr. Coyote's pursuit of a normal social life.

14   As the Court is no doubt aware, Defendant has a virtual monopoly of manufacture and sale of goods required by Mr. Coyote's work. It is our contention that Defendant has used its market advantage to the detriment of the consumer of such specialized products as itching powder, giant kites, Burmese tiger traps, anvils, and two-hundred-foot-long rubber bands. Much as he has come to mistrust Defendant's products, Mr. Coyote has no other domestic source of supply to which to turn. One can only wonder what our trading partners in Western Europe and Japan would make of such a situation, where a giant company is allowed to victimize the consumer in the most reckless and wrongful manner over and over again.

15   Mr. Coyote respectfully requests that the Court regard these larger economic implications and assess punitive damages in the amount of seventeen million dollars. In addition, Mr. Coyote seeks actual damages (missed meals, medical expenses, days lost from professional occupation) of one million dollars; general damages (mental suffering, injury to reputation) of twenty million dollars; and attorney's fees of seven hundred and fifty thousand dollars. Total damages: thirty-eight million seven hundred and fifty thousand dollars. By awarding Mr. Coyote the full amount, this Court will censure Defendant, its directors, officers, shareholders, successors, and assigns, in the only language they understand, and reaffirm the right of the individual predator to equal protection under the law.

Questions for Discussion

1. In Roadrunner cartoons, what is Wile E. Coyote's "work"? Why is it specifically identified only in the last sentence?

2. What is ridiculous about Coyote's suit against Acme?

3. What is this parody of a suit satirizing? What similarly frivolous actual suits do you know of?

4. What is the effect of the detailed description of each step of a process that, in the cartoon, would take only a few seconds? What emotion does the detailed description of Coyote's injuries evoke?

5. The attorney claims that Coyote's injuries have been "a major impediment to Mr. Coyote's pursuit of a normal social life." What would you expect his social life to be?

6. Explain the irony of the attorney's claim that "company is allowed to victimize the consumer in the most reckless and wrongful manner *over and over again*."

Suggestions for Exploring, Writing, and Persuading

1. Write a closing statement for the defense of Acme.

2. Where would you draw the line between company liability and user responsibility? That is, to what extent should a company be held responsible for the safety of its products, and to what extent should the consumer be responsible for his or her own safety?

3. Selecting as your client a person—real or fictional—or an animal—cartoon or actual—, write a similar legal brief suing a company for damages that resulted from the customer's misuse of a product.

4. Write an essay comparing the satiric tone and ironic inversions of "Coyote v. Acme" with those of Swift's "A Modest Proposal."

FICON

Katherine Anne Porter (1890–1980)

Katherine Anne Porter was born in Texas and attended convent schools there and in Louisiana. She worked as a journalist in Chicago and in Mexico. Porter considered herself an artist, and in her short stories, short novels, and one full-length novel, Ship of Fools, *she proves her claim. Her mastery of style, even in her early stories, is at least partly a result of her almost endless polishing. Literary critics repeatedly praise her craftsmanship with language and her command of multiple-layered point of view. Through her skillful use of point of view, Porter probes deeply into the minds and hearts of her characters, revealing their dreams and aspirations and their disappointments and disillusionment. While most of Porter's works reflect events and locations from her own life, the character with whom she is most often identified is Miranda Gay. The seven short stories grouped together under the heading "The Old Order" in chronological order are "The Source," "The Journey," "The Witness," "The Circus," "The Last Leaf," "The Fig Tree," and "The Grave." These stories trace many of the people, events, and perceptions that shape Miranda into the young woman portrayed at the end of "The Grave" and in two longer stories—"Old Mortality" and "Pale Horse, Pale Rider."*

THE GRAVE   (1935)

1   The grandfather, dead for more than thirty years, had been twice disturbed in his long repose by the constancy and possessiveness of his widow. She removed his bones first to Louisiana and then to Texas as if she had set out to find her own burial place, knowing well she would never return to the places she had left. In Texas she set up a small cemetery in a corner of her first farm, and as the family connection grew, and oddments of relations came over from Kentucky to settle, it contained at last about twenty graves. After the grandmother's death, part of her land was to be sold for the benefit of certain of her children, and the cemetery happened to lie in the part set aside for sale. It was necessary to take up the bodies and bury them again in the family plot in the big new public cemetery, where the grandmother had been buried. At last her husband was to lie beside her for eternity, as she had planned.

2   The family cemetery had been a pleasant small neglected garden of tangled rose bushes and ragged cedar trees and cypress, the simple flat stones rising out of uncropped sweet-smelling wild grass. The graves were lying open and empty one burning day when Miranda and her

brother Paul, who often went together to hunt rabbits and doves, propped their twenty-two Winchester rifles carefully against the rail fence, climbed over and explored among the graves. She was nine years old and he was twelve.

3   They peered into the pits all shaped alike with such purposeful accuracy, and looking at each other with pleased adventurous eyes, they said in solemn tones: "These were graves!" trying by words to shape a special, suitable emotion in their minds, but they felt nothing except an agreeable thrill of wonder: they were seeing a new sight, doing something they had not done before. In them both there was also a small disappointment at the entire commonplaceness of the actual spectacle. Even if it had once contained a coffin for years upon years, when the coffin was gone a grave was just a hole in the ground. Miranda leaped into the pit that had held her grandfather's bones. Scratching around aimlessly and pleasurably as any young animal, she scooped up a lump of earth and weighed it in her palm. It had a pleasantly sweet, corrupt smell, being mixed with the cedar needles and small leaves, and as the crumbs fell apart, she saw a silver dove no larger than a hazel nut, with spread wings and a neat fan-shaped tail. The breast had a deep round hollow in it. Turning it up to the fierce sunlight, she saw that the inside of the hollow was cut in little whorls. She scrambled out, over the pile of loose earth that had fallen back into one end of the grave, calling to Paul that she had found something, he must guess what....His head appeared smiling over the rim of another grave. He waved a closed hand at her. "I've got something too!" They ran to compare treasures, making a game of it, so many guesses each, all wrong, and a final show-down with opened palms. Paul had found a thin wide gold ring carved with intricate flowers and leaves. Miranda was smitten at sight of the ring and wished to have it. Paul seemed more impressed by the dove. They made a trade, with some little bickering. After he had got the dove in his hand, Paul said, "Don't you know what this is? This is a screw head for a *coffin!*... I'll bet nobody else in the world has one like this!"

4   Miranda glanced at it without covetousness. She had the gold ring on her thumb; it fitted perfectly. "Maybe we ought to go now," she said, "maybe one of the niggers 'll see us and tell somebody." They knew the land had been sold, the cemetery was no longer theirs, and they felt like trespassers. They climbed back over the fence, slung their rifles loosely under their arms—they had been shooting at targets with various kinds of firearms since they were seven years old—and set out to look for the rabbits and doves or whatever small game might happen along. On these expeditions Miranda always followed at Paul's heels along the path, obeying instructions about handling her gun when going through fences; learning how to stand it up properly so it would not slip and fire unexpectedly; how to wait her time for a shot and not just bang away in the air without looking, spoiling shots for Paul, who really could hit things if given a chance. Now and then, in her excitement at seeing birds whizz up suddenly before her face, or a rabbit leap across her very toes, she

lost her head, and almost without sighting she flung her rifle up and pulled the trigger. She hardly ever hit any sort of mark. She had no proper sense of hunting at all. Her brother would be often completely disgusted with her. "You don't care whether you get your bird or not," he said. "That's no way to hunt." Miranda could not understand his indignation. She had seen him smash his hat and yell with fury when he had missed his aim. "What I like about shooting," said Miranda, with exasperating inconsequence, "is pulling the trigger and hearing the noise."

5   "Then, by golly," said Paul, "whyn't you go back to the range and shoot at bulls-eyes?"

6   "I'd just as soon," said Miranda, "only like this, we walk round more."

7   "Well, you just stay behind and stop spoiling my shots," said Paul, who, when he made a kill, wanted to be certain he had made it. Miranda, who alone brought down a bird once in twenty rounds, always claimed as her own any game they got when they fired at the same moment. It was tiresome and unfair and her brother was sick of it.

8   "Now, the first dove we see, or the first rabbit, is mine," he told her. "and the next will be yours. Remember that and don't get smarty."

9   "What about snakes?" asked Miranda idly. "Can I have the first snake?"

10   Waving her thumb gently and watching her gold ring glitter, Miranda lost interest in shooting. She was wearing her summer roughing outfit: dark blue overalls, a light blue shirt, a hired-man's straw hat, and thick brown sandals. Her brother had the same outfit except his was a sober hickory-nut color. Ordinarily Miranda preferred her overalls to any other dress, though it was making rather a scandal in the countryside, for the year was 1903, and in the back country the law of female decorum had teeth in it. Her father had been criticized for letting his girls dress like boys and go careering around astride barebacked horses. Big sister Maria, the really independent and fearless one, in spite of her rather affected ways, rode at a dead run with only a rope knotted around her horse's nose. It was said that the motherless family was running down, with the Grandmother no longer there to hold it together. It was known that she had discriminated against her son Harry in her will, and that he was in straits about money. Some of his old neighbors reflected with vicious satisfaction that now he would probably not be so stiffnecked, nor have any more high-stepping horses either. Miranda knew this, though she could not say how. She had met along the road old women of the kind who smoked corn-cob pipes, who had treated her grandmother with most sincere respect. They slanted their gummy old eyes side-ways at the granddaughter and said, "Ain't you ashamed of yoself, Missy? It's aginst the Scriptures to dress like that. Whut yo Pappy thinkin about?" Miranda, with her powerful social sense, which was like a fine set of antennae radiating from every pore of her skin, would feel ashamed because she knew well it was rude and ill-bred to shock anybody, even bad-tempered old crones, though she had faith in her father's judgment and was perfectly comfortable in the clothes. Her father had said, "They're just what you need, and

they'll save your dresses for school..." This sounded quite simple and natural to her. She had been brought up in rigorous economy. Wastefulness was vulgar. It was also a sin. These were truths; she had heard them repeated many times and never once disputed.

11   Now the ring, shining with the serene purity of fine gold on her rather grubby thumb, turned her feelings against her overalls and sockless feet, toes sticking through the thick brown leather straps. She wanted to go back to the farmhouse, take a good cold bath, dust herself with plenty of Maria's violet talcum powder—provided Maria was not present to object, of course—put on the thinnest, most becoming dress she owned, with a big sash, and sit in a wicker chair under the trees...These things were not all she wanted, of course; she had vague stirrings of desire for luxury and a grand way of living which could not take precise form in her imagination but were founded on family legend of past wealth and leisure. These immediate comforts were what she could have, and she wanted them at once. She lagged rather far behind Paul, and once she thought of just turning back without a word and going home. She stopped, thinking that Paul would never do that to her, and so she would have to tell him. When a rabbit leaped, she let Paul have it without dispute. He killed it with one shot.

12   When she came up with him, he was already kneeling, examining the wound, the rabbit trailing from his hands. "Right through the head," he said complacently, as if he had aimed for it. He took out his sharp, competent bowie knife and started to skin the body. He did it very cleanly and quickly. Uncle Jimbilly knew how to prepare the skins so that Miranda always had fur coats for her dolls, for though she never cared much for her dolls she liked seeing them in fur coats. The children knelt facing each other over the dead animal. Miranda watched admiringly while her brother stripped the skin away as if he were taking off a glove. The flayed flesh emerged dark scarlet, sleek, firm; Miranda with thumb and finger felt the long fine muscles with the silvery flat strips binding them to the joints. Brother lifted the oddly bloated belly. "Look," he said, in a low amazed voice. "It was going to have young ones."

13   Very carefully he slit the thin flesh from the center ribs to the flanks, and a scarlet bag appeared. He slit again and pulled the bag open, and there lay a bundle of tiny rabbits, each wrapped in a thin scarlet veil. The brother pulled these off and there they were, dark gray, their sleek wet down lying in minute even ripples, like a baby's head just washed, their unbelievably small delicate ears folded close, their little blind faces almost featureless.

14   Miranda said, "Oh, I want to *see*," under her breath. She looked and looked—excited but not frightened, for she was accustomed to the sight of animals killed in hunting—filled with pity and astonishment and a kind of shocked delight in the wonderful little creatures for their own sakes, they were so pretty. She touched one of them ever so carefully, "Ah, there's blood running over them," she said and began to tremble without knowing why. Yet she wanted most deeply to see and to know. Having

seen, she felt at once as if she had known all along. The very memory of her former ignorance faded, she had always known just this. No one had ever told her anything outright, she had been rather unobservant of the animal life around her because she was so accustomed to animals. They seemed simply disorderly and unaccountably rude in their habits, but altogether natural and not very interesting. Her brother had spoken as if he had known about everything all along. He may have seen all this before. He had never said a word to her, but she knew now a part at least of what he knew. She understood a little of the secret, formless intuitions in her own mind and body, which had been clearing up, taking form, so gradually and so steadily she had not realized that she was learning what she had to know. Paul said cautiously, as if he were talking about something forbidden. "They were just about ready to be born." His voice dropped on the last word. "I know," said Miranda, "like kittens. I know, like babies." She was quietly and terribly agitated, standing again with her rifle under her arm, looking down at the bloody heap. "I don't want the skin," she said, "I won't have it." Paul buried the young rabbits again in their mother's body, wrapped the skin around her, carried her to a clump of sage bushes, and hid her away. He came out again at once and said to Miranda, with an eager friendliness, a confidential tone quite unusual in him, as if he were taking her into an important secret on equal terms: "Listen now. Now you listen to me, and don't ever forget. Don't you ever tell a living soul that you saw this. Don't tell a soul. Don't tell Dad because I'll get into trouble. He'll say I'm leading you into things you ought not to do. He's always saying that. So now don't you go and forget and blab out sometime the way you're always doing...Now, that's a secret. Don't you tell."

15   Miranda never told, she did not even wish to tell anybody. She thought about the whole worrisome affair with confused unhappiness for a few days. Then it sank quietly in her mind and was heaped over by accumulated thousands of impressions, for nearly twenty years. One day she was picking her path among the puddles and crushed refuse of a market street in a strange city of a strange country, when without warning, plain and clear in its true colors as if she looked through a frame upon a scene that had not stirred nor changed since the moment it happened, the episode of that far-off day leaped from its burial place before her mind's eye. She was so reasonlessly horrified she halted suddenly staring, the scene before her eyes dimmed by the vision back of them. An Indian vendor had held up before her a tray of dyed sugar sweets, in the shapes of all kinds of small creatures: birds, baby chicks, baby rabbits, lambs, baby pigs. They were in gay colors and smelled of vanilla, maybe....It was a very hot day and the smell in the market, with its piles of raw flesh and wilting flowers, was like the mingled sweetness and corruption she had smelled that other day in the empty cemetery at home: the day she had remembered always until now vaguely as the time she and her brother had found treasure in the opened graves. Instantly upon this thought the dreadful vision faded, and she saw clearly her brother, whose childhood

face she had forgotten, standing again in the blazing sunshine, again twelve years old, a pleased sober smile in his eyes, turning the silver dove over and over in his hands.

Questions for Discussion

1. Why are the graves empty? What is the double significance of their being empty?

2. List and explain the objects and phrases in the story that suggest death and/or rebirth.

3. We see this event through the double perception of Miranda's consciousness. Here she is first described at age nine, but at the end of the story she recalls the incident twenty years later. What triggers this memory? Why is she "reasonlessly horrified" by the memory? Why does the "dreadful vision" fade into a memory of her brother Paul's "childhood face..., a pleased sober smile in his eyes"?

4. The story of the discoveries in the grave is framed by the description of moving the remains of Miranda's grandfather and the final scene in the Indian market. What significance do these framing scenes have?

Suggestions for Exploring, Writing, and Persuading

1. This story describes events in Miranda's life that shape her as an adult. Analyze the significance of a transforming event in your life.

2. After carefully rereading the descriptions in "The Grave" of the empty graves, the ring, the dove, and the rabbit, write an essay explaining and illustrating what each symbolizes.

3. Write an essay explaining how and why this story might be described as ending in an epiphany.

F. Scott Fitzgerald (1896–1940)

A native of St. Paul, Minnesota, educated at Princeton, Francis Scott Key Fitzgerald published his highly successful first novel, This Side of Paradise, *in 1920. Soon thereafter, he and his fashionable wife, Zelda, embraced an extravagant and hedonistic lifestyle of partying with the newly rich Americans of what Fitzgerald dubbed "the jazz age." Most of his fiction, including the short story collections* Flappers and Philosophers *(1920) and* Tales of the Jazz Age *(1922), chronicles the enthusiastic pursuit of pleasure among the wealthy partygoers he and Zelda encountered. He is perhaps best known for his novels, including* The Great Gatsby *(1925), surely one of the gems of modern American fiction, and* Tender Is the Night *(1934).*

WINTER DREAMS (1922)

I

1   Some of the caddies were poor as sin and lived in one-room houses with a neurasthenic cow in the front yard, but Dexter Green's father owned the second best grocery-store in Black Bear—the best one was "The Hub," patronized by the wealthy people from Sherry Island—and Dexter caddied only for pocket-money.

2   In the fall when the days became crisp and gray, and the long Minnesota winter shut down like the white lid of a box, Dexter's skis moved over the snow that hid the fairways of the golf course. At these times the country gave him a feeling of profound melancholy—it offended him that the links should lie in enforced fallowness, haunted by ragged sparrows for the long season. It was dreary, too, that on the tees where the gay colors fluttered in summer there were now only the desolate sand-boxes knee-deep in crusted ice. When he crossed the hills the wind blew cold as misery, and if the sun was out he tramped with his eyes squinted up against the hard dimensionless glare.

3   In April the winter ceased abruptly. The snow ran down into Black Bear Lake scarcely tarrying for the early golfers to brave the season with red and black balls. Without elation, without an interval of moist glory, the cold was gone.

4   Dexter knew that there was something dismal about this Northern spring, just as he knew there was something gorgeous about the fall. Fall made him clinch his hands and tremble and repeat idiotic sentences to himself, and make brisk abrupt gestures of command to imaginary audiences and armies. October filled him with hope which November raised to a sort of ecstatic triumph, and in this mood the fleeting brilliant impressions of the summer at Sherry Island were ready grist to his mill. He became a golf champion and defeated Mr. T. A. Hedrick in a marvellous match played a hundred times over the fairways of his imagination, a match each detail of which he changed about untiringly—sometimes he won with almost laughable ease, sometimes he came up magnificently from behind. Again, stepping from a Pierce-Arrow automobile, like Mr. Mortimer Jones, he strolled frigidly into the lounge of the Sherry Island Golf Club—or perhaps, surrounded by an admiring crowd, he gave an exhibition of fancy diving from the spring-board of the club raft....Among those who watched him in open-mouthed wonder was Mr. Mortimer Jones.

5   And one day it came to pass that Mr. Jones—himself and not his ghost—came up to Dexter with tears in his eyes and said that Dexter was the ——— best caddy in the club, and wouldn't he decide not to quit if Mr. Jones made it worth his while, because every other ——— caddy in the club lost one ball a hole for him—regularly———

6   "No, sir," said Dexter decisively, "I don't want to caddy any more." Then, after a pause: "I'm too old."

7   "You're not more than fourteen. Why the devil did you decide just this morning that you wanted to quit? You promised that next week you'd go over to the State tournament with me."

8   "I decided I was too old."

9   Dexter handed in his "A Class" badge, collected what money was due him from the caddy master, and walked home to Black Bear Village.

10   "The best —— caddy I ever saw," shouted Mr. Mortimer Jones over a drink that afternoon. "Never lost a ball! Willing! Intelligent! Quiet! Honest! Grateful!"

11   The little girl who had done this was eleven—beautifully ugly as little girls are apt to be who are destined after a few years to be inexpressibly lovely and bring no end of misery to a great number of men. The spark, however, was perceptible. There was a general ungodliness in the way her lips twisted down at the corners when she smiled, and in the— Heaven help us!—in the almost passionate quality of her eyes. Vitality is born early in such women. It was utterly in evidence now, shining through her thin frame in a sort of glow.

12   She had come eagerly out on to the course at nine o'clock with a white linen nurse and five small new golf-clubs in a white canvas bag which the nurse was carrying. When Dexter first saw her she was standing by the caddy house, rather ill at ease and trying to conceal the fact by engaging her nurse in an obviously unnatural conversation graced by startling and irrelevant grimaces from herself.

13   "Well, it's certainly a nice day, Hilda," Dexter heard her say. She drew down the corners of her mouth, smiled, and glanced furtively around, her eyes in transit falling for an instant on Dexter.

14   Then to the nurse:

15   "Well, I guess there aren't very many people out here this morning, are there?"

16   The smile again—radiant, blatantly artificial—convincing.

17   "I don't know what we're supposed to do now," said the nurse, looking nowhere in particular.

18   "Oh, that's all right. I'll fix it up."

19   Dexter stood perfectly still, his mouth slightly ajar. He knew that if he moved forward a step his stare would be in her line of vision—if he moved backward he would lose his full view of her face. For a moment he had not realized how young she was. Now he remembered having seen her several times the year before—in bloomers.

20   Suddenly, involuntarily, he laughed, a short abrupt laugh—then, startled by himself, he turned and began to walk quickly away.

21   "Boy!"

22   Dexter stopped.

23   "Boy——"

24   Beyond question he was addressed. Not only that, but he was treated to that absurd smile, that preposterous smile—the memory of which at least a dozen men were to carry into middle age.

25   "Boy, do you know where the golf teacher is?"

26   "He's giving a lesson."

27   "Well, do you know where the caddy-master is?"

28   "He isn't here yet this morning."

29   "Oh." For a moment this baffled her. She stood alternately on her right and left foot.

30   "We'd like to get a caddy," said the nurse. "Mrs. Mortimer Jones sent us out to play golf, and we don't know how without we get a caddy."

31   Here she was stopped by an ominous glance from Miss Jones, followed immediately by the smile.

32   "There aren't any caddies here except me," said Dexter to the nurse, "and I got to stay here in charge until the caddy-master gets here."

33   "Oh."

34   Miss Jones and her retinue now withdrew, and at a proper distance from Dexter became involved in a heated conversation, which was concluded by Miss Jones taking one of the clubs and hitting it on the ground with violence. For further emphasis she raised it again and was about to bring it down smartly upon the nurse's bosom, when the nurse seized the club and twisted it from her hands.

35   "You damn little mean old *thing!*" cried Miss Jones wildly.

36   Another argument ensued. Realizing that the elements of the comedy were implied in the scene, Dexter several times began to laugh, but each time restrained the laugh before it reached audibility. He could not resist the monstrous conviction that the little girl was justified in beating the nurse.

37   The situation was resolved by the fortuitous appearance of the caddy-master, who was appealed to immediately by the nurse.

38   "Miss Jones is to have a little caddy, and this one says he can't go."

39   "Mr. McKenna said I was to wait here till you came," said Dexter quickly.

40   "Well, he's here now." Miss Jones smiled cheerfully at the caddy-master. Then she dropped her bag and set off at a haughty mince toward the first tee.

41   "Well?" The caddy-master turned to Dexter. "What you standing there like a dummy for? Go pick up the young lady's clubs."

42   "I don't think I'll go out to-day," said Dexter.

43   "You don't———"

44   "I think I'll quit."

45   The enormity of his decision frightened him. He was a favorite caddy, and the thirty dollars a month he earned through the summer were not to be made elsewhere around the lake. But he had received a strong emotional shock, and his perturbation required a violent and immediate outlet.

46   It is not so simple as that, either. As so frequently would be the case in the future, Dexter was unconsciously dictated to by his winter dreams.

II

47   Now, of course, the quality and the seasonability of these winter dreams varied, but the stuff of them remained. They persuaded Dexter several years later to pass up a business course at the State university—his father, prospering now, would have paid his way—for the precarious advantage of attending an older and more famous university in the East, where he was bothered by his scanty funds. But do not get the impression, because his winter dreams happened to be concerned at first with musings on the rich, that there was anything merely snobbish in the boy. He wanted not association with glittering things and glittering people—he wanted the glittering things themselves. Often he reached out for the best without knowing why he wanted it—and sometimes he ran up against the mysterious denials and prohibitions in which life indulges. It is with one of those denials and not with his career as a whole that this story deals.

48   He made money. It was rather amazing. After college he went to the city from which Black Bear Lake draws its wealthy patrons. When he was only twenty-three and had been there not quite two years, there were already people who liked to say: "Now *there's* a boy—". All about him rich men's sons were peddling bonds precariously, or investing patrimonies precariously, or plodding through the two dozen volumes of the "George Washington Commercial Course," but Dexter borrowed a thousand dollars on his college degree and his confident mouth, and bought a partnership in a laundry.

49   It was a small laundry when he went into it but Dexter made a specialty of learning how the English washed fine woollen golf-stockings without shrinking them, and within a year he was catering to the trade that wore knickerbockers. Men were insisting that their Shetland hose and sweaters go to his laundry just as they had insisted on a caddy who could find golf-balls. A little later he was doing their wives' lingerie as well—and running five branches in different parts of the city. Before he was twenty-seven he owned the largest string of laundries in his section of the country. It was then that he sold out and went to New York. But the part of his story that concerns us goes back to the days when he was making his first big success.

50   When he was twenty-three Mr. Hart—one of the gray-haired men who like to say "Now there's a boy"—gave him a guest card to the Sherry Island Golf Club for a week-end. So he signed his name one day on the register, and that afternoon played golf in a foursome with Mr. Hart and Mr. Sandwood and Mr. T. A. Hedrick. He did not consider it necessary to remark that he had once carried Mr. Hart's bag over this same links, and that he knew every trap and gully with his eyes shut—but he found himself glancing at the four caddies who trailed them, trying to catch a gleam or gesture that would remind him of himself, that would lessen the gap which lay between his present and his past.

51   It was a curious day, slashed abruptly with fleeting, familiar impressions. One minute he had the sense of being a trespasser—in the next he

was impressed by the tremendous superiority he felt toward Mr. T. A. Hedrick, who was a bore and not even a good golfer any more.

52 Then, because of a ball Mr. Hart lost near the fifteenth green, an enormous thing happened. While they were searching the stiff grasses of the rough there was a clear call of "Fore!" from behind a hill in their rear. And as they all turned abruptly from their search a bright new ball sliced abruptly over the hill and caught Mr. T. A. Hedrick in the abdomen.

53 "By Gad!" cried Mr. T. A. Hedrick, "they ought to put some of these crazy women off the course. It's getting to be outrageous."

54 A head and a voice came up together over the hill:

55 "Do you mind if we go through?"

56 "You hit me in the stomach!" declared Mr. Hedrick wildly.

57 "Did I?" The girl approached the group of men. "I'm sorry. I yelled 'Fore!'"

58 Her glance fell casually on each of the men—then scanned the fairway for her ball.

59 "Did I bounce into the rough?"

60 It was impossible to determine whether this question was ingenuous or malicious. In a moment, however, she left no doubt, for as her partner came up over the hill she called cheerfully:

61 "Here I am! I'd have gone on the green except that I hit something."

62 As she took her stance for a short mashie shot, Dexter looked at her closely. She wore a blue gingham dress, rimmed at throat and shoulders with a white edging that accentuated her tan. The quality of exaggeration, of thinness, which had made her passionate eyes and down-turning mouth absurd at eleven, was gone now. She was arrestingly beautiful. The color in her cheeks was centered like the color in a picture—it was not a "high" color, but a sort of fluctuating and feverish warmth, so shaded that it seemed at any moment it would recede and disappear. This color and the mobility of her mouth gave a continual impression of flux, of intense life, of passionate vitality—balanced only partially by the sad luxury of her eyes.

63 She swung her mashie impatiently and without interest, pitching the ball into a sand-pit on the other side of the green. With a quick, insincere smile and a careless "Thank you!" she went on after it.

64 "That Judy Jones!" remarked Mr. Hedrick on the next tee, as they waited—some moments—for her to play on ahead. "All she needs is to be turned up and spanked for six months and then to be married off to an old-fashioned cavalry captain."

65 "My God, she's good-looking!" said Mr. Sandwood, who was just over thirty.

66 "Good-looking!" cried Mr. Hedrick contemptuously, "she always looks as if she wanted to be kissed! Turning those big cow-eyes on every calf in town!"

67 It was doubtful if Mr. Hedrick intended a reference to the maternal instinct.

68 "She'd play pretty good golf if she'd try," said Mr. Sandwood.

69 "She has no form," said Mr. Hedrick solemnly.

70 "She has a nice figure," said Mr. Sandwood.

71   "Better thank the Lord she doesn't drive a swifter ball," said Mr. Hart, winking at Dexter.

72   Later in the afternoon the sun went down with a riotous swirl of gold and varying blues and scarlets, and left the dry, rustling night of Western summer. Dexter watched from the veranda of the Golf Club, watched the even overlap of the waters in the little wind, silver molasses under the harvest-moon. Then the moon held a finger to her lips and the lake became a clear pool, pale and quiet. Dexter put on his bathing-suit and swam out to the farthest raft, where he stretched dripping on the wet canvas of the springboard.

73   There was a fish jumping and a star shining and the lights around the lake were gleaming. Over on a dark peninsula a piano was playing the songs of last summer and of summers before that—songs from "Chin-Chin" and "The Count of Luxemburg" and "The Chocolate Soldier"—and because the sound of a piano over a stretch of water had always seemed beautiful to Dexter he lay perfectly quiet and listened.

74   The tune the piano was playing at that moment had been gay and new five years before when Dexter was a sophomore at college. They had played it at a prom once when he could not afford the luxury of proms, and he had stood outside the gymnasium and listened. The sound of the tune precipitated in him a sort of ecstasy and it was with that ecstasy he viewed what happened to him now. It was a mood of intense appreciation, a sense that, for once, he was magnificently attune to life and that everything about him was radiating a brightness and a glamour he might never know again.

75   A low, pale oblong detached itself suddenly from the darkness of the Island, spitting forth the reverberate sound of a racing motor-boat. Two white streamers of cleft water rolled themselves out behind it and almost immediately the boat was beside him, drowning out the hot tinkle of the piano in the drone of its spray. Dexter raising himself on his arms was aware of a figure standing at the wheel, of two dark eyes regarding him over the lengthening space of water—then the boat had gone by and was sweeping in an immense and purposeless circle of spray round and round in the middle of the lake. With equal eccentricity one of the circles flattened out and headed back toward the raft.

76   "Who's that?" she called, shutting off her motor. She was so near now that Dexter could see her bathing-suit, which consisted apparently of pink rompers.

77   The nose of the boat bumped the raft, and as the latter tilted rakishly he was precipitated toward her. With different degrees of interest they recognized each other.

78   "Aren't you one of those men we played through this afternoon?" she demanded.

79   He was.

80   "Well, do you know how to drive a motor-boat? Because if you do I wish you'd drive this one so I can ride on the surf-board behind. My name is Judy Jones"—she favored him with an absurd smirk—rather, what tried

to be a smirk, for, twist her mouth as she might, it was not grotesque, it was merely beautiful—"and I live in a house over there on the Island, and in that house there is a man waiting for me. When he drove up at the door I drove out of the dock because he says I'm his ideal."

81   There was a fish jumping and a star shining and the lights around the lake were gleaming. Dexter sat beside Judy Jones and she explained how her boat was driven. Then she was in the water, swimming to the float-ing surfboard with a sinuous crawl. Watching her was without effort to the eye, watching a branch waving or a sea-gull flying. Her arms, burned to butternut, moved sinuously among the dull platinum ripples, elbow appearing first, casting the forearm back with a cadence of falling water, then reaching out and down, stabbing a path ahead.

82   They moved out into the lake; turning, Dexter saw that she was kneel-ing on the low rear of the now uptilted surf-board.

83   "Go faster," she called, "fast as it'll go."

84   Obediently he jammed the lever forward and the white spray mounted at the bow. When he looked around again the girl was standing up on the rushing board, her arms spread wide, her eyes lifted toward the moon.

85   "It's awful cold," she shouted. "What's your name?"

86   He told her.

87   "Well, why don't you come to dinner to-morrow night?"

88   His heart turned over like the fly-wheel of the boat, and, for the sec-ond time, her casual whim gave a new direction to his life.

III

89   Next evening while he waited for her to come down-stairs, Dexter peopled the soft deep summer room and the sun-porch that opened from it with the men who had already loved Judy Jones. He knew the sort of men they were—the men who when he first went to college had entered from the great prep schools with graceful clothes and the deep tan of healthy summers. He had seen that, in one sense, he was better than these men. He was newer and stronger. Yet in acknowledging to himself that he wished his children to be like them he was admitting that he was but the rough, strong stuff from which they eternally sprang.

90   When the time had come for him to wear good clothes, he had known who were the best tailors in America, and the best tailors in America had made him the suit he wore this evening. He had acquired that particular reserve peculiar to his university, that set it off from other universities. He recognized the value to him of such a mannerism and he had adopted it; he knew that to be careless in dress and manner required more confi-dence than to be careful. But carelessness was for his children. His mother's name had been Krimslich. She was a Bohemian of the peasant class and she had talked broken English to the end of her days. Her son must keep to the set patterns.

91   At a little after seven Judy Jones came down-stairs. She wore a blue silk afternoon dress, and he was disappointed at first that she had not put

on something more elaborate. This feeling was accentuated when, after a brief greeting, she went to the door of a butler's pantry and pushing it open called: "You can serve dinner, Martha." He had rather expected that a butler would announce dinner, that there would be a cocktail. Then he put these thoughts behind him as they sat down side by side on a lounge and looked at each other.

92   "Father and mother won't be here," she said thoughtfully.

93   He remembered the last time he had seen her father, and he was glad the parents were not to be here to-night—they might wonder who he was. He had been born in Keeble, a Minnesota village fifty miles farther north, and he always gave Keeble as his home instead of Black Bear Village. Country towns were well enough to come from if they weren't inconveniently in sight and used as footstools by fashionable lakes.

94   They talked of his university, which she had visited frequently during the past two years, and of the near-by city which supplied Sherry Island with its patrons, and whither Dexter would return next day to his prospering laundries.

95   During dinner she slipped into a moody depression which gave Dexter a feeling of uneasiness. Whatever petulance she uttered in her throaty voice worried him. Whatever she smiled at—at him, at a chicken liver, at nothing—it disturbed him that her smile could have no root in mirth, or even in amusement. When the scarlet corners of her lips curved down, it was less a smile than an invitation to a kiss.

96   Then, after dinner, she led him out on the dark sun-porch and deliberately changed the atmosphere.

97   "Do you mind if I weep a little?" she said.

98   "I'm afraid I'm boring you," he responded quickly.

99   "You're not. I like you. But I've just had a terrible afternoon. There was a man I cared about, and this afternoon he told me out of a clear sky that he was poor as a church-mouse. He'd never even hinted it before. Does this sound horribly mundane?"

100   "Perhaps he was afraid to tell you."

101   "Suppose he was," she answered. "He didn't start right. You see, if I'd thought of him as poor—well, I've been mad about loads of poor men, and fully intended to marry them all. But in this case, I hadn't thought of him that way, and my interest in him wasn't strong enough to survive the shock. As if a girl calmly informed her fiancé that she was a widow. He might not object to widows, but——

102   "Let's start right," she interrupted herself suddenly. "Who are you, anyhow?"

103   For a moment Dexter hesitated. Then:

104   "I'm nobody," he announced. "My career is largely a matter of futures."

105   "Are you poor?"

106   "No," he said frankly, "I'm probably making more money than any man my age in the Northwest. I know that's an obnoxious remark, but you advised me to start right."

107   There was a pause. Then she smiled and the corners of her mouth drooped and an almost imperceptible sway brought her closer to him, looking up into his eyes. A lump rose in Dexter's throat, and he waited breathless for the experiment, facing the unpredictable compound that would form mysteriously from the elements of their lips. Then he saw— she communicated her excitement to him, lavishly, deeply, with kisses that were not a promise but a fulfillment. They aroused in him not hunger demanding renewal but surfeit that would demand more surfeit...kisses that were like charity, creating want by holding back nothing at all.

108   It did not take him many hours to decide that he had wanted Judy Jones ever since he was a proud, desirous little boy.

IV

109   It began like that—and continued, with varying shades of intensity, on such a note right up to the dénouement. Dexter surrendered a part of himself to the most direct and unprincipled personality with which he had ever come in contact. Whatever Judy wanted, she went after with the full pressure of her charm. There was no divergence of method, no jockeying for position or premeditation of effects—there was a very little mental side to any of her affairs. She simply made men conscious to the highest degree of her physical loveliness. Dexter had no desire to change her. Her deficiencies were knit up with a passionate energy that transcended and justified them.

110   When, as Judy's head lay against his shoulder that first night, she whispered, "I don't know what's the matter with me. Last night I thought I was in love with a man and to-night I think I'm in love with you————" —it seemed to him a beautiful and romantic thing to say. It was the exquisite excitability that for the moment he controlled and owned. But a week later he was compelled to view this same quality in a different light. She took him in her roadster to a picnic supper, and after supper she disappeared, likewise in her roadster, with another man. Dexter became enormously upset and was scarcely able to be decently civil to the other people present. When she assured him that she had not kissed the other man, he knew she was lying—yet he was glad that she had taken the trouble to lie to him.

111   He was, as he found before the summer ended, one of a varying dozen who circulated about her. Each of them had at one time been favored above all others—about half of them still basked in the solace of occasional sentimental revivals. Whenever one showed signs of dropping out through long neglect, she granted him a brief honeyed hour, which encouraged him to tag along for a year or so longer. Judy made these forays upon the helpless and defeated without malice, indeed half unconscious that there was anything mischievous in what she did.

112   When a new man came to town every one dropped out—dates were automatically cancelled.

113   The helpless part of trying to do anything about it was that she did it all herself. She was not a girl who could be "won" in the kinetic sense—she was proof against cleverness, she was proof against charm; if any of these

assailed her too strongly she would immediately resolve the affair to a physical basis, and under the magic of her physical splendor the strong as well as the brilliant played her game and not their own. She was entertained only by the gratification of her desires and by the direct exercise of her own charm. Perhaps from so much youthful love, so many youthful lovers, she had come, in self-defense, to nourish herself wholly from within.

114   Succeeding Dexter's first exhilaration came restlessness and dissatisfaction. The helpless ecstasy of losing himself in her was opiate rather than tonic. It was fortunate for his work during the winter that those moments of ecstasy came infrequently. Early in their acquaintance it had seemed for a while that there was a deep and spontaneous mutual attraction—that first August, for example—three days of long evenings on her dusky veranda, of strange wan kisses through the late afternoon, in shadowy alcoves or behind the protecting trellises of the garden arbors, of mornings when she was fresh as a dream and almost shy at meeting him in the clarity of the rising day. There was all the ecstasy of an engagement about it, sharpened by his realization that there was no engagement. It was during those three days that, for the first time, he had asked her to marry him. She said "maybe some day," she said "kiss me," she said "I'd like to marry you," she said "I love you"—she said—nothing.

115   The three days were interrupted by the arrival of a New York man who visited at her house for half September. To Dexter's agony, rumor engaged them. The man was the son of the president of a great trust company. But at the end of a month it was reported that Judy was yawning. At a dance one night she sat all evening in a motor-boat with a local beau, while the New Yorker searched the club for her frantically. She told the local beau that she was bored with her visitor, and two days later he left. She was seen with him at the station, and it was reported that he looked very mournful indeed.

116   On this note the summer ended. Dexter was twenty-four, and he found himself increasingly in a position to do as he wished. He joined two clubs in the city and lived at one of them. Though he was by no means an integral part of the stag-lines at these clubs, he managed to be on hand at dances where Judy Jones was likely to appear. He could have gone out socially as much as he liked—he was an eligible young man, now, and popular with down-town fathers. His confessed devotion to Judy Jones had rather solidified his position. But he had no social aspirations and rather despised the dancing men who were always on tap for the Thursday or Saturday parties and who filled in at dinners with the younger married set. Already he was playing with the idea of going East to New York. He wanted to take Judy Jones with him. No disillusion as to the world in which she had grown up could cure his illusion as to her desirability.

117   Remember that—for only in the light of it can what he did for her be understood.

118   Eighteen months after he first met Judy Jones he became engaged to another girl. Her name was Irene Scheerer, and her father was one of the men who had always believed in Dexter. Irene was light-haired and sweet

and honorable, and a little stout, and she had two suitors whom she pleasantly relinquished when Dexter formally asked her to marry him.

119   Summer, fall, winter, spring, another summer, another fall—so much he had given of his active life to the incorrigible lips of Judy Jones. She had treated him with interest, with encouragement, with malice, with indifference, with contempt. She had inflicted on him the innumerable little slights and indignities possible in such a case—as if in revenge for having ever cared for him at all. She had beckoned him and yawned at him and beckoned him again and he had responded often with bitterness and narrowed eyes. She had brought him ecstatic happiness and intolerable agony of spirit. She had caused him untold inconvenience and not a little trouble. She had insulted him, and she had ridden over him, and she had played his interest in her against his interest in his work-for fun. She had done everything to him except to criticise him—this she had not done—it seemed to him only because it might have sullied the utter indifference she manifested and sincerely felt toward him.

120   When autumn had come and gone again it occurred to him that he could not have Judy Jones. He had to beat this into his mind but he convinced himself at last. He lay awake at night for a while and argued it over. He told himself the trouble and the pain she had caused him, he enumerated her glaring deficiencies as a wife. Then he said to himself that he loved her, and after a while he fell asleep. For a week, lest he imagined her husky voice over the telephone or her eyes opposite him at lunch, he worked hard and late, and at night he went to his office and plotted out his years.

121   At the end of a week he went to a dance and cut in on her once. For almost the first time since they had met he did not ask her to sit out with him or tell her that she was lovely. It hurt him that she did not miss these things—that was all. He was not jealous when he saw that there was a new man to-night. He had been hardened against jealousy long before.

122   He stayed late at the dance. He sat for an hour with Irene Scheerer and talked about books and about music. He knew very little about either. But he was beginning to be master of his own time now, and he had a rather priggish notion that he—the young and already fabulously successful Dexter Green—should know more about such things.

123   That was in October, when he was twenty-five. In January, Dexter and Irene became engaged. It was to be announced in June, and they were to be married three months later.

124   The Minnesota winter prolonged itself interminably, and it was almost May when the winds came soft and the snow ran down into Black Bear Lake at last. For the first time in over a year Dexter was enjoying a certain tranquility of spirit. Judy Jones had been in Florida, and afterward in Hot Springs, and somewhere she had been engaged, and somewhere she had broken it off. At first, when Dexter had definitely given her up, it had made him sad that people still linked them together and asked for news of her, but when he began to be placed at dinner next to Irene

Scheerer people didn't ask him about her any more—they told him about her. He ceased to be an authority on her.

125   May at last. Dexter walked the streets at night when the darkness was damp as rain, wondering that so soon, with so little done, so much of ecstasy had gone from him. May one year back had been marked by Judy's poignant, unforgivable, yet forgiven turbulence—it had been one of those rare times when he fancied she had grown to care for him. That old penny's worth of happiness he had spent for this bushel of content. He knew that Irene would be no more than a curtain spread behind him, a hand moving among gleaming tea-cups, a voice calling to children...fire and loveliness were gone, the magic of nights and the wonder of the varying hours and seasons...slender lips, down-turning, dropping to his lips and bearing him up into a heaven of eyes....The thing was deep in him. He was too strong and alive for it to die lightly.

126   In the middle of May when the weather balanced for a few days on the thin bridge that led to deep summer he turned in one night at Irene's house. Their engagement was to be announced in a week now-no one would be surprised at it. And to-night they would sit together on the lounge at the University Club and look on for an hour at the dancers. It gave him a sense of solidity to go with her—she was so sturdily popular, so intensely "great."

127   He mounted the steps of the brownstone house and stepped inside.

128   "Irene," he called.

129   Mrs. Scheerer came out of the living-room to meet him.

130   "Dexter," she said, "Irene's gone up-stairs with a splitting headache. She wanted to go with you but I made her go to bed."

131   "Nothing serious, I———"

132   "Oh, no. She's going to play golf with you in the morning. You can spare her for just one night, can't you, Dexter?"

133   Her smile was kind. She and Dexter liked each other. In the living-room he talked for a moment before he said good-night.

134   Returning to the University Club, where he had rooms, he stood in the doorway for a moment and watched the dancers. He leaned against the door-post, nodded at a man or two—yawned.

135   "Hello, darling."

136   The familiar voice at his elbow startled him. Judy Jones had left a man and crossed the room to him—Judy Jones, a slender enamelled doll in cloth of gold: gold in a band at her head, gold in two slipper points at her dress's hem. The fragile glow of her face seemed to blossom as she smiled at him. A breeze of warmth and light blew through the room. His hands in the pockets of his dinner-jacket tightened spasmodically. He was filled with a sudden excitement.

137   "When did you get back?" he asked casually.

138   "Come here and I'll tell you about it."

139   She turned and he followed her. She had been away—he could have wept at the wonder of her return. She had passed through enchanted

streets, doing things that were like provocative music. All mysterious happenings, all fresh and quickening hopes, had gone away with her, come back with her now.

140   She turned in the doorway.

141   "Have you a car here? If you haven't, I have."

142   "I have a coupé."

143   In then, with a rustle of golden cloth. He slammed the door. Into so many cars she had stepped—like this—like that—her back against the leather, so—her elbow resting on the door—waiting. She would have been soiled long since had there been anything to soil her—except herself—but this was her own self outpouring.

144   With an effort he forced himself to start the car and back into the street. This was nothing, he must remember. She had done this before, and he had put her behind him, as he would have crossed a bad account from his books.

145   He drove slowly down-town and, affecting abstraction, traversed the deserted streets of the business section, peopled here and there where a movie was giving out its crowd or where consumptive or pugilistic youth lounged in front of pool halls. The clink of glasses and the slap of hands on the bars issued from saloons, cloisters of glazed glass and dirty yellow light.

146   She was watching him closely and the silence was embarrassing, yet in this crisis he could find no casual word with which to profane the hour. At a convenient turning he began to zigzag back toward the University Club.

147   "Have you missed me?" she asked suddenly.

148   "Everybody missed you."

149   He wondered if she knew of Irene Scheerer. She had been back only a day—her absence had been almost contemporaneous with his engagement.

150   "What a remark!" Judy laughed sadly—without sadness. She looked at him searchingly. He became absorbed in the dashboard.

151   "You're handsomer than you used to be," she said thoughtfully. "Dexter, you have the most rememberable eyes."

152   He could have laughed at this, but he did not laugh. It was the sort of thing that was said to sophomores. Yet it stabbed at him.

153   "I'm awfully tired of everything, darling." She called every one darling, endowing the endearment with careless, individual comraderie. "I wish you'd marry me."

154   The directness of this confused him. He should have told her now that he was going to marry another girl, but he could not tell her. He could as easily have sworn that he had never loved her.

155   "I think we'd get along," she continued, on the same note, "unless probably you've forgotten me and fallen in love with another girl."

156   Her confidence was obviously enormous. She had said, in effect, that she found such a thing impossible to believe, that if it were true he had merely committed a childish indiscretion—and probably to show off. She would forgive him, because it was not a matter of any moment but rather something to be brushed aside lightly.

157   "Of course you could never love anybody but me," she continued. "I like the way you love me. Oh, Dexter, have you forgotten last year?"

158   "No, I haven't forgotten."

159   "Neither have I!"

160   Was she sincerely moved—or was she carried along by the wave of her own acting?

161   "I wish we could be like that again," she said, and he forced himself to answer:

162   "I don't think we can."

163   "I suppose not....I hear you're giving Irene Scheerer a violent rush."

164   There was not the faintest emphasis on the name, yet Dexter was suddenly ashamed.

165   "Oh, take me home," cried Judy suddenly; "I don't want to go back to that idiotic dance—with those children."

166   Then, as he turned up the street that led to the residence district, Judy began to cry quietly to herself. He had never seen her cry before.

167   The dark street lightened, the dwellings of the rich loomed up around them, he stopped his coupé in front of the great white bulk of the Mortimer Joneses house, somnolent, gorgeous, drenched with the splendor of the damp moonlight. Its solidity startled him. The strong walls, the steel of the girders, the breadth and beam and pomp of it were there only to bring out the contrast with the young beauty beside him. It was sturdy to accentuate her slightness—as if to show what a breeze could be generated by a butterfly's wing.

168   He sat perfectly quiet, his nerves in wild clamor, afraid that if he moved he would find her irresistibly in his arms. Two tears had rolled down her wet face and trembled on her upper lip.

169   "I'm more beautiful than anybody else," she said brokenly, "why can't I be happy?" Her moist eyes tore at his stability—her mouth turned slowly downward with an exquisite sadness: "I'd like to marry you if you'll have me, Dexter. I suppose you think I'm not worth having, but I'll be so beautiful for you, Dexter."

170   A million phrases of anger, pride, passion, hatred, tenderness fought on his lips. Then a perfect wave of emotion washed over him, carrying off with it a sediment of wisdom, of convention, of doubt, of honor. This was his girl who was speaking, his own, his beautiful, his pride.

171   "Won't you come in?" He heard her draw in her breath sharply.

172   Waiting.

173   "All right," his voice was trembling, "I'll come in."

V

174   It was strange that neither when it was over nor a long time afterward did he regret that night. Looking at it from the perspective of ten years, the fact that Judy's flare for him endured just one month seemed of little importance. Nor did it matter that by his yielding he subjected himself to a deeper agony in the end and gave serious hurt to Irene Scheerer and to Irene's parents, who had befriended him. There was nothing sufficiently pictorial about Irene's grief to stamp itself on his mind.

175　　Dexter was at bottom hard-minded. The attitude of the city on his action was of no importance to him, not because he was going to leave the city, but because any outside attitude on the situation seemed superficial. He was completely indifferent to popular opinion. Nor, when he had seen that it was no use, that he did not possess in himself the power to move fundamentally or to hold Judy Jones, did he bear any malice toward her. He loved her, and he would love her until the day he was too old for loving—but he could not have her. So he tasted the deep pain that is reserved only for the strong, just as he had tasted for a little while the deep happiness.

176　　Even the ultimate falsity of the grounds upon which Judy terminated the engagement that she did not want to "take him away" from Irene—Judy, who had wanted nothing else—did not revolt him. He was beyond any revulsion or any amusement.

177　　He went East in February with the intention of selling out his laundries and settling in New York—but the war came to America in March and changed his plans. He returned to the West, handed over the management of the business to his partner, and went into the first officers' training-camp in late April. He was one of those young thousands who greeted the war with a certain amount of relief, welcoming the liberation from webs of tangled emotion.

VI

178　　This story is not his biography, remember, although things creep into it which have nothing to do with those dreams he had when he was young. We are almost done with them and with him now. There is only one more incident to be related here, and it happens seven years farther on.

179　　It took place in New York, where he had done well—so well that there were no barriers too high for him. He was thirty-two years old, and, except for one flying trip immediately after the war, he had not been West in seven years. A man named Devlin from Detroit came into his office to see him in a business way, and then and there this incident occurred, and closed out, so to speak, this particular side of his life.

180　　"So you're from the Middle West," said the man Devlin with careless curiosity. "That's funny—I thought men like you were probably born and raised on Wall Street. You know—wife of one of my best friends in Detroit came from your city. I was an usher at the wedding."

181　　Dexter waited with no apprehension of what was coming.

182　　"Judy Simms," said Devlin with no particular interest; "Judy Jones she was once."

183　　"Yes, I knew her." A dull impatience spread over him. He had heard, of course, that she was married—perhaps deliberately he had heard no more.

184　　"Awfully nice girl," brooded Devlin meaninglessly, "I'm sort of sorry for her."

185　　"Why?" Something in Dexter was alert, receptive, at once.

186   "Oh, Lud Simms has gone to pieces in a way. I don't mean he ill-uses her, but he drinks and runs around————"

187   "Doesn't she run around?"

188   "No, Stays at home with her kids."

189   "Oh."

190   "She's a little too old for him," said Devlin.

191   "Too old!" cried Dexter. "Why, man, she's only twenty-seven."

192   He was possessed with a wild notion of rushing out into the streets and taking a train to Detroit. He rose to his feet spasmodically.

193   "I guess you're busy," Devlin apologized quickly. "I didn't realize————"

194   "No, I'm not busy," said Dexter, steadying his voice. "I'm not busy at all. Not busy at all. Did you say she was—twenty-seven? No, I said she was twenty-seven."

195   "Yes, you did," agreed Devlin dryly.

196   "Go on, then. Go on."

197   "What do you mean?"

198   "About Judy Jones."

199   Devlin looked at him helplessly.

200   "Well, that's—I told you all there is to it. He treats her like the devil. Oh, they're not going to get divorced or anything. When he's particularly outrageous she forgives him. In fact, I'm inclined to think she loves him. She was a pretty girl when she first came to Detroit."

201   A pretty girl! The phrase struck Dexter as ludicrous.

202   "Isn't she—a pretty girl, any more?"

203   "Oh, she's all right."

204   "Look here," said Dexter, sitting down suddenly, "I don't understand. You say she was a 'pretty girl' and now you say she's 'all right.' I don't understand what you mean—Judy Jones wasn't a pretty girl, at all. She was a great beauty. Why, I knew her, I knew her. She was————"

205   Devlin laughed pleasantly.

206   "I'm not trying to start a row," he said. "I think Judy's a nice girl and I like her. I can't understand how a man like Lud Simms could fall madly in love with her, but he did." Then he added: "Most of the women like her."

207   Dexter looked closely at Devlin, thinking wildly that there must be a reason for this, some insensitivity in the man or some private malice.

208   "Lots of women fade just like *that*," Devlin snapped his fingers. "You must have seen it happen. Perhaps I've forgotten how pretty she was at her wedding. I've seen her so much since then, you see. She has nice eyes."

209   A sort of dullness settled down upon Dexter. For the first time in his life he felt like getting very drunk. He knew that he was laughing loudly at something Devlin had said, but he did not know what it was or why it was funny. When, in a few minutes, Devlin went he lay down on his lounge and looked out the window at the New York sky-line into which the sun was sinking in dull lovely shades of pink and gold.

210   He had thought that having nothing else to lose he was invulnerable at last—but he knew that he had just lost something more, as surely as if he had married Judy Jones and seen her fade away before his eyes.

211   The dream was gone. Something had been taken from him. In a sort of panic he pushed the palms of his hands into his eyes and tried to bring up a picture of the waters lapping on Sherry Island and the moonlit veranda, and gingham on the golf-links and the dry sun and the gold color of her neck's soft down. And her mouth damp to his kisses and her eyes plaintive with melancholy and her freshness like new fine linen in the morning. Why, these things were no longer in the world! They had existed and they existed no longer.

212   For the first time in years the tears were streaming down his face. But they were for himself now. He did not care about mouth and eyes and moving hands. He wanted to care, and he could not care. For he had gone away and he could never go back any more. The gates were closed, the sun was gone down, and there was no beauty but the gray beauty of steel that withstands all time. Even the grief he could have borne was left behind in the country of illusion, of youth, of the richness of life, where his winter dreams had flourished.

213   "Long ago," he said, "long ago, there was something in me, but now that thing is gone. Now that thing is gone, that thing is gone. I cannot cry. I cannot care. That thing will come back no more."

Questions for Discussion

1. Why does Dexter quit his caddying job? What characteristic of his personality is first revealed by this action?

2. List the things that attract Dexter to Judy. Then compare these to the qualities that attract Dexter to Irene.

3. What were Judy Jones's "casual whims," and how do they affect Dexter's life? Explain how "the helpless ecstasy of himself in her" is an "opiate rather than a tonic."

4. What knowledge does Dexter acquire at the end of the story? Why is this knowledge so important to him? How does it change him?

5. Explain the meaning and the implications of the title.

Suggestions for Exploring, Writing, and Persuading

1. If you have ever acted on impulse in a way that changed your life, either for a short while or forever, describe this action and analyze why you made that particular choice.

2. Dexter Green's dreams were "winter dreams." In an essay, describe your own dreams and explain why you would label them winter, spring, summer, or fall.

3. In an essay, persuade the reader that Dexter's behavior toward Judy is or is not typical of individuals who are infatuated. Or recommend a better course of behavior for Dexter.

4. Analyze Judy Jones's personality and motivation, from her attitudes as a child of eleven on the golf course to her later role as wife.

5. In an essay, compare the two women in Dexter's life.

6. Write a character analysis of Dexter, exploring his impulsiveness, his goals, and his talents.

William Faulkner (1897–1962)

Born near Oxford, Mississippi, Faulkner used his home state as the setting for many of his short stories and novels. He invented an imaginary county—Yoknapatawpha—and peopled it with a variety of characters worthy of Shakespeare, from the noble members of the Sartoris family and the intellectual Quenton Compson to the Snopes family, most of whom are sneaky and self-serving. His most famous novels include The Sound and the Fury *(1929);* Light in August *(1932);* Absalom, Absalom! *(1936); and the Snopes trilogy:* The Hamlet *(1940),* The Town *(1957), and* The Mansion *(1958). In 1950, Faulkner was awarded the Nobel Prize for Literature.*

A ROSE FOR EMILY   (1930)

I

1   When Miss Emily Grierson died, our whole town went to her funeral: the men through a sort of respectful affection for a fallen monument, the women mostly out of curiosity to see the inside of her house, which no one save an old manservant—a combined gardener and cook—had seen in at least ten years.

2   It was a big, squarish frame house that had once been white, decorated with cupolas and spires and scrolled balconies in the heavily lightsome style of the seventies, set on what had once been our most select street. But garages and cotton gins had encroached and obliterated even the august names of that neighborhood; only Miss Emily's house was left, lifting its stubborn and coquettish decay above the cotton wagons and the gasoline pumps—an eyesore among eyesores. And now Miss Emily had gone to join the representatives of those august names where they lay in the cedar-bemused cemetery among the ranked and anonymous graves of Union and Confederate soldiers who fell at the battle of Jefferson.

3   Alive, Miss Emily had been a tradition, a duty, and a care; a sort of hereditary obligation upon the town, dating from that day in 1894 when Colonel Sartoris, the mayor—he who fathered the edict that no Negro woman should appear on the streets without an apron—remitted her taxes, the dispensation dating from the death of her father on into perpetuity. Not that Miss Emily would have accepted charity. Colonel Sartoris

invented an involved tale to the effect that Miss Emily's father had loaned money to the town, which the town, as a matter of business, preferred this way of repaying. Only a man of Colonel Sartoris' generation and thought could have invented it and only a woman could have believed it.

4   When the next generation, with its more modern ideas, became mayors and aldermen, this arrangement created some little dissatisfaction. On the first of the year they mailed her a tax notice. February came, and there was no reply. They wrote her a formal letter, asking her to call at the sheriff's office at her convenience. A week later the mayor wrote her himself, offering to call or to send his car for her, and received in reply a note on paper of an archaic shape, in a thin, flowing calligraphy in faded ink, to the effect that she no longer went out at all. The tax notice was also enclosed, without comment.

5   They called a special meeting of the Board of Aldermen. A deputation waited upon her, knocked at the door through which no visitor had passed since she ceased giving china painting lessons eight or ten years earlier. They were admitted by the old Negro into a dim hall from which a stairway mounted into still more shadow. It smelled of dust and disuse—a close, dank smell. The Negro led them into the parlor. It was furnished in heavy, leather-covered furniture. When the Negro opened the blinds of one window, they could see that the leather was cracked; and when they sat down, a faint dust rose sluggishly about their thighs, spinning with slow motes in the single sun-ray. On a tarnished gilt easel before the fireplace stood a crayon portrait of Miss Emily's father.

6   They rose when she entered—a small, fat woman in black, with a thin gold chain descending to her waist and vanishing into her belt, leaning on an ebony cane with a tarnished gold head. Her skeleton was small and spare; perhaps that was why what would have been merely plumpness in another was obesity in her. She looked bloated, like a body long submerged in motionless water, and of that pallid hue. Her eyes, lost in the fatty ridges of her face, looked like two small pieces of coal pressed into a lump of dough as they moved from one face to another while the visitors stated their errand.

7   She did not ask them to sit. She just stood in the door and listened quietly until the spokesman came to a stumbling halt. Then they could hear the invisible watch ticking at the end of the gold chain.

8   Her voice was dry and cold. "I have no taxes in Jefferson. Colonel Sartoris explained it to me. Perhaps one of you can gain access to the city records and satisfy yourselves."

9   "But we have. We are the city authorities, Miss Emily. Didn't you get a notice from the sheriff, signed by him?"

10   "I received a paper, yes," Miss Emily said. "Perhaps he considers himself the sheriff...I have no taxes in Jefferson."

11   "But there is nothing on the books to show that, you see. We must go by the—"

12   "See Colonel Sartoris. I have no taxes in Jefferson."

13   "But, Miss Emily—"

14   "See Colonel Sartoris." (Colonel Sartoris had been dead almost ten years.) "I have no taxes in Jefferson. Tobe!" The Negro appeared. "Show these gentlemen out."

II

15   So she vanquished them, horse and foot, just as she had vanquished their fathers thirty years before about the smell. That was two years after her father's death and a short time after her sweetheart—the one we believed would marry her—had deserted her. After her father's death she went out very little; after her sweetheart went away, people hardly saw her at all. A few of the ladies had the temerity to call, but were not received, and the only sign of life about the place was the Negro man—a young man then—going in and out with a market basket.

16   "Just as if a man—any man—could keep a kitchen properly," the ladies said; so they were not surprised when the smell developed. It was another link between the gross, teeming world and the high and mighty Griersons.

17   A neighbor, a woman, complained to the mayor, Judge Stevens, eighty years old.

18   "But what will you have me do about it, madam?" he said.

19   "Why, send her word to stop it," the woman said. "Isn't there a law?"

20   "I'm sure that won't be necessary," Judge Stevens said. "It's probably just a snake or a rat that nigger of hers killed in the yard. I'll speak to him about it."

21   The next day he received two more complaints, one from a man who came in diffident deprecation. "We really must do something about it, Judge. I'd be the last one in the world to bother Miss Emily, but we've got to do something." That night the Board of Aldermen met—three graybeards and one younger man, a member of the rising generation.

22   "It's simple enough," he said. "Send her word to have her place cleaned up. Give her a certain time to do it in, and if she don't..."

23   "Dammit, sir," Judge Stevens said, "will you accuse a lady to her face of smelling bad?"

24   So the next night, after midnight, four men crossed Miss Emily's lawn and slunk about the house like burglars, sniffing along the base of the brickwork and at the cellar openings while one of them performed a regular sowing motion with his hand out of a sack slung from his shoulder. They broke open the cellar door and sprinkled lime there, and in all the outbuildings. As they recrossed the lawn, a window that had been dark was lighted and Miss Emily sat in it, the light behind her, and her upright torso motionless as that of an idol. They crept quietly across the lawn and into the shadow of the locusts that lined the street. After a week or two the smell went away.

25   That was when people had begun to feel really sorry for her. People in our town, remembering how old lady Wyatt, her great-aunt, had gone com-

pletely crazy at last, believed that the Griersons held themselves a little too high for what they really were. None of the young men were quite good enough for Miss Emily and such. We had long thought of them as a tableau, Miss Emily a slender figure in white in the background, her father a spraddled silhouette in the foreground, his back to her and clutching a horsewhip, the two of them framed by the back-flung front door. So when she got to be thirty and was still single, we were not pleased exactly, but vindicated; even with insanity in the family she wouldn't have turned down all of her chances if they had really materialized.

26   When her father died, it got about that the house was all that was left to her; and in a way, people were glad. At last they could pity Miss Emily. Being left alone, and a pauper, she had become humanized. Now she too would know the old thrill and the old despair of a penny more or less.

27   The day after his death all the ladies prepared to call at the house and offer condolence and aid, as is our custom. Miss Emily met them at the door, dressed as usual and with no trace of grief on her face. She told them that her father was not dead. She did that for three days, with the ministers calling on her, and the doctors, trying to persuade her to let them dispose of the body. Just as they were about to resort to law and force, she broke down, and they buried her father quickly.

28   We did not say she was crazy then. We believed she had to do that. We remembered all the young men her father had driven away, and we knew that with nothing left, she would have to cling to that which had robbed her, as people will.

III

29   She was sick for a long time. When we saw her again, her hair was cut short, making her look like a girl, with a vague resemblance to those angels in colored church windows—sort of tragic and serene.

30   The town had just let the contracts for paving the sidewalks, and in the summer after her father's death they began the work. The construction company came with niggers and mules and machinery, and a foreman named Homer Barron, a Yankee—a big, dark, ready man, with a big voice and eyes lighter than his face. The little boys would follow in groups to hear him cuss the niggers, and the niggers singing in time to the rise and fall of picks. Pretty soon he knew everybody in town. Whenever you heard a lot of laughing anywhere about the square, Homer Barron would be in the center of the group. Presently we began to see him and Miss Emily on Sunday afternoons driving in the yellow-wheeled buggy and the matched team bays from the livery stable.

31   At first we were glad that Miss Emily would have an interest, because the ladies all said, "Of course a Grierson would not think seriously of a Northerner, a day laborer." But there were still others, older people, who said that even grief could not cause a real lady to forget *noblesse oblige*— without calling it *noblesse oblige*. They just said, "Poor Emily. Her kinsfolk should come to her." She had some kin in Alabama; but years ago

her father had fallen out with them over the estate of old lady Wyatt, the crazy woman, and there was no communication between the two families. They had not even been represented at the funeral.

32   And as soon as the old people said, "Poor Emily," the whispering began. "Do you suppose it's really so?" they said to one another. "Of course it is. What else could..." This behind their hands; rustling of craned silk and satin behind jalousies closed upon the sun of Sunday afternoon as the thin, swift clop-clop-clop of the matched team passed: "Poor Emily."

33   She carried her head high enough—even when we believed that she was fallen. It was as if she demanded more than ever the recognition of her dignity as the last Grierson; as if it had wanted that touch of earthiness to reaffirm her imperviousness. Like when she bought the rat poison, the arsenic. That was over a year after they had begun to say "Poor Emily," and while the two female cousins were visiting her.

34   "I want some poison," she said to the druggist. She was over thirty then, still a slight woman, though thinner than usual, with cold, haughty black eyes in a face the flesh of which was strained across the temples and about the eyesockets as you imagine a lighthouse-keeper's face ought to look. "I want some poison," she said.

35   "Yes, Miss Emily. What kind? For rats and such? I'd recom—"

36   "I want the best you have. I don't care what kind."

37   The druggist named several. "They'll kill anything up to an elephant. But what you want is—"

38   "Arsenic," Miss Emily said, "Is that a good one?"

39   "Is...arsenic? Yes, ma'am. But what you want—"

40   "I want arsenic."

41   The druggist looked down at her. She looked back at him, erect, her face like a strained flag. "Why, of course," the druggist said. "If that's what you want. But the law requires you to tell what you are going to use it for."

42   Miss Emily just stared at him, her head tilted back in order to look him eye for eye, until he looked away and went and got the arsenic and wrapped it up. The Negro delivery boy brought her the package; the druggist didn't come back. When she opened the package at home there was written on the box, under the skull and bones: "For rats."

IV

43   So the next day we all said, "She will kill herself"; and we said it would be the best thing. When she had first begun to be seen with Homer Barron, we had said, "She will marry him." Then we said, "She will persuade him yet," because Homer himself had remarked—he liked men, and it was known that he drank with the younger men in the Elks' Club—that he was not a marrying man. Later we said, "Poor Emily" behind the jalousies as they passed on Sunday afternoon in the glittering buggy, Miss Emily with her head high and Homer Barron with his hat cocked and a cigar in his teeth, reins and whip in a yellow glove.

44   Then some of the ladies began to say that it was a disgrace to the town and a bad example to the young people. The men did not want to interfere, but at last the ladies forced the Baptist minister—Miss Emily's people were Episcopal—to call upon her. He would never divulge what happened during that interview, but he refused to go back again. The next Sunday they again drove about the streets, and the following day the minister's wife wrote to Miss Emily's relations in Alabama.

45   So she had blood-kin under her roof again and we sat back to watch the developments. At first nothing happened. Then we were sure that they were to be married. We learned that Miss Emily had been to the jeweler's and ordered a man's toilet set in silver, with the letters H. B. on each piece. Two days later we learned that she had bought a complete outfit of men's clothing, including a nightshirt, and we said, "They are married." We were really glad. We were glad because the two female cousins were even more Grierson than Miss Emily had ever been.

46   So we were not surprised when Homer Barron—the streets had been finished some time since—was gone. We were a little disappointed that there was not a public blowing-off, but we believed that he had gone on to prepare for Miss Emily's coming, or to give her a chance to get rid of the cousins. (By that time it was a cabal, and we were all Miss Emily's allies to help circumvent the cousins.) Sure enough, after another week they departed. And, as we had expected all along, within three days Homer Barron was back in town. A neighbor saw the Negro man admit him at the kitchen door at dusk one evening.

47   And that was the last we saw of Homer Barron. And of Miss Emily for some time. The Negro man went in and out with the market basket, but the front door remained closed. Now and then we would see her at a window for a moment, as the men did that night when they sprinkled the lime, but for almost six months she did not appear on the streets. Then we knew that this was to be expected too; as if that quality of her father which had thwarted her woman's life so many times had been too virulent and too furious to die.

48   When we next saw Miss Emily, she had grown fat and her hair was turning gray. During the next few years it grew grayer and grayer until it attained an even pepper-and-salt iron-gray, when it ceased turning. Up to the day of her death at seventy-four it was still that vigorous iron-gray, like the hair of an active man.

49   From that time on her front door remained closed, save for a period of six or seven years, when she was about forty, during which she gave lessons in china-painting. She fitted up a studio in one of the downstairs rooms, where the daughters and granddaughters of Colonel Sartoris' contemporaries were sent to her with the same regularity and in the same spirit that they were sent to church on Sundays with a twenty-five-cent piece for the collection plate. Meanwhile her taxes had been remitted.

50   Then the newer generation became the backbone and the spirit of the town, and the painting pupils grew up and fell away and did not

send their children to her with boxes of color and tedious brushes and pictures cut from the ladies' magazines. The front door closed upon the last one and remained closed for good. When the town got free postal delivery, Miss Emily alone refused to let them fasten the metal numbers above her door and attach a mailbox to it. She would not listen to them.

51   Daily, monthly, yearly we watched the Negro grow grayer and more stooped, going in and out with the market basket. Each December we sent her a tax notice, which would be returned by the post office a week later, unclaimed. Now and then we would see her in one of the downstairs windows—she had evidently shut up the top floor of the house—like the carven torso of an idol in a niche, looking or not looking at us, we could never tell which. Thus she passed from generation to generation—dear, inescapable, impervious, tranquil, and perverse.

52   And so she died. Fell ill in the house filled with dust and shadows, with only a doddering Negro man to wait on her. We did not even know she was sick; we had long since given up trying to get any information from the Negro. He talked to no one, probably not even to her, for his voice had grown harsh and rusty, as if from disuse.

53   She died in one of the downstairs rooms, in a heavy walnut bed with a curtain, her gray head propped on a pillow yellow and moldy with age and lack of sunlight.

V

54   The Negro met the first of the ladies at the front door and let them in, with their hushed, sibilant voices and their quick curious glances, and then he disappeared. He walked right through the house and out the back and was not seen again.

55   The two female cousins came at once. They held the funeral on the second day, with the town coming to look at Miss Emily beneath a mass of bought flowers, with the crayon face of her father musing profoundly above the bier and the ladies sibilant and macabre; and the very old men—some in their brushed confederate uniforms—on the porch and the lawn, talking of Miss Emily as if she had been a contemporary of theirs, believing that they had danced with her and courted her perhaps, confusing time with its mathematical progression, as the old do, to whom all the past is not a diminishing road but, instead, a huge meadow which no winter ever quite touches, divided from them now by the narrow bottleneck of the most recent decade of years.

56   Already we knew that there was one room in that region above stairs which no one had seen in forty years, and which would have to be forced. They waited until Miss Emily was decently in the ground before they opened it.

57   The violence of breaking down the door seemed to fill this room with pervading dust. A thin, acrid pall as of the tomb seemed to lie everywhere upon this room decked and furnished as for a bridal: upon the valance

curtains of faded rose color, upon the rose-shaded lights, upon the dressing table, upon the delicate array of crystal and the man's toilet things backed with tarnished silver, silver so tarnished that the monogram was obscured. Among them lay a collar and tie, as if they had just been removed, which, lifted, left upon the surface a pale crescent in the dust. Upon a chair hung the suit, carefully folded; beneath it the two mute shoes and the discarded socks.

58   The man himself lay in the bed.

59   For a long while we just stood there, looking down at the profound and fleshless grin. The body had apparently once lain in the attitude of an embrace, but now the long sleep that outlasts love, that conquers even the grimace of love, had cuckolded him. What was left of him, rotted beneath what was left of the nightshirt, had become inextricable from the bed in which he lay; and upon him and upon the pillow beside him lay that even coating of the patient and biding dust.

60   Then we noticed that in the second pillow was the indentation of a head. One of us lifted something from it, and leaning forward, that faint and invisible dust dry and acrid in the nostrils, we saw a long strand of iron-gray hair.

Questions for Discussion

1. From whose point of view is the story told? How would you describe the narrator's attitude toward Miss Emily?

2. What is the relationship between the town and Miss Emily? In what sense(s) is she a "tradition, a duty, and a care"? Why does Colonel Sartoris feel obliged to remit her taxes and to make up an excuse for doing so?

3. What does Miss Emily's ability to vanquish the authorities of Jefferson, to make them back down on taxes and on the smell, reveal about her attitudes and personality?

4. What does the description of the parlor reveal about the house and about Miss Emily?

5. What does the last sentence of the story reveal? What hints of the ending make it believable, if shocking?

Suggestions for Exploring, Writing, and Persuading

1. Write an essay about a person you know who has refused to adapt to changing times.

2. The question of whether Tobe, the Negro servant, knew about what happened to Homer constantly comes up. Write a persuasive essay in which you argue that he did know but did not inform the authorities and why. Or write a persuasive essay in which you convince

your reader that he did not know anything about Homer and the reasons.

3. In terms of the time and the environment in which she lives, explain Miss Emily's treatment by, and response to, the two men in her life.

4. Write a persuasive essay in which you argue one of the following:
   Convince a jury that Miss Emily is or is not guilty of murder.

   After researching psychological disorders, support or refute the idea that Miss Emily was insane.

Arna Bontemps (1902–1973)

Bontemps was born in Alexandria, Louisiana, but moved to Los Angeles, California, as a child. Because his parents resented their African American heritage, they sent him to white schools, and he lived in white neighborhoods. Bontemps learned about his culture from his great-uncle Buddy. As a result of his upbringing, Bontemps spent the rest of his life trying to rectify omissions in the history books and trying to increase interest in African American literature and culture.

A Summer Tragedy   (1933)

1   Old Jeff Patton, the black share farmer, fumbled with his bow tie. His fingers trembled, and the high, stiff collar pinched his throat. A fellow loses his hand for such vanities after thirty or forty years of simple life. Once a year, or maybe twice if there's a wedding among his kin-folks, he may spruce up; but generally fancy clothes do nothing but adorn the wall of the big room and feed the moths. That had been Jeff Patton's experience. He had not worn his stiff-bosomed shirt more than a dozen times in all his married life. His swallowtailed coat lay on the bed beside him, freshly brushed and pressed, but it was as full of holes as the overalls in which he worked on week days. The moths had used it badly. Jeff twisted his mouth into a hideous toothless grimace as he contended with the obstinate bow. He stamped his good foot and decided to give up the struggle.

2   "Jennie," he called.

3   "What's that, Jeff?" His wife's shrunken voice came out of the adjoining room like an echo. It was hardly bigger than a whisper.

4   "I reckon you'll have to he'p me wid this heah bow tie, baby," he said meekly. "Dog if I can hitch it up."

5   Her answer was not strong enough to reach him, but presently the old woman came to the door, feeling her way with a stick. She had a wasted, dead-leaf appearance. Her body, as scrawny and gnarled as a stringbean, seemed less than nothing in the ocean of frayed and faded petticoats that surrounded her. These hung an inch or two above the tops of her heavy, unlaced shoes and showed little grotesque piles where the stockings had fallen down from her negligible legs.

6   "You oughta could do a heap mo' wid a thing like that 'n me—beingst as you got yo' good sight."

7   "Looks like I *oughta* could," he admitted. "But ma fingers is gone democrat on me. I get all mixed up in the looking glass an' can't tell whicha way to twist the devilish thing."

8   Jennie sat on the side of the bed and old Jeff Patton got down on one knee while she tied the bow knot. It was a slow and painful ordeal for each of them in this position. Jeff's bones cracked, his knee ached, and it was only after a half dozen attempts that Jennie worked a semblance of a bow into the tie.

9   "I got to dress maself now," the old woman whispered. "These is ma old shoes an' stockings, and I ain't so much as unwrapped ma dress."

10   "Well, don't worry 'bout me no mo', baby," Jeff said. "That 'bout finishes me. All I gotta do now is slip on that old coat 'n ves' an' I'll be fixed to leave."

11   Jennie disappeared again through the dim passage into the shed room. Being blind was no handicap to her in that black hole. Jeff heard the cane placed against the wall beside the door and knew that his wife was on easy ground. He put on his coat, took a battered top hat from the bed post, and hobbled to the front door. He was ready to travel. As soon as Jennie could get on her Sunday shoes and her old black silk dress, they would start.

12   Outside the tiny log house the day was warm and mellow with sunshine. A host of wasps was humming with busy excitement in the trunk of a dead sycamore. Grey squirrels were searching through the grass for hickory nuts and blue jays were in the trees, hopping from branch to branch. Pine woods stretched away to the left like a black sea. Among them were scattered scores of log houses like Jeff's, houses of black share farmers. Cows and pigs wandered freely among the trees. There was no danger of loss. Each farmer knew his own stock and knew his neighbor's as well as he knew his neighbor's children.

13   Down the slope to the right were the cultivated acres on which the colored folks worked. They extended to the river, more than two miles away, and they were today green with the unmade cotton crop. A tiny thread of a road, which passed directly in front of Jeff's place, ran through these green fields like a pencil mark.

14   Jeff, standing outside the door with his absurd hat in his left hand, surveyed the wide scene tenderly. He had been forty-five years on these acres. He loved them with the unexplained affection that others have for the countries to which they belong.

15   The sun was hot on his head, his collar still pinched his throat, and the Sunday clothes were intolerably hot. Jeff transferred the hat to his right hand and began fanning with it. Suddenly the whisper that was Jennie's voice came out of the shed room.

16   "You can bring the car round front whilst you's waitin'," it said feebly. There was a tired pause; then it added, "I'll soon be fixed to go."

17   "A'right, baby," Jeff answered. "I'll get it in a minute."

18   But he didn't move. A thought struck him that made his mouth fall open. The mention of the car brought to his mind, with new intensity, the trip he and Jennie were about to take. Fear came into his eyes; excitement took his breath. Lord, Jesus!

19   "Jeff...Oh Jeff," the old woman's whisper called.

20   He awakened with a jolt. "Hunh, baby?"

21   "What you doin'?"

22   "Nuthin. Jes studyin'. I jes been turnin' things round 'n round in ma mind."

23   "You could be gettin' the car," she said.

24   "Oh yes, right away, baby."

25   He started round to the shed, limping heavily on his bad leg. There were three frizzly chickens in the yard. All his other chickens had been killed or stolen recently. But the frizzly chickens had been saved somehow. That was fortunate indeed, for these curious creatures had a way of devouring "poison" from the yard and in that way protecting against conjure and bad luck and spells. But even the frizzly chickens seemed now to be in a stupor. Jeff thought they had some ailment; he expected all three of them to die shortly.

26   The shed in which the old model-T Ford stood was only a grass roof held up by four corner poles. It had been built by tremulous hands at a time when the little rattle-trap car had been regarded as a peculiar treasure. And, miraculously, despite wind and downpour, it still stood.

27   Jeff adjusted the crank and put his weight on it. The engine came to life with a sputter and bang that rattled the old car from radiator to tail light. Jeff hopped into the seat and put his foot on the accelerator. The sputtering and banging increased. The rattling became more violent. That was good. It was good banging, good sputtering and rattling, and it meant that the aged car was still in running condition. She could be depended on for this trip.

28   Again Jeff's thought halted as if paralyzed. The suggestion of the trip fell into the machinery of his mind like a wrench. He felt dazed and weak. He swung the car out into the yard, made a half turn, and drove around to the front door. When he took his hands off the wheel, he noticed that he was trembling violently. He cut off the motor and climbed to the ground to wait for Jennie.

29   A few moments later she was at the window, her voice rattling against the pane like a broken shutter.

30   "I'm ready, Jeff."

31   He did not answer, but limped into the house and took her by the arm. He led her slowly though the big room, down the step, and across the yard.

32   "You reckon I'd oughta lock the do'?" he asked softly.

33   They stopped and Jennie weighed the question. Finally she shook her head.

34   "Ne' mind the do'," she said. "I don't see no cause to lock up things."

35   "You right," Jeff agreed. "No cause to lock up."

36   Jeff opened the door and helped his wife into the car. A quick shudder passed over him. Jesus! Again he trembled.

37   "How come you shaking so?" Jennie whispered.

38   "I don't know," he said.

39   "You mus' be scairt, Jeff."

40   "No, baby, I ain't scairt."

41   He slammed the door after her and went around to crank up again. The motor started easily. Jeff wished that it had not been so responsive. He would have liked a few more minutes in which to turn things around in his head. As it was, with Jennie chiding him about being afraid, he had to keep going. He swung the car into the little pencil-mark road and started off toward the river, driving very slowly, very cautiously.

42   Chugging across the green countryside, the small, battered Ford seemed tiny indeed. Jeff felt a familiar excitement, a thrill, as they came down the first slope to the immense levels on which the cotton was growing. He could not help reflecting that the crops were good. He knew what that meant, too; he had made forty-five of them with his own hands. It was true that he had worn out nearly a dozen mules, but that was the fault of old man Stevenson, the owner of the land. Major Stevenson had the odd notion that one mule was all a share farmer needed to work a thirty-acre plot. It was an expensive notion, the way it killed mules from overwork, but the old man held to it. Jeff thought it killed a good many share farmers as well as mules, but he had no sympathy for them. He had always been strong, and he had been taught to have no patience with weakness in men. Women or children might be tolerated if they were puny, but a weak man was a curse. Of course, his own children—

43   Jeff's thought halted there. He and Jennie never mentioned their dead children any more. And naturally he did not wish to dwell upon them in his mind. Before he knew it, some remark would slip out of his mouth and that would make Jennie feel blue. Perhaps she would cry. A woman like Jennie could not easily throw off the grief that comes from losing five grown children within two years. Even Jeff was still staggered by the blow. His memory had not been much good recently. He frequently talked to himself. And, although he had kept it a secret he knew that his courage had left him. He was terrified by the least unfamiliar sound at night. He was reluctant to venture far from home in the daytime. And that habit of trembling when he felt fearful was now far beyond his control. Sometimes he became afraid and trembled without knowing what had frightened him. The feeling would just come over him like a chill.

44   The car rattled slowly over the dusty road. Jennie sat erect and silent, with a little absurd hat pinned to her hair. Her useless eyes seemed very large and very white in their deep sockets. Suddenly Jeff heard her voice, and he inclined his head to catch the words.

45   "Is we passed Delia Moore's house yet?" she asked.

46   "Not yet," he said.

47   "You must be drivin' mighty slow, Jeff."

48   "We jes as well take our time, baby."

49   There was a pause. A little puff of steam was coming out of the radiator of the car. Heat wavered above the hood. Delia Moore's house was nearly half a mile away. After a moment Jennie spoke again.

50   "You ain't really scairt, is you, Jeff?"

51   "Nah, baby, I ain't scairt."

52   "You know how we agreed—we gotta keep on goin'."

53   Jewels of perspiration appeared on Jeff's forehead. His eyes rounded, blinked, became fixed on the road.

54   "I don't know," he said with a shiver. "I reckon it's the only thing to do."

55   "Hm."

56   A flock of guinea fowls, pecking in the road, were scattered by the passing car. Some of them took to their wings; others hid under bushes. A blue jay, swaying on a leafy twig, was annoying a roadside squirrel. Jeff held an even speed till he came near Delia's place. Then he slowed down noticeably.

57   Delia's house was really no house at all, but an abandoned store building converted into a dwelling. It sat near a crossroads, beneath a single black cedar tree. There Delia, a catlike old creature of Jennie's age, lived alone. She had been there more years than anybody could remember, and long ago had won the disfavor of such women as Jennie. For in her young days Delia had been gayer, yellower, and saucier than seemed proper in those parts. Her ways with menfolks had been dark and suspicious. And the fact that she had had as many husbands as children did not help her reputation.

58   "Yonder's old Delia," Jeff said as they passed.

59   "What she doin'?"

60   "Jes sittin' in the do'," he said.

61   "She see us?"

62   "Hm," Jeff said. "Musta did."

63   That relieved Jennie. It strengthened her to know that her old enemy had seen her pass in her best clothes. That would give the old she-devil something to chew her gums and fret about, Jennie thought. Wouldn't she have a fit if she didn't find out? Old evil Delia! This would be just the thing for her. It would pay her back for being so evil. It would also pay her, Jennie thought, for the way she used to grin at Jeff—long ago when her teeth were good.

64   The road became smooth and red, and Jeff could tell by the smell of the air that they were nearing the river. He could see the rise where the road turned and ran along parallel to the stream. The car chugged on monotonously. After a long silent spell, Jennie leaned against Jeff and spoke.

65   "How many bale o' cotton you think we got standin'?" she said.

66   Jeff wrinkled his forehead as he calculated.

67   "'Bout twenty-five, I reckon."

68   "How many you make las' year?"

69   "Twenty-eight," he said. "How come you ask that?"

70   "I's jes thinkin'," Jennie said quietly.

71   "It don't make a speck o' diff'ence though," Jeff reflected. "If we get much or if we get little, we still gonna be in debt to old man Stevenson when he gets through counting up agin us. It's took us a long time to learn that."

72   Jennie was not listening to these words. She had fallen into a trance-like meditation. Her lips twitched. She chewed her gums and rubbed her old gnarled hands nervously. Suddenly, she leaned forward, buried her face in the nervous hands, and burst into tears. She cried aloud in a dry, cracked voice that suggested the rattle of fodder on dead stalks. She cried aloud like a child, for she had never learned to suppress a genuine sob. Her slight old frame shook heavily and seemed hardly able to sustain such violent grief.

73   "What's the matter, baby?" Jeff asked awkwardly. "Why you cryin' like all that?"

74   "I's jes thinkin'," she said.

75   "So you the one what's scairt now, hunh?"

76   "I ain't scairt, Jeff. I's jes thinkin' 'bout leavin' eve'thing like this— eve'thing we been used to. It's right sad-like."

77   Jeff did not answer, and presently Jennie buried her face and continued crying.

78   The sun was almost overhead. It beat down furiously on the dusty wagon path road, on the parched roadside grass, and the tiny battered car. Jeff's hands, gripping the wheel, became wet with perspiration; his forehead sparkled. Jeff's lips parted and his mouth shaped a hideous grimace. His face suggested the face of a man being burned. But the torture passed and his expression softened again.

79   "You mustn't cry, baby," he said to his wife. "We gotta be strong. We can't break down."

80   Jennie waited a few seconds, then said, "You reckon we oughta do it, Jeff? You reckon we oughta go 'head an' do it really?"

81   Jeff's voice choked; his eyes blurred. He was terrified to hear Jennie say the thing that had been in his mind all morning. She had egged him on when he had wanted more than anything in the world to wait, to reconsider, to think things over a little longer. Now *she* was getting cold feet. Actually, there was no need of thinking the question through again. It would only end in making the same painful decision once more. Jeff knew that. There was no need of fooling around longer.

82   "We jes as well to do like we planned," he said. "They ain't nuthin else for us now—it's the bes' thing."

83   Jeff thought of the handicaps, the near impossibility, of making another crop with his leg bothering him more and more each week. Then there was always the chance that he would have another stroke, like the one that had made him lame. Another one might kill him. The least it could do would be to leave him helpless. Jeff gasped...Lord, Jesus! He could not bear to think of being helpless, like a baby, on Jennie's hands. Frail, blind Jennie.

84   The little pounding motor of the car worked harder and harder. The puff of steam from the cracked radiator became large. Jeff realized that

they were climbing a little rise. A moment later the road turned abruptly and he looked down upon the face of the river.

85   "Jeff."

86   "Hunh?"

87   "Is that the water I hear?"

88   "Hm. That's it."

89   "Well, which way you goin' now?"

90   "Down this-a way," he answered. "The road runs 'long-side o' the water a lil piece."

91   She waited a while calmly. Then she said, "Drive faster."

92   "A'right, baby," Jeff said.

93   The water roared in the bed of the river. It was fifty or sixty feet below the level of the road. Between the road and the water there was a long smooth slope, sharply inclined. The slope was dry; the clay had been hardened by prolonged summer heat. The water below, roaring in a narrow channel, was noisy and wild.

94   "Jeff."

95   "Hunh?"

96   "How far you goin'?"

97   "Jes a lil piece down the road."

98   "You ain't scairt is you, Jeff?"

99   "Nah, baby," he was trembling. "I ain't scairt."

100   "Remember how we planned it, Jeff. We gotta do it like we said. Brave-like."

101   "Hm."

102   Jeff's brain darkened. Things suddenly seemed unreal, like figures in a dream. Thoughts swam in his mind foolishly, hysterically, like little blind fish in a pool within a dense cave. They rushed, crossed one another, jostled, collided, retreated, and rushed again. Jeff soon became dizzy. He shuddered violently and turned to his wife.

103   "Jennie, I can't do it. I can't." His voice broke pitifully.

104   She did not appear to be listening. All the grief had gone from her face. She sat erect, her unseeing eyes wide open, strained and frightful. Her glossy black skin had become dull. She seemed as thin and as sharp and bony as a starved bird. Now, having suffered and endured the sadness of tearing herself away from beloved things, she showed no anguish. She was absorbed with her own thoughts, and she didn't even hear Jeff's voice shouting in her ear.

105   Jeff said nothing more. For an instant there was light in his cavernous brain. That chamber was, for less than a second, peopled by characters he knew and loved. They were simple, healthy creatures, and they behaved in a manner that he could understand. They had quality. But since he had already taken leave of them long ago, the remembrance did not break his heart again. Young Jeff Patton was among them, the Jeff Patton of fifty years ago who went down to New Orleans with a crowd of country boys to the Mardi Gras doings. The gay young crowd—boys

with candy-striped shirts and rouged brown girls in noisy silks—was like a picture in his head. Yet it did not make him sad. On that very trip Slim Burns had killed Joe Beasley—the crowd had been broken up. Since then Jeff Patton's work had been the Greenbrier Plantation. If there had been other Mardi Gras carnivals, he had not heard of them. Since then there had been no time; the years had fallen on him like waves. Now he was old, worn out. Another paralytic stroke like the one he had already suffered would put him on his back for keeps. In that condition, with a frail blind woman to look after him, he would be worse off than if he were dead.

106   Suddenly Jeff's hands became steady. He actually felt brave. He slowed down the motor of the car and carefully pulled off the road. Below, the water of the stream boomed, a soft thunder in the deep channel. Jeff ran the car onto the clay slope, pointed it directly toward the stream, and put his foot heavily on the accelerator. The little car leaped furiously down the steep incline toward the water. The movement was nearly as swift and direct as a fall. The two old black folks, sitting quietly side by side, showed no excitement. In another instant the car hit the water and dropped immediately out of sight.

107   A little later it lodged in the mud of a shallow place. One wheel of the crushed and upturned little Ford became visible above the rushing water.

Questions for Discussion

1. What does "gone democrat" mean?
2. Why does Bontemps take so much time to describe the old couple, the setting, and the model-T Ford?
3. Analyze the feelings of Jeff Patton. Why does Jeff shiver or feel dazed? What does his saying, "Women or children might be tolerated if they were puny, but a weak man was a curse" reveal about his concept of what it means to be a man?
4. Analyze the feelings of Jennie Patton. Why does she want to get even with Delia Moore? Why does she cry?
5. What events in their lives cause Jeff and Jennie to despair? What is Mr. Stevenson's role in their decision?
6. What details foreshadow the ending?

Suggestions for Exploring, Writing, and Persuading

1. Bontemps says that "fear came into [Jeff Patton's] eyes; excitement took his breath." Sometimes fear is accompanied by excitement. Examine some activity that evokes both thrill and fear.
2. Jeff Patton thinks to himself, "Now he was old, worn out." Discuss why and how elderly people in some cultures are treated as if they are "worn out." Or write an essay contrasting such treatment of the elderly with the belief of some cultures that the elderly must be treated with respect.

3. Compare the attitude toward the elderly in this story with that shown in Capote's "A Christmas Memory."

4. Write an essay convincing your reader Jeff and Jennie would or would not be likely to face a similar decision today.

5. Write an argumentative essay on one of the following:

   Jeff and Jennie should have hung on a little—hope springs eternal.

   Jeff and Jennie did the right thing.

Chinua Achebe (b. 1930)

Chinua Achebe, a Nigerian novelist and man of letters who writes in English, is among the most highly respected and influential contemporary African authors. Achebe's early novels, Things Fall Apart *(1959),* No Longer at Ease *(1962), and* Arrow of Gold *(1964), explore the conflict between traditional tribal customs and the European values introduced by colonists. His later novels,* A Man of the People *(1964) and* Anthills of the Savannah *(1988), expose the corruption and conflicts in postcolonial Nigerian politics.* Morning Yet on Creation Day *(1975) is a collection of essays.* Home and Exile *(2000) is one of his most recent works.*

DEAD MEN'S PATH   (1953)

1   Michael Obi's hopes were fulfilled much earlier than he had expected. He was appointed headmaster of Ndume Central School in January 1949. It had always been an unprogressive school, so the Mission authorities decided to send a young and energetic man to run it. Obi accepted this responsibility with enthusiasm. He had many wonderful ideas and this was an opportunity to put them into practice. He had had sound secondary school education which designated him a "pivotal teacher" in the official records and set him apart from the other headmasters in the mission field. He was outspoken in his condemnation of the narrow views of these older and often less-educated ones.

2   "We shall make a good job of it, shan't we?" he asked his young wife when they first heard the joyful news of his promotion.

3   "We shall do our best," she replied. "We shall have such beautiful gardens and everything will be just *modern* and delightful...." In their two years of married life she had become completely infected by his passion for "modern methods" and his denigration of "these old and superannuated people in the teaching field who would be better employed as traders in the Onitsha market." She began to see herself already as the admired wife of the young headmaster, the queen of the school.

4   The wives of the other teachers would envy her position. She would set the fashion in everything.... Then, suddenly, it occurred to her that there might not be other wives. Wavering between hope and fear, she asked her husband, looking anxiously at him.

5   "All our colleagues are young and unmarried," he said with enthusiasm which for once she did not share. "Which is a good thing," he continued.

6   "Why?"

7   "Why? They will give all their time and energy to the school."

8   Nancy was downcast. For a few minutes she became skeptical about the new school; but it was only for a few minutes. Her little personal misfortune could not blind her to her husband's happy prospects. She looked at him as he sat folded up in a chair. He was stoop-shouldered and looked frail. But he sometimes surprised people with sudden bursts of physical energy. In his present posture, however, all his bodily strength seemed to have retired behind his deep-set eyes, giving them an extraordinary power of penetration. He was only twenty-six, but looked thirty or more. On the whole, he was not unhandsome.

9   "A penny for your thoughts, Mike," said Nancy after a while, imitating the woman's magazine she read.

10   "I was thinking what a grand opportunity we've got at last to show these people how a school should be run."

11   Ndume School was backward in every sense of the word. Mr. Obi put his whole life into the work, and his wife hers too. He had two aims. A high standard of teaching was insisted upon, and the school compound was to be turned into a place of beauty. Nancy's dream-gardens came to life with the coming of the rains, and blossomed. Beautiful hibiscus and allamanda hedges in brilliant red and yellow marked out the carefully tended school compound from the rank neighborhood bushes.

12   One evening as Obi was admiring his work he was scandalized to see an old woman from the village hobble right across the compound, through a marigold flower-bed and the hedges. On going up there he found faint signs of an almost disused path from the village across the school compound to the bush on the other side.

13   "It amazes me," said Obi to one of his teachers who had been three years in the school, "that you people allowed the villagers to make use of this footpath. It is simply incredible." He shook his head.

14   "The path," said the teacher apologetically, "appears to be very important to them. Although it is hardly used, it connects the village shrine with their place of burial."

15   "And what has that got to do with the school?" asked the headmaster.

16   "Well, I don't know," replied the other with a shrug of the shoulders. "But I remember there was a big row some time ago when we attempted to close it."

17   "That was some time ago. But it will not be used now," said Obi as he walked away. "What will the Government Education Officer think of this when he comes to inspect the school next week? The villagers might, for all I know, decide to use the schoolroom for a pagan ritual during the inspection."

18   Heavy sticks were planted closely across the path at the two places where it entered and left the school premises. These were further strengthened with barbed wire.

19   Three days later the village priest of *Ani* called on the headmaster. He was an old man and walked with a slight stoop. He carried a stout walking-stick which he usually tapped on the floor, by way of emphasis, each time he made a new point in his argument.

20   "I have heard," he said after the usual exchange of cordialities, "that our ancestral footpath has recently been closed...."

21   "Yes," replied Mr. Obi. "We cannot allow people to make a highway of our school compound."

22   "Look here, my son," said the priest bringing down his walking-stick, "this path was here before you were born and before your father was born. The whole life of this village depends on it. Our dead relatives depart by it and our ancestors visit us by it. But most important, it is the path of children coming in to be born...."

23   Mr. Obi listened with a satisfied smile on his face.

24   "The whole purpose of our school," he said finally, "is to eradicate just such beliefs as that. Dead men do not require footpaths. The whole idea is just fantastic. Our duty is to teach your children to laugh at such ideas."

25   "What you say may be true," replied the priest, "but we follow the practices of our fathers. If you reopen the path we shall have nothing to quarrel about. What I always say is: let the hawk perch and let the eagle perch." He rose to go.

26   "I am sorry," said the young headmaster. "But the school compound cannot be a thoroughfare. It is against our regulations. I would suggest your constructing another path, skirting our premises. We can even get our boys to help in building it. I don't suppose the ancestors will find the little detour too burdensome."

27   "I have no more words to say," said the old priest, already outside.

28   Two days later a young woman in the village died in childbed. A diviner was immediately consulted and he prescribed heavy sacrifices to propitiate ancestors insulted by the fence.

29   Obi woke up next morning among the ruins of his work. The beautiful hedges were torn up not just near the path but right round the school, the flowers trampled to death and one of the school buildings pulled down...That day, the white Supervisor came to inspect the school and wrote a nasty report on the state of the premises but more seriously about the "tribal-war situation developing between the school and the village, arising in part from the misguided zeal of the new headmaster."

Questions for Discussion

1. Why is Obi infatuated with "modern" ways and disdainful of the "narrow views" of "less educated" people? Why does his wife go along with these ideas? Why is she "downcast" at first? What do their names suggest?

2. What are his two goals? Explain how and why each goal is or is not fulfilled.

3. What is the essence of the argument about the path? What is the village priest's position? Explain whether his argument has merit.

4. Explain what the priest means when he says, "let the hawk perch and let the eagle perch."

5. Why do the local people vandalize the garden and the school grounds? What is their justification?

6. How do the headmaster's goals backfire in an ironic way?

Suggestions for Exploring, Writing, and Persuading

1. In an essay, discuss what is lost when traditions are destroyed in the name of progress.

2. Discuss in detail an instance you know of where those seeking progress or development came into conflict with the old and traditional.

3. Write a character analysis of Nancy and/or Michael.

4. Michael says, "'Dead men do not require footpaths.'" The priest thinks just the opposite. Research other rituals for the dead, such as the Greeks' use of coins on the eyes of the dead. Then write a documented essay on two or three of these rituals.

Bharati Mukherjee (b. 1940)

Born in Calcutta to wealthy parents, Mukherjee moved to Britain when she was eight and knew she wanted to become a writer when she was ten. She received a B.A. from the University of Calcutta and an M.A, in English and Ancient Indian Culture from the University of Baroda. Mukherjee earned an M.F.A. in creative writing and Ph.D. from the University of Iowa. After her marriage to Clark Blaize, she wrote two books with her husband: Days and Nights in Calcutta *(1977) and* The Sorrow and the Terror: The Haunting Legacy of the Air India Tragedy *(1987). Writing about the immigrant experience in America and about Indian women and their mistreatment, Mukherjee has published* The Tiger's Daughter *(1972),* Wife *(1975),* The Holder of the World *(1993), and* Leave It To Me *(1997). Currently, she is a professor at the University of California, Berkeley.*

THE MANAGEMENT OF GRIEF   (1988)

1   A woman I don't know is boiling tea the Indian way in my kitchen. There are a lot of women I don't know in my kitchen, whispering and moving tactfully. They open doors, rummage through the pantry, and try not to ask me where things are kept. They remind me of when my sons were small, on Mother's Day or when Vikram and I were tired, and they

would make big, sloppy omelets. I would lie in bed pretending I didn't hear them.

2   Dr. Sharma, the treasurer of the Indo-Canada Society, pulls me into the hallway. He wants to know if I am worried about money. His wife, who has just come up from the basement with a tray of empty cups and glasses, scolds him. "Don't bother Mrs. Bhave with mundane details." She looks so monstrously pregnant her baby must be days overdue. I tell her she shouldn't be carrying heavy things. "Shaila," she says, smiling, "this is the fifth." Then she grabs a teenager by his shirttails. He slips his Walkman off his head. He has to be one of her four children; they have the same domed and dented foreheads. "What's the official word now?" she demands. The boy slips the headphones back on. "They're acting evasive, Ma. They're saying it could be an accident or a terrorist bomb."

3   All morning, the boys have been muttering, Sikh bomb, Sikh bomb. The men, not using the word, bow their heads in agreement. Mrs. Sharma touches her forehead at such a word. At least they've stopped talking about space debris and Russian lasers.

4   Two radios are going in the dining room. They are tuned to different stations. Someone must have brought the radios down from my boys' bedrooms. I haven't gone into their rooms since Kusum came running across the front lawn in her bathrobe. She looked so funny, I was laughing when I opened the door.

5   The big TV in the den is being whizzed through American networks and cable channels.

6   "Damn!" some man swears bitterly. "How can these preachers carry on like nothing's happened?" I want to tell him we're not that important. You look at the audience, and at the preacher in his blue robe with his beautiful white hair, the potted palm trees under a blue sky, and you know they care about nothing.

7   The phone rings and rings. Dr. Sharma's taken charge. "We're with her," he keeps saying. "Yes, yes, the doctor has given calming pills. Yes, yes, pills are having necessary effect." I wonder if pills alone explain this calm. Not peace, just a deadening quiet. I was always controlled, but never repressed. Sound can reach me, but my body is tensed, ready to scream. I hear their voices all around me. I hear my boys and Vikram cry. "Mommy, Shaila!" and their screams insulate me, like headphones.

8   The woman boiling water tells her story again and again. "I got the news first. My cousin called from Halifax before six A.M., can you imagine. He'd gotten up for prayers and his son was studying for medical exam and heard on a rock channel that something had happened to a plane. They said first it had disappeared from the radar, like a giant eraser just reached out. His father called me, so I said to him, what do you mean 'something bad'? You mean a hijacking? And he said, *Behn*, there is no confirmation of anything yet, but check with your neighbors because a lot of them must be on that plane. So I called poor Kusum straight-away. I knew Kusum's husband and daughter were booked to go yesterday."

9   Kusum lives across the street from me. She and Satish had moved less than a month ago. They said they needed a bigger place. All the people, the Sharmas and friends from the Indo-Canada Society, had been there for the housewarming. Satish and Kusum made tandoori on their big gas grill and even the white neighbors piled their plates high with that luridly red, charred, juicy chicken. Their younger daughter had danced, and even our boys had broken away from the Stanley Cup telecast to put in a reluctant appearance. Everyone took pictures for their albums and for the community newspapers—another of our families had made it big in Toronto—and now I wonder how many of those happy faces are gone. "Why does God give us so much if all along He intends to take it away?" Kusum asks me.

10   I nod. We sit on carpeted stairs, holding hands like children. "I never once told him that I loved him," I say. I was too much the well-brought-up woman. I was so well brought up I never felt comfortable calling my husband by his first name.

11   "It's all right," Kusum says. "He knew. My husband knew. They felt it. Modern young girls have to say it because what they feel is fake."

12   Kusum's daughter Pam runs in with an overnight case. Pam's in her McDonald's uniform. "Mummy! You have to get dressed!" Panic makes her cranky. "A reporter's on his way here."

13   "Why?"

14   "You want to talk to him in your bathrobe?" She starts to brush her mother's long hair. She's the daughter who's always in trouble. She dates Canadian boys and hangs out in the mall, shopping for tight sweaters. The younger one, the goody-goody one according to Pam, the one with voice so sweet that when she sang *bhajans* for Ethiopian relief even a frugal man like my husband wrote out a hundred-dollar check, *she* was on that plane. *She* was going to spend July and August with grandparents because Pam wouldn't go. Pam said she'd rather waitress at McDonald's. "If it's a choice between Bombay and Wonderland, I'm picking Wonderland," she'd said.

15   "Leave me alone," Kusum yells. "You know what I want to do? If I didn't have to look after you now, I'd hang myself."

16   Pam's young face goes blotchy with pain. "Thanks," she says, "don't let me stop you."

17   "Hush," pregnant Mrs. Sharma scolds Pam. "Leave your mother alone. Mr. Sharma will tackle the reporters and fill out the forms. He'll know what has to be said."

18   Pam stands her ground. "You think I don't know what Mummy's thinking? *Why her?* That's what. That's sick! Mummy wishes my little sister were alive and I were dead."

19   Kusum's hand in mine is trembly hot. We continue to sit on the stairs.

20   She calls before she arrives, wondering if there's anything I need. Her name is Judith Templeton and she's an appointee of the provincial gov-

ernment. "Multiculturalism?" I ask, and she says "partially," but that her mandate is bigger. "I've been told you knew many of the people on that flight," she says. "Perhaps if you'd agree to help us reach the others...?"

21 She gives me time at least to put on tea water and pick up the mess in the front room. I have a few *samosas* from Kusum's housewarming that I could fry up, but then I think, why prolong this visit?

22 Judith Templeton is much younger than she sounded. She wears a blue suit with a white blouse and a polka-dot tie. Her blond hair is cut short, her only jewelry is pearl-drop earrings. Her briefcase is new and expensive looking, a gleaming cordovan leather. She sits with it across her lap. When she looks out the front windows onto the street, her contact lenses seem to float in front of her light blue eyes.

23 "What sort of help do you want from me?" I ask. She has refused the tea, out of politeness, but I insist, along with some slightly stale biscuits.

24 "I have no experience," she admits. "That is, I have an M.S.W. and I've worked in liaison with accident victims, but I mean I have no experience with a tragedy of this scale—"

25 "Who could?" I ask.

26 "—and with the complications of culture, language, and custom. Someone mentioned that Mrs. Bhave is a pillar—because you've taken it more calmly."

27 At this, perhaps, I frown, for she reaches forward, almost to take my hand. "I hope you understand my meaning, Mrs. Bhave. There are hundreds of people in Metro directly affected, like you, and some of them speak no English. There are some widows who've never handled money or gone on a bus, and there are old parents who still haven't eaten or gone outside their bedrooms. Some houses and apartments have been looted. Some wives are still hysterical. Some husbands are in shock and profound depression. We want to help, but our hands are tied in so many ways. We have to distribute money to some people, and there are legal documents— these things can be done. We have interpreters, but we don't always have the human touch, or maybe the right human touch. We don't want to make mistakes, Mrs. Bhave, and that's why we'd like to ask you to help us."

28 "More mistakes, you mean," I say.

29 "Police matters are not in my hands," she answers.

30 "Nothing I can do will make any difference," I say. "We must all grieve in our own way."

31 "But you are coping very well. All the people said, Mrs. Bhave is the strongest person of all. Perhaps if the others could see you, talk with you, it would help them."

32 "By the standards of the people you call hysterical, I am behaving very oddly and very badly, Miss Templeton." I want to say to her, *I wish I could scream, starve, walk into Lake Ontario, jump from a bridge.* "They would not see me as a model. I do not see myself as a model."

33 I am a freak. No one who has ever known me would think of me reacting this way. This terrible calm will not go away.

34   She asks me if she may call again, after I get back from a long trip that we all must make. "Of course," I say. "Feel free to call, anytime."

35   Four days later, I find Kusum squatting on a rock overlooking a bay in Ireland. It isn't a big rock, but it juts sharply out over water. This is as close as we'll ever get to them. June breezes balloon out her sari and unpin her knee-length hair. She has the bewildered look of a sea creature whom the tides have stranded.

36   It's been one hundred hours since Kusum came stumbling and screaming across my lawn. Waiting around the hospital, we've heard many stories. The police, the diplomats, they tell us things thinking that we're strong, that knowledge is helpful to the grieving, and maybe it is. Some, I know, prefer ignorance, or their own versions. The plane broke into two, they say. Unconsciousness was instantaneous. No one suffered. My boys must have just finished their breakfasts. They loved eating on planes, they loved the smallness of plates, knives, and forks. Last year they saved the airline salt and pepper shakers. Half an hour more and they would have made it to Heathrow.

37   Kusum says that we can't escape our fate. She says that all those people—our husbands, my boys, her girl with the nightingale voice, all those Hindus, Christians, Sikhs, Muslims, Parsis, and atheists on that plane—were fated to die together off this beautiful bay. She learned this from a swami in Toronto.

38   I have my Valium.

39   Six of us "relatives"—two widows and four widowers—chose to spend the day today by the waters instead of sitting in a hospital room and scanning photographs of the dead. That's what they call us now: relatives. I've looked through twenty-seven photos in two days. They're very kind to us, the Irish are very understanding. Sometimes understanding means freeing a tourist bus for this trip to the bay, so we can pretend to spy our loved ones through the glassiness of waves or in sun-speckled cloud shapes.

40   I could die here, too, and be content.

41   "What is that, out there?" She's standing and flapping her hands, and for a moment I see a head shape bobbing in the waves. She's standing in the water, I on the boulder. The tide is low, and a round, black headsized rock has just risen from the waves. She returns, her sari end dripping and ruined, and her face is a twisted remnant of hope, the way mine was a hundred hours ago, still laughing but inwardly knowing that nothing but the ultimate tragedy could bring two women together at six o'clock on a Sunday morning. I watch her face sag into blankness.

42   "That water felt warm, Shaila," she says at length.

43   "You can't," I say. "We have to wait for our turn to come."

44   I haven't eaten in four days, haven't brushed my teeth.

45   "I know," she says. "I tell myself I have no right to grieve. They are in a better place than we are. My swami says depression is a sign of our selfishness."

46   Maybe I'm selfish. Selfishly I break away from Kusum and run, sandals slapping against stones, to the water's edge. What if my boys aren't lying pinned under the debris? What if they aren't stuck a mile below that innocent blue chop? What if, given the strong currents...

47   Now I've ruined my sari, one of my best. Kusum has joined me, knee deep in water that feels to me like a swimming pool. I could settle in the water, and my husband would take my hand and the boys would slap water in my face just to see me scream.

48   "Do you remember what good swimmers my boys were, Kusum?"

49   "I saw the medals," she says.

50   One of the widowers, Dr. Ranganathan from Montreal, walks out to us, carrying his shoes in one hand. He's an electrical engineer. Someone at the hotel mentioned his work is famous around the world, something about the place where physics and electricity come together. He has lost a huge family, something indescribable. "With some good luck," Dr. Ranganathan suggests to me, "a good swimmer could make it safely to some island. It is quite possible that there may be many, many microscopic islets scattered around."

51   "You're not just saying that?" I tell Dr. Ranganathan about Vinod, my elder son. Last year he took diving as well.

52   "It's a parent's duty to hope," he says. "It is foolish to rule out possibilities that have not been tested. I myself have not surrendered hope."

53   Kusum is sobbing once again. "Dear lady," he says, laying his free hand on her arm, and she calms down.

54   "Vinod is how old?" he asks me. He's very careful, as we all are. *Is*, not was.

55   "Fourteen. Yesterday he was fourteen. His father and uncle were going to take him down to the Taj and give him a big birthday party. I couldn't go with them because I couldn't get two weeks off from my stupid job in June." I process bills for a travel agent. June is a big travel month.

56   Dr. Ranganathan whips the pockets of his suit jacket inside out. Squashed roses, in darkening shades of pink, float on the water. He tore the roses off creepers in somebody's garden. He didn't ask anyone if he could pluck the roses, but now there's been an article about it in the local papers. When you see an Indian person, it says, please give them flowers.

57   "A strong youth of fourteen," he says, "can very likely pull to safety a younger one."

58   My sons, though four years apart, were very close. Vinod wouldn't let Mithun drown. *Electrical engineering*, I think, foolishly perhaps: this man knows important secrets of the universe, things closed to me. Relief spins me lightheaded. No wonder my boys' photographs haven't turned up in the gallery of photos of the recovered dead. "Such pretty roses," I say.

59   "My wife loved pink roses. Every Friday I had to bring a bunch home. I used to say, Why? After twenty-odd years of marriage you're still needing proof positive of my love?" He has identified his wife and three of his children. Then others from Montreal, the lucky ones, intact families with

no survivors. He chuckles as he wades back to shore. Then he swings around to ask me a question. "Mrs. Bhave, you are wanting to throw in some roses for your loved ones? I have two big ones left."

60   But I have other things to float: Vinod's pocket calculator; a half-painted model B-52 for my Mithun. They'd want them on their island. And for my husband? For him I let fall into the calm, glassy waters a poem I wrote in the hospital yesterday. Finally he'll know my feelings for him. "Don't tumble, the rocks are slippery," Dr. Ranganathan cautions. He holds out a hand for me to grab.

61   Then it's time to get back on the bus, time to rush back to our waiting posts on hospital benches. Kusum is one of the lucky ones. The lucky ones flew here, identified in multiplicate their loved ones, then will fly to India with the bodies for proper ceremonies. Satish is one of the few males who surfaced. The photos of faces we saw on the walls in an office at Heathrow and here in the hospital are mostly of women. Women have more body fat, a nun said to me matter-of-factly. They float better.

62   Today I was stopped by a young sailor on the street. He had loaded bodies, he'd gone into the water when—he checks my face for signs of strength—when the sharks were first spotted. I don't blush, and he breaks down. "It's all right," I say. "Thank you." I heard about the sharks from Dr. Ranganathan. In his orderly mind, science brings understanding, it holds no terror. It is the shark's duty. For every deer there is a hunter, for every fish a fisherman.

63   The Irish are not shy; they rush to me and give me hugs and some are crying. I cannot imagine reactions like that on the streets of Toronto. Just strangers, and I am touched. Some carry flowers with them and give them to any Indian they see.

64   After lunch, a policeman I have gotten to know quite well catches hold of me. He says he thinks he has a match for Vinod. I explain what a good swimmer Vinod is.

65   "You want me with you when you look at the photos?" Dr. Ranganathan walks ahead of me into the picture gallery. In these matters he is a scientist and I am grateful. It is a new perspective. "They have performed miracles," he says. "We are indebted to them."

66   The first day or two the policemen showed us relatives only one picture at a time; now they're in a hurry, they're eager to lay out the possibles, and even the probables.

67   The face on the photo is of a boy much like Vinod; the same intelligent eyes, the same thick brows dipping into a V. But this boy's features, even his cheeks, are puffier, wider, mushier.

68   "No." My gaze is pulled by other pictures. There are five other boys who look like Vinod.

69   The nun assigned to console me rubs the first picture with a fingertip. "When they've been in the water for a while, love, they look a little heavier." The bones under the skin are broken, they said on the first day—try to adjust your memories. It's important.

70   "It's not him. I'm his mother. I'd know."

71   "I know this one!" Dr. Ranganathan cries out, and suddenly from the back of the gallery. "And this one!" I think he senses that I don't want to find my boys. "They are the Kutty brothers. They were also from Montreal." I don't mean to be crying. On the contrary, I am ecstatic. My suitcase in the hotel is packed heavy with dry clothes for my boys.

72   The policeman starts to cry. "I am so sorry. I am so sorry, ma'am. I really thought we had a match."

73   With the nun ahead of us and the policeman behind, we, the unlucky ones without our children's bodies, file out of the makeshift gallery.

74   From Ireland most of us go on to India. Kusum and I take the same direct flight to Bombay, so I can help her clear customs quickly. But we have to argue with a man in uniform. He has large boils on his face. The boils swell and glow with sweat as we argue with him. He wants Kusum to wait in line and he refuses to take authority because his boss is on a tea break. But Kusum won't let her coffins out of sight, and I shan't desert her though I know that my parents, elderly and diabetic, must be waiting in a stuffy car in a scorching lot.

75   "You bastard!" I scream at the man with the popping boils. Other passengers press closer. "You think we're smuggling contraband in those coffins!"

76   Once upon a time we were well-brought-up women; we were dutiful wives who kept our heads veiled, our voices shy and sweet.

77   In India, I become, once again, an only child of rich, ailing parents. Old friends of the family come to pay their respects. Some are Sikh, and inwardly, involuntarily, I cringe. My parents are progressive people; they do not blame communities for a few individuals.

78   In Canada it is a different story now.

79   "Stay longer," my mother pleads. "Canada is a cold place. Why would you want to be by yourself?" I stay.

80   Three months pass. Then another.

81   "Vikram wouldn't have wanted you to give up things!" they protest. They called my husband by the name he was born with. In Toronto he'd changed to Vik so the men he worked with at his office would find his name as easy as Rod or Chris. "You know, the dead aren't cut off from us!"

82   My grandmother, the spoiled daughter of a rich zamindar, shaved her head with rusty razor blades when she was widowed at sixteen. My grandfather died of childhood diabetes when he was nineteen, and she saw herself as the harbinger of bad luck. My mother grew up without parents, raised indifferently by an uncle, while her true mother slept in a hut behind the main estate house and took her food with the servants. She grew up a rationalist. My parents abhor mindless mortification.

83   The zamindar's daughter kept stubborn faith in Vedic rituals; my parents rebelled. I am trapped between two modes of knowledge. At thirty-six, I am too old to start over and too young to give up. Like my husband's spirit, I flutter between worlds.

84   Courting aphasia, we travel. We travel with our phalanx of servants and poor relatives. To hill stations and to beach resorts. We play contract bridge in dusty gymkhana clubs. We ride stubby ponies up crumbly mountain trails. At tea dances, we let ourselves be twirled twice round the ballroom. We hit the holy spots we hadn't made time for before. In Varanasi, Kalighat, Rishikesh, Hardwar, astrologers and palmists seek me out and for a fee offer me cosmic consolations.

85   Already the widowers among us are being shown new bride candidates. They cannot resist the call of custom, the authority of their parents and older brothers. They must marry; it is the duty of a man to look after a wife. The new wives will be young widows with children, destitute but of good family. They will make loving wives, but the men will shun them. I've had calls from the men over crackling Indian telephone lines. "Save me," they say, these substantial, educated, successful men of forty. "My parents are arranging a marriage for me." In a month they will have buried one family and returned to Canada with a new bride and partial family.

86   I am comparatively lucky. No one here thinks of arranging a husband for an unlucky widow.

87   Then, on the third day of the sixth month into this odyssey, in an abandoned temple in a tiny Himalayan village, as I make my offering of flowers and sweetmeats to the god of a tribe of animists, my husband descends to me. He is squatting next to a scrawny sadhu in moth-eaten robes. Vikram wears the vanilla suit he wore the last time I hugged him. The sadhu tosses petals on a butter-fed flame, reciting Sanskrit mantras and sweeps his face of flies. My husband takes my hands in his.

88   *You're beautiful*, he starts. Then, *What are you doing here?*

89   *Shall I stay?* I ask. He only smiles, but already the image is fading. *You must finish alone what we started together.* No seaweed wreathes his mouth. He speaks too fast, just as he used to when we were an envied family in our pink split-level. He is gone.

90   In the windowless altar room, smoky with joss sticks and clarified butter lamps, a sweaty hand gropes for my blouse. I do not shriek. The sadhu arranges his robe. The lamps hiss and sputter out.

91   When we come out of the temple, my mother says, "Did you feel something weird in there?"

92   My mother has no patience with ghosts, prophetic dreams, holy men, and cults.

93   "No," I lie. "Nothing."

94   But she knows that she's lost me. She knows that in days I shall be leaving.

95   Kusum's put up her house for sale. She wants to live in an ashram in Hardwar. Moving to Hardwar was her swami's idea. Her swami runs two ashrams, the one in Hardwar and another here in Toronto.

96   "Don't run away," I tell her.

97   "I'm not running away," she says. "I'm pursuing inner peace. You think you or that Ranganathan fellow are better off?"

98   Pam's left for California. She wants to do some modeling, she says. She says when she comes into her share of the insurance money she'll open a yoga-cum-aerobics studio in Hollywood. She sends me postcards so naughty I daren't leave them on the coffee table. Her mother has withdrawn from her and the world.

99   The rest of us don't lose touch, that's the point. Talk is all we have, says Dr. Ranganathan, who has also resisted his relatives and returned to Montreal and to his job, alone. He says, Whom better to talk with than other relatives? We've been melted down and recast as a new tribe.

100   He calls me twice a week from Montreal. Every Wednesday night and every Saturday afternoon. He is changing jobs, going to Ottawa. But Ottawa is over a hundred miles away, and he is forced to drive two hundred and twenty miles a day from his home in Montreal. He can't bring himself to sell his house. The house is a temple, he says; the king-sized bed in the master bedroom is a shrine. He sleeps on a folding cot. A devotee.

101   There are still some hysterical relatives. Judith Templeton's list of those needing help and those who've "accepted" is in nearly perfect balance. Acceptance means you speak of your family in the past tense and you make active plans for moving ahead with your life. There are courses at Seneca and Ryerson we could be taking. Her gleaming leather briefcase is full of college catalogues and lists of cultural societies that need our help. She has done impressive work, I tell her.

102   "In the textbooks on grief management," she replies—I am her confidante. I realize, one of the few whose grief has not sprung bizarre obsessions— "there are stages to pass through: rejection, depression, acceptance, reconstruction." She has compiled a chart and finds that six months after the tragedy, none of us still rejects reality, but only a handful are reconstructing. "Depressed acceptance" is the plateau we've reached. Remarriage is a major step in reconstruction (though she's a little surprised, even shocked, over *how* quickly some of the men have taken on new families). Selling one's house and changing jobs and cities is healthy.

103   How to tell Judith Templeton that my family surrounds me, and that like creatures in epics, they've changed shapes? She sees me as calm and accepting but worries that I have no job, no career. My closest friends are worse off than I. I cannot tell her my days, even my nights, are thrilling.

104   She asks me to help with families she can't reach at all. An elderly couple in Agincourt whose sons were killed just weeks after they had brought their parents over from a village in Punjab. From their names, I know they are Sikh. Judith Templeton and a translator have visited them twice with offers of money for airfare to Ireland, with bank forms, power-of-attorney forms, but they have refused to sign, or to leave their tiny apartment. Their sons' money is frozen in the bank. Their sons' investment apartments have been trashed by tenants, the furnishings sold off. The parents fear that anything they sign or any money they receive will end the company's or the country's obligations to them. They fear they are selling their sons for two airline tickets to a place they've never seen.

105   The high-rise apartment is a tower of Indians and West Indians, with a sprinkling of Orientals. The nearest bus-stop kiosk is lined with women in saris. Boys practice cricket in the parking lot. Inside the building, even I wince a bit from the ferocity of onion fumes, the distinctive and immediate Indianness of frying ghee, but Judith Templeton maintains a steady flow of information. These poor old people are in imminent danger of losing their place and all their services.

106   I say to her, "They are Sikh. They will not open up to a Hindu woman." And what I want to add is, as much as I try not to, I stiffen now at the sight of beards and turbans. I remember a time when we all trusted each other in this new country, it was only the new country we worried about.

107   The two rooms are dark and stuffy. The lights are off, and an oil lamp sputters on the coffee table. The bent old lady has let us in, and her husband is wrapping a white turban over his oiled, hip-length hair. She immediately goes into the kitchen, and I hear the most familiar sound of an Indian home, tap water hitting and filling a teapot.

108   They have not paid their utility bills, out of fear and inability to write a check. The telephone is gone, electricity and gas and water are soon to follow. They have told Judith their sons will provide. They are good boys and they have always earned and looked after their parents.

109   We converse a bit in Hindi. They do not ask about the crash and I wonder if I should bring it up. If they think I am here merely as a translator, then they may feel insulted. There are thousands of Punjabi speakers, Sikhs, in Toronto to do a better job. And so I say to the old lady, "I too have lost my sons, and my husband, in the crash."

110   Her eyes immediately fill with tears. The man mutters a few words which sound like a blessing. "God provides and God takes away," he says.

111   I want to say, But only men destroy and give back nothing. "My boys and my husband are not coming back," I say. "We have to understand that."

112   Now the old woman responds. "But who is to say? Man alone does not decide these things." To this her husband adds his agreement.

113   Judith asks about the bank papers, the release forms. With a stroke of the pen, they will have a provincial trustee to pay their bills, invest their money, send them a monthly pension.

114   "Do you know this woman?" I ask them.

115   The man raises his hand from the table, turns it over, and seems to regard each finger separately before he answers. "This young lady is always coming here, we make tea for her, and she leaves papers for us to sign." His eyes scan a pile of papers in the corner of the room. "Soon we will be out of tea, then will she go away?"

116   The old lady adds, "I have asked my neighbors and no one else gets *angrezi* visitors. What have we done?"

117   "It's her job," I try to explain. "The government is worried. Soon you will have no place to stay, no lights, no gas, no water."

118   "Government will get its money. Tell her not to worry, we are honorable people."

119   I try to explain the government wishes to give money, not take. He raises his hand. "Let them take," he says. "We are accustomed to that. That is no problem."

120   "We are strong people," says the wife. "Tell her that."

121   "Who needs all this machinery?" demands the husband. "It is unhealthy, the bright lights, the cold air on a hot day, the cold food, the four gas rings. God will provide, not government."

122   "When our boys return," the mother says.

123   Her husband sucks his teeth. "Enough talk," he says.

124   Judith breaks in. "Have you convinced them?" The snaps on her cordovan briefcase go off like firecrackers in that quiet apartment. She lays the sheaf of legal papers on the coffee table. "If they can't write their names, an X will do—I've told them that."

125   Now the old lady has shuffled to the kitchen and soon emerges with a pot of tea and two cups. "I think my bladder will go first on a job like this," Judith says to me, smiling. "If only there was some way of reaching them. Please thank her for the tea. Tell her she's very kind."

126   I nod in Judith's direction and tell them in Hindi, "She thanks you for the tea. She thinks you are being very hospitable but she doesn't have the slightest idea what it means."

127   I want to say, Humor her. I want to say, My boys and my husband are with me too, more than ever. I look in the old man's eyes and I can read his stubborn, peasant's message: *I have protected this woman as best I can. She is the only person I have left. Give to me or take from what you will, but I will not sign for it. I will not pretend that I accept.*

128   In the car, Judith, says, "You see what I'm up against? I'm sure they're lovely people, but their stubbornness and ignorance are driving me crazy. They think signing a paper is signing their sons' death warrants, don't they?"

129   I am looking out the window. I want to say, *In our culture, it is a parent's duty to hope.*

130   "Now Shaila, this next woman is a real mess. She cries day and night, and she refuses all medical help. We may have to—"

131   "Let me out at the subway," I say.

132   "I beg your pardon?" I can feel those blue eyes staring at me.

133   It would not be like her to disobey. She merely disapproves, and slows at a corner to let me out. Her voice is plaintive. "Is there anything I said? Anything I did?"

134   I could answer her suddenly in a dozen ways, but I choose not to. "Shaila? Let's talk about it," I hear, then slam the door.

135   A wife and mother begins her life in a new country, and that life is cut short. Yet her husband tells her: Complete what we have started. We, who stayed out of politics and came half way around the world to avoid religious and political feuding, have been the first in the New World to die from it. I no longer know what we started, nor how to complete it. I write letters to the editors of local papers and to members of Parliament. Now at least they admit it was a bomb. One MP answers back, with sympathy,

but with a challenge. You want to make a difference? Work on a campaign. Work on mine. Politicize the Indian voter.

136   My husband's old lawyer helps me set up a trust. Vikram was a saver
and a careful investor. He had saved the boys' boarding school and college fees. I sell the pink house at four times what we paid for it and take
a small apartment downtown. I am looking for a charity to support.

137   We are deep in the Toronto winter, gray skies, icy pavements. I stay
indoors, watching television. I have tried to assess my situation, how best
to live my life, to complete what we began so many years ago. Kusum has
written me from Hardwar that her life is now serene. She has seen Satish
and has heard her daughter sing again. Kusum was on a pilgrimage, passing through a village, when she heard a young girl's voice, singing one of
her daughter's favorite *bhajans*. She followed the music through the
squalor of a Himalayan village, to a hut where a young girl, an exact replica
of her daughter, was fanning coals under the kitchen fire. When she
appeared, the girl cried out, "Ma!" and ran away. What did I think of that?

138   I think I can only envy her.

139   Pam didn't make it to California, but writes me from Vancouver. She
works in a department store, giving makeup hints to Indian and Oriental
girls. Dr. Ranganathan has given up his commute, given up his house and
job, and accepted an academic position in Texas, where no one knows
his story and he has vowed not to tell it. He calls me now once a week.

140   I wait, I listen and I pray, but Vikram has not returned to me. The
voices and the shapes and the nights filled with visions ended abruptly
several weeks ago.

141   I take it as a sign.

142   One rare, beautiful, sunny day last week, returning from a small errand
on Yonge Street, I was walking through the park from the subway to my
apartment. I live equidistant from the Ontario Houses of Parliament and
the University of Toronto. The day was not cold, but something in the
bare trees caught my attention. I looked up from the gravel, into the
branches and the clear blue sky beyond. I thought I heard the rustling of
larger forms, and I waited a moment for voices. Nothing.

143   "What?" I asked.

144   Then as I stood in the path looking north to Queen's Park and west to
the university, I heard the voices of my family one last time. *Your time
has come*, they said. *Go, be brave.*

145   I do not know where this voyage I have begun will end. I do not know
which direction I will take. I dropped the package on a park bench and
started walking.

Questions for Discussion

1. Why does the narrator, Mrs. Bhave, focus on the fact that she never
told her husband she loved him or called him by his first name?

2. Joan Templeton, the social worker, asks the narrator for help because she has heard that Mrs. Bhave has "taken it more calmly." How does Mrs. Bhave feel about this observation? In what ways is Templeton's depiction of Mrs. Bhave false?

3. The narrator says, "'Nothing I can do will make any difference....We must all grieve in our own way.'" What are the stages of grief according to Kübler-Ross? How does Mrs. Bhave deal with each stage?

4. Explain why the narrator says, "'I'm a freak.'"

5. Mrs. Bhave calls the custom agent in India a "bastard." How do her words give her relief from her frustration? How is this outburst related to "Once upon a time we were well-brought up women; we were dutiful wives who kept our heads veiled, our voices shy and sweet."

Suggestions for Exploring, Writing, and Persuading

1. In an essay argue for or against the government's trying to help people grieve over a major tragedy such as a plane wreck, hurricane, or earthquake.

2. Discuss in detail the misunderstanding between the government and the grieving in Mukherjee's story. What are the attitudes of the recipients to the government's attempt to help?

3. Compare Mukherjee's question, "Why does God give us so much if all along He intends to take it away?" with a similar expression in Weisel's "Yom Kippur."

4. Mukherjee states that "knowledge is helpful to the grieving. . . . Some, I know, prefer ignorance, or their own versions." In an essay agree, disagree, or modify this statement.

Madison Smartt Bell (b. 1957)

A prolific young writer, Madison Smartt Bell by the age of thirty-four had published six novels and two collections of short stories. His fiction creates a dark world of often violent characters who frequently, like the narrator-protagonist of "Customs of the Country," live or die in the face of apparent hopelessness. Among Bell's novels are Waiting for the World *(1985);* The Year of Silence *(1987);* Save Me, Joe Louis *(1993);* Soldier's Joy, *which received a Lillian Smith Award; and* All Souls' Rising, *which received a National Book Award nomination.*

CUSTOMS OF THE COUNTRY   (1988)

1   I don't remember much about that place anymore. It was nothing but somewhere I came to put in some pretty bad time, though that was not

what I had planned on when I went there. I had it in mind to improve things, but I didn't think you could fairly claim that's what I did. So that's one reason I might just as soon forget about it. And I didn't stay there all that long, not more than about nine months or so, about the same time, come to think, that the child I was there to try to get back had lived inside my body.

2   It was a cluster-housing thing a little ways north out of town from Roanoke, on a two-lane road that crossed the railroad cut and went about a mile farther up through the woods. The buildings looked something like a motel, a little raw still, though they weren't new. My apartment was no more than a place that would barely look all right and yet cost me little enough so I had something left over to give the lawyer. There was fresh paint on the walls and the trim in the kitchen and bathroom was in fair shape. And it was real quiet mostly, except that the man next door used to beat up his wife a couple of times a week. The place was soundproof enough I couldn't usually hear talk but I could hear yelling plain as day and when he got going good he would slam her bang into our common wall. If she hit in just the right spot it would send my pots and pans flying off the pegboard where I'd hung them above the stove.

3   Not that it mattered to me that the pots fell down, except for the noise and the time it took to pick them up again. Living alone like I was, I didn't have the heart to do much cooking and if I did fix myself something I mostly used an old iron skillet that hung there on the same wall. All the others I only had out for show. The whole apartment was done about the same way, made into something I kept spotless and didn't much care to use. I wore my hands out scrubbing everything clean and then saw to it that it stayed that way. I sewed slipcovers for that threadbare batch of Goodwill furniture I'd put in the place, and I hung curtains and found some sunshiny posters to tack on the walls, and I never cared a damn about any of it. It was an act, and I wasn't putting it on for me or for Davey, but for all the other people I expected to come to see it and judge it. And however good I could get it looking, it never felt quite right.

4   I felt even less at home there than I did at my job, which was waitressing three snake-bends of the counter at the Truckstops of America out at the I-81 interchange. The supervisor was a man named Tim that used to know my husband Patrick from before we had tne trouble. He was nice about letting me take my phone calls there and giving me time off to see the lawyer, and in most other ways he was a decent man to work for, except that now and then he would have a tantrum over something or other and try to scream the walls down. Still, it never went beyond yelling, and he always acted sorry once he got through. The other waitress on my shift was an older lady named Prissy, and I liked her all right in spite of the name.

5   We were both on a swing shift that rolled over every ten days, which was the main thing I didn't like about that job. The six-to-two I hated the worst because it would have me getting back to my apartment building around three in the morning, not the time it looked its best. It was the

kind of place where at that time of night I could expect to find the deputies out there looking for somebody, or else some other kind of trouble. I never got to know the neighbors any too well, but a lot of them were pretty sorry—small-time criminals, dope dealers and thieves, none of them much good at whatever it was they did. There was one check forger that I knew of, and a man who would break into the other apartments looking for whiskey. One thing and another, along that line.

6   The man next door, the one that beat up his wife, didn't do crimes or work either that I ever heard. He just seemed to lay around the place, maybe drawing some kind of welfare. There wasn't a whole lot of him, he was just a stringy little man, hair and mustache a dishwater-brown, cheap green tatoos running up his arms. Maybe he was stronger than he looked, but I did wonder how come his wife would take it from him, since she was about a head taller and must have outweighed him an easy ten pounds. I might have thought she was whipping on him—stranger things have been known to go on—but she was the one that seemed like she might break out crying if you looked at her crooked. She was a big fine-looking girl with a lovely shape, and long brown hair real smooth and straight and shiny. I guess she was too hammered down most of the time to pay much attention to how she dressed, but still she had pretty brown eyes, big and long-lashed and soft, sort of like a cow's eyes, except I never saw a cow that looked that miserable.

7   At first I thought maybe I might make a friend of her, she was about the only one around there I felt like I might want to. Our paths crossed pretty frequent, either around the apartment building or in the Kwik Sack back toward town, where I'd find her running the register some days. But she was shy of me, shy of anybody I suppose. She would flinch if you did so much as say hello. So after a while I quit trying. She'd get hers about twice a week, maybe other times I wasn't around to hear it happen. It's a wonder all the things you can learn to ignore, and after a month or so I was that accustomed I barely noticed when they would start in. I would just wait till I thought they were good and through, and then get up and hang those pans back on the wall where they were supposed to go. And all the while I would just be thinking about some other thing, like what might be going on with my Davey.

8   The place where he had been fostered out was not all that far away, just about ten or twelve miles up the road, out there in the farm country. The people were named Baker. I never got to first names with them, just called them Mr. and Mrs. They were older than me, both just into their forties, and they didn't have any children of their own. The place was only a small farm but Mr. Baker grew tobacco on the most of it and I'm told he made it a paying thing. Mrs. Baker kept a milk cow or two and she grew a garden and canned in the old-time way. Thrifty people. They were real sweet to Davey and he seemed to like being with them pretty well. He had been staying there almost the whole two years, which was lucky too, since most children usually got moved around a whole lot more than that.

9   And that was the trouble, like the lawyer explained to me, it was just too good. Davey was doing too well out there. He'd made out better in the first grade than anybody would have thought. So nobody really felt like he needed to be moved. The worst of it was the Bakers had got to like him well enough they were saying they wanted to adopt him if they could. Well, it would have been hard enough for me without that coming into it.

10   Even though he was so close, I didn't go out to see Davey near as much as I would have liked to. The lawyer kept telling me it wasn't a good idea to look like I was pressing too hard. Better take it easy till all the evaluations came in and we had our court date and all. Still, I would call and go on out there maybe a little more than once a month, most usually on the weekends, since that seemed to suit the Bakers better. They never acted like it was any trouble, and they were always pleasant to me, or polite might be a better word yet. The way it sometimes seemed they didn't trust me did bother me a little. I would have liked to take him out to the movies a time or two, but I could see plain enough the Bakers wouldn't have been easy about me having him off their place.

11   But I can't remember us having a bad time, any of those times I went. He was always happy to see me, though he'd be quiet when we were in the house, with Mrs. Baker hovering. So I would get us outside quick as ever I could and, once we were out, we would just play like both of us were children. There was an open pasture, a creek with a patch of woods, a hay barn where we would play hide-and-go-seek. I don't know what all else we did, silly things mostly. That was how I could get near him the easiest, he didn't get a whole lot of playing in, way out there. The Bakers weren't what you would call playful and there weren't any other children living near. So that was the thing I could give him that was all mine to give. When the weather was good we would stay outside together most all the day and he would just wear me out. But over the winter those visits seemed to get shorter and shorter, like the days.

12   Davey called me Momma still, but I suppose he had come to think your mother was something more like a big sister or just some kind of a friend. Mrs. Baker was the one doing for him all the time. I don't know just what he remembered from before, or if he remembered any of the bad part. He would always mind me but he never acted scared around me, and if anybody says he did they lie. But I never really did get to know what he had going on in the back of his mind about the past. At first I worried the Bakers might have been talking against me, but after I had seen a little more of them I knew they wouldn't have done anything like that, wouldn't have thought it right. So I expect whatever Davey knew about the other time he remembered on his own. He never mentioned Patrick hardly and I think he really had forgotten about him. Thinking back I guess he never saw that much of Patrick even when we were all living together. But Davey had Patrick's mark all over him, the same eyes and the same red hair.

13   Patrick had thick wavy hair the shade of an Irish setter's, and a big rolling mustache the same color. Maybe that was his best feature, but he

was a good-looking man altogether, still is I suppose, though the prison haircut don't suit him. If he ever had much of a thought in his head I suspect he had knocked it clean out with dope, yet he was always fun to be around. I wasn't but seventeen when I married him and I didn't have any better sense myself. Right to the end I never thought anything much was the matter, all his vices looked so small to me. He was good-tempered almost all the time, and good with Davey when he did notice him. Never once did he raise his hand to either one of us. In little ways he was unreliable, late, not showing up at all, gone out of the house for days sometimes. Hindsight shows me he ran with other women, but I managed not to know anything about that at the time. He had not quite finished high school and the best job he could hold was being an orderly down at the hospital, but he made a good deal of extra money stealing pills out of there and selling them on the street.

14   That was something else I didn't allow myself to think on much back then. Patrick never told me a lot about it anyhow, always acted real mysterious about whatever he was up to in that line. He would disappear on one of his trips and come back with a whole mess of money, and I would spend up my share and be glad I had it too. I never thought much about where it was coming from, the money or the pills either one. He used to keep all manner of pills around the house, Valium and ludes and a lot of different kinds of speed, and we both took what we felt like whenever we felt in the mood. But what Patrick made the most on was Dilaudid. I used to take it without ever knowing what it really was, but once everything fell in on us I found out it was a bad thing, bad as heroin they said, and not much different, and it was what they gave Patrick most of his time for.

15   I truly was surprised to find out that it was the strongest dope we had, because I never really even felt like it made you all that high. You would just take one and kick back on a long slow stroke and whatever trouble you might have, it would not be able to find you. It came on like nothing but it was the hardest habit to lose, and I was a long time shaking it. I might be thinking about it yet if I would let myself, and there were times, all through the winter I spent in that apartment, I'd catch myself remembering the feeling.

16   You couldn't call it a real bad winter, there wasn't much snow or anything, but I was cold just about all the time, except when I was at work. All I had in the apartment was some electric baseboard heaters, and they cost too much for me to leave them running very long at a stretch. I'd keep it just warm enough so I couldn't see my breath, and spent my time in a hot bathtub or under a big pile of blankets on the bed. Or else I would just be cold.

17   There was some kind of strange quietness about that place all during the cold weather. If the phone rang it would make me jump. Didn't seem like there was any TV or radio ever playing next door. The only sound coming out of there was Susan getting beat up once in a while. That was her name, a sweet name, I think. I found it out from hearing him say it, which he used to do almost every time before he started on her. "Su-*san*,"

he'd call out, loud enough I could hear him through the wall. He'd do it a time or two, he might have been calling her to him, and I suppose she went. After that would come a bad silence that reminded you of a snake being somewhere around. Then a few minutes' worth of hitting sounds and then the big slam as she hit the wall, and the clatter of my pots falling on the floor. He'd throw her at the wall maybe once or twice, usually when he was about to get rough. By the time the pots had quit spinning on the floor it would be real quiet over there again, and the next time I saw Susan she'd be walking in that ginger way people have when they're hiding a hurt, and if I said hello to her she'd give a little jump and look away.

18   After a while I quit paying it much mind, it didn't feel any different to me than hearing the news on the radio. All their carrying on was not any more to me than a bump in the rut I had worked myself into, going back and forth from the job, cleaning that apartment till it hurt, calling up the lawyer about once a week to find out what was happening, which never was much. He was forever trying to get our case before some particular doctor or social worker or judge who'd be more apt to help us than another, so he said. I would call him up from the TOA, all eager to hear what news he had, and every time it was another delay. In the beginning I used to talk it all over with Tim or Prissy after I hung up, but after a while I got out of the mood to discuss it. I kept ahead making those calls but every one of them just wore out my hope a little more, like a drip of water wearing down a stone. And little by little I got in the habit of thinking that nothing really was going to change.

19   Somehow or other that winter passed by, with me going from one phone call to the next, going out to wait on that TOA counter, coming home to shiver and hold hands with myself and lie awake all through the night, or the day, depending what shift I was on. It was springtime, well into warm weather, before anything really happened at all. That was when the lawyer called *me*, for a change, and told me he had some people lined up to see me at last.

20   Well, I was all ready for them to come visit, come see how I'd fixed up my house and all the rest of my business to get set for having Davey back with me again. But as it turned out, nobody seemed to feel like they were called on to make that trip. "I don't think that will be necessary" was what one of them said, I don't recall which. They both talked about the same, in voices that sounded like filling out forms.

21   So all I had to do was drive downtown a couple of times and see them in their offices. That child psychologist was the first and I doubt he kept me more than half an hour. I couldn't tell the point of most of the questions he asked. My second trip I saw the social worker, who turned out to be a black lady once I got down there, though I never could have told it over the phone. Her voice sounded like it was coming out of the TV. She looked me in the eye while she was asking her questions, but I couldn't tell a thing about what she thought. It wasn't till I was back in the apartment that I understood that she must have already had her mind made up.

22   That came to me in a sort of a flash, while I was standing in the kitchen washing out a cup. Soon as I walked back in the door I saw my coffee mug left over from breakfast, and I kicked myself for letting it sit out. I was giving it a hard scrub with a scouring pad when I realized it didn't matter anymore. I might just as well have dropped it on the floor and got what kick I could out of watching it smash, because it wasn't going to make any difference to anybody now. But all the same I rinsed it and set it in the drainer, careful as if it was an eggshell. Then I stepped backward out of the kitchen and took a long look around that cold shabby place and thought it might be for the best that nobody was coming. How could I have expected it to fool anybody else when it wasn't even good enough to fool me? A lonesomeness came over me, I felt like I was floating all alone in the middle of cold air, and then I began to remember some things I would just as soon as have not.

23   No, I never did like to think about this part, but I have had to think about it time and again, with never a break for a long, long time, because I needed to get to understand it at least well enough to believe it never would ever happen anymore. And I had come to believe that, in the end. If I hadn't, I never would have come back at all. I had found a way to trust myself again, though it took me a full two years to do it, and though of course it still didn't mean that anybody else would trust me.

24   What had happened was that Patrick went off on one of his mystery trips and stayed gone a deal longer than usual. Two nights away, I was used to that, but on the third I did start to wonder. He normally would have called at least, if he was going to be gone that long of a stretch. But I didn't hear a peep until about halfway through the fourth day. And it wasn't Patrick himself that called, but one of those public-assistance lawyers from downtown.

25   Seemed like the night before Patrick had got himself stopped on the interstate loop down there. The troopers said he was driving like a blind man, and he was so messed up on whiskey and ludes I suppose he must have been pretty near blind at that. Well, maybe he would have just lost his license or something like that, only that the backseat of the car was loaded up with all he had lately stole out of the hospital.

26   So it was bad. It was so bad my mind just could not contain it, and every hour it seemed to be getting worse. I spent the next couple of days running back and forth between the jail and that lawyer, and I had to haul Davey along with me wherever I went. He was too little for school and I couldn't find anybody to take him right then, though all that running around made him awful cranky. Patrick was just grim, he would barely speak. He already knew pretty well for sure that he'd be going to prison. The lawyer had told him there wasn't no use in getting a bondsman, he might just as well stay on in there and start pulling his time. I don't know how much he really saved himself that way, though, since what they ended up giving him was twenty-five years.

27   That was when all my troubles found me, quick. Two days after Patrick got arrested, I came down real sick with something. I thought at first it

was a bad cold or the flu. My nose kept running and I felt so wore out I couldn't hardly get up off the bed and yet at the same time I felt real restless, like all my nerves had been scraped bare. Well, I didn't really connect it up to the fact that I'd popped the last pill in the house a couple of days before. What was really the matter was me coming off that Dilaudid, but I didn't have any notion of that at the time.

28   I was laying there in bed not able to get up and about ready to jump right out of my skin at the same time when Davey got the drawer underneath the stove open. Of course he was getting restless himself with all that had been going on, and me not able to pay him much mind. All our pots and pans were down in that drawer then, and he began to take them out one at a time and throw them on the floor. It made a hell of a racket, and the shape I was in, I felt like he must be doing it on purpose to devil me. I called out to him and asked him to quit. Nice at first: "You stop that, now, Davey. Momma don't feel good." But he kept right ahead. All he wanted was to have my attention, I know, but my mind wasn't working right just then. I knew I should get up and just go lead him away from there, but I couldn't seem to get myself to move. I had a picture of myself doing the right thing, but I just wasn't doing it. I was still lying there calling to him to quit and he was still banging those pots around and before long I was screaming at him outright, and starting to cry at the same time. But he never stopped a minute. I guess I had scared him some already and he was just locked into doing it, or maybe he wanted to drown me out. Every time he flung a pot it felt like I was getting shot at. And the next thing I knew I got myself in the kitchen someway and I was snatching him up off the floor.

29   To this day I don't remember doing it, though I have tried and tried. I thought if I could call it back then maybe I could root it out of myself and be shed of it for good and all. But all I ever knew was one minute I was grabbing a hold of him and the next he was laying on the far side of the room with his right leg folded up funny where it was broke, not even crying, just looking surprised. And I knew that it had to be me that threw him over there because as sure as hell is real there was nobody else around that could have done it.

30   I drove him to the hospital myself. I laid him straight on the front seat beside me and drove with one hand all the way so I could hold on to him with the other. He was real quiet and real brave the whole time, never cried the least bit, just kept a tight hold on my hand with his. Well, after a while, we got there and they ran him off somewhere to get his leg set and pretty soon the doctor came back out and asked me how it had happened.

31   It was the same hospital where Patrick had worked and I even knew that doctor a little bit. Not that being connected to Patrick would have done me a whole lot of good around there at that time. Still, I have often thought since then that things might have come out better for me and Davey both if I just could have lied to that man, but I was not up to telling a lie that anybody would be apt to believe. All I could do was start to

scream and jabber like a crazy person, and it ended up I stayed in that hospital quite a few days myself. They took me for a junkie and I guess I really was one too, though I hadn't known it till that very day. And I never saw Davey again for a whole two years, not till the first time they let me go out to the Bakers'.

32   Sometimes you don't get but one mistake, if the one you pick is bad enough. Do as much as step in the road one time without looking, and your life could be over with then and there. But during those two years I taught myself to believe that this mistake of mine could be wiped out, that if I struggled hard enough with myself and the world I could make it like it never had been.

33   Three weeks went by after I went to see that social worker, and I didn't have any idea what was happening, or if anything was. Didn't call anybody, I expect I was afraid to. Then one day the phone rang for me out there at the TOA. It was the lawyer and I could tell right off from the sound of his voice I wasn't going to care for his news. Well, he told me all the evaluations had come in now, sure enough and they weren't running in our favor. They weren't against *me*, he made sure to say that, it was more like they were *for* the Bakers. And his judgment was it wouldn't pay me anything if we went on to court. It looked like the Bakers would get Davey for good anyhow, and they were likely to be easier about visitation if there wasn't any big tussle. But if I drug them into court, then we would have to start going back over the whole case history—

34   That was the word he used, *case history*, and it was around about there that I hung up. I went walking stiff-legged back across to the counter and just let myself sort of drop on a stool. Prissy had been covering my station while I was on the phone and she came right over to me then.

35   "What is it?" she said. I guess she could tell it was something by the look on my face.

36   "I lost him," I said.

37   "Oh, hon, you know I'm so sorry," she said. She reached out for my hand but I snatched it back. I know she meant it well but I just was not in the mood to be touched.

38   "There's no forgiveness," I said. I felt bitter about it. It had been a hard road for me to come as near forgiving myself as I ever could. And Davey forgave me, I really knew that, I could tell it in the way he acted when we were together. And if us two could do it, I didn't feel like it ought to be anybody else's business but ours. Tim walked up then and Prissy whispered something to him, and then he took a step nearer to me.

39   "I'm sorry," he told me.

40   "Not like I am," I said. "You don't know the meaning of the word."

41   "Go ahead and take off the rest of your shift if you feel like it," he said. "I'll wait on these tables myself, need be."

42   "I don't know it would make any difference," I said.

43   "Better take it easy on yourself," he said. "No use in taking it so hard. You're just going to have to get used to it."

44   "Is that a fact?" I said. And I lit myself a cigarette and turned my face away. We had been pretty busy, it was lunchtime, and the people were getting restless seeing all of us standing around there not doing a whole lot about bringing them their food. Somebody called out something to Tim, I didn't hear just what it was, but it set off one of his temper fits.

45   "Go on and get out of here if that's how you feel," he said. He was getting red in the face and waving his arms around to include everybody there in what he was saying. "Go on and clear out of here, every last one of you, and we don't care if you never come back. There's not one of you couldn't stand to miss a meal anyhow. Take a look at yourselves, you're all fat as hogs..."

46   It seemed like he might be going to keep it up a good while, and he had already said I could leave, so I hung up my apron and got my purse and I left. It was the first time he ever blew up at the customers that way, it had always been me or Prissy or one of the cooks. I never did find out what came of it all because I never went back to that place again.

47   I drove home in such a poison mood I barely knew I was driving a car or that there were any others on the road. I was ripe to get killed or kill somebody, and I wouldn't have cared much either way. I kept thinking about what Tim had said about having to get used to it. It came to me that I was used to it already, I really hadn't been all that surprised. That's what I'd been doing all those months, just gradually getting used to losing my child forever.

48   When I got back to the apartment I just fell in a chair and sat there staring across at the kitchen wall. It was in my mind to pack my traps and leave that place, but I hadn't yet figured out where I could go. I sat there a good while, I guess. The door was ajar from me not paying attention, but it wasn't cold enough out to make any difference. If I turned my head that way I could see a slice of the parking lot. I saw Susan drive up and park and come limping toward the building with an armload of groceries. Because of the angle I couldn't see her go into their apartment but I heard the door open and shut and after that it was quiet as a tomb. I kept on sitting there thinking about how used to everything I had got. There must have been generous numbers of other people too, I thought, who had got themselves accustomed to all kinds of things. Some were used to taking the pain and the rest were used to serving it up. About half of the world was screaming in misery, and it wasn't anything but a habit.

49   When I started to hear the hitting sounds come toward me through the wall, a smile came on my face like it was cut there with a knife. I'd been expecting it, you see, and the mood I was in I felt satisfied to see what I had expected was going to happen. So I listened a little more carefully than I'd been inclined to do before. It was *hit hit hit* going along together with a groan and a hiss of the wind being knocked out of her. I had to strain pretty hard to hear that breathing part, and I could hear him grunt too, when he got in a good one. There was about three minutes of that with some little breaks, and then a longer pause. When she hit the wall it

was the hardest she had yet, I think. It brought down every last one of my pots at one time, including the big iron skillet that was the only one I ever used.

50   It was the first time they'd managed to knock that skillet down, and I was so impressed that I went over and stood looking down at it like I needed to make sure it was a real thing. I stared at the skillet so long it went out of focus and started looking more like a big black hole in the floor. That's when it dawned on me that this was one thing I didn't really have to keep on being used to.

51   It took three or four knocks before he came to the door, but that didn't worry me at all. I had faith, I knew he was going to come. I meant to stay right there till he did. When he came, he opened the door wide and stood there with his arms folded and his face all stiff with his secrets. It was fairly dark behind him, they had all the curtains drawn. I had that skillet held out in front of me in both my hands, like maybe I had come over to borrow a little hot grease or something. It was so heavy it kept wanting to dip down toward the floor like a water witch's rod. When I saw he wasn't expecting anything, I twisted the skillet back over my shoulder like baseball players do their bat, and I hit him bang across the face as hard as I knew how. He went down and out at the same time and fetched up on his back clear in the middle of the room.

52   Then I went in after him with the skillet cocked and ready in case he made to get up. But he didn't look like there was a whole lot of fight left in him right then. He was awake, at least partly awake, but his nose was just spouting blood and it seemed like I'd knocked out a few of his teeth. I wish I could tell you I was sorry or glad, but I didn't feel much of anything really, just that high lonesome whistle in the blood I used to get when I took all that Dilaudid. Susan was sitting on the floor against the wall, leaning down on her knees and sniveling. Her eyes were red but she didn't have any bruises where they showed. He never did hit her on the face, that was the kind he was. There was a big crack coming down the wall behind her and I remember thinking it probably wouldn't be too much longer before it worked through to my side.

53   "I'm going to pack and drive over to Norfolk," I told her. I hadn't thought of it before but once it came out my mouth I knew it was what I would do. "You can ride along with me if you want to. With your looks you could make enough money serving drinks to the sailors to buy that Kwik Sack and blow it up."

54   She didn't say anything, just raised her head up and stared at me kind of bug-eyed. And after a minute I turned around and went out. It didn't take me any time at all to get ready. All I had was a suitcase and a couple of boxes of other stuff. The sheets and blankets I just pulled off the bed and stuffed in the trunk all in one big wad. I didn't care a damn about that furniture, I would have lit it on fire on a dare.

55   When I was done I stuck my head back into the other apartment. The door was still open like I had left it. What was she doing but kneeling

down over that son of a bitch and trying to clean off his face with a washrag. I noticed he was making a funny sound when he breathed, and his nose was still bleeding pretty quick, so I thought maybe I had broke it. Well, I can't say that worried me much.

56   "Come on now if you're coming, girl," I said. She looked up at me, not telling me one word, just giving me a stare out of those big cow eyes of hers like I was the one had been beating on her that whole winter through. And I saw then that they were both of them stuck in their groove and that she would not be the one to step out of it. So I pulled back out of the doorway and went on down the steps to my car.

57   I was speeding on the road to Norfolk, doing seventy, seventy-five. I'd have liked to gone faster if the car had been up to it. I can't say I felt sorry for busting that guy, though I didn't enjoy the thought of it either. I just didn't know what difference it had made, and chances were it had made none at all. Kind of a funny thing, when you thought about it that way. It was the second time in my life I'd hurt somebody bad, and the other time I hadn't meant to do it at all. This time I'd known what I was doing for sure, but I still didn't know what I'd done.

Questions for Discussion

1. Why does the narrator clean up the apartment even though she says she does not care how it looks and does not feel at home there? How does she feel when the expected social worker and other experts do not come to her apartment?

2. What events led the narrator to abuse Davey?

3. What does the narrator mean when she says, "That's what I'd been doing all those months, just gradually getting used to losing my child forever"? How has she attempted to get used to losing her child? How successful has she been?

4. What kind of future can the narrator anticipate?

5. How would this story be different if it were told from another point of view? Could it be as effective?

Suggestions for Exploring, Writing, and Persuading

1. What factors are most often the causes of child abuse? In an essay, propose methods for stopping child abuse or treatments for abused children.

2. Is the narrator, a child abuser and drug addict, simply an evil person, or does she have some redeeming qualities? Do you feel sympathy for her? If you do, explain how the writer has caused you to do so. If you have no sympathy for the narrator, explain why, citing specific passages from the story.

3. In spite of her husband's abuse, Susan is very tender toward him and refuses to leave him. Using research on spousal abuse, explain the reasons for Susan's behavior in a documented essay.

4. Argue whether the narrator should be given custody of her son.

Eric Skipper (b. 1967)

Born in Burlington, North Carolina, Eric Skipper attended The Georgia Institute of Technology and Florida State University. A student of Hispanic literature and culture, he has worked with Mexican immigrants, traveled extensively in Puerto Rico and Spain, and lectured on Spanish literature at various national conferences. Skipper currently teaches Spanish at Augusta State University in Georgia. "The Runt," his second published work of fiction, first appeared in The Roanoke Review.

THE RUNT   (2001)

1   The summer after my second year of college I found myself overseeing a crew of Mexican migrant workers in a small farming community called Garrett. I had envisioned a sexier form of employment, perhaps on the shrimp docks of New Orleans or a ranch in Arizona or Texas, but low traveling funds and a copy of *Farmer's Bulletin* which happened into my hands ultimately kept me in the state.

2   Garrett is in south Georgia, which is the dry, flat part of the state. Farmers consider its location ideal on two counts. It is close enough to Valdosta or Tallahassee for a same-day trip when parts or equipment are needed, but far enough away to deter workers from making same-night quests for debauchery. The population, on average, is one-fourth Mexican; the number rises during the harvest season and drops during the off-months. The Garrett community, made up mostly of farmers and their families, is very tolerant of the migrant workers and views them as a vital ingredient of the economic landscape. They work hard and for cheap, for the most part. Mexican-on-Mexican crime is generally ignored by local authorities. Conflicts that cross cultural lines are usually blown out of proportion for a day or two, but then are forgotten just as quickly and the community resumes its prosaic, work-a-day routine.

3   A fat, bleary-eyed man named Moss picked me up at the bus station in Valdosta and introduced himself as my new foreman. During the drive to Garrett he informed me that I would be staying in town, in a small apartment connected to the back of one Mr. Banks's house. I protested smally, telling him that I hoped to live near the Mexicans in order to improve my Spanish.

4   "Believe me," he said, regarding me with those large, bleary eyes, "you don't want to live in that hell-hole. Do yourself a favor and stay in town. You'll get plenty chance to practice your Spanish."

5   I followed Moss's advice and took up residence at 120 Fuller Street. The Banks house was one of several stately residences on the street. It sat directly across from the Methodist church and was three blocks from the town's main strip. Mr. Banks—a squat, pallid-faced man with glasses and wispy white hair—seemed friendly enough at first. He assured me I would have the utmost privacy. Then he proceeded to inform me that his previous boarder used to eat six meals a day, drank a cheap brand of vodka, and caught the clap from a local girl. He said all this with a voice that was a little hungry-sounding.

6   "I'm an active practitioner of witchcraft," I told him.

7   It seemed to hold him at bay. Mr. Banks forced a weak smile, dismissed himself, and went back around the hedgerow toward the front of the house. I don't know if he kept tabs on me during the next three months, but I never caught a trace of him except when I paid the rent.

8   After arranging my room I went out for dinner. Coming from the Banks house the tops of the town's old brick buildings, the courthouse belfry, and two church steeples are visible. From that angle and distance the establishment of Garrett makes for an appeasing view. But once down-town the magical quality disappears and drab reality, in the form of bro-ken sidewalks and deserted buildings—a few of them completely gutted—sets in. I had supper in a trailer-diner called Rhonda's and went back to my flat and read until I fell asleep.

9   It was still dark when Moss came to pick me up the next morning.

10   "You've wrangled yourself a plumb easy job," he told me when we arrived at the fields. His breath had the rotten smell of stale tobacco and whisky. Suddenly I felt like the chicken-fried steak from Rhonda's was stuck in my esophagus. Moss flipped on the cab light and handed me a grid sheet.

11   "You put the names of the workers here. Out here you put a mark for each bucket they fill so we know how much to pay them at the end of the day. Make sure they fill them to the top. Keep an eye out for bruised fruit. Especially the tomatoes. Sometimes they get careless and just toss them in the bucket."

12   I nodded and said that it sounded easy enough.

13   "I know it sounds rather simplistic," Moss continued, "but somebody's got to do it. Somebody's got to be here to tell them when to take breaks and when to go back to work. Somebody's got to make sure they show up in the morning. You'll pay them at the end of the day. I'll give you a bank this afternoon. The schedule goes like this..." Moss laid out the day for me. I expressed my amusement at the fact that there was a break from eleven-thirty to two for "siesta."

14   Moss explained, "It keeps them out of the sun during the hottest part of the day."

15   We got out of Moss's truck. Murky light had begun to crawl up the east-ern sky. The morning air was warm and balmy. The tomato plants had a strong acrid smell that grew stronger when an occasional breeze stirred

the leaves. A pair of headlights came bouncing down the rutted road that parted the fields. Moss looked at his watch. "Right on time."

16   A battered pick-up pulled up and nine sleepy Mexicans tumbled out of it.

17   "Who's missing?" asked Moss.

18   A young, athletic-looking Mexican with longish hair said, "Joaqúin." He looked at me. "Who is he?"

19   "This is Willis," said Moss. "He's come here to whip your sorry asses into shape."

20   The Mexican grinned and flashed a gold tooth. "She-it!" he said twangily.

21   The Mexicans filed automatically toward Moss's truck and each took two five-gallon buckets from the back. They straggled toward the edge of the field while pulling on canvas gloves. After a few moments of shoving and bickering, each took a row and bent silently to work. The leathery plants rustled in response. The ripe tomatoes made soft plopping noises in the buckets.

22   Moss said, "They're like little kids. They're funny in their ways sometimes." He hiccuped and pounded his chest with a beefy hand. He shrugged. "It's a different culture and they do things different. Leave them be and they usually work things out among themselves. Now, the one that asked about you—his name is Mauricio. He's a good kid and his English is pretty good. Actually, there's not a bad one in the lot. I'd set up shop under one of these trees if I were you. Help me unload these buckets, will you?"

23   We took several stacks of buckets from the truck bed and put them under an oak tree. Moss pulled out a folding chair and handed it to me along with a clipboard and a whistle on a string. He turned and pointed across the field at a dense line of trees.

24   "Sometimes they like to go to the river during break. Use the whistle when you need to. I'll be back by eleven to pick up what they've picked. We'll go get lunch in town. There's a great little place called Rhonda's."

25   Within a couple of days I learned all the Mexicans' names and there developed a healthy affection between us, expressed mostly through cursing or vulgarities. Needless to say, I was never able to use the Spanish I learned that summer in a practical setting. I grew bored watching the Mexicans' straw hats bobbing in the fields and got a membership at the local library and commenced a summer of wide and varied reading. This is not to say that I ceased to give proper attention to my Mexicans. They were an entertaining clan, to say the least. During breaks Mauricio took great pleasure in relating the latest drunk-fest or amorous episode that had taken place in Village Heights, the trailer park in which most of Garrett's Mexicans lived. I was certain Mauricio embellished a good deal because of the outlandish nature of his stories. A fifth of tequila does not increase one's stamina and a deer stand is not a viable place for making love. The other workers, who knew minimal English, if any, had no way of keeping him in check. Nevertheless, they crowded around Mauricio and myself grinning and nodding as if they understood every word.

26   One worker in particular caught my attention from the first day. He was a skinny, black boy named Rafa. He could not have been more than sixteen, though he swore he was twenty. His complexion was rough and his eyes were large and black and mouse-like in their nervousness. There was always a lazy idiot's grin pasted across his thick, purple lips. His limbs were loose and gangly and he seemed to flop about whenever he went into motion. He was a very slow worker, the slowest in fact, and the lazy vacant smile gave the impression that somehow he was proud of the fact. He was last in line for everything: last to drop down from the old blue pick-up in the mornings, last to climb back in at eleven-thirty for the siesta break, last to collect his pay at the end of the day. The thing that perturbed me the most was the fact that he served as the butt of his coworkers' every joke. He was a proverbial goat for all occasions.

27   One morning after a week on the job I witnessed a terrible thing. One of the Mexicans—a sloppy, bearded man named Octavio—had lost a bet on some sporting event the night before. That morning he beat Rafa to near unconsciousness, out of principle it seemed. When he finished, he stepped back and laughed roughly. Then he commenced to cleaning his bloody knuckles on his shirttails. The other Mexicans picked up the laughter where Octavio had left it. They stepped over and around the lank form that lay in the dust and patted Octavio on the back and congratulated him. They ushered him toward the field like a boxer's entourage. I shivered despite the morning heat.

28   I helped Rafa over to my tree where he lay on the ground. He made croaking noises and rolled from side to side.

29   "Are you okay?" I asked.

30   "Jes, okay!" he grunted. He grinned up at me lazily.

31   In twenty minutes he was standing and ready to go back to work. I handed him his straw hat, which had been crushed during the fight.

32   "Take it easy," I said. I pointed at his eye, which was swollen shut. I spoke slowly, touched him on the shoulder. "That doesn't look so good. You'd better clean it up a little. Rest some more until you feel better."

33   He was a pathetic sight. His shirt had been ripped open and fresh welts stood up on his neck and chest. His lower lip was split open and shiny with fresh blood. He took his shapeless hat and pressed it down over his stiff black hair so the brim drooped limply over his eyes. He did not bother to tilt his head so he could see me when he spoke.

34   "Jew no tell Mister Moss nothing, okay?"

35   "You speak English," I said. "Why didn't you say so?"

36   Rafa did not respond. He stood there waiting. All I could see were his smiling cut mouth and his narrow, black chin smeared with drying blood.

37   "Sure, I won't tell Moss anything," I said finally.

38   Rafa retrieved his buckets and limped across the field. One of the workers raised his head and said something, and there resulted a chorus of laughter. Out in the open the laughter had a faint, metallic quality, like pebbles dropping into a pail. As I watched Rafa join the others, I tried to

make sense of it. I came to the conclusion that I did not understand the mistreatment, but I resolved to do something nice for the kid.

39   That same afternoon Mauricio invited me to Village Heights for supper and drinking. After hearing the stories, curiosity had gotten the better of me and I accepted. That evening I stopped by Billy's Bait & Supply—one of those big country stores that carries almost every item imaginable—and purchased a straw cowboy hat for Rafa. I sized it by finding one that fit me and buying the next size down. It was a good hat, arrow shaped with a red feather protruding from the wide black band. I also bought a six-pack of beer and I set off walking.

40   I arrived at Village Heights in ten minutes. It was a squalid little community comprised of thirty or so run-down trailers facing in all directions and arranged in no particular order. It sat just outside the city limits and low off the road behind a narrow stretch of cedars and pines, as if whoever had put it there did not want it to be visible from the road. Ash heaps and rusty vehicles dotted the landscape. Clusters of spindly pines grew up here and there, and the grass grew tall and stiff against the trailers and brushed against the sides when the wind blew. The atmosphere was a festive one. Everyone was outside. Small, brown children ran about throwing and chasing balls and playing tag. Groups of men were clustered here and there, chatting or tinkering with cars. The spicy smells of meals cooking drifted smokily from the open doors of trailers. Brassy ranchero and cumbia music competed from several directions.

41   "Hey, gringo!"

42   Mauricio and several other Mexicans were standing near the open hood of a rusty Mustang. Mauricio approached and shook my hand.

43   "Maybe jew know some of these guys."

44   I nodded. Three of the Mexicans worked with our picking crew. The bearded Octavio was one of them. I shook hands with each of them, seven in all including Mauricio.

45   Mauricio noticed the new hat. "Ah. Jew buy one, I see."

46   I fingered the rigid brim of the hat, turning it in my hands. "This is for Rafa. His took a beating today. It wasn't in very good shape to begin with."

47   A shadow crossed Mauricio's face. "Rafa live there," he said, motioning toward the road. Then he pointed at the nearest trailer, a dingy yellow one with a square of cardboard in place of one of the windows. "This is my house," he said. "Come in and see. You meet now my wife."

48   I followed Mauricio toward the trailer and some of the other Mexicans fell in behind me. A faint, high-pitched whimpering came from beneath the trailer. I stopped.

49   "You got pups," I said.

50   "Jes," Mauricio said proudly. He moved from the steps and lifted one of the tin underpinnings. "Come see."

51   I squatted next to Mauricio and peered into the darkness under the trailer. A brown and white mongrel bitch was sprawled on her side in the cool dirt. Her puppies squirmed and writhed against her warm belly,

suckling in one heavy mass. I reached my hand in and the mongrel began licking it slowly. She regarded me with wet, affectionate eyes.

52   "How many are there?" I asked.

53   "I don't know."

54   "Look at this little one," I said. I lifted by the scruff the only pup that was not participating in the feast. It drew its hind legs up and began whimpering hysterically. It was smaller and darker than the others. Its eyelids were still clamped shut. I cupped it against my chest and caressed it with my fingers.

55   "You know you can feed him with an eyedropper," I said. "He'll drink that way. He's still plenty lively."

56   Mauricio nodded. "Strong one live, weak one die," he said. "I no can do nothing." His face was pleasant but unyielding.

57   I made a little crease between the warm, wriggling bodies and placed the runt facing his mother's teats. He quickly disappeared beneath the squirming bodies of his livelier brothers and sisters. So he would not suffocate. I fished him out and put him on the edge where I had found him.

58   "Feed him warm milk with an eye dropper," I repeated. "He can live yet."

59   "Jes." Mauricio stood up and dropped the tin into place. "Come inside. Meet my wife."

60   I followed him up the steps into the trailer. Three of the Mexicans, including Octavio, were already sitting in the small living room. The others were gone. The walls of the living room were decorated with calendars and colorful drapery. The vinyl sofa that sat against one wall was torn in several places and the arms were peppered with cigarette burns. Several cheap, vinyl-colored kitchen chairs sat about the perimeter of the room. In the kitchen a broad-hipped, dark woman flitted adroitly about, transferring dishes from the stove to the table. Mauricio nodded in that direction.

61   "This is my wife, Yolanda."

62   Yolanda looked up from her steamy work and smiled at me. A few strands of hair were plastered to her moist forehead. Her large face was petal-shaped; her laughing, black eyes gave me the feeling that we shared in some secret.

63   I nodded. "Willis," I said.

64   "Give her the beer," said Mauricio. "She put in refrigerator." He spoke to Yolanda in Spanish. She laughed aloud and took my six-pack. She opened a bottle of Tecate and gave it to me.

65   "Please, sit," said Mauricio. "We eat now."

66   There was not room for all of us. Mauricio and I sat down. Octavio joined us and Yolanda took the seat closest to the stove. The other two Mexicans prepared their plates at the table and went to sit in the living room. The table was laden with steaming dishes, a couple of which I did not recognize. We served ourselves.

67   "This *real* Mexican food," Mauricio told me. "Not like the food you get in a restaurant." He proceeded to identify nearly everything I put on my plate. "This—*real* enchilada; this—*real* chorizo; this here—*real* chiles rellenos." There was a plate of lettuce and freshly sliced tomatoes. "This,"

said Mauricio, picking up a cold slab of tomato and plopping it in his mouth, "this come from work."

68   It was the best food I had eaten since I arrived in Garrett. We ate quietly, ravenously, and drank long swigs of beer. Yolanda kept getting up to bring us more tortillas and beer. I noticed that Octavio's manners matched his appearance. He ate hunched over his plate so that all that was visible was the top of his dirty, matted head. He shoved food onto his tortilla with his round fingers and alternately made snorting and slurping noises. There was a warm, wet towel for us to clean our hands. I was happy to see that Octavio did not use it, as he occasionally cleaned his dripping beard on his shirtsleeve.

69   Mauricio said, "See this. I am one lucky man. *Buena suerte*, yeah? I have the good food, and I have *this*." He whacked Yolanda's rump as she was sitting down. "You like this one, eh?"

70   Yolanda smiled coyly across the table at me.

71   Octavio gave one final snort and shoved his chair noisily away from the table. His eyes glazed over and his mouth curved into a satisfied smile. He slid down low in his chair and regarded us through half-closed eyelids. I swear he began to make a low growling noise, like the purring of a large cat. The noise did not let up once. I looked at his plate. He had mopped it clean with a tortilla so it looked like it had never been touched.

72   Yolanda giggled. Mauricio said, "Big man eat big, no?"

73   I nodded toward Octavio and the men in the living room. "Do they live here with you?"

74   "Jes," said Mauricio. "It make five of us."

75   "Do the others work?"

76   "Sometime. Sometime they here all day."

77   Yolanda got up with a stack of dirty dishes and began plunging them vigorously into the sudsy water in the sink.

78   As we spoke I noticed that Octavio's slotted eyes were focused on the new hat which I had left on the counter. Every so often his eyes glinted and shifted over to me as his fleshy lips flattened into an increased smile. The purring never stopped.

79   "Where does Rafa live?" I asked. "I want to take the hat to him before it gets late."

80   "You come back, jes?" Mauricio implored. He pointed at the row of cabinets over the sink. "I have here *real* tequila."

81   I went outside. Lilac-colored light was diminishing over the fields in the west. The buzz sawing of crickets rose and fell in perfect intervals. Most of the children had gone inside but the men were still standing about in their small groups. Their forms were dark and anonymous in the fading light. Now and then the glower of a cigarette exposed one of their brooding faces. As I walked past them their voices were tinny and peaceful in the dark.

82   I found Rafa's trailer, number eighteen. I strode across the warped plywood of the porch and knocked on the door. There came a hollow booming of footsteps. An unfamiliar Mexican appeared at the door. The yellow light from inside flooded past his square frame.

83   "Is Rafa home?" I asked.

84   The man retreated inside and shortly Rafa's bruised, smiling face appeared at the door. He did not seem surprised to see me.

85   "Buenas noches," I said. "I brought you something."

86   Rafa's good eye flickered upon the hat I offered him. Then it resumed the flat, somber quality that matched his voice.

87   "Thank you. It is one good hat."

88   "It's nothing," I said. "I've been at Mauricio's eating dinner. We're going to drink tequila now. Come join us. Mauricio won't mind."

89   Rafa regarded me with a puzzled expression that I almost mistook for one of amusement. It was hard to tell with that grin. "No," he said. "No tequila for me." He stood there holding the hat against his chest, grinning stupidly and regarding me with his one good eye. His lip had swollen considerably, and the cut on it had opened a quarter inch and turned black.

90   "Suit yourself. You're not a pretty sight for going out anyway." I instinctively reached out and patted his thin shoulder. "If you change your mind, you know where we'll be."

91   "Jes," he said.

92   "Well, goodnight."

93   Rafa closed the door and I stood on the porch for a moment thinking that he had not even tried on the hat. I thought about knocking again, but decided against it.

94   I went back to Mauricio's and learned never to doubt the veracity of his stories again. We began doing shots of mescal. Mauricio and I made a grand ordeal of sharing the worm on the bottom. Mauricio played cumbia music and tried to teach me to dance. We must have made a pathetic sight because he was trying to dance the woman's part. All the while he was telling me, "Now jew do it. Now jew do it." He finally turned me over to Yolanda. The smell of her perfume and the feel of her broad, swinging hips made me feel dizzy. She kept leaning back and regarding me with those black, shining eyes. Her complexion was a bit rutty and over-done with make-up, but the smiling, eager expression superseded it. Octavio climbed on the flimsy kitchen table and began spinning in circles. When a heavy-set man named José tried to join him the table collapsed and Octavio hit his head on the broken refrigerator handle. It did not even faze him. He sat on the floor grinning and holding the back of his bleeding head and saying, "Lu, lu, lu, lu, lu, lu!"

95   If I had been in a bigger town I might have been picked up for public drunkenness during the walk home. Instead all I got were a few honks from passers-by and some unoriginal obscenities from a carful of cruising teenagers. Once I got home I was cognizant enough to be thankful that the next day was Sunday. I lay down on my bed fully clothed. The first thing I saw upon closing my eyes was Yolanda's wide, tapered face and laughing eyes.

96   When I returned to work on Monday I was not surprised to see Octavio wearing the hat I had given Rafa, and Rafa wearing his old one. Octavio looked ridiculous in the new hat. It was too small for his big head but he

had jammed it on anyway. It pinched and pulled his skin upward and gave his eyes a slanted Oriental's look. To make matters worse, Rafa's lip looked like it had been freshly burst open. And while the swelling in his injured eye had gone down, his opposite cheekbone was now blue and puffy. I was annoyed but tried to forget about it.

97   Due to the exceptional heat, the Mexicans took their morning break by the large river which twisted through the middle of the fields. The river was crowded by thick growth of cypress and oaks and its shade was damp and pleasant. The water stayed muddy from irrigating. Since it moved quickly it also stayed very cold. On hot afternoons some the Mexicans would go for a swim. After twenty minutes in the sun their clothes would be dry again.

98   When I blew the whistle for the nine o'clock break the Mexicans moved toward the line of lush green foliage that parted the thousands of acres that we harvested along with other crews. When I arrived a few of them were already wading barefoot on the slippery rocks where the water swirled and lapped against the craggy black rocks that jutted out of the water.

99   I sat on the high embankment overlooking the river beside Mauricio. As we watched down on the horseplay Mauricio poked me with an elbow.

100   "How jew feeling today, boss?"

101   "Fine, today," I said. "Yesterday was a different story though. I didn't get up till noon."

102   "Jew no like the mescal, eh?"

103   "It's fine when I'm drinking it."

104   Mauricio laughed. "When jew leave Octavio run naked outside. He scare the neighbors."

105   "Well, I'm glad I got out when I did."

106   While we were talking a splashing battle began. Within a few seconds it had escalated to a full-fledged war. The Mexicans that were standing on the bank got wet and began jumping in to exact revenge. The water boiled with flailing limbs as they climbed on each other's backs and tried to push one another into the deep part of the river. I saw Octavio drag Rafa to the deep water and hold his head under. The longer he held Rafa's head the less horseplay there was. The Mexicans stopped their rough-housing and began whooping and shouting encouragement. Octavio snatched the boy's head out of the water long enough for him to gasp briefly and submerged it again.

107   "Tell him to stop," I told Mauricio.

108   Mauricio held up a hand as if to silence me. The hooting and shouting continued.

109   I slid down the embankment and splashed into the water. "Let go of him," I said. I shoved Octavio hard and he sprawled backwards into the water. Rafa came up coughing and sputtering. He limped over to the bank where he flopped down on the sand and continued to cough and wheeze. When he caught his breath and saw me standing in the water an expression of alarm came into his face. The Mexicans had grown silent and I

could feel them watching me. A bird overhead sounded three shrill notes. I looked at my watch.

110   "Break's over," I said.

111   The Mexicans resumed their work. The sun climbed up the sky. I shifted my chair close to the trunk of the poplar I was sitting under. Periodically one of the Mexicans would lug his buckets full of tomatoes over to check them in. I tried to concentrate on Clark's *The Ox-Bow Incident* but my thoughts kept turning to Rafa.

112   When he finally came to check in, I demanded angrily, "What's wrong with you? Why do you take it?"

113   He gave me that lazy grin and didn't answer.

114   "For Christ's sake," I exclaimed. "Buck up. Don't let them run all over you."

115   I felt like giving him a good shaking. I grabbed both his shoulders, but then stopped. I reached into my pocket and withdrew a jack knife. It was curved, with a bone handle grooved for gripping. It had been a gift from my father. I seized Rafa's hand and placed the knife in it.

116   The insipid smile faded from Rafa's lips and his eyes flashed intently. He opened the knife and tilted it so the shiny blade glinted in the sun.

117   "Next time that troll messes with you, whip it out," I instructed. "Don't use it, for God's sake, but—at least it will make him think." I clapped him hard on the shoulder. "Grow a spine, for Christ's sake! Don't act like a señorita."

118   Rafa looked at the knife for a long time before folding it and sliding it into his pocket. He looked at me and his eyes shone with sharpness and purpose. They were a man's eyes, weighted with responsibility.

119   "It is one good knife," he said. He turned to the stacks of buckets, separated two of them, and strode across the field.

120   At eleven-thirty I whistled for the siesta break. I called Mauricio aside as he came from the field. "Why is everybody down on the kid?"

121   Mauricio regarded me questioningly for a moment and then broke into an easy laugh. "The river? It happen all the time. They like to play."

122   "I'm not just talking about the river," I said. I felt the anger beginning to well in me again.

123   "Rafa still one little kid," said Mauricio. "We make him grow up. We make him one man." He watched me closely and chuckled. "Jew no worry. He okay."

124   As the Mexicans piled into the old pick-up, I saw Octavio clamp a large hand around the back of Rafa's neck. He shoved the boy aside and climbed onto the tailgate ahead of him. I caught a glimpse of Rafa's face and saw that he was not smiling.

125   A week passed without a major incident. I felt I had played a part in bringing relative peace to our crew and rewarded myself by buying a bicycle at a garage sale. I rewarded Moss actually. I didn't want to burden him with transporting me to and from work the rest of the summer, although I don't think he would have minded. Riding the bicycle felt good

and the extra time in the sun turned me a walnut shade of brown. Every so often I felt obliged to step back and marvel at my exquisite freedom. I had my own place and was making money. I ate and read what I wanted, and the bicycle enabled me to come and go as I pleased. I had supper with Mauricio again and found Yolanda as captivating as ever. When I left she kissed me and left a burning sensation on my lips that lasted an hour. Garrett, Georgia, was certainly no New Orleans or Arizona, but it had a strange way of growing on you.

126   One afternoon Moss's truck came tearing in from the main road. It jerked to a stop beside my tree and the swirling dust from the road enveloped it momentarily.

127   Moss got out of the truck. He waved a clipboard at the dust. "I got a couple of discrepancies with the numbers."

128   "I'll take a look." I blew my whistle for the four o'clock break and watched the Mexicans move slowly toward the river and disappear into the foliage. I thought about asking Moss to walk across the field with me, but then I looked at his flushed, swollen face and his sweat-soaked shirt and thought better of it.

129   "How are they treating you?" Moss asked.

130   "Things are under control," I said.

131   Moss squinted after the Mexicans as they retreated into the trees. "They're funny in their ways," he mused. "They got their own codes and such."

132   I took the clipboard from Moss and winked at him. "Let's see what you've got. It's probably your math again."

133   After Moss drove away I was about to blow my whistle when the Mexicans came trailing out of the trees. They never started back to work without me telling them. I sensed something was wrong and started across the field in a half-run. I drew near and saw the confused look on Mauricio's face. He stepped in front of me and grabbed my arm.

134   "He no want to," he cried. "He no want to do it."

135   I made a quick head count, and tore away from Mauricio's grasp. I sprinted toward the river. I found Octavio curled in a ball on the bank. He was shivering and making a high-pitched whimpering noise like a wounded beast. His arm was sliced open. The blood that ran from it had formed a dark circle in the sand. He was oblivious to the cut. He stared at the water with bolted eyes.

136   "Where is he?" I demanded. I slid down the embankment and lifted Octavio by the shirt. "Where is he?" When he did not respond I struck him hard across the face. "Where is he?"

137   Octavio offered no resistance. He slouched against my grasp and continued to whimper as if I had never touched him. His glazed eyes remained fixed on the water.

138   I looked at the water and saw Rafa's straw hat bobbing against some rocks. I let go of Octavio and crawled numbly up the embankment. The other Mexicans stood in a huddle twenty yards from the trees.

139   "What happened?" I asked Mauricio.

140   His voice was frightened and distant. "They start to play like last time. Rafa take out one knife." He looked at me earnestly. "Octavio no want to do it."

141   I looked across the field, at the neat tree-tufts along the horizon. "Did Octavio use the knife?" I asked.

142   Mauricio shook his head. "One rock."

143   "Where is the knife?"

144   "In the water, I think."

145   I looked at the sky. It was overcast with silver, rugged-looking clouds. The air was too muggy for rain. The tomato plants rustled in a breeze and their smell came up sharp and peppery. The Mexicans stood behind Mauricio like a throng of damp puppies. They looked back and forth between Mauricio and myself with wide, frightened eyes.

146   "I'll call Moss in a few minutes," I said. "I'll think of what to tell him. Octavio can't go to a hospital. We'll have to patch him up ourselves."

147   Mauricio regarded me gratefully. "Jes, we fix it!"

148   "Go get him, then get these guys back to work."

149   After the Mexicans had hauled Octavio out of the gorge I picked up an empty bucket and returned to the river alone. The battered old hat was gone from the rocks. I walked downstream a hundred yards and could not find it. I went back up to the river, and as I washed the blood from the sand I felt as if I were covering up my own crime.

Questions for Discussion

1. Explain why, in this South Georgia town, "Mexican-on-Mexican crime" would be ignored. What attitude is suggested by the townspeople's ignoring Mexican-on-Mexican crime and their thinking that Mexicans are "like little kids"?

2. Why didn't Willis, the narrator, stop Octavio from beating Rafa instead of choosing just to be nice to him? Why doesn't he retrieve the cowboy hat from Octavio?

3. Explain Moss's claim about the Mexicans, "It's a different culture and they do things different. Leave them be and they usually work things out among themselves." What does this statement suggest about Moss? Why does Willis ignore it?

4. What is the significance of Willis's calling the laborers "my Mexicans"?

5. Why does Octavio beat Rafa? Why do the others then treat Octavio as a hero and laugh at Rafa? What tendency of some people is suggested by this situation?

6. How are the other laborers' attitudes toward Rafa mirrored by Mauricio's attitude toward the runt puppy?

7. Why does Willis give Rafa the new hat? The knife? Explain whether he should have anticipated the results of his gifts.

8. Why does Willis help to cover up the crime? Should he feel as though he is "covering up [his] own crime"? How much responsibility should Willis take for what has happened?

Suggestions for Exploring, Writing, and Persuading

1. If you have ever experienced a similar dilemma in which you had to make a decision without full knowledge of the cultural customs of those affected by your decision, write an essay describing the situation and telling how you resolved it.

2. In an essay, describe what you would have done if you had been in Willis's place, or write a character analysis of Willis.

3. Write an essay examining the effect structure and foreshadowing have on the story.

4. Compare the lone puppy with Rafa. What characteristics do they have in common? Then in an essay, define what you consider to be a runt.

5. In an essay, argue whether Willis acted properly or that he should not have interfered with the Mexicans' lives.

6. Conduct a mock trial where you decide whether Willis is an accessory to a crime.

POETRY

William Shakespeare (1564–1616)

The biography of William Shakespeare precedes Othello.

SONNET 73   (1609)

That time of year thou mayst in me behold
When yellow leaves, or none, or few, do hang
Upon those boughs which shake against the cold,
Bare ruined choirs, where late the sweet birds sang.
5   In me thou seest the twilight of such day
As after sunset fadeth in the west;
Which by and by black night doth take away,
Death's second self that seals up all in rest.
In me thou seest the glowing of such fire,
10 That on the ashes of his youth doth lie,
As the deathbed whereon it must expire,

Consumed with that which it was nourished by.
   This thou perceiv'st, which makes thy love more strong,
   To love that well, which thou must leave ere long.

Questions for Discussion

1. What three analogies does the speaker use in the poem?
2. What do these analogies suggest about the speaker's attitude toward growing old?
3. How does the concluding couplet change your perception of the speaker's attitude?

Suggestions for Exploring, Writing, and Persuading

1. Write an essay in which you explain what it would mean to you to grow old with someone or to love someone who is near death.
2. In an essay, argue that love is stronger when one of the lovers fears the imminent loss of the other OR that love that lasts into old age is deeper and "more strong."
3. Reread this poem; then write an essay analyzing the tone. Is it morbid, hopeful, or matter of fact?

Percy Bysshe Shelley (1792–1822)

Shelley, born in Field Place, Sussex, England, was adored by his six brothers and sisters; consequently, he demanded adoration in later years. He was expelled from Oxford along with his friend Thomas Jefferson Hogg because of his revolutionary philosophy. From that point on, Shelley led a fascinating life, marrying twice and enjoying a friendship with Romantic hero George Gordon, Lord Byron. He is known for his propaganda writing, lovely lyrics, and intellectual convictions.

OZYMANDIAS   (1818)

I met a traveller from an antique land
Who said: Two vast and trunkless legs of stone
Stand in the desert...Near them, on the sand,
Half sunk, a shattered visage lies, whose frown,
5   And wrinkled lip, and sneer of cold command,
Tell that its sculptor well those passions read
Which yet survive, stamped on these lifeless things,
The hand that mocked them, and the heart that fed:
And on the pedestal these words appear:
10   "My name is Ozymandias, king of kings:

Look on my works, ye Mighty, and despair!"
Nothing beside remains. Round the decay
Of that colossal wreck, boundless and bare
The lone and level sands stretch far away.

Questions for Discussion

1. What kind of king must Ozymandias have been?
2. Explain the metaphorical suggestions of "shattered visage" and "the heart that fed"?
3. How did the sculptor mock Ozymandias? What is ironic about the inscription on the pedestal?
4. Are *hand* and *heart* in line 8 synecdoche or metonymy?
5. What is the form of this poem?
6. What is the theme of "Ozymandias"?

Suggestions for Exploring, Writing, and Persuading

1. Write your epitaph. Then discuss the effect this epitaph might have on later generations of your family or on society in general.
2. Ozymandias is the Greek name for Ramses II, an Egyptian ruler who erected a huge statue in his likeness. In later generations, however, the statue does not reflect a favorable image of Ramses II. Select one work of art or one artist and discuss how this art reflects its era.
3. In an essay, show how Shelley uses the tight form of the sonnet and the vivid metaphorical devices to create his powerful theme.

Edwin Arlington Robinson (1869–1935)

Edwin Arlington Robinson's life provided him with a wealth of material for his poetic portraits of lonely and tragic misfits. After a series of financial and physical tragedies decimated his family, Robinson moved to Greenwich Village in New York City, where for a time he was practically destitute. Although he received Pulitzer prizes for his later work, primarily book-length blank verse poems on the Arthurian legends, Robinson is best remembered for his Tilbury Town poems, portraits of imaginary misfits who inhabit a town based on his hometown of Gardiner, Maine.

RICHARD CORY   (1897)

Whenever Richard Cory went down town,
We people on the pavement looked at him:
He was a gentleman from sole to crown,
Clean favored, and imperially slim.

5   And he was always quietly arrayed,
And he was always human when he talked;
But still he fluttered pulses when he said,
"Good-morning," and he glittered when he walked.

And he was rich—yes, richer than a king—
10   And admirably schooled in every grace:
In fine, we thought that he was everything
To make us wish that we were in his place.

So on we worked, and waited for the light,
And went without the meat, and cursed the bread;
15   And Richard Cory, one calm summer night,
Went home and put a bullet through his head.

Questions for Discussion

1. From what point of view is the poem written? Explain how Robinson's use of this point of view allows him to withhold information about Richard Cory. How does a similar point of view achieve a similar result in Faulkner's "A Rose for Emily"?
2. What do the people see when they look at Richard Cory?
3. What is the tone of the poem?

Suggestions for Exploring, Writing, and Persuading

1. Situations and appearances are sometimes deceiving. Using the poem as the basis for an essay, discuss why the public makes assumptions about the seemingly rich lives of public figures.
2. Write an essay on the symbols, images, and sound devices used in this poem—the overall symbolism of kingship; the metonymy and metaphor; the alliteration, assonance, consonance, rhyme, and rhythm. Explain how these devices help to emphasize the observers' misperception of Richard Cory.

Paul Laurence Dunbar (1872–1906)

Paul Dunbar was born in Dayton, Ohio, to former slaves; however, his father, Joshua, escaped to Canada and fought in the Union army. Dunbar later wrote for The Tattler, *printed by his classmate, Orville Wright. Wanting more than Dayton could offer, Dunbar toured Europe giving readings of his poetry. He wrote poems, among them the collection* Oak and Ivy *(1892); novels, such as* The Sport of Gods *(1902); and musicals, including* Dream Lovers: An Operatic Romance *(1898). Dunbar gained recognition for his diverse accomplishments and for the use of dialect in his poems.*

*His themes include the overt oppression of African Ameri-
cans in all aspects of life and the ramifications of brutality
imposed on the human soul.*

WE WEAR THE MASK   (1913)

We wear the mask that grins and lies,
It hides our cheeks and shades our eyes,—
This debt we pay to human guile;
With torn and bleeding hearts we smile,
5   And mouth with myriad subtleties.
Why should the world be overwise,
In counting all our tears and sighs?
Nay, let them only see us, while
    We wear the mask.

10   We smile, but, O great Christ, our cries
To Thee from tortured souls arise.
We sing, but oh, the clay is vile
Beneath our feet, and long the mile;
But let the world dream otherwise,
15   We wear the mask.

Questions for Discussion

1. To whom does the word *we* refer?

2. What does the speaker mean by "with torn and bleeding hearts we smile"? At another point the speaker refers to "tortured souls" and says, "the clay is vile." What is the tone and how is it revealed?

3. Why does the speaker say African Americans wish to mask their true feelings? Do all people mask their feelings? Why is there a certain amount of fear involved in exposing the true feelings behind the mask?

4. What does Dunbar mean by "let the world dream otherwise, / We wear the mask"? Why does he use the word *dream?*

Suggestions for Exploring, Writing, and Persuading

1. Does the poem have to refer to just one racial or ethnic group? Discuss cultural, racial, or ethnic groups that wear masks. Then write an essay on why or how one group wears masks.

2. In an essay, discuss to what degree men and women wear masks that conceal parts of themselves from the opposite sex.

3. Explain why people have to hide behind masks. What is there in society that causes people to conceal their true identities?

4. In an essay, argue that everyone does or does not wear a mask.

John McCrae (1872–1918)

Canadian John McCrae had resigned from the military in 1904 and pursued a successful career as a physician, but in 1914, when Canada declared war on Germany, McCrae, then forty-one years old, immediately joined the war effort. After fighting on the Western Front, he was assigned to the medical corps in France. He was still on active duty when he died of pneumonia in 1918. His only book of poetry, In Flanders Fields and Other Poems, *was published in 1919, but "In Flanders Fields," a poem written immediately after the battlefield death of a close friend, had been published in* Punch, *the English magazine, in 1915 and was already the most popular poem about World War I.*

IN FLANDERS FIELDS   (1915)

In Flanders fields the poppies blow
Between the crosses, row on row,
That mark our place; and in the sky
The larks, still bravely singing, fly
5   Scarce heard amid the guns below.

We are the Dead. Short days ago,
We lived, felt dawn, saw sunset glow,
Loved, and were loved, and now we lie
In Flanders fields.

10   Take up our quarrel with the foe:
To you from failing hands we throw
The torch; be yours to hold it high.
If ye break faith with us who die
We shall not sleep, though poppies grow
In Flanders fields.

Questions for Discussion

1. Who are the speakers in this poem?
2. What are Flanders fields?
3. How does nature provide a contrast to the activities of the men?
4. What is the challenge issued in the third verse?

Suggestions for Exploring, Writing, and Persuading

1. Using McCrae's poem as a pattern, write a poem using the first person plural to represent those who died in the September 11, 2001, attacks.
2. One theme of the poem is that life goes on in spite of death and during war. Using this theme, write an essay describing what has happened to you since September 11, 2001.

3. Write an essay from the point of view of the dead at the twin towers, the Pentagon, the Pennsylvania crash, or the Iraq war in which you clarify who the real foe is and how America has "[taken] up [their] quarrel with the foe."

4. Write an essay interpreting the symbols in this poem.

5. Select at least two of the poems about war and write an essay comparing their tone, theme, or symbolism.

Robert Frost (1874–1963)

A biographical note on Robert Frost can be found in the unit on Men and Women.

DESIGN   (1936)

I found a dimpled spider, fat and white,
On a white heal-all, holding up a moth
Like a white piece of rigid satin cloth—
Assorted characters of death and blight
5   Mixed ready to begin the morning right,
Like the ingredients of a witches' broth—
A snow-drop spider, a flower like a froth,
And dead wings carried like a paper kite.

What had that flower to do with being white,
10   The wayside blue and innocent heal-all?
What brought the kindred spider to that height,
Then steered the white moth thither in the night?
What but design of darkness to appall?—
If design govern in a thing so small.

Question for Discussion

1. The traditional Italian sonnet asks a question in the octave and answers it in the sestet. In "Design," Frost changes the traditional form by asking questions in the sestet. What do these questions imply? How does Frost's reversal of the traditional form emphasize the meaning of the poem?

Suggestions for Exploring, Writing, and Persuading

1. Write an essay on Frost's use of ironic inversion.

2. In an essay argue whether Frost's conclusion that the flower, the spider, and the moth are part of the "design of darkness to appall" is or is not valid.

ONCE BY THE PACIFIC   (1936)

The shattered water made a misty din.
Great waves looked over others coming in,
And thought of doing something to the shore
That water never did to land before.
5   The clouds were low and hairy in the skies,
Like locks blown forward in the gleam of eyes.
You could not tell, and yet it looked as if
The shore was lucky in being backed by cliff,
The cliff in being backed by continent;
10   It looked as if a night of dark intent
Was coming, and not only a night, an age.
Someone had better be prepared for rage.
There would be more than ocean-water broken
Before God's last *Put out the Light* was spoken.

Questions for Discussion

1. How does the personification of the ocean make the poem threatening?
2. What is the threat implied in the last five lines of the poem?

Suggestions for Exploring, Writing, and Persuading

1. Select an example from nature that reflects your opinion of what the world is like and write an essay supporting your choice.
2. Use these two poems to write an essay about Frost's frightening view of the world.
3. Contrast the view of the natural world in this poem with a more optimistic view in another of Frost's poems.

Claude McKay (1890–1948)

Claude McKay's poetry reflects his childhood in Jamaica and his adult life in America. His work is associated with the Harlem Renaissance, but he was often in conflict with the writers of that movement because of his political views. During the course of his life, McKay wrote lyrical poems, dialect poems, and sonnets.

IF WE MUST DIE   (1922)

If we must die, let it not be like hogs
Hunted and penned in an inglorious spot,

While round us bark the mad and hungry dogs,
Making their mock at our accursed lot.
5 If we must die, O let us nobly die,
So that our precious blood may not be shed
In vain; then even the monsters we defy
Shall be constrained to honor us though dead!
O kinsmen! we must meet the common foe!
10 Though far outnumbered let us show us brave,
And for their thousand blows deal one deathblow!
What though before us lies the open grave?
Like men we'll face the murderous, cowardly pack,
Pressed to the wall, dying, but fighting back!

Questions for Discussion

1. Whom does McKay refer to as "we" in the poem? McKay uses the terms *kinsmen* and the *common foe*. Is his poem only about African Americans?

2. McKay has negative words for those he wants to oppose: "mad and hungry dogs," "the monsters," and "murderous, cowardly pack." Do you think McKay is being too biased or slanted? What is the effect of this loaded language?

Suggestions for Exploring, Writing, and Persuading

1. Is there any cause for which you would be willing to die? Discuss.

2. Martin Luther King Jr. preached nonviolence; however, Claude McKay, writing a generation earlier, preached violence. Using the poem as the basis for discussion, comment on McKay's justification for not backing down from retaliation or violence.

3. In an essay, argue that violence is more effective than nonviolence or that nonviolence is more effective.

4. Write an essay examining the loaded language in a current speech about politics or war.

Wilfred Owen (1893–1918)

Wilfred Owen is recognized as one of the greatest English war poets. He joined the British Army in 1915, fought as an officer in World War I, and was killed in that war on November 4, 1918, just seven days before it ended. Most of Owen's poems, which powerfully evoke the terror and inhumanity of war, were not published until after his death.

DULCE ET DECORUM EST   (1920)

Bent double, like old beggars under sacks,
Knock-kneed, coughing like hags, we cursed through sludge,
Till on the haunting flares we turned our backs
And towards our distant rest began to trudge.
5   Men marched asleep. Many had lost their boots
But limped on, blood-shod. All went lame; all blind;
Drunk with fatigue; deaf even to the hoots
Of tired, outstripped Five-Nines that dropped behind.
Gas! GAS! Quick, boys!—An ecstasy of fumbling,
10   Fitting the clumsy helmets just in time;
But someone still was yelling out and stumbling
And flound'ring like a man in fire or lime...
Dim, through the misty panes and thick green light,
As under a green sea, I saw him drowning.

15   In all my dreams, before my helpless sight,
He plunges at me, guttering, choking, drowning.

If in some smothering dreams you too could pace
Behind the wagon that we flung him in,
And watch the white eyes writhing in his face,
20   His hanging face, like a devil's sick of sin;
If you could hear, at every jolt, the blood
Come gargling from the froth-corrupted lungs,
Obscene as cancer, bitter as the cud
Of vile, incurable sores on innocent tongues,—
25   My friend, you would not tell with such high zest
To children ardent for some desperate glory,
The old Lie: *Dulce et decorum est*
Pro patria mori.

Questions for Discussion

1. This poem's last sentence, from Horace, *Odes*, III, ii, 13, means "It is sweet and proper to die for one's country." How does the realistic portrayal of war in the first stanza contrast with the patriotic sentiments the speaker attacks in the last few lines of the poem?
2. Why does Owen use the Latin quotation at the end?

Suggestions for Exploring, Writing, and Persuading

1. Write a thorough analysis of this poem, examining how its tone changes from stanza to stanza and how imagery, sound, diction, and syntax develop tone.

2. In an essay, argue that war is sometimes justified or that war should be the last resort.

3. Write an essay describing the circumstances that, in your opinion, justify going to war.

e. e. cummings (1894–1962)

[E]dward [E]stlin [C]ummings spent his early life in Cambridge, Massachusetts. During World War I, he spent several months in a French concentration camp as a political prisoner, an experience he recalls in his first book, The Enormous Room *(1922). Best known for his poetry, which is highly experimental in typography and punctuation, cummings published twelve books of poems, including* Tulips and Chimneys *(1923),* 50 Poems *(1940), and* 95 Poems *(1958). His* Poems 1923–1954 *earned a special citation from the National Book Awards.*

BUFFALO BILL'S DEFUNCT   (1923)

Buffalo Bill's
defunct
    who used to
    ride a watersmooth-silver
5   stallion
and break onetwothreefourfive pigeonsjustlikethat
                    Jesus
he was a handsome man
         and what i want to know is
10 how do you like your blueeyed boy
Mister Death

Questions for Discussion

1. What is the effect of cummings's using the word *defunct* instead of *dead?*

2. Why are the words run together in line 6?

Suggestion for Exploring, Writing, and Persuading

1. Research the cowboy of the 1800s and early 1900s. Then, write an epistolary essay to Mr. Death in which you explain what has been lost or gained by Buffalo Bill's death or the death of the cowboy spirit epitomized by Buffalo Bill.

ANYONE LIVED IN A PRETTY HOW TOWN   (1940)

anyone lived in a pretty how town
(with up so floating many bells down)
spring summer autumn winter
he sang his didn't he danced his did.

5   Women and men(both little and small)
cared for anyone not at all
they sowed their isn't they reaped their same
sun moon stars rain

children guessed(but only a few
10   and down they forgot as up they grew
autumn winter spring summer)
that noone loved him more by more

when by now and tree by leaf
she laughed his joy she cried his grief
15   bird by snow and stir by still
anyone's any was all to her

someones married their everyones
laughed their cryings and did their dance
(sleep wake hope and then)they
20   said their nevers they slept their dream

stars rain sun moon
(and only the snow can begin to explain
how children are apt to forget to remember
with up so floating many bells down)

25   one day anyone died i guess
(and noone stooped to kiss his face)
busy folk buried them side by side
little by little and was by was

all by all and deep by deep
30   and more by more they dream their sleep
noone and anyone earth by april
wish by spirit and if by yes.

Women and men(both dong and ding)
summer autumn winter spring
35   reaped their sowing and went their came
sun moon stars rain

Questions for Discussion

1. List and interpret the repeated lines that emphasize the passage of
   time and the cycle of life.

2. What lines in the poem reveal the sadness and loneliness of the people?

3. Either alone or in groups, interpret each verse of the poem.

Suggestions for Exploring, Writing, and Persuading

1. Compare the people in this poem with J. Alfred Prufrock from T. S. Eliot's poem in the Quest unit.

2. Using the interpretations from question 3 above, write an essay on the joys and sorrows of "noone and anyone."

Langston Hughes (1902–1967)

Hughes's biography can be found in the Family Unit.

DRAMA FOR WINTER NIGHT (FIFTH AVENUE)   (1925)

You can't sleep here,
My good man,
You can't sleep here.
This is the house of God.
5   The usher opens the church door and he goes out.

You can't sleep in this car, old top,
Not here.
If Jones found you
He'd give you to the cops.
10   Get-the-hell out now,
This ain't home.
You can't stay here.
The chauffeur opens the door and he gets out.

Lord! You can't let a man lie
25   In the streets like this.
Find an officer quick.
Send for an ambulance.
Maybe he is sick but
He can't die on this corner,
20   Not here!
He can't die here.
Death opens a door.

Oh, God,
Lemme git by St. Peter.
25   Lemme sit down on the steps of your throne.
Lemme rest somewhere.
What did yuh say, God?
What did yuh say?

You can't sleep here. . . .
30 Bums can't stay. . . .
The man's raving.
Get him to the hospital quick.
He's attracting a crowd.,
He can't die on this corner.
35 No, no, not here.

Questions for Discussion

1. Identify the speaker in each verse.

2. Explain the irony of the open doors.

3. What is the significance of the man's "ravings" about God and St. Peter?

4. Why do the speakers want the homeless person not to die in their vicinity? Why do they not offer to help him?

Suggestions for Exploring, Writing, and Persuading

1. What is your reaction to the people who would not allow a homeless man a place to sleep? Do you blame the homeless man? Who is at fault in this situation?

2. Is the poem realistic in its indictment of our society? To what degree is it true that a homeless man would not be allowed to sleep in a church, in a car, or on the street? What message is Hughes sending about the homeless? You might consider in your essay the NIMBY (Not In My Backyard) syndrome.

3. Write an essay in which you support one or more ways to alleviate homelessness.

Countee Cullen (1903–1948)

A New Yorker by birth, Cullen was a Phi Beta Kappa graduate of New York University. He wrote his first collection of poems, Color *(1925), while he was in college. Cullen also wrote a novel,* One Way to Heaven *(1932), and a version of Euripides's play* Medea. *A member of the Harlem Renaissance, Cullen later turned to teaching to earn a living.*

INCIDENT   (1925)

(FOR ERIC WALROND)

Once riding in old Baltimore,
    Heart-filled, head-filled with glee,

I saw a Baltimorean
   Keep looking straight at me.

5 Now I was eight and very small,
   And he was no whit bigger,
And so I smiled, but he poked out
   His tongue, and called me, "Nigger."

I saw the whole of Baltimore
10   From May until December;
Of all the things that happened there
   That's all that I remember.

Questions for Discussion

1. Why does the speaker remember only this incident from a seven-month stay in the city?
2. Explain the significance of the tone of the poem.

Suggestions for Exploring, Writing, and Persuading

1. If you have had a similar experience, describe it in a narrative essay.
2. Discuss the impact that a word such as *nigger* or another derogatory term can have on the self-esteem of an individual or a group.
3. Write an essay on the power of language. Explain, for example, the ways in which language can be used to "demonize" or "glorify" a person or a group of people.

Randall Jarrell (1914–1965)

Randall Jarrell was an American poet and critic. While some of his poems like the following one present a bleak, almost tragic vision, others present an innocent, almost childlike one. Early war poems such as "The Death of the Ball Turret Gunner" arose out of Jarrell's brief service as a pilot in World War II. Jarrell failed as a pilot, partially because he was bored by having to stay in formation and fly at one unvarying speed.

THE DEATH OF THE BALL TURRET GUNNER   (1945)

From my mother's sleep I fell into the State,
And I hunched in its belly till my wet fur froze.
Six miles from earth, loosed from its dream of life,
I woke to black flak and the nightmare fighters.
5 When I died they washed me out of the turret with a hose.

Questions for Discussion

1. Why does Jarrell name the soldier the Ball Turret Gunner instead of giving him a real name?

2. What does the first line mean? What does it suggest about the gunner and his relationship to the military? Why do you think Jarrell chose to write this poem in the first person?

3. Consider the metaphor, "till my wet fur froze." What does Jarrell mean and what is usually associated with wet fur?

4. Note the references to "sleep," "dream," and "nightmare" in the poem. What do they suggest about the speaker's consciousness?

5. In the last line, to whom does "they" refer? Why does Jarrell use an unclear pronoun? What is the emotional effect of this line?

Suggestion for Exploring, Writing, and Persuading

1. Discuss in an essay what message about war and death this poem offers. How is this message different from the traditional myth of war?

Henry Reed (1914–1986)

Born in Birmingham, England, and educated at Birmingham University, Reed spent a year in the Royal Army Ordnance Corps during World War II. Out of this military experience grew his most famous book of poems, Lessons of the War *(1945). After the war, he produced more poems, subsequently published in* A Map of Verona *(1946), and several successful comic plays for radio. The poem included here is, in its mocking tone, typical of his war poems.*

NAMING OF PARTS   (1945)

Today we have naming of parts. Yesterday,
We had daily cleaning. And tomorrow morning,
We shall have what to do after firing. But today,
Today we have naming of parts. Japonica
5   Glistens like coral in all of the neighboring gardens,
        And today we have naming of parts.

This is the lower sling swivel. And this
Is the upper sling swivel, whose use you will see,
When you are given your slings. And this is the piling swivel,
10   Which in your case you have not got. The branches
Hold in the gardens their silent, eloquent gestures,
        Which in our case we have not got.

This is the safety-catch, which is always released
With an easy flick of the thumb. And please do not let me
15 See anyone using his finger. You can do it quite easy
If you have any strength in your thumb. The blossoms
Are fragile and motionless, never letting anyone see
    Any of them using their finger.

And this you can see is the bolt. The purpose of this
20 Is to open the breech, as you see. We can slide it
Rapidly backwards and forwards: we call this
Easing the spring. And rapidly backwards and forwards
The early bees are assaulting and fumbling the flowers:
    They call it easing the Spring.

25 They call it easing the Spring: it is perfectly easy
If you have any strength in your thumb: like the bolt,
And the breech, and the cocking-piece, and the point of balance,
Which in our case we have not got; and the almond-blossom
Silent in all of the gardens and the bees going backwards and forwards,
30   For today we have naming of parts.

Questions for Discussion

1. How would you describe the language in the opening lines of each stanza? What tone or feeling does the language convey?
2. How do the closing lines of each stanza differ in language and tone from the other lines? How do you account for this difference in tone?
3. What seems to be the situation? How does the speaker in the closing lines of each stanza react to the situation?
4. Why is the naming of the parts of a gun important to war even if the soldiers don't have the guns yet? How are the soldiers being conditioned to the war?

Suggestion for Exploring, Writing, and Persuading

1. Many children have been told how to use a gun. In an essay, explain how this action affects their attitudes toward human lives.

Dylan Thomas (1914–1953)

Dylan Thomas was a Welsh poet known for his extraordinary reading voice. His most famous poems, exuberant and rich in sound and imagery, are nevertheless constructed with painstaking care, as the deceptively simple villanelle "Do Not Go Gentle into That Good Night" illustrates.

Do Not Go Gentle into That Good Night   (1945)

Do not go gentle into that good night,
Old age should burn and rave at close of day;
Rage, rage against the dying of the light.

Though wise men at their end know dark is right,
5   Because their words had forked no lightning they
Do not go gentle into that good night.

Good men, the last wave by, crying how bright
Their frail deeds might have danced in a green bay,
Rage, rage against the dying of the light.

10   Wild men who caught and sang the sun in flight,
And learn, too late, they grieved it on its way,
Do not go gentle into that good night.

Grave men, near death, who see with blinding sight
Blind eyes could blaze like meteors and be gay,
15   Rage, rage against the dying of the light.

And you, my father, there on the sad height,
Curse, bless, me now with your fierce tears, I pray.
Do not go gentle into that good night.
Rage, rage against the dying of the light.

Questions for Discussion

1. What is the effect of Thomas's repeating the two lines "Do not go gentle into that good night" and "Rage, rage against the dying of the light"?

2. Each of the middle stanzas describes a different kind of man facing death. Besides resisting death, what do the men have in common?

3. How effective is the longer, more specific last stanza after the first five? Why are the first five stanzas necessary if the main subject is the father's death?

4. Why does the speaker ask his father to "curse, bless" him? What does the speaker mean?

5. This poem is a *villanelle*, a form that is extremely difficult and rare in English poetry because of its rigidly patterned rhyme scheme. How does the extremely rigid form contribute to the tone of Thomas's poem?

Suggestions for Exploring, Writing, and Persuading

1. Write an essay urging someone you love to fight for life.

2. Thomas repeats, "Rage, rage against the dying of the light." He obviously feels that everyone should live life to the fullest and challenge old age and eventual death. Write an essay on whether you would agree or disagree.

Derek Walcott (b. 1930)

Born in Saint Lucia of mixed heritage, Walcott received a B.A. from the University of the West Indies in Jamaica. He began writing at an early age and became a prolific writer. His books of poetry include Epitaph for the Young: A Poem in XII Cantos *(1949),* The Caribbean Poetry of Derek Walcott, *and the* Art of Romare Beardon *(1983),* The Arkansas Testament *(1987),* Omeros *(1989), and* The Bounty *(1997). In addition, he has written plays:* Ione: A Play with Music *(1957),* Dream on Monkey Mountain *(1967), and* Odyssey: A Stage Version *(1993). In 1992, he won the Nobel Prize in literature. Trying to find a creative means of synthesizing opposites in order to fashion a Caribbean identity of the recent past, Walcott wrote of the contrasts in life: black and white, British and West Indian, colonizer and colonized.*

THE YOUNG WIFE   (1987)
(FOR NIGEL)

Make all your sorrow neat.
Plump pillows, soothe the corners
of her favourite coverlet.
Write to her mourners.

5   At dusk, after the office,
travel an armchair's ridge,
the valley of the shadow in the sofas,
the drapes' dead foliage.

Ah, but the mirror—the mirror
10 which you believe has seen
the traitor you feel you are—
clouds, though you wipe it clean!

The buds on the wallpaper
do not shake at the muffled sobbing
15 the children must not hear,
or the drawers you dare not open.

She has gone with that visitor
that sat beside her, like wind
clicking shut the bedroom door;
20   arm in arm they went,

leaving her wedding photograph in
its lace frame, a face smiling at
itself. And the telephone
without a voice. The weight

25   we bear on this heavier side
of the grave brings no comfort.
But the vow that was said
in white lace has brought

you now to the very edge
30   of that promise; now, for some,
the hooks in the hawthorn hedge
break happily into blossom

and the heart into grief.
The sun slants on a kitchen floor.
35   You keep setting a fork and knife
at her place for supper.

The children close in the space
made by a chair removed,
and nothing takes her place,
40   loved and now deeper loved.

The children accept your answer.
They startle you when they laugh.
She sits there smiling that cancer
kills everything but Love.

Questions for Discussion

1. How is the husband in the poem attempting to cope with the death of
   his young wife?

2. Why does the husband want to make sorrow neat? Is this realistic?
   Explain.

3. What are the little reminders of his loss?

4. Explain why the wife is "loved and now deeper loved."

5. Explain the last two lines of the poem.

6. Explain the following allusions in the poem:
       "the valley of the shadow in the sofas"
       "the mirror...clouds, though you wipe it clean!"
       "the vow that was said / in white lace has brought / you now to the
       very edge / of that promise"

Suggestions for Exploring, Writing, and Persuading

1. Walcott writes that earth is the "heavier side / of the grave [and] brings no comfort." Explain.
2. The speaker refers to various objects he associates with the dead wife. Write an essay analyzing the mixture of emotions aroused by an object you associate with someone who died.

Mary Oliver (b. 1935)

Mary Oliver, whose poetry has won the Pulitzer Prize and the National Book Award, has lived in Ohio and New England. Among her books are No Voyage and Other Poems *(1963);* New and Selected Poems *(1992);* A Poetry Handbook *(1995);* Blue Pastures *(1995), essays about nature; and* Winter Hours: Prose, Prose Poems, and Poems *(1999). Her book-length poem,* The Leaf and the Cloud, *appears in* The Best American Poetry *for 1999 and 2000. Oliver was awarded the Catharine Osgood Foster Chair for Distinguished Teaching at Bennington College. In her vivid and distinctive images, she shares both the inspiration and the wisdom found in nature.*

UNIVERSITY HOSPITAL, BOSTON   (1983)

The trees on the hospital lawn
are lush and thriving. They too
are getting the best of care,
like you, and the anonymous many,
5   in the clean rooms high above this city,
where day and night the doctors keep
arriving, where intricate machines
chart with cool devotion
the murmur of the blood,
10   the slow patching-up of bone,
the despair of the mind.

When I come to visit and we walk out
into the light of a summer day,
we sit under the trees—
15   buckeyes, a sycamore and one
black walnut brooding
high over a hedge of lilacs
as old as the red-brick building
behind them, the original
20   hospital built before the Civil War.
We sit on the lawn together, holding hands
while you tell me: you are better.

How many young men, I wonder,
came here, wheeled on cots off the slow trains
25   from the red and hideous battlefields
to lie all summer in the small and stuffy chambers
while doctors did what they could, longing
for tools still unimagined, medicines still unfound,
wisdoms still unguessed at, and how many died
30   staring at the leaves of the trees, blind
to the terrible effort around them to keep them alive?
I look into your eyes

which are sometimes green and sometimes gray,
and sometimes full of humor, but often not,
35   and tell myself, you are better,
because my life without you would be
a place of parched and broken trees.
Later, walking the corridors down to the street,
I turn and step inside an empty room.
40   Yesterday someone was here with a gasping face.
Now the bed is made all new,
the machines have been rolled away. The silence
continues, deep and neutral,
as I stand there, loving you.

Questions for Discussion

1. In what ways do the machines in hospitals "chart with cool devotion"? Why is their presence comforting?

2. What impression do the images of the first stanza convey about healing in a hospital? How do these images contrast to those in the second stanza describing the hospital grounds?

3. How do the trees contrast with the lives of the patients in the hospital? What would the narrator's life be like if the patient were to die?

Suggestion for Exploring, Writing, and Persuading

1. Using the poem as the basis for an essay, discuss the vulnerability of both the patient and the friend.

Billy Collins (b. 1941)

Award-winning poet Billy Collins was born in New York. Among his books of poetry are Pokerface *(1977),* The Art of Drowning *(1995),* The Apple That Astonished Paris *(1988),* Questions About Angels *(1991), which was selected for the Edward Hirsch National Poetry Series, and* Picnic, Lightning

(1998). In 1971, he received a Ph.D. from the University of California, Riverside; he presently teaches at Herbert H. Lehman College of the City University of New York. Collins was appointed Poet Laureate of the United States for 2001–2003 and has been named to serve as Poet Laureate of the state of New York during 2004–2006. His most recent collections of poems include Sailing Around the Room: New and Selected Poems *(2001) and* Nine Horses *(2002).*

FORGETFULNESS   (1991)

The name of the author is the first to go
followed obediently by the title, the plot,
the heartbreaking conclusion, the entire novel
which suddenly becomes one you have never read, never
    even heard of,

5 as if, one by one, the memories you used to harbor
decided to retire to the southern hemisphere of the brain,
to a little fishing village where there are no phones.

Long ago you kissed the names of the nine Muses goodbye
and watched the quadratic equation pack its bag,
10 and even now as you memorize the order of the planets,

something else is slipping away, a state flower perhaps,
the address of an uncle, the capital of Paraguay.

Whatever it is you are struggling to remember
it is not poised on the tip of your tongue,
15 not even lurking in some obscure corner of your spleen.
It has floated away down a dark mythological river
whose name begins with an *L* as far as you can recall,
well on your own way to oblivion where you will join those
who have even forgotten how to swim and how to ride a
    bicycle.

20 No wonder you rise in the middle of the night
to look up the date of a famous battle in a book on war.
No wonder the moon in the window seems to have drifted
out of a love poem that you used to know by heart.

Questions for Discussion

1. To whom does "you" refer in Collins's poem?
2. What kinds of things has the speaker forgotten?
3. Explain Collins's pun on "harbor" in the second verse.
4. What is the mythological river that begins with *L*?

5. Does this poem relate only to the elderly? When have you experienced the kind of forgetfulness the speaker describes? How does such forgetfulness make you feel?

6. Compare Collins's comments about forgetfulness with Mary's comment in Frost's poem "Death of the Hired Man": "I know just how it feels to think of the right thing to say too late."

Suggestions for Exploring, Writing, and Persuading

1. Write an essay, either humorous or serious, explaining your own forgetfulness or that of someone you know.

2. In an essay, argue that forgetfulness is not a laughing matter.

3. Although Collins doesn't talk about Alzheimer's disease, forgetfulness may be the beginning of this debilitating disease. If you had a parent with this disease, argue whether you would take care of this parent at home, put him or her in an assisted living facility, or propose another solution.

Sharon Olds (b. 1942)

Sharon Olds, a San Francisco-born poet, was educated at Stanford and Columbia universities. She has won a National Book Critics Circle Award for her poetry. Her books of poems include Satan Says *(1980);* Dead and the Living *(1983);* The Gold Cell *(1987), which includes the following poem;* The Father *(1992);* The Wellspring *(1995); and* Blood, Tin, Straw *(1999). Her poetry has appeared in* The New Yorker, The Paris Review, *and* Ploughshares. *She teaches poetry workshops at New York University.*

ON THE SUBWAY   (1987)

The boy and I face each other.
His feet are huge, in black sneakers
laced with white in a complex pattern like a
set of intentional scars. We are stuck on
5   opposite sides of the car, a couple of
molecules stuck in a rod of light
rapidly moving through darkness. He has the
casual cold look of a mugger,
alert under hooded lids. He is wearing
10 red, like the inside of the body
exposed. I am wearing dark fur, the
whole skin of an animal taken and
used. I look at his raw face,
he looks at my fur coat, and I don't

15   know if I am in his power—
he could take my coat so easily, my
briefcase, my life—
or if he is in my power, the way I am
living off his life, eating the steak
20   he does not eat, as if I am taking
the food from his mouth. And he is black
and I am white, and without meaning or
trying to I must profit from his darkness,
the way he absorbs the murderous beams of the
25   nation's heart, as black cotton
absorbs the heat of the sun and holds it. There is
no way to know how easy this
white skin makes my life, this
life he could take so easily and
30   break across his knee like a stick the way his
own back is being broken, the
rod of his soul that at birth was dark and
fluid and rich as the heart of a seedling
ready to thrust up into any available light.

Questions for Discussion

1. Examine the images of color and light in the poem. How are they important in creating the tone of the poem?

2. List the images of hurt and pain the speaker uses to describe the life of the man she meets. How do these and other images create a striking contrast between the speaker's life and that of the stranger?

3. Explain the contradiction of the speaker's saying:

   > . . .I don't
   >
   > know if I am in his power—
   >
   > . . . .
   >
   > or if he is in my power. . .

   To be in another's control can be very frightening. Who is in control of the lives in this poem—the boy, the speaker, both, or neither?

Suggestions for Exploring, Writing, and Persuading

1. Write an essay explaining how the rich similes and metaphors add to the visual effect of the poem and the depth of meaning.

2. Using the poem as background, analyze the factors leading to the fear the black man may have of the white woman.

3. Discuss the meaning of the last three lines of the poem. According to Olds, what has happened to the rod of the black man's soul?

Adam Zagajewski (b. 1945)

Zagajewski is a prolific and award-winning writer of poetry, fiction, and essays. Born in Poland and raised in Silesia and Cracow, he graduated from the Jagiellonian University. His early poetry, published in Communique *(1972) and* Meat Shops *(1975), features political and social issues; but later poetry, in* Traveling to Lowe *(1985) and* The Canvas *(1986), deals with the searching of young intellectuals. His novels, such as* Warm and Cold *(1975),* The Thin Line *(1983), and* Absolute Pitch, *published only in German translation, present the spiritual problems of the modern artist. His often autobiographical essays are included in* The Unpresented World *(1974),* Solidarity and Solitude *(1986),* Two Cities *(1991), and* In the Beauty of Others *(1998).*

TRY TO PRAISE THE MUTILATED WORLD   (2002)

TRANSLATED FROM THE POLISH BY CLARE CAVANAGH

Try to praise the mutilated world.
Remember June's long days,
and wild strawberries, drops of wine, the dew.
The nettles that methodically overgrow
5   the abandoned homesteads of exiles.
You must praise the mutilated world.
You watched the stylish yachts and ships;
one of them had a long trip ahead of it,
while salty oblivion awaited others.
10   You've seen the refugees heading nowhere,
you've heard the executioners sing joyfully.
You should praise the mutilated world.
Remember the moments when we were together
in a white room and the curtain fluttered.
15   Return in thought to the concert where music flared.
You gathered acorns in the park in autumn
and leaves eddied over the earth's scars.
Praise the mutilated world
and the gray feather a thrush lost,
20   and the gentle light that strays and vanishes
and returns.

Questions for Discussion

1. Why does the speaker call the world "mutilated"? Who mutilated the world—when, and how? In what way can this world be "praised"?

2. What is the implication of the last two lines?

3. What is the tone of the poem? What words and images set this tone?

4. Why does Zagajewski advise praising the world even though it is mutilated? Explain why the poet wants the reader to remember pleasant things. Is this act of remembrance in fact a denial of reality?

5. What recent events could be appropriately included in this poem?

Suggestions for Exploring, Writing, and Persuading

1. Write an essay describing what you consider recurring mutilations or what you consider the major mutilations of the modern world.

2. List the kinds of mutilation described in the poem. Then divide these into slight mutilations and major mutilations. In an essay, contrast and illustrate these forms of mutilation. Then give your interpretation of what Zagajewski is implying by these contrasts.

3. In an expository essay, explain what Zagajewski is saying about grief and loss.

Samuel Wharton (b. 1977)

Samuel Wharton received his undergraduate degree from Cornell College in Iowa and an M.F.A. in creative writing from Emerson College in Boston in 2003. "Riveaulx Abbey, Winter" is from his master's thesis, "The Barrens." Wharton lives in Austin, Texas.

RIEVAULX ABBEY, WINTER   (2004)

So little remains reaching for the sky: a wall,
unbuttressed; some halved columns;
that one row of stones arching
from tower to nave. We trudge around
5   the perimeter, through ankle-deep drifts,
some grass still crunching underfoot.
To walk inward, into that inside-now-outside,
would be a violation, though other groups
have wandered in across the transepts,
10   jumped the chapterhouse's broken walls.
Within the dormitory's outline: people pretending
to piss down the open holes of the garderobes,
spitting on the cold pallets where hundreds
of years of Cistercians found their peace
15   in unheated cells. This monastery grew rich
off wool and wheat—for that
it was destroyed, a small monument
to the years of the Dissolution.
What's here now is anonymous.

20 People zoom and click,
myself included. Isn't this how to document history—
take a picture and stare later at its flatness?
Because what *is* permanent, if not this yellow
light slanting back to the hillsides,
25 that one small tree perched atop a wall,
the few more flakes beginning to drift down, again?

Questions for Discussion

1. The speaker says, "To walk inward, that inside now outside, / would be a violation." What does he mean? How does he react to the tourists' tramping through this ancient, holy place?

2. What contrast does the poem make between past and present?

3. What does the speaker regard as permanent? Why?

Suggestion for Exploring, Writing, and Persuading

1. In an essay discuss how tourists and/or the tourist business distort and demean local, natural, and historic sites.

DRAMA

William Shakespeare (1564–1616)

William Shakespeare is generally regarded as the greatest writer ever to have written in English. Though Shakespeare also produced an often-admired sequence of 154 sonnets and several narrative poems, his extraordinary reputation rests primarily on his plays. Notable for their sheer number and diversity, the thirty-seven plays include thirteen comedies, ten tragedies, ten history plays, and four romances.

Using language that is rich and highly allusive yet conversational and informal, the plays reveal not only a sure sense of dramatic structure and tension but also a love of human diversity. As a member of an acting company that performed both in the outdoor Globe playhouse and in the indoor Blackfriars, Shakespeare was intimately familiar with the theater of his time and with its conventions. Among the most highly regarded of his plays are the comedies As You Like It, All's Well That Ends Well, *and* Twelfth

Night; *the history plays* Henry IV, Part I *and* Henry IV, Part II; *the tragedies* Hamlet, Othello, King Lear, *and* Macbeth; *and* The Tempest, *a romance generally thought to have been Shakespeare's last play.* Othello *displays the richness of language, character, and dramatic tension for which Shakespeare is justly celebrated.*

ABOUT TRAGEDY

Shakespeare's Othello *is a tragedy. In its most general literary usage, the term tragedy refers to a particular kind of play in which a good person through some character flaw destroys himself or herself.*

The most famous definition of tragedy comes from the ancient Greek philosopher Aristotle (384–322 B.C.). In his Poetics, *Aristotle defines tragedy as*

> a representation *(mimesis)* of an action *(praxis)* that is serious, complete, and of a certain magnitude [...] presented, not narrated [i.e., a drama, not a story] [...] with incidents arousing pity and fear in such a way as to accomplish a purgation *(katharsis)* of such emotions. (296)

*The purpose of tragedy, according to Aristotle, then, is to make the audience feel "pity and fear" in order somehow to purge or cleanse these emotions. The most important elements of tragedy are plot and character. The plot must present an action that is complete, with a clear beginning and an ending that gives a sense of finality, and must be unified, so that every part contributes to the whole. The best plots feature reversal (**peripeteia**), a not improbable but unexpected 180-degree change in situation, and recognition (**anagnorisis**), the tragic hero's sudden understanding of his or her fate and its implications. A **tragic hero**, Aristotle maintains, must be good but flawed, must be aristocratic, must be believable, and must behave consistently.*

Shakespeare, writing for a different audience in a different kind of theater at a different time, produced tragedies that are rich in language and character development but less dramatically unified than Aristotle prescribes. For example, Shakespeare did not hesitate to insert into his tragedies scenes containing the broadest farce, an impropriety of which Aristotle would almost certainly have disapproved. It is a testimony to Shakespeare's dramatic genius that he could include in his tragedies such richly comic scenes without disrupting their dramatic tension. Of all Shakespeare's tragedies, Othello *is the most Aristotelian in its unity. Shakespearean in its puns and plays on words and in the diversity and fullness of such characters as Othello, Iago, Emilia, and Desdemona,* Othello *moves inexorably to its tragic conclusion.*

Work Cited

Aristotle. "The Art of Poetry." From *Aristotle*. Sel. and trans. Philip
Wheelwright. New York: Odyssey, 1951.

OTHELLO, THE MOOR OF VENICE   (1604)

The Names of the Actors

Othello:	the Moor
Brabantio:	[a senator,] father to Desdemona
Cassio:	an honorable lieutenant [to Othello]
Iago:	[Othello's ancient,] a villain
Roderigo:	a gulled gentleman
Duke of Venice	
Senators [of Venice]	
Montano:	Governor of Cyprus
Gentlemen of Cyprus	
Lodovico and Gratiano:	[kinsmen to Brabantio,] two noble Venetians
Sailors	
Clown	
Desdemona:	[daughter to Brabantio and wife to Othello]
Emilia:	wife to Iago
Bianca:	a courtesan [and mistress to Cassio]
A Messenger	
A Herald	
A Musician	
Servants, Attendants, Officers, Senators, Musicians, Gentlemen	

SCENE

Venice; a seaport in Cyprus

1.1

(Enter Roderigo and Iago.)

RODERIGO:

1   Tush, never tell me! I take it much unkindly
    That thou, Iago, who has had my purse

3   As if the strings were thine, shouldst know of this.

_____

1.1 Location: Venice. A street.   1 never tell me (An expression of incredulity, like
"tell me another one.")   **3 this** i.e., Desdemona's elopement

4   IAGO: 'Sblood, but you'll not hear me.
    If ever I did dream of such a matter,
    Abhor me.
    RODERIGO:
    Thou toldst me thou didst hold him in thy hate.
    IAGO: Despise me
    If I do not. Three great ones of the city,
    In personal suit to make me his lieutenant,
11 Off-capped to him; and by the faith of man,
    I know my price, I am worth no worse a place.
    But he, as loving his own pride and purposes,
14 Evades them with a bombast circumstance
15 Horribly stuffed with epithets of war,
    And, in conclusion,
17 Nonsuits my mediators. For, "Certes," says he,
    "I have already chose my officer."
    And what was he?
20 Forsooth, a great arithmetician,
    One Michael Cassio, a Florentine,
22 A fellow almost damned in a fair wife,
    That never set a squadron in the field
24 Nor the division of a battle knows
25 More than a spinster unless the bookish theoric,
26 Wherein the togaed consuls can propose
    As masterly as he. Mere prattle without practice
    Is all his soldiership. But he, sir, had th' election;
29 And I, of whom his eyes had seen the proof
    At Rhodes, at Cyprus, and on other grounds
31 Christened and heathen, must be beeled and calmed
32 By debitor and creditor. This countercaster,
33 He, in good time, must his lieutenant be,
34 And I—God bless the mark!—his Moorship's ancient.

---

4 'Sblood by His (Christ's) blood   **11 him** i.e., Othello   **14 bombast circumstance**
wordy evasion. (*Bombast* is cotton padding.)   **15 epithets of war** military expressions
17 Nonsuits rejects the petition of. **Certes** certainly   **20 arithmetician** i.e., a man
whose military knowledge is merely theoretical, based on books of tactics   **22 A [...]**
wife (Cassio does not seem to be married, but his counterpart in Shakespeare's source
does have a woman in his house. See also 4.1.131.)   **24 division of a battle** disposition
of a military unit   **25 a spinster** i.e., a housewife, one whose regular occupation is spinning. **theoric** theory   **26 togaed** wearing the toga. **consuls** counselors, senators.
propose discuss   **29 his** i.e., Othello's   **31 Christened** Christian. **beeled and calmed**
left to leeward without wind, becalmed. (A sailing metaphor.)   **32 debitor and creditor** (A name for a system of bookkeeping, here used as a contemptuous nickname for
Cassio.) **countercaster** i.e., bookkeeper, one who tallies with *counters*, or "metal disks."
(Said contemptuously.)   **33 in good time** opportunely, i.e., forsooth   **34 God bless
the mark** (Perhaps originally a formula to ward off evil; here an expression of impatience.) **ancient** standard-bearer, ensign

RODERIGO:

35   By heaven, I rather would have been his hangman.

IAGO:

Why, there's no remedy. 'Tis the curse of service;

37   Preferment goes by letter and affection,

38   And not by old gradation, where each second

Stood heir to th' first. Now, sir, be judge yourself

40   Whether I in any just term am affined

To love the Moor.

RODERIGO: I would not follow him then.

43   IAGO: O sir, content you.

I follow him to serve my turn upon him.

We cannot all be masters, nor all masters

46   Cannot be truly followed. You shall mark

Many a duteous and knee-crooking knave

That, doting on his own obsequious bondage,

Wears out his time, much like his master's ass,

50   For naught but provender, and when he's old, cashiered.

51   Whip me such honest knaves. Others there are

52   Who, trimmed in forms and visages of duty,

Keep yet their hearts attending on themselves,

And, throwing but shows of service on their lords,

55   Do well thrive by them, and when they have lined their coats,

Do themselves homage. These fellows have some soul,

And such a one do I profess myself. For, sir,

59   It is as sure as you are Roderigo,

Were I the Moor I would not be Iago.

In following him, I follow but myself—

Heaven is my judge, not I for love and duty,

62   But seeming so for my peculiar end.

For when my outward action doth demonstrate

64   The native act and figure of my heart

65   In compliment extern, 'tis not long after

But I will wear my heart upon my sleeve

67   For daws to peck at. I am not what I am.

---

35 his hangman the executioner of him   **37 Preferment** promotion. **letter and affec-tion** personal influence and favoritism   **38 old gradation** step-by-step seniority, the tra-ditional way   **40 term** respect. **affined** bound   **43 content you** don't you worry about that   **46 truly** faithfully   **50 cashiered** dismissed from service   **51 Whip me** whip, as far as I'm concerned   **52 trimmed [...] duty** dressed up in the mere form and show of dutifulness   **55 lined their coats** i.e., stuffed their purses   **56 Do themselves homage** i.e., attend to self-interest solely   **59 Were [...] Iago** i.e., if *I* were able to assume com-mand, *I* certainly would not choose to remain a subordinate, or, *I* would keep a suspicious eye on a flattering subordinate   **62 peculiar** particular, personal   **64 native** innate. **figure** shape, intent   **65 compliment extern** outward show (conforming in this case to the inner workings and intention of the heart)   **67 daws** small crowlike birds, proverbially stupid and avaricious. **I am not what I am** i.e., I am not one who wears his heart on his sleeve

RODERIGO:

68   What a full fortune does the thick-lips owe

60   If he can carry 't thus!

IAGO: Call up her father.

Rouse him, make after him, poison his delight,

Proclaim him in the streets; incense her kinsmen,

72   And, though he in a fertile climate dwell,

73   Plague him with flies. Though that his joy be joy,

74   Yet throw such chances of vexation on 't

75   As it may lose some color.

RODERIGO: Here is her father's house. I'll call aloud.

IAGO:

77   Do, with like timorous accent and dire yell

78   As when, by night and negligence, the fire

Is spied in populous cities.

RODERIGO:

What ho, Brabantio! Signor Brabantio, ho!

IAGO:

Awake! What ho, Brabantio! Thieves, thieves, thieves!

Look to your house, your daughter, and your bags!

83   Thieves, thieves!

(Brabantio [enters] above [at a window].)

BRABANTIO:

What is the reason of this terrible summons?

85   What is the matter there?

RODERIGO: Signor, is all your family within?

IAGO: Are your doors locked?

BRABANTIO: Why, wherefore ask you this?

IAGO:

89   Zounds, sir, you're robbed. For shame, put on your gown!

Your heart is burst; you have lost half your soul.

Even now, now, very now, an old black ram

92   Is tupping your white ewe. Arise, arise!

93   Awake the snorting citizens with the bell,

94   Or else the devil will make a grandsire of you.

Arise, I say!

---

68 full swelling. **thick-lips** (Elizabethans often applied the term "Moor" to Negroes.)
owe own   **69 carry 't thus** carry this off   **72–73 though [...] flies** though he seems
prosperous and happy now, vex him with misery   **73 Though [...] be joy** although he
seems fortunate and happy. (Repeats the idea of line 72.)   **74 chances of vexation** vex-
ing changes   **75 As it may** that may cause it to. **some color** some of its fresh gloss
77 timorous frightening   **78 and negligence** i.e., by negligence   **83 s.d. at a window**
(This stage direction, from the Quarto, probably calls for an appearance on the gallery
above and rearstage.)   **85 the matter** your business   **89 Zounds** by His (Christ's)
wounds   **92 tupping** covering, copulating with. (Said of sheep.)   **93 snorting** snoring
94 the devil (The devil was conventionally pictured as black.)

BRABANTIO: What, have you lost your wits?

RODERIGO: Most reverend signor, do you know my voice?

BRABANTIO: Not I. What are you?

RODERIGO: My name is Roderigo.

BRABANTIO: The worser welcome.

I have charged thee not to haunt about my doors.

In honest plainness thou hast heard me say

My daughter is not for thee; and now, in madness,

104   Being full of supper and distempering drafts,

105   Upon malicious bravery dost thou come

106   To start my quiet.

RODERIGO: Sir, sir, sir—

BRABANTIO: But thou must needs be sure

109   My spirits and my place have in their power

To make this bitter to thee.

RODERIGO: Patience, good sir.

BRABANTIO:

What tell'st thou me of robbing? This is Venice;

113   My house is not a grange.

RODERIGO: Most grave Brabantio,

115   In simple and pure soul I come to you.

IAGO: Zounds, sir, you are one of those that will not serve God if the

devil bid you. Because we come to do you service and you think we

118   are ruffians, you'll have your daughter covered with a Barbary horse;

119   you'll have your nephews neigh to you; you'll have coursers for

120   cousins and jennets for germans.

BRABANTIO: What profane wretch art thou?

IAGO: I am one, sir, that comes to tell you your daughter and the Moor

are now making the beast with two backs.

BRABANTIO: Thou art a villain.

125   IAGO: You are a senator.

BRABANTIO:

126   This thou shalt answer. I know thee, Roderigo.

RODERIGO:

Sir, I will answer anything. But I beseech you,

128   If't be your pleasure and most wise consent—

As partly I find it is—that your fair daughter,

130   At this odd-even and dull watch o' the night,

---

104 distempering intoxicating   **105 Upon malicious bravery** with hostile intent to defy me   **106 start** startle, disrupt   **109 My spirits and my place** my temperament and my authority of office. **have in** have it in   **113 grange** isolated country house   **115 simple** sincere   **118 Barbary** from northern Africa (and hence associated with Othello)   **119 nephews** i.e., grandsons. **coursers** powerful horses   **120 cousins** kinsmen. **jennets** small Spanish horses. **germans** near relatives   **125 a senator** (Said with mock politeness, as though the word itself were an insult.)   **126 answer** be held accountable for   **128 wise** well-informed   **130 odd-even** between one day and the next, i.e., about midnight

131   Transported with no worse nor better guard
132   But with a knave of common hire, a gondolier,
     To the gross clasps of a lascivious Moor—
134   If this be known to you and your allowance
135   We then have done you bold and saucy wrongs.
136   But if you know not this, my manners tell me
     We have your wrong rebuke. Do not believe
138   That, from the sense of all civility,
139   I thus would play and trifle with your reverence.
     Your daughter, if you have not given her leave,
     I say again, hath made a gross revolt,
142   Tying her duty, beauty, wit, and fortunes
143   In an extravagant and wheeling stranger
144   Of here and everywhere. Straight satisfy yourself.
     If she be in her chamber or your house,
     Let loose on me the justice of the state
     For thus deluding you.
148   BRABANTIO: Strike on the tinder, ho!
     Give me a taper! Call up all my people!
150   This accident is not unlike my dream.
     Belief of it oppresses me already.
     Light, I say, light!   (*Exit [above].*)
     IAGO: Farewell, for I must leave you.
154   It seems not meet nor wholesome to my place
155   To be producted—as, if I stay, I shall—
     Against the Moor. For I do know the state,
157   However this may gall him with some check,
158   Cannot with safety cast him, for he's embarked
159   With such loud reason to the Cyprus wars,
160   Which even now stands in act, that, for their souls,
161   Another of his fathom they have none
162   To lead their business; in which regard,
     Though I do hate him as I do hell pains,
164   Yet for necessity of present life
     I must show out a flag and sign of love,

---

131 with by   **132 But with a knave** than by a low fellow, a servant   **134 allowance** permission   **135 saucy** insolent   **138 from** contrary to. **civility** good manners, decency   **139 your reverence** the respect due to you   **142 wit** intelligence   **143 extravagant** expatriate, wandering far from home. **wheeling** roving about, vagabond **stranger** foreigner   **144 Straight** straightway   **148 tinder** charred linen ignited by a spark from flint and steel, used to light torches or *tapers* (lines 145, 171)   **150 accident** occurrence, event   **154 meet** fitting. **place** position (as ensign)   **155 producted** produced (as a witness)   **157 gall** rub; oppress. **check** rebuke   **158 cast** dismiss. **embarked** engaged   **159 loud reason** unanimous shout of confirmation (in the Senate)   **160 stands in act** are going on. **for their souls** to save themselves   **161 fathom** i.e., ability, depth of experience   **162 in which regard** out of regard for which   **164 life** livelihood

Which is indeed but sign. That you shall surely find him,
167   Lead to the Sagittary the raisèd search,
168   And there will I be with him. So farewell. (*Exit*)

(*Enter [below] Brabantio [in his nightgown] with servants and torches.*)

BRABANTIO:
It is too true an evil. Gone she is;
170   And what's to come of my despisèd time
Is naught but bitterness. Now, Roderigo,
Where didst thou see her?—O unhappy girl!—
With the Moor, sayst thou?—Who would be a father!—
How didst thou know 'twas she?—O, she deceives me
Past thought!—What said she to you?—Get more tapers.
Raise all my kindred.—Are they married, think you?
RODERIGO: Truly, I think they are.
BRABANTIO:
O heaven! How got she out? O treason of the blood!
Fathers, from hence trust not your daughters' minds
180   By what you see them act. Is there not charms
181   By which the property of youth and maidhood
182   May be abused? Have you not read, Roderigo,
Of some such thing?
RODERIGO: Yes, sir, I have indeed.
BRABANTIO: Call up my brother.—O, would you had had her!—
Some one way, some another.—Do you know
Where we may apprehend her and the Moor?
RODERIGO:
188   I think I can discover him, if you please
To get good guard and go along with me.
BRABANTIO:
Pray you, lead on. At every house I'll call;
191   I may command at most.—Get weapons, ho!
And raise some special officers of night.-
193   On, good Roderigo. I will deserve your pains.   (*Exeunt.*)

1.2

(*Enter Othello, Iago, attendants with torches.*)

IAGO: Though in the trade of war I have slain men,

---

167 Sagittary (An inn or house where Othello and Desdemona are staying, named for its sign of Sagittarius, or Centaur.) **raisèd search** search party roused out of sleep   **168 s.d. night-gown** dressing gown. (This costuming is specified in the Quarto text.)   **170 time** i.e., remainder of life   **180 charms** spells   **181 property** special quality, nature   **182 abused** deceived
188 discover reveal, uncover   **191 command** demand assistance   **193 deserve** show gratitude for

2   Yet do I hold it very stuff o' the conscience
3   To do no contrived murder. I lack iniquity
     Sometimes to do me service. Nine or ten times
5   I had thought t' have yerked him here under the ribs.
     OTHELLO: 'Tis better as it is.
     IAGO: Nay, but he prated,
     And spoke such scurvy and provoking terms
     Against your honor
     That, with the little godliness I have,
11   I did full hard forbear him. But, I pray you, sir,
     Are you fast married? Be assured of this,
13   That the magnifico is much beloved,
14   And hath in his effect a voice potential
     As double as the Duke's. He will divorce you,
     Or put upon you what restraint or grievance
     The law, with all his might to enforce it on,
18   Will give him cable.
     OTHELLO: Let him do his spite.
20   My services which I have done the seigniory
21   Shall out-tongue his complaints. 'Tis yet to know—
     Which, when I know that boasting is an honor,
     I shall promulgate—I fetch my life and being
24   From men of royal siege, and my demerits
25   May speak unbonneted to as proud a fortune
     As this that I have reached. For know, Iago,
     But that I love the gentle Desdemona,
28   I would not my unhousèd free condition
29   Put into circumscription and confine
30   For the sea's worth. But look, what lights come yond?

     (Enter Cassio [and certain officers] with torches.)

     IAGO: Those are the raisèd father and his friends.
     You were best go in.
     OTHELLO: Not I. I must be found.
34   My parts, my title, and my perfect soul

1.2 Location: Venice. Another street, before Othello's lodgings.   2 very stuff
essence, basic material (continuing the metaphor of *trade* from line 1)
3 contrived premeditated   **5 yerked** stabbed. **him** i.e., Roderigo   **11 I [...] him** *I*
restrained myself with great difficulty from assaulting him   **13 magnifico** Venetian
grandee, i.e., Brabantio   **14 in his effect** at his command. **potential** powerful
18 cable i.e., scope   **20 seigniory** Venetian government   **21 yet to know** not yet
widely known   **24 siege** i.e., rank. (Literally, seat used by a person of distinction.)
demerits deserts   **25 unbonneted** without removing the hat, i.e., on equal terms (? Or
"with hat off," "in all due modesty.")   **28 unhousèd** unconfined, undomesticated
29 circumscription and confine restriction and confinement   **30 the sea's worth** all
the riches at the bottom of the sea. **s.d. officers** (The Quarto text calls for "Cassio with
lights, officers with torches.")   **34 My [...] soul** my natural gifts, my position or reputation, and my unflawed conscience

Shall manifest me rightly. Is it they?

36 IAGO: By Janus, I think no.

OTHELLO: The servants of the Duke? And my lieutenant?
The goodness of the night upon you, friends!
What is the news?

CASSIO: The Duke does greet you, General,
And he requires your haste-post-haste appearance
Even on the instant.

43 OTHELLO: What is the matter, think you?

CASSIO:

44   Something from Cyprus, as I may divine.

45   It is a business of some heat. The galleys

46   Have sent a dozen sequent messengers
This very night at one another's heels,

48   And many of the consuls, raised and met,
Are at the Duke's already. You have been hotly called for;
When, being not at your lodging to be found,

51   The Senate hath sent about three several quests
To search you out.

OTHELLO: 'Tis well I am found by you.
I will but spend a word here in the house
And go with you.   (*Exit.*)

56 CASSIO: Ancient, what makes he here?

IAGO:

57   Faith, he tonight hath boarded a land carrack.

58   If it prove lawful prize, he's made forever.

CASSIO:
I do not understand.

IAGO: He's married.

CASSIO: To who?

(*Enter Othello.*)

IAGO:

62   Marry, to—Come,—Captain, will you go?

63 OTHELLO: Have with you.

CASSIO:

64   Here comes another troop to seek for you.

(*Enter Brabantio, Roderigo, with officers and torches.*)

---

36 Janus Roman two-faced god of beginnings   **43 matter** business   **44 divine** guess
45 heat urgency   **46 sequent** successive   **48 consuls** senators   **51 about** all over the
city. **several** separate   **56 makes** does   **57 boarded** gone aboard and seized as an act
of piracy (with sexual suggestion).**carrack** large merchant ship   **58 prize** booty
62 Marry (An oath, originally "by the Virgin Mary"; here used with wordplay on *married*.)
63 Have with you i.e., let's go   **64 s.d. officers and torches** (The Quarto text calls for
"others with lights and weapons.")

IAGO:

65   It is Brabantio. General, be advised.

He comes to bad intent.

OTHELLO: Holla! Stand there!

RODERIGO:

Signor, it is the Moor.

BRABANTIO: Down with him, thief!

(They draw on both sides.)

IAGO:

You, Roderigo! Come, sir, I am for you.

OTHELLO:

71   Keep up your bright swords, for the dew will rust them.

Good signor, you shall more command with years.

Than with your weapons.

BRABANTIO:

O thou foul thief, where hast thou stowed my daughter?

Damned as thou art, thou hast enchanted her!

76   For I'll refer me to all things of sense,

If she in chains of magic were not bound

Whether a maid so tender, fair, and happy,

So opposite to marriage that she shunned

The wealthy curlèd darlings of our nation,

Would ever have, t' incur a general mock,

82   Run from her guardage to the sooty bosom

Of such a thing as thou—to fear, not to delight.

84   Judge me the world if 'tis not gross in sense

That thou hast practiced on her with foul charms,

86   Abused her delicate youth with drugs or minerals

87   That weakens motion. I'll have 't disputed on;

'Tis probable and palpable to thinking.

89   I therefore apprehend and do attach thee

For an abuser of the world, a practicer

91   Of arts inhibited and out of warrant.—

Lay hold upon him! If he do resist,

Subdue him at his peril.

OTHELLO: Hold your hands,

95   Both you of my inclining and the rest.

Were it my cue to fight, I should have known it

Without a prompter.—Whither will you that I go

---

65 be advised be on your guard   **71 Keep up** keep in the sheath   **76 refer me** submit my case. **things of sense** common sense understandings, or, creatures possessing common sense   **82 her guardage** my guardianship of her   **84 gross in sense** obvious   **86 minerals** i.e., poisons   **87 weakens motion** impair the vital faculties. **disputed on** argued in court by professional counsel, debated by experts   **89 attach** arrest   **91 arts inhibited** prohibited arts, black magic   **95 inclining** following, party

To answer this your charge?

BRABANTIO: To prison, till fit time

100   Of law and course of direct session
Call thee to answer.

OTHELLO: What if I do obey?
How may the Duke be therewith satisfied,
Whose messengers are here about my side
Upon some present business of the state
To bring me to him?

OFFICER: 'Tis true, most worthy signor.
The Duke's in council, and your noble self,
I am sure, is sent for.

BRABANTIO: How? The Duke in council?

111   In this time of the night? Bring him away.

112   Mine's not an idle cause. The Duke himself,
Or any of my brothers of the state,
Cannot but feel this wrong as 'twere their own;
For if such actions may have passage free,
Bondslaves and pagans shall our statesmen be.   (*Exeunt.*)

1.3

(*Enter Duke [and] Senators [and sit at a table, with lights], and Officers.*)

[*The Duke and Senators are reading dispatches.*]

DUKE:

1   There is no composition in these news
That gives them credit.

3 FIRST SENATOR: Indeed, they are disproportioned.
My letters say a hundred and seven galleys.

DUKE:

And mine, a hundred forty.

SECOND SENATOR: And mine, two hundred.

7   But though they jump not on a just account—

8   As in these cases, where the aim reports
'Tis oft with difference—yet do they all confirm
A Turkish fleet, and bearing up to Cyprus.

DUKE:

Nay, it is possible enough to judgment.

---

100 course of direct session regular or specially convened legal proceedings   **111 away** right along   **112 idle** trifling   **115 have passage free** are allowed to go unchecked
1.3 Location: Venice. A council chamber. s.d. Enter [...] Officers (The Quarto text calls for the Duke and senators to "sit at a table with lights and attendants.")   **1 composition** consistency   **3 disproportioned** inconsistent   **7 jump** agree. **just** exact   **8 the aim** conjecture

12   I do not so secure me in the error
     But the main article I do approve
     In fearful sense.

SAILOR (*within*):   What ho, what ho, what ho!

(Enter Sailor.)

OFFICER: A messenger from the galleys.
DUKE: Now, what's the business?
SAILOR:

18   The Turkish preparation makes for Rhodes.
     So was I bid report here to the state
     By Signor Angelo.

DUKE:

21   How say you by this change?

FIRST SENATOR: This cannot be
23   By no assay of reason. 'Tis a pageant
24   To keep us in false gaze. When we consider
     Th' importancy of Cyprus to the Turk,
     And let ourselves again but understand
     That, as it more concerns the Turk than Rhodes,
28   So may he with more facile question bear it,
29   For that it stands not in such warlike brace,
30   But altogether lacks th' abilities
31   That Rhodes is dressed in—if we make thought of this,
32   We must not think the Turk is so unskillful
33   To leave the latest which concerns him first,
     Neglecting an attempt of ease and gain
35   To wake and wage a danger profitless,

DUKE:

     Nay, in all confidence, he's not for Rhodes.

OFFICER: Here is more news.

(Enter a Messenger.)

MESSENGER: The Ottomites, reverend and gracious,
     Steering with due course toward the isle of Rhodes,
40   Have there injointed them with an after fleet.

FIRST SENATOR:

     Ay, so I thought. How many, as you guess?

12–13 I do not [...] approve *I* do not take such (false) comfort in the discrepancies that
I fail to perceive the main point, i.e., that the Turkish fleet is threatening   **18 preparation** fleet prepared for battle   **21 by** about   **23 assay** test. **pageant** mere show   **24 in
false gaze** looking the wrong way   **28 So may [...] it** so also he (the Turk) can more
easily capture it (Cyprus)   **29 For that** since. **brace** state of defense   **30 abilities**
means of self-defense   **31 dressed in** equipped with   **32 unskillful** deficient in judgment   **33 latest** last   **35 wake** stir up. **wage** risk   **40 injointed them** joined themselves. **after** second, following

MESSENGER:

42   Of thirty sail; and now they do restem
43   Their backward course, bearing with frank appearance
      Their purposes toward Cyprus. Signor Montano,
45   Your trusty and most valiant servitor,
46   With his free duty recommends you thus,
      And prays you to believe him.
DUKE: 'Tis certain then for Cyprus.
      Marcus Luccicos, is not he in town?
FIRST SENATOR: He's now in Florence.
DUKE:
      Write from us to him, post-post-haste. Dispatch.
FIRST SENATOR: Here comes Brabantio and the valiant Moor.

      (*Enter Brabantio, Othello, Cassio, Iago, Roderigo, and officers.*)

DUKE:
53   Valiant Othello, we must straight employ you
54   Against the general enemy Ottoman.
55   (*To Brabantio.*) I did not see you; welcome, gentle signor.
      We lacked your counsel and your help tonight.
BRABANTIO:
      So did I yours. Good Your Grace, pardon me;
58   Neither my place nor aught I heard of business
      Hath raised me from my bed, nor doth the general care
60   Take hold on me, for my particular grief
61   Is of so floodgate and o'erbearing nature
62   That it engluts and swallows other sorrows
63   And it is still itself.
DUKE: Why, what's the matter?
BRABANTIO: My daughter! O, my daughter!
DUKE AND SENATORS: Dead?
BRABANTIO: Ay, to me.
68   She is abused, stol'n from me, and corrupted
      By spells and medicines bought of mountebanks;
      For nature so preposterously to err,
71   Being not deficient, blind, or lame of sense,
72   Sans witchcraft could not.

42-43 restem [...] course retrace their original course   **43 frank appearance** undis-
guised intent   **45 servitor** officer under your command   **46 free duty** freely given and
loyal service. **recommends** commends himself and reports to   **53 straight** straightway
54 general enemy universal enemy to all Christendom   **55 gentle** noble   **58 place**
official position   **60 particular** personal   **61 floodgate** i.e., overwhelming (as when
floodgates are opened)   **62 engluts** engulfs   **63 is still itself** remains undiminished
68 abused deceived   **71 deficient** defective. **lame of sense** deficient in sensory perception   **72 Sans** without

DUKE:
>Whoe'er he be that in this foul proceeding
>Hath thus beguiled your daughter of herself,
>And you of her, the bloody book of law
>You shall yourself read in the bitter letter

77   After your own sense—yea, though our proper son

78   Stood in your action.

BRABANTIO: Humbly I thank Your Grace.
>Here is the man, this Moor, whom now it seems
>Your special mandate for the state affairs
>Hath hither brought.

ALL: We are very sorry for 't.

DUKE (*to Othello*): What, in your own part, can you say to this?

BRABANTIO: Nothing, but this is so.

OTHELLO:
>Most potent, grave, and reverend signors,

87   My very noble and approved good masters:
>That I have ta'en away this old man's daughter,
>It is most true; true, I have married her.

90   The very head and front of my offending

91   Hath this extent, no more. Rude am I in my speech,
>And little blessed with the soft phrase of peace;

93   For since these arms of mine had seven years' pith,

94   Till now some nine moons wasted, they have used

95   Their dearest action in the tented field;
>And little of this great world can I speak
>More than pertains to feats of broils and battle,
>And therefore little shall I grace my cause
>In speaking for myself. Yet, by your gracious patience,

100   I will a round unvarnished tale deliver
>Of my whole course of love—what drugs, what charms,
>What conjuration, and what mighty magic,

103   For such proceeding I am charged withal,
>I won his daughter.

BRABANTIO: A maiden never bold;

106   Of spirit so still and quiet that her motion
>Blushed at herself; and she, in spite of nature,

108   Of years, of country, credit, everything,

---

77 **After [...] sense** according to your own interpretation. **our proper** my own   **78 Stood [...] action** were under your accusation   **87 approved** proved, esteemed   **90 head and front** height and breadth, entire extent   **91 Rude** unpolished   **93 since [...] pith** i.e., since I was seven. **pith** strength, vigor   **94 Till [...] wasted** until some nine months ago (since when Othello has evidently not been on active duty, but in Venice)   **95 dearest** most valuable   **100 round** plain   **103 withal** with   **106–107 her [...] herself** i.e., she blushed easily at herself. (*Motion* can suggest the impulse of the soul or of the emotions, or physical movement.)   **108 years** i.e., difference in age. **credit** virtuous reputation

To fall in love with what she feared to look on!
It is a judgment maimed and most imperfect
111   That will confess perfection so could err
Against all rules of nature, and must be driven
113   To find out practices of cunning hell
114   Why this should be. I therefore vouch again
115   That with some mixtures powerful o'er the blood,
116   Or with some dram conjured to this effect,
He wrought upon her.
DUKE: To vouch this is no proof,
119   Without more wider and more overt test
120   Than these thin habits and poor likelihoods
121   Of modern seeming do prefer against him.
FIRST SENATOR: But Othello, speak.
123   Did you by indirect and forcèd courses
Subdue and poison this young maid's affections?
125   Or came it by request and such fair question
As soul to soul affordeth?
OTHELLO: I do beseech you,
Send for the lady to the Sagittary
And let her speak of me before her father.
If you do find me foul in her report,
The trust, the office I do hold of you
Not only take away, but let your sentence
Even fall upon my life.
DUKE: Fetch Desdemona hither.
OTHELLO:
Ancient, conduct them. You best know the place.

(Exeunt Iago and attendants.)

And, till she come, as truly as to heaven
137   I do confess the vices of my blood,
138   So justly to your grave ears I'll present
How I did thrive in this fair lady's love,
And she in mine.
DUKE: Say it, Othello.
OTHELLO:
Her father loved me, oft invited me,
143   Still questioned me the story of my life
From year to year—the battles, sieges, fortunes

---

111 confess concede (that)   **113 practices** plots   **114 vouch** assert   **115 blood** passions   **116 dram** [...] **effect** dose made by magical spells to have this effect   **119 more
wider** fuller. **test** testimony   **120 habits** garments, i.e., appearances. **poor likelihoods**
weak inferences   **121 modern seeming** commonplace assumption. **prefer** bring forth
123 forcèd courses means used against her will   **125 question** conversation   **137 blood**
passions, human nature   **138 justly** truthfully, accurately   **143 Still** continually

That I have passed.
I ran it through, even from my boyish days
To th' very moment that he bade me tell it,
Wherein I spoke of most disastrous chances,
149 Of moving accidents by flood and field,
150 Of hairbreadth scapes i' th' imminent deadly breach,
Of being taken by the insolent foe
And sold to slavery, of my redemption thence,
153 And portance in my travels' history,
154 Wherein of antres vast and deserts idle,
155 Rough quarries, rocks, and hills whose heads touch heaven,
156 It was my hint to speak—such was my process—
And of the Cannibals that each other eat,
158 The Anthropophagi, and men whose heads
Do grow beneath their shoulders. These things to hear
Would Desdemona seriously incline;
But still the house affairs would draw her thence,
Which ever as she could with haste dispatch
She'd come again, and with a greedy ear
Devour up my discourse. Which I, observing,
165 Took once a pliant hour, and found good means
To draw from her a prayer of earnest heart
167 That I would all my pilgrimage dilate,
168 Whereof by parcels she had something heard,
169 But not intentively. I did consent,
And often did beguile her of her tears,
When I did speak of some distressful stroke
That my youth suffered. My story being done,
She gave me for my pains a world of sighs.
174 She swore, in faith, 'twas strange, 'twas passing strange,
'Twas pitiful, 'twas wondrous pitiful.
She wished she had not heard it, yet she wished
177 That heaven had made her such a man. She thanked me,
And bade me, if I had a friend that loved her,
I should but teach him how to tell my story,
180 And that would woo her. Upon this hint I spake.
She loved me for the dangers I had passed,
And I loved her that she did pity them.

---

149 moving accidents stirring happenings   **150 imminent** [...] **breach** death-threatening gaps made in a fortification   **153 portance** conduct   **154 antres** caverns. **idle** barren, desolate   **155 Rough quarries** rugged rock formations   **156 hint** occasion, opportunity   **158 Anthropophagi** man-eaters. (A term from Pliny's *Natural History*.)
165 pliant well-suiting   **167 dilate** relate in detail   **168 by parcels** piecemeal
169 intentively with full attention, continuously   **174 passing** exceedingly   **177 made her** created her to be   **180 hint** opportunity. (Othello does not mean that she was dropping hints.)

This only is the witchcraft I have used.
Here comes the lady. Let her witness it.

(Enter Desdemona, Iago, [and] attendants.)

DUKE:
I think this tale would win my daughter too.
Good Brabantio,

187   Take up this mangled matter at the best.
Men do their broken weapons rather use
Than their bare hands.

BRABANTIO: I pray you, hear her speak.
If she confess that she was half the wooer,
Destruction on my head if my bad blame
Light on the man!—Come hither, gentle mistress.
Do you perceive in all this noble company
Where most you owe obedience?

DESDEMONA: My noble Father,
I do perceive here a divided duty.

198   To you I am bound for life and education;
199   My life and education both do learn me
200   How to respect you. You are the lord of duty;
I am hitherto your daughter. But here's my husband,
And so much duty as my mother showed
To you, preferring you before her father,

204   So much I challenge that I may profess
Due to the Moor my lord.

BRABANTIO: God be with you! I have done.
Please it Your Grace, on to the state affairs.

208   I had rather to adopt a child than get it.
Come hither, Moor.   *(He joins the hands of Othello and Desdemona.)*

210   I here do give thee that with all my heart
211   Which, but thou hast already, with all my heart
212   I would keep from thee.—For your sake, jewel,
I am glad at soul I have no other child,

214   For thy escape would teach me tyranny,
215   To hang clogs on them.—I have done, my lord.

DUKE:
216   Let me speak like yourself, and lay a sentence
217   Which, as a grece or step, may help these lovers

---

187 **Take [...] best** make the best of a bad bargain   198 **education** upbringing
199 **learn** teach   200 **of duty** to whom duty is due   204 **challenge** claim   208 **get**
beget   210 **with all my heart** wherein my whole affection has been engaged
211 **with all my heart** willingly, gladly   212 **For your sake** on your account
214 **escape** elopement   215 **clogs** (Literally, blocks of wood fastened to the legs of
criminals or convicts to inhibit escape.)   216 **like yourself** i.e., as you would, in your
proper temper. **lay a sentence** apply a maxim   217 **grece** step

Into your favor.

219 When remedies are past, the griefs are ended

220 By seeing the worst, which late on hopes depended.

221 To mourn a mischief that is past and gone

222 Is the next way to draw new mischief on.

223 What cannot be preserved when fortune takes,

224 Patience her injury a mockery makes.

The robbed that smiles steals something from the thief;

226 He robs himself that spends a bootless grief.

BRABANTIO:

So let the Turk of Cyprus us beguile,

We lose it not, so long as we can smile.

229 He bears the sentence well that nothing bears

But the free comfort which from thence he hears,

But he bears both the sentence and the sorrow

That, to pay grief, must of poor patience borrow.

233 These sentences, to sugar or to gall,

Being strong on both sides, are equivocal.

But words are words. I never yet did hear

236 That the bruisèd heart was piercèd through the ear.

I humbly beseech you, proceed to th' affairs of state.

DUKE: The Turk with a most mighty preparation makes for Cyprus.

239 Othello, the fortitude of the place is best known to you; and though

240 we have there a substitute of most allowed sufficiency, yet opinion,

a sovereign mistress of effects, throws a more safer voice on you.

242 You must therefore be content to slubber the gloss of your

243 new fortunes with this more stubborn and boisterous expedition.

OTHELLO:

The tyrant custom, most grave senators,

Hath made the flinty and steel couch of war

246 My thrice-driven bed of down. I do agnize

A natural and prompt alacrity

248 I find in hardness, and do undertake

---

219 remedies hopes of remedy   **220 which [...] depended** which griefs were sustained until recently by hopeful anticipation   **221 mischief** misfortune, injury   **222 next** nearest   **223 What** whatever   **224 Patience [...] makes** patience laughs at the injury inflicted by fortune (and thus eases the pain)   **226 spends a bootless grief** indulges in unavailing grief   **229–232 He bears [...] borrow** a person well bears out your maxim who can enjoy its platitudinous comfort, free of all genuine sorrow, but anyone whose grief bankrupts his poor patience is left with your saying and his sorrow, too. (*Bears the sentence* also plays on the meaning, "receives judicial sentence.")   **233–234 These [...] equivocal** these fine maxims are equivocal, either sweet or bitter in their application   **236 piercèd [...] ear** i.e., surgically lanced and cured by mere words of advice   **239 fortitude** strength   **240 substitute** deputy. **allowed** acknowledged   **240–241 opinion [...] on you** general opinion, an important determiner of affairs, chooses you as the best man   **242 slubber** soil, sully   **243 stubborn** harsh, rough   **246 thrice-driven** thrice sifted, winnowed. **agnize** know in myself, acknowledge   **248 hardness** hardship

These present wars against the Ottomites.
250   Most humbly therefore bending to your state,
I crave fit disposition for my wife,
252   Due reference of place and exhibition,
253   With such accommodation and besort
254   As levels with her breeding.

DUKE:
Why, at her father's.

BRABANTIO: I will not have it so.

OTHELLO:
                    Nor I.

DESDEMONA: Nor I. I would not there reside,
To put my father in impatient thoughts
By being in his eye. Most gracious Duke,
261   To my unfolding lend your prosperous ear,
262   And let me find a charter in your voice,
T' assist my simpleness.

DUKE: What would you, Desdemona?

DESDEMONA:
That I did love the Moor to live with him,
266   My downright violence and storm of fortunes
267   May trumpet to the world. My heart's subdued
Even to the very quality of my lord.
I saw Othello's visage in his mind,
270   And to his honors and his valiant parts
Did I my soul and fortunes consecrate.
So that, dear lords, if I be left behind
273   A moth of peace, and he go to the war,
274   The rites for why I love him are bereft me,
And I a heavy interim shall support
276   By his dear absence. Let me go with him.

OTHELLO:
277   Let her have your voice.
Vouch with me, heaven, I therefor beg it not
To please the palate of my appetite,
280   Nor to comply with heat—the young affects

---

250 bending [...] state bowing or kneeling to your authority   252 reference [...] exhibition provision of appropriate place to live and allowance of money   253 accommodation suitable provision. besort attendance   254 levels equals, suits. breeding social position, upbringing   261 unfolding explanation, proposal. prosperous propitious   262 charter privilege, authorization   266 My [...] fortunes my plain and total breach of social custom, taking my future by storm and disrupting my whole life   267–268 My heart's [...] lord my heart is brought wholly into accord with Othello's virtues; I love him for his virtues   270 parts qualities   273 moth i.e., one who consumes merely   274 rites rites of love (with a suggestion, too, of "rights," sharing)   276 dear (1) heartfelt (2) costly   277 voice consent   280 heat sexual passion. young affects passions of youth, desires

281 In me defunct—and proper satisfaction,
282 But to be free and bounteous to her mind.
283 And heaven defend your good souls that you think
I will your serious and great business scant
When she is with me. No, when light-winged toys
286 Of feathered Cupid seel with wanton dullness
287 My speculative and officed instruments,
288 That my disports corrupt and taint my business,
Let huswives make a skillet of my helm,
290 And all indign and base adversities
291 Make head against my estimation!

DUKE:
Be it as you shall privately determine,
Either for her stay or going. Thè affair cries haste,
And speed must answer it.

A SENATOR: You must away tonight.

DESDEMONA:
Tonight, my lord?

DUKE: This night.

OTHELLO: With all my heart.

DUKE:
At nine i' the morning here we'll meet again.
Othello, leave some officer behind,
And he shall our commission bring to you,
302 With such things else of quality and respect
303 As doth import you.

OTHELLO: So please Your Grace, my ancient;
A man he is of honesty and trust.
To his conveyance I assign my wife,
With what else needful Your Good Grace shall think
To be sent after me.

DUKE: Let it be so.
Good night to everyone. (*To Brabantio.*) And, noble signor,
If virtue no delighted beauty lack,
Your son-in-law is far more fair than black.

311 FIRST SENATOR:
Adieu, brave Moor. Use Desdemona well.

BRABANTIO:
Look to her, Moor, if thou hast eyes to see.
She has deceived her father, and may thee.

---

281 proper personal   **282 free** generous   **283 defend** forbid. **think** should think   **286 seel**
i.e., making blind (as in falconry, by sewing up the eyes of the hawk during training)
287 speculative [...] instruments eyes and other faculties used in the performance of duty
288 That so that. **disports** sexual pastimes. **taint** impair   **290 indign** unworthy, shameful
291 Make head raise an army. **estimation** reputation   **302 of quality and respect** of
importance and relevance   **303 import** concern   **311 delighted** capable of delighting

(Exeunt [Duke, Brabantio, Cassio, Senators and officers].)

OTHELLO:
My life upon her faith! Honest Iago,
My Desdemona must I leave to thee.
I prithee, let thy wife attend on her,
319   And bring them after in the best advantage.
Come, Desdemona. I have but an hour
321   Of love, of worldly matters and direction,
322   To spend with thee. We must obey the time.

([Exit with Desdemona].)

RODERIGO: Iago—
IAGO: What sayst thou, noble heart?
RODERIGO: What will I do, think'st thou?
IAGO: Why, go to bed and sleep.
327   RODERIGO: I will incontinently drown myself.
IAGO: If thou dost, I shall never love thee after. Why,
thou silly gentleman?
RODERIGO: It is silliness to live when to live is torment;
331   and then have we a prescription to die when death is
our physician.
333   IAGO: O villainous! I have looked upon the
world for four times seven years, and, since I could distinguish
betwixt a benefit and an injury, I never found man
that knew how to love himself. Ere I would say I
337   would drown myself for the love of a guinea hen, I
would change my humanity with a baboon.
RODERIGO: What should I do? I confess it is my shame
340   to be so fond, but it is not in my virtue to amend it.
341   IAGO: Virtue? A fig! 'Tis in ourselves that we are thus
or thus. Our bodies are our gardens, to the which our
wills are gardeners; so that if we will plant nettles or
344   sow lettuce, set hyssop and weed up thyme, supply it
345   with one gender of herbs or distract it with many,
346   either to have it sterile with idleness or manured with
347   industry—why, the power and corrigible authority of
348   this lies in our wills. If the beam of our lives had not

---

319 in [...] advantage at the most favorable opportunity   **321 direction** instructions
322 the time the urgency of the present crisis   **327 incontinently** immediately, without self-restraint   **331 prescription** (1) right based on long-established custom (2) doctor's prescription   **333 villainous** i.e., what perfect nonsense   **337 guinea hen** (A slang term for a prostitute.)   **340 fond** infatuated. **virtue** strength, nature   **341 fig** (To give a fig is to thrust the thumb between the first and second fingers in a vulgar and insulting gesture)   **344 hyssop** a herb of the mint family   **345 gender** kind. **distract it with** divide it among   **346 idleness** want of cultivation   **347 corrigible authority** power to correct   **348 beam** balance

349 one scale of reason to poise another of sensuality, the
350 blood and baseness of our natures would conduct us
to most preposterous conclusions. But we have reason
352 to cool our raging motions, our carnal stings, our
353 unbitted lusts, whereof I take this that you call love to
354 be a sect or scion.

RODERIGO: It cannot be.

IAGO: It is merely a lust of the blood and a permission
of the will. Come, be a man. Drown thyself? Drown
cats and blind puppies. I have professed me thy friend,
and I confess me knit to thy deserving with cables of
360 perdurable toughness. I could never better stead thee
than now. Put money in thy purse. Follow thou the
362 wars; defeat thy favor with an usurped beard. I say,
put money in thy purse. It cannot be long that Desdemona should continue her love to the Moor—put
money in thy purse—nor he his to her. It was a vio-
366 lent commencement in her, and thou shalt see an
answerable sequestration—put but money in thy purse.
368 These Moors are changeable in their wills—fill thy
purse with money. The food that to him now is as
370 luscious as locusts shall be to him shortly as bitter as
371 coloquintida. She must change for youth; when she is
sated with his body, she will find the error of her
choice. She must have change, she must. Therefore
put money in thy purse. If thou wilt needs damn thy-
375 self, do it a more delicate way than drowning. Make
376 all the money thou canst. If sanctimony and a frail vow
377 betwixt an erring barbarian and a supersubtle Venetian be not too hard for my wits and all the tribe of
hell, thou shalt enjoy her. Therefore make money.
380 A pox of drowning thyself! It is clean out of the way.
381 Seek thou rather to be hanged in compassing thy joy
than to be drowned and go without her.

383 RODERIGO: Wilt thou be fast to my hopes if I depend on
384 the issue?

---

349 poise counterbalance   **350 blood** natural passions   **352 motions** appetites
353 unbitted unbridled, uncontrolled   **354 sect or scion** cutting or offshoot
360 perdurable very durable. **stead** assist   **362 defeat thy favor** disguise your face.
usurped (The suggestion is that Roderigo is not man enough to have a beard of his
own.)   **366–367 an answerable sequestration** a corresponding separation or
estrangement   **368 wills** carnal appetites   **370 locusts** fruit of the carob tree (see
Matthew 3:4), or perhaps honeysuckle   **371 coloquintida** colocynth or bitter apple, a
purgative   **375 Make** raise, collect   **376 sanctimony** sacred ceremony   **377 erring**
wandering, vagabond, unsteady   **380 clean [...] way** entirely unsuitable as a course of
action   **381 compassing** encompassing, embracing   **383 fast** true   **384 issue** (successful) outcome

IAGO: Thou art sure of me. Go, make money. I have
    told thee often, and I retell thee again and again, I hate
387   the Moor. My cause is hearted; thine hath no less reason.
388   Let us be conjunctive in our revenge against him.
    If thou canst cuckold him, thou dost thyself a pleasure,
    me a sport. There are many events in the womb of tim
391   which will get delivered. Traverse, go, provide thy money.
    We will have more of this tomorrow. Adieu.

RODERIGO: Where shall we meet i' the morning?

IAGO: At my lodging.

395 RODERIGO: I'll be with thee betimes.   *(He starts to leave.)*

IAGO: Go to, farewell.—Do you hear, Roderigo?

RODERIGO: What say you?

IAGO: No more of drowning, do you hear?

RODERIGO: I am changed.

IAGO: Go to, farewell. Put money enough in your purse.

RODERIGO: I'll sell my land.   *(Exit.)*

IAGO:
    Thus do I ever make my fool my purse;
    For I mine own gained knowledge should profane
404   If I would time expend with such a snipe
    But for my sport and profit. I hate the Moor;
406   And it is thought abroad that twixt my sheets
407   He's done my office. I know not if 't be true;
    But I, for mere suspicion in that kind,
409   Will do as if for surety. He holds me well;
    The better shall my purpose work on him.
411   Cassio's a proper man. Let me see now:
412   To get his place and to plume up my will
    In double knavery—How, how?—Let's see:
414   After some time, to abuse Othello's ear
415   That he is too familiar with his wife.
416   He hath a person and a smooth dispose
    To be suspected, framed to make women false.
418   The Moor is of a free and open nature,
    That thinks men honest that but seem to be so,
420   And will as tenderly be led by the nose
    As asses are.

---

387 hearted fixed in the heart, heartfelt   **388 conjunctive** united   **391 Traverse** (A military marching term.)   **395 betimes** early   **404 snipe** woodcock, i.e., fool   **406 it is thought abroad** it is rumored   **407 my office** i.e., my sexual function as husband   **409 do [...] surety** act as if on certain knowledge. **holds me well** regards me favorably   **411 proper** handsome   **412 plume up** put a feather in the cap of, i.e., glorify, gratify   **414 abuse** deceive   **415 he** i.e., Cassio   **416 dispose** disposition   **418 free** frank, generous. **open** unsuspicious   **420 tenderly** readily

I have 't. It is engendered. Hell and night
Must bring this monstrous birth to the world's light.

(Exit.)

2.1

(Enter Montano and two Gentlemen.)

MONTANO: What from the cape can you discern at sea?
FIRST GENTLEMAN:
2   Nothing at all. It is a high-wrought flood.
3   I cannot, twixt the heaven and the main,
       Descry a sail.
MONTANO:
       Methinks the wind hath spoke aloud at land;
       A fuller blast ne'er shook our battlements.
7   If it hath ruffianed so upon the sea,
8   What ribs of oak, when mountains melt on them,
9   Can hold the mortise? What shall we hear of this?
SECOND GENTLEMAN:
10   A segregation of the Turkish fleet.
       For do but stand upon the foaming shore,
12   The chidden billow seems to pelt the clouds;
13   The wind-shaked surge, with high and monstrous mane,
14   Seems to cast water on the burning Bear
       And quench the guards of th' ever-fixèd pole.
16   I never did like molestation view
17   On the enchafèd flood.
18 MONTANO: If that the Turkish fleet
19   Be not ensheltered and embayed, they are drowned;
20   It is impossible to bear it out.

(Enter a [Third] Gentleman.)

THIRD GENTLEMAN: News, lads! Our wars are done.
       The desperate tempest hath so banged the Turks

2.1 Location: A seaport in Cyprus. An open place near the quay.   2 high-wrought flood very agitated sea   **3 main** ocean (also at line 42)   **7 ruffianed** raged   **8 mountains** i.e., of water   **9 hold the mortise** hold their joints together. (A mortise is the socket hollowed out in fitting timbers.)   **10 segregation** dispersal   **12 chidden** i.e., rebuked, repelled (by the shore), and thus shot into the air   **13 monstrous mane** (The surf is like the mane of a wild beast.)   **14 the burning Bear** i.e., the constellation Ursa Minor or the Little Bear, which includes the polestar (and hence regarded as the *guards of th' ever-fixèd pole* in the next line; sometimes the term *guards* is applied to the two "pointers" of the Big Bear or Dipper, which may be intended here.)   **16 like molestation** comparable disturbance   **17 enchafèd** angry   **18 If that** if   **19 embayed** sheltered by a bay   **20 bear it out** survive, weather the storm

23   That their designment halts. A noble ship of Venice
24   Hath seen a grievous wreck and sufferance
       On most part of their fleet.
MONTANO: How? Is this true?
THIRD GENTLEMAN: This ship is here put in,
28   A Veronesa; Michael Cassio,
       Lieutenant to the warlike Moor Othello,
       Is come on shore; the Moor himself at sea,
       And is in full commission here for Cyprus.
MONTANO:
       I am glad on 't. 'Tis a worthy governor.
THIRD GENTLEMAN:
       But this same Cassio, though he speak of comfort
34   Touching the Turkish loss, yet he looks sadly
       And prays the Moor be safe, for they were parted
       With foul and violent tempest.
MONTANO: Pray heaven he be,
       For I have served him, and the man commands
39   Like a full soldier. Let's to the seaside, ho!
       As well to see the vessel that's come in
       As to throw out our eyes for brave Othello,
42   Even till we make the main and the' aerial blue
43   An indistinct regard.
THIRD GENTLEMAN: Come, let's do so,
45   For every minute is expectancy
46   Of more arrivance.

       (Enter Cassio.)

CASSIO:
       Thanks, you the valiant of this warlike isle,
48   That so approve the Moor! O, let the heavens
       Give him defense against the elements,
       For I have lost him on a dangerous sea.
MONTANO: Is he well shipped?
CASSIO:
       His bark is stoutly timbered, and his pilot
53   Of very expert and approved allowance;
54   Therefore my hopes, not surfeited to death,

---

23 designment design, enterprise. **halts** is lame   **24 wreck** shipwreck. **sufferance**
damage, disaster   **28 Veronesa** i.e., fitted out in Verona for Venetian service, or possibly
Verennessa (the Folio spelling), i.e., *verrinessa*, a cutter (from *verrinare*, "to cut
through")   **34 sadly** gravely   **39 full** perfect   **42 the main [...] blue** the sea and the
sky   **43 An indistinct regard** indistinguishable in our view   **45 is expectancy** gives
expectation   **46 arrivance** arrival   **48 approve** admire, honor   **53 approved**
allowance tested reputation   **54 surfeited to death** i.e., overextended, worn thin
through repeated application or delayed fulfillment

55 Stand in bold cure.

            (*A cry*) within: "A sail, a sail, a sail!"

CASSIO: What noise?

A GENTLEMAN:

58 The town is empty. On the brow o' the sea

    Stand ranks of people, and they cry "A sail!"

CASSIO:

60 My hopes do shape him for the governor.

                 (*A shot within.*)

SECOND GENTLEMAN:

61 They do discharge their shot of courtesy;

    Our friends at least.

CASSIO: I pray you, sir, go forth,

    And give us truth who 'tis that is arrived.

SECOND GENTLEMAN: I shall. (*Exit.*)

MONTANO:

    But, good Lieutenant, is your general wived?

CASSIO:

    Most fortunately. He hath achieved a maid

68 That paragons description and wild fame,

69 One that excels the quirks of blazoning pens,

70 And in th' essential vesture of creation

    Does tire the enginer.

    (Enter [Second] Gentleman.)

72   How now? Who has put in?

SECOND GENTLEMAN:

    'Tis one Iago, ancient to the General.

CASSIO:

    He's had most favorable and happy speed.

    Tempests themselves, high seas, and howling winds,

76 The guttered rocks and congregated sands—

77 Traitors ensteeped to clog the guiltless keel—

78 As having sense of beauty, do omit

79 Their mortal natures, letting go safely by

    The divine Desdemona.

MONTANO: What is she?

---

55 in bold cure in strong hopes of fulfillment   **58 brow o' the sea** cliff-edge   **60 My [...] for** I hope it is   **61 discharge [...] courtesy** fire a salute in token of respect and courtesy   **68 paragons** surpasses. **wild fame** extravagant report   **69 quirks** witty conceits. **blazoning** setting forth as though in heraldic language   **70–71 in [...] enginer** in her real, God-given, beauty, (she) defeats any attempt to praise her. **enginer** engineer, i.e, poet, one who devises. **s.d. Second Gentleman** (So identified in the Quarto text here and in lines 58, 61, 68, and 96; the Folio calls him a gentleman.)   **72 put in** i.e., to harbor   **76 guttered** jagged, trenched   **77 ensteeped** lying under water   **78 As** as if. **omit** forbear to exercise   **79 mortal** deadly

CASSIO:

    She that I spake of, our great captain's captain,

    Left in the conduct of the bold Iago,

84   Whose footing here anticipates our thoughts

85   A sennight's speed. Great Jove, Othello guard,

    And swell his sail with thine own powerful breath,

87   That he may bless this bay with his tall ship,

    Make love's quick pants in Desdemona's arms,

    Give renewed fire to our extincted spirits,

    And bring all Cyprus comfort!

(Enter Desdemona, Iago, Roderigo, and Emilia.)

      O, behold,

    The riches of the ship is come on shore!

    You men of Cyprus, let her have your knees.

(The gentleman make curtsy to Desdemona.)

    Hail to thee, lady! And the grace of heaven

    Before, behind thee, and on every hand

    Enwheel thee round!

DESDEMONA: I thank you, valiant Cassio.

    What tidings can you tell me of my lord?

CASSIO:

    He is not yet arrived, nor know I aught.

    But that he's well and will be shortly here.

DESDEMONA:

    O, but I fear—How lost you company?

CASSIO:

    The great contention of the sea and skies

    Parted our fellowship.

              (Within) "A sail, a sail!" *(A shot.)*

              But hark. A sail!

SECOND GENTLEMAN:

    They give their greeting to the citadel.

    This likewise is a friend.

CASSIO: See for the news.

(Exit Second Gentleman.)

    Good Ancient, you are welcome. *(Kissing Emilia.)*

        Welcome, mistress.

    Let it not gall your patience, good Iago,

112   That I extend my manners; 'tis my breeding

    That gives me this bold show of courtesy.

---

84 footing landing   **85 sennight's** week's   **87 tall** splendid, gallant   **112 extend** give
scope to. **breeding** training in the niceties of etiquette

IAGO:

> Sir, would she give you so much of her lips
> As of her tongue she often bestows on me,
> You would have enough.

117 DESDEMONA: Alas, she has no speech!

IAGO: In faith, too much.

119 I find it still, when I have list to sleep.
Marry, before your ladyship, I grant,
She puts her tongue a little in her heart
122 And chides with thinking.

EMILIA: You have little cause to say so.

IAGO:

124 Come on, come on. You are pictures out of doors,
125 Bells in your parlors, wildcats in your kitchens,
126 Saints in your injuries, devils being offended,
127 Players in your huswifery, and huswives in your beds.

DESDEMONA: O, fie upon thee, slanderer!

IAGO:

129 Nay, it is true, or else I am a Turk.
You rise to play, and go to bed to work.

EMILIA:

You shall not write my praise.

IAGO: No, let me not.

DESDEMONA:

What wouldst write of me, if thou shouldst praise me?

IAGO:

O gentle lady, do not put me to 't,
135 For I am nothing if not critical.

DESDEMONA:

136 Come on, essay.—There's one gone to the harbor?

IAGO: Ay, madam.

DESDEMONA:

I am not merry, but I do beguile
139 The thing I am by seeming otherwise.
Come, how wouldst thou praise me?

IAGO:

I am about it, but indeed my invention
142 Comes from my pate as birdlime does from frieze—

---

117 she has no speech i.e., she's not a chatterbox, as you allege   **119 still** always. **list** desire   **122 with thinking** i.e., in her thoughts only   **124 pictures out of doors** i.e., silent and well-behaved in public   **125 Bells** i.e., jangling, noisy, and brazen. **in your kitchens** i.e., in domestic affairs. (Ladies would not do the cooking.)   **126 Saints** martyrs   **127 Players** idlers, triflers, or deceivers. **huswifery** housekeeping. **huswives** hussies (i.e., women are "busy" in bed, or unduly thrifty in dispensing sexual favors)   **129 A Turk** an infidel, not to be believed   **135 critical** censorious   **136 essay** try   **139 The thing I am** i.e., my anxious self   **142 birdlime** sticky substance used to catch small birds. **frieze** coarse woolen cloth

143   It plucks out brains and all. But my Muse labors,
       And thus she is delivered:
       If she be fair and wise, fairness and wit,
146   The one's for use, the other useth it.

DESDEMONA:
147   Well praised! How if she be black and witty?

IAGO:
       If she be black, and thereto have a wit,
149   She'll find a white that shall her blackness fit.

DESDEMONA:
       Worse and worse.

EMILIA: How if fair and foolish?
       She never yet was foolish that was fair,
153   For even her folly helped her to an heir.

154   DESDEMONA: These are old fond paradoxes to make fools
       laugh i' th' alehouse. What miserable praise hast thou
156   for her that's foul and foolish?

IAGO:
157   There's none so foul and foolish thereunto,
158   But does foul pranks which fair and wise ones do.

DESDEMONA: O heavy ignorance! Thou praisest the worst
       best. But what praise couldst thou bestow on a deserving
       woman indeed, one that, in the authority of her merit,
162   did justly put on the vouch of very malice itself?

IAGO:
       She that was ever fair, and never proud,
       Had tongue at will, and yet was never loud,
165   Never lacked gold and yet went never gay,
166   Fled from her wish, and yet said, "Now I may,"
       She that being angered, her revenge being nigh,
168   Bade her wrong stay and her displeasure fly,
       She that in wisdom never was so frail
170   To change the cod's head for the salmon's tail,
       She that could think and ne'er disclose her mind,
       See suitors following and not look behind,
       She was a wight, if ever such wight were—

DESDEMONA: To do what?

_____

143 labors (1) exerts herself (2) prepares to deliver a child (with a following pun on
delivered in line 144)   **146 The one's [...] it** i.e., her cleverness will make use of her
beauty   **147 black** dark-complexioned, brunette   **149 a white** a fair person (with
wordplay on "wight," a person). **fit** (with sexual suggestion of mating)   **153 folly** (with
added meaning of "lechery, wantonness"). **to an heir** i.e., to bear a child   **154 fond** foolish   **156 foul** ugly   **157 thereunto** in addition   **158 foul** sluttish   **162 put [...]**
vouch compel the approval   **165 gay** extravagantly clothed   **166 Fled [...] may**
avoided temptation where the choice was hers   **168 Bade [...] stay** i.e., resolved to put
up with her injury patiently   **170 To [...] tail** i.e., to exchange a lackluster husband for a
sexy lover (?) (*Cod's head* is slang for "penis," and *tail*, for "pudendum.")

IAGO:

175   To suckle fools and chronicle small beer.

DESDEMONA: O most lame and impotent conclusion! Do
not learn of him, Emilia, though he be thy husband.

178   How say you, Cassio? Is he not a most profane and

179   liberal counselor?

180   CASSIO: He speaks home, madam. You may relish him

181   more in the soldier than in the scholar.

(Cassio and Desdemona stand together, conversing intimately.)

182   IAGO *(aside)*: He takes her by the palm. Ay, well said,
whisper. With as little a web as this will I ensnare as
great a fly as Cassio. Ay, smile upon her, do; I will

185   gyve thee in thine own courtship. You say true; 'tis so,
indeed. If such tricks as these strip you out of your
lieutenantry, it had been better you had not kissed
your three fingers so oft, which now again you are

189   most apt to play the sir in. Very good; well kissed! An
excellent courtesy! 'Tis so, indeed. Yet again your fingers

191   to your lips? Would they were clyster pipes for your
sake! *(Trumpet within.)* The Moor! I know his trumpet.

CASSIO: 'Tis truly so.

DESDEMONA: Let's meet him and receive him.

CASSIO: Lo, where he comes!

(Enter Othello and attendants.)

OTHELLO:

      O my fair warrior!

DESDEMONA: My dear Othello!

OTHELLO:

      It gives me wonder great as my content
      To see you here before me. O my soul's joy,
      If after every tempest come such calms,
      May the winds blow till they have wakened death,
      And let the laboring bark climb hills of seas
      Olympus-high, and duck again as low
      As hell's from heaven! If it were now to die,
      'Twere now to be most happy, for I fear
      My soul hath her content so absolute

---

175 suckle fools breastfeed babies. chronicle small beer i.e., keep petty household
accounts, keep track of trivial matters   178 profane irreverent, ribald   179 liberal
licentious, free-spoken   180 home right to the target. (A term from fencing.) relish
appreciate   181 in in the character of   182 well said well done   185 gyve fetter,
shackle. courtship courtesy, show of courtly manners. You say true i.e., that's right, go
ahead   189 the sir i.e., the fine gentleman   191 clyster pipes tubes used for enemas
and douches

That not another comfort like to this
208   Succeeds in unknown fate.

DESDEMONA: The heavens forbid
But that our loves and comforts should increase
Even as our days do grow!

OTHELLO:
Amen to that, sweet powers!
I cannot speak enough of this content.
It stops me here; it is too much of joy.
And this, and this, the greatest discords be

(They kiss.)
215
That e'er our hearts shall make!

IAGO *(aside)*: O, you are well tuned now!
218   But I'll set down the pegs that make this music,
219   As honest as I am.

OTHELLO: Come, let us to the castle.
News, friends! Our wars are done, the Turks are drowned.
How does my old acquaintance of this isle?—
223   Honey, you shall be well desired in Cyprus;
I have found great love amongst them. O my sweet,
225   I prattle out of fashion, and I dote
In mine own comforts.—I prithee, good Iago,
227   Go to the bay and disembark my coffers.
228   Bring thou the master to the citadel;
He is a good one, and his worthiness
230   Does challenge much respect.—Come, Desdemona.—
Once more, well met at Cyprus!

(Exeunt Othello and Desdemona [and all but Iago and Roderigo].)

IAGO *(to an attendant)*: Do thou meet me presently at
the harbor. *(To Roderigo.)* Come hither. If thou be'st
234   valiant—as, they say, base men being in love have
then a nobility in their natures more than is native to
236   them—list me. The Lieutenant tonight watches on
237   the court of guard. First, I must tell thee this:
Desdemona is directly in love with him.

RODERIGO: With him? Why, 'tis not possible.
240   IAGO: Lay thy finger thus, and let thy soul be instructed.

---

208 Succeeds [...] fate i.e., can follow in the unknown future   **215 s.d. They kiss** (The direction is from the Quarto.)   **218 set down** loosen (and hence untune the instrument)
219 As [...] I am for all my supposed honesty   **223 desired** welcomed   **225 out of fashion** irrelevantly, incoherently (?)   **227 coffers** chests, baggage   **228 master** ship's captain   **230 challenge** lay claim to, deserve   **234 base men** even lowly born men
236 list listen to   **237 court of guard** guardhouse. (Cassio is in charge of the watch.)
240 thus i.e., on your lips

Mark me with what violence she first loved the Moor,
242 but for bragging and telling her fantastical lies. To love
him still for prating? Let not thy discreet heart think it.
Her eye must be fed; and what delight shall she have
to look on the devil? When the blood is made dull with
246 the act of sport, there should be, again to inflame it
247 and to give satiety a fresh appetite, loveliness in favor,
248 sympathy in years, manners, and beauties all which
the Moor is defective in. Now, for want of these
250 required conveniences, her delicate tenderness will
251 find itself abused, begin to heave the gorge, disrelish
252 and abhor the Moor. Very nature will instruct her in it
and compel her to some second choice. Now, sir, this
254 granted—as it is a most pregnant and unforced
255 position—who stands so eminent in the degree of this
256 fortune as Cassio does? A knave very voluble, no
257 further conscionable than in putting on the mere form
258 of civil and humane seeming for the better compass-
259 ing of his salt and most hidden loose affection. Why,
260 none, why, none. A slipper and subtle knave, a finder
261 out of occasions, that has an eye can stamp and
262 counterfeit advantages, though true advantage never
present itself; a devilish knave. Besides, the knave is
handsome, young, and hath all those requisites in him
265 that folly and green minds look after. A pestilent
266 complete knave, and the woman hath found him already.
RODERIGO: I cannot believe that in her. She's full of
268 most blessed condition.
269 IAGO: Blessed fig's end! The wine she drinks is made of
grapes. If she had been blessed, she would never have
271 loved the Moor. Blessed pudding! Didst thou not see
her paddle with the palm of his hand? Didst not mark that?
RODERIGO: Yes, that I did; but that was but courtesy.
274 IAGO: Lechery, by this hand. An index, an obscure prologue to the history of lust and foul thoughts. They
met so near with their lips that their breaths embraced

---

242 **but** only   246 **the act of sport** sex   247 **favor** appearance   248 **sympathy** correspondence, similarity   250 **required conveniences** things conducive to sexual compat-
ibility   251 **abused** cheated, revolted. **heave the gorge** experience nausea   252 **Very**
nature her very instincts   254 **pregnant** evident, cogent   255 **in [...] of** as next in line
for   256 **voluble** facile, glib   257 **conscionable** conscientious, conscience-bound
258 **humane** polite, courteous   259 **salt** licentious. **affection** passion   260 **slipper** slippery   261 **an eye can stamp** an eye that can coin, create   262 **advantages** favorable
opportunities   265 **folly** wantonness. **green** immature   266 **found him** sized him up,
perceived his intent   268 **condition** disposition   269 **fig's end** (See 1.3.341 for the vulgar
gesture of the fig.)   271 **pudding** sausage   274 **index** table of contents. **obscure** (i.e.,
the *lust and foul thoughts*, line 275, are secret, hidden from view)

together. Villainous thoughts, Roderigo! When these
278   mutualities so marshal the way, hard at hand comes
279   the master and main exercise, th' incorporate conclusion. Pish! But, sir, be you ruled by me. I have brought
281   you from Venice. Watch you tonight; for the command,
I'll lay't upon you. Cassio knows you not. I'll not
be far from you. Do you find some occasion to
284   anger Cassio, either by speaking too loud, or tainting
his discipline, or from what other course you please,
286   which the time shall more favorably minister.
RODERIGO: Well.
288 IAGO: Sir, he's rash and very sudden in choler, and haply
may strike at you. Provoke him that he may, for even
290   out of that will I cause these of Cyprus to mutiny,
291   whose qualification shall come into no true taste again
but by the displanting of Cassio. So shall you have a
shorter journey to your desires by the means I shall
294   then have to prefer them, and the impediment most
profitably removed, without the which there were no
expectation of our prosperity.
RODERIGO: I will do this, if you can bring it to any opportunity.
298 IAGO: I warrant thee. Meet me by and by at the citadel.
I must fetch his necessaries ashore. Farewell.
RODERIGO: Adieu. (*Exit.*)
IAGO: That Cassio loves her, I do well believe 't;
302   That she loves him, 'tis apt and of great credit.
The Moor, howbeit that I endure him not,
Is of a constant, loving, noble nature,
And I dare think he'll prove to Desdemona
A most dear husband. Now, I do love her too,
Not out of absolute lust—though peradventure
308   I stand accountant for as great a sin—
309   But partly led to diet my revenge
For that I do suspect the lusty Moor
Hath leaped into my seat, the thought whereof
Doth, like a poisonous mineral, gnaw my innards;
And nothing can or shall content my soul
Till I am evened with him, wife for wife,
Or failing so, yet that I put the Moor

---

278 **mutualities** exchanges, intimacies. **hard at hand** closely following   279 **incorpo-**
rate carnal   281 **Watch you** stand watch   281-282 **for the command [...] you** I'll
arrange for you to be appointed, given orders   284 **tainting** disparaging   286 **minister**
provide   288 **choler** wrath **haply** perhaps   290 **mutiny** riot   291 **qualification**
appeasement. **true taste** i.e., acceptable state   294 **prefer** advance   298 **warrant**
assure. **by and by** immediately   302 **apt** probable. **credit** credibility   308 **accountant**
accountable   309 **diet** feed

At least into a jealousy so strong

That judgment cannot cure. Which thing to do,

318 If this poor trash of Venice, whom I trace

319 For his quick hunting, stand the putting on,

320 I'll have our Michael Cassio on the hip,

321 Abuse him to the Moor in the rank garb—

322 For I fear Cassio with my nightcap too—

Make the Moor thank me, love me, and reward me

For making him egregiously an ass

325 And practicing upon his peace and quiet

Even to madness. 'Tis here, but yet confused.

Knavery's plain face is never seen till used.   (*Exit.*)

2.2

(*Enter Othello's Herald with a proclamation.*)

HERALD: It is Othello's pleasure, our noble and valiant
general, that, upon certain tidings now arrived, im-

3 porting the mere perdition of the Turkish fleet, every

4 man put himself into triumph: some to dance, some to
make bonfires, each man to what sport and revels his

6 addiction leads him. For, besides these beneficial
news, it is the celebration of his nuptial. So much was

8 his pleasure should be proclaimed. All offices are open,
and there is full liberty of feasting from this present
hour of five till the bell have told eleven. Heaven bless
the isle of Cyprus and our noble general Othello!

(*Exit.*)

2.3

(*Enter Othello, Desdemona, Cassio, and attendants.*)

OTHELLO:

Good Michael, look you to the guard tonight.

2 Let's teach ourselves that honorable stop

3 Not to outsport discretion.

---

318 trace i.e., train, or follow (?), or perhaps *trash*, a hunting term, meaning to put
weights on a hunting dog in order to slow him down   **319 For** to make more eager.
stand [...] on respond properly when I incite him to quarrel   **320 on the hip** at my
mercy, where I can throw him. (A wrestling term.)   **321 Abuse** slander. **rank garb**
coarse manner, gross fashion   **322 with my nightcap** i.e., as a rival in my bed, as one
who gives me cuckold's horns   **325 practicing upon** plotting against   **2.2 Location:
Cyprus. A street.   3 mere perdition** complete destruction   **4 triumph** public celebration   **6 addiction** inclination   **8 offices** rooms where food and drink are kept
2.3. Location: Cyprus. The citadel.   2 stop restraint   **3 outsport** celebrate beyond
the bounds of

CASSIO:
Iago hath direction what to do,
But notwithstanding, with my personal eye
Will I look to 't.

OTHELLO: Iago is most honest.
8   Michael, good night. Tomorrow with your earliest
Let me have speech with you. (*To Desdemona.*)
Come, my dear love,
11   The purchase made, the fruits are to ensue;
That profit's yet to come 'tween me and you.—
Good night.

(*Exit [Othello, with Desdemona and attendants].*)

(*Enter Iago.*)

CASSIO: Welcome, Iago. We must to the watch.
15   IAGO: Not this hour, Lieutenant; 'tis not yet ten o' the
16   clock. Our general cast us thus early for the love of his
17   Desdemona; who let us not therefore blame. He hath
          not yet made wanton the night with her, and she is
          sport for Jove.

CASSIO: She's a most exquisite lady.

IAGO: And, I'll warrant her, full of game.

CASSIO: Indeed, she's a most fresh and delicate creature.

23   IAGO: What an eye she has! Me thinks it sounds a parley
          to provocation.

CASSIO: An inviting eye, and yet methinks right modest.

26   IAGO: And when she speaks, is it not an alarum to love?

CASSIO: She is indeed perfection.

IAGO: Well, happiness to their sheets! Come, Lieutenant,
29   I have a stoup of wine, and here without are a brace of
30   Cyprus gallants that would fain have a measure to the
          health of black Othello.

CASSIO: Not tonight, good Iago. I have very poor and un-
          happy brains for drinking. I could well wish courtesy
          would invent some other custom of entertainment.

35   IAGO: O, they are our friends. But one cup! I'll drink for you.

CASSIO: I have drunk but one cup tonight and that was
37   craftily qualified too, and behold what innovation it

---

8 **with your earliest** at your earliest convenience   **11–12 The purchase [...] you** i.e.,
though married, we haven't yet consummated our love   **15 Not this hour** not for an
hour yet   **16 cast** dismissed   **17 who** i.e., Othello   **23 sounds a parley** calls for a conference, issues an invitation   **26 alarum** signal calling men to arms (continuing the military metaphor of *parley,* line 23)   **29 stoup** measure of liquor, two quarts. **without**
outside. **brace** pair   **30 fain have a measure** gladly drink a toast   **35 for you** in your
place. (Iago will do the steady drinking to keep the gallants company while Cassio has
only one cup.)   **37 qualified** diluted. **innovation** disturbance, insurrection

38 makes here. I am unfortunate in the infirmity and
dare not task my weakness with any more.
IAGO: What, man? 'Tis a night of revels. The gallants
desire it.
CASSIO: Where are they?
IAGO: Here at the door. I pray you, call them in.
44 CASSIO: I'll do 't, but it dislikes me.   (*Exit.*)
IAGO: If I can fasten but one cup upon him,
With that which he hath drunk tonight already,
47 He'll be as full of quarrel and offense
As my young mistress' dog. Now, my sick fool Roderigo,
Whom love hath turned almost the wrong side out,
50 To Desdemona hath tonight caroused
51 Potations pottle-deep; and he's to watch.
52 Three lads of Cyprus—noble swelling spirits,
53 That hold their honors in a wary distance,
54 The very elements of this warlike isle—
Have I tonight flustered with flowing cups,
56 And they watch too. Now, 'mongst this flock of drunkards
Am I to put our Cassio in some action
That may offend the isle. But here they come.

(*Enter Cassio, Montano, and gentlemen; [servants following with wine].*)

59 If consequence do but approve my dream,
60 My boat sails freely both with wind and stream.
61 CASSIO: 'Fore God, they have given me a rouse already,
MONTANO: Good faith, a little one; not past a pint, as I am a soldier.
IAGO: Some wine, ho!
65   (*He sings.*) "And let me the cannikin clink, clink,
And let me the cannikin clink.
A soldier's a man,
68   O, man's life's but a span;
Why, then, let a soldier drink."
Some wine, boys!
CASSIO: 'Fore God, an excellent song.
IAGO: I learned it in England, where indeed they are
73 most potent in potting. Your Dane, your German,

---

38 here i.e., in my head   **44 it dislikes me** i.e., I'm reluctant   **47 offense** readiness to take offense   **50 caroused** drunk off   **51 pottle-deep** to the bottom of the tankard. **watch** stand watch   **52 swelling** proud   **53 hold [...] distance** i.e., are extremely sensitive of their honor   **54 very elements** typical sort   **56 watch** are members of the guard **59 If [...] dream** if subsequent events will only substantiate my scheme   **60 stream** current   **61 rouse** full draft of liquor   **65 cannikin** small drinking vessel   **68 span** brief span of time. (Compare Psalm 39:5 as rendered in the Book of Common Prayer: "Thou hast made my days as it were a span long.")   **73 potting** drinking

and your swag-bellied Hollander—drink, ho!—are
nothing to your English.

CASSIO: Is your Englishman so exquisite in his drinking?

77 IAGO: Why, he drinks you, with facility, your Dane

78   dead drunk; he sweats not to overthrow your Almain;
he gives your Hollander a vomit ere the next pottle
can be filled.

CASSIO: To the health of our general!

82 MONTANO: I am for it, Lieutenant, and I'll do you justice.

IAGO: O sweet England!   (*He sings.*)
        "King Stephen was and-a worthy peer,
            His breeches cost him but a crown;
        He held them sixpence all too dear,

87   With that he called the tailor lown.
        He was a wight of high renown,
            And thou art but of low degree.
        'Tis pride that pulls the country down;

91   Then take thy auld cloak about thee."
Some wine, ho!

CASSIO: 'Fore God, this is a more exquisite song than
the other.

IAGO: Will you hear't again?

CASSIO: No, for I hold him to be unworthy of his place
that does those things. Well, God's above all; and
there be souls must be saved, and there be souls must
not be saved.

IAGO: It's true, good Lieutenant.

CASSIO: For mine own part—no offense to the General,

102   nor any man of quality—I hope to be saved.

IAGO: And so do I too, Lieutenant.

CASSIO: Ay, but, by your leave, not before me; the lieutenant is to be saved before the ancient. Let's have no
more of this; let's to our affairs.—God forgive us our
sins!—Gentlemen, let's look to our business. Do not
think, gentlemen, I am drunk. This is my ancient; this
is my right hand, and this is my left. I am not drunk
now. I can stand well enough, and speak well enough.

GENTLEMEN: Excellent well.

CASSIO: Why, very well then; you must not think then
that I am drunk.   (*Exit.*)

MONTANO:

114   To th' platform, masters. Come, let's set the watch.
                    (*Exeunt Gentlemen.*)

---

77 **drinks you** drinks. **your Dane** your typical Dane   78 **sweats not** i.e., need not exert
himself. **Almain** German   82 **I'll [...] justice** i.e., I'll drink as much as you   87 **lown** lout,
rascal   91 **auld** old   102 **quality** rank   114 **set the watch** mount the guard

IAGO:

You see this fellow that is gone before.

He's a soldier fit to stand by Caesar

And give direction; and do but see his vice.

118 'Tis to his virtue a just equinox,

The one as long as the other. 'Tis pity of him.

I fear the trust Othello puts him in,

On some odd time of his infirmity,

Will shake this island.

MONTANO: But is he often thus?

IAGO:

'Tis evermore the prologue to his sleep.

125 He'll watch the horologe a double set,

If drink rock not his cradle.

MONTANO: It were well

The General were put in mind of it.

Perhaps he sees it not, or his good nature

Prizes the virtue that appears in Cassio

And looks not on his evils. Is not this true?

(Enter Roderigo.)

IAGO *(aside to him)*: How now, Roderigo?

I pray you, after the Lieutenant; go.   *(Exit Roderigo.)*

MONTANO:

And 'tis great pity that the noble Moor

135 Should hazard such a place as his own second

136 With one of an engraffed infirmity.

It were an honest action to say so

To the Moor.

IAGO: Not I, for this fair island.

I do love Cassio well and would do much

To cure him of this evil.   *(Cry within:* "Help! Help!"*)*

But, hark! What noise?

142 *(Enter Cassio, pursuing Roderigo.)*

CASSIO: Zounds, you rogue! You rascal!

MONTANO: What's the matter, Lieutenant?

CASSIO: A knave teach me my duty? I'll beat the knave

146 into a twiggen bottle.

RODERIGO: Beat me?

---

118 just equinox exact counterpart. (*Equinox* is an equal length of days and nights.)
125 watch [...] set stay awake twice around the clock or *horologe*   **135–136 hazard [...]
With** risk giving such an important position as his second in command to   **136 engraffed**
engrafted, inveterate   **142 s.d. pursuing** (The Quarto text reads, "driving in.")
146 twiggen wicker-covered. (Cassio vows to assail Roderigo until his skin resembles
wickerwork or until he has driven Roderigo through the holes in a wickerwork.)

CASSIO: Dost thou prate, rogue?   (*He strikes Roderigo.*)

MONTANO: Nay, good Lieutenant.   (*Restraining him.*)

I pray you, sir, hold your hand.

CASSIO: Let me go, sir, or I'll knock you o'er

152   the mazard.

MONTANO: Come, come, you're drunk.

CASSIO: Drunk?   (*They fight.*)

IAGO (*aside to Roderigo*):

155   Away, I say. Go out and cry a mutiny.

(*Exit Roderigo.*)

Nay, good Lieutenant—God's will, gentlemen—

Help, ho!—Lieutenant—sir—Montano—sir—

158   Help, masters!—Here's a goodly watch indeed!

(*A bell rings.*)

159   Who's that which rings the bell?—Diablo, ho!

160   The town will rise. God's will, Lieutenant, hold!

You'll be ashamed forever.

(*Enter Othello and attendants [with weapons].*)

OTHELLO:

What is the matter here?

MONTANO: Zounds, I bleed still.

I am hurt to th' death. He dies! (*He thrusts at Cassio.*)

OTHELLO: Hold, for your lives!

IAGO:

Hold, ho!

Lieutenant—sir—Montano—gentlemen—

Have you forgot all sense of place and duty?

Hold! The General speaks to you. Hold, for shame!

OTHELLO:

Why, how now, ho! From whence ariseth this?

170   Are we turned Turks, and to ourselves do that

Which heaven hath forbid the Ottomites?

For Christian shame, put by this barbarous brawl!

173   He that stirs next to carve for his own rage

174   Holds his soul light; he dies upon his motion.

Silence that dreadful bell. It frights the isle

176   From her propriety. What is the matter, masters?

---

152 **mazard** i.e., head. (Literally, a drinking vessel.)   155 **mutiny** riot   158 **masters** sirs. **s.d. A bell rings** (This direction is from the Quarto, as are *Exit Roderigo* pat line 133, *They fight* at line 154, and *with weapons* at line 161.)   159 **Diablo** the devil   160 **rise** grow riotous   170–171 **to ourselves [...] Ottomites** inflict on ourselves the harm that heaven has prevented the Turks from doing (by destroying their fleet)   173 **carve for** i.e., indulge, satisfy with his sword   174 **Holds [...] light** i.e., places little value on his life. **upon his motion** if he moves   176 **propriety** proper state or condition

Honest Iago, that looks dead with grieving,
Speak. Who began this? On thy love, I charge thee.

IAGO:

I do not know. Friends all but now, even now,
180   In quarter and in terms like bride and groom
181   Devesting them for bed; and then, but now—
As if some planet had unwitted men—
Swords out, and tilting one at others' breasts
184   In opposition bloody. I cannot speak
185   Any beginning to this peevish odds;
And would in action glorious I had lost
Those legs that brought me to a part of it!

OTHELLO:

188   How comes it, Michael, you are thus forgot?

CASSIO: I pray you, pardon me. I cannot speak.

OTHELLO:

190   Worthy Montano, you were wont be civil;
191   The gravity and stillness of your youth
The world hath noted, and your name is great
193   In mouths of wisest censure. What's the matter
194   That you unlace your reputation thus
195   And spend your rich opinion for the name
Of a night-brawler? Give me answer to it.

MONTANO:

Worthy Othello, I am hurt to danger.
Your officer, Iago, can inform you—
199   While I spare speech, which something now offends me—
Of all that I do know; nor know I aught
By me that's said or done amiss this night,
Unless self-charity be sometimes a vice,
And to defend ourselves it be a sin
When violence assails us.

OTHELLO: Now, by heaven,
206   My blood begins my safer guides to rule,
207   And passion, having my best judgment collied,
208   Essays to lead the way. Zounds, if I stir,
Or do but lift this arm, the best of you
Shall sink in my rebuke. Give me to know
211   How this foul rout began, who set it on;

---

180 In quarter in friendly conduct, within bounds. **in terms** on good terms   **181 Devesting them** undressing themselves   **184 speak** explain   **185 peevish odds** childish quarrel   **188 are thus forgot** have forgotten yourself thus   **190 wont** be accustomed to be   **191 stillness** sobriety   **193 censure** judgment   **194 unlace** undo, lay open (as one might loose the strings of a purse containing reputation)   **195 opinion** reputation   **199 something** somewhat. **offends** pains   **206 blood** passion (of anger). **guides** i.e., reason   **207 collied** darkened   **208 Essays** undertakes   **211 rout** riot

212 And he that is approved in this offense,
Though he had twinned with me, both at a birth,
214 Shall lose me. What? In a town of war
Yet wild, the people's hearts brim full of fear,
216 To manage private and domestic quarrel?
217 In night, and on the court and guard of safety?
'Tis monstrous. Iago, who began 't?

MONTANO (*to Iago*):
219 If partially affined, or leagued in office,
Thou dost deliver more or less than truth,
Thou art no soldier.

IAGO: Touch me not so near.
I had rather have this tongue cut from my mouth
Than it should do offense to Michael Cassio;
Yet, I persuade myself, to speak the truth
Shall nothing wrong him. Thus it is, General.
Montano and myself being in speech,
There comes a fellow crying out for help,
And Cassio following him with determined sword
230 To execute upon him. Sir, this gentleman
                    (*indicating Montano*)
231 Steps in to Cassio and entreats his pause.
Myself the crying fellow did pursue,
Lest by his clamor—as it so fell out—
The town might fall in fright. He, swift of foot,
235 Outran my purpose, and I returned, the rather
For that I heard the clink and fall of swords
And Cassio high in oath, which till tonight
I ne'er might say before. When I came back—
For this was brief—I found them close together
At blow and thrust, even as again they were
When you yourself did part them.
More of this matter cannot I report.
243 But men are men; the best sometimes forget.
Though Cassio did some little wrong to him,
245 As men in rage strike those that wish them best,
Yet surely Cassio, I believe, received
From him that fled some strange indignity,
248 Which patience could not pass.

---

212 approved in found guilty of   **214 town of** town garrisoned for   **216 manage**
undertake   **217 on [...] safety** at the main guardhouse or headquarters and on watch
219 partially affined made partial by some personal relationship. **leagued in office** in
league as fellow officers   **230 execute** give effect to (his anger)   **231 his pause** him to
stop   **235 rather** sooner   **243 forget** forget themselves   **245 those [...] best** i.e.,
even those who are well disposed   **248 pass** pass over, overlook

OTHELLO: I know, Iago,
Thy honesty and love doth mince this matter,
Making it light to Cassio. Cassio, I love thee,
But nevermore be officer of mine.

(Enter Desdemona, attended.)

Look if my gentle love be not raised up.
I'll make thee an example.
DESDEMONA:
What is the matter, dear?
OTHELLO: All's well now, sweeting;
Come away to bed. *(To Montano.)* Sir, for your hurts,
258 Myself will be your surgeon.—Lead him off.

(Montano is led off.)

Iago, look with care about the town
And silence those whom this vile brawl distracted.
Come, Desdemona. 'Tis the soldiers' life
To have their balmy slumbers waked with strife.

(Exit [with all but Iago and Cassio].)

IAGO: What, are you hurt, Lieutenant?
CASSIO: Ay, past all surgery.
IAGO: Marry, God forbid!
CASSIO: Reputation, reputation, reputation! O, I have
lost my reputation! I have lost the immortal part of
myself, and what remains is bestial. My reputation,
Iago, my reputation!
IAGO: As I am an honest man, I thought you had
received some bodily wound; there is more sense in
that than in reputation. Reputation is an idle and most
273   false imposition, oft got without merit and lost without deserving. You have lost no reputation at all,
unless you repute yourself such a loser. What, man,
276   there are more ways to recover the General again. You
277   are but now cast in his mood—a punishment more in
278   policy than in malice, even so as one would beat his
279   offenseless dog to affright an imperious lion. Sue to
him again and he's yours.

---

258 **be your surgeon** i.e., make sure you receive medical attention   273 **false imposition** thing artificially imposed and of no real value   276 **recover** regain favor with
277 **cast in his mood** dismissed in a moment of anger   277–278 **in policy** done for
expediency's sake and as a public gesture   278–279 **would [...] lion** i.e., would make an
example of a minor offender in order to deter more important and dangerous offenders
279 **Sue** petition

CASSIO: I will rather sue to be despised than to deceive

282   so good a commander with so slight, so drunken, and

283   so indiscreet an officer. Drunk? And speak parrot?
And squabble? Swagger? Swear? And discourse fustian with one's own shadow? O thou invisible spirit
of wine, if thou hast no name to be known by, let us
call thee devil!

IAGO: What was he that you followed with your sword?
What had he done to you?

CASSIO: I know not.

IAGO: Is 't possible?

CASSIO: I remember a mass of things, but nothing

293   distinctly; a quarrel, but nothing wherefore. O God,
that men should put an enemy in their mouths to steal
away their brains! That we should with joy, pleasance,

296   revel, and applause transform ourselves into beasts!

IAGO: Why, but you are now well enough. How came
you thus recovered?

CASSIO: It hath pleased the devil drunkenness to give
place to the devil wrath. One unperfectness shows me
another, to make me frankly despise myself.

302   IAGO: Come, you are too severe a moraler. As the time,
the place, and the condition of this country stand, I
could heartily wish this had not befallen; but since it is
as it is, mend it for your own good.

CASSIO: I will ask him for my place again; he shall tell

307   me I am a drunkard. Had I as many mouths as Hydra,
such an answer would stop them all. To be now a
sensible man, by and by a fool, and presently a beast!
O, strange! Every inordinate cup is unblessed, and the
ingredient is a devil.

IAGO: Come, come, good wine is a good familiar
creature, if it be well used. Exclaim no more against it.
And, good Lieutenant, I think you think I love you.

315   CASSIO: I have well approved it, sir. I drunk!

316   IAGO: You or any man living may be drunk at a time,
man. I'll tell you what you shall do. Our general's wife

318   is now the general—I may say so in this respect, for
that he hath devoted and given up himself to the

---

282 **slight** worthless   283 **speak parrot** talk nonsense, rant. (*Discourse fustian*, lines
284-285, has much the same meaning.)   293 **wherefore** why   296 **applause** desire for
applause   302 **moraler** moralizer   307 **Hydra** the Lernaean Hydra, a monster with
many heads and the ability to grow two heads when one was cut off, slain by Hercules as
the second of his twelve labors   315 **approved** proved   316 **at a time** at one time or
another   318-319 **in [...] that** in view of this fact, that

320   contemplation, mark, and denotement of her parts
           and graces. Confess yourself freely to her; importune
           her help to put you in your place again. She is of so
323   free, so kind, so apt, so blessed a disposition, she
           holds it a vice in her goodness not to do more than she
           is requested. This broken joint between you and her
326   husband entreat her to splinter; and, my fortunes
327   against any lay worth naming, this crack of your love
           shall grow stronger than it was before.
       CASSIO: You advise me well.
330   IAGO: I protest, in the sincerity of love and honest
           kindness.
332   CASSIO: I think it freely; and betimes in the morning I
           will beseech the virtuous Desdemona to undertake for
334   me. I am desperate of my fortunes if they check me here.
       IAGO: You are in the right. Good night, Lieutenant. I
           must to the watch.
       CASSIO: Good night, Honest Iago.   (*Exit Cassio.*)
       IAGO:
           And what's he then that says I play the villain,
339   When this advice is free I give, and honest,
340   Probal to thinking, and indeed the course
           To win the Moor again? For 'tis most easy
342   Th' inclining Desdemona to subdue
343   In any honest suit; she's framed as fruitful
344   As the free elements. And then for her
           To win the Moor—were't to renounce his baptism,
           All seals and symbols of redeemèd sin—
           His soul is so enfettered to her love
           That she may make, unmake, do what she list,
349   Even as her appetite shall play the god
350   With his weak function. How am I then a villain,
351   To counsel Cassio to this parallel course
352   Directly to his good? Divinity of hell!
353   When devils will the blackest sins put on,
354   They do suggest at first with heavenly shows,

---

320 mark, and denotement (Both words mean "observation.") **parts** qualities
323 free generous   **326 splinter** bind with splints   **327 lay** stake, wager
330 protest insist, declare   **332 freely** unreservedly   **334 check** repulse   **339 free**
(1) free from guile (2) freely given   **340 Probal** probable, reasonable   **342 inclining**
favorably disposed. **subdue** persuade   **343 framed as fruitful** created as generous
344 free elements i.e., earth, air, fire, and water, unrestrained and spontaneous
349 her appetite her desire, or, perhaps, his desire for her   **350 function** exercise of
faculties (weakened by his fondness for her)   **351 parallel** corresponding to these facts
and to his best interests   **352 Divinity of hell** inverted theology of hell (which seduces
the soul to its damnation)   **353 put on** further, instigate   **354 suggest** tempt

As I do now. For whiles this honest fool
Plies Desdemona to repair his fortune,
And she for him pleads strongly to the Moor,
I'll pour this pestilence into his ear,
359   That she repeals him for her body's lust;
And by how much she strives to do him good,
She shall undo her credit with the Moor.
362   So will I turn her virtue into pitch,
And out of her own goodness make the net
That shall enmesh them all.

(Enter Roderigo.)

How now, Roderigo?
RODERIGO: I do follow here in the chase, not like a
367   hound that hunts, but one that fills up the cry. My
money is almost spent; I have been tonight exceedingly well cudgeled; and I think the issue will be I shall
370   have so much experience for my pains, and so,
with no money at all and a little more wit, return again
to Venice.
IAGO:
How poor are they that have not patience!
What wound did ever heal but by degrees?
Thou know'st we work by wit, and not by witchcraft,
And wit depends on dilatory time.
Does't not go well? Cassio hath beaten thee,
378   And thou, by that small hurt, hast cashiered Cassio.
379   Though other things grow fair against the sun,
Yet fruits that blossom first will first be ripe.
Content thyself awhile. By the Mass, 'tis morning!
Pleasure and action make the hours seem short.
Retire thee; go where thou art billeted.
Away, I say! Thou shalt know more hereafter.
Nay, get thee gone.   *(Exit Roderigo.)*
Two things are to be done.
387   My wife must move for Cassio to her mistress;
I'll set her on;
Myself the while to draw the Moor apart
390   And bring him jump when he may Cassio find
Soliciting his wife. Ay, that's the way.
392   Dull not device by coldness and delay.   *(Exit.)*

---

359 repeals him attempts to get him restored   **362 pitch** i.e., (1) foul blackness (2) a
snaring substance   **367 fills up the cry** merely takes part as one of the pack   **370 so**
much just so much and no more   **378 cashiered** dismissed from service   **379–380**
Though [...] ripe i.e., plans that are well prepared and set expeditiously in motion will
soonest ripen into success   **387 move** plead   **390 jump** precisely   **392 device** plot.
coldness lack of zeal

3.1

(Enter Cassio [and] Musicians.)

1   CASSIO: Masters, play here—I will content your pains—
       Something that's brief, and bid "Good morrow, General."
                                              (They play.)

       ([Enter] Clown)

     CLOWN: Why, masters, have your instruments been in
4   Naples, that they speak i' the nose thus?
     A MUSICIAN: How, sir, how?
     CLOWN: Are these, I pray you, wind instruments?
     A MUSICIAN: Ay, marry, are they, sir.
     CLOWN: O, thereby hangs a tail.
     A MUSICIAN: Whereby hangs a tale, sir?
10   CLOWN: Marry, sir, by many a wind instrument that I know.
       But, masters, here's money for you. *(He gives money.)*
       And the General so likes your music that he desires
13   you, for love's sake, to make no more noise with it.
     A MUSICIAN: Well, sir, we will not.
15   CLOWN: If you have any music that may not be heard,
       to 't again; but, as they say, to hear music the General
       does not greatly care.
     A MUSICIAN: We have none such, sir.
19   CLOWN: Then put up your pipes in your bag, for I'll away.
       Go, vanish into air, away!   *(Exeunt Musicians.)*
     CASSIO: Dost thou hear, mine honest friend?
     CLOWN: No, I hear not your honest friend; I hear you.
23   CASSIO: Prithee, keep up thy quillets. There's a poor
       piece of gold for thee. *(He gives money.)* If the gentle-
       woman that attends the General's wife be stirring, tell
26   her there's one Cassio entreats her a little favor of
       speech. Wilt thou do this?
28   CLOWN: She is stirring, sir. If she will stir hither, I
29   shall seem to notify unto her.
     CASSIO:
       Do, good my friend.   *(Exit Clown.)*

**3.1 Location: Before the chamber of Othello and Desdemona.   1 content your
pains** reward your efforts   **4 speak i' the nose** (1) sound nasal (2) sound like one
whose nose has been attacked by syphilis. (Naples was popularly supposed to have a
high incidence of venereal disease.)   **10 wind instrument** (With a joke on flatulence.
The *tail*, line 8, that hangs nearby the *wind instrument* suggests the penis.)   **13 for
love's sake** (1) out of friendship and affection (2) for the sake of lovemaking in Othello's
marriage   **15 may not** cannot   **19 I'll away** (Possibly a misprint, or a snatch of
song?)46   **23 keep up** do not bring out, do not use. **quillets** quibbles, puns   **26-27 a
little [...] speech** the favor of a brief talk   **28 stir** bestir herself (with a play on
stirring, "rousing herself from rest")   **29 seem** deem it good, think fit

(Enter Iago.)

31   In happy time, Iago.

IAGO: You have not been abed, then?

CASSIO: Why, no. The day had broke

Before we parted. I have made bold, Iago,

To send in to your wife. My suit to her

Is that she will to virtuous Desdemona

Procure me some access.

IAGO: I'll send her to you presently;

And I'll devise a means to draw the Moor

Out of the way, that your converse and business

May be more free.

CASSIO:

I humbly thank you for 't.   *(Exit Iago).*

I never knew

44   A Florentine more kind and honest.

(Enter Emilia.)

EMILIA: Good morrow, good Lieutenant. I am sorry

46   For your displeasure; but all will sure be well.

The General and his wife are talking of it,

48   And she speaks for you stoutly. The Moor replies

49   That he you hurt is of great fame in Cyprus

50   And great affinity, and that in wholesome wisdom

51   He might not but refuse you; but he protests he loves you

And needs no other suitor but his likings

53   To take the safest occasion by the front

To bring you in again.

CASSIO: Yet I beseech you,

If you think fit, or that it may be done,

Give me advantage of some brief discourse

With Desdemona alone.

EMILIA: Pray you, come in.

I will bestow you where you shall have time

61   To speak your bosom freely.

CASSIO: I am much bound to you.   *(Exeunt.)*

3.2

(Enter Othello, Iago, and Gentlemen.)

OTHELLO *(giving letters)*: These letters give, Iago, to the pilot,

---

31 In happy time i.e., well met   **44 Florentine** i.e., even a fellow Florentine. (Iago is a
Venetian; Cassio is a Florentine.)   **46 displeasure** fall from favor   **48 stoutly** spirit-
edly   **49 fame** reputation, importance   **50 affinity** kindred, family connection
51 protests insists   **53 occasion [...] front** opportunity by the forelock   **61 bosom**
inmost thoughts   **3.2 Location: The citadel.**

2   And by him do my duties to the Senate.

3   That done, I will be walking on the works;

4   Repair there to me.

IAGO: Well, my good lord, I'll do't.

OTHELLO:

       This fortification, gentlemen, shall we see't?

7 GENTLEMEN: We'll wait upon your lordship.   (*Exeunt.*)

3.3

       (*Enter Desdemona, Cassio, and Emilia.*)

DESDEMONA:

       Be thou assured, good Cassio, I will do
       All my abilities in thy behalf.

EMILIA:

       Good madam, do. I warrant it grieves my husband
       As if the cause were his.

DESDEMONA:

       O, that's an honest fellow. Do not doubt, Cassio,
       But I will have my lord and you again
       As friendly as you were.

CASSIO: Bounteous madam,
       Whatever shall become of Michael Cassio,
       He's never anything but your true servant.

DESDEMONA:

       I know't. I thank you. You do love my lord;
       You have known him long, and be you well assured

13   He shall in strangeness stand no farther off

14   Than in a politic distance.

CASSIO: Ay, but lady,
       That policy may either last so long,

17   Or feed upon such nice and waterish diet,

18   Or breed itself so out of circumstance,

19   That, I being absent and my place supplied,
       My general will forget my love and service.

DESDEMONA:

21   Do not doubt that. Before Emilia here

22   I give thee warrant of thy place. Assure thee,

---

2 do my duties convey my respects   **3 works** breastworks, fortifications   **4 Repair** return, come   **7 wait upon** attend   **3.3 Location: The garden of the citadel.** **13 strangeness** aloofness   **14 politic** required by wise policy   **17 Or [...] diet** or sustain itself at length upon such trivial and meager technicalities   **18 breed [...] circumstance** continually renew itself so out of chance events, or yield so few chances for my being pardoned   **19 supplied** filled by another person   **21 doubt** fear **22 warrant** guarantee

If I do vow a friendship I'll perform it
To the last article. My lord shall never rest.
25   I'll watch him tame and talk him out of patience;
26   His bed shall seem a school, his board a shrift;
I'll intermingle everything he does
With Cassio's suit. Therefore be merry, Cassio,
29   For thy solicitor shall rather die
30   Than give thy cause away.

(Enter Othello and Iago [at a distance].)

EMILIA: Madam, here comes my lord.
CASSIO: Madam, I'll take my leave.
DESDEMONA: Why, stay, and hear me speak.
CASSIO:
    Madam, not now. I am very ill at ease,
    Unfit for mine own purposes.
36   DESDEMONA: Well, do your discretion.   *(Exit Cassio.)*
IAGO: Ha? I like not that.
OTHELLO: What dost thou say?
IAGO:
    Nothing, my lord; or if—I know not what.
OTHELLO: Was not that Cassio parted from my wife?
IAGO:
    Cassio, my lord? No, sure, I cannot think it,
    That he would steal away so guiltylike,
    Seeing you coming.
OTHELLO: I do believe 'twas he.
DESDEMONA: How now, my lord?
    I have been talking with a suitor here.
    A man that languishes in your displeasure.
OTHELLO: Who is 't you mean?
DESDEMONA:
    Why, your lieutenant, Cassio. Good my lord,
    If I have any grace or power to move you,
51   His present reconciliation take;
    For if he be not one that truly loves you,
53   That errs in ignorance and not in cunning,
    I have no judgment in an honest face.
    I prithee, call him back.
OTHELLO: Went he hence now?
DESDEMONA: Yes, faith, so humbled
    That he hath left part of his grief with me

---

25 watch him tame tame him by keeping him from sleeping (A term from falconry.) **out of patience** past his endurance   **26 board** dining table. **shrift** confessional   **29 solicitor** advocate   **30 away** up   **36 do your discretion** act according to your own discretion   **51 His [...] take** let him be reconciled to you right away   **53 in cunning** wittingly

To suffer with him. Good love, call him back.

OTHELLO:

Not now, sweet Desdemon. Some other time.

DESDEMONA: But shall 't be shortly?

OTHELLO: The sooner, sweet, for you.

DESDEMONA: Shall 't be tonight at supper?

OTHELLO: No, not tonight.

65 DESDEMONA: Tomorrow dinner, then?

OTHELLO: I shall not dine at home.

I meet the captains at the citadel.

DESDEMONA:

Why, then, tomorrow night, or Tuesday morn,
Or Tuesday noon, or night, or Wednesday morn.
I prithee, name the time, but let it not
Exceed three days. I' faith, he's penitent;

72 And yet his trespass, in our common reason—
73 Save that, they say, the wars must make example
74 Out of her best—is not almost a fault
75 T'incur a private check. When shall he come?
Tell me, Othello. I wonder in my soul
What you would ask me that I should deny,

78 Or stand so mammering on. What? Michael Cassio,
That came a-wooing with you, and so many a time,
When I have spoke of you dispraisingly,
Hath ta'en your part—to have so much to do

82 To bring him in! By 'r Lady, I could do much—

OTHELLO:

Prithee, no more. Let him come when he will;
I will deny thee nothing.

DESDEMONA: Why, this is not a boon.

'Tis as I should entreat you wear your gloves,
Or feed on nourishing dishes, or keep you warm,

88 Or sue to you to do a peculiar profit
To your own person. Nay, when I have a suit

90 Wherein I mean to touch your love indeed,
91 It shall be full of poise and difficult weight,
And fearful to be granted.

OTHELLO: I will deny thee nothing.

94 Whereon, I do beseech thee, grant me this,
To leave me but a little to myself.

---

65 dinner (the noontime meal)   **72 common reason** everyday judgments   **73-74 Save
[...] best** were it not that, as the saying goes, military discipline requires making an
example of the very best men. (*Her* refers to *wars* as a singular concept.)   **74 not
almost** scarcely   **75 a private check** even a private reprimand   **78 mammering
on** wavering about   **82 bring him in** restore him to favor   **88 peculiar** particular, personal   **90 touch** test   **91 poise** weight, heaviness; or equipoise, delicate balance involving hard choice   **94 Whereon** in return for which

DESDEMONA:

    Shall I deny you? No. Farewell, my lord.

OTHELLO:

97   Farewell, my Desdemona. I'll come to thee straight.

DESDEMONA:

98   Emilia, come.—Be as your fancies teach you;

    Whate'er you be, I am obedient.   (*Exit [with Emilia].*)

OTHELLO:

100   Excellent wretch! Perdition catch my soul

101   But I do love thee! And when I love thee not,

    Chaos is come again.

IAGO: My noble lord—

OTHELLO: What doest thou say, Iago?

IAGO:

    Did Michael Cassio, when you wooed my lady,

    Know of your love?

OTHELLO:

    He did, from first to last. Why dost thou ask?

IAGO:

    But for a satisfaction of my thought;

    No further harm.

OTHELLO: Why of thy thought, Iago?

IAGO:

    I did not think he had been acquainted with her.

OTHELLO:

    O, yes, and went between us very oft.

IAGO: Indeed?

OTHELLO:

    Indeed? Ay, indeed. Discern'st thou aught in that? Is he not honest?

IAGO: Honest, my lord?

OTHELLO: Honest. Ay, honest?

IAGO: My lord, for aught I know.

OTHELLO: What dost thou think?

IAGO: Think, my lord?

OTHELLO:

    "Think, my lord?" By heaven, thou echo'st me,

    As if there were some monster in thy thought

    Too hideous to be shown. Thou dost mean something.

    I heard thee say even now, thou lik'st not that,

    When Cassio left my wife. What didst not like?

125   And when I told thee he was of my counsel

---

97 straight straightway   **98 fancies** inclinations   **100 wretch** (A term of affectionate endearment.)   **101–102 And [...] again,** i.e., my love for you will last forever, until the end of time when chaos will return. (But with an unconscious, ironic suggestion that, if anything should induce Othello to cease loving Desdemona, the result would be chaos.)   **125 of my counsel** in my confidence

In my whole course of wooing, thou criedst "Indeed?"

127 And didst contract and purse thy brow together
And didst contract and purse thy brow together
As if thou then hadst shut up in thy brain

129 Some horrible conceit. If thou dost love me,
Show me thy thought.

IAGO: My lord, you know I love you.

OTHELLO: I think thou dost;

133 And for I know thou'rt full of love and honesty,
And weigh'st thy words before thou giv'st them breath,

135 Therefore these stops of thine fright me the more;
For such things in a false disloyal knave

137 Are tricks of custom, but in a man that's just

138 They're close dilations, working from the heart

139 That passion cannot rule.

140 IAGO: For Michael Cassio,
I dare be sworn I think that he is honest.

OTHELLO:
I think so too.

IAGO: Men should be what they seem;

144 Or those that be not, would they might seem none!

OTHELLO:
Certain, men should be what they seem.

IAGO:
Why, then, I think Cassio's an honest man.

OTHELLO: Nay, yet there's more in this.
I prithee, speak to me as to thy thinkings,
As thou dost ruminate, and give thy worst of thoughts
The worst of words.

IAGO: Good my lord, pardon me.
Though I am bound to every act of duty,

153 I am not bound to that all slaves are free to.
Utter my thoughts? Why, say they are vile and false,
As where's that palace where into foul things
Sometimes intrude not? Who has that breast so pure
But some uncleanly apprehensions

158 Keep leets and law days, and in sessions sit

159 With meditations lawful?

OTHELLO:

160 Thou dost conspire against thy friend, Iago,

---

127 purse knit   **129 conceit** fancy   **133 for** because   **135 stops** pauses   **137 of custom** customary   **138 close dilations** secret or involuntary expressions or delays   **139 That passion cannot rule** i.e., that are too passionately strong to be restrained (referring to the workings), or, that cannot rule its own passions (referring to the heart).   **140 For** as for   **144 none** i.e., not to be men, or not seem to be honest   **153 that** that which. **free to** free with respect to   **158 Keep leets and law days** i.e., hold court, set up their authority in one's heart. (*Leets* are a kind of manor court; *law days* are the days courts sit in session, or those sessions.)   **159 With** along with. **lawful** innocent   **160 thy friend** i.e., Othello

If thou but think'st him wronged and mak'st his ear
A stranger to thy thoughts.

IAGO: I do beseech you,
164   Though I perchance am vicious in my guess—
As I confess it is my nature's plague
166   To spy into abuses, and oft my jealousy
167   Shapes faults that are not—that your wisdom then,
168   From one that so imperfectly conceits,
Would take no notice, nor build yourself a trouble
170   Out of his scattering and unsure observance.
It were not for your quiet nor your good,
Nor for my manhood, honesty, and wisdom,
To let you know my thoughts.

OTHELLO: What dost thou mean?

IAGO:
Good name in man and woman, dear my lord,
176   Is the immediate jewel of their souls.
Who steals my purse steals trash; 'tis something, nothing;
'Twas mine, 'tis his, and has been slave to thousands;
But he that filches from me my good name
Robs me of that which not enriches him
And makes me poor indeed.

OTHELLO: By heaven, I'll know thy thoughts.

IAGO:
183   You cannot, if my heart were in your hand,
Nor shall not, whilst 'tis in my custody.

OTHELLO: Ha?

IAGO: O, beware, my lord, of jealousy.
187   It is the green-eyed monster which doth mock
The meat it feeds on. That cuckold lives in bliss
189   Who, certain of his fate, loves not his wronger;
190   But O, what damnèd minutes tells he o'er
Who dotes, yet doubts, suspects, yet fondly loves!

OTHELLO: O misery!

193   IAGO: Poor and content is rich, and rich enough,
194   But riches fineless is as poor as winter
To him that ever fears he shall be poor.
Good God, the souls of all my tribe defend

---

164 vicious wrong   **166 jealousy** suspicious nature   **167 then** on that account
168 one i.e., myself, Iago. **conceits** judges, conjectures   **170 scattering** random
176 immediate essential, most precious   **183 if** even if   **187–188 doth mock [...] on**
mocks and torments the heart of its victim, the man who suffers jealousy   **189 his
wronger** i.e., his faithless wife. (The unsuspecting cuckold is spared the misery of loving
his wife only to discover she is cheating on him.)   **190 tells** counts   **193 Poor [...]
enough** to be content with what little one has is the greatest wealth of all. (Proverbial.)
194 fineless boundless

From jealousy!

OTHELLO: Why, why is this?
Think'st thou I'd make a life of jealousy,
200 To follow still the changes of the moon
With fresh suspicions? No! To be once in doubt
202 Is once to be resolved. Exchange me for a goat
When I shall turn the business of my soul
204 To such exsufflicate and blown surmises
205 Matching thy inference. 'Tis not to make me jealous
To say my wife is fair, feeds well, loves company,
Is free of speech, sings, plays, and dances well;
Where virtue is, these are more virtuous.
Nor from mine own weak merits will I draw
210 The smallest fear or doubt of her revolt,
For she had eyes, and chose me. No, Iago,
I'll see before I doubt; when I doubt, prove;
And on the proof, there is no more but this—
Away at once with love or jealousy.

IAGO:
I am glad of this, for now I shall have reason
To show the love and duty that I bear you
With franker spirit. Therefore, as I am bound,
Receive it from me. I speak not yet of proof.
Look to your wife; observe her well with Cassio.
220 Wear your eyes thus, not jealous nor secure.
I would not have your free and noble nature,
222 Out of self-bounty, be abused. Look to 't.
I know our country disposition well;
In Venice they do let God see the pranks
They dare not show their husbands; their best conscience
Is not to leave 't undone, but keep 't unknown.

OTHELLO: Dost thou say so?

IAGO:
She did deceive her father, marrying you;
And when she seemed to shake and fear your looks,
She loved them most.

OTHELLO: And so she did.

232 IAGO: Why, go to, then!

200–201 To follow [...] suspicions to be constantly imagining new causes for suspicion, changing incessantly like the moon   **202 once** once and for all. **resolved** free of doubt, having settled the matter   **204 exsufflicate and blown** inflated and blown up, rumored about, or spat out and fly-blown, hence loathsome, disgusting   **205 inference** description or allegation   **210 doubt [...] revolt** fear of her unfaithfulness   **220 not** neither. **secure** free from uncertainty   **222 self-bounty** inherent or natural goodness and generosity. **abused** deceived   **232 go to** (An expression of impatience.)

233   She that, so young, could give out such a seeming,
234   To seel her father's eyes up close as oak,
      He thought 'twas witchcraft! But I am much to blame.
      I humbly do beseech you of your pardon
      For too much loving you.
238   OTHELLO: I am bound to thee forever.
      IAGO:
      I see this hath a little dashed your spirits.
      OTHELLO: Not a jot, not a jot.
      IAGO: I' faith, I fear it has.
      I hope you will consider what is spoke
      Comes from my love. But I do see you're moved.
      I am to pray you not to strain my speech
245   To grosser issues nor to larger reach
      Than to suspicion.
      OTHELLO: I will not.
      IAGO: Should you do so, my lord,
249   My speech should fall into such vile success
      Which my thoughts aimed not. Cassio's my worthy friend.
      My lord, I see you're moved.
      OTHELLO: No, not much moved.
253   I do not think but Desdemona's honest.
      IAGO:
      Long live she so! And long live you to think so!
      OTHELLO:
      And yet, how nature erring from itself—
      IAGO:
      Ay, there's the point! As—to be bold with you—
257   Not to affect many proposèd matches
258   Of her own clime, complexion, and degree,
      Whereto we see in all things nature tends—
260   Foh! One may smell in such a will most rank,
261   Foul disproportion, thoughts unnatural.
262   But pardon me. I do not in position
      Distinctly speak of her, though I may fear
264   Her will, recoiling to her better judgment,
265   May fall to match you with her country forms
266   And happily repent.

---

233 seeming false appearance   **234 seel** blind. (A term from falconry.) **oak** (A close-grained wood.)   **238 bound** indebted (but perhaps with ironic sense of "tied")   **245 issues** significance. **reach** meaning, scope   **249 success** effect, result   **253 honest** chaste   **257 affect** prefer, desire   **258 clime [...] degree** country, color, and social position   **260 will** sensuality, appetite   **261 disproportion** abnormality   **262 position** argument, proposition   **264 recoiling** reverting. **better** i.e., more natural and reconsidered   **265 fall [...] forms** undertake to compare you with Venetian norms of handsomeness   **266 happily repent** haply repent her marriage

OTHELLO: Farewell, farewell!
    If more thou dost perceive, let me know more.
    Set on thy wife to observe. Leave me, Iago.
IAGO (*going*): My lord, I take my leave.
OTHELLO:
    Why did I marry? This honest creature doubtless
    Sees and knows more, much more, than he unfolds.
IAGO (*returning*):
    My Lord, I would I might entreat your honor
274   To scan this thing no farther. Leave it to time.
    Although 'tis fit that Cassio have his place—
    For, sure, he fills it up with great ability—
    Yet, if you please to hold him off awhile,
278   You shall by that perceive him and his means.
279   Note if your lady strain his entertainment
    With any strong or vehement importunity;
    Much will be seen in that. In the meantime,
282   Let me be thought too busy in my fears—
    As worthy cause I have to fear I am—
284   And hold her free, O do beseech your honor.
285 OTHELLO: Fear not my government.
    IAGO: I once more take my leave.   (*Exit.*)
    OTHELLO:
    This fellow's of exceeding honesty,
288   And knows all qualities, with a learnèd spirit,
289   Of human dealings. If I do prove her haggard,
290   Though that her jesses were my dear heartstrings,
291   I'd whistle her off and let her down the wind
292   To prey at fortune. Haply, for I am black
293   And have not those soft parts of conversation
294   That chamberers have, or for I am declined
    Into the vale of years—yet that's not much—
296   She's gone. I am abused, and my relief
    Must be to loathe her. O curse of marriage,
    That we can call these delicate creatures ours
    And not their appetites! I had rather be a toad
    And live upon the vapor of a dungeon
    Than keep a corner in the thing I love
    For others' uses. Yet, 'tis the plague of great ones;

---

274 scan scrutinize   **278 his means** the method he uses (to regain his post)   **279 strain his entertainment** urge his reinstatement   **282 busy** interfering   **284 hold her free** regard her as innocent   **285 government** self-control, conduct   **288 qualities** natures, types   **289 haggard** wild (like a wild female hawk)   **290 jesses** straps fastened around the legs of a trained hawk   **291 I'd [...] wind** i.e., I'd let her go forever. (To release a hawk downwind was to invite it not to return.)   **292 prey at fortune** fend for herself in the wild. **Haply, for** perhaps, because   **293 soft [...] conversation** pleasing graces of social behavior   **294 chamberers** gallants   **296 abused** deceived

303   Prerogatived are they less than the base.
       'Tis destiny unshunnable, like death.
305   Even then this forkèd plague is fated to us
306   When we do quicken. Look where she comes.

(Enter Desdemona and Emilia.)

If she be false, O, then heaven mocks itself!
I'll not believe 't.
DESDEMONA: How now, my dear Othello?
310   Your dinner, and the generous islanders
311   By you invited, do attend your presence.
OTHELLO:
I am to blame.
DESDEMONA: Why do you speak so faintly?
Are you not well?
OTHELLO:
I have a pain upon my forehead here.
DESDEMONA:
316   Faith, that's with watching. 'Twill away again.

(She offers her handkerchief.)

Let me but bind it hard, within this hour
It will be well.
319   OTHELLO: Your napkin is too little.
320   Let it alone. Come, I'll go in with you.

(He puts the handkerchief from him, and it drops.)

DESDEMONA:
I am very sorry that you are not well.

(Exit [with Othello].)

EMILIA *(picking up the handkerchief)*: I am glad I have found this napkin.
This was her first remembrance from the Moor.
324   My wayward husband hath a hundred times
Wooed me to steal it, but she so loves the token—
For he conjured her she should ever keep it—
That she reserves it evermore about her
328   To kiss and talk to. I'll have the work ta'en out,

---

303 Prerogatived privileged (to have honest wives). **the base** ordinary citizens.
(Socially prominent men are especially prone to the unavoidable destiny of being cuckolded and to the public shame that goes with it.)   **305 forkèd** (An allusion to the horns
of the cuckold.)   **306 quicken** receive life. (*Quicken* may also mean to swarm with maggots as the body festers, as in 4.2.76, in which case lines 305-306 suggest that *even then*, in
death, we are cuckolded by *forkèd* worms.)   **310 generous** noble   **311 attend** await
316 watching too little sleep   **319 napkin** handkerchief   **320 Let it alone** i.e., never
mind   **324 wayward** capricious   **328 work ta'en out** design of the embroidery copied

And give 't Iago. What he will do with it
Heaven knows, not I;
331   I nothing but to please his fantasy.

(Enter Iago.)

IAGO:
How now? What do you here alone?
EMILIA:
Do not you chide. I have a thing for you.
IAGO:
334   You have a thing for me? It is a common thing-
EMILIA: Ha?
IAGO: To have a foolish wife.
EMILIA:
O, is that all? What will you give me now
For that same handkerchief?
IAGO: What handkerchief?
EMILIA: What handkerchief?
Why, that the Moor first gave to Desdemona;
That which so often you did bid me steal.
IAGO: Hast stolen it from her?
EMILIA:
No, faith. She let it drop by negligence,
345   And to th' advantage, I, being here, took 't up.
Look, here 'tis.
IAGO: A good wench! Give it me.
EMILIA: What will you do with 't, that you have been so earnest
To have me filch it?
IAGO (*snatching it*): Why, what is that to you?
EMILIA:
If it be not for some purpose of import,
Give 't me again. Poor lady, she'll run mad
353   When she shall lack it.
354   IAGO: Be not acknown on 't.
I have use for it. Go, leave me. (*Exit Emilia.*)
356   I will in Cassio's lodging lose this napkin
And let him find it. Trifles light as air
Are to the jealous confirmations strong
As proofs of Holy Writ. This may do something.
The Moor already changes with my poison.
361   Dangerous conceits are in their natures poisons,

---

331 fantasy whim   **334 common thing** (With bawdy suggestion; *common* suggests coarseness and availability to all comers, and *thing* is a slang term for the pudendum.) **345 to th' advantage** taking the opportunity   **353 lack** miss   **354 Be [...] on 't** do not confess knowledge of it   **356 lose** (The Folio spelling, *loose*, is a normal spelling for "lose," but may also contain the idea of "let go," "release.")   **361 conceits** fancies, ideas

362   Which at the first are scarce found to distaste,
363   But with a little act upon the blood
Burn like the mines of sulfur.

(Enter Othello.)

I did say so.
366   Look where he comes! Not poppy nor mandragora
Nor all the drowsy syrups of the world
Shall ever medicine thee to that sweet sleep
369   Which thou owedst yesterday.
OTHELLO: Ha, ha, false to me?
IAGO:
Why, how now, General? No more of that.
OTHELLO:
Avaunt! Begone! Thou hast set me on the rack.
I swear 'tis better to be much abused
Than but to know 't a little.
IAGO: How now, my lord?
OTHELLO:
What sense had I of her stolen hours of lust?
I saw 't not, thought it not, it harmed not me.
378   I slept the next night well, fed well, was free and merry;
I found not Cassio's kisses on her lips.
380   He that is robbed, not wanting what is stolen,
Let him not know 't and he's not robbed at all.
IAGO: I am sorry to hear this.
OTHELLO:
I had been happy if the general camp,
384   Pioners and all, had tasted her sweet body,
385   So I had nothing known. O, now, forever
Farewell the tranquil mind! Farewell content!
387   Farewell the plumèd troops and the big wars
That makes ambition virtue! Oh, farewell!
Farewell the neighing steed and the shrill trump,
The spirit-stirring drum, th' ear-piercing fife,
391   The royal banner, and all quality,
392   Pride, pomp, and circumstance of glorious war!
393   And O, you mortal engines, whose rude throats
394   Th' immortal Jove's dread clamors counterfeit,
Farewell! Othello's occupation's gone.

---

362 **distaste** be distasteful   363 **act** action, working   366 **mandragora** an opiate
made of the mandrake root   369 **thou owedst** you did own   378 **free** carefree
380 **wanting** missing   384 **Pioners** diggers of mines, the lowest grade of soldiers
385 **So** provided   387 **big** stately   391 **quality** character, essential nature   392 **Pride**
rich display. **circumstance** pageantry   393 **mortal engines** i.e., cannon. (*Mortal* means
"deadly.")   394 **Jove's dread clamors** i.e., thunder

IAGO: Is 't possible, my lord?

OTHELLO:

> Villain, be sure thou prove my love a whore!
> Be sure of it. Give me the ocular proof,
> Or, by the worth of mine eternal soul,
> Thou hadst been better have been born a dog
> Than answer my waked wrath!

IAGO: Is 't come to this?

OTHELLO:

> Make me to see 't, or at least so prove it
404 That the probation bear no hinge nor loop
> To hang a doubt on, or woe upon thy life!

IAGO: My noble lord—

OTHELLO:

> If thou dost slander her and torture me,
408 Never pray more; abandon all remorse;
409 On horror's head horrors accumulate;
410 Do deeds to make heaven weep, all earth amazed;
> For nothing canst thou to damnation add
> Greater than that.

IAGO: O grace! O heaven forgive me!

> Are you a man? Have you a soul or sense?
415 God b' wi' you; take mine office. O wretched fool,
416 That lov'st to make thine honesty a vice!
> O monstrous world! Take note, take note, O world,
> To be direct and honest is not safe.
419 I thank you for this profit, and from hence
420 I'll love no friend, sith love breeds such offense.

421 OTHELLO: Nay, stay. Thou shouldst be honest.

IAGO:

> I should be wise, for honesty's a fool
> And loses that it works for.

OTHELLO: By the world,

> I think my wife be honest and think she is not;
426 I think that thou art just and think thou are not.
> I'll have some proof. My name, that was as fresh
428 As Dian's visage, is now begrimed and black
> As mine own face. If there be cords, or knives,
> Poison, or fire, or suffocating streams,

---

404 probation proof   **408 remorse** pity, penitent hope for salvation   **409 horrors accumulate** add still more horrors   **410 amazed** confounded with horror   **415 O wretched fool** (Iago addresses himself as a fool for having carried honesty too far.)   **416 vice** failing, something overdone   **419 profit** profitable instruction. **hence** henceforth   **420 sith** since. **offense** i.e., harm to the one who offers help and friendship   **421 Thou shouldst be** It appears that you are. (But Iago replies in the sense of "ought to be.")   **426 that** what   **428 Dian** Diana, goddess of the moon and of chastity

I'll not endure it. Would I were satisfied!

IAGO:

    I see, sir, you are eaten up with passion.

    I do repent me that I put it to you.

    You would be satisfied?

OTHELLO: Would? Nay, and I will.

IAGO:

    And may; but how? How satisfied, my lord?

437   Would you, the supervisor, grossly gape on?

    Behold her topped?

OTHELLO: Death and damnation! O!

IAGO:

    It were a tedious difficulty, I think,

441   To bring them to that prospect. Damn them then,

442   If ever mortal eyes do see them bolster

443   More than their own. What then? How then?

    What shall I say? Where's satisfaction?

    It is impossible you should see this,

446   Were they as prime as goats, as hot as monkeys,

447   As salt as wolves in pride, and fools as gross

    As ignorance made drunk. But yet I say,

449   If imputation and strong circumstances

    Which lead directly to the door of truth

    Will give you satisfaction, you might have 't.

OTHELLO:

    Give me a living reason she's disloyal.

IAGO: I do not like the office.

454   But sith I am entered in this cause so far,

455   Pricked to 't by foolish honesty and love,

    I will go on. I lay with Cassio lately,

    And being troubled with a raging tooth

    I could not sleep. There are a kind of men

    So loose of soul that in their sleeps will mutter

    Their affairs. One of this kind is Cassio.

    In sleep I heard him say, "Sweet Desdemona,

    Let us be wary, let us hide our loves!"

    And then, sir, would he grip and wring my hand,

    Cry "O sweet creature!", then kiss me hard,

    As if he plucked up kisses by the roots

    That grew upon my lips; then laid his leg

    Over my thigh, and sighed, and kissed, and then

---

437 **supervisor** onlooker   441 **Damn them then** i.e., they would have to be really incorrigible   442 **bolster** go to bed together, share a bolster   443 **More** other. **own** own eyes   446 **prime** lustful   447 **salt** wanton, sensual. **pride** heat   449 **imputation** [...] **circumstances** strong circumstantial evidence   454 **sith** since   455 **Pricked** spurred

Cried, "Cursèd fate that gave thee to the Moor!"

OTHELLO:

O monstrous! Monstrous!

IAGO: Nay, this was but his dream.

OTHELLO:

471 But this denoted a foregone conclusion.

472 'Tis a shrewd doubt, though it be but a dream.

IAGO:

And this may help to thicken other proofs

That do demonstrate thinly.

OTHELLO: I'll tear her all to pieces.

IAGO:

Nay, but be wise. Yet we see nothing done;

She may be honest yet. Tell me but this:

Have you not sometimes seen a handkerchief

479 Spotted with strawberries in your wife's hand?

OTHELLO:

I gave her such a one. 'Twas my first gift.

IAGO:

I know not that; but such a handkerchief—

I am sure it was your wife's—did I today

See Cassio wipe his beard with.

OTHELLO: If it be that—

IAGO:

If it be that, or any that was hers,

It speaks against her with the other proofs.

OTHELLO:

487 O, that the slave had forty thousand lives!

One is too poor, too weak for my revenge.

Now do I see 'tis true. Look here, Iago,

490 All my fond love thus do I blow to heaven.

'Tis gone.

Arise, black vengeance, from the hollow hell!

493 Yield up, O love, thy crown and hearted throne

494 To tyrannous hate! Swell, bosom, with thy freight,

495 For 'tis of aspics' tongues!

496 IAGO: Yet be content.

OTHELLO: O, blood, blood, blood!

IAGO:

Patience, I say. Your mind perhaps may change.

----

471 foregone conclusion concluded experience or action   **472 shrewd doubt** suspicious circumstance   **479 Spotted with strawberries** embroidered with a strawberry pattern   **487 the slave** i.e., Cassio   **490 fond** foolish (but also suggesting "affectionate")   **493 hearted** fixed in the heart   **494 freight** burden   **495 aspics'** venomous serpents'   **496 content** calm

OTHELLO:

499   Never, Iago. Like to the Pontic Sea,
        Whose icy current and compulsive course
        Ne'er feels retiring ebb, but keeps due on
502   To the Propontic and the Hellespont,
        Even so my bloody thoughts with violent pace
        Shall ne'er look back, ne'er ebb to humble love,
505   Till that a capable and wide revenge
506   Swallow them up. Now, by yond marble heaven,
        (*Kneeling*) In the due reverence of a sacred vow
        I here engage my words.

IAGO: Do not rise yet.

510   (*He kneels.*) Witness, you ever-burning lights above,
511   You elements that clip us round about,
        Witness that here Iago doth give up
513   The execution of his wit, hands, heart,
        To wronged Othello's service. Let him command,
515   And to obey shall be in me remorse,
516   What bloody business ever.   (*They rise.*)

OTHELLO: I greet thy love,
        Not with vain thanks, but with acceptance bounteous,
519   And will upon the instant put thee to 't.
        Within these three days let me hear thee say
        That Cassio's not alive.

IAGO: My friend is dead;
        'Tis done at your request. But let her live.

OTHELLO:

524   Damn her, lewd minx! O, damn her, damn her!
        Come, go with me apart. I will withdraw
        To furnish me with some swift means of death
        For the fair devil. Now art thou my lieutenant.

IAGO: I am your own forever.   (*Exeunt.*)

3.4

(*Enter Desdemona, Emilia, and Clown.*)

1   DESDEMONA: Do you know, sirrah, where Lieutenant
2   Cassio lies?

---

499 Pontic Sea Black Sea   **502 Propontic** Sea of Marmora, between the Black Sea and the Aegean. **Hellespont** Dardanelles, straits where the Sea of Marmora joins with the Aegean   **505 capable** ample, comprehensive   **506 marble** i.e., gleaming like marble and unrelenting   **510 s.d. He kneels** (In the Quarto text, Iago kneels here after Othello has knelt at line 506.)   **511 clip** encompass   **513 execution** exercise, action. **wit** mind   **515 remorse** pity (for Othello's wrongs)   **516 ever** soever   **519 to 't** to the proof   **524 minx** wanton   **3.4. Location: Before the citadel.**   **1 sirrah** (A form of address to an inferior.)   **2 lies** lodges. (But the Clown makes the obvious pun.)

CLOWN: I dare not say he lies anywhere.

DESDEMONA: Why, man?

CLOWN: He's a soldier, and for me to say a soldier lies, 'tis stabbing.

DESDEMONA: Go to. Where lodges he?

CLOWN: To tell you where he lodges is to tell you where I lie.

DESDEMONA: Can anything be made of this?

11 CLOWN: I know not where he lodges, and for me to devise a lodging and say he lies here, or he lies there, were to lie in mine own throat.

DESDEMONA: Can you inquire him out, and be edified by report?

CLOWN: I will catechize the world for him; that is, make questions, and by them answer.

16 DESDEMONA: Seek him, bid him come hither. Tell him I have moved my lord on his behalf and hope all will be well.

CLOWN: To do this is within the compass of man's wit, and therefore I will attempt the doing it. (*Exit Clown.*)

DESDEMONA:
    Where should I lose that handkerchief, Emilia?

EMILIA: I know not, madam.

DESDEMONA:
    Believe me, I had rather have lost my purse
23   Full of crusadoes; and but my noble Moor
    Is true of mind and made of no such baseness
    As jealous creatures are, it were enough
    To put him to ill thinking.

EMILIA: Is he not jealous?

DESDEMONA:
    Who, he? I think the sun where he was born
29   Drew all such humors from him.

EMILIA   Look where he comes.

    (*Enter Othello.*)

DESDEMONA:
    I will not leave him now till Cassio
    Be called to him. How is 't with you, my lord?

OTHELLO:
    Well, my good lady. (*Aside.*) O, hardness to dissemble!—
    How do you, Desdemona?

DESDEMONA: Well, my good lord.

OTHELLO:
    Give me your hand. (*She gives her hand.*) This hand is moist, my

---

11 lie [...] throat (1) lie egregiously and deliberately (2) use the windpipe to speak a lie **16 moved** petitioned **23 crusadoes** Portuguese gold coins **29 humors** (Refers to the four bodily fluids thought to determine temperament.)

lady.

DESDEMONA: It yet hath felt no age nor known no sorrow.

39 OTHELLO: This argues fruitfulness and liberal heart.

Hot, hot, and moist. This hand of yours requires

41 A sequester from liberty, fasting and prayer,

42 Much castigation, exercise devout;

For here's a young and sweating devil here

That commonly rebels. 'Tis a good hand,

45 A frank one.

DESDEMONA: You may indeed say so,

For 'twas that hand that gave away my heart.

OTHELLO:

48 A liberal hand. The hearts of old gave hands,

49 But our new heraldry is hands, not hearts.

DESDEMONA:

I cannot speak of this. Come now, your promise.

51 OTHELLO: What promise, chuck?

DESDEMONA:

I have sent to bid Cassio come speak with you.

OTHELLO:

53 I have a salt and sorry rheum offends me;

Lend me thy handkerchief.

DESDEMONA: Here, my lord. (*She offers a handkerchief.*)

OTHELLO:

That which I gave you.

DESDEMONA: I have it not about me.

OTHELLO: Not?

DESDEMONA: No, faith, my lord.

OTHELLO:

That's a fault. That handkerchief

Did an Egyptian to my mother give.

62 She was a charmer, and could almost read

The thoughts of people. She told her, while she kept it

'Twould make her amiable and subdue my father

Entirely to her love, but if she lost it

Or made a gift of it, my father's eye

Should hold her loathèd and his spirits should hunt

68 After new fancies. She, dying, gave it me,

---

39 argues gives evidence of. **fruitfulness** generosity, amorousness, and fecundity. **liberal** generous and sexually free   **41 sequester** separation, sequestration   **42 castigation** corrective discipline. **exercise devout** i.e., prayer, religious meditation, etc.   **45 frank** generous, open (with sexual suggestion)   **48 The hearts [...] hands** i.e., in former times, people would give their hearts when they gave their hands to something   **49 But [...] hearts** i.e., in our decadent times, the joining of hands is no longer a badge to signify the giving of hearts   **51 chuck** (A term of endearment.)   **53 salt [...] rheum** distressful head cold or watering of the eyes   **62 charmer** sorceress   **68 fancies** loves

And bid me, when my fate would have me wived,
70   To give it her. I did so; and take heed on 't;
Make it a darling like your precious eye.
72   To lose 't or give 't away were such perdition
As nothing else could match.

DESDEMONA: Is 't possible?

OTHELLO:
'Tis true. There's magic in the web of it.
A sibyl, that had numbered in the world
77   The sun to course two hundred compasses,
78   In her prophetic fury sewed the work;
The worms were hallowed that did breed the silk,
80   And it was dyed in mummy which the skillful
81   Conserved of maiden's hearts.

DESDEMONA: I' faith! Is 't true?

OTHELLO:
Most veritable. Therefore look to 't well.

DESDEMONA: Then would to God that I had never seen 't!

OTHELLO: Ha? Wherefore?

DESDEMONA:
86   Why do you speak so startingly and rash?

OTHELLO:
87   Is 't lost? Is 't gone? Speak, is 't out o' the way?

DESDEMONA: Heaven bless us!

OTHELLO: Say you?

90   DESDEMONA: It is not lost; but what an if it were?

OTHELLO: How?

DESDEMONA:
I say it is not lost.

OTHELLO: Fetch 't, let me see 't.

DESDEMONA:
Why, so I can, sir, but I will not now.
This is a trick to put me from my suit.
Pray you, let Cassio be received again.

OTHELLO:
Fetch me the handkerchief! My mind misgives.

DESDEMONA: Come, come,
99   You'll never meet a more sufficient man.

OTHELLO:
The handkerchief!

---

70 her i.e., to my wife   **72 perdition** loss   **77 compasses** annual circlings. (The *sibyl*, or prophetess, was two hundred years old.)   **78 prophetic fury** frenzy of prophetic inspiration. **work** embroidered pattern   **80 mummy** medicinal or magical preparation drained from mummified bodies   **81 Conserved of** prepared or preserved out of **86 startingly and rash** disjointedly and impetuously, excitedly   **87 out o' the way** lost, misplaced   **90 an if** if   **99 sufficient** able, complete

101 DESDEMONA: I pray, talk me of Cassio.
     OTHELLO:
     The handkerchief!
103 DESDEMONA: A man that all his time
     Hath founded his good fortunes on your love,
     Shared dangers with you—
     OTHELLO: The handkerchief!
     DESDEMONA: I' faith, you are to blame.
     OTHELLO: Zounds!   (*Exit Othello.*)
     EMILIA: Is not this man jealous?
     DESDEMONA: I ne'er saw this before.
     Sure, there's some wonder in this handkerchief.
     I am most unhappy in the loss of it.
     EMILIA:
113 'Tis not a year or two shows us a man.
114 They are all but stomachs, and we all but food;
115 They eat us hungerly, and when they are full
     They belch us.

     (*Enter Iago and Cassio.*)

     Look you, Cassio and my husband.
     IAGO (*to Cassio*): There is no other way; 'tis she must do 't.
119 And, lo, the happiness! Go and importune her.
     DESDEMONA:
     How now, good Cassio? What's the news with you?
     CASSIO:
     Madam, my former suit. I do beseech you
122 That by your virtuous means I may again
     Exist and be a member of his love
124 Whom I, with all the office of my heart,
     Entirely honor. I would not be delayed.
126 If my offense be of such mortal kind
127 That nor my service past, nor present sorrows,
     Nor purposed merit in futurity
     Can ransom me into his love again,
130 But to know so must be my benefit;
     So shall I clothe me in a forced content,
132 And shut myself up in some other course,
133 To fortune's alms.

---

101 talk talk to   **103 all his time** throughout his career   **113 'Tis [...] man** i.e., you
can't really know a man even in a year or two of experience (?), or, real men come along
seldom (?)   **114 but** nothing but   **115 hungerly** hungrily   **119 the happiness** in
happy time, fortunately met   **122 virtuous** efficacious   **124 office** loyal service
126 mortal fatal   **127 nor [...] nor** neither [...] nor   **130 But [...] benefit** merely to
know that my case is hopeless will have to content me (and will be better than uncertainty)   **132 shut [...] in** confine myself to   **133 To fortune's alms** throwing myself on
the mercy of fortune

DESMONA: Alas, thrice-gentle Cassio,
135 My advocation is not now in tune.
My lord is not my lord; nor should I know him,
137 Were he in favor as in humor altered.
So help me every spirit sanctified
As I have spoken for you all my best
140 And stood within the blank of his displeasure
For my free speech! You must awhile be patient.
What I can do I will, and more I will
Than for myself I dare. Let that suffice you.
IAGO:
Is my lord angry?
EMILIA: He went hence but now.
And certainly in strange unquietness.
IAGO:
Can he be angry? I have seen the cannon
When it hath blown his ranks into the air,
And like the devil from his very arm
Puffed his own brother—and is he angry?
151 Something of moment then. I will go meet him.
There's matter in 't indeed, if he be angry.
DESMONA:
I prithee, do so. *(Exit [Iago].)*
154 Something, sure of state,
155 Either from Venice, or some unhatched practice
Made demonstrable here in Cyprus to him,
157 Hath puddled his clear spirit; and in such cases
Men's natures wrangle with inferior things,
Though great ones are their object. 'Tis even so;
160 For let our finger ache, and it indues
Our other, healthful members even to a sense
Of pain. Nay, we must think men are not gods,
163 Nor of them look for such observancy
164 As fits the bridal. Beshrew me much, Emilia,
165 I was, unhandsome warrior as I am,
166 Arraigning his unkindness with my soul;
167 But now I find I had suborned the witness,
And he's indicted falsely.

---

135 advocation advocacy **137 favor** appearance. **humor** mood **140 within the blank** within point-blank range. (The *blank* is the center of the target.) **151 of moment** of immediate importance, momentous **154 of state** concerning state affairs **155 unhatched practice** as yet unexecuted or undiscovered plot **157 puddled** muddied **160 indues** brings to the same condition **163 observancy** attentiveness **164 bridal** wedding (when a bridegroom is newly attentive to his bride). **Beshrew me** (A mild oath.) **165 unhandsome** insufficient, unskillful **166 with** before the bar of **167 suborned the witness** induced the witness to give false testimony

EMILIA: Pray heaven it be
State matters, as you think, and no conception
171   Nor no jealous toy concerning you.

DESDEMONA:
Alas the day! I never gave him cause.

EMILIA:
But jealous souls will not be answered so;
They are not ever jealous for the cause,
175   But jealous for they're jealous. It is a monster
176   Begot upon itself, born on itself.

DESDEMONA:
Heaven keep that monster from Othello's mind!

EMILIA: Lady, amen.

DESDEMONA:
I will go seek him. Cassio, walk hereabout.
If I do find him fit, I'll move your suit
And seek to effect it to my uttermost.

CASSIO:
I humbly thank your ladyship.

(Exit [Desdemona with Emilia].)

(Enter Bianca.)

BIANCA:
183   Save you, friend Cassio!
184   CASSIO: What make you from home?
How is 't with you, my most fair Bianca?
I' faith, sweet love, I was coming to your house.

BIANCA:
And I was going to your lodging, Cassio.
What, keep a week away? Seven days and nights?
189   Eightscore-eight hours? And lovers' absent hours
190   More tedious than the dial eightscore times?
O weary reckoning!

CASSIO: Pardon me, Bianca.
I have this while with leaden thoughts been pressed;
194   But I shall, in a more continuate time,
195   Strike off this score of absence. Sweet Bianca,

(giving her Desdemona's handkerchief)

196   Take me this work out.

---

171 toy fancy   **175 for** because   **176 Begot upon itself** generated solely from itself
183 Save God save.   **184 make** do   **189 Eightscore-eight** one hundred sixty-eight,
the number of hours in a week   **190 the dial** a complete revolution of the clock
194 continuate uninterrupted   **195 Strike [...] score** settle this account   **196 Take
[...] out** copy this embroidery for me

BIANCA: O Cassio, whence came this?

198   This is some token from a newer friend.
To the felt absence now I feel a cause.
Is 't come to this? Well, well.

CASSIO: Go to, woman!
Throw your vile guesses in the devil's teeth,
From whence you have them. You are jealous now
That this is from some mistress, some remembrance.
No, by my faith, Bianca.

BIANCA: Why, whose is it?

CASSIO:
I know not, neither. I found it in my chamber.

208   I like the work well. Ere it be demanded—
209   As like enough it will—I would have it copied.
Take it and do 't, and leave me for this time.

BIANCA: Leave you? Wherefore?

CASSIO:
I do attend here on the General,

213   And think it no addition, nor my wish,
To have him see me womaned.

BIANCA: Why, I pray you?

CASSIO: Not that I love you not.

BIANCA: But that you do not love me.

218   I pray you, bring me on the way a little,
And say if I shall see you soon at night.

CASSIO:
'Tis but a little way that I can bring you,
For I attend here; but I'll see you soon.

BIANCA:
'Tis very good. I must be circumstanced.

(Exeunt omnes.)

4.1

(Enter Othello and Iago.)

IAGO: Will you think so?

OTHELLO: Think so, Iago?

IAGO: What,
To kiss in private?

OTHELLO: An unauthorized kiss!

IAGO:
Or to be naked with her friend in bed

---

198 friend mistress   **208 demanded** inquired for   **209 like** likely   **213 addition** i.e., addition to my reputation   **218 bring** accompany   **4.1 Location: Before the citadel.**

An hour or more, not meaning any harm?

OTHELLO:
Naked in bed, Iago, and not mean harm?
It is hypocrisy against the devil.
They that mean virtuously and yet do so,
The devil their virtue tempts, and they tempt heaven.

IAGO:
12   If they do nothing, 'tis a venial slip.
But if I give my wife a handkerchief—

OTHELLO: What then?

IAGO:
Why then, 'tis hers, my lord, and being hers,
She may, I think, bestow 't on any man.

OTHELLO:
She is protectress of her honor too.
May she give that?

IAGO:
Her honor is an essence that's not seen;
20   They have it very oft that have it not.
But, for the handkerchief—

OTHELLO:
By heaven, I would most gladly have forgot it.
Thou saidst—O, it comes o'er my memory
24   As doth the raven o'er the infectious house,
Boding to all—he had my handkerchief.

IAGO: Ay, what of that?

OTHELLO: That's not so good now.

IAGO: What
If I had said I had seen him do you wrong?
30   Or heard him say—as knaves by such abroad,
Who having, by their own importunate suit,
32   Or voluntary dotage of some mistress,
33   Convincèd or supplied them, cannot choose
But they must blab—

OTHELLO: Hath he said anything?

IAGO:
He hath, my lord; but, be you well assured,
No more than he'll unswear.

OTHELLO: What hath he said?

IAGO:
Faith, that he did—I know not what he did.

OTHELLO: What? What?

---

12 venial pardonable   **20 They have it** i.e., they enjoy a reputation for it   **24 raven [...] house** (Allusion to the belief that the raven hovered over a house of sickness or infection, such as one visited by the plague.)   **30 abroad** around about   **32 voluntary dotage** willing infatuation   **33 Convincèd or supplied** seduced or sexually gratified

IAGO:
> Lie—

OTHELLO: With her?

IAGO: With her, on her; what you will.

OTHELLO: Lie with her? Lie on her? We say "lie on her"
45 when they belie her. Lie with her? Zounds, that's fulsome.
    —Handkerchief—confessions—handkerchief!
47 —To confess and be hanged for his labor—first to be
48 hanged and then to confess.—I tremble at it. Nature
    would not invest herself in such shadowing passion
50 without some instruction. It is not words that shakes
    me thus. Pish! Noses, ears, and lips.—Is 't possible?
    —Confess—handkerchief!—O devil!

(Falls in a trance.)

IAGO: Work on,
> My medicine, work! Thus credulous fools are caught,
> And many worthy and chaste dames even thus,
> All guiltless, meet reproach.—What, ho! My lord!
> My lord, I say! Othello!

(Enter Cassio.)

>   How now, Cassio?

CASSIO: What's the matter?

IAGO:
> My lord is fall'n into an epilepsy.
> This is his second fit. He had one yesterday.

CASSIO:
> Rub him about the temples.

IAGO: No, forbear.
64 The lethargy must have his quiet course.
> If not, he foams at mouth, and by and by
> Breaks out to savage madness. Look, he stirs.
> Do you withdraw yourself a little while.
> He will recover straight. When he is gone,
69 I would on great occasion speak with you.

(Exit Cassio.)

> How is it, General? Have you not hurt your head?

---

45 belie slander. **fulsome** foul   **47–48 first [...] to confess** (Othello reverses the proverbial *confess and be hanged;* Cassio is to be given no time to confess before he dies.)   **48–50 Nature [...] instruction** i.e., without some foundation in fact, nature would not have dressed herself in such an overwhelming passion that comes over me now and fills my mind with images, or in such a lifelike fantasy as Cassio had in his dream of lying with Desdemona   **50 words** mere words   **64 lethargy** coma. **his** its **69 on great occasion** on a matter of great importance

OTHELLO:

71   Dost thou mock me?

IAGO: I mock you not, by heaven.
         Would you would bear your fortune like a man!

OTHELLO:
         A hornèd man's a monster and a beast.

IAGO:
         There's many a beast then in a populous city,

76   And many a civil monster.

OTHELLO: Did he confess it?

IAGO: Good sir, be a man.

79   Think every bearded fellow that's but yoked
80   May draw with you. There's millions now alive
81   That nightly lie in those unproper beds
82   Which they dare swear peculiar. Your case is better.
         O, 'tis the spite of hell, the fiend's arch-mock,
84   To lip a wanton in a secure couch
         And to suppose her chaste! No, let me know,
86   And knowing what I am, I know what she shall be.

OTHELLO: O, thou art wise. 'Tis certain.

IAGO: Stand you awhile apart;

89   Confine yourself but in a patient list.
         Whilst you were here o'erwhelmèd with your grief—
         A passion most unsuiting such a man—
92   Cassio came hither. I shifted him away,
93   And laid good 'scuse upon your ecstasy,
         Bade him anon return and here speak with me,
95   The which he promised. Do but encave yourself
96   And mark the fleers, the gibes, and notable scorns
         That dwell in every region of his face;
         For I will make him tell the tale anew,
         Where, how, how oft, how long ago, and when
100   He hath and is again to cope your wife.
         I say, but mark his gesture. Marry, patience!
102   Or I shall say you're all-in-all in spleen,
         And nothing of a man.

OTHELLO: Dost thou hear, Iago?

---

71 mock me (Othello takes Iago's question about hurting his head to be a mocking reference to the cuckold's horns)   **76 civil** i.e., dwelling in a city   **79 yoked** (1) married (2) put into the yoke of infamy and cuckoldry   **80 draw with you** pull as you do, like oxen who are yoked, i.e., share your fate as cuckold   **81 unproper** not exclusively their own **82 peculiar** private, their own. **better** i.e., because you know the truth   **84 lip** kiss. **secure** free from suspicion   **86 what I am** i.e., a cuckold. **she shall be** will happen to her   **89 in [...] list** within the bounds of patience   **92 shifted him away** used a dodge to get rid of him   **93 ecstasy** trance   **95 encave** conceal   **96 fleers** sneers. **notable** obvious   **100 cope** encounter with, have sex with   **102 all-in-all in spleen** utterly governed by passionate impulses

I will be found most cunning in my patience;
But dost thou hear?—most bloody.

IAGO: That's not amiss;

108   But yet keep time in all. Will you withdraw?

(Othello stands apart.)

Now will I question Cassio of Bianca,
110   A huswife that by selling her desires.
Buys herself bread and clothes. It is a creature
That dotes on Cassio—as 'tis the strumpet's plague
To beguile many and be beguiled by one.
114   He, when he hears of her, cannot restrain
From the excess of laughter. Here he comes.

(Enter Cassio.)

As he shall smile, Othello shall go mad;
117   And his unbookish jealousy must conster
Poor Cassio's smiles, gestures, and light behaviors
Quite in the wrong.—How do you now, Lieutenant?

CASSIO:
120   The worser that you give me the addition
121   Whose want even kills me.

IAGO:
Ply Desdemona well and you are sure on 't.
(Speaking lower.) Now, if this suit lay in Bianca's power,
How quickly should you speed!

125   CASSIO *(laughing)*: Alas, poor caitiff!

OTHELLO *(aside)*: Look how he laughs already!

IAGO:
I never knew a woman love man so.

CASSIO:
Alas, poor rogue! I think, i' faith, she loves me.

OTHELLO:
Now he denies it faintly, and laughs it out.

IAGO:
Do you hear, Cassio?

OTHELLO: Now he importunes him
132   To tell it o'er. Go to! Well said, well said.

IAGO:
She gives it out that you shall marry her.
Do you intend it?

CASSIO: Ha, ha, ha!

---

108 keep time keep yourself steady (as in music)   **110 huswife** hussy   **114 restrain** refrain   **117 unbookish** uninstructed. **conster** construe   **120 addition** title
121 Whose want the lack of which   **125 caitiff** wretch   **132 Go to** (An expression of remonstrance.) **Well said** well done

OTHELLO:

136   Do you triumph, Roman? Do you triumph?

137   CASSIO: I marry her? What? A customer? Prithee, bear
some charity to my wit; do not think it so unwhole-
some. Ha, ha, ha!

140   OTHELLO: So, so, so, so! They laugh that win.

141   IAGO: Faith, the cry goes that you shall marry her.
CASSIO: Prithee, say true.

143   IAGO: I am a very villain else.

144   OTHELLO: Have you scored me? Well.
CASSIO: This is the monkey's own giving out. She is
persuaded I will marry her out of her own love and

147   flattery, not out of my promise.

148   OTHELLO: Iago beckons me. Now he begins the story.
CASSIO: She was here even now; she haunts me in every

150   place. I was the other day talking on the seabank with

151   certain Venetians, and thither comes the bauble, and,

152   by this hand, she falls thus about my neck—
                    [He embraces Iago.]
OTHELLO: Crying, "O dear Cassio!" as it were; his ges-
ture imports it.
CASSIO: So hangs and lolls and weeps upon me, so shakes
and pulls me. Ha, ha, ha!
OTHELLO: Now he tells how she plucked him to my

158   chamber. O, I see that nose of yours, but not that dog
I shall throw it to.
CASSIO: Well, I must leave her company.

161   IAGO: Before me, look where she comes.

(Enter Bianca [with Othello's handkerchief].)

162   CASSIO: 'Tis such another fitchew! Marry, a perfumed
one. What do you mean by this haunting of me?

164   BIANCA: Let the devil and his dam haunt you! What did
you mean by that same handkerchief you gave me
even now? I was a fine fool to take it. I must take out

167   the work? A likely piece of work, that you should find

---

136 Roman (The Romans were noted for their *triumphs* or triumphal processions.)
137 customer i.e.,prostitute   **137–138 bear [...] wit** be more charitable to my judgment   **140 They [...] win** i.e., they that laugh last laugh best   **141 cry** rumor   **143 I
[...] else** call me a complete rogue if I'm not telling the truth   **144 scored me** scored off
me, beaten me, made up my reckoning, branded me   **147 flattery** self-flattery, self-
deception   **148 beckons** signals   **150 seabank** seashore   **151 bauble** plaything
152 by this hand I make my vow   **158-159 not [...] to** (Othello imagines himself cutting off Cassio's nose and throwing it to a dog.)   **161 Before me** i.e., on my soul
162 'Tis [...] fitchew what a polecat she is! Just like all the others. **fitchew** (Polecats
were often compared with prostitutes because of their rank smell and presumed lechery.)
164 dam mother   **167 A likely [...] work** a fine story

it in your chamber and know not who left it there!
This is some minx's token, and I must take out the
170 work? There; give it your hobbyhorse. [*She gives him
the handkerchief.*] Wheresoever you had it, I'll take out
no work on't.

CASSIO: How now, my sweet Bianca? How now? How now?

174 OTHELLO: By heaven, that should be my handkerchief!

BIANCA: If you'll come to supper tonight, you may; if
176 you will not, come when you are next prepared for.

(*Exit.*)

IAGO: After her, after her.

CASSIO: Faith, I must. She'll rail in the streets else.

IAGO: Will you sup there?

CASSIO: Faith, I intend so.

IAGO: Well, I may chance to see you, for I would very fain speak with you.

CASSIO: Prithee, come. Will you?

183 IAGO: Go to. Say no more.   (*Exit Cassio.*)

OTHELLO (*advancing*): How shall I murder him, Iago?

IAGO: Did you perceive how he laughed at his vice?

OTHELLO: O, Iago!

IAGO: And did you see the handkerchief?

OTHELLO: Was that mine?

IAGO: Yours, by this hand. And to see how he prizes
the foolish woman your wife! She gave it him, and he
hath given it his whore.

OTHELLO: I would have him nine years a-killing. A fine
woman! A fair woman! A sweet woman!

IAGO: Nay, you must forget that.

OTHELLO: Ay, let her rot and perish, and be damned
tonight, for she shall not live. No, my heart is turned
to stone; I strike it, and it hurts my hand. O, the world
hath not a sweeter creature! She might lie by an emperor's side and command him tasks.

200 IAGO: Nay, that's not your way.

OTHELLO: Hang her! I do but say what she is. So delicate
with her needle! An admirable musician! O, she will
sing the savageness out of a bear. Of so high and plen-
204 teous wit and invention!

IAGO: She's the worse for all this.

OTHELLO: O, a thousand, a thousand times! And then,
207 of so gentle a condition!

---

170 hobbyhorse harlot   **174 should be** must be   **176 when [...] for** when I'm ready
for you (i.e., never)   **183 Go to** (An expression of remonstrance.)   **200 your way** i.e.
the way you should think of her   **204 invention** imagination   **207 gentle a condition**
wellborn and well-bred

208 IAGO: Ay, too gentle.

OTHELLO: Nay, that's certain. But yet the pity of it, Iago!
O, Iago, the pity of it, Iago!

211 IAGO: If you are so fond over her iniquity, give her patent
to offend, for if it touch not you it comes near nobody.

213 OTHELLO: I will chop her into messes.
Cuckold me?

IAGO: O, 'tis foul in her.

OTHELLO: With mine officer?

IAGO: That's fouler.

OTHELLO: Get me some poison, Iago, this night. I'll not

218 expostulate with her, lest her body and beauty unprovide my mind again. This night, Iago.

IAGO: Do it not with poison. Strangle her in her bed,
even the bed she hath contaminated.

OTHELLO: Good, good! The justice of it pleases. Very good.

223 IAGO: And for Cassio, let me be his undertaker. You shall
hear more by midnight.

OTHELLO:
Excellent good. [*A trumpet within.*] What trumpet is that same?

IAGO: I warrant, something from Venice.

(Enter Lodovico, Desdemona, and attendants.)

'Tis Lodovico. This comes from the Duke.
See, your wife's with him.

LODOVICO:
God save you, worthy General!

230 OTHELLO: With all my heart, sir.

LODOVICO (*giving him a letter*):
The duke and the senators of Venice greet you.

OTHELLO:
I kiss the instrument of their pleasures.

(He opens the letter, and reads.)

DESDEMONA:
And what's the news, good cousin Lodovico?

IAGO:
I am very glad to see you, signor. Welcome to Cyprus.

LODOVICO:
I thank you. How does Lieutenant Cassio?

IAGO: Lives, sir.

---

208 gentle generous, yielding (to other men)   **211 fond** foolish. **patent** license
213 messes portions of meat, i.e., bits   **218–219 unprovide** weaken, render unfit
223 be his undertaker undertake to dispatch him   **230 With all my heart** i.e., I thank
you most heartily

DESDEMONA:

238   Cousin, there's fall'n between him and my lord

An unkind breach; but you shall make all well.

OTHELLO: Are you sure of that?

DESDEMONA: My lord?

OTHELLO (*reads*): "This fail you not to do, as you will—"

LODOVICO:

He did not call; he's busy in the paper.

Is there division twixt my lord and Cassio?

DESDEMONA:

A most unhappy one. I would do much

245   T' atone them, for the love I bear to Cassio.

OTHELLO: Fire and brimstone!

DESDEMONA: My lord?

OTHELLO: Are you wise?

DESDEMONA:

What, is he angry?

LODOVICO: Maybe the letter moved him;

For, as I think, they do command him home,

252   Deputing Cassio in his government.

253 DESDEMONA: By my troth, I am glad on 't.

OTHELLO: Indeed?

DESDEMONA: My lord?

256 OTHELLO: I am glad to see you mad.

DESDEMONA: Why, sweet Othello—

OTHELLO (*striking her*): Devil!

DESDEMONA: I have not deserved this.

LODOVICO:

My lord, this would not be believed in Venice,

261   Though I should swear I saw 't. 'Tis very much.

Make her amends; she weeps.

OTHELLO: O devil, devil!

264   If that the earth could teem with woman's tears,

265   Each drop she falls would prove a crocodile.

Out of my sight!

DESDEMONA: I will not stay to offend you.   (*Going.*)

LODOVICO: Truly, an obedient lady.

I do beseech your lordship, call her back.

OTHELLO: Mistress!

DESDEMONA (*returning*): My lord?

---

238 unkind unnatural, contrary to their natures; hurtful   **245 atone** reconcile   **252 government** office   **253 on 't** of it   **256 I am [...] mad** i.e., I am glad to see that you are insane enough to rejoice in Cassio's promotion (? Othello bitterly plays on Desdemona's *I am glad.*)   **261 very much** too much, outrageous   **264 teem** breed, be impregnated   **265 falls** lets fall. **crocodile** (Crocodiles were supposed to weep hypocritical tears for their victims.)

272   OTHELLO: What would you with her, sir?

LODOVICO: Who, I, my lord?

OTHELLO:

Ay, you did wish that I would make her turn.
Sir, she can turn, and turn, and yet go on
And turn again; and she can weep, sir, weep;
277   And she's obedient, as you say, obedient,
Very obedient.—Proceed you in your tears.—
279   Concerning this, sir—O well—painted passion!—
I am commanded home.—Get you away;
I'll send for you anon.—Sir, I obey the mandate
And will return to Venice.—Hence, avaunt!

(Exit Desdemona.)

Cassio shall have my place. And, sir, tonight
I do entreat that we may sup together.
285   You are welcome, sir, to Cyprus.—Goats and monkeys!

(Exit.)

LODOVICO:

Is this the noble Moor whom our full Senate
Call all in all sufficient? Is this the nature
Whom passion could not shake? Whose solid virtue
The shot of accident nor dart of chance
Could neither graze nor pierce?

IAGO: He is much changed.

LODOVICO:

Are his wits safe? Is he not light of brain?

IAGO:

293   He's that he is. I may not breathe my censure
What he might be. If what he might he is not,
I would to heaven he were!

LODOVICO: What, strike his wife?

IAGO:

Faith, that was not so well; yet would I knew
That stroke would prove the worst!

299   LODOVICO: Is it his use?

300   Or did the letters work upon his blood
And new-create his fault?

---

272 What [...] sir (Othello implies that Desdemona is pliant and will do a *turn*, lines
274-276, for any man.)   **277 obedient** (With much the same sexual connotation as *turn*
in lines 274-276.)   **279 passion** i.e., grief   **285 Goats and monkeys** (See 3.3.446.)
293–295 I may [...] were i.e., I dare not venture an opinion as to whether he's of
unsound mind, as you suggest, but, if he isn't, then it might be better to wish he were in
fact insane, since only that could excuse his wild behavior   **299 use** custom
300 blood passions

IAGO: Alas, alas!
    It is not honesty in me to speak
    What I have seen and known. You shall observe him,
305   And his own courses will denote him so
    That I may save my speech. Do but go after,
    And mark how he continues.

LODOVICO:
    I am sorry that I am deceived in him. (*Exeunt.*)

4.2

    (*Enter Othello and Emilia.*)

OTHELLO: You have seen nothing then?

EMILIA:
    Nor ever heard, nor ever did suspect.

OTHELLO:
    Yes, you have seen Cassio and she together.

EMILIA:
    But then I saw no harm, and then I heard
    Each syllable that breath made up between them.

OTHELLO: What, did they never whisper?

EMILIA: Never, my lord.

OTHELLO: Nor send you out o' the way?

EMILIA: Never.

OTHELLO:
    To fetch her fan, her gloves, her mask, nor nothing?

EMILIA: Never, my lord.

OTHELLO: That's strange.

EMILIA:
    I durst, my lord, to wager she is honest,
14   Lay down my soul at stake. If you think other,
15   Remove your thought; it doth abuse your bosom.
    If any wretch have put this in your head,
17   Let heaven requite it with the serpent's curse!
    For if she be not honest, chaste, and true,
    There's no man happy; the purest of their wives
    Is foul as slander.

OTHELLO: Bid her come hither. Go.

    (*Exit Emilia.*)

---

305 courses will denote actions will reveal   **4.2 Location: The citadel.**   **14 at stake** as the wager   **15 abuse your bosom** deceive you   **17 the serpent's curse** the curse pronounced by God on the serpent for deceiving Eve, just as some man has done to Othello and Desdemona. (See Genesis 3:14.)

22   She says enough; yet she's a simple bawd
23   That cannot say as much. This is a subtle whore,
24   A closet lock and key of villainous secrets.
      And yet she'll kneel and pray; I have seen her do't.

(Enter Desdemona and Emilia.)

DESDEMONA: My lord, what is your will?
OTHELLO: Pray you, chuck, come hither.
DESDEMONA:
      What is your pleasure?
OTHELLO: Let me see your eyes.
      Look in my face.
DESDEMONA: What horrible fancy's this?
32   OTHELLO *(to Emilia)*: Some of your function, mistress.
33   Leave procreants alone and shut the door;
      Cough or cry "hem" if anybody come.
35   Your mystery, your mystery! Nay, dispatch.

(Exit Emilia.)

DESDEMONA *(kneeling)*:
      Upon my knees, what doth your speech import?
      I understand a fury in your words,
      But not the words.
OTHELLO:
      Why, what art thou?
DESDEMONA: Your wife, my lord, your true
      And loyal wife.
OTHELLO:
43   Come, swear it, damn thyself,
      Lest, being like one of heaven, the devils themselves
      Should fear to seize thee. Therefore be double damned:
      Swear thou art honest.
DESDEMONA: Heaven doth truly know it
OTHELLO:
      Heaven truly knows that thou art false as hell.
DESDEMONA:
      To whom, my lord? With whom? How am I false?
OTHELLO [*weeping*]:
      Ah, Desdemon! Away, away, away!
DESDEMONA:
      Alas the heavy day! Why do you weep?

22-23 she's [...] much i.e., any procuress or go-between who couldn't make up as plausible
a story as Emilia's would have to be pretty stupid   **23 This** i.e., Desdemona   **24 closet
lock and key** i.e, concealer   **32 Some [...] function** i.e., practice your chosen profession,
that of bawd (by guarding the door)   **33 procreants** mating couples   **35 mystery** trade,
occupation   **43 being [...] heaven** looking like an angel

51   Am I the motive of these tears, my lord?
      If haply you my father do suspect
      An instrument of this your calling back,
      Lay not your blame on me. If you have lost him,
      I have lost him too.

OTHELLO: Had it pleased heaven
57   To try me with affliction, had they rained
      All kinds of sores and shames on my bare head,
      Steeped me in poverty to the very lips,
      Given to captivity me and my utmost hopes,
      I should have found in some place of my soul
      A drop of patience. But, alas, to make me
63   A fixèd figure for the time of scorn
64   To point his slow and moving finger at!
      Yet could I bear that too, well, very well.
66   But there where I have garnered up my heart,
      Where either I must live or bear no life,
68   The fountain from the which my current runs
      Or else dries up to be discarded thence!
70   Or keep it as a cistern for foul toads
71   knot and gender in! Turn thy complexion there,
72   Patience, thou young and rose-lipped cherubin—
      Ay, there look grim as hell!

DESDEMONA:
74   I hope my noble lord esteems me honest.

OTHELLO:
75   O, ay, as summer flies are in the shambles,
76   That quicken even with blowing. O thou weed,
      Who art so lovely fair and smell'st so sweet
      That the sense aches at thee, would thou hadst ne'er been born!

DESDEMONA:
79   Alas, what ignorant sin have I committed?

OTHELLO:
      Was this fair paper, this most goodly book,
      Made to write "whore" upon? What committed?
82   Committed? O thou public commoner!
      I should make very forges of my cheeks,

---

51 motive cause   **57 they** i.e., heavenly powers   **63 time of scorn** i.e., scornful world
64 his its. **slow and moving finger** i.e., hour hand of the clock, moving so slowly it
seems hardly to move at all. (Othello envisages himself as being eternally pointed at by
the scornful world as the numbers on a clock are pointed at by the hour hand.)   **66 garnered** stored   **68 fountain** spring   **70 cistern** cesspool   **71 knot** couple. **gender**
engender. **Turn [...] there** change your color, grow pale, at such a sight   **72–73
Patience [...] hell** (Even Patience, that rose-lipped cherub, will look grim and pale at
this spectacle.)   **74 honest** chaste   **75 shambles** slaughterhouse   **76 quicken** come
to life. **with blowing** i.e., with the puffing up of something rotten in which maggots are
breeding   **79 ignorant sin** sin in ignorance   **82 commoner** prostitute

That would to cinders burn up modesty,
Did I but speak thy deeds. What committed?
86   Heaven stops the nose at it and the moon winks;
87   The bawdy wind, that kisses all it meets,
88   Is hushed within the hollow mine of earth
And will not hear 't. What committed?
Impudent strumpet!

DESDEMONA: By heaven, you do me wrong.

OTHELLO:
Are not you a strumpet?

DESDEMONA: No, as I am a Christian.
94   If to preserve this vessel for my lord
From any other foul unlawful touch
Be not to be a strumpet, I am none.

OTHELLO: What, not a whore?

DESDEMONA: No, as I shall be saved.

OTHELLO: Is 't possible?

DESDEMONA:
O, heaven forgive us!

101   OTHELLO: I cry you mercy, then.
I took you for that cunning whore of Venice
That married with Othello. (*Calling out.*) You, mistress,
That have the office opposite to Saint Peter
And keep the gate of hell!

(*Enter Emilia.*)

You, you, ay, you!
107   We have done our course. There's money for your pains.

(*He gives money.*)

I pray you, turn the key and keep our counsel.   (*Exit.*)

EMILIA:
109   Alas, what does this gentleman conceive?
How do you, madam? How do you, my good lady?

111   DESDEMONA: Faith, half asleep.

EMILIA:
Good madam, what's the matter with my lord?

DESDEMONA: With who?

EMILIA: Why, with my lord, madam.

DESDEMONA:
Who is thy lord?

EMILIA: He that is yours, sweet lady.

_____

86 **winks** closes her eyes. (The moon symbolizes chastity.)   87 **bawdy** kissing one and
all   88 **mine** cave (where the winds were thought to dwell)   94 **vessel** body   101 **cry
you mercy** beg your pardon   107 **course** business (with an indecent suggestion of
"trick," turn at sex)   109 **conceive** suppose, think   111 **half asleep** i.e., dazed

DESDEMONA:

    I have none. Do not talk to me, Emilia.

    I cannot weep, nor answers have I none

119   But what should go by water. Prithee, tonight

    Lay on my bed my wedding sheets, remember;

    And call thy husband hither.

EMILIA: Here's a change indeed!   (*Exit.*)

DESDEMONA:

    'Tis meet I should be used so, very meet.

124   How have I been behaved, that he might stick

125   The small'st opinion on my least misuse?

    (*Enter Iago and Emilia.*)

IAGO:

    What is your pleasure, madam? How is 't with you?

DESDEMONA:

    I cannot tell. Those that do teach young babes

    Do it with gentle means and easy tasks.

    He might have chid me so, for, in good faith,

    I am a child to chiding.

IAGO: What is the matter, lady?

EMILIA:

    Alas, Iago, my lord hath so bewhored her,

    Thrown such despite and heavy terms upon her,

    That true hearts cannot bear it.

DESDEMONA: Am I that name, Iago?

IAGO: What name, fair lady?

DESDEMONA:

    Such as she said my lord did say I was.

EMILIA:

    He called her whore. A begger in his drink

139   Could not have laid such terms upon his callet.

IAGO: Why did he so?

DESDEMONA (*weeping*):

    I do not know. I am sure I am none such.

IAGO: Do not weep, do not weep. Alas the day!

EMILIA:

    Hath she forsook so many noble matches,

    Her father and her country and her friends,

    To be called whore? Would it not make one weep?

DESDEMONA:

    It is my wretched fortune.

147 IAGO: Beshrew him for 't!

---

119 go by water be expressed by tears   **124 stick** attach   **125 opinion** censure. **least misuse** slightest misconduct   **139 callet** whore   **147 Beshrew** curse

148   How comes this trick upon him?

DESDEMONA: Nay, heaven doth know.

EMILIA:

150   I will be hanged if some eternal villain,
151   Some busy and insinuating rogue,
152   Some cogging, cozening slave, to get some office,
       Have not devised this slander. I will be hanged else.

IAGO:

       Fie, there is no such man. It is impossible.

DESDEMONA:

       If any such there be, heaven pardon him!

EMILIA:

156   A halter pardon him! And hell gnaw his bones!
       Why should he call her whore? Who keeps her company?
158   What place? What time? What form? What likelihood?
       The Moor's abused by some most villainous knave,
       Some base notorious knave, some scurvy fellow.
161   O heaven, that such companions thou'dst unfold,
       And put in every honest hand a whip
       To lash the rascals naked through the world
       Even from the east to th' west!

165   IAGO: Speak within door.

EMILIA:

166   O, fie upon them! Some such squire he was
167   That turned your wit the seamy side without
       And made you to suspect me with the Moor.

IAGO:

169   You are a fool. Go to.

DESDEMONA: Alas, Iago,
       What shall I do to win my lord again?
       Good friend, go to him; for, by this light of heaven,
       I know not how I lost him. Here I kneel.   (*She kneels.*)
       If e'er my will did trespass 'gainst his love,
175   Either in discourse of thought or actual deed,
176   Or that mine eyes, mine ears, or any sense
177   Delighted them in any other form;
178   Or that I do not yet, and ever did,
       And ever will—though he do shake me off
       To beggarly divorcement love him dearly,

---

148 trick strange behavior, delusion   **150 eternal** inveterate   **151 insinuating** ingra-
tiating, fawning, wheedling   **152 cogging** cheating. **cozening** defrauding   **156 halter**
hangman's noose   **158 form** appearance, circumstance   **161 that** would that.
companions fellows. **unfold** expose   **165 within door** i.e., not so loud   **166 squire**
fellow   **167 seamy side without** wrong side out   **169 Go to** i.e., that's enough
175 discourse of thought process of thinking   **176 that** if. (Also in line 178.)
177 Delighted them took delight   **178 yet** still

181   Comfort forswear me! Unkindness may do much,
182   And his unkindness may defeat my life,
      But never taint my love. I cannot say "whore."
184   It does abhor me now I speak the word;
185   To do the act that might the addition earn
186   Not the world's mass of vanity could make me.
              (She rises.)

IAGO:

187   I pray you, be content. 'Tis but his humor.
      The business of the state does him offense,
      And he does chide with you.
DESDEMONA: If 'twere no other—
IAGO: It is but so, I warrant.   *(Trumpets within.)*
      Hark, how these instruments summon you to supper!
193   The messengers of Venice stays the meat.
      Go in, and weep not. All things shall be well.

                    (Exeunt Desdemona and Emilia.)

(Enter Roderigo.)

      How now, Roderigo?
RODERIGO: I do not find that thou deal'st justly with me.
IAGO: What in the contrary?
198   RODERIGO: Every day thou dafft'st me with some device,
      Iago, and rather, as it seems to me now, keep'st
200   from me all conveniency than suppliest me with the
201   least advantage of hope. I will indeed no longer
202   endure it, nor am I yet persuaded to put up in peace
      what already I have foolishly suffered.
IAGO: Will you hear me, Roderigo?
RODERIGO: Faith, I have heard too much, for your words
      and performances are no kin together.
IAGO: You charge me most unjustly.
RODERIGO: With naught but truth. I have wasted myself
      out of my means. The jewels you have had from me to
210   deliver Desdemona would half have corrupted a votarist.
      You have told me she hath received them and returned
212   me expectations and comforts of sudden respect and
      acquaintance, but I find none.
IAGO: Well, go to, very well.

---

181 Comfort forswear may heavenly comfort forsake   **182 defeat** destroy   **184 abhor**
(1) fill me with abhorrence (2) make me whorelike   **185 addition** title   **186 vanity**
showy splendor   **187 humor** mood   **193 stays the meat** are waiting to dine   **198 thou
dafft'st me** you put me off **device** excuse, trick   **200 conveniency** advantage, opportunity   **201 advantage** increase   **202 put up** submit to, tolerate   **210 deliver** deliver to
votarist nun   **212 sudden respect** immediate consideration

215 RODERIGO: "Very well"! "Go to"! I cannot go to, man,
       nor 'tis not very well. By this hand, I think it is scurvy,
217   and begin to find myself fopped in it.
    IAGO: Very well.
219 RODERIGO: I tell you 'tis not very well. I will make myself
       known to Desdemona. If she will return me my jewels,
       I will give over my suit and repent my unlawful solicita-
222   tion; if not, assure yourself I will seek satisfaction of you.
223 IAGO: You have said now?
    RODERIGO: Ay, and said nothing but what I protest
225   intendment of doing.
    IAGO: Why, now I see there's mettle in thee, and even
       from this instant do build on thee a better opinion
       than ever before. Give me thy hand, Roderigo. Thou
       hast taken against me a most just exception; but yet I
       protest I have dealt most directly in thy affair.
    RODERIGO: It hath not appeared.
    IAGO: I grant indeed it hath not appeared, and your
       suspicion is not without wit and judgment. But,
       Roderigo, if thou hast that in thee indeed which I have
       greater reason to believe now than ever—I mean
       purpose, courage, and valor—this night show it. If
       thou the next night following enjoy not Desdemona,
       take me from this world with treachery and devise
239   engines for my life.
    RODERIGO: Well, what is it? Is it within reason and compass?
    IAGO: Sir, there is especial commission come from Venice
       to depute Cassio in Othello's place.
    RODERIGO: Is that true? Why, then Othello and Desdemona
       return again to Venice.
    IAGO: O, no; he goes into Mauritania and takes away
       with him the fair Desdemona, unless his abode be
       lingered here by some accident; wherein none can be
248   so determinate as the removing of Cassio.
    RODERIGO: How do you mean, removing of him?
    IAGO: Why, by making him uncapable of Othello's
       place—knocking out his brains.
    RODERIGO: And that you would have me to do?
    IAGO: Ay, if you dare do yourself a profit and a right.

---

215 I cannot go to (Roderigo changes Iago's *go to*, an expression urging patience, to *I cannot go to*, "I have no opportunity for success in wooing.")   **217 fopped** fooled, duped   **219 not very well** (Roderigo changes Iago's *very well*, "all right then," to *not very well*, "not at all good.")   **222 satisfaction** repayment. (The term normally means settling of accounts in a duel.)   **223 You [...] now** have you finished?   **225 intendment** intention   **239 engines for** plots against   **248 determinate** conclusive

254 He sups tonight with a harlotry, and thither will I go to
him. He knows not yet of his honorable fortune. If
you will watch his going thence, which I will fashion
257 to fall out between twelve and one, you may take him
at your pleasure. I will be near to second your attempt,
and he shall fall between us. Come, stand not amazed
at it, but go along with me. I will show you such a
necessity in his death that you shall think yourself
262 bound to put it on him. It is now high suppertime,
263 and the night grows to waste. About it.

RODERIGO: I will hear further reason for this.

IAGO: And you shall be satisfied.   (*Exeunt.*)

4.3

(*Enter Othello, Lodovico, Desdemona, Emilia, and attendants.*)

LODOVICO:
I do beseech you, sir, trouble yourself no further.

OTHELLO:
O, pardon me; 'twill do me good to walk.

LODOVICO:
Madam, good night. I humbly thank your ladyship.

DESDEMONA:
Your honor is most welcome.

OTHELLO: Will you walk, sir?
O, Desdemona!

DESDEMONA: My lord?

OTHELLO: Get you to bed on th' instant. I will be returned forthwith. Dismiss your attendant there. Look 't be done.

DESDEMONA: I will my lord.

(*Exit [Othello, with Lodovico and attendants].*)

EMILIA: How goes it now? He looks gentler than he did.

DESDEMONA:
12   He says he will return incontinent,
And hath commanded me to go to bed,
And bid me to dismiss you.

EMILIA: Dismiss me?

DESDEMONA:
It was his bidding. Therefore, good Emilia,
Give me my nightly wearing, and adieu.
We must not now displease him.

EMILIA: I would you had never seen him!

---

254 harlotry slut   **257 fall out** occur   **262 high** fully   **263 grows to waste** wastes
away   **4.3. Location: The citadel.**   **12 incontinent** immediately

DESDEMONA:
> So would not I. My love doth so approve him

21 > That even his stubbornness, his checks, his frowns—
> Prithee, unpin me—have grace and favor in them.

(Emilia prepares Desdemona for bed.)

EMILIA: I have laid those sheets you bade me on the bed.

DESDEMONA:

24 > All's one. Good faith, how foolish are our minds!
> If I do die before thee, prithee shroud me
> In one of these same sheets.

27 EMILIA: Come, come, you talk.

DESDEMONA:
> My mother had a maid called Barbary.

29 > She was in love, and he she loved proved mad
> And did forsake her. She had a song of "Willow."
> An old thing 'twas, but it expressed her fortune,
> And she died singing it. That song tonight

33 > Will not go from my mind; I have much to do
> But to go hang my head all at one side
> And sing it like poor Barbary. Prithee, dispatch.

36 EMILIA: Shall I go fetch your nightgown?

DESDEMONA: No, unpin me here.

38 > This Lodovico is a proper man.

EMILIA: A very handsome man.

DESDEMONA: He speaks well.

EMILIA: I know a lady in Venice would have walked barefoot to Palestine for a touch of his nether lip.

DESDEMONA *(singing)*:
> "The poor soul sat sighing by a sycamore tree,

44 > Sing all a green willow;
> Her hand on her bosom, her head on her knee,
> Sing willow, willow, willow.
> The fresh streams ran by her and murmured her moans;
> Sing willow, willow, willow;
> Her salt tears fell from her, and softened the stones-"
>   Lay by these.
> *(Singing.)* "Sing willow, willow, willow—"

52 > Prithee, hie thee. He'll come anon.
> *(Singing.)* "Sing all a green willow must be my garland.
> Let nobody blame him; his scorn I approve—"

---

21 stubbornness roughness. **checks** rebukes   **24 All's one** all right. It doesn't really matter   **27 talk** i.e., prattle   **29 mad** wild, i.e., faithless   **33–34 I [...] hang** I can scarcely keep myself from hanging   **36 nightgown** dressing gown   **38 proper** handsome   **44 willow** (A conventional emblem of disappointed love.)   **52 hie thee** hurry. **anon** right away

Nay, that's not next.—Hark! Who is 't that knocks?

EMILIA: It's the wind.

DESDEMONA (*singing*):

"I called my love false love; but what said he then?

Sing willow, willow, willow;

If I court more women, you'll couch with more men."

So, get thee gone. Good night. Mine eyes do itch;

Doth that bode weeping?

EMILIA: 'Tis neither here nor there.

DESDEMONA: I have heard it said so. O, these men, these men!

Dost thou in conscience think—tell me, Emilia—

65   That there be women do abuse their husbands

In such gross kind?

EMILIA: There be some such, no question.

DESDEMONA:

Wouldst thou do such a deed for all the world?

EMILIA:

Why, would not you?

DESDEMONA: No, by this heavenly light!

EMILIA:

Nor I neither by this heavenly light;

I might do 't as well i' the dark.

DESDEMONA: Wouldst thou do such a deed for all the world?

EMILIA:

The world's a huge thing. It is a great price

For a small vice.

DESDEMONA:

Good troth, I think thou wouldst not.

EMILIA: By my troth, I think I should, and undo 't when

I had done. Marry, I would not do such a thing for a

79   joint ring, nor for measures of lawn, nor for gowns,

80   petticoats, nor caps, nor any petty exhibition. But for

81   all the whole world! Uds pity, who would not make

her husband a cuckold to make him a monarch? I

should venture purgatory for 't.

DESDEMONA:

Beshrew me if I would do such a wrong

For the whole world.

EMILIA: Why, the wrong is but a wrong i' the world, and

having the world for your labor, 'tis a wrong in your

own world, and you might quickly make it right.

DESDEMONA:

I do not think there is any such woman.

----

65 abuse deceive   **79 joint ring** a ring made in separate halves. **lawn** fine linen
80 exhibition gift   **81 Uds** God's

EMILIA: Yes, a dozen, and as many

91   To th' vantage as would store the world they played for.

    But I do think it is their husbands' faults

93   If wives do fall. Say that they slack their duties

94   And pour our treasures into foreign laps,

    Or else break out in peevish jealousies,

96   Throwing restraint upon us? Or say they strike us,

97   Or scant our former having in despite?

98   Why, we have galls, had though we have some grace,

    Yet have we some revenge. Let husbands know

100   Their wives have sense like them. They see, and smell,

    And have their palates both for sweet and sour,

    As husbands have. What is it that they do

103   When they change us for others? Is it sport?

104   I think it is. And doth affection breed it?

    I think it doth. Is 't frailty that thus errs?

    It is so, too. And have not we affections,

    Desires for sport, and frailty, as men have?

    Then let them use us well; else let them know,

    The ills we do, their ills instruct us so.

DESDEMONA:

110   Good night, good night. God me such uses send

111   Not to pick bad from bad, but by bad mend!

(Exeunt.)

5.1

(Enter Iago and Roderigo.)

IAGO:

1   Here stand behind this bulk. Straight will he come.

2   Wear thy good rapier bare, and put it home.

    Quick, quick! Fear nothing. I'll be at thy elbow.

    It makes us or it mars us. Think on that,

---

91 To th' vantage in addition, to boot. **store** populate. **played** (1) gambled (2) sported sexually   **93 duties** marital duties   **94 pour [...] laps** i.e., are unfaithful, give what is rightfully ours (semen) to other women   **96 Throwing [...] us** i.e., jealously restricting our freedom to see other men   **97 scant [...] despite** reduce our allowance to spite us **98 have galls** i.e., are capable of resenting injury and insult   **100 sense** physical sense **103 sport** sexual pastime   **104 affection** passion   **110 uses** habit, practice   **111 Not [...] mend** i.e, not to learn bad conduct from others' badness (as Emilia has suggested women learn from men), but to mend my ways by perceiving what badness is, making spiritual benefit out of evil and adversity   **5.1 Location: A street in Cyprus.**   **1 bulk** framework projecting from the front of a shop   **2 bare** unsheathed

And fix most firm thy resolution.

RODERIGO:
Be near at hand. I may miscarry in 't.

IAGO:
Here, at thy hand. Be bold, and take thy stand.

(Iago stands aside. Roderigo conceals himself.)

RODERIGO:
I have no great devotion to the deed;
And yet he hath given me satisfying reasons.
'Tis but a man gone. Forth, my sword! He dies.

(He draws.)

IAGO:
11   I have rubbed this young quat almost to the sense,
And he grows angry. Now, whether he kill Cassio
Or Cassio him, or each do kill the other,
14   Every way makes my gain. Live Roderigo,
He calls me to a restitution large
16   Of gold and jewels that I bobbed from him
As gifts to Desdemona.
It must not be. If Cassio do remain,
He hath a daily beauty in his life
That makes me ugly; and besides, the Moor
21   May unfold me to him; there stand I in much peril.
No, he must die. Be 't so. I hear him coming.

(Enter Cassio.)

RODERIGO (*coming forth*):
I know his gait, 'tis he.—Villain, thou diest!

(He attacks Cassio.)

CASSIO:
That thrust had been mine enemy indeed,
25   But that my coat is better than thou know'st.
26   I will make proof of thine.
(He draws, and wounds Roderigo.)

RODERIGO: O, I am slain! *(He falls.)*
(Iago, from behind, wounds Cassio in the leg, and exit.)

CASSIO:
I am maimed forever. Help, ho! Murder! Murder!

---

11 quat pimple, pustule. **to the sense** to the quick   **14 Live Roderigo** if Roderigo lives
16 bobbed swindled   **21 unfold** expose   **25 coat** (Possibly a garment of mail under
the outer clothing, or simply a tougher coat than Roderigo expected.)   **26 proof** a test

(Enter Othello.)

OTHELLO:
  The voice of Cassio! Iago keeps his word.

RODERIGO: O, villain that I am!

OTHELLO: It is even so.

CASSIO: O, help, ho! Light! A surgeon!

OTHELLO:
  'Tis he. O brave Iago, honest and just,
  That hast such noble sense of thy friend's wrong!
35 Thou teachest me. Minion, your dear lies dead,
36 And your unblest fate hies. Strumpet, I come.
37 Forth of my heart those charms, thine eyes, are blotted;
  Thy bed, lust-stained, shall with lust's blood be spotted.
    (Exit Othello.)

(Enter Lodovico and Gratiano.)

CASSIO:
39 What ho! No watch? No passage? Murder! Murder!

GRATIANO:
  'Tis some mischance. The voice is very direful.

CASSIO: O, help!

LODOVICO: Hark!

RODERIGO: O wretched villain!

LODOVICO:
44 Two or three groan. 'Tis heavy night;
  These may be counterfeits. Let's think 't unsafe
46 To come in to the cry without more help.

    (They remain near the entrance.)

RODERIGO:
  Nobody come? Then shall I bleed to death.

    (Enter Iago [in his shirtsleeves, with a light].)

LODOVICO: Hark!

GRATIANO:
  Here's one comes in his shirt, with light and weapons.

IAGO:
50 Who's there? Whose noise is this that cries on murder?

LODOVICO:
  We do not know.

IAGO: Did not you hear a cry?

---

35 Minion hussy (i.e., Desdemona)   **36 hies** hastens on   **37 Forth of** from out
39 passage people passing by   **44 heavy** thick, dark   **46 come in to** approach
50 cries on cries out

CASSIO:
Here, here! for heaven's sake, help me!

IAGO: What's the matter?
(*He moves toward Cassio.*)

GRATIANO (*to Lodovico*):
This is Othello's ancient, as I take it.

LODOVICO (*to Gratiano*):
The same indeed, a very valiant fellow.

IAGO (*to Cassio*):
57   What are you here that cry so grievously?

CASSIO:
58   Iago? O, I am spoiled, undone by villains!
Give me some help.

IAGO:
O me, Lieutenant! What villains have done this?

CASSIO:
I think that one of them is hereabout,
62   And cannot make away.

IAGO: O treacherous villains!
(*To Lodovico and Gratiano.*) What are you there? Come
in, and give me some help.   (*They advance.*)

RODERIGO: O, help me there!

CASSIO:
That's one of them.

IAGO: O murderous slave! O villain!
(*He stabs Roderigo.*)

RODERIGO:
O damned Iago! O inhuman dog!

IAGO:
Kill men i' the dark?—Where be these bloody thieves?—
How silent is this town!—Ho! Murder, murder!—
(*To Lodovico and Gratiano.*) What may you be? Are you of good
or evil?

74   LODOVICO: As you shall prove us, praise us.

IAGO: Signor Lodovico?

LODOVICO: He, sir.

IAGO:
77   I cry you mercy. Here's Cassio hurt by villains.

GRATIANO: Cassio?

IAGO: How is 't, brother?

CASSIO: My leg is cut in two.

IAGO: Marry, heaven forbid!

---

57 What who (also at lines 64 and 72)   **58 spoiled** ruined, done for   **62 make** get
74 praise appraise   **77 I cry you mercy** I beg your pardon

Light, gentlemen! I'll bind it with my shirt.

(He hands them the light, and tends to Cassio's wound.)

(Enter Bianca.)

BIANCA:
What is the matter, ho? Who is 't that cried?

IAGO: Who is 't that cried?

BIANCA: O my dear Cassio!
My sweet Cassio! O Cassio, Cassio, Cassio!

IAGO:
O notable strumpet! Cassio, may you suspect
Who they should be that have thus mangled you?

CASSIO: No.

GRATIANO:
I am sorry to find you thus. I have been to seek you.

IAGO:
91   Lend me a garter. *(He applies a tourniquet.)* So.—O, for a chair,
To bear him easily hence!

BIANCA:
Alas, he faints! O Cassio, Cassio, Cassio!

IAGO:
Gentlemen all, I do suspect this trash
To be a party in this injury.—
Patience awhile, good Cassio.—Come, come;
Lend me a light. *(He shines the light on Roderigo.)*
Know we this face or no?
Alas, my friend and my dear countryman
Roderigo! No.—Yes, sure.—O heaven! Roderigo!

GRATIANO: What, of Venice?

IAGO: Even he, sir. Did you know him?

GRATIANO: Know him? Ay.

IAGO:
104   Signor Gratiano? I cry your gentle pardon.
105   These bloody accidents must excuse my manners
That so neglected you.

GRATIANO: I am glad to see you.

IAGO:
How do you, Cassio? O, a chair, a chair!

GRATIANO: Roderigo!

IAGO:
110   He, he, 'tis he. *(A litter is brought in.)* O, that's well said;
the chair.
Some good man bear him carefully from hence;

---

91 chair litter   **104 gentle** noble   **105 accidents** sudden events   **110 well said**
well done

I'll fetch the General's surgeon. (*To Bianca.*) For you, mistress,
114 Save you your labor.—He that lies slain here, Cassio,
115 Was my dear friend. What malice was between you?
CASSIO:
　　None in the world, nor do I know the man.
IAGO (*to Bianca*):
117 What, look you pale?—O, bear him out o' th' air.

(*Cassio and Roderigo are borne off.*)

118 Stay you, good gentlemen.—Look you pale, mistress?—
119 Do you perceive the gastness of her eye?—
120 Nay, if you stare, we shall hear more anon.—
　　Behold her well; I pray you, look upon her.
　　Do you see, gentlemen? Nay, guiltiness
　　Will speak, though tongues were out of use.

(*Enter Emilia.*)

EMILIA:
　　'Las, what's the matter? What's the matter, husband?
IAGO:
　　Cassio hath here been set on in the dark
　　By Roderigo and fellows that are scaped.
　　He's almost slain, and Roderigo dead.
EMILIA:
　　Alas, good gentleman! Alas, good Cassio!
IAGO:
　　This is the fruits of whoring. Prithee, Emilia,
130 Go know of Cassio where he supped tonight.
　　(*To Bianca.*) What, do you shake at that?
BIANCA:
　　He supped at my house, but I therefore shake not.
IAGO:
　　O, did he so? I charge you go with me.
EMILIA: O, fie upon thee, strumpet!
BIANCA:
135 I am no strumpet, but of life as honest
　　As you that thus abuse me.
EMILIA: As I? Faugh! Fie upon thee!
IAGO:
138 Kind gentlemen, let's go see poor Cassio dressed.-
　　Come, mistress, you must tell's another tale.

---

114 Save [...] labor i.e., never you mind tending Cassio　**115 malice** enmity　**117 bear [...] air** (Fresh air was thought to be dangerous for a wound.)　**118 Stay you** (Lodovico and Gratiano are evidently about to leave.)　**119 gastness** terror　**120 stare** (Iago pretends to interpret Bianca's wild looks as an involuntary confession of guilt.)　**130 know** learn　**135 honest** chaste　**138 Cassio dressed** Cassio's wounds dressed

Emilia, run you to the citadel
And tell my lord and lady what hath happed.—
Will you go on afore? (*Aside.*) This is the night
143   That either makes me or fordoes me quite.   (*Exeunt.*)

5.2

(*Enter Othello [with a light], and Desdemona in her bed.*)

OTHELLO:
1   It is the cause, it is the cause, my soul.
Let me not name it to you, you chaste stars!
It is the cause. Yet I'll not shed her blood,
Nor scar that whiter skin of hers than snow,
5   And smooth as monumental alabaster.
Yet she must die, else she'll betray more men.
7   Put out the light, and then put out the light.
8   If I quench thee, thou flaming minister,
I can again thy former light restore,
10   Should I repent me; but once put out thy light,
11   Thou cunning'st pattern of excelling nature,
12   I know not where is that Promethean heat
13   That can thy light relume. When I have plucked thy rose,
I cannot give it vital growth again;
It needs must wither. I'll smell thee on the tree.
                              (*He kisses her.*)
O balmy breath, that dost almost persuade
Justice to break her sword! One more, one more.
Be thus when thou art dead, and I will kill thee,
And love thee after. One more, and that's the last.
                              (*He kisses her.*)
So sweet was ne'er so fatal. I must weep,
21   But they are cruel tears. This sorrow's heavenly;
22   It strikes where it doth love. She wakes.
DESDEMONA: Who's there? Othello?
OTHELLO: Ay, Desdemona.
DESDEMONA: Will you come to bed, my lord?

---

143 **fordoes** undoes, ruins   **5.2 Location:** A bedchamber in the citadel. **s.d. in her bed** (Either the curtains are drawn back to reveal the bed in a recessed area backstage, or the bed is "thrust out" onstage as the scene begins.)   **1 cause** i.e., cause of justice, the offense itself, which Othello must correct as an agent of justice   **5 monumental** i.e., used in making tombs and funeral monuments   **7 the light [...] light** the torch or lamp [...] Desdemona's life   **8 flaming minister** torch or lamp that serves me   **10 repent me** change my mind   **11 Thou [...] pattern** you skillfully wrought perfect example   **12 Promethean heat** divine fire (Alluding to the theft of fire from heaven by Prometheus.)   **13 relume** rekindle   **21 cruel** unrelenting   **22 It [...] love** (Compare Hebrews 12:6: "For whom the Lord loveth he chasteneth.")

OTHELLO: Have you prayed tonight, Desdemon?

DESDEMONA: Ay, my lord.

OTHELLO:

28   If you bethink yourself of any crime
      Unreconciled as yet to heaven and grace,
30   Solicit for it straight.

DESDEMONA:
      Alack, my lord, what may you mean by that?

OTHELLO:
      Well, do it, and be brief. I will walk by.
      I would not kill thy unpreparèd spirit.
34   No, heaven forfend! I would not kill thy soul.

DESDEMONA:
      Talk you of killing?

OTHELLO: Ay, I do.

DESDEMONA: Then heaven
      Have mercy on me!

OTHELLO: Amen, with all my heart!

DESDEMONA:
      If you say so, I hope you will not kill me.

OTHELLO: Humh!

DESDEMONA:
      And yet I fear you; for you're fatal then
      When your eyes roll so. Why I should fear I know not,
      Since guiltiness I know not; but yet I feel I fear.

OTHELLO:
      Think on thy sins.

46   DESDEMONA: They are loves I bear to you.

OTHELLO: Ay, and for that thou diest.

DESDEMONA:
      That death's unnatural that kills for loving.
      Alas, why gnaw you so your nether lip?
      Some bloody passion shakes your very frame.
      These are portents; but yet I hope, I hope,
52   They do not point on me.

OTHELLO: Peace, and be still!

DESDEMONA: I will so. What's the matter?

OTHELLO:
      That handkerchief which I so loved and gave thee
      Thou gav'st to Cassio.

DESDEMONA: No, by my life and soul!
      Send for the man and ask him.

---

28 **crime** sin   30 **Solicit** petition, pray. **straight** immediately   34 **forfend** forbid
46 **They are [...] you** i.e., if I sinned, it was in loving you more than my father or more
than God   52 **point on** point at, predict what is to happen to

OTHELLO:

Sweet soul, take heed, take heed of perjury.

Thou art on thy deathbed.

DESDEMONA:

Ay, but not yet to die.

62   OTHELLO: Yes, presently.

Therefore confess thee freely of thy sin;

For to deny each article with oath

65   Cannot remove nor choke the strong conception

66   That I do groan withal. Thou art to die.

DESDEMONA:

Then Lord have mercy on me!

OTHELLO: I say, amen.

DESDEMONA:

And have you mercy too! I never did

70   Offend you in my life; never loved Cassio

71   But with such general warranty of heaven

As I might love. I never gave him token.

OTHELLO:

By heaven, I saw my handkerchief in 's hand.

74   O perjured woman! Thou dost stone my heart,

And makes me call what I intend to do

A murder, which I thought a sacrifice.

I saw the handkerchief.

DESDEMONA: He found it, then.

I never gave it him. Send for him hither;

Let him confess a truth.

OTHELLO: He hath confessed.

DESDEMONA: What, my lord?

OTHELLO:

That he hath used thee.

DESDEMONA: How? Unlawfully?

OTHELLO: Ay.

DESDEMONA:

He will not say so.

OTHELLO: No, his mouth is stopped;

88   Honest Iago hath ta'en order for't.

DESDEMONA:

O, my fear interprets. What, is he dead?

OTHELLO:

Had all his hairs been lives, my great revenge

Had stomach for them all.

DESDEMONA:

Alas, he is betrayed and I undone!   (*She weeps.*)

---

62 presently immediately   **65 conception** (1) belief in your guilt (2) plan in my mind
66 groan withal (1) groan at in sorrow (2) as in giving birth   **70 Offend** wrong   **71 warranty** sanction   **74 stone** turn to stone, harden   **88 ta'en order** taken measures

OTHELLO:

    Out, strumpet! Weep'st thou for him to my face?

DESDEMONA:

    O, banish me, my lord, but kill me not!

OTHELLO: Down, strumpet!

DESDEMONA:

    Kill me tomorrow; let me live tonight!

OTHELLO: Nay, if you strive—

DESDEMONA:

    But half an hour!

99   OTHELLO: Being done, there is no pause.

DESDEMONA:

    But while I say one prayer!

OTHELLO: It is too late.

                                (Smothers her.)

EMILIA (*at the door*):

    My lord, my lord! What, ho! My lord, my lord!

OTHELLO:

    What noise is this? Not dead? Not yet quite dead?

    I that am cruel am yet merciful;

    I would not have thee linger in thy pain.

                           (He dispatches her.)

    So, so.

EMILIA (*within*): What, ho! My lord, my lord!

OTHELLO: Who's there?

EMILIA (*within*):

    O, good my lord, I would speak a word with you!

OTHELLO:

    Yes, 'tis Emilia.—By and by—She's dead.

    'Tis like she comes to speak of Cassio's death.—

112   The noise was here. Ha! No more moving?

    Still as the grave. Shall she come in? Were 't good?—

    I think she stirs again. No. What's best to do?

    If she come in, she'll sure speak to my wife.

    My wife! My wife! What wife? I have no wife.

    O, insupportable! O heavy hour!

    Methinks it should be now a huge eclipse

    Of sun and moon, and that th' affrighted globe

120   Should yawn at alteration.

EMILIA (*within*):   I do beseech you

    That I may speak with you, O, good my lord!

---

99 Being done i.e., since justice has begun its relentless course   **112 here** (The Folio's *high* is possible, suggesting that the commotion of the attack on Cassio was loud.) **120 yawn** gape in amazement, i.e., move in an earthquake. (According to Pliny, earthquakes often happen during eclipses.) **at alteration** at these cataclysmic events in nature, well suited to express the horror of Desdemona's death

OTHELLO:

　　I had forgot thee. O, come in, Emilia.—
124　Soft, by and by. Let me the curtains draw—
　　　　(*He closes the bed-curtains and opens the door.*)
　　Where art thou?

　　　　　　　(*Enter Emilia.*)

　　　　　　　　What's the matter with thee now?

EMILIA:

　　O, my good lord, yonder's foul murders done!

OTHELLO: What, now?

EMILIA: But now, my lord.

OTHELLO:

130　It is the very error of the moon;
　　She comes more nearer earth than she was wont,
　　And makes men mad.

EMILIA:

　　Cassio, my lord, hath killed a young Venetian
　　Called Roderigo.

OTHELLO: Roderigo killed?
　　And Cassio killed?

EMILIA:　　　　　　No, Cassio is not killed.

OTHELLO:

　　Not Cassio killed? Then murder's out of tune,
　　And sweet revenge grows harsh.

DESDEMONA: O, falsely, falsely murdered!

EMILIA: O Lord, what cry is that?

OTHELLO: That? What?

EMILIA:

143　Out and alas, that was my lady's voice.

　　　　　　(*She opens the bed-curtains.*)

　　Help, help, ho, help! O lady, speak again!
　　Sweet Desdemona! O sweet mistress, speak!

DESDEMONA: A guiltless death I die.

EMILIA: O, who hath done this deed?

DESDEMONA: Nobody; I myself. Farewell.
　　Commend me to my kind lord. O, farewell! (*She dies.*)

OTHELLO:

　　Why, how should she be murdered?

EMILIA:　　　　　　　　　　Alas, who knows?

OTHELLO:

　　You heard her say herself it was not I.

---

124 Soft wait a minute　**130 error** aberration, irregularity　**143 Out** (A cry of dismay, intensifying *alas.*)

EMILIA:

She said so. I must needs report the truth.

OTHELLO:

She's like a liar gone to burning hell!

'Twas I that killed her.

EMILIA: O, the more angel she,

And you the blacker devil!

OTHELLO:

158   She turned to folly, and she was a whore.

EMILIA:

159   Thou dost belie her, and thou art a devil.

OTHELLO: She was false as water.

EMILIA: Thou art rash as fire to say

That she was false. O, she was heavenly true!

OTHELLO:

163   Cassio did top her. Ask thy husband else.

O, I were damned beneath all depth in hell

But that I did proceed upon just grounds

To this extremity. Thy husband knew it all.

EMILIA: My husband?

OTHELLO: Thy husband.

EMILIA: That she was false to wedlock?

OTHELLO:

Ay, with Cassio. Nay, had she been true,

If heaven would make me such another world

172   Of one entire and perfect chrysolite,

I'd not have sold her for it.

EMILIA: My husband?

OTHELLO:

Ay, 'twas he that told me on her first.

An honest man he is, and hates the slime

That sticks on filthy deeds.

EMILIA: My husband?

OTHELLO:

179   What needs this iterance, woman? I say thy husband.

EMILIA:

180   O mistress, villainy hath made mocks with love!

My husband say she was false?

OTHELLO: He, woman;

I say thy husband. Dost understand the word?

My friend, thy husband, honest, honest Iago.

EMILIA:

If he say so, may his pernicious soul

---

158 folly i.e., wantonness, fleshly sin   **159 belie** slander   **163 else** i.e., if you don't believe me   **172 chrysolite** precious topaz   **179 iterance** iteration, repetition **180 made mocks with** derided, made sport of

Rot half a grain a day! He lies to th' heart.

She was too fond of her most filthy bargain.

OTHELLO: Ha?   (*He draws.*)

EMILIA: Do thy worst!

This deed of thine is no more worthy heaven

Than thou wast worthy her.

192   OTHELLO: Peace, you were best.

EMILIA:

Thou hast not half that power to do me harm

194   As I have to be hurt. O gull! O dolt!

As ignorant as dirt! Thou hast done a deed—

I care not for thy sword; I'll make thee known,

Though I lost twenty lives.—Help! Help, ho, help!

The Moor hath killed my mistress! Murder, murder!

(Enter Montano, Gratiano, and Iago.)

MONTANO:

What is the matter? How now, General?

EMILIA:

O, are you come, Iago? You have done well,

That men must lay their murders on your neck.

GRATIANO: What is the matter?

EMILIA (*to Iago*):

Disprove this villain, if thou be'st a man.

He says thou toldst him that his wife was false.

I know thou didst not; thou'rt not such a villain.

Speak, for my heart is full.

IAGO:

I told him what I thought, and told no more

208   Than what he found himself was apt and true.

EMILIA:

But did you ever tell him she was false?

IAGO: I did.

EMILIA:

You told a lie, an odious, damnèd lie!

Upon my soul, a lie, a wicked lie.

She false with Cassio? Did you say with Cassio?

IAGO:

214   With Cassio, mistress. Go to, charm your tongue.

EMILIA:

I will not charm my tongue; I am bound to speak.

My mistress here lies murdered in her bed—

ALL: O heavens forfend!

_____

192 you were best it would be best for you   **194 to be hurt** i.e, to endure hurt. **gull** dupe   **208 apt** plausible   **214 charm** keep silent (as though by a magic spell)

EMILIA:
  And your reports have set the murder on.

OTHELLO:
  Nay, stare not, masters. It is true indeed.

GRATIANO: 'Tis a strange truth.

MONTANO:
  O monstrous act!

EMILIA: Villainy, villainy, villainy!
  I think upon 't—I think I smell 't! O villainy!
224 I thought so then—I'll kill myself for grief—
  O villainy, villainy!

IAGO:
  What, are you mad? I charge you, get you home.

EMILIA:
  Good gentlemen, let me have leave to speak.
  'Tis proper I obey him, but not now.
  Perchance, Iago, I will ne'er go home.

OTHELLO:
230 O! O! O!   (*Othello falls on the bed.*)

EMILIA: Nay, lay thee down and roar,
  For thou hast killed the sweetest innocent
233 That e'er did lift up eye.

OTHELLO (*rising*):   O, she was foul!
  I scarce did know you, uncle. There lies your niece,
  Whose breath indeed these hands have newly stopped.
237 I know this act shows horrible and grim.

GRATIANO:
  Poor Desdemon! I am glad thy father's dead.
  Thy match was mortal to him, and pure grief
240 Shore his old thread in twain. Did he live now,
241 This sight would make him do a desperate turn,
  Yea, curse his better angel from his side,
243 And fall to reprobance.

OTHELLO:
  'Tis pitiful. But yet Iago knows.
  That she with Cassio hath the act of shame
  A thousand times committed. Cassio confessed it;
247 And she did gratify his amorous works
248 With that recognizance and pledge of love
  Which I first gave her. I saw it in his hand;

---

224 then (Perhaps at 3.3.347-349 and 4.2.150-169.)   **230 s.d. Othello [...] bed** (This
direction is from the Quarto, as also *He kisses her* at line 19 and *She dies* at line 149.)
233 lift up eye i.e., lift her eyes to heaven   **237 shows** looks   **240 Shore [...] thread**
sheared the thread of his old age (as Atropos, one of the three Fates, was thought to do)
241 turn deed   **243 reprobance** damnation, i.e., suicide   **247 gratify** reward
248 recognizance token

It was a handkerchief, an antique token
My father gave my mother.

EMILIA: O God! O heavenly God!

IAGO:
Zounds, hold your peace.

EMILIA: 'Twill out, 'twill out! I peace?

255   No, I will speak as liberal as the north.
Let heaven and men and devils, let them all,
All, all, cry shame against me, yet I'll speak.

IAGO:
Be wise, and get you home.

EMILIA: I will not.

           (Iago threatens Emilia.)

GRATIANO: Fie,
Your sword upon a woman?

EMILIA:
O thou dull Moor! That handkerchief thou speak'st of
I found by fortune and did give my husband;
For often, with a solemn earnestness,

265   More than indeed belonged to such a trifle,
He begged of me to steal 't.

IAGO: Villainous whore!

EMILIA:
She give it Cassio? No, alas! I found it,
And I did give 't my husband.

IAGO: Filth, thou liest!

EMILIA:
By heaven, I do not, I do not, gentlemen.

272   O murderous coxcomb! What should such a fool
Do with so good a wife?

274   OTHELLO: Are there no stones in heaven

275   But what serves for the thunder?—Precious villain!

           *(He runs at Iago; Montano disarms Othello, Iago, from behind, stabs
           Emilia.)*

GRATIANO:
The woman falls! Sure he hath killed his wife.

EMILIA:
Ay, ay. O, lay me by my mistress' side.
           (Exit Iago.)

---

255 liberal as the north freely as the north wind (blows)   **265 belonged** was
appropriate   **272 coxcomb** fool. (Addressed to Othello.)   **274 stones** bolts, such as
those used for thunderbolts   **275 Precious** i.e., arrant, utter, **s.d. He [...] Emilia** (The
Quarto text reads, "The Moor runs at Iago. Iago kills his wife." The Quarto also specifies
the exit of Iago at line 277 and the death of Emilia at line 293.)

GRATIANO:
    He's gone, but his wife's killed.
MONTANO:
    'Tis a notorious villain. Take you this weapon,
    Which I have here recovered from the Moor.
    Come, guard the door without. Let him not pass,
    But kill him rather. I'll after that same villain,
    For 'tis a damnèd slave.

    *(Exit [with all but Othello and Emilia, who has been laid by Desde-
    mona's side].)*

OTHELLO: I am not valiant neither,
285   But every puny whipster gets my sword.
286   But why should honor outlive honesty?
    Let it go all.
EMILIA: What did thy song bode, lady?
    Hark, canst thou hear me? I will play the swan,
    And die in music. *(She sings.)* "Willow, willow, willow."
    Moor, she was chaste. She loved thee, cruel Moor.
    So come my soul to bliss as I speak true.
    So speaking as I think, alas, I die.   *(She dies.)*
OTHELLO:
    I have another weapon in this chamber;
295   It was a sword of Spain, the ice-brook's temper—
    O, here it is. *(He finds a sword.)* Uncle, I must come forth.
GRATIANO *(within)*:
    If thou attempt it, it will cost thee dear.
    Thou hast no weapon, and perforce must suffer.
OTHELLO:
    Look in upon me then and speak with me,
300   Or, naked as I am, I will assault thee.

    (Enter Gratiano.)

GRATIANO:
    What is the matter?
OTHELLO: Behold, I have a weapon;
    A better never did itself sustain
    Upon a soldier's thigh. I have seen the day
    That, with this little arm and this good sword,
    I have made my way through more impediments
307   Than twenty times your stop. But O, vain boast!
    Who can control his fate? 'Tis not so now.

---

285 whipster contemptible fellow (one who is always ready to whip out his sword)
286 honor i.e., the bravery for which one enjoys a soldier's reputation. **honesty** true
integrity   **295 the ice-brook's temper** tempered in ice-cold water   **300 naked**
unarmed   **307 stop** power (to stop)

Be not afraid, though you do see me weaponed;
310   Here is my journey's end, here is my butt
311   And very seamark of my utmost sail.

(Gratiano steps back.)

312   Do you go back dismayed? 'Tis a lost fear;
313   Man but a rush against Othello's breast
       And he retires. Where should Othello go?

(He turns to Desdemona.)

       Now, how dost thou look now? O ill-starred wench!
316   Pale as thy smock! When we shall meet at compt,
       This look of thine will hurl my soul from heaven,
       And fiends will snatch at it. Cold, cold, my girl?
319   Even like thy chastity. O cursèd, cursèd slave!
       Whip me, ye devils,
       From the possession of this heavenly sight!
       Blow me about in winds! Roast me in sulfur!
       Wash me in steep-down gulfs of liquid fire!
       O Desdemon! Dead, Desdemon! Dead! O! O!

(Enter Lodovico, Cassio [carried in a litter], Montano, and Iago [prisoner], with officers.)

LODOVICO:
   Where is this rash and most unfortunate man?
OTHELLO:
   That's he that was Othello. Here I am.
LODOVICO:
   Where is that viper? Bring the villain forth.

(Iago is led forward.)

OTHELLO:
328   I look down towards his feet; but that's a fable.
       If that thou be'st a devil, I cannot kill thee.

(He wounds Iago.)

LODOVICO:
   Wrench his sword from him.   *(Othello is disarmed.)*
IAGO: I bleed, sir, but not killed.
OTHELLO:
   I am not sorry neither. I'd have thee live,

---

310 butt goal, limit (An archery term.)   **311 seamark** beacon (marking his destination or limit)   **312 lost** wasted, unneeded   **313 Man [...] rush** wield no more than a reed
316 compt account, judgment day   **319 slave** i.e., Othello himself   **324 s.d. in a litter** (The Quarto specifies that Cassio is "in a chair.")   **328 towards his feet** i.e., to see if they are cloven, as the devil's are fabled to be

333   For in my sense 'tis happiness to die.

LODOVICO:

    O thou Othello that was once so good,

335   Fall'n in the practice of a cursèd slave,

    What shall be said to thee?

OTHELLO: Why, anything.

    An honorable murderer, if you will,

    For naught I did in hate, but all in honor.

LODOVICO:

    This wretch hath part confessed his villainy.

341   Did you and he consent in Cassio's death?

OTHELLO: Ay.

CASSIO:

    Dear General, I never gave you cause.

OTHELLO:

    I do believe it, and I ask your pardon.

    Will you, I pray, demand that demi-devil

    Why he hath thus ensnared my soul and body?

IAGO:

    Demand me nothing. What you know, you know.

    From this time forth I never will speak word.

LODOVICO: What, not to pray?

350 GRATIANO: Torments will ope your lips.

OTHELLO: Well, thou dost best.

LODOVICO:

    Sir, you shall understand what hath befall'n,

    Which, as I think, you know not. Here is a letter

    Found in the pocket of the slain Roderigo;

    And here another. (*He produces letters.*) The one of them imports

    The death of Cassio, to be undertook

    By Roderigo.

OTHELLO: O villain!

359 CASSIO: Most heathenish and most gross!

LODOVICO (*showing another paper*):

360   Now here's another discontented paper

    Found in his pocket too. And this, it seems,

    Roderigo meant t' have sent this damnèd villain;

363   But that belike Iago in the interim

364   Came in and satisfied him.

OTHELLO: O thou pernicious caitiff!—

    How came you, Cassio, by that handkerchief

    That was my wife's?

---

333 in my sense to one who feels as I do   **335 in the practice** through the plotting, into the snare. **slave** villain   **341 consent** agree   **350 Torments** torture   **359 gross** monstrous   **360 discontented** full of discontent   **363 belike** most likely   **364 Came [...] him** interposed and gave him satisfactory explanation

CASSIO: I found it in my chamber;
And he himself confessed but even now
That there he dropped it for a special purpose
371 Which wrought to his desire.
OTHELLO: O fool, fool, fool!
CASSIO:
There is besides in Roderigo's letter
How he upbraids Iago, that he made him
375 Brave me upon the watch, whereon it came
376 That I was cast; and even but now he spake,
After long seeming dead, Iago hurt him,
Iago set him on.
LODOVICO (*to Othello*):
You must forsake this room and go with us.
380 Your power and your command is taken off,
And Cassio rules in Cyprus. For this slave,
If there be any cunning cruelty
383 That can torment him much and hold him long,
384 It shall be his. You shall close prisoner rest
Till that the nature of your fault be known
To the Venetian state.—Come, bring away.
OTHELLO:
387 Soft you; a word or two before you go.
I have done the state some service, and they know 't.
No more of that. I pray you, in your letters,
390 When you shall these unlucky deeds relate,
Speak of me as I am; nothing extenuate,
Nor set down aught in malice. Then must you speak
Of one that loved not wisely but too well;
394 Of one not easily jealous but, being wrought,
395 Perplexed in the extreme; of one whose hand,
396 Like the base Indian, threw a pearl away
397 Richer than all his tribe; of one whose subdued eyes,
Albeit unusèd to the melting mood,
Drops tears as fast as the Arabian trees
400 Their medicinable gum. Set you down this;
And say besides that in Aleppo once,
Where a malignant and a turbaned Turk

---

371 wrought [...] desire worked out as he wished, fitted in with his plan **375 Brave**
defy. **whereon it came** whereof it came about **376 cast** dismissed **380 taken off**
taken away **383 hold him long** keep him alive a long time (during his torture) **384
rest** remain **387 Soft you** one moment **390 unlucky** unfortunate **394 wrought**
worked upon, worked into a frenzy **395 Perplexed** distraught **396 Indian** (This
reading from the Quarto pictures an ignorant savage who cannot recognize the value of a
precious jewel. The Folio reading, *Iudean* or *Judean*, i.e., infidel or disbeliever, may refer
to Herod, who slew Miriamne in a fit of jealousy, or to Judas Iscariot, the betrayer of
Christ.) **397 subdued** i.e., overcome by grief **400 gum** i.e., myrrh

Beat a Venetian and traduced the state,
I took by th' throat the circumcisèd dog
And smote him, thus.   (*He stabs himself.*)

406   LODOVICO: O bloody period!

GRATIANO: All that is spoke is marred.

OTHELLO:

I kissed thee ere I killed thee. No way but this,
Killing myself, to die upon a kiss.

(*He kisses Desdemona and dies.*)

CASSIO:

This did I fear, but thought he had no weapon;
For he was great of heart.

412   LODOVICO (*to Iago.*):   O Spartan dog,
413   More fell than anguish, hunger, or the sea!
Look on the tragic loading of this bed.
This is thy work. The object poisons sight;
416   Let it be hid. Gratiano, keep the house,

(*The bed curtains are drawn.*)

417   And seize upon the fortunes of the Moor,
418   For they succeed on you. (*To Cassio.*) To you, Lord Governor,
418   Remains the censure of this hellish villain,
The time, the place, the torture. O, enforce it!

---

405 s.d. He stabs himself (This direction is in the Quarto text).   **406 period** termination, conclusion   **412 Spartan dog** (Spartan dogs were noted for their savagery and silence.)   **413 fell** cruel   **416 Let it be hid** i.e., draw the bed curtains. (No stage direction specifies that the dead are to be carried offstage at the end of the play.) **keep** remain in   **417 seize upon** take legal possession of   **418 succeed on** pass as though by inheritance to   **419 censure** sentencing

Questions for Discussion

Act I

1. What are Iago's motives for disliking Othello? What does he mean by "'Tis in ourselves that we are thus or thus" (1.3.341)? Why does Iago tell Roderigo he hates Othello, then advise Othello of danger in the next scene?

2. How does Iago feel about Othello's ethnic background? Support your answer with quotations from the play.

3. When Brabantio and Roderigo draw swords to attack Othello, the latter says, "Keep up your bright swords, for the dew will rust them" (1.2.71). What does this line reveal about Othello's character?

4. What are the qualities in Othello that cause Desdemona to fall in love with him?

5. What in Iago's character makes him particularly dangerous?

6. Why does Othello trust Iago more than he trusts Desdemona?

Act II

1. Why must Othello punish Cassio so severely? Is Cassio to blame? Is Othello punishing Cassio unjustly?

2. Why is Iago adept when talking to Roderigo but inept in producing flattering verses to please Desdemona? How do Iago's apparent ineptness in flattery and bluntness of speech serve his purpose?

3. What seems to be Iago's attitude toward women and sexuality? How does the imagery he uses reveal this attitude?

4. Why does Shakespeare have the ordinarily deceptive Iago reveal his true character in his soliloquies?

Act III

1. How does Iago lead Othello to begin doubting and suspecting Cassio?

2. Iago says in 3.3.360, "The Moor already changes with my poison." When Othello begins to doubt Desdemona, how else does his character change? Does his language change? If so, how does that reveal a character change? See 3.3.287–306 and 3.3.383—95.

3. Explain the significance of the handkerchief.

4. Iago has what he initially sought—the position of lieutenant. Why then does he continue his efforts to destroy Othello?

5. Explain the foreshadowing of Othello's speech:
   Perdition catch my soul
   But I do love thee! And when I love thee not,
   Chaos is come again. (3.3.100–02)

6. Explain the truth and the irony of Iago's speech:
   Who steals my purse steals trash; 'tis something, nothing;
   'Twas mine, 'tis his, and has been slave to thousands;
   But he that filches from me my good name
   Robs me of that which not enriches him
   And makes me poor indeed. (3.3.177–81)

Act IV

1. How does Iago manipulate Cassio into incriminating himself and Desdemona?

2. Do Othello's speech and actions in this act make sense? What has happened to him? How does Lodovico's speech in 4.1.286–90 reflect the extent of Othello's fall?

3. Does Desdemona show the slightest sign of disobedience or unfaithfulness to Othello? How innocent is she? How does she respond to bad treatment from him? Support your response with references to the text. See, in particular, 4.3.63–66 and 4.3.84–85.

4. In what ways is Emilia a dramatic foil for Desdemona?

Act V

1. Why does Othello say, "Put out the light, and then put out the light" (5.2.7)?

2. How does Othello feel about killing Desdemona as he prepares to do so? See his soliloquy at 5.2.1–22.

3. How does Othello's speech at 5.2.302–24 reflect the extent of his fall?

4. What is Othello's motivation to kill Desdemona? Would he have been justified in doing so even if he had incontrovertible evidence of her infidelity? What flaw in his character leads him to fall into Iago's trap?

5. Why, after having explained his motives in soliloquies and conversations earlier in the play, does Iago now (5.2.348) say, "From this time forth I never will speak word"?

6. In what sense is Othello's death a triumph? Has he managed to retain any of his former dignity?

Suggestions for Exploring, Writing, and Persuading

1. Examine Iago's motivation. Is there any adequate motive that can explain the intensity of his malevolence? Is his evil ultimately explainable? Is it diabolic?

2. Analyze the means by which Iago poisons Othello's mind.

3. Examine in detail the change Othello undergoes. How does jealousy change not only his attitude toward Desdemona and Cassio but also his language, his sleep, and his attitudes toward his work as a soldier—his entire personality?

4. Discuss in detail how imagery defines one or more of the major characters—Iago, Desdemona, Othello, or Cassio. For example, you might choose to show how Iago's use of animal imagery reveals his character.

5. In *Poetics*, Aristotle describes the tragic hero as a good man who holds a high position and falls because of a flaw within himself. Write an essay explaining how Othello does or does not fit this definition.

Casebook on Amy Tan

WRITING ABOUT FEAR AND LOSS

The two excerpts from Amy Tan's novels *The Hundred Secret Senses* and *The Bonesetter's Daughter* are excellent examples of the theme of fear and loss. They are connected to each other through the characters and Tan's physical, emotional, and cultural experiences that determine the revelations about the self. The three articles will allow you to write critically about this theme using both primary and secondary sources. They will also provide insight into Chinese and Chinese American feelings of alienation.

Amy Tan (b. 1952)

Amy Tan was born in Oakland, California, several years after her mother and father emigrated from China. Upon the deaths of her father and brother in 1967 and 1968, the family began a haphazard journey through Europe before settling in Switzerland. For the next seven years, Tan attended five schools before graduating with honors from San Jose State University, where she later earned an M.A. in linguistics. In 1989 her first novel, The Joy Luck Club, *was published and through word-of-mouth endorsements by independent booksellers became a surprise bestseller. The* Joy Luck Club *received numerous awards and was adapted into a feature film in 1994. Tan is also author of* The Kitchen God's Wife *(1991),* The Hundred Secret Senses*

(1995), a number of short stories and essays, and two children's books. Her most recent novel is The Bonesetter's Daughter *(2002).*

YOUNG GIRL'S WISH

1   My first morning in China, I awake in a dark hotel room in Guilin and see a figure leaning over my bed, staring at me with the concentrated look of a killer. I'm about to scream, when I hear my sister Kwan saying, in Chinese, "Sleeping on your side—so *this* is the reason your posture is so bad. From now on, you must sleep on your back. Also, do exercises."

2   She snaps on the light and proceeds to demonstrate, hands on hips, twisting at the waist like a sixties P.E. teacher. I wonder how long she's been standing by my bed, waiting for me to waken so she can present her latest bit of unsolicited advice. Her bed is already made.

3   I look at my watch and say, in a grumpy voice, "Kwan, it's only five in the morning."

4   "This is China. Everyone else is up. Only you're asleep."

5   "Not anymore."

6   We've been in China less than eight hours, and already she's taking control of my life. We're on her terrain; we have to go by her rules, speak her language. She's in Chinese heaven.

7   Snatching my blankets, she laughs. "Libby-ah, hurry and get up." Kwan has never been able to correctly pronounce my name, Olivia. "I want to go see my village and surprise everyone. I want to watch Big Ma's mouth fall open and hear her words of surprise: 'Hey, I thought I chased you away. Why are you back?'"

8   Kwan pushes open the window. We're staying at the Sheraton Guilin, which faces the Li River. Outside it's still dark. I can hear the *trnnng! trnnng!* of what sounds like a noisy pachinko parlor. I go to the window and look down. Peddlers on tricycle carts are ringing their bells, greeting one another as they haul their baskets of grain, melons, and turnips to market. The boulevard is bristling with the shadows of bicycles and cars, workers and schoolchildren—the whole world chirping and honking, shouting and laughing, as though it were the middle of the day. On the handlebar of a bicycle dangle the gigantic heads of four pigs, roped through the nostrils, their white snouts curled in death grins.

9   "Look." Kwan points down the street to a set of stalls lit by low-watt bulbs. "We can buy breakfast there, cheap and good. Better than paying nine dollars each for hotel food—and for what? Doughnut, orange juice, bacon, who wants it?"

10   I recall the admonition in our guidebooks to steer clear of food sold by street venders. "Nine dollars, that's not much," I reason.

11   "Wah! You can't think this way anymore. Now you're in China. Nine dollars is lots of money here, one week's salary."

12   "Yeah, but cheap food might come with food poisoning."

13   Kwan gestures to the street. "You look. All those people there, do they have food poisoning?"

14   Kwan is right. Who am I to begrudge carrying home a few parasites? I slip some warm clothes on and go into the hallway to knock on my husband's door. Simon answers immediately, fully dressed. "I couldn't sleep," he admits.

15   In five minutes, the three of us are on the sidewalk. We pass dozens of food stalls, some with portable propane burners, others with makeshift grills. In front of the stalls, customers squat in semicircles eating noodles and dumplings. Kwan chooses a vender who is slapping what look like floury pancakes onto the sides of a blazing-hot oil drum. "Give me three," she says, in Chinese. The vender pries the pancakes off with his blackened fingers, and Simon and I yelp as we toss the hot pancakes up and down like circus jugglers.

16   "How much?" Kwan opens her change purse.

17   "Six yuan," the pancake vender tells her.

18   I calculate the cost is a little more than a dollar, dirt cheap. By Kwan's estimation, this is tantamount to extortion. "Wah!" She points to another customer. "You charged him only fifty fen a pancake."

19   "Of course! He's a local worker. You three are tourists."

20   "What are you saying! I'm also local."

21   "You?" The vender snorts and gives her a cynical once-over. "From where, then?"

22   "Changmian."

23   His eyebrows rise in suspicion. "Really, now! Who do you know in Changmian?"

24   Kwan rattles off some names.

25   The vender slaps his thigh. "Wu Ze-min? You know Wu Ze-min?"

26   "Of course. As children, we lived across the lane from each other. I haven't seen him in over thirty years."

27   "His daughter married my son."

28   "Nonsense!"

29   The man laughs. "It's true. Two years ago. My wife and my mother opposed the match—just because the girl was from Changmian. But they have old countryside ideas, they still believe Changmian is cursed. Not me, I'm not superstitious, not anymore. And now a baby's been born, last spring, a girl, but I don't mind."

30   "Hard to believe Wu Ze-min's a grandfather. How is he?"

31   "Lost his wife twenty years ago, when they were sent to the cowsheds for counter-revolutionary thinking. They smashed his hands, but not his mind. Later he married another woman, Yang Ling-fang."

32   "That's not possible! She was the little sister of an old schoolmate of mine. I still see her as a tender young girl."

33   "Not so tender anymore. She's got *jiaoban* skin, tough as leather, been through plenty of hardships, let me tell you."

34   Kwan and the vender continue to gossip while Simon and I eat our pancakes. They taste like a cross between focaccia and a green-onion

omelette. By now Kwan and the vender act like old friends, and he advises her how to get a good price on a driver to take us to Changmian.

35   "All right, older brother," Kwan says, "how much do I owe you?"

36   "Six yuan."

37   "Wah! Still six yuan? Too much, too much. I'll give you two, no more than that."

38   "Make it three, then."

39   Kwan grunts, settles up, and we leave. When we're half a block away, I whisper to Simon, "That man said Changmian is cursed."

40   Kwan overhears me. "*Tst!* That's just a story, a thousand years old. Only stupid people still think Changmian is a bad-luck place to live."

41   I translate for Simon, then ask, "What kind of bad luck?"

42   "You don't want to know."

43   I am about to insist she tell me, when Simon points to an open-air market overflowing with wicker baskets of thick-skinned pomelos, dried beans, cassia tea, chilies.

44   I inhale deeply and imagine that I'm filling my lungs with the very air that inspired my ancestors, whoever they might have been. Because we arrived late the night before, we haven't yet seen the Guilin landscape, its fabled karst peaks, its magical limestone caves, and all the other sites listed in our guidebook as the reasons this is known in China as "the most beautiful place on earth."

45   Looking up toward cloud level, we see the amazing peaks, which resemble prehistoric shark's teeth, the clichéd subject of every Chinese calendar and scroll painting. But tucked in the gums of these ancient stone formations is the blight of high-rises, their stucco exteriors grimy with industrial pollution, their signboards splashed with garish red and gilt characters. Between these are lower buildings from an earlier era, all of them painted a proletarian toothpaste-green. And here and there is the rubble of prewar houses and impromptu garbage dumps. The whole scene gives Guilin the look and stench of a pretty face marred by tawdry lipstick, gapped teeth, and an advanced case of periodontal disease.

46   "Boy, oh boy," whispers Simon. "If Guilin is China's most beautiful city, I can't wait to see what the cursed village of Changmian looks like."

47   We catch up with Kwan. "Everything is entirely different, no longer the same." Kwan must be sad to see how horribly Guilin has changed over the past thirty years. But then she says, in a proud and marvelling voice, "So much progress, everything is so much better."

48   A couple of blocks farther on, we come upon a bird market. Hanging from tree limbs are hundreds of decorative cages containing singing finches, and exotic birds with gorgeous plumage, punk crests, and fan-like tails. On the ground are cages of huge birds, perhaps eagles or hawks, magnificent, with menacing talons and beaks. There are also the ordinary fowl—chickens and ducks, destined for the stewpot.

49   I see a man hissing at me. "*Sssss!*" He sternly motions me to come over. What is he, the secret police?

50 The man solemnly reaches underneath a table and brings out a cage. "You like," he says, in English. Facing me is a snowy-white owl with milk-chocolate highlights. It looks like a fat Siamese cat with wings. The owl blinks its golden eyes and I fall in love.

51 "Hey, Simon, Kwan, come here. Look at this."

52 "One hundred dollar, U.S.," the man says. "Very cheap."

53 Simon shakes his head and says in a weird combination of pantomime and broken English: "Take bird on plane, not possible, customs official will say stop, not allowed, must pay big fine—"

54 "How much?" the man asks brusquely. "You say. I give you morning price, best price."

55 "There's no use bargaining," Kwan tells the man in Chinese. "We're tourists. We can't bring birds back to the United States, no matter how cheap."

56 "Aaah, who's talking about bringing it back?" the man replies in rapid Chinese. "Buy it today, then take it to that restaurant, over there. For a small price, they can cook it tonight for your dinner."

57 "Oh, my God!" I turn to Simon. "He's selling this owl as food!"

58 "That's disgusting. Tell him he's a fucking goon."

59 "You tell him!"

60 "I can't speak Chinese."

61 The man must think I am urging my husband to buy me an owl for din-ner. "You're very lucky I even have *one*. The cat-eagle is rare, very rare," he brags. "Took me three weeks to catch it."

62 "I don't believe this," I tell Simon. "I'm going to be sick."

63 Then I hear Kwan saying, "A cat-eagle is not that rare, just hard to catch. Besides, I hear the flavor is ordinary."

64 "To be honest," says the man, "it's not as pungent as, say, a pangolin. But you eat a cat-eagle to give you strength and ambition, not to be fussy over taste. Also, it's good for improving your eyesight. One of my cus-tomers was nearly blind. After he ate a cat-eagle, he could see his wife for the first time in twenty years. The customer came back and cursed me: 'Shit! She's ugly enough to scare a monkey. Fuck your mother for let-ting me eat that cat-eagle!'"

65 Kwan laughs heartily. "Yes, yes, I've heard this about cat-eagles. It's a good story." She pulls out her change purse and holds up a hundred-yuan note.

66 "Kwan, what are you doing?" I cry. "We are *not* going to eat this owl!"

67 The man waves away the hundred yuan. "Only American money," he says firmly. "One hundred *American* dollars."

68 Kwan pulls out an American ten-dollar bill.

69 "Kwan!" I shout.

70 The man shakes his head, refusing the ten. Kwan shrugs, then starts to walk away. The man shouts to her to give him fifty, then. She comes back and holds out a ten and a five, and says, "That's my last offer."

71 "This is insane!" Simon mutters.

72   The man sighs, then relinquishes the cage, complaining, "What a shame, so little money for so much work. Look at my hands, three weeks of climbing and cutting down bushes to catch this bird."

73   As we walk away, I grab Kwan's free arm: "There's no way I'm going to let you eat this owl. I don't care if we are in China."

74   "Shh! Shh! You'll scare him!" Kwan pulls the cage out of my reach. She gives me a maddening smile, then walks over to a concrete wall, overlooking the river and sets the cage on top. She meows to the owl. "Oh, little friend, you want to go to Changmian? You want to climb with me to the top of the mountain, let my little sister watch you fly away?" The owl twists his head and blinks.

75   I almost cry with joy and guilt. Why do I think such bad things about Kwan?

76   "See that?" I hear Kwan say. "Over there." She's pointing to a cone-shaped peak off in the distance. "Just outside my village stands a sharp-headed mountain, taller than that one, even. We call it Young Girl's Wish, after a slave girl who ran away to the top of it, then flew off with a phoenix who was her lover." Kwan looks at me. "It's a story, just superstition."

77   I'm amused that she thinks she has to explain.

78   Kwan continues, "Yet all the girls in our village believed in that tale, not because they were stupid but because they wanted to hope for a better life. We thought that if we climbed to the top and made a wish, it might come true. So we raised little hatchlings, and when the birds were ready to fly we climbed to the top of Young Girl's Wish and let them go. The birds would then fly to where the phoenixes lived and tell them our wishes." Kwan sniffs. "Big Ma told me the peak was named Young Girl's Wish because a crazy girl climbed to the top. But when she tried to fly, she fell all the way down and lodged herself so firmly into the earth she became a boulder. Big Ma said that's why you can see so many boulders at the bottom of that peak—they're all the stupid girls who followed her kind of crazy thinking, wishing for hopeless things."

79   I laugh. Kwan stares at me fiercely, as if I were Big Ma, the aunt who raised her. "You can't stop young girls from wishing. No! Everyone must dream. To stop dreaming—well, that's like saying you can never change your fate. Isn't that true?"

80   "I suppose."

81   "So now you guess what I wished for."

82   "I don't know. What?"

83   "Come on, you guess."

84   "A handsome husband."

85   "No."

86   "A car."

87   Kwan laughs and slaps my arm. "You guessed wrong! O.K., I'll tell you." She looks toward the mountain peaks. "Before I left for America, I raised three birds, not just one, so I could make three wishes at the top of the peak. I told myself, If these three wishes come true, my life is complete, I

can die happy. My first wish: to have a sister I could love with all my heart, only that, and I would ask for nothing more from her. My second wish: to return to China with my sister. My third wish"—Kwan's voice now quavers—"for Big Ma to see this and say she was sorry she sent me away."

88   This is the first time Kwan's ever shown me how deeply she can resent someone who's treated her wrong. "I opened the cage," she continues, "and let my three birds go free." She flings out her hand in demonstration. "But one of them beat its wings uselessly, drifting in half-circles, before it fell like a stone all the way to the bottom. Now you see, two of my wishes have already happened: I have you, and together we are in China. Last night, I realized my third wish would never come true. Big Ma will never tell me she is sorry."

89   She holds up the cage with the owl. "But now I have a beautiful cat-eagle that can carry with him my new wish. When he flies away, all my old sadnesses will go with him. Then both of us will be free."

90   Actually, Kwan is my half sister, but I never mention that publicly. That would be an insult, as if she deserved only fifty per cent of my love. She was born in China. I was born in San Francisco, after our father immigrated there and married my mother.

91   Mom calls herself "American mixed grill, a bit of everything white, fatty, and fried." She was born in Moscow, Idaho, where she was a champion baton twirler and once won a county-fair prize for growing a deformed potato that had the profile of Jimmy Durante. She told me she dreamed she'd one day grow up to be different—thin, exotic, and noble, like Luise Rainer, who won an Oscar playing O-lan in "The Good Earth." When Mom moved to San Francisco and became a Kelly girl instead, she did the next-best thing. She married our father. Mom thinks that her marrying out of the Anglo race makes her a liberal. "When Jack and I met," she still tells people, "there were laws against mixed marriages. We broke the law for love." She neglects to mention that those laws didn't apply in California.

92   None of us, including my mom, even knew that Kwan existed until shortly before my father died, of renal failure. I was not quite four when he passed away. But I still remember the last day I saw him in the hospital.

93   I was sitting on a sticky vinyl chair, eating a bowl of strawberry Jell-O cubes that my father had given me from his lunch tray. He was propped up in bed, breathing hard. Mom would cry one minute, then act cheerful. The next thing I remember, my father was whispering and Mom leaned in close to listen. Her mouth opened wider and wider. Then her head turned sharply toward me, all twisted with horror.

94   "Your daughter?" I heard my mom say. "Bring her back?"

95   What I remember after that is a jumble: the bowl of Jell-O crashing to the floor, Mom staring at a photo, then me seeing the black-and-white snapshot of a skinny baby with patchy hair.

96   It turned out that my father had been a university student in Guilin. He used to buy live frogs for his supper at the outdoor market from a young

woman named Li Chen. He later married her, and in 1944 she gave birth to a daughter. In 1948, my father's first wife died, of a lung disease, perhaps t.b. He went to Hong Kong to search for work and left Kwan in the care of his wife's younger sister, Li Bin-bin, who lived in a small mountain village called Changmian. He sent money for their support—but in 1949, after the Communists took over, it was impossible for my father to return. What else could he do? With a heavy heart, he left for America to start a new life and forget about the sadness he left behind.

97   Eleven years later, while he was dying in the hospital, the ghost of his first wife appeared at the foot of his bed. "Claim back your daughter," she warned, "or suffer the consequences after death!"

98   Looking back, I can imagine how my mom must have felt when she first heard this. Another wife? A daughter in China? We were a modern American family. We spoke English. Sure, we ate Chinese food, but take-out, like everyone else. And we lived in a ranch-style house in Daly City. My father worked for the Government Accounting Office. My mother went to P.T.A. meetings. She had never heard my father talk about Chinese superstitions before; they attended church and bought life insurance instead.

99   After my father died, my mother kept telling everyone how he had treated her "just like a Chinese empress." She made all sorts of grief-stricken promises to God and my father's grave. My mother vowed never to remarry. She vowed to teach us children to do honor to the family name. She vowed to find my father's firstborn child, Kwan, and bring her to the United States. The last promise was the only one she kept.

100   I was nearly six when Kwan arrived.

101   We head to the hotel, in search of a car that will take one local, two tourists, and a cat-eagle to Changmian village. By nine, we've procured the services of a driver, an amiable young man who knows how to do the capitalist hustle. "Clean, cheap, fast," he declares, in Chinese. And then he makes an aside for Simon's benefit.

102   "What'd he say?" Simon asks.

103   "He's letting you know he speaks English."

104   Our driver reminds me of the slick Hong Kong youths who hang out in the trendy pool halls of San Francisco, the same pomaded hair, his inch-long pinkie nail, perfectly manicured, symbolizing that his lucky life is one without backbreaking work. He flashes us a smile, revealing a set of nicotine-stained teeth. "You call me Rocky," he says, in heavily accented English. "Like famous movie star." He opens the door with a flourish, and we climb into a black Nissan, a late-model sedan that, curiously, lacks seat belts and safety headrests. Do the Japanese think Chinese lives aren't worth saving? "China has either better drivers or no liability lawyers," Simon concludes.

105   Rocky happily assumes we like loud music and slips in a Eurythmics tape, a gift from one of his other "excellent American customers." And so, with Kwan in the front seat and Simon, the owl, and me in back, we

start our journey to Changmian, blasted by the beat of "Sisters Are Doing It for Themselves."

106   Rocky's excellent American customers have also taught him select phrases, which he recites to us: "Where you go? I know it. Jump in, let's go." "Go faster? Too fast? No way, José." "How far? Not far. Too far." "Park car? Wait a sec. Back in flash." "Not lost. No problem. Chill out."

107   Rocky explains that he is teaching himself English so he can one day go to America.

108   "My idea," he says, in Chinese, "is to become a famous movie actor, specializing in martial arts. Of course, I don't expect a big success from the start. Maybe I'll have to take a job as a taxi-driver. But I'm hardworking. In America, people don't know how to be as hardworking as we Chinese. We also know how to suffer. What's unbearable to Americans would be ordinary for me. Don't you think that's true, older sister?"

109   Kwan gives an ambiguous "Hmm." I wonder whether she is thinking of her brother-in-law, a former chemist, who immigrated to the States and now works as a dishwasher because he's too scared to speak English, lest people think he is stupid. Just then Simon's eyes grow round, and I shout, "Holy shit!" as the car nearly sideswipes two schoolgirls holding hands. Rocky blithely goes on about his dream.

110   "When I live in America, I'll save most of my money, spend only a little on food, cigarettes, maybe the movies every now and then, and, of course, a car for my taxi business. My needs are simple. Even if I don't become a movie star, I can still come back to China and live like a rich man."

111   He looks at us through the rearview mirror and gives us a thumbs-up. A second later, Simon grips the front seat, and I shout, "Holy Jesus shit!" We are about to hit a young woman on a bicycle with her baby perched on the handlebar. At the last possible moment, the cyclist wobbles to the right and out of our way.

112   Rocky laughs. "Chill out," he says. And then he explains, in Chinese, why we shouldn't worry. Kwan turns around and translates for Simon: "He said in China if driver run over somebody, driver always at fault, no matter how careless other person."

113   Simon looks at me. "This is supposed to reassure us? Did something get lost in the translation?"

114   "It doesn't make any sense," I tell Kwan, as Rocky veers in and out of traffic. "A dead pedestrian is a dead pedestrian, no matter whose fault it is."

115   "*Tst!* This American thinking," Kwan replies. The owl swings his head and stares at me, as if to say, Wise up, gringa, this is China, your American ideas don't work here. "In China," Kwan goes on, "you always responsible for someone else, no matter what. You get run over, this my fault, you my little sister. Now you understand?"

116   We drive by a strip of shops selling rattan furniture and straw hats. And then we're in the outskirts of town, both sides of the road lined with mile after mile of identical one-room restaurants. Some are in the stages of being built, their walls layers of brick, mud plaster, and whitewash.

They advertise the same specialties: orange soda pop and steamy-hot noodle soup. Idle waitresses squat outside, watching our car whizz by.

117   A few miles farther on, the restaurants give way to simple wooden stalls with thatched roofs, and, even farther, peddlers, without any shelter, stand by the road, yelling at the top of their lungs, waving their string bags of pomelos, their bottles of homemade hot sauce.

118   As the stretches between villages grow longer, Kwan falls asleep, her head bobbing lower and lower. She half awakens with a snort every time we hit a pothole. After a while, she emits long, rhythmical snores, blissfully unaware that Rocky is driving faster and faster down the two-lane road. Each time he accelerates, the owl opens his wings slightly, then settles down again in the cramped cage. I'm gripping my knees, then sucking air between clenched teeth whenever Rocky swings into the left lane.

119   We are now tailgating a truck filled with soldiers in green uniforms. They wave to us. Rocky honks his horn, then swerves sharply to pass. As we go by the truck, I can see an oncoming bus bearing down on us, the urgent blare of its horn growing louder and louder. "Oh, my God, oh, my God," I whimper. I close my eyes, and Simon grabs my hand. The car jerks back into the right lane. I hear a *whoosh*, then the blare of the bus horn receding.

120   "That's it," I say in a tense whisper. "I'm going to tell him to slow down."

121   "I don't know, Olivia. He might be offended."

122   I glare at Simon. "What? You'd rather die than be rude?"

123   He affects an attitude of nonchalance. "They all drive like that."

124   "So mass suicide makes it O.K.?"

125   "Well, we haven't seen any accidents."

126   Simon stares at me. At that moment, Rocky brakes abruptly. Kwan and the owl awake with a flutter of arms and wings. Rocky rolls down the window and sticks out his head. He curses under his breath, then starts punching the car horn with the heel of his hand.

127   After a few minutes, we see the source of our delay: an accident, a bad one, to judge from the spray of glass, metal, and personal belongings that litters the road. The smells of spilled gasoline and scorched rubber hang in the air. Just as I am about to say to Simon, "See?" our car inches past a black minivan, belly up, its doors splayed like the broken wings of a squashed insect. A tire lies in a nearby vegetable field. Seconds later, we go by the other half of the impact: a red-and-white bus. The large front window is smashed, the hound-nosed hood twisted and smeared with a hideous swath of blood. About fifty gawkers, farm tools still in hand, mill around, staring and pointing at various parts of the crumpled bus as if it were a science exhibit. And then I see a dozen or so injured people, some clutching themselves and bellowing in pain, others lying quietly in shock. Or perhaps they are already dead.

128   "Shit, I can't believe this," says Simon. "There's no ambulance, no doctors."

129   "Stop the car," I order Rocky, in Chinese. "We should help them." Why did I say that? What can I possibly do? I can barely look at the victims, let alone touch them.

130   "*Ai-ya.*" Kwan stares at the field. "So many yin people." Yin people? Kwan believes she can see ghosts, those who have died and now dwell in the World of Yin. Is she now saying there are dead people out there? The owl coos mournfully, and my hands turn slippery-cold.

131   Rocky keeps his eyes on the road ahead, driving forward, leaving the tragedy behind us. "We'd be of no use," he says, in Chinese. "We have no medicine, no bandages. Besides, it's not good to interfere, especially since you're foreigners. Don't worry, the police will be along soon."

132   I'm secretly relieved he isn't heeding my instructions.

133   "You're Americans," he continues, his voice deep with Chinese authority. "You're not used to seeing tragedies. You pity us, yes, because you can later go home to a comfortable life and forget what you've seen. For us, this type of disaster is commonplace. We have so many people, no room left for pity."

134   "Would someone please tell me what's going on!" Simon exclaims. "Why aren't we stopping?"

135   "Don't ask questions," I snap. "Remember?"

136   When we get back on the open road, Kwan gives Rocky some advice. He solemnly nods, then slows down.

137   "What'd she say?" Simon asks.

138   "Chinese logic. If we're killed, no payment. And in the next life, he'll owe us big time."

139   Another three hours pass. I know we have to be getting close to Changmian. Kwan is pointing out landmarks. "There! There!" she cries huskily, bouncing up and down like a little child. "Those two peaks. The village they surround is called Wife Waiting for Husband's Return. But where is the tree? What happened to the tree? Next to that house, there was a very big tree, maybe a thousand years old."

140   She scans ahead. "That place there! We used to hold a big market. But now look, it's just an empty field. And there—that mountain up ahead! That's the one we called Young Girl's Wish."

141   Kwan laughs, but the next second she seems puzzled. "Funny, now that mountain looks so small. Why is that? Did it shrink, washed down by the rain? Or maybe the peak was worn down by too many girls running up there to make a wish. Or maybe it's because I've become too American and now. I see things with different eyes, everything looking smaller poorer, not as good."

142   All at once, Kwan shouts to Rocky to turn down a small dirt road we have just passed. He makes an abrupt U-turn, knocking Simon and me into each other, and causing the owl to shriek. We are rumbling along a rutted lane, past fields with pillows of moist red dirt. "Turn left, turn left!" Kwan orders. She has her hands clasped in her lap. "Too many years, too many years," she says, as if chanting.

143   We approach a stand of trees, and then, as soon as Kwan announces, "Changmian," I see it: a village nestled between two jagged peaks, their

hillsides a velvety moss-green with folds deepening into emerald. More comes into view: crooked rows of buildings whitewashed with lime, their pitched tile roofs laid in the traditional pattern of dragon coils. Surrounding the village are well-tended fields and mirrorlike ponds neatly divided by stone walls and irrigation trenches. We jump out of the car. Miraculously, Changmian has avoided the detritus of modernization. I see no tin roofs or electrical power lines. In contrast to other villages we've passed, the outlying lands here haven't become dumping grounds for garbage, the alleys aren't lined with crumpled cigarette packs or pink plastic bags. Clean stone pathways crisscross the village, then thread up a cleft between the two peaks and disappear through a stone archway. In the distance is another pair of tall peaks, dark jade in color, and beyond those the purple shadows of two more. Simon and I stare at each other, wide-eyed.

144   I feel as though we've stumbled on a fabled misty land, half memory, half illusion. Are we in Chinese Nirvana? Changmian looks like the carefully cropped photos found in travel brochures advertising "a charmed world of the distant past, where visitors can step back in time." There must be something wrong, I keep warning myself. Around the corner we'll stumble on reality: the fast-food market, the tire junkyard, the signs indicating this village is really a Chinese fantasyland for tourists.

145   "I feel like I've seen this place before," I whisper to Simon.

146   "Me, too. Maybe it was in a documentary." He laughs. "Or a car commercial."

147   I gaze at the mountains and realize why Changmian seems so familiar. It's the setting for Kwan's stories, the ones that filter into my dreams. There they are: the archways, the cassia trees, the hills leading to Thistle Mountain. And being here, I feel as if the membrane separating the two halves of my life has finally been shed.

148   From out of nowhere we hear squeals and cheers. Fifty tiny schoolchildren race toward the perimeter of a fenced-in yard. As we draw closer, the children shriek, turn on their heels, and run back to the school building, laughing. After a few seconds, they come screaming toward us like a flock of birds, followed by their smiling teacher. They stand at attention, and then shout all together, in English, "A-B-C! One-two-three! How are you! Hello goodbye!"

149   We continue along the path. Two young men on bicycles slow down and stop to stare at us. We keep walking and round a corner. Kwan gasps. Farther up the path, in front of an arched gateway, stand a dozen smiling people. Kwan puts her hand to her mouth, then runs toward them. When she reaches the group, she grabs each person's hand between her two palms, then hails a stout woman and slaps her on the back.

150   "Fat!" Kwan says. "You've grown unbelievably fat!"

151   "Hey, look at you—what happened to your hair? Did you ruin it on purpose?"

152   "This is the style! What, have you been in the countryside so long you don't recognize good style?"

153   "Oh, listen to her, she's still bossy, I can tell."

154   "You were always the bossy one, not—"

155   Kwan stops in midsentence, transfixed by a stone wall. You would think it's the most fascinating sight she's ever seen.

156   "Big Ma," she murmurs. "What's happened? How can this be?"

157   A man in the crowd guffaws. "Ha! She was so anxious to see you she got up early this morning, then jumped on a bus to meet you in Guilin. And now look—you're here, she's there. Won't she be mad!"

158   Everyone laughs, except Kwan. She walks closer to the wall, calling hoarsely, "Big Ma, Big Ma." Several people whisper, and everyone draws back, frightened.

159   "Uh-oh," I say.

160   "Why is Kwan crying?" Simon whispers.

161   "Big Ma, oh, Big Ma." Tears are streaming down Kwan's cheeks. "You must believe me, this is not what I wished. How unlucky that you died on the day that I've come home." A few women gasp and cover their mouths.

162   I walk over to Kwan. "What are you saying? Why do you think she's dead?"

163   "Why is everyone so freaked?" Simon glances about.

164   I hold up my hand. "I'm not sure." I turn back to her. "Kwan?" I say gently. "Kwan?" But she does not seem to hear me. She is looking tenderly at the wall, laughing and crying.

165   "Yes, I knew this," she is saying. "Of course, I knew. In my heart, I knew all the time."

166   In the afternoon, the villagers hold an uneasy homecoming party for Kwan in the community hall. The news has spread through Changmian that Kwan has seen Big Ma's ghost. Yet she has not announced this to the village, and since there is no proof that Big Ma has died, there is no reason to call off a food-laden celebration that evidently took her friends days to prepare. During the festivities, Kwan does not brag about her car, her sofa, her English. She listens quietly as her former childhood playmates recount major events of their lives: the birth of twin sons, a railway trip to a big city, and the time a group of student intellectuals was sent to Changmian for reëducation during the Cultural Revolution.

167   "They thought they were smarter than us," recounts one woman, whose hands are gnarled by arthritis. "They wanted us to raise a fast-growing rice, three crops a year instead of two. They gave us special seeds. They brought us insect poison. Then the little frogs that swam in the rice fields and ate the insects, they all died. And the ducks that ate the frogs, they all died, too. Then the rice died."

168   A man with bushy hair shouts, "So we said, 'What good is it to plant three crops of rice that fail rather than two that are successful?'"

169   The woman with arthritic hands continues: "These same intellectuals tried to breed our mules! Ha! Can you believe it? For two years, every week, one of us would ask them, 'Any luck?' And they'd say, 'Not yet, not

yet.' And we'd try to keep our faces serious but encouraging. 'Try harder, comrade,' we'd say. 'Don't give up.'"

170   We are still laughing when a young boy runs into the hall, shouting that an official from Guilin has arrived in a fancy black car. Silence. The official comes into the hall, and everyone stands. He solemnly holds up the identity card of Li Bin-bin and asks if she belonged to the village. Several people glance nervously at Kwan. She walks slowly toward the official, looks at the identity card, and nods. The official makes an announcement, and a ripple of moans and then wails fills the room.

171   Simon leans toward me. "What's wrong?"

172   "Big Ma's dead. She was killed in that bus accident we saw this morning."

173   Simon and I walk over and each put a hand on one of Kwan's shoulders. She feels so small.

174   "I'm sorry," Simon stammers.

175   Kwan gives him a teary smile. As Li Bin-bin's closest relative, she has volunteered to perform the necessary bureaucratic ritual of bringing the body back to the village the next day. The three of us are returning to Guilin.

176   As soon as Rocky sees us, he stubs out his cigarette and turns off the car radio. Someone must have told him the news. "What a tragedy," he says. "I'm sorry, big sister, I should have stopped. I'm to blame—"

177   Kwan waves off his apologies. "No one's to blame. Anyway, regrets are useless, always too late."

178   When Rocky opens the car door, we see that the owl is still in his cage on the backseat. Kwan lifts the cage gently and stares at the bird. "No need to climb the mountain anymore," she says. She sets the cage on the ground, then opens its door. The owl sticks out his head, hops to the edge of the doorway and onto the ground. He twists his head and, with a great flap of wings, takes off toward the peaks. Kwan watches him until he disappears.

179   As Rocky warms the engine, I ask Kwan, "When we passed the bus accident this morning, did you see someone who looked like Big Ma? Is that how you knew she'd died?"

180   "What are you saying? I didn't know she was dead until I saw her yin self standing by the wall."

181   "Then why did you tell her that you knew?"

182   Kwan frowns, puzzled. "I knew what?"

183   "You were telling her you knew, in your heart you knew it was true. Weren't you talking about the accident?"

184   "Ah," she says, understanding at last. "No, not the accident." She sighs. "I told Big Ma that what *she* was saying was true."

185   "What did she say?"

186   Kwan turns to the window, and I can see the reflection of her stricken face. "She said she was wrong about the story of Young Girl's Wish. She said all my wishes had already come true. She was always sorry she sent me away. But she could never tell me this. Otherwise, I wouldn't have left her for a chance at a better life."

187   I search for some way to console Kwan. "At least you can still see her," I say.

188   "Ah?"

189   "I mean as a yin person. She can visit you."

190   Kwan stares out the car window. "But it's not the same. We can no longer make new memories together. We can't change the past. Not until the next lifetime." She exhales heavily, releasing all her unsaid words.

Questions for Discussion

1. Why is Kwan in "Chinese heaven" at the beginning of the story?

2. Describe the street scenes in Guilin. What does Olivia mean when she says that the city of Guilin was "a pretty face marred by tawdry lipstick, gapped teeth, and an advanced case of periodontal disease"?

3. Explain the importance of the "cat-eagle" and what Kwan wants to do with it.

4. List some of the foreshadowing elements and explain what they foreshadow.

5. What is the tale of the "Young Girl's Wish"? What are Kwan's three wishes?

6. Explain Kwan's and Olivia's relationship. How did Olivia discover this relationship?

7. Who are "yin people"? What other Chinese legends does the story include?

8. How does Kwan know that Big Ma is dead before anyone else does?

9. Why doesn't Kwan brag about her American possessions after Big Ma's death?

10. What is the significance of the owl at the end of the story?

HEART   (2001)

1   These are the things I must not forget.

2   I was raised with the Liu clan in the rocky Western Hills south of Peking. The oldest recorded name of our village was Immortal Heart. Precious Auntie taught me how to write this down on my chalkboard. *Watch now, Doggie,* she ordered, and drew the character for "heart": *See this curving stroke? That's the bottom of the heart, where blood gathers and flows. And the dots, those are the two veins and the artery that carry the blood in and out.* As I traced over the character, she asked: *Whose dead heart gave shape to this word? How did it begin, Doggie? Did it belong to a woman? Was it drawn in sadness?*

3   I once saw the heart of a fresh-killed pig. It was red and glistening. And I had already seen plenty of chicken hearts in a bowl, waiting to be

cooked. They looked like tiny lips and were the same color as Precious Auntie's scars. But what did a woman heart look like? "Why do we have to know whose heart it was?" I asked as I wrote the character.

4   And Precious Auntie flapped her hands fast: *A person should consider how things begin. A particular beginning results in a particular end.*

5   I remember her often talking about this, how things begin. Since then I have wondered about the beginning and end of many things. Like Immortal Heart village. And the people who lived there, myself included. By the time I was born, Immortal Heart was no longer lucky. The village lay between hills in a valley that dropped into a deep limestone ravine. The ravine was shaped like the curved chamber of a heart, and the heart's artery and veins were the three streams that once fed and drained the ravine. But they had gone dry. So had the divine springs. Nothing was left of the waterways but cracked gullies and the stench of a fart.

6   Yet the village began as a sacred place. According to legend, a visiting emperor himself had planted a pine tree in the middle of the valley. The tree was to honor his dead mother, and his respect for his mother was so great he vowed that the tree would live forever. When Precious Auntie first saw the tree, it was already more than three thousand years old.

7   Rich and poor alike made a pilgrimage to Immortal Heart. They hoped that the tree's vital energy would rub off on them. They stroked the trunk, patted the leaves, then prayed for baby sons or big fortunes, a cure for dying, an end to curses. Before leaving, they chipped off some bark, snapped off some twigs. They took them away as souvenirs. Precious Auntie said this was what killed the tree, too much admiration. When the tree died, the souvenirs lost their strength. And because the dead tree was no longer immortal, it was no longer famous, nor was our village. That tree was not even ancient, people said afterward, maybe only two or three hundred years old. As for the story about the emperor honoring his mother? That was a fake feudal legend to make us think the corrupt were sincere. Those complaints came out the same year that the old Ching Dynasty fell down and the new Republic sprang up.

8   The nickname of our village is easy for me to remember: Forty-six Kilometers from Reed Moat Bridge. Reed Moat Bridge is the same as Marco Polo Bridge, what people now call the turnoff point to and from Peking. GaoLing's probably forgotten the old name, but I have not. During my girlhood, the directions to get to Immortal Heart went like this: "First find the Reed Moat Bridge, then walk backward forty-six kilometers."

9   That joke made it sound as if we lived in a pitiful little hamlet of twenty or thirty people. Not so. When I was growing up, nearly two thousand people lived there. It was crowded, packed from one edge of the valley to the other. We had a brick maker, a sack weaver, and a dye mill. We had twenty-four market days, six temple fairs, and a primary school that GaoLing and I went to when we were not helping our family at home. We had all kinds of peddlers who went from house to house, selling fresh bean curd and steamed buns, twisted dough and colorful candies. And

we had lots of people to buy those goods. A few coppers, that was all you needed to make your stomach as happy as a rich man's.

10   The Liu clan had lived in Immortal Heart for six centuries. For that amount of time, the sons had been inkstick makers who sold their goods to travelers. They had lived in the same courtyard house that had added rooms, and later wings, when one mother four hundred years ago gave birth to eight sons, one a year. The family home grew from a simple three-pillar house to a compound with wings stretching five pillars each. In later generations, the number of sons was less, and the extra rooms became run-down and were rented to squabbling tenants. Whether those people laughed at coarse jokes or screamed in pain, it did not matter, the sounds were the same, ugly to hear.

11   All in all, our family was successful but not so much that we caused great envy. We ate meat or bean curd at almost every meal. We had new padded jackets every winter, no holes. We had money to give for the temple, the opera, the fair. But the men of our family also had ambitions. They were always looking for more. They said that in Peking, more people wrote important documents. Those important documents required more good ink. Peking was where more of the big money was. Around 1920, Father, my uncles, and their sons went there to sell the ink. From then on, that was where they lived most of the time, in the back room of a shop in the old Pottery-Glazing District.

12   In our family, the women made the ink. We stayed home. We all worked—me, GaoLing, my aunts and girl cousins, everybody. Even the babies and Great-Granny had a job of picking out stones from the dried millet we boiled for breakfast. We gathered each day in the ink-making studio. According to Great-Granny, the studio began as a grain shed that sat along the front wall of the courtyard house. Over the years, one generation of sons added brick walls and a tile roof. Another strengthened the beams and lengthened it by two pillars. The next tiled the floors and dug pits for storing the ingredients. Then other descendants made a cellar for keeping the inksticks away from the heat and cold. "And now look," Great-Granny often bragged. "Our studio is an ink palace."

13   Because our ink was the best quality, we had to keep the tables and the floors clean year-round. With the dusty yellow winds from the Gobi, this was not easy to do. The window openings had to be covered with both glass and thick paper. In the summer, we hung netting over the doorways to keep out the insects. In the winter, it was sheep hides to keep out the snow.

14   Summer was the worst season for ink-making. Heat upon heat. The fumes burned our eyes and nostrils and lungs. From watching Precious Auntie tie her scarf over her marred face, we got the idea of putting a wet cloth over our mouths. I can still smell the ingredients of our ink. There were several kinds of fragrant soot: pine, cassia, camphor, and the wood of the chopped-down Immortal Tree. Father hauled home several big logs of it after lightning cracked the dead tree right down the middle, expos-

ing its heart, which was nearly hollow because of beetles eating it inside out. There was also a glue of sticky paste mixed with many oils—serpentine, camphor, turpentine, and tung wood. Then we added a sweet poisonous flower that helped resist insects and rats. That was how special our ink was, all those lasting smells.

15   We made the ink a little at a time. If a fire broke out, as it had a couple of hundred years before, all the supplies and stock would not be lost at once. And if a batch was too sticky or too wet, too soft or not black enough, it was easier to find out who was to blame. Each of us had at least one part in a long list of things to do. First there was burning and grinding, measuring and pouring. Then came stirring and molding, drying and carving. And finally, wrapping and counting, storing and stacking. One season I had to wrap, only that. My mind could wander but my fingers still moved like small machines. Another season I had to use very fine tweezers to pluck bugs that had fallen onto the sticks. Whenever GaoLing did this, she left too many dents. Precious Auntie's job was to sit at a long table and press the sooty mixture into the stone molds. As a result, the tips of her fingers were always black. When the ink was dry, she used a long, sharp tool to carve the good-luck words and drawings into the sticks. Her calligraphy was even better than Father's.

16   It was boring work, but we were proud of our secret family recipe. It yielded just the right color and hardness. An inkstick of ours could last ten years or more. It did not dry out and crumble, or grow soggy with moisture. And if the sticks were stored in the coolness of a root cellar, as ours were, they could last from one great period of history to another. Those who used our ink said the same. It didn't matter how much heat or moisture or dirt from fingers soaked into the page, their words lasted, black and strong.

17   Mother claimed the ink was why our hair remained the blackest black. It was better for the hair than drinking black-sesame-seed soup. "Work hard all day making ink, look young at night while you sleep." That was our joke, and Great-Granny often boasted: "My hair is as black as the burnt shell of a horse chestnut and my face as wrinkly white as the meat inside." Great-Granny had a clever tongue. One time she added, "Better than having white hair and a burnt face," and everyone laughed, even though Precious Auntie was in the room.

18   In later years, however, Great-Granny's tongue was not so sharp or fast. Often she said with a worried brow, "Have you seen Hu Sen?" You could say yes, you could say no, and a moment later, she chirped like a bird, "Hu Sen? Hu Sen?" always requesting her dead grandson, very sad to hear.

19   Toward the end of her life, Great-Granny had thoughts that were like crumbling walls, stones without mortar. A doctor said her inner wind was cold and her pulse was slow, a shallow stream about to freeze. He advised foods with more heat. But Great-Granny only grew worse. Precious Auntie suspected that a tiny flea had crawled into her ear and was feasting on her brain. Confusion Itch was the name of the malady, Precious Auntie said.

It is the reason people often scratch their heads when they cannot remember. Her father had been a doctor, and she had seen other patients with the same problem. Yesterday, when I could not remember Precious Auntie's name, I wondered if a flea had run in my ear! But now that I am writing down so many things, I know I don't have Great-Granny's disease. I can recall the smallest details even though they were long ago and far away.

20   The compound where we lived and worked—that comes back to me as if I were now standing before the gate. It was on Pig's Head Lane. The road started at the east, near the market square where pigs heads were sold. From the square, it hooked to the north and ran past the former location of the once famous Immortal Tree. Then it tightened into the little crooked alley where one compound bumped into another. The end of Pig's Head Lane was a narrow perch of earth above the deepest part of the ravine. Precious Auntie told me that the perch was originally made by a warlord thousands of years before. He dreamed that the insides of the mountain were made of jade. So he ordered everyone to dig, dig, don't stop. Men, women, and children dredged for his dream. By the time the warlord died, the children were old, with crooked backs, and half the mountain lay on its side.

21   Behind our compound, the perch became a cliff. And way down, if you fell head over toes, was the bottom of the ravine. The Liu family had once owned twenty *mu* of land behind the compound. But over the centuries, with each heavy rainfall, the walls of the ravine had collapsed and widened, rumbled and deepened. Each decade, those twenty *mu* of land grew smaller and smaller and the cliff crept closer to the back of our house.

22   The moving cliff gave us the feeling we had to look behind us to know what lay ahead. We called it the End of the World. Sometimes the men of our family argued among themselves whether we still owned the land that had crashed down into the ravine. One uncle said, "What you own is the spit that travels from your own mouth to the bottom of that wasteland." And his wife said, "Don't talk about this anymore. You're only inviting disaster." For what lay beyond and below was too unlucky to say out loud: unwanted babies, suicide maidens, and beggar ghosts. Everyone knew this.

23   I went to the cliff many times with my brothers and GaoLing when we were younger. We liked to roll spoiled melons and rotten cabbages over the edge. We watched them fall and splat, hitting skulls and bones. At least that was what we thought they had hit. But one time we climbed down, sliding on our bottoms, grabbing onto roots, descending into the underworld. And when we heard rustling sounds in the brush, we screamed so loud our ears hurt. The ghost turned out to be a scavenger dog. And the skulls and bones, they were just boulders and broken branches. But though we saw no bodies, all around were bright pieces of clothing: a sleeve, a collar, a shoe, and we were sure they belonged to the dead. And then we smelled it: the stink of ghosts. A person needs to smell that only once to know what it is. It rose from the earth. It wafted toward us on the

wings of a thousand flies. The flies chased us like a storm cloud, and as we scrambled back up, First Brother kicked loose a stone that gouged out a piece of Second Brother's scalp. We could not hide this wound from Mother, and when she saw it, she beat us all, then told us that if we ever went down to the End of the World again, we might as well stand outside the walls of the compound forever and not bother to come in.

24   The walls of the Liu home were made of rocks exposed from the washed-down earth. The rocks were stacked and held together with a mud, mortar, and millet paste, then plastered over with lime. They were sweaty damp in summer, moldy damp in winter. And in the many rooms of that house, here and there was always another roof leak or drafty hole in the wall. And yet when I remember that house, I have a strange home-sickness for it. Only there do I have a memory of secret places, warm or cool, of darkness where I hid and pretended I could escape to somewhere else.

25   Within those walls, many families of different positions and generations lived together at the same time, from landlord to tenants, Great-Granny to smallest niece. I guess we were thirty or more people, half of which was the Liu clan. Liu Jin Sen was the eldest of four sons. He was the one I called Father. My uncles and their wives called him Eldest Brother. My cousins called him Eldest Uncle. And by position my uncles were Big Uncle and Little Uncle, and their wives were Big Aunt and Little Aunt. When I was very small, I used to think Father and Mother were called Eldest because they were much taller than my uncles and aunts. First Brother and Second Brother were also large-boned, as was Gao-Ling, and for a long time I did not know why I was so short.

26   Baby Uncle was the fourth son, the youngest, the favorite. His name was Liu Hu Sen. He was my real father, and he would have married Precious Auntie, if only he had not died on their wedding day.

27   Precious Auntie was born in a bigger town down in the foothills, a place called Zhou's Mouth of the Mountain, named in honor of Emperor Zhou of the Shang Dynasty, whom everyone now remembers as a tyrant.

28   Our family sometimes went to the Mouth of the Mountain for temple fairs and operas. If we traveled by road, it was only about ten kilometers from Immortal Heart. If we walked through the End of the World, it was half that distance but a more dangerous way to go, especially in the summertime. That was when the big rains came. The dry ravine filled, and before you could run to the cliffs, climb up, and cry out, "Goddess of Mercy," the gullies ran by like thieves, grabbing you and whatever else was not deeply rooted in the soil. Once the rain stopped, the floodwaters drained fast and the mouths of the caves swallowed the dirt and the trees, the bodies and the bones. They went down the mountain's throat, into its stomach, intestines, and finally the bowels, where everything got stuck. *Constipated,* Precious Auntie once explained to me. *Now you see why there are so many bones and hills: Chicken Bone Hill, Old Cow Hill, Dragon Bone Hill. Of course, it's not just dragon bones in Dragon Bone*

Hill. Some are from ordinary creatures, bear, elephant, hippopotamus.
Precious Auntie drew a picture of each of these animals on my chalkboard, because we had never talked about them before.

29   *I have a bone, probably from a turtle,* she told me. She fished it from
a tuck in her sleeve. It looked like a dried turnip with pockmarks. *My
father almost ground this up for medicine. Then he saw there was writing on it.* She turned the bone over, and I saw strange characters running
up and down. *Until recently, these kinds of bones weren't so valuable,
because of the scratches. Bone diggers used to smooth them with a file
before selling them to medicine shops. Now the scholars call these oracle bones, and they sell for twice as much. And the words on here?
They're questions to the gods.*

30   "What does it say?" I asked.

31   Who knows? The words were different then. But it must be something
that should have been remembered. Otherwise, why did the gods say it,
why did a person write it down?

32   "Where are the answers?"

33   Those are the cracks. The diviner put a hot nail to the bone, and it
cracked like a tree hit by lightning. Then he interpreted what the cracks
meant.

34   She took back the divining bone. *Someday, when you know how to
remember, I'll give this to you to keep. But for now you'll only forget
where you put it. Later we can go looking for more dragon bones, and
if you find one with writing on it, you can keep it for yourself.*

35   In the Mouth of the Mountain, every poor man collected dragon bones
when he had a chance. So did the women, but if they found one, they had
to say a man found it instead, because otherwise the bone was not worth
as much. Later, middlemen went around the village buying the dragon
bones, and then they took them to Peking and sold them to medicine
shops for high prices, and the shops sold them to sick people for higher
prices yet. The bones were well known for curing anything, from wasting diseases to stupidity. Plenty of doctors sold them. And so did Precious
Auntie's father. He used bones to heal bones.

36   For nine hundred years, Precious Auntie's family had been bonesetters. That was the tradition. Her father's customers were mostly men and
boys who were crushed in the coal mines and limestone quarries. He
treated other maladies when necessary, but bonesetting was his specialty.
He did not have to go to a special school to be a bone doctor. He learned
from watching his father, and his father learned from his father before
him. That was their inheritance. They also passed along the secret location for finding the best dragon bones, a place called the Monkey's Jaw.
An ancestor from the time of the Sung Dynasty had found the cave in the
deepest ravines of the dry riverbed. Each generation dug deeper and
deeper, with one soft crack in the cave leading to another farther in. And
the secret of the exact location was also a family heirloom, passed from
generation to generation, father to son, and in Precious Auntie's time,
father to daughter to me.

37   I still remember the directions to our cave. It was between the Mouth of the Mountain and Immortal Heart, far from the other caves in the foothills, where everyone else went to dig up dragon bones. Precious Auntie took me there several times, always in the spring or the autumn, never summer or winter. To get there, we went down into the End of the World and walked along the middle of the ravine, away from the walls, where the grown-ups said there were things that were too bad to see. Sometimes we passed by a skein of weeds, shards of a bowl, a quagmire of twigs. In my childish mind, those sights became parched flesh, a baby's skullcap, a soup of maiden bones. And maybe they were, because sometimes Precious Auntie put her hands over my eyes.

38   Of the three dry streambeds, we took the one that was the artery of the heart. And then we stood in front of the cave itself, a split in the mountain only as tall as a broom. Precious Auntie pulled aside the dead bushes that hid the cave. And the two of us took big breaths and went in. In words, it is hard to say how we made our way in, like trying to describe how to get inside an ear. I had to twist my body in an unnatural way far to the left, then rest a foot on a little ledge that I could reach only by crooking my leg close to my chest. By then I was crying and Precious Auntie was grunting to me, because I could not see her black fingers to know what she was saying. I had to follow her huffs and handclaps, crawling like a dog so I would not hit my head or fall down. When we finally reached the larger part of the cave, Precious Auntie lighted the candle lamp and hung it on a long pole with footrests, which had been left by one of her clan from long ago.

39   On the floor of the cave were digging tools, iron wedges of different sizes, hammers and claws, as well as sacks for dragging out the dirt. The walls of the cave were many layers, like an eight-treasure rice pudding cut in half, with lighter, crumbly things on top, then a thicker muddy part like bean paste below, and growing heavier toward the bottom. The highest layer was easiest to chip. The lowest was like rock. But that was where the best bones were found. And after centuries of people's digging through the bottom there was now an overhang waiting to crash down. The inside of the cave looked like the molars of a monkey that could bite you in two, which was why it was called the Monkey's Jaw.

40   While we rested, Precious Auntie talked with her inky hands. *Stay away from that side of the monkey's teeth. Once they chomped down on an ancestor, and he was ground up and gobbled with stone. My father found his skull over there. We put it back right away. Bad luck to separate a man's head from his body.*

41   Hours later, we would climb back out of the Monkey's Jaw with a sack of dirt and, if we had been lucky, one or two dragon bones. Precious Auntie held them up to the sky and bowed, thanking the gods. She believed the bones from this cave were the reason her family had become famous as bonesetters.

42   *When I was a girl*, she said once as we walked home, *I remember lots of desperate people coming to see my father. He was their last chance.*

If a man could not walk, he could not work. And if he could not work, his family could not eat. Then he would die, and that would be the end of his family line and all that his ancestors had worked for.

43   For those desperate customers, Precious Auntie's father had remedies of three kinds: modern, try-anything, and traditional. The modern was the Western medicine of missionaries. The try-anything was the spells and chants of rogue monks. As for the traditional, that included the dragon bones, as well as seahorses and seaweed, insect shells and rare seeds, tree bark and bat dung, all of the highest quality. Precious Auntie's father was so talented that patients from the five surrounding mountain villages traveled to the Famous Bonesetter from the Mouth of the Mountain (whose name I will write down, once I remember it).

44   Skilled and famous though he was, he could not prevent all tragedies. When Precious Auntie was four, her mother and older brothers died of an intestine-draining disease. So did most of the other relatives from both sides of the family, dead just three days after they attended a red-egg ceremony and drank from a well infected with the body of a suicide maiden. The bonesetter was so ashamed he could not save his own family members that he spent his entire fortune and went into a lifetime of debt to hold their funerals.

45   *Because of grief,* Precious Auntie said with her hands, *he spoiled me, let me do whatever a son might do. I learned to read and write, to ask questions, to play riddles, to write eight-legged poems, to walk alone and admire nature. The old biddies used to warn him that it was dangerous that I was so boldly happy, instead of shy and cowering around strangers. And why didn't he bind my feet, they asked. My father was used to seeing pain of the worst kinds. But with me, he was helpless. He couldn't bear to see me cry.*

46   So Precious Auntie freely followed her father around in his study and shop. She soaked the splints and plucked the moss. She polished the scales and tallied the accounts. A customer could point to any jar in the shop and she could read the name of its contents, even the scientific words for animal organs. As she grew older, she learned to bleed a wound with a square nail, to use her own saliva for cleansing sores, to apply a layer of maggots for eating pus, and to wrap torn flaps with woven paper. By the time she passed from childhood to maidenhood, she had heard every kind of scream and curse. She had touched so many bodies, living, dying, and dead, that few families considered her for a bride. And while she had never been possessed by romantic love, she recognized the throes of death. *When the ears grow soft and flatten against the head,* she once told me, *then it's too late. A few seconds later, the last breath hisses out. The body turns cold.* She taught me many facts like that.

47   For the most difficult cases, she helped her father put the injured man on a light latticework pallet of rattan. Her father lifted and lowered this by pulleys and rope, and she guided the pallet into a tub filled with salt water. There the man's crushed bones floated and were fitted into place.

Afterward, Precious Auntie brought her father rattan strips that had been soaked soft. He bent them into a splint so the limb could breathe but remain still. Toward the end of the visit, the bonesetter opened his jar of dragon bones and used a narrow chisel to chip off a sliver tiny as a finger-nail clipping. Precious Auntie ground this into a powder with a silver ball. The powder went into a paste for rubbing or a potion for drinking. Then the lucky patient went home. Soon he was back in the quarries all day long.

48   One day, at dinnertime, Precious Auntie told me a story with her hands that only I could understand. *A rich lady came to my father and told him to unbind her feet and mold them into more modern ones. She said she wanted to wear high-heeled shoes. "But don't make the new feet too big," she said, "not like a slave girl's or a foreigner's. Make them naturally small like hers." And she pointed to my feet.*

49   I forgot that Mother and my other aunts were at the dinner table, and I said aloud, "Do bound feet look like the white lilies that the romantic books describe?" Mother and my aunts, who still had bound feet, gave me a frowning look. How could I talk so openly about a woman's most private parts? So Precious Auntie pretended to scold me with her hands for asking such a question, but what she really said was this: *They're usually crimped like flower-twist bread. But if they're dirty and knotty with calluses, they look like rotten ginger roots and smell like pig snouts three days dead.*

50   In this way, Precious Auntie taught me to be naughty, just like her. She taught me to be curious, just like her. She taught me to be spoiled. And because I was all these things, she could not teach me to be a better daughter, though in the end, she tried to change my faults.

51   I remember how she tried. It was the last week we were together. She did not speak to me for days. Instead she wrote and wrote and wrote. Finally she handed me a bundle of pages laced together with cord. *This is my true story*, she told me, *and yours as well.* Out of spite, I did not read most of those pages. But when I did, this is what I learned.

52   One late-autumn day, when Precious Auntie was nineteen by her Chinese age, the bonesetter had two new patients. The first was a screaming baby from a family who lived in Immortal Heart. The second was Baby Uncle. They would both cause Precious Auntie everlasting sorrow, but in two entirely different ways.

53   The bawling baby was the youngest son of a big-chested man named Chang, a coffinmaker who had grown rich in times of plagues. The carvings on the outside of his coffins were of camphor wood. But the insides were cheap pine, painted and lacquered to look and smell like the better golden wood.

54   Some of that same golden wood had fallen from a stack and knocked the baby's shoulder out of its socket. That's why the baby was howling, Chang's wife reported with a frightened face. Precious Auntie recognized this nervous woman. Two years before, she had sat in the bonesetter's

shop because her eye and jaw had been broken by a stone that must have fallen out of the open sky. Now she was back with her husband, who was slapping the baby's leg, telling him to stop his racket. Precious Auntie shouted at Chang: "First the shoulder, now you want to break his leg as well." Chang scowled at her. Precious Auntie picked up the baby. She rubbed a little bit of medicine inside his cheeks. Soon the baby quieted, yawned once, and fell asleep. Then the bonesetter snapped the small shoulder into place.

55   "What's the medicine?" the coffinmaker asked Precious Auntie. She didn't answer.

56   "Traditional things," the bonesetter said. "A little opium, a little herbs, and a special kind of dragon bone we dig out from a secret place only our family knows."

57   "Special dragon bone, eh?" Chang dipped his finger in the medicine bowl, then dabbed inside his cheek. He offered some to Precious Auntie, who sniffed in disgust, and then he laughed and gave Precious Auntie a bold look, as if he already owned her and could do whatever he pleased.

58   Right after the Changs and their baby left, Baby Uncle limped in.

59   He had been injured by his nervous horse, he explained to the bonesetter. He had been traveling from Peking to Immortal Heart, and during a rest, the horse startled a rabbit, then the rabbit startled the horse, and the horse stepped on Baby Uncle's foot. Three broken toes resulted, and Baby Uncle rode his bad horse to the Mouth of the Mountain, straight to the Famous Bonesetter's shop.

60   Baby Uncle sat in the blackwood examination chair. Precious Auntie was in the back room and could see him through the parted curtain. He was a thin young man of twenty-two. His face was refined but he did not act pompous or overly formal, and while his gown was not that of a rich gentleman, he was well groomed. She heard him joke about his accident: "My mare was so crazy with fright I thought she was going to gallop straight to the underworld with me stuck astride." When Precious Auntie stepped into the room, she said, "But fate brought you here instead." Baby Uncle fell quiet. When she smiled, he forgot his pain. When she put a dragon bone poultice on his naked foot, he decided to marry her. That was Precious Auntie's version of how they fell in love.

61   I have never seen a picture of my real father, but Precious Auntie told me that he was very handsome and smart, yet also shy enough to make a girl feel tender. He looked like a poor scholar who could rise above his circumstances, and surely he would have qualified for the imperial examinations if they had not been canceled several years before by the new Republic.

62   The next morning, Baby Uncle came back with three stemfuls of lychees for Precious Auntie as a gift of appreciation. He peeled off the shell of one, and she ate the white-fleshed fruit in front of him. The morning was warm for late autumn, they both remarked. He asked if he could recite a poem he had written that morning: "You speak," he said, "the lan-

guage of shooting stars, more surprising than sunrise, more brilliant than the sun, as brief as sunset. I want to follow its trail to eternity."

63   In the afternoon, the coffinmaker Chang brought a watermelon to the bonesetter. "To show my highest appreciation," he said. "My baby son is already well, able to pick up bowls and smash them with the strength of three boys."

64   Later that week, unbeknownst one to the other, each man went to a different fortune-teller. The two men wanted to know if their combination of birthdates with Precious Auntie's was lucky. They asked if there were any bad omens for a marriage.

65   The coffinmaker went to a fortune-teller in Immortal Heart, a man who walked about the village with a divining stick. The marriage signs were excellent, the fortune-teller said. See here, Precious Auntie was born in a Rooster year, and because Chang was a Snake, that was nearly the best match possible. The old man said that Precious Auntie also had a lucky number of strokes in her name (I will write the number down here when I remember her name). And as a bonus, she had a mole in position eleven, near the fatty part of her cheek, indicating that only sweet words fell from her obedient mouth. The coffinmaker was so happy to hear this that he gave the fortune-teller a big tip.

66   Baby Uncle went to a fortune-teller in the Mouth of the Mountain, an old lady with a face more wrinkled than her palm. She saw nothing but calamity. The first sign was the mole on Precious Auntie's face. It was in position twelve, she told Baby Uncle, and it dragged down her mouth, meaning that her life would always bring her sadness. Their combination of birth years was also inharmonious, she a fire Rooster and he a wood Horse. The girl would ride his back and peck him apart piece by piece. She would consume him with her insatiable demands. And here was the worst part. The girl's father and mother had reported the date of her birth was the sixteenth day of the seventh moon. But the fortune-teller had a sister-in-law who lived near the bonesetter, and she knew better. She had heard the newborn's wails, not on the sixteenth day, but on the fifteenth, the only day when unhappy ghosts are allowed to roam the earth. The sister-in-law said the baby sounded like this: "*Wu-wu, wu-wu,*" not like a human but like a haunted one. The fortune-teller confided to Baby Uncle that she knew the girl quite well. She often saw her on market days, walking by herself. That strange girl did fast calculations in her head and argued with merchants. She was arrogant and headstrong. She was also educated, taught by her father to know the mysteries of the body. The girl was too curious, too questioning, too determined to follow her own mind. Maybe she was possessed. Better find another marriage match, the fortune-teller said. This one would lead to disaster.

67   Baby Uncle gave the fortune-teller more money, not as a tip, but to make her think harder. The fortune-teller kept shaking her head. But after Baby Uncle had given a total of a thousand coppers, the old lady finally had another thought. When the girl smiled, which was often, her mole

was in a luckier position, number eleven. The fortune-teller consulted an almanac, matched it to the hour of the girl's birth. Good news. The Hour of the Rabbit was peace-loving. Her inflexibility was just a bluff. And any leftover righteousness could be beaten down with a strong stick. It was further revealed that the fortune-teller's sister-in-law was a gossip known for exaggeration. But just to make sure the marriage went well, the fortune-teller sold Baby Uncle a Hundred Different Things charm that covered bad dates, bad spirits, bad luck, and hair loss. "But even with this, don't marry in the Dragon Year. Bad year for a Horse."

68   The first marriage proposal came from Chang's matchmaker, who went to the bonesetter and related the good omens. She boasted of the coffin-maker's respect, as an artisan descended from noted artisans. She described his house, his rock gardens, his fish ponds, the furniture in his many rooms, how the wood was of the best color, purple like a fresh bruise. As to the mat-ter of a dowry, the coffinmaker was willing to be more than generous. Since the girl was to be a second wife and not a first, couldn't her dowry be a jar of opium and a jar of dragon bones? This was not much, yet it was priceless, and therefore not insulting to the girl's worth.

69   The bonesetter considered the offer. He was growing old. Where would his daughter go when he died? And what other man would want her in his household? She was too spirited, too set in her ways. She had no mother to teach her the manners of a wife. True, the coffinmaker would not have been his first choice of son-in-law, if he had had another, but he did not want to stand in the way of his daughter's future happiness. He told Pre-cious Auntie about the generous offer from the coffinmaker.

70   To this, Precious Auntie huffed. "The man's a brute," she said. "I'd rather eat worms than be his wife."

71   The bonesetter had to give Chang's matchmaker an awkward answer: "I'm sorry," he said, "but my daughter cried herself sick, unable to bear the thought of leaving her worthless father." The lie would have been swallowed without disgrace, if only the offer from Baby Uncle's match-maker had not been accepted the following week.

72   A few days after the future marriage was announced, the coffinmaker went back to the Mouth of the Mountain and surprised Precious Auntie as she was returning from the well. "You think you can insult me, then walk away laughing?"

73   "Who insulted whom? You asked me to be your concubine, a servant to your wife. I'm not interested in being a slave in a feudal marriage."

74   As she tried to leave, Chang pinched her neck, saying he should break it, then shook her as if he truly might snap off her head like a winter twig. But instead he threw her to the ground, cursing her and her dead mother's private parts.

75   When Precious Auntie recovered her breath, she sneered, "Big words, big fists. You think you can scare a person into being sorry?"

76   And he said these words, which she never forgot: "You'll soon be sorry every day of your miserable life."

77   Precious Auntie did not tell her father or Hu Sen what had happened. No sense in worrying them. And why lead her future husband to wonder if Chang had a reason to feel insulted? Too many people had already said she was too strong, accustomed to having her own way. And perhaps this was true. She had no fear of punishment or disgrace. She was afraid of almost nothing.

78   A month before the wedding, Baby Uncle came to her room late at night. "I want to hear your voice in the dark," he whispered. "I want to hear the language of shooting stars." She let him into her *k'ang* and he eagerly began the nuptials. But as Baby Uncle caressed her, a wind blew over her skin and she began to tremble and shake. For the first time, she was afraid, she realized, frightened by unknown joy.

79   The wedding was supposed to take place in Immortal Heart village, right after the start of the new Dragon Year. It was a bare spring day. Slippery pockets of ice lay on the ground. In the morning, a traveling photographer came to the bonesetter's shop in the Mouth of the Mountain. He had broken his arm the month before, and his payment was a photograph of Precious Auntie on her wedding day. She wore her best winter jacket, one with a high fur-lined collar, and an embroidered cap. She had to stare a long time into the camera, and as she did so, she thought of how her life would soon change forever. Though she was happy, she was also worried. She sensed danger, but she could not name what it was. She tried to look far into the future, but she could see nothing.

80   For the journey to the wedding, she changed her clothes to her bridal costume, a red jacket and skirt, the fancy headdress with a scarf that she had to drape over her head once she left her father's home. The bonesetter had borrowed money to rent two mule carts, one to carry gifts for the groom's family, the other for the bride's trunks of blankets and clothes.

81   There was an enclosed sedan chair for the bride herself, and the bonesetter also had to hire four sedan carriers, two carters, a flute player, and two bodyguards to watch out for bandits. For his daughter, he had procured only the best: the fanciest sedan chair, the cleanest carts, the strongest guards with real pistols and gunpowder. In one of the carts was the dowry, the jar of opium and the jar of dragon bones, the last of his supply. He assured his daughter many times not to worry about the cost. After her wedding, he could go to the Monkey's Jaw and gather more bones.

82   Halfway between the villages, two bandits wearing hoods sprang out of the bushes. "I'm the famous Mongol Bandit!" the larger one bellowed. Right away, Precious Auntie recognized the voice of Chang the coffin-maker. What kind of ridiculous joke was this? But before she could say anything, the guards threw down their pistols, the carriers dropped their poles, and Precious Auntie was thrown to the floor of the sedan and knocked out.

83   When she came to, she saw Baby Uncle's face in a haze. He had lifted her out of the sedan. She looked around and saw that the wedding trunks had been ransacked and the guards and carriers had fled. And then she noticed

her father lying in a ditch, his head and neck at an odd angle, the life gone from his face. Was she in a dream? "My father," she moaned. "I want to go to him." As she bent over the body, unable to make sense of what had happened, Baby Uncle picked up a pistol that one of the guards had dropped.

84   "I swear I'll find the demons who caused my bride so much grief," he shouted, and then he fired the pistol toward heaven, startling his horse.

85   Precious Auntie did not see the kick that killed Baby Uncle, but she heard it, a terrible crack, like the opening of the earth when it was born. For the rest of her life she was to hear it in the breaking of twigs, the crackling of fire, whenever a melon was cleaved in the summer.

86   That was how Precious Auntie became a widow and an orphan in the same day. "This is a curse," she murmured, as she stared down at the bodies of the men she loved. For three sleepless days after their deaths, Precious Auntie apologized to the corpses of her father and Baby Uncle. She talked to their still faces. She touched their mouths, though this was forbidden and caused the women of the house to fear that the wronged ghosts might either possess her or decide to stay.

87   On the third day, Chang arrived with two coffins. "He killed them!" Precious Auntie cried. She picked up a fire poker and tried to strike him. She beat at the coffins. Baby Uncle's brothers had to wrestle her away. They apologized to Chang for the girl's lunacy, and Chang replied that grief of this magnitude was admirable. Because Precious Auntie continued to be wild with admirable grief, the women of the house had to bind her from elbows to knees with strips of cloth. Then they laid her on Baby Uncle's *k'ang*, where she wiggled and twisted like a butterfly stuck in its cocoon until Great-Granny forced her to drink a bowl of medicine that made her body grow limp. For two days and nights, she dreamed she was with Baby Uncle, lying on the *k'ang* as his bride.

88   When she revived, she was alone in the dark. Her arms and legs had been unbound, but they were weak. The house was quiet. She went searching for her father and Baby Uncle. When she reached the main hall, the bodies were gone, already buried in Chang's wooden handiwork. Weeping, she wandered about the house and vowed to join them in the yellow earth. In the ink-making studio, she went looking for a length of rope, a sharp knife, matches she could swallow, anything to cause pain greater than she felt. And then she saw a pot of black resin. She lowered a dipper into the liquid and put it in the maw of the stove. The oily ink became a soup of blue flames. She tipped the ladle and swallowed.

89   Great-Granny was the first to hear the thump-bumping sounds in the studio. Soon the other women of the household were there as well. They found Precious Auntie thrashing on the floor, hissing air out of a mouth blackened with blood and ink. "Like eels are swimming in the bowl of her mouth," Mother said. "Better if she dies."

90   But Great-Granny did not let this happen. Baby Uncle's ghost had come to her in a dream and warned that if Precious Auntie died, he and his ghost bride would roam the house and seek revenge on those who had not pitied

her. Everyone knew there was nothing worse than a vengeful ghost. They caused rooms to stink like corpses. They turned bean curd rancid in a moment's breath. They let wild creatures climb over the walls and gates. With a ghost in the house, you could never get a good night's sleep.

91   Day in and day out, Great-Granny dipped cloths into ointments and laid these over Precious Auntie's wounds. She bought dragon bones, crushed them, and sprinkled them into her swollen mouth. And then she noticed that another part of Precious Auntie had become swollen: her womb.

92   Over the next few months, Precious Auntie wounds changed from pus to scars, and her womb grew like a gourd. She had once been a fine-looking girl. Now all except blind beggars shuddered at the sight of her. One day, when it was clear she was going to survive, Great-Granny said to her speechless patient: "Now that I've saved your life, where will you and your baby go? What will you do?"

93   That night, the ghost of Baby Uncle came once again to Great-Granny, and the next morning, Great-Granny told Precious Auntie: "You are to stay and be nursemaid to this baby. First Sister will claim it as hers and raise it as a Liu. To those you meet, we'll say you're a distant relation from Peking, a cousin who lived in a nunnery until it burned down and nearly took you with it. With that face, no one will recognize you."

94   And that's what happened. Precious Auntie stayed. I was the reason she stayed, her only reason to live. Five months after my birth in 1916, GaoLing was born to Mother, who had been forced by Great-Granny to claim me as her own. How could Mother say she had two babies five months apart? That was impossible. So Mother decided to wait. Exactly nine months after my birth, and on a very lucky date in 1917, GaoLing was born for sure.

95   The grown-ups knew the truth of our births. The children knew only what they were supposed to pretend. And though I was smart I was stupid. I did not ever question the truth. I did not wonder why Precious Auntie had no name. To others she was Nursemaid. To me, she was Precious Auntie. And I did not know who she really was until I read what she wrote.

96   "I am your mother," the words said.

97   I read that only after she died. Yet I have a memory of her telling me with her hands, I can see her saying this with her eyes. When it is dark, she says this to me in a clear voice I have never heard. She speaks in the language of shooting stars.

Questions for Discussion

1. Explain the duties of a bonesetter.
2. Give examples of the geographically descriptive names of the Chinese cities and areas.
3. Why did Precious Auntie consider Chang's proposal of marriage an insult?

4. What did Chang and Baby Uncle have in common and what were their differences? What were the results of their commonalities? Why did Precious Auntie choose Baby Uncle instead of Chang, the coffin-maker?

5. How did Precious Auntie lose the ability to speak?

6. In what ways is Lu Ling dependent on her nursemaid, Precious Auntie?

7. What indicators early in the story suggest the true relationship between Precious Auntie and Lu Ling?

8. Explain the metaphor in the last line.

AMY TAN: A CRITICAL COMPANION[1]

E. D. HUNTLEY

Like a growing number of contemporary writers, Amy Tan crafts novels that resist facile and definitive classification into any of the conventional fictional genres. That the books are novels is widely acknowledged, although Tan has said that she intended *The Joy Luck Club* to be a collection of short stories. Readers and critics alike do, however, agree that Tan's work incorporates or echoes other genres including nonfiction and poetry. In fact, a significant source of the charm and artistry of the three Tan novels is their shape as fictional narratives that embrace elements of biography and autobiography, history and mythology, folk tale and Asian talk story, personal reminiscence and memoir. Tan's novels reify and reinterpret traditional genres by casting them in a variety of modes—realistic, comic, tragic, tragicomic, allegorical, fantastic, naturalistic, and heroic—that metamorphose seamlessly into each other in Tan's signature narrative style. Commentary is juxtaposed with memory, fable with history, pidgin English with California-speak, American culture with Chinese tradition, past with present in a collision of stories and voices and personalities, filtered through the point of view of an Asian American author who lives between worlds, who inhabits that border country known only to those in whose minds and sensibilities cultures clash and battle for dominance. Although Amy Tan's prose style is distinctively her own, she also owes a literary debt to other writers who, like her, inhabit the border country that shapes and inspires so many minority writers-writers who derive their voices and narrative structures from their experiences in the neighborhoods of America's diaspora cultures.

Asian American Literature: A Definition

In 1982, Elaine Kim's ground-breaking study, *Asian American Literature: An Introduction to the Writings and Social Context*, essentially brought an entire body of little-known literature into the American liter-

[1] E. D. Huntley, *Amy Tan: A Critical Companion* (Westport, CT: Greenwood Press, 1998), 219-31, 115-21.

ary consciousness, and helped Asian American literature gain recognition as a significant body of writing with both a "new tradition" of literary creation and a discernible—and very fluid—canon. In her work, Kim defined Asian American literature as "published creative writings in English by Americans of Chinese, Japanese, Korean, and Filipino descent" (xi). Although that definition lost its currency as immigrants from Cambodia, Vietnam, India, Pakistan, and other Asian countries began to make their homes in the United States and to write about their experiences, one crucial element of Kim's definition still holds true. Asian American literature is the creative work of writers of Asian descent who identify themselves as Americans and who view their own experiences and the world through the dual lenses of their American identities and their ethnic roots. More specifically, Asian American literature "elucidates the social history of Asians in the United States" (xiii). Although, as Kim points out, Asian American literature "shares with most other literature thematic concerns such as love, desire for personal freedom and acceptance, and struggles against oppression and injustice" (xii–xiii), this body of literature also is the product of other distinctive cultural forces. Like African American writing, fiction, poetry, and drama by Asian Americans is shaped by racism—both overt and disguised—and its corollaries, prejudice and discrimination. Moreover, for most Asian American writers, the Old Country and its culture are neither ancient nor buried history but very much alive and integral to the present, either in their own lives or in those of their parents and grandparents. The immigrant experience looms large in the writing of Asian Americans, and with that experience comes questions about marginality and life on the border, as well as explorations of issues of biculturalism and language, and decisions about identity.

The Asian American Literary Tradition

The history of Asian Americans goes back to the nineteenth century when thousands of men left their families and homes in China, Japan, Korea, and the Philippines to seek their fortunes in the United States, a country that the Chinese referred to as *gum san* or "the Gold Mountain." Seeking opportunity and possibly wealth, these men found ready work on the railroad, in gold- and silver-mining towns, and in lumber camps in the Western United States, industriously setting about making lives for themselves and for the picture brides from China and Japan who eventually traveled to the United States to marry men they had never met. The earliest official immigrant arrivals seem to have been men from Guangdong Province in China, although there exist records of Chinese sailors who stopped briefly in Baltimore in the late eighteenth century. Perhaps because they were first to arrive, the Chinese formed the largest Asian immigrant group, and they became the first Asians to experience institutionalized discrimination when the Chinese Exclusion Act of 1882 was passed by Congress, barring the majority of Chinese from entering the United States. The only exceptions to the ban were businessmen, diplomats, teachers, and students. When the law expired, it was renewed for another decade. Similar laws passed in 1902 and 1904 made the Chinese exclusion permanent, and Chinese who were already in the United States not only were denied citizenship but also were abused, publicly denounced in the press and from the pulpit, vilified, and physically attacked and even killed. Not until 1943 was exclusion legally ended with the passage of the Magnuson Act, which allowed 105 Chinese immigrants to enter the United States legally each year and gave Chinese the privilege of earning citizenship through naturalization. The older generation that is portrayed in Amy Tan's novels represents that group of new Chinese immigrants—especially the women who had long been denied entry—who entered the United States after the war in the years immediately following the Magnuson Act.

Not surprisingly, Asian immigrants—whose straight black hair and yellow-brown skin made them look different and who spoke languages that had no relation to Indo-European—seemed exotic and thus oddly fascinating to most Americans who were of European ancestry. Consequently, a number of stereotypical Asian characters became fixtures in certain forms of popular entertainment and literature. Racist images—the result of fear, ignorance, and xenophobia—were dominant, disseminated, and encouraged in a culture that feared that the increasing numbers of Chinese laborers, who were willing to work long hours at difficult tasks for low wages, posed a threat to employment opportunities for white men. Many of these fictional Asians were "inscrutable," humorlessly industrious, humble, patient, and inclined to say "Ah so" in response to nearly any comment or question that they presumably did not understand. The few who differed were aristocratic mandarins whose haughty demeanor and elegant carriage hinted at long acquaintance with a more ceremonious way of life in a mythical Old China. For decades, Charlie Chan, Fu Manchu, and Anna May Wong were the only Asians that many Americans had ever encountered, and their images remained indelibly etched into the American imagination and popular culture until well into the twentieth century.

Despite the popularity of Asian stock characters on stage and screen and in fiction, literary work by authors of Asian ancestry, while not unknown, was not particularly accessible or available, and much of what was published rapidly went out of print. Before their arrival in the United States, most Asian immigrants had belonged to economic or social classes that, in their home countries, would have provided them with little or no exposure to education, and certainly not to art and poetry, although a few might have learned some rudimentary reading and writing. On their arrival in America, they found employment that required them to labor up to twenty hours each day, often seven days a week, focusing all of their energies on the struggle to earn livelihoods for themselves as well as for their families who remained in China or Japan or Korea. Ignored on the job, and left to socialize among themselves, few Asian immigrants learned much English beyond the few phrases that were essential to basic communication in their jobs. Overworked, underpaid, housed in barely habitable structures in labor camps, deprived of educational opportunities, and widely discriminated against, most Asian immigrants endured bleak and joyless existences that stifled all creative or imaginative impulses. Hence, the dearth of imaginative writing from the earliest Asian Americans. Early immigrant writing—when it existed at all—generally took the form of letters and journals in languages other than English. Creative efforts, which were rare, resulted mainly in unfamiliar poetic genres such as *haiku* or *tanka*. In a poignantly significant series of attempts at artistic expression, anonymous Chinese immigrants who were detained at the Angel Island Detention Center after the passage of the Exclusion Act scrawled poetry on the walls, giving vent to their emotions and disappointments (Lim and Ling 5).

Although the Exclusion Act was directed at Chinese immigrants, negative Asian stereotypes were applied indiscriminately for decades not only to Chinese but also to Japanese, Korean, and Filipino immigrants. World War II changed those perceptions when international hostilities and American military losses in the Pacific unleashed waves of anti-Japanese propaganda, accompanied by sympathy for China and the Philippines. Because China was suffering the ravages of America's enemy, the Japanese army, the Chinese in America found themselves suddenly accepted as members of a "model minority" that was praised for loyalty to the United States.

In spite of the obstacles that barred the way to an Asian literary tradition in the United States, a few pieces of writing—chiefly memoirs—by Asians did appear as early as the end of the nineteenth century. The authors—mainly Chinese—had come to the United States as students, diplomats, or merchants, and were thus exempt from the Exclusion Act. Among the early books was a series of volumes by Western-educated young men of different countries, including two from China and Korea. These books, which were commissioned by the D. Lothrop Publishing Company, focused on elucidating for the benefit of the average American reader the cultural mores and traditional customs of the writers' native countries. Other autobiographies, written in the 1930s and 1940s, attempted to perform much the same anthropological function—to describe and explain to Western readers the more attractive elements of life in China: dress, food, festivals, sports, rituals and ceremonies, leisure activities, and daily life. Common to all of these personal accounts of life in China was their limited focus on the experiences of a privileged class, the members of which had nothing in common with the hordes of Asian laborers who spent their days patiently enduring their work in America's railroads, mines, and lumber camps. These early autobiographics and memoirs entranced American readers with descriptions of Chinese houses furnished with silk carpets and decorated with jade and porcelain artifacts, surrounded by gardens burgeoning with exotic blooms, meticulously maintained by happy, smiling servants who existed to make life easy and pleasant for the family who owned the house and land.

Among the most widely read of the Asian memoir-writers between the wars were three immigrant Chinese authors whose work is representative of the style of immigrant writing that American readers—and critics and reviewers—found not only acceptable but also immensely fascinating. The most prolific of these writers was Lin Yutang, who churned out scores of essays that are most notable for their gentle self-deprecating humor—at the expense not only of the author but also of his fellow Chinese—and for their genially superficial treatment of cultural issues and questions.

In a writing career that spanned about forty years, Lin Yutang claimed that his main purpose was to explain China and her people to Western readers. That he succeeded in reaching his target audience is evident in the popularity of his works, especially *My Country and My People* (1935), a book that went through four editions. The appeal of Lin's book for the majority of readers from the 1930s through the 1960s lies in its validation of a popular myth—the stereotype of the gently bred Chinese as naive, unworldly people who desired nothing more than to focus their energies and time on artistic and literary activities, and who submitted docilely to colonial rule because they lacked the motivation to govern themselves. Not surprisingly, more than a few Asian American readers took exception to Lin Yutang's portraits of China and the Chinese, claiming that Lin's books privileged a tiny percentage of the Chinese population—the affluent classes—and ignored the reality of the impoverished majority from whose ranks most Chinese immigrants came.

With a literary output that was far less voluminous than Lin Yutang's, Pardee Lowe and Jade Snow Wong nevertheless published highly regarded and extremely well-received memoirs of their experiences as Chinese immigrants growing up in America. Like Lin Yutang's books, Pardee Lowe's *Father and Glorious Descendant* (1943) and Jade Snow Wong's *Fifth Chinese Daughter* (1945 and 1950) describe an ethnic world in which existing stereotypes are confirmed and sanitized. Both books provided the predominantly white readership of the war years with a picture of Chinese American life that was both intriguing and easy to accept as genuine because it conformed to the mythical China that already existed in the popular American consciousness. Because he had enlisted in the U.S. Army, Lowe was praised for his patriotism and for the message of accommodation and assimilation that he disseminated through his memoirs.

As valuable as these works are in the history of Asian writing in the United States, they focus mainly on those immigrants whose antecedents had belonged to the privileged classes, and the prose and images appear dated to the late twentieth-century reader. The world of Lowe and Wong is populated with tea-sipping, poetry-writing aristocrats in beautiful, alien settings that exist only in a world that has receded into memory or survives only in the pages of forgotten volumes on neglected library shelves.

After the successes of Lowe and Wong, little by Asian American writers appeared for over two decades. In 1963, however, Virginia Lee's *The House That Tai Ming Built* revived the semi-autobiographical strain of immigrant writing popularized by Lowe and Wang. Like her predecessors, Lee portrayed a Chinese culture that did not represent the experience of the majority of Chinese Americans; nevertheless, like those earlier writers, Lee is important in the history of Asian American literary production. In their introduction to the first anthology of Asian American writing, Kaiyu Hsu and Helen Palubinskas comment on the work of Lowe, Wong, and Lee, which they describe as autobiographical and suggestive of

> the Chinese culture described in the connoisseurs' manuals of Chinese jade or oolong tea, and the stereotype of the Chinese immigrant, either withdrawn and totally Chinese, or quietly assimilated and unobtrusively American. (10)

Hsu and Palubinskas also caution against dismissing those early memoirs as irrelevant, pointing out that they have value for the student of Asian American literature. They assert that the three volumes of memoirs have a genuine claim to be considered landmarks in the development of a literary tradition by Asian Americans because "the authors wrote about the Chinese in America as they saw and understood them." Hsu and Palubinskas go on to issue a challenge: "Other Chinese-American writers, if they have different perceptions, should come forth with their stories" (10). Less than a decade after the publication of Lee's book, a vocal group of those "other [...] writers" emerged onto the American literary scene. But before they did so, their work was anticipated by Louis Chu whose 1961 novel, *Eat a Bowl of Tea*, first articulated some of the major concerns that would inform the work of later Asian writers.

Eat a Bowl of Tea is remarkable for its early treatment of the debilitating effects of racism and the patriarchal culture in Asian American communities. Set in 1947, two years after the War Bride Act of 1945 opened U.S. immigration to Chinese women, the novel examines the conflict between old-world patriarchal immigrant elders and their American-born children, a struggle that Ruth Hsiao describes as involving "emotionally damaged sons and daughters locked in battles of independence with their fathers or with the tradition that gives the fathers power" (54). Louis Chu foregrounds a nascent antipatriarchal movement through a complicated plot that portrays the traditional authoritarian father as a mere parody of the traditional patriarch. Hsiao points out that many consider Chu to be "a herald of the new Asian American sensibility" (153), although she criticizes his novel for suggesting in the end that patriarchy is an incurable condition in bicultural Asian communities and for positing "the birth of a new age patriarchy" (152). Nonetheless, it is clear that Chu does indeed prefigure not only the work of the writer-activists who would follow him in the next decade, but also the even more significant explosion of writing by Asian women that would mark the 1980s and 1990s.

The new Asian American writers of the 1970s were neither completely Asian nor definitively Western, but considered themselves to be members of a distinct new culture or set of cultures. Frank Chin, one of the new writers, articulated his position vis-à-vis the dominant landscape into which he was expected to assimilate by explaining the cultural force behind his writing:

> The sensibility, the kind of sensibility that is neither Chinese of China nor white-American. The sensibility derived from the peculiar experience of a Chinese born in this country some thirty years ago, with all the stigmas attached to his race, but felt by himself alone as an individual human being. (quoted in Hsu and Palubinskas 47)

The "sensibility" of which Chin speaks was shared by his peers, all of whom had grown up in a kind of ethnic limbo, belonging by heritage to a culture and homeland in which they were strangers, yet living and maturing in a culture that persisted in viewing them as Other, as alien and marginal. These writers incorporated their paradoxical condition—they were bicultural yet estranged from both cultures—into their poetry, fiction, and drama, producing a body of work that reflected a new Asian American voice that refused to mythologize ethnic origins or perpetuate stereotypes, yet avoided complete assimilation and in fact embraced difference on its own terms. For many of these writers, a crucial initiative of the decade was the attempt to redefine Asian American manhood and to counteract through their published writing what they perceived to have been the progressive cultural and psychological emasculation of the Asian male by the dominant culture.

Central to the activity of the 1970s was the work of a group called the Combined Asian Resources Project (CARP), whose members—Chin, Jeffery Paul Chan, Lawson Fusao Inada, Nathan Lee, Benjamin R. Tong, and Shawn Hsu Wong—actively sought publishing venues and performance spaces for the works of Asian American writers, created a collection of materials about those writers, found support for reissuing out-of-print works by the earliest Asian American writers, and sponsored literary conferences that focused on literary texts by Asian Americans. In addition, several valuable anthologies of writing by Asian Americans were published in the 1970s. The three best known of these anthologies are *Asian American Authors* (1972), edited by Kai-yu Hsu and Helen Palubinskas; *Aiiieeeee! An Anthology of Asian-American Writers* (1974), edited by CARP members Frank Chin, Jeffery Paul Chan, Lawson Fusao Inada, and Shawn Hsu Wong; and *Asian American Heritage: An Anthology of Prose and Poetry* (1974), edited by David Hsin-fu Wand.

Although these anthologies made some Asian writing more accessible to larger numbers of readers, Asian American literature had its first significant impact on the popular American consciousness in 1976 when Maxine Hong Kingston published *The Woman Warrior*, her rivetingly powerful memoir about growing up Chinese in America. Kingston's book was well-received in literary circles, winning the National Book Critics Circle Award for the best nonfiction of 1976, and paved the way for the young writers of the next decade to prove conclusively that the Asian

American voice had a powerful resonance far beyond Chinatown or Little Tokyo or the neighborhood enclaves of Korean or Filipino immigrants. Unfortunately, Kingston was condemned by some Asian American writers who accused her of trying to "cash in" on the "feminist fad," of writing only for financial gain by creating "white-pleasing autobiography passing for pop cultural anthropology" (Kim 198). However, Kingston's detractors, although articulate and vocal, are few—limited mainly to a few male writers of Asian descent who have continued to argue that the tremendous sales and widespread popularity enjoyed by Asian American women writers undermines the masculinity of their male colleagues.

Kingston ushered in the 1980s with *China Men* (1980), winning the American Book Award. During that decade, Asian American writers earned recognition for the excellence and importance of their work. Among poets, Cathy Song won the Yale Series of Younger Poets competition for *Picture Bride* in 1982, Garrett Hongo was awarded the Lamont Poetry prize of the Academy of American Poets in 1987, and Li-Young Lee was invited to read his poetry on National Public Radio. A new generation of playwrights graced the American stage: Genny Lim's *Island* (1985) was featured on National Public Television, and David Henry Hwang entranced Broadway audiences and won several Tony Awards for *M. Butterfly* in 1988. Into the growing market for and interest in Asian American writing came Amy Tan and *The Joy Luck Club* in 1989. The publication of that novel helped to catapult Asian American fiction into the literary mainstream when it appeared on national bestseller lists and became a featured book-club selection. By the end of the decade, many writers, including David Mura, Jessica Hagedorn, Philip Kan Gotanda, Ping Chong, Gish Jen, and Cynthia Kadohata discovered their work—along with that of Kingston and Tan—in textbook anthologies and on required reading lists for literature courses. Years later, the final pieces of evidence that Asian American writing has entrenched itself in the popular mind are the popular film versions of works by writers as diverse as Tan and Hwang, and memoir-writer Le-Ly Hayslip.

Partly because of the volume of their work and certainly because they write about subjects that resonate with so many mainstream readers, Chinese American women writers have been largely but inadvertently responsible for the new and sudden popularity of Asian American writing, a development that is made more startling because Chinese women were an almost invisible minority in American society until the early 1950s. Because most of them were kept out of the United States by laws specifically excluding Chinese women (including those who were married to American-born Chinese men) from immigration quotas, these women were outnumbered by Chinese men by approximately twenty to one. Given those numbers, we should not be surprised at the relatively small number of Chinese women writers in the first half of the twentieth century—in fact, we should be amazed that so many of the significant early Chinese American writers were women.

Chinese American Women Writers

The earliest successful Chinese American women authors were the Eurasian sisters Edith and Winnifred Eaton, daughters of an English artist and his Chinese wife. Although born in England, both Edith and Winnifred emigrated to the United States as adults, and it was as Americans that they began their writing careers. Despite their Caucasian features, the Eaton sisters used Asian pseudonyms: Edith became Sui Sin Far, Cantonese for "Narcissus," and Winnifred became the faux-Japanese Onoto Watanna. The sisters' choices are intriguing, particularly because Edith decided to emphasize their Chinese heritage despite the Chinese Exclusion Act and widespread prejudice against the Chinese, while Winnifred, by contrast, assumed the more acceptable Japanese identity. During the decades before World War II, the Japanese enjoyed widespread respect in the United States, and Winnifred enhanced the prestige of her assumed identity by claiming that her mother belonged to a noble Japanese family from Nagasaki.

The Eaton sisters' writing paralleled their pseudonymous identities. As Sui Sin Far, Edith wrote in defense of the much maligned Chinese, taking up the fight against racism and injustice, attempting in her short stories to portray Chinese characters sympathetically and without resorting to prevalent stereotypes. Her ironic examinations of American culture are not limited to the plight of the Chinese immigrant; she also focuses attention on prejudice based on gender and class, or on that cultural phenomenon that she exemplified—the individual of mixed heritage who belongs neither to one culture nor to the other. Winnifred's career was markedly different from that of her sister. Onoto Watanna's "Japanese novels" were romances set in exotic Orientalized landscapes, featuring delicate, winsome Japanese women and influential powerful men—often white men— to whom the heroine must appeal for help or protection. Unlike Edith, who used her pen as a weapon of protest, Winnifred's writing foregrounded and supported the status quo with its prejudices and cultural assumptions. So popular were Onoto Watanna's novels that they were translated into several European languages and went through several printings. They were adapted for the stage as well, and Winnifred eventually moved on to a highly successful career as a Hollywood scriptwriter.

Japan's attack on Pearl Harbor destroyed American readers' fascination with things Japanese and created a new acceptance of the Chinese, who were suddenly recognized as fellow victims of Japan's aggression. Several women—immigrants, American-born Chinese, American-raised Chinese—wrote novels and personal accounts about the devastating effects of the war on China, and about the strength and resilience of the Chinese people. Amy Ling points out that much of the war literature has a specifically defined purpose: "demonstration to the United States, a country superior in arms and supplies, that China was a worthy ally" ("Chinese American" 227). Among these writers were the three daughters of Lin Yutang—Adet and Anor, both of whom would have literary careers, and Mei-mei, the youngest and most Americanized. Also beginning their writing careers with personal accounts of the war were Han Suyin, Mai-mai Sze, and Helena Kuo. Although the war pieces received attention from readers who were chiefly concerned with discovering how the war was affecting some of America's Asian friends, it was Jade Snow Wong's *Fifth Chinese Daughter* that garnered the popularity and wide readership that the other works did not.

When the Exclusion Act was finally repealed in 1943, the increase in Chinese emigrating to the United States included significant numbers of women, and, as a result, the number of Chinese American women writers increased. Amy Ling and Elaine Kim, among others, have pointed out that despite the growing numbers of writers, Asian Americans' novels continued for a time to cater to the tastes of the predominantly white readership, looking with polite disfavor on Asian culture and enthusiastically embracing the American lifestyle.

There are two interesting exceptions to the tendency among early Asian writers in America to apologize for their ethnic backgrounds while commenting approvingly on Western culture. Han Suyin and Chuang Hua deserve mention for unapologetically examining the precarious balancing act performed by not only individuals who have both Asian and European or American blood but also Asians who are involved in interracial relationships. Herself of mixed blood, Han Suyin is a prolific writer with nearly two dozen titles—written over nearly half a century—in her oeuvre. Central to her most powerful novels are the problematic relationships between couples of different—and often antagonistic—ethnic and cultural backgrounds; and she underscores the tensions in such relationships by setting her novels in inherently contested territory that is unfamiliar to most of her readers. In Han Suyin's fiction, the cultural clashes involve Eurasian, American, Chinese, English, and Indian characters in settings as geographically diverse as Nepal, China under communism, and Hong Kong. Another writer, Chuang Hua, focuses her experimental novel, *Crossings* (1968), on life in that border country between cultures. Her protagonist, a Chinese woman who has grown up in England and the United States and spends time in France, falls in love with a European journalist, and their doomed affair is played out against the backdrop of the Korean War, which pits China and America against each other. Formally and structurally, Hua's novel is a forerunner of Maxine Hong Kingston's and Amy Tan's multiple genre approach to storytelling. In *Crossings*, the line of the narrative is ruptured time and again by autobiographical reminiscences, biographical elements, recounted dreams and nightmares, interior monologues, resulting in what Amy Ling calls "a highly original expression of the Chinese American hyphenated condition" (235).

As noted earlier, Maxine Hong Kingston's *Woman Warrior* took the American literary establishment as well as the reading public by surprise in 1975. In her text—which has been labeled variously talk-story memoir, autobiography, biography, novel—Kingston rejects the traditional linear fictional narrative structure, privileging instead a polyvocal mosaic of genres and styles that work together by both completing and contradicting each other, thus illustrating through content as well as form the collision between distinct and complex cultures. Writing about Kingston's work as the beginning of a new tradition in Asian American writing, Marlene Goldman points out that "Kingston's novel constitutes an alternative system for organizing experience, an activity directly related to the inscription of identity" (225). Kingston herself asserts that although *Woman Warrior* privileges women's circular narratives based on cultural memory and "old myths," the work itself is "much more American than Chinese" with characters who are "American people" (179). Indeed, the central theme in all of Kingston's writing is the attempt to sort out what being Chinese American means through the exploration of her experiences as an American-born child of immigrant parents.

By the time Amy Tan published her first novel, Maxine Hong Kingston had already introduced the general reading public to the talk-story narrative style. With her multiperspectival text, Tan was not only working in the traditions of her Chinese heritage and her Western training, but she also was following in the literary footsteps of a significant and powerful Asian American writer who had already begun to mine the rich vein of oral and written literary genres and traditions that exists within America's immigrant communities.

Plot Development

The plot of *The Hundred Secret Senses* follows two narrative threads: Olivia's search for an integrated self, and Kwan's desire to undo the damage of a century-old mistake. Although the two are closely related, the connections between them do not immediately become obvious but emerge gradually as elements of each plot come to light and reveal echoes of the other.

Borrowing a technique from the classical epic, Amy Tan begins the novel *in medias res*, or—colloquially translated—in the middle of the action. Over a century earlier in China, Kwan—with the very best intentions—told a lie, fabricating a story that had the unforeseen effect of disrupting the lives of two people and abruptly terminating the romance that had begun between them. The plot that has Kwan at its center is the history of her previous existence as Nunumu; the events of her life gradually reveal the incidents that lead inexorably toward the mistake that separates Miss Banner and Yiban. Now in California, Kwan is devoting her energies to the cause of rectifying her mistake and reuniting the lovers. Meanwhile, in the narrative of Olivia's efforts to discover what she wants her life to become, Olivia and Simon already are separated and have initiated the legal transactions that will lead to divorce. Both women tell their stories, but whereas Olivia's narratives suggest interior monologues with a pervasive component of self-questioning and no identifiable audience, Kwan's stories—which are embedded in Olivia's—are clearly addressed to Olivia.

As Olivia sorts through the emotional chaos resulting from her separation from Simon, she repeatedly is reminded of the events of their courtship, the early years of their marriage, and their more recent attempts to revive the companionship they felt when they were younger. Because Simon was and is her first and only love, Olivia is not dealing well with the break-up of her marriage, and Kwan, who is still the protective older sister although they are both adults, worries constantly about Olivia, inviting her to dinner, dropping in for brief visits, offering the opinion that the separation is a mistake and that Olivia and Simon should reconcile. In the first half of the novel, each overture by Kwan prompts Olivia to remember a story that Kwan has told her, and each story told by Kwan in turn somehow returns the narrative to Olivia's emotional dilemma. With each new story, the outlines of connections become clearer. Initially, it appears that Kwan wants to bring the couple back together because she was responsible for the evening during which Elza—a *yin* person and Simon's first love who had been dead for a while—supposedly told Simon to forget her and to find happiness with Olivia. But Kwan's stories and everyday conversation are laced with oblique references to her belief that the rightness of Olivia's and Simon's union was determined by events in the distant past, and eventually Kwan manages to persuade Simon and Olivia to join her on a trip to China where, she points out mysteriously, they will discover the true pattern of their lives.

During the China trip, Olivia's and Kwan's narratives abruptly change. Removed from the familiar and confronted with a new culture, Olivia curtails her litany of past rejections and begins instead to detail events as they happen; and because she is in China, Olivia no longer has to rely on her memory of Kwan's stories—China is all around her to be experienced. Kwan, for her part, increases the number and frequency of her stories about Nunumu and Miss Banner, adding stories that Olivia has never heard—for instance, the story of Yiban and the last days in the Ghost Merchant's house, or the tale of the flight to the mountains. Early in the novel, Kwan's stories emerge as Olivia's memories, but in the final chapters, Kwan tells her stories in the immediate present. Gone is the slow gentle rhythm of memory; each tale now is urgent, immediate, triggered by the sight of a mountain or the taste of a special dish or, ultimately, the very palpable presence of a music box that Kwan claims to have hidden in a cave over a century earlier. Kwan's final stories clarify connections: Olivia and Simon are Miss Banner and Yiban, and Kwan has brought them to Changmian to reunite them. The novel ends with an epilogue narrated by Olivia. She and Simon are working toward reconciliation. More important, they have a daughter who was conceived in China, and who is— Olivia firmly believes—Kwan's final gift to them.

Narrative Strategies

Tan employs the juxtaposition of past and present as a narrative device for her story of the indestructibility of love and loyalty. Past and present are so closely interrelated that Olivia ultimately admits to being occasionally confused about whether an event actually occurred or is merely an episode in one of Kwan's frequently recounted stories. Toward the end of the novel, as Olivia and Kwan turn over the contents of the ancient music box that the latter says she hid in a cave more than a hundred years earlier, Olivia's logical mind races from one explanation to another. Always the rational American woman of the 1990s, Olivia is inclined to doubt what her senses suggest; nevertheless, she cannot dismiss the fact of Kwan's unflinching candor. In their time together, Olivia has never known Kwan to lie; in fact, Kwan says only what she truly believes to be true. And although Olivia knows that she should believe Kwan even now, another question surfaces: "[I]f I believe what she says, does that mean I now believe she has *yin* eyes?" (320). At that moment, Olivia realizes what she has known, has in fact believed all along—since childhood—that Kwan does remember events, the memory of which defies rational explanation.

Events in the past clearly and significantly influence the lives of both Olivia and Kwan. They are sisters, thanks to Jack Yee's two marriages and the shameful act of thievery that provided him with the wherewithal to abandon a wife and child, to discard an identity, and to begin a new life and new family in America. Through her conversations with her *yin* friends about Olivia's marital problems, Kwan bridges the chronological gap between her two lives, and Olivia is forced to endure advice and comments on her marriage from a certain Lao Lu, a friend of Kwan's from the Taiping days in the Ghost Merchant's house. Not even Olivia's marriage is immune to the influence of the past: after nearly two decades of marriage, Simon still appears to be obsessed with his first love who was killed in an avalanche.

During the visit to China, Kwan becomes more and more insistent that she and Olivia have had a previous life together, and when the sisters are together on the mountain, Olivia begins to half believe that she does indeed recognize in her present circumstances a series of strong resonances from another time. Whether these frissons of memory are remnants of Kwan's stories or genuine recollections from Olivia's past is immaterial. What is clear is that Olivia finds the more distinctive elements of the Guilin landscape disturbingly familiar.

Present and past finally collide on a rain-drenched mountain just beyond Changmian. Assailed from all directions by a cascade of sensory and emotional stimuli (Kwan's final story about her last hours in the nineteenth century, a hilly landscape that possesses a dreamlike familiarity combined with jarring strangeness, Simon's disappearance into the cold mist, Kwan's rediscovery of the music box that she last saw when she was Nunumu, and finally Kwan's revelation of the truth about Simon and Elza), Olivia is drawn into an admission that her history with Kwan could have begun near this mountain in an earlier century. It remains only for Olivia to unearth the jars full of duck eggs that Kwan says Nunumu buried during the Taiping troubles. As Olivia holds the ancient crumbling duck eggs in her cupped hands, the act liberates her from the doubts that have undermined all of her relationships. And although Kwan vanishes into the Changmian caves and is never found despite an intensive and protracted search, Olivia believes that the daughter who is born to her and Simon nine months later is a gift from Kwan. The child is not Kwan, exactly, but she is connected with Kwan in some mysterious way—and in that little girl, the past and the present are fused into wholeness and the future.

As she does in her other novels, Tan relies on formal storytelling as a narrative strategy in *The Hundred Secret Senses*. Both Kwan's nineteenth-century existence as Nunumu and her twentieth-century childhood in Changmian before her emigration to America emerge through narrative set pieces that Kwan performs as though they are legends or folktales, artifacts of an oral tradition that she feels impelled to pass on to Olivia who is her captive audience.

Tan uses the flashback technique to superb effect in the novel. New words, chance remarks, familiar objects and mementos, the taste of traditional Chinese dishes, and celebrations trigger Kwan's recollections, prompting her to narrate vignettes, brief tales, events, the particulars of specific episodes in her former lives. In one instance, when she overhears the neighborhood children referring to her as "a retard" and forces Olivia to define the word, Kwan suddenly is reminded of Miss Banner's early attempts to speak Chinese, and she tells Olivia that Nunumu initially thought that Miss Banner's inability to speak or understand Chinese indicated a lack of intelligence. On occasion, Kwan says, Nunumu actually laughed at Miss Banner's feeble attempts to converse in the vernacular. The memory prompts Kwan immediately to launch into an account of Miss Banner's first garbled description of her early life. Because Miss Banner cannot speak adequate Chinese, she ends up thoroughly confusing Nunumu by telling an impossibly surrealistic story about her origins, but Nunumu's patience with her mistress eventually results in her success at teaching Miss Banner how to view the world "exactly as a Chinese person" would (49).

By providing multiple versions of and varying perspectives on events that are central to the novel, Tan explores the ways through which storytellers create meaning on many levels and from different points of view. In some cases, the plurality of versions is the inadvertent result of misunderstandings, incomplete information, or even partial fabrication; in other cases, variant editions of a story signal the storyteller's intent to deceive. Tan seems to be suggesting that the truth exists both in each version of a story and somewhere in the unspoken narrative or in the spaces between stories.

A hallmark of *The Hundred Secret Senses* is the novel's precarious position somewhere between the real and the surreal, between the prosaic and the magical. When Kwan as Nunumu first hears Miss Banner's life story told in fractured stumbling Chinese, she forms the impression that

Miss Banner has come from a peculiarly skewed and topsy-turvy universe. Miss Banner's little brothers chase a chicken into a deep hole and fall all the way to the other side of the world; her father picks scented money that grows like flowers and makes people happy; her mother puffs out her neck like a rooster, calls for her sons, and climbs down the hole that has swallowed them. After her mother's disappearance, Miss Banner's father takes her first to a palace governed by little Jesuses, and later to an island ruled by mad dogs. At length, the father vanishes and Miss Banner lives with a succession of uncles, including one who cuts off pieces of China and sails off on a floating island. The reality—which Kwan learns after Miss Banner becomes more fluent in Chinese—is that Miss Banner's brothers died of chicken pox and her mother of a goiter disease; her father was an opium trader who put her in a school for Jesus-worshipping children in India; father and daughter left India for Malacca; and the uncles were actually a series of lovers. Tan's clever juxtaposition of fact and whimsy complements the surrealism that pervades the entire novel and validates for the reader the simultaneous existence of twentieth century and nineteenth century, Chinese and American, Kwan and Nunumu, and the *yin* people in Tan's fictional universe.

Tan also employs multiple versions of a story to create uncertainty and to describe a world in which no definite answers are possible. Jack Yee, the shadowy father that Kwan and Olivia barely remember, is an enigma to both daughters, but for different reasons. In Olivia's version of Jack's story—passed on to her by the American-born adults in the family—Jack was a good-looking university student in Guilin who was forced to marry a young market vendor when she became pregnant with his child. Five years later, when his wife died of a lung disease, the grief-stricken Jack left his young daughter with an aunt and went to Hong Kong to begin a new life. Before he could send for his beloved daughter, the Communist takeover in China destroyed all hope for a reunion between father and child, and the despondent Jack emigrated to America. Kwan's arrival replaces the sad story with an even more disturbing one. According to Kwan, her mother did not die of a lung disease; she died of "heartsickness" when her husband abandoned her with a four-year-old daughter and another child on the way. Kwan tells Olivia that all the water in her mother's belly "poured out as tears from her eyes.[...] That poor starving baby in her belly ate a hole in my mother's heart, and they both died" (14). In this way, years later, Olivia learns what Kwan has always known. Their father had no legal or hereditary claim to the name Jack Yee. The name belonged to the owner of a stolen overcoat that the young university student who became their father purloined from a drunken man who had been trying to sell it for whatever cash he could get. In the coat's pockets were immigration permits, academic records, notification of admission to an American university, a ticket for passage on a ship, and cash—documents that would facilitate a new life in a wealthy country full of opportunity, far away from poverty, factory work, a pregnant wife, and a child. Donning the coat and the spectacles he found in one pocket, and appropriating the documents, the student became Jack Yee. But Amy Tan does not privilege Kwan's version. Kwan, in fact, prefaces her tale by saying that she heard it from Li Bin-bin, her mother's sister who raised her—and who, under the circumstances, would be unlikely to feel kindly toward the bogus Jack Yee. Thus the question remains: Who is the man behind the identity of Jack Yee? Kwan says that she has never known his true name, and she clearly knows almost nothing of his origins. And by extension, then, who are Olivia and Kwan? Who are their true ancestors? And who are Miss Banner and Nunumu? And, ultimately, how are all of these individuals connected?

Finally, Tan employs the many-layered triple narrative to interrogate the accounts of actual historical events, perhaps even to suggest that such accounts are unstable because they are the productions of gendered, class-defined, or racially constructed language. The Taiping Rebellion of the mid-nineteenth century is well known to Sinologists as well as to historians and geographers, but the standard texts tend toward factual, Westernized accounts of military battles, descriptions of territory gained or lost, and tallies of victories and defeats. Kwan's version of the Rebellion privileges the perspective of a half-blind orphan who notices far more than battles between Manchu and Hakka. For one-eyed Nunumu, the Rebellion means the loss of her entire family, and life in a half-deserted village populated only by the elderly and the very young, the physically and mentally disabled, and the cowardly; the Heavenly King and his armies succeed only in bringing her hunger and cold, and a life of servitude in a house full of missionaries. Nunumu's experiences factor the personal element into a historical equation, revealing the frequently overlooked truth that military and political battles are always won or lost at the expense of thousands of individuals whose lives are forever disrupted by the ambitions of a powerful minority and their followers.

Works Cited

Goldman, Marlene. "Naming the Unspeakable: The Mapping of Female Identity in Maxine Hong Kingston's *The Woman Warrior.*" *International Women's Writing: New Landscapes of Identity*. Eds. Anne E. Brown and Marjanne E. Goozé. Westport, CT: Greenwood Press, 1995. 223–32.

Hsaio, Ruth. "Facing the Incurable: Patriarchy in *Eat a Bowl of Tea.*" In *Reading the Literature of Asian America*. Eds. Shirley Geok-lin Lim and Amy Ling. Philadelphia: Temple University Press, 1992. 151–62.

Kim, Elaine. *Asian American Literature: An Introduction to the Writings and their Social Context*. Philadelphia: Temple University Press, 1982.

Lim, Shirley G., and Amy Ling. *Reading the Literatures of Asian America*. Philadelphia: Temple University Press, 1992.

Ling, Amy. *Between Worlds: Women Writers of Chinese Ancestry*. New York: Pergamon, 1990.

Chinese American Women, Language, and Moving Subjectivity[1]

Victoria Chen

To imagine a language means to imagine a form of life.

Wittgenstein, *Philosophical Investigations*

Philosophical Investigations

It was not until the 1970s that Asian American literature became recognized as a separate canon and a "new tradition" of writing. While this "new" form of expression created a new political consciousness and identity, the images and stories that abound in pioneer literature such as Maxine Hong Kingston's *The Woman Warrior* and *China Men* are paradoxically located in "recovered" ethnic history. More recently, Amy Tan's *The Joy Luck Club* also takes the reader through a journey back to a specific set of ethnic memories as the mothers in the stories interweave their experiences struggling for survival and dignity in China and for coherence and hope in America. Part of the reason for the celebration of Asian American women's literature is that it provides an alternative way to think about issues such as language, subjectivity, cultural voice, and ethnic/gender identity.

For Chinese American women such as Kingston, Tan, and the female characters in *The Joy Luck Club*, speaking in a double voice and living in a bicultural world characterize their dual cultural enmeshment. While striving to maintain a relationship with their Chinese immigrant parents, the Chinese American daughters also live in a society where one is expected to speak in a "standard" form of English and to "succeed" in the middle class Euro-American way. For Kingston and Tan, writing about their immigrant mothers' neglected pasts and their own tumultuous presents becomes a powerful way to recreate their own identities as Chinese Americans and to confront the dilemma of living biculturally in a society that insists on a homogeneous identity. If a language indeed is intrinsically connected with a form of life, and speaking and writing in a given language necessitates one to participate in that cultural world, how then do these Chinese American women authors position themselves in linguistic/cultural borderlands through the use of language? What are some forms of language and life that make their storytelling possible and intelligible? How do different languages function in their own lives and in their storytelling? How do they use languages to interweave and mediate their multiple identities? This essay attempts to address some of these issues. I will draw upon essays written by and about Kingston and Tan as well as narratives from *The Joy Luck Club* and *The Woman Warrior* in my discussion.

[1]From *Women & Language* 18.1 (Spring 1995). Copyright 1995 by *Women & Language*.

Amy Tan (1991) in her essay "Mother Tongue" discusses that as some-one who has always loved language, she celebrates using "all the Eng-lishes I grew up with" in her living and her writing. The English that she hears from her mother, despite its "imperfection," has become their "lan-guage of intimacy, a different sort of English that relates to family talk, the language I grew up with." There is a discrepancy, both linguistically and culturally, between the "standard" English that she learns from school and uses in her professional world and the "simple" and "broken" English that is used in her interaction with her mother. However, as Tan points out, speaking her mother's version of English gives her bicultural insight and strength, and she sees the beauty and wisdom in her mother's language: "Her language, as I hear it, is vivid, direct, full of observation and imagery"; "I wanted to capture what language ability tests can never reveal: her intent, her passion, her imagery, the rhythms of her speech and the nature of her thoughts." Kingston also grew up in two languages, her family's Chinese dialect and the public American English in which she was educated. *The Woman Warrior* reveals the disjunction that Kingston expe-rienced in moving between these two languages. While her mother marked her growing up with stories of nameless Chinese women, multiple cultural ghosts, Kingston wrote, "To make my waking life American-normal [...] I push the deformed into my dreams, which are in Chinese, the language of impossible stories." The entire book is devoted to Kingston's ongoing struggle to enter the Chinese cultural world composed of impossible sto-ries and to figure out what it meant to be a Chinese American woman in this society.

Tan's *The Joy Luck Club* is a segmented novel, set in San Francisco in the 1980s, powerfully blending the voices of four Chinese immigrant mothers and their American-born daughters. The book opens with a story of a swan and a woman sailing across an ocean toward America saying, "In America I will have a daughter just like me. But over there [...] nobody will look down on her, because I will make her speak only perfect Amer-ican English. And over there she will always be too full to swallow any sorrow! She will know my meaning.[...]" The tale symbolizes not only the geographic separation from the woman's motherland but also the alien-ation later felt by both the mother and daughter in America. The woman's desire for her daughter to speak perfect American English foregrounds the problems and difficulties of communicating and translating between the different languages that they speak. The American dream eventually eludes the immigrant woman beyond her best intentions. Mastering this imaginary perfect English for the American-born daughter turns out not to be a simple ticket to American success. This linguistic competency, ironically, signifies her departure from her mother (and her motherland), deepening the chasm between generations and cultures. Moreover, learn-ing to speak perfect American English may also entail the complex jour-ney of "successful" acculturation which often masks the racism and sexism that belie the American dream.

Although Tan's essay celebrates the two Englishes with which she grew up, and that dual languages and cultures can indeed enrich and enlighten one's life, coherence and double voice do not always come without personal struggle and emotional trauma. As we enter the hyphenated world of the "Chinese-American" women in *The Joy Luck Club,* much of the mothers' and daughters' conversations seem to be focused on debating, negotiating, and wandering between the two disparate cultural logics. Lindo shared her daughter's concern that she cannot say whether her Chinese or American face is better: "I think about our two faces. I think about my intentions. Which one is American? Which one is Chinese? Which one is better? If you show one, you must always sacrifice the other." Tan (1990), in her essay "The Language of Discretion," pointed out a special kind of double bind attached to knowing two languages and vehemently rebelled against seeing cultural descriptions as dichotomous categories: "It's dangerous business, this sorting out of language and behavior. Which one is English? Which is Chinese? [...] Reject them all!" "Having listened to both Chinese and English, I also tend to be suspicious of any comparisons between Chinese and English languages." Tan argued: "Typically, one language—that of the person doing the comparing—is often used as the standard, the benchmark for a logical form of explanation."

Speaking a language is inherently political. In the case of Chinese American women, while straddling and juggling along the fault lines of gender and culture, the truth is that the two Englishes that Tan cherished are not valued equally in this society. Despite the creative use of imaginative metaphors in her English, as Tan humorously presented, her mother would never score high in a standard English test that insists on one correct way of linguistic construction. It is no secret that in much of our social discourse and communication practice, the myth persists that what counts as the "normal" standards and criteria for comparing and discussing cultural difference is still the mainstream Eurocentric mode of thinking and doing. In her writing about Asian American women's experience of racism, Shah (1994) said, "For me, the experience of 'otherness,' the formative discrimination in my life, has resulted from culturally different people thinking they were culturally central; thinking that *my* house smelled funny, that *my* mother talked weird, that *my* habits were strange. They were normal; I wasn't." Similarly, in a discussion of the difficult dialogues between black and white women, Houston (1994) points out that when a white woman says "We're all alike," she usually means "I can see how you, a black woman, are like me, a white woman." She does not mean "I can see how I am like you." In other words, whether explicitly or implicitly, "just people" often means "just white people."

Language and identity are always positioned within a hierarchical power structure in which the Chinese American immigrants' form of life has never been granted a status equal to that of their European counterparts in the history of this country. It is one thing to embrace the philosophical wisdom of "having the best of both worlds" but another to confront the real ongoing struggle between languages and identities that most Chinese Americans experience. Bicultural identity cannot be reduced to two neutral, pristine, and equal linguistic domains that one simply picks and chooses to participate in without personal, relational, social, and political consequences. We need to understand the tension and conflict between generations of Chinese American women within the ideological cultural context of racial and sexual inequality and their ongoing contestation of their positions in it.

Through Tan's storytelling in *The Joy Luck Club*, the meaning of "perfect English" is transformed from the mother's naive American dream to the daughter's awakening bicultural disillusionment, as the daughter June laments: "These kinds of explanations made me feel my mother and I spoke two different languages, which we did. I talked to her in English, she answered back in Chinese," and later, "My mother and I never really understood one another. We translated each other's meanings and I seemed to hear less than what was said, while my mother heard more." The lack of shared languages and cultural logics remains a central theme throughout all the narratives in Tan's book. This absence transcends the simple linguistic dichotomies or cultural misunderstandings; both mothers and daughters are negotiating their relational and social positions and contesting their identities as Chinese American women in the languages that can enhance or undermine their power, legitimacy, and voice.

In a similar vein, in *The Woman Warrior* Kingston describes "abnormal" discourse as constructed and experienced by both parents and children in her family. The children in Kingston's family often spoke in English language which their parents "didn't seem to hear"; "the Chinese can't hear American at all; the language is too soft and Western music unhearable." Exasperated and bemused by their Chinese aunt's behavior, the children told each other that "Chinese people are very weird." Angry at the fact that the Chinese were unable, unwilling, or did not see the need to explain things to the children, Kingston writes, "I thought talking and not talking made the differences between sanity and insanity. Insane people were the ones who couldn't explain themselves." While the Chinese American children were frustrated by the impenetrable wisdom spoken or unspoken in the Chinese language, the parents teased the children about the way they spoke in the "ghost's" language and of the craziness and absurdity of doing things in American ways. Insane and absurd in what language(s) and from what cultural perspective(s)? Who has the authority to tell Kingston that Chinese girls are worthless growing up in a society that is supposed to be more egalitarian and liberating for women? What constitutes "normal" and "abnormal" discourse for Chinese American women? What price do they have to pay for being a full participant in either or both cultural worlds?

One intriguing feature in learning to speak and hear incommensurate languages is the process of adjudicating conflicting voices. In Chinese

American families, communication can often be characterized by a lack of a shared universe of discourse or a set of mutually intelligible vocabularies. For Kingston, even attempting to engage in a meaningful dialogue with her parents about her confusions and their conflicts became a problem, as she told us, "I don't know any Chinese I can ask without getting myself scolded or teased." Silent and silenced, Kingston was angry at the sexist trivialization of her intellectual interests and academic accomplishment. She writes, "I've stopped checking 'bilingual' on job applications. I could not understand any of the dialects the interviewer at China Airlines tried on me, and he didn't understand me either." Family language almost became a "burden" as Kingston strived to make sense of what it meant to occupy two linguistic and cultural spaces as a Chinese American woman in a patriarchal system. Could her surrender allude to the disappointment and frustration that Chinese Americans as a group feel within the larger society?

In Tan's novel, when one of the daughters, June, did not comply with her mother's wishes, her mother shouted at her in Chinese: "Only two kinds of daughters. Those who are obedient and those who follow their own mind! Only one kind of daughter can live in this house. Obedient daughter!" The mother's injunction is an enactment of her personal power within the family structure, and in this language and cultural logic, June is powerless even if she could speak "perfect" American English, which would give her positional power in a different situation.

Toward the end of the book when Kingston finally confronted her mother with her long list of feelings of guilt being a Chinese American daughter, the linguistic gap and cultural intranslatability resonated throughout their shouting match. Angry, frustrated, hurt, sad, and disappointed, Kingston realized that the confrontation was futile: "And suddenly I got very confused and lonely because I was at the moment telling her my list, and in the telling, it grew. No higher listener. No listener but myself." Once again, their voices did not intermesh, and neither could enter the cultural logic that was specifically structured within the primary language that they spoke. There was no possibility for Kingston to articulate her silence, nor was there space for displaying her mother's good intentions. The celebration of the multiple languages and polyphonic voices seemed elusive. Two generations of women were ultimately torn apart and yet inextricably bonded by the unspeakable cultural tongue. Each in their own way sounded strange, incoherent, crazy, abnormal, and stubborn to the other.

The end of the story of the swan in *The Joy Luck Club* says, "Now the woman was old. And she had a daughter who grew up speaking only English and swallowing more Coca-Cola than sorrow. For a long time now the woman had wanted to give her daughter the single swan feather and tell her, 'This feather may look worthless, but it comes from afar and carries with it all my good intentions.' And she waited, year after year, for the day she could tell her daughter this in perfect American English." As one of the mothers Lindo lamented, "I wanted my children to have the best combination, American circumstances and Chinese character. How could I know these two things do not mix?"

If indeed Chinese Americans are steeped in two languages and two forms of life, one public and dominant, another private and submerged, what is the symbolic significance of using these languages as constructed from various social positions? For the immigrant parents, educating their American-born children to speak the family language is a way to continue the cultural tradition and to instill ethnic pride. Speaking a private language is also an attempt to mark one's difference from the mainstream culture and to resist racism, hegemony, and the overwhelming power of homogenization in this society. In Tan's and Kingston's storytelling, speaking Chinese also becomes simply functional for the older immigrants who do not want to participate or/and are not perceived as full participants in the public language. As a result, they remain outsiders within the system; their use of private language marks the central feature of their identity.

Although for many American-born Chinese, using family language can affirm their cultural ties to their ancestors, Kingston also grew up hearing all the derogatory comments about girls in Chinese, the language of foreign and impossible stories to her ear. While speaking her family dialect gives her a sense of connection and intimacy, the private language also symbolizes the oppression, confusion, frustration, madness, and silence that were associated with her coming of age. Using English to speak and write signifies Kingston's rebellion against the patriarchal tradition; it forced her to take a non-Chinese and non-female position in her family and community. For Chinese American women, speaking English affirms their public identity and gives them a legitimate cultural voice to claim for a space in this society. English gives them a means to assert their independence and a tool to fight against sexism and racism that they encounter. Trinh Minh-ha, in an interview, insisted that identity remains as a political/personal strategy of resistance and survival; "the reflexive question asked [...] is no longer: who am I? but when, where, how am I (so and so)?"

It is important to remember that a discussion of uses of language needs to be understood in a political context. Chinese Americans strive for polyphonic coherence within a society that celebrates conformity and homogeneity despite its rhetoric of diversity and pluralism. To mainstream ears, Chinese languages may sound a cacophony of unfamiliar tones and words; this unintelligibility can be associated with foreignness, exotic cultural others, lack of education, or powerlessness. This perceived absence of a shared language and culture (and therefore of disparate social and national interests) can lead to hostility or discrimination toward Chinese Americans.

Through the use of language we create and maintain our social relationships. We accomplish this goal only if an intersubjective discourse exists so that our words and actions are intelligible to others within the community. In Chinese American bicultural experience, this shared language often cannot be taken for granted. In *The Woman Warrior*, Kingston confronted her mother about telling her that she was ugly all the time, to which her mother replied, "That's what we're supposed to say. That's what Chinese say. We like to say the opposite." Here in the mother's language, "truth" is characterized by the logic of the opposite; this "indirect" approach works only if one knows how to hear the statement within the context of a certain kind of relationship. Saying the opposite is what the mother felt obligated to perform; in fact, it was the only language that she could use in order to demonstrate her affection and care for her daughter. Unfortunately, lacking the cultural insight to reverse the logic of her mother's statement, Kingston felt shamed, outraged, and was in turn accused by her mother of not being able to "tell a joke from real life"; her mother shouts at her, "You're not so smart. Can't even tell real from false." Real from false in what language? Where does the humor of this apparent joke for the mother—and humiliation for the daughter—lie in perfect American English?

In *The Joy Luck Club*, the young women's innocence, ignorance, and apathy toward their mother's language seemed to frighten the mothers. June tried to understand her three aunties at the mah jong table:

> And then it occurs to me. They are frightened. In me, they see their own daughters, just as ignorant, just as unmindful of all the truths and hopes they have brought to America. They see daughters who grow impatient when their mothers talk in Chinese, who think they are stupid when they explain things in fractured English. They see that joy and luck do not mean the same to their daughters, that to these closed American-born minds "joy luck" is not a word, it does not exist. They see daughters who will bear grandchildren born without any connecting hope passed from generation to generation

Failure to translate between languages can cost emotional turmoil; it can also silence someone who depends on the English translation to negotiate or accomplish his/her goals. In one of the stories in *The Joy Luck Club*, the daughter Lena was unable to translate her mother's words to her Caucasian stepfather who did not speak Chinese. Since Lena understood the Chinese words spoken by her mother but not the implications, she made up something in her translation and as a result rewrote her mother's story in that episode. Tan intentionally constructed this scene to illustrate the nature of the mother-daughter relationship. Lena was ignorant of both the story that her mother was hinting at and of the Chinese language that her mother was speaking. Kingston's and Tan's writings are characterized by untold stories written in untranslatable language between the two generations of women. McAlister (1992) argued that by failing to translate between languages and stories, Chinese American daughters can participate in the silencing of their mothers. This position seems incongruous in view of Tan's overall agenda in her storytelling.

By having all the women narrate their own stories, Tan treats language not just as a tool to reflect upon the past or to celebrate the present, but as a political means to allow Chinese American women to articulate their silenced lives, their otherwise voiceless positions in this society.

Tan writes *The Joy Luck Club* in a language that demands the reader recognize the distinctness of each character, each story and voice, and each mother-daughter relationship. The women in her creation are not just nameless, faceless, or interchangeable Chinese Americans. The interrelated narratives make sense only if readers can discern the specificities of each woman's story as located within the novel. Therefore, "Tan confronts an Orientalist discourse that depends on the sameness of Chinese difference." By granting subjectivity to each woman, Tan compels each to tell her own story in her own words, thus (re)creating the meanings of her life. The mother-daughter tensions as constructed in their own discourse are fraught with complexities of racial, gender, and class issues, not just the simple binary opposition of Americanness and Chineseness, mothers and daughters.

The ability to tell one's own story, to speak one's mind, is the best antidote to powerlessness. Tan's writing instills agency and visibility in Chinese American women. The silence is broken, and their new voices are constructed in collective storytelling, a language of community, without denying or erasing the different positions such collaboration encounters. In a similar vein, Kingston gave the no name woman in her mother's storytelling a voice and a life, a permanent place in American culture; she immortalized this silent woman through her writing: "My aunt haunts me—her ghost drawn to me because now, after fifty years of neglect, I alone devote pages of paper to her." Both Tan and Kingston allow their female characters to reclaim and recreate their identity. "Storytelling heals past experiences of loss and separation; it is also a medium for rewriting stories of oppression and victimization into parables of self-affirmation and individual empowerment." It is possible to celebrate the present without forgetting the past. In an interview when Kingston was contrasting her own American voice in *Tripmaster Monkey* and her translation of Chinese voices in her previous two books, she said, "When I wrote *The Woman Warrior* and *China Men*, as I look back on it, I was trying to find an American language that would translate the speech of the people who are living their lives with the Chinese language. They carry on their adventures and their emotional life and everything in Chinese. I had to find a way to translate all that into a graceful American language, which is my language." Perhaps the boundary between Kingston's two languages/voices is not so clear; of *Tripmaster Monkey*, [a Chinese poet] she said that "I was writing in the tradition of the past." "And I spent this lifetime working on roots. So what they were saying was that I was their continuity."

Both Kingston's and Tan's writings point to the multiplicity and instability of cultural identity for Chinese American women, oscillating and crisscrossing between different Englishes and Chinese dialects that they speak. Although cultural borderlands can be a useful metaphor for "home" for these individuals, we must realize that this home does not rest in a fixed location, nor is it constructed in any one unified language or perfect American English. Neither of the authors is searching for a definitive Chinese American voice. Through interweaving their own bicultural tongues and multiple imaginative voices, Kingston and Tan focus on women's experiences in their writings and position their uses of languages as central to our understanding of Chinese American women's bicultural world.

Ultimately we see the transformation of double voice in both *The Woman Warrior* and *The Joy Luck Club*. As Trinh put it nicely, "the fact one is always marginalized in one's own language and areas of strength is something that one has to learn to live with." Therefore, fragmentation in one's identity becomes "a way of living with differences without turning them into opposites, nor trying to assimilate them out of insecurity." Chinese American women need to cultivate not simply multiple subjectivities but also the ability to move between different languages and positions. As Trinh suggested, this fluidity is a form of challenge and reconstruction of power relations, and women need to learn to use language as a poetic arena of struggle of possibility for transformation. "Ethnic identity is twin skin to linguistic identity—I am my language." Unless Chinese American women acknowledge and celebrate all the Englishes that they grew up with, they cannot accept the legitimacy of their bicultural identity. When asked if she still felt the same contradictions that the protagonist did in *The Woman Warrior*, Kingston said "No, no. I feel much more integrated [...] It takes decades of struggle. When you are a person who comes from a multicultural background it just means that you have more information coming in from the universe. And it's your task to figure out how it all integrates, figure out its order and its beauty. It's a harder, longer struggle."

THE SALON INTERVIEW[1]

AMY TAN: THE SPIRIT WITHIN

"My sister Kwan believes she has yin eyes. She sees those who have died and now dwell in the World of Yin, ghosts who leave the mists just to visit her kitchen on Balboa Street in San Francisco. 'Libby-ah,' she'll say to me. 'Guess who I see yesterday, you guess.' And I don't have to guess that she's talking about someone dead."

So begins Amy Tan's third novel, *The Hundred Secret Senses*. Although it has flown up the best-seller lists in the month since its release, the book is a risky departure for the 43-year-old writer, with its emphasis on spirits, magical time-shifts and other unearthly phenomena.

Tan spoke enthusiastically about her book, but admitted that she feared it would be ridiculed as "Chinese superstition." She sat for an

[1] 12 Nov. 1995.

interview on the balcony of her San Francisco home, where she surreptitiously lit up a cigarette.

"I don't smoke in public, it's not a good image, it's not a good role model," she apologized. "Not that I actively set out to be one."

With her tiny Yorkshire terrier, Babbazo, snugly ensconced in her lap, Tan, a brilliant smile often belying the frankness of her words, talked about the burdens of fame, the world of Yin, and her struggles with her own emotional demons.

Q. Have you felt the need to be a role model ever since the success of your first book, *The Joy Luck Club*, in 1989?

A. I don't feel the need to be a role model, it's just something that's been thrust upon me. Teachers and a lot of Asian American organizations, for example, say to me, "We need you to come and speak to us because you're a role model."

Q. Are you comfortable with that?

A. No. Placing on writers the responsibility to represent a culture is an onerous burden. Someone who writes fiction is not necessarily writing a depiction of any generalized group, they're writing a very specific story. There's also a danger in balkanizing literature, as if it should be read as sociology, or politics, or that it should answer questions like, "What does *The Hundred Secret Senses* have to teach us about Chinese culture?" As opposed to treating it as literature—as a story, language, memory.

Q. Are you finding more or less of that pressure to be categorized?

A. It's lessening in the United States. Other Asian American writers just shudder when they are compared to me; it really denigrates the uniqueness of their own work. I find it happening less here partly because people are more aware now of the flaws of political correctness—that literature has to do something to educate people. I don't see myself, for example, writing about cultural dichotomies, but about human connections. All of us go through angst and identity crises. And even when you write in a specific context, you still tap into that subtext of emotions that we all feel about love and hope, and mothers and obligations and responsibilities.

Q. Speaking of mothers, do you get a hard time from relatives or close friends who think they see themselves in your books? Any accusations of personal secrets being told or confidences betrayed?

A. I did, at one point. One relative felt that the story of my grandmother should not have been revealed. My grandmother was the woman (in *The Kitchen God's Wife*) who had been raped, forced to be a concubine, and finally killed herself. My mother, though, got equally angry at the relative and said, "For so many years, I carried this shame on my back, and my mother suffered, because she couldn't say anything to anybody." And she said, "It's not too late; tell the world, tell the world what happened to her." And I take her mandate to be the one that is in my heart, the one that I should follow.

Q. In *The Hundred Secret Senses*, you draw much more on the world of the spirit than in your previous books. Was that a theme that you had always wanted to tackle as a writer, or did more personal experiences compel you to address it?

A. It's been a part of my life for at least the past 20 years. I've had a lot of death in my life, of people who have been close to me. So I've long thought about how life is influenced by death, how it influences what you believe in and what you look for. Yes, I think I was pushed in a way to write this book by certain spirits—the yin people—in my life. They've always been there, I wouldn't say to help, but to kick me in the ass to write.

Q. Yin people?

A. Yin people is the term Kwan uses, because "ghosts" is politically incorrect. People have such terrible assumptions about ghosts—you know, phantoms that haunt you, that make you scared, that turn the house upside down. Yin people are not in our living presence but are around, and kind of guide you to insights. Like in Las Vegas when the bells go off, telling you you've hit the jackpot. Yin people ring the bells, saying, "Pay attention." And you say, "Oh, I see now." Yet I'm a fairly skeptical person. I'm educated, I'm reasonably sane, and I know that this subject is fodder for ridicule.

Q. Does that worry you?

A. To write the book, I had to put that aside. As with any book. I go through the anxiety, "What will people think of me for writing something like this?" But ultimately, I have to write what I have to write about, including the question of life continuing beyond our ordinary senses.

Q. You have a very optimistic way of looking at life and death. But these concerns have also been a cause for deep distress in your life, including bouts with serious depression.

A. Some of it is probably biochemical, but I think it's also in my family tree. I mean, my grandmother killed herself; she certainly had depression in her life. And anyone, like my mother, who witnessed her own mother killing herself, is going to be prone to the same disease. My own father died of a brain tumor when I was 14. My brother died of the same disease. I didn't do anything about it for a long time, because, like many people, I worried about altering my psyche with drugs. As a writer, I was especially concerned with that. A lot of writers believe that the trauma and the angst that you feel is an essential part of the craft.

Q. And depression is still not respectable—especially taking medication for it.

A. People look at me as this very, I don't know, Confucius-like wise person—which I'm not. They don't see all the shit that I've been through (laughs). And going back to the question of being a role model, well, my life hasn't been perfect. I needed help.

Q. What do you take?

A. Zoloft. I don't think it's made me a Pollyanna. I can still get angry and upset, but I don't fall into the abyss. I'm grateful that I have some traction now. It doesn't change essentially who you are, but it fixes things just the way insulin does for people with diabetes.

Q. In *The Hundred Secret Senses*, the central character, Kwan, is packed off to a California mental hospital for seeing "ghosts." She is somewhat weird, often embarrassing, and doesn't exactly look like Joan Chen. Where did Kwan come from?

A. Kwan comes strictly from my imagination, from that world of yin that I write about. I don't know anybody in my life like Kwan, although I feel Kwan-like characters all round me. I would find myself laughing and wondering where these ideas came from. You can call it imagination, I suppose. But I was grateful for wherever they came from.

Q. Olivia, Kwan's American half-sister is not so happy-go-lucky. Pained, needy, she accidentally pulls heads off pet turtles and has a hard time with other people.

A. I took my own skepticism and embedded it into Olivia. Some of her—or the questions that trouble her—are drawn from friends who have the usual existential questions about life and relationships and work and success, and "Why are we here?" and "Why are we with this person?" I've already had interviewers wondering if Olivia's relationship with her husband, Simon, is like my marriage, and I think, "Wait a minute, that's not my husband, that's not my relationship." Certainly all of us have gone through fights with partners in our life, but that's not drawn from my relationships per se. But I know that I'm going to be subject to that assumption.

Q. You write that Olivia's mother suffers "from a kind heart compounded by seasonal rashes of volunteerism." She thinks of her step-daughter

Kwan "as a foreign exchange student she would host for a year." In other words, she's a somewhat self-centered ditz—like some of your other less-than-appealing Caucasian characters, in *The Joy Luck Club*, for example. Is there a problem between you and white characters?

A. (Laughs). No. Some of these characters have to be foils. I needed a mother who was kind of undependable, so that Kwan could become that fount of love that Olivia is looking for. There was no intention—unless there is something subconscious—in trying to depict a Caucasian mother as not so great. I'd have to go through psychotherapy to explore that one. No, some of my best friends are Caucasian.

Man Must Die

Gael Fowler

1   The short story "Heart," written by the Chinese-American author Amy Tan, illustrates the theme of grief and loss resulting from the deaths of close family members. Three tragic deaths portrayed in this story are the loss of a child, a spouse, and a parent. The narrator, Lu Ling, reveals her nursemaid's experiences with these types of losses throughout the story. Lu Ling and Precious Auntie, her nursemaid, have a terrible argument toward the end of the story, and Lu Ling speaks harshly to her servant. Lu Ling realizes that she has been unkind to her friend and wants to apologize for her cruel behavior. Lu Ling discovers Precious Auntie dead in a ravine and mourns the loss of the woman she has known as her nursemaid. Later, she learns that Precious Auntie was actually her biological mother. Both mother and daughter experience tragic losses and have to deal with intense grief throughout their lives.

2   The most painful event that a parent can ever experience is the death of his child. In this story, Precious Auntie's father is an extremely gifted bonesetter who fails to save his four sons from a deadly disease. The loss of his children is devastating to him, and as a result "he spent his entire fortune and went into a lifetime of debt to pay for their

funerals" (Tan 826). The death of Precious Auntie's brothers causes her father to be plagued with grief for the remainder of his life. The bone-setter survives the death of his sons by living through the happiness of his daughter. According to Precious Auntie, "he spoiled me, let me do whatever a son might do" (Tan 826). She also comments, "My father was used to seeing pain of the worst kinds. But with me he was helpless. He couldn't bear to see me cry" (Tan 826). Losing four sons is extremely difficult for the bonesetter, but this tragedy results in the birth of a stronger relationship with his daughter as he struggles to endure the pain.

3   The loss of an intended spouse is also a catastrophic and traumatic experience. On the day of Precious Auntie's marriage to Baby Uncle, a horse kicks Baby Uncle in the head. This fatal blow changes Precious Auntie's life drastically. She continually hears the horrendous sound of the accident "in the breaking of twigs, the crackling of fire, [and] whenever a melon was split in two" (Tan 832). Precious Auntie is hysterical for days and weeks after her lover's death. She even tries to commit suicide in order "to cause pain greater than what she already felt" (Tan 832). Fortunately, Precious Auntie has a daughter who gives her a purpose for living during the remainder of her years.

4   Losing a mother or a father is extremely desolating for a child. When a parent dies, a child feels as if a vital part of her existence is missing. Precious Auntie never really knows her mother because she loses her mother at a young age. Therefore, her relationship with her father becomes that much closer. Seeing her father "lying [dead] in a ditch" (Tan 832) is the worst nightmare that Precious Auntie can imagine. For days, she "apologized to the [corpse] of her father" (Tan 832) because she feels responsible for her father's death. Even though Precious

Auntie cannot prevent the accident that kills her father, she lives the rest of her life with agonizing feelings of guilt.

5   Death has always been a dominant theme in literature. Amy Tan's excellence at portraying basic literary themes is seen throughout her writing. According to Elaine Kim, Asian authors like Tan write masterfully about the topics of "'love, desire for personal freedom and acceptance, and struggles against oppression and injustice'" (qtd. in Huntley 835). Several of Tan's stories depict the lives of common people who experience severe tragedies, such as the loss of loved ones. Some people, like the bonesetter, lose a child. Many people like Precious Auntie will watch in horror as their lovers or parents slip away from them. A few unfortunate people like Lu Ling will even have to learn devastating secrets about their family relationships. Amy Tan addresses these classic themes of literature by delving into her own personal and cultural history. Amy Tan's style of writing is perfectly described with the following statement by E.D. Huntley:

> Tan's novels reify and reinterpret traditional
> genres by casting them in a variety of modes—
> realistic, comic, tragic, tragicomic,
> allegorical, fantastic, naturalistic, and
> heroic—that metamorphose seamlessly into each
> other in Tan's signature narrative style." (834)

Amy Tan's greatest strength as an author is the ability to make readers identify with her characters by writing from her heart.

[New page]   Works Cited

Henderson, Gloria Mason, Bill Day, and Sandra Stevenson Waller, eds. <u>Literature and Ourselves</u>. 5th ed. New York: Longman, 2006.

Huntley, E. D. <u>Amy Tan: A Critical Companion</u>. Westport,

Connecticut: Greenwood P, 1998. Henderson, Day, and Waller.

834-49.

Tan, Amy. "Heart." <u>The New Yorker</u>. 25 Dec. 2000-1 Jan. 2001:

134-52. Henderson, Day, and Waller. 818-33.

Suggestions for Exploring, Writing, and Persuading

1. Most people have an image of a childhood place that, when revisited as an adult, turns out different from memories and expectations. Think back to your childhood and write an essay describing an event that left you happier, sadder, or wiser.

2. Using one or more of the critical essays in the casebook, write an essay explaining Simon's role in "Young Girl's Wish."

3. "Young Girl's Wish" and "Heart" portray grief and loss on many levels. Choose one or more stages of grief and write an essay explaining this theme as it relates to these two selections. Use one or more of the critical essays.

4. When Lu Ling complains that her (apparent) mother does not love her, Precious Auntie says, "If she didn't love you, why did she bother to criticize you for your own good?" In an essay, discuss the degree to which criticism is an expression of love.

5. In a researched essay, discuss the differences in marriage customs between Lu Ling's culture and your own. Alternatively, research marriage customs in the Far and Near East. Then write an essay categorizing these customs.

Fear and Loss: Suggestions for Writing

1. One consistent theme in many of the works in this unit is that death is the ultimate equalizer, as everyone has to die. Discuss the use of this theme in one or more of the works.

2. Write an essay on racial, cultural, or gender vulnerability, examining one of the selections that deals with a race, culture, or gender other than your own. You may use any one of the secondary sources contained in the casebook.

3. Use two of the short stories to show how people try to deal with their own fear or loss by clinging to others.

4. Select at least two poems that deal with the reaction of the living to the death of a loved one. Write an essay discussing the survivors' emotions.

5. Human beings often react violently when they realize their own vulnerability. Using one or more of the selections in this unit to illustrate and support your points, classify and describe these violent reactions.

6. Write an essay using three poems that illustrate three types of fear.

7. People are constantly susceptible to fears, prejudice, discrimination, and abuse of one sort or another. Describe an incident in which you were a victim of, or a witness to, one of these kinds of vulnerability.

8. Four of the works in this unit—Faulkner's "A Rose for Emily," Robinson's "Richard Cory," Dunbar's "We Wear the Mask," and McCrae's "In Flander's Field"—are written in first person plural. After carefully rereading each work, analyze each author's reasons for choosing this particular point of view.

9. In Eric Skipper's "The Runt," Willis is told not to interfere in the Mexicans' affairs. In "Young Girl's Wish," Olivia and Kwan are told by Rocky, the cab driver, not to interfere because they are foreigners. What do these statements imply?

10. After carefully studying Cooper's definition of terrorism, write an essay in which you give your definition.

11. Several works in this unit deal with misunderstandings because of cultural or generational differences. Select at least two works in this unit and write a comparison of their differences in dealing with the same problem.

12. Because of the development of new methods of destruction and complex geopolitical forces, the twenty-first century faces new and frightening situations. Write an essay in which you

    Describe or classify these new sources of terror

    Examine the causes of the new sources of terror, or

    Recommend ways of coping with fear or terror

Fear and Loss: Writing About Film

1. Select a short lyric poem and design a silent screenplay to depict the images of the poem in such a way that they imply the meaning of the poem. Your screenplay should state in images the words of the poem you want to depict. Be sure to describe how each shot is framed (closeup, medium, or long shot), what exactly the camera sees, how the camera moves, how the images cut together, and what important design elements such as colors, details, props, or effects you want to include. Don't worry too much about telling the story of the poem, but try to create images that will work as visual poetry that honors the written poem.

2. Many contemporary films touch on the theme of loss (*Memento; Mystic River; Crouching Tiger, Hidden Dragon; The Others; About Schmidt; White Oleander; The Notebook; Titanic*). View or re-view a

loss-themed film, watching for specific cinematic methods: What design elements contribute to creating a mood of mourning or unhappiness? What scene is central to understanding how the main character is affected by loss or misfortune? How do the design elements assist the script in making this a particularly effective scene? What is the effect of the music?

3. There are several film versions of *Othello*. Watch two; then compare the bedroom scenes in which Othello murders Desdemona. Is one more effective than the other? Which filmmaking element is most effective: pace, framing, camera movement, setting? No doubt the actors must make convincing choices as well. What are the actors doing that make you believe they are Othello and Desdemona? What information in the text justifies your judgment?

4. In light of the popularity of disaster movies, it is obvious that some part of human nature enjoys being scared. View one or more of the disaster movies—*Armageddon*, *Towering Inferno*, *28 Days Later*, *Twister*, *The Day After Tomorrow*, *Independence Day*, the *Perfect Storm*—to mention only a few. Then analyze the scenes that seem designed to terrify the audience and one of the following:

   The use of camera effects, such as close-ups that reveal only a small portion of the scene or the person in order to keep the audience in suspense or panoramic views that zoom in in order to make the audience feel that they too are sinking, being tossed by waves or wind, etc.

   The score and the ways that it increases terror

   The quality of acting

   The resolution

Freedom and Responsibility

A scene from *Minority Report*. 20th Century Fox/Dreamworks/The Kobal Collection.

W e are accustomed to celebrating our freedom as Americans without much thought. Seldom do we stop to realize what that freedom means or requires of us. The most seminal of American documents, the Declaration of Independence, espouses a doctrine that even today in this country seems astoundingly revolutionary— the idea that governments "derive their just powers from the consent of the governed" and that when they fail to serve their purpose in protecting citizens' rights, those citizens have the right, even the responsibility, to overthrow such governments. When Martin Luther King Jr. led peaceful protests against the segregation and brutal treatment of African Americans, he was simply acting on ideas contained in Jefferson's great founding document.

Often we fail to realize the extent to which those great American values, freedom and equality, both of which originate in the Declaration of Independence, may be mutually exclusive. As Kurt Vonnegut's "Harrison Bergeron" demonstrates, an exact and universal equality may not only reduce our freedom but also produce a world that is culturally sterile. Asserting our freedom, as the fate of Harrison Bergeron illustrates, may be very costly. In John Updike's "A & P," Sammy's refusal to conform and his assertion of independence cost him his job. Also, in Vaclav Havel's "The Trial," a Czech rock band, guilty only of failure to conform to government-prescribed norms, faces trial as a menace to society. Nowhere is the terrible cost of freedom more graphically exemplified than in Ursula Le Guin's "The Ones Who Walk Away from Omelas," where the freedom and comfortable lives of a whole society depend on the brutal suffering of a single poor wretch. One person's freedom may mean another's subjugation.

What, then, are the limits to freedom? To what degree should we be subject to our government, and to what degree should the government be subject to us? Sometimes the desire for freedom may compete with personal responsibilities to family and community. In "On the Rainy River," Tim O'Brien faces an agonizing choice. If he goes to Canada because of his opposition to the Vietnam War, he fears being perceived by his parents, friends, and neighbors as a coward, not a principled objector. On the other hand, to fight in a war he considers wrong will violate his conscience. Hence, O'Brien's story raises extremely important issues. When must we submerge our individuality in deference to the community? Where does our individual freedom end, and where do the perceived needs of the community begin? When should communal decisions, expressed as government policy, supersede individual conscience?

Writing About Freedom and Responsibility

In writing about the selections in Freedom and Responsibility, you will have a wide variety of choices. As you study the types of essays and subjects, you will probably notice that several of the stories and essays use satire or irony. You might start by reviewing the definitions of these two terms included in the glossary. Then you might use Jonathan Swift's "A Modest Proposal," which offers a perfect example of a caustic satire written about a real-life situation, to write a **definition essay**, an essay illustrating the literary devices that Swift uses to make his points, or a researched paper about the situation in Ireland that is the subject of Swift's satire. If you prefer to write about short stories, and especially if you enjoy fantasy, you might choose Vonnegut's "Harrison Bergeron," which combines satire with humor; you might examine the real-life tendencies that he satirizes and explore the ways in which the author uses humor in his satire.

After reviewing the questions from the introduction on Writing About Poetry, you might write an essay comparing or classifying the choices and lack of choices recognized by the speakers in Randall Jarrell's "The Woman at the Washington Zoo" or Anne Sexton's "Ringing the Bells." Or you might discuss problems faced by immigrants portrayed in Pat Mora's "Immigrants" and Dwight Okita's "In Response to Executive Order 9066." As in any of the thematic units, you might write an essay examining the distinctive tone or the sound and metaphorical devices used by the poets to create the overall effects they desire. Or you might compare Shapiro's "The Conscientious Objector" to one of Tim O'Brien's stories in terms of freedom and duties.

All sections in this unit suggest arguments that might appeal to your sense of freedom and the responsibility that goes with freedom. For example, in "Letter From Birmingham City Jail," King feels he has a responsibility to confront the clergy and other leaders about his concerns. But what are the boundaries of his responsibilities? As you read these selections, ask yourself these questions, many of which lead to good arguments. Do the townspeople have the right to put all the evil and wrong on one person in LeGuin's "Those Who Walk Away From Omelas"? Could the same thing happen in a small town in America as happens in Omelas? What responsibilities do children/teens have toward parents? Although Sammy in "A&P" chooses to quit his job because of the three young ladies, does he really have an obligation to stay because of his parents' reputation in that New England town? Will he indeed feel "how hard the world was going to be to [him] hereafter"?

If your professor asks you to use the casebook on Tim O'Brien to write a documented paper, you should, of course, begin by reading the stories. You might list ideas for topics as you read and then add to the list when you have completed your reading and have a more complete view of the possibilities. After writing down some of your own ideas for future reference, you should then read the critical essays. Using this technique will help you remember which ideas were yours and which the essays influenced. When Nick Hembree was asked to write a documented essay using some of the stories and critical essays in the casebook, he began by trying to detail the interesting and provocative techniques used by O'Brien. He also wanted to emphasize the meanings of the stories. Nick decided to use three of the stories to write an essay about the nature of truth and its general elusiveness and complexity. He e-mailed the first draft of the essay to his professor, who made a few suggestions. Then he polished the final draft, checked his documentation, and proofread it before e-mailing it to the professor. After you have read the O'Brien stories, you will probably enjoy reading Nick's essay to see if your perceptions are similar to his.

E S S A Y S

Jonathan Swift (1667–1745)

*Though Jonathan Swift's parents were English, he was born
in Dublin and became one of the most ardent defenders of
Ireland. As dean of St. Patrick's Cathedral in Dublin from
1726 to 1739, Swift was a major force in the religious and
political affairs of Ireland. A man of great intellect, Swift is
recognized as a true master of style and as one of the world's
foremost satirists. His most famous work,* Gulliver's Travels,
*satirizes many of the social, political, and religious prac-
tices of his time. "A Modest Proposal" reveals the extreme
hardships the peasants of Ireland suffered at the hands of
greedy English landlords.*

A MODEST PROPOSAL   (1729)

FOR PREVENTING THE CHILDREN OF POOR PEOPLE IN IRELAND FROM BEING A BURDEN TO THEIR PARENTS OR COUNTRY, AND FOR MAKING THEM BENEFICIAL TO THE PUBLIC

1   It is a melancholy object to those who walk through this great town,
or travel in the country, when they see the streets, the roads and cabin-
doors crowded with beggars of the female sex, followed by three, four,
or six children, all in rags, and importuning every passenger for an alms.
These mothers, instead of being able to work for their honest livelihood,
are forced to employ all their time in strolling, to beg sustenance for their
helpless infants, who, as they grow up, either turn thieves for want of
work, or leave their dear native country to fight for the Pretender in
Spain, or sell themselves to the Barbadoes.

2   I think it is agreed by all parties that this prodigious number of children, in the arms, or on the backs, or at the heels of their mothers, and
frequently of their fathers, is in the present deplorable state of the kingdom a very great additional grievance; and therefore whoever could find
out a fair, cheap, and easy method of making these children sound and
useful members of the commonwealth would deserve so well of the public as to have his statue set up for a preserver of the nation.

3   But my intention is very far from being confined to provide only for
the children of professed beggars; it is of a much greater extent, and shall
take in the whole number of infants at a certain age who are born of parents in effect as little able to support them as those who demand our
charity in the streets.

4   As to my own part, having turned my thoughts for many years upon
this important subject, and maturely weighed the several schemes of

other projectors, I have always found them grossly mistaken in their computation. It is true a child just dropped from its dam may be supported by her milk for a solar year with little other nourishment, at most not above the value of two shillings, which the mother may certainly get, or the value in scraps, by her lawful occupation of begging, and it is exactly at one year old that I propose to provide for them, in such a manner as, instead of being a charge upon their parents, or the parish, or wanting food and raiment for the rest of their lives, they shall, on the contrary, contribute to the feeding and partly to the clothing of many thousands.

5   There is likewise another great advantage in my scheme, that it will prevent those voluntary abortions, and that horrid practice of women murdering their bastard children, alas, too frequent among us, sacrificing the poor innocent babes, I doubt, more to avoid the expense than the shame, which would move tears and pity in the most savage and inhuman breast.

6   The number of souls in Ireland being usually reckoned one million and a half, of these I calculate there may be about two hundred thousand couples whose wives are breeders, from which number I subtract thirty thousand couples who are able to maintain their own children, although I apprehend there cannot be so many under the present distresses of the kingdom, but this being granted, there will remain an hundred and seventy thousand breeders. I again subtract fifty thousand for those women who miscarry, or whose children die by accident or disease within the year. There only remain an hundred and twenty thousand children of poor parents annually born: the question therefore is, how this number shall be reared, and provided for, which, as I have already said, under the present situation of affairs is utterly impossible by all the methods hitherto proposed, for we can neither employ them in handicraft or agriculture; we neither build houses (I mean in the country), nor cultivate land: they can very seldom pick up a livelihood by stealing until they arrive at six years old, except where they are of towardly parts, although I confess they learn the rudiments much earlier, during which time they can however be properly looked upon only as probationers, as I have been informed by a principal gentleman in the County of Cavan, who protested to me that he never knew above one or two instances under the age of six, even in a part of the kingdom so renowned for the quickest proficiency in that art.

7   I am assured by our merchants that a boy or a girl before twelve years old, is no saleable commodity, and even when they come to this age, they will not yield above three pounds, or three pounds and half-a-crown at most on the Exchange, which cannot turn to account either to the parents or the kingdom, the charge of nutriment and rags having been at least four times that value.

8   I shall now therefore humbly propose my own thoughts, which I hope will not be liable to the least objection.

9   I have been assured by a very knowing American of my acquaintance in London, that a young healthy child well nursed is at a year old a most delicious, nourishing and wholesome food, whether stewed, roasted,

baked, or boiled, and I make no doubt that it will equally serve in a fricassee, or a ragout.

10   I do therefore humbly offer it to public consideration, that of the hundred and twenty thousand children already computed, twenty thousand may be reserved for breed, whereof only one fourth part to be males, which is more than we allow to sheep, black-cattle, or swine, and my reason is that these children are seldom the fruits of marriage, a circumstance not much regarded by our savages, therefore one male will be sufficient to serve four females. That the remaining hundred thousand may at a year old be offered in sale to the persons of quality, and fortune, through the kingdom, always advising the mother to let them suck plentifully in the last month, so as to render them plump, and fat for a good table. A child will make two dishes at an entertainment for friends, and when the family dines alone, the fore or hind quarter will make a reasonable dish, and seasoned with a little pepper or salt will be very good boiled on the fourth day, especially in winter.

11   I have reckoned upon a medium, that a child just born will weigh twelve pounds, and in a solar year if tolerably nursed increaseth to twenty-eight pounds.

12   I grant this food will be somewhat dear, and therefore very proper for landlords, who, as they have already devoured most of the parents, seem to have the best title to the children.

13   Infant's flesh will be in season throughout the year, but more plentiful in March, and a little before and after, for we are told by a grave author,1 an eminent French physician, that fish being a prolific diet, there are more children born in Roman Catholic countries about nine months after Lent than at any other season; therefore reckoning a year after Lent, the markets will be more glutted than usual, because the number of Popish infants is at least three to one in this kingdom, and therefore it will have one other collateral advantage by lessening the number of Papists among us.

14   I have already computed the charge of nursing a beggar's child (in which list I reckon all cottagers, labourers, and four-fifths of the farmers) to be about two shillings *per annum*, rags included, and I believe no gentleman would repine to give ten shillings for the carcass of a good fat child, which, as I have said, will make four dishes of excellent nutritive meat, when he hath only some particular friend or his own family to dine with him. Thus the Squire will learn to be a good landlord and grow popular among his tenants, the mother will have eight shillings net profit, and be fit for work until she produces another child.

15   Those who are more thrifty (as I must confess the times require) may flay the carcass; the skin of which artificially dressed, will make admirable gloves for ladies, and summer boots for fine gentlemen.

16   As to our city of Dublin, shambles may be appointed for this purpose, in the most convenient parts of it, and butchers we may be assured will not be wanting, although I rather recommend buying the children alive, and dressing them hot from the knife, as we do roasting pigs.

17   A very worthy person, a true lover of his country, and whose virtues I highly esteem, was lately pleased, in discoursing on this matter to offer a refinement upon my scheme. He said that many gentlemen of this kingdom, having of late destroyed their deer, he conceived that the want of venison might be well supplied by the bodies of young lads and maidens, not exceeding fourteen years of age, nor under twelve, so great a number of both sexes in every county being now ready to starve, for want of work and service: and these to be disposed of by their parents if alive, or otherwise by their nearest relations. But with due deference to so excellent a friend, and so deserving a patriot, I cannot be altogether in his sentiments. For as to the males, my American acquaintance assured me from frequent experience that their flesh was generally tough and lean, like that of our schoolboys, by continual exercise, and their taste disagreeable, and to fatten them would not answer the charge. Then as to the females, it would, I think with humble submission, be a loss to the public, because they soon would become breeders themselves: and besides, it is not improbable that some scrupulous people might be apt to censure such a practice (although indeed very unjustly) as a little bordering upon cruelty, which I confess, hath always been with me the strongest objection against any project, howsoever well intended.

18   But in order to justify my friend, he confessed that this expedient was put into his head by the famous Psalmanazar, a native of the island Formosa, who came from thence to London, above twenty years ago, and in conversation told my friend that in his country when any young person happened to be put to death, the executioner sold the carcass to persons of quality, as a prime dainty, and that, in his time, the body of a plump girl of fifteen, who was crucified for an attempt to poison the emperor, was sold to his Imperial Majesty's Prime Minister of State, and other great Mandarins of the Court, in joints from the gibbet, at four hundred crowns. Neither indeed can I deny that if the same use were made of several plump young girls in this town who, without one single groat to their fortunes, cannot stir abroad without a chair, and appear at the playhouse and assemblies in foreign fineries, which they never will pay for, the kingdom would not be the worse.

19   Some persons of a desponding spirit are in great concern about that vast number of poor people, who are aged, diseased, or maimed, and I have been desired to employ my thoughts what course may be taken to ease the nation of so grievous an encumbrance. But I am not in the least pain upon that matter, because it is very well known that they are every day dying, and rotting, by cold, and famine, and filth, and vermin, as fast as can be reasonably expected. And as to the younger labourers they are now in almost as hopeful a condition. They cannot get work, and consequently pine away from want of nourishment, to a degree that if at any time they are accidentally hired to common labour, they have not strength to perform it; and thus the country and themselves are in a fair way of being soon delivered from the evils to come.

20   I have too long digressed, and therefore shall return to my subject. I think the advantages by the proposal which I have made are obvious and many, as well as of the highest importance.

21   For first, as I have already observed, it would greatly lessen the number of Papists, with whom we are yearly over-run, being the principal breeders of the nation, as well as our most dangerous enemies, and who stay at home on purpose with a design to deliver the kingdom to the Pretender, hoping to take their advantage by the absence of so many good Protestants, who have chosen rather to leave their country than stay at home and pay tithes against their conscience to an idolatrous Episcopal curate.

22   Secondly, the poorer tenants will have something valuable of their own, which by law may be made liable to distress, and help to pay their landlord's rent, their corn and cattle being already seized, and money a thing unknown.

23   Thirdly, whereas the maintenance of an hundred thousand children, from two years old, and upwards, cannot be computed at less than ten shillings a piece *per annum*, the nation's stock will be thereby increased fifty thousand pounds *per annum* besides the profit of a new dish, introduced to the tables of all gentlemen of fortune in the kingdom, who have any refinement in taste, and the money will circulate among ourselves, the goods being entirely of our own growth and manufacture.

24   Fourthly, the constant breeders, besides the gain of eight shillings sterling *per annum*, by the sale of their children, will be rid of the charge of maintaining them after the first year.

25   Fifthly, this food would likewise bring great custom to taverns, where the vintners will certainly be so prudent as to procure the best receipts for dressing it to perfection, and consequently have their houses frequented by all the fine gentlemen, who justly value themselves upon their knowledge in good eating; and a skilful cook, who understands how to oblige his guests, will contrive to make it as expensive as they please.

26   Sixthly, this would be a great inducement to marriage, which all wise nations have either encouraged by rewards, or enforced by laws and penalties. It would increase the care and tenderness of mothers towards their children, when they were sure of a settlement for life, to the poor babes, provided in some sort by the public to their annual profit instead of expense. We should soon see an honest emulation among the married women, which of them could bring the fattest child to the market. Men would become as fond of their wives, during the time of their pregnancy, as they are now of their mares in foal, their cows in calf, or sows when they are ready to farrow, nor offer to beat or kick them (as it is too frequent a practice) for fear of a miscarriage.

27   Many other advantages might be enumerated. For instance, the addition of some thousand carcasses in our exportation of barrelled beef; the propagation of swine's flesh, and improvement in the art of making good bacon, so much wanted among us by the great destruction of pigs, too frequent at our tables, which are no way comparable in taste or magnificence

to a well-grown, fat, yearling child, which roasted whole will make a considerable figure at a Lord Mayor's feast, or any other public entertainment.

28   Supposing that one thousand families in this city would be constant customers for infants' flesh, besides others who might have it at merry meetings, particularly weddings and christenings; I compute that Dublin would take off annually about twenty thousand carcasses, and the rest of the kingdom (where probably they will be sold somewhat cheaper) the remaining eighty thousand.

29   I can think of no one objection that will possibly be raised against this proposal, unless it should be urged that the number of people will be thereby much lessened in the kingdom. This I freely own, and it was indeed one principal design in offering it to the world. I desire the reader will observe, that I calculate my remedy *for this one individual Kingdom of* Ireland, *and for no other that ever was, is, or, I think, ever can be upon earth.* Therefore let no man talk to me of other expedients: *Of taxing our absentees at five shillings a pound: Of using neither clothes, nor household furniture, except what is of our own growth and manufacture: Of utterly rejecting the materials and instruments that promote foreign luxury: Of curing the expensiveness of pride, vanity, idleness, and gaming in our women: Of introducing a vein of parsimony, prudence, and temperance: Of learning to love our country, wherein we differ even from* Laplanders, *and the inhabitants of* Topinamboo: *Of quitting our animosities and factions, nor act any longer like the* Jews, *who were murdering one another at the very moment their city was taken: Of being a little cautious not to sell our country and consciences for nothing: Of teaching landlords to have at least one degree of mercy towards their tenants.* Lastly, *of putting a spirit of honesty, industry, and skill into our shopkeepers, who, if a resolution could now be taken to buy only our native goods, would immediately unite to cheat and exact upon us in the price, the measure and the goodness, nor could ever yet be brought to make one fair proposal of just dealing, though often and earnestly invited to it.*

30   Therefore I repeat, let no man talk to me of these and the like expedients, till he hath at least a glimpse of hope that there will ever be some hearty and sincere attempt to put them in practice.

31   But as to myself, having been wearied out for many years with offering vain, idle, visionary thoughts, and at length utterly despairing of success, I fortunately fell upon this proposal, which as it is wholly new, so it hath something solid and real, of no expense and little trouble, full in our own power, and whereby we can incur no danger in disobliging England. For this kind of commodity will not bear exportation, the flesh being of too tender a consistence to admit a long continuance in salt, *although perhaps I could name a country which would be glad to eat up our whole nation without it.*

32   After all I am not so violently bent upon my own opinion as to reject any offer, proposed by wise men, which shall be found equally innocent, cheap, easy and effectual. But before some thing of that kind shall be

advanced in contradiction to my scheme, and offering a better, I desire the author, or authors, will be pleased maturely to consider two points. First, as things now stand, how they will be able to find food and raiment for a hundred thousand useless mouths and backs? And secondly, there being a round million of creatures in human figure, throughout this kingdom, whose whole subsistence put into a common stock would leave them in debt two millions of pounds sterling; adding those who are beggars by profession, to the bulk of farmers, cottagers, and labourers with their wives and children, who are beggars in effect; I desire those politicians who dislike my overture, and may perhaps be so bold to attempt an answer, that they will first ask the parents of these mortals whether they would not at this day think it a great happiness to have been sold for food at a year old, in the manner I prescribe, and thereby have avoided such a perpetual scene of misfortunes as they have since gone through, by the oppression of landlords, the impossibility of paying rent without money or trade, the want of common sustenance, with neither house nor clothes to cover them from the inclemencies of weather, and the most inevitable prospect of entailing the like, or greater miseries upon their breed for ever.

33   I profess in the sincerity of my heart that I have not the least personal interest in endeavouring to promote this necessary work, having no other motive than the *public good of my country, by advancing our trade, providing for infants, relieving the poor, and giving some pleasure to the rich.* I have no children by which I can propose to get a single penny; the youngest being nine years old, and my wife past child-bearing.

Questions for Discussion

1. What is the tone of this essay?
2. At what point in the essay does Swift's narrator present his shocking proposal?
3. Why would older children not be just as good as younger children for Swift's plan?
4. Outline the "advantages" of the "Modest Proposal," according to the narrator.
5. List the other suggestions for solving Ireland's problem included in paragraph 29. Swift, in other essays, had suggested all of these solutions. Why does the narrator reject them?
6. Would the money and benefits from the sale of children indeed "trickle down" to the less fortunate or the most needy?

Suggestions for Exploring, Writing, and Persuading

1. Write a character sketch of the narrator of this proposal.
2. Write your own modest proposal: an ironic solution to a current problem. Follow Swift's style: build a case, state your proposal, list and

explain the advantages with one or more disadvantages, and end with the statement that the proposal is "solid and real, of no expense and little trouble." Possible topics might be the treatment of the homeless or the elderly, deadbeat fathers (or mothers), or drug dealers.

3. Analyze Swift's essay as an indictment of both the Irish and the English.

4. Someone has said that the more things change, the more they stay the same. Apply this saying to the situation Swift is discussing and to a similar situation today.

5. In what ways are we metaphorically cannibals today?

Thomas Jefferson (1743–1826)

Thomas Jefferson, the third president of the United States and author of the Declaration of Independence, was truly a Renaissance man—a statesman, a scientist, an architect, and an author. The son of a successful planter and a member of the famous Randolph family of Virginia, Jefferson spent most of his life in Virginia. As an architect, he designed both his home, Monticello, and the buildings of the University of Virginia. Jefferson is considered by many historians to be the foremost symbol of the American desire for individual freedom.

THE DECLARATION OF INDEPENDENCE (1776)

1 When in the course of human events, it becomes necessary for one people to dissolve the political bands which have connected them with another, and to assume among the powers of the earth, the separate and equal station to which the Laws of Nature and of Nature's God entitle them, a decent respect to the opinions of mankind requires that they should declare the causes which impel them to the separation.

2 We hold these truths to be self-evident, that all men are created equal, that they are endowed by their Creator with certain inalienable rights, that among these are life, liberty, and the pursuit of happiness. That to secure these rights, governments are instituted among men, deriving their just powers from the consent of the governed. That whenever any form of government becomes destructive of these ends, it is the right of the people to alter or to abolish it, and to institute new government, laying its foundation on such principles and organizing its powers in such form, as to them shall seem most likely to effect their safety and happiness. Prudence, indeed, will dictate that governments long established should not be changed for light and transient causes; and accordingly all experience hath shown, that mankind are more disposed to suffer, while evils are sufferable, than to right themselves by abolishing the forms to which they are accustomed. But when a long train of abuses and usurpations, pursuing invariably the same object, evinces a design to reduce them under absolute despotism, it is their right, it is their duty, to throw off

such government, and to provide new guards for their future security. Such has been the patient sufferance of these Colonies; and such is now the necessity which constrains them to alter their former systems of government. The history of the present King of Great Britain is a history of repeated injuries and usurpations, all having in direct object the establishment of an absolute tyranny over these States. To prove this, let facts be submitted to a candid world.

3   He has refused his assent to laws, the most wholesome and necessary for the public good.

4   He has forbidden his Governors to pass laws of immediate and pressing importance, unless suspended in their operation till his assent should be obtained; and when so suspended, he has utterly neglected to attend to them.

5   He has refused to pass other laws for the accommodation of large districts of people, unless those people would relinquish the right of representation in the legislature, a right inestimable to them and formidable to tyrants only.

6   He has called together legislative bodies at places unusual, uncomfortable, and distant from the depository of their public records, for the sole purpose of fatiguing them into compliance with his measures.

7   He has dissolved representative houses repeatedly, for opposing with manly firmness his invasions on the rights of the people.

8   He has refused for a long time, after such dissolutions, to cause others to be elected; whereby the legislative powers, incapable of annihilation, have returned to the people at large for their exercise; the State remaining in the meantime exposed to all the dangers of invasion from without and convulsions within.

9   He has endeavoured to prevent the population of these states; for that purpose obstructing the laws for naturalization of foreigners; refusing to pass others to encourage their migration hither, and raising the conditions of new appropriations of lands.

10   He has obstructed the administration of justice, by refusing his assent to laws for establishing judiciary powers.

11   He has made judges dependent on his will alone, for the tenure of their office, and the amount and payment of their salaries.

12   He has erected a multitude of new offices, and sent hither swarms of officers to harass our people, and eat out their substance.

13   He has kept among us, in times of peace, standing armies without the consent of our legislatures.

14   He has affected to render the military independent of and superior to the civil power.

15   He has combined with others to subject us to a jurisdiction foreign of our constitution, and unacknowledged by our laws; giving his assent to their acts of pretended legislation:

16   For quartering large bodies of armed troops among us:

17   For protecting them, by a mock trial, from punishment for any murders which they should commit on the inhabitants of these States:

18   For cutting off our trade with all parts of the world:

19   For imposing taxes on us without our consent:

20   For depriving us in many cases of the benefits of trial by jury:

21   For transporting us beyond seas to be tried for pretended offenses:

22   For abolishing the free system of English laws in a neighbouring Province, establishing therein an arbitrary government, and enlarging its boundaries so as to render it at once an example and fit instrument for introducing the same absolute rule into these Colonies:

23   For taking away our Charters, abolishing our most valuable laws, and altering fundamentally the forms of our governments:

24   For suspending our own legislatures, and declaring themselves invested with power to legislate for us in all cases whatsoever.

25   He has abdicated government here, by declaring us out of his protection and waging war against us.

26   He has plundered our seas, ravaged our coasts, burnt our towns, and destroyed the lives of our people.

27   He is at this time transporting large armies of foreign mercenaries to complete the works of death, desolation, and tyranny, already begun with circumstances of cruelty and perfidy scarcely paralleled in the most barbarous ages, and totally unworthy the head of a civilized nation.

28   He has constrained our fellow citizens taken captive on the high seas to bear arms against their country, to become the executioners of their friends and brethren, or to fall themselves by their hands.

29   He has excited domestic insurrections amongst us, and has endeavored to bring on the inhabitants of our frontiers, the merciless Indian savages, whose known rule of warfare, is an undistinguished destruction of all ages, sexes, and conditions.

30   In every stage of these oppressions we have petitioned for redress in the most humble terms: our repeated petitions have been answered only by repeated injury. A prince whose character is thus marked by every act which may define a tyrant is unfit to be the ruler of a free people.

31   Nor have we been wanting in attention to our British brethren. We have warned them from time to time of attempts by their legislature to extend an unwarrantable jurisdiction over us. We have reminded them of the circumstances of our emigration and settlement here. We have appealed to their native justice and magnanimity, and we have conjured them by the ties of our common kindred to disavow these usurpations, which would inevitably interrupt our connections and correspondence. They too have been deaf to the voice of justice and of consanguinity. We must, therefore, acquiesce in the necessity, which denounces our separation, and hold them, as we hold the rest of mankind, enemies in war, in peace friends.

32   We, therefore, the Representatives of the United States of America, in General Congress assembled, appealing to the Supreme Judge of the world for the rectitude of our intentions, do, in the name, and by authority of the good people of these Colonies, solemnly publish and declare, That these United Colonies are, and of right ought to be, Free and Independent States; that they are absolved from all allegiance to the British

Crown, and that all political connection between them and the state of Great Britain, is and ought to be totally dissolved; and that as Free and Independent States, they have full power to levy war, conclude peace, contract alliances, establish commerce, and to do all other acts and things which Independent States may of right do. And for the support of this declaration, with a firm reliance on the protection of Divine Providence, we mutually pledge to each other our lives, our fortunes, and our sacred honor.

Questions for Discussion

1. Since the outcome of the rebellion will be determined by war in any case, why do Jefferson and his fellow patriots feel compelled to explain their reasons for rebellion?
2. What are the premises of Jefferson's argument?
3. What, according to Jefferson, is the purpose of government?
4. What are the abuses of power with which the Declaration charges King George III of England?

Suggestions for Exploring, Writing, and Persuading

1. To what degree have governments and government agencies in the United States today—local, state, and federal—failed in their purpose and ignored the source of their power?
2. Jefferson says that when government ceases to be responsive to the people, the people have the right to abolish the government. What offenses would cause you to advocate overthrowing the government? Discuss.
3. Jefferson says government derives its "just powers from the consent of the governed." In what ways have government agencies treated you as a subject rather than a person who is the source of their authority? Discuss.

Abraham Lincoln (1809–1865)

Abraham Lincoln, the sixteenth president of the United States, led his country through the difficult times of the Civil War. With the Emancipation Proclamation on January 1, 1863, Lincoln declared that all slaves were free. Even before he became president, Lincoln was noted for his powerful speeches; probably his most famous is The Gettysburg Address, delivered on November 19, 1863, at the site of the Battle of Gettysburg in honor of those who had died there for their country. This speech combines the best of Lincoln's rhetorical abilities in a powerful tribute and challenge. On

April 14, 1865, while attending a performance of Our American Cousin *at Ford's Theatre in Washington, D.C., Lincoln was assassinated.*

THE GETTYSBURG ADDRESS (1863)

1   Four score and seven years ago our fathers brought forth on this continent a new nation, conceived in liberty and dedicated to the proposition that all men are created equal. Now we are engaged in a great civil war, testing whether that nation or any nation so conceived and so dedicated can long endure. We are met on a great battlefield of that war. We have come to dedicate a portion of that field as a final resting-place for those who here gave their lives that the nation might live. It is altogether fitting and proper that we should do this. But in a larger sense, we cannot dedicate, we cannot consecrate, we cannot hallow this ground. The brave men, living and dead, who struggled here have consecrated it far above our poor power to add or detract. The world will little note nor long remember what we say here, but it can never forget what they did here. It is for us the living rather to be dedicated here to the unfinished work which they who fought here have thus far so nobly advanced. It is rather for us to be here dedicated to the great task remaining before us— that from these honored dead we take increased devotion to that cause for which they gave the last full measure of devotion—that we here highly resolve that these dead shall not have died in vain, that this nation under God shall have a new birth of freedom, and that government of the people, by the people, for the people shall not perish from the earth.

Questions for Discussion

1. Why does Lincoln say that "we cannot consecrate, we cannot hallow this ground"? Explain.

2. What is the irony of his statement that "The world will little note nor long remember what we say here"?

3. Notice the many examples of parallel structure in this famous speech. How does this parallelism affect the meaning of Lincoln's speech?

Suggestions for Exploring, Writing, and Persuading

1. Write a speech in which you dedicate the sites of the September 11, 2001, attacks on the World Trade Centers, the Pentagon, or the Pennsylvania site.

2. In an essay, defend Lincoln's description of the American government as "of the people, by the people, for the people."

3. Write an essay comparing Lincoln's challenge here with that in McCrae's "In Flanders Fields."

Harriet Jacobs (1813–1897)

Harriet Jacobs was born into slavery in North Carolina and was orphaned as a child. Her owner's wife taught her to read, but her owner abused her. Consequently, she ran away and hid in a crawlspace in her grandmother's home. In 1842, she escaped to the North and became active in the antislavery movement. Her Incidents in the Life of a Slave Girl, *published in Boston in 1860, is a forceful and revealing account of the abuse endured by female slaves.*

THE SLAVE WHO DARED TO FEEL LIKE A MAN   (1860)

1   Two years had passed since I entered Dr. Flint's family, and those years had brought much of the knowledge that comes from experience, though they had afforded little opportunity for any other kinds of knowledge.

2   My grandmother had, as much as possible, been a mother to her orphan grandchildren. By perseverance and unwearied industry, she was now mistress of a snug little home, surrounded with the necessaries of life. She would have been happy could her children have shared them with her. There remained but three children and two grandchildren, all slaves. Most earnestly did she strive to make us feel that it was the will of God: that He had seen fit to place us under such circumstances; and though it seemed hard, we ought to pray for contentment.

3   It was a beautiful faith, coming from a mother who could not call her children her own. But I, and Benjamin, her youngest boy, condemned it. We reasoned that it was much more the will of God that we should be situated as she was. We longed for a home like hers. There we always found sweet balsam for our troubles. She was so loving, so sympathizing! She always met us with a smile, and listened with patience to all our sorrows. She spoke so hopefully, that unconsciously the clouds gave place to sunshine. There was a grand big oven there, too, that baked bread and nice things for the town, and we knew there was always a choice bit in store for us.

4   But, alas! even the charms of the old oven failed to reconcile us to our hard lot. Benjamin was now a tall, handsome lad, strongly and gracefully made, and with a spirit too bold and daring for a slave. My brother William, now twelve years old, had the same aversion to the word master that he had when he was an urchin of seven years. I was his confidant. He came to me with all his troubles. I remember one instance in particular. It was on a lovely spring morning, and when I marked the sunlight dancing here and there, its beauty seemed to mock my sadness. For my master, whose restless, craving, vicious nature roved about day and night, seeking whom to devour, had just left me, with stinging, scorching words; words that scathed ear and brain like fire. O, how I despised him! I thought how glad I should be, if some day when he walked the earth, it would open and swallow him up, and disencumber the world of a plague.

5   When he told me that I was made for his use, made to obey his command in *every* thing; that I was nothing but a slave, whose will must and should surrender to his, never before had my puny arm felt half so strong.

6   So deeply was I absorbed in painful reflections afterwards, that I neither saw nor heard the entrance of any one, till the voice of William sounded close beside me. "Linda," he said, "what makes you look so sad? I love you. O, Linda, isn't this a bad world? Every body seems so cross and unhappy. I wish I had died when poor father did."

7   I told him that every body was *not* cross, or unhappy; that those who had pleasant homes, and kind friends, and who were not afraid to love them, were happy. But we, who were slave-children, without father or mother, could not expect to be happy. We must be good; perhaps that would bring us contentment.

8   "Yes," he said, "I try to be good; but what's the use? They are all the time troubling me." Then he proceeded to relate his afternoon's difficulty with young master Nicholas. It seemed that the brother of master Nicholas had pleased himself with making up stories about William. Master Nicholas said he should be flogged, and he would do it. Whereupon he went to work; but William fought bravely, and the young master, finding he was getting the better of him, undertook to tie his hands behind him. He failed in that likewise. By dint of kicking and fisting, William came out of the skirmish none the worse for a few scratches.

9   He continued to discourse on his young master's *meanness;* how he whipped the *little* boys, but was a perfect coward when a tussle ensued between him and white boys of his own size. On such occasions he always took to his legs. William had other charges to make against him. One was his rubbing up pennies with quicksilver, and passing them off for quarters of a dollar on an old man who kept a fruit stall. William was often sent to buy fruit, and he earnestly inquired of me what he ought to do under such circumstances. I told him it was certainly wrong to deceive the old man, and that it was his duty to tell him of the impositions practised by his young master. I assured him the old man would not be slow to comprehend the whole, and there the matter would end. William thought it might with the old man, but not with *him.* He said he did not mind the smart of the whip, but he did not like the *idea* of being whipped.

10   While I advised him to be good and forgiving I was not unconscious of the beam in my own eye. It was the very knowledge of my own shortcomings that urged me to retain, if possible, some sparks of my brother's God-given nature. I had not lived fourteen years in slavery for nothing. I had felt, seen, and heard enough, to read the characters, and question the motives, of those around me. The war of my life had begun; and though one of God's most powerless creatures, I resolved never to be conquered. Alas, for me!

11   If there was one pure, sunny spot for me, I believed it to be in Benjamin's heart, and in another's, whom I loved with all the ardor of a girl's first love. My owner knew of it, and sought in every way to render me

miserable. He did not resort to corporal punishment, but to all the petty, tyrannical ways that human ingenuity could devise.

12   I remember the first time I was punished. It was in the month of February. My grandmother had taken my old shoes, and replaced them with a new pair. I needed them; for several inches of snow had fallen, and it still continued to fall. When I walked through Mrs. Flint's room, their creaking grated harshly on her refined nerves. She called me to her, and asked what I had about me that made such a horrid noise. I told her it was my new shoes. "Take them off," said she; "and if you put them on again, I'll throw them into the fire."

13   I took them off, and my stockings also. She then sent me a long distance, on an errand. As I went through the snow, my bare feet tingled. That night I was very hoarse; and I went to bed thinking the next day would find me sick, perhaps dead. What was my grief on waking to find myself quite well!

14   I had imagined if I died, or was laid up for some time, that my mistress would feel a twinge of remorse that she had so hated "the little imp," as she styled me. It was my ignorance of that mistress that gave rise to such extravagant imaginings.

15   Dr. Flint occasionally had high prices offered for me; but he always said, "She don't belong to me. She is my daughter's property, and I have no right to sell her." Good, honest man! My young mistress was still a child, and I could look for no protection from her. I loved her, and she returned my affection. I once heard her father allude to her attachment to me; and his wife promptly replied that it proceeded from fear. This put unpleasant doubts into my mind. Did the child feign what she did not feel? or was her mother jealous of the mite of love she bestowed on me? I concluded it must be the latter. I said to myself, "Surely, little children are true."

16   One afternoon I sat at my sewing, feeling unusual depression of spirits. My mistress had been accusing me of an offence, of which I assured her I was perfectly innocent; but I saw, by the contemptuous curl of her lip, that she believed I was telling a lie.

17   I wondered for what wise purpose God was leading me through such thorny paths, and whether still darker days were in store for me. As I sat musing thus, the door opened softly, and William came in. "Well, brother," said I, "what is the matter this time?"

18   "O Linda, Ben and his master have had a dreadful time!" said he.

19   My first thought was that Benjamin was killed. "Don't be frightened, Linda," said William; "I will tell you all about it."

20   It appeared that Benjamin's master had sent for him, and he did not immediately obey the summons. When he did, his master was angry, and began to whip him. He resisted. Master and slave fought, and finally the master was thrown. Benjamin had cause to tremble; for he had thrown to the ground his master—one of the richest men in town. I anxiously awaited the result.

21   That night I stole to my grandmother's house, and Benjamin also stole thither from his master's. My grandmother had gone to spend a day or two with an old friend living in the country.

22   "I have come," said Benjamin, "to tell you good by. I am going away."

23   I inquired where.

24   "To the north," he replied.

25   I looked at him to see whether he was in earnest. I saw it all in his firm, set mouth. I implored him not to go, but he paid no heed to my words. He said he was no longer a boy, and every day made his yoke more galling. He had raised his hand against his master, and was to be publicly whipped for the offence. I reminded him of the poverty and hardships he must encounter among strangers. I told him he might be caught and brought back; and that was terrible to think of.

26   He grew vexed, and asked if poverty and hardships with freedom, were not preferable to our treatment in slavery. "Linda," he continued, "we are dogs here; foot-balls, cattle, every thing that's mean. No, I will not stay. Let them bring me back. We don't die but once."

27   He was right; but it was hard to give him up. "Go," said I, "and break your mother's heart."

28   I repented of my words ere they were out.

29   "Linda," said he, speaking as I had not heard him speak that evening, "how *could* you say that? Poor mother! be kind to her, Linda; and you, too, cousin Fanny."

30   Cousin Fanny was a friend who had lived some years with us.

31   Farewells were exchanged, and the bright, kind boy, endeared to us by so many acts of love, vanished from our sight.

32   It is not necessary to state how he made his escape. Suffice it to say, he was on his way to New York when a violent storm overtook the vessel. The captain said he must put into the nearest port. This alarmed Benjamin, who was aware that he would be advertised in every port near his own town. His embarrassment was noticed by the captain. To port they went. There the advertisement met the captain's eye. Benjamin so exactly answered its description, that the captain laid hold on him, and bound him in chains. The storm passed, and they proceeded to New York. Before reaching that port Benjamin managed to get off his chains and throw them overboard. He escaped from the vessel, but was pursued, captured, and carried back to his master.

33   When my grandmother returned home and found her youngest child had fled, great was her sorrow; but, with characteristic piety, she said, "God's will be done." Each morning, she inquired if any news had been heard from her boy. Yes, news *was* heard. The master was rejoicing over a letter, announcing the capture of his human chattel.

34   That day seems but as yesterday, so well do I remember it. I saw him led through the streets in chains, to jail. His face was ghastly pale, yet full of determination. He had begged one of the sailors to go to his mother's house and ask her not to meet him. He said the sight of her distress would

take from him all self-control. She yearned to see him, and she went; but she screened herself in the crowd, that it might be as her child had said.

35   We were not allowed to visit him; but we had known the jailer for years, and he was a kind-hearted man. At midnight he opened the jail door for my grandmother and myself to enter, in disguise. When we entered the cell not a sound broke the stillness. "Benjamin, Benjamin!" whispered my grandmother. No answer. "Benjamin!" she again faltered. There was a jingle of chains. The moon had just risen, and cast an uncertain light through the bars of the window. We knelt down and took Benjamin's cold hands in ours. We did not speak. Sobs were heard, and Benjamin's lips were unsealed; for his mother was weeping on his neck. How vividly does memory bring back that sad night! Mother and son talked together. He asked her pardon for the suffering he had caused her. She said she had nothing to forgive; she could not blame his desire for freedom. He told her that when he was captured, he broke away, and was about casting himself into the river, when thoughts of *her* came over him, and he desisted. She asked if he did not also think of God. I fancied I saw his face grow fierce in the moonlight. He answered, "No, I did not think of him. When a man is hunted like a wild beast he forgets there is a God, a heaven. He forgets every thing in his struggle to get beyond the reach of the bloodhounds."

36   "Don't talk so, Benjamin," said she. "Put your trust in God. Be humble, my child, and your master will forgive you."

37   "Forgive me for *what*, mother? For not letting him treat me like a dog? No! I will never humble myself to him. I have worked for him for nothing all my life, and I am repaid with stripes and imprisonment. Here I will stay till I die, or till he sells me."

38   The poor mother shuddered at his words. I think he felt it; for when he next spoke, his voice was calmer. "Don't fret about me, mother. I ain't worth it," said he. "I wish I had some of your goodness. You bear every thing patiently, just as though you thought it was all right. I wish I could."

39   She told him she had not always been so; once, she was like him; but when sore troubles came upon her, and she had no arm to lean upon, she learned to call on God, and he lightened her burdens. She besought him to do likewise.

40   We overstaid our time, and were obliged to hurry from the jail.

41   Benjamin had been imprisoned three weeks, when my grandmother went to intercede for him with his master. He was immovable. He said Benjamin should serve as an example to the rest of his slaves; he should be kept in jail till he was subdued, or be sold if he got but one dollar for him. However, he afterwards relented in some degree. The chains were taken off, and we were allowed to visit him.

42   As his food was of the coarsest kind, we carried him as often as possible a warm supper, accompanied with some little luxury for the jailer.

43   Three months elapsed, and there was no prospect of release or of a purchaser. One day he was heard to sing and laugh. This piece of indecorum was told to his master, and the overseer was ordered to re-chain him.

He was now confined in an apartment with other prisoners, who were covered with filthy rags. Benjamin was chained near them, and was soon covered with vermin. He worked at his chains till he succeeded in getting out of them. He passed them through the bars of the window, with a request that they should be taken to his master, and he should be informed that he was covered with vermin.

44   This audacity was punished with heavier chains, and prohibition of our visits.

45   My grandmother continued to send him fresh changes of clothes. The old ones were burned up. The last night we saw him in jail his mother still begged him to send for his master, and beg his pardon. Neither persuasion nor argument could turn him from his purpose. He calmly answered, "I am waiting his time."

46   Those chains were mournful to hear.

47   Another three months passed, and Benjamin left his prison walls. We that loved him waited to bid him a long and last farewell. A slave trader had bought him. You remember, I told you what price he brought when ten years of age. Now he was more than twenty years old, and sold for three hundred dollars. The master had been blind to his own interest. Long confinement had made his face too pale, his form too thin; moreover, the trader had heard something of his character, and it did not strike him as suitable for a slave. He said he would give any price if the handsome lad was a girl. We thanked God that he was not.

48   Could you have seen that mother clinging to her child, when they fastened the irons upon his wrists; could you have heard her heart-rending groans, and seen her bloodshot eyes wander wildly from face to face, vainly pleading for mercy; could you have witnessed that scene as I saw it, you would exclaim, *Slavery is damnable!*

49   Benjamin, her youngest, her pet, was forever gone! She could not realize it. She had had an interview with the trader for the purpose of ascertaining if Benjamin could be purchased. She was told it was impossible, as he had given bonds not to sell him till he was out of the state. He promised that he would not sell him till he reached New Orleans.

50   With a strong arm and unvaried trust, my grandmother began her work of love. Benjamin must be free. If she succeeded, she knew they would still be separated; but the sacrifice was not too great. Day and night she labored. The trader's price would treble that he gave; but she was not discouraged.

51   She employed a lawyer to write to a gentleman, whom she knew, in New Orleans. She begged him to interest himself for Benjamin, and he willingly favored her request. When he saw Benjamin, and stated his business, he thanked him; but said he preferred to wait a while before making the trader an offer. He knew he had tried to obtain a high price for him, and had invariably failed. This encouraged him to make another effort for freedom. So one morning, long before day, Benjamin was missing. He was riding over the blue billows, bound for Baltimore.

52   For once his white face did him a kindly service. They had no suspicion that it belonged to a slave; otherwise, the law would have been followed out to the letter, and the *thing* rendered back to slavery. The brightest skies are often overshadowed by the darkest clouds. Benjamin was taken sick, and compelled to remain in Baltimore three weeks. His strength was slow in returning; and his desire to continue his journey seemed to retard his recovery. How could he get strength without air and exercise? He resolved to venture on a short walk. A by-street was selected, where he thought himself secure of not being met by any one that knew him; but a voice called out, "Halloo, Ben, my boy! what are you doing *here?*"

53   His first impulse was to run; but his legs trembled so that he could not stir. He turned to confront his antagonist, and behold, there stood his old master's next door neighbor! He thought it was all over with him now; but it proved otherwise. That man was a miracle. He possessed a goodly number of slaves, and yet was not quite deaf to that mystic clock, whose ticking is rarely heard in the slaveholder's breast.

54   "Ben, you are sick," said he. "Why, you look like a ghost. I guess I gave you something of a start. Never mind, Ben, I am not going to touch you. You had a pretty tough time of it, and you may go on your way rejoicing for all me. But I would advise you to get out of this place plaguy quick, for there are several gentlemen here from our town." He described the nearest and safest route to New York, and added, "I shall be glad to tell your mother I have seen you. Good by, Ben."

55   Benjamin turned away, filled with gratitude, and surprised that the town he hated contained such a gem—a gem worthy of a purer setting.

56   This gentleman was a Northerner by birth, and had married a southern lady. On his return, he told my grandmother that he had seen her son, and of the service he had rendered him.

57   Benjamin reached New York safely, and concluded to stop there until he had gained strength enough to proceed further. It happened that my grandmother's only remaining son had sailed for the same city on business for his mistress. Through God's providence, the brothers met. You may be sure it was a happy meeting. "O Phil," exclaimed Benjamin, "I am here at last." Then he told him how near he came to dying, almost in sight of free land, and how he prayed that he might live to get one breath of free air. He said life was worth something now, and it would be hard to die. In the old jail he had not valued it; once, he was tempted to destroy it; but something, he did not know what, had prevented him; perhaps it was fear. He had heard those who profess to be religious declare there was no heaven for self-murderers; and as his life had been pretty hot here, he did not desire a continuation of the same in another world. "If I die now," he exclaimed, "thank God, I shall die a freeman!"

58   He begged my uncle Phillip not to return south; but stay and work with him, till they earned enough to buy those at home. His brother told him it would kill their mother if he deserted her in her trouble. She had pledged her house, and with difficulty had raised money to buy him. Would he be bought?

59   "No, never!" he replied. "Do you suppose, Phil, when I have got so far out of their clutches, I will give them one red cent? No! And do you suppose I would turn mother out of her home in her old age? That I would let her pay all those hard-earned dollars for me, and never to see me? For you know she will stay south as long as her other children are slaves. What a good mother! Tell her to buy *you*, Phil. You have been a comfort to her, and I have been a trouble. And Linda, poor Linda; what'll become of her? Phil, you don't know what a life they lead her. She has told me something about it, and I wish old Flint was dead, or a better man. When I was in jail, he asked her if she didn't want *him* to ask my master to forgive me, and take me home again. She told him, No; that I didn't want to go back. He got mad, and said we were all alike. I never despised my own master half as much as I do that man. There is many a worse slaveholder than my master; but for all that I would not be his slave."

60   While Benjamin was sick, he had parted with nearly all his clothes to pay necessary expenses. But he did not part with a little pin I fastened in his bosom when we parted. It was the most valuable thing I owned, and I thought none more worthy to wear it. He had it still.

61   His brother furnished him with clothes, and gave him what money he had.

62   They parted with moistened eyes; and as Benjamin turned away, he said, "Phil, I part with all my kindred." And so it proved. We never heard from him again.

63   Uncle Phillip came home; and the first words he uttered when he entered the house were, "Mother, Ben is free! I have seen him in New York." She stood looking at him with a bewildered air. "Mother, don't you believe it?" he said, laying his hand softly upon her shoulder. She raised her hands, and exclaimed, "God be praised! Let us thank him." She dropped on her knees, and poured forth her heart in prayer. Then Phillip must sit down and repeat to her every word Benjamin had said. He told her all; only he forbore to mention how sick and pale her darling looked. Why should he distress her when she could do him no good?

64   The brave old woman still toiled on, hoping to rescue some of her other children. After a while she succeeded in buying Phillip. She paid eight hundred dollars, and came home with the precious document that secured his freedom. The happy mother and son sat together by the old hearthstone that night, telling how proud they were of each other, and how they would prove to the world that they could take care of themselves, as they had long taken care of others. We all concluded by saying, "He that is *willing* to be a slave, let him be a slave."

Questions for Discussion

1. Why did the grandmother try to convince her children and grandchildren that they should be content to be slaves?

2. What does Linda imply about her master in saying that his "restless, craving, vicious nature roved about day and night, seeking whom to devour"?

3. Explain the irony of the title. List the qualities that make Benjamin ill suited to be a slave.

4. What does the ordeal in the jail reveal about Benjamin's character?

5. What does Linda mean when she says of Benjamin's master that he had been "blind to his own interest"?

6. Why does Benjamin refuse to be bought by his mother?

7. Why did the slave owner's neighbor treat Benjamin kindly and report his whereabouts to his mother? Do you think this behavior typical of slave owners? Explain.

Suggestions for Exploring, Writing, and Persuading

1. Benjamin asks Linda "if poverty and hardships with freedom, were not preferable to our treatment in slavery." What would your answer be? Write an essay defending your position.

2. Discuss the last sentence in the essay. Who is willing to be a slave? Why?

3. Benjamin says, "When a man is hunted like a wild beast, he forgets there is a God." Compare Benjamin's attitude to Pinhas's attitude in Wiesel's "Yom Kippur."

4. The grandmother and Benjamin represent two distinctly different ways of dealing with injustice: passive contentment and resistance. Which would you be most likely to choose? Defend your answer in an essay.

5. Phil neglects to tell his mother "how sick and pale" Benjamin looked in order to spare his mother's feelings. Why? Explain whether you would hide the truth in order to spare someone pain.

Martin Luther King Jr. (1929-1968)

Martin Luther King Jr., an ordained minister at the age of eighteen, was born in Atlanta, Georgia. He received degrees from Morehouse College, Crozer Theological Seminary, and Boston University. A leader of the civil rights movement, King organized the Montgomery, Alabama, bus boycott after Rosa Parks refused to give up her seat on a bus to a white person. He was also the founder and president of the Southern Christian Leadership Conference (SCLC), which espoused his philosophy of nonviolence. This letter from jail was written in response to the local clergy who had questioned King's approach and methodology.

LETTER FROM BIRMINGHAM CITY JAIL   (1963)

1   My dear Fellow Clergymen,

2   While confined here in Birmingham city jail, I came across your recent statement calling our present activities "unwise and untimely." Seldom,

if ever, do I pause to answer criticism of my work and ideas. If I sought to answer all of the criticisms that cross my desk, my secretaries would be engaged in little else in the course of the day, and I would have no time for constructive work. But since I feel that you are men of genuine good will and your criticisms are sincerely set forth, I would like to answer your statement in what I hope will be patient and reasonable terms.

3   I think I should give the reason for my being in Birmingham, since you have been influenced by the argument of "outsiders coming in." I have the honor of serving as president of the Southern Christian Leadership Conference, an organization operating in every southern state, with headquarters in Atlanta, Georgia. We have some eighty-five affiliate organizations all across the South—one being the Alabama Christian Movement for Human Rights. Whenever necessary and possible we share staff, educational and financial resources with our affiliates. Several months ago our local affiliate here in Birmingham invited us to be on call to engage in a nonviolent direct-action program if such were deemed necessary. We readily consented and when the hour came we lived up to our promises. So I am here, along with several members of my staff, because we were invited here. I am here because I have basic organizational ties here.

4   Beyond this, I am in Birmingham because injustice is here. Just as the eighth century prophets left their little villages and carried their "thus saith the Lord" far beyond the boundaries of their hometowns; and just as the Apostle Paul left his little village of Tarsus and carried the gospel of Jesus Christ to practically every hamlet and city of the Graeco-Roman world, I too am compelled to carry the gospel of freedom beyond my particular hometown. Like Paul, I must constantly respond to the Macedonian call for aid.

5   Moreover, I am cognizant of the interrelatedness of all communities and states. I cannot sit idly by in Atlanta and not be concerned about what happens in Birmingham. Injustice anywhere is a threat to justice every-where. We are caught in an inescapable network of mutuality, tied in a single garment of destiny. Whatever affects one directly affects all indirectly. Never again can we afford to live with the narrow, provincial "outside agitator" idea. Anyone who lives in the United States can never be considered an outsider anywhere in this country.

6   You deplore the demonstrations that are presently taking place in Birmingham. But I am sorry that your statement did not express a similar concern for the conditions that brought the demonstrations into being. I am sure that each of you would want to go beyond the superficial social analyst who looks merely at effects, and does not grapple with underlying causes. I would not hesitate to say that it is unfortunate that so-called demonstrations are taking place in Birmingham at this time, but I would say in more emphatic terms that it is even more unfortunate that the white power structure of this city left the Negro community with no other alternative.

7   In any nonviolent campaign there are four basic steps: (1) collection of the facts to determine whether injustices are alive, (2) negotiation, (3)

self-purification, and (4) direct action. We have gone through all of these steps in Birmingham. There can be no gainsaying of the fact that racial injustice engulfs this community.

8   Birmingham is probably the most thoroughly segregated city in the United States. Its ugly record of police brutality is known in every section of this country. Its injust treatment of Negroes in the courts is a notorious reality. There have been more unsolved bombings of Negro homes and churches in Birmingham than any city in this nation. These are the hard, brutal and unbelievable facts. On the basis of these conditions Negro leaders sought to negotiate with the city fathers. But the political leaders consistently refused to engage in good faith negotiation.

9   Then came the opportunity last September to talk with some of the leaders of the economic community. In these negotiating sessions certain promises were made by the merchants—such as the promise to remove the humiliating racial signs from the stores. On the basis of these promises Rev. Shuttlesworth and the leaders of the Alabama Christian Movement for Human Rights agreed to call a moratorium on any type of demonstrations. As the weeks and months unfolded we realized that we were the victims of a broken promise. The signs remained. Like so many experiences of the past we were confronted with blasted hopes, and the dark shadow of a deep disappointment settled upon us. So we had no alternative except that of preparing for direct action, whereby we would present our very bodies as a means of laying our case before the conscience of the local and national community. We were not unmindful of the difficulties involved. So we decided to go through a process of self-purification. We started having workshops on nonviolence and repeatedly asked ourselves the questions, "Are you able to accept blows without retaliating?" "Are you able to endure the ordeals of jail?" We decided to set our direct-action program around the Easter season, realizing that with the exception of Christmas, this was the largest shopping period of the year. Knowing that a strong economic withdrawal program would be the by-product of direct action, we felt that this was the best time to bring pressure on the merchants for the needed changes. Then it occurred to us that the March election was ahead and so we speedily decided to postpone action until after election day. When we discovered that Mr. Connor was in the run-off, we decided again to postpone action so that the demonstrations could not be used to cloud the issues. At this time we agreed to begin our nonviolent witness the day after the run-off.

10   This reveals that we did not move irresponsibly into direct action. We too wanted to see Mr. Connor defeated; so we went through postponement after postponement to aid in this community need. After this we felt that direct action could be delayed no longer.

11   You may well ask, "Why direct action? Why sit-ins, marches, etc.? Isn't negotiation a better path?" You are exactly right in your call for negotiation. Indeed, this is the purpose of direct action. Nonviolent direct action seeks to create such a crisis and establish such creative tension that a

community that has constantly refused to negotiate is forced to confront the issue. It seeks so to dramatize the issue that it can no longer be ignored. I just referred to the creation of tension as a part of the work of the nonviolent resister. This may sound rather shocking. But I must confess that I am not afraid of the word tension. I have earnestly worked and preached against violent tension, but there is a type of constructive nonviolent tension that is necessary for growth. Just as Socrates felt that it was necessary to create a tension in the mind so that individuals could rise from the bondage of myths and half-truths to the unfettered realm of creative analysis and objective appraisal, we must see the need of having nonviolent gadflies to create the kind of tension in society that will help men to rise from the dark depths of prejudice and racism to the majestic heights of understanding and brotherhood. So the purpose of the direct action is to create a situation so crisis-packed that it will inevitably open the door to negotiation. We, therefore, concur with you in your call for negotiation. Too long has our beloved Southland been bogged down in the tragic attempt to live in monologue rather than dialogue.

12   One of the basic points in your statement is that our acts are untimely. Some have asked, "Why didn't you give the new administration time to act?" The only answer that I can give to this inquiry is that the new administration must be prodded about as much as the outgoing one before it acts. We will be sadly mistaken if we feel that the election of Mr. Boutwell will bring the millennium to Birmingham. While Mr. Boutwell is much more articulate and gentle than Mr. Connor, they are both segregationists, dedicated to the task of maintaining the status quo. The hope I see in Mr. Boutwell is that he will be reasonable enough to see the futility of massive resistance to desegregation. But he will not see this without pressure from the devotees of civil rights. My friends, I must say to you that we have not made a single gain in civil rights without determined legal and nonviolent pressure. History is the long and tragic story of the fact that privileged groups seldom give up their privileges voluntarily. Individuals may see the moral light and voluntarily give up their unjust posture; but as Reinhold Niebuhr has reminded us, groups are more immoral than individuals.

13   We know through painful experience that freedom is never voluntarily given by the oppressor; it must be demanded by the oppressed. Frankly, I have never yet engaged in a direct action movement that was "well-timed," according to the timetable of those who have not suffered unduly from the disease of segregation. For years now I have heard the words "Wait!" It rings in the ear of every Negro with a piercing familiarity. This "Wait" has almost always meant "Never." It has been a tranquilizing thalidomide, relieving the emotional stress for a moment, only to give birth to an ill-formed infant of frustration. We must come to see with the distinguished jurist of yesterday that "justice too long delayed is justice denied." We have waited for more than 340 years for our constitutional and God-given rights. The nations of Asia and Africa are moving with jetlike speed toward the goal of political independence, and we still

creep at horse and buggy pace toward the gaining of a cup of coffee at a lunch counter. I guess it is easy for those who have never felt the stinging darts of segregation to say, "Wait." But when you have seen vicious mobs lynch your mothers and fathers at will and drown your sisters and brothers at whim; when you have seen hate-filled policemen curse, kick, brutalize and even kill your black brothers and sisters with impunity; when you see the vast majority of your twenty million Negro brothers smothering in an airtight cage of poverty in the midst of an affluent society; when you suddenly find your tongue twisted and your speech stammering as you seek to explain to your six-year-old daughter why she can't go to the public amusement park that has just been advertised on television, and see tears welling up in her little eyes when she is told that Funtown is closed to colored children, and see the depressing clouds of inferiority begin to form in her little mental sky, and see her begin to distort her little personality by unconsciously developing a bitterness toward white people; when you have to concoct an answer for a five-year-old son asking in agonizing pathos: "Daddy, why do white people treat colored people so mean?"; when you take a cross-country drive and find it necessary to sleep night after night in the uncomfortable corners of your automobile because no motel will accept you; when you are humiliated day in and day out by nagging signs reading "white" and "colored"; when your first name becomes "nigger" and your middle name becomes "boy" (however old you are) and your last name becomes "John," and when your wife and mother are never given the respected title "Mrs."; when you are harried by day and haunted by night by the fact that you are a Negro, living constantly at tiptoe stance never quite knowing what to expect next, and plagued with inner fears and outer resentments; when you are forever fighting a degenerating sense of "nobodiness"; then you will understand why we find it difficult to wait. There comes a time when the cup of endurance runs over, and men are no longer willing to be plunged into an abyss of injustice where they experience the blackness of corroding despair. I hope, sirs, you can understand our legitimate and unavoidable impatience.

14   You express a great deal of anxiety over our willingness to break laws. This is certainly a legitimate concern. Since we so diligently urge people to obey the Supreme Court's decision of 1954 outlawing segregation in the public schools, it is rather strange and paradoxical to find us consciously breaking laws. One may well ask, "How can you advocate breaking some laws and obeying others?" The answer is found in the fact that there are two types of laws: there are *just* and there are *unjust* laws. I would agree with Saint Augustine that "An unjust law is no law at all."

15   Now what is the difference between the two? How does one determine when a law is just or unjust? A just law is a man-made code that squares with the moral law or the law of God. An unjust law is a code that is out of harmony with the moral law. To put it in the terms of Saint Thomas Aquinas, an unjust law is a human law that is not rooted in eternal and natural law. Any law that uplifts human personality is just. Any law that

degrades human personality is unjust. All segregation statutes are unjust because segregation distorts the soul and damages the personality. It gives the segregator a false sense of superiority, and the segregated a false sense of inferiority. To use the words of Martin Buber, the great Jewish philosopher, segregation substitutes an "I-it" relationship for the "I-thou" relationship, and ends up relegating persons to the status of things. So segregation is not only politically, economically and sociologically unsound, but it is morally wrong and sinful. Paul Tillich has said that sin is separation. Isn't segregation an existential expression of man's tragic separation, an expression of his awful estrangement, his terrible sinfulness? So I can urge men to disobey segregation ordinances because they are morally wrong.

16   Let us turn to a more concrete example of just and unjust laws. An unjust law is a code that a majority inflicts on a minority that is not binding on itself. This is difference made legal. On the other hand a just law is a code that a majority compels a minority to follow that it is willing to follow itself. This is sameness made legal.

17   Let me give another explanation. An unjust law is a code inflicted upon a minority which that minority had no part in enacting or creating because they did not have the unhampered right to vote. Who can say that the legislature of Alabama which set up the segregation laws was democratically elected? Throughout the state of Alabama all types of conniving methods are used to prevent Negroes from becoming registered voters and there are some counties without a single Negro registered to vote despite the fact that the Negro constitutes a majority of the population. Can any law set up in such a state be considered democratically structured?

18   These are just a few examples of unjust and just laws. There are some instances when a law is just on its face and unjust in its application. For instance, I was arrested Friday on a charge of parading without a permit. Now there is nothing wrong with an ordinance which requires a permit for a parade, but when the ordinance is used to preserve segregation and to deny citizens the First Amendment privilege of peaceful assembly and peaceful protest, then it becomes unjust.

19   I hope you can see the distinction I am trying to point out. In no sense do I advocate evading or defying the law as the rabid segregationist would do. This would lead to anarchy. One who breaks an unjust law must do it *openly*, *lovingly* (not hatefully as the white mothers did in New Orleans when they were seen on television screaming, "nigger, nigger, nigger"), and with a willingness to accept the penalty. I submit that an individual who breaks a law that conscience tells him is unjust, and willingly accepts the penalty by staying in jail to arouse the conscience of the community over its injustice, is in reality expressing the very highest respect for law.

20   Of course, there is nothing new about this kind of civil disobedience. It was seen sublimely in the refusal of Shadrach, Meshach and Abednego to obey the laws of Nebuchadnezzar because a higher moral law was

involved. It was practiced superbly by the early Christians who were willing to face hungry lions and the excruciating pain of chopping blocks,
before submitting to certain unjust laws of the Roman Empire. To a
degree academic freedom is a reality today because Socrates practiced
civil disobedience.

21   We can never forget that everything Hitler did in Germany was "legal"
and everything the Hungarian freedom fighters did in Hungary was "illegal." It was "illegal" to aid and comfort a Jew in Hitler's Germany. But I am
sure that if I had lived in Germany during that time I would have aided and
comforted my Jewish brothers even though it was illegal. If I lived in a
Communist country today where certain principles dear to the Christian
faith are suppressed, I believe I would openly advocate disobeying these
anti-religious laws. I must make two honest confessions to you, my Christian and Jewish brothers. First, I must confess that over the last few years
I have been gravely disappointed with the white moderate. I have almost
reached the regrettable conclusion that the Negro's great stumbling block
in the stride toward freedom is not the White Citizen's Counciler or the
Ku Klux Klanner, but the white moderate who is more devoted to "order"
than to justice; who prefers a negative peace which is the absence of tension to a positive peace which is the presence of justice; who constantly
says, "I agree with you in the goal you seek, but I can't agree with your
methods of direct action"; who paternalistically feels that he can set the
timetable for another man's freedom; who lives by the myth of time and
who constantly advised the Negro to wait until a "more convenient season." Shallow understanding from people of good will is more frustrating
than absolute misunderstanding from people of ill will. Lukewarm acceptance is much more bewildering than outright rejection.

22   I had hoped that the white moderate would understand that law and
order exist for the purpose of establishing justice, and that when they fail
to do this they become dangerously structured dams that block the flow
of social progress. I had hoped that the white moderate would understand that the present tension of the South is merely a necessary phase
of the transition from an obnoxious negative peace, where the Negro pas-
sively accepted his unjust plight, to a substance-filled positive peace,
where all men will respect the dignity and worth of human personality.
Actually, we who engage in nonviolent direct action are not the creators
of tension. We merely bring to the surface the hidden tension that is
already alive. We bring it out in the open where it can be seen and dealt
with. Like a boil that can never be cured as long as it is covered up but
must be opened with all its pus-flowing ugliness to the natural medicines
of air and light, injustice must likewise be exposed, with all of the tension its exposing creates, to the light of human conscience and the air of
national opinion before it can be cured.

23   In your statement you asserted that our actions, even though peaceful, must be condemned because they precipitate violence. But can this
assertion be logically made? Isn't this like condemning the robbed man

because his possession of money precipitated the evil act of robbery? Isn't this like condemning Socrates because his unswerving commitment to truth and his philosophical delvings precipitated the misguided popular mind to make him drink the hemlock? Isn't this like condemning Jesus because His unique God-consciousness and never-ceasing devotion to his will precipitated the evil act of crucifixion? We must come to see, as federal courts have consistently affirmed, that it is immoral to urge an individual to withdraw his efforts to gain his basic constitutional rights because the quest precipitates violence. Society must protect the robbed and punish the robber.

24   I had also hoped that the white moderate would reject the myth of time. I received a letter this morning from a white brother in Texas which said: "All Christians know that the colored people will receive equal rights eventually, but it is possible that you are in too great of a religious hurry. It has taken Christianity almost two thousand years to accomplish what it has. The teachings of Christ take time to come to earth." All that is said here grows out of a tragic misconception of time. It is the strangely irrational notion that there is something in the very flow of time that will inevitably cure all ills. Actually time is neutral. It can be used either destructively or constructively. I am coming to feel that the people of ill will have used time much more effectively than the people of good will. We will have to repent in this generation not merely for the vitriolic words and actions of the bad people, but for the appalling silence of the good people. We must come to see that human progress never rolls in on wheels of inevitability. It comes through the tireless efforts and persistent work of men willing to be co-workers with God, and without this hard work time itself becomes an ally of the forces of social stagnation. We must use time creatively, and forever realize that the time is always ripe to do right. Now is the time to make real the promise of democracy, and transform our pending national elegy into a creative psalm of brotherhood. Now is the time to lift our national policy from the quicksand of racial injustice to the solid rock of human dignity.

25   You spoke of our activity in Birmingham as extreme. At first I was rather disappointed that fellow clergymen would see my nonviolent efforts as those of the extremist. I started thinking about the fact that I stand in the middle of two opposing forces in the Negro community. One is a force of complacency made up of Negroes who, as a result of long years of oppression, have been so completely drained of self-respect and a sense of "somebodiness" that they have adjusted to segregation, and, of a few Negroes in the middle class who, because of a degree of academic and economic security, and because at points they profit by segregation, have unconsciously become insensitive to the problems of the masses. The other force is one of bitterness and hatred, and comes perilously close to advocating violence. It is expressed in the various black nationalist groups that are springing up over the nation, the largest and best known being Elijah Muhammad's Muslim movement. This movement is nourished by the

contemporary frustration over the continued existence of racial discrimination. It is made up of people who have lost faith in America, who have absolutely repudiated Christianity, and who have concluded that the white man is an incurable "devil." I have tried to stand between these two forces, saying that we need not follow the "do-nothingism" of the complacent or the hatred and despair of the black nationalist. There is the more excellent way of love and nonviolent protest. I'm grateful to God that, through the Negro church, the dimension of nonviolence entered our struggle. If this philosophy had not emerged, I am convinced that by now many streets of the South would be flowing with floods of blood. And I am further convinced that if our white brothers dismiss us as "rabble-rousers" and "outside agitators," those of us who are working through the channels of nonviolent direct action, and refuse to support our nonviolent efforts, millions of Negroes, out of frustration and despair, will seek solace and security in black nationalist ideologies, a development that will lead inevitably to a frightening racial nightmare.

26   Oppressed people cannot remain oppressed forever. The urge for freedom will eventually come. This is what happened to the American Negro. Something within has reminded him of his birthright of freedom; something without has reminded him that he can gain it. Consciously and unconsciously, he has been swept in by what the Germans call the *Zeitgeist*, and with his black brothers of Africa, and his brown and yellow brothers of Asia, South America and the Caribbean, he is moving with a sense of cosmic urgency toward the promised land of racial justice. Recognizing this vital urge that has engulfed the Negro community, one should readily understand public demonstrations. The Negro has many pent-up resentments and latent frustrations. He has to get them out. So let him march sometime; let him have his prayer pilgrimages to the city hall; understand why he must have sit-ins and freedom rides. If his repressed emotions do not come out in these nonviolent ways, they will come out in ominous expressions of violence. This is not a threat; it is a fact of history. So I have not said to my people "get rid of your discontent." But I have tried to say that this normal and healthy discontent can be channelized through the creative outlet of nonviolent direct action. Now this approach is being dismissed as extremist. I must admit that I was initially disappointed in being so categorized.

27   But as I continued to think about the matter I gradually gained a bit of satisfaction from being considered an extremist. Was not Jesus an extremist in love—"Love your enemies, bless them that curse you, pray for them that despitefully use you." Was not Amos an extremist for justice—"Let justice roll down like waters and righteousness like a mighty stream." Was not Paul an extremist for the gospel of Jesus Christ—"I bear in my body the marks of the Lord Jesus." Was not Martin Luther an extremist—"Here I stand; I can do none other so help me God." Was not John Bunyan an extremist—"I will stay in jail to the end of my days before I make a butchery of my conscience." Was not Abraham Lincoln an

extremist—"This nation cannot survive half slave and half free." Was not Thomas Jefferson an extremist—"We hold these truths to be self-evident, that all men are created equal." So the question is not whether we will be extremists but what kind of extremist will we be. Will we be extremists for hate or will we be extremists for love? Will we be extremists for the preservation of injustice—or will we be extremists for the cause of justice? In that dramatic scene on Calvary's hill, three men were crucified. We must not forget that all three were crucified for the same crime—the crime of extremism. Two were extremists for immorality, and thusly fell below their environment. The other, Jesus Christ, was an extremist for love, truth and goodness, and thereby rose above his environment. So, after all, maybe the South, the nation and the world are in dire need of creative extremists.

28   I had hoped that the white moderate would see this. Maybe I was too optimistic. Maybe I expected too much. I guess I should have realized that few members of a race that has oppressed another race can understand or appreciate the deep groans and passionate yearnings of those that have been oppressed and still fewer have the vision to see that injustice must be rooted out by strong, persistent and determined action. I am thankful, however, that some of our white brothers have grasped the meaning of this social revolution and committed themselves to it. They are still all too small in quantity, but they are big in quality. Some like Ralph McGill, Lillian Smith, Harry Golden and James Dabbs have written about our struggle in eloquent, prophetic and understanding terms. Others have marched with us down nameless streets of the South. They have languished in filthy roach-infested jails, suffering the abuse and brutality of angry policemen who see them as "dirty nigger-lovers." They, unlike so many of their moderate brothers and sisters, have recognized the urgency of the moment and sensed the need for powerful "action" antidotes to combat the disease of segregation.

29   Let me rush on to mention my other disappointment. I have been so greatly disappointed with the white church and its leadership. Of course, there are some notable exceptions. I am not unmindful of the fact that each of you has taken some significant stands on this issue. I commend you, Rev. Stallings, for your Christian stance on this past Sunday, in welcoming Negroes to your worship service on a non-segregated basis. I commend the Catholic leaders of this state for integrating Springhill College several years ago.

30   But despite these notable exceptions I must honestly reiterate that I have been disappointed with the church. I do not say that as one of the negative critics who can always find something wrong with the church. I say it as a minister of the gospel, who loves the church; who was nurtured in its bosom; who has been sustained by its spiritual blessing and who will remain true to it as long as the cord of life shall lengthen.

31   I had the strange feeling when I was suddenly catapulted into the leadership of the bus protest in Montgomery several years ago that we would have the support of the white church. I felt that the white ministers,

priests and rabbis of the South would be some of our strongest allies. Instead, some have been outright opponents, refusing to understand the freedom movement and misrepresenting its leaders; all too many others have been more cautious than courageous and have remained silent behind the anesthetizing security of the stained-glass windows.

32   In spite of my shattered dreams of the past, I came to Birmingham with the hope that the white religious leadership of this community would see the justice of our cause, and with deep moral concern, serve as the channel through which our just grievances would get to the power structure. I had hoped that each of you would understand. But again I have been disappointed. I have heard numerous religious leaders of the South call upon their worshippers to comply with a desegregation decision because it is the *law*, but I have longed to hear white ministers say, "Follow this decree because integration is morally *right* and the Negro is your brother." In the midst of blatant injustices inflicted upon the Negro, I have watched white churches stand on the sideline and merely mouth pious irrelevancies and sanctimonious trivialities. In the midst of a mighty struggle to rid our nation of racial and economic injustice, I have heard so many ministers say, "Those are social issues with which the gospel has no concern," and I have watched so many churches commit themselves to a completely otherworldly religion which made a strange distinction between body and soul, the sacred and the secular.

33   So here we are moving toward the exit of the twentieth century with a religious community largely adjusted to the status quo, standing as a taillight behind other community agencies rather than a headlight leading men to higher levels of justice.

34   I have traveled the length and breadth of Alabama, Mississippi and all the other southern states. On sweltering summer days and crisp autumn mornings I have looked at her beautiful churches with their lofty spires pointing heavenward. I have beheld the impressive outlay of her massive religious education buildings. Over and over again I have found myself asking: "What kind of people worship here? Who is their God? Where were their voices when the lips of Governor Barnett dripped with words of interposition and nullification? Where were they when Governor Wallace gave the clarion call for defiance and hatred? Where were their voices of support when tired, bruised and weary Negro men and women decided to rise from the dark dungeons of complacency to the bright hills of creative protest?"

35   Yes, these questions are still in my mind. In deep disappointment, I have wept over the laxity of the church. But be assured that my tears have been tears of love. There can be no deep disappointment where there is not deep love. Yes, I love the church; I love her sacred walls. How could I do otherwise? I am in the rather unique position of being the son, the grandson and the great-grandson of preachers. Yes, I see the church as the body of Christ. But, oh! How we have blemished and scarred that body through social neglect and fear of being nonconformists.

36   There was a time when the church was very powerful. It was during that period when the early Christians rejoiced when they were deemed worthy to suffer for what they believed. In those days the church was not merely a thermometer that recorded the ideas and principles of popular opinion; it was a thermostat that transformed the mores of society. Wherever the early Christians entered a town the power structure got disturbed and immediately sought to convict them for being "disturbers of the peace" and "outside agitators." But they went on with the conviction that they were "a colony of heaven," and had to obey God rather than man. They were small in number but big in commitment. They were too God-intoxicated to be "astronomically intimidated." They brought an end to such ancient evils as infanticide and gladiatorial contests.

37   Things are different now. The contemporary church is often a weak, ineffectual voice with an uncertain sound. It is so often the arch-supporter of the status quo. Far from being disturbed by the presence of the church, the power structure of the average community is consoled by the church's silent and often vocal sanction of things as they are.

38   But the judgment of God is upon the church as never before. If the church of today does not recapture the sacrificial spirit of the early church, it will lose its authentic ring, forfeit the loyalty of millions, and be dismissed as an irrelevant social club with no meaning for the twentieth century. I am meeting young people every day whose disappointment with the church has risen to outright disgust.

39   Maybe again, I have been too optimistic. Is organized religion too inextricably bound to the status quo to save our nation and the world? Maybe I must turn my faith to the inner spiritual church, the church within the church, as the true *ecclesia* and the hope of the world. But again I am thankful to God that some noble souls from the ranks of organized religion have broken loose from the paralyzing chains of conformity and joined us as active partners in the struggle for freedom. They have left their secure congregations and walked the streets of Albany, Georgia, with us. They have gone through the highways of the South on tortuous rides for freedom. Yes, they have gone to jail with us. Some have been kicked out of their churches, and lost support of their bishops and fellow ministers. But they have gone with the faith that right defeated is stronger than evil triumphant. These men have been the leaven in the lump of the race. Their witness has been the spiritual salt that has preserved the true meaning of the gospel in these troubled times. They have carved a tunnel of hope through the dark mountain of disappointment.

40   I hope the church as a whole will meet the challenge of this decisive hour. But even if the church does not come to the aid of justice, I have no despair about the future. I have no fear about the outcome of our struggle in Birmingham, even if our motives are presently misunderstood. We will reach the goal of freedom in Birmingham and all over the nation, because the goal of America is freedom. Abused and scorned though we may be, our destiny is tied up with the destiny of America. Before the Pilgrims

landed at Plymouth, we were here. Before the pen of Jefferson etched across the pages of history the majestic words of the Declaration of Independence, we were here. For more than two centuries our foreparents labored in this country without wages; they made cotton king; and they built the homes of their masters in the midst of brutal injustice and shameful humiliation—and yet out of a bottomless vitality they continued to thrive and develop. If the inexpressible cruelties of slavery could not stop us, the opposition we now face will surely fail. We will win our freedom because the sacred heritage of our nation and the eternal will of God are embodied in our echoing demands.

41   I must close now. But before closing I am impelled to mention one other point in your statement that troubled me profoundly. You warmly commended the Birmingham police force for keeping "order" and "preventing violence." I don't believe you would have so warmly commended the police force if you had seen its angry violent dogs literally biting six unarmed, nonviolent Negroes. I don't believe you would so quickly commend the policemen if you would observe their ugly and inhuman treatment of Negroes here in the city jail; if you would watch them push and curse old Negro women and young Negro girls; if you would see them slap and kick old Negro men and young boys; if you will observe them, as they did on two occasions, refuse to give us food because we wanted to sing our grace together. I'm sorry that I can't join you in your praise for the police department.

42   It is true that they have been rather disciplined in their public handling of the demonstrators. In this sense they have been rather publicly "nonviolent." But for what purpose? To preserve the evil system of segregation. Over the last few years I have consistently preached that nonviolence demands that the means we use must be as pure as the ends we seek. So I have tried to make it clear that it is wrong to use immoral means to attain moral ends. But now I must affirm that it is just as wrong, or even more so, to use moral means to preserve immoral ends. Maybe Mr. Connor and his policemen have been rather publicly nonviolent, as Chief Pritchett was in Albany, Georgia, but they have used the moral means of nonviolence to maintain the immoral end of flagrant racial injustice. T. S. Eliot has said that there is no greater treason than to do the right deed for the wrong reason.

43   I wish you had commended the Negro sit-inners and demonstrators of Birmingham for their sublime courage, their willingness to suffer and their amazing discipline in the midst of the most inhuman provocation. One day the South will recognize its real heroes. They will be the James Merediths, courageously and with a majestic sense of purpose facing jeering and hostile mobs and the agonizing loneliness that characterizes the life of the pioneer. They will be old, oppressed, battered Negro women, symbolized in the seventy-two-year-old woman of Montgomery, Alabama, who rose up with a sense of dignity and with her people decided not to ride the segregated buses, and responded to one who inquired about her tiredness

with ungrammatical profundity: "My feet is tired, but my soul is rested." They will be the young high school and college students, young ministers of the gospel and a host of their elders courageously and nonviolently sitting-in at lunch counters and willingly going to jail for conscience's sake. One day the South will know that when these disinherited children of God sat down at lunch counters they were in reality standing up for the best in the American dream and the most sacred values in our Judeo-Christian heritage, and thusly, carrying our whole nation back to those great wells of democracy which were dug deep by the Founding Fathers in the formulation of the Constitution and the Declaration of Independence.

44   Never before have I written a letter this long (or should I say a book?). I'm afraid that it is much too long to take your precious time. I can assure you that it would have been much shorter if I had been writing from a comfortable desk, but what else is there to do when you are alone for days in the dull monotony of a narrow jail cell other than write long letters, think strange thoughts, and pray long prayers?

45   If I have said anything in this letter that is an overstatement of the truth and is indicative of an unreasonable impatience, I beg you to forgive me. If I have said anything in this letter that is an understatement of the truth and is indicative of my having a patience that makes me patient with anything less than brotherhood, I beg God to forgive me.

46   I hope this letter finds you strong in the faith. I also hope that circumstances will soon make it possible for me to meet each of you, not as an integrationist or a civil rights leader, but as a fellow clergyman and a Christian brother. Let us all hope that the dark clouds of racial prejudice will soon pass away and the deep fog of misunderstanding will be lifted from our fear-drenched communities and in some not too distant tomorrow the radiant stars of love and brotherhood will shine over our great nation with all of their scintillating beauty.

47   Yours for the cause of Peace and Brotherhood,

48   Martin Luther King Jr.

Questions for Discussion

1. What are the conditions King and others in Birmingham are protesting? How does King respond to the charge that he is an "outside agitator"?

2. What are the four basic steps in a nonviolent action campaign? How were they carried out in Birmingham?

3. How does King use the word *untimely?* How does he prove invalid the charge that the demonstrations are untimely? Explain how "wait" becomes "never."

4. Under what circumstances does King consider breaking the law justified? What precedents does he cite for doing so? Discuss the dichotomy between *just* and *unjust* law and the difference between "*difference* made legal" and "*sameness* made legal."

5. Explain King's claim that "Injustice anywhere is a threat to justice everywhere."

6. Explain the "tension in the mind" that King discusses. How can it "help men to rise from the dark depths of prejudice and racism to the majestic heights of understanding and brotherhood"?

7. King was accused of extremism. Which do you consider more extreme, King's essay or the Declaration of Independence? Justify your answer.

Suggestions for Exploring, Writing, and Persuading

1. Agree or disagree with this statement: If the cause is right or just, I would participate in a boycott, march, or other nonviolent action.

2. Select one of the following quotations from King's letter and agree or disagree with it:

   • History is the long and tragic story of the fact that privileged groups seldom give up their privileges voluntarily.
   • Shallow understanding from people of good will is more frustrating than absolute misunderstanding from people of ill will. Lukewarm acceptance is much more bewildering than outright rejection.

3. Both the Bible and the Declaration of Independence influenced King. In an essay, show how King's letter reflects the ideas and styles of these documents.

4. Analyze the style of this letter, showing how the rhythmic cadences of a sermon, the rhetorical questions, and the metaphors help to make the letter persuasive.

5. Write an essay explaining how poverty can be "an airtight cage."

6. King says that if people's frustrations and contained anger are not released, people will resort to violence, yet he preached nonviolence. Discuss this concept.

7. Argue for or against this statement: Churches and their leaders have a moral responsibility to speak out against hatred and injustice and to speak for love and justice.

Vaclav Havel (b. 1936)

In such plays as The Garden Party *(1963) and* The Memorandum *(1966) and in a provocative collection of essays,* Protocols *(1966), Czech writer Havel, early in his career, angered the ruling Communist party of Czechoslovakia. In 1976, after attending the trial of a nonconformist Czech rock group,* The Plastic People of the Universe, *Havel became more overtly critical of his country's government and took a leading role in founding Charter 77, a loosely organized group of Czech dissidents. Havel's involvement in Charter 77, along with his portraying in his plays and poems the absurd, mechanical conformity of Czech society under communism, led the Czech government to imprison him from 1979 to 1983. After helping to lead the overthrow of Czech communism in the "velvet revolution" of 1989, Havel was elected president of Czechoslovakia, and, in 1993, when Slovakia and the Czech Republic became separate nations, he was elected to the presidency of the Czech Republic and served in that office until 2003. He has been an articulate international spokesman for human rights.*

THE TRIAL (1976)

1   It doesn't often happen and when it does it usually happens when least expected: somewhere, something slips out of joint and suddenly a particular event, because of an unforeseen interplay between its inner premises and more or less fortuitous external circumstances, crosses the threshold of its usual place in the everyday world, breaks through the shell of what it is supposed to be and what it seems, and reveals its innermost symbolic significance. And something originally quite ordinary suddenly casts a surprising light on the time and the world we live in, and dramatically highlights its fundamental questions.

2   On the surface of things, nothing special happened. The trial took place on schedule, lasted as long as it was supposed to, and turned out as intended: with the conviction of the defendants. Yet everything one saw here was clearly and compellingly more than that, so much so that even those who had the least reason to admit it could feel it. This sensation was in the air from the start, and it intensified relentlessly from hour to hour. The strangest thing of all was that nothing could be done about it. Once begun, the game had to be played out, only to reveal, ultimately, how terribly entangled those who started it had become in the web of their own prestige: rather than simply calling a halt and admitting their error, they let this disgraceful spectacle carry on to the end.

3   The players in this spectacle found themselves in a paradoxical situation. The more candidly they played their role, the more clearly they revealed its unpremeditated significance, and thus they gradually became co-creators of a drama utterly different from the one they thought they were playing in, or wanted to play in.

4   What was the public prosecutor originally supposed to have been in this trial? Undoubtedly a plausible spokesman and guardian of society's interests, convincingly demonstrating how offensive, vulgar, immoral, and antisocial the defendants' creative work was.

5   But what did this man become? The symbol of an inflated, narrow-minded power, persecuting everything that does not fit into its sterile notions of life, everything unusual, risky, self-taught, and unbribable,

everything that is too artless and too complex, too accessible and too mysterious, everything in fact that is different from itself. He was a mouthpiece for the world of spiritual manipulation, opportunism, emotional sterility, banality, and moral prudery. In short, he represented the world of the "masters," those masters who for as long as we can remember—whether they spoke in religious, liberal, patriotic, or socialist platitudes—have always tried to turn artists into lackeys, and whom artists have always rebelled against, or at least ridiculed. At the same time this cramped, unimaginative, and humorless man stood cloaked in the garb that "masters" traditionally don when they try to deal with an unclassifiable creative phenomenon: the garb of histrionic disgust at moral degeneration and lack of respect for traditional values.

6   What did Ivan Jirous and his friends in the dock wish to be? Certainly not heroes who, like Dimitrov, would rise from the dock to become prosecutors and condemn the world that was trying to condemn them. I doubt they had any other aim in mind than persuading the court of their innocence and defending their right to compose and sing the songs they wanted. What did the author of the scenario want them to be? Repulsive, long-haired hooligans from the "underworld," as they were treated by the director of Czechoslovak Television, to be rejected in disgust by all serious people.

7   But what did they ultimately become? The unintentional personification of those forces in man that compel him to search for himself, to determine his own place in the world freely, and in his own way, not to make deals with his heart and not to cheat his conscience, to call things by their true names and to penetrate—as Pavel Zajíček said at the trial—to the "deeper level of being," and to do so at one's own risk, aware that at any time one may come up against the disfavor of the "masters," the incomprehension of the dull-witted, or their own limitations.

8   And what, finally, did the presiding judge try to be? My feeling is that at the outset, she simply wanted to be an objective arbiter, listening without prejudice to the arguments of the prosecution and the defense, the testimony of the witnesses and the defendants, and come to a just decision.

9   But what did the trial turn her into? The tragic symbol of a judiciary incapable of maintaining its independence and handing down the kind of verdicts that flow from the human, civil, and legal conscience of the judges; a judiciary fully aware of how it is manipulated by power, but incapable of defying that power and so, ultimately, accepting the pitiful role of a subordinated employee of the "masters."

10   And what was the whole trial meant to be? Obviously no more than an ordinary element in the practice of justice that traditionally converts human lives, actions, and crimes into a boring pile of documents, files, reports, and articles, a routine treatment of one of hundreds of similar crimes. This superficial similarity to ordinary criminal cases, by the way, was maintained for some time. A great deal of time was spent hearing dozens of written and oral eyewitness accounts that dealt at great length with questions such as

whether, at a concert of "The Plastic People of the Universe" in Bojanovice or Postupice, the doors to the hall were open or closed.

11   Soon, however, this facade of judicial thoroughness and objectivity began to appear as a mere smokescreen to hide what the trial really was: an impassioned debate about the meaning of human existence, an urgent questioning of what one should expect from life, whether one should silently accept the world as it is presented to one and slip obediently into one's prearranged place in it, or whether one has the strength to exercise free choice in the matter; whether one should be "reasonable" and take one's place in the world, or whether one has the right to resist in the name of one's own human convictions.

12   For a long time, I sought, without much success, for the best way to characterize this process of "slipping out of joint."

13   Was it depressing? Of course it was: what other feelings could have been aroused when the most humanly authentic impression was made by those who sat in the dock, surrounded by policemen and even taken to the toilet in handcuffs? Or by the fact that the defense lawyers presented an excellent and exhaustive defense, the accused pleaded their innocence convincingly, and the case for the prosecution gradually fell into disarray, all in a situation where—as every one must have known—the accused had already been found guilty long before? And anyway, the whole case was depressing simply because it had slipped out of joint. How could it have been otherwise, when this controversy over the meaning of human life took place here, in the district court for the Prague-West region, and when no one present could do the one thing that was appropriate in this situation: stand up and shout: "Enough of this comedy! Case dismissed!"?

14   Was it moving? Naturally. There were moments when a lump came to one's throat, such as when Svatopluk Karásek said quietly that if Jirous was found guilty, he wanted to be found guilty, too. From the legal point of view, this was obvious nonsense, but at that moment and in those circumstances, it was so humanly right that it told us more in a single second about the essence of the case than a whole pile of official documents.

15   At times it was tense, at times disturbing, at times agonizing (there were moments when one felt like shouting); very often, on the contrary, it flung one back into the world of sheer absurdity.

16   But none of this does justice to the experience. At a deeper level it was, oddly enough, not depressing at all. There was even something elevating about it. This was perhaps because of the very awareness that we were participants in a unique illumination of the world. But chiefly, I suppose, it was the exciting realization that there are still people among us who assume the existential responsibility for their own truth and are willing to pay a high price for it. (Whereas those who judge them can only depend on the collective backing of a colossal social power and would rather send someone to prison for no reason at all than risk even a minor blemish on their record.)

910 Freedom and Responsibility

Somewhere deep down, however, I discerned yet another element in this experience, perhaps the most important of all. It was something that aroused me, a challenge that was all the more urgent for being unintentional. It was the challenge of example. Suddenly, much of the wariness and caution that marks my behavior seemed petty to me. I felt an increased revulsion toward all forms of guile, all attempts at painlessly worming one's way out of vital dilemmas. Suddenly, I discovered in myself more determination in one direction, and more independence in another. Suddenly, I felt disgusted with a whole world, in which—as I realized then—I still have one foot: the world of emergency exits.

18 As we have seen, if a certain event slips out of joint—and if it does so in the deeper sense that I have in mind here—then inevitably something slips out of joint in ourselves, too: a new view of the world gives us a new view of our own human potential, of what we are and might be. Abruptly jerked out of our "routine humanness," we stand once more face to face with the most important question of all: How do we settle accounts with ourselves?

19 I would probably not be writing about this challenging aspect of things at all were I not convinced that it is not simply a product of my tendency to dramatize (for which I am often taken to task, by the way). But it was not. The universality of this feeling was underlined as well by the fact that it seeped out of the hermetically sealed courtroom into the corridors and stairwells of the courthouse. Only the exalting awareness of an important, shared experience, and only the urgency of the challenge that everyone felt in it, could have explained the rapid genesis of that very special, improvised community that came into being here for the duration of the trial, and which was definitely something more than an accidental assembly of friends of the accused and people who were interested in the trial. For instance, a new and quite unusual etiquette appeared: no one bothered with introductions, getting acquainted, or feeling one another out. The usual conventions were dropped and the usual reticence disappeared, and this happened right before the eyes of several squads of those "others" (though they wore no uniforms, they were identifiable at once). Dozens of things were discussed that many of us, in other circumstances, might have been afraid to talk about even with one other person. It was a community of people who were not only more considerate, communicative, and trusting toward each other, they were in a strange way democratic. A distinguished, elderly gentleman, a former member of the praesidium of the Communist Party of Czechoslovakia, spoke with long-haired youths he'd never seen in his life before, and they spoke uninhibitedly with him, though they had known him only from photographs. In this situation, all reserve and inner reticence seemed to lose its point; in this atmosphere, all the inevitable "buts" seemed ridiculous, insignificant, and evasive. Everyone seemed to feel that at a time when all the chips are down, there are only two things one can do: gamble everything, or throw in the cards.

20 On the second day of the trial, when I left the courthouse on Karmelitská Street and walked to the Malá Strana Café (where we all went, us and

the "others"), and I was still so full of impressions that I could scarcely think of anything else, I met a certain Czech film director of the middle generation. When he asked me how I was, I replied, none too logically, that I had just been at a trial of the Czech underground. He asked whether it was about those drugs. I said that it had nothing to do with drugs at all, and I tried, succinctly, to explain the essence of things. When I had finished, he nodded and then said, "Apart from that, what else are you up to?"

21   Perhaps I'm doing him an injustice, but at that moment, I was overwhelmed by an intense feeling that this dear man belonged to a world that I no longer wish to have anything to do with—and Mr. Public Prosecutor Kovařík, pay attention, because here comes a vulgar word—I mean the world of cunning shits.

Questions for Discussion

1. Havel says the trial "turned out as intended: with the conviction of the defendants," and "the accused had already been found guilty long before." What does he mean?

2. Why does Havel call the parties in the trial "players"? Why and how are the prosecutors representative of the "masters"? To what degree are prosecutors the "guardian[s] of society's interests"?

3. Havel says artists have always rebelled against "the masters." Cite examples of such rebellion and of its cost to the artists themselves.

4. Judging from various clues in the essay, what are Ivan Jirous and his band on trial for?

5. In the course of the trial, what do Ivan and his friends come to symbolize?

6. Havel describes the trial at different times as "depressing," "moving," "intense," and "disgusting." Explain why he feels each of these emotions.

7. What does Havel mean by "people who assume the existential responsibility for their own truth and are willing to pay a high price for it"?

8. How did this trial build community among the spectators?

9. What does Havel mean by "the world of emergency exits"?

10. Why was Havel disgusted at the film director he met after the second day of the trial?

Suggestions for Exploring, Writing, and Persuading

1. Havel sums up the trial as being about a fundamental choice:

  . . . whether one should silently accept the world as it is presented to one and slip obediently into one's prearranged place in it, or whether one has the strength to exercise free choice in the matter, whether one should be "reasonable" and take one's place in the world, or whether one has the right to resist in the name of one's own human conscience.

In an essay, explain your position on this issue and give your reasons, supporting them with examples from your own experience.

2. Argue in an essay whether you would be willing to go along with unethical actions in order to preserve your job or position in your community or group.

3. Discuss in detail a situation where you had "one foot" in "the world of emergency exits." Explain how or whether you used an exit and how using it or rejecting it made you feel.

4. Imagine you are the prosecutor or a defendant in the trial Havel is discussing. Write a speech you would present to the judge, arguing your position.

5. From an event in today's news, write an essay showing that "something originally quite ordinary casts a surprising light on the time and the world we live in, and dramatically highlights its fundamental questions."

FICTION

Kurt Vonnegut Jr. (b. 1922)

Kurt Vonnegut Jr., a self-acknowledged pessimist, is one of America's foremost science fiction writers. In his short stories and novels, he satirizes the dilemmas people have created: unimaginably destructive wars, out-of-control technology, pollution, and racism. His most famous novels are Cat's Cradle *(1963), which ends with the freezing of the world, and* Slaughterhouse-Five *(1969), inspired by his experiences as a prisoner of war in Germany during the Dresden bombings. Vonnegut's novel* Timequake *(1999), and an autobiography,* Fates Worse Than Death *(1991), are his latest works. Vonnegut also writes essays, plays, and television adaptations of his works. He is a popular speaker on college campuses, where he challenges students to become critical thinkers.*

HARRISON BERGERON   (1961)

1   The year was 2081, and everybody was finally equal. They weren't only equal before God and the law. They were equal every which way. Nobody was smarter than anybody else. Nobody was better looking than anybody

else. Nobody was stronger or quicker than anybody else. All this equality was due to the 211th, 212th, and 213th Amendments to the Constitution, and to the unceasing vigilance of agents of the United States Handicapper General.

2   Some things about living still weren't quite right, though. April, for instance, still drove people crazy by not being springtime. And it was in that clammy month that the H-G men took George and Hazel Bergeron's fourteen-year-old son, Harrison, away.

3   It was tragic, all right, but George and Hazel couldn't think about it very hard. Hazel had a perfectly average intelligence, which meant she couldn't think about anything except in short bursts. And George, while his intelligence was way above normal, had a little mental handicap radio in his ear. He was required by law to wear it at all times. It was tuned to a government transmitter. Every twenty seconds or so, the transmitter would send out some sharp noise to keep people like George from taking unfair advantage of their brains.

4   George and Hazel were watching television. There were tears on Hazel's cheeks, but she'd forgotten for the moment what they were about.

5   On the television screen were ballerinas.

6   A buzzer sounded in George's head. His thoughts fled in panic, like bandits from a burglar alarm.

7   "That was a really pretty dance, that dance they just did," said Hazel.

8   "Huh?" said George.

9   "That dance—it was nice," said Hazel.

10   "Yup," said George. He tried to think a little about the ballerinas. They weren't really very good—no better than anybody else would have been, anyway. They were burdened with sashweights and bags of birdshot, and their faces were masked, so that no one, seeing a free and graceful gesture or a pretty face, would feel like something the cat drug in. George was toying with the vague notion that maybe dancers shouldn't be handicapped. But he didn't get very far with it before another noise in his ear radio scattered his thoughts.

11   George winced. So did two out of the eight ballerinas.

12   Hazel saw him wince. Having no mental handicap herself, she had to ask George what the latest sound had been.

13   "Sounded like somebody hitting a milk bottle with a ball peen hammer," said George.

14   "I'd think it would be real interesting, hearing all the different sounds," said Hazel, a little envious. "All the things they think up."

15   "Um," said George.

16   "Only, if I was Handicapper General, you know what I would do?" said Hazel. Hazel, as a matter of fact, bore a strong resemblance to the Handicapper General, a woman named Diana Moon Glampers. "If I was Diana Moon Glampers," said Hazel, "I'd have chimes on Sunday—just chimes. Kind of in honor of religion."

17   "I could think, if it was just chimes," said George.

18   "Well—maybe make 'em real loud," said Hazel. "I think I'd make a good Handicapper General."

19   "Good as anybody else," said George.

20   "Who knows better'n I do what normal is?" said Hazel.

21   "Right," said George. He began to think glimmeringly about his abnormal son who was now in jail, about Harrison, but a twenty-one-gun salute in his head stopped that.

22   "Boy!" said Hazel, "that was a doozy, wasn't it?"

23   It was such a doozy that George was white and trembling, and tears stood on the rims of his red eyes. Two of the eight ballerinas had collapsed to the studio floor, were holding their temples.

24   "All of a sudden you look so tired," said Hazel. "Why don't you stretch out on the sofa, so's you can rest your handicap bag on the pillows, honeybunch." She was referring to the forty-seven pounds of birdshot in a canvas bag, which was padlocked around George's neck. "Go on and rest the bag for a little while," she said. "I don't care if you're not equal to me for a while."

25   George weighed the bag with his hands. "I don't mind it," he said. "I don't notice it any more. It's just a part of me."

26   "You been so tired lately—kind of wore out," said Hazel. "If there was just some way we could make a little hole in the bottom of the bag, and just take out a few of them lead balls. Just a few."

27   "Two years in prison and two thousand dollars fine for every ball I took out," said George. "I don't call that a bargain."

28   "If you could just take a few out when you came home from work," said Hazel. "I mean—you don't compete with anybody around here. You just set around."

29   "If I tried to get away with it," said George, "then other people'd get away with it—and pretty soon we'd be right back to the dark ages again, with everybody competing against everybody else. You wouldn't like that, would you?"

30   "I'd hate it," said Hazel.

31   "There you are," said George. "The minute people start cheating on laws, what do you think happens to society?"

32   If Hazel hadn't been able to come up with an answer to this question, George couldn't have supplied one. A siren was going off in his head.

33   "Reckon it'd fall all apart," said Hazel.

34   "What would?" said George blankly.

35   "Society," said Hazel uncertainly. "Wasn't that what you just said?"

36   "Who knows?" said George.

37   The television program was suddenly interrupted for a news bulletin. It wasn't clear at first as to what the bulletin was about, since the announcer, like all announcers, had a serious speech impediment. For about half a minute, and in a state of high excitement, the announcer tried to say, "Ladies and gentlemen—"

38   He finally gave up, handed the bulletin to a ballerina to read.

39 "That's all right—" Hazel said of the announcer, "he tried. That's the big thing. He tried to do the best he could with what God gave him. He should get a nice raise for trying so hard."

40 "Ladies and gentlemen—" said the ballerina, reading the bulletin. She must have been extraordinarily beautiful, because the mask she wore was hideous. And it was easy to see that she was the strongest and most graceful of all the dancers, for her handicap bags were as big as those worn by two-hundred-pound men.

41 And she had to apologize at once for her voice, which was a very unfair voice for a woman to use. Her voice was a warm, luminous, timeless melody. "Excuse me—" she said, and she began again, making her voice absolutely uncompetitive.

42 "Harrison Bergeron, age fourteen," she said in a grackle squawk, "has just escaped from jail, where he was held on suspicion of plotting to overthrow the government. He is a genius and an athlete, is underhandicapped, and should be regarded as extremely dangerous."

43 A police photograph of Harrison Bergeron was flashed on the screen—upside down, then sideways, upside down again, then right side up. The picture showed the full length of Harrison against a background calibrated in feet and inches. He was exactly seven feet tall.

44 The rest of Harrison's appearance was Halloween and hardware. Nobody had ever borne heavier handicaps. He had outgrown hindrances faster than the H-G men could think them up. Instead of a little ear radio for a mental handicap, he wore a tremendous pair of earphones, and spectacles with thick wavy lenses. The spectacles were intended to make him not only half blind, but to give him whanging headaches besides.

45 Scrap metal was hung all over him. Ordinarily, there was a certain symmetry, a military neatness to the handicaps issued to strong people, but Harrison looked like a walking junkyard. In the race of life, Harrison carried three hundred pounds.

46 And to offset his good looks, the H-G men required that he wear at all times a red rubber ball for a nose, keep his eyebrows shaved off, and cover his even white teeth with black caps at snaggle-tooth random.

47 "If you see this boy," said the ballerina, "do not—I repeat, do not—try to reason with him."

48 There was the shriek of a door being torn from its hinges.

49 Screams and barking cries of consternation came from the television set. The photograph of Harrison Bergeron on the screen jumped again and again, as though dancing to the tune of an earthquake.

50 George Bergeron correctly identified the earthquake, and well he might have—for many was the time his own home had danced to the same crashing tune. "My God—" said George, "that must be Harrison."

51 The realization was blasted from his mind instantly by the sound of an automobile collision in his head.

52 When George could open his eyes again, the photograph of Harrison was gone. A living, breathing Harrison filled the screen.

53   Clanking, clownish, and huge, Harrison stood in the center of the studio. The knob of the uprooted studio door was still in his hand. Ballerinas, technicians, musicians, and announcers cowered on their knees before him, expecting to die.

54   "I am the Emperor!" cried Harrison. "Do you hear? I am the Emperor! Everybody must do what I say at once!" He stamped his foot and the studio shook.

55   "Even as I stand here—" he bellowed, "crippled, hobbled, sickened— I am a greater ruler than any man who ever lived! Now watch me become what I *can* become!"

56   Harrison tore the straps of his handicap harness like wet tissue paper, tore straps guaranteed to support five thousand pounds.

57   Harrison's scrap-iron handicaps crashed to the floor.

58   Harrison thrust his thumbs under the bar of the padlock that secured his head harness. The bar snapped like celery. Harrison smashed his headphones and spectacles against the wall.

59   He flung away his rubber-ball nose, revealed a man that would have awed Thor, the god of thunder.

60   "I shall now select my Empress!" he said, looking down on the cowering people. "Let the first woman who dares rise to her feet claim her mate and her throne!"

61   A moment passed, and then a ballerina arose, swaying like a willow.

62   Harrison plucked the mental handicap from her ear, snapped off her physical handicaps with marvellous delicacy. Last of all, he removed her mask.

63   She was blindingly beautiful.

64   "Now—" said Harrison, taking her hand, "shall we show the people the meaning of the word dance? Music!" he commanded.

65   The musicians scrambled back into their chairs, and Harrison stripped them of their handicaps, too. "Play your best," he told them, "and I'll make you barons and dukes and earls."

66   The music began. It was normal at first—cheap, silly, false. But Harrison snatched two musicians from their chairs, waved them like batons as he sang the music as he wanted it played. He slammed them back into their chairs.

67   The music began again and was much improved.

68   Harrison and his Empress merely listened to the music for a while— listened gravely, as though synchronizing their heartbeats with it.

69   They shifted their weights to their toes.

70   Harrison placed his big hands on the girl's tiny waist, letting her sense the weightlessness that would soon be hers.

71   And then, in an explosion of joy and grace, into the air they sprang!

72   Not only were the laws of the land abandoned, but the law of gravity and the laws of motion as well.

73   They reeled, whirled, swiveled, flounced, capered, gamboled, and spun.

74   They leaped like deer on the moon.

75   The studio ceiling was thirty feet high, but each leap brought the dancers nearer to it.

76   It became their obvious intention to kiss the ceiling.

77   They kissed it.

78   And then, neutralizing gravity with love and pure will, they remained suspended in air inches below the ceiling, and they kissed each other for a long, long time.

79   It was then that Diana Moon Glampers, the Handicapper General, came into the studio with a double-barreled ten-gauge shotgun. She fired twice, and the Emperor and the Empress were dead before they hit the floor.

80   Diana Moon Glampers loaded the gun again. She aimed it at the musicians and told them they had ten seconds to get their handicaps back on.

81   It was then that the Bergerons' television tube burned out.

82   Hazel turned to comment about the blackout to George. But George had gone out into the kitchen for a can of beer.

83   George came back in with the beer, paused while a handicap signal shook him up. And then he sat down again. "You been crying?" he said to Hazel.

84   "Yup," she said.

85   "What about?" he said.

86   "I forget," she said. "Something real sad on television."

87   "What was it?" he said.

88   "It's all kind of mixed up in my mind," said Hazel.

89   "Forget sad things," said George.

90   "I always do," said Hazel.

91   "That's my girl," said George. He winced. There was the sound of a rivetting gun in his head.

92   "Gee—I could tell that one was a doozy," said Hazel.

93   "You can say that again," said George.

94   "Gee—" said Hazel, "I could tell that one was a doozy."

Questions for Discussion

1. Why is it significant that the same thing happens every normal day?

2. What is Vonnegut saying about equality as a viable ideal?

3. What are the effects of enforced equality in this story? What is lost in this society because of enforced equality?

4. Discuss the symbolic importance of the television's going black.

5. What is the effect of seeing the story through George's and Hazel's eyes? How would the story be different if told from Harrison's point of view?

6. Why are the ballerina's numerous handicaps significant? What might her "mask" symbolize? Why does she continue "dancing" in spite of all her burdens? Explain why the kiss at the ceiling is an important symbol.

7. Think about the kinds of handicaps Harrison wears that diminish his natural talents. How might such handicaps relate to prejudice?

8. What is the significance of Hazel's repeating herself at the end of the story?

Suggestions for Exploring, Writing, and Persuading

1. Discuss current trends in education or society that parallel the kind of equality established in this story.

2. Write an essay explaining what effect 213 amendments would have on the U.S. Constitution.

3. The society of "Harrison Bergeron" extends to its logical conclusion Jefferson's premise that "all men are created equal." In what ways does the society described in this story violate other principles enunciated in the Declaration of Independence?

4. Write an essay comparing George and Harrison.

5. George Bergeron says, "'The minute people start cheating on laws, what do you think happens to society?'" Hazel responds, "'Reckon it'd fall all apart.'" Argue for or against Hazel's assessment.

6. "Harrison Bergeron" makes a statement about the clash between equality and competition. In an essay, discuss the conflict between equality and competition in a free society.

7. What does Diana symbolize? What does her leadership say about tyranny? Consider, too, the other kinds of tyranny exercised in this story. What about the tyranny of television? Of technology? Of ignorance? Write an essay about Diana or about a modern tyranny.

Philip K. Dick (1928–1982)

A prolific writer of novels and short stories, primarily in the field of science fiction, Philip K. Dick died before his reputation reached its peak. In one five-year period during his lifetime beginning in 1959, Dick published sixteen novels and was awarded the Hugo Award. Since his death in 1982, readers have become even more fascinated by his philosophically intriguing future worlds. As a result, many of his stories and novels have been made into movies. In 1982, his novel Blade Runner *was made into a movie staring Harrison Ford. His short story "We Can Remember It for You Wholesale" was adapted into the 1990 movie* Total Recall; *and in 2002, Tom Cruise starred in* Minority Report, *the movie adaptation of the story included here. A 2005 production of Dick's* A Scanner Darkly *has been announced.*

MINORITY REPORT   (1956)

1   THE
first thought Anderton had when he saw the young man was: *I'm getting bald. Bald and fat and old.* But he didn't say it aloud. Instead, he pushed back his chair, got to his feet, and came resolutely around the side of his desk, his right hand rigidly extended. Smiling with forced amiability, he shook hands with the young man.

2   "Witwer?" he asked, managing to make this query sound gracious.

3   "That's right," the young man said. "But the name's Ed to you, of course. That is, if you share my dislike for needless formality." The look on his blond, overly-confident face showed that he considered the matter settled. It would be Ed and John: Everything would be agreeably cooperative right from the start.

4   "Did you have much trouble finding the building?" Anderton asked guardedly, ignoring the too-friendly overture. *Good God, he had to hold on to something.* Fear touched him and he began to sweat. Witwer was moving around the office as if he already owned it—as if he were measuring it for size. Couldn't he wait a couple of days—a decent interval?

5   "No trouble," Witwer answered blithely, his hands in his pockets. Eagerly, he examined the voluminous files that lined the wall. "I'm not coming into your agency blind, you understand. I have quite a few ideas of my own about the way Precrime is run."

6   Shakily, Anderton lit his pipe. "How is it run? I should like to know."

7   "Not badly," Witwer said. "In fact, quite well."

8   Anderton regarded him steadily. "Is that your private opinion? Or is it just cant?"

9   Witwer met his gaze guilelessly. "Private and public. The Senate's pleased with your work. In fact, they're enthusiastic." He added, "As enthusiastic as very old men can be."

10   Anderton winced, but outwardly he remained impassive. It cost him an effort, though. He wondered what Witwer *really* thought. What was actually going on in that closecropped skull? The young man's eyes were blue, bright—and disturbingly clever. Witwer was nobody's fool. And obviously he had a great deal of ambition.

11   "As I understand it," Anderton said cautiously, "you're going to be my assistant until I retire."

12   "That's my understanding, too," the other replied, without an instant's hesitation.

13   "Which may be this year, or next year—or ten years from now." The pipe in Anderton's hand trembled. "I'm under no compulsion to retire. I founded Precrime and I can stay on here as long as I want. It's purely *my* decision."

14   Witwer nodded, his expression still guileless. "Of course."

15   With an effort, Anderton cooled down a trifle. "I merely wanted to get things straight."

16   "From the start," Witwer agreed. "You're the boss. What you say goes." With every evidence of sincerity, he asked: "Would you care to show me the organization? I'd like to familiarize myself with the general routine as soon as possible."

17   As they walked along the busy, yellowlit tiers of offices, Anderton said: "You're acquainted with the theory of precrime, of course. I presume we can take that for granted."

18   "I have the information publicly available," Witwer replied. "With the aid of your precog mutants, you've boldly and successfully abolished the postcrime punitive system of jails and fines. As we all realize, punishment was never much of a deterrent, and could scarcely have afforded comfort to a victim already dead."

19   They had come to the descent lift. As it carried them swiftly downward, Anderton said: "You've probably grasped the basic legalistic drawback to precrime methodology. We're taking in individuals who have broken no law."

20   "But they surely will," Witwer affirmed with conviction.

21   "Happily they *don't*—because we get them first, before they can commit an act of violence. So the commission of the crime itself is absolute metaphysics. We claim they're culpable. They, on the other hand, eternally claim they're innocent. And, in a sense, they *are* innocent."

22   The lift let them out, and they again paced down a yellow corridor. "In our society we have no major crimes." Anderton went on, "but we do have a detention camp full of would-be criminals."

23   Doors opened and closed, and they were in the analytical wing. Ahead of them rose impressive banks of equipment—the data-receptors, and the computing mechanisms that studied and restructured the incoming material. And beyond the machinery sat the three precogs, almost lost to view in the maze of wiring.

24   "There they are," Anderton said dryly. "What do you think of them?"

25   In the gloomy half-darkness the three idiots sat babbling. Every incoherent utterance, every random syllable, was analyzed, compared, reassembled in the form of visual symbols, transcribed on conventional punchcards, and ejected into various coded slots. All day long the idiots babbled, imprisoned in their special high-backed chairs, held in one rigid position by metal bands, and bundles of wiring, clamps. Their physical needs were taken care of automatically. They had no spiritual needs. Vegetable-like, they muttered and dozed and existed. Their minds were dull, confused, lost in shadows.

26   But not the shadows of today. The three gibbering, fumbling creatures, with their enlarged heads and wasted bodies, were contemplating the future. The analytical machinery was recording prophecies, and as the three precog idiots talked, the machinery carefully listened.

27   For the first time Witwer's face lost its breezy confidence. A sick, dismayed expression crept into his eyes, a mixture of shame and moral shock. "It's not—pleasant," he murmured. "I didn't realize they were so—" He groped in his mind for the right word, gesticulating. "So—deformed."

28   "Deformed and retarded," Anderton instantly agreed. "Especially the girl, there. Donna is forty-five years old. But she looks about ten. The talent absorbs everything; the esp-lobe shrivels the balance of the frontal area. But what do we care? We get their prophecies. They pass on what we need. They don't understand any of it, but *we* do."

29   Subdued, Witwer crossed the room to the machinery. From a slot he collected a stack of cards. "Are these names that have come up?" he asked.

30   "Obviously." Frowning, Anderton took the stack from him. "I haven't had a chance to examine them," he explained, impatiently concealing his annoyance.

31   Fascinated, Witwer watched the machinery pop a fresh card into the now empty slot. It was followed by a second—and a third. From the whirring disks came one card after another. "The precogs must see quite far into the future," Witwer exclaimed.

32   "They see a quite limited span," Anderton informed him. "One week or two ahead at the very most. Much of their data is worthless to us— simply not relevant to our line. We pass it on to the appropriate agencies. And they in turn trade data with us. Every important bureau has its cellar of treasured *monkeys*."

33   "Monkeys?" Witwer stared at him uneasily. "Oh, yes, I understand. See no evil, speak no evil, et cetera. Very amusing."

34   "Very *apt*." Automatically, Anderton collected the fresh cards which had been turned up by the spinning machinery. "Some of these names will be totally discarded. And most of the remainder record petty crimes: thefts, income tax evasion, assault, extortion. As I'm sure you know, Precrime has cut down felonies by ninety-nine and decimal point eight percent. We seldom get actual murder or treason. After all, the culprit knows we'll confine him in the detention camp a week before he gets a chance to commit the crime."

35   "When was the last time an actual murder was committed?" Witwer asked.

36   "Five years ago," Anderton said, pride in his voice.

37   "How did it happen?"

38   "The criminal escaped our teams. We had his name—in fact, we had all the details of the crime, including the victim's name. We knew the exact moment, the location of the planned act of violence. But in spite of us he was able to carry it out." Anderton shrugged. "After all, we can't get all of them." He riffled the cards. "But we do get most."

39   "One murder in five years." Witwer's confidence was returning. "Quite an impressive record...something to be proud of."

40   Quietly Anderton said: "I *am* proud. Thirty years ago I worked out the theory—back in the days when the self-seekers were thinking in terms of quick raids on the stock market. I saw something legitimate ahead— something of tremendous social value."

41   He tossed the packet of cards to Wally Page, his subordinate in charge of the monkey block. "See which ones we want," he told him. "Use your own judgment."

42   As Page disappeared with the cards, Witwer said thoughtfully: "It's a big responsibility."

43   "Yes, it is," agreed Anderton. "If we let one criminal escape—as we did five years ago—we've got a human life on our conscience. We're solely responsible. If we slip up, somebody dies." Bitterly, he jerked three new cards from the slot. "It's a public trust."

44   "Are you ever tempted to—" Witwer hesitated. "I mean, some of the men you pick up must offer you plenty."

45   "It wouldn't do any good. A duplicate file of cards pops out at Army GHQ. It's check and balance. They can keep their eye on us as continuously as they wish." Anderton glanced briefly at the top card. "So even if we wanted to accept a—"

46   He broke off, his lips tightening.

47   "What's the matter?" Witwer asked curiously.

48   Carefully, Anderton folded up the top card and put it away in his pocket. "Nothing," he muttered. "Nothing at all."

49   The harshness in his voice brought a flush to Witwer's face. "You really don't like me," he observed.

50   "True," Anderton admitted. "I don't. But—"

51   He couldn't believe he disliked the young man that much. It didn't seem possible: it *wasn't* possible. Something was wrong. Dazed, he tried to steady his tumbling mind.

52   On the card was his name. Line one—an already accused future murderer! According to the coded punches, Precrime Commissioner John A. Anderton was going to kill a man—and within the next week.

53   With absolute, overwhelming conviction, he didn't believe it.

54   I N the outer office, talking to Page, stood Anderton's slim and attractive young wife, Lisa. She was engaged in a sharp, animated discussion of policy, and barely glanced up as Witwer and her husband entered.

55   "Hello, darling," Anderton said.

56   Witwer remained silent. But his pale eyes flickered slightly as they rested on the brown-haired woman in her trim police uniform. Lisa was now an executive official of Precrime but once, Witwer knew, she had been Anderton's secretary.

57   Noticing the interest on Witwer's face Anderton paused and reflected. To plant the card in the machines would require an accomplice on the inside—someone who was closely connected with Precrime and had access to the analytical equipment. Lisa was an improbable element. But the possibility did exist.

58   Of course, the conspiracy could be large-scale and elaborate, involving far more than a "rigged" card inserted somewhere along the line. The original data itself might have been tampered with. Actually, there was no telling how far back the alteration went. A cold fear touched him as he began to see the possibilities. His original impulse—to tear open the

machines and remove all the data—was uselessly primitive. Probably the tapes agreed with the card: He would only incriminate himself further.

59   He had approximately twenty-four hours. Then, the Army people would check over their cards and discover the discrepancy. They would find in their files a duplicate of the card he had appropriated. He had only one of two copies, which meant that the folded card in his pocket might just as well be lying on Page's desk in plain view of everyone.

60   From outside the building came the drone of police cars starting out on their routine round-ups. How many hours would elapse before one of them pulled up in front of *his* house?

61   "What's the matter, darling?" Lisa asked him uneasily. "You look as if you've just seen a ghost. Are you all right?"

62   "I'm fine," he assured her.

63   Lisa suddenly seemed to become aware of Ed Witwer's admiring scrutiny. "Is this gentleman your new co-worker, darling?" she asked.

64   Warily, Anderton introduced his new associate. Lisa smiled in friendly greeting.

65   Did a covert awareness pass between them? He couldn't tell. God, he was beginning to suspect everybody—not only his wife and Witwer, but a dozen members of his staff.

66   "Are you from New York?" Lisa asked.

67   "No," Witwer replied. "I've lived most of my life in Chicago. I'm staying at a hotel—one of the big downtown hotels. Wait—I have the name written on a card somewhere."

68   While he self-consciously searched his pockets, Lisa suggested: "Perhaps you'd like to have dinner with us. We'll be working in close cooperation, and I really think we ought to get better acquainted."

69   Startled, Anderton backed off. What were the chances of his wife's friendliness being benign, accidental? Witwer would be present the balance of the evening, and would now have an excuse to trail along to Anderton's private residence. Profoundly disturbed, he turned impulsively, and moved toward the door.

70   "Where are you going?" Lisa asked, astonished.

71   "Back to the monkey block," he told her "I want to check over some rather puzzling data tapes before the Army sees them." He was out in the corridor before she could think of a plausible reason for detaining him.

72   Rapidly, he made his way to the ramp at its far end. He was striding down the outside stairs toward the public sidewalk, when Lisa appeared breathlessly behind him.

73   "What on earth has come over you?" Catching hold of his arm, she moved quickly in front of him. "I *knew* you were leaving," she exclaimed, blocking his way. "What's wrong with you? Everybody thinks you're—" She checked herself. "I mean, you're acting so erratically."

74   People surged by them—the usual afternoon crowd. Ignoring them, Anderton pried his wife's fingers from his arm. "I'm getting out," he told her. "While there's still time."

75   "But...why?"

76   "I'm being framed—deliberately and maliciously. This creature is out to get my job. The Senate is getting at me *through* him."

77   Lisa gazed up at him, bewildered. "But he seems like such a nice young man."

78   "Nice as a water moccasin."

79   Lisa's dismay turned to disbelief. "I don't believe it. Darling, all this strain you've been under—" Smiling uncertainly, she faltered: "It's not really credible that Ed Witwer is trying to frame you. How could he, even if he wanted to? Surely Ed wouldn't—"

80   "Ed?"

81   "That's his name, isn't it?"

82   Her brown eyes flashed in startled, wildly incredulous protest. "Good heavens, you're suspicious of everybody. You actually believe I'm mixed up with it in some way, don't you?"

83   He considered. "I'm not sure."

84   She drew closer to him, her eyes accusing. "That's not true. You really believe it. Maybe you *ought* to go away for a few weeks. You desperately need a rest. All this tension and trauma, a younger man coming in. You're acting paranoiac. Can't you see that? People plotting against you. Tell me, do you have any actual proof?"

85   Anderton removed his wallet and took out the folded card. "Examine this carefully," he said, handing it to her.

86   The color drained out of her face, and she gave a little harsh, dry gasp.

87   "The set-up is fairly obvious," Anderton told her, as levelly as he could. "This will give Witwer a legal pretext to remove me right now. He won't have to wait until I resign." Grimly, he added: "They know I'm good for a few years yet."

88   "But—"

89   "It will end the check and balance system. Precrime will no longer be an independent agency. The Senate will control the police, and after that—" His lips tightened. "They'll absorb the Army too. Well, it's out-wardly logical enough. *Of course* I feel hostility and resentment toward Witwer—*of course* I have a motive.

90   "Nobody likes to be replaced by a younger man, and find himself turned out to pasture. It's all really quite plausible—except that I haven't the remotest intention of killing Witwer. But I can't prove that. So what can I do?"

91   Mutely, her face very white, Lisa shook her head. "I—I don't know. Darling, if only—"

92   "Right now," Anderton said abruptly, "I'm going home to pack my things. That's about as far ahead as I can plan."

93   "You're really going to—to try to hide out?"

94   "I am. As far as the Centaurian-colony planets, if necessary. It's been done successfully before, and I have a twenty-four-hour start." He turned resolutely. "Go back inside. There's no point in your coming with me."

95   "Did you imagine I would?" Lisa asked huskily.

96   Startled, Anderton stared at her. "Wouldn't you?" Then with amazement, he murmured: "No, I can see you don't believe me. You still think I'm imagining all this." He jabbed savagely at the card. "Even with that evidence you still aren't convinced."

97   "No," Lisa agreed quickly, "I'm not. You didn't look at it closely enough, darling. Ed Witwer's name isn't on it."

98   Incredulous, Anderton took the card from her.

99   "Nobody says you're going to kill Ed Witwer," Lisa continued rapidly, in a thin, brittle voice. "The card *must* be genuine, understand? And it has nothing to do with Ed. He's not plotting against you and neither is anybody else."

100   Too confused to reply, Anderton stood studying the card. She was right. Ed Witwer was not listed as his victim. On line five, the machine had neatly stamped another name.

LEOPOLO KAPLAN

101   Numbly, he pocketed the card. He had never heard of the man in his life.

102   T H E house was cool and deserted, and almost immediately Anderton began making preparations for his journey. While he packed, frantic thoughts passed through his mind.

103   Possibly he was wrong about Witwer—but how could he be sure? In any event, the conspiracy against him was far more complex than he had realized. Witwer, in the over-all picture, might be merely an insignificant puppet animated by someone else—by some distant, indistinct figure only vaguely visible in the background.

104   It had been a mistake to show the card to Lisa. Undoubtedly, she would describe it in detail to Witwer. He'd never get off Earth, never have an opportunity to find out what life on a frontier planet might be like.

105   While he was thus preoccupied, a board creaked behind him. He turned from the bed, clutching a weather-stained winter sports jacket, to face the muzzle of a gray-blue A-pistol.

106   "It didn't take you long," he said, staring with bitterness at the tight-lipped, heavyset man in a brown overcoat who stood holding the gun in his gloved hand. "Didn't she even hesitate?"

107   The intruder's face registered no response. "I don't know what you're talking about," he said. "Come along with me."

108   Startled, Anderton laid down the sports jacket. "You're not from my agency? You're not a police officer?"

109   Protesting and astonished, he was hustled outside the house to a waiting limousine. Instantly three heavily armed men closed in behind him. The door slammed and the car shot off down the highway, away from the

city. Impassive and remote, the faces around him jogged with the motion of the speeding vehicle as open fields, dark and somber, swept past.

110   Anderton was till trying futilely to grasp the implications of what had happened, when the car came to a rutted side road, turned off, and descended into a gloomy sub-surface garage. Someone shouted an order. The heavy metal lock grated shut and overhead lights blinked on. The driver turned off the car motor.

111   "You'll have reason to regret this," Anderton warned hoarsely, as they dragged him from the car. "Do you realize who I am?"

112   "We realize," the man in the brown overcoat said.

113   At gun-point, Anderton was marched upstairs, from the clammy silence of the garage into a deep-carpeted hallway. He was apparently, in a luxurious private residence, set out in the war-devoured rural area. At the far end of the hallway he could make out a room—a book-lined study simply but tastefully furnished. In a circle of lamplight, his face partly in shadows, a man he had never met sat waiting for him.

114   As Anderton approached, the man nervously slipped a pair of rimless glasses in place, snapped the case shut, and moistened his dry lips. He was elderly, perhaps seventy or older, and under his arm was a slim silver cane. His body was thin, wiry, his attitude curiously rigid. What little hair he had was dusty brown—a carefully-smoothed sheen of neutral color above his pale, bony skull. Only his eyes seemed really alert.

115   "Is this Anderton?" he inquired querulously, turning to the man in the brown overcoat. "Where did you pick him up?"

116   "At his home," the other replied. "He was packing—as we expected."

117   The man at the desk shivered visibly. "Packing." He took off his glasses and jerkily returned them to their case. "Look here," he said bluntly to Anderton, "what's the matter with you? Are you hopelessly insane? How could you kill a man you've never met?"

118   The old man, Anderton suddenly realized was Leopold Kaplan.

119   "First, I'll ask you a question," Anderton countered rapidly. "Do you realize what you've done? I'm Commissioner of Police. I can have you sent up for twenty years."

120   He was going to say more, But a sudden wonder cut him short.

121   "*How did you find out?*" he demanded. Involuntarily, his hand went to his pocket, where the folded card was hidden. "It won't be for another—"

122   "I wasn't notified through your agency," Kaplan broke in, with angry impatience. "The fact that you've never heard of me doesn't surprise me too much. Leopold Kaplan, General of the Army of the Federated West-bloc Alliance." Begrudgingly, he added. "Retired, since the end of the Anglo-Chinese War, and the abolishment of AFWA."

123   It made sense. Anderton had suspected that the Army processed its duplicate cards immediately, for its own protection. Relaxing somewhat, he demanded: "Well? You've got me here. What next?"

124   "Evidently," Kaplan said, "I'm not going to have you destroyed, or it would have shown up on one of those miserable little cards. I'm curious

about you. It seemed incredible to me that a man of your stature could contemplate the cold-blooded murder of a total stranger. There must be something more here. Frankly, I'm puzzled. If it represented some kind of Police strategy—" He shrugged his thin shoulders. "Surely you wouldn't have permitted the duplicate card to reach us."

125 "Unless," one of his men suggested, "it's a deliberate plant."

126 Kaplan raised his bright, bird-like eyes and scrutinized Anderton. "What do you have to say?"

127 "That's exactly what it is," Anderton said, quick to see the advantage of stating frankly what he believed to be the simple truth. "The prediction on the card was deliberately fabricated by a clique inside the police agency. The card is prepared and I'm netted. I'm relieved of my authority automatically. My assistant steps in and claims he prevented the murder in the usual efficient Precrime manner. Needless to say, there is no murder or intent to murder."

128 "I agree with you that there will be no murder," Kaplan affirmed grimly. "You'll be in police custody. I intend to make certain of that."

129 Horrified, Anderton protested: "You're taking me back there? If I'm in custody, I'll never be able to prove—"

130 "I don't care what you prove or don't prove," Kaplan interrupted. "All I'm interested in is having you out of the way." Frigidly, he added: "For my own protection."

131 "He was getting ready to leave," one of the men asserted.

132 "That's right," Anderton said, sweating. "As soon as they get hold of me I'll be confined in the detention camp. Witwer will take over—lock, stock and barrel." His face darkened. "And my wife. They're acting in concert, apparently."

133 For a moment Kaplan seemed to waver. "It's possible," he conceded, regarding Anderton steadily. Then he shook his head. "I can't take the chance. If this is a frame against you. I'm sorry. But it's simply not my affair." He smiled slightly. "However, I wish you luck." To the men he said: "Take him to the police building and turn him over to the highest authority." He mentioned the name of the acting commissioner, and waited for Anderton's reaction.

134 "Witwer!" Anderton echoed, incredulous.

135 Still smiling slightly, Kaplan turned and clicked on the console radio in the study. "Witwer has already assumed authority. Obviously, he's going to create quite an affair out of this."

136 There was a brief static hum, and then, abruptly, the radio blared out into the room—a noisy professional voice, reading a prepared announcement.

137 "...all citizens are warned not to shelter or in any fashion aid or assist this dangerous marginal individual. The extraordinary circumstance of an escaped criminal at liberty and in a position to commit an act of violence is unique in modern times. All citizens are hereby notified that legal statues still in force implicate any and all persons failing to cooperate fully with the police in their task of apprehending John Allison Anderton.

To repeat: The Precrime Agency of the Federal Westbloc Government is in the process of locating and neutralizing its former Commissioner, John Allison Anderton, who, through the methodology of the precrime-system, is hereby declared a potential murderer and as such forfeits his rights to freedom and all its privileges."

138   "It didn't take him long," Anderton muttered, appalled. Kaplan snapped off the radio and the voice vanished.

139   "Lisa must have gone directly to him," Anderton speculated bitterly.

140   "Why should he wait?" Kaplan asked. "You made your intentions clear."

141   He nodded to his men. "Take him back to town. I feel uneasy having him so close. In that respect I concur with Commissioner Witwer. I want him neutralized as soon as possible."

142   COLD
light rain beat against the pavement, as the car moved through the dark streets of New York City toward the police building.

143   "You can see his point," one of the men said to Anderton. "If you were in his place you'd act just as decisively."

144   Sullen and resentful, Anderton stared straight ahead.

145   "Anyhow," the man went on, "you're just one of many. Thousands of people have gone to that detention camp. You won't be lonely. As a matter of fact, you may not want to leave."

146   Helplessly, Anderton watched pedestrians hurrying along the rain-swept side-walks. He felt no strong emotion. He was aware only of an overpowering fatigue. Dully, he checked off the street numbers: they were getting near the police station.

147   "This Witwer seems to know how to take advantage of an opportunity," one of the men observed conversationally. "Did you ever meet him?"

148   "Briefly," Anderton answered.

149   "He wanted your job—so he framed you. Are you sure of that?"

150   Anderton grimaced. "Does it matter?"

151   "I was just curious." The man eyed him languidly. "So you're the ex-Commissioner of Police. People in the camp will be glad to see you coming. They'll remember you."

152   "No doubt," Anderton agreed.

153   "Witwer sure didn't waste any time.

154   "Kaplan's lucky—with an official like that in charge." The man looked at Anderton almost pleadingly. "You're really convinced it's a plot, eh?"

155   "Of course."

156   "You wouldn't harm a hair of Kaplan's head? For the first time in history, Precrime goes wrong? An innocent man is framed by one of those cards. Maybe there've been other innocent people—right?"

157   "It's quite possible," Anderton admitted listlessly.

158   "Maybe the whole system can break down. Sure, you're not going to commit a murder—and maybe none of them were. Is that why you told Kaplan you wanted to keep yourself outside? Were you hoping to prove the system wrong? I've got an open mind, if you want to talk about it."

159   Another man leaned over, and asked, "Just between the two of us, is there really anything to this plot stuff? Are you really being framed?"

160   Anderton sighed. At that point he wasn't certain, himself. Perhaps he was trapped in a closed, meaningless time-circle with no motive and no beginning. In fact, he was almost ready to concede that he was the victim of a weary, neurotic fantasy, spawned by growing insecurity. Without a fight, he was willing to give himself up. A vast weight of exhaustion lay upon him. He was struggling against the impossible—and all the cards were stacked against him.

161   The sharp squeal of tires roused him. Frantically, the driver struggled to control the car, tugging at the wheel and slamming on the brakes, as a massive bread truck loomed up from the fog and ran directly across the lane ahead. Had he gunned the motor instead he might have saved himself. But too late he realized his error. The car skidded, lurched, hesitated for a brief instant, and then smashed head on into the bread truck.

162   Under Anderton the seat lifted up and flung him face-forward against the door. Pain, sudden, intolerable, seemed to burst in his brain as he lay gasping and trying feebly to pull himself to his knees. Somewhere the crackle of fire echoed dismally, a patch of hissing brilliance winking in the swirls of mist making their way into the twisted hulk of the car.

163   Hands from outside the car reached for him. Slowly he became aware that he was being dragged through the rent that had been the door. A heavy seat cushion was shoved brusquely aside, and all at once he found himself on his feet, leaning heavily against a dark shape and being guided into the shadows of an alley a short distance from the car.

164   In the distance, police sirens wailed.

165   "You'll live," a voice grated in his ear, low and urgent. It was a voice he had never heard before, as unfamiliar and harsh as the rain beating into his face. "Can you hear what I'm saying?"

166   "Yes," Anderton acknowledged. He plucked aimlessly at the ripped sleeve of his shirt. A cut on his cheek was beginning to throb. Confused, he tried to orient himself. "You're not—"

167   "Stop talking and listen." The man was heavyset, almost fat. Now his big hands held Anderton propped against the wet brick wall of the building, out of the rain and the flickering light of the burning car. "We had to do it that way," he said. "It was the only alternative. We didn't have much time. We thought Kaplan would keep you at his place longer."

168   "Who are you?" Anderton managed.

169   The moist, rain-streaked face twisted into a humorless grin. "My name's Fleming. You'll see me again. We have about five seconds before the police get here. Then we're back where we started." A flat packet was stuffed into Anderton's hands. "That's enough loot to keep you going. And there's a full set of identification in there. We'll contact you from time to time." His grin increased and became a nervous chuckle. "Until you've proved your point."

170   Anderton blinked. "It is a frameup, then?"

171   "Of course." Sharply, the man swore. "You mean they got you to believe it, too?"

172   "I thought—" Anderton had trouble talking; one of his front teeth seemed to be loose. "Hostility toward Witwer...replaced, my wife and a younger man, natural resentment...."

173   "Don't kid yourself," the other said. "You know better than that. This whole business was worked out carefully. They had every phase of it under control. The card was set to pop the day Witwer appeared. They've already got the first part wrapped up. Witwer is Commissioner, and you're a hunted criminal."

174   "Who's behind it?"

175   "Your wife."

176   Anderton's head spun. "You're positive?"

177   The man laughed. "You bet your life."

178   He glanced quickly around. "Here come the police. Take off down this alley. Grab a bus, get yourself into the slum section, rent a room and buy a stack of magazines to keep you busy. Get other clothes—You're smart enough to take care of yourself. Don't try to leave Earth. They've got all the intersystem transports screened. If you can keep low for the next seven days, you're made."

179   "Who are you?" Anderton demanded.

180   Fleming let go of him. Cautiously, he moved to the entrance of the alley and peered out. The first police car had come to rest on the damp pavement; its motor spinning tinnily, it crept suspiciously toward the smouldering ruin that had been Kaplan's car. Inside the wreck the squad of men were stirring feebly, beginning to creep painfully through the tangle of steel and plastic out into the cold rain.

181   "Consider us a protective society," Fleming said softly, his plump, expressionless face shining with moisture. "A sort of police force that watches the police. To see," he added, "that everything stays on an even keel."

182   His thick hand shot out. Stumbling, Anderton was knocked away from him, half-falling into the shadows and damp debris that littered the alley.

183   "Get going," Fleming told him sharply. "And don't discard that packet." As Anderton felt his way hesitantly toward the far exit of the alley, the man's last words drifted to him. "Study it carefully and you may still survive."

184   **T H E**
identification cards described him as Ernest Temple, an unemployed electrician, drawing a weekly subsistence from the State of New York, with a wife and four children in Buffalo and less than a hundred dollars in assets. A sweat-stained green card gave him permission to travel and to maintain no fixed address. A man looking for work needed to travel. He might have to go a long way.

185   As he rode across town in the almost empty bus, Anderton studied the description of Ernest Temple. Obviously, the cards had been made out with him in mind, for all the measurements fitted. After a time he wondered about the fingerprints and the brain-wave pattern. They couldn't

possibly stand comparison. The walletful of cards would get him past only the most cursory examinations.

186   But it was something. And with the ID cards came ten thousand dollars in bills. He pocketed the money and cards, then turned to the neatly-typed message in which they had been enclosed.

187   At first he could make no sense of it. For a long time he studied it, perplexed.

The existence of a majority logically implies a corresponding minority.

188   The bus had entered the vast slum region, the tumbled miles of cheap hotels and broken-down tenements that had sprung up after the mass destruction of the war. It slowed to a stop, and Anderton got to his feet. A few passengers idly observed his cut cheek and damaged clothing. Ignoring them, he stepped down onto the rain-swept curb.

189   Beyond collecting the money due him, the hotel clerk was not interested. Anderton climbed the stairs to the second floor and entered the narrow, musty-smelling room that now belonged to him. Gratefully, he locked the door and pulled down the window shades. The room was small but clean. Bed, dresser, scenic calendar, chair, lamp, a radio with a slot for the insertion of quarters.

190   He dropped a quarter into it and threw himself heavily down on the bed. All main stations carried the police bulletin. It was novel, exciting, something unknown to the present generation. An escaped criminal! The public was avidly interested.

191   "...this man has used the advantage of his high position to carry out an initial escape," the announcer was saying, with professional indignation. "Because of his high office he had access to the previewed data and the trust placed in him permitted him to evade the normal process of detection and re-location. During the period of his tenure he exercised his authority to send countless potentially guilty individuals to their proper confinement, thus sparing the lives of innocent victims. This man, John Allison Anderton, was instrumental in the original creation of the Pre-crime system, the prophylactic pre-detection of criminals through the ingenious use of mutant precogs, capable of previewing future events and transferring orally that data to analytical machinery. These three precogs, in their vital function...."

192   The voice faded out as he left the room and entered the tiny bathroom. There, he stripped off his coat, and shirt, and ran hot water in the wash bowl. He began bathing the cut on his cheek. At the drugstore on the corner he had bought iodine and Bandaids, a razor, comb, toothbrush, and other small things he would need. The next morning he intended to find a second-hand clothing store and buy more suitable clothing. After all, he was now an unemployed electrician, not an accident-damaged Commissioner of Police.

193   In the other room the radio blared on. Only subconsciously aware of it, he stood in front of the cracked mirror, examining a broken tooth.

194   "...the system of three precogs finds its genesis in the computers of the middle decades of this century. How are the results of an electronic computer checked? By feeding the data to a second computer of identical design. But two computers are not sufficient. If each computer arrived at a different answer it is impossible to tell *a priori* which is correct. The solution, based on a careful study of statistical method, is to utilize a third computer to check the results of the first two. In this manner, a so-called majority report is obtained. It can be assumed with fair probability that the agreement of two out of three computers indicates which of the alternative results is accurate. It would not be likely that two computers would arrive at identically incorrect solutions—"

195   Anderton dropped the towel he was clutching and raced into the other room. Trembling, he bent to catch the blaring words of the radio.

196   "...unanimity of all three precogs is a hoped-for but seldom-achieved phenomenon, acting-Commissioner Witwer explains. It is much more common to obtain a collaborative majority report of two precogs, plus a minority report of some slight variation, usually with reference to time and place, from the third mutant. This is explained by the theory of *multiple-futures*. If only one time-path existed, precognitive information would be of no importance, since no possibility would exist, in possessing this information, of altering the future. In the Precrime Agency's work we must first of all assume—"

197   Frantically, Anderton paced around the tiny room. Majority report— only two of the precogs had concurred on the material underlying the card. That was the meaning of the message enclosed with the packet. The report of the third precog, the minority report, was somehow of importance.

198   Why?

199   His watch told him that it was after midnight. Page would be off duty. He wouldn't be back in the monkey block until the next afternoon. It was a slim chance, but worth taking. Maybe Page would cover for him, and maybe not. He would have to risk it.

200   He had to see the minority report.

201   **BETWEEN**
noon and one o'clock the rubbish-littered streets swarmed with people. He chose that time, the busiest part of the day, to make his call. Selecting a phonebooth in a patron-teeming super drugstore, he dialed the familiar police number and stood holding the cold receiver to his ear. Deliberately, he had selected the aud, not the vid line: in spite of his second-hand clothing and seedy, unshaven appearance, he might be recognized.

202   The receptionist was new to him. Cautiously, he gave Page's extension. If Witwer were removing the regular staff and putting in his satellites, he might find himself talking to a total stranger.

203   "Hello," Page's gruff voice came.

204   Relieved, Anderton glanced around. Nobody was paying any attention to him. The shoppers wandered among the merchandise, going about their daily routines. "Can you talk?" he asked. "Or are you tied up?"

205   There was a moment of silence. He could picture Page's mild face torn with uncertainty as he wildly tried to decide what to do. At last came halting words. "Why—are you calling here?"

206   Ignoring the question, Anderton said, "I didn't recognize the receptionist. New personnel?"

207   "Brand-new," Page agreed, in a thin, strangled voice. "Big turnovers, these days."

208   "So I hear." Tensely, Anderton asked, "How's your job? Still safe?"

209   "Wait a minute." The receiver was put down and the muffled sound of steps came in Anderton's ear. It was followed by the quick slam of a door being hastily shut. Page returned. "We can talk better now," he said hoarsely.

210   "How much better?"

211   "Not a great deal. Where are you?"

212   "Strolling through Central Park," Anderton said. "Enjoying the sunlight." For all he knew, Page had gone to make sure the line-tap was in place. Right now, an airborne police team was probably on its way. But he had to take the chance. "I'm in a new field," he said curtly. "I'm an electrician these days."

213   "Oh?" Page said, baffled.

214   "I thought maybe you had some work for me. If it can be arranged, I'd like to drop by and examine your basic computing equipment. Especially the data and analytical banks in the monkey block."

215   After a pause, Page said: "It—might be arranged. If it's really important."

216   "It is," Anderton assured him. "When would be best for you?"

217   "Well," Page said, struggling. "I'm having a repair team come in to look at the intercom equipment. The acting-Commissioner wants it improved, so he can operate quicker. You might trail along."

218   "I'll do that. About when?"

219   "Say four o'clock. Entrance B, level 6. I'll—meet you."

220   "Fine," Anderton agreed, already starting to hang up. "I hope you're still in charge, when I get there."

221   He hung up and rapidly left the booth. A moment later he was pushing through the dense pack of people crammed into the nearby cafeteria. Nobody would locate him there.

222   He had three and a half hours to wait. And it was going to seem a lot longer. It proved to be the longest wait of his life before he finally met Page as arranged.

223   The first thing Page said was: "You're out of your mind. Why in hell did you come back?"

224   "I'm not back for long." Tautly, Anderton prowled around the monkey block, systematically locking one door after another. "Don't let anybody in. I can't take chances."

225   "You should have quit when you were ahead." In an agony of apprehension, Page followed after him. "Witwer is making hay, hand over fist. He's got the whole country screaming for your blood."

226   Ignoring him, Anderton snapped open the main control bank of the analytical machinery. "Which of the three monkeys gave the minority report?"

227   "Don't question me—I'm getting out." On his way to the door Page halted briefly, pointed to the middle figure, and then disappeared. The door closed; Anderton was alone.

228   The middle one. He knew that one well. The dwarfed, hunched-over figure had sat buried in its wiring and relays for fifteen years. As Anderton approached, it didn't look up. With eyes glazed and blank, it contemplated a world that did not yet exist, blind to the physical reality that lay around it.

229   "Jerry" was twenty-four years old. Originally, he had been classified as a hydrocephalic idiot but when he reached the age of six the psych testers had identified the precog talent, buried under the layers of tissue corrosion. Placed in a government-operated training school, the latent talent had been cultivated. By the time he was nine the talent had advanced to a useful stage. "Jerry," however, remained in the aimless chaos of idiocy; the burgeoning faculty had absorbed the totality of his personality.

230   Squatting down, Anderton began dis-assembling the protective shields that guarded the tape-reels stored in the analytical machinery. Using schematics, he traced the leads back from the final stages of the integrated computers, to the point where "Jerry's" individual equipment branched off. Within minutes he was shakily lifting out two half-hour tapes: recent rejected data not fused with majority reports. Consulting the code chart, he selected the section of tape which referred to his particular card.

231   A tape scanner was mounted nearby. Holding his breath, he inserted the tape, activated the transport, and listened. It took only a second. From the first statement of the report it was clear what had happened. He had what he wanted; he could stop looking.

232   "Jerry's" vision was misphased. Because of the erratic nature of precognition, he was examining a time-area slightly different from that of his companions. For him, the report that Anderton would commit a murder was an event to be integrated along with everything else. That assertion—and Anderton's reaction—was one more piece of datum.

233   Obviously, "Jerry's" report superseded the majority report. Having been informed that he would commit a murder, Anderton would change his mind and not do so. The preview of the murder had cancelled out the murder; prophylaxis had occurred simply in his being informed. Already, a new time-path had been created. But "Jerry" was outvoted.

234   Trembling, Anderton rewound the tape and clicked on the recording head. At high speed he made a copy of the report, restored the original, and removed the duplicate from the transport. Here was the proof that the card was invalid: *obsolete*. All he had to do was show it to Witwer....

235   His own stupidity amazed him. Undoubtedly, Witwer had seen the report; and in spite of it, had assumed the job of Commissioner, had kept the police teams out. Witwer didn't intend to back down: he wasn't concerned with Anderton's innocence.

236   What, then, could he do? Who else would be interested?

237   "You damn fool!" a voice behind him grated, wild with anxiety.

238   Quickly, he turned. His wife stood at one of the doors, in her police uniform, her eyes frantic with dismay. "Don't worry," he told her briefly, displaying the reel of tape. "I'm leaving."

239   Her face distorted, Lisa rushed frantically up to him. "Page said you were here, but I couldn't believe it. He shouldn't have let you in. He just doesn't understand what you are."

240   "What am I?" Anderton inquired caustically. "Before you answer, maybe you better listen to this tape."

241   "I don't want to listen to it! I just want you to get out of here! Ed Witwer knows somebody's down here. Page is trying to keep him occupied, but—" She broke off, her head turned stiffly to one side. "He's here now! He's going to force his way in."

242   "Haven't you got any influence? Be gracious and charming. He'll probably forget about me."

243   Lisa looked at him in bitter reproach. "There's a ship parked on the roof. If you want to get away...." Her voice choked and for an instant she was silent. Then she said, "I'll be taking off in a minute or so. If you want to come—"

244   "I'll come," Anderton said. He had no other choice. He had secured his tape, his proof, but he hadn't worked out any method of leaving. Gladly, he hurried after the slim figure of his wife as she strode from the block, through a side door and down a supply corridor, her heels clicking loudly in the deserted gloom.

245   "It's a good fast ship," she told him over her shoulder. "It's emergency fueled—ready to go. I was going to supervise some of the teams."

246   **B E H I N D**
the wheel of the high-velocity police cruiser, Anderton outlined what the minority report tape contained. Lisa listened without comment, her face pinched and strained, her hands clasped tensely in her lap. Below the ship, the war-ravaged rural countryside spread out like a relief map, the vacant regions between cities craterpitted and dotted with the ruins of farms and small industrial plants.

247   "I wonder," she said, when he had finished, "how many times this has happened before."

248   "A minority report? A great many times."

249   "I mean, one precog misphased. Using the report of the others as data—superseding them." Her eyes dark and serious, she added, "Perhaps a lot of the people in the camps are like you."

250   "No," Anderton insisted. But he was beginning to feel uneasy about it, too. "I was in a position to see the card, to get a look at the report. That's what did it."

251   "But—" Lisa gestured significantly. "Perhaps all of them would have reacted that way. We could have told them the truth."

252   "It would have been too great a risk," he answered stubbornly.

253   Lisa laughed sharply. "Risk? Chance? Uncertainty? With precogs around?"

254   Anderton concentrated on steering the fast little ship. "This is a unique case," he repeated. "And we have an immediate problem. We can tackle the theoretical aspects later on. I have to get this tape to the proper people—before your bright young friend demolishes it."

255   "You're taking it to Kaplan?"

256   "I certainly am." He tapped the reel of tape which lay on the seat between them. "He'll be interested. Proof that his life isn't in danger ought to be of vital concern to him."

257   From her purse, Lisa shakily got out her cigarette case. "And you think he'll help you."

258   "He may—or he may not. It's a chance worth taking."

259   "How did you manage to go underground so quickly?" Lisa asked. "A completely effective disguise is difficult to obtain."

260   "All it takes is money," he answered evasively.

261   As she smoked, Lisa pondered. "Probably Kaplan will protect you," she said. "He's quite powerful."

262   "I thought he was only a retired general."

263   "Technically—that's what he is. But Witwer got out the dossier on him. Kaplan heads an unusual kind of exclusive veterans' organization. It's actually a kind of club, with a few restricted members. High officers only—an international class from both sides of the war. Here in New York they maintain a great mansion of a house, three glossy-paper publications, and occasional TV coverage that costs them a small fortune."

264   "What are you trying to say?"

265   "Only this. You've convinced me that you're innocent. I mean, it's obvious that you *won't* commit a murder. But you must realize now that the original report, the majority report, *was not a fake*. Nobody falsified it. Ed Witwer didn't create it. There's no plot against you, and there never was. If you're going to accept this minority report as genuine you'll have to accept the majority one, also."

266   Reluctantly, he agreed. "I suppose so."

267   "Ed Witwer," Lisa continued, "is acting in complete good faith. He really believes you're a potential criminal—and why not? He's got the majority report sitting on his desk, but you have that card folded up in your pocket."

268   "I destroyed it," Anderton said, quietly.

269   Lisa leaned earnestly toward him. "Ed Witwer isn't motivated by any desire to get your job," she said. "He's motivated by the same desire that has always dominated you. He believes in Precrime. He wants the system to continue. I've talked to him and I'm convinced he's telling the truth."

270   Anderton asked, "Do you want me to take this reel to Witwer? If I do—he'll destroy it."

271   "Nonsense," Lisa retorted. "The originals have been in his hands from the start. He could have destroyed them any time he wished."

272   "That's true." Anderton conceded. "Quite possibly he didn't know."

273   "Of course he didn't. Look at it this way. If Kaplan gets hold of that tape, the police will be discredited. Can't you see why? It would prove that the majority report was an error. Ed Witwer is absolutely right. You have to be taken in—if Precrime is to survive. You're thinking of your own safety. But think, for a moment, about the system." Leaning over, she stubbed out her cigarette and fumbled in her purse for another. "Which means more to you—your own personal safety or the existence of the system?"

274   "My safety," Anderton answered, without hesitation.

275   "You're positive?"

276   "If the system can survive only by imprisoning innocent people, then it deserves to be destroyed. My personal safety is important because I'm a human being. And furthermore—"

277   From her purse, Lisa got out an incredibly tiny pistol. "I believe," she told him huskily, "that I have my finger on the firing release. I've never used a weapon like this before. But I'm willing to try."

278   After a pause, Anderton asked: "You want me to turn the ship around? Is that it?"

279   "Yes, back to the police building. I'm sorry. If you could put the good of the system above your own selfish—"

280   "Keep your sermon," Anderton told her. "I'll take the ship back. But I'm not going to listen to your defense of a code of behavior no intelligent man could subscribe to."

281   Lisa's lips pressed into a thin, bloodless line. Holding the pistol tightly, she sat facing him, her eyes fixed intently on him as he swung the ship in a broad arc. A few loose articles rattled from the glove compartment as the little craft turned on a radical slant, one wing rising majestically until it pointed straight up.

282   Both Anderton and his wife were supported by the constraining metal arms of their seats. But not so the third member of the party.

283   Out of the corner of his eye, Anderton saw a flash of motion. A sound came simultaneously, the clawing struggle of a large man as he abruptly lost his footing and plunged into the reinforced wall of the ship. What followed happened quickly. Fleming scrambled instantly to his feet, lurching and wary, one arm lashing out for the woman's pistol. Anderton was too startled to cry out. Lisa turned, saw the man—and screamed. Fleming knocked the gun from her hand, sending it clattering to the floor.

284   Grunting, Fleming shoved her aside and retrieved the gun. "Sorry," he gasped, straightening up as best he could. "I thought she might talk more. That's why I waited."

285   "You were here when—" Anderton began—and stopped. It was obvious that Fleming and his men had kept him under surveillance. The existence of Lisa's ship had been duly noted and factored in, and while Lisa

had debated whether it would be wise to fly him to safety, Fleming had crept into the storage compartment of the ship.

286   "Perhaps," Fleming said, "you'd better give me that reel of tape." His moist, clumsy fingers groped for it. "You're right—Witwer would have melted it down to a puddle."

287   "Kaplan, too?" Anderton asked numbly, still dazed by the appearance of the man.

288   "Kaplan is working directly with Witwer. That's why his name showed on line five of the card. Which one of them is the actual boss, we can't tell. Possibly neither." Fleming tossed the tiny pistol away and got out his own heavy-duty military weapon. "You pulled a real flub in taking off with this woman. I told you she was back of the whole thing."

289   "I can't believe that," Anderton protested. "If she—"

290   "You've got no sense. This ship was warmed up by Witwer's order. They wanted to fly you out of the building so that we couldn't get to you. With you on your own, separated from us, you didn't stand a chance."

291   A strange look passed over Lisa's stricken features. "It's not true," she whispered. "Witwer never saw this ship. I was going to supervise—"

292   "You almost got away with it," Fleming interrupted inexorably. "We'll be lucky if a police patrol ship isn't hanging on us. There wasn't time to check." He squatted down as he spoke, directly behind the woman's chair. "The first thing is to get this woman out of the way. We'll have to drag you completely out of this area. Page tipped off Witwer on your new disguise, and you can be sure it has been widely broadcast."

293   Still crouching, Fleming seized hold of Lisa. Tossing his heavy gun to Anderton, he expertly tilted her chin up until her temple was shoved back against the seat. Lisa clawed frantically at him; a thin, terrified wail rose in her throat. Ignoring her, Fleming closed his great hands around her neck and began relentlessly to squeeze.

294   "No bullet wound," he explained, gasping. "She's going to fall out— natural accident. It happens all the time. But in this case, her neck will be broken *first*."

295   It seemed strange that Anderton waited so long. As it was, Fleming's thick fingers were cruelly embedded in the woman's pale flesh before he lifted the butt of the heavyduty pistol and brought it down on the back of Fleming's skull. The monstrous hands relaxed. Staggered, Fleming's head fell forward and he sagged against the wall of the ship. Trying feebly to collect himself, he began dragging his body upward. Anderton hit him again, this time above the left eye. He fell back, and lay still.

296   Struggling to breathe, Lisa remained for a moment huddled over, her body swaying back and forth. Then, gradually, the color crept back into her face.

297   "Can you take the controls?" Anderton asked, shaking her, his voice urgent.

298   "Yes, I think so." Almost mechanically she reached for the wheel. "I'll be all right. Don't worry about me."

299   "This pistol," Anderton said, "is Army ordnance issue. But it's not from the war. It's one of the useful new ones they've developed. I could be a long way off but there's just a chance—"

300   He climbed back to where Fleming lay spread out on the deck. Trying not to touch the man's head, he tore open his coat and rummaged in his pockets. A moment later Fleming's sweat-sodden wallet rested in his hands.

301   Tod Fleming, according to his identification, was an Army Major attached to the Internal Intelligence Department of Military Information. Among the various papers was a document signed by General Leopold Kaplan, stating that Fleming was under the special protection of his own group—the International Veterans' League.

302   Fleming and his men were operating under Kaplan's orders. The bread truck, the accident, had been deliberately rigged.

303   It meant that Kaplan had deliberately kept him out of police hands. The plan went back to the original contact in his home, when Kaplan's men had picked him up as he was packing. Incredulous, he realized what had really happened. Even then, they were making sure they got him before the police. From the start, it had been an elaborate strategy to make certain that Witwer would fail to arrest him.

304   "You were telling the truth," Anderton said to his wife, as he climbed back in the seat. "Can we get hold of Witwer?"

305   Mutely, she nodded. Indicating the communications circuit of the dashboard, she asked: "What—did you find?"

306   "Get Witwer for me. I want to talk to him as soon as I can. It's very urgent."

307   Jerkily, she dialed, got the closed-channel mechanical circuit, and raised police headquarters in New York. A visual panorama of petty police officials flashed by before a tiny replica of Ed Witwer's features appeared on the screen.

308   "Remember me?" Anderton asked him.

309   Witwer blanched. "Good God. What happened? Lisa, are you bringing him in?" Abruptly his eyes fastened on the gun in Anderton's hands. "Look," he said savagely, "don't do anything to her. Whatever you may think, she's not responsible."

310   "I've already found that out," Anderton answered. "Can you get a fix on us? We may need protection getting back."

311   "*Back!*" Witwer gazed at him unbelievingly. "You're coming in? You're giving yourself up?"

312   "I am, yes." Speaking rapidly, urgently, Anderton added, "There's something you must do immediately. Close off the monkey block. Make certain nobody gets it—Page or anyone else. *Especially Army people.*"

313   "Kaplan," the miniature image said.

314   "What about him?"

315   "He was here. He—he just left."

316   Anderton's heart stopped beating. "What was he doing?"

317   "Picking up data. Transcribing duplicates of our precog reports on you. He insisted he wanted them solely for his protection."

318   "Then he's already got it," Anderton said. "It's too late."

319   Alarmed, Witwer almost shouted: "Just what do you mean? What's happening?"

320   "I'll tell you," Anderton said heavily, "when I get back to my office."

321   WITWER

met him on the roof on the police building. As the small ship came to rest, a cloud of escort ships dipped their fins and sped off. Anderton immediately approached the blond-haired young man.

322   "You've got what you wanted," he told him. "You can lock me up, and send me to the detention camp. But that won't be enough."

323   Witwer's blue eyes were pale with uncertainty. "I'm afraid I don't understand—"

324   "It's not my fault. I should never have left the police building. Where's Wally Page?"

325   "We've already clamped down on him," Witwer replied. "He won't give us any trouble."

326   Anderton's face was grim.

327   "You're holding him for the wrong reason," he said. "Letting me into the monkey block was no crime. But passing information to Army is. You've had an Army plant working here." He corrected himself, a little lamely, "I mean, I have."

328   "I've called back the order on you. Now the teams are looking for Kaplan."

329   "Any luck?"

330   "He left here in an Army truck. We followed him, but the truck got into a militarized Barracks. Now they've got a big wartime R-3 tank blocking the street. It would be civil war to move it aside."

331   Slowly, hesitantly, Lisa made her way from the ship. She was still pale and shaken and on her throat an ugly bruise was forming.

332   "What happened to you?" Witwer demanded. Then he caught sight of Fleming's inert form lying spread out inside. Facing Anderton squarely, he said: "Then you've finally stopped pretending this is some conspiracy of mine."

333   "I have."

334   "You don't think I'm—" He made a disgusted face. "*Plotting* to get your job."

335   "Sure you are. Everybody is guilty of that sort of thing. And I'm plotting to keep it. But this is something else—and you're not responsible."

336   "Why do you assert," Witwer inquired, "that it's too late to turn yourself in? My God, we'll put you in the camp. The week will pass and Kaplan will still be alive."

337   "He'll be alive, yes," Anderton conceded. "But he can prove he'd be just as alive if I were walking the streets. He has the information that proves the majority report obsolete. He can break the Precrime system."

He finished, "Heads or tails, he wins—and we lose. The Army discredits us; their strategy paid off."

338   "But why are they risking so much? What exactly do they want?"

339   "After the Anglo-Chinese War, the Army lost out. It isn't what it was in the good old AFWA days. They ran the complete show, both military and domestic. And they did their own police work."

340   "Like Fleming," Lisa said faintly.

341   "After the war, the Westbloc was demilitarized. Officers like Kaplan were retired and discarded. Nobody likes that." Anderton grimaced. "I can sympathize with him. He's not the only one. But we couldn't keep on running things that way. We had to divide up the authority."

342   "You say Kaplan has won," Witwer said. "Isn't there anything we can do?"

343   "I'm not going to kill him. We know it and he knows it. Probably he'll come around and offer us some kind of deal. We'll continue to function, but the Senate will abolish our real pull. You wouldn't like that, would you?"

344   "I should say not," Witwer answered emphatically. "One of these days I'm going to be running this agency." He flushed. "Not immediately, of course."

345   Anderton's expression was somber. "It's too bad you publicized the majority report. If you had kept it quiet, we could cautiously draw it back in. But everybody's heard about it. We can't retract it now."

346   "I guess not," Witwer admitted awkwardly. "Maybe I—don't have this job down as neatly as I imagined."

347   "You will, in time. You'll be a good police officer. You believe in the status quo. But learn to take it easy." Anderton moved away from them. "I'm going to study the data tapes of the majority report. I want to find out exactly how I was supposed to kill Kaplan." Reflectively, he finished: "It might give me some ideas."

348   The data tapes of the precogs "Donna" and "Mike" were separately stored. Choosing the machinery responsible for the analysis of "Donna," he opened the protective shield and laid out the contents. As before, the code informed him which reels were relevant and in a moment he had the tape-transport mechanism in operation.

349   It was approximately what he had suspected. This was the material utilized by "Jerry"—the superseded time-path. In it Kaplan's Military Intelligence agents kidnapped Anderton as he drove home from work. Taken to Kaplan's villa, the organization GHQ of the International Veterans' League. Anderton was given an ultimatum: voluntarily disband the Precrime system or face open hostilities with Army.

350   In this discarded time-path, Anderton, as Police Commissioner, had turned to the Senate for support. No support was forth-coming. To avoid civil war, the Senate had ratified the dismemberment of the police system, and decreed a return to military law "to cope with the emergency." Taking a corps of fanatic police, Anderton had located Kaplan and shot him, along with other officials of the Veterans' League. Only Kaplan had died. The others had been patched up. And the coup had been successful.

351   This was "Donna." He rewound the tape and turned to the material previewed by "Mike." It would be identical; both precogs had combined to present a unified picture. "Mike" began as "Donna" had begun: Anderton had become aware of Kaplan's plot against the police. But something was wrong. Puzzled, he ran the tape back to the beginning. Incomprehensibly, it didn't jibe. Again he relayed the tape, listening intently.

352   The "Mike" report was quite different from the "Donna" report.

353   An hour later, he had finished his examination, put away the tapes, and left the monkey block. As soon as he emerged, Witwer asked. "What's the matter? I can see something's wrong."

354   "No," Anderton answered slowly, still deep in thought. "Not exactly wrong." A sound came to his ears. He walked vaguely over to the window and peered out.

355   The street was crammed with people. Moving down the center lane was a four-column line of uniformed troops. Rifles, helmets...marching soldiers in their dingy wartime uniforms, carrying the cherished pennants of AFWA flapping in the cold afternoon wind.

356   "An Army rally," Witwer explained bleakly. "I was wrong. They're not going to make a deal with us. Why should they? Kaplan's going to make it public."

357   Anderton felt no surprise. "He's going to read the minority report?"

358   "Apparently. They're going to demand the Senate disband us, and take away our authority. They're going to claim we've been arresting innocent men—nocturnal police raids, that sort of thing. Rule by terror."

359   "You suppose the Senate will yield?"

360   Witwer hesitated. "I wouldn't want to guess."

361   "I'll guess," Anderton said. "They will. That business out there fits with what I learned downstairs. We've got ourselves boxed in and there's only one direction we can go. Whether we like it or not, we'll have to take it." His eyes had a steely glint.

362   Apprehensively, Witwer asked: "What is it?"

363   "Once I say it, you'll wonder why you didn't invent it. Very obviously, I'm going to have to fulfill the publicized report. I'm going to have to kill Kaplan. That's the only way we can keep them from discrediting us."

364   "But," Witwer said, astonished, "the majority report has been superseded."

365   "I can do it," Anderton informed him, "but it's going to cost. You're familiar with the statutes governing first-degree murder?"

366   "Life imprisonment."

367   "At least. Probably, you could pull a few wires and get it commuted to exile. I could be sent to one of the colony planets, the good old frontier."

368   "Would you—prefer that?"

369   "Hell, no," Anderton said heartily. "But it would be the lesser of the two evils. And it's got to be done."

370   "I don't see how you can kill Kaplan."

371   Anderton got out the heavy-duty military weapon Fleming had tossed to him. "I'll use this."

372 "They won't stop you?"

373 "Why should they? They've got that minority report that says I've changed my mind."

374 "Then the minority report is incorrect?"

375 "No," Anderton said, "It's absolutely correct. But I'm going to murder Kaplan anyhow."

376 **H E**

had never killed a man. He had never even seen a man killed. And he had been Police Commissioner for thirty years. For this generation, deliberate murder had died out. It simply didn't happen.

377 A police car carried him to within a block of the Army rally. There, in the shadows of the back seat, he painstakingly examined the pistol Fleming had provided him. It seemed to be intact. Actually, there was no doubt of the outcome. He was absolutely certain of what would happen within the next half hour. Putting the pistol back together, he opened the door of the parked car and stepped warily out.

378 Nobody paid the slightest attention to him. Surging masses of people pushed eagerly forward, trying to get within hearing distance of the rally. Army uniforms predominated and at the perimeter of the cleared area, a line of tanks and major weapons was displayed—formidable armament still in production.

379 Army had erected a metal speaker's stand and ascending steps. Behind the stand hung the vast AFWA banner, emblem of the combined powers that had fought in the war. By a curious corrosion of time, the AFWA Veterans' League included officers from the wartime enemy. But a general was a general and fine distinctions had faded over the years.

380 Occupying the first rows of seats sat the high brass of the AFWA command. Behind them came junior commissioned officers. Regimental banners swirled in a variety of colors and symbols. In fact, the occasion had taken on the aspect of a festive pageant. On the raised stand itself sat stern-faced dignitaries of the Veterans' League, all of them tense with expectancy. At the extreme edges, almost unnoticed, waited a few police units, ostensibly to keep order. Actually, they were informants making observations. If order were kept, the Army would maintain it.

381 The late-afternoon wind carried the muffled booming of many people packed tightly together. As Anderton made his way through the dense mob he was engulfed by the solid presence of humanity. An eager sense of anticipation held everybody rigid. The crowd seemed to sense that something spectacular was on the way. With difficulty, Anderton forced his way past the rows of seats and over to the tight knot of Army officials at the edge of the platform.

382 Kaplan was among them. But he was now General Kaplan.

383 The vest, the gold pocket watch, the cane, the conservative business suit—all were gone. For this event, Kaplan had got his old uniform from its mothballs. Straight and impressive, he stood surrounded by what had been his general staff. He wore his service bars, his medals, his boots, his

decorative short-sword, and his visored cap. It was amazing how transformed a bald man became under the stark potency of an officer's peaked and visored cap.

384   Noticing Anderton, General Kaplan broke away from the group and strode to where the younger man was standing. The expression on his thin, mobile countenance showed how incredulously glad he was to see the Commissioner of Police.

385   "This is a surprise," he informed Anderton, holding out his small gray-gloved hand. "It was my impression you had been taken in by the acting Commissioner."

386   "I'm still out," Anderton answered shortly, shaking hands. "After all, Witwer has that same reel of tape." He indicated the package Kaplan clutched in his steely fingers and met the man's gaze confidently.

387   In spite of his nervousness, General Kaplan was in good humor. "This is a great occasion for the Army," he revealed. "You'll be glad to hear I'm going to give the public a full account of the spurious charge brought against you."

388   "Fine," Anderton answered noncommittally.

389   "It will be made clear that you were unjustly accused." General Kaplan was trying to discover what Anderton knew. "Did Fleming have an opportunity to acquaint you with the situation?"

390   "To some degree," Anderton replied. "You're going to read only the minority report? That's all you've got there?"

391   "I'm going to compare it to the majority report." General Kaplan signalled an aide and a leather briefcase was produced.

392   "Everything is here—all the evidence we need," he said. "You don't mind being an example, do you? Your case symbolizes the unjust arrests of countless individuals." Stiffly, General Kaplan examined his wristwatch. "I must begin. Will you join me on the platform?"

393   "Why?"

394   Coldly, but with a kind of repressed vehemence, General Kaplan said: "So they can see the living proof. You and I together—the killer and his victim. Standing side by side, exposing the whole sinister fraud which the police have been operating."

395   "Gladly," Anderton agreed. "What are we waiting for?"

396   Disconcerted, General Kaplan moved toward the platform. Again, he glanced uneasily at Anderton, as if visibly wondering why he had appeared and what he really knew. His uncertainty grew as Anderton willingly mounted the steps of the platform and found himself a seat directly beside the speaker's podium.

397   "You fully comprehend what I'm going to be saying?" General Kaplan demanded. "The exposure will have considerable repercussions. It may cause the Senate to reconsider the basic validity of the Precrime system."

398   "I understand," Anderton answered, arms folded. "Let's go."

399   A hush had descended on the crowd. But there was a restless, eager stirring when General Kaplan obtained the briefcase and began arranging his material in front of him.

400   "The man sitting at my side," he began, in a clean, clipped voice, "is familiar to you all. You may be surprised to see him, for until recently he was described by the police as a dangerous killer."

401   The eyes of the crowd focused on Anderton. Avidly, they peered at the only potential killer they had ever been privileged to see at close range.

402   "Within the last few hours, however," General Kaplan continued, "the police order for his arrest has been cancelled; because former Commissioner Anderton voluntarily gave himself up? No, that is not strictly accurate. He is sitting here. He has not given himself up, but the police are no longer interested in him. John Allison Anderton is innocent of any crime in the past, present, and future. The allegations against him were patent frauds, diabolical distortions of a contaminated penal system based on a false premise—a vast, impersonal engine of destruction grinding men and women to their doom."

403   Fascinated, the crowd glanced from Kaplan to Anderton. Everyone was familiar with the basic situation.

404   "Many men have been seized and imprisoned under the so-called prophylactic Precrime structure," General Kaplan continued, his voice gaining feeling and strength. "Accused not of crimes they have committed, *but of crimes they will commit*. It is asserted that these men, if allowed to remain free, will at some future time commit felonies."

405   "But there can be no valid knowledge about the future. As soon as precognitive information is obtained, *it cancels itself out*. The assertion that this man will commit a future crime is paradoxical. The very act of possessing this data renders it spurious. In every case, without exception, the report of the three police precogs has invalidated their own data. If no arrests had been made, there would still have been no crimes committed."

406   Anderton listened idly, only half-hearing the words. The crowd, however, listened with great interest. General Kaplan was now gathering up a summary made from the minority report. He explained what it was and how it had come into existence.

407   From his coat pocket, Anderton slipped out his gun and held it in his lap. Already, Kaplan was laying aside the minority report, the precognitive material obtained from "Jerry." His lean, bony fingers groped for the summary of first, "Donna," and after that, "Mike."

408   "This was the original majority report," he explained. "The assertion, made by the first two precogs, that Anderton would commit a murder. Now here is the automatically invalidated material. I shall read it to you." He whipped out his rimless glasses, fitted them to his nose, and started slowly to read.

409   A queer expression appeared on his face. He halted, stammered, and abruptly broke off. The papers fluttered from his hands. Like a cornered animal, he spun, crouched, and dashed from the speaker's stand.

410   For an instant his distorted face flashed past Anderton. On his feet now, Anderton raised the gun, stepped quickly forward, and fired. Tangled up in the rows of feet projecting from the chairs that filled the platform.

Kaplan gave a single shrill shriek of agony and fright. Like a ruined bird, he tumbled, fluttering and flailing, from the platform to the ground below. Anderton stepped to the railing, but it was already over.

411   Kaplan, as the majority report had asserted, was dead. His thin chest was a smoking cavity of darkness, crumbling ash that broke loose as the body lay twitching.

412   Sickened, Anderton turned away, and moved quickly between the rising figures of stunned Army officers. The gun, which he still held, guaranteed that he would not be interfered with. He leaped from the platform and edged into the chaotic mass of people at its base. Stricken, horrified, they struggled to see what had happened. The incident, occurring before their very eyes, was incomprehensible. It would take time for acceptance to replace blind terror.

413   At the periphery of the crowd, Anderton was seized by the waiting police. "You're lucky to get out," one of them whispered to him as the car crept cautiously ahead.

414   "I guess I am," Anderton replied remotely. He settled back and tried to compose himself. He was trembling and dizzy. Abruptly, he leaned forward and was violently sick.

415   "The poor devil," one the cops murmured sympathetically.

416   Through the swirls of misery and nausea, Anderton was unable to tell whether the cop was referring to Kaplan or to himself.

417   **F O U R**
burly policemen assisted Lisa and John Anderton in the packing and loading of their possessions. In fifty years, the ex-Commissioner of Police had accumulated a vast collection of material goods. Somber and pensive, he stood watching the procession of crates on their way to the waiting trucks.

418   By truck they would go directly to the field—and from there to Centaurus X by inter-system transport. A long trip for an old man. But he wouldn't have to make it back.

419   "There goes the second from the last crate," Lisa declared, absorbed and preoccupied by the task. In sweater and slacks, she roamed through the barren rooms, checking on last-minute details. "I suppose we won't be able to use these new atronic appliances. They're still using electricity on Centten."

420   "I hope you don't care too much," Anderton said.

421   "We'll get used to it," Lisa replied, and gave him a fleeting smile. "Won't me?"

422   "I hope so. You're positive you'll have no regrets. If I thought—"

423   "No regrets," Lisa assured him. "Now suppose you help me with this crate."

424   As they boarded the lead truck, Witwer drove up in a patrol car. He leaped out and hurried up to them, his face looking strangely haggard. "Before you take off," he said to Anderton, "you'll have to give me a break-down on the situation with the precogs. I'm getting inquiries from

the Senate. They want to find out if the middle report, the retraction, was an error—or what." Confusedly, he finished: "I still can't explain it. The minority report was wrong, wasn't it?"

425 "Which minority report?" Anderton inquired, amused.

426 Witwer blinked. "Then that *is* it. I might have known."

427 Seated in the cabin of the truck, Anderton got out his pipe and shook tobacco into it. With Lisa's lighter he ignited the tobacco and began operations. Lisa had gone back to the house, wanting to be sure nothing vital had been overlooked.

428 "There were three minority reports," he told Witwer, enjoying the young man's confusion. Someday, Witwer would learn not to wade into situations he didn't fully understand. Satisfaction was Anderton's final emotion. Old and worn-out as he was, he had been the only one to grasp the real nature of the problem.

429 "The three reports were consecutive," he explained. "The first was 'Donna.' In that time-path, Kaplan told me of the plot, and I promptly murdered him. 'Jerry,' phased slightly ahead of 'Donna,' used her report as data. He factored in my knowledge of the report. In that, the second time-path, all I wanted to do was to keep my job. It wasn't Kaplan I wanted to kill. It was my own position and life I was interested in."

430 "And 'Mike' was the third report? That came *after* the minority report?" Witwer corrected himself. "I mean, it came last?"

431 " 'Mike' was the last of the three, yes. Faced with the knowledge of the first report, I had decided *not* to kill Kaplan. That produced report two. But faced with *that* report, I changed my mind back. Report two, situation two, was the situation Kaplan wanted to create. It was to the advantage of the police to recreate position one. And by that time I was thinking of the police. I had figured out what Kaplan was doing. The third report invalidated the second one in the same way the second one invalidated the first. That brought us back where we started from."

432 Lisa came over, breathless and gasping. "Let's go—we're all finished here." Lithe and agile, she ascended the metal rungs of the truck and squeezed in beside her husband and the driver. The latter obediently started up his truck and the others followed.

433 "Each report was different," Anderton concluded. "Each was unique. But two of them agreed on one point. If left free, *I would kill Kaplan.* That created the illusion of a majority report. Actually, that's all it was— an illusion. 'Donna' and 'Mike' previewed the same event—but in two totally different time-paths, occurring under totally different situations. 'Donna' and 'Jerry,' the so-called minority report and half of the majority report, were incorrect. Of the three, 'Mike' was correct— since no report came after his, to invalidate him. That sums it up."

434 Anxiously, Witwer trotted along beside the truck, his smooth, blond face creased with worry. "Will it happen again? Should we overhaul the set-up?"

435 "It can happen in only one circumstance," Anderton said. "My case was unique, since I had access to the data. It *could* happen again—but only

to the next Police Commissioner. So watch your step." Briefly, he grinned, deriving no inconsiderable comfort from Witwer's strained expression. Beside him, Lisa's red lips twitched and her hand reached out and closed over his.

436   "Better keep your eyes open," he informed young Witwer. "It might happen to you at any time."

Questions for Discussion

1. Explain the concept of precrime. What makes its existence possible? What is the function of the precogs? What detail about the conclusions of the precogs is concealed from almost everyone?

2. In the story only two out of three precogs' visions, the Majority Report, are necessary to determine guilt. The Minority Report is suppressed. What are the dangers of such suppression?

3. What are the advantages of the precrime system? Its disadvantages? What are some of the dilemmas?

4. Who are Leopold Kaplan and Fleming? What role do they play in the story?

5. What is the role of the army in this society? Why are the former generals dissatisfied with their role?

6. Anderton at one point argues, "If the system can survive only by imprisoning innocent people, then it deserves to be destroyed." Discuss the implications of this argument.

7. Explain Anderton's decision to commit a murder that he had no intention of committing.

Suggestions for Exploring, Writing, and Persuading

1. Write an argumentative essay supporting the view that a precrime system, while not perfect, would be desirable because it would eliminate most violent crime, OR arguing that because precogs are not infallible, a reduction in the crime rate is not sufficient justification for imprisoning people who have not committed a crime.

2. After reading the Patriot Act, answer the following questions. How far should government go in detaining people who are only potentially dangerous? What is lost or gained when governments detain suspicious people under such laws as the Patriot Act?

3. Discuss whether governments are ever justified in using people as the government in the story uses the precogs. If they are justified, when and why? If not, why not?

4. Witmer claims that "'punishment was never much of a deterrent and could scarcely have afforded comfort to a victim already dead.'" Support or refute this point of view.

5. Although this story is fairly long, making a full-length film from it obviously required some additions and changes to the plot. Also in the decades between the original publication in 1956 and the release of the movie in 2002, technology changed dramatically. After reading the story carefully and watching the film, write a comparison-contrast essay on one of the following:

- select a character, such as Anderton, as he is described in the story and as he is portrayed in the film version
- compare a futuristic device described in the story—such as the way knowledge is retrieved from the precogs—with the version in the film
- analyze a twist in the plot that is omitted or added in the film version

Ursula K. Le Guin (b. 1929)

Ursula K. Le Guin is one of America's most prolific writers and one of the hardest to classify. She has written poetry, short stories, novels, and children's books. At times, the genres seem to overlap, for her fiction is beautifully lyric, often symbolic, and philosophically titillating. Though she is usually classified as a writer of science fiction or fantasy, Le Guin's works are also realistic. Her fiction is sometimes based on recorded mythology, but often the myths are Le Guin originals. Her most famous and most admired novels are those included in The Earthsea Series—A Wizard of Earthsea (1968), The Tombs of Atuan (1971), The Farthest Shore (1972), Tehanu (1990), and The Other Wind (2001)— and the Hainish Series, which includes two of her most famous novels—The Left Hand of Darkness (1969) and The Dispossessed (1974). Her most recent publication is The Wave in the Mind: Talks and Essays on the Writer, the Reader, and the Imagination (2004).

THE ONES WHO WALK AWAY FROM OMELAS   (1973)

1   With a clamor of bells that set the swallows soaring, the Festival of Summer came to the city Omelas, bright-towered by the sea. The rigging of the boats in harbor sparkled with flags. In the streets between houses with red roofs and painted walls, between old moss-grown gardens and under avenues of trees, past great parks and public buildings, processions moved. Some were decorous: old people in long stiff robes of mauve and grey, grave master workmen, quiet, merry women carrying their babies and chatting as they walked. In other streets the music beat faster, a shimmering of gong and tambourine, and the people went dancing, the procession was a dance. Children dodged in and out, their high calls rising like the swallows' crossing flights over the music and the singing. All the processions wound towards the northside of the city, where on the great water-meadow called the Green Fields boys and girls,

naked in the bright air, with mud-stained feet and ankles and long, lithe arms, exercised their restive horses before the race. The horses wore no gear at all but a halter without bit. Their manes were braided with streamers of silver, gold, and green. They flared their nostrils and pranced and boasted to one another; they were vastly excited, the horse being the only animal who has adopted our ceremonies as his own. Far off to the north and west the mountains stood up half encircling Omelas on her bay. The air of morning was so clear that the snow still crowning the Eighteen Peaks burned with white-gold fire across the miles of sunlit air, under the dark blue of the sky. There was just enough wind to make the banners that marked the race-course snap and flutter now and then. In the silence of the broad green meadows one could hear the music winding through the city streets, farther and nearer and ever approaching, a cheerful faint sweetness of the air that from time to time trembled and gathered together and broke into the great joyous clanging of the bells.

2   Joyous! How is one to tell about joy? How describe the citizens of Omelas?

3   They were not simple folk, you see, though they were happy. But we do not say the words of cheer much any more. All smiles have become archaic. Given a description such as this one tends to make certain assumptions. Given a description such as this one tends to look next for the King, mounted on a splendid stallion and surrounded by his noble knights, or perhaps in a golden litter borne by great-muscled slaves. But there was no king. They did not use swords, or keep slaves. They were not barbarians. I do not know the rules and laws of their society, but I suspect that they were singularly few. As they did without monarchy and slavery, so they also got on without the stock exchange, the advertisement, the secret police, and the bomb. Yet I repeat that these were not simple folk, not dulcet shepherds, noble savages, bland utopians. They were not less complex than us. The trouble is that we have a bad habit, encouraged by pedants and sophisticates, of considering happiness as something rather stupid. Only pain is intellectual, only evil interesting. This is the treason of the artist: a refusal to admit the banality of evil and the terrible boredom of pain. If you can't lick 'em, join 'em. If it hurts, repeat it. But to praise despair is to condemn delight, to embrace violence is to lose hold of everything else. We have almost lost hold; we can no longer describe a happy man, nor make any celebration of joy. How can I tell you about the people of Omelas? They were not naïve and happy children—though their children were, in fact, happy. They were mature, intelligent, passionate adults whose lives were not wretched. O miracle! but I wish I could describe it better. I wish I could convince you. Omelas sounds in my words like a city in a fairy tale, long ago and far away, once upon a time. Perhaps it would be best if you imagined it as your own fancy bids, assuming it will rise to the occasion, for certainly I cannot suit you all. For instance, how about technology? I think that there would be no cars or helicopters in and above the streets; this follows from the fact

that the people of Omelas are happy people. Happiness is based on a just discrimination of what is necessary, what is neither necessary nor destructive, and what is destructive. In the middle category, however—that of the unnecessary but undestructive, that of comfort, luxury, exuberance, etc.—they could perfectly well have central heating, subway trains, washing machines, and all kinds of marvelous devices not yet invented here, floating light-sources, fuelless power, a cure for the common cold. Or they could have none of that: it doesn't matter. As you like it. I incline to think that people from towns up and down the coast have been coming in to Omelas during the last days before the Festival on very fast little trains and double-decked trams, and that the train station of Omelas is actually the handsomest building in town, though plainer than the magnificent Farmer's Market. But even granted trains, I fear that Omelas so far strikes some of you as goody-goody. Smiles, bells, parades, horses, bleh. If so, please add an orgy. If an orgy would help, don't hesitate. Let us not, however, have temples from which issue beautiful nude priests and priestesses already half in ecstasy and ready to copulate with any man or woman, lover or stranger, who desires union with the deep godhead of the blood, although that was my first idea. But really it would be better not to have any temples in Omelas—at least, not manned temples. Religion yes, clergy no. Surely the beautiful nudes can just wander about, offering themselves like divine soufflés to the hunger of the needy and the rapture of the flesh. Let them join the processions. Let tambourines be struck above the copulations, and the glory of desire be proclaimed upon the gongs, and (a not unimportant point) let the offspring of these delightful rituals be beloved and looked after by all. One thing I know there is none of in Omelas is guilt. But what else should there be? I thought at first there were no drugs, but that is puritanical. For those who like it, the faint insistent sweetness of *drooz* may perfume the ways of the city, *drooz* which first brings a great lightness and brilliance to the mind and limbs, and then after some hours a dreamy languor, and wonderful visions at least of the very arcana and inmost secrets of the Universe, as well as exciting the pleasure of sex beyond all belief; and it is not habit-forming. For more modest tastes I think there ought to be beer. What else, what else belongs in the joyous city? The sense of victory, surely, the celebration of courage. But as we did without clergy, let us do without soldiers. The joy built upon successful slaughter is not the right kind of joy; it will not do; it is fearful and it is trivial. A boundless and generous contentment, a magnanimous triumph felt not against some outer enemy but in communion with the finest and fairest in the souls of all men everywhere and the splendor of the world's summer: this is what swells the hearts of the people of Omelas, and the victory they celebrate is that of life. I really don't think many of them need to take *drooz*.

4   Most of the processions have reached the Green Fields by now. A marvelous smell of cooking goes forth from the red and blue tents of the provisioners. The faces of small children are amiably sticky; in the benign

grey beard of a man a couple of crumbs of rich pastry are entangled. The youths and girls have mounted their horses and are beginning to group around the starting line of the course. An old woman, small, fat, and laughing, is passing out flowers from a basket, and tall young men wear her flowers in their shining hair. A child of nine or ten sits at the edge of the crowd, alone, playing on a wooden flute. People pause to listen, and they smile, but they do not speak to him, for he never ceases playing and never sees them, his dark eyes wholly rapt in the sweet, thin magic of the tune.

5   He finishes, and slowly lowers his hands holding the wooden flute.

6   As if that little private silence were the signal, all at once a trumpet sounds from the pavilion near the starting line: imperious, melancholy, piercing. The horses rear on their slender legs, and some of them neigh in answer. Sober-faced, the young riders stroke the horses' necks and soothe them, whispering, "Quiet, quiet, there my beauty, my hope...." They begin to form in rank along the starting line. The crowds along the race-course are like a field of grass and flowers in the wind. The Festival of Summer has begun.

7   Do you believe? Do you accept the festival, the city, the joy? No? Then let me describe one more thing.

8   In a basement under one of the beautiful public buildings of Omelas, or perhaps in the cellar of one of its spacious private homes, there is a room. It has one locked door, and no window. A little light seeps in dustily between cracks in the boards, secondhand from a cobwebbed window somewhere across the cellar. In one corner of the little room a couple of mops, with stiff, clotted, foul-smelling heads, stand near a rusty bucket. The floor is dirt, a little damp to the touch, as cellar dirt usually is. The room is about three paces long and two wide: a mere broom closer or disused tool room. In the room a child is sitting. It could be a boy or a girl. It looks about six, but actually is nearly ten. It is feeble-minded. Perhaps it was born defective, or perhaps it has become imbecile through fear, malnutrition, and neglect. It picks its nose and occasionally fumbles vaguely with its toes or genitals, as it sits hunched in the corner farthest from the bucket and the two mops. It is afraid of the mops. It finds them horrible. It shuts its eyes, but it knows the mops are still standing there; and the door is locked; and nobody will come. The door is always locked; and nobody ever comes, except that sometimes—the child has no understanding of time or interval—sometimes the door rattles terribly and opens, and a person, or several people, are there. One of them may come in and kick the child to make it stand up. The others never come close, but peer in at it with frightened, disgusted eyes. The food bowl and the water jug are hastily filled, the door is locked, the eyes disappear. The people at the door never say anything, but the child, who has not always lived in the tool room, and can remember sunlight and its mother's voice, sometimes speaks. "I will be good," it says. "Please let me out. I will be good!" They never answer. The child used to scream for help at night, and cry a good deal, but now it only makes a kind of whining, "eh-haa, eh-haa," and it speaks less and less often. It is so thin there are no calves

to its legs; its belly protrudes; it lives on a half-bowl of corn meal and grease a day. It is naked. Its buttocks and thighs are a mass of festered sores, as it sits in its own excrement continually.

9   They all know it is there, all the people of Omelas. Some of them have come to see it, others are content merely to know it is there. They all know that it has to be there. Some of them understand why, and some do not, but they all understand that their happiness, the beauty of their city, the tenderness of their friendships, the health of their children, the wisdom of their scholars, the skill of their makers, even the abundance of their harvest and the kindly weathers of their skies, depend wholly on this child's abominable misery.

10   This is usually explained to children when they are between eight and twelve, whenever they seem capable of understanding; and most of those who come to see the child are young people, though often enough an adult comes, or comes back, to see the child. No matter how well the matter has been explained to them, these young spectators are always shocked and sickened at the sight. They feel disgust, which they had thought themselves superior to. They feel anger, outrage, impotence, despite all the explanations. They would like to do something for the child. But there is nothing they can do. If the child were brought up into the sunlight out of that vile place, if it were cleaned and fed and comforted, that would be a good thing, indeed; but if it were done, in that day and hour all the prosperity and beauty and delight of Omelas would wither and be destroyed. Those are the terms. To exchange all the goodness and grace of every life in Omelas for that single, small improvement: to throw away the happiness of thousands for the chance of the happiness of one: that would be to let guilt within the walls indeed.

11   The terms are strict and absolute; there may not even be a kind word spoken to the child.

12   Often the young people go home in tears, or in a tearless rage, when they have seen the child and faced this terrible paradox. They may brood over it for weeks or years. But as time goes on they begin to realize that even if the child could be released, it would not get much good of its freedom: a little vague pleasure of warmth and food, no doubt, but little more. It is too degraded and imbecile to know any real joy. It has been afraid too long ever to be free of fear. Its habits are too uncouth for it to respond to humane treatment. Indeed, after so long it would probably be wretched without walls about it to protect it, and darkness for its eyes, and its own excrement to sit in. Their tears at the bitter injustice dry when they begin to perceive the terrible justice of reality, and to accept it. Yet it is their tears and anger, the trying of their generosity and the acceptance of their helplessness, which are perhaps the true source of the splendor of their lives. Theirs is no vapid, irresponsible happiness. They know that they, like the child, are not free. They know compassion. It is the existence of the child, and their knowledge of its existence, that makes possible the nobility of their archi-

tecture, the poignancy of their music, the profundity of their science. It is because of the child that they are so gentle with children. They know that if the wretched one were not there snivelling in the dark, the other one, the flute-player, could make no joyful music as the young riders line up in their beauty for the race in the sunlight of the first morning of summer.

13   Now do you believe in them? Are they not more credible? But there is one more thing to tell, and this is quite incredible.

14   At times one of the adolescent girls or boys who go to see the child does not go home to weep or rage, does not, in fact, go home at all. Sometimes also a man or woman much older falls silent for a day or two, and then leaves home. These people go out into the street, and walk down the street alone. They keep walking, and walk straight out of the city of Omelas, through the beautiful gates. They keep walking across the farmlands of Omelas. Each one goes alone, youth or girl, man or woman. Night falls; the traveler must pass down village streets, between the houses with yellow-lit windows, and on out into the darkness of the fields. Each alone, they go west or north, towards the mountains. They go on. They leave Omelas, they walk ahead into the darkness, and they do not come back. The place they go towards is a place even less imaginable to most of us than the city of happiness. I cannot describe it at all. It is possible that it does not exist. But they seem to know where they are going, the ones who walk away from Omelas.

Questions for Discussion

1. What descriptive details might lead you to infer that Omelas is a utopia? How does Le Guin involve you in making her description of Omelas believable? What is the significance of telling you what the people are *not?*

2. Le Guin's narrator accuses writers and artists of having a bias against happiness and joy, of seeing happiness as simple-minded. Which writers whom you have read in this anthology seem to have such a bias?

3. Why does the happiness of Omelas depend on the misery of a feeble-minded child locked in a closet? Why is the child referred to as "it"?

4. Why are the young offended, and why do some eventually walk away from Omelas? Why does the story emphasize the people who stay and the title emphasize those who walk away?

5. Omelas has religion but no clergy. What is the logic behind this proposal? Similarly, Omelas has no soldiers. Why?

Suggestions for Exploring, Writing, and Persuading

1. Should the prosperity of the majority be considered over the "rights" of the minority? What are the alternatives? Apply this story to a situation in the United States today.

2. Write an essay explaining why you would or would not walk away from Omelas.

3. What are the parallels between Third World countries and the child? Write an argumentative essay in which you discuss whether superpowers have any obligations to Third World countries or whether the rights of Third World countries should or should not be protected.

John Updike (b. 1932)

Born in Reading, Pennsylvania, John Updike attended Harvard and wrote for and was later editor of the Harvard Lampoon. *As a Knox Fellow, he traveled and studied in England; as a Fulbright Lincoln Lecturer, he traveled to Ghana, Nigeria, Tanzania, Kenya, and Ethiopia. His short story collections include* The Same Door *(1958) and* Pigeon Feathers *(1959); his poetry includes* The Carpentered Hen and Other Tame Creatures *(1958). However, Updike is best known for his novels.* The Poorhouse Fair *(1959) won the Rosenthal Foundation Award, and* The Witches of Eastwick *(1984) was later made into a movie. The Rabbit series, which won Updike critical acclaim includes:* Rabbit, Run *(1960);* Rabbit Redux *(1971);* Rabbit Is Rich *(1981), which won the Pulitzer Prize in 1982; and* Rabbit at Rest *(1990). Among his recent works are* In the Beauty of the Lilies *(1996),* Beach at Bay *(1998), and* Seek My Face *(2002). His many awards and honors include a National Book Award for* The Centaur *(1963). In addition, he is one of the very few artists to have been awarded both the National Medal of Arts (1989) and the National Medal for the Humanities (2003) at the White House. In 1998, Updike was awarded the National Book Foundation Medal for Distinguished Contribution to American Letters.*

A & P (1959)

1   In walks these three girls in nothing but bathing suits. I'm in the third checkout slot, with my back to the door, so I don't see them until they're over by the bread. The one that caught my eye first was the one in the plaid green two-piece. She was a chunky kid, with a good tan and a sweet broad soft-looking can with those two crescents of white just under it, where the sun never seems to hit, at the top of the backs of her legs. I stood there with my hand on a box of HiHo crackers trying to remember if I rang it up or not. I ring it up again and the customer starts giving me hell. She's one of these cash-register-watchers, a witch about fifty with rouge on her cheekbones and no eyebrows, and I know it made her day to trip me up. She'd been watching cash registers for fifty years and probably never seen a mistake before.

2   By the time I got her feathers smoothed and her goodies into a bag—she gives me a little snort in passing, if she'd been born at the right time

they would have burned her over in Salem—by the time I get her on her way the girls had circled around the bread and were coming back, without a pushcart, back my way along the counters, in the aisle between the checkouts and the Special bins. They didn't even have shoes on. There was this chunky one, with the two-piece—it was bright green and the seams on the bra were still sharp and her belly was still pretty pale so I guessed she just got it (the suit)—there was this one, with one of those chubby berry-faces, the lips all bunched together under her nose, this one, and a tall one, with black hair that hadn't quite frizzed right, and one of these sunburns right across under the eyes, and a chin that was too long—you know, the kind of girl other girls think is very "striking" and "attractive" but never quite makes it, as they very well know, which is why they like her so much—and then the third one, that wasn't quite so tall. She was the queen. She kind of led them, the other two peeking around and making their shoulders round. She didn't look around, not this queen, she just walked straight on slowly, on these long white prima-donna legs. She came down a little hard on her heels, as if she didn't walk in her bare feet that much, putting down her heels and then letting the weight move along to her toes as if she was testing the floor with every step, putting a little deliberate extra action into it. You never know for sure how girls' minds work (do you really think it's a mind in there or just a little buzz like a bee in a glass jar?) but you got the idea she had talked the other two into coming in here with her, and now she was showing them how to do it, walk slow and hold yourself straight.

3   She had on a kind of dirty-pink—beige maybe, I don't know—bathing suit with a little nubble all over it and, what got me, the straps were down. They were off her shoulders looped loose around the cool tops of her arms, and I guess as a result the suit had slipped a little on her, so all around the top of the cloth there was this shining rim. If it hadn't been there you wouldn't have known there could have been anything whiter than those shoulders. With the straps pushed off, there was nothing between the top of the suit and the top of her head except just *her*, this clean bare plane of the top of her chest down from the shoulder bones like a dented sheet of metal tilted in the light. I mean, it was more than pretty.

4   She had sort of oaky hair that the sun and salt had bleached, done up in a bun that was unravelling, and a kind of prim face. Walking into the A & P with your straps down, I suppose it's the only kind of face you *can* have. She held her head so high her neck, coming up out of those white shoulders, looked kind of stretched, but I didn't mind. The longer her neck was, the more of her there was.

5   She must have felt in the corner of her eye me and over my shoulder Stokesie in the second slot watching, but she didn't tip. Not this queen. She kept her eyes moving across the racks, and stopped, and turned so slow it made my stomach rub the inside of my apron, and buzzed to the other two, who kind of huddled against her for relief, and then they all

three of them went up the cat-and-dog-food-breakfast-cereal-macaroni-rice-raisins-seasonings-spreads-spaghetti-soft-drinks-crackers-and-cook-ies aisle. From the third slot I look straight up this aisle to the meat counter, and I watched them all the way. The fat one with the tan sort of fumbled with the cookies, but on second thought she put the package back. The sheep pushing their carts down the aisle—the girls were walk-ing against the usual traffic (not that we have one-way signs or any-thing)—were pretty hilarious. You could see them, when Queenie's white shoulders dawned on them, kind of jerk, or hop, or hiccup, but their eyes snapped back to their own baskets and on they pushed. I bet you could set off dynamite in an A & P and the people would by and large keep reaching and checking oatmeal off their lists and muttering "Let me see, there was a third thing, began with A, asparagus, no, ah, yes, applesauce!" or whatever it is they do mutter. But there was no doubt, this jiggled them. A few houseslaves in pin curlers even looked around after pushing their carts past to make sure what they had seen was correct.

6   You know, it's one thing to have a girl in a bathing suit down on the beach, where what with the glare nobody can look at each other much anyway, and another thing in the cool of the A & P, under the fluorescent lights, against all those stacked packages, with her feet paddling along naked over our checkerboard green-and-cream rubber-tile floor.

7   "Oh Daddy," Stokesie said beside me. "I feel so faint."

8   "Darling," I said. "Hold me tight." Stokesie's married, with two babies chalked up on his fuselage already, but as far as I can tell that's the only difference. He's twenty-two, and I was nineteen this April.

9   "Is it done?" he asks, the responsible married man finding his voice. I forgot to say he thinks he's going to be manager some sunny day, maybe in 1990 when it's called the Great Alexandrov and Petrooshki Tea Com-pany or something.

10   What he meant was, our town is five miles from a beach, with a big summer colony out on the Point, but we're right in the middle of town, and the women generally put on a shirt or shorts or something before they get out of the car into the street. And anyway these are usually women with six children and varicose veins mapping their legs and nobody, including them, could care less. As I say, we're right in the mid-dle of town, and if you stand at our front doors you can see two banks and the Congregational church and the newspaper store and three real-estate offices and about twenty-seven old freeloaders tearing up Central Street because the sewer broke again. It's not as if we're on the Cape; we're north of Boston and there's people in this town haven't seen the ocean for twenty years.

11   The girls had reached the meat counter and were asking McMahon something. He pointed, they pointed, and they shuffled out of sight behind a pyramid of Diet Delight peaches. All that was left for us to see was old McMahon patting his mouth and looking after them sizing up their joints. Poor kids, I began to feel sorry for them, they couldn't help it.

12   Now here comes the sad part of the story, at least my family says it's sad, but I don't think it's so sad myself. The store's pretty empty, it being Thursday afternoon, so there was nothing much to do except lean on the register and wait for the girls to show up again. The whole store was like a pinball machine and I didn't know which tunnel they'd come out of. After a while they come around out of the far aisle, around the light bulbs, records at discount of the Caribbean Six or Tony Martin Sings or some such gunk you wonder they waste the wax on, sixpacks of candy bars, and plastic toys done up in cellophane that fall apart when a kid looks at them anyway. Around they come, Queenie still leading the way, and holding a little gray jar in her hand. Slots Three through Seven are unmanned and I could see her wondering between Stokes and me, but Stokesie with his usual luck draws an old party in baggy gray pants who stumbles up with four giant cans of pineapple juice (what do these bums *do* with all that pineapple juice? I've often asked myself) so the girls come to me. Queenie puts down the jar and I take it into my fingers icy cold. Kingfish Fancy Herring Snacks in Pure Sour Cream: 49¢. Now her hands are empty, not a ring or a bracelet, bare as God made them, and I wonder where the money's coming from. Still with that prim look she lifts a folded dollar bill out of the hollow at the center of her nubbled pink top. The jar went heavy in my hand. Really, I thought that was so cute.

13   Then everybody's luck begins to run out. Lengel comes in from haggling with a truck full of cabbages on the lot and is about to scuttle into that door marked MANAGER behind which he hides all day when the girls touch his eye. Lengel's pretty dreary, teaches Sunday school and the rest, but he doesn't miss that much. He comes over and says, "Girls, this isn't the beach."

14   Queenie blushes, though maybe it's just a brush of sunburn I was noticing for the first time, now that she was so close. "My mother asked me to pick up a jar of herring snacks." Her voice kind of startled me, the way voices do when you see the people first, coming out so flat and dumb yet kind of tony, too, the way it ticked over "pick up" and "snacks." All of a sudden I slid right down her voice into her living room. Her father and the other men were standing around in ice-cream coats and bow ties and the women were in sandals picking up herring snacks on toothpicks off a big glass plate and they were all holding drinks the color of water with olives and sprigs of mint in them. When my parents have somebody over they get lemonade and if it's a real racy affair Schlitz in tall glasses with "They'll Do It Every Time" cartoons stencilled on.

15   "That's all right," Lengel said. "But this isn't the beach." His repeating this struck me as funny, as if it had just occurred to him, and he had been thinking all these years the A & P was a great big dune and he was the head lifeguard. He didn't like my smiling—as I say he doesn't miss much—but he concentrates on giving the girls that sad Sunday-school-superintendent stare.

16   Queenie's blush is no sunburn now, and the plump one in plaid, that I liked better from the back—a really sweet can—pipes up. "We weren't doing any shopping. We just came in for the one thing."

17   "That makes no difference," Lengel tells her, and I could see from the way his eyes went that he hadn't noticed she was wearing a two-piece before. "We want you decently dressed when you come in here."

18   "We *are* decent," Queenie says suddenly, her lower lip pushing, getting sore now that she remembers her place, a place from which the crowd that runs the A & P must look pretty crummy. Fancy Herring Snacks flashed in her very blue eyes.

19   "Girls, I don't want to argue with you. After this come in here with your shoulders covered. It's our policy." He turns his back. That's policy for you. Policy is what the kingpins want. What the others want is juvenile delinquency.

20   All this while, the customers had been showing up with their carts but, you know, sheep, seeing a scene, they had all bunched up on Stokesie, who shook open a paper bag as gently as peeling a peach, not wanting to miss a word. I could feel in the silence everybody getting nervous, most of all Lengel, who asks me, "Sammy, have you rung up their purchase?"

21   I thought and said "No" but it wasn't about that I was thinking. I go through the punches, 4, 9, GROC, TOT—it's more complicated than you think, and after you do it often enough, it begins to make a little song, that you hear words to, in my case "Hello (*bing*) there, you (*gung*) happy *pee*-pul (*splat*)!"—the *splat* being the drawer flying out. I uncrease the bill, tenderly as you may imagine, it just having come from between the two smoothest scoops of vanilla I had ever known were there, and pass a half and a penny into her narrow pink palm, and nestle the herrings in a bag and twist its neck and hand it over, all the time thinking.

22   The girls, and who'd blame them, are in a hurry to get out, so I say "I quit" to Lengel quick enough for them to hear, hoping they'll stop and watch me, their unsuspected hero. They keep right on going, into the electric eye; the door flies open and they flicker across the lot to their car, Queenie and Plaid and Big Tall Goony-Goony (not that as raw material she was so bad), leaving me with Lengel and a kink in his eyebrow.

23   "Did you say something, Sammy?"

24   "I said I quit."

25   "I thought you did."

26   "You didn't have to embarrass them."

27   "It was they who were embarrassing us."

28   I started to say something that came out "Fiddle-de-doo." It's a saying of my grandmother's, and I know she would have been pleased.

29   "I don't think you know what you're saying," Lengel said.

30   "I know you don't," I said. "But I do." I pull the bow at the back of my apron and start shrugging it off my shoulders. A couple customers that had been heading for my slot begin to knock against each other, like scared pigs in a chute.

31   Lengel sighs and begins to look very patient and old and gray. He's been a friend of my parents for years. "Sammy, you don't want to do this to your Mom and Dad," he tells me. It's true, I don't. But it seems to me

that once you begin a gesture it's fatal not to go through with it. I fold the apron, "Sammy" stitched in red on the pocket, and put it on the counter, and drop the bow tie on top of it. The bow tie is theirs, if you've ever wondered. "You'll feel this for the rest of your life," Lengel says, and I know that's true, too, but remembering how he made that pretty girl blush makes me so scrunchy inside I punch the No Sale tab and the machine whirs "pee-pul" and the drawer splats out. One advantage to this scene taking place in summer, I can follow this up with a clean exit, there's no fumbling around getting your coat and galoshes, I just saunter into the electric eye in my white shirt that my mother ironed the night before, and the door heaves itself open, and outside the sunshine is skating around on the asphalt.

32   I look around for my girls, but they're gone, of course. There wasn't anybody but some young married screaming with her children about some candy they didn't get by the door of a powder-blue Falcon station wagon. Looking back in the big windows, over the bags of peat moss and aluminum lawn furniture stacked on the pavement, I could see Lengel in my place in the slot, checking the sheep through. His face was dark gray and his back stiff, as if he'd just had an injection of iron, and my stomach kind of fell as I felt how hard the world was going to be to me hereafter.

Questions for Discussion

1. Describe Sammy's feelings about his job.

2. Other than the obvious physical attraction, what is appealing to Sammy about the three girls "in nothing but bathing suits"? What does Sammy see as the significance of their wearing bathing suits in the A & P?

3. How do Sammy's customers behave? Why does Sammy call them sheep?

4. Describe Sammy's family. Explain whether he has any obligation to them.

Suggestions for Exploring, Writing, and Persuading

1. In an essay, analyze Sammy's reasons for quitting his job at the A & P.

2. Explain why you agree or disagree with Sammy's parents that his quitting his job is "sad."

3. Write an essay arguing that, under the circumstances, Sammy does or does not make the right choice.

4. Write a detailed contrast of the lifestyles of Sammy's family, the A & P customers, and the girls.

POETRY

William Blake (1757–1827)

William Blake was an English mystical poet and engraver. He sought to release Christianity from the constraints of early industrial materialism, Enlightenment rationalism, and puritanical sexual repression. He developed his own philosophical and mythological system expressed in such long, complex, and extremely difficult prophetic works as The Book of Thel *(1789) and* Jerusalem *(1804–1820). Much more accessible are the lyrics in* Songs of Innocence *(1789) and its companion volume,* Songs of Experience *(1794), poems that express Blake's sympathy with the oppressed and his rage at the human institutions that perpetuate oppression.*

LONDON   (1794)

I wander through each chartered street,
Near where the chartered Thames does flow,
And mark in every face I meet
Marks of weakness, marks of woe.

5   In every cry of every man,
In every infant's cry of fear,
In every voice, in every ban,
The mind-forged manacles I hear.

How the chimney-sweeper's cry
10 Every black'ning church appalls
And the hapless soldier's sigh
Runs in blood down palace walls.

But most through midnight streets I hear
How the youthful harlot's curse
15 Blasts the new born infant's tear
And blights with plagues the marriage hearse.

Questions for Discussion

1. What does Blake mean by calling the London streets and the Thames River "chartered"?

2. Look up the word *appalls*. What different meanings of the word seem appropriate here?

3. What is the "youthful harlot's curse"? What are the "plagues"?

4. How, according to Blake's poem, is the revolt of the oppressed expressed?

Suggestions for Exploring, Writing, and Persuading

1. Observe the faces of the people in a city near you. What "marks of weakness, marks of woe" as well as marks of strength and marks of happiness do you find in these faces? Discuss in an essay.

2. Discuss what Blake means by "The mind-forged manacles I hear." Or write an essay describing one or more of the "mind-forged manacles" that some hear today.

William Wordsworth (1770–1850)

William Wordsworth was a leading poet of the Romantic movement in England. His collaboration with Samuel Taylor Coleridge on the book of poems Lyrical Ballads *in 1798 is often cited as the beginning of the Romantic movement in England. Wordsworth rebelled against the order and restraint of the Enlightenment, supported the French Revolution, and sought in nature and in the lives of ordinary people an answer to the complexity and materialism of industrial England. In his poetry, he tried to use the plain language of ordinary people. As the supreme English nature poet, Wordsworth changed forever the view of nature in his culture and in ours.*

THE WORLD IS TOO MUCH WITH US   (1807)

The world is too much with us; late and soon,
Getting and spending, we lay waste our powers;
Little we see in Nature that is ours;
We have given our hearts away, a sordid boon!
5   This Sea that bares her bosom to the moon;
The winds that will be howling at all hours,
And are up-gathered now like sleeping flowers;
For this, for everything, we are out of tune;
It moves us not. Great God! I'd rather be
10 A Pagan suckled in a creed outworn;
So might I, standing on this pleasant lea,
Have glimpses that would make me less forlorn;
Have sight of Proteus rising from the sea;
Or hear old Triton blow his wreathed horn.

Questions for Discussion

1. According to Wordsworth, what has the world made us "out of tune" for? In what sense have we "given our hearts away"?

2. What does Wordsworth mean by "a Pagan suckled in a creed out-worn"? Why would he prefer being a pagan?

3. Proteus was an ancient Greek god of the sea who could change his shape whenever and however he wished. Triton, another ancient Greek sea god, had the upper body of a man and the lower body of a fish. In what ways might the sight of Proteus and the sound of Triton's horn be consoling to the poem's speaker?

4. Compare the theme and subject of this poem to those of Hopkins's "God's Grandeur" in the Quest unit.

Suggestions for Exploring, Writing, and Persuading

1. Wordsworth speaks of a former time when nature still awed humanity and life was simple. He says, however, "We have given our hearts away, a sordid boon!" Write an essay arguing that his assessment is or is not correct.

2. Wordsworth's poem seems to suggest that the cliché, "Life was much simpler in the past" is true. In an essay defend your position on this subject.

Rudyard Kipling (1865–1936)

Born in Bombay, India, Kipling was educated in England; in 1882, he returned to India to work as an editor of a newspaper. In 1889, he went back to England to continue his writing career. Some of his early poems were collected in Departmental Ditties *(1886) and* Barrack-Room Ballads *(1892); his short stories from this period were* Soldiers Three *(1888) and* Plain Tales from the Hills *(1888). His novel,* The Light That Failed *(1890), met with success. Kipling's stories of India made him a popular writer because of his romantic notions of the Englishman and the Indian people. These views are reflected in some of his poems such as "Mandalay," "The White Man's Burden," "Gunga Din" and in* Recessional *(1897). After marrying an American, Kipling moved to Vermont, where he lived for four years and wrote the children's stories* The Jungle Book *(1894),* Second Jungle Book *(1895),* Captains Courageous *(1897),* Kim *(1901), and* Just So Stories *(1902). In 1900, he returned to England and continued to write. His later works include* Puck of Pook's Hill *(1906) and his famous poem "If" (1910). Kipling was England's first Nobel Prize winner in literature (1907).*

If
(1910)

If you can keep your head when all about you
Are losing theirs and blaming it on you,
If you can trust yourself when all men doubt you

But make allowance for their doubting too,
5   If you can wait and not be tired by waiting,
Or being lied about, don't deal in lies,
Or being hated, don't give way to hating,
And yet don't look too good, nor talk too wise:

If you can dream—and not make dreams your
10   master,
If you can think—and not make thoughts your aim;
If you can meet with Triumph and Disaster
And treat those two impostors just the same;
If you can bear to hear the truth you've spoken
15   Twisted by knaves to make a trap for fools,
Or watch the things you gave your life to, broken,
And stoop and build 'em up with worn-out tools:

If you can make one heap of all your winnings
And risk it all on one turn of pitch-and-toss,
20   And lose, and start again at your beginnings
And never breathe a word about your loss;
If you can force your heart and nerve and sinew
To serve your turn long after they are gone,
And so hold on when there is nothing in you
25   Except the Will which says to them: "Hold on!"

If you can talk with crowds and keep your virtue,
Or walk with kings—nor lose the common touch,
If neither foes nor loving friends can hurt you;
If all men count with you, but none too much,
30   If you can fill the unforgiving minute
With sixty seconds' worth of distance run,
Yours is the Earth and everything that's in it,
And—which is more—you'll be a Man, my son!

Questions for Discussion

1. How many sentences make up this poem? Examine the sentence structure and explain the effect of this structure on the poem.

2. Look at each one of the "If" clauses and try to select one noun that names the characteristic you would have if you could accomplish the task described.

Suggestions for Exploring, Writing, and Persuading

1. Make a list of the qualities that you consider most important to manhood and to womanhood. Then write an essay explaining why those lists are or are not the same.

2. Compare the qualities suggested here with those described by Maya Angelou in "Phenomenal Woman."

3. Use the nouns you listed for the question above to write an expository essay about what qualities, according to Kipling, would make "a Man." Alternatively, use these nouns or others that you add to write an essay describing what you consider the qualities that make any person— whether male or female—a responsible and admirable adult.

4. Argue whether the qualities that made a man in 1910 are or are not relevant in the twenty-first century.

Stephen Crane (1871–1900)

In his brief life, Stephen Crane produced a remarkable variety of literature. The son of a Methodist minister, Crane was born in Newark, New Jersey, and attended Lafayette College and Syracuse University. As a newspaper reporter, he traveled to Cuba and to Greece. His first novel, Maggie: A Girl of the Streets *(1893), shocked readers with its realistic depiction of slum life in the Bowery of New York, and his second,* The Red Badge of Courage *(1895), considered his masterpiece, told a remarkably true-to-life story about the American Civil War. Crane's poems, usually written in free verse, have been described as miniature parables.*

A MAN SAID TO THE UNIVERSE   (1899)

A man said to the universe:
"Sir, I exist!"
"However," replied the universe,
"The fact has not created in me
5   A sense of obligation."

Questions for Discussion

1. What does the man's statement imply about his opinion of himself?

2. Explain what this brief poem suggests about man's responsibility for his own fate.

Suggestions for Exploring, Writing, and Persuading

1. Write an epistolary essay from the man in response to the universe.

2. Write an essay in which the universe details the man's responsibilities for his own behavior and his obligations, or lack of obligations, to other human beings.

Langston Hughes (1902–1967)

The biography of Langston Hughes appears in the Family unit.

I, Too   (1925)

I, too, sing America.

I am the darker brother.
They send me to eat in the kitchen
When company comes,
5   But I laugh,
And eat well,
And grow strong.

Tomorrow,
I'll be at the table
10   When company comes.
Nobody'll dare
Say to me,
"Eat in the kitchen,"
Then.

15   Besides,
They'll see how beautiful I am
And be ashamed—
I, too, am America.

Questions for Discussion

1. Why does Hughes call himself a "brother"? Why not a cousin, uncle, or man?
2. What is the irony of eating well in the kitchen?
3. When is "tomorrow"?
4. To whom is Hughes referring by using the term "they"?
5. What American poet is Hughes answering in this poem?

Suggestion for Exploring, Writing, and Persuading

1. Hughes's poem was published in 1925. Hughes says, "They'll see how beautiful I am / And be ashamed—." Write an essay arguing that people of your generation should or should not be ashamed of their treatment of those who differ from them.

W. H. Auden (1907–1973)

W. H. Auden, a major twentieth-century poet who was born in England, became a citizen of the United States in 1946. A precocious writer, he published Poems *in 1930 and* Orators *in 1932. Also in the 1930s, Auden experimented with different forms of drama, including verse plays and plays that used music. A winner of many literary prizes, he was praised for his expertise in lyrical poetry and for his technical proficiency. Auden, who influenced many of the poets of his age, is noted as a poet, critic, essayist, and playwright.*

THE UNKNOWN CITIZEN   (1940)

(To JS/07/M/378 This Marble Monument Is Erected by the State)

He was found by the Bureau of Statistics to be
One against whom there was no official complaint,
And all the reports on his conduct agree
That, in the modern sense of an old-fashioned word, he was a saint,
5   For in everything he did he served the Greater Community.
Except for the War till the day he retired
He worked in a factory and never got fired
But satisfied his employers, Fudge Motors Inc.
Yet he wasn't a scab or odd in his views,
10   For his Union reports that he paid his dues,
(Our report on his Union shows it was sound)
And our Social Psychology workers found
That he was popular with his mates and liked a drink.
The Press are convinced that he bought a paper every day
15   And that his reactions to advertisements were normal in every way.
Policies taken out in his name prove that he was fully insured,
And his Health-card shows he was once in hospital but left it cured.
Both Producers Research and High-Grade Living declare
He was fully sensible to the advantages of the Installment Plan
20   And had everything necessary to the Modern Man,
A phonograph, a radio, a car and a frigidaire.
Our researchers into Public Opinion are content
That he held the proper opinions for the time of year;
When there was peace, he was for peace; when there was war, he went.
25   He was married and added five children to the population,
Which our Eugenist says was the right number for a parent of his
    generation.
And our teachers report that he never interfered with their education.
Was he free? Was he happy? The question is absurd:
Had anything been wrong, we should certainly have heard.

Questions for Discussion

1. What, according to the poem, is the modern sense of the word "saint"?
   In what ways is this man saintly?

2. What adjectives seem best to describe the "unknown citizen"? In what ways is he unknown?

3. What does the name of the unknown citizen's employer suggest?

4. Explain the implication of the statement that because he "was fully sensible to the advantages of the Installment Plan," he "had everything necessary to the Modern Man."

5. Why does the speaker call the questions "Was he free? Was he happy?" absurd? How would you answer these questions about the unknown citizen?

6. What is Auden mocking in this poem?

Suggestions for Exploring, Writing, and Persuading

1. Write an essay about your efforts or the efforts of your peers to conform and appear "normal in every way."

2. In an essay, describe the character traits that the speaker admired. Explain why you agree or disagree with the speaker's choices.

Karl Shapiro (1913–2000)

American poet and literary critic Karl Shapiro was born in Baltimore, Maryland. He is known for his independence and iconoclasm. He disliked and opposed the great modern poets Ezra Pound, William Butler Yeats, and T. S. Eliot, regarding Eliot's Christianity as a sellout to an outmoded worldview. Shapiro taught at many universities, including Johns Hopkins, the University of Nebraska, the University of Illinois at Chicago, and the University of California, Davis. His collections of poems include V-Letter and Other Poems *(1945), a collection of poems about World War II that won a Pulitzer Prize;* Poems of a Jew *(1958); and* The Bourgeois Poet *(1964).*

THE CONSCIENTIOUS OBJECTOR   (1978)

The gates clanged and they walked you into jail
More tense than felons but relieved to find
The hostile world shut out, flags that dripped
From every mother's windowpane, obscene
5   The bloodlust sweating from the public heart,
The dog authority slavering at your throat.
A sense of quiet, of pulling down the blind
Possessed you. Punishment you felt was clean.

The decks, the catwalks, and the narrow light
10 Composed a ship. This was a mutinous crew

Troubling the captains for plain decencies,
A *Mayflower* brim with pilgrims headed out
To establish new theocracies to west,
A Noah's ark coasting the topmost seas
15   Ten miles above the sodomites and fish.
These inmates loved the only living doves.

Like all men hunted from the world you made
A good community, voyaging the storm
To no safe Plymouth or green Ararat;
20   Trouble or calm, the men with Bibles prayed,
The gaunt politicals construed our hate.
The opposite of all armies, you were best
Opposing uniformity and yourselves;
Prison and personality were your fate.
25   You suffered not so physically but knew
Maltreatment, hunger, ennui of the mind.
Well might the soldier kissing the hot beach
Erupting in his face damn all your kind.
Yet you who saved neither yourselves nor us
30   Are equally with those who shed the blood
The heroes of our cause. Your conscience is
What we come back to in the armistice.

Questions for Discussion

1. Define a conscientious objector.
2. Why and how is the prisoner "relieved" to be in prison?
3. What are the implications of Shapiro's comparing the prisoners to the pilgrims and to Noah on the ark?
4. Explain this statement: "Like all men hunted from the world you made / A good community."

Suggestions for Exploring, Writing, and Persuading

1. In an essay, contrast the conscientious objector to the "unknown citizen" of Auden's poem.
2. O'Brien in "On the Rainy River" describes his agonizing decision to allow himself to be drafted. In an essay, discuss the relative merits of O'Brien's decision and the conscientious objector's decision.
3. The speaker says, "Well might the soldier . . . damn all your kind" but also says, "Yet you who saved neither yourselves nor us / Are equally with those who shed the blood / The heroes of our cause." Explain this apparent contradiction. In an essay, support one of these statements.

4. Research people who went to Canada rather than go to Vietnam to fight. In a documented essay, explain whether you would call them conscientious objectors, heroes, or traitors.

Randall Jarrell (1914–1965)

The biography of Randall Jarrell appears in the Fear and Loss unit.

THE WOMAN AT THE WASHINGTON ZOO   (1960)

The saris go by me from the embassies.
Cloth from the moon. Cloth from another planet.
They look back at the leopard like the leopard.

And I....
5   this print of mine, that has kept its color
Alive through so many cleanings; this dull null
Navy I wear to work, and wear from work, and so
To my bed, so to my grave, with no
Complaints, no comment: neither from my chief,
10   The Deputy Chief Assistant, nor his chief—
Only I complain....this serviceable
Body that no sunlight dyes, no hand suffuses
But, dome-shadowed, withering among columns,
Wavy beneath fountains—small, far-off, shining
15   In the eyes of animals, these beings trapped
As I am trapped but not, themselves, the trap,
Aging, but without knowledge of their age,
Kept safe here, knowing not of death, for death—
Oh, bars of my own body, open, open!
20   The world goes by my cage and never sees me.
And there come not to me, as come to these,
The wild beasts, sparrows pecking the llamas' grain,
Pigeons settling on the bears' bread, buzzards
Tearing the meat the flies have clouded....
25   Vulture,
When you come for the white rat that the foxes left,
Take off the red helmet of your head, the black
Wings that have shadowed me, and step to me as man:
The wild brother at whose feet the white wolves fawn,
30   To whose hand of power the great lioness
Stalks, purring....
           You know what I was,
You see what I am: change me, change me!

Questions for Discussion

1. How does the speaker contrast with the other women she sees? What does she mean by "They look back at the leopard like the leopard"?
2. How does such repetition as "so / To my bed, so to my grave" reveal the speaker's feeling of entrapment?
3. How does the speaker compare herself to the animals she sees?
4. Briefly paraphrase the speaker's concluding apostrophe to the vulture. Why would she choose to address this short speech to such a bird?

Suggestions for Exploring, Writing, and Persuading

1. Would you have noticed the woman at the zoo? Why are some people almost invisible while others are not? Write an essay classifying people according to their degree of visibility.
2. How does the speaker feel about her condition? How do sound, diction, syntax, and imagery develop her feeling?
3. What does Jarrell's narrator mean by "Oh, bars of my own body, open, open!"? Using this poem and Blake's "London," write an essay about the cages and/or bars that people build for themselves.
4. At one point the woman thinks, "change me, change me!" To what extent is she not free to change? Discuss.
5. Both the conscientious objector in Shapiro's poem and the woman in the zoo are imprisoned, one literally and one figuratively. In an essay classify the types of prisons that confine us.

Anne Sexton (1928–1974)

Anne Sexton believed that as a child she had been unwanted and rejected. Before she was twenty years old, she married Alfred Muller Sexton III. In 1954, shortly after the birth of her first daughter, Sexton suffered her first mental breakdown. The birth of her second daughter in 1955 was followed by a second breakdown. The psychiatrist who treated her at this time convinced her that she was intelligent and talented, and he encouraged her to write poetry. Sexton found a form of salvation in writing poems about her tendency toward suicide, her mental breakdowns, and the problems she faced as a woman. In 1974, after a lifetime of feeling that death was calling her, Sexton committed suicide. The following poem was included in her first collection, To Bedlam and Part Way Back *(1960).*

RINGING THE BELLS   (1960)

And this is the way they ring
the bells in Bedlam

and this is the bell-lady
who comes each Tuesday morning
5   to give us a music lesson
and because the attendants make you go
and because we mind by instinct,
like bees caught in the wrong hive,
we are the circle of the crazy ladies
10   who sit in the lounge of the mental house
and smile at the smiling woman
who passes us each a bell,
who points at my hand
that holds my bell, E flat,
15   and this is the gray dress next to me
who grumbles as if it were special
to be old, to be old,
and this is the small hunched squirrel girl
on the other side of me
20   who picks at the hairs over her lip.
who picks at the hairs over her lip all day,
and this is how the bells really sound,
as untroubled and clean
as a workable kitchen,
25   and this is always my bell responding
to my hand that responds to the lady
who points at me, E flat;
and although we are no better for it,
they tell you to go. And you do.

Questions for Discussion

1. What is the music lesson supposed to do for the "crazy ladies"? What does it actually do for them?
2. How does the speaker feel about the music lesson? Explain how the structure and diction of the poem reveal feeling. What does Sexton's use of anaphora add to the poem?
3. What does the animal imagery reveal about the women in the poem?

Suggestions for Exploring, Writing, and Persuading

1. Research the symptoms of Alzheimer's disease. Then write an essay comparing some of these symptoms to the symptoms of the "crazy ladies" in the poem.
2. In an essay explain Sexton's claim that they are "like bees caught in the wrong hive."
3. After researching music therapy, argue that Sexton probably is or is not accurate in claiming "we are no better for" the music.

Adrienne Rich (b. 1929)

Adrienne Rich has won a Guggenheim fellowship and a National Book Award for her highly regarded poems, which often advocate the liberation of oppressed groups, especially women. From the clear and traditional A Change of Worlds *(1951) to the highly polemical* An Atlas of What's Difficult *(1992), her poems have become more difficult and more aggressively feminist. Among her many other volumes of poetry are* The Dream of a Common Language *(1978);* The Fact of a Doorframe: Poems Selected and New, 1950–1984 *(1984);* Time's Power: Poems 1985–1988 *(1989);* An Atlas of the Difficult World: Poems 1988–1991 *(1991);* Dark Fields of the Republic: Poems 1991–1995 *(1995);* Midnight Salvage: Poems 1995–1998 *(1999); and* Fox: Poems 1998–2000 *(2001). In 1997, Adrienne Rich was awarded the Wallace Stevens Award for outstanding and proven mastery in the art of poetry.*

AUNT JENNIFER'S TIGERS   (1951)

Aunt Jennifer's tigers prance across a screen,
Bright topaz denizens of a world of green.
They do not fear the men beneath the tree;
They pace in sleek chivalric certainty.

5   Aunt Jennifer's fingers fluttering through her wool
Find even the ivory needle hard to pull.
The massive weight of Uncle's wedding band
Sits heavily upon Aunt Jennifer's hand.

When Aunt is dead, her terrified hands will lie
10 Still ringed with ordeals she was mastered by.
The tigers in the panel that she made
Will go on prancing, proud and unafraid.

Linda Pastan (b. 1932)

Linda Pastan was born in New York City but presently lives in Potomac, Maryland. After attending Radcliffe College, she earned an M.A. from Brandeis University. Her works include A Perfect Circle of Sun *(1971),* The Five Stages of Grief *(1978),* Carnival Evening: New and Selected Poems 1968-1998, *and* The Last Uncle *(2002). Pastan has received many awards, including a Pushcart Prize, a Dylan Thomas Award, and the Di Castagnola Award. From 1991 through 1994, Pastan was the Poet Laureate of Maryland.*

ETHICS   (1981)

In ethics class so many years ago
our teacher asked this question every fall:

if there were a fire in a museum
which would you save, a Rembrandt painting
5   or an old woman who hadn't many
years left anyhow? Restless on hard chairs
caring little for pictures or old age
we'd opt one year for life, the next for art
and always half-heartedly. Sometimes
10   the woman borrowed my grandmother's face
leaving her usual kitchen to wander
some drafty, half imagined museum.
One year, feeling clever, I replied
why not let the woman decide herself?
15   Linda, the teacher would report, eschews
the burdens of responsibility.
This fall in a real museum I stand
before a real Rembrandt, old woman,
or nearly so, myself. The colors
20   within this frame are darker than autumn,
darker even than winter—the browns of earth,
though earth's most radiant elements burn
through the canvas. I know now that woman
and painting and season are almost one
25   and all beyond saving by children.

Questions for Discussion

1. Who is the speaker in this poem? How has her point of view changed as she aged?
2. Why does Linda, according to the teacher, "[eschew] / the burdens of responsibility"? Why is her "clever reply" not really an answer?
3. What point does Pastan make about freedom and responsibility?
4. Explain her final statement.
5. What is the tone of the poem?
6. Discuss the significance of the title.

Suggestions for Exploring, Writing, and Persuading

1. Select another ethical dilemma, one you have faced or might have to face, and write an essay explaining why it is an ethical problem, what choice you would make, and why.
2. What other ethical problems are "beyond saving by children"? Write an essay about one and persuade your audience that you are right.
3. Explain in an essay what the stakes are in the choices in Pastan's poem. Then explain what choice you would make and why.

Pat Mora (b. 1942)

Pat Mora, a Southwestern poet from El Paso, Texas, was educated at Texas Western College and University of Texas, El Paso. Of Mexican American parentage, she has written several books of poems, including Borders *(1986), which includes the following poem. Her poems and her memoirs about her family,* Voices from the Garden: Voces del Jardin *(1997), explore her heritage and the theme of identity, especially of female identity.*

IMMIGRANTS (1986)

wrap their babies in the American flag,
feed them mashed hot dogs and apple pie,
name them Bill and Daisy,
buy them blonde dolls that blink blue
5   eyes or a football and tiny cleats
before the baby can even walk,
speak to them in thick English,
    hallo, babee, hallo,
whisper in Spanish or Polish
10 when the babies sleep, whisper
in a dark parent bed, that dark
parent fear, "Will they like
our boy, our girl, our fine american
boy, our fine american girl?"

Questions for Discussion

1. What American qualities do the immigrants seek for their children? Why?

2. Why do immigrants "whisper in Spanish or Polish / when the babies sleep"?

3. What is the source of the immigrants' anxiety?

4. The United States is often described as a "melting pot." What does this poem imply may be melted away?

Suggestions for Exploring, Writing, and Persuading

1. Explain the advantages and disadvantages of individuals' conforming to the society to which they have immigrated.

2. In an essay, discuss the responsibilities of immigrants to their new country and the responsibilities of citizens to newcomers.

3. Argue that all immigrants in the United States should or should not be expected to learn English.

4. Write an essay describing the ways in which the attitudes of some Americans toward immigrants have changed since September 11, 2001.

5. Mora speaks of the ultimate fear of the immigrant parents: that their children will not fit in despite all attempts to Americanize them. Discuss your attitude or the attitudes of your community toward people who are from different countries or different cultures.

Joy Harjo (b. 1951)

Joy Harjo, a Creek Indian born in Tulsa, Oklahoma, has won wide acclaim for her poetry. Her books of poetry include The Woman Who Fell from the Sky *(1994), which received the Oklahoma Book Arts Award;* In Mad Love and War *(1990), which received an American Book Award; and* What Moon Drove Me to This? *(1997). Harjo has received many honors such as the William Carlos Williams Award, National Endowment for the Arts fellowships, and the American Indian Distinguished Achievement in the Arts Award. She lives in Albuquerque, New Mexico, where she recites her poetry and plays saxophone with her band, Joy Harjo and the Real Revolution. Most of her poems deal with her Creek heritage or the struggles of her people to avoid assimilation. Harjo's style usually mirrors the rhythm of the Creek language.*

THE WOMAN HANGING FROM THE THIRTEENTH FLOOR WINDOW   (1983)

She is the woman hanging from the 13th floor
window. Her hands are pressed white against the
concrete moulding of the tenement building. She
hangs from the 13th floor window in east Chicago,
5   with a swirl of birds over her head. They could
be a halo, or a storm of glass waiting to crush her.

She thinks she will be set free.

The woman hanging from the 13th floor window
on the east side of Chicago is not alone.
10   She is a woman of children, of the baby, Carlos,
and of Margaret, and of Jimmy who is the oldest.
She is her mother's daughter and her father's son.
She is several pieces between the two husbands
she has had. She is all the women of the apartment
15   building who stand watching her, watching themselves.

When she was young she ate wild rice on scraped down
plates in warm wood rooms. It was in the farther
north and she was the baby then. They rocked her.

She sees Lake Michigan lapping at the shores of
20   herself. It is a dizzy hole of water and the rich
live in tall glass houses at the edge of it. In some
places Lake Michigan speaks softly, here, it just sputters
and butts itself against the asphalt. She sees
other buildings just like hers. She sees other
25   women hanging from many-floored windows
counting their lives in the palms of their hands
and in the palms of their children's hands.

She is the woman hanging from the 13th floor window
on the Indian side of town. Her belly is soft from
30   her children's births, her worn levis swing down below
her waist, and then her feet, and then her heart.
She is dangling.

The woman hanging from the 13th floor hears voices.
They come to her in the night when the lights have gone
35   dim. Sometimes they are little cats mewing and scratching
at the door, sometimes they are her grandmother's voice,
and sometimes they are gigantic men of light whispering
to her to get up, to get up, to get up. That's when she wants
to have another child to hold onto in the night, to be able
40   to fall back into dreams.

And the woman hanging from the 13th floor window
hears other voices. Some of them scream out from below
for her to jump, they would push her over. Others cry softly
from the sidewalks, pull their children up like flowers and gather
45   them into their arms. They would help her, like themselves.

But she is the woman hanging from the 13th floor window,
and she knows she is hanging by her own fingers, her
own skin, her own thread of indecision.

She thinks of Carlos, of Margaret, of Jimmy.
50   She thinks of her father, and of her mother.
She thinks of all the women she has been, of all
the men. She thinks of the color of her skin, and
of Chicago streets, and of waterfalls and pines.
She thinks of moonlight nights, and of cool spring storms.
55   Her mind chatters like neon and northside bars.
She thinks of the 4 a.m. lonelinesses that have folded
her up like death, discordant, without logical and
beautiful conclusion. Her teeth break off at the edges.
She would speak.
60   The woman hangs from the 13th floor window crying for
the lost beauty of her own life. She sees the

sun falling west over the grey plane of Chicago.
She thinks she remembers listening to her own life
break loose, as she falls from the 13th floor
65   window on the east side of Chicago, or as she
climbs back up to claim herself again.

Questions for Discussion

1. Explain the significance of the "13th floor window," "a tenement build-ing...in east Chicago," and "on the Indian side of town"?
2. Why does the hanging woman represent all the watching women? What do the references to the children mean in the overall context of the poem?
3. Explain why the woman thinks she "will be set free."
4. Why does Harjo end the poem with two choices? What do you think she is saying about freedom and responsibility?

Suggestions for Exploring, Writing, and Persuading

1. Using the poem to support your opinion, write an essay explaining what the woman's decision is and why she makes that decision.
2. From the poem, select one passage that makes a political statement. Write an essay that discusses the significance of this passage, or write an essay that argues whether you agree or disagree with the passage.
3. Write an essay analyzing the vivid similes, personification, and metaphors used to describe this woman's situation.

Dwight Okita (b. 1958)

Dwight Okita, a native of Chicago, is a poet of Japanese American descent. His mother spent World War II in a relo-cation center, one of ten such centers in the Western states. In response to the Japanese attack on Pearl Harbor, the United States government, without due process, forced more than 100,000 Japanese Americans into these centers. Okita's Crossing with the Light *was published in paperback in 1992.*

IN RESPONSE TO EXECUTIVE ORDER 9066: ALL AMERICANS OF JAPANESE DESCENT MUST REPORT TO RELOCATION CENTERS   (1983)

Dear Sirs:
Of course I'll come. I've packed my galoshes
and three packets of tomato seeds. Janet calls them
"love apples." My father says where we're going
5   they won't grow.

I am a fourteen-year-old girl with bad spelling
and a messy room. If it helps any, I will tell you
I have always felt funny using chopsticks
and my favorite food is hot dogs.
10   My best friend is a white girl named Denise—
we look at boys together. She sat in front of me
all through grade school because of our names:
O'Connor, Ozawa. I know the back of Denise's head very well.
I tell her she's going bald. She tells me I copy on tests.
15   We're best friends.

I saw Denise today in Geography class.
She was sitting on the other side of the room.
"You're trying to start a war," she said, "giving secrets away
to the Enemy, Why can't you keep your big mouth shut?"
20   I didn't know what to say.
I gave her a packet of tomato seeds
and asked her to plant them for me, told her
when the first tomato ripened
she'd miss me.

Questions for Discussion

1. What seems to be the speaker's attitude toward the executive order to report to a relocation center? Why does she say that she likes hot dogs and feels uncomfortable using chopsticks?

2. Contrast the relationship between the speaker and Denise in stanza 2 with their relationship in stanza 3. What has happened to their friendship? Why does Denise sit on the other side of the room?

3. How does the speaker's attitude here compare to that of the speaker in "Immigrants"?

4. Why does the speaker give Denise tomato seeds?

Suggestions for Exploring, Writing, and Persuading

1. Discuss some of the consequences of relocation centers as shown by this letter from the fourteen-year-old Japanese girl and by the behavior of her friend Denise.

2. How appropriate is it to refer to people born in the United States as Japanese Americans, African Americans, Native Americans, and so forth? In what ways is the United States a melting pot of different cultures homogenized and blended? In what ways is it a stew of different cultures maintaining their distinctiveness? Discuss.

3. Write an essay arguing that the situation of the detainees at Guantanamo Bay is or is not similar to that of the Japanese during World War II.

DRAMA

Susan Glaspell (1882–1948)

Susan Glaspell wrote many plays for the Provincetown Players in Cape Cod, Massachusetts. She won a Pulitzer Prize for Alison's House *(1931), a play based loosely on the family and lifestyle of Emily Dickinson.* Trifles *(1916), written in ten days for the Provincetown Players, was inspired by a murder trial that Glaspell encountered while she was a reporter for a Des Moines newspaper. One year later she wrote the short story version, "A Jury of Her Peers."*

TRIFLES
(1916)

Characters

GEORGE HENDERSON:	*county attorney*
HENRY:	*sheriff*
LEWIS HALE:	*a neighboring farmer*
MRS. PETERS	
MRS. HALE	

SCENE

The kitchen in the now abandoned farmhouse of John Wright, a gloomy kitchen, and left without having been put in order—unwashed pans under the sink, a loaf of bread outside the breadbox, a dish towel on the table—other signs of incompleted work. At the rear the outer door opens and the Sheriff comes in followed by the County Attorney and Hale. The Sheriff and Hale are men in middle life, the County Attorney is a young man; all are much bundled up and go at once to the stove. They are followed by two women—the Sheriff's wife first; she is a slight wiry woman, a thin nervous face. Mrs. Hale is larger and would ordinarily be called more comfortable looking, but she is disturbed now and looks fearfully about as she enters. The women have come in slowly, and stand close together near the door.

COUNTY ATTORNEY *(Rubbing his hands)*: This feels good. Come up to the fire, ladies.

MRS. PETERS *(After taking a step forward)*: I'm not—cold.

SHERIFF *(Unbuttoning his overcoat and stepping away from the stove as if to mark the beginning of official business)*: Now, Mr. Hale, before we move things about, you explain to Mr. Henderson just what you saw when you came here yesterday morning.

COUNTY ATTORNEY: By the way, has anything been moved? Are things just as you left them yesterday?

SHERIFF *(Looking about)*: It's just the same. When it dropped below
10   zero last night I thought I'd better send Frank out this morning to make a fire for us—no use getting pneumonia with a big case on, but I told him not to touch anything except the stove—and you know Frank.

COUNTY ATTORNEY: Somebody should have been left here yesterday.

SHERIFF: Oh—yesterday. When I had to send Frank to Morris Center for that man who went crazy—I want you to know I had my hands full yesterday, I knew you could get back from Omaha by today and as long as I went over everything here myself—

COUNTY ATTORNEY: Well, Mr. Hale, tell just what happened when you came here yesterday morning.

20   HALE: Harry and I had started to town with a load of potatoes. We came along the road from my place and as I got here I said, "I'm going to see if I can't get John Wright to go in with me on a party telephone." I spoke to Wright about it once before and he put me off, saying folks talked too much anyway, and all he asked was peace and quiet—I guess you know about how much he talked himself; but I thought maybe if I went to the house and talked about it before his wife, though I said to Harry that I didn't know as what his wife wanted made much difference to John—

COUNTY ATTORNEY: Let's talk about that later, Mr. Hale. I do want to talk
30   about that, but tell now just what happened when you got to the house.

HALE: I didn't hear or see anything; I knocked at the door, and still it was all quiet inside. I knew they must be up, it was past eight o'clock. So I knocked again, and I thought I heard somebody say, "Come in." I wasn't sure, I'm not sure yet, but I opened the door—this door *(Indicating the door by which the two women are still standing)* and there in that rocker—*(Pointing to it)* sat Mrs. Wright.

COUNTY ATTORNEY: What—was she doing?

HALE: She was rockin' back and forth. She had her apron in her hand and was kind of—pleating it.

40   COUNTY ATTORNEY: And how did she—look?

HALE: Well, she looked queer.

COUNTY ATTORNEY: How do you mean—queer?

HALE: Well, as if she didn't know what she was going to do next. And kind of done up.

COUNTY ATTORNEY: How did she seem to feel about your coming?

HALE: Why, I don't think she minded—one way or other. She didn't pay much attention. I said, "How do, Mrs. Wright, it's cold, ain't it?" and she said, "Is it?"—and went on kind of pleating at her apron. Well, I was surprised; she didn't ask me to come up to the stove, or to set
50   down, but just sat there, not even looking at me, so I said, "I want to see John." And then she—laughed. I guess you would call it a laugh.

I thought of Harry and the team outside, so I said a little sharp: "Can't I see John?" "No," she says, kind o' dull like. "Ain't he home?" says I. "Yes," says she, "He's home." "Then why can't I see him?" I asked her, out of patience. "'Cause he's dead," says she. *"Dead?"* says I. She just nodded her head, not getting a bit excited, but rockin' back and forth. "Why—where is he?" says I, not knowing what to say. She just pointed upstairs—like that *(Himself pointing to the room above)* I got up, with the idea of going up there. I walked
60   from there to here—then I says, "Why, what did he die of?" "He died of a rope round his neck," says she, and just went on pleatin' at her apron. Well, I went out and called Harry. I thought I might—need help. We went upstairs and there he was lyin'—

COUNTY ATTORNEY: I think I'd rather have you go into that upstairs, where you can point it all out. Just go on now with the rest of the story.

HALE: Well, my first thought was to get that rope off. It looked...*(Stops, his face twitches)*...but Harry, he went up to him, and he said, "No, he's dead all right, and we'd better not touch anything." So we went back down stairs. She was still sitting that same way. "Has anybody
70   been notified?" I asked. "No," says she, unconcerned. "Who did this, Mrs. Wright?" said Harry. He said it businesslike—and she stopped pleatin' of her apron. "I don't know," she says. "You don't *know?*" says Harry. "No," says she. "Weren't you sleepin' in the bed with him?" says Harry. "Yes," says she, "but I was on the inside." "Somebody slipped a rope around his neck and strangled him and you didn't wake up?" says Harry. "I didn't wake up," she said after him. We must 'a looked as if we didn't see how that could be, for after a minute she said, "I sleep sound." Harry was going to ask her more questions but I said maybe we ought to let her tell her story first to
80   the coroner, or the sheriff, so Harry went fast as he could to Rivers' place, where there's a telephone.

COUNTY ATTORNEY: And what did Mrs. Wright do when she knew that you had gone for the coroner?

HALE: She moved from that chair to this one over here *(Pointing to a small chair in the corner)* and just sat there with her hands held together and looking down. I got a feeling that I ought to make some conversation, so I said I had come in to see if John wanted to put in a telephone, and at that she started to laugh, and then she stopped and looked at me—scared. *(The County Attorney, who has had his note-*
90   *book out, makes a note.)* I dunno, maybe it wasn't scared. I wouldn't like to say it was. Soon Harry got back, and then Dr. Lloyd came, and you, Mr. Peters, and so I guess that's all I know that you don't.

COUNTY ATTORNEY *(Looking around)*: I guess we'll go upstairs first— and then out to the barn and around there. *(To the Sheriff)* You're convinced that there was nothing important here—nothing that would point to any motive.

SHERIFF: Nothing here but kitchen things.

(The County Attorney, after again looking around the kitchen, opens the door of a cupboard closet. He gets up on a chair and looks on a shelf. Pulls his hand away, sticky.)

COUNTY ATTORNEY: Here's a nice mess.

(The women draw nearer.)

MRS. PETERS *(To the other woman)*: Oh, her fruit; it did freeze. *(To the County Attorney)* She worried about that when it turned so cold. She said the fire'd go out and her jars would break.

SHERIFF: Well, can you beat the women! Held for murder and worryin' about her preserves.

COUNTY ATTORNEY: I guess before we're through she may have something more serious than preserves to worry about.

HALE: Well, women are used to worrying over trifles.

(The two women move a little closer together.)

COUNTY ATTORNEY *(With the gallantry of a young politician)*: And yet, for all their worries, what would we do without the ladies? *(The women do not unbend. He goes to the sink, takes a dipperful of water from the pail and pouring it into a basin, washes his hands. Starts to wipe them on the roller towel, turns it for a cleaner place.)* Dirty towels! *(Kicks his foot against the pans under the sink.)* Not much of a housekeeper, would you say, ladies?

MRS. HALE *(Stiffly)*: There's a great deal of work to be done on a farm.

COUNTY ATTORNEY: To be sure. And yet *(With a little bow to her)* I know there are some Dickson county farmhouses which do not have such roller towels.

(He gives it a pull to expose its full length again.)

MRS. HALE: Those towels get dirty awful quick. Men's hands aren't always as clean as they might be.

COUNTY ATTORNEY: Ah, loyal to your sex, I see. But you and Mrs. Wright were neighbors. I suppose you were friends, too.

MRS. HALE *(Shaking her head)*: I've not seen much of her of late years. I've not been in this house—it's more than a year.

COUNTY ATTORNEY: And why was that? You didn't like her?

MRS. HALE: I liked her all well enough. Farmers' wives have their hands full, Mr. Henderson. And then—

COUNTY ATTORNEY: Yes—?

MRS. HALE *(Looking about)*: It never seemed a very cheerful place.

COUNTY ATTORNEY: No—it's not cheerful. I shouldn't say she had the homemaking instinct.

MRS. HALE: Well, I don't know as Wright had, either.

COUNTY ATTORNEY: You mean that they didn't get on very well?

MRS. HALE: No, I don't mean anything. But I don't think a place'd be any
cheerfuller for John Wright's being in it.

COUNTY ATTORNEY: I'd like to talk more of that a little later. I want to get
the lay of things upstairs now.

(He goes to the left, where three steps lead to a stair door.)

SHERIFF: I suppose anything Mrs. Peters does'll be all right. She was to
take in some clothes for her, you know, and a few little things. We
left in such a hurry yesterday.

COUNTY ATTORNEY: Yes, but I would like to see what you take, Mrs.
140   Peters, and keep an eye out for anything that might be of use to us.

MRS. PETERS: Yes, Mr. Henderson.

*(The women listen to the men's steps on the stairs, then look about
the kitchen.)*

MRS. HALE: I'd hate to have men coming into my kitchen, snooping
around and criticizing.

*(She arranges the pans under sink which the County Attorney had
shoved out of place.)*

MRS. PETERS: Of course it's no more than their duty.

MRS. HALE: Duty's all right, but I guess that deputy sheriff that came out
to make the fire might have got a little of this on. *(Gives the roller
towel a pull.)* Wish I'd thought of that sooner. Seems mean to talk
about her for not having things slicked up when she had to come
away in such a hurry.

MRS. PETERS: *(Who has gone to a small table in the left rear corner of*
150   *the room, and lifted one end of a towel that covers a pan.)*: She had
bread set.

(Stands still.)

MRS. HALE *(Eyes fixed on a loaf of bread beside the breadbox, which is
on a low shelf at the other side of the room. Moves slowly to ward
it)*: She was going to put this in there. *(Picks up loaf, then abruptly
drops it. In a manner of returning to familiar things)* It's a shame
about her fruit. I wonder if it's all gone. *(Gets up on the chair and
looks.)* I think there's some here that's all right, Mrs. Peters. Yes—
here; *(Holding it toward the window)* this is cherries, too. *(Looking
again)* I declare I believe that's the only one. *(Gets down, bottle in
her hand. Goes to the sink and wipes it off on the outside.)* She'll
160   feel awful bad after all her hard work in the hot weather. I remember
the afternoon I put up my cherries last summer.

*(She puts the bottle on the big kitchen table, center of the room. With
a sigh, is about to sit down in the rocking-chair. Before she is seated
realizes what chair it is; with a slow look at it, steps back. The chair
which she has touched rocks back and forth.)*

MRS. PETERS: Well, I must get those things from the front room closet. *(She goes to the door at the right, but after looking into the other room, steps back.)* You coming with me, Mrs. Hale? You could help me carry them.

(They go in the other room; reappear, Mrs. Peters carrying a dress and skirt, Mrs. Hale following with a pair of shoes.)

MRS. PETERS: My, it's cold in there.

(She puts the clothes on the big table, and hurries to the stove.)

MRS. HALE *(Examining her skirt)*:   Wright was close. I think maybe that's why she kept so much to herself. She didn't even belong to the Ladies Aid. I suppose she felt she couldn't do her part, and then you don't enjoy things when you feel shabby. She used to wear pretty
170   clothes and be lively, when she was Minnie Foster, one of the town girls singing in the choir. But that—oh, that was thirty years ago. This all you was to take in?

MRS. PETERS: She said she wanted an apron. Funny thing to want, for there isn't much to get you dirty in jail, goodness knows. But I suppose just to make her feel more natural. She said they was in the top drawer in this cupboard. Yes, here. And then her little shawl that always hung behind the door. *(Opens stair door and looks)* Yes, here it is.

(Quickly shuts door leading upstairs.)

MRS. HALE *(Abruptly moving toward her.)*: Mrs. Peters?
MRS. PETERS: Yes, Mrs. Hale?
MRS. HALE: Do you think she did it?
180   MRS. PETERS: *(In a frightened voice.)*: Oh, I don't know.
MRS. HALE: Well, I don't think she did. Asking for an apron and her little shawl. Worrying about her fruit.
MRS. PETERS *(Starts to speak, glances up, where footsteps are heard in the room above. In a low voice)*: Mr. Peters says it looks bad for her. Mr. Henderson is awful sarcastic in a speech and he'll make fun of her sayin' she didn't wake up.
MRS. HALE: Well, I guess John Wright didn't wake when they was slipping that rope under his neck.
MRS. PETERS: No, it's strange. It must have been done awful crafty and still. They say it was such a—funny way to kill a man, rigging it all
190   up like that.
MRS. HALE: That's just what Mr. Hale said. There was a gun in the house. He says that's what he can't understand.
MRS. PETERS: Mr. Henderson said coming out that what was needed for the case was a motive; something to show anger, or—sudden feeling.
MRS. HALE *(Who is standing by the table)*: Well, I don't see any signs of anger around here. *(She puts her hand on the dish towel which lies*

on the table, stands looking down at table, one half of which is clean, the other half messy.) It's wiped to here. *(Makes a move as if to finish work, then turns and looks at loaf of bread outside the breadbox. Drops towel. In that voice of coming back to familiar* 200   *things)* Wonder how they are finding things upstairs. I hope she had it a little more redup there. You know, it seems kind of *sneaking.* Locking her up in town and then coming out here and trying to get her own house to turn against her!

MRS. PETERS: But Mrs. Hale, the law is the law.

MRS. HALE: I s'pose 'tis. *(Unbuttoning her coat)* Better loosen up your things, Mrs. Peters. You won't feel them when you go out.

(Mrs. Peters takes off her fur tippet, goes to hang it on hook at back of room, stands looking at the under part of the small corner table.)

MRS. PETERS: She was piecing a quilt.

(She brings the large sewing basket and they look at the bright pieces.)

MRS. HALE: It's log cabin pattern. Pretty, isn't it? I wonder if she was goin' to quilt it or just knot it?

(Footsteps have been heard coming down the stairs. The Sheriff enters followed by Hale and the County Attorney.)

SHERIFF: They wonder if she was going to quilt it or just knot it!

(The men laugh; the women look abashed.)

210   COUNTY ATTORNEY *(Rubbing his hands over the stove)*: Frank's fire didn't do much up there, did it? Well, let's go out to the barn and get that cleared up.

(The men go outside.)

MRS. HALE *(Resentfully)*: I don't know as there's anything so strange, our takin' up our time with little things while we're waiting for them to get the evidence. *(She sits down at the big table smoothing out a block with decision.)* I don't see as it's anything to laugh about.

MRS. PETERS *(Apologetically)*: Of course they've got awful important things on their minds.

(Pulls up a chair and joins Mrs. Hale at the table.)

MRS. HALE *(Examining another block)*: Mrs. Peters, look at this one. 220   Here, this is the one she was working on, and look at the sewing! All the rest of it has been so nice and even. And look at this! It's all over the place! Why, it looks as if she didn't know what she was about!

(After she has said this they look at each, then start to glance back at the door. After an instant Mrs. Hale has pulled at a knot and ripped the sewing.)

MRS. PETERS: Oh, what are you doing, Mrs. Hale?

MRS. HALE *(Mildly)*: Just pulling out a stitch or two that's not sewed very good. *(Threading a needle)* Bad sewing always made me fidgety.

MRS. PETERS *(Nervously)*: I don't think we ought to touch things.

MRS. HALE: I'll just finish up this end. *(Suddenly stopping and leaning forward)* Mrs. Peters?

230 MRS. PETERS: Yes, Mrs. Hale?

MRS. HALE: What do you suppose she was so nervous about?

MRS. PETERS: Oh—I don't know. I don't know as she was nervous. I sometimes sew awful queer when I'm just tired. *(Mrs. Hale starts to say something, looks at Mrs. Peters, then goes on sewing.)* Well, I must get these things wrapped up. They may be through sooner than we think. *(Putting apron and other things together)* I wonder where I can find a piece of paper, and string.

MRS. HALE: In that cupboard, maybe.

MRS. PETERS: *(Looking in cupboard)*: Why, here's a birdcage. *(Holds it up)* Did she have a bird, Mrs. Hale?

240 MRS. HALE: Why, I don't know whether she did or not—I've not been here for so long. There was a man around last year selling canaries cheap, but I don't know as she took one; maybe she did. She used to sing real pretty herself.

MRS. PETERS *(Glancing around)*: Seems funny to think of a bird here. But she must have had one, or why would she have a cage? I wonder what happened to it.

MRS. HALE: I s'pose maybe the cat got it.

MRS. PETERS: No, she didn't have a cat. She's got that feeling some people have about cats—being afraid of them. My cat got in her room 250 and she was real upset and asked me to take it out.

MRS. HALE: My sister Bessie was like that. Queer, ain't it?

MRS. PETERS *(Examining the cage)*: Why, look at this door. It's broke. One hinge is pulled apart.

MRS. HALE *(Looking too)*: Looks as if someone must have been rough with it.

MRS. PETERS: Why, yes.

(She brings the cage forward and puts it on the table.)

MRS. HALE: I wish if they're going to find any evidence they'd be about it. I don't like this place.

260 MRS. PETERS: But I'm awful glad you came with me, Mrs. Hale. It would be lonesome for me sitting here alone.

MRS. HALE: It would, wouldn't it? *(Dropping her sewing)* But I tell you what I do wish, Mrs. Peters. I wish I had come over sometimes when *she* was here. I—*(Looking round the room)*—wish I had.

MRS. PETERS: But of course you were awful busy, Mrs. Hale—your house and your children.

MRS. HALE: I could've come. I stayed away because it weren't cheerful—
and that's why I ought to have come. I—I've never liked this place.
Maybe because it's down in a hollow and you don't see the road. I
270   dunno what it is but it's a lonesome place and always was. I wish I
had come over to see Minnie Foster sometimes. I can see now—

(Shakes her head).

MRS. PETERS: Well, you mustn't reproach yourself, Mrs. Hale. Somehow
we just don't see how it is with other folks until—something comes
up.

MRS. HALE: Not having children makes less work—but it makes a quiet
house, and Wright out to work all day, and no company when he did
come in. Did you know John Wright, Mrs. Peters?

MRS. PETERS: Not to know him; I've seen him in town. They say he was a
good man.

MRS. HALE: Yes—good; he didn't drink, and kept his word as well as
most, I guess, and paid his debts. But he was a hard man, Mrs.
280   Peters. Just to pass the time of day with him—*(Shivers)* Like a raw
wind that gets to the bone. *(Pauses, her eye falling on the cage)* I
should think she would'a wanted a bird. But what do you suppose
went with it?

MRS. PETERS: I don't know, unless it got sick and died.

*(She reaches over and swings the broken door, swings it again. Both
women watch it.)*

MRS. HALE: You weren't raised round here, were you? *(Mrs. Peters
shakes her head).* You didn't know—her?

MRS. PETERS: Not till they brought her yesterday.

MRS. HALE: She—come to think of it, she was kind of a like a bird herself—
real sweet and pretty, but kind of timid and—fluttery. How—she—
290   did—change. *(Silence, then as if struck by a happy thought and
relieved to get back to everyday things).* Tell you what, Mrs. Peters,
why don't you take the quilt in with you? It might take up her mind.

MRS. PETERS: Why, I think that's a real nice idea, Mrs. Hale. There
couldn't possibly be an objection to it, could there? Now, just what
would I take? I wonder if her patches are in here—and her things.

(They look in the sewing basket.)

MRS. HALE: Here's some red. I expect this has got sewing things in it.
(Brings out a fancy box) What a pretty box. Looks like something
somebody would give you. Maybe her scissors are in here. *(Opens
box. Suddenly puts her hand to her nose)* Why—*(Mrs. Peters bends
nearer, then turns her face away).* There's something wrapped up
300   in this piece of silk.

MRS. PETERS: Why, this isn't her scissors.

MRS. HALE *(Lifting the silk)*: Oh, Mrs. Peters—it's—

(Mrs. Peters bends closer).

MRS. PETERS: It's the bird.

MRS. HALE *(Jumping up)*: But, Mrs. Peters—look at it! Its neck! Look at its neck! It's all—other side *to.*

MRS. PETERS: Somebody—wrung—its—neck.

(Their eyes meet. A look of growing comprehension, of horror. Steps are heard outside. Mrs. Hale slips the box under quilt pieces, and sinks into her chair. Enter Sheriff and County Attorney. Mrs. Peters rises.)

COUNTY ATTORNEY: *(As one turning from serious things to little pleasantries)*: Well, ladies, have you decided whether she was going to quilt it or knot it?

310   MRS. PETERS: We think she was going to—knot it.

COUNTY ATTORNEY: Well, that's interesting, I'm sure. *(Seeing the bird-cage)* Has the bird flown?

MRS. HALE *(Putting more quilt pieces over the box)*: We think the—cat got it.

COUNTY ATTORNEY *(Preoccupied)*: Is there a cat?

(Mrs. Hale glances in a quick covert way at Mrs. Peters.)

MRS. PETERS: Well, not now. They're superstitious, you know. They leave.

COUNTY ATTORNEY: *(To Sheriff Peters, continuing an interrupted conversation)*: No sign at all of anyone having come from the outside. Their own rope. Now let's go up again and go over it piece by piece. *(They start upstairs)*. It would have to have been someone who knew just the—

(Mrs. Peters sits down. The two women sit there not looking at one another, but as if peering into something and at the same time holding back. When they talk now it is in the manner of feeling their way over strange ground, as if afraid of what they are saying, but as if they can not help saying it.)

320   MRS. HALE: She liked the bird. She was going to bury it in that pretty box.

MRS. PETERS *(In a whisper)*: When I was a girl—my kitten—there was a boy took a hatchet, and before my eyes—and before I could get there—*(Covers her face an instant)* If they hadn't held me back I would have—*(Catches herself, looks upstairs where steps are heard, falters weakly)*—hurt him.

MRS. HALE *(With a slow look around her)*: I wonder how it would seem never to have had any children around. *(Pause)* No, Wright wouldn't like the bird—a thing that sang. She used to sing. He killed that, too.

MRS. PETERS *(Moving uneasily)*: We don't know who killed the bird.

330   MRS. HALE: I knew John Wright.

MRS. PETERS: It was an awful thing was done in this house that night, Mrs. Hale. Killing a man while he slept, slipping a rope around his neck that choked the life out of him.

MRS. HALE: His neck. Choked the life out of him.

(Her hand goes out and rests on the birdcage.)

MRS. PETERS *(With rising voice)*: We don't know who killed him. We don't know.

MRS. HALE *(Her own feeling not interrupted)*: If there'd been years and years of nothing, then a bird to sing to you, it would be awful—still, after the bird was still.

340   MRS. PETERS *(Something within her speaking)*: I know what stillness is. When we homesteaded in Dakota, and my first baby died—after he was two years old, and me with no other then—

MRS. HALE *(Moving)*: How soon do you suppose they'll be through, looking for the evidence?

MRS. PETERS: I know what stillness is. *(Pulling herself back)* The law has got to punish crime, Mrs. Hale.

MRS. HALE *(Not as if answering that)*: I wish you'd seen Minnie Foster when she wore a white dress with blue ribbons and stood up there in the choir and sang. *(A look around the room)* Oh, I *wish* I'd come

350   over here once in a while! That was a crime! That was a crime! Who's going to punish that?

MRS. PETERS *(Looking upstairs)*: We mustn't—take on.

MRS. HALE: I might have known she needed help! I know how things can be—for women. I tell you, it's queer, Mrs. Peters. We live close together and we live far apart. We all go through the same things— it's all just a different kind of the same thing. *(Brushes her eyes; noticing the bottle of fruit, reaches out for it)* If I was you I wouldn't tell her her fruit was gone. Tell her it *ain't.* Tell her it's all right. Take this in to prove it to her. She—she may never know whether it was broke or not.

MRS. PETERS *(Takes the bottle, looks about for something to wrap it in; takes petticoat from the clothes brought from the other room, very

360   nervously begins winding this around the bottle. In a false voice)*: My, it's a good thing the men couldn't hear us. Wouldn't they just laugh! Getting all stirred up over a little thing like a—dead canary. As if that could have anything to do with—with—wouldn't they *laugh!*

(The men are heard coming down stairs).

MRS. HALE *(Under her breath)*: Maybe they would—maybe they wouldn't.

COUNTY ATTORNEY: No, Peters, it's all perfectly clear except a reason for doing it. Something to show—something to make a story about—a thing that would connect up with this strange way of doing it—

(The women's eyes meet for an instant. Enter Hale from outer door).

HALE: Well, I've got the team around. Pretty cold out there.

370   COUNTY ATTORNEY: I'm going to stay here a while myself. *(To the Sheriff)* You can send Frank out for me, can't you? I want to go over everything. I'm not satisfied that we can't do better.

SHERIFF: Do you want to see what Mrs. Peters is going to take in?

(The County Attorney goes to the table, picks up the apron, laughs.)

COUNTY ATTORNEY: Oh, I guess they're not very dangerous things the ladies have picked out. *(Moves a few things about, disturbing the quilt pieces which cover the box. Steps back)* No, Mrs. Peters doesn't need supervising. For that matter, a sheriff's wife is married to the law. Ever think of it that way, Mrs. Peters?

MRS. PETERS: Not—just that way.

380 SHERIFF *(Chuckling)*: Married to the law. *(Moves toward the other room)* I just want you to come in here a minute, George. We ought to take a look at these windows.

COUNTY ATTORNEY *(Scoffingly)*: Oh, windows!

SHERIFF: We'll be right out, Mr. Hale.

(Hale goes outside. The Sheriff follows the County Attorney into the other room. Then Mrs. Hale rises, hands tight together, looking intensely at Mrs. Peters, whose eyes make a slow turn, finally meeting Mrs. Hale's. A moment Mrs. Hale holds her, then her own eyes point the way to where the box is concealed. Suddenly Mrs. Peters throws back quilt pieces and tries to put the box in the bag she is wearing. It is too big. She opens box, starts to take bird out, cannot touch it, goes to pieces, stands there helpless. Sound of a knob turning in the other room. Mrs. Hale snatches the box and puts it in the pocket of her big coat. Enter County Attorney and Sheriff)

COUNTY ATTORNEY: *(Facetiously)*: Well, Henry, at least we found out that she was not going to quilt it. She was going to—what is it you call it, ladies?

MRS. HALE: *(Her hand against her pocket)*: We call it—knot it, Mr. Henderson.

Curtain.

Questions for Discussion

1. When Lewis Hale tells how he found John Wright's body, Hale's story is loose and rambling. How does County Attorney Henderson react to Hale's story? What does Henderson's reaction reveal about him? How much does Henderson learn from Hale's story? What can you learn from Hale's story that Henderson fails to learn?

2. Explain the irony of the sheriff's saying, "Nothing here but kitchen things" and the irony of the play's title.

3. In what ways are the men in the story condescending to the women?

4. Putting together all the signs in the play, what conclusions can you draw about who killed Mr. Wright and about the killer's motive?

5. Glaspell changed the title of the play, *Trifles*, when she wrote the short story, "A Jury of Her Peers." Which title is more appropriate and why?

Suggestions for Exploring, Writing, and Persuading

1. Do you think people of the same sex communicate better with each other than with those of the opposite sex? Write an essay in which you explain your position.

2. In an essay, contrast the men's manner and approach to the investigation with that of the women. Why are the women able to solve the murder when the men are not?

3. For what reasons do Mrs. Peters and Mrs. Hale decide to withhold evidence from the men? Do these reasons justify their becoming, in effect, Minnie's judge and jury?

4. Starting with the bird in the cage, explain how the various objects in the kitchen are symbolic of Minnie's life after her marriage.

5. From the clues given, write a character analysis of the dead man, John Wright.

6. In class, conduct a trial in which Minnie Wright is charged with murdering John Wright. Then write a brief for the prosecution or for the defense, or write an argument supporting your verdict.

Casebook
on Tim O'Brien

WRITING ABOUT WAR

Perhaps more vividly and convincingly than any other writer, Tim O'Brien, in his stories and novels on Vietnam, graphically illustrates William Tecumseh Sherman's statement, "War is hell." This casebook, containing three of O'Brien's stories as well as critical analyses of O'Brien's work, enables you to explore in class discussion and in writing the soul-searching, sometimes gut-wrenching dilemma of young men unwillingly drafted to fight in the Vietnam War, a war many did not believe in and very few understood.

Tim O'Brien (b.1946)

Upon graduation from Macalester College in Minnesota in 1968, O'Brien was drafted into the infantry and, though he strongly opposed the war, went to Vietnam as a foot soldier. During part of his time in Vietnam, O'Brien and his platoon were stationed at My Lai, where, the previous year, panicking American soldiers had killed in cold blood every living thing in the village. Vietnam has been the primary focus of O'Brien's fiction. His books include If I Die in a Combat Zone, Box Me Up and Ship Me Home *(1973);* Northern Lights *(1975);* Going After Cacciato *(1978), which won the* National Book Award; The Things They Carried *(1990) a collection of interconnected stories, including the four printed here;* In the Lake of the Woods *(1990), which, in an effort to portray the tragic truth of the My Lai massacre, mixes fact and fiction; and* Tomcat in Love *(1998), a comic novel.*

ON THE RAINY RIVER   (1990)

1   This is one story I've never told before. Not to anyone. Not to my parents, not to my brother or sister, not even to my wife. To go into it, I've always thought, would only cause embarrassment for all of us, a sudden need to be elsewhere, which is the natural response to a confession. Even now, I'll admit, the story makes me squirm. For more than twenty years I've had to live with it, feeling the shame, trying to push it away, and so by this act of remembrance, by putting the facts down on paper, I'm hoping to relieve at least some of the pressure on my dreams. Still, it's a hard story to tell. All of us, I suppose, like to believe that in a moral emergency we will behave like the heroes of our youth, bravely and forthrightly, without thought of personal loss or discredit. Certainly that was my conviction back in the summer of 1968. Tim O'Brien: a secret hero. The Lone Ranger. If the stakes ever became high enough—if the evil were evil enough, if the good were good enough—I would simply tap a secret reservoir of courage that had been accumulating inside me over the years. Courage, I seemed to think, comes to us in finite quantities, like an inheritance, and by being frugal and stashing it away and letting it earn interest, we steadily increase our moral capital in preparation for that day when the account must be drawn down. It was a comforting theory. It dispensed with all those bothersome little acts of daily courage; it offered hope and grace to the repetitive coward; it justified the past while amortizing the future.

2   In June of 1968, a month after graduating from Macalester College, I was drafted to fight a war I hated. I was twenty-one years old. Young, yes, and politically naive, but even so the American war in Vietnam seemed to me wrong. Certain blood was being shed for uncertain reasons. I saw no unity of purpose, no consensus on matters of philosophy or history or law. The very facts were shrouded in uncertainty: Was it a civil war? A war of national liberation or simple aggression? Who started it, and when, and why? What really happened to the USS *Maddox* on that dark night in the Gulf of Tonkin? Was Ho Chi Minh a Communist stooge, or a nationalist savior, or both, or neither? What about the Geneva Accords? What about SEATO and the Cold War? What about dominoes? America was divided on these and a thousand other issues, and the debate had spilled out across the floor of the United States Senate and into the streets, and smart men in pinstripes could not agree on even the most fundamental matters of public policy. The only certainty that summer was moral confusion. It was my view then, and still is, that you don't make war without knowing why. Knowledge, of course, is always imperfect, but it seemed to me that when a nation goes to war it must have reasonable confidence

in the justice and imperative of its cause. You can't fix your mistakes. Once people are dead, you can't make them undead.

3   In any case those were my convictions, and back in college I had taken a modest stand against the war. Nothing radical, no hothead stuff, just ringing a few doorbells for Gene McCarthy, composing a few tedious, uninspired editorials for the campus newspaper. Oddly, though, it was almost entirely an intellectual activity. I brought some energy to it, of course, but it was the energy that accompanies almost any abstract endeavor; I felt no personal danger; I felt no sense of an impending crisis in my life. Stupidly, with a kind of smug removal that I can't begin to fathom, I assumed that the problems of killing and dying did not fall within my special province.

4   The draft notice arrived on June 17, 1968. It was a humid afternoon, I remember, cloudy and very quiet, and I'd just come in from a round of golf. My mother and father were having lunch out in the kitchen. I remember opening up the letter, scanning the first few lines, feeling the blood go thick behind my eyes. I remember a sound in my head. It wasn't thinking, just a silent howl. A million things all at once—I was too *good* for this war. Too smart, too compassionate, too everything. It couldn't happen. I was above it. I had the world dicked—Phi Beta Kappa and summa cum laude and president of the student body and a full-ride scholarship for grad studies at Harvard. A mistake, maybe—a foul-up in the paperwork. I was no soldier. I hated Boy Scouts. I hated camping out. I hated dirt and tents and mosquitoes. The sight of blood made me queasy, and I couldn't tolerate authority, and I didn't know a rifle from a slingshot. I was a *liberal,* for Christ sake: If they needed fresh bodies, why not draft some back-to-the-stone-age hawk? Or some dumb jingo in his hard hat and Bomb Hanoi button, or one of LBJ's pretty daughters, or Westmoreland's whole handsome family—nephews and nieces and baby grandson. There should be a law, I thought. If you support a war, if you think it's worth the price, that's fine, but you have to put your own precious fluids on the line. You have to head for the front and hook up with an infantry unit and help spill the blood. And you have to bring along your wife, or your kids, or your lover. A law, I thought.

5   I remember the rage in my stomach. Later it burned down to a smoldering self-pity, then to numbness. At dinner that night my father asked what my plans were.

6   "Nothing," I said. "Wait."

7   I spent the summer of 1968 working in an Armour meatpacking plant in my hometown of Worthington, Minnesota. The plant specialized in pork products, and for eight hours a day I stood on a quarter-mile assembly line—more properly, a disassembly line—removing blood clots from the necks of dead pigs. My job title, I believe, was Declotter. After slaughter, the hogs were decapitated, split down the length of the belly, pried open, eviscerated, and strung up by the hind hocks on a high conveyer belt. Then gravity took over. By the time a carcass reached my spot on the line, the

fluids had mostly drained out, everything except for thick clots of blood in the neck and upper chest cavity. To remove the stuff, I used a kind of water gun. The machine was heavy, maybe eighty pounds, and was suspended from the ceiling by a heavy rubber cord. There was some bounce to it, and elastic up-and-down give, and the trick was to maneuver the gun with your whole body, not lifting with the arms, just letting the rubber cord do the work for you. At one end was a trigger; at the muzzle end was a small nozzle and a steel roller brush. As a carcass passed by, you'd lean forward and swing the gun up against the clots and squeeze the trigger, all in one motion, and the brush would whirl and water would come shooting out and you'd hear a quick splattering sound as the clots dissolved into a fine red mist. It was not pleasant work. Goggles were a necessity, and a rubber apron, but even so it was like standing for eight hours a day under a lukewarm blood-shower. At night I'd go home smelling of pig. It wouldn't go away. Even after a hot bath, scrubbing hard, the stink was always there—like old bacon, or sausage, a dense greasy pig-stink that soaked deep into my skin and hair. Among other things, I remember, it was tough getting dates that summer. I felt isolated; I spent a lot of time alone. And there was also that draft notice tucked away in my wallet.

8   In the evenings I'd sometimes borrow my father's car and drive aimlessly around town, feeling sorry for myself, thinking about the war and the pig factory and how my life seemed to be collapsing toward slaughter. I felt paralyzed. All around me the options seemed to be narrowing, as if I were hurtling down a huge black funnel, the whole world squeezing in tight. There was no happy way out. The government had ended most graduate school deferments; the waiting lists for the National Guard and Reserves were impossibly long; my health was solid; I didn't qualify for CO status—no religious grounds, no history as a pacifist. Moreover, I could not claim to be opposed to war as a matter of general principle. There were occasions, I believed, when a nation was justified in using military force to achieve its ends, to stop a Hitler or some comparable evil, and I told myself that in such circumstances I would've willingly marched off to the battle. The problem, though, was that a draft board did not let you choose your war.

9   Beyond all this, or at the very center, was the raw fact of terror. I did not want to die. Not ever. But certainly not then, not there, not in a wrong war. Driving up Main Street, past the courthouse and the Ben Franklin store, I sometimes felt the fear spreading inside me like weeds. I imagined myself dead. I imagined myself doing things I could not do—charging an enemy position, taking aim at another human being.

10   At some point in mid-July I began thinking seriously about Canada. The border lay a few hundred miles north, an eight-hour drive. Both my conscience and my instincts were telling me to make a break for it, just take off and run like hell and never stop. In the beginning the idea seemed purely abstract, the word Canada printing itself out in my head; but after a time I could see particular shapes and images, the sorry details of my

own future—a hotel room in Winnipeg, a battered old suitcase, my father's eyes as I tried to explain myself over the telephone. I could almost hear his voice, and my mother's. Run, I'd think. Then I'd think, Impossible. Then a second later I'd think, *Run.*

11   It was a kind of schizophrenia. A moral split. I couldn't make up my mind. I feared the war, yes, but I also feared exile. I was afraid of walking away from my own life, my friends and my family, my whole history, everything that mattered to me. I feared losing the respect of my parents. I feared the law. I feared ridicule and censure. My hometown was a conservative little spot on the prairie, a place where tradition counted, and it was easy to imagine people sitting around a table down at the old Gobbler Café on Main Street, coffee cups poised, the conversation slowly zeroing in on the young O'Brien kid, how the damned sissy had taken off for Canada. At night, when I couldn't sleep, I'd sometimes carry on fierce arguments with those people. I'd be screaming at them, telling them how much I detested their blind, thoughtless, automatic acquiescence to it all, their simple-minded patriotism, their prideful ignorance, their love-it-or-leave-it platitudes, how they were sending me off to fight a war they didn't understand and didn't want to understand. I held them responsible. By God, yes, I *did.* All of them—I held them personally and individually responsible—the polyestered Kiwanis boys, the merchants and farmers, the pious churchgoers, the chatty housewives, the PTA and the Lions club and the Veterans of Foreign Wars and the fine upstanding gentry out at the country club. They didn't know Bao Dai from the man in the moon. They didn't know history. They didn't know the first thing about Diem's tyranny, or the nature of Vietnamese nationalism, or the long colonialism of the French—this was all too damned complicated, it required some reading—but no matter, it was a war to stop the Communists, plain and simple, which was how they liked things, and you were a treasonous pussy if you had second thoughts about killing or dying for plain and simple reasons.

12   I was bitter, sure. But it was so much more than that. The emotions went from outrage to terror to bewilderment to guilt to sorrow and then back again to outrage. I felt a sickness inside me. Real disease.

13   Most of this I've told before, or at least hinted at, but what I have never told is the full truth. How I cracked. How at work one morning, standing on the pig line, I felt something break open in my chest. I don't know what it was. I'll never know. But it was real, I know that much, it was a physical rupture—a cracking-leaking-popping feeling. I remember dropping my water gun. Quickly, almost without thought, I took off my apron and walked out of the plant and drove home. It was midmorning, I remember, and the house was empty. Down in my chest there was still that leaking sensation, something very warm and precious spilling out, and I was covered with blood and hog-stink, and for a long while I just concentrated on holding myself together. I remember taking a hot shower. I remember packing a suitcase and carrying it out to the kitchen, standing very still

for a few minutes, looking carefully at the familiar objects all around me. The old chrome toaster, the telephone, the pink and white Formica on the kitchen counters. The room was full of bright sunshine. Everything sparkled. My house, I thought. My life. I'm not sure how long I stood there, but later I scribbled out a short note to my parents.

14   What it said, exactly, I don't recall now. Something vague. Taking off, will call, love Tim.

15   I drove north.

16   It's a blur now, as it was then, and all I remember is a sense of high velocity and the feel of the steering wheel in my hands. I was riding on adrenaline. A giddy feeling, in a way, except there was the dreamy edge of impossibility to it—like running a dead-end maze—no way out—it couldn't come to a happy conclusion and yet I was doing it anyway because it was all I could think of to do. It was pure flight, fast and mindless. I had no plan. Just hit the border at high speed and crash through and keep on running. Near dusk I passed through Bemidji, then turned northeast toward International Falls. I spent the night in the car behind a closed-down gas station a half mile from the border. In the morning, after gassing up, I headed straight west along the Rainy River, which separates Minnesota from Canada, and which for me separated one life from another. The land was mostly wilderness. Here and there I passed a motel or bait shop, but otherwise the country unfolded in great sweeps of pine and birch and sumac. Though it was still August, the air already had the smell of October, football season, piles of yellow-red leaves, everything crisp and clean. I remember a huge blue sky. Off to my right was the Rainy River, wide as a lake in places, and beyond the Rainy River was Canada.

17   For a while I just drove, not aiming at anything, then in the late morning I began looking for a place to lie low for a day or two. I was exhausted, and scared sick, and around noon I pulled into an old fishing resort called the Tip Top Lodge. Actually it was not a lodge at all, just eight or nine tiny yellow cabins clustered on a peninsula that jutted northward into the Rainy River. The place was in sorry shape. There was a dangerous wooden dock, an old minnow tank, a flimsy tar paper boathouse along the shore. The main building, which stood in a cluster of pines on high ground, seemed to lean heavily to one side, like a cripple, the roof sagging toward Canada. Briefly, I thought about turning around, just giving up, but then I got out of the car and walked up to the front porch.

18   The man who opened the door that day is the hero of my life. How do I say this without sounding sappy? Blurt it out—the man saved me. He offered exactly what I needed, without questions, without any words at all. He took me in. He was there at the critical time—a silent, watchful presence. Six days later, when it ended, I was unable to find a proper way to thank him, and I never have, and so, if nothing else, this story represents a small gesture of gratitude twenty years overdue.

19   Even after two decades I can close my eyes and return to that porch at the Tip Top Lodge. I can see the old guy staring at me. Elroy Berdahl: eighty-one years old, skinny and shrunken and mostly bald. He wore a

flannel shirt and brown work pants. In one hand, I remember, he carried a green apple, a small paring knife in the other. His eyes had the bluish gray color of a razor blade, the same polished shine, and as he peered up at me I felt a strange sharpness, almost painful, a cutting sensation, as if his gaze were somehow slicing me open. In part, no doubt, it was my own sense of guilt, but even so I'm absolutely certain that the old man took one look and went right to the heart of things—a kid in trouble. When I asked for a room, Elroy made a little clicking sound with his tongue. He nodded, led me out to one of the cabins, and dropped a key in my hand. I remember smiling at him. I also remember wishing I hadn't. The old man shook his head as if to tell me it wasn't worth the bother.

20   "Dinner at five-thirty," he said. "You eat fish?"

21   "Anything," I said.

22   Elroy grunted and said, "I'll bet."

23   We spent six days together at the Tip Top Lodge. Just the two of us. Tourist season was over, and there were no boats on the river, and the wilderness seemed to withdraw into a great permanent stillness. Over those six days Elroy Berdahl and I took most of our meals together. In the mornings we sometimes went out on long hikes into the woods, and at night we played Scrabble or listened to records or sat reading in front of his big stone fireplace. At times I felt the awkwardness of an intruder, but Elroy accepted me into his quiet routine without fuss or ceremony. He took my presence for granted, the same way he might've sheltered a stray cat—no wasted sighs or pity—and there was never any talk about it. Just the opposite. What I remember more than anything is the man's willful, almost ferocious silence. In all that time together, all those hours, he never asked the obvious questions: Why was I there? Why alone? Why so preoccupied? If Elroy was curious about any of this, he was careful never to put it into words.

24   My hunch, though, is that he already knew. At least the basics. After all, it was 1968, and guys were burning draft cards, and Canada was just a boat ride away. Elroy Berdahl was no hick. His bedroom, I remember, was cluttered with books and newspapers. He killed me at the Scrabble board, barely concentrating, and on those occasions when speech was necessary he had a way of compressing large thoughts into small, cryptic packets of language. One evening, just at sunset, he pointed up at an owl circling over the violet-lighted forest to the west.

25   "Hey, O'Brien," he said. "There's Jesus."

26   The man was sharp—he didn't miss much. Those razor eyes. Now and then he'd catch me staring out at the river, at the far shore, and I could almost hear the tumblers clicking in his head. Maybe I'm wrong, but I doubt it.

27   One thing for certain, he knew I was in desperate trouble. And he knew I couldn't talk about it. The wrong word—or even the right word— and I would've disappeared. I was wired and jittery. My skin felt too tight. After supper one evening I vomited and went back to my cabin and lay down for a few moments and then vomited again; another time, in the mid-

dle of the afternoon, I began sweating and couldn't shut it off. I went through whole days feeling dizzy with sorrow. I couldn't sleep; I couldn't lie still. At night I'd toss around in bed, half awake, half dreaming, imagining how I'd sneak down to the beach and quietly push one of the old man's boats out into the river and start paddling my way toward Canada. There were times when I thought I'd gone off the psychic edge. I couldn't tell up from down, I was just falling, and late in the night I'd lie there watching weird pictures spin through my head. Getting chased by the Border Patrol—helicopters and searchlights and barking dogs—I'd be crashing through the woods, I'd be down on my hands and knees—people shouting out my name—the law closing in on all sides—my hometown draft board and the FBI and the Royal Canadian Mounted Police. It all seemed crazy and impossible. Twenty-one years old, an ordinary kid with all the ordinary dreams and ambitions, and all I wanted was to live the life I was born to—a mainstream life—I loved baseball and hamburgers and cherry Cokes—and now I was off on the margins of exile, leaving my country forever, and it seemed so impossible and terrible and sad.

28   I'm not sure how I made it through those six days. Most of it I can't remember. On two or three afternoons, to pass some time, I helped Elroy get the place ready for winter, sweeping down the cabins and hauling in the boats, little chores that kept my body moving. The days were cool and bright. The nights were very dark. One morning the old man showed me how to split and stack firewood, and for several hours we just worked in silence out behind his house. At one point, I remember, Elroy put down his maul and looked at me for a long time, his lips drawn as if framing a difficult question, but then he shook his head and went back to work. The man's self-control was amazing. He never pried. He never put me in a position that required lies or denials. To an extent, I suppose, his reticence was typical of that part of Minnesota, where privacy still held value, and even if I'd been walking around with some horrible deformity—four arms and three heads—I'm sure the old man would've talked about everything except those extra arms and heads. Simple politeness was part of it. But even more than that, I think, the man understood that words were insufficient. The problem had gone beyond discussion. During that long summer I'd been over and over the various arguments, all the pros and cons, and it was no longer a question that could be decided by an act of pure reason. Intellect had come up against emotion. My conscience told me to run, but some irrational and powerful force was resisting, like a weight pushing me toward the war. What it came down to, stupidly, was a sense of shame. Hot, stupid shame. I did not want people to think badly of me. Not my parents, not my brother and sister, not even the folks down at the Gobbler Café. I was ashamed to be there at the Tip Top Lodge. I was ashamed of my conscience, ashamed to be doing the right thing.

29   Some of this Elroy must've understood. Not the details, of course, but the plain fact of crisis.

30   Although the old man never confronted me about it, there was one occasion when he came close to forcing the whole thing out into the open. It was early evening, and we'd just finished supper, and over coffee and dessert I asked him about my bill, how much I owed so far. For a long while the old man squinted down at the tablecloth.

31   "Well, the basic rate," he said, "is fifty bucks a night. Not counting meals. This makes four nights, right?"

32   I nodded. I had three hundred and twelve dollars in my wallet.

33   Elroy kept his eyes on the tablecloth. "Now that's an onseason price. To be fair, I suppose we should knock it down a peg or two." He leaned back in his chair. "What's a reasonable number, you figure?"

34   "I don't know," I said. "Forty?"

35   "Forty's good. Forty a night. Then we tack on food—say another hundred? Two hundred sixty total?"

36   "I guess."

37   He raised his eyebrows. "Too much?"

38   "No, that's fair. It's fine. Tomorrow, though...I think I'd better take off tomorrow."

39   Elroy shrugged and began clearing the table. For a time he fussed with the dishes, whistling to himself as if the subject had been settled. After a second he slapped his hands together.

40   "You know what we forgot?" he said. "We forgot wages. Those odd jobs you done. What we have to do, we have to figure out what your time's worth. Your last job—how much did you pull in an hour?"

41   "Not enough," I said.

42   "A bad one?"

43   "Yes. Pretty bad."

44   Slowly then, without intending any long sermon, I told him about my days at the pig plant. It began as a straight recitation of the facts, but before I could stop myself I was talking about the blood clots and the water gun and how the smell had soaked into my skin and how I couldn't wash it away. I went on for a long time. I told him about wild hogs squealing in my dreams, the sounds of butchery, slaughter-house sounds, and how I'd sometimes wake up with that greasy pig-stink in my throat.

45   When I was finished, Elroy nodded at me.

46   "Well, to be honest," he said, "when you first showed up here, I wondered about all that. The aroma, I mean. Smelled like you was awful damned fond of pork chops." The old man almost smiled. He made a snuffling sound, then sat down with a pencil and a piece of paper. "So what'd this crud job pay? Ten bucks an hour? Fifteen?"

47   "Less."

48   Elroy shook his head. "Let's make it fifteen. You put in twenty-five hours here, easy. That's three hundred seventy-five bucks total wages. We subtract the two hundred sixty for food and lodging, I still owe you a hundred and fifteen."

49   He took four fifties out of his shirt pocket and laid them on the table.

50   "Call it even," he said.

51   "No."

52   "Pick it up. Get yourself a haircut."

53   The money lay on the table for the rest of the evening. It was still there when I went back to my cabin. In the morning, though, I found an envelope tacked to my door. Inside were the four fifties and a two-word note that said EMERGENCY FUND.

54   The man knew.

55   Looking back after twenty years, I sometimes wonder if the events of that summer didn't happen in some other dimension, a place where your life exists before you've lived it, and where it goes afterward. None of it ever seemed real. During my time at the Tip Top Lodge I had the feeling that I'd slipped out of my own skin, hovering a few feet away while some poor yo-yo with my name and face tried to make his way toward a future he didn't understand and didn't want. Even now I can see myself as I was then. It's like watching an old home movie: I'm young and tan and fit. I've got hair—lots of it. I don't smoke or drink. I'm wearing faded blue jeans and a white polo shirt. I can see myself sitting on Elroy Berdahl's dock near dusk one evening, the sky a bright shimmering pink, and I'm finishing up a letter to my parents that tells what I'm about to do and why I'm doing it and how sorry I am that I'd never found the courage to talk to them about it. I ask them not to be angry. I try to explain some of my feelings, but there aren't enough words, and so I just say that it's a thing that has to be done. At the end of the letter I talk about the vacations we used to take up in this north country, at a place called Whitefish Lake, and how the scenery here reminds me of those good times. I tell them I'm fine. I tell them I'll write again from Winnipeg or Montreal or wherever I end up.

56   On my last full day, the sixth day, the old man took me out fishing on the Rainy River. The afternoon was sunny and cold. A stiff breeze came in from the north, and I remember how the little fourteen-foot boat made sharp rocking motions as we pushed off from the dock. The current was fast. All around us, I remember, there was a vastness to the world, an unpeopled rawness, just the trees and the sky and the water reaching out toward nowhere. The air had the brittle scent of October.

57   For ten or fifteen minutes Elroy held a course upstream, the river choppy and silver-gray, then he turned straight north and put the engine on full throttle. I felt the bow lift beneath me. I remember the wind in my ears, the sound of the old outboard Evinrude. For a time I didn't pay attention to anything, just feeling the cold spray against my face, but then it occurred to me that at some point we must've passed into Canadian waters, across that dotted line between two different worlds, and I remember a sudden tightness in my chest as I looked up and watched the far shore come at me. This wasn't a daydream. It was tangible and real. As we came in toward land, Elroy cut the engine, letting the boat fishtail lightly about twenty yards off shore. The old man didn't look at me or speak. Bending down, he

opened up his tackle box and busied himself with a bobber and a piece of wire leader, humming to himself, his eyes down.

58   It struck me then that he must've planned it. I'll never be certain, of course, but I think he meant to bring me up against the realities, to guide me across the river and to take me to the edge and to stand a kind of vigil as I chose a life for myself.

59   I remember staring at the old man, then at my hands, then at Canada. The shoreline was dense with brush and timber. I could see tiny red berries on the bushes. I could see a squirrel up in one of the birch trees, a big crow looking at me from a boulder along the river. That close—twenty yards—and I could see the delicate latticework of the leaves, the texture of the soil, the browned needles beneath the pines, the configurations of geology and human history. Twenty yards. I could've done it. I could've jumped and started swimming for my life. Inside me, in my chest. I felt a terrible squeezing pressure. Even now, as I write this, I can still feel that tightness. And I want you to feel it—the wind coming off the river, the waves, the silence, the wooded frontier. You're at the bow of a boat on the Rainy River. You're twenty-one years old, you're scared, and there's a hard squeezing pressure in your chest.

60   What would you do?

61   Would you jump? Would you feel pity for yourself? Would you think about your family and your childhood and your dreams and all you're leaving behind? Would it hurt? Would it feel like dying? Would you cry, as I did?

62   I tried to swallow it back. I tried to smile, except I was crying.

63   Now, perhaps, you can understand why I've never told this story before. It's not just the embarrassment of tears. That's part of it, no doubt, but what embarrasses me much more, and always will, is the paralysis that took my heart. A moral freeze: I couldn't decide, I couldn't act, I couldn't comport myself with even a pretense of modest human dignity.

64   All I could do was cry. Quietly, not bawling, just the chest-chokes.

65   At the rear of the boat Elroy Berdahl pretended not to notice. He held a fishing rod in his hands, his head bowed to hide his eyes. He kept humming a soft, monotonous little tune. Everywhere, it seemed, in the trees and water and sky, a great worldwide sadness came pressing down on me, a crushing sorrow, sorrow like I had never known it before. And what was so sad, I realized, was that Canada had become a pitiful fantasy. Silly and hopeless. It was no longer a possibility. Right then, with the shore so close, I understood that I would not do what I should do. I would not swim away from my hometown and my country and my life. I would not be brave. That old image of myself as a hero, as a man of conscience and courage, all that was just a threadbare pipe dream. Bobbing there on the Rainy River, looking back at the Minnesota shore, I felt a sudden swell of helplessness come over me, a drowning sensation, as if I had toppled overboard and was being swept away by the silver waves. Chunks of my

own history flashed by. I saw a seven-year-old boy in a white cowboy hat and a Lone Ranger mask and a pair of holstered six-shooters; I saw a twelve-year-old Little League shortstop pivoting to turn a double play; I saw a sixteen-year-old kid decked out for his first prom, looking spiffy in a white tux and a black bow tie, his hair cut short and flat, his shoes freshly polished. My whole life seemed to spill out into the river, swirling away from me, everything I had ever been or ever wanted to be. I couldn't get my breath; I couldn't stay afloat; I couldn't tell which way to swim. A hallucination, I suppose, but it was as real as anything I would ever feel. I saw my parents calling to me from the far shoreline. I saw my brother and sister, all the townsfolk, the mayor and the entire Chamber of Commerce and all my old teachers and girlfriends and high school buddies. Like some weird sporting event: everybody screaming from the side-lines, rooting me on—a loud stadium roar. Hotdogs and popcorn—stadium smells, stadium heat. A squad of cheer-leaders did cartwheels along the banks of the Rainy River; they had megaphones and pompoms and smooth brown thighs. The crowd swayed left and right. A marching band played fight songs. All my aunts and uncles were there, and Abraham Lincoln, and Saint George, and a nine-year-old girl named Linda who had died of a brain tumor back in fifth grade, and several members of the United States Senate, and a blind poet scribbling notes, and LBJ, and Huck Finn, and Abbie Hoffman, and all the dead soldiers back from the grave, and the many thousands who were later to die—villagers with terrible burns, little kids without arms or legs—yes, and the Joint Chiefs of Staff were there, and a couple of popes, and a first lieutenant named Jimmy Cross, and the last surviving veteran of the American Civil War, and Jane Fonda dressed up as Barbarella, and an old man sprawled beside a pigpen, and my grandfather, and Gary Cooper, and a kind-faced woman carrying an umbrella and a copy of Plato's *Republic*, and a million ferocious citizens waving flags of all shapes and colors—people in hard hats, people in headbands—they were all whooping and chanting and urging me toward one shore or the other. I saw faces from my distant past and distant future. My wife was there. My unborn daughter waved at me, and my two sons hopped up and down, and a drill sergeant named Blyton sneered and shot up a finger and shook his head. There was a choir in bright purple robes. There was a cabbie from the Bronx. There was a slim young man I would one day kill with a hand grenade along a red clay trail outside the village of My Khe.

66   The little aluminum boat rocked softly beneath me. There was the wind and the sky.

67   I tried to will myself overboard.

68   I gripped the edge of the boat and leaned forward and thought, *Now.*

69   I did try. It just wasn't possible.

70   All those eyes on me—the town, the whole universe—and I couldn't risk the embarrassment. It was as if there were an audience to my life, that swirl of faces along the river, and in my head I could hear people screaming at me. Traitor! they yelled. Turncoat! Pussy! I felt myself blush.

I couldn't tolerate it. I couldn't endure the mockery, or the disgrace, or the patriotic ridicule. Even in my imagination, the shore just twenty yards away, I couldn't make myself be brave. It had nothing to do with morality. Embarrassment, that's all it was.

71   And right then I submitted.

72   I would go to the war—I would kill and maybe die—because I was embarrassed not to.

73   That was the sad thing. And so I sat in the bow of the boat and cried.

74   It was loud now. Loud, hard crying.

75   Elroy Berdahl remained quiet. He kept fishing. He worked his line with the tips of his fingers, patiently, squinting out at his red and white bobber on the Rainy River. His eyes were flat and impassive. He didn't speak. He was simply there, like the river and the late-summer sun. And yet by his presence, his mute watchfulness, he made it real. He was the true audience. He was a witness, like God, or like the gods, who look on in absolute silence as we live our lives, as we make our choices or fail to make them.

76   "Ain't biting," he said.

77   Then after a time the old man pulled in his line and turned the boat back toward Minnesota.

78   I don't remember saying goodbye. That last night we had dinner together, and I went to bed early, and in the morning Elroy fixed breakfast for me. When I told him I'd be leaving, the old man nodded as if he already knew. He looked down at the table and smiled.

79   At some point later in the morning it's possible that we shook hands—I just don't remember—but I do know that by the time I'd finished packing the old man had disappeared. Around noon, when I took my suitcase out to the car, I noticed that his old black pickup truck was no longer parked in front of the house. I went inside and waited for a while, but I felt a bone certainty that he wouldn't be back. In a way, I thought, it was appropriate. I washed up the breakfast dishes, left his two hundred dollars on the kitchen counter, got into the car, and drove south toward home.

80   The day was cloudy. I passed through towns with familiar names, through the pine forests and down to the prairie, and then to Vietnam, where I was a soldier, and then home again. I survived, but it's not a happy ending. I was a coward. I went to the war.

Questions for Discussion

1. Explain O'Brien's youthful theory about courage.

2. Describe O'Brien's summer job. How does it influence his decision? What causes him to leave the job and drive north?

3. Explain O'Brien's imagery of the pig stench and relate it to the stench of war.

4. In what way is the Tip Top Lodge misnamed? In what way is the name appropriate?

5. O'Brien chose to allow himself to be drafted and sent to Vietnam. Why does he now consider his decision cowardly?

6. Why did O'Brien oppose the war in Vietnam? Referring to the summer of 1968 when he received his draft notice, O'Brien says, "The only certainty that summer was moral confusion." What does he mean? What are some of the uncertainties that contributed to his opposition to the war?

7. What is a conscientious objector? Why does O'Brien not apply for conscientious objector status?

8. How does the fishing trip on Rainy River precipitate O'Brien's decision not to flee to Canada?

9. What does Elroy Berdahl do for O'Brien that causes O'Brien to regard Berdahl as "the hero of [his] life"?

How to Tell a True War Story   (1990)

1   This is true.

2   I had a buddy in Vietnam. His name was Bob Kiley, but everybody called him Rat.

3   A friend of his gets killed, so about a week later Rat sits down and writes a letter to the guy's sister. Rat tells her what a great brother she had, how together the guy was, a number one pal and comrade. A real soldier's soldier, Rat says. Then he tells a few stories to make the point, how her brother would always volunteer for stuff nobody else would volunteer for in a million years, dangerous stuff, like doing recon or going out on these really badass night patrols. Stainless steel balls, Rat tells her. The guy was a little crazy, for sure, but crazy in a good way, a real daredevil, because he liked the challenge of it, he liked testing himself, just man against gook. A great, great guy, Rat says.

4   Anyway, it's a terrific letter, very personal and touching. Rat almost bawls writing it. He gets all teary telling about the good times they had together, how her brother made the war seem almost fun, always raising hell and lighting up villes and bringing smoke to bear every which way. A great sense of humor, too. Like the time at this river when he went fishing with a whole damn crate of hand grenades. Probably the funniest thing in world history, Rat says, all that gore, about twenty zillion dead gook fish. Her brother, he had the right attitude. He knew how to have a good time. On Halloween, this real hot spooky night, the dude paints up his body all different colors and puts on this weird mask and hikes over to a ville and goes trick-or-treating almost stark naked, just boots and balls and an M–16. A tremendous human being, Rat says. Pretty nutso sometimes, but you could trust him with your life.

5   And then the letter gets very sad and serious. Rat pours his heart out. He says he loved the guy. He says the guy was his best friend in the world. They were like soul mates, he says, like twins or something, they had a whole lot in common. He tells the guy's sister he'll look her up when the war's over.

6   So what happens?

7   Rat mails the letter. He waits two months. The dumb cooze never writes back.

8   A true war story is never moral. It does not instruct, nor encourage virtue, nor suggest models of proper human behavior, nor restrain men from doing the things men have always done. If a story seems moral, do not believe it. If at the end of a war story you feel uplifted, or if you feel that some small bit of rectitude has been salvaged from the larger waste, then you have been made the victim of a very old and terrible lie. There is no rectitude whatsoever. There is no virtue. As a first rule of thumb, therefore, you can tell a true war story by its absolute and uncompromising allegiance to obscenity and evil. Listen to Rat Kiley. Cooze, he says. He does not say bitch. He certainly does not say woman, or girl. He says cooze. Then he spits and stares. He's nineteen years old—it's too much for him—so he looks at you with those big sad gentle killer eyes and says cooze, because his friend is dead, and because it's so incredibly sad and true: she never wrote back.

9   You can tell a true war story if it embarrasses you. If you don't care for obscenity, you don't care for the truth; if you don't care for the truth, watch how you vote. Send guys to war, they come home talking dirty.

10   Listen to Rat: "Jesus Christ, man, I write this beautiful fuckin' letter, I slave over it, and what happens? The dumb cooze never writes back."

11   The dead guy's name was Curt Lemon. What happened was, we crossed a muddy river and marched west into the mountains, and on the third day we took a break along a trail junction in deep jungle. Right away, Lemon and Rat Kiley started goofing. They didn't understand about the spookiness. They were kids; they just didn't know. A nature hike, they thought, not even a war, so they went off into the shade of some giant trees—quadruple canopy, no sunlight at all—and they were giggling and calling each other yellow mother and playing a silly game they'd invented. The game involved smoke grenades, which were harmless unless you did stupid things, and what they did was pull out the pin and stand a few feet apart and play catch under the shade of those huge trees. Whoever chickened out was a yellow mother. And if nobody chickened out, the grenade would make a light popping sound and they'd be covered with smoke and they'd laugh and dance around and then do it again.

12   It's all exactly true.

13   It happened, to *me*, nearly twenty years ago, and I still remember that trail junction and those giant trees and a soft dripping sound somewhere beyond the trees. I remember the smell of moss. Up in the canopy there were tiny white blossoms, but no sunlight at all, and I remember the shadows spreading out under the trees where Curt Lemon and Rat Kiley were playing catch with smoke grenades. Mitchell Sanders sat flipping his yo-yo. Norman Bowker and Kiowa and Dave Jensen were dozing, or half dozing, and all around us were those ragged green mountains.

14   Except for the laughter things were quiet.

15   At one point, I remember, Mitchell Sanders turned and looked at me, not quite nodding, as if to warn me about something, as if he already *knew*, then after a while he rolled up his yo-yo and moved away.

16   It's hard to tell you what happened next.

17   They were just goofing. There was a noise, I suppose, which must've been the detonator, so I glanced behind me and watched Lemon step from the shade into bright sunlight. His face was suddenly brown and shining. A handsome kid, really. Sharp gray eyes, lean and narrow-waisted, and when he died it was almost beautiful, the way the sunlight came around him and lifted him up and sucked him high into a tree full of moss and vines and white blossoms.

18   In any war story, but especially a true one, it's difficult to separate what happened from what seemed to happen. What seems to happen becomes its own happening and has to be told that way. The angles of vision are skewed. When a booby trap explodes, you close your eyes and duck and float outside yourself. When a guy dies, like Curt Lemon, you look away and then look back for a moment and then look away again. The pictures get jumbled; you tend to miss a lot. And then afterward, when you go to tell about it, there is always that surreal seemingness, which makes the story seem untrue, but which in fact represents the hard and exact truth as it *seemed*.

19   In many cases a true war story cannot be believed. If you believe it, be skeptical. It's a question of credibility. Often the crazy stuff is true and the normal stuff isn't, because the normal stuff is necessary to make you believe the truly incredible craziness.

20   In other cases you can't even tell a true war story. Sometimes it's just beyond telling.

21   I heard this one, for example, from Mitchell Sanders. It was near dusk and we were sitting at my foxhole along a wide muddy river north of Quang Ngai. I remember how peaceful the twilight was. A deep pinkish red spilled out on the river, which moved without sound, and in the morning we would cross the river and march west into the mountains. The occasion was right for a good story.

22   "God's truth," Mitchell Sanders said. "A six-man patrol goes up into the mountains on a basic listening-post operation. The idea's to spend a week up there, just lie low and listen for enemy movement. They've got a radio along, so if they hear anything suspicious—anything—they're supposed to call in artillery or gunships, whatever it takes. Otherwise they keep strict field discipline. Absolute silence. They just listen."

23   Sanders glanced at me to make sure I had the scenario. He was playing with his yo-yo, dancing it with short, tight little strokes of the wrist.

24   His face was blank in the dusk.

25   "We're talking regulation, by-the-book LP. These six guys, they don't say boo for a solid week. They don't got tongues. *All* ears."

26   "Right," I said.

27   "Understand me?"

28   "Invisible."

29   Sanders nodded.

30   "Affirm," he said. "Invisible. So what happens is, these guys get themselves deep in the bush, all camouflaged up, and they lie down and wait
and that's all they do, nothing else, they lie there for seven straight days
and just listen. And man, I'll tell you—it's spooky. This is mountains. You
don't *know* spooky till you been there. Jungle, sort of, except it's way up
in the clouds and there's always this fog—like rain, except it's not raining—everything's all wet and swirly and tangled up and you can't see
jack, you can't find your own pecker to piss with. Like you don't even
have a body. Serious spooky. You just go with the vapors—the fog sort of
takes you in...And the sounds, man. The sounds carry forever. You hear
stuff nobody should *ever* hear."

31   Sanders was quiet for a second, just working the yo-yo, then he smiled
at me.

32   "So after a couple days the guys start hearing this real soft, kind of
wacked-out music. Weird echoes and stuff. Like a radio or something, but
it's not a radio, it's this strange gook music that comes right out of the
rocks. Faraway, sort of, but right up close, too. They try to ignore it. But
it's a listening post, right? So they listen. And every night they keep hearing that crazyass gook concert. All kinds of chimes and xylophones. I
mean, this is wilderness—no way, it can't be real—but there it *is*, like the
mountains are tuned in to Radio fucking Hanoi. Naturally they get nervous. One guy sticks Juicy Fruit in his ears. Another guy almost flips.
Thing is, though, they can't report music. They can't get on the horn and
call back to base and say, 'Hey, listen, we need some firepower, we got to
blow away this weirdo gook rock band.' They can't do that. It wouldn't go
down. So they lie there in the fog and keep their mouths shut. And what
makes it extra bad, see, is the poor dudes can't horse around like normal.
Can't joke it away. Can't even talk to each other except maybe in whispers, all hush-hush, and that just revs up the willies. All they do is listen."

33   Again there was some silence as Mitchell Sanders looked out on the
river. The dark was coming on hard now, and off to the west I could see
the mountains rising in silhouette, all the mysteries and unknowns.

34   "This next part," Sanders said quietly, "you won't believe."

35   "Probably not," I said.

36   "You won't. And you know why?" He gave me a long, tired smile.
"Because it happened. Because every word is absolutely dead-on true."

37   Sanders made a sound in his throat, like a sigh, as if to say he didn't
care if I believed him or not. But he did care. He wanted me to feel the
truth, to believe by the raw force of feeling. He seemed sad, in a way.

38   "These six guys," he said, "they're pretty fried out by now, and one
night they start hearing voices. Like at a cocktail party. That's what it
sounds like, this big swank gook cocktail party somewhere out there in
the fog. Music and chitchat and stuff. It's crazy, I know, but they hear the
champagne corks. They hear the actual martini glasses. Real hoity-toity,
all very civilized, except this isn't civilization. This is Nam.

39   "Anyway, the guys try to be cool. They just lie there and groove, but after a while they start hearing—you won't believe this—they hear chamber music. They hear violins and cellos. They hear this terrific mama-san soprano. Then after a while they hear gook opera and a glee club and the Haiphong Boys Choir and a barbershop quartet and all kinds of weird chanting and Buddha-Buddha stuff. And the whole time, in the background, there's still that cocktail party going on. All these different voices. Not human voices, though. Because it's the mountains. Follow me? The rock—it's *talking*. And the fog, too, and the grass and the goddamn mongooses. Everything talks. The trees talk politics, the monkeys talk religion. The whole country. Vietnam. The place talks. It talks. Understand? Nam—it truly *talks*.

40   "The guys can't cope. They lose it. They get on the radio and report enemy movement—a whole army, they say—and they order up the firepower. They get arty and gunships. They call in air strikes. And I'll tell you, they fuckin' crash that cocktail party. All night long, they just smoke those mountains. They make jungle juice. They blow away trees and glee clubs and whatever else there is to blow away. Scorch time. They walk napalm up and down the ridges. They bring in the Cobras and F-4s, they use Willie Peter and HE and incendiaries. It's all fire. They make those mountains burn.

41   "Around dawn things finally get quiet. Like you never even *heard* quiet before. One of those real thick, real misty days—just clouds and fog, they're off in this special zone—and the mountains are absolutely dead-flat silent. Like *Brigadoon*—pure vapor, you know? Everything's all sucked up inside the fog. Not a single sound, except they still *hear* it.

42   "So they pack up and start humping. They head down the mountain, back to base camp, and when they get there they don't say diddly. They don't talk. Not a word, like they're deaf and dumb. Later on this fat bird colonel comes up and asks what the hell happened out there. What'd they hear? Why all the ordnance? The man's ragged out, he gets down tight on their case. I mean, they spent six trillion dollars on firepower, and this fatass colonel wants answers, he wants to know what the fuckin' story is.

43   "But the guys don't say zip. They just look at him for a while, sort of funny like, sort of amazed, and the whole war is right there in that stare. It says everything you can't ever say. It says, man, you got *wax* in your ears. It says, poor bastard, you'll never know—wrong frequency—you don't *even* want to hear this. Then they salute the fucker and walk away, because certain stories you don't ever tell."

44   You can tell a true war story by the way it never seems to end. Not then, not ever. Not when Mitchell Sanders stood up and moved off into the dark.

45   It all happened.

46   Even now, at this instant, I remember that yo-yo. In a way, I suppose, you had to be there, you had to hear it, but I could tell how desperately Sanders wanted me to believe him, his frustration at not quite getting the details right, not quite pinning down the final and definitive truth.

47   And I remember sitting at my foxhole that night, watching the shadows of Quang Ngai, thinking about the coming day and how we would cross the river and march west into the mountains, all the ways I might die, all the things I did not understand.

48   Late in the night Mitchell Sanders touched my shoulder. "Just came to me," he whispered. "The moral, I mean. Nobody listens. Nobody hears nothin'. Like that fatass colonel. The politicians, all the civilian types. Your girlfriend. My girlfriend. Everybody's sweet little virgin girlfriend. What they need is to go out on LP. The vapors, man. Trees and rocks— you got to *listen* to your enemy."

49   And then again, in the morning, Sanders came up to me. The platoon was preparing to move out, checking weapons, going through all the little rituals that preceded a day's march. Already the lead squad had crossed the river and was filing off toward the west.

50   "I got a confession to make," Sanders said. "Last night, man, I had to make up a few things."

51   "I know that."

52   "The glee club. There wasn't any glee club."

53   "Right."

54   "No opera."

55   "Forget it, I understand."

56   "Yeah, but listen, it's still true. Those six guys, they heard wicked sound out there. They heard sound you just plain won't believe."

57   Sanders pulled on his rucksack, closed his eyes for a moment, then almost smiled at me. I knew what was coming.

58   "All right," I said, "what's the moral?"

59   "Forget it."

60   "No, go ahead."

61   For a long while he was quiet, looking away, and the silence kept stretching out until it was almost embarrassing. Then he shrugged and gave me a stare that lasted all day.

62   "Hear that quiet, man?" he said. "That quiet—just listen. There's your moral."

63   In a true war story, if there's a moral at all, it's like the thread that makes the cloth. You can't tease it out. You can't extract the meaning without unraveling the deeper meaning. And in the end, really, there's nothing much to say about a true war story, except maybe "Oh."

64   True war stories do not generalize. They do not indulge in abstraction or analysis.

65   For example: War is hell. As a moral declaration the old truism seems perfectly true, and yet because it abstracts, because it generalizes, I can't believe it with my stomach. Nothing turns inside.

66   It comes down to gut instinct. A true war story, if truly told, makes the stomach believe.

67   This one does it for me. I've told it before—many times, many versions—but here's what actually happened.

68   We crossed that river and marched west into the mountains. On the third day, Curt Lemon stepped on a booby-trapped 105 round. He was playing catch with Rat Kiley, laughing, and then he was dead. The trees were thick; it took nearly an hour to cut an LZ for the dustoff.

69   Later, higher in the mountains, we came across a baby VC water buffalo. What it was doing there I don't know—no farms or paddies—but we chased it down and got a rope around it and led it along to a deserted village where we set up for the night. After supper Rat Kiley went over and stroked its nose.

70   He opened up a can of C rations, pork and beans, but the baby buffalo wasn't interested.

71   Rat shrugged.

72   He stepped back and shot it through the right front knee. The animal did not make a sound. It went down hard, then got up again, and Rat took careful aim and shot off an ear. He shot it in the hindquarters and in the little hump at its back. He shot it twice in the flanks. It wasn't to kill; it was to hurt. He put the rifle muzzle up against the mouth and shot the mouth away. Nobody said much. The whole platoon stood there watching, feeling all kinds of things, but there wasn't a great deal of pity for the baby water buffalo. Curt Lemon was dead. Rat Kiley had lost his best friend in the world. Later in the week he would write a long personal letter to the guy's sister, who would not write back, but for now it was a question of pain. He shot off the tail. He shot away chunks of meat below the ribs. All around us there was the smell of smoke and filth and deep greenery, and the evening was humid and very hot. Rat went to automatic. He shot randomly, almost casually, quick little spurts in the belly and butt. Then he reloaded, squatted down, and shot it in the left front knee. Again the animal fell hard and tried to get up, but this time it couldn't quite make it. It wobbled and went down sideways. Rat shot it in the nose. He bent forward and whispered something, as if talking to a pet, then he shot it in the throat. All the while the baby buffalo was silent, or almost silent, just a light bubbling sound where the nose had been. It lay very still. Nothing moved except the eyes, which were enormous, the pupils shiny black and dumb.

73   Rat Kiley was crying. He tried to say something, but then cradled his rifle and went off by himself.

74   The rest of us stood in a ragged circle around the baby buffalo. For a time no one spoke. We had witnessed something essential, something brand-new and profound, a piece of the world so startling there was not yet a name for it.

75   Somebody kicked the baby buffalo.

76   It was still alive, though just barely, just in the eyes.

77   "Amazing," Dave Jensen said. "My whole life, I never seen anything like it."

78   "Never?"

79   "Not hardly. Not once."

80   Kiowa and Mitchell Sanders picked up the baby buffalo. They hauled it across the open square, hoisted it up, and dumped it in the village well.

81   Afterward, we sat waiting for Rat to get himself together.

82   "Amazing," Dave Jensen kept saying. "A new wrinkle. I never seen it before."

83   Mitchell Sanders took out his yo-yo. "Well, that's Nam," he said. "Garden of Evil. Over here, man, every sin's real fresh and original."

84   How do you generalize?

85   War is hell, but that's not the half of it, because war is also mystery and terror and adventure and courage and discovery and holiness and pity and despair and longing and love. War is nasty; war is fun. War is thrilling; war is drudgery. War makes you a man; war makes you dead.

86   The truths are contradictory. It can be argued, for instance, that war is grotesque. But in truth war is also beauty. For all its horror, you can't help but gape at the awful majesty of combat. You stare out at tracer rounds unwinding through the dark like brilliant red ribbons. You crouch in ambush as a cool, impassive moon rises over the nighttime paddies. You admire the fluid symmetries of troops on the move, the harmonies of sound and shape and proportion, the great sheets of metal-fire streaming down from a gunship, the illumination rounds, the white phosphorus, the purply orange glow of napalm, the rocket's red glare. It's not pretty, exactly. It's astonishing. It fills the eye. It commands you. You hate it, yes, but your eyes do not. Like a killer forest fire, like cancer under a microscope, any battle or bombing raid or artillery barrage has the aesthetic purity of absolute moral indifference—a powerful, implacable beauty—and a true war story will tell the truth about this, though the truth is ugly.

87   To generalize about war is like generalizing about peace. Almost everything is true. Almost nothing is true. At its core, perhaps, war is just another name for death, and yet any soldier will tell you, if he tells the truth, that proximity to death brings with it a corresponding proximity to life. After a firefight, there is always the immense pleasure of aliveness. The trees are alive. The grass, the soil—everything. All around you things are purely living, and you among them, and the aliveness makes you tremble. You feel an intense, out-of-the-skin awareness of your living self—your truest self, the human being you want to be and then become by the force of wanting it. In the midst of evil you want to be a good man. You want decency. You want justice and courtesy and human concord, things you never knew you wanted. There is a kind of largeness to it, a kind of godliness. Though it's odd, you're never more alive than when you're almost dead. You recognize what's valuable. Freshly, as if for the first time, you love what's best in yourself and in the world, all that might be lost. At the hour of dusk you sit at your foxhole and look out on a wide river turning pinkish red, and at the mountains beyond, and although in the morning you must cross the river and go into the mountains and do terrible things and maybe die, even so, you find yourself studying the fine colors on the river, you feel wonder and awe at the setting of the sun, and

you are filled with a hard, aching love for how the world could be and always should be, but now is not.

88   Mitchell Sanders was right. For the common soldier, at least, war has the feel—the spiritual texture—of a great ghostly fog, thick and permanent. There is no clarity. Everything swirls. The old rules are no longer binding, the old truths no longer true. Right spills over into wrong. Order blends into chaos, love into hate, ugliness into beauty, law into anarchy, civility into savagery. The vapors suck you in. You can't tell where you are, or why you're there, and the only certainty is overwhelming ambiguity.

89   In war you lose your sense of the definite, hence your sense of truth itself, and therefore it's safe to say that in a true war story nothing is ever absolutely true.

90   Often in a true war story there is not even a point, or else the point doesn't hit you until twenty years later, in your sleep, and you wake up and shake your wife and start telling the story to her, except when you get to the end you've forgotten the point again. And then for a long time you lie there watching the story happen in your head. You listen to your wife's breathing. The war's over. You close your eyes. You smile and think, Christ, what's the *point?*

91   This one wakes me up.

92   In the mountains that day, I watched Lemon turn sideways. He laughed and said something to Rat Kiley. Then he took a peculiar half step, moving from shade into bright sunlight, and the booby-trapped 105 round blew him into a tree. The parts were just hanging there, so Dave Jensen and I were ordered to shinny up and peel him off. I remember the white bone of an arm. I remember pieces of skin and something wet and yellow that must've been the intestines. The gore was horrible, and stays with me. But what wakes me up twenty years later is Dave Jensen singing "Lemon Tree" as we threw down the parts.

93   You can tell a true war story by the questions you ask. Somebody tells a story, let's say, and afterward you ask, "Is it true?" and if the answer matters, you've got your answer.

94   For example, we've all heard this one. Four guys go down a trail. A grenade sails out. One guy jumps on it and takes the blast and saves his three buddies.

95   Is it true?

96   The answer matters.

97   You'd feel cheated if it never happened. Without the grounding reality, it's just a trite bit of puffery, pure Hollywood, untrue in the way all such stories are untrue. Yet even if it did happen—and maybe it did, anything's possible—even then you know it can't be true, because a true war story does not depend upon that kind of truth. Absolute occurrence is irrelevant. A thing may happen and be a total lie; another thing may not hap-

pen and be truer than the truth. For example: Four guys go down a trail. A grenade sails out. One guy jumps on it and takes the blast, but it's a killer grenade and everybody dies anyway. Before they die, though, one of the dead guys says, "The fuck you do *that* for?" and the jumper says, "Story of my life, man," and the other guy starts to smile but he's dead.

98   That's a true story that never happened.

99   Twenty years later, I can still see the sunlight on Lemon's face. I can see him turning, looking back at Rat Kiley, then he laughed and took that curious half step from shade into sunlight, his face suddenly brown and shining, and when his foot touched down, in that instant, he must've thought it was the sunlight that was killing him. It was not the sunlight. It was a rigged 105 round. But if I could ever get the story right, how the sun seemed to gather around him and pick him up and lift him high into a tree, if I could somehow re-create the fatal whiteness of that light, the quick glare, the obvious cause and effect, then you would believe the last thing Curt Lemon believed, which for him must've been the final truth.

100   Now and then, when I tell this story, someone will come up to me afterward and say she liked it. It's always a woman. Usually it's an older woman of kindly temperament and humane politics. She'll explain that as a rule she hates war stories; she can't understand why people want to wallow in all the blood and gore. But this one she liked. The poor baby buffalo, it made her sad. Sometimes, even, there are little tears. What I should do, she'll say, is put it all behind me. Find new stories to tell.

101   I won't say it but I'll think it.

102   I'll picture Rat Kiley's face, his grief, and I'll think, *You dumb cooze*.

103   Because she wasn't listening.

104   It *wasn't* a war story. It was a *love* story.

105   But you can't say that. All you can do is tell it one more time, patiently, adding and subtracting, making up a few things to get at the real truth. No Mitchell Sanders, you tell her. No Lemon, no Rat Kiley. No trail junction. No baby buffalo. No vines or moss or white blossoms. Beginning to end, you tell her, it's all made up. Every goddamn detail—the mountains and the river and especially that poor dumb baby buffalo. None of it happened. *None* of it. And even if it did happen, it didn't happen in the mountains, it happened in this little village on the Batangan Peninsula, and it was raining like crazy, and one night a guy named Stink Harris woke up screaming with a leech on his tongue. You can tell a true war story if you just keep on telling it.

106   And in the end, of course, a true war story is never about war. It's about sunlight. It's about the special way that dawn spreads out on a river when you know you must cross the river and march into the mountains and do things you are afraid to do. It's about love and memory. It's about sorrow. It's about sisters who never write back and people who never listen.

Questions for Discussion

1. How does war appear to affect the men's behavior? What do they do that they would not have done at home?

2. Why would a story that instructs on moral virtues, teaches the right way to do things, and causes a listener or reader to "feel uplifted" not be "a true war story"? What does O'Brien mean when he says the "stomach [must] believe" for a war story to be true? How do the stories the narrator tells exemplify what he says about the nature of a "true war story"?

3. Mitchell Sanders tells a story about a platoon on a listening post hearing strange music from a village. What about the music makes the men uncomfortable? What does the narrator mean when he comments that the trees, the monkeys, the fog, the grass—"everything talks"? Why did the men call down air strikes on the village from which the music emanates? Do you think they should have been held accountable for doing so? Why or why not?

4. Mitchell Sanders says of his story that he had made up the parts about the "glee club" and the "opera." Why does the narrator still regard Sanders' story as true? What does Sanders mean when he says the meaning of his story is in the "quiet"?

5. Why does Rat Kiley shoot and torture the baby water buffalo? Why does he cry as he does so? Why do the men watch in silence? Elie Wiesel, who wrote the story "Yom Kippur" printed in the Grief and Loss unit of this text, who spent part of his childhood in a Nazi concentration camp, and whose family died in the camp, has written and spoken at length against indifference and against refusal to get involved in stopping violence or injustice. Do you think the men of Rat Kiley's unit should be held accountable for their failure to stop Kiley from shooting the buffalo? Why or why not?

6. The narrator describes war as having "a powerful, implacable beauty" that is simultaneously an "ugly" "truth." What does he mean?

7. What does the narrator mean by "in the end...a true war story is never about war"?

8. Explain whether you think O'Brien is telling the truth about war.

THE MAN I KILLED   (1990)

1   His jaw was in his throat, his upper lip and teeth were gone, his one eye was shut, his other eye was a star-shaped hole, his eyebrows were thin and arched like a woman's, his nose was undamaged, there was a slight tear at the lobe of one ear, his clean black hair was swept upward into a cowlick at the rear of the skull, his forehead was lightly freckled, his fingernails were clean, the skin at his left cheek was peeled back in three ragged strips, his right cheek was smooth and hairless, there was a butterfly on his chin, his neck was open to the spinal cord and the blood there

was thick and shiny and it was this wound that had killed him. He lay face-up in the center of the trail, a slim, dead, almost dainty young man. He had bony legs, a narrow waist, long shapely fingers. His chest was sunken and poorly muscled—a scholar, maybe. His wrists were the wrists of a child. He wore a black shirt, black pajama pants, a gray ammunition belt, a gold ring on the third finger of his right hand. His rubber sandals had been blown off. One lay beside him, the other a few meters up the trail. He had been born, maybe, in 1946 in the village of My Khe near the central coast-line of Quang Ngai Province, where his parents farmed, and where his family had lived for several centuries, and where, during the time of the French, his father and two uncles and many neighbors had joined in the struggle for independence. He was not a Communist. He was a citizen and a soldier. In the village of My Khe, as in all of Quang Ngai, patriotic resistance had the force of tradition, which was partly the force of legend, and from his earliest boyhood the man I killed would have listened to stories about the heroic Trung sisters and Tran Hung Dao's famous rout of the Mongols and Le Loi's final victory against the Chinese at Tot Dong. He would have been taught that to defend the land was a man's highest duty and highest privilege. He had accepted this. It was never open to question. Secretly, though, it also frightened him. He was not a fighter. His health was poor, his body small and frail. He liked books. He wanted someday to be a teacher of mathematics. At night, lying on his mat, he could not picture himself doing the brave things his father had done, or his uncles, or the heroes of the stories. He hoped in his heart that he would never be tested. He hoped the Americans would go away. Soon, he hoped. He kept hoping and hoping, always, even when he was asleep.

2   "Oh, man, you fuckin' trashed the fucker," Azar said. "You scrambled his sorry self, look at that, you *did*, you laid him out like Shredded fuckin' Wheat."

3   "Go away," Kiowa said.

4   "I'm just saying the truth. Like oatmeal."

5   "Go," Kiowa said.

6   "Okay, then. I take it back," Azar said. He started to move away, then stopped and said, "Rice Krispies, you know? On the dead test, this particular individual gets A-plus."

7   Smiling at this, he shrugged and walked up the trail toward the village behind the trees.

8   Kiowa kneeled down.

9   "Just forget that crud," he said. He opened up his canteen and held it out for a while and then sighed and pulled it away. "No sweat, man. What else could you do?"

10   Later, Kiowa said, "I'm serious. Nothing *anybody* could do. Come on, stop staring."

11   The trail junction was shaded by a row of trees and tall brush. The slim young man lay with his legs in the shade. His jaw was in his throat. His one eye was shut and the other was a star-shaped hole.

12   Kiowa glanced at the body.

13   "All right, let me ask a question," he said. "You want to trade places with him? Turn it all upside down—you *want* that? I mean, be honest."

14   The star-shaped hole was red and yellow. The yellow part seemed to be getting wider, spreading out at the center of the star. The upper lip and gum and teeth were gone. The man's head was cocked at a wrong angle, as if loose at the neck, and the neck was wet with blood.

15   "Think it over," Kiowa said.

16   Then later he said, "Tim, it's a *war*. The guy wasn't Heidi—he had a weapon, right? It's a tough thing, for sure, but you got to cut out that staring."

17   Then he said, "Maybe you better lie down a minute."

18   Then after a long empty time he said, "Take it slow. Just go wherever the spirit takes you."

19   The butterfly was making its way along the young man's forehead, which was spotted with small dark freckles. The nose was undamaged. The skin on the right cheek was smooth and fine-grained and hairless. Frail-looking, delicately boned, the young man would not have wanted to be a soldier and in his heart would have feared performing badly in battle. Even as a boy growing up in the village of My Khe, he had often worried about this. He imagined covering his head and lying in a deep hole and closing his eyes and not moving until the war was over. He had no stomach for violence. He loved mathematics. His eyebrows were thin and arched like a woman's, and at school the boys sometimes teased him about how pretty he was, the arched eyebrows and long shapely fingers, and on the playground they mimicked a woman's walk and made fun of his smooth skin and his love for mathematics. The young man could not make himself fight them. He often wanted to, but he was afraid, and this increased his shame. If he could not fight little boys, he thought, how could he ever become a soldier and fight the Americans with their airplanes and helicopters and bombs? It did not seem possible. In the presence of his father and uncles, he pretended to look forward to doing his patriotic duty, which was also a privilege, but at night he prayed with his mother that the war might end soon. Beyond anything else, he was afraid of disgracing himself, and therefore his family and village. But all he could do, he thought, was wait and pray and try not to grow up too fast.

20   "Listen to me," Kiowa said. "You feel terrible, I know that."

21   Then he said, "Okay, maybe I *don't* know."

22   Along the trail there were small blue flowers shaped like bells. The young man's head was wrenched sideways, not quite facing the flowers, and even in the shade a single blade of sunlight sparkled against the buckle of his ammunition belt. The left cheek was peeled back in three ragged strips. The wounds at his neck had not yet clotted, which made him seem animate even in death, the blood still spreading out across his shirt.

23   Kiowa shook his head.

24   There was some silence before he said, "Stop *staring*."

25   The young man's fingernails were clean. There was a slight tear at the lobe of one ear, a sprinkling of blood on the forearm. He wore a gold ring on the

third finger of his right hand. His chest was sunken and poorly muscled—a scholar, maybe. His life was now a constellation of possibilities. So, yes, maybe a scholar. And for years, despite his family's poverty, the man I killed would have been determined to continue his education in mathematics. The means for this were arranged, perhaps, through the village liberation cadres, and in 1964 the young man began attending classes at the university in Saigon, where he avoided politics and paid attention to the problems of calculus. He devoted himself to his studies. He spent his nights alone, wrote romantic poems in his journal, took pleasure in the grace and beauty of differential equations. The war, he knew, would finally take him, but for the time being he would not let himself think about it. He had stopped praying; instead, now, he waited. And as he waited, in his final year at the university, he fell in love with a classmate, a girl of seventeen, who one day told him that his wrists were like the wrists of a child, so small and delicate, and who admired his narrow waist and the cowlick that rose up like a bird's tail at the back of his head. She liked his quiet manner; she laughed at his freckles and bony legs. One evening, perhaps, they exchanged gold rings.

26   Now one eye was a star.

27   "You okay?" Kiowa said.

28   The body lay almost entirely in shade. There were gnats at the mouth, little flecks of pollen drifting above the nose. The butterfly was gone. The bleeding had stopped except for the neck wounds.

29   Kiowa picked up the rubber sandals, clapping off the dirt, then bent down to search the body. He found a pouch of rice, a comb, a fingernail clipper, a few soiled piasters, a snapshot of a young woman standing in front of a parked motorcycle. Kiowa placed these items in his rucksack along with the gray ammunition belt and rubber sandals.

30   Then he squatted down.

31   "I'll tell you the straight truth," he said. "The guy was dead the second he stepped on the trail. Understand me? We all had him zeroed. A good kill—weapon, ammunition, everything." Tiny beads of sweat glistened at Kiowa's forehead. His eyes moved from the sky to the dead man's body to the knuckles of his own hands. "So listen, you best pull your shit together. Can't just sit here all day."

32   Later he said, "Understand?"

33   Then he said, "Five minutes, Tim. Five more minutes and we're moving out."

34   The one eye did a funny twinkling trick, red to yellow. His head was wrenched sideways, as if loose at the neck, and the dead young man seemed to be staring at some distant object beyond the bell-shaped flowers along the trail. The blood at the neck had gone to a deep purplish black. Clean fingernails, clean hair—he had been a soldier for only a single day. After his years at the university, the man I killed returned with his new wife to the village of My Khe, where he enlisted as a common rifleman with the 48th Vietcong Battalion. He knew he would die quickly. He knew he would see a flash of light. He knew he would fall dead and wake up in the stories of his village and people.

35   Kiowa covered the body with a poncho.

36   "Hey, you're looking better," he said. "No doubt about it. All you needed was time—some mental R&R."

37   Then he said, "Man, I'm sorry."

38   Then later he said, "Why not talk about it?"

39   Then he said, "Come on, man, talk."

40   He was a slim, dead, almost dainty young man of about twenty. He lay with one leg bent beneath him, his jaw in his throat, his face neither expressive nor inexpressive. One eye was shut. The other was a star-shaped hole.

41   "Talk," Kiowa said.

Questions for Discussion

1. What is the effect of O'Brien's opening "The Man I Killed" with sometimes gruesome details about the dead man? Why does O'Brien mix ordinary and brutal details?

2. Why does the narrator discuss in detail the past life of the dead Vietnamese, a past that is obviously fictional, as the narrator could have no way of knowing it? What effect does O'Brien create by using these details?

3. Kiowa insists that the narrator had no choice but to kill the Vietnamese soldier. Explain whether you agree or disagree.

4. How does the narrator feel about the death of the Vietnamese soldier? If he had no choice, why does he dwell so extensively on the killing?

The Undying Uncertainty of the Narrator in Tim O'Brien's *The Things They Carried*[1]

Steven Kaplan, University of Southern Colorado

Before the United States became militarily involved in defending the sovereignty of South Vietnam, it had to, as one historian recently put it, "invent" (Baritz 142–43) the country and the political issues at stake there. The Vietnam War was in many ways a wild and terrible work of fiction written by some dangerous and frightening storytellers. First the United States decided what constituted good and evil, right and wrong, civilized and uncivilized, freedom and oppression for Vietnam, according to American standards; then it traveled the long physical distance to Vietnam and attempted to make its own notions about these things clear to the Vietnamese people—ultimately by brute, technological force. For the U.S. military and government, the Vietnam that they had in effect invented became fact. For the soldiers that the government then sent

[1]*Critique* 35.1 (Fall 1993): 43-52, online, Galileo, Academic Search Premier, 15 Feb. 2002.

there, however, the facts that their government had created about who was the enemy, what were the issues, and how the war was to be won were quickly overshadowed by a world of uncertainty. Ultimately, trying to stay alive long enough to return home in one piece was the only thing that made any sense to them. As David Halberstam puts it in his novel, *One Very Hot Day*, the only fact of which an American soldier in Vietnam could be certain was that "yes was no longer yes, no was no longer no, maybe was more certainly maybe" (127). Almost all of the literature on the war, both fictional and nonfictional, makes clear that the only certain thing during the Vietnam War was that nothing was certain. Philip Beidler has pointed out in an impressive study of the literature of that war that "most of the time in Vietnam, there were some things that seemed just too terrible and strange to be true and others that were just too terrible and true to be strange" (4).

The main question that Beidler's study raises is how, in light of the overwhelming ambiguity that characterized the Vietnam experience, could any sense or meaning be derived from what happened and, above all, how could this meaning, if it were found, be conveyed to those who had not experienced the war? The answer Beidler's book offers, as Beidler himself recently said at a conference on writing about the war, is that "words are all we have. In the hands of true artists . . . they may yet preserve us against the darkness" (Lomperis 87). Similarly, for the novelist Tim O'Brien, the language of fiction is the most accurate means for conveying, as Beidler so incisively puts it, "what happened [in Vietnam] . . . what might have happened, what could have happened, what should have happened, and maybe also what can be kept from happening or what can be made to happen" (87). If the experience of Vietnam and its accompanying sense of chaos and confusion can be shown at all, then for Tim O'Brien it will not be in the fictions created by politicians but in the stories told by writers of fiction.

One of Tim O'Brien's most important statements about the inherent problems of understanding and writing about the Vietnam experience appears in a chapter of his novel, *Going After Cacciato*, appropriately titled "The Things They Didn't Know." The novel's protagonist, Paul Berlin, briefly interrupts his fantasy about chasing the deserter Cacciato, who is en route from Vietnam to Paris, to come to terms with the fact that although he is physically in Vietnam and fighting a war, his understanding of where he is and what he is doing there is light-years away. At the center of the chapter is a long catalogue of the things that Berlin and his comrades did not know about Vietnam, and the chapter closes with the statement that what "they" knew above all else were the "uncertainties never articulated in war stories" (319). In that chapter Tim O'Brien shows that recognizing and exploring the uncertainties about the war is perhaps the closest one can come to finding anything certain at all. Paul Berlin, in his fantasy about escaping the war and chasing Cacciato to Paris, is in fact attempting to confront and, as far as possible, understand the uncertainties of the

Vietnam War through the prism of his imagination. Once inside his make-believe world, Berlin has the opportunity to explore all of the things that he did not know about the war: The elusive enemy suddenly becomes his partner in a long debate about the meaning of the war; he explores the mysterious tunnels of the Vietcong; one of the victims of the war becomes Berlin's tour guide as he and his fellow soldiers go after Cacciato; and, most important of all, Berlin is given a chance to test and ultimately reject his own thoughts of desertion by imagining how he would react to the desertion of another soldier.

In his most recent work of fiction, *The Things They Carried*,[2] Tim O'Brien takes the act of trying to reveal and understand the uncertainties about the war one step further, by looking at it through the imagination. He completely destroys the fine line dividing fact from fiction and tries to show, even more so than in *Cacciato*, that fiction (or the imagined world) can often be truer, especially in the case of Vietnam, than fact. In the first chapter, an almost documentary account of the items referred to in the book's title, O'Brien introduces the reader to some of the things, both imaginary and concrete, emotional and physical, that the average foot soldier had to carry through the jungles of Vietnam. All of the "things" are depicted in a style that is almost scientific in its precision. We are told how much each subject weighs, either psychologically or physically, and, in the case of artillery, we are even told how many ounces each round weighed:

> As PFCs or Spec 4s, most of them were common grunts and carried the standard M-16 gas operated assault rifle. The weapon weighed 7.5 pounds, 8.2 pounds with its full 20-round magazine. Depending on numerous factors, such as topography and psychology, the rifleman carried anywhere from 12 to 20 magazines, usually in cloth bandoliers, adding on another 8.4 pounds at minimum, 14 pounds at maximum. (Carried 7)

Even the most insignificant details seem worth mentioning. One main character is not just from Oklahoma City but from "Oklahoma City, Oklahoma" (5), as if mentioning the state somehow makes the location more factual, more certain. More striking than this obsession with even the minutest detail, however, is the academic tone that at times makes the narrative sound like a government report. We find such transitional phrases as "for instance" (5) and "in addition" (7), and whole paragraphs are dominated by sentences that begin with "because" (5). These strengthen our impression that the narrator is striving, above all else, to convince us of the reality, of the concrete certainty, of the things they carried.

In the midst of this factuality and certainty, however, are signals that all the information in this opening chapter will not amount to much: that the certainties are merely there to conceal uncertainties and that the

[2]The reviewers of this book are split on whether to call it a novel or a collection of short stories. In a recent interview, I asked Tim O'Brien what he felt was the most adequate designation. He said that *The Things They Carried* is neither a collection of stories nor a novel; he preferred to call it a work of fiction.

words following the frequent "becauses" do not provide an explanation of anything. We are told in the opening page that the most important thing that First Lieutenant Jimmy Cross carried were some letters from a girl he loved. The narrator, one of Cross's friends in the war and now a forty-three-year-old writer named Tim O'Brien, tells us that the girl did not love Cross, but that he constantly indulged in "hoping" and "pretending" (3) in an effort to turn her love into fact. We are also told "she was a virgin," but this is immediately qualified by the statement that "he was almost sure" of this (3). On the next page, Cross becomes increasingly uncertain as he sits at "night and wonder(s) if Martha was a virgin" (4). Shortly after this, Cross wonders who had taken the pictures he now holds in his hands "because he knew she had boyfriends" (5), but we are never told how he "knew" this. At the end of the chapter, after one of Cross's men has died because Cross was too busy thinking of Martha, Cross sits at the bottom of his foxhole crying, not so much for the member of his platoon who has been killed "but mostly it was for Martha, and for himself, because she belonged to another world, and because she was . . . a poet and a virgin and uninvolved" (17).

This pattern of stating facts and then quickly calling them into question that is typical of Jimmy Cross's thoughts in these opening pages characterizes how the narrator portrays events throughout this book; the facts about an event are given; they then are quickly qualified or called into question; from this uncertainty emerges a new set of facts about the same subject that are again called into question—on and on, without end. O'Brien catalogues the weapons that the soldiers carried, down to their weight, thus making them seem important and their protective power real. However, several of these passages are introduced by the statement that some of these same weapons were also carried by the character Ted Lavender; each of the four sections of the first chapter that tells us what he carried is introduced by a qualifying phrase that reveals something about which Lavender himself was not at all certain when he was carrying his weapons: "Until he was shot . . . " (4, 7, 10).

Conveying the average soldier's sense of uncertainty about what actually happened in Vietnam by presenting the what-ifs and maybes as if they were facts, and then calling these facts back into question again, can be seen as a variation of the haunting phrase used so often by American soldiers to convey their own uncertainty about what happened in Vietnam: "there it is." They used it to make the unspeakable and indescribable and the uncertain real and present for a fleeting moment. Similarly, O'Brien presents facts and stories that are only temporarily certain and real; the strange "balance" in Vietnam between "crazy and almost crazy" (20) always creeps back in and forces the mind that is remembering and retelling a story to remember and retell it one more time in a different form, adding different nuances, and then to tell it again one more time.

Storytelling in this book is something in which "the whole world is rearranged" (39) in an effort to get at the "full truth" (49) about events that themselves deny the possibility of arriving at something called the "full," meaning certain and fixed, "truth." By giving the reader facts and then calling those facts into question, by telling stories and then saying that those stories happened (147), and then that they did not happen (203), and then that they might have happened (204), O'Brien puts more emphasis in *The Things They Carried* on the question that he first posed in *Going After Cacciato:* how can a work of fiction become paradoxically more real than the events upon which it is based, and how can the confusing experiences of the average soldier in Vietnam be conveyed in such a way that they will acquire at least a momentary sense of certainty? In *The Things They Carried*, this question is raised even before the novel begins. The book opens with a reminder: "This is a work of fiction. Except for a few details regarding the author's own life, all the incidents, names, and characters are imaginary." Two pages later we are told that "this book is lovingly dedicated to the men of Alpha Company, and in particular to Jimmy Cross, Norman Bowker, Rat Kiley, Mitchell Sanders, Henry Dobbins, and Kiowa." We discover only a few pages after this dedication that those six men are the novel's main characters.

These prefatory comments force us simultaneously to consider the unreal (the fictions that follow) as real because the book is dedicated to the characters who appear in it, and the "incidents, names, and characters" are unreal or "imaginary." O'Brien informs us at one point that in telling these war stories he intends to get at the "full truth" (49) about them; yet from the outset he has shown us that the full truth as he sees it is in itself something ambiguous. Are these stories and the characters in them real or imaginary, or does the "truth" hover somewhere between the two? A closer look at the book's narrative structure reveals that O'Brien is incapable of answering the questions that he initially raises, because the very act of writing fiction about the war, of telling war stories, as he practices it in *The Things They Carried*, is determined by the nature of the Vietnam War and ultimately by life in general where "the only certainty is overwhelming ambiguity" (88).

The emphasis on ambiguity behind O'Brien's narrative technique in *The Things They Carried* is thus similar to the pattern used by Joseph Conrad's narrator, Marlow, in *Heart of Darkness*, so incisively characterized by J. Hillis Miller as a lifting of veils to reveal a truth that is quickly obscured again by the dropping of a new veil (158). Over and over again, O'Brien tells us that we are reading "the full and exact truth" (181), and yet, as we make our way through this book and gradually find the same stories being retold with new facts and from a new perspective, we come to realize that there is no such thing as the full and exact truth. Instead, the only thing that can be determined at the end of the story is its own indeterminacy.

O'Brien calls telling stories in this manner "Good Form" in the title of one of the chapters of *The Things They Carried:* This is good form because "telling stories" like this "can make things present" (204). The stories in this book are not truer than the actual things that happened in

Vietnam because they contain some higher, metaphysical truth: "True war stories do not generalize. They do not indulge in abstractions or analysis" (84). Rather, these stories are true because the characters and events within them are being given a new life each time they are told and retold. This approach to storytelling echoes Wolfgang Iser's theory of representation in his essay "Representation: A Performative Act":

> Whatever shape or form these various (philosophical or fictional) conceptualizations (of life) may have, their common denominator is the attempt to explain origins. In this respect they close off those very potentialities that literature holds open. Of course literature also springs from the same anthropological need, since it stages what is inaccessible, thus compensating for the impossibility of knowing what it is to be. But literature is not an explanation of origins; it is a staging of the constant deferment of explanation, which makes the origin explode into its multifariousness.
>
> It is at this point that aesthetic semblance makes its full impact. Representation arises out of and thus entails the removal of difference, whose irremovability transforms representation into a performative act of staging something. This staging is almost infinitely variable, for in contrast to explanations, no single staging could ever remove difference and so explain origin. On the contrary, its very multiplicity facilitates an unending mirroring of what man is, because no mirrored manifestation can ever coincide with our actual being. (245)

When we conceptualize life, we attempt to step outside ourselves and look at who we are. We constantly make new attempts to conceptualize our lives and uncover our true identities because looking at who we might be is as close as we can come to discovering who we actually are. Similarly, representing events in fiction is an attempt to understand them by detaching them from the "real world" and placing them in a world that is being staged. In *The Things They Carried*, Tim O'Brien desperately struggles to make his readers believe that what they are reading is true because he wants them to step outside their everyday reality and participate in the events that he is portraying; he wants us to believe in his stories to the point where we are virtually in the stories so that we might gain a more thorough understanding of, or feeling for, what is being portrayed in them. Representation as O'Brien practices it in this book is not a mimetic act but a "game," as Iser also calls it in a more recent essay, "The Play of the Text," a process of acting things out:

> Now since the latter [the text] is fictional, it automatically invokes a convention-governed contract between author and reader indicating that the textual world is to be viewed not as reality but as if it were reality. And so whatever is repeated in the text is not meant to denote the world, but merely a world enacted. This may well repeat an identifiable reality, but it contains one all-important difference: what happens within it is relieved of the consequences inherent in the real world referred to. Hence in disclosing itself, fictionality signalizes that everything is only to be taken as if it were what it seems to be, to be taken—in other words—as play. (251)

In *The Things They Carried*, representation includes staging what might have happened in Vietnam while simultaneously questioning the accuracy and credibility of the narrative act itself. The reader is thus made fully aware of being made a participant in a game, in a "performative act," and thereby also is asked to become immediately involved in the incredibly frustrating act of trying to make sense of events that resist understanding. The reader is permitted to experience at first hand the uncertainty that characterized being in Vietnam. We are being forced to "believe" (79) that the only "certainty" was the "overwhelming ambiguity."

This process is nowhere clearer than in a chapter appropriately called "How to Tell A True War Story." O'Brien opens this chapter by telling us "This Is True." Then he takes us through a series of variations of the story about how Curt Lemon stepped on a mine and was blown up into a tree. The only thing true or certain about the story, however, is that it is being constructed and then deconstructed and then reconstructed right in front of us. The reader is given six different versions of the death of Curt Lemon, and each version is so discomforting that it is difficult to come up with a more accurate statement to describe his senseless death than "there it is," or as O'Brien puts it—"in the end, really there's nothing much to say about a true war story, except maybe 'oh'" (84).

Before we learn in this chapter how Curt Lemon was killed, we are told the "true" story that Rat Kiley apparently told to the character-narrator O'Brien about how Kiley wrote to Lemon's sister and "says he loved the guy. He says the guy was his best friend in the world" (76). Two months after writing the letter, Kiley has not heard from Lemon's sister, and so he writes her off as a "dumb cooze" (76). This is what happened according to Kiley, and O'Brien assures us that the story is "incredibly sad and true" (77). However, when Rat Kiley tells a story in another chapter we are warned that he

> swore up and down to its truth, although in the end, I'll admit, that doesn't amount to much of a warranty. Among the men in Alpha Company, Rat had a reputation for exaggeration and overstatement, a compulsion to rev up the facts, and for most of us it was normal procedure to discount sixty or seventy percent of anything he had to say. (101)

Rat Kiley is an unreliable narrator, and his facts are always distorted, but this does not affect storytelling truth as far as O'Brien is concerned. The passage above on Rat Kiley's credibility as a storyteller concludes: "It wasn't a question of deceit. Just the opposite: he wanted to heat up the truth, to make it burn so hot that you would feel exactly what he felt" (101). This summarizes O'Brien's often confusing narrative strategy in *The Things They Carried;* the facts about what actually happened, or whether anything happened at all, are not important. They cannot be important because they themselves are too uncertain, too lost in a world in which certainty had vanished somewhere between the "crazy and almost crazy." The important thing is that any story about the war, any "true war story," must "burn so hot" when it is told that it becomes alive for the listener-reader in the act of its telling.

In Rat Kiley's story about how he wrote to Curt Lemon's sister, the details we are initially given are exaggerated to the point where, in keeping with O'Brien's fire metaphor, they begin to heat up. Curt Lemon, we are told, "would always volunteer for stuff nobody else would volunteer for in a million years" (75). And once Lemon went fishing with a crate of hand grenades, "the funniest thing in world history...about twenty zillion dead gook fish" (76). But the story does not get so hot that it burns, it does not become so "incredibly sad and true," as O'Brien puts it, until we find out at the story's close that, in Rat's own words, "I write this beautiful fuckin' letter, I slave over it, and what happens? The dumb cooze never writes back" (77). It is these words and not the facts that come before them that make the story true for O'Brien.

At the beginning of this chapter, O'Brien asks us several times to "Listen to Rat," to listen how he says things more than to what he says. And of all of the words that stand out in his story, it is the word "cooze," (which is repeated four times in two pages), that makes his story come alive for O'Brien. "You can tell a true war story by its absolute and uncompromising allegiance to obscenity and evil" (76). This is just one way that O'Brien gives for determining what constitutes a true war story. The unending list of possibilities includes reacting to a story with the ambiguous words "Oh" and "There it is." Rat Kiley's use of "cooze" is another in the sequence of attempts to utter some truth about the Vietnam experience and, by extension, about war in general. There is no moral to be derived from this word, such as war is obscene or corrupt: "A true war story is never moral. It does not instruct" (76). There is simply the real and true fact that the closest thing to certainty and truth in a war story is a vague utterance, a punch at the darkness, an attempt to rip momentarily through the veil that repeatedly re-covers the reality and truth of what actually happened.

It is thus probably no coincidence that in the middle of this chapter on writing a true war story, O'Brien tells us that "Even now, at this instant," Mitchell Sanders's "yo-yo" is the main thing he can remember from the short time encompassing Lemon's death (83). This object, associated with games and play, becomes a metaphor for the playful act of narration that O'Brien practices in this book, a gamestory that he plays by necessity. The only way to tell a true war story, according to O'Brien, is to keep telling it "one more time, patiently, adding and subtracting, making up a few things to get at the real truth" (91), which ultimately is impossible because the real truth, the full truth, as the events themselves, are lost forever in "a great ghostly fog, thick and permanent" (88). You only "tell a true war story" "if you just keep on telling it" (91) because "absolute occurrence is irrelevant" (89). The truth, then, is clearly not something that can be distinguished or separated from the story itself, and the reality or non-reality of the story's events is not something that can be determined from a perspective outside of the story. As the critic Geoffrey Hartman says about poetry: "To keep a poem in mind is to keep it there, not to resolve it into available meanings" (274). Similarly, for O'Brien it is not the fact that a story happened that makes it true and worth remembering, any more than the story itself can be said to contain a final truth. The important thing is that a story becomes so much a part of the present that "there is nothing to remember (while we are reading it) except the story" (40). This is why O'Brien's narrator is condemned, perhaps in a positive sense, to telling and then retelling numerous variations of the same story over and over and over again. This is also why he introduces each new version of a story with such comments as: "This one does it for me. I have told it before many times, many versions—but here is what actually happened" (85). What actually happened, the story's truth, can only become apparent for the fleeting moment in which it is being told; that truth will vanish back into the fog just as quickly as the events that occurred in Vietnam were sucked into a realm of uncertainty the moment they occurred.

O'Brien demonstrates nothing new about trying to tell war stories— that the "truths" they contain "are contradictory" (87), elusive, and thus indeterminate. Two hundred years ago, Goethe, as he tried to depict the senseless bloodshed during the allied invasion of revolutionary France, also reflected in his autobiographical essay "Campaign in France" on the same inevitable contradictions that arise when one speaks of what happened or might have happened in battle. Homer's *Iliad* is, of course, the ultimate statement on the contradictions inherent in war. However, what is new in O'Brien's approach in *The Things They Carried* is that he makes the axiom that in war "almost everything is true. Almost nothing is true" (87) the basis for the act of telling a war story.

The narrative strategy that O'Brien uses in this book to portray the uncertainty of what happened in Vietnam is not restricted to depicting war, and O'Brien does not limit it to the war alone. He concludes his book with a chapter titled "The Lives of the Dead" in which he moves from his experiences in Vietnam back to when he was nine years old. On the surface, the book's last chapter is about O'Brien's first date, his first love, a girl named Linda who died of a brain tumor a few months after he had taken her to see the movie *The Man Who Never Was*. What this chapter is really about, however, as its title suggests, is how the dead (which also includes people who may never have actually existed) can be given life in a work of fiction. In a story, O'Brien tells us, "memory and imagination and language combine to make spirits in the head. There is the illusion of aliveness" (260). Like the man who never was in the film of that title, the people that never were except in memories and the imagination can become real or alive, if only for a moment, through the act of storytelling.

According to O'Brien, when you tell a story, really tell it, "you objectify your own experience. You separate it from yourself" (178). By doing this you are able to externalize "a swirl of memories that might otherwise have ended in paralysis or worse" (179). However, the storyteller does not just escape from the events and people in a story by placing them on paper; as we have seen, the act of telling a given story is an on-going and never-ending process. By constantly involving and then re-involving the reader in the task of determining what "actually" happened in a given situation, in a story, and by forcing the reader to experience the impossibility of ever knowing with any certainty what actually happened, O'Brien liberates himself from the lonesome responsibility of remembering and trying to understand events. He also creates a community of individuals immersed in the act of experiencing the uncertainty or indeterminacy of all events, regardless of whether they occurred in Vietnam, in a small town in Minnesota (253–73), or somewhere in the reader's own life.

O'Brien thus saves himself, as he puts it in the last sentence of his book, from the fate of his character Norman Bowker who, in a chapter called "Speaking of Courage," kills himself because he cannot find some lasting meaning in the horrible things he experienced in Vietnam. O'Brien saves himself by demonstrating in this book that the most important thing is to be able to recognize and accept that events have no fixed or final meaning and that the only meaning that events can have is one that emerges momentarily and then shifts and changes each time that the events come alive as they are remembered or portrayed.

The character Norman Bowker hangs himself in the locker room of the local YMCA after playing basketball with some friends (181), partially because he has a story locked up inside of himself that he feels he cannot tell because no one would want to hear it. It is the story of how he failed to save his friend Kiowa[3] from drowning in a field of human excrement: "A good war story, he thought, but it was not a war for war stories, not for talk of valor, and nobody in town wanted to know about the stink. They wanted good intentions and good deeds" (169). Bowker's dilemma is remarkably similar to that of Krebs in Hemingway's story "Soldier's Home": "At first Krebs [...] did not want to talk about the war at all. Later he felt the need to talk but no one wanted to hear about it. His town had heard too many atrocity stories to be thrilled by actualities" (Hemingway 145).

O'Brien, after his war, took on the task "of grabbing people by the shirt and explaining exactly what had happened to me" (179). He explains in *The Things They Carried* that it is impossible to know "exactly what had happened." He wants us to know all of the things he/they/we did not know about Vietnam and will probably never know. He wants us to feel the sense of uncertainty that his character/narrator Tim O'Brien experiences twenty years after the war when he returns to the place where his friend Kiowa sank into a "field of shit" and tries to find "something meaningful and right" (212) to say but ultimately can only say, "well...there it is" (212). Each time we, the readers of *The Things They Carried*, return to Vietnam through O'Brien's labyrinth of stories, we become more and

---

[3]In the "Notes" to this chapter, O'Brien typically turns the whole story upside down "in the interest of truth" and tells us that Norman Bowker was not responsible for Kiowa's horrible death: "That part of the story is my own" (182). This phrase could be taken to mean that this part of the story is his own creation or that he was the one responsible for Kiowa's death.

more aware that this statement is the closest we probably ever will come to knowing the "real truth," the undying uncertainty of the Vietnam War.

Works Cited

Baritz, Loren. *Backfire: A History of How American Culture Led Us into Vietnam and Made Us Fight the Way We Did*. New York: Morrow, 1985.

Beidler, Philip. *American Literature and the Experience of Vietnam*. Athens: University of Georgia Press, 1982.

Halberstam, David. *One Very Hot Day*. New York: Houghton, 1967.

Hartman, Geoffrey. *Criticism in the Wilderness: The Study of Literature Today*. New Haven: Yale UP, 1980.

Hemingway, Ernest. *Short Stories*. New York: Scribner, 1953.

Iser, Wolfgang. *Prospecting: From Reader Response to Literary Anthropology*. Baltimore, MD: Johns Hopkins University Press, 1989.

Lomperis, Timothy, *"Reading the Wind": The Literature of the Vietnam War: An Interpretative Critique*. Durham, N.C.: Duke University Press, 1989.

Miller, J. Hillis. "Heart of Darkness Revisited." In *Heart of Darkness: A Case Study in Contemporary Criticism*, edited by Ross C. Murfin. New York: St. Martin's, 1989.

O'Brien, Tim. *Going After Cacciato*. New York: Dell, 1978.

——. *The Things They Carried*. Boston: Houghton, 1990.

"HOW TO TELL A TRUE WAR STORY": METAFICTION IN *THE THINGS THEY CARRIED*[1]

CATHERINE CALLOWAY

Tim O'Brien's most recent book, *The Things They Carried*, begins with a litany of items that the soldiers "hump" in the Vietnam War—assorted weapons, dog tags, flak jackets, car plugs, cigarettes, insect repellent, letters, can openers, C-rations, jungle boots, maps, medical supplies, and explosives as well as memories, reputations, and personal histories. In addition, the reader soon learns, the soldiers also carry stories: stories that connect "the past to the future" (40), stories that can "make the dead talk" (261), stories that "never seem . . . to end" (83), stories that are "beyond telling" (79), and stories "that swirl back and forth across the border between trivia and bedlam, the mad and the mundane" (101). Although perhaps few of the stories in *The Things They Carried* are as brief as the well-known Vietnam War tale related by Michael Herr in *Dispatches*—"Patrol went up the mountain. One man came back. He died before he could tell us what happened," (6)—many are in their own way

[1]*Critique* 36.4 (Summer 1995): 249—57, online, Galileo, Academic Search Premier, 15 Jan. 2002 .

as enigmatic. The tales included in O'Brien's twenty-two chapters range from several lines to many pages and demonstrate well the impossibility of knowing the reality of the war in absolute terms. Sometimes stories are abandoned, only to be continued pages or chapters later. At other times, the narrator begins to tell a story, only to have another character finish the tale. Still other stories are told as if true accounts, only for their validity to be immediately questioned or denied. O'Brien draws the reader into the text, calling the reader's attention to the process of invention and challenging him to determine which, if any, of the stories are true. As a result, the stories become epistemological tools, multidimensional windows through which the war, the world, and the ways of telling a war story can be viewed from many different angles and visions.

The epistemological ambivalence of the stories in *The Things They Carried* is reinforced by the book's ambiguity of style and structure. What exactly is *The Things They Carried* in terms of technique? Many reviewers refer to the work as a series of short stories, but it is much more than that. *The Things They Carried* is a combat novel, yet it is not a combat novel. It is also a blend of traditional and untraditional forms—a collection, Gene Lyons says, of "short stories, essays, anecdotes, narrative fragments, jokes, fables, biographical and autobiographical sketches, and philosophical asides" (52). It has been called both "a unified narrative with chapters that stand perfectly on their own" (Coffey 60) and a series of "22 discontinuous sections" (Bawer A 13).

Also ambiguous is the issue of how much of the book is autobiography. The relationship between fiction and reality arises early in the text when the reader learns the first of many parallels that emerge as the book progresses: that the protagonist and narrator, like the real author of *The Things They Carried*, is named Tim O'Brien. Both the real and the fictional Tim O'Brien are in their forties and are natives of Minnesota, writers who graduated Phi Beta Kappa from Macalester College, served as grunts in Vietnam after having been drafted at age twenty-one, attended graduate school at Harvard University, and wrote books entitled *If I Die in a Combat Zone* and *Going After Cacciato*. Other events of the protagonist's life are apparently invention. Unlike the real Tim O'Brien, the protagonist has a nine-year-old daughter named Kathleen and makes a return journey to Vietnam years after the war is over.[2] However, even the other supposedly fictional characters of the book sound real because of an epigraph preceding the stories that states, "This book is lovingly dedicated to the men of Alpha Company, and in particular to Jimmy Cross, Norman Bowker, Rat Kiley, Mitchell Sanders, Henry Dobbins, and Kiowa," leading the reader to wonder if the men of Alpha Company are real or imaginary.

---

[2]Biographical information on the real Tim O'Brien is taken from published facts of his life. See, for instance, Michael Coffey, "Tim O'Brien," *Publishers Weekly*, 237, 16 Feb. 1990, 60-61, and Everett C. Wilkie Jr., "Tim O'Brien." *Dictionary of Literary Biography Yearbook: 1980*, eds. Karen L. Rood, Jean W. Ross, and Richard Ziegfeld (Detroit: Gale, 1981), 286–90.

Clearly O'Brien resists a simplistic classification of his latest work. In both the preface to the book and in an interview with Elizabeth Mehren, he terms *The Things They Carried* "fiction . . . a novel" (Mehren El), but in an interview with Martin Naparsteck, he refers to the work as a "sort of half novel, half group of stories. It's part nonfiction, too," he insists (7). And, as Naparsteck points out, the work "resists easy categorization: it is part novel, part collection of stories, part essays, part journalism; it is, more significantly, all at the same time" (1).

As O'Brien's extensive focus on storytelling indicates, *The Things They Carried* is also a work of contemporary metafiction, what Robert Scholes first termed fabulation or "ethically controlled fantasy" (3). According to Patricia Waugh,

> Metafiction is a term given to fictional writing which self-consciously and systematically draws attention to its status as an artefact in order to pose questions about the relationship between fiction and reality. In providing a critique of their own methods of construction, such writings not only examine the fundamental structures of narrative fiction, they also explore the possible fictionality of the world outside the literary fictional text. (2)

Like O'Brien's earlier novel, the critically acclaimed *Going After Cacciato*,[3] *The Things They Carried* considers the process of writing; it is, in fact, as much about the process of writing as it is the text of a literary work. By examining imagination and memory, two main components that O'Brien feels are important to a writer of fiction (Schroeder 143), and by providing so many layers of technique in one work, O'Brien delves into the origins of fictional creation. In focusing so extensively on what a war story is or is not, O'Brien writes a war story as he examines the process of writing one. To echo what Philip Beidler has stated about *Going After Cacciato*, "the form" of *The Things They Carried* thus becomes "its content" (172); the medium becomes the message.

"I'm forty-three years old, and a writer now," O'Brien's protagonist states periodically throughout the book, directly referring to his role as author and to the status of his work as artifice. "Much of it [the war] is hard to remember," he comments. "I sit at this typewriter and stare through my words and watch Kiowa sinking into the deep muck of a shit field, or Curt Lemon hanging in pieces from a tree, and as I write about these things, the remembering is turned into a kind of rehappening" (36). The "rehappening" takes the form of a number of types of stories: some happy, some sad, some peaceful, some bloody, some wacky. We learn of Ted Lavender, who is "zapped while zipping" (17) after urinating, of the paranoid friendship of Dave Jensen and Lee Strunk, of the revenge plot against Bobby Jorgenson, an unskilled medic who almost accidentally kills the narrator, of the moral confusion of the protagonist who fishes on the Rainy River and dreams of desertion to Canada, and Mary Ann

---

[3]O'Brien, *Going After Cacciato* (New York: Delta/Seymour Lawrence, 1978). *Going After Cacciato* received the National Book Award in 1979.

Bell, Mark Fossie's blue-eyed, blonde, seventeen-year-old girlfriend, who is chillingly attracted to life in a combat zone.

Some stories only indirectly reflect the process of writing; other selections include obvious metafictional devices. In certain sections of the book, entire chapters are devoted to discussing form and technique. A good example is "Notes," which elaborates on "Speaking of Courage," the story that precedes it. The serious reader of the real Tim O'Brien's fiction recognizes "Speaking of Courage" as having first been published in the Summer 1976 issue of *Massachusetts Review*.[4] This earlier version of the story plays off chapter 14 of *Going After Cacciato*, "Upon Almost Winning the Silver Star," in which the protagonist, Paul Berlin, is thinking about how he might have won the Silver Star for bravery in Vietnam had he had the courage to rescue Frenchie Tucker, a character shot while searching a tunnel. However, in *The Things They Carried*'s version of "Speaking of Courage," the protagonist is not Paul Berlin, but Norman Bowker, who wishes he had had the courage to save Kiowa, a soldier who dies in a field of excrement during a mortar attack.[5] Such shifts in character and events tempt the reader into textual participation, leading him to question the ambiguous nature of reality. Who really did not win the Silver Star for bravery? Paul Berlin, Norman Bowker, or Tim O'Brien? Who actually needed saving? Frenchie Tucker or Kiowa? Which version of the story, if either, is accurate? The inclusion of a metafictional chapter presenting the background behind the tale provides no definite answers or resolutions. We learn that Norman Bowker, who eventually commits suicide, asks the narrator to compose the story and that the author has revised the tale for inclusion in *The Things They Carried* because a postwar story is more appropriate for the later book than for *Going After Cacciato*. However, O'Brien's admission that much of the story is still invention compels the reader to wonder about the truth. The narrator assures us that the truth is that "Norman did not experience a failure of nerve that night [...] or lose the Silver Star for valor" (182). Can

[4]*Massachusetts Review* 17 (Spring 1976): 243–53. The earlier version of the story has also been published in *Prize Stories 1978: The O'Henry Awards*. Ed. and intro. William Abrahams (Garden City: Doubleday, 1978), 159–68. A later version of "Speaking of Courage" appeared in *Granta* 29 (Winter 1989): 135–154, along with "Notes."

[5]O'Brien frequently makes changes between versions of his stories that are published in literary magazines and chapters of his books. The version of "Spin" that was published in the Spring 1990 issue of *The Quarterly* (3–13), for example, combines several of the individual stories from *The Things They Carried* into one longer tale. In addition, O'Brien makes changes between the hardback and paperback versions of his books. In both the "Field Trip" chapter of the hardback edition of *The Things They Carried* and the short story version of "Field Trip" (*McCalls* 17, Aug. 1990: 78–79), the narrator returns Kiowa's hatchet to the site of Kiowa's death, but in the paperback edition of *The Things They Carried* (New York: Penguin, 1990), the narrator carries a pair of Kiowa's moccasins. For references to changes in O'Brien's earlier works, see my "Pluralities of Vision: *Going After Cacciato* and Tim O'Brien's Short Fiction," *America Rediscovered: Critical Essays on Literature and Film of the Vietnam War*, eds. Owen W. Gilman Jr. and Lorrie Smith (New York: Garland, 1990), 213-24.

even this version be believed? Was there really a Norman Bowker, or is he, too, only fictional?

Even more significant, the reader is led to question the reality of many, if not all, of the stories in the book. The narrator insists that the story of Curt Lemon's death, for instance, is "all exactly true" (77), then states eight pages later that he has told Curt's story previously—"many times, many versions" (85)—before narrating yet another version. As a result, any and all accounts of the incident are questionable. Similarly, the reader is led to doubt the validity of many of the tales told by other characters in the book. The narrator remarks that Rat Kiley's stories, such as the one about Mary Ann Bell in "Sweetheart of the Song Tra Bong," are particularly ambiguous:

> For Rat Kiley [...] facts were formed by sensation, not the other way around, and when you listened to one of his stories, you'd find yourself performing rapid calculations in your head, subtracting superlatives, figuring the square root of an absolute and then multiplying by maybe. (101)

Still other characters admit the fictionality of their stories. Mitchell Sanders, in the ironically titled "How to Tell a True War Story," confesses to the protagonist that although his tale is the truth, parts of it are pure invention. "Last night, man," Sanders states, "I had to make up a few things [...] The glee club. There wasn't any glee club...No opera," either (83–84). "But," he adds, "it's still true" (84).

O'Brien shares the criteria with which the writer or teller and the reader or listener must be concerned by giving an extended definition of what a war story is or is not. The chapter "How to Tell a True War Story" focuses most extensively on the features that might be found in a "true" war tale. "A true war story is never moral," the narrator states. "It does not instruct, nor encourage virtue, nor suggest models of proper human behavior, nor restrain men from doing the things men have always done" (76).

Furthermore, a true war story has an "absolute and uncompromising allegiance to obscenity and evil" (76), is embarrassing, may not be believable, seems to go on forever, does "not generalize" or "indulge in abstraction or analysis" (84), does not necessarily make "a point" (88), and sometimes cannot even be told. True war stories, the reader soon realizes, are like the nature of the Vietnam War itself; "the only certainty is overwhelming ambiguity" (88). "The final and definitive truth" (83) cannot be derived, and any "truths are contradictory" (87).

By defining a war story so broadly, O'Brien writes more stories, interspersing the definitions with examples from the war to illustrate them. What is particularly significant about the examples is that they are given in segments, a technique that actively engages the readers in the process of textual creation. Characters who are mentioned as having died early in the work are brought back to life through flashbacks in other parts of the text so that we can see who these characters are, what they are like, and how they die. For instance, in the story "Spin," the narrator first refers to the death of Curt Lemon, a soldier blown apart by a booby trap, but the reader does not learn the details of the tragedy until four stories later, in "How to Tell a True War Story." Even then, the reader must piece together the details of Curt's death throughout that particular tale. The first reference to Lemon appears on the third page of the story, when O'Brien matter-of-factly states, "The dead guy's name was Curt Lemon" (77). Lemon's death is briefly mentioned a few paragraphs later, but additional details surrounding the incident are not given at once but are revealed gradually throughout the story, in between digressive stories narrated by two other soldiers, Rat Kiley and Mitchell Sanders. Each fragment about Curt's accident illustrates the situation more graphically. Near the beginning of the tale, O'Brien describes the death somewhat poetically. Curt is "a handsome kid, really. Sharp grey eyes, lean and narrow-waisted, and when he died it was almost beautiful, the way the sunlight came around him and lifted him up and sucked him high into a tree full of moss and vines and white blossoms" (78). Lemon is not mentioned again for seven pages, at which time O'Brien illustrates the effect of Lemon's death upon the other soldiers by detailing how Rat Kiley, avenging Curt's death, mutilates and kills a baby water buffalo. When later in the story Lemon's accident is narrated for the third time, the reader is finally told what was briefly alluded to in the earlier tale "Spin": how the soldiers had to peel Curt Lemon's body parts from a tree.

The story of Curt Lemon does not end with "How to Tell a True War Story" but is narrated further in two other stories, "The Dentist" and "The Lives of the Dead." In "The Lives of the Dead," for example, Curt is resurrected through a story of his trick-or-treating in Vietnamese hootches on Halloween for whatever goodies he can get: "candles and joss sticks and a pair of black pajamas and statuettes of the smiling Buddha" (268). To hear Rat Kiley tell it, the narrator comments, "you'd never know that Curt Lemon was dead. He was still out there in the dark, naked and painted up, trick-or-treating, sliding from hootch to hootch in that crazy white ghost mask" (268). To further complicate matters, in "The Lives of the Dead," O'Brien alludes to a soldier other than Curt, Stink Harris, from a previous literary work, *Going After Cacciato*, written over a decade before *The Things They Carried*. Thus, the epistemological uncertainty in the stories is mirrored by the fact that O'Brien presents events that take place in a fragmented form rather than in a straightforward, linear fashion. The reader has to piece together information, such as the circumstances surrounding the characters' deaths, in the same manner that the characters must piece together the reality of the war, or, for that matter, Curt Lemon's body.

The issue of truth is particularly a main crux of the events surrounding "The Man I Killed," a story that O'Brien places near the center of the book. Gradually interspersed throughout the stories that make up *The Things They Carried* are references to a Vietnamese soldier, "A slim, dead, dainty young man of about twenty" (40) with "a star-shaped hole" (141) in his face, who is first mentioned in the story "Spin" and whose death still haunts the narrator long after the end of the war. Nine chapters after "Spin," in "The Man I Killed," the protagonist graphically describes the dead Vietnamese youth as well as creates a personal history for him; he envisions the young man to have been a reluctant soldier who hated violence and "loved mathematics" (142), a university-educated man who "had been a soldier for only a single day" (144) and who, like the narrator, perhaps went to war only to avoid "disgracing himself, and therefore his family and village" (142).[6] "Ambush," the story immediately following "The Man I Killed," provides yet another kaleidoscopic fictional frame of the incident, describing in detail the events that lead up to the narrator's killing of the young soldier and ending with a version of the event that suggests that the young man does not die at all. The reader is forced to connect the threads of the story in between several chapters that span over a hundred pages; not until a later chapter, "Good Form," where the protagonist narrates three more stories of the event, does the reader fully question the truth of the incident. In the first version in "Good Form," the narrator reverses the details of the earlier stories and denies that he was the thrower of the grenade that killed the man. "Twenty years ago I watched a man die on a trail near the village of My Khe," he states. "I did not kill him. But I was present, you see, and my presence was guilt enough" (203). However, he immediately admits that "Even that story is made up" (203) and tells instead what he terms "the happening-truth":

> I was once a soldier. There were many bodies, real bodies with real faces, but I was young then and I was afraid to look. And now, twenty years later, I'm left with faceless responsibility and faceless grief. (203)

In still a third version, "the happening-truth" is replaced with "the story-truth." According to the protagonist, the Vietnamese soldier

> was a slim, dead, almost dainty young man of about twenty. He lay in the center of a red clay trail near the village of My Khe. His jaw was in his throat. His one eye was shut, the other eye was a star-shaped hole. I killed him. (204)

But the reader wonders, did the narrator kill the young man? When the narrator's nine-year-old daughter demands, "Daddy, tell the truth . . . did you ever kill anybody?" the narrator reveals that he "can say, honestly, 'Of course not,'" or he "can say, honestly, 'Yes'" (204).

According to Inger Christensen, one of the most important elements of metafiction is "the novelist's message" (10). At least one reviewer has reduced O'Brien's message in *The Things They Carried* to the moral "'Death sucks'" (Melmoth H6); the book, however, reveals an even greater thematic concern. "Stories can save us," asserts the protagonist in "The Lives of the Dead," the concluding story of the text (255), where fiction is used as a means of resurrecting the deceased. In this multiple narrative, O'Brien juxtaposes tales of death in Vietnam with an account of the death of Linda, a nine-year-old girl who had a brain tumor. As the pro-

---

[6]O'Brien develops the figure of the young Vietnamese youth who opposes the war more fully in *Going After Cacciato*, where Li Van Hgoc, a Vietnamese major, has been imprisoned in a tunnel complex for ten years for fleeing from the war and refusing to fight. The major, in a sense, mirrors Paul Berlin and the Third Squad. Theoretically, the soldiers have one main factor in common with Li Van Hgoc; they are all deserters from the war.

tagonist tells Linda's story, he also comments on the nature and power of fiction. Stories, he writes, are "a kind of dreaming, [where] the dead sometimes smile and sit up and return to the world" (255). The narrator of "The Lives of the Dead" thus seeks to keep his own friends alive through the art of storytelling. "As a writer now," he asserts,

> I want to save Linda's life. Not her body—her life [...] in a story I can steal her soul. I can revive, at least briefly, that which is absolute and unchanging [...] in a story, miracles can happen. Linda can smile and sit up. She can reach out, touch my wrist, and say, "Timmy, stop crying." (265)

Past, present, and future merge into one story as through fiction O'Brien zips "across the surface of [...] [his] own history, moving fast, riding the melt beneath the blades, doing loops and spins . . . as Tim trying to save Timmy's life with a story" (273). His story mirrors his own creative image of history, "a blade tracing loops on ice" (265), as his metafictive narrative circles on three levels: the war of a little boy's soul as he tries to understand the death of a friend, the Vietnam War of a twenty-three-year-old infantry sergeant, and the war of "guilt and sorrow" (265) faced by "a middle-aged writer" (265) who must deal with the past.

In focusing so extensively on the power of fiction and on what a war story is or is not in *The Things They Carried*, O'Brien writes a multidimensional war story even as he examines the process of writing one. His tales become stories within stories or multilayered texts within texts within texts. The book's genius is a seeming inevitability of form that perfectly embodies its theme—the miracle of vision—the eternally protean and volatile capacity of the imagination, which may invent that which it has the will and vision to conceive.[7] "In the end," the narrator states,

> a true war story is never about war. It's about sunlight. It's about the special way that dawn spreads out on a river when you know you must cross the river and march into the mountains and do things you are afraid to do. It's about love and memory. It's about sorrow. It's about sisters who never write back and people who never listen. (91)

How, then, can a true war story be told? Perhaps the best way, O'Brien says, is to "just keep on telling it" (91).

Works Cited

Bawer, Bruce. "Confession or Fiction? Stories from Vietnam." *Wall Street Journal* 215, 23 Mar. 1990: A13.

Beidler, Philip D. *American Literature and the Experience of Vietnam*. Athens: University of Georgia Press, 1982.

Christensen, Inger. *The Meaning of Metafiction*. Bergen: Universitetsforlaget, 1981.

[7]This theme is also a main theme of *Going After Cacciato*, which examines issues such as how war affects the imagination and how the imagination affects war, how reality cannot be escaped even in the imagination, how the imagination is used to invent rather than to discover, how the imagination must be used as a responsible tool, and how the imagination can be a force for remaking reality.

Herr, Michael. *Dispatches*. New York: Vintage, 1977.

Lyons, Gene. "No More Bugles, No More Drums." *Entertainment Weekly* 23 Feb. 1990: 50–52.

Mehren, Elizabeth. "Short War Stories." *Los Angeles Times* 11 Mar. 1990: E1, E12.

Melmoth, John. "Muck and Bullets." *The Sunday Times* (London) 20 May 1990: H6.

Naparsteck, Martin. "An Interview with Tim O'Brien." *Contemporary Literature* 32 (Spring 1991): 1–11.

O'Brien, Tim. *The Things They Carried*. New York: Houghton, 1990.

Scholes, Robert. *Fabulation and Metafiction*. Urbana: University of Illinois Press, 1983.

Schroeder, Eric James. "Two Interviews: Talks with Tim O'Brien and Robert Stone." *Modern Fiction Studies 30* (Spring 1984): 135–64.

Waugh, Patricia. *Metafiction: The Theory and Practice of Self-Conscious Fiction*. New York: Methuen, 1984.

GETTING IT RIGHT: THE SHORT FICTION OF TIM O'BRIEN[1]

DANIEL ROBINSON

But it's true even if it didn't happen—

—KEN KESEY

In his introduction to *Men at War*, Ernest Hemingway states that a "writer's job is tell the truth. His standard of fidelity to the truth should be so high that his inventions . . . should produce a truer account than anything factual can be" (xi). Tim O'Brien, for whose writing the Vietnam War is the informing principle, returns to this notion of truth in his short fiction.[2] His stories revolve around multiple centers of interest—at once stories in the truest sense, with a core of action and character, and also metafictional stories on the precise nature of writing war stories.

For O'Brien, like Hemingway in his introduction, the notion of absolute fidelity to facts almost becomes a non sequitur when considering truth. Facts might provide a chronology of events (and even then, we may disagree on the validity of the facts), but alone they cannot reveal the hidden truths found in a true war story. As Hemingway writes, facts "can be observed badly; but when a good writer is creating something,

---

[1]*Critique* 40.3 (Spring 1999): 257–64, online, Galileo, Academic Search Premier, 15 Jan. 2002 .

[2]In this essay, I consider only those stories of Tim O'Brien's that were previously published as separate short stories and are substantially different from any counterparts in later novels. Thus, I exclude stories that appeared in *Going After Cacciato* in much the same form as when they were published earlier as well as those stories in *The Things They Carried* that were not separately published.

he has time and scope to make of it an absolute truth" (xi–xii). That is also true for O'Brien: He sometimes writes stories that contradict the facts of other stories; yet the essential, underlying truth of each story is intact and illuminating. Those truths lie as much in the fragmented, impressionistic stories he tells as in the narrative technique he chooses for the telling.

O'Brien does not deliver Vietnam in neatly packaged truisms. The same words that rang obscene for Frederic Henry in Hemingway's *A Farewell to Arms*, "abstract words such as glory, honor, courage, or hallow," become empty in O'Brien's fiction. Those words imply a rational order to war that does not exist, and the absence of those words mirrors the horror of a world at its most irrational. As O'Brien writes in "How to Tell a True War Story," "[O]ften in a true war story there is not even a point" (88). What O'Brien prefers are the images that make "the stomach believe" (89), images of men at war who are too afraid not to kill.

The true reasons that bring O'Brien's characters to Vietnam are far from the abstract words that Frederic Henry dismisses and equally far from the Hollywood notion of heroism so prevalent in war movies prior to American involvement in Vietnam. The average age of the company of foot soldiers O'Brien writes about is nineteen or twenty, and most were probably drafted, as is the case of the fictional Tim O'Brien through whom author O'Brien often tells his stories. Thus, we see boys becoming men before they have had the opportunity to understand what manhood involves. And among the many things each soldier carried—the weapons, charms, diseases, and emotions—they "carried the soldier's greatest fear, which was the fear of blushing. Men killed, and died, because they were embarrassed not to" ("Things" 20-21). Even the enemy soldiers, the Viet Cong, exhibit that moral dichotomy and fight out of fear as much as nationalism:

> In the presence of his father and uncles, he pretended to look forward to doing his patriotic duty, which was also a privilege, but at night he prayed with his mother that the war might end soon. Beyond anything else, he was afraid of disgracing himself, and therefore his family and village. ("Man" 142)

However, quite different from most of O'Brien's characters driven by fear is Azar, the nineteen-year-old draftee who straps a puppy to a Claymore antipersonnel mine and blows the dog to pieces. Azar, still a teenager, loves Vietnam because it makes him "feel like a kid again." "The Vietnam experience," he says, "I mean, wow, I love this shit" ("Ghost" 237). O'Brien's characters choose war for entirely negative reasons, not for unselfish love of country or of basic freedoms but from fear of embarrassment and cowardice or the love of war as if it were a child's game. Even the decision to go to Vietnam is determined not through an examination of positive motives but, again, for negative reasons: "I would go to the war . . . because I was embarrassed not to. . . . I was a coward. I went to war" ("River" 63).

That inability in O'Brien's characters to establish a positive purpose in their reasons for going to war mirrors the historical ambiguities surrounding American involvement in Vietnam. Like the chaotic and morally ambiguous war they fight, O'Brien's characters are unsure of their purpose or even their actions. Azar explains blowing up the puppy as simple childish exuberance: "What's everybody so upset about? I mean, Christ, I'm just a boy" ("Spin" 40). After one of his men dies, "Lieutenant Jimmy Cross led his men into the village of Than Ke. They burned everything. They shot chickens and dogs, they trashed the village well, they called in artillery and watched the wreckage, then they marched for several hours through the hot afternoon" to a place where they set up camp for the night ("Things" 16). Those men act not from forethought but from some measure of selective emotion: Azar, the sadist, experiences delight from torturing the puppy and, in "The Ghost Soldiers," torture—prankstering a medic on guard duty who had nearly allowed another soldier to die through inaction; and the troop, following Lavender's sniper-death, razes the nearest village not for some strategic reason but out of an apparent need for revenge. The chauvinistic clichés that so often accompany patriotic fervor are missing. These characters have no center around which they can construct a reason for their involvement, and the only absolute is that resupply helicopters will arrive soon with more things for them to carry: For "all the ambiguities of Vietnam, all the mysteries and unknowns, there was at least the single abiding certainty that they would never be at a loss for things to carry" ("Things" 16).

As Lorrie Smith writes in "Disarming the War Story," "The 'story' of World War II . . . has meaning for our culture as a heroic quest, and it forms a coherent narrative in which the soldier's sacrifices are redemptive" (90). All of that coherence of purpose is lost in O'Brien's stories of Vietnam, as his characters stumble through a landscape of disjointed experiences and realities. And though we may, as Smith asserts, "feel acutely the disjunction between ideals and realities" (90) when we attempt to consider Vietnam in terms of heroic quests, coherent actions, and redemptive sacrifices, O'Brien's characters seldom articulate any distinctions. For them, the realities are too overpowering to place against any abstract notions based upon cultural and societal ideals. Only Lt. Jimmy Cross, in "The Things They Carried," and Tim,[3] in "On the Rainy River," consider that disjunction, and then only in personal terms, excluding any real notion of established codes.

One often expects writers of war stories to present antithetical abstractions in a concrete form to establish some moral or ethical base. O'Brien, however, fuses abstracts such as reality and surreality and right

---

[3]Any use of "Tim" in this essay refers to the fictional character, and the use of "O'Brien" refers to Tim O'Brien the author. In an interview with Steven Kaplan, O'Brien discusses the similarities and differences between him and his fictional character: "Everything I have written has come partly out of my own concerns . . . but the story lines themselves, the events . . . the characters . . . the places . . . are almost all invented. . . . Ninety percent or more of the material . . . is invented, and I invented ninety percent of a new Tim O'Brien, maybe even more than that" (95).

and wrong in an effort to emphasize the lack of firm moral ground supporting his characters in a war lacking in definable purposes. To stop his own pain at seeing his best friend blown up, Rat Kiley systematically dismembers a baby water buffalo by shooting pieces from its body—its mouth, tail, ears, nose—until all that remains alive and moving are its eyes. The reaction by Rat's stunned comrades is restrained amazement: "A new wrinkle. I never seen it before. . . . Well, that's Nam" (86). A group of Green Berets keep a pile of enemy bones stacked in a corner of their barracks underneath a sign that reads, "ASSEMBLE YOUR OWN GOOK!! FREE SAMPLE KIT!" ("Sweetheart" 119). That distillation of moral or ethical standards, an "aesthetic purity of moral indifference" ("True" 87), illustrates a general loss of humanity in any war, but possibly more so in a war that lacks any underlying absolutes, any real reasons for having gone to war. Thus the moral confusion Tim feels (in "On the Rainy River") after finding out he has been drafted becomes a moral indifference once exposed to the brutalities and absurdities of war.

Those apparent indifferences extend even to how the soldiers deal with the death of their comrades. When a man dies, he is not killed, but "greased. . . . offed, lit up, zapped." ("Things" 19). Somehow, by verbally denying the reality of death through hyperbolic misnomers, they reject the death itself. At one point in "The Lives of the Dead," Tim's unit enters a village it has calmly watched being bombed and burned by air strikes for thirty minutes. When the unit enters, the only person in the village is a dead old man who is missing an arm and whose face is covered by swarming flies and gnats. Each man, as he walks past the dead Vietnamese, offers a greeting and shakes the remaining hand: "How-dee-doo. . . . Gimme five. . . . A real honor. . . . Pleased as punch" (256). After Tim refuses to introduce himself or even offer a toast to the old man's health, he is ridiculed for not showing respect for his elders: "Maybe it's too real for you?" he is asked. "That's right," he replies. "Way too real" (256). It is only his fourth day, and Tim soon realizes that he must develop the cynical sense of humor he will eventually need to cope with the realities of death. Paul Berlin, on his first day in Vietnam, in "Where Have You Gone, Charming Billy?" watches one of his comrades die of a heart attack brought on by the fear of dying. In his attempt to deal with witnessing his first death, he tries to transform the event into something that had not happened. Eventually, however, as the realities of the experience eat at him, he places the death in comic terms by imagining the official death notification:

SORRY TO INFORM YOU THAT YOUR SON BILLY BOY WAS YESTERDAY SCARED TO DEATH IN ACTION IN THE REPUBLIC OF VIETNAM, VALIANTLY SUCCUMBING TO A HEART ATTACK SUFFERED WHILE UNDER ENORMOUS STRESS. . . . (130)

Berlin finally concludes that the death will make "a good joke" and "a funny war story" for his father (132). Not superficial male posturing, but overwhelming fear forces O'Brien's characters purposefully to detach themselves from death. They use any method possible, from keeping the dead alive through absurd ceremonial greetings to parodying government form letters to, as Albert Wilhelm writes, "keep the horrors of war at bay" (221).

Ironically, one of the deaths that breaks through the fabricated veneer of insulation is the death of an enemy in "The Man I Killed." In explicit detail bordering on the religious, Tim vividly recalls the man he killed— maybe the first man or maybe just the first he had an opportunity to study afterwards. Azar dismisses the death in the common distancing dialogue discussed above, "Oh, man, you fuckin' trashed the fucker. . . . You laid him out like Shredded fuckin' Wheat. . . . Rice Krispies, you know? On the dead test, this particular individual gets A-plus" (140); And Kiowa tries moving Tim beyond his dumbstruck staring at the bloody corpse to talk about his emotions. Only here and in "Speaking of Courage," where Norman Bowker, back home in Iowa on the Fourth of July, recounts the death of Kiowa in a swampy field, is the examination of death not covered under false layers of fear. O'Brien the writer must now dredge up those deaths that Tim the young soldier tried so hard to bury, which may explain why O'Brien returns to Vietnam in his fiction with such force and passion: he is reliving the horrors he suppressed decades earlier.

As in "The Man I Killed" and "Speaking of Courage," O'Brien often uses a spiraling narrative technique to draw out the realism of death, even if this characters continue to refute that death. O'Brien revolves those stories around a specific death, as Joseph Heller revolves the first part of *Catch–22* around Snowden's death, covering the same ground yet illuminating the moment's particular horror with each movement back to the death. The effect is at once numbing and oddly positive. We sense the overwhelming totality of death on the one hand, but we also imagine the narrator attempting to place a new order to his story, one that will somehow exclude the death. In "The Man I Killed," the effect is an increasing horror at seeing the dead man; whereas in "Speaking of Courage," Norman realizes that he failed to save his friend's life. "The Things They Carried" revolves around the sniper death of Lavender, and in so doing shows Lt. Jimmy Cross's movement from the innocence of his insular world in which, to keep the war at a distance, he pretends that a girl back home in the United States is in love with him. However, with Lavender's death, he must face the reality that his lack of focus in leading his men may in part have caused that death. As many initiations do, Cross's initiation into the realities surrounding him results also in his need to destroy something of his past, which he does when he burns Martha's letters and photographs.

Kiowa's death becomes the center point for Norman Bowker in "Speaking of Courage" and is also the death around which the action revolves in "In the Field." Ironically, here two other soldiers feel the responsibility for Kiowa's death, which adds an interesting layer of multiplicity of perception to O'Brien's stories. O'Brien further explores that notion of multiplicity of perception through Jimmy Cross's drafting a letter to Kiowa's parents. His first draft places blame on some ubiquitous "They" who sent him and his men to bivouac in a tactically indefensible position; in his second draft, he accepts the blame; and finally, he revises the letter to express "an officer's condolences. No apologies necessary" (197–98). All three drafts are accurate and true, underscoring the inability to write about war in absolute terms.

O'Brien's cyclical pattern that places death as the center point around which many of his stories revolve reinforces a permanence to war that a more linear narrative structure would necessarily exclude. O'Brien's characters cannot leave the deaths behind them and trudge on through a strictly chronological story. "The bad stuff," O'Brien writes in "Spin," "never stops happening: it lives in its own dimension, replaying itself over and over" (36). And even when the war is over, it is not over; even though "the war occurred half a lifetime ago, . . . the remembering makes it now" (40). So the cyclical pattern established in many of these stories continues to revolve long after the story stops, and the things they carried during the war become eclipsed by the things they carry following the war.

The deaths, of course, form the most visually unforgettable parts of O'Brien's stories. They are, first of all, not Hollywood war deaths: They are not scripted to show grace under pressure or to elevate the human reaction to the horrors of war. O'Brien's characters do not die filled with the notions of courage, honor, and camaraderie: they just die. Ted Lavender dies while zipping up his pants after urinating on a bus; Kiowa dies from drowning in the muddy human filth of a village's sewage field; Billy Boy Watkins dies of a heart attack brought on by the fear of dying after stepping on a land mine; Lemon dies from stepping on a land mine while playing an innocent game of catch and is literally blown into a nearby tree; and Jorgenson, who dies after eluding enemy patrols and taking a midnight swim, swallows bad water. None of the deaths are the deaths of heroes; and like the ritualized shooting of the water buffalo following Lemon's death, they serve to show a major theme connecting O'Brien's work—how isolated events of cruelty define war. Azar killing the puppy, Bowker shooting the water buffalo, a little girl dancing to an unheard rhythm outside her burned-out hut following a napalm raid, the first enemy killed, and the singular deaths of friends accrue as acts of cruelty to, as O'Brien says, "touch [the] reader's heart more than a grandiose description of the fire bombing of a village, or the napalming of a village, where you don't see corpses, you don't know the corpses, you don't witness the death in any detail. It is somehow made abstract, bloodless" (Kaplan 102). By focusing on the character—the individual coming in close contact with what death looks like—and allowing the surrounding scenes and events to take secondary importance, O'Brien increases the absurdity and horror. His plots are determined not by incident and event, but by the changing moral attitudes and development of his characters.

Likewise, "declarations about war, such as war is hell" (Kaplan 101) or war is immoral seem, in O'Brien's fiction, just as hollow as the declarations of war that place men in battle. These declarations, while possibly true, are little more than abstract generalities that fail to turn something deep within the reader. "A true war story," as O'Brien wrote, "if truly told, makes the stomach believe" (84). A true war story, then, may not have a point, and it certainly does not exist in the narrative vacuum of beginning-middle-end, but it functions at a level of truth beyond that found in the story's words. Often, you doubt whether an O'Brien story can be true. Can a man actually transport his girlfriend to an isolated medical post in the Central Highlands and then lose her to the war as she slowly matriculates into the jungle? Some things, Pederson says in "Keeping Watch by Night," "you just see and you got to believe in what you see" (66). A true war story has no moral, no instruction, no virtue, no suggestion of proper behavior; there is only a revelation of the possible evil in the nature of man: "You can tell a true war story," O'Brien tells us, "by its absolute and uncompromising allegiance to obscenity and evil" ("True" 76). True war stories, as O'Brien writes in his nonfiction narrative *If I Die in a Combat Zone*, offer "simple, unprofound scraps of truth" that lack any lessons to teach about war. The writer, then, according to O'Brien, must "simply tell stories" (32). However, within that apparent lack of pretense to message lies the phenomenological truths of O'Brien's fiction, which strike much deeper than, as Lorrie Smith writes, an exploitation of "war's larger political implications" (94). By suppressing the abstract in favor of the concrete, O'Brien allows his stories to exist as commentary through the "complex tangles and nuances of actual experience" (Calloway 222).

Beyond that, moreover, as O'Brien tells Steven Kaplan, "good stories somehow have to do with an awakening into a new world, something new and true, where someone is jolted out of ... complacency and forced to confront a new set of circumstances or a new self" (99). The archetypal pattern that O'Brien here alludes to of initiation into the complexities of the real world forms an underlying basis of much of O'Brien's fiction. Paul Berlin's witnessing Billy Boy's death signals his loss of innocence, his transition into manhood, and an unwelcome realization of the world's potential for cruelty. And Tim, who may realize that his only options are kill or be killed, cannot be comforted by that knowledge as his world of relative innocence is shattered by the realities of this new world he inhabits. Correspondingly, that separation between men and boys is also shown by the physical appearance of the soldiers as they trudge along under the weight of all they carry: "The most recent arrivals had pasty skin burnt at the shoulder blades and clavicle and neck; their boots were not yet red with clay, and they walked more carefully than the rest, and they looked more vulnerable" ("Spin" 36). As their appearance evolves and their movements change, so, too, their character changes in the "effort to establish a new order" to their life (Kaplan 99)—one in which the vulnerability of youth is replaced by the cynicism and hardness of manhood.

That also may be why O'Brien still returns to Vietnam in his fiction—because he is still trying to make sense of the new order established in his life over twenty years ago. In his stories, in the futile attempt to regain what he had before the war, he can still dream alive the people who died; unfortunately, though, that also necessitates his reliving their deaths. That need may be what still hits O'Brien: "twenty years later, in your sleep, and you wake up and shake your wife and start telling the story to her, except when you get to the end you've forgotten the point again. And then for a long time you lie there watching the story happen in your head. You listen to your wife's breathing. The war's over. You close your eyes. You smile and think, Christ, what's the point?" ("True" 88–89). The point, however, is all in the telling, as is the healing. In his stories, O'Brien answers his characters' desire to make sense out of their experiences: Kiowa imploring Tim to just talk after killing an enemy soldier instead of dumbly staring at the corpse, or Rat Kiley—not wanting to have to listen to the silence of the night—asking Kiowa to tell once again how Lavender fell like a sack of cement, or the platoon waiting once more for Rat to tell his story about the sweetheart of Song Tra Bong. O'Brien's characters, like O'Brien himself, carry their stories with them, sometimes damning the unimaginable weight of relived experience and sometimes extolling the outlet allowed through storytelling, which becomes at times a life-support system and a salvation from the moral complexities of the war.

Those moral complexities required of O'Brien "an innovative form rather than the conventional chronological narrative" (Slabey 206). In presenting stories from a war that lacked a traditional progression or a logical structure, O'Brien demands more from his writing than strict realism can provide. He blurs the distinctions in his stories to present truths coalesced in memory and imagination to, "get things right"—not in the absolute terms of packaged truisms and simplistic judgments but through the inner landscape of experiential truth telling.

Works Cited

Beidler, Philip D. *Re-Writing America: Vietnam Authors in Their Generation.* Athens: University of Georgia Press, 1991.

Calloway, Catherine. "Pluralities of Vision: *Going After Cacciato* and *Tim O'Brien's* Short Fiction." In *America Rediscovered,* edited by Gilman and Smith, 213–22.

Gilman, Owen W., and Lorrie Smith, eds. *America Rediscovered: Critical Essays on Literature and Film of the Vietnam War.* New York: Garland, 1990.

Kaplan, Steven. "An Interview with *Tim O'Brien*." *Missouri Review* *14.3* (1991): 95–108.

O'Brien, Tim. "The Ghost Soldiers." O'Brien, *Things* 215–44.

———. "How to Tell a True War Story." O'Brien, *Things*, 73–92.

———. "In the Field." O'Brien, *Things*, 183-200.

———. "Keeping Watch by Night." *Redbook* 148 (Dec. 1976): 65–67.

———. "The Lives of the Dead." O'Brien, *Things*, 253–73.

———. "The Man I Killed." O'Brien, *Things*, 137–44.

———. "On the Rainy River." O'Brien, *Things*, 41–64.

———. "Speaking of Courage." O'Brien, *Things*, 155–74.

———. "Spin." O'Brien, *Things*, 33–40.

———. "Style." O'Brien, *Things*, 151–54.

———. "Sweetheart of Song Tra Bong." O'Brien, *Things*, 99–126.

———. "The Things They Carried." O'Brien, *Things*, 1–26.

———. *The Things They Carried.* New York: Penguin, 1991.

———. "Where Have You Gone, Charming Billy?" *Redbook* 145 (May 1975): 81, 127–32.

Slabey, Robert M. "*Going After Cacciato:* Tim O'Brien's 'Separate Peace.'" In *America Rediscovered,* edited by Gilman and Smith, 205–11.

Smith, Lorrie. "Disarming the War Story." In *America Rediscovered,* edited by Gilman and Smith, 87–99.

Wilhelm, Albert. "Ballad Allusions in Tim O'Brien's 'Where Have You Gone, Charming Billy?'" *Studies in Short Fiction* 28.2 (Spring 1991): 218–22.

Dreams of Truth, Reality, and War

Nick Hembree

1   Tim O'Brien seamlessly blends fact and fiction in his stories set in the Vietnam conflict, weaving a horridly beautiful tapestry of war and of life. He creates truths that transcend what is and what is not, and in his own words, "[w]hat stories can do, I guess, is make things present" ("Good Form" 180). Many critics of his work agree that his masterful storytelling ability confers some special sense of what it was like to be there, deep in the foggy mountains and torrid jungles of Vietnam. Catherine Calloway says, "Clearly O'Brien resists a simplistic classification of his latest work [The Things They Carried]" (1032), and Daniel Robinson comments, "[Tim O'Brien] sometimes writes stories that contradict the facts of other stories; yet the essential underlying truth of each story is intact and illuminating" (1039).

2   As O'Brien himself often repeats throughout his works, there are no morals to his stories—only truths. A moral is a simple truism that can be applied to a limited situation; a truth, on the other hand, allows those who understand it properly to be more aware of the nature of humanity. With that idea in mind, O'Brien probes deeply into his own inner psyche in "On the Rainy River," delving deeply into powerful emotional currents that sweep past all of the thoughts and ideals that he

has tried to construct around them. He begins the story with an explanation of why he has never told this particular tale to anyone before:

> To go into it, I always thought, would only
> cause embarrassment for all of us, a sudden
> need to be elsewhere, which is the natural
> response to a confession. . .For nearly twenty
> years I've had to live with it, feeling the
> shame, trying to push it away, and so by this
> act of remembrance, by putting the facts down
> on paper, I hope to relieve at least some of
> the pressure of my dreams. (994)

3   This passage gives the reader some small idea of how profoundly O'Brien's acts in the story have affected even his present day life. The price of cowardice to one's self is one not easily repaid, as O'Brien discovers from the events of his past. Morally and intellectually against the fighting in Vietnam, Tim O'Brien has found himself suddenly with a draft notice and having finally to come to grips with who he is and what he is personally going to do about the war, yet indecision is the only solution he can come up with, and "[b]eyond all this, or at the very center, was the raw fact of terror" (966), the terror of facing death for a reason that cannot be understood or believed in. Eventually, O'Brien heads north in a vain attempt to escape his reality, only to find the Canadian border, and the ultimate need to make a decision to run from the war or to take a part in it. At the very end of the story, the choice is made: "[e]ven in my imagination, the shore [of Canada] just twenty yards away, I couldn't make myself be brave. It had nothing to do with morality. Embarrassment, that's all it was" (1005). It is nice to believe in ideals of what is right and what is wrong, but in the end,

sometimes we simply do what our overwhelming internal forces drive us to, for better or for worse. Tim O'Brien would likely argue for the worst, yet the past has already been, and we can only take care of the present.

4   Of all his stories, "On the Rainy River" rings with the clearest sound of fact, yet this is not always the case with O'Brien's writings. In fact, one of his greatest attributes as a writer is his excellent use of metafiction, drawing the reader's attention to a fundamental truth that might otherwise be missed. All throughout the story "How to Tell a True War Story," in <u>The Things They Carried</u>, O'Brien repeats the account of how Curt Lemon came to die: "he must've thought it was the sunlight killing him. It was not the sunlight. It was a rigged 105 round" (1015). Every time he repeats the story, it comes a small step closer to a truth, becoming more full with the telling, yet also becoming less believable. Rat Kiley, a friend of Curt, writes to his sister after he dies, expressing his love and anguish for Curt, yet the "dumb cooze" never writes back, despite Rat's pouring his heart out into the letter. The reader later learns that Curt is the same man who trick-or-treated completely nude (save only his boots and gun) in a small Vietnamese village, and he is also the same man who traipses about the jungle, as if on a school field trip instead of a military mission. Later on, after Curt's death, Rat mercilessly tortures a water buffalo, shooting it in various places and watching it collapse, as all of his fellow soldiers sit back and watch, sickened at the display, yet simply letting it pass. Finally, O'Brien tells of how whenever he tells this particular story, someone will always come up and say to him how touching it was and that he should also move on with his life, but "[a]ll you can do is tell it one more time, patiently, adding and subtracting, making up a few things to get at the real truth ... No Lemon, no Rat Kiley. No

trail junction. No baby buffalo" (1015). Simply telling the facts can be a poor way of getting people to understand what the speaker is trying to tell them; rather, it is when he changes the way that he tells a story, the exact details of it, that he can more easily allow people to understand truth, and not simple truisms or facts.

5   Yet another technique that O'Brien uses in his writings is that of complete focus upon one thing all throughout a story, such as in "The Man I Killed," as well as a complete rejection of the facts to his readers, making them completely uncertain that the story has any factual base yet at the same time, reinforcing the abstract idea behind the story. In "The Man I Killed," O'Brien begins with telling the physical details of a dead body lying on a trail, a man stripped of his very life, moving on to personal details of the Vietnamese youth that he could not possibly know, such as where he was born, where he went to school, who his fiancée was. Throughout the story, a mental image of what the youth was like slowly collects in the reader's mind: "He was not a fighter. His health was poor, his body small and frail. He liked books. He wanted someday to be a teacher of mathematics" (1017). There is nothing especially evil about the youth, as he was not unlike O'Brien himself, afraid of war, but more afraid to fight tradition and ridicule; nevertheless, he has been killed, and O'Brien sits and ponders the death of the youth, wondering who the young Vietnamese boy was, what his future might have been. However, in another short story in The Things They Carried, O'Brien refutes the fact that the incident ever occurred, yet at the same time making it clear that the story truth is more real than the happening-truth:

>   Here is the happening-truth. I was once a
>   soldier. There were many bodies, real bodies
>   with real faces, but I was young then and I

was afraid to look. And now, twenty years
later, I'm left with faceless responsibility
and faceless grief.

Here is the story-truth. He was a slim,
dead, almost dainty young man of about twenty. He
lay in the center of a red clay trail near the
village of My Khe. His jaw was in his throat. His
one eye was shut, the other eye was a star-shaped
hole. I killed him. ("Good Form" 180)

O'Brien manages again to twist reality and fiction into
something more real than either, and transcending both, reaching
for some celestial absolute that tantalizes the mind.

6   Tim O'Brien's use of fiction and storytelling is a work of
genius, extracting and manipulating its reader's thoughts and
feelings in an incredibly powerful way. His stories do not have
morals; as he says in "How to Tell a True War Story": "A true war
story is never moral. It does not instruct, nor encourage virtue,
nor suggest models of proper human behavior, nor restrain men
from doing the things that men have always done" (1007). A good
story merely tells truth, and O'Brien has done the job elegantly
in his savagely beautiful The Things They Carried, a book that
should be read by anyone who wants to understand better the
workings of the human mind under the stresses of war and
conflict, be they physical, mental, or emotional.

[New page]   Works Cited

Calloway, Catherine. "'How To Tell a True War Story':
    Metafiction in the Things They Carried." Critique 36.4
    (Summer 1995): 249ff. Henderson, Day, and Waller. 1030-38.
Henderson, Gloria Mason, Bill Day, and Sandra Stevenson Waller,
    eds. Literature and Ourselves. 5th Ed. New York: Longman,
    2006.

O'Brien, Tim. "Good Form." In <u>The Things They Carried</u>, 179–80.

New York: Broadway Books, 1990.

---. "How to Tell a True War Story." <u>The Things They Carried</u>.

New York: Broadway Books, 1990. Henderson, Day, and Waller.

1006–20.

---. "The Man I Killed." <u>The Things They Carried</u>. New York:

Broadway Books, 1990. Henderson, Day, and Waller. 1016–20.

---. "On the Rainy River." <u>The Things They Carried</u>. New York:

Broadway Books, 1990. Henderson, Day, and Waller. 994–1005.

Robinson, "Getting It Right: The Short Fiction of Tim O'Brien."

<u>Critique</u> 40.3 (Spring 1999): 257ff. Henderson, Day, and

Waller. 1038–46.

Suggestions for Exploring, Writing, and Persuading

1. If you have been in a war or in a confrontational situation comparable to war, write a war story that is "true," according to O'Brien's criteria.

2. Using one or more of the critical essays in this casebook, write an essay analyzing a situation in which "story-truth" is truer than "happening-truth."

3. Discuss in detail a situation where you felt responsible for a wrong you did not commit.

4. The men in O'Brien's stories have both extraordinary restrictions on their freedom and simultaneously the freedom to commit acts they would never consider at home. In a researched essay, using O'Brien's stories, analyze how war changes men's sense of freedom and responsibility. Use one or more of the secondary sources in this casebook.

5. Write an argumentative essay assessing responsibility for the brutal violence the men commit.

6. Using the stories and critical essays, write a researched essay arguing the truth of the narrator's assertion that "the truths [about war] are contradictory."

7. The narrator says of war, "The old rules are no longer binding, the old truths no longer hold true. Right spills over into wrong." Develop this idea in an essay.

8. Analyze a moral dilemma you have faced and give the reason(s) for your final decision.

9. Research the draft system in the 1960s. When did this system start? When did it end? Write an essay on your findings.

10. O'Brien says that he thought, "There should be a law....If you support a war, if you think it's worth the price,...you have to put your own precious fluids on the line. You have to head for the front and hook up with an infantry unit and help spill the blood." Write an essay explaining why you agree or disagree with this statement. You may want to use one or more of the critical essays.

11. In an essay, analyze the moral dilemma O'Brien describes in "On the Rainy River."

12. Write a character sketch of Elroy Berdahl, explaining his wisdom and understanding.

Freedom and Responsibility: Suggestions for Writing

1. Using one selection from this unit, discuss how the author shows the delicate balance between freedom and responsibility.

2. Choose one short story from this section and relate what that work says about the responsibilities a person has to others in society.

3. When is a person obligated to disobey government regulations or laws? Using at least one work from this section, write an essay answering this question.

4. Select one of the stories in this unit and defend the protagonist's decision to defy or to obey the government.

5. Use one or more of the works in this unit to discuss how one's responsibilities change during a lifetime.

6. From your own experience or knowledge, explain how one's own freedom may be limited by the obligation to allow others to be free.

7. Write an essay describing the responsibilities to others that members of a civilized and organized society are expected to fulfill. Or write an essay describing the results, in the United States or in another country, of a failure to fulfill such responsibilities.

8. In an essay, discuss the ways in which individuals let their desire to be accepted limit their freedom.

9. Vonnegut implies that laws have to be followed if society does not want to fall apart. Apply, in an essay, this theory to the work of Virginia Woolf, Martin Luther King Jr., or Harriet Jacobs.

10. Write about an ethical problem characters in a work other than Linda in Pastan's poem "Ethics" must solve. You might select, for example, "Minority Report" or "Trifles."

11. Several of the narrators or characters in the poems in this unit are imprisoned, either literally or figuratively. In an essay argue one of the following:

    Sometimes prison is preferable to another choice.

    Many individuals create their own prisons.

    Often people fail to realize that they lack freedom.

Freedom and Responsibility: Writing About Film

1. The Western movie genre is often concerned with themes of freedom
   and responsibility. In fact, the western frontier was a metaphor for a
   land where a man (rarely a woman) could be free and discover his true
   nature. View a classic Western made between 1938 and 1958
   (*Stagecoach, Drums Along the Mohawk, The Man Who Shot Liberty
   Valence, My Darling Clementine, Red River, High Noon, The
   Searchers*). Then watch a contemporary Western (*Unforgiven, Young
   Guns, Dances with Wolves, Tombstone, The Last of the Mohicans,
   Wild, Wild West*) and consider how the films from different periods
   reflect different cultural beliefs about freedom and responsibility in
   regard to the land, white "civilization," native and/or Hispanic people,
   cowboys, violence, and man/woman relationships.

2. An event that occurs in the plot of most American films is a choice
   made by the main character. This choice ultimately determines the
   outcome of the film and is central to determining the point of view of
   the film. Watch one or two films and see if you can locate the scene in
   which the character makes such a decision. Is it a reasoned choice or
   an emotional choice? How much control does the character have up
   to that point? After that point? In an essay, analyze the scene, explaining why it is or is not effectively presented. Have you ever experienced
   a similar choice-making/transformative event? If so, describe it in
   detail; if not, explain the difference between your real-life experience
   and the fictional story-world of the film.

3. Select one of the following movies—*Apocalypse Now, Full Metal
   Jacket, The Thin Red Line, Saving Private Ryan, Platoon, Glory, The
   Deer Hunter, Courage Under Fire, Das Boot, We Were Soldiers, Black
   Hawk Down, The Patriot, Braveheart*, or *MASH*—and, after review-
   ing it, carefully write on one of the following:

   The theme of freedom and responsibility as portrayed in this film

   The relation of the theme to modern times

   Special camera techniques used in the portrayal of battle scenes

   The use of humor as a technique for emphasizing the horrors of
   war

Imagination and Reality

A scene from *The Matrix Reloaded*. Interfoto USA/SIPA.

Wherever we look, we are encouraged to dream. Virtually every program or commercial we see on television asks us to imagine ourselves as somehow different from what we are—as healthier, more attractive, richer, or happier. Even so-called "reality shows" lead us to imagine ourselves as tougher or stronger or more popular. We are indeed a society of dreamers, always seeking, like Jay Gatsby in F. Scott Fitzgerald's great novel, a brighter future, always pursuing "the American dream," whatever that may be.

Accustomed as we are, then, to living with our dreams, to regarding them and treating them as if they were real, it seems artificial, even inaccurate, to make a sharp distinction between imagination and "reality." Among metaphysicians, philosophers who theorize about the nature of reality, many, often referred to as idealists, consider reality to consist of the life of the mind—our thoughts, our feelings, our sensations, our dreams, our imaginings; the physical universe, in this view, is simply a construct of the perceiving mind, perhaps even a mere illusion.

So we see in many of the works in this unit, if not in most literature, indeed most art, a blurring or perhaps even a reversal of the distinction between imagination and reality. In John Keats's "Ode on a Grecian Urn," for example, the design on the urn takes on a heightened kind of reality, a static frozen world "far above" our daily struggles, a world where, as the poem says, "Beauty is truth, truth beauty." With its final line, "That is all we know on earth and all we need to know," Keats's poem reverses our usual concepts of imagination and reality. In Joyce Carol Oates's story "Valentine," the details of the protagonist's daily life—her math teacher's appearance, her classmates, the geography of the city where she lives—merge with the fantastic images of her dream to create an experience that appears to be half dream, half actual experience. In Woody Allen's "The Kugelmass Episode," Kugelmass, like many of us, selfishly escapes into a fantasy world only to find himself consumed by this world as it turns into a comic nightmare. Tom Stoppard's post-modern play *The Real Inspector Hound*, using a play within the play, wreaks havoc on our perception of reality. A theater critic, who is reviewing a play within Stoppard's play, suddenly becomes a character in the play he is reviewing. Stoppard keeps his audience and readers constantly confused as to who is who and what is what.

In David James Duncan's "My One Conversation with Collin Walcott," the jazz quartet Oregon in an outdoor concert on the rocky Oregon coast plays so intensely that an approaching thunderstorm seems to become a part of the music, paying tribute to the power of art, the splendor of the

human imagination. This is a powerful symbol for the nature of art itself
and for the human imagination, which transmutes the physical world into
an imagined world often more intensely real than the world it transforms.

Writing About Imagination and Reality

If you are asked to write about the theme of Imagination and Reality, you
might begin by asking yourself about the nature of reality. Several of the
works in this section use science fiction or fantasy to explore the nature
of truth. You might choose to explore what Ray Bradbury is implying
about our present by showing us one version of the future in "There Will
Come Soft Rains." You might compare "The Vietnam Wall," as described
in Alberto Rios's poem, to another monument of war such as the memorial to World War II veterans or the tomb of the unknown soldier to show
the realities of war.

Another aspect of Imagination and Reality involves the creation of lit-
erary works. You might use the works in this unit to form a definition of
a literary genre. If you choose to describe poetry, you might use Archibald
MacLeish's "Ars Poetica" as a starting point, or you might examine what
Billy Collins is saying about poetry in his poem and analyze Lawrence
Ferlinghetti's description of what it means to be a poet in "Constantly
Risking Absurdity." Or you might ask what qualities of poetry allow John
Keats to explore the meaning of beauty in his "Ode on a Grecian Urn."

You could choose to write argumentative essays on a number of topics. You might use David James Duncan's essay "My One Conversation
with Collin Walcott" to decide whether music as an art form is or is not
more valuable than another art form such as paintings or films. This question about music might also apply to Louise Erdrich's "Naked Woman
Playing Chopin: A Fargo Romance." Or you might debate the issue of
whether a painting is more real than the world it represents, using W. H.
Auden's "Musée des Beaux Arts" as a beginning point. You might argue
whether the things Victor Hernandez Cruz discusses about poetry in
"today is a day of great joy" will ever come true in the United States.
Using Woody Allen's "The Kugelmass Episode," you might argue whether
fantasies are a benefit or a deterrent to productive lives. Argumentation
can be used effectively in this unit on Imagination and Reality.

When Kim Prevett was assigned a documented essay using the casebook on Joyce Carol Oates, she first read the two stories. She decided to
write her essay before reading what other writers said about the stories
because she did not want the other essays to influence her own interpretation. She was having difficulty deciding what to write about until
she noticed the many parallels in the two stories. Once she had decided
to discuss these similarities, she wrote the body paragraphs of her essay.
When the first draft was finished, Kim read the critical essays. In these
she found several ideas that paralleled or illustrated some of her points,

and she selected several quotations to add to her essay. Like many other writers, Kim found the introductory and concluding paragraphs much more difficult to write. For help with the introduction, she went to a biography of Oates, where she found an effective quotation. She asked her professor for help with ideas for the conclusion, finally deciding to stress the dreamlike qualities and the mystery and horror mentioned in her introduction. Before submitting her essay, Kim checked to make sure that her quotations were accurate and that her paraphrases reflected the authors' ideas without quoting them. Her final essay is included at the end of the casebook on Joyce Carol Oates.

Essays

Ursula K. LeGuin (b. 1929)

The biography of Ursula LeGuin appears in the Freedom and Responsibility unit.

THE CHILD AND THE SHADOW   (1975)

1　Once upon a time, says Hans Christian Andersen, there was a kind, shy, learned young man from the North, who came south to visit the hot countries, where the sun shines fiercely and all shadows are very black.

2　Now across the street from the young man's window is a house, where he once glimpses a beautiful girl tending beautiful flowers on the balcony. The young man longs to go speak to her, but he's too shy. One night, while his candle is burning behind him, casting his shadow onto the balcony across the way, he "jokingly" tells his shadow to go ahead, go on into that house. And it does. It enters the house across the street and leaves him.

3　The young man's a bit surprised, naturally, but he doesn't do anything about it. He presently grows a new shadow and goes back home. And he grows older, and more learned; but he's not a success. He talks about beauty and goodness, but nobody listens to him.

4　Then one day when he's a middle-aged man, his shadow comes back to him—very thin and rather swarthy, but elegantly dressed. "Did you go into the house across the street?" the man asks him, first thing; and the shadow says, "Oh, yes, certainly." He claims that he saw everything, but he's just boasting. The man knows what to ask. "Were the rooms like the starry sky when one stands on the mountaintops?" he asks, and all the shadow can say is, "Oh, yes, everything was there." He doesn't know how to answer. He never got in any farther than the anteroom, being, after all, only a shadow. "I should have been annihilated by that flood of light had I penetrated into the room where the maiden lived," he says.

5　He is, however, good at blackmail and such arts; he is a strong unscrupulous fellow, and he dominates the man completely. They go traveling, the shadow as master and the man as servant. They meet a princess who suffers "because she sees too clearly." She sees that the shadow casts no shadow and distrusts him, until he explains that the man is really his shadow, which he allows to walk about by itself. A peculiar arrangement, but logical; the princess accepts it. When she and the shadow engage to marry, the man rebels at last. He tries to tell the princess the truth, but the shadow gets there first, with explanations: "The poor fellow is crazy, he thinks he's a man and I'm his shadow!"—"How dreadful," says the princess. A mercy killing is definitely in order. And while the shadow and the princess get married, the man is executed.

6   Now that is an extraordinarily cruel story. A story about insanity, ending in humiliation and death.

7   Is it a story for children? Yes, it is. It's a story for anybody who's listening.

8   If you listen, what do you hear?

9   The house across the street is the House of Beauty, and the maiden is the Muse of Poetry; the shadow tells us that straight out. And that the princess who sees too clearly is pure, cold reason, is plain enough. But who are the man and the shadow? That's not so plain. They aren't allegorical figures. They are symbolic or archetypal figures, like those in a dream. Their significance is multiple, inexhaustible. I can only hint at the little I'm able to see of it.

10   The man is all that is civilized—learned, kindly, idealistic, decent. The shadow is all that gets suppressed in the process of becoming a decent, civilized adult. The shadow is the man's thwarted selfishness, his unadmitted desires, the swearwords he never spoke, the murders he didn't commit. The shadow is the dark side of his soul, the unadmitted, the inadmissible.

11   And what Andersen is saying is that this monster is an integral part of the man and cannot be denied—not if the man wants to enter the House of Poetry.

12   The man's mistake is in not following his shadow. It goes ahead of him, as he sits there at his window, and he cuts it off from himself, telling it, "jokingly," to go on without him. And it does. It goes on into the House of Poetry, the source of all creativity—leaving him outside, on the surface of reality.

13   So, good and learned as he is, he can't do any good, can't act, because he has cut himself off at the roots. And the shadow is equally helpless; it can't get past the shadowy anteroom to the light. Neither of them, without the other, can approach the truth.

14   When the shadow returns to the man in middle life, he has a second chance. But he misses it, too. He confronts his dark self at last, but instead of asserting equality or mastery, he lets it master him. He gives in. He does, in fact, become the shadow's shadow, and his fate then is inevitable. The Princess Reason is cruel in having him executed, and yet she is just.

15   Part of Andersen's cruelty is the cruelty of reason—of psychological realism, radical honesty, the willingness to see and accept the consequences of an act or a failure to act. There is a sadistic depressive streak in Andersen also, which is his own shadow; it's there, it's part of him, but not all of him, nor is he ruled by it. His strength, his subtlety, his creative genius, come precisely from his acceptance of and cooperation with the dark side of his own soul. That's why Andersen the fabulist is one of the great realists of literature.

16   Now I stand here, like the princess herself, and tell you what the story of the shadow means to me at age forty-five. But what did it mean to me when I first read it, at age ten or eleven? What does it mean to children? Do they "understand" it? Is it "good" for them—this bitter, complex study of a moral failure?

17   I don't know. I hated it when I was a kid. I hated all the Andersen stories with unhappy endings. That didn't stop me from reading them, and rereading them. Or from remembering them...so that after a gap of over thirty years, when I was pondering this talk, a little voice suddenly said inside my left ear, "You'd better dig out that Andersen story, you know, about the shadow."

18   At age ten I certainly wouldn't have gone on about reason and repression and all that. I had no critical equipment, no detachment, and even less power of sustained thought than I have now. I had somewhat less conscious mind than I have now. But I had as much, or more, of an unconscious mind, and was perhaps in better touch with it than I am now. And it was to that, to the unknown depths in me, that the story spoke; and it was the depths which responded to it and, nonverbally, irrationally, understood it, and learned from it.

19   The great fantasies, myths, and tales are indeed like dreams: they speak *from* the unconscious *to* the unconscious, in the *language* of the unconscious—symbol and archetype. Though they use words, they work the way music does: they short-circuit verbal reasoning, and go straight to the thoughts that lie too deep to utter. They cannot be translated fully into the language of reason, but only a Logical Positivist, who also finds Beethoven's Ninth Symphony meaningless, would claim that they are therefore meaningless. They are profoundly meaningful, and usable— practical—in terms of ethics; of insight; of growth.

20   Reduced to the language of daylight, Andersen's story says that a man who will not confront and accept his shadow is a lost soul. It also says something specifically about itself, about art. It says that if you want to enter the House of Poetry, you have to enter it in the flesh, the solid, imperfect, unwieldy body, which has corns and colds and greeds and passions, the body that casts a shadow. It says that if the artist tries to ignore evil, he will never enter into the House of Light.

21   That's what one great artist said to me about shadows. Now if I may move our candle and throw the shadows in a different direction, I'd like to interrogate a great psychologist on the same subject. Art has spoken, let's hear what science has to say. Since art is the subject, let it be the psychologist whose ideas on art are the most meaningful to most artists, Carl Gustav Jung.

22   Jung's terminology is notoriously difficult, as he kept changing meanings the way a growing tree changes leaves. I will try to define a few of the key terms in an amateurish way without totally misrepresenting them. Very roughly, then, Jung saw the ego, what we usually call the self, as only a part of the Self, the part of it which we are consciously aware

of. The ego "revolves around the Self as the earth around the Sun," he says. The Self is transcendent, much larger than the ego; it is not a private possession, but collective—that is, we share it with all other human beings, and perhaps with all beings. It may indeed be our link with what is called God. Now this sounds mystical, and it is, but it's also exact and practical. All Jung is saying is that we are fundamentally alike; we all have the same general tendencies and configurations in our psyche, just as we all have the same general kind of lungs and bones in our body. Human beings all look roughly alike; they also think and feel alike. And they are all part of the universe.

23   The ego, the little private individual consciousness, knows this, and it knows that if it's not to be trapped in the hopeless silence of autism it must identify with something outside itself, beyond itself, larger than itself. If it's weak, or if it's offered nothing better, what it does is identify with the "collective consciousness." That is Jung's term for a kind of lowest common denominator of all the little egos added together, the mass mind, which consists of such things as cults, creeds, fads, fashions, status-seeking, conventions, received beliefs, advertising, popcult, all the isms, all the ideologies, all the hollow forms of communication and "togetherness" that lack real communion or real sharing. The ego, accepting these empty forms, becomes a member of the "lonely crowd." To avoid this, to attain real community, it must turn inward, away from the crowd, to the source: it must identify with *its own* deeper regions, the great unexplored regions of the Self. These regions of the psyche Jung calls the "collective unconscious," and it is in them, where we all meet, that he sees the source of true community; of felt religion; of art, grace, spontaneity, and love.

24   How do you get there? How do you find your own private entrance to the collective unconscious? Well, the first step is often the most important, and Jung says that the first step is to turn around and follow your own shadow.

25   Jung saw the psyche as populated with a group of fascinating figures, much livelier than Freud's grim trio of Id, Ego, Superego; they're all worth meeting. The one we're concerned with is the shadow.

26   The shadow is on the other side of our psyche, the dark brother of the conscious mind. It is Cain, Caliban, Frankenstein's monster, Mr. Hyde. It is Vergil who guided Dante through hell, Gilgamesh's friend Enkidu, Frodo's enemy Gollum. It is the Doppelgänger. It is Mowgli's Grey Brother; the werewolf; the wolf, the bear, the tiger of a thousand folktales; it is the serpent, Lucifer. The shadow stands on the threshold between the conscious and the unconscious mind, and we meet it in our dreams, as sister, brother, friend, beast, monster, enemy, guide. It is all we don't want to, can't, admit into our conscious self, all the qualities and tendencies within us which have been repressed, denied, or not used. In describing Jung's psychology, Jolande Jacobi wrote that "the development of the shadow runs parallel to that of the ego; qualities which the

ego does not need or cannot make use of are set aside or repressed, and thus they play little or no part in the conscious life of the individual. Accordingly, a child has no real shadow, but his shadow becomes more pronounced as his ego grows in stability and range."[1] Jung himself said, "Everyone carries a shadow, and the less it is embodied in the individual's conscious life, the blacker and denser it is."[2] The less you look at it, in other words, the stronger it grows, until it can become a menace, an intolerable load, a threat within the soul.

27   Unadmitted to consciousness, the shadow is projected outward, onto others. There's nothing wrong with me—it's *them*. I'm not a monster, other people are monsters. All foreigners are evil. All communists are evil. All capitalists are evil. It was the cat that made me kick him, Mommy.

28   If the individual wants to live in the real world, he must withdraw his projections; he must admit that the hateful, the evil, exists within himself. This isn't easy. It is very hard not to be able to blame anybody else. But it may be worth it. Jung says, "If he only learns to deal with his own shadow he has done something real for the world. He has succeeded in shouldering at least an infinitesimal part of the gigantic, unsolved social problems of our day."[3]

29   Moreover, he has grown toward true community, and self-knowledge and creativity. For the shadow stands on the threshold. We can let it bar the way to the creative depths of the unconscious, or we can let it lead us to them. For the shadow is not simply evil. It is inferior, primitive, awkward, animallike, childlike; powerful, vital, spontaneous. It's not weak and decent, like the learned young man from the North; it's dark and hairy and unseemly; but, without it, the person is nothing. What is a body that casts no shadow? Nothing, a formlessness, two-dimensional, a comic-strip character. The person who denies his own profound relationship with evil denies his own reality. He cannot do, or make; he can only undo, unmake.

30   Jung was especially interested in the second half of life, when this conscious confrontation with a shadow that's been growing for thirty or forty years can become imperative—as it did for the poor fellow in the Andersen story. As Jung says, the child's ego and shadow are both still ill defined; a child is likely to find his ego in a ladybug, and his shadow lurking horribly under his bed. But I think that when in pre-adolescence and adolescence the conscious sense of self emerges, often quite overwhelmingly, the shadow darkens right with it. The normal adolescent ceases to project so blithely as the little child did; he realizes that you can't blame everything on the bad guys with the black Stetsons. He begins to take responsibility for his acts and feelings. And with it he often shoulders a terrible load of guilt. He sees his shadow as much blacker, more

[1]Jolande Jacobi, *The Psychology of C. G. Jung* (New Haven: Yale University Press, 1962), 107.

[2]Carl Gustav Jung, *Psychology and Religion: West and East*, Bollingen Series XX, *The Collected Works of C. G. Jung*, vol. 11 (New York: Pantheon Books, 1958), 76.

[3]Jung, *Psychology and Religion*, 83.

wholly evil, than it is. The only way for a youngster to get past the paralyzing self-blame and self-disgust of this stage is really to look at that
shadow, to face it, warts and fangs and pimples and claws and all—to
accept it as himself—as *part* of himself. The ugliest part, but not the
weakest. For the shadow is the guide. The guide inward and out again;
downward and up again; there, as Bilbo the Hobbit said, and back again.
The guide of the journey to self-knowledge, to adulthood, to the light.

31   "Lucifer" means the one who carries the light.

32   It seems to me that Jung described, as the individual's imperative need
and duty, that journey which Andersen's learned young man failed to
make.

33   It also seems to me that most of the great works of fantasy are about
that journey; and that fantasy is the medium best suited to a description
of that journey, its perils and rewards. The events of a voyage into the
unconscious are not describable in the language of rational daily life: only
the symbolic language of the deeper psyche will fit them without trivial-
izing them.

34   Moreover, the journey seems to be not only a psychic one, but a moral
one. Most great fantasies contain a very strong, striking moral dialectic,
often expressed as a struggle between the Darkness and the Light. But
that makes it sound simple, and the ethics of the unconscious—of the
dream, the fantasy, the fairy tale—are not simple at all. They are, indeed,
very strange.

35   Take the ethics of the fairy tale, where the shadow figure is often
played by an animal—horse, wolf, bear, snake, raven, fish. In her article
"The Problem of Evil in Fairytales," Mary Louise von Franz—a Jungian—
points out the real strangeness of morality in folktales. There *is no right
way* to act when you're the hero or heroine of a fairy tale. There is no
system of conduct, there are no standards of what a nice prince does and
what a good little girl doesn't do. I mean, do good little girls usually push
old ladies into baking ovens, and get rewarded for it? Not in what we call
"real life," they don't. But in dreams and fairy tales they do. And to judge
Gretel by the standards of conscious, daylight virtue is a complete and
ridiculous mistake.

36   In the fairy tale, though there is no "right" and "wrong," there is a different standard, which is perhaps best called "appropriateness." Under
no conditions can we say that it is morally right and ethically virtuous to
push an old lady into a baking oven. But, under the conditions of fairy tale,
in the language of the archetypes, we can say with perfect conviction that
it may be *appropriate* to do so. Because, in those terms, the witch is not
an old lady, nor is Gretel a little girl. Both are psychic factors, elements of
the complex soul. Gretel is the archaic child-soul, innocent, defenseless;
the witch is the archaic crone, the possessor and destroyer, the mother
who feeds you cookies and who must be destroyed before she eats you
like a cookie, so that you can grow up and be a mother too. And so on and
so on. All explanations are partial. The archetype is unexhaustible. And

children understand it as fully and surely as adults do—often more fully, because they haven't got minds stuffed full of the one-sided, shadowless half-truths and conventional moralities of the collective consciousness.

37   Evil, then, appears in the fairy tale not as something diametrically opposed to good, but as inextricably involved with it, as in the yang-yin symbol. Neither is greater than the other, nor can human reason and virtue separate one from the other and choose between them. The hero or heroine is the one who sees what is appropriate to be done, because he or she sees the *whole*, which is greater than either evil or good. Their heroism is, in fact, their certainty. They do not act by rules; they simply know the way to go.

38   In this labyrinth where it seems one must trust to blind instinct, there is, von Franz points out, one—only one—consistent rule or "ethic": "Anyone who earns the gratitude of animals, or whom they help for any reason, invariably wins out. This is the only unfailing rule that I have been able to find."

39   Our instinct, in other words, is not blind. The animal does not reason, but it sees. And it acts with certainty; it acts "rightly," appropriately. That is why all animals are beautiful. It is the animal who knows the way, the way home. It is the animal within us, the primitive, the dark brother, the shadow soul, who is the guide.

40   There is often a queer twist to this in folktales, a kind of final secret. The helpful animal, often a horse or a wolf, says to the hero, "When you have done such-and-so with my help, then you must kill me, cut off my head." And the hero must trust his animal guide so wholly that he is willing to do so. Apparently the meaning of this is that when you have followed the animal instincts far enough, then they must be sacrificed, so that the true self, the whole person, may step forth from the body of the animal, reborn. That is von Franz's explanation, and it sounds fair enough; I am glad to have any explanation of that strange episode in so many tales, which has always shocked me. But I doubt that that's all there is to it—or that any Jungian would pretend it was. Neither rational thought nor rational ethics can "explain" these deep strange levels of the imagining mind. Even in merely reading a fairy tale, we must let go our daylight convictions and trust ourselves to be guided by dark figures, in silence; and when we come back, it may be very hard to describe where we have been.

41   In many fantasy tales of the nineteenth and twentieth centuries the tension between good and evil, light and dark, is drawn absolutely clearly, as a battle, the good guys on one side and the bad guys on the other, cops and robbers, Christians and heathens, heroes and villains. In such fantasies I believe the author has tried to force reason to lead him where reason cannot go, and has abandoned the faithful and frightening guide he should have followed, the shadow. These are false fantasies, rationalized fantasies. They are not the real thing. Let me, by way of exhibiting the real thing, which is always much more interesting than the fake one, discuss *The Lord of the Rings* for a minute.

42   Critics have been hard on Tolkien for his "simplisticness," his division of the inhabitants of Middle Earth into the good people and the evil people. And indeed he does this, and his good people tend to be entirely good, though with endearing frailties, while his Orcs and other villains are altogether nasty. But all this is a judgment by daylight ethics, by conventional standards of virtue and vice. When you look at the story as a psychic journey, you see something quite different, and very strange. You see then a group of bright figures, each one with its black shadow. Against the Elves, the Orcs. Against Aragorn, the Black Rider. Against Gandalf, Saruman. And above all, against Frodo, Gollum. Against him— and with him.

43   It is truly complex, because both the figures are already doubled. Sam is, in part, Frodo's shadow, his inferior part. Gollum is two people, too, in a more direct, schizophrenic sense; he's always talking to himself, Slinker talking to Stinker, Sam calls it. Sam understands Gollum very well, though he won't admit it and won't accept Gollum as Frodo does, letting Gollum be their guide, trusting him. Frodo and Gollum are not only both hobbits; they are the same person—and Frodo knows it. Frodo and Sam are the bright side, Smeagol-Gollum the shadow side. In the end Sam and Smeagol, the lesser figures, drop away, and all that is left is Frodo and Gollum, at the end of the long quest. And it is Frodo the good who fails, who at the last moment claims the Ring of Power for himself; and it is Gollum the evil who achieves the quest, destroying the Ring, and himself with it. The Ring, the archetype of the Integrative Function, the creative-destructive, returns to the volcano, the eternal source of creation and destruction, the primal fire. When you look at it that way, can you call it a simple story? I suppose so. *Oedipus Rex* is a fairly simple story, too. But it is not simplistic. It is the kind of story that can be told only by one who has turned and faced his shadow and looked into the dark.

44   That it is told in the language of fantasy is not an accident, or because Tolkien was an escapist, or because he was writing for children. It is a fantasy because fantasy is the natural, the appropriate, language for the recounting of the spiritual journey and the struggle of good and evil in the soul.

45   That has been said before—by Tolkien himself, for one—but it needs repeating. It needs lots of repeating, because there is still, in this country, a deep puritanical distrust of fantasy, which comes out often among people truly and seriously concerned about the ethical education of children. Fantasy, to them, is escapism. They see no difference between the Batmen and Supermen of the commercial dope-factories and the timeless archetypes of the collective unconscious. They confuse fantasy, which in the psychological sense is a universal and essential faculty of the human mind, with infantilism and pathological regression. They seem to think that shadows are something that we can simply do away with, if we can only turn on enough electric lights. And so they see the

irrationality and cruelty and strange amoralities of fairy tale, and they say: "But this is very bad for children, we must teach children right from wrong, with realistic books, books that are true to life!"

46   I agree that children need to be—and usually want very much to be—taught right from wrong. But I believe that realistic fiction for children is one of the very hardest media in which to do it. It's hard not to get entangled in the superficialities of the collective consciousness, or simplistic moralism, in projections of various kinds, so that you end up with the baddies and the goodies all over again. Or you get that business about "there's a little bit of bad in the best of us and a little bit of good in the worst of us," a dangerous banalization of the fact, which is that there is incredible potential for good and for evil in every one of us. Or writers are encouraged to merely capitalize on sensationalism, upsetting the child reader without themselves being really involved in the violence of the story, which is shameful. Or you get the "problem books." The problem of drugs, of divorce, of race prejudice, of unmarried pregnancy, and so on—as if evil were a problem, something that can be solved, that has an answer, like a problem in fifth grade arithmetic. If you want the answer, you just look in the back of the book.

47   *That* is escapism, that posing evil as a "problem," instead of what it is: all the pain and suffering and waste and loss and injustice we will meet all our lives long, and must face and cope with over and over and over, and admit, and live with, in order to live human lives at all.

48   But what, then, is the naturalistic writer for children to do? Can he present the child with evil as an *insoluble* problem—something neither the child nor any adult can do anything about at all? To give the child a picture of the gas chambers of Dachau, or the famines of India, or the cruelties of a psychotic parent, and say, "Well, baby, this is how it is, what are you going to make of it?"—that is surely unethical. If you suggest that there is a "solution" to these monstrous facts, you are lying to the child. If you insist that there isn't, you are overwhelming him with a load he's not strong enough yet to carry.

49   The young creature does need protection and shelter. But it also needs the truth. And it seems to me that the way you can speak absolutely honestly and factually to a child about both good and evil is to talk about himself. Himself, his inner self, his deep, the deepest Self. That is something he can cope with; indeed, his job in growing up is to become himself. He can't do this if he feels the task is hopeless, nor can he if he's led to think there isn't any task. A child's growth will be stunted and perverted if he is forced to despair or if he is encouraged in false hope, if he is terrified or if he is coddled. What he needs to grow up is reality, the wholeness which exceeds all our virtue and all our vice. He needs knowledge; he needs self-knowledge. He needs to see himself and the shadow he casts. That is something he can face, his own shadow; and he can learn to control it and to be guided by it. So that, when he grows up into his strength and responsibility as an adult in society, he will be less inclined, perhaps,

either to give up in despair or to deny what he sees, when he must face the evil that is done in the world, and the injustices and grief and suffering that we all must bear, and the final shadow at the end of all.

50   Fantasy is the language of the inner self. I will claim no more for fantasy than to say that I personally find it the appropriate language in which to tell stories to children—and others. But I say that with some confidence, having behind me the authority of a very great poet, who put it much more boldly. "The great instrument of moral good," Shelley said, "is the imagination."

Questions for Discussion

1. Look up symbol and archetype in the glossary. Using the definitions, discuss LeGuin's interpretation of Andersen's story.

2. According to LeGuin, what is the difference between Jung's "'collective consciousness'" and his "'collective unconscious'"?

3. LeGuin describes the shadow as "Cain, Caliban, Frankenstein's monster, Mr. Hyde . . . ; Vergil . . . , Gilgamesh's friend Enkidu, Frodo's enemy Gollum . . . ; the Doppelganger . . . ; Mowgli's Grey Brother; the werewolf; the wolf, the bear, the tiger of a thousand folktales . . . ; the serpent, Lucifer." Working in groups, see how many of these references each group can identify without the help of your professor.

4. What is the journey that LeGuin describes in paragraphs 30 through 34?

5. LeGuin calls fantasies in which the lines between good and evil are clearly drawn "false fantasies." Why?

6. Explain why you agree or disagree with LeGuin's definition of evil in paragraphs 46 and 47.

7. LeGuin believes that fantasy is "the appropriate language in which to tell stories to children—and others." What are her reasons? Explain why you agree or disagree.

Suggestions for Exploring, Writing, and Persuading

1. LeGuin says, "[T]he shadow is not simply evil. It is inferior, primitive, animal-like, childlike; powerful, vital, spontaneous." Why is it nevertheless essential?

2. In this essay, Le Guin describes fantasy as "the natural, the appropriate, language for the recounting of the spiritual journey and the struggle of good and evil in the soul." Using one or more works from this unit, oppose or support this statement.

3. Reread LeGuin's interpretation of Tolkein's *Lord of the Rings*. Then write an essay applying her interpretation to Peter Jackson's film version of the trilogy.

David James Duncan (b. 1952)

A native of Oregon, David James Duncan is a novelist, essayist, and environmental activist. He has published two novels, The River Why *(1983) and* The Brothers K *(1993), which won an American Library Best Books award and was listed as a* New York Times *notable book. His other books include* River Teeth: Stories and Writings *(1995), from which "My One Conversation with Collin Walcott" comes, and* My Story as Told by Water *(2001), a collection of essays on threats to our environment, which was a National Book Award finalist. Duncan's deep concern for environmental preservation is apparent in essays he has written for* Harper's, Gray's Sporting Journal, *and* Sierra, *the publication of the Sierra Club.*

MY ONE CONVERSATION WITH COLLIN WALCOTT (1995)

FOR GLEN MOORE, RALPH TOWNER AND PAUL MCCANDLESS

1   In the mid–1980's, during a severe August drought, I stopped by to gab with my neighbor, Jon (who pronounces it "Yawn"), and happened to arrive at his house just as his Baldwin upright piano (Yawn called it his "Ax") was heading out the door into the local piano-tuner's van. As I grabbed a corner and helped lift, I learned that a jazz quartet called Oregon was going to be playing an outdoor concert the following night, and that Yawn's Ax was headed off to serve as one of the two "concert grands" the band had requested. When I learned that a free tuning went with the loan, I said, "Hey!"—and a short time later the piano-tuner's van was jouncing up my mud-rut drive-way, destined to make my motheaten, hymn-beaten, five-owner Jansen upright Oregon's second "concert grand."

2   In defense of these pianos I should explain that we lived, geographically, on a decidedly rural portion of the Oregon coast, which implies that, culturally, we lived in what the national jargon would term a vacuum. On Forest Service maps we were a green thumb-print with a few blue veins (the creeks) running through us. On highway maps we were nothing at all—solid color without symbols or words. But there, nevertheless, we were, smack in the middle of Downtown Vacuum, our various oddball houses sprouting like Cubist mushrooms from the abandoned dairy pastures, clearcuts and river valleys. And somehow or other these internationally renowned musicians had found us and decided, despite our pianos, to play some music.

3   The place Oregon played was called Cascade Head—a twelve-hundred-foot "mountain" whose eastern end is actually a ridge buried in the Coast Range, and whose western end is actually a cape amputated by the Pacific into a serrated series of basalt cliffs and inaccessible coves. The concert took place at a little arts center named Sitka (after the local spruce trees), in a grassy outdoor alder-and-spruce-ringed bowl.

4   Because it was necessary to park at the bottom of the Head and hike a steep half-mile to reach this bowl, the arriving faces had that benign quality faces get when the psychic umbilicus connecting humans to cars is severed. And they grew more benign when, in a building behind the concert bowl, they discovered a local restaurateur catering wine and imported beer, and the baker from the co-op serving up delectable carbos. Meanwhile the local ocean was serving up a low summer fog that crept eastward through the trees like a spectator with no ticket. The fog cooled things fast, but with most of the rest of North America smoggy or humid and pushing 100 degrees that day, I heard no complainers. We sat on green grass in gray light, those who'd brought blankets sharing with those who hadn't. The band was on time, and already warming up.

5   For a while I bustled around the crowd like a demented father, pointing out my enstaged and honored piano to everybody I knew. My friends mostly gawked at it, then winced, so my pride soon grew containable. I sat, and began to check out the band.

6   Though I'd heard many, maybe all, of their recordings, I'd never seen Oregon in person. I eyed Glen Moore first, since he was the guy standing closest to my Jansen. He was wearing bright red pointy-toed genie slippers and even brighter maroon pants, but to judge by his smile he'd done it on purpose. Instead of plucking, tuning or even touching his stand-up bass, he just goofed around with a friend's baby daughter, zooming her low over the stage, *nnnrowwing* her round and round the spotlights. His bass, at least, looked ready for action: it sported a snarling gargoyle head and appeared to be at least a thousand years old.

7   Ralph Towner stood with his back to us, adjusting the valves or something on a Prophet 5 synthesizer, tuning six- and twelve-string guitars, blowing warm air through a flügelhorn, playing deft warm-up scales on Yawn's Ax. (I noticed Yawn not ten feet away, chest puffed, eyes glistening, pointing out his shining Ax to other concert-goers. But Yawn had an excuse: the Ax really is a nice piano.) When Towner finished the Prophet 5's valve job and showed his face, he looked a little as if he'd been working swingshift at United Grocers. But half an hour or so into the concert his fatigue, or whatever it was, had vanished, and I realized the United Grocers' look must have been merely the pre-fix appearance of a man whose body has become hopelessly addicted to the making of music.

8   Paul McCandless, in contrast to Moore and Towner, looked alert and fiery from the start, even in dirty, unlaced tennis shoes. His name and face brought to mind some indomitable, straitlaced, nineteenth-century Scottish missionary who'd set out to convert the heathen world to God knows what, but by a stroke of luck had instead been converted himself, to unlaced heathen horn-playing.

9   Then there was the percussionist, Collin Walcott—a man whose name had me expecting a contemporary of Dickens, Trollope, or Thackeray, but who instead sat buddha-style in the middle of things, his long bald head shining, his face solemn and focused, his manner comfortably, contradictorily

Oriental. He had a synthesized drum set just to his north—the first I'd ever seen—its heads and cymbals full-sized in sound, but no bigger than tea saucers. He had five different tablas to his south, a sitar to his east and a bewildering semicircle of rattles, chimes, clackers, bells, whistles, finger-drums, triangles and unnameable noisemakers to his west. He was the first Western "jazz" percussionist I'd ever seen sit flat on the floor like an East Indian. And after a night of watching him play in that position, the thought of the standard drummer perched on a steel stool, convulsively whacking with both feet at a high hat and drum, seemed a trifle inane.

10   The concert began in a cool gray dusk. Sunset consisted of a few minutes during which the fog and white alderbark turned golden. Then it grew dark, the cool turned decidedly cold, and we listeners began to need the music not only as a source of pleasure but as a source of heat. A little later the no-see-'ums came out in clouds, convening mostly beneath the spotlights, so that the band needed their music to transcend the fact that they were being devoured alive. A little after that the baby girl Moore had taken on the pre-concert zoom got tired and needed the music to calm her to sleep. A heater, an insect-antidote, a lullabye: Oregon's music served many purposes that night. But what it did last it did best. What it did last—so it seemed to me—was bring on its own annihilation. But we'll cross, or stumble into, that chasm when we come to it.

11   There is something uncanny about live music, about watching living, breathing musicians as their music is being born. For all its technical perfection, a recording is just what it says it is: an accurate but lifeless replica of a living event. It leaves out the flickering hands, bending bodies, skilled, exerted breathing; the sharp, almost desperate inhalations by the horn players; the *screek* of the pick against the wound strings of the guitar; the nods, fleet smiles, deft understandings flickering back and forth between performers. These visual nuances are satisfying in themselves, but also guide a live listener toward the intent of every silence and sound. And there is a cumulative effect to the best live music. One piece sheds light on another, like stories in a strong collection, till your ears begin to master a lexicon. And when song after song reaches climax after climax, energy is not only generated, it's congealed, distilled, intensified, like sunlight passing through a magnifying glass. The sounds burn clear through the mind and hit you somewhere deeper. That, at least, is the alchemy concert-goers hope for. What can't be described, of course, is what a band does to put a listener in this state. We call it *music* but so what? *Music* is just a word for something we love largely because it consists of things that words can't express. Likewise, the *heart* is just a word for something in us that music sometimes touches. But once these two somethings, heart and music, do touch, there is only one of them.

12   Music is the food whose peculiarity it is to enter us through the ears. Music is an inexpressible from outside us touching an inexpressible within, causing the frenetic persona that normally wedges itself between

outside and inside, creating twoness, to vanish. Gospel musicians used to shout out certain words when they felt inexpressibles touching, maybe *hallelujah*, or *amen*, which literally means simply, "It is so." These were magic words once, both of them. Then people learned to shout them when they weren't feeling anything in particular, and the words took revenge by becoming hokey as hell. They still are hokey. But during Oregon's performance that night I longed for the presence of such a word: beery shouts and clapping seemed far from sufficient to acknowledge the beauty of what we were receiving.

13   Maybe two hours into the concert Oregon played a Towner composition called "The Rapids" that had inexpressibles touching all over the mountainside. It is so. In fact it is, or was, so much so that just as the music was fading, a green brilliance flashed through the fog, and just as we began applauding there was a polite peal of thunder. Everybody laughed. Like a shouted *hallelujah*, genuine "thunderous applause" at a genuine Oregon concert on the Oregon coast seemed hokey. But it happened. And right afterward, when I sniffed the air, I sensed more about to happen. Something electric was going on. Something meteorologically electric. It hadn't rained in two months, and the satellite picture in the paper that morning had shown a North Pacific cloudless clear to Japan. But as a Caucasian I am part Asian, as a part-Asian I'm part Hindu, and when my Hindu part sniffed the air and saw more faint green flashes, it began to suspect that the fog was now much more than fog, and that Indra, the Rainmaker, was hiding in it, drawn by the music, listening closely.

14   We found out later that there had been a lone backpacker up on Cascade Head that night. Knowing nothing of the upcoming concert, this young man had toiled up a swale to a point maybe a quarter-mile beyond and five hundred feet above our little declivity in the spruce and alder grove, pitched his tent in open meadow, cooked his dinner on a tiny propane stove and leaned back against the ridge to study the stars—when astonishing sounds began to pour up out of the fog. He had no idea who or even where the musicians were. But the long swale's acoustics, he said, were great. And because he was perched above the fogline, he was aware of things we never suspected down in our bowl. He saw, for instance, the way the Head jutted out into the Pacific, its entire seaward face crumbling, thanks to old storm batterings. He saw that the general source of the music was not—as it seemed to us—a cozy, sheltered glade, but a tenuous, fogbound fold in that same battered, seaward face. And he saw the moment when, far out in the ocean, gigantic whorls of vapor began to rise up off the fogbank, drift inland and upward toward the summit of the Head and gather there, darkening, congealing, intensifying, till they became a towering, blue-black entity that bore no relation to vapor. This thunderhead, he said, formed above the sea off our solitary headland like a listener created by the music itself. And when it moved in to listen more closely, when thunderhead met Cascade Head and they too

began trying to become one thing, the entire sky above our niche began
to spark and rumble. It is so.

15   The band began a song called "Taos"—a composition as indescribable
as any piece of music. To get a handle on what happened next, I'll
describe something that isn't music, which this music was something
like. Let's say that "Taos" is a wordless narrative describing a seven-
minute-long natural event. Say it takes place in uninhabited desert, perhaps somewhere (as the name suggests) outside Taos, New Mexico. Say
it takes place, like our concert, late in the evening. The sun is just vanishing. The sky is cloudless. Things are cooling after a day of sweltering
heat. The shadows, once long and black, turn blue, then gray as the sun
vanishes, then grow indistinct...

16   The music begins, like everything on this planet, with the water: Walcott's tablas dripping a steady, assonant stream of drops, Moore's bass *tok-
tok-tok*ing in high, percussive overtones, Towner's Prophet also pouring
out something percussive, quiet and wet. It sounds as though there is a
seep, a tiny spring, hidden in the scorched rocks and warm shadows. And
when McCandless kindles a little tin whistle we realize there's a bird,
too—some solitary, nameless desert bird the music brings so near to life
that we feel its heartbeat. The bird drinks at the seep, then seems to go
wandering, and the mood is so benign, the chords so simple, that you
think the song is about almost nothing—a little divertimento. But then the
overtones end, the bass gropes deeper, the tablas give way to an insistent,
staccato cymbal beat, the bird keeps flitting along, and though there is no
increase in volume and no dissonance—nothing diminished or augmented
or even minor to warn you—there comes a moment when you realize that
the day has ended, the desert nights are cold and the little bird's flitting is
in deadly earnest. What is it looking for? Or who? Moore's bass stays deep,
the volume low, the mode insistently simple, almost heraldic, as in a
medieval chant. The whole band joins in a chord that seems to believe in
but can't quite find resolution. The tin bird cries out in panic now. Then
the cymbals crash, the mouth of an immense desert cave comes into view
and the bass erupts—two astounding, tympanic tones rising from the
depths of the cavern. The bird's cries grow frantic. And finally it comes:
resolution, the same tremendous bass notes, but doubled, booming out in
fours now, and the flickering cymbals are the wingbeats of the little bird,
the piercing tin whistle its joy, and the synthesizer the answering voices
of its thousand sisters and brothers, bursting from the cave's mouth in a
cloud. Again and again the four tremendous bass notes. Again and again
the ecstatic birds, swirling round their lost brother in a cloud that finally
vanishes, with a beautiful echo, back into the cavern...

17   There is the description, the handle. Here is what happened as the
music was played:

18   The very first time Moore's bass groped deep, all around us, all over
the Head, the thunder joined in—the pitch, the timing and tone, the volume of the peal all so perfectly wedded to the music that some of us

couldn't take it in. The acid-retreads among us gaped reverentially at the bass's gargoyle head. The scientists peered up into the trees, trying to make out the gargantuan hidden speakers that would let them chalk it up to the marvels of technology. But the next time the bass dove for the cavern notes, the thunder was there again: a perfectly pitched, perfectly played crescendo. This time no one missed it. Towner turned an incredulous face toward his campadres. McCandless, mouth full of whistle, bulged his eyes and nodded. Moore threw back his head and laughed. Walcott just played on. Brilliant green flashes shot through the cloud. And to the end of the song the guest musician, the thunderhead, played its part to perfection. Call it weather, call it coincidence, call it Khizr or Indra or anything you choose, we heard it as pure music, it came from all over that mountain, and it turned us inside out. Then the music became visible: just as the desert birds began swirling back into their cave a real wind swirled down upon us, the real trees began to churn and the early dying leaves from a thousand alders whirled round us like birds. The song ended, the air filled with ozone, and our bodies remained so full of the sense of listening that the music in us refused to die. *It is so.* We cheered ourselves hoarse, applauded till our hands stung like hail. Then Moore, sensing too late the impending downpour, said, "If you'd like to hear us again, you can catch us in October—in Greece."

19   Like the auntie who gives you the same dang pair of socks each Christmas, the god Indra, when pleased, can think of just one gift. Cascade Head gets a hundred inches of rain per annum, the stage had no roof and we wanted more concert, so a greater godly gift, under the circumstances, seemed like no rain at all. But gods will be gods, and when musicians please one they must accept the consequences, though their instruments, amps and bare heads be exposed to the sky.

20   Trying to dispel some of the energy they'd brought down upon us, Oregon set out on a courageous but ill-advised coda—a contemplative little piece, with Walcott on sitar and Towner on guitar. Thunder smashed it into meaningless fragments. Wind blew the shards away. The first few drops fell, enormous and warm. Then came the downpour, the cold gusts, the crowd's insane, frenetic cheering. The stage was a puddle in seconds. Spotlights started exploding. An alert technician doused everything electric but the lights. Most of the audience fled, whooping and shouting, but a score or so of us altruists and piano-owners ran down to the stage, hoping to help.

21   It was a deluge, a real Ark-launcher. Everyone was soaked through in seconds. A couple of tall guys jumped up, grabbed the whipping canvas canopy, pulled it over the stage and lashed it, but the wind drove the rain straight in under it. Water ran down the amplifiers, drenched the instruments, stung our faces, and despite our incurable elation we could see that, for the musicians, it was a disaster. Walcott cased up his sitar first, Towner his guitars. A stage-hand packed up the Prophet 5. Moore—with admirable carelessness—tossed a tarp over his priceless gargoyle and

turned to help McCandless, the two of them popping woodwinds into cases quick as bagboys sacking grocks. My friend Yawn was a marvelous sight, staggering round under the bank of exploding spotlights like King Lear in Act Five, roaring, "*My Ax! O God! My Ax!*" till a bunch of brawny volunteers muscled it into the piano-tuner's van. I checked my own piano: its top was off and nowhere to be seen; a microphone was dangling down inside; a soggy blanket had been draped over the treble cleff, but I could hear rain dripping like coffee through a filter, thumping the soundboard, soaking the felts. Moore hadn't played a note on it. I was going to need that free tuning. I didn't care. I stretched the sopping blanket down over the bass clef—just to keep the damage symmetrical—and wandered over toward Walcott.

22   He was hunched in the midst of his forty or fifty instruments, piling, covering and desperately packing them away. Out on the lawn a few Zorbas were still dancing and screaming, and a woman in a sopped T-shirt, bouncing in bra-less stereo, shrieked, "*The ultimate Oregon concert!*" It came out sounding like a faked hallelujah. In the face of the real storm, even words of would-be ecstasy felt wordy. Walcott looked miserable. A lot of his life was splayed out in the rain. There would be warping and water damage. I asked if there was anything I could do. He looked up and, in a tone incongruously calm, dry and New Yawkish for a man so wet and Oriental, said, "Yeah. Make it stop."

23   I nodded, then solemnly set about doing a pseudo-Hopi anti-rain chant as I hopped in a puddle on one foot.

24   Walcott seemed marginally amused at best.

25   But a minute or so later, the rain stopped.

26   That was my one conversation with Collin Walcott. And there won't be another. The following December, right after we'd all failed to "catch them in Greece," he was killed in a car wreck en route to a concert in East Germany. It is written that "the Believing Mind is the Buddha-nature." And I believe. But when I think of Walcott sitting cross-legged amid his instruments like a serious child surrounded by toys he lived only to give away, I feel nothing but loss. Yes, the Believing Mind is the Buddha-nature. But in disguise. And what a disguise! In the face of a real storm, even buddhistic words feel wordy. Yet my instruments, my toys, are words. And when I learned that this wonderful maker of music was gone, I was moved to make some sentences in an attempt, however hopeless, to give as Collin Walcott had given.

27   The clouds, that August night, dispersed shortly after the music ended. And in bright sunlight the following morning, that solitary backpacker came down off the Head, looking for some sign of the marvels he'd witnessed. He found an old cedar stage covered with fresh-fallen alder leaves. He found, in the grass, the fast-fading imprints of a few hundred human bottoms. No native tribe ever left a cleaner camp. And after the grandeur he'd witnessed, this cleanliness confused the backpacker. How

much had he heard? How much had he dreamed? Would anything he'd
heard remain free of dream later?

28   Spotting the Sitka caretaker, he rushed over and cried, "Last night!
That *music!* Who *were* those guys?"

29   But when he was told, "A band called Oregon," he just shook his head
and laughed. Laughed, then failed, as I have, to tell how for one long song,
one sweet seven minutes, he'd watched them play, like an instrument, an
entire headland and sky.

Questions for Discussion

1. What is unusual about the setting for "Oregon's" concert?

2. How could the band's music be a "heater, an insect-antidote, a lullabye"?

3. What, according to the narrator, is the difference between live and
   recorded music?

4. What does the narrator mean by "inexpressibles touching"?

5. The narrator says, "and to the end of the song, the great musician, the
   thunderhead, played its part to perfection" and "for one long song, one
   sweet seven minutes, [the backpacker had] watched [the band] play,
   like an instrument, an entire headland and sky." How do you account
   for this fantastic correspondence between art and nature? How much
   of it is real and how much illusion?

Suggestions for Exploring, Writing, and Persuading

1. Write an essay from the point of view of the backpacker, describing
   the concert in detail.

2. Citing examples from your own experience, write an essay contrasting live music and recorded music.

3. Describe a concert you attended where the music had a similar cosmic impact similar to the events Duncan describes.

FICTION

Mark Twain (1835–1910)

*Mark Twain is the pseudonym adopted by Samuel Lang-
horne Clemens. Twain grew up on the banks of the Mississippi River in Hannibal, Missouri, a locale that forms the*

backdrop for two of his finest novels, The Adventures of Tom Sawyer *(1876) and* The Adventures of Huckleberry Finn *(1885). By the time he published his first story at the age of thirty, Twain had already worked as a printer's apprentice, a riverboat pilot on the Mississippi River, and a reporter on the wild frontier in the 1860s in Nevada and California. In addition to* Tom Sawyer *and* Huckleberry Finn, *his books include* Innocents Abroad *(1869), a hilarious account of Americans in Europe;* Roughing It *(1872), comic nonfiction about his work as a reporter in the American West; and such cynical but thought-provoking later fiction as "The Man That Corrupted Hadleyburg" (1900) and* The Mysterious Stranger, *published posthumously in 1916.*

A FABLE   (1909)

1   Once upon a time an artist who had painted a small and very beautiful picture placed it so that he could see it in the mirror. He said, "This doubles the distance and softens it, and it is twice as lovely as it was before."

2   The animals out in the woods heard of this through the housecat, who was greatly admired by them because he was so learned, and so refined and civilized, and so polite and high-bred, and could tell them so much which they didn't know before, and were not certain about afterward. They were much excited about this new piece of gossip, and they asked questions, so as to get at a full understanding of it. They asked what a picture was, and the cat explained.

3   "It is a flat thing," he said; "wonderfully flat, marvelously flat, enchantingly flat and elegant. And, oh, so beautiful!"

4   That excited them almost to a frenzy, and they said they would give the world to see it. Then the bear asked:

5   "What is it that makes it so beautiful?"

6   "It is the looks of it," said the cat.

7   This filled them with admiration and uncertainty, and they were more excited than ever. Then the cow asked:

8   "What is a mirror?"

9   "It is a hole in the wall," said the cat. "You look in it, and there you see the picture, and it is so dainty and charming and ethereal and inspiring in its unimaginable beauty that your head turns round and round, and you almost swoon with ecstasy."

10   The ass had not said anything as yet; he now began to throw doubts. He said there had never been anything as beautiful as this before, and probably wasn't now. He said that when it took a whole basketful of sesquipedalian adjectives to whoop up a thing of beauty, it was time for suspicion.

11   It was easy to see that these doubts were having an effect upon the animals, so the cat went off offended. The subject was dropped for a couple of days, but in the meantime curiosity was taking a fresh start, and there was a revival of interest perceptible. Then the animals assailed the ass for

spoiling what could possibly have been a pleasure to them, on a mere suspicion that the picture was not beautiful, without any evidence that such was the case. The ass was not troubled; he was calm, and said there was one way to find out who was in the right, himself or the cat: he would go and look in that hole, and come back and tell what he found there. The animals felt relieved and grateful, and asked him to go at once—which he did.

12   But he did not know where he ought to stand; and so, through error, he stood between the picture and the mirror. The result was that the picture had no chance, and didn't show up. He returned home and said:

13   "The cat lied. There was nothing in that hole but an ass. There wasn't a sign of a flat thing visible. It was a handsome ass, and friendly, but just an ass, and nothing more."

14   The elephant asked:

15   "Did you see it good and clear? Were you close to it?"

16   "I saw it good and clear, O Hathi, King of Beasts. I was so close that I touched noses with it."

17   "This is very strange," said the elephant; "the cat was always truthful before—as far as we could make out. Let another witness try. Go, Baloo, look in the hole, and come and report."

18   So the bear went. When he came back, he said:

19   "Both the cat and the ass have lied; there was nothing in the hole but a bear."

20   Great was the surprise and puzzlement of the animals. Each was now anxious to make the test himself and get at the straight truth. The elephant sent them one at a time.

21   First, the cow. She found nothing in the hole but a cow.

22   The tiger found nothing in it but a tiger.

23   The lion found nothing in it but a lion.

24   The leopard found nothing in it but a leopard.

25   The camel found a camel, and nothing more.

26   Then Hathi was wroth, and said he would have the truth, if he had to go and fetch it himself. When he returned, he abused his whole subjectry for liars, and was in an unappeasable fury with the moral and mental blindness of the cat. He said that anybody but a near-sighted fool could see that there was nothing in the hole but an elephant.

MORAL, BY THE CAT

27   You can find in a text whatever you bring, if you will stand between it and the mirror of your imagination. You may not see your ears, but they will be there.

Questions for Discussion

1. Why does the artist position the picture across from the mirror?

2. Explain why the other animals believe the cat to be "learned," "refined," and "high-bred."

3. Why does the cat refer to the mirror as "a hole in the wall"?

4. For what reasons does the ass not believe the cat? What does he see in the mirror? What is the significance of his being the first to question the cat?

5. What does Twain mean by "You may not see your ears, but they will be there"?

Suggestions for Exploring, Writing, and Persuading

1. Twain says that "you can find in a text whatever you bring, if you will stand between it and the mirror of your imagination." In an essay, explain how you found meaning in a text because of your own personal experience.

2. Write your own fable about how to appreciate a work of art.

3. To what degree do you agree with Twain's suggestion that we see ourselves in a work of art? Select one work from this unit and write an essay relating what Twain suggests to that work.

Ray Bradbury (b. 1920)

One of America's most prolific writers of science fiction and fantasy, Ray Bradbury was born in Waukegan, Illinois, but has spent most of his life in Los Angeles, California. His novels and short stories have won numerous awards, including the Nebula, O. Henry Memorial, Prometheus, Benjamin Franklin, and Aviation-Space Writers and World Fantasy Lifetime Achievement Awards. His works have often been adapted for television and film. The most notable adaptations include The Martian Chronicles, *a 1980 miniseries;* Fahrenheit 451 *(1966), adapted from the 1953 novel;* The Illustrated Man *(1969);* It Came from Outer Space *(1953) and* It Came from Outer Space II *(1996);* Quest *(1983); and* Something Wicked This Way Comes *(1983), from the 1962 novel.*

THERE WILL COME SOFT RAINS   (1950)

1   In the living room the voice-clock sang, *Tick-tock, seven o'clock, time to get up, time to get up, seven o'clock!* as if it were afraid that nobody would. The morning house lay empty. The clock ticked on, repeating and repeating its sounds into the emptiness. *Seven-nine, breakfast time, seven-nine!*

2   In the kitchen the breakfast stove gave a hissing sigh and ejected from its warm interior eight pieces of perfectly browned toast, eight eggs sunnyside up, sixteen slices of bacon, two coffees, and two cool glasses of milk.

3   "Today is August 4, 2026," said a second voice from the kitchen ceiling, "in the city of Allendale, California." It repeated the date three times for memory's sake. "Today is Mr. Featherstone's birthday. Today is the anniversary of Tilita's marriage. Insurance is payable, as are the water, gas, and light bills."

4   Somewhere in the walls, relays clicked, memory tapes glided under electric eyes.

5   *Eight-one, tick-tock, eight-one o'clock, off to school, off to work, run, run, eight-one!* But no doors slammed, no carpets took the soft tread of rubber heels. It was raining outside. The weather box on the front door sang quietly: "Rain, rain, go away; rubbers, raincoats for today..." And the rain tapped on the empty house, echoing.

6   Outside, the garage chimed and lifted its door to reveal the waiting car. After a long wait the door swung down again.

7   At eight-thirty the eggs were shriveled and the toast was like stone. An aluminum wedge scraped them into the sink, where hot water whirled them down a metal throat which digested and flushed them away to the distant sea. The dirty dishes were dropped into a hot washer and emerged twinkling dry.

8   *Nine-fifteen*, sang the clock, *time to clean.*

9   Out of warrens in the wall, tiny robot mice darted. The rooms were acrawl with the small cleaning animals, all rubber and metal. They thudded against chairs, whirling their mustached runners, kneading the rug nap, sucking gently at hidden dust. Then, like mysterious invaders, they popped into their burrows. Their pink electric eyes faded. The house was clean.

10   *Ten o'clock.* The sun came out from behind the rain. The house stood alone in a city of rubble and ashes. This was the one house left standing. At night the ruined city gave off a radioactive glow which could be seen for miles.

11   *Ten-fifteen.* The garden sprinklers whirled up in golden founts, filling the soft morning air with scatterings of brightness. The water pelted windowpanes, running down the charred west side where the house had been burned evenly free of its white paint. The entire west face of the house was black, save for five places. Here the silhouette in paint of a man mowing a lawn. Here, as in a photograph, a woman bent to pick flowers. Still farther over, their images burned on wood in one titanic instant, a small boy, hands flung into the air; higher up, the image of a thrown ball, and opposite him a girl, hands raised to catch a ball which never came down.

12   The five spots of paint—the man, the woman, the children, the ball—remained. The rest was a thin charcoaled layer.

13   The gentle sprinkler rain filled the garden with falling light.

14   Until this day, how well the house had kept its peace. How carefully it had inquired, "Who goes there? What's the password?" and, getting no answer from lonely foxes and whining cats, it had shut up its windows and drawn shades in an old-maidenly preoccupation with self-protection which bordered on a mechanical paranoia.

15   It quivered at each sound, the house did. If a sparrow brushed a window, the shade snapped up. The bird, startled, flew off! No, not even a bird must touch the house!

16   The house was an altar with ten thousand attendants, big, small, servicing, attending, in choirs. But the gods had gone away, and the ritual of the religion continued senselessly, uselessly.

17   *Twelve noon.*

18   A dog whined, shivering, on the front porch.

19   The front door recognized the dog voice and opened. The dog, once huge and fleshy, but now gone to bone and covered with sores, moved in and through the house, tracking mud. Behind it whirred angry mice, angry at having to pick up mud, angry at inconvenience.

20   For not a leaf fragment blew under the door but what the wall panels flipped open and the copper scrap rats flashed swiftly out. The offending dust, hair, or paper, seized in miniature steel jaws, was raced back to the burrows. There, down tubes which fed into the cellar, it was dropped into the sighing vent of an incinerator which sat like evil Baal in a dark corner.

21   The dog ran upstairs, hysterically yelping to each door, at last realizing, as the house realized, that only silence was here.

22   It sniffed the air and scratched the kitchen door. Behind the door, the stove was making pancakes which filled the house with a rich baked odor and the scent of maple syrup.

23   The dog frothed at the mouth, lying at the door, sniffing, its eyes turned to fire. It ran wildly in circles, biting at its tail, spun in a frenzy, and died. It lay in the parlor for an hour.

24   *Two o'clock*, sang a voice.

25   Delicately sensing decay at last, the regiments of mice hummed out as softly as blown gray leaves in an electrical wind.

26   *Two-fifteen.*

27   The dog was gone.

28   In the cellar, the incinerator glowed suddenly and a whirl of sparks leaped up the chimney.

29   *Two thirty-five.*

30   Bridge tables sprouted from patio walls. Playing cards fluttered onto pads in a shower of pips. Martinis manifested on an oaken bench with egg-salad sandwiches. Music played.

31   But the tables were silent and the cards untouched.

32   At four o'clock the tables folded like great butterflies back through the paneled walls.

33   *Four-thirty.*

34   The nursery walls glowed.

35   Animals took shape: yellow giraffes, blue lions, pink antelopes, lilac panthers cavorting in crystal substance. The walls were glass. They looked out upon color and fantasy. Hidden films clocked through well-oiled sprockets, and the walls lived. The nursery floor was woven to

resemble a crisp, cereal meadow. Over this ran aluminum roaches and iron crickets, and in the hot still air butterflies of delicate red tissue wavered among the sharp aromas of animal spoors! There was the sound like a great matted yellow hive of bees within a dark bellows, the lazy bumble of a purring lion. And there was the patter of okapi feet and the murmur of a fresh jungle rain, like other hoofs, falling upon the summer-starched grass. Now the walls dissolved into distances of parched weed, mile on mile, and warm endless sky. The animals drew away into thorn brakes and water holes.

36   It was the children's hour.

37   *Five o'clock.* The bath filled with clear hot water.

38   *Six, seven, eight o'clock.* The dinner dishes manipulated like magic tricks, and in the study a *click*. In the metal stand opposite the hearth where a fire now blazed up warmly, a cigar popped out, half an inch of soft gray ash on it, smoking, waiting.

39   *Nine o'clock.* The beds warmed their hidden circuits, for nights were cool here.

40   *Nine-five.* A voice spoke from the study ceiling:

41   "Mrs. McClellan, which poem would you like this evening?"

42   The house was silent.

43   The voice said at last, "Since you express no preference, I shall select a poem at random." Quiet music rose to back the voice. "Sara Teasdale. As I recall, your favorite....

> There will come soft rains and the smell of the ground,
> And swallows circling with their shimmering sound;
>
> And frogs in the pools singing at night,
> And wild plum trees in tremulous white;
>
> Robins will wear their feathery fire,
> Whistling their whims on a low fence-wire;
>
> And not one will know of the war, not one
> Will care at last when it is done.
>
> Not one would mind, neither bird nor tree,
> If mankind perished utterly;
>
> And Spring herself, when she woke at dawn
> Would scarcely know that we were gone."

44   The fire burned on the stone hearth and the cigar fell away into a mound of quiet ash on its tray. The empty chairs faced each other between the silent walls, and the music played.

45   At ten o'clock the house began to die.

46   The wind blew. A falling tree bough crashed through the kitchen window. Cleaning solvent, bottled, shattered over the stove. The room was ablaze in an instant!

47   "Fire!" screamed a voice. The house lights flashed, water pumps shot water from the ceilings. But the solvent spread on the linoleum, licking, eating, under the kitchen door, while the voices took it up in chorus: "Fire, fire, fire!"

48   The house tried to save itself. Doors sprang tightly shut, but the windows were broken by the heat and the wind blew and sucked upon the fire.

49   The house gave ground as the fire in ten billion angry sparks moved with flaming ease from room to room and then up the stairs. While scurrying water rats squeaked from the walls, pistoled their water, and ran for more. And the wall sprays let down showers of mechanical rain.

50   But too late. Somewhere, sighing, a pump shrugged to a stop. The quenching rain ceased. The reserve water supply which had filled baths and washed dishes for many quiet days was gone.

51   The fire crackled up the stairs. It fed upon Picassos and Matisses in the upper halls, like delicacies, baking off the oily flesh, tenderly crisping the canvases into black shavings.

52   Now the fire lay in beds, stood in windows, changed the colors of drapes!

53   And then, reinforcements.

54   From attic trapdoors, blind robot faces peered down with faucet mouths gushing green chemical.

55   The fire backed off, as even an elephant must at the sight of a dead snake. Now there were twenty snakes whipping over the floor, killing the fire with a clear cold venom of green froth.

56   But the fire was clever. It had sent flame outside the house, up through the attic to the pumps there. An explosion! The attic brain which directed the pumps was shattered into bronze shrapnel on the beams.

57   The fire rushed back into every closet and felt of the clothes hung there.

58   The house shuddered, oak bone on bone, its bared skeleton cringing from the heat, its wire, its nerves revealed as if a surgeon had torn the skin off to let the red veins and capillaries quiver in the scalded air. Help, help! Fire! Run, run! Heat snapped mirrors like the first brittle winter ice. And the voices wailed, Fire, fire, run, run, like a tragic nursery rhyme, a dozen voices, high, low, like children dying in a forest, alone, alone. And the voices fading as the wires popped their sheathings like hot chestnuts. One, two, three, four, five voices died.

59   In the nursery the jungle burned. Blue lions roared, purple giraffes bounded off. The panthers ran in circles, changing color, and ten million animals, running before the fire, vanished off toward a distant steaming river....

60   Ten more voices died. In the last instant under the fire avalanche, other choruses, oblivious, could be heard announcing the time, playing music, cutting the lawn by remote-control mower, or setting an umbrella frantically out and in, the slamming and opening front door, a thousand things happening, like a clock shop when each clock strikes the hour insanely before or after the other, a scene of maniac confusion, yet unity; singing,

screaming, a few last cleaning mice darting bravely out to carry the horrid ashes away! And one voice, with sublime disregard for the situation, read poetry aloud in the fiery study, until all the film spools burned, until all the wires withered and the circuits cracked.

61   The fire burst the house and let it slam flat down, puffing out skirts of spark and smoke.

62   In the kitchen, an instant before the rain of fire and timber, the stove could be seen making breakfasts at a psychopathic rate, ten dozen eggs, six loaves of toast, twenty dozen bacon strips, which, eaten by fire, started the stove working again, hysterically hissing!

63   The crash. The attic smashing into kitchen and parlor. The parlor into cellar, cellar into sub-cellar. Deep freeze, armchair, film tapes, circuits, beds, and all like skeletons thrown in a cluttered mound deep under.

64   Smoke and silence. A great quantity of smoke.

65   Dawn showed faintly in the east. Among the ruins, one wall stood alone. Within the wall, a last voice said, over and over again and again, even as the sun rose to shine upon the heaped rubble and steam:

66   "Today is August 5, 2026, today is August 5, 2026, today is..."

Questions for Discussion

1. What early details suggest that this is a futuristic story about a technologically advanced civilization?

2. Explain what the author means when he writes that "the gods had gone away, and the ritual of the religion continued senselessly, uselessly."

3. List the clues to the desolation and devastation that Bradbury gives even before paragraph 10. What has caused the destruction?

4. What is the significance of the starving dog's death before the robots finish making the pancakes?

5. Reread paragraph 16. Then explain the analogy in this paragraph.

6. Using the silhouettes and the possessions within the house, describe the family that lived here.

7. What is the effect of the personification of the fire?

8. What is Bradbury suggesting may be a result of technological advances?

Suggestions for Exploring, Writing, and Persuading

1. Make a list of mechanical devices or technological advances, such as the car (buying, washing, detailing, servicing), that have become like religions with rituals that are performed on a regular basis. Then choose one and explain how its rituals promote it to religious or, at least, cult status.

2. Persuade your audience that a particular technological advance other than the computer has most improved society in America.

3. After carefully rereading the story and Teasdale's poem, write an essay explaining why, in your opinion, Bradbury chose this poem's opening words as the title and included the poem in the story.

Woody Allen (b. 1935)

Born Allen Stewart Konigsberg, Woody. Allen exhibited an early interest in writing and at the age of seventeen joined NBC as a staff writer. There he wrote for The Garry Moore Show *and Sid Caesar's* Your Show of Shows. *His first screenplay,* What's New, Pussycat? *(1964), decided his future as a director. Since then he has written, directed, and starred in many of his own films as an Academy Award-winning filmmaker; he is one of the few directors with total control over production. Many of Allen's films and stories are parodies, science fiction, and spoofs of nineteenth-century Russian novels; they often use wordplay, allusions, and juxtapositions of unusual elements. "The Kugelmass Episode," first published in the* New Yorker, *won an O. Henry Award as one of the best stories of 1978.*

THE KUGELMASS EPISODE   (1977)

1   Kugelmass, a professor of humanities at City College, was unhappily married for the second time. Daphne Kugelmass was an oaf. He also had two dull sons by his first wife, Flo, and was up to his neck in alimony and child support.

2   "Did I know it would turn out so badly?" Kugelmass whined to his analyst one day. "Daphne had promise. Who suspected she'd let herself go and swell up like a beach ball? Plus she had a few bucks, which is not in itself a healthy reason to marry a person, but it doesn't hurt, with the kind of operating nut I have. You see my point?"

3   Kugelmass was bald and as hairy as a bear, but he had soul.

4   "I need to meet a new woman," he went on. "I need to have an affair. I may not look the part, but I'm a man who needs romance. I need softness, I need flirtation. I'm not getting younger, so before it's too late I want to make love in Venice, trade quips at '21,' and exchange coy glances over red wine and candlelight. You see what I'm saying?"

5   Dr. Mandel shifted in his chair and said, "An affair will solve nothing. You're so unrealistic. Your problems run much deeper."

6   "And also this affair must be discreet," Kugelmass continued. "I can't afford a second divorce. Daphne would really sock it to me."

7   "Mr. Kugelmass—"

8   "But it can't be anyone at City College, because Daphne also works there. Not that anyone on the faculty at C.C.N.Y. is any great shakes, but some of those co-eds..."

9   "Mr. Kugelmass—"

10   "Help me. I had a dream last night. I was skipping through a meadow holding a picnic basket and the basket was marked 'Options.' And then I saw there was a hole in the basket."

11   "Mr. Kugelmass, the worst thing you could do is act out. You must simply express your feelings here, and together we'll analyze them. You have been in treatment long enough to know there is no overnight cure. After all, I'm an analyst, not a magician."

12   "Then perhaps what I need is a magician," Kugelmass said, rising from his chair. And with that he terminated his therapy.

13   A couple of weeks later, while Kugelmass and Daphne were moping around in their apartment one night like two pieces of old furniture, the phone rang.

14   "I'll get it," Kugelmass said. "Hello."

15   "Kugelmass?" a voice said. "Kugelmass, this is Persky."

16   "Who?"

17   "Persky. Or should I say The Great Persky?"

18   "Pardon me?"

19   "I hear you're looking all over town for a magician to bring a little exotica into your life? Yes or no?"

20   "Sh-h-h," Kugelmass whispered. "Don't hang up. Where are you calling from, Persky?"

21   Early the following afternoon, Kugelmass climbed three flights of stairs in a broken-down apartment house in the Bushwick section of Brooklyn. Peering through the darkness of the hall, he found the door he was looking for and pressed the bell. I'm going to regret this, he thought to himself.

22   Seconds later, he was greeted by a short, thin, waxy-looking man.

23   "*You're* Persky the Great?" Kugelmass said.

24   "The Great Persky. You want a tea?"

25   "No, I want romance. I want music. I want love and beauty."

26   "But not tea, eh? Amazing. O.K., sit down."

27   Persky went to the back room, and Kugelmass heard the sounds of boxes and furniture being moved around. Persky reappeared, pushing before him a large object on squeaky roller-skate wheels. He removed some old silk handkerchiefs that were lying on its top and blew away a bit of dust. It was a cheap-looking Chinese cabinet, badly lacquered.

28   "Persky," Kugelmass said, "what's your scam?"

29   "Pay attention," Persky said. "This is some beautiful effect. I developed it for a Knights of Pythias date last year, but the booking fell through. Get into the cabinet."

30   "Why, so you can stick it full of swords or something?"

31   "You see any swords?"

32   Kugelmass made a face and, grunting, climbed into the cabinet. He couldn't help noticing a couple of ugly rhinestones glued onto the raw plywood just in front of his face. "If this is a joke," he said.

33   "Some joke. Now, here's the point. If I throw any novel into this cabinet with you, shut the doors, and tap it three times, you will find yourself projected into that book."

34   Kugelmass made a grimace of disbelief.

35   "It's the emess," Persky said "My hand to God. Not just a novel, either. A short story, a play, a poem. You can meet any of the women created by the world's best writers. Whoever you dreamed of. You could carry on all you like with a real winner. Then when you've had enough you give a yell, and I'll see you're back here in a split second."

36   "Persky, are you some kind of outpatient?"

37   "I'm telling you it's on the level," Persky said.

38   Kugelmass remained skeptical. "What are you telling me—that this cheesy homemade box can take me on a ride like you're describing?"

39   "For a double sawbuck."

40   Kugelmass reached for his wallet. "I'll believe this when I see it," he said.

41   Persky tucked the bills in his pants pocket and turned toward his bookcase. "So who do you want to meet? Sister Carrie?[1] Hester Prynne?[2] Ophelia?[3] Maybe someone by Saul Bellow?[4] Hey, what about Temple Drake?[5] Although for a man your age she'd be a workout."

42   "French. I want to have an affair with a French lover."

43   "Nana?"[6]

44   "I don't want to have to pay for it."

45   "What about Natasha in *War and Peace?*"

46   "I said French. I know! What about Emma Bovary?[7] That sounds to me perfect."

47   "You got it Kugelmass. Give me a holler when you've had enough." Persky tossed in a paperback copy of Flaubert's novel.

48   "You sure this is safe?" Kugelmass asked as Persky began shutting the cabinet doors.

49   "Safe. Is anything safe in this crazy world?" Persky rapped three times on the cabinet and then flung open the doors.

50   Kugelmass was gone. At the same moment, he appeared in the bedroom of Charles and Emma Bovary's house at Yonville. Before him was a beautiful woman, standing alone with her back turned to him as she folded some linen. I can't believe this, thought Kugelmass, staring at the doctor's ravishing wife. This is uncanny. I'm here. It's her.

51   Emma turned in surprise. "Goodness, you startled me," she said. "Who are you?" She spoke in the same fine English translation as the paperback.

[1]Sister Carrie, a character in Theodore Dreiser's novel of the same name, becomes a prostitute.
[2]Hester Prynne, a character in Hawthorne's *The Scarlet Letter*, wears an "A" for adultery.
[3]Ophelia in Shakespeare's *Hamlet* is the young woman whom Hamlet loves.
[4]Saul Bellow is a contemporary American novelist.
[5]In William Faulkner's novel *Sanctuary*, Popeye rapes Temple Drake with a corncob.
[6]Nana is the sensuous heroine of Zola's *Nana*.
[7]Emma Bovary is the faithless wife in Flaubert's *Madame Bovary*.

52   It's simply devastating, he thought. Then, realizing that it was he whom she had addressed, he said, "Excuse me. I'm Sidney Kugelmass. I'm from City College. A professor of humanities. C.C.N.Y.? Uptown. I—oh, boy!"

53   Emma Bovary smiled flirtatiously and said, "Would you like a drink? A glass of wine, perhaps?"

54   She is beautiful, Kugelmass thought. What a contrast with the troglodyte who shared his bed! He felt a sudden impulse to take this vision into his arms and tell her she was the kind of woman he had dreamed of all his life.

55   "Yes, some wine," he said hoarsely. "White. No, red. No, white. Make it white."

56   "Charles is out for the day," Emma said, her voice full of playful implication.

57   After the wine, they went for a stroll in the lovely French countryside. "I've always dreamed that some mysterious stranger would appear and rescue me from the monotony of this crass rural existence," Emma said, clasping his hand. They passed a small church. "I love what you have on," she murmured. "I've never seen anything like it around here. It's so...so modern."

58   "It's called a leisure suit," he said romantically. "It was marked down." Suddenly he kissed her. For the next hour they reclined under a tree and whispered together and told each other deeply meaningful things with their eyes. Then Kugelmass sat up. He had just remembered he had to meet Daphne at Bloomingdale's. "I must go," he told her. "But don't worry, I'll be back."

59   "I hope so," Emma said.

60   He embraced her passionately, and the two walked back to the house. He held Emma's face cupped in his palms, kissed her again, and yelled, "O.K., Persky! I got to be at Bloomingdale's by three-thirty."

61   There was an audible pop, and Kugelmass was back in Brooklyn.

62   "So? Did I lie?" Persky asked triumphantly.

63   "Look, Persky, I'm right now late to meet the ball and chain at Lexington Avenue, but when can I go again? Tomorrow?"

64   "My pleasure. Just bring a twenty. And don't mention this to anybody."

65   "Yeah. I'm going to call Rupert Murdoch."[8]

66   Kugelmass hailed a cab and sped off to the city. His heart danced on point. I am in love, he thought, I am the possessor of a wonderful secret. What he didn't realize was that at this very moment students in various classrooms across the country were saying to their teachers, "Who is this character on page 100? A bald Jew is kissing Madame Bovary?" A teacher in Sioux Falls, South Dakota, sighed and thought, Jesus, these kids, with their pot and acid. What goes through their minds!

67   Daphne Kugelmass was in the bathroom-accessories department at Bloomingdale's when Kugelmass arrived breathlessly. "Where've you been?" she snapped. "It's four-thirty."

68   "I got held up in traffic," Kugelmass said.

[8]Rupert Murdoch is a wealthy Australian publisher and owner of several sensational tabloids.

69   Kugelmass visited Persky the next day, and in a few minutes was again passing magically to Yonville. Emma couldn't hide her excitement at seeing him. The two spent hours together, laughing and talking about their different backgrounds. Before Kugelmass left, they made love. "My God, I'm doing it with Madame Bovary!" Kugelmass whispered to himself. "Me, who failed freshman English."

70   As the months passed, Kugelmass saw Persky many times and developed a close and passionate relationship with Emma Bovary. "Make sure and always get me into the book before page 120," Kugelmass said to the magician one day. "I always have to meet her before she hooks up with this Rodolphe character."

71   "Why?" Persky asked. "You can't beat his time?"

72   "Beat his time. He's landed gentry. Those guys have nothing better to do than flirt and ride horses. To me, he's one of those faces you see in the pages of *Women's Wear Daily*. With the Helmut Berger hairdo. But to her he's hot stuff."

73   "And her husband suspects nothing?"

74   "He's out of his depth. He's a lacklustre little paramedic who's thrown in his lot with a jitterbug. He's ready to go to sleep by ten, and she's putting on her dancing shoes. Oh, well...See you later."

75   And once again Kugelmass entered the cabinet and passed instantly to the Bovary estate at Yonville. "How you doing, cupcake?" he said to Emma.

76   "Oh, Kugelmass," Emma sighed. "What I have to put up with. Last night at dinner, Mr. Personality dropped off to sleep in the middle of the dessert course. I'm pouring my heart out about Maxim's and the ballet, and out of the blue I hear snoring."

77   "It's O.K., darling. I'm here now," Kugelmass said, embracing her. I've earned this, he thought, smelling Emma's French perfume and burying his nose in her hair. I've suffered enough. I've paid enough analysts. I've searched till I'm weary. She's young and nubile, and I'm here a few pages after Leon and just before Rodolphe. By showing up during the correct chapters, I've got the situation knocked.

78   Emma, to be sure, was just as happy as Kugelmass. She had been starved for excitement, and his tales of Broadway night life, of fast cars and Hollywood and TV stars, enthralled the young French beauty.

79   "Tell me again about O. J. Simpson," she implored that evening, as she and Kugelmass strolled past Abbé Bournisien's church.

80   "What can I say? The man is great. He sets all kinds of rushing records. Such moves. They can't touch him."

81   "And the Academy Awards?" Emma said wistfully. "I'd give anything to win one."

82   "First you've got to be nominated."

83   "I know. You explained it. But I'm convinced I can act. Of course, I'd want to take a class or two. With Strasberg maybe. Then if I had the right agent—"

84   "We'll see, we'll see. I'll speak to Persky."

85   That night, safely returned to Persky's flat, Kugelmass brought up the idea of having Emma visit him in the big city.

86   "Let me think about it," Persky said. "Maybe I could work it. Stranger things have happened." Of course, neither of them could think of one.

87   "Where the hell do you go all the time?" Daphne Kugelmass barked at her husband as he returned home late that evening. "You got a chippie stashed somewhere?"

88   "Yeah, sure, I'm just the type," Kugelmass said wearily. "I was with Leonard Popkin. We were discussing Socialist agriculture in Poland. You know Popkin. He's a freak on the subject."

89   "Well, you've been very odd lately," Daphne said. "Distant. Just don't forget about my father's birthday. On Saturday?"

90   "Oh, sure, sure," Kugelmass said, heading for the bathroom.

91   "My whole family will be there. We can see the twins. And Cousin Hamish. You should be more polite to Cousin Hamish—he likes you."

92   "Right, the twins," Kugelmass said, closing the bathroom door and shutting out the sound of his wife's voice. He leaned against it and took a deep breath. In a few hours, he told himself, he would be back in Yonville again, back with his beloved. And this time, if all went well, he would bring Emma back with him.

93   At three-fifteen the following afternoon, Persky worked his wizardry again. Kugelmass appeared before Emma, smiling and eager. The two spent a few hours at Yonville with Binet and then remounted the Bovary carriage. Following Persky's instructions, they held each other tightly, closed their eyes, and counted to ten. When they opened them, the carriage was just drawing up at the side door of the Plaza Hotel, where Kugelmass had optimistically reserved a suite earlier in the day.

94   "I love it! It's everything I dreamed it would be," Emma said as she swirled joyously around the bedroom, surveying the city from their window. "There's F.A.O. Schwarz. And there's Central Park, and the Sherry is which one? Oh, there—I see. It's too divine."

95   On the bed there were boxes from Halston and Saint Laurent. Emma unwrapped a package and held up a pair of black velvet pants against her perfect body.

96   "The slacks suit is by Ralph Lauren," Kugelmass said. "You'll look like a million bucks in it. Come on, sugar, give us a kiss."

97   "I've never been so happy!" Emma squealed as she stood before the mirror. "Let's go out on the town. I want to see *Chorus Line* and the Guggenheim and this Jack Nicholson character you always talk about. Are any of his flicks showing?"

98   "I cannot get my mind around this," a Stanford professor said. "First a strange character named Kugelmass, and now she's gone from the book. Well, I guess the mark of a classic is that you can reread it a thousand times and always find something new."

99   The lovers passed a blissful weekend. Kugelmass had told Daphne he would be away at a symposium in Boston and would return Monday. Savoring each moment, he and Emma went to the movies, had dinner in Chinatown, passed two hours at a discothèque, and went to bed with a TV movie. They slept till noon on Sunday, visited SoHo, and ogled celebrities at Elaine's. They had caviar and champagne in their suite on Sunday night and talked until dawn. That morning, in the cab taking them to Persky's apartment, Kugelmass thought, It was hectic, but worth it. I can't bring her here too often, but now and then it will be a charming contrast with Yonville.

100   At Persky's, Emma climbed into the cabinet, arranged her new boxes of clothes neatly around her, and kissed Kugelmass fondly. "My place next time," she said with a wink. Persky rapped three times on the cabinet. Nothing happened.

101   "Hmmm," Persky said, scratching his head. He rapped again, but still no magic. "Something must be wrong," he mumbled.

102   "Persky, you're joking!" Kugelmass cried. "How can it not work?"

103   "Relax, relax. Are you still in the box, Emma?"

104   "Yes."

105   Persky rapped again—harder this time.

106   "I'm still here, Persky."

107   "I know, darling. Sit tight."

108   "Persky, we *have* to get her back," Kugelmass whispered. "I'm a married man, and I have a class in three hours. I'm not prepared for anything more than a cautious affair at this point."

109   "I can't understand it," Persky muttered. "It's such a reliable little trick."

110   But he could do nothing. "It's going to take a little while," he said to Kugelmass. "I'm going to have to strip it down. I'll call you later."

111   Kugelmass bundled Emma into a cab and took her back to the Plaza. He barely made it to his class on time. He was on the phone all day, to Persky and to his mistress. The magician told him it might be several days before he got to the bottom of the trouble.

112   "How was the symposium?" Daphne asked him that night.

113   "Fine, fine," he said, lighting the filter end of a cigarette.

114   "What's wrong? You're as tense as a cat."

115   "Me? Ha, that's a laugh. I'm as calm as a summer night. I'm just going to take a walk." He eased out the door, hailed a cab, and flew to the Plaza.

116   "This is no good," Emma said. "Charles will miss me."

117   "Bear with me, sugar," Kugelmass said. He was pale and sweaty. He kissed her again, raced to the elevators, yelled at Persky over a pay phone in the Plaza lobby, and just made it home before midnight.

118   "According to Popkin, barley prices in Kraków have not been this stable since 1971," he said to Daphne, and smiled wanly as he climbed into bed.

119   The whole week went by like that.

120   On Friday night, Kugelmass told Daphne there was another symposium he had to catch, this one in Syracuse. He hurried back to the Plaza, but the second weekend there was nothing like the first. "Get me back

into the novel or marry me," Emma told Kugelmass. "Meanwhile, I want to get a job or go to class, because watching TV all day is the pits."

121   "Fine. We can use the money," Kugelmass said. "You consume twice your weight in room service."

122   "I met an Off Broadway producer in Central Park yesterday, and he said I might be right for a project he's doing," Emma said.

123   "Who is this clown?" Kugelmass asked.

124   "He's not a clown. He's sensitive and kind and cute. His name's Jeff Something-or-Other, and he's up for a Tony."

125   Later that afternoon, Kugelmass showed up at Persky's drunk.

126   "Relax," Persky told him. "You'll get a coronary."

127   "Relax. The man says relax. I've got a fictional character stashed in a hotel room, and I think my wife is having me tailed by a private shamus."

128   "O.K., O.K. We know there's a problem." Persky crawled under the cabinet and started banging on something with a large wrench.

129   "I'm like a wild animal." Kugelmass went on. "I'm sneaking around town, and Emma and I have had it up to here with each other. Not to mention a hotel tab that reads like the defense budget."

130   "So what should I do? This is the world of magic," Persky said. "It's all nuance."

131   "Nuance, my foot. I'm pouring Dom Pérignon and black eggs into this little mouse, plus her wardrobe, plus she's enrolled at the Neighborhood Playhouse and suddenly needs professional photos. Also, Persky, Professor Fivish Kopkind, who teaches Comp Lit and who has always been jealous of me, has identified me as the sporadically appearing character in the Flaubert book. He's threatened to go to Daphne. I see ruin and alimony; jail. For adultery with Madame Bovary, my wife will reduce me to beggary."

132   "What do you want me to say? I'm working on it night and day. As far as your personal anxiety goes, that I can't help you with. I'm a magician, not an analyst."

133   By Sunday afternoon, Emma had locked herself in the bathroom and refused to respond to Kugelmass's entreaties. Kugelmass stared out the window at the Wollman Rink and contemplated suicide. Too bad this is a low floor, he thought, or I'd do it right now. Maybe if I ran away to Europe and started life over....Maybe I could sell the *International Herald Tribune*, like those young girls used to.

134   The phone rang. Kugelmass lifted it to his ear mechanically.

135   "Bring her over," Persky said. "I think I got the bugs out of it."

136   Kugelmass's heart leaped. "You're serious?" he said. "You got it licked?"

137   "It was something in the transmission. Go figure."

138   "Persky, you're a genius. We'll be there in a minute. Less than a minute."

139   Again the lovers hurried to the magician's apartment, and again Emma Bovary climbed into the cabinet with her boxes. This time there was no kiss. Persky shut the doors, took a deep breath, and tapped the box three

times. There was the reassuring popping noise, and when Persky peered inside, the box was empty. Madame Bovary was back in her novel. Kugelmass heaved a great sigh of relief and pumped the magician's hand.

140   "It's over," he said. "I learned my lesson. I'll never cheat again, I swear it." He pumped Persky's hand again and made a mental note to send him a necktie.

141   Three weeks later, at the end of a beautiful spring afternoon, Persky answered his doorbell. It was Kugelmass, with a sheepish expression on his face.

142   "O.K., Kugelmass," the magician said. "Where to this time?"

143   "It's just this once," Kugelmass said. "The weather is so lovely, and I'm not getting any younger. Listen, you've read *Portnoy's Complaint?*[9] Remember The Monkey?"[10]

144   "The price is now twenty-five dollars, because the cost of living is up, but I'll start you off with one freebie, due to all the trouble I caused you."

145   "You're good people," Kugelmass said, combing his few remaining hairs as he climbed into the cabinet again. "This'll work all right?"

146   "I hope. But I haven't tried it much since all that unpleasantness."

147   "Sex and romance," Kugelmass said from inside the box. "What we go through for a pretty face."

148   Persky tossed in a copy of *Portnoy's Complaint* and rapped three times on the box. This time, instead of a popping noise there was a dull explosion, followed by a series of crackling noises and a shower of sparks. Persky leaped back, was seized by a heart attack, and dropped dead. The cabinet burst into flames, and eventually the entire house burned down.

149   Kugelmass, unaware of this catastrophe, had his own problems. He had not been thrust into *Portnoy's Complaint*, or into any other novel, for that matter. He had been projected into an old textbook, *Remedial Spanish,* and was running for his life over a barren, rocky terrain as the word *tener* ("to have")—a large and hairy irregular verb—raced after him on its spindly legs.

[9]*Portnoy's Complaint* is a novel by Philip Roth that, when it was first published, was a favorite of undergraduates because of its sexual explicitness.

[10]The Monkey is a sexually athletic young woman in *Portnoy's Complaint.*

Questions for Discussion

1. Why does Kugelmass want to have a love affair?

2. Why does Persky mention as choices such characters as Hester Prynne, Ophelia, Temple Drake, or Nana? How do these allusions add depth to the humor of the story?

3. Why does Kugelmass return to Persky after the Madam Bovary affair?

4. What is the irony of the ending?

5. What relationship between life and art does this story suggest? In what ways does it give new meaning to the term "escapist literature"?

Suggestions for Exploring, Writing, and Persuading

1. Imagine yourself or a friend transported to a story or play in this anthology, and write a narrative—comic, serious, or frightening—describing the incident and its results.

2. Cast yourself as a character in a recent movie and explain your reasons for selecting that character.

3. In an essay argue that escaping into other identities through reading or through film is or is not a constructive way to spend time. Or argue that whether it is or is not constructive depends on the book or film selection.

4. Select a recent movie in which a character swaps bodies with another character or becomes an older or younger version of him or herself. Then write an essay showing the effect of such a transformation on the self-concept of the character.

5. Kugelmass is given the option of meeting and loving any woman in any work of literature. If you were given the option of so choosing any man or woman, whom would you choose? Why?

6. If you have read *Madame Bovary*, choose a scene before the entry of Rodolphe and rewrite it, adding Kugelmass. If you have not read *Madame Bovary*, write an imagined scene set in either France or New York City from the point of view of Emma Bovary as she is seen in Allen's story.

7. At the end of Allen's story, Kugelmass becomes a character with "few remaining hairs" being chased by "a large and hairy irregular verb" in a remedial Spanish book. Compare his situation to becoming a character in a Stephen King novel or a similar work.

Louise Erdrich (b. 1954)

Award-winning writer Louise Erdrich is a native of Minnesota. Her mother is French and Ojibwe Indian. As Erdrich was growing up, her parents worked at the Bureau of Indian Affairs School in Wahpeton, North Dakota. Her grandfather was the Tribal Chairman of the Turtle Mountain Reservation in North Dakota, and Erdrich is a member of the Turtle Mountain Band of Chippewa. She was married to author Michael Dorris, and in addition to his three adopted children, they had three children. Her fiction is influenced by the stories she heard as a child and by the perceptions she has gained as a mother. Her works include nonfiction, such as The Blue Jay's Dance: A Birth Year *(1995), and fiction, such as* Love Medicine *(1984),* The Bingo Palace *(1994), and* Tales of Burning Love *(1996). Erdrich published her first children's book,* Grandmother's Pigeon, *in 1996. She won the Wordcraft circle writer of the year award in 2000 for her children's book* The Birchbark House *(1900).*

NAKED WOMAN PLAYING CHOPIN   (1998)
A FARGO ROMANCE

1   The street that runs along the Red River follows the curves of a stream that is muddy and shallow, full of brush, silt, and oxbows that throw the whole town off the strict clean grid laid out by railroad plat. The river floods most springs and drags local back yards into its flow, even though its banks are strengthened with riprap and piled high with concrete torn from reconstructed streets and basements. It is a hopelessly complicated river, one that freezes deceptively, breaks rough, drowns one or two every year in its icy flow. It is a dead river in some places, one that harbors only carp and bullheads. Wild in others, it lures moose down from Canada into the city limits. At one time, when the land along its banks was newly broken, paddleboats and barges of grain moved grandly from its source to Winnipeg, for the river flows inscrutably north. And, over on the Minnesota side, across from what is now church land and the town park, a farm spread generously up and down the river and back into wide hot fields.

2   The bonanza farm belonged to Easterners who had sold a foundry in Vermont and with their money bought the flat vastness that lay along the river. They raised astounding crops when the land was young—rutabagas that weighed sixty pounds, wheat unbearably lush, corn on cobs like truncheons. Then there were six grasshopper years during which even the handles on the hoes and rakes were eaten and a cavalry soldier, too, was partially devoured while he lay drunk in the insects' path. The enterprise suffered losses on a grand scale. The farm was split among four brothers, eventually, who then sold off half each so that, by the time Berndt Vogel escaped the trench war of Europe where he'd been chopped mightily but inconclusively in six places by a British cavalry sabre and then kicked by a horse so that his jaw never shut right again, there was just one beautiful and peaceful swatch of land about to go for grabs. In the time it took him to gather—by forswearing women, drinking low beers only, and working twenty-hour days—the money to retrieve the farm from the local bank, its price had dropped further and further, as the earth rose up in a great ship of destruction. Sails of dust carried half of Berndt's lush dirt over the horizon, but enough remained for him to plant and reap six fields.

3   So Berndt survived. On his land there stood an old hangar-like barn, with only one small part still in use—housing a cow, chickens, one

depressed pig. Berndt kept the rest in decent repair, not only because as a good German he must waste nothing that came his way, but also because he saw in those grand, dust-filled shafts of light something that he could worship. It had once housed teams of great blue Percherons and Belgian draft horses. Only one horse was left, old and made of brutal velvet, but the others still moved in the powerful synchronicity of his dreams. He fussed over the remaining mammoth and imagined his farm one day entire, vast and teeming, crews of men under his command, a cookhouse, a bunkhouse, equipment, a woman and children sturdily determined to their toil, and a garden in which seeds bearing the scented pinks and sharp red geraniums of his childhood were planted and thrived.

4   How surprised he was to find, one afternoon, as though sown by the wind and summoned by his dreams, a woman standing barefoot, starved and frowsy in the doorway of his barn. She was a pale flower, nearly bald and dressed in a rough shift. He blinked stupidly at the vision. Light poured around her like smoke and swirled at her gesture of need. She spoke.

5   *"Ich habe Hunger."*

6   By the way she said it, he knew she was a Swabian and therefore—he tried to thrust the thought from his mind—liable to have certain unruly habits in bed. He passed his hand across his eyes. Through the gown of nearly transparent muslin he could see that her breasts were, excitingly, bound tightly to her chest with strips of cloth. He blinked hard. Looking directly into her eyes, he experienced the vertigo of confronting a female who did not blush or look away but held him with an honest human calm. He thought at first that she must be a loose woman, fleeing a brothel— had Fargo got so big? Or escaping an evil marriage, perhaps. He didn't know she was from God.

7   In the center of the town on the other side of the river there stood a convent made of yellow bricks. Hauled halfway across Minnesota from Little Falls by pious drivers, they still held the peculiar sulfurous moth gold of the clay outside that town. The word "Fleisch" was etched in shallow letters on each one: Fleisch Company Brickworks. Donated to the nuns at cost. The word, of course, was covered by mortar each time a brick was laid. However, because she had organized a few discarded bricks behind the convent into the base for a small birdbath, one of the younger nuns knew, as she gazed at the mute order of the convent's wall, that she lived within the secret repetition of that one word.

8   She had once been Agnes DeWitt and now was Sister Cecellia, shorn, houseled, clothed in black wool and bound in starched linen of heatless white. She not only taught but lived music, existed for those hours when she could be concentrated in her being—which was half music, half divine light, flesh only to the degree that she could not admit otherwise. At the piano keyboard, absorbed into the notes that rose beneath her hands, she existed in her essence, a manifestation of compelling sound. Her hands were long and thick-veined, very white, startling against her habit. She rubbed them with lard and beeswax nightly to keep them supple. During

the day, when she graded papers or used the blackboard her hands twitched and drummed, patterned and repatterned difficult fingerings. She was no trouble to live with and her obedience was absolute. Only, and with increasing concentration, she played Brahms, Beethoven, Debussy, Schubert, and Chopin.

9   It wasn't that she neglected her other duties; rather, it was the playing itself—distilled of longing—that disturbed her sisters. In her music Sister Cecellia explored profound emotions. She spoke of her faith and doubt, of her passion as the bride of Christ, of her loneliness, shame, ultimate redemption. The Brahms she played was thoughtful, the Schubert confounding. Debussy was all contrived nature and yet as gorgeous as a meadowlark. Beethoven contained all messages, but her crescendos lacked conviction. When it came to Chopin, however, she did not use the flowery ornamentation or the endless trills and insipid floribunda of so many of her day. Her playing was of the utmost sincerity. And Chopin, played simply, devastates the heart. Sometimes a pause between the piercing sorrows of minor notes made a sister scrubbing the floor weep into the bucket where she dipped her rag so that the convent's boards, washed in tears, seemed to creak in a human tongue. The air of the house thickened with sighs.

10   Sister Cecellia, however, was emptied. Thinned. It was as though her soul were neatly removed by a drinking straw and siphoned into the green pool of quiet that lay beneath the rippling cascade of notes. One day, exquisite agony built and released, built higher, released more forcefully until slow heat spread between her fingers, up her arms, stung at the points of her bound breasts, and then shot straight down.

11   Her hands flew off the keyboard—she crouched as though she had been shot, saw yellow spots, and experienced a peaceful wave of oneness in which she entered pure communion. She was locked into the music, held there safely, entirely understood. Such was her innocence that she didn't know she was experiencing a sexual climax, but believed, rather, that what she felt was the natural outcome of this particular nocturne played to the utmost of her skills—and so it came to be. Chopin's spirit became her lover. His flats caressed her. His whole notes sank through her body like clear pebbles. His atmospheric trills were the flicker of a tongue. His pauses before the downward sweep of notes nearly drove her insane.

12   The Mother Superior knew something had to be done when she herself woke, her face bathed with sweat and tears, to the insinuating soft largo of the Prelude in E Minor. In those notes she remembered the death of her mother and sank into an endless afternoon of her loss. The Mother Superior then grew, in her heart, a weed of rage against the God who had taken a mother from a seven-year-old child whose world she was, entirely, without question—heart, arms, guidance, soul—until by evening she felt fury steaming from the hot marrow of her bones and stopped herself.

13   "Oh, God, forgive me," the Superior prayed. She considered humunculation, but then rushed down to the piano room instead, and with all of

the strength in her wide old arms gathered and hid from Cecellia every piece of music but the Bach.

14   After that, for some weeks, there was relief. Sister Cecellia turned to the Two-Part Inventions. Her fingers moved on the keys with the precision of an insect building its nest. She played each as though she were constructing an airtight box. Stealthily, once Cecellia had moved on to Bach's other works, the Mother Superior removed from the music cabinet and destroyed the Goldberg Variations—clearly capable of lifting subterranean complexities into the mind. Life in the convent returned to normal. The cook, to everyone's gratitude, stopped preparing the rancid, goose-fat-laced beet soup of her youth and stuck to overcooked string beans, cabbage, potatoes. The floors stopped groaning and absorbed fresh wax. The doors ceased to fly open for no reason and closed discreetly. The water stopped rushing through the pipes as the sisters no longer took continual advantage of the new plumbing to drown out the sounds of their emotions.

15   And then one day Sister Cecellia woke with a tightness in her chest. Pain shot through her and the red lump in her rib cage beat like a wild thing caught in a snare of bones. Her throat shut. She wept. Her hands, drawn to the keyboard, floated into a long appoggiatura. Then, crash, she was inside a thrusting mazurka. The music came back to her. There was the scent of faint gardenias—his hothouse boutonnière. The silk of his heavy brown hair. His sensuous drawing-room sweat. His voice—she heard it—avid and light. It was as if the composer himself had entered the room. Who knows? Surely there was no more desperate, earthly, exacting heart than Cecellia's. Surely something, however paltry, lies beyond the grave.

16   At any rate, she played Chopin. Played him in utter naturalness until the Mother Superior was forced to shut the cover to the keyboard and gently pull the stool away. Cecellia lifted the lid and played upon her knees. The poor scandalized dame dragged her from the keys. Cecellia crawled back. The Mother, at her wit's end, sank down and urged the young woman to pray. She herself spoke first in fear and then in certainty, saying that it was the very Devil who had managed to find a way to Cecellia's soul through the flashing doors of sixteenth notes. Her fears were confirmed when, not moments later, the gentle sister raised her arms and fists and struck the keys as though the instrument were stone and from the rock her thirst would be quenched. But only discord emerged.

17   "My child, my dear child," the Mother comforted, "come away and rest yourself."

18   The younger nun, breathing deeply, refused. Her severe gray eyes were rimmed in a smoky red. Her lips bled purple. She was in torment. "There is no rest," she declared. She unpinned her veil and studiously dismantled her habit, folding each piece with reverence and setting it upon the piano bench. The Mother remonstrated with Cecellia in the most tender and compassionate tones. However, just as in the depth of her playing the vir-

gin had become the woman, so now the woman in the habit became a woman to the bone. She stripped down to her shift, but no further.

19   "He wouldn't want me to go out unprotected," she told her Mother Superior.

20   "God?" the older woman asked, bewildered.

21   "Chopin," Cecellia answered.

22   Kissing her dear Mother's trembling fingers, Cecellia knelt. She made a true genuflection, murmured an act of contrition, and then walked away from the convent made of bricks with the secret word pressed between yellow mortar, and from the music, her music, which the Mother Superior would from then on keep under lock and key.

23   So it was Sister Cecellia, or Agnes DeWitt of rural Wisconsin, who appeared before Berndt Vogel in the cavern of the barn and said in her mother's dialect, for she knew a German when she met one, that she was hungry. She wanted to ask whether he had a piano, but it was clear to her that he wouldn't and at any rate she was exhausted.

24   "*Jetzt muss ich schlafen,*" she said after eating half a plate of scalded oatmeal with new milk.

25   So he took her to his bed, the only bed there was, in the corner of the otherwise empty room. He went out to the barn he loved, covered himself with hay, and lay awake all night listening to the rustling of mice and sensing the soundless predatory glide of the barn owls and the stiff erratic flutter of bats. By morning, he had determined to marry her if she would have him, just so that he could unpin and then unwind the long strip of cloth that bound her torso. She refused his offer, but she did speak to him of who she was and where from, and in that first summary she gave of her life she concluded that she must never marry again, for not only had she wed herself soul to soul to Christ, but she had already been unfaithful—with her phantom lover, the Polish composer. She had already lived out too grievous a destiny to become a bride again. By explaining this to Berndt, however, she had merely moved her first pawn in a long game of words and gestures that the two would play over the course of many months. What she didn't know was that she had opened to a dogged and ruthless opponent.

26   Berndt Vogel's passion engaged him, mind and heart. He prepared himself. Having dragged Army caissons through hip-deep mud after the horses died in torment, having seen his best friend suddenly uncreated into a mass of shrieking pulp, having lived intimately with pouring tumults of eager lice and rats plump with a horrifying food, he was rudimentarily prepared for the suffering he would experience in love. She, however, had also learned her share of discipline. Moreover—for the heart of her gender is stretched, pounded, molded, and tempered for its hot task from birth—she was a woman.

27   The two struck a temporary bargain, and set up housekeeping. She still slept in the indoor bed. He stayed in the barn. A month passed. Three. Six.

Each morning she lit the stove and cooked, then heated water in a big tank for laundry and swept the cool linoleum floors. Monday she sewed. She baked all day Tuesday. On Wednesdays she churned and scrubbed. She sold the butter and the eggs Thursdays. Killed a chicken every Friday. Saturdays she walked into town and practiced the piano in the school basement. Sunday she played the organ for Mass and then at the close of the day started the next week's work. Berndt paid her. At first she spent her salary on clothing. When with her earnings she had acquired shoes, stockings, a full set of cotton underclothing and then a woollen one, too, and material for two housedresses—one patterned with twisted leaves and tiny blue berries, and the other of an ivy lattice print—and a sweater and, at last, a winter coat, after she had earned a blanket, quilted overalls, a pair of boots, she decided on a piano.

28   This is where Berndt thought he could maneuver her into marriage, but she proved too cunning for him. It was early in the evening and the yard was pleasant with the sound of grasshoppers. The two sat on the porch drinking glasses of sugared lemon water. Every so often, in the ancient six-foot grasses that survived at the margin of the yard, a firefly signalled or a dove cried out its five hollow notes.

29   They drank slowly, she in her sprigged-berry dress that skimmed her waist. He noted with disappointment that she wore normal underclothing now, had stopped binding her breasts. Perhaps, he thought, he could persuade her to resume her old ways, at least occasionally, just for him. It was a wan hope. She looked so comfortable, so free. She'd taken on a little weight and lost her anemic pallor. Her arms were brown, muscular. In the sun, her straight fine hair glinted with green-gold sparks of light and her eyes were deceptively clear.

30   "I can teach music," she told him. She had decided that her suggestion must sound merely practical, a money-making ploy. She did not express any pleasure or zeal, though at the very thought each separate tiny muscle in her hands ached. "It would be a way of bringing in some money."

31   He was left to absorb this. He might have believed her casual proposition, except that her restless fingers gave her away, and he noted their insistent motions. She was playing the Adagio of the "Pathétique" on the tablecloth, a childhood piece that nervously possessed her from time to time.

32   "You would need a piano," he told her. She nodded and held his gaze in that aloof and unbearably sexual way that had first skewered him.

33   "It's the sort of thing a husband gives his wife," he dared.

34   Her fingers stopped moving. She cast down her eyes in contempt.

35   "I can use the school instrument. I've spoken to the school principal already."

36   Berndt looked at the Moon-shaped bone of her ankle, at her foot in the brown, thick-heeled shoe she'd bought. He ached to hold her foot in his lap, untie her oxford shoe with his teeth, cover her calf with kisses, and breathe against the delicate folds of berry cloth.

37   He offered marriage once again. His heart. His troth. His farm. She spurned the lot. She would simply walk into town. He let her know that he would like to buy the piano, it wasn't that, but there was not a store for many miles where it could be purchased. She knew better and with exasperated heat described the way that she would, if he would help financially, go about locating and then acquiring the best piano for the best price. She vowed that she would purchase the instrument not in Fargo but in Minneapolis. From there, she could have it hauled for less than the freight markup. She would make her arrangements in one day and return by night in order not to spend one extra dime either on food she couldn't carry or on a hotel room. When he resisted to the last, she told him that she was leaving. She would find a small room in town and there she would acquire students, give lessons.

38   She betrayed her desperation. Some clench of her fingers gave her away, and it was as much Berndt's unconfused love of her and wish that she might be happy as any worry she might leave him that finally caused him to agree. In the six months that he'd known Agnes DeWitt she had become someone to reckon with, and even he, who understood desperation and self-denial, was finding her proximity most difficult. He worked himself into exhaustion, and his farm prospered. Sleeping in the barn was difficult, but he had set into one wall a bunk room for himself and his hired man and installed a stove that burned red hot on cold nights; only, sometimes, as he looked sleepily into the glowering flanks of iron, he could not keep his own fingers from moving along the rough mattress in faint imitation of the way he would, if he ever could, touch her hips. He, too, was practicing.

39   The piano moved across the August desert of drought-sucked wheat like a shield, a dark upended black thing, an ebony locust. Agnes made friends with a hauler out of Morris and he gave her a slow-wagon price. Both were to accompany into Fargo the last grand piano made by Caramacchione. It had been shipped to Minneapolis, unsold until Agnes entered with her bean sock of money. She accompanied the instrument back to the farm during the dog days. Hot weather was beloved by this particular piano. It tuned itself on muggy days. And so, as it moved across the flat expanse, Miss Agnes DeWitt mounted the back of the wagon and played to the clouds.

40   They had to remove one side of the house to get the piano into the front room, and it took six strong men a full day to do the job. By the time the instrument was settled into place by the window, Berndt was persuaded of its necessary presence, and proud. He sent the men away, although the side of the house was still open to the swirling light of stars. Dark breezes moved the curtains; he asked her to play for him. She did, the music gripped her, and she did not, could not, stop.

41   Late that night she turned from the last chord of the simple Nocturne in C Minor into the silence of Berndt's listening presence. Three slow

claps from his large hands died in the waiting quiet. His eyes rested upon her and she returned his gaze with a long and mysterious stare of gentle regard. The side of the house admitted a great swatch of Moonlight. Spiders built their webs of phosphorescence across black space. Berndt ticked through what he knew—she would not marry him because she had been married and unfaithful, in her mind at least. He was desperate not to throw her off, repel her, damage the mood set by the boom of nighthawks flying in, swooping out, by the rustle of black oak and willow, by the scent of the blasted petals of summer's last wild roses. His courage was at its lowest ebb. Fraught with sheer need and emotion he stood before Agnes, finally, and asked in a low voice, *"Schlaf mit mir. Bitte, Schlaf mit mir."*

42   Agnes looked into his face, openly at last, showing him the great weight of feeling she carried. As she had for her Mother Superior, she removed her clothing carefully and folded it, only she did not stop undressing at her shift but continued until she had slipped off her large tissuey bloomers and seated herself naked at the piano. Her body was a pale blush of silver, and her hands, when they began to move, rose and fell with the simplicity of water.

43   It became clear to Berndt Vogel, as the music slowly wrapped around him, that he was engaged in something that he would have had to pay a whore in Fargo—if there really were any whores in Fargo—a great sum to perform. A snake of hair wound down her spine. Her pale buttocks seemed to float off the invisible bench. Her legs moved like a swimmer's, and he thought he heard her moan. He watched her fingers spin like white shadows across the keys, and found that his body was responding as though he lay fully twined with her underneath a quilt of music and stars. His breath came short, shorter, rasping and ragged. Beyond control, he gasped painfully and gave himself into some furtive cleft of halftones and anger that opened beneath the ice of high keys.

44   Shocked, weak and wet, Berndt rose and slipped through the open side wall. He trod aimless crop lines until he could allow himself to collapse in the low fervor of night wheat. It was true, wasn't it, that the heart was a lying cheat? And as the songs Chopin invented were as much him as his body, so it followed that Berndt had just watched the woman he loved make love to a dead man. Now, as he listened to the music, he thought of returning. Imagined the meal of her white shoulders. Shut his eyes and entered the confounding depth between her legs.

45   Then followed their best years. Together, they constructed a good life in which the erotic merged into the daily so that every task and even small kindness was charged with a sexual humor. Some mornings the two staggered from the bedroom disoriented, still half drunk on the unlikely eagerness of the other's body. These frenzied periods occurred every so often, like spells in the weather. They would be drawn, sink, disappear into their greed, until the cow groaned for milking or the hired man swore

and banged on the outside gate. If nothing else intervened, they'd stop from sheer exhaustion. Then they would look at one another oddly, quest-ingly, as if the other person were a complete stranger, and gradually resume their normal interaction, which was off-hand and distracted, but upheld by the assurance of people who thought alike.

46   Agnes gave music lessons, and although the two weren't married, even the Catholics and the children came to her. This was because it was well-known that Miss DeWitt's first commitment had been to Christ. It was understandable that she would have no other marriage. Although she did not take the Holy Eucharist on her tongue, she was there at church each Sunday morning, faithful and devout, to play the organ. There, she, of course, played Bach, with a purity of intent purged of any subterranean feeling, strictly, and for God.

47   So when the river began to rise one spring, Berndt had already gone where life was deepest many times, and he did not particularly fear the rain. But what began as a sheer mist became an even sprinkle and then developed into a slow, pounding shower that lasted three days, then four, then on the fifth day, when it should have tapered off, increased.

48   The river boiled along swiftly, a gray soup still contained, just barely, within its high banks. On day six the rain stopped, or seemed to. The storm had moved upstream. All day while the sun shone pleasantly the river heaved itself up, tore into its flow new trees and boulders, created tip-ups, washouts, areas of singing turbulence, and crawled, like an infant, toward the farm. Berndt rushed around uneasily, pitching hay into the high loft, throwing chickens up after the hay, wishing he could throw the horse up as well, and the house, and—because Agnes wrung her hands—the piano. But the piano was earth-anchored and well-tuned by the rainy air, so, instead of worrying, Agnes practiced.

49   Once the river started to move, it gained confidence. It had no prob-lem with fences or gates, wispy windbreaks, ditches. It simply levelled or attained the level of whatever stood in its path. Water jumped up the lawn and collected behind the sacks of sand that Berndt had desperately filled and laid. The river tugged itself up the porch and into the house from one side. From the other side it undermined an already weak foun-dation that had temporarily shored up the same wall once removed to make way for the piano. The river tore against the house and then, like a child tipping out a piece of candy from a box, it surged underneath and rocked the floor, and the piano crashed through the weakened wall.

50   It landed in the swift current of the yard, Agnes with it. Berndt saw only the white treble clef of her dress as she spun away, clutching the curved lid. It bobbed along the flower beds first, and then, as muscular new eddies caught it, touched down on the shifting lanes of Berndt's wheat fields, and farther, until the revolving instrument and the woman on it reached the original river and plunged in. They were carried not more than a hundred feet before the piano lost momentum and sank. As

it went down, Agnes thought at first of crawling into its box, nestling for safety among the cold, dead strings. But, as she struggled with the hinged cover, she lost her grip and was swept north. She should have drowned, but there was a snag of rope, a tree, two men in a fishing skiff risking themselves to save a valuable birding dog. They pulled Agnes out and dumped her in the bottom of the boat, impatient to get the dog. She gagged, coughed, and passed out in a roil of feet and fishing tackle.

51   When she came to, she was back in the convent, which was on high ground and open to care for victims of the flood. Berndt was not among the rescued. When the river went down and the heat rose, he was found snagged in a tip-up of roots, tethered to his great blue steaming horse. As Agnes recovered her strength, did she dream of him? Think of him entering her and her receiving him? Long for the curve of his hand on her breast? Yes and no. She thought again of music. Chopin. Berndt. Chopin.

52   He had written a will, in which he declared her his common-law wife and left to her the farm and all upon it. There, she raised Rosecomb Bantams, Dominikers, Reds. She bought another piano and played with an isolated intensity that absorbed her spirit.

53   A year or so after Berndt's death, her students noticed that she would stop in the middle of a lesson and smile out the window as though welcoming a long-expected visitor. One day the neighbor children went to pick up the usual order of eggs and were most struck to see the white-and-black-flecked Dominikers flapping up in alarm around Miss DeWitt as she stood magnificent upon the green grass.

54   Tall, slender, legs slightly bowed, breasts jutting a bit to either side, and the flare of hair flicking up the center of her—naked. She looked at the children with remote kindness. Asked, "How many dozen?" Walked off to gather the eggs.

55   That episode made the gossip-table rounds. People put it off to Berndt's death and a relapse of nerves. She lost only a Lutheran student or two. She continued playing the organ for Mass, and at home, in the black, black nights, Chopin. And if she was asked, by an innocent pupil too young to understand the meaning of discretion, why she sometimes didn't wear clothes, Miss DeWitt would answer that she removed her clothing when she played the music of a particular bare-souled composer. She would nod meditatively and say in her firmest manner that when one enters into such music, one should be naked. And then she would touch the keys.

Questions for Discussion

1. Explain how the description of the river at the beginning helps to define the story and foreshadow what happens.

2. Why does Agnes's playing Chopin disturb the other sisters in the convent?

3. What is the Mother Superior's role in the story? What does she hope to accomplish by hiding the music and dragging Sister Cecellia away from the piano? Why did she then keep the music under lock and key after Sister Cecellia left?

4. Why does Agnes refuse to marry Berndt? What do marriage and Berndt mean to her? Why then does she agree to sleep with him?

5. Explain Erdrich's description of Agnes's relationship to music: "She not only taught but lived music, existed for those hours when she could be concentrated in her being—which was half music, half divine light, flesh only to the degree that she could not admit otherwise."

6. How can music speak "of her faith and doubt, of her passion as the bride of Christ, of her loneliness, shame, ultimate redemption"?

7. Explain why, even though Agnes has not agreed to marry him, Berndt agrees to sleep in the barn and to remove one wall so that Agnes can get her piano into the house.

8. Explain how music can be for Agnes both a religious and a sexual experience.

Suggestions for Exploring, Writing, and Persuading

1. As Mother Superior did, many authority figures try to change what they feel is inappropriate behavior by forbidding it. Does this method work? In an essay, analyze why or why not.

2. If you have ever been absorbed in something to the point of obsession, then write an essay explaining how and why you were obsessed.

3. Select a piece of music that expresses your "faith and doubt," your "loneliness, shame, ultimate redemption," or your joy and explain how music can express such feelings.

POETRY

John Keats (1795–1821)

John Keats was, along with William Wordsworth, Samuel Taylor Coleridge, Lord Byron, and Percy Bysshe Shelley, one of the leading poets of the Romantic period in England. Nearly all of his greatest poems were written in one year, 1818-1819, and published in Lamia, Isabella, and Other

Poems (1820). Keats's poetry celebrates beauty in rich, lush images; his magnificent collected letters, a work of art in their own right, gained increasing attention in the twentieth century. Keats was stricken with tuberculosis and died at the age of twenty-five.

ODE ON A GRECIAN URN   (1819)

I

Thou still unravish'd bride of quietness,
   Thou foster-child of silence and slow time,
Sylvan historian, who canst thus express
   A flowery tale more sweetly than our rhyme:
5   What leaf-fring'd legend haunts about thy shape
     Of deities or mortals, or of both,
       In Tempe or the dales of Arcady?
What men or gods are these? What maidens loth?
What mad pursuit? What struggle to escape?
10   What pipes and timbrels? What wild ecstasy?

II

Heard melodies are sweet, but those unheard
   Are sweeter; therefore, ye soft pipes, play on;
Not to the sensual ear, but, more endear'd,
   Pipe to the spirit ditties of no tone:
15   Fair youth, beneath the trees, thou canst not leave
     Thy song, nor ever can those trees be bare;
       Bold Lover, never, never canst thou kiss,
Though winning near the goal—yet, do not grieve;
   She cannot fade, though thou hast not thy bliss,
20   For ever wilt thou love, and she be fair!

III

Ah, happy, happy boughs! that cannot shed
   Your leaves, nor ever bid the Spring adieu;
And, happy melodist, unwearied,
   For ever piping songs for ever new;
25   More happy love! more happy, happy love!
     For ever warm and still to be enjoy'd,
       For ever panting, and for ever young;
All breathing human passion far above,
   That leaves a heart high-sorrowful and cloy'd,
30   A burning forehead, and a parching tongue.

IV

Who are these coming to the sacrifice?
  To what green altar, O mysterious priest,
Lead'st thou that heifer lowing at the skies,
  And all her silken flanks with garlands drest?
35 What little town by river or sea shore,
  Or mountain-built with peaceful citadel,
    Is emptied of this folk, this pious morn?
And, little town, thy streets for evermore
  Will silent be; and not a soul to tell
40   Why thou art desolate, can e'er return.

V

O Attic shape! Fair attitude! with brede
  Of marble men and maidens overwrought,
With forest branches and the trodden weed;
  Thou, silent form, dost tease us out of thought
45 As doth eternity: Cold Pastoral!
  When old age shall this generation waste,
    Thou shalt remain, in midst of other woe
Than ours, a friend to man, to whom thou say'st,
  'Beauty is truth, truth beauty,'—that is all
50   Ye know on earth, and all ye need to know.

Questions for Discussion

1. Keats begins by addressing an urn or vase. What does he mean when he calls the urn a "still unravish'd bride of quietness," a "foster-child of silence and slow time," and a "Sylvan historian"?

2. How can "unheard" melodies be "sweeter" than "heard" ones?

3. At the beginning of the second stanza, Keats addresses the "pipes," and midway through the second stanza, he addresses lovers. In the third stanza, Keats addresses "happy boughs" and in the fourth, a priest. Where did he find the pipes, the lovers, the boughs, and the priest? What do they all have in common?

4. How can the speaker say to the lovers, "For ever wilt thou love, and she be fair"?

Suggestion for Exploring, Writing, and Persuading

1. Supporting your answer with references to your own experience, argue for or against the statement: "'Beauty is truth, truth beauty.'"

Archibald MacLeish (1892–1982)

Archibald MacLeish was an American scholar, teacher, poet, essayist, critic, and playwright. He served for five years (1939–1944) as Librarian of Congress. Primarily known for his short poems, MacLeish also received a Pulitzer Prize for J.B., a verse dramatization of the biblical story of Job. Though MacLeish was not one of the first Imagists, his "Ars Poetica" is often mentioned as one of the best examples of Imagist writing.

ARS POETICA   (1926)

A poem should be palpable and mute
As a globed fruit,

Dumb
As old medallions to the thumb,
5   Silent as the sleeve-worn stone
Of casement ledges where the moss has grown—

A poem should be wordless
As the flight of birds.

A poem should be motionless in time
10   As the Moon climbs,

Leaving, as the Moon releases
Twig by twig the night-entangled trees,

Leaving, as the Moon behind the winter leaves,
Memory by memory the mind—
15   A poem should be motionless in time
As the Moon climbs.

A poem should be equal to:
Not true.

For all the history of grief
20   An empty doorway and a maple leaf.

For love
The leaning grasses and two lights above the sea—

A poem should not mean
But be.

Questions for Discussion

1. Explain each of the three statements that MacLeish makes about poetry.

2. What pictures do the similes and metaphors provide? In what ways do these devices communicate, even more clearly than expository writing can, a definition of poetry?

Suggestions for Exploring, Writing, and Persuading

1. Both Collins and MacLeish use poetic form to give their definitions of poetry. In a comparison-contrast essay, examine these definitions of poetry. If possible, explain the poets' selection of the poetic form for their definitions.

2. Write your own definition of a poem in poem or essay form.

Countee Cullen (1903–1948)

A brief biography of Countee Cullen precedes "Incident" in the Fear and Loss Unit.

YET DO I MARVEL   (1925)

I doubt not God is good, well-meaning, kind,
And did he stoop to quibble could tell why
The little buried mole continues blind,
Why flesh that mirrors him must some day die,
5   Make plain the reason tortured Tantalus
Is baited with the fickle fruit, declare
If merely brute caprice dooms Sisyphus
To struggle up a never-ending stair.

Inscrutable His ways are and immune
10   To catechism by a mind too strewn
With petty cares to slightly understand
What awful brain compels His awful hand;
Yet do I marvel at this curious thing:
To make a poet black, and bid him sing!

Questions for Discussion

1. What acts of God puzzle the narrator?

2. To Cullen, what is the most "inscrutable" and "curious" of all of God's creations? Explain why.

3. Research the myths of Tantalus and Sisyphus and explain the last four lines of the octave.

4. What limitations does Cullen suggest the human brain has?

5. Explain the double meaning of the word *awful* in line 12.

6. Taking into consideration the time in which the poet lived, explain the last two lines.

Suggestions for Exploring, Writing, and Persuading

1. In an essay, explain what you think is the most curious or inscrutable event of the last two years.

2. How does Cullen use the traditional form of the English sonnet to present his question rather than to answer it?

W. H. Auden (1907–1973)

A brief biography of W. H. Auden precedes "The Unknown Citizen" in the Freedom and Responsibility Unit.

Musée des Beaux Arts (1940)

About suffering they were never wrong,
The Old Masters: how well they understood
Its human position; how it takes place
While someone else is eating or opening a window or just walking
5   dully along;
How, when the aged are reverently, passionately waiting
For the miraculous birth, there always must be
Children who did not specially want it to happen, skating
On a pond at the edge of the wood:
10 They never forgot
That even the dreadful martyrdom must run its course
Anyhow in a corner, some untidy spot
Where the dogs go on with their doggy life and the torturer's horse
Scratches its innocent behind on a tree.
15 In Brueghel's *Icarus*, for instance: how everything turns away
Quite leisurely from the disaster; the ploughman may
Have heard the splash, the forsaken cry,
But for him it was not an important failure; the sun shone
As it had to on the white legs disappearing into the green
20 Water; and the expensive delicate ship that must have seen
Something amazing, a boy falling out of the sky,
Had somewhere to get to and sailed calmly on.

Questions for Discussion

1. What is "the miraculous birth"? Why do the children "not specially want it to happen"?

2. What can the "Old Masters" reveal about suffering?

3. What is the "dreadful martyrdom" and why must it "run its course"?

4. Find a reproduction of Brueghel's *The Fall of Icarus*. The background of this painting depicts the fall of Icarus after he has disregarded the

1110 Imagination and Reality

advice of his father, Daedalus, and flown too close to the sun, melting the wax that held his wings together. Explain how the painting supports Auden's claim about the "Old Masters."

Suggestions for Exploring, Writing, and Persuading

1. Write an essay describing a work of art that you admire, explaining what special meaning it has for you.

2. Auden says, "About suffering they [the Old Masters] were never wrong." Select one work of art—poetry, fiction, drama, painting, sculpture, or music—and discuss what it says about human suffering.

3. MacLeish, in "Ars Poetica," says, "A poem should not mean / But be." Compare MacLeish's definition with Auden's meaning in "Muéee des Beaux Arts." What does Auden say about being?

Lawrence Ferlinghetti (b. 1919)

Lawrence Ferlinghetti is an American poet, novelist, and playwright who was an important member of the Beat movement. He opened the first paperback bookstore in the United States, a shop that became a center for jazz performances and poetry readings. Many of his poems use irony and sarcasm to protest the status quo. Ferlinghetti believes that poetry can improve society.

CONSTANTLY RISKING ABSURDITY (1958)

Constantly risking absurdity
                    and death
    whenever he performs
                above the heads
5   of his audience
    the poet like an acrobat
            climbs on rime
                to a high wire of his own making
    and balancing on eyebeams
10   above a sea of faces
            paces his way
                    to the other side of day
    performing entrechats
                    and sleight-of-foot tricks
15   and other high theatrics
                    and all without mistaking
            any thing
                for what it may not be
    For he's the super realist
20   who must perforce perceive

<pre>
            taut truth
                        before the taking of each stance or step
          in his supposed advance
                        toward that still higher perch
25   where Beauty stands and waits
                        with gravity
                            to start her death-defying leap
          And he
            a little charleychaplin man
30   who may or may not catch
               her fair eternal form
                        spreadeagled in the empty air
            of existence
</pre>

Questions for Discussion

1. In one long sentence Ferlinghetti compares the poet to the high-wire acrobat. In what ways are they alike? Why do they both take risks?

2. What effect does the reading aloud of "must perforce perceive / taut truth" have on the speed of the poem? How is this speed relevant to that of a tightrope walker?

3. Why is a poet a "super realist"?

4. Explain the use of "charleychaplin." Describe the image conveyed by this allusion.

5. What effect does the arrangement of the lines have on the meaning of the poem?

6. What is the tone of the poem?

Suggestions for Exploring, Writing, and Persuading

1. In an expository essay, describe the skills and talents that make a person a poet.

2. Write an argumentative essay agreeing or disagreeing with this statement: The profession of poet is costly for the person who chooses it.

3. Argue in an essay that the risks Ferlinghetti describes a poet as taking apply to anyone who pours his or her soul into a work of art.

Audre Lorde (1934–1992)

Born to Granadian parents, Audre Lorde attended school and lived most of her life in New York. Inarticulate as a small child, she spoke in rhythm or in poetry form to express herself. Lorde wrote about subjects that lead to confrontation. As a feminist poet, she portrays strong African American women who challenge the status quo.

THE ART OF RESPONSE   (1986)

The first answer was incorrect
the second was
sorry   the third trimmed its toenails
on the Vatican steps
5   the fourth went mad
the fifth
nursed a grudge until it bore twins
that drank poisoned grape juice in Jonestown
the sixth wrote a book about it
10   the seventh
argued a case before the Supreme Court
against taxation on Girl Scout Cookies
the eighth held a news conference
while four Black babies
15   and one other   picketed New York City
for a hospital bed to die in
the ninth and tenth swore
Revenge on the Opposition
and the eleventh dug their graves
20   next to Eternal Truth
the twelfth
processed funds from a Third World country
that provides doctors for Central Harlem
the thirteenth
25   refused
the fourteenth sold cocaine and shamrocks
near a toilet in the Big Apple circus
the fifteenth
changed the question.

Questions for Discussion

1. How does Lorde build the "art" of answering a question? What is the
   significance of the fifteenth's response?

2. Why isn't the question to which all are responding ever given?

3. Select one response and discuss its humor or its deeper implications.

Suggestions for Exploring, Writing, and Persuading

1. Write an essay explaining what you think the question is and why. Or
   explain what the question is and what the fifteenth person's change is.

2. Explain how responding to essay questions on an exam can be an
   art form.

Seamus Heaney (b. 1939)

Seamus Heaney was born in County Derry in Northern Ireland, where his father was a farmer and cattle dealer; this locale has been influential in his writing. He has described his move away from the farm as a removal from "the earth of farm labour to the heaven of education." At St. Columb's College and Queen's University, Belfast, he learned Latin, Irish, and Anglo-Saxon, languages that have influenced his poetry. In addition to poetry, Heaney writes incisive literary criticism. He has taught at several universities, including the University of California at Berkeley, Carysfort College, and Harvard University. In 1995, Heaney was awarded the Nobel Prize in Literature.

DIGGING

(1966)

Between my finger and my thumb
The squat pen rests; snug as a gun.
Under my window, a clean rasping sound
When the spade sinks into gravelly ground:
5   My father, digging. I look down

Till his straining rump among the flowerbeds
Bends low, comes up twenty years away
Stooping in rhythm through potato drills
Where he was digging.
10   The coarse boot nestled on the lug, the shaft
Against the inside knee was levered firmly.
He rooted out tall tops, buried the bright edge deep
To scatter new potatoes that we picked
Loving their cool hardness in our hands.
15   By God, the old man could handle a spade.
Just like his old man.
My grandfather cut more turf in a day
Than any other man on Toner's bog.
Once I carried him milk in a bottle
20   Corked sloppily with paper. He straightened up
To drink it, then fell to right away
Nicking and slicing neatly, heaving sods
Over his shoulder, going down and down
For the good turf. Digging.
25   The cold smell of potato mould, the squelch and slap
Of soggy peat, the curt cuts of an edge
Through living roots awaken in my head.
But I've no spade to follow men like them.
Between my finger and my thumb
30   The squat pen rests.
I'll dig with it.

Questions for Discussion

1. The speaker describes his father's and his grandfather's digging. What are they digging for? What is the speaker's attitude toward them?

2. Explain the speaker's metaphorical parallel of the shovel and the pen.

3. What is the narrator digging for?

Suggestions for Exploring, Writing, and Persuading

1. Read Whitelock's "Future Connected By" in the Family unit. In an essay, show the similarities and differences between this poem and "Digging."

2. Write an essay detailing the parallels between the narrator's writing and the father's digging.

3. Compare this poem to Ferlinghetti's description of the poet.

Billy Collins (b. 1941)

A brief biography of Billy Collins appears in the Fear and Loss Unit.

POEM   (1988)

Some poems name their subjects.
The titles are *On* this or *On* that,
or they hang like small marquees
indicating what is playing inside:
5   "Celibacy," "Ostriches at Dusk."

Other poems fall into it as they go along.
You trip over a word while carrying
a tray of vocabulary out to the pool
only to discover that broken glass
10   is a good topic.
Still others have no subject
other than themselves to gnaw on.
The fly lands on the swatter.
The movie runs backwards
15   and catches fire in the projector.
This species apes us well
by talking only about itself.

Such is often the case with poems
afflicted by the same plain title
20   as this one:
a sign by the road announcing a bump.

Questions for Discussion

1. What does Collins mean by "You trip over a word while carrying / a tray of vocabulary"?

2. Why does Collins claim "broken glass is a good subject"?

3. What is Collins implying about "us" in the last two lines of the third stanza?

4. Explain Collins's concluding metaphor: "a sign by the road announcing a bump."

Suggestions for Exploring, Writing, and Persuading

1. Either alone or in groups, prepare a "tray of vocabulary" and try to trip your classmates with these words.

2. Compare this definition of poetry to those by Victor Hernández Cruz and Archibald MacLeish.

Victor Hernández Cruz (b. 1949)

Cruz was born in Aguas Buenas, Puerto Rico, but moved with his parents to New York in 1955. A high school dropout, Cruz has written many books of poetry, including Snaps *(1969),* Tropicalization *(1976),* Mainland *(1973), and* Rhythm, Content, and Flavor: New and Selected Poems *(1989). His 1991 book,* Red Beans, *was the winner of the* Publishers Weekly *"Ten Best Books of the Year" Award.* Panoramas *(1997) is a collection of poems, essays, and stories. Cruz belongs to a movement called "neo-rican" or "nuyorican," composed of writers who use English with accents of Spanish and African American idiomatic expressions. His poems are written in simple language, free of pretense. Cruz now lives and writes in his native Puerto Rico.*

TODAY IS A DAY OF GREAT JOY   (1989)

when they stop poems
in the mail & clap
their hands & dance to
them
5   when women become pregnant
by the side of poems
the strongest sounds making
the river go along

it is a great day

10   as poems fall down to
movie crowds in restaurants
in bars

when poems start to
knock down walls to
15   choke politicians
when poems scream &
begin to break the air

that is the time of
true poets that is
20   the time of greatness

a true poet aiming
poems & watching things
fall to the ground

it is a great day

Questions for Discussion

1. What kinds of poems do people sing and dance to?
2. What kinds of poems knock down walls? What kind of walls?
3. Choose a clause beginning with *when* or *as* and explain the joy of that idea.
4. Cruz describes "a true poet aiming / poems & watching things / fall to the ground." What does he mean? At whom is he aiming poems? What does Cruz imply is the purpose of poems?

Suggestions for Exploring, Writing, and Persuading

1. Using one of Cruz's four functions of poetry (to create, destroy, communicate, or reveal), write an essay explaining how this function applies to drama, fiction, or essay.
2. In Russia and in Ireland, poetry and the poet are revered. Explain why the same homage is not paid to poets in America.
3. Write an essay in which you explain each of the metaphors Cruz uses to portray the unique power and joy of poetry.

Alberto Ríos (b. 1952)

Ríos, a highly respected modern Hispanic American writer, was born in Nogales, Arizona, to an English mother and a Mexican American father. He has received the Walt Whitman Award of the Academy of American Poets (1981), the Western States Book Award (1984), the Pushcart Prize IX (1989), and the Mountain Plains Library Author of the Year Award (1991). Ríos has published both poetry and fiction: Whispering to Fool the Wind *(1981) and* The Iguana Killer *(1984).*

THE VIETNAM WALL   (1985)

I

Have seen it
And I like it: The magic,
The way like cutting onions
5   It brings water out of nowhere.
Invisible from one side, a scar
Into the skin of the ground
From the other, a black winding
Appendix line.
10   A dig.
        An archaeologist can explain.
The walk is slow at first
Easy, a little black marble wall
Of a dollhouse,
15   A smoothness, a shine
The boys in the street want to give.
One name. And then more
Names, long lines, lines of names until
They are the shape of the U.N. building
20   Taller than I am: I have walked
Into a grave.
And everything I expect has been taken away, like that, quick:
        The names are not alphabetized.
        They are in the order of dying,
25   An alphabet of—somewhere—screaming.
I start to walk out. I almost leave
But stop to look up names of friends,
My own name. There is somebody
Severiano Ríos.
30   Little kids do not make the same noise
Here, junior high school boys don't run
Or hold each other in headlocks.
No rules, something just persists
Like pinching on St. Patrick's Day
35   Every year for no green.
        No one knows why.
Flowers are forced
Into the cracks
Between sections.
40   Men have cried
At this wall.
I have
Seen them.

Questions for Discussion

1. Why is the wall "a scar / Into the skin of the ground"?

2. In what ways is the Vietnam Wall a grave that the speaker has walked into? Why *into*?

3. Explain in what ways his expectations have been overwhelmed by reality.

4. Why does he stop to look up his own name? Explain Ríos's statement that the names are "in the order of dying, / An alphabet of—somewhere—screaming."

5. What do his references to "little kids" or "junior high school boys" have to do with the monument to the Vietnam War?

6. What is the "something" that "just persists"?

Suggestions for Exploring, Writing, and Persuading

1. Explain how art without language can sometimes speak louder than language.

2. If you have ever visited a monument, write your reaction to that monument as an art form or as an expression of humanity.

3. Write an essay on what kind of monument would cause grown "men [to] cry."

DRAMA

Tom Stoppard (b. 1937)

Born "Tom Strassler" in Czechoslovakia, Stoppard and his family left that country when the Nazis invaded in 1939, then moved to England in 1946. During his late twenties, Stoppard wrote a variety of plays for stage, radio, and television, beginning with A Walk on the Water *(1963). When* Rosencrantz and Guildenstern Are Dead *opened in London in 1966, critics hailed him as one of the most important of contemporary playwrights. In addition to* Rosencrantz and Guildenstern Are Dead, *which re-tells the story of Shakespeare's* Hamlet, *focusing on two lesser characters who are killed in the power struggle between Hamlet and his uncle, several other Stoppard plays have won high praise:* Travesties *(1974), which borrows from the plot of Oscar Wilde's* The Importance of Being Ernest; Arcadia *(1993); and* The Invention of Love *(1997). His screenplays include* The Human Factor *(1979,* Billy Bathgate *(1991),* and Shakespeare in Love *(1998), for which he won an Academy Award.*

The Real Inspector Hound (1968)

The first thing is that the audience appear to be confronted by their own reflection in a huge mirror. Impossible. However, back there in the gloom—not at the footlights—a bank of plush seats and pale smudges of faces. (The total effect having been established, it can be progressively faded out as the play goes on, until the front row remains to remind us of the rest and then, finally, merely two seats in that row—one of which is now occupied by Moon[1] *Between* Moon *and the auditorium is an acting area which represents, in as realistic an idiom as possible, the drawing-room of Muldoon Manor. French windows[2] at one side. A telephone fairly well upstage (i.e., towards* Moon*). The* body *of a man lies sprawled face down on the floor in front of a large settee. This settee must be a size and design to allow it to be wheeled over the body, hiding it completely. Silence. The room. The* body*.* Moon*.*

Moon *stares blankly ahead. He turns his head to one side then the other, then up, then down—waiting. He picks up his programme and reads the front cover. He turns over the page and reads.*

He turns over the page and reads.

He turns over the page and reads.

He turns over the page and reads.

He looks at the back cover and reads.

He puts it down and crosses his legs and looks about. He stares front. Behind him and to one side, barely visible, a man enters and sits down: Birdboot*.*

Pause. Moon *picks up his programme, glances at the front cover and puts it down impatiently. Pause....Behind him there is the crackle of a chocolate-box, absurdly loud.* Moon *looks round. He and* Birdboot *see each other. They are clearly known to each other. They acknowledge each other with constrained waves.* Moon *looks straight ahead.* Birdboot *comes down to join him.*

Note: *Almost always,* Moon *and* Birdboot *converse in tones suitable for an auditorium, sometimes a whisper. However good the acoustics might be, they will have to have microphones where they are sitting. The effect must be not of sound picked up, amplified and flung out at the audience, but of sound picked up, carried, and gently dispersed around the auditorium.*

[1]Stoppard told Kenneth Tynan: "Moon is a person to whom things happen. Boot is rather more aggressive."

[2]A pair of windows, reaching to the ground, open like doors between room and garden.

Anyway, BIRDBOOT, *with a box of Black Magic,*[3] *makes his way down to join* MOON *and plumps himself down next to him, plumpish middle-aged* BIRDBOOT *and younger taller, less-relaxed* MOON.

BIRDBOOT (*Sitting down; conspiratorially.*): Me and the lads[4] have had a meeting in the bar and decided it's first-class family entertainment but if it goes on beyond half-past ten it's self-indulgent—pass it on...(*And laughs jovially.*) I'm on my own tonight, don't mind if I join you?

MOON: Hello, Birdboot.

BIRDBOOT: Where's Higgs?

MOON: I'm standing in.

MOON AND BIRDBOOT: Where's Higgs?

MOON: Every time.

10   BIRDBOOT: What?

MOON: It is as if we only existed one at a time, combining to achieve continuity. I keep space warm for Higgs. My presence defines his absence, his absence confirms my presence, his presence precludes mine....When Higgs and I walk down this aisle together to claim our common seat, the oceans will fall into the sky and the trees will hang with fishes.

BIRDBOOT (*He has not been paying attention, looking around vaguely, now catches up.*): Where's Higgs?

MOON: The very sight of me with a complimentary ticket[5] is enough.

20   The streets are impassable tonight, the country is rising and the cry goes up from hill to hill—Where—is—Higgs? (*Small pause.*) Perhaps he's dead at last, or trapped in a lift somewhere, or succumbed to amnesia, wandering the land with his turn-ups[6] stuffed with ticket-stubs. (BIRDBOOT *regards him doubtfully for a moment.*)

BIRDBOOT: Yes....Yes, well I didn't bring Myrtle tonight—not exactly her cup of tea, I thought, tonight.

MOON: Over her head, you mean?

BIRDBOOT: Well, no—I mean it's a sort of a *thriller,* isn't it?

MOON: Is it?

30   BIRDBOOT: That's what I heard. Who killed thing?—no one will leave the house.

MOON: I suppose so. Underneath.

BIRDBOOT: *Underneath?!?* It's a whodunnit, man!—Look at it!

(*They look at it. The room. The* BODY. *Silence.*)

Has it started yet?

MOON: Yes.

(*Pause. They look at it.*)

[3]Brand of chocolates.
[4]i.e., the other theater critics.
[5]As issued to a theater critic.
[6]Trouser leg cuffs.

BIRDBOOT: Are you sure?

MOON: It's a pause.

BIRDBOOT: You can't start with a *pause*! If you want my opinion there's
40   total panic back there. (*Laughs and subsides.*) Where's Higgs
tonight, then?

MOON: It will follow me to the grave and become my epitaph—Here lies
Moon the second string: where's Higgs? ...Sometimes I dream of revolution, a bloody *coup d'etat*[7] by the second rank—troupes of actors
slaughtered by their understudies, magicians sawn in half by inde-
fatigably smiling glamour girls, cricket teams wiped out by maraud-
ing bands of twelfth men[8]—I dream of champions chopped down by
rabbitpunching sparring partners while eternal bridesmaids turn and
rape the bridegrooms over the sausage rolls and parliamentary private secretaries plant bombs in the Minister's Humber[9]—comedians
50   die on provincial stages, robbed of their feeds[10] by mutely triumphant stooges[11]—

—and—march—

—an army of assistants and deputies, the seconds-in-command, the
runners-up, the right-hand men—storming the palace gates wherein
the second son has already mounted the throne having committed
regicide with a croquet-mallet—stand-ins of the world stand up!—
(*Beat.*)[12] Sometimes I dream of Higgs.

(*Pause.* BIRDBOOT *regards him doubtfully. He is at a loss, and grasps
reality in the form of his box of chocolates.*)

BIRDBOOT (*Chewing into mike.*): Have a chocolate!

MOON: What kind?

60 BIRDBOOT (*Chewing into mike.*): Black Magic.

MOON: No thanks.

(*Chewing stops dead.*)

(*Of such tiny victories and defeats...*)

BIRDBOOT: I'll give you a tip, then. Watch the girl.

MOON: You think she did it?

BIRDBOOT: No, no—the *girl*, watch her.

MOON: What girl?

BIRDBOOT: You won't know her, I'll give you a nudge.

MOON: *You* know her, do you?

BIRDBOOT (*Suspiciously, bridling.*): What's *that* supposed to mean?

MOON: I beg your pardon?

---

[7]Revolution (French).

[8]Reserve players on cricket teams with eleven members.

[9](Make of) car assigned to a government minister.

[10]Cue lines.

[11]Foils or subordinate partners.

[12]Short pause.

70   BIRDBOOT: I'm trying to tip you a wink—give you a nudge as good as a
        tip—for God's sake, Moon, what's the matter with you?—you could
        do yourself some good, spotting her first time out—she's new, from
        the provinces,[13] going straight to the top. I don't want to put words
        into your mouth but a word from us and we could make her.
      MOON: I suppose you've made dozens of them, like that.
      BIRDBOOT (*Instantly outraged.*): I'll have you know I'm a family man
        devoted to my homely but good-natured wife, and if you're suggest-
        ing—
      MOON: No, no—
80   BIRDBOOT: —A man of my scrupulous morality—
      MOON: I'm sorry—
      BIRDBOOT: —falsely besmirched.
      MOON: Is that her?
        (*For* MRS. DRUDGE *has entered.*)
      BIRDBOOT: —don't be absurd, wouldn't be seen dead with the old—ah.
        (Mrs. Drudge *is the char,[14] middle-aged, turbanned. She heads
        straight for the radio, dusting on the trot.*)
      MOON (*Reading his programme.*): Mrs. Drudge the Help.
      RADIO (*Without preamble, having been switched on by* MRS. DRUDGE):
        We interrupt our programme for a special police message.
        (MRS. DRUDGE *stops to listen.*)
90   The search still goes on for the escaped madman who is on the run
        in Essex.
      MRS. DRUDGE (*Fear and dismay.*): Essex!
      RADIO: County police led by Inspector Hound have received a report
        that the man has been seen in the desolate marshes around Muldoon
        Manor.
        (*Fearful gasp from* MRS. DRUDGE.)
        The man is wearing a darkish suit with a lightish shirt. He is of
        medium height and build and youngish. Anyone seeing a man
        answering to his description and acting suspiciously, is advised to
        phone the nearest police station.
        (*A man answering this description has appeared behind* MRS.
        DRUDGE. *He is acting suspiciously. He creeps in. He creeps out.* MRS.
        DRUDGE *does not see him. He does not see the body.*)
100   That is the end of the police message.
        (MRS. DRUDGE *turns off the radio and resumes her cleaning. She does
        not see the body. Quite fortuitously, her view of the body is always
        blocked, and when it isn't she has her back to it. However, she is dust-
        ing and polishing her way towards it.*)
      BIRDBOOT: So that's what they say about me, is it?

---

[13]Working in theaters outside London.
[14]Charwoman, house cleaner.

MOON: What?

BIRDBOOT: Oh, I know what goes on behind my back—sniggers—slanders—hole-in-corner innuendo—What have you heard?

MOON: Nothing.

BIRDBOOT (*Urbanely.*): Tittle tattle. Tittle, my dear fellow, tattle. I take no notice of it—the sly envy of scandal mongers—I can afford to ignore them, I'm a respectable married man—

110   MOON: Incidentally—

BIRDBOOT: Water off a duck's back, I assure you.

MOON: Who was that lady I saw you with last night?

BIRDBOOT (*Unexpectedly stung into fury.*): How dare you! (*More quietly.*) How dare you. Don't you come here with your slimy insinuations! My wife Myrtle understands perfectly well that a man of my critical standing is obliged occasionally to mingle with the world of the footlights, simply by way of keeping *au fait*[15] with the latest—

MOON: I'm sorry—

BIRDBOOT: That a critic of my scrupulous integrity should be vilified and pilloried in the stocks[16] of common gossip—

120   MOON: Ssssh—

BIRDBOOT: I have nothing to hide!—why, if this should reach the ears of my beloved Myrtle—

MOON: Can I have a chocolate?

BIRDBOOT: What? Oh—(*Mollified.*) Oh yes—my dear fellow—yes, let's have a chocolate—No point in—yes, good show. (*Pops chocolate into his mouth and chews.*) Which one do you fancy?—Cherry? Strawberry? Coffee cream? Turkish delight?

MOON: I'll have montelimar.

(*Chewing stops.*)

BIRDBOOT: Ah. Sorry. (*Just missed that one.*)

130   MOON: Gooseberry fondue?

BIRDBOOT: No.

MOON: Pistacchio fudge? Nectarine cluster? Hickory nut praline? Chateau Neuf du Pape '55 cracknell?

BIRDBOOT: I'm afraid not....Caramel?

MOON: Yes, all right.

BIRDBOOT: Thanks very much. (*He gives* Moon *a chocolate. Pause.*) Incidentally, old chap, I'd be grateful if you didn't mention—I mean, you know how these misunderstandings get about....

MOON: What?

BIRDBOOT: The fact is, Myrtle simply doesn't *like* the theatre....

---

[15]In touch (French).

[16]Slandered and abused. The pillory was a wooden framework with holes for the head and hands of an offender condemned to be exposed to public ridicule; the stocks was a similar framework with holes for feet and occasionally hands in which offenders were confined in a sitting position.

(*He tails off hopelessly.* MRS. DRUDGE, *whose discovery of the body has been imminent, now—by way of tidying the room—slides the couch over the corpse, hiding it completely. She resumes dusting and humming.*)

140   MOON: By the way, congratulations, Birdboot.

BIRDBOOT: What?

MOON: At the Theatre Royal. Your entire review reproduced in neon!

BIRDBOOT (*Pleased.*): Oh...that old thing.

MOON: You've seen it, of course.

BIRDBOOT (*Vaguely.*): Well, I was passing....

MOON: I definitely intend to take a second look when it has settled down.

BIRDBOOT: As a matter of fact I have a few colour transparencies—I don't know whether you'd care to...?

150   MOON: Please, please—love to, love to...

(BIRDBOOT *hands over a few colour slides and a battery-powered viewer which* MOON *holds up to his eyes as he speaks.*)

Yes...yes...lovely...awfully sound. It has scale, it has colour, it is, in the best sense of the word, electric. Large as it is, it is a small masterpiece—I would go so far as to say—kinetic[17] without being pop, and having said that, I think it must be said that here we have a review that adds a new dimension to the critical scene. I urge you to make haste to the Theatre Royal, for this is the stuff of life itself. (*Handing back the slides, morosely.*) All I ever got was "Unforgettable" on the posters for...What was it?

BIRDBOOT: Oh—yes—I know...Was that you? I thought it was Higgs.

(*The phone rings.* MRS. DRUDGE *seems to have been waiting for it to do so and for the last few seconds has been dusting it with an intense concentration. She snatches it up.*)

160   MRS. DRUDGE (*Into phone.*): Hello, the drawing-room of Lady Muldoon's country residence one morning in early spring?... He*llo*!—the draw— Who? Who did you wish to speak to? I'm afraid there is no one of that name here, this is all very mysterious and I'm sure it's leading up to something, I hope nothing is amiss for we, that is Lady Muldoon and her houseguests, are here cut off from the world, including Magnus, the wheelchair-ridden half-brother of her ladyship's husband Lord Albert Muldoon who ten years ago went out for a walk on the cliffs and was never seen again—and all alone, for they had no children.

MOON: Derivative,[18] of course.

170   BIRDBOOT: But quite sound.

MRS. DRUDGE: Should a stranger enter our midst, which I very much doubt, I will tell him you called. Good-bye.

---

[17]In motion.

[18]i.e., of such other plays as Agatha Christie's *The Mousetrap.*

(*She puts down the phone and catches sight of the previously seen suspicious character who has now entered again, more suspiciously than ever, through the french windows. He senses her stare, freezes, and straightens up.*)

SIMON: Ah!—hello there! I'm Simon Gascoyne, I hope you don't mind, the door was open so I wandered in. I'm a friend of Lady Muldoon, the lady of the house, having made her acquaintance through a mutual friend, Felicity Cunningham, shortly after moving into this neighbourhood just the other day.

MRS. DRUDGE: I'm Mrs. Drudge. I don't live in but I pop in on my bicycle when the weather allows to help in the running of charming though
180   somewhat isolated Muldoon Manor. Judging by the time (*she glances at the clock*) you did well to get here before high water cut us off for all practical purposes from the outside world.

SIMON: I took the short cut over the cliffs and followed one of the old smugglers' paths through the treacherous swamps that surround this strangely inaccessible house.

MRS. DRUDGE: Yes, many visitors have remarked on the topographical quirk in the local strata whereby there are no roads leading from the Manor, though there *are* ways of getting *to* it, weather allowing.

SIMON: Yes, well I must say it's a lovely day so far.

190   MRS. DRUDGE: Ah, but now that the cuckoo-beard is in bud there'll be fog before the sun hits Foster's Ridge.

SIMON: I say, it's wonderful how you country people really know weather.

MRS. DRUDGE (*Suspiciously.*): Know whether what?

SIMON (*Glancing out of the window.*): Yes, it does seem to be coming on a bit foggy.

MRS. DRUDGE: The fog is very treacherous around here—it rolls off the sea without warning, shrouding the cliffs in a deadly mantle of blind man's buff.[19]

200   SIMON: Yes, I've heard it said.

MRS. DRUDGE: I've known whole week-ends when Muldoon Manor, as this lovely old Queen Anne[20] House is called, might as well have been floating on the pack ice for all the good it would have done phoning the police. It was on such a week-end as this that Lord Muldoon who had lately brought his beautiful bride back to the home of his ancestors, walked out of this house ten years ago, and his body was never found.

SIMON: Yes, indeed, poor Cynthia.

MRS. DRUDGE: His name was Albert.

---

[19]A game in which a blindfolded person has to catch and identify others not blindfolded.

[20]Built in the reign of Queen Anne (1702–14), or in the architectural style of that period.

210   SIMON: Yes indeed, poor Albert. But tell me, is Lady Muldoon about?

MRS. DRUDGE: I believe she is playing tennis on the lawn with Felicity Cunningham.

SIMON (*Startled.*): Felicity Cunningham?

MRS. DRUDGE: A mutual friend, I believe you said. A happy chance. I will tell them you are here.

SIMON: Well, I can't really stay as a matter of fact—please don't disturb them—I really should be off.

MRS. DRUDGE: They would be very disappointed. It is some time since we have had a four for pontoon bridge[21] at the Manor, and I don't

220   play cards myself.

SIMON: There is another guest, then?

MRS. DRUDGE: Major Magnus, the crippled half-brother of Lord Muldoon who turned up out of the blue from Canada just the other day, completes the house-party.

(MRS. DRUDGE *leaves on this,* SIMON *is undecided.*)

MOON (*Ruminating quietly.*): I think I must be waiting for Higgs to die.

BIRDBOOT: What?

MOON: Half afraid that I will vanish when he does.

(*The phone rings.* SIMON *picks it up.*)

SIMON: Hello?

MOON: I wonder if it's the same for Puckeridge?

230   BIRDBOOT AND SIMON (*Together.*): Who?

MOON: Third string.

BIRDBOOT: Your stand-in?

MOON: Does he wait for Higgs and I to write each other's obituary—does he dream—?

SIMON: To whom did you wish to speak?

BIRDBOOT: What's he like?

MOON: Bitter.

SIMON: There is no one of that name here.

BIRDBOOT: No—as a critic, what's Puckeridge like as a critic?

240   MOON (*Laughs poisonously.*): Nobody knows—

SIMON: You must have got the wrong number!

MOON: —there's always been me and Higgs.

(SIMON *replaces the phone and paces nervously. Pause.* BIRDBOOT *consults his programme.*)

BIRDBOOT: Simon Gascoyne. It's not him, of course.

MOON: What?

BIRDBOOT: I said it's not him.

MOON: Who is it, then?

---

[21]Pontoon (otherwise vingt-et-un) and bridge are two quite different card games. A pontoon bridge, crossing a river, is supported by a line of barges, rafts, or hollow metal cylinders.

BIRDBOOT: My guess is Magnus.

MOON: In disguise, you mean?

BIRDBOOT: What?

250 MOON: You think he's Magnus in disguise?

BIRDBOOT: I don't think you're concentrating, Moon.

MOON: I thought you said—

BIRDBOOT: You keep chattering on about Higgs and Puckeridge—what's the matter with you?

MOON (*Thoughtfully.*): I wonder if they talk about me...?
(*A strange impulse makes* SIMON *turn on the radio.*)

RADIO: Here is another police message. Essex county police are still searching in vain for the madman who is at large in the deadly marshes of the coastal region. Inspector Hound who is mastermind-ing the operation, is not available for comment but it is widely
260 believed that he has a secret plan....Meanwhile police and volunteers are combing the swamps with loud-hailers, shouting, "Don't be a madman, give yourself up." That is the end of the police message.
(SIMON *turns off the radio. He is clearly nervous.* MOON *and* BIRDBOOT *are on separate tracks.*)

BIRDBOOT (*Knowingly.*): Oh yes....

MOON: Yes, I should think my name is seldom off Puckeridge's lips...sad, really. I mean, it's no life at all, a stand-in's stand-in.

BIRDBOOT: Yes...yes....

MOON: Higgs never gives me a second thought. I can tell by the way he nods.

BIRDBOOT: Revenge, of course.

270 MOON: What?

BIRDBOOT: Jealousy.

MOON: Nonsense—there's nothing *personal* in it—

BIRDBOOT: The paranoid grudge—

MOON (*Sharply first, then starting to career...*): It is merely that it is not enough to wax at another's wane,[22] to be held in reserve, to be on hand, on call, to step in or not at all, the substitute—the near offer—the temporary-acting—for I am Moon, continuous Moon, in my own shoes, Moon in June, April, September and no member of the human race keeps warm my bit of space—yes, I can tell by the way he nods.

280 BIRDBOOT: Quite mad, of course.

MOON: What?

BIRDBOOT: The answer lies out there in the swamps.

MOON: Oh.

[22]Increase and decrease, respectively. Cf. Isaac Watts's hymn *Jesus shall reign where'er the sun*, lines 3–4: "His kingdom stretch from shore to shore,/Till moons shall wax and wane no more."

BIRDBOOT: The skeleton in the cupboard is coming home to roost.

MOON: Oh yes. (*He clears his throat...for both he and* BIRDBOOT *have a "public" voice, a critic voice which they turn on for sustained pronouncements of opinion.*) Already in the opening stages we note the classic impact of the catalystic figure—the outsider—plunging through to the centre of an ordered world and setting up the disruptions—the shock waves—which unless I am much mistaken, will strip these comfortable people—these crustaceans in the rock pool of society—strip them of their shells and leave them exposed as the trembling raw meat which, at heart, is all of us. But there is more to it than that—

BIRDBOOT: I agree—keep your eye on Magnus.

(*A tennis ball bounces through the french windows, closely followed by* FELICITY, *who is in her twenties. She wears a pretty tennis outfit, and carries a racket.*)

FELICITY (*Calling behind her.*): Out!

(*It takes her a moment to notice* SIMON *who is standing shiftily to one side.* MOON *is stirred by a memory.*)

MOON: I say, Birdboot....

BIRDBOOT: That's the one.

FELICITY (*Catching sight of* SIMON.): You!

(FELICITY'S *manner at the moment is one of great surprise but some pleasure.*)

SIMON (*Nervously.*): Er, yes—hello again.

FELICITY: What are you doing here?

SIMON: Well, I....

MOON: She's—

BIRDBOOT: Sssh....

SIMON: No doubt you're surprised to see me.

FELICITY: Honestly, darling, you really are extraordinary.

SIMON: Yes, well, here I am.

FELICITY: You must have been desperate to see me—I mean, I'm *flattered*, but couldn't it wait till I got back?

SIMON (*Bravely.*): There is something you don't know.

FELICITY: What is it?

SIMON: Look, about the things I said—it may be that I got carried away a little—we both did—

FELICITY (*Stiffly.*): What are you trying to say?

SIMON: I love another!

FELICITY: I see.

SIMON: I didn't make any promises—I merely—

FELICITY: You don't have to say any more—

SIMON: Oh, I didn't want to hurt you—

FELICITY: Of all the nerve!

SIMON: Well, I—

FELICITY: You philandering coward—

SIMON: Let me explain—

FELICITY: This is hardly the time and place—you think you can barge in anywhere, whatever I happen to be doing—

SIMON: But I want you to know that my admiration for you is sincere—I don't want you to think that I didn't mean those things I said—

FELICITY: I'll kill you for this, Simon Gascoyne!

(*She leaves in tears, passing* MRS. DRUDGE *who has entered in time to overhear her last remark.*)

MOON: It was her.

BIRDBOOT: I told you—straight to the top—

330 MOON: No, no—

BIRDBOOT: Sssh....

SIMON (*To* MRS. DRUDGE.): Yes, what is it?

MRS. DRUDGE: I have come to set up the card table, sir.

SIMON: I don't think I can stay.

MRS. DRUDGE: Oh, Lady Muldoon *will* be disappointed.

SIMON: Does she know I'm here?

MRS. DRUDGE: Oh yes, sir, I just told her and it put her in quite a tizzy.

SIMON: Really?...Well, I suppose now that I've cleared the air....Quite a tizzy, you say...really...really...

(*He and* MRS. DRUDGE *start setting up for card game. Mrs. Drudge Leaves when this is done.*)

340 MOON: Felicity!—she's the one.

BIRDBOOT: Nonsense—red herring.

MOON: I mean, it was *her*!

BIRDBOOT (*Exasperated.*): *What* was?

MOON: That lady I saw you with last night!

BIRDBOOT (*Inhales with fury.*): Are you suggesting that a man of my scrupulous integrity would trade his pen for a mess of potage?![23] Simply because in the course of my profession I happen to have struck up an acquaintance—to have, that is, a warm regard, if you like, for a fellow toiler in the vineyard of greasepaint—I find it

350 simply intolerable to be pillified and villoried—

MOON: I never implied—

BIRDBOOT: —to find myself the object of uninformed malice, the petty slanders of little men—

MOON: I'm sorry—

BIRDBOOT: —to suggest that my good opinion in a journal of unimpeachable integrity is at the disposal of the first coquette who gives me what I want—

MOON: Ssssh—

---

[23]In the Old Testament, Esau sold his birthright for "a mess of pottage" (dish of soup); see Genevan Bible, Genesis 25.

BIRDBOOT: A ladies' man! ...Why, Myrtle and I have been together now
360   for—Christ!—who's *that*?
           (*Enter* LADY CYNTHIA MULDOON *through french windows. A beautiful
           woman in her thirties. She wears a cocktail dress, is formally coif-
           fured, and carries a tennis racket.*)
           (*Her effect on* BIRDBOOT *is also impressive. He half rises and sinks
           back agape.*)
CYNTHIA (*Entering.*): Simon!
           (*A dramatic freeze between her and* SIMON.)
MOON:Lady Muldoon.
BIRDBOOT: No, I mean—who *is* she?
SIMON (*Coming forward.*): Cynthia!
CYNTHIA: Don't say anything for a moment—just hold me.
           (*He seizes her and glues his lips to hers, as they say. While their lips
           are glued—*)
BIRDBOOT: She's *beautiful*—a vision of eternal grace, a poem...
MOON: I think she's got her mouth open.
           (CYNTHIA *breaks away dramatically.*)
CYNTHIA: We can't go on meeting like this!
SIMON: We have nothing to be ashamed of!
370 CYNTHIA: But darling, this is madness!
SIMON: Yes!—I am mad with love for you!
CYNTHIA: Please—remember where we are!
SIMON: Cynthia, I love you!
CYNTHIA: Don't—I love Albert!
SIMON: He's dead! [*Shaking her.*] Do you understand me—Albert's dead!
CYNTHIA: No—I'll never give up hope! Let me go! We are not free!
SIMON: I don't care, we were meant for each other—had we but met in
           time.
CYNTHIA: You're a cad, Simon! You will use me and cast me aside as you
380   have cast aside so many others.
SIMON: No, Cynthia!—you can make me a better person!
CYNTHIA: You're ruthless—so strong, so cruel—
           (*Ruthlessly he kisses her.*)
MOON: The son she never had, projected in this handsome stranger
           and transformed into lover—youth, vigour, the animal, the athlete
           as aesthete—breaking down the barriers at the deepest level of
           desire.
BIRDBOOT: By jove, I think you're right. Her mouth *is* open.
           (CYNTHIA *breaks away.* MRS. DRUDGE *has entered.*)
CYNTHIA: Stop—can't you see you're making a fool of yourself!
SIMON: I'll kill anyone who comes between us!
CYNTHIA: Yes, what is it, Mrs. Drudge?
390 MRS. DRUDGE: Should I close the windows, my lady? The fog is begin-
           ning to roll off the sea like a deadly—

CYNTHIA: Yes, you'd better. It looks as if we're in for one of those days. Are the cards ready?

MRS. DRUDGE: Yes, my lady.

CYNTHIA: Would you tell Miss Cunningham we are waiting.

MRS. DRUDGE: Yes, my lady.

CYNTHIA: And fetch the Major down.

MRS. DRUDGE: I think I hear him coming downstairs now. (*As she leaves.*)

(*She does: the sound of a wheelchair approaching down several flights of stairs with landings in between. It arrives bearing* MAGNUS *at about 15 m.p.h., knocking* SIMON *over violently.*)

CYNTHIA: Simon!

400 MAGNUS (*Roaring.*): Never had a chance! Ran under the wheels!

CYNTHIA: Darling, are you all right?

MAGNUS: I have witnesses!

CYNTHIA: Oh, Simon—say something!

SIMON (*Sitting up suddenly.*): I'm most frightfully sorry.

MAGNUS (*Shouting yet.*): How long have you been a pedestrian?

SIMON: Ever since I could walk.

CYNTHIA: Can you walk now...?

(SIMON *rises and walks.*)

Thank God! Magnus, this is Simon Gascoyne.

MAGNUS: What's he doing here?

410 CYNTHIA: He just turned up.

MAGNUS: Really? How do you like it here?

SIMON (*To* CYNTHIA.): I could stay for ever.

(FELICITY *enters.*)

FELICITY: So—you're still here.

CYNTHIA: Of course he's still here. We're going to play cards. There's no need to introduce you two, is there, for I recall now that you, Simon, met me through Felicity, our mutual friend.

FELICITY: Yes, Simon is an old friend, though not as old as you, Cynthia dear.

SIMON: Yes, I haven't seen Felicity since—

420 FELICITY: Last night.

CYNTHIA: Indeed? Well, you deal, Felicity. Simon, you help me with the sofa. Will you partner Felicity, Magnus, against Simon and me?

MAGNUS (*Aside.*): Will Simon and you always be partnered against me, Cynthia?

CYNTHIA: What do you mean, Magnus?

MAGNUS: You are a damned attractive woman, Cynthia.

CYNTHIA: Please! Please! Remember Albert!

MAGNUS: Albert's dead, Cynthia—and you are still young. I'm sure he would have wished that you and I—

430 CYNTHIA: No, Magnus, this is not to be!

MAGNUS: It's Gascoyne, isn't it? I'll kill him if he comes between us!

CYNTHIA (*Calling.*): Simon!

(*The sofa is shoved towards the card table, once more revealing the corpse, though not to the players.*)

BIRDBOOT: Simon's for the chop[24] all right.

CYNTHIA: Right! Who starts?

MAGNUS: I do. No bid.

CYNTHIA: Did I hear you say you saw Felicity last night, Simon?

SIMON: Did I—Ah yes, yes, quite—your turn, Felicity.

FELICITY: I've had my turn, haven't I, Simon?—now, it seems, it's Cynthia's turn.

440   CYNTHIA: That's my trick, Felicity dear.

FELICITY: Hell hath no fury like a woman scorned, [25] Simon.

SIMON: Yes, I've heard it said.

FELICITY: So I hope you have not been cheating, Simon.

SIMON (*Standing up and throwing down his cards.*): No, Felicity, it's just that I hold the cards![26]

CYNTHIA: Well done, Simon!

(MAGNUS *pays* SIMON, *while* CYNTHIA *deals.*)

FELICITY: Strange how Simon appeared in the neighbourhood from nowhere. We know so little about him.

SIMON: It doesn't always pay to show your hand!

450   CYNTHIA: Right! Simon, it's your opening on the minor bid.[27]

(SIMON *plays.*)

CYNTHIA: Hm, let's see....(*Plays.*)

FELICITY: I hear there's a dangerous madman on the loose.

CYNTHIA: Simon?

SIMON: Yes—yes—sorry. (*Plays.*)

CYNTHIA: I meld.

FELICITY: Yes—personally, I think he's been hiding out in the deserted cottage (*Plays.*) on the cliffs.

SIMON: Flush!

CYNTHIA: No! Simon—your luck's in tonight!

460   FELICITY We shall see—the night is not over yet, Simon Gascoyne! (*She exits.*)

(MAGNUS *pays* SIMON *again.*)

SIMON (*To* MAGNUS.): So you're the crippled half-brother of Lord Muldoon who turned up out of the blue from Canada just the other day, are you? It's taken you a long time to get here. What did you do—walk? Oh, I say, I'm most frightfully sorry!

[24]Will be cut down (slang).

[25]Cf. Congreve, *The Mourning Bride* 3.7: "Heaven has no rage, like love to hatred turned, / Nor Hell a fury, like a woman scorned."

[26]Have the advantage (slang).

[27]Term used in certain card games, as also "meld" and "flush," below.

MAGNUS: Care for a spin round the rose garden, Cynthia?

CYNTHIA: No, Magnus, I must talk to Simon.

SIMON: My round, I think, Major.

MAGNUS: You think so?

SIMON: Yes, Major—I do.

470 MAGNUS: There's an old Canadian proverb handed down from the Bladfoot Indians, which says: He who laughs last laughs longest.

SIMON: Yes, I've heard it said.

(SIMON *turns away to* CYNTHIA.)

MAGNUS: Well, I think I'll go and oil my gun.[28] (*He exits.*)

CYNTHIA: I think Magnus suspects something. And Felicity...Simon, was there anything between you and Felicity?

SIMON: No, no—it's over between her and me, Cynthia—it was a mere passing fleeting thing we had—but now that I have found you—

CYNTHIA: If I find that you have been untrue to me—if I find that you have falsely seduced me from my dear husband Albert—I will kill

480 you, Simon Gascoyne!

(MRS. DRUDGE *has entered silently to witness this. On this tableau, pregnant with significance, the act ends, the body still undiscovered. Perfunctory applause.*)

(MOON *and* BIRDBOOT *seem to be completely preoccupied, becoming audible, as it were.*)

MOON: Camps it around the Old Vic in his opera cloak and passes me the tat.[29]

BIRDBOOT: Do you believe in love at first sight?

MOON: It's not that I think I'm a better critic—

BIRDBOOT: I feel my whole life changing—

MOON: I am but it's not that.

BIRDBOOT: Oh, the world will laugh at me, I know....

MOON: It is not that they are much in the way of shoes to step into....

BIRDBOOT:...call me an infatuated old fool...

490 MOON:....They are not.

BIRDBOOT:.... condemn me....

MOON: He is standing in my light, that is all.

BIRDBOOT:...betrayer of my class...

MOON:...an almost continuous eclipse, interrupted by the phenomenon of Moonlight.

BIRDBOOT: I don't care, I'm a goner.

MOON: And I dream....

BIRDBOOT: The Blue Angel[30] all over again.

---

[28]Go to the lavatory (slang).

[29]Leaves me the drudgery (*tat* is slang for rubbish or junk). "Old Vic": famous London theater.

[30]A novel (1932) by Heinrich Mann, adapted as a film starring Marlene Dietrich, which tells of an old man's infatuation for a heartless young singer.

MOON:...of the day his temperature climbs through the top of his head. . . .

500 BIRDBOOT: Ah, the sweet madness of love . . .

MOON:...of the spasm on the stairs. . . .

BIRDBOOT: Myrtle, farewell . . .

MOON:...dreaming of the stair he'll never reach—

BIRDBOOT:...for I only live but once. . . .

MOON: Sometimes I dream that I've killed him.

BIRDBOOT:What?

MOON: What?

> (*They pull themselves together.*)

BIRDBOOT: Yes . . . yes. . . . A beautiful performance, a collector's piece. I shall say so.

510 MOON: A very promising debut. I'll put in a good word.

BIRDBOOT: It would be as hypocritical of me to withhold praise on grounds of personal feelings, as to withhold censure.

MOON: You're right. Courageous.

BIRDBOOT: Oh, I know what people will say—There goes Birdboot buttering up his latest—

MOON: Ignore them—

BIRDBOOT: But I rise above that—The fact is I genuinely believe her performance to be one of the summits in the range of contemporary theatre.

520 MOON: Trim-buttocked, that's the word for her.

BIRDBOOT: —the radiance, the inner sadness—

MOON: Does she actually come across with it?

BIRDBOOT: The part as written is a mere cypher but she manages to make Cynthia a real person—

MOON: *Cynthia?*

BIRDBOOT: And should she, as a result, care to meet me over a drink, simply by way of er—thanking me, as it were—

MOON: Well, you fickle old bastard!

BIRDBOOT (*Aggressively.*): Are you suggesting...?

> (BIRDBOOT *shudders to a halt and clears his throat.*)

530 BIRDBOOT: Well now—shaping up quite nicely, wouldn't you say?

MOON: Oh yes, yes. A nice trichotomy[31] of forces. One must reserve judgement of course, until the confrontation, but I think it's pretty clear where we're heading.

BIRDBOOT: I agree. It's Magnus a mile off.

> (*Small pause.*)

MOON: What's Magnus a mile off?

BIRDBOOT: If we knew that we wouldn't be here.

---

[31]Division into three.

MOON (*Clears throat.*): Let me at once say that it has *élan* while at the same time avoiding *éclat*.[32] Having said that, and I think it must be said, I am bound to ask—does this play know where it is going?

540 BIRDBOOT: Well, it seems open and shut to me, Moon—Magnus is not what he pretends to be and he's got his next victim marked down—

MOON: Does it, I repeat, declare its affiliations? There are moments, and I would not begrudge it this, when the play, if we can call it that, and I think on balance we can, aligns itself uncompromisingly on the side of life. *Je suis*, it seems to be saying, *ergo sum*.[33] But is that enough? I think we are entitled to ask. For what in fact is this play concerned with? It is my belief that here we are concerned with what I have referred to else where as the nature of identity. I think we are entitled to ask—and here one is irresistibly

550 reminded of Voltaire's cry, "*Voila*"[34]—I think we are entitled to ask—*Where is God?*

BIRDBOOT (*Stunned.*): Who?

MOON: Go—od.

BIRDBOOT (*Peeping furtively into his programme.*): God?

MOON: I think we are entitled to ask.

(*The phone rings.*)

(*The set re-illumines to reveal* CYNTHIA, FELICITY, *and* MAGNUS *about to take coffee, which is being taken round by* MRS. DRUDGE. SIMON *is missing. The body lies in position.*)

MRS. DRUDGE (*Into phone.*): The same, half an hour later? . . . No, I'm sorry—there's no one of that name here. (*She replaces phone and goes round with coffee. To* CYNTHIA.) Black or white, my lady?

CYNTHIA: White please.

(MRS. DRUDGE *pours.*)

560 MRS. DRUDGE (*To* FELICITY.): Black or white, miss?

FELICITY: White please.

(MRS. DRUDGE *pours.*)

MRS. DRUDGE (*To* MAGNUS.): Black or white, Major?

MAGNUS: White please.

(*Ditto.*)

MRS. DRUDGE (*To* CYNTHIA.): Sugar, my lady?

CYNTHIA: Yes please.

(*Puts sugar in.*)

[32]Brilliant display (French). "*Élan*": vivacity (French).
[33]Cf. Descartes's *Le Discourse de la Methode*: "*Cogito, ergo sum*" (I think, therefore I am—Latin). "*Je suis*": I am (French).
[34]The French philosopher and author François Marie Arouet de Voltaire is not on record as saying any such thing.

MRS. DRUDGE (*To* FELICITY.): Sugar, miss?

FELICITY: Yes please.

   (*Ditto.*)

MRS. DRUDGE (*To* MAGNUS.): Sugar, Major?

MAGNUS: Yes please.

   (*Ditto.*)

570   MRS. DRUDGE (*To* CYNTHIA.): Biscuit, my lady?

CYNTHIA: No thank you.

BIRDBOOT (*Writing elaborately in his notebook.*): The second act, however, fails to fulfil the promise....

FELICITY: If you ask me, there's something funny going on.

   (MRS. DRUDGE'S *approach to* FELICITY *makes* FELICITY *jump to her feet
   in impatience. She goes to the radio while* MAGNUS *declines his biscuit, and* MRS. DRUDGE *leaves.*)

RADIO: We interrupt our programme for a special police message.
   The search for the dangerous madman who is on the loose in
   Essex has now narrowed to the immediate vicinity of Muldoon
   Manor. Police are hampered by the deadly swamps and the fog,
   but believe that the madman spent last night in a deserted cottage
   on the cliffs. The public is advised to stick together and make
580   sure none of their number is missing. That is the end of the police
   message.

   (FELICITY *turns off the radio nervously. Pause.*)

CYNTHIA: Where's Simon?

FELICITY: Who?

CYNTHIA: Simon. Have you seen him?

FELICITY: No.

CYNTHIA Have you, Magnus?

MAGNUS: No.

CYNTHIA: Oh.

FELICITY: Yes, there's something foreboding in the air, it is as if one of
590   *us*—

CYNTHIA: Oh, Felicity, the house is locked up tight—no one can get in—
   and the police are practically on the doorstep.

FELICITY: I don't know—it's just a feeling.

CYNTHIA: It's only the fog.

MAGNUS: Hound will never get through on a day like this.

CYNTHIA (*Shouting at him.*): Fog!

FELICITY: He means the Inspector.

CYNTHIA: Is he bringing a dog?

FELICITY: Not that I know of.

600   MAGNUS: —never get through the swamps. Yes, I'm afraid the madman
   can show his hand in safety now.

   (*A mournful baying hooting is heard in the distance, scary.*)

CYNTHIA: What's that?!

FELICITY (*Tensely.*): It sounded like the cry of a gigantic Hound![35]

MAGNUS: Poor devil!

CYNTHIA: Ssssh!

(*They listen. The sound is repeated, nearer.*)

FELICITY: There it is again!

CYNTHIA: It's coming this way—it's right outside the house!

(MRS. DRUDGE *enters.*)

MRS. DRUDGE: Inspector Hound!

CYNTHIA: A *police* dog?

(*Enter* INSPECTOR HOUND. *On his feet are his swamp boots. These are two inflatable—and inflated—pontoons with flat bottoms about two feet across. He carries a foghorn.*)

610   HOUND: Lady Muldoon?

CYNTHIA: Yes.

HOUND: I came as soon as I could. Where shall I put my foghorn and my swamp boots?

CYNTHIA: Mrs. Drudge will take them out. Be prepared, as the Force's[36] motto has it, eh, Inspector? How very resourceful!

HOUND (*Divesting himself of boots and foghorn.*): It takes more than a bit of weather to keep a policeman from his duty.

(MRS. DRUDGE *leaves with chattels. A pause.*)

CYNTHIA: Oh—er, Inspector Hound—Felicity Cunningham, Major Magnus Muldoon.

620   HOUND: Good evening.

(*He and* CYNTHIA *continue to look expectantly at each other.*)

CYNTHIA AND HOUND (*Together.*): Well?—Sorry—

CYNTHIA: No, do go on.

HOUND: Thank you. Well, tell me about it in your own words—take your time, begin at the beginning and don't leave anything out.

CYNTHIA: I beg your pardon?

HOUND: Fear nothing. You are in safe hands now. I hope you haven't touched anything.

CYNTHIA: I'm afraid I don't understand.

HOUND: I'm Inspector Hound.

630   CYNTHIA: Yes.

HOUND: Well, what's it all about?

CYNTHIA: I really have no idea.

HOUND: How did it begin?

CYNTHIA: What?

---

[35]Cf. Sir Arthur Conan Doyle, *Hound of the Baskervilles:* "Mr. Holmes, they were the footprints of a gigantic hound!"

[36]"Be prepared" is the motto of the Boy Scouts, not the British police force.

HOUND: The...thing.

CYNTHIA: What thing?

HOUND (*Rapidly losing confidence but exasperated.*): The trouble!

CYNTHIA: There hasn't *been* any trouble!

HOUND: Didn't you phone the police?

640   CYNTHIA: No.

FELICITY: I didn't.

MAGNUS: What for?

HOUND: I see. (*Pause.*) This puts me in a very difficult position.
(*A steady pause.*) Well, I'll be getting along, then. (*He moves towards the door.*)

CYNTHIA: I'm terribly sorry.

HOUND (*Stiffly.*): That's perfectly all right.

CYNTHIA: Thank you so much for coming.

HOUND: Not at all. You never know, there might have been a serious matter.

CYNTHIA: Drink?

HOUND: More serious than that, even.

650   CYNTHIA (*Correcting.*): Drink before you go?

HOUND: No thank you. (*Leaves.*)

CYNTHIA (*Through the door.*): I do hope you find him.

HOUND (*Reappearing at once.*): Find who, Madam?—out with it!

CYNTHIA: I thought you were looking for the lunatic.

HOUND: And what do you know about that?

CYNTHIA: It was on the radio.

HOUND: Was it, indeed? Well, that's what I'm here about, really. I didn't want to mention it because I didn't know how much you knew. No point in causing unnecessary panic, even with a murderer in our midst.

660   FELICITY: Murderer, did you say?

HOUND: Ah—so that was not on the radio?

CYNTHIA: Whom has he murdered, Inspector?

HOUND: Perhaps no one—yet. Let us hope we are in time.

MAGNUS: You believe he is in our midst, Inspector?

HOUND: I do. If anyone of you have recently encountered a youngish good-looking fellow in a smart suit, white shirt, hatless, well-spoken—someone possibly claiming to have just moved into the neighbourhood, someone who on the surface seems as sane as you or I, then now is the time to speak!

670   FELICITY: I—

HOUND: Don't interrupt!

FELICITY: Inspector—

HOUND: Very well.

CYNTHIA: No. Felicity!

HOUND: Please, Lady Cynthia, we are all in this together. I must ask you to put yourself completely in my hands.

CYNTHIA: Don't, Inspector. I love Albert.

HOUND: I don't think you quite grasp my meaning.

MAGNUS: Is one of us in danger, Inspector?

680 HOUND: Didn't it strike you as odd that on his escape the madman made a beeline for Muldoon Manor? It is my guess that he bears a deep-seated grudge against someone in this very house! Lady Muldoon— where is your husband?

CYNTHIA: My husband?—you don't mean—?

HOUND: I don't know—but I have a reason to believe that one of you is the real McCoy![37]

FELICITY: The real what?

HOUND: William Herbert McCoy who as a young man, meeting the madman in the street and being solicited for sixpence for a cup of tea,
690 replied, "Why don't you do a decent day's work, you shifty old bag of horse manure," in Canada all those many years ago and went on to make his fortune. (*He starts to pace intensely.*) The madman was a mere boy at the time but he never forgot that moment, and thenceforth carried in his heart the promise of revenge! (*At which point he finds himself standing on top of the corpse. He looks down carefully.*)

HOUND: Is there anything you have forgotten to tell me?

(*They all see the corpse for the first time.*)

FELICITY: So the madman has struck!

CYNTHIA: Oh—it's horrible—horrible—

HOUND: Yes, just as I feared. Now you see the sort of man you are pro-
700 tecting.

CYNTHIA: I can't believe it!

FELICITY: I'll have to tell him, Cynthia—Inspector, a stranger of that description has indeed appeared in our midst—Simon Gascoyne. Oh, he had charm, I'll give you that, and he took me in completely. I'm afraid I made a fool of myself over him, and so did Cynthia.

HOUND: Where is he now?

MAGNUS: He must be around the house—he couldn't get away in these conditions.

HOUND: You're right. Fear naught, Lady Muldoon—I shall apprehend the
710 man who killed your husband.

---

[37]The genuine article (slang).

CYNTHIA: My husband? I don't understand.

HOUND: Everything points to Gascoyne.

CYNTHIA: But who's that? (*The corpse.*)

HOUND: Your husband.

CYNTHIA: No, it's not.

HOUND: Yes, it is.

CYNTHIA: I tell you it's not.

HOUND: *I'm* in charge of this case!

CYNTHIA: But that's not my husband.

720   HOUND: Are you sure?

CYNTHIA: For goodness sake!

HOUND: Then who is it?

CYNTHIA: I don't know.

HOUND: Anybody?

FELICITY: I've never seen him before.

MAGNUS: Quite unlike anybody I've ever met.

HOUND: This case is becoming an utter shambles.

CYNTHIA: But what are we going to do?

HOUND (*Snatching the phone.*): I'll phone the police!

730   CYNTHIA: But you are the police!

HOUND: Thank God I'm here—the lines have been cut!

CYNTHIA: You mean—?

HOUND: Yes!—we're on our own, cut off from the world and in grave
    danger!

FELICITY: You mean—?

HOUND: Yes!—I think the killer will strike again!

MAGNUS: You mean—?

HOUND: Yes! One of us ordinary mortals thrown together by fate and cut off
    by the elements, is the murderer! He must be found—search the house!
    (*All depart speedily in different directions leaving a momentarily
    empty stage.* SIMON *strolls on.*)

740   SIMON (*Entering, calling.*): Anyone about?—funny....
    (*He notices the corpse and is surprised. He approaches it and turns
    it over. He stands up and looks about in alarm.*)

BIRDBOOT: This is where Simon gets the chop.
    (*There is a shot.* SIMON *falls dead.*)
    (INSPECTOR HOUND *runs on and crouches down by* SIMON's *body.*
    CYNTHIA *appears at the french windows. She stops there and
    stares.*)

CYNTHIA: What happened, Inspector?!
    (HOUND *turns to face her.*)

HOUND: He's dead....Simon Gascoyne, I presume. Rough justice even for
    a killer—unless—unless—We assumed that the body could not have
    been lying there before Simon Gascoyne entered the house...but...

[*he slides the sofa over the body*] there's your answer. And now—
who killed Simon Gascoyne? And why?
(*"Curtain," freeze, applause, exeunt.*)

MOON: Why not?

BIRDBOOT: Exactly. Good riddance.

750   MOON: Yes, getting away with murder must be quite easy provided that
one's motive is sufficiently inscrutable.

BIRDBOOT: Fickle young pup! He was deceiving her right, left and
centre.

MOON (*Thoughtfully.*): Of course. I'd still have Puckeridge behind *me*—

BIRDBOOT: She needs someone steadier, more mature—

MOON: —And if I could, so could he—

BIRDBOOT: Yes, I know of this rather nice hotel, very discreet, run by a
man of the world—

MOON: Uneasy lies the head that wears the crown.[38]

BIRDBOOT: Breakfast served in one's room and no questions asked.

760   MOON: Does Puckeridge dream of me?

BIRDBOOT (*Pause.*): Hello—what's happened?

MOON: What? Oh yes—what do you make of it, so far?

BIRDBOOT (*Clears throat.*): It is at this point that the play for me
comes alive. The groundwork has been well and truly laid, and the
author has taken the trouble to learn from the masters of the
genre. He has created a real situation, and few will doubt his ability to resolve it with a startling denouement. Certainly that is
what it so far lacks, but it has a beginning, a middle and I have no

770   doubt it will prove to have an end. For this let us give thanks, and
double thanks for a good clean show without a trace of smut. But
perhaps even all this would be for nothing were it not for a
performance which I consider to be one of the summits in the
range of contemporary theatre. In what is possibly the finest
Cynthia since the war—

MOON: If we examine this more closely, and I think close examination is
the least tribute that this play deserves, I think we will find that
within the austere framework of what is seen to be on one level a
country-house week-end, and what a useful symbol that is, the
author has given us—yes, I will go far—he has given us the human
condition—

780   BIRDBOOT: More talent in her little finger—

MOON: An uncanny ear that might have belonged to a Van Gogh[39]—

---

[38]*2 Henry IV* 3.1.31.

[39]The painter Vincent Van Gogh, in his madness, severed his ear and sent it to his
brother.

BIRDBOOT: —a public scandal that the Birthday Honours[40] to date have neglected—

MOON: Faced as we are with such ubiquitous obliquity, it is hard, it is hard indeed, and therefore I will not attempt, to refrain from invoking the names of Kafka, Sartre, Shakespeare, St. Paul, Beckett, Birkett, Pinero, Pirandello, Dante, and Dorothy L. Sayers.[41]

BIRDBOOT: A rattling good evening out. I was held.

(*The phone starts to ring on the empty stage.* MOON *tries to ignore it.*)

790   MOON: Harder still—Harder still if possible—Harder still if it is possible to be—Neither do I find it easy—Dante and Dorothy L. Sayers. Harder still—

BIRDBOOT: Others taking part included—*Moon!*

(*For* MOON *has lost patience and is bearing down on the ringing phone. He is frankly irritated.*)

MOON (*Picking up phone, barks.*): Hel—lo! (*Pause, turns to* BIRDBOOT, *quietly.*) It's for you. (*Pause.*)

(BIRDBOOT *gets up. He approaches cautiously.* MOON *gives him the phone and moves back to his seat.* BIRDBOOT *watches him go. He looks round and smiles weakly, expiating himself.*)

BIRDBOOT (*Into phone.*): Hello....(*Explosion.*) Oh, for God's sake, Myrtle!—I've told you never to phone me at work! (*He is naturally embarrassed, looking about with surreptitious fury.*) What? Last night? Good God, woman, this is hardly the time to—I assure you, Myrtle, there is absolutely nothing going on between me and—I took her to dinner simply by way of keeping *au fait* with the world of the

800   paint and the motley[42] —Yes, I promise—Yes, I do—Yes, I *said* yes— I *do*—and you are mine too, Myrtle—darling—I can't—(*Whispers.*) *I'm not alone*—(Up.) No, she's not!—(*He looks around furtively, licks his lips and mumbles.*) All *right!* I love your little pink ears and you are my own fluffy bunnyboo—Now for God's sake—Goodbye, Myrtle—(*Puts down phone.*)

(BIRDBOOT *mops his brow with his handkerchief. As he turns, a tennis ball bounces in through the french windows, followed by* FELICITY, *as before, in tennis outfit. The lighting is as it was. Everything is as it was. It is, let us say, the same moment of time.*)

---

[40]Titles given on the British sovereign's official birthday.

[41]British detective story writer and translator of Dante's *Divine Comedy*. Franz Kafka, German novelist of Czech origin. Jean-Paul Sartre, French philosopher and writer. William Shakespeare, English playwright. St. Paul of Tarsus, Christian apostle. Samuel Beckett, Irish playwright and novelist. Lord Birkett of Ulverston, lord justice of British Court of Appeal. Sir Arthur Pinero, British dramatist. Luigi Pirandello, Italian dramatist. Dante Alighieri, Italian poet.

[42]i.e., theater (literally, greasepaint and the particolored costume of the jester).

FELICITY (*Calling.*): Out! (*She catches sight of* BIRDBOOT *and is amazed.*) You!

BIRDBOOT: Er, yes—hello again.

FELICITY: What are you doing here?!

810 BIRDBOOT: Well, I...

FELICITY: Honestly, darling, you really are extraordinary—

BIRDBOOT: Yes, well, here I am. [*He looks round sheepishly.*)

FELICITY: You must have been desperate to see me—I mean, I'm flattered, but couldn't it wait till I got back?

BIRDBOOT: No, no, you've got it all wrong—

FELICITY: What is it?

BIRDBOOT: And about last night—perhaps I gave you the wrong impression—got carried away a bit, perhaps—

FELICITY (*Stiffly.*): What are you trying to say?

820 BIRDBOOT: I want to call it off.

FELICITY: I see.

BIRDBOOT: I didn't promise anything—and the fact is, I have my reputation—people do talk—

FELICITY: You don't have to say any more—

BIRDBOOT: And my wife, too—I don't know how she got to hear of it, but—

FELICITY: Of all the nerve! To march in here and—

BIRDBOOT: I'm sorry you had to find out like this—the fact is I didn't mean it this way—

FELICITY: You philandering coward!

830 BIRDBOOT: I'm sorry—but I want you to know that I meant those things I said—oh yes—shows brilliant promise—I shall say so—

FELICITY: I'll kill you for this, Simon Gascoyne!

(*She leaves in tears, passing* MRS. DRUDGE *Who has entered in time to overhear her last remark.*)

BIRDBOOT (*Wide-eyed.*): Good God. . . .

MRS. DRUDGE: I have come to set up the card table, sir.

BIRDBOOT (*Wildly.*): I can't stay for a game of *cards*!

MRS. DRUDGE: Oh, Lady Muldoon *will* be disappointed.

BIRDBOOT: You mean...you mean, she wants to meet me. . . ?

MRS. DRUDGE: Oh yes, sir, I just told her and it put her in quite a tizzy.

BIRDBOOT: Really? Yes, well, a man of my influence is not to be sneezed

840   at—I think I have some small name for the making of reputations— mmm, yes, quite a tizzy, you say?

(MRS. DRUDGE *is busied with the card table.* BIRDBOOT *stands marooned and bemused for a moment.*)

MOON (*From his seat.*): Birdboot!—(*A tense whisper*). Birdboot!

(BIRDBOOT *looks round vaguely.*)

What the hell are you doing?

BIRDBOOT: Nothing.

MOON: Stop making an ass of yourself. Come back.

BIRDBOOT: Oh, I know what you're thinking—but the fact is I genuinely consider her performance to be one of the summits—

(CYNTHIA *enters as before.* MRS. DRUDGE *has gone.*)

CYNTHIA: Darling!

BIRDBOOT: Ah, good evening—may I say that I genuinely consider—

850   CYNTHIA: Don't say anything for a moment—just hold me.

(*She falls into his arms.*)

BIRDBOOT: All right! (*They kiss.*) My God!—she *does* have her mouth open! Dear lady, from the first moment I saw you, I felt my whole life changing—

CYNTHIA (*Breaking free.*): We can't go on meeting like this!

BIRDBOOT: I am not ashamed to proclaim nightly my love for you!—but fortunately that will not be necessary—I know of a very good hotel, discreet—run by a man of the world—

CYNTHIA: But darling, this is madness!

BIRDBOOT: Yes! I am mad with love.

860   CYNTHIA: Please!—remember where we are!

BIRDBOOT: I don't care! Let them think what they like, I love you!

CYNTHIA: Don't—I love Albert!

BIRDBOOT: He's dead. (*Shaking her.*) Do you understand me—Albert's dead!

CYNTHIA: No—I'll never give up hope! Let me go! We are not free!

BIRDBOOT: You mean Myrtle? She means nothing to me—nothing!— she's all cocoa and blue nylon fur slippers—not a spark of creative genius in her whole slumping knee-length-knickered body—

CYNTHIA: You're a cad, Simon! You will use me and cast me aside as you

870   have cast aside so many others!

BIRDBOOT: No, Cynthia—now that I have found you—

CYNTHIA: You're ruthless—so strong—so cruel—

(BIRDBOOT *seizes her in an embrace, during which* MRS. DRUDGE *enters, and* MOON'S *fevered voice is heard.*)

MOON: Have you taken leave of your tiny mind?

(*Cynthia breaks free.*)

CYNTHIA: Stop—can't you see you're making a fool of yourself!

MOON: She's right.

BIRDBOOT (*To* MOON.): You keep out of this.

CYNTHIA: Yes, what is it, Mrs. Drudge?

MRS. DRUDGE: Should I close the windows, my lady? The fog—

CYNTHIA: Yes, you'd better.

880   MOON: Look, they've got your number—

BIRDBOOT: I'll leave in my own time, thank you very much.

MOON: It's the finish of you, I suppose you know that—

BIRDBOOT: I don't need your twopenny Grubb Street prognostications[43]— I have found something bigger and finer—

MOON (*Bemused, to himself.*): If only it were Higgs....

CYNTHIA:...And fetch the Major down.

MRS. DRUDGE: I think I hear him coming down stairs now.

> (*She leaves. The sound of a wheelchair's approach as before.* BIRDBOOT *prudently keeps out of the chair's former path but it enters from the next wing down and knocks him flying. A babble of anguish and protestation.*)

CYNTHIA: Simon—say something!

BIRDBOOT: That reckless bastard [*as he sits up*].

890 CYNTHIA: Thank God!—

MAGNUS: What's *he* doing here?

CYNTHIA: He just turned up.

MAGNUS: Really? How do you like it here?

BIRDBOOT: I couldn't take it night after night.

> (FELICITY *enters.*)

FELICITY: So—you're still here.

CYNTHIA: Of course he's still here. We're going to play cards. There is no need to introduce you two, is there, for I recall now that you, Simon, met me through Felicity, our mutual friend.

FELICITY: Yes, Simon is an old friend—

900 BIRDBOOT: Ah—yes—well, I like to give young up and comers the benefit of my—er—Of course, she lacks technique as yet—

FELICITY: Last night.

BIRDBOOT: I'm not talking about last night!

CYNTHIA: Indeed? Well, you deal, Felicity. Simon, you help me with the sofa.

BIRDBOOT (*To* MOON.): Did you see that? Tried to kill me. I told you it was Magnus—not that it *is* Magnus.

MOON: Who did it, you mean?

BIRDBOOT: What?

910 MOON: You think it's not Magnus who did it?

BIRDBOOT: Get a grip on yourself, Moon—the facts are staring you in the face. He's after Cynthia for one thing.

MAGNUS: It's Gascoyne, isn't it?

BIRDBOOT: Over my dead body!

MAGNUS: If he comes between us...

MOON (*Angrily.*): For God's sake sit down!

CYNTHIA: Simon!

---

[43]Forecasts of literary hack. Grub Street in London was inhabited by hack writers in the 17th and 18th centuries.

BIRDBOOT: She needs me, Moon. I've got to make up a four.[44]
(CYNTHIA *and* BIRDBOOT *move the sofa as before, and they all sit at the table.*)

CYNTHIA: Right! Who starts?

920   MAGNUS: I do. I'll dummy for a no-bid ruff and double my holding on South's queen. (*While he moves cards.*)

CYNTHIA: Did I hear you say you saw Felicity last night, Simon?

BIRDBOOT: Er—er—

FELICITY: Pay twenty-ones or trump my contract. (*Discards.*) Cynthia's turn.

CYNTHIA: I'll trump your contract with five dummy no-trumps there (*discards*), and I'll move West's rook for the re-bid with a banker ruff on his second trick there. (*Discards.*) Simon?

BIRDBOOT: Would you mind doing that again?

930   CYNTHIA: And I'll ruff your dummy with five no-bid trumps there, (*discards*) and I support your re-bid with a banker for the solo ruff in the dummy trick there. (*Discards.*)

BIRDBOOT (*Standing up and throwing down his cards.*): And I call your bluff!

CYNTHIA: Well done, Simon!
(MAGNUS *pays* BIRDBOOT *while* CYNTHIA *deals.*)

FELICITY: Strange how Simon appeared in the neighbourhood from nowhere, we know so little about him.

CYNTHIA: Right, Simon, it's your opening on the minor bid. Hmm. Let's see. I think I'll overbid the spade convention with two no-trumps

940   and King's gambit offered there—[*discards*] and West's dummy split double to Queen's Bishop four there!

MAGNUS (*As he plays cards.*): Faites vos jeux. Rien ne va plus. Rouge et noir.[45] Zero.

CYNTHIA: Simon?

BIRDBOOT (*Triumphant, leaping to his feet.*): And I call your bluff!

CYNTHIA: (*Imperturbably.*) I meld.

FELICITY: I huff.

MAGNUS: I ruff.

BIRDBOOT: I bluff.

950   CYNTHIA: Twist.

FELICITY: Bust.

MAGNUS: Check.

BIRDBOOT: Snap.

CYNTHIA: How's that?

---

[44]For a game of cards. In what follows, the players employ a nonsensical medley of terms from a variety of card games, interspersed with terms from chess ("rook," "king's gambit," "check"), roulette ("Faites vos jeux." "Rien he va plus." "Rouge et noir"), and cricket ("How's that?" "Not out").

[45]Place your bets. No more betting. Red and black (French).

FELICITY: Not out.

MAGNUS: Double top.

BIRDBOOT: Bingo!

CYNTHIA: No! Simon—your luck's in tonight.

FELICITY: We shall see—the night is not over yet, Simon Gascoyne! (*She*
960   *quickly exits.*)

BIRDBOOT (*Looking after* FELICITY.): Red herring—smell it a mile off.
(*To* MAGNUS.) Oh, yes, she's as clean as a whistle, I've seen it a thousand times. And I've seen you before too, haven't I? Strange—there's
something about you—

MAGNUS: Care for a spin round the rose garden, Cynthia?

CYNTHIA: No, Magnus, I must talk to Simon.

BIRDBOOT: There's nothing for you there, you know.

MAGNUS: You think so?

BIRDBOOT: Oh, yes, she knows which side her bread is buttered. I am a
970   man not without a certain influence among those who would reap
the limelight—she's not going to throw me over for a heavily disguised cripple.

MAGNUS: There's an old Canadian proverb—

BIRDBOOT: Don't give me that—I tumbled to you right from the start—oh,
yes, you chaps are not as clever as you think. . . . Sooner or later you
make your mistake. . . . Incidentally, where was it I saw you? . . . I've
definitely—

MAGNUS (*Leaving.*): Well, I think I'll go and oil my gun. (*Exits.*)

BIRDBOOT (*After* MAGNUS.): Double bluff!—(*To* Cynthia.) I've seen it a
thousand times.

980 CYNTHIA: I think Magnus suspects something. And Felicity? Simon, was
there anything between you and Felicity?

BIRDBOOT: No, no—that's all over now. I merely flattered her a little over
a drink, told her she'd go far, that sort of thing. Dear me, the fuss
that's been made over a simple flirtation—

CYNTHIA (*As* MRS. DRUDGE *enters behind.*): If I find you have falsely
seduced me from my dear husband Albert, I will kill you, Simon
Gascoyne!

(*The* "curtain" *as before.* MRS. DRUDGE *and* CYNTHIA *leave.* BIRDBOOT
starts to follow them.)

MOON: *Birdboot!*

(BIRDBOOT *stops.*)

MOON: For God's sake pull yourself together.

BIRDBOOT: I can't help it.

990 MOON: What do you think you're doing? You're turning it into a complete farce!

BIRDBOOT: I know, I know—but I can't live without her. (*He is making
erratic neurotic journeys about the stage.*) I shall resign my position,
of course. I don't care I'm a gonner, I tell you—(*He has arrived at the
body. He looks at it in surprise, hesitates, bends and turns it over.*)

MOON: Birdboot, think of your family, your friends—your high standing the world of letters—I say, what are you doing?

(BIRDBOOT *is staring at the body's face.*)

BIRDBOOT: . . . leave it alone. Come and sit down—what's the matter
1000   with you?

BIRDBOOT (*Dead-voiced.*): It's Higgs.

MOON: What?

BIRDBOOT: It's Higgs.

(*Pause.*)

MOON: Don't be silly.

BIRDBOOT: I tell you it's Higgs!

(MOON *half rises. Bewildered.*)

I don't understand. . . . He's dead.

MOON: Dead?

BIRDBOOT: Who would want to . . . ?

MOON: He must have been lying there all the time. . . .
1010   BIRDBOOT:. . .kill Higgs?

MOON: But what's he doing here? I was standing in tonight. . . .

BIRDBOOT (*Turning.*): Moon? . . .

MOON (*In wonder, quietly.*): So it's me and Puckeridge now.

BIRDBOOT: *Moon.* . . . ?

MOON (*Faltering.*): But I swear I. . . .

BIRDBOOT: I've got it—

MOON: But I didn't—

BIRDBOOT (*Quietly.*): My God . . . so that was it. . . . (*Up.*) Moon—now I see—

MOON: —I swear I didn't—
1020   BIRDBOOT: Now—finally—I see it all—

(*There is a shot and* BIRDBOOT *falls dead.*)

MOON: Birdboot! (*He runs on, to* BIRDBOOT's *body.*)

(CYNTHIA *appears at the french windows. She stops and stares. All as before.*)

CYNTHIA: Oh my God—what happened, Inspector?

MOON: (*Almost to himself.*) He's dead. . . . (*He rises.*) That's a bit rough, isn't it?—A bit extreme!—He may have had his faults—I admit he was a fickle old . . . Who did this, and why?

(MOON *turns to face her. He stands up and makes swiftly for his seat. Before he gets there he is stopped by the sound of voices.*)

(SIMON *and* HOUND *are occupying the critics' seats.*)

(MOON *freezes.*)

SIMON: To say that it is without pace, point, focus, interest, drama, wit or originality is to say simply that it does not happen to be my cup of tea. One has only to compare this ragbag with the masters of the genre to see that here we have a trifle that is not my cup of tea at all.

1030   HOUND: I'm sorry to be blunt but there is no getting away from it. It lacks pace. A complete ragbag.

SIMON: I will go further. Those of you who were fortunate enough to be at the Comedie Française[46] on Wednesday last, will not need to be reminded that hysterics are no substitute for *éclat.*

HOUND: It lacks *élan.*

SIMON: Some of the cast seem to have given up acting altogether, apparently aghast, with every reason, at finding themselves involved in an evening that would, and indeed will, make the angels weep.[47]

HOUND: I am not a prude but I fail to see any reason for the shower of

1040   filth and sexual allusion foisted on to an unsuspecting public in the guise of modernity at all costs. . . .

(*Behind* MOON, FELICITY, MAGNUS, *and* MRS. DRUDGE *have made their entrances, so that he turns to face their semicircle.*)

MAGNUS (*Pointing to* BIRDBOOT's *body.*): Well, Inspector, is this your man?

MOON (*Warily.*): . . . Yes. . . . Yes. . . .

CYNTHIA: It's Simon . . .

MOON: Yes . . . yes . . . poor. . . . (*Up.*) Is this some kind of a joke?

MAGNUS: If it is, Inspector, it's in very poor taste.

(MOON *pulls himself together and becomes galvanic, a little wild, in grief for* BIRDBOOT.)

MOON: All right! I'm going to find out who did this! I want every one to go to the positions they occupied when the shot was fired—(*They move; hysterically.*). No one will leave the house! (*They move back.*)

1050   MAGNUS: I think we all had the opportunity to fire the shot, Inspector—

MOON (*Furious.*): I am not—

MAGNUS: —but which of us would want to?

MOON: Perhaps you, Major Magnus!

MAGNUS: Why should I want to kill him?

MOON: Because he was on to you—yes, he tumbled you right from the start—and you shot him just when he was about to reveal that you killed—(MOON *points, pauses and then crosses to* HIGGS's *body and falters*)—killed—(*He turns* HIGGS *over.*)—this . . . chap.

MAGNUS: But what motive would there be for killing him? (*Pause.*) Who

1060   is this chap? (*Pause.*) Inspector?

MOON (*Rising.*): I don't know. Quite unlike anyone I've ever met. (*Long pause.*) Well . . . now . . .

---

[46]State Theater in Paris, France.

[47]Cf. *Measure for Measure* 2.2.117–22: "But man, proud man, / ...like an angry ape / Plays such fantastic tricks before high heaven / As makes the angels weep."

MRS. DRUDGE: Inspector?

MOON (*Eagerly.*): Yes? Yes, what is it, dear lady?

MRS. DRUDGE: Happening to enter this room earlier in the day to close the windows, I chanced to overhear a remark made by the deceased Simon Gascoyne to her ladyship, viz.—"I will kill anyone who comes between us."

MOON: Ah—yes—well, that's it, then. This . . . chap . . . (*Pointing.*) was
1070   obviously killed by (*Pointing.*) er . . . by (*Pause.*) Simon.

CYNTHIA: But he didn't come between us!

MAGNUS: And who, then, killed Simon?

MRS. DRUDGE: Subsequent to that reported remark, I also happened to be in earshot of a remark made by Lady Muldoon to the deceased, to the effect, "I will kill you, Simon Gascoyne!" I hope you don't mind my mentioning it.

MOON: Not at all. I'm glad you did. It is from these chance remarks that we in the force build up our complete picture before moving in to make the arrest. It will not be long now, I fancy, and I must warn
1080   you, Lady Muldoon that anything you say—

CYNTHIA: Yes!—I hated Simon Gascoyne, for he had me in his power!— But I didn't kill him!

MRS. DRUDGE: Prior to that, Inspector, I also chanced to overhear a remark made by Miss Cunningham, no doubt in the heat of the moment, but it stuck in my mind as these things do, viz., "I will kill you for this, Simon Gascoyne!"

MOON: Ah! The final piece of the jigsaw! I think I am now in a position to reveal the mystery. This man (*The corpse.*) was, of course, McCoy, the Canadian who, as we heard, meeting Gascoyne in the street and being
1090   solicited for sixpence for a toffee apple, smacked him across the ear, with the cry, "How's that for a grudge to harbour, you sniffling little workshy!"[48] all those many years ago. Gascoyne bided his time, but in due course tracked McCoy down to this house, having, on the way, met, in the neighbourhood, a simple ambitious girl from the provinces. He was charming, persuasive—told her, I have no doubt, that she would go straight to the top—and she, flattered by his sophis- tication, taken in by his promises to see her all right[49] on the night, gave in to his simple desires. Perhaps she loved him. We shall never know. But in the very hour of her promised triumph, his eye fell on
1100   another—yes, I refer to Lady Cynthia Muldoon. From the moment he caught sight of her there was no other woman for him—he was in her spell, willing to sacrifice anything, even you, Felicity Cunningham. It was only today—unexpectedly finding him here—that you learned the truth. There was a bitter argument which ended with your promise to kill him—a promise that you carried out in this very room at your first opportunity! And I must warn you that anything you say—

[48]Idler.
[49]Look after her (slang).

FELICITY: But it doesn't make sense!

MOON: Not at first glance, *perhaps*.

MAGNUS: Could not Simon have been killed by the same person who
1110   killed McCoy?

FELICITY: But why should any of us want to kill a perfect stranger?

MAGNUS: Perhaps he was not a stranger to *one* of us.

MOON (*Faltering.*): But Simon was the madman, wasn't he?

MAGNUS: We only have your word for that, Inspector. We only have your
word for a lot of things. For instance—McCoy. Who is he? Is his
name McCoy? Is there any truth in that fantastic and implausible
tale of the insult inflicted in the Canadian streets? Or is there something else, something quite unknown to us, behind all this? Suppose
for a moment that the madman, having killed this unknown stranger
1120   for private and inscrutable reasons of his own, was disturbed before
he could dispose of the body, so having cut the telephone wires he
decided to return to the scene of the crime, masquerading as—
Police Inspector Hound!

MOON: But . . . I'm not mad . . . I'm almost sure I'm not mad. . . .

MAGNUS:...only to discover that in the house was a man, Simon Gascoyne, who recognized the corpse as a man against whom you had
held a deep-seated grudge—!

MOON: But I didn't kill—I'm almost sure I—

MAGNUS: I put it to you!—are you the real Inspector Hound?!

1130   MOON: You know damn well I'm not! What's it all about?

MAGNUS: I thought as much.

MOON: I only dreamed . . . sometimes I dreamed—

CYNTHIA: So it was you!

MRS. DRUDGE: The madman!

FELICITY: The killer!

CYNTHIA: Oh, it's horrible, horrible.

MRS. DRUDGE: The stranger in our midst!

MAGNUS: Yes, we had a shrewd suspicion he would turn up here—and
he walked into the trap!

1140   MOON: What *trap*?

MAGNUS: I am not the real Magnus Muldoon!—It was a mere sub-
terfuge!—and (*Standing up and removing his moustaches.*) I now
reveal myself as—

CYNTHIA: You mean—?

MAGNUS: Yes!—I am the real Inspector Hound!

MOON (*Pause.*): Puckeridge!

MAGNUS (*With pistol.*): Stand where you are, or I shoot!

MOON (*Backing.*): Puckeridge! You killed Higgs—and Birdboot tried to
tell me—

1150   MAGNUS: Stop in the name of the law!

(MOON *turns to run.* MAGNUS *fires.* MOON *drops to his knees.*)

I have waited a long time for this moment.

CYNTHIA: So you are the real Inspector Hound.

MAGNUS: Not only that!—I have been leading a double life—at *least*!

CYNTHIA: You mean—?

MAGNUS: Yes!—It's been ten long years, but don't you know me?

CYNTHIA: You mean—?

MAGNUS: Yes!—it is me, Albert!—who lost his memory and joined the force, rising by merit to the rank of Inspector, his past blotted out—until fate cast him back into the home he left behind, back to the beautiful woman he had brought here as his girlish bride—in short, my darling, my memory has returned and your long wait is

1160 over!

CYNTHIA: Oh, Albert!

(*They embrace.*)

MOON (*With a trace of admiration.*): Puckeridge . . . you cunning bastard. (MOON *dies.*)

THE END

Questions for Discussion

1. What is the effect of two things going on at the same time at the beginning: the theater critics, Moon and Birdboot, conversing in the audience while the play is taking place on the stage?

2. How meaningful is the dialogue and conversation between characters?

3. Explain the things that preoccupy the two critics. Why does Moon use foreign words and pompous prose when speaking? What makes Birdboot a good critic, despite his womanizing, and Moon a second string?

4. What motivates characters' actions in the play? Specifically, consider the motives of Moon, Birdboot, Simon Gascoyne, Cynthia, Felicity, and Magnus.

5. Explain the meaning of Magnus's statement that he has "been leading a double life at least." What roles has he played? What are the implications of all these role reversals? What do they suggest about the nature of human identity?

6. How does the set as described in the opening stage direction reinforce the play's blurring of the distinction between actors and audience, between imagination and reality?

7. How does the play compare or contrast to most mysteries? How does the traditional mystery end? What does the traditional ending suggest about the nature of reality? Why is such an ending satisfying? What do you know about the murders and murderer at the end of Stoppard's play? Have the murderers been identified and caught? What is the effect of the uncertainty of the ending?

8. What are the implications in the play about the nature of reality?

Suggestions for Exploring, Writing, and Persuading

1. In an essay contrast Stoppard's play to a traditional mystery such as Agatha Christie's *The Mousetrap*.

2. Write an essay arguing that, in one way or another, virtually all the characters are complicit in murder.

3. Use Stoppard's play to argue that our perceptions of reality are unreliable.

4. If you have read or seen a performance of Pirandello's *Six Characters in Search of an Author*, compare his portrayal of levels of reality with Stoppard's.

5. Use Stoppard's play to argue that most of our conversation is banal and actually communicates very little of consequence.

6. With the deaths of Moon and Birdboot, what do you think Stoppard is saying about theater critics? Write an essay in which you argue that film and theater critics are or are not useful to playwrights or to audiences.

7. Explain the significance of Moon's and Birdboot's names. Or examine the names of all the characters. Then show how Stoppard's selection of names suggests their personalities and creates humor.

CASEBOOK ON JOYCE CAROL OATES

WRITING ABOUT IMAGINATION AND REALITY

Focusing on the dreams and imaginings of young girls that render them both hopeful and vulnerable, this casebook will allow you to explore in discussion and writing two complementary yet quite different stories by Joyce Carol Oates. The critical essays that follow should suggest ways of reading Oates's stories as well as some possible comparisons to Flannery O'Connor, two of whose works are featured in another casebook in the Quest unit, the final unit in this textbook.

Joyce Carol Oates (b. 1938)

Joyce Carol Oates, a highly skilled and extraordinarily productive American writer of poems, criticism, and fiction, is best known for her more than twenty darkly violent novels. From Them *(1969), which won a National Book Award, to* Beasts *(2002) and* The Falls *(2004), Oates's novels represent an unusually large body of distinguished achievement. Born a Roman Catholic in Lockport, New York, Oates depicts a world devoid of saving grace. A realistic writer whose characters speak a colloquial dialogue full of allusions to popular culture, Oates explores the surrealistic, nightmarish encounters that haunt the empty, lost souls she creates.*

WHERE ARE YOU GOING, WHERE HAVE YOU BEEN? (1970)

FOR BOB DYLAN

1   Her name was Connie. She was fifteen and she had a quick nervous giggling habit of craning her neck to glance into mirrors, or checking other people's faces to make sure her own was all right. Her mother, who noticed everything and knew everything and who hadn't much reason any longer to look at her own face, always scolded Connie about it. "Stop gawking at yourself, who are you? You think you're so pretty?" she would say. Connie would raise her eyebrows at these familiar complaints and look right through her mother, into a shadowy vision of herself as she was right at that moment: she knew she was pretty and that was everything. Her mother had been pretty once too, if you could believe those old snapshots in the album, but now her looks were gone and that was why she was always after Connie.

2   "Why don't you keep your room clean like your sister? How've you got your hair fixed—what the hell stinks? Hair spray? You don't see your sister using that junk."

3   Her sister June was twenty-four and still lived at home. She was a secretary in the high school Connie attended, and if that wasn't bad enough—with her in the same building—she was so plain and chunky and steady that Connie had to hear her praised all the time by her mother and her mother's sisters. June did this, June did that, she saved money and helped clean the house and cooked and Connie couldn't do a thing, her mind was all filled with trashy daydreams. Their father was away at work most of the time and when he came home he wanted supper and he read the newspaper at supper and after supper he went to bed. He didn't bother talking much to them, but around his bent head Connie's mother kept picking at her until Connie wished her mother was dead and she herself was dead and it was all over. "She makes me want to throw up sometimes," she complained to her friends. She had a high, breathless, amused voice which made everything she said sound a little forced, whether it was sincere or not.

4   There was one good thing: June went places with girl friends of hers, girls who were just as plain and steady as she, and so when Connie wanted to do that her mother had no objections. The father of Connie's best girl friend drove the girls the three miles to town and left them off at a shopping plaza, so that they could walk through the stores or go to a movie, and when he came to pick them up again at eleven he never bothered to ask what they had done.

5   They must have been familiar sights, walking around that shopping plaza in their shorts and flat ballerina slippers that always scuffed the sidewalk, with charm bracelets jingling on their thin wrists; they would lean together to whisper and laugh secretly if someone passed by who amused or interested them. Connie had long dark blond hair that drew anyone's eye to it, and she wore part of it pulled up on her head and puffed out and the rest of it she let fall down her back. She wore a pull-over jersey blouse that looked one way when she was at home and another way when she was away from home. Everything about her had two sides to it, one for home and one for anywhere that was not home: her walk that could be childlike and bobbing, or languid enough to make anyone think she was hearing music in her head, her mouth which was pale and smirking most of the time, but bright and pink on these evenings out, her laugh which was cynical and drawling at home—"Ha, ha, very funny"—but high-pitched and nervous anywhere else, like the jingling of the charms on her bracelet.

6   Sometimes they did go shopping or to a movie, but sometimes they went across the highway, ducking fast across the busy road, to a drive-in restaurant where older kids hung out. The restaurant was shaped like a big bottle, though squatter than a real bottle, and on its cap was a revolving figure of a grinning boy who held a hamburger aloft. One night in mid-summer they ran across, breathless with daring, and right away someone leaned out a car window and invited them over, but it was just a boy from high school they didn't like. It made them feel good to be able to ignore him. They went up through the maze of parked and cruising cars to the bright-lit, fly-infested restaurant, their faces pleased and expectant as if they were entering a sacred building that loomed out of the night to give them what haven and what blessing they yearned for. They sat at the counter and crossed their legs at the ankles, their thin shoulders rigid with excitement, and listened to the music that made everything so good: the music was always in the background like music at a church service, it was something to depend upon.

7   A boy named Eddie came in to talk with them. He sat backwards on his stool, turning himself jerkily around in semi-circles and then stopping and turning again, and after a while he asked Connie if she would like something to eat. She said she did and so she tapped her friend's arm on her way out—her friend pulled her face up into a brave droll look—and Connie said she would meet her at eleven, across the way. "I just hate to leave her like that," Connie said earnestly, but the boy said that she wouldn't be alone for long. So they went out to his car and on the way Connie couldn't help but let her eyes wander over the windshields and faces all around her, her face gleaming with a joy that had nothing to do with Eddie or even this place; it might have been the music. She drew her shoulders up and sucked in her breath with the pure pleasure of being alive, and just at that moment she happened to glance at a face just a few feet from hers. It was a boy with shaggy black hair, in a convertible jalopy

painted gold. He stared at her and then his lips widened into a grin. Connie slit her eyes at him and turned away, but she couldn't help glancing back and there he was still watching her. He wagged a finger and laughed and said, "Gonna get you, baby," and Connie turned away again without Eddie noticing anything.

8   She spent three hours with him, at the restaurant where they ate hamburgers and drank Cokes in wax cups that were always sweating, and then down an alley a mile or so away, and when he left her off at five to eleven only the movie house was still open at the plaza. Her girl friend was there, talking with a boy. When Connie came up the two girls smiled at each other and Connie said, "How was the movie?" and the girl said, "*You* should know." They rode off with the girl's father, sleepy and pleased, and Connie couldn't help but look at the darkened shopping plaza with its big empty parking lot and its signs that were faded and ghostly now, and over at the drive-in restaurant where cars were still circling tirelessly. She couldn't hear the music at this distance.

9   Next morning June asked her how the movie was and Connie said, "So-so."

10   She and that girl and occasionally another girl went out several times a week that way, and the rest of the time Connie spent around the house— it was summer vacation—getting in her mother's way and thinking, dreaming, about the boys she met. But all the boys fell back and dissolved into a single face that was not even a face, but an idea, a feeling, mixed up with the urgent insistent pounding of the music and the humid night air of July. Connie's mother kept dragging her back to the daylight by finding things for her to do or saying, suddenly, "What's this about the Pettinger girl?"

11   And Connie would say nervously, "Oh, her. That dope." She always drew thick clear lines between herself and such girls, and her mother was simple and kindly enough to believe her. Her mother was so simple, Connie thought, that it was maybe cruel to fool her so much. Her mother went scuffling around the house in old bedroom slippers and complained over the telephone to one sister about the other, then the other called up and the two of them complained about the third one. If June's name was mentioned her mother's tone was approving, and if Connie's name was mentioned it was disapproving. This did not really mean she disliked Connie and actually Connie thought that her mother preferred her to June because she was prettier, but the two of them kept up a pretense of exasperation, a sense that they were tugging and struggling over something of little value to either of them. Sometimes, over coffee, they were almost friends, but something would come up—some vexation that was like a fly buzzing suddenly around their heads—and their faces went hard with contempt.

12   One Sunday Connie got up at eleven—none of them bothered with church—and washed her hair so that it could dry all day long, in the sun. Her parents and sister were going to a barbecue at an aunt's house and Connie said no, she wasn't interested, rolling her eyes to let her mother know just what she thought of it. "Stay home alone then," her mother said

sharply. Connie sat out back in a lawn chair and watched them drive away, her father quiet and bald, hunched around so that he could back the car out, her mother with a look that was still angry and not at all softened through the windshield, and in the back seat poor old June all dressed up as if she didn't know what a barbecue was, with all the running yelling kids and the flies. Connie sat with her eyes closed in the sun, dreaming and dazed with the warmth about her as if this were a kind of love, the caresses of love, and her mind slipped over onto thoughts of the boy she had been with the night before and how nice he had been, how sweet it always was, not the way someone like June would suppose but sweet, gentle, the way it was in movies and promised in songs; and when she opened her eyes she hardly knew where she was, the back yard ran off into weeds and a fence-line of trees and behind it the sky was perfectly blue and still. The asbestos "ranch house" that was now three years old startled her—it looked small. She shook her head as if to get awake.

13   It was too hot. She went inside the house and turned on the radio to drown out the quiet. She sat on the edge of her bed, barefoot, and listened for an hour and a half to a program called XYZ Sunday Jamboree, record after record of hard, fast, shrieking songs she sang along with, interspersed by exclamations from "Bobby King": "An' look here you girls at Napoleon's—Son and Charley want you to pay real close attention to this song coming up!"

14   And Connie paid close attention herself, bathed in a glow of slow-pulsed joy that seemed to rise mysteriously out of the music itself and lay languidly about the airless little room, breathed in and breathed out with each gentle rise and fall of her chest.

15   After a while she heard a car coming up the drive. She sat up at once, startled, because it couldn't be her father so soon. The gravel kept crunching all the way in from the road—the driveway was long—and Connie ran to the window. It was a car she didn't know. It was an open jalopy, painted a bright gold that caught the sunlight opaquely. Her heart began to pound and her fingers snatched at her hair, checking it, and she whispered "Christ. Christ," wondering how bad she looked. The car came to a stop at the side door and the horn sounded four short taps as if this were a signal Connie knew.

16   She went into the kitchen and approached the door slowly, then hung out the screen door, her bare toes curling down off the step. There were two boys in the car and now she recognized the driver: he had shaggy, shabby black hair that looked crazy as a wig and he was grinning at her.

17   "I ain't late, am I?" he said.

18   "Who the hell do you think you are?" Connie said.

19   "Toldja I'd be out, didn't I?"

20   "I don't even know who you are."

21   She spoke sullenly, careful to show no interest or pleasure, and he spoke in a fast bright monotone. Connie looked past him to the other boy, taking her time. He had fair brown hair, with a lock that fell onto his forehead. His

sideburns gave him a fierce, embarrassed look, but so far he hadn't even bothered to glance at her. Both boys wore sunglasses. The driver's glasses were metallic and mirrored everything in miniature.

22   "You wanta come for a ride?" he said.

23   Connie smirked and let her hair fall loose over one shoulder.

24   "Don'tcha like my car? New paint job," he said. "Hey."

25   "What?"

26   "You're cute."

27   She pretended to fidget, chasing flies away from the door.

28   "Don'tcha believe me, or what?" he said.

29   "Look, I don't even know who you are," Connie said in disgust.

30   "Hey, Ellie's got a radio, see. Mine's broke down." He lifted his friend's arm and showed her the little transistor the boy was holding, and now Connie began to hear the music. It was the same program that was playing inside the house.

31   "Bobby King?" she said.

32   "I listen to him all the time. I think he's great."

33   "He's kind of great," Connie said reluctantly.

34   "Listen, that guy's *great*. He knows where the action is."

35   Connie blushed a little, because the glasses made it impossible for her to see just what this boy was looking at. She couldn't decide if she liked him or if he was just a jerk, and so she dawdled in the doorway and wouldn't come down or go back inside. She said "What's all that stuff painted on your car?"

36   "Can'tcha read it?" He opened the door very carefully, as if he was afraid it might fall off. He slid out just as carefully, planting his feet firmly on the ground, the tiny metallic world in his glasses slowing down like gelatine hardening and in the midst of it Connie's bright green blouse. "This here is my name, to begin with," he said. ARNOLD FRIEND was written in tarlike black letters on the side, with a drawing of a round grinning face that reminded Connie of a pumpkin, except it wore sunglasses. "I wanta introduce myself, I'm Arnold Friend and that's my real name and I'm gonna be your friend, honey, and inside the car's Ellie Oscar, he's kinda shy." Ellie brought his transistor radio up to his shoulder and balanced it there. "Now these numbers are a secret code, honey," Arnold Friend explained. He read off the numbers 33, 19, 17 and raised his eyebrows at her to see what she thought of that, but she didn't think much of it. The left rear fender had been smashed and around it was written, on the gleaming gold background: DONE BY CRAZY WOMAN DRIVER. Connie had to laugh at that. Arnold Friend was pleased at her laughter and looked up at her. "Around the other side's a lot more—you wanta come and see them?"

37   "No."

38   "Why not?"

39   "Why should I?"

40   "Don'tcha wanta see what's on the car? Don'tcha wanta go for a ride?"

41   "I don't know."

42   "Why not?"

43   "I got things to do."

44   "Like what?"

45   "Things."

46   He laughed as if she had said something funny. He slapped his thighs. He was standing in a strange way, leaning back against the car as if he were balancing himself. He wasn't tall, only an inch or so taller than she would be if she came down to him. Connie liked the way he was dressed, which was the way all of them dressed: tight faded jeans stuffed into black, scuffed boots, a belt that pulled his waist in and showed how lean he was, and a white pull-over shirt that was a little soiled and showed the hard small muscles of his arms and shoulders. He looked as if he probably did hard work, lifting and carrying things. Even his neck looked muscular. And his face was a familiar face, somehow: the jaw and chin and cheeks slightly darkened, because he hadn't shaved for a day or two, and the nose long and hawk-like, sniffing as if she were a treat he was going to gobble up and it was all a joke.

47   "Connie, you ain't telling the truth. This is your day set aside for a ride with me and you know it," he said, still laughing. The way he straightened and recovered from his fit of laughing showed that it had been all fake.

48   "How do you know what my name is?" she said suspiciously.

49   "It's Connie."

50   "Maybe and maybe not."

51   "I know my Connie," he said, wagging his finger. Now she remembered him even better, back at the restaurant, and her cheeks warmed at the thought of how she sucked in her breath just at the moment she passed him—how she must have looked to him. And he had remembered her. "Ellie and I come out here especially for you," he said. "Ellie can sit in back. How about it?"

52   "Where?"

53   "Where what?"

54   "Where're we going?"

55   He looked at her. He took off the sunglasses and she saw how pale the skin around his eyes was, like holes that were not in shadow but instead in light. His eyes were chips of broken glass that catch the light in an amiable way. He smiled. It was as if the idea of going for a ride somewhere, to some place, was a new idea to him.

56   "Just for a ride, Connie sweetheart."

57   "I never said my name was Connie," she said.

58   "But I know what it is. I know your name and all about you, lots of things," Arnold Friend said. He had not moved yet but stood still leaning back against the side of his jalopy. "I took a special interest in you, such a pretty girl, and found out all about you like I know your parents and sister are gone somewheres and I know where and how long they're going to be gone, and I know who you were with last night, and your best girl friend's name is Betty. Right?"

59   He spoke in a simple lilting voice, exactly as if he were reciting the words to a song. His smile assured her that everything was fine. In the car, Ellie turned up the volume on his radio and did not bother to look around at them.

60   "Ellie can sit in the back seat," Arnold Friend said. He indicated his friend with a casual jerk of his chin, as if Ellie did not count and she should not bother with him.

61   "How'd you find out all that stuff?" Connie said.

62   "Listen: Betty Schultz and Tony Fitch and Jimmy Pettinger and Nancy Pettinger," he said, in a chant. "Raymond Stanley and Bob Hutter—"

63   "Do you know all those kids?"

64   "I know everybody."

65   "Look, you're kidding. You're not from around here."

66   "Sure."

67   "But—how come we never saw you before?"

68   "Sure you saw me before," he said. He looked down at his boots, as if he were a little offended. "You just don't remember."

69   "I guess I'd remember you," Connie said.

70   "Yeah?" He looked up at this, beaming. He was pleased. He began to mark time with the music from Ellie's radio, tapping his fists lightly together. Connie looked away from his smile to the car, which was painted so bright it almost hurt her eyes to look at it. She looked at that name, ARNOLD FRIEND. And up at the front fender was an expression that was familiar—MAN THE FLYING SAUCERS. It was an expression kids had used the year before, but didn't use this year. She looked at it for a while as if the words meant something to her that she did not yet know.

71   "What're you thinking about? Huh?" Arnold Friend demanded. "Not worried about your hair blowing around in the car, are you?"

72   "No."

73   "Think I maybe can't drive good?"

74   "How do I know?"

75   "You're a hard girl to handle. How come?" he said. "Don't you know I'm your friend? Didn't you see me put my sign in the air when you walked by?"

76   "What sign?"

77   "My sign." And he drew an X in the air, leaning out toward her. They were maybe ten feet apart. After his hand fell back to his side the X was still in the air, almost visible. Connie let the screen door close and stood perfectly still inside it, listening to the music from her radio and the boy's blend together. She stared at Arnold Friend. He stood there so stiffly relaxed, pretending to be relaxed, with one hand idly on the door handle as if he were keeping himself up that way and had no intention of ever moving again. She recognized most things about him, the tight jeans that showed his thighs and buttocks and the greasy leather boots and the tight shirt, and even that slippery friendly smile of his, that sleepy dreamy smile that all the boys used to get across ideas they didn't want to put

into words. She recognized all this and also the singsong way he talked, slightly mocking, kidding, but serious and a little melancholy, and she recognized the way he tapped one fist against the other in homage to the perpetual music behind him. But all these things did not come together.

78   She said suddenly, "Hey, how old are you?"

79   His smile faded. She could see then that he wasn't a kid, he was much older—thirty, maybe more. At this knowledge her heart began to pound faster.

80   "That's a crazy thing to ask. Can'tcha see I'm your own age?"

81   "Like hell you are."

82   "Or maybe a couple years older, I'm eighteen."

83   "Eighteen?" she said doubtfully.

84   He grinned to reassure her and lines appeared at the corners of his mouth. His teeth were big and white. He grinned so broadly his eyes became slits and she saw how thick the lashes were, thick and black as if painted with a black tarlike material. Then he seemed to become embarrassed, abruptly, and looked over his shoulder at Ellie. "*Him*, he's crazy," he said. "Ain't he a riot, he's a nut, a real character." Ellie was still listening to the music. His sunglasses told nothing about what he was thinking. He wore a bright orange shirt unbuttoned halfway to show his chest, which was a pale, bluish chest and not muscular like Arnold Friend's. His shirt collar was turned up all around and the very tips of the collar pointed out past his chin as if they were protecting him. He was pressing the transistor radio up against his ear and sat there in a kind of daze, right in the sun.

85   "He's kinda strange," Connie said.

86   "Hey, she says you're kinda strange! Kinda strange!" Arnold Friend cried. He pounded on the car to get Ellie's attention. Ellie turned for the first time and Connie saw with shock that he wasn't a kid either—he had a fair, hairless face, cheeks reddened slightly as if the veins grew too close to the surface of his skin, the face of a forty-year-old baby. Connie felt a wave of dizziness rise in her at this sight and she stared at him as if waiting for something to change the shock of the moment, make it all right again. Ellie's lips kept shaping words, mumbling along, with the words blasting in his ear.

87   "Maybe you two better go away," Connie said faintly.

88   "What? How come?" Arnold Friend cried. "We come out here to take you for a ride. It's Sunday." He had the voice of the man on the radio now. It was the same voice, Connie thought. "Don'tcha know it's Sunday all day and honey, no matter who you were with last night today you're with Arnold Friend and don't you forget it!—Maybe you better step out here," he said, and this last was in a different voice. It was a little flatter, as if the heat was finally getting to him.

89   "No. I got things to do."

90   "Hey."

91   "You two better leave."

92   "We ain't leaving until you come with us."

93   "Like hell I am—"

94   "Connie, don't fool around with me. I mean, I mean, don't fool *around*," he said, shaking his head. He laughed incredulously. He placed his sunglasses on top of his head, carefully, as if he were indeed wearing a wig, and brought the stems down behind his ears. Connie stared at him, another wave of dizziness and fear rising in her so that for a moment he wasn't even in focus but was just a blur, standing there against his gold car, and she had the idea that he had driven up the driveway all right but had come from nowhere before that and belonged nowhere and that everything about him and even about the music that was so familiar to her was only half real.

95   "If my father comes and sees you—"

96   "He ain't coming. He's at the barbecue."

97   "How do you know that?"

98   "Aunt Tillie's. Right now they're—uh—they're drinking. Sitting around," he said vaguely, squinting as if he were staring all the way to town and over to Aunt Tillie's backyard. Then the vision seemed to get clear and he nodded energetically. "Yeah. Sitting around. There's your sister in a blue dress, huh? And high heels, the poor sad bitch—nothing like you, sweetheart! And your mother's helping some fat woman with the corn, they're cleaning the corn—husking the corn—"

99   "What fat woman?" Connie cried.

100 "How do I know what fat woman. I don't know every goddam fat woman in the world!" Arnold Friend laughed.

101 "Oh, that's Mrs. Hornby....Who invited her?" Connie said. She felt a little light-headed. Her breath was coming quickly.

102 "She's too fat. I don't like them fat. I like them the way you are, honey," he said, smiling sleepily at her. They stared at each other for awhile, through the screen door. He said softly, "Now what you're going to do is this: you're going to come out that door. You're going to sit up front with me and Ellie's going to sit in the back, the hell with Ellie, right? This isn't Ellie's date. You're my date. I'm your lover, honey."

103 "What? You're crazy—"

104 "Yes, I'm your lover. You don't know what that is but you will," he said. "I know that too. I know all about you. But look: it's real nice and you couldn't ask for nobody better than me, or more polite. I always keep my word. I'll tell you how it is, I'm always nice at first, the first time. I'll hold you so tight you won't think you have to try to get away or pretend anything because you'll know you can't. And I'll come inside you where it's all secret and you'll give in to me and you'll love me—"

105 "Shut up! You're crazy!" Connie said. She backed away from the door. She put her hands against her ears as if she'd heard something terrible, something not meant for her. "People don't talk like that, you're crazy," she muttered. Her heart was almost too big now for her chest and its pumping made sweat break out all over her. She looked out to see Arnold

Friend pause and then take a step toward the porch lurching. He almost fell. But, like a clever drunken man, he managed to catch his balance. He wobbled in his high boots and grabbed hold of one of the porch posts.

106   "Honey?" he said. "You still listening?"

107   "Get the hell out of here!"

108   "Be nice, honey. Listen."

109   "I'm going to call the police—"

110   He wobbled again and out of the side of his mouth came a fast spat curse, an aside not meant for her to hear. But even this "Christ!" sounded forced. Then he began to smile again. She watched this smile come, awkward as if he were smiling from inside a mask. His whole face was a mask, she thought wildly, tanned down onto his throat but then running out as if he had plastered make-up on his face but had forgotten about his throat.

111   "Honey—? Listen, here's how it is. I always tell the truth and I promise you this: I ain't coming in that house after you."

112   "You better not! I'm going to call the police if you—if you don't—"

113   "Honey," he said, talking right through her voice, "honey, I'm not coming in there but you are coming out here. You know why?"

114   She was panting. The kitchen looked like a place she had never seen before, some room she had run inside but which wasn't good enough, wasn't going to help her. The kitchen window had never had a curtain, after three years, and there were dishes in the sink for her to do—probably—and if you ran your hand across the table you'd probably feel something sticky there.

115   "You listening, honey? Hey?"

116   "—going to call the police—"

117   "Soon as you touch the phone I don't need to keep my promise and can come inside. You won't want that."

118   She rushed forward and tried to lock the door. Her fingers were shaking. "But why lock it," Arnold Friend said gently, talking right into her face. "It's just a screen door. It's just nothing." One of his boots was at a strange angle, as if his foot wasn't in it. It pointed out to the left, bent at the ankle. "I mean, anybody can break through a screen door and glass and wood and iron or anything else if he needs to, anybody at all and specially Arnold Friend. If the place got lit up with a fire honey you'd come running out into my arms, right into my arms and safe at home—like you knew I was your lover and'd stopped fooling around. I don't mind a nice shy girl but I don't like no fooling around." Part of those words were spoken with a slight rhythmic lilt, and Connie somehow recognized them— the echo of a song from last year, about a girl rushing into her boy friend's arms and coming home again—

119   Connie stood barefoot on the linoleum floor, staring at him. "What do you want?" she whispered.

120   "I want you," he said.

121   "What?"

122   "Seen you that night and thought, that's the one, yes sir. I never needed to look any more."

123   "But my father's coming back. He's coming to get me. I had to wash my hair first—" She spoke in a dry, rapid voice, hardly raising it for him to hear.

124   "No, your daddy is not coming and yes, you had to wash your hair and you washed it for me. It's nice and shining and all for me, I thank you, sweetheart," he said, with a mock bow, but again he almost lost his balance. He had to bend and adjust his boots. Evidently his feet did not go all the way down; the boots must have been stuffed with something so that he would seem taller. Connie stared out at him and behind him Ellie in the car, who seemed to be looking off toward Connie's right, into nothing. This Ellie said, pulling the words out of the air one after another as if he were just discovering them, "You want me to pull out the phone?"

125   "Shut your mouth and keep it shut," Arnold Friend said, his face red from bending over or maybe from embarrassment because Connie had seen his boots. "This ain't none of your business."

126   "What—what are you doing? What do you want?" Connie said. "If I call the police they'll get you, they'll arrest you—"

127   "Promise was not to come in unless you touch that phone, and I'll keep that promise," he said. He resumed his erect position and tried to force his shoulders back. He sounded like a hero in a movie, declaring something important. He spoke too loudly and it was as if he were speaking to someone behind Connie. "I ain't made plans for coming in that house where I don't belong but just for you to come out to me, the way you should. Don't you know who I am?"

128   "You're crazy," she whispered. She backed away from the door but did not want to go into another part of the house, as if this would give him permission to come through the door. "What do you...You're crazy, you ..."

129   "Huh? What're you saying, honey?"

130   Her eyes darted everywhere in the kitchen. She could not remember what it was, this room.

131   "This is how it is, honey: you come out and we'll drive away, have a nice ride. But if you don't come out we're gonna wait till your people come home and then they're all going to get it."

132   "You want that telephone pulled out?" Ellie said. He held the radio away from his ear and grimaced, as if without the radio the air was too much for him.

133   "I toldja shut up, Ellie," Arnold Friend said, "you're deaf, get a hearing aid, right? Fix yourself up. This little girl's no trouble and's gonna be nice to me, so Ellie keep to yourself, this ain't your date—right? Don't hem in on me. Don't hog. Don't crush. Don't bird dog. Don't trail me," he said in a rapid meaningless voice, as if he were running through all the expressions he'd learned but was no longer sure which one of them was in style, then rushing on to new ones, making them up with his eyes closed, "Don't crawl under my fence, don't squeeze in my chipmunk hole, don't sniff my

glue, suck my popsicle, keep your own greasy fingers on yourself!" He shaded his eyes and peered in at Connie, who was backed against the kitchen table. "Don't mind him honey he's just a creep. He's a dope. Right? I'm the boy for you and like I said you come out here nice like a lady and give me your hand, and nobody else gets hurt, I mean, your nice old bald-headed daddy and your mummy and your sister in her high heels. Because listen: why bring them in this?"

134   "Leave me alone," Connie whispered.

135   "Hey, you know that old woman down the road, the one with the chickens and stuff—you know her?"

136   "She's dead!"

137   "Dead? What? You know her?" Arnold Friend said.

138   "She's dead—"

139   "Don't you like her?"

140   "She's dead—she's—she isn't here any more—"

141   "But don't you like her, I mean, you got something against her? Some grudge or something?" Then his voice dipped as if he were conscious of a rudeness. He touched the sunglasses perched on top of his head as if to make sure they were still there. "Now you be a good girl."

142   "What are you going to do?"

143   "Just two things, or maybe three," Arnold Friend said. "But I promise it won't last long and you'll like me that way you get to like people you're close to. You will. It's all over for you here, so come on out. You don't want your people in any trouble, do you?"

144   She turned and bumped against a chair or something, hurting her leg, but she ran into the back room and picked up the telephone. Something roared in her ear, a tiny roaring, and she was so sick with fear that she could do nothing but listen to it—the telephone was clammy and very heavy and her fingers groped down to the dial but were too weak to touch it. She began to scream into the phone, into the roaring. She cried out, she cried for her mother, she felt her breath start jerking back and forth in her lungs as if it were something Arnold Friend were stabbing her with again and again with no tenderness. A noisy sorrowful wailing rose all about her and she was locked inside it the way she was locked inside the house.

145   After a while she could hear again. She was sitting on the floor with her wet back against the wall.

146   Arnold Friend was saying from the door, "That's a good girl. Put the phone back."

147   She kicked the phone away from her.

148   "No, honey. Pick it up. Put it back right."

149   She picked it up and put it back. The dial tone stopped.

150   "That's a good girl. Now come outside."

151   She was hollow with what had been fear, but what was now just an emptiness. All that screaming had blasted it out of her. She sat, one leg cramped under her, and deep inside her brain was something like a pinpoint of light that kept going and would not let her relax. She thought,

I'm not going to see my mother again. She thought, I'm not going to sleep in my bed again. Her bright green blouse was all wet.

152   Arnold Friend said, in a gentle—loud voice that was like a stage voice, "The place where you came from ain't there any more, and where you had in mind to go is cancelled out. This place you are now—inside your daddy's house—is nothing but a cardboard box I can knock down any time. You know that and always did know it. You hear me?"

153   She thought, I have got to think. I have to know what to do.

154   "We'll go out to a nice field, out in the country here where it smells so nice and it's sunny," Arnold Friend said. "I'll have my arms around you so you won't need to try to get away and I'll show you what love is like, what it does. The hell with this house! It looks solid all right," he said. He ran a fingernail down the screen and the noise did not make Connie shiver, as it would have the day before. "Now put your hand on your heart, honey. Feel that? That feels solid too but we know better, be nice to me, be sweet like you can because what else is there for a girl like you but to be sweet and pretty and give in?—and get away before her people come back?"

155   She felt her pounding heart. Her hand seemed to enclose it. She thought for the first time in her life that it was nothing that was hers, that belonged to her, but just a pounding, living thing inside this body that wasn't really hers either.

156   "You don't want them to get hurt," Arnold Friend went on. "Now get up, honey. Get up all by yourself."

157   She stood up.

158   "Now turn this way. That's right. Come over here to me—Ellie, put that away, didn't I tell you? You dope. You miserable creepy dope," Arnold said. His words were not angry but only part of an incantation. The incantation was kindly. "Now come out through the kitchen to me honey and let's see a smile, try it, you're a brave sweet little girl and now they're eating corn and hotdogs cooked to bursting over an outdoor fire, and they don't know one thing about you and never did and honey you're better than them because not a one of them would have done this for you."

159   Connie felt the linoleum under her feet; it was cool. She brushed her hair back out of her eyes. Arnold Friend let go of the post tentatively and opened his arms for her, his elbows pointing in toward each other and his wrists limp, to show that this was an embarrassed embrace and a little mocking, he didn't want to make her self-conscious.

160   She put out her hand against the screen. She watched herself push the door slowly open as if she were safe back somewhere in the other doorway, watching this body and this head of long hair moving out into the sunlight where Arnold Friend waited.

161   "My sweet little blue-eyed girl," he said, in a half-sung sigh that had nothing to do with her brown eyes but was taken up just the same by the vast sunlit reaches of the land behind him and on all sides of him, so much land that Connie had never seen before and did not recognize except to know that she was going to it.

Questions for Discussion

1. How and why does Connie's mother's constant nagging cause her to react the way she does? What do Connie's reactions suggest about her character?

2. What is most important to Connie?

3. Why does Arnold Friend fake laughter and pretend to be a teenager even though he must know Connie will see through his charade? What attracts Connie to Arnold and Ellie? What frightens her?

4. How does Arnold know so much about Connie? How does Arnold convince Connie that she is powerless before him?

5. What does the evidence in the story suggest will happen to Connie?

VALENTINE   (1999)

1   In upstate New York in those years there were snowstorms so wild and fierce they could change the world, within a few hours, to a place you wouldn't know. First came the heavy black thunderheads over Lake Erie, then the wind hammering overhead like a freight train, then the snowflakes erupting, flying, swirling like crazed atoms. If there'd been a sun it was extinguished, gone. Night and day were reversed, the fallen snow emitted such a radium-glare.

2   I was fifteen years old living in the Red Rock section of Buffalo with an aunt, an older sister of my mother's, and her husband who was retired from the New York Central Railroad with a disability pension. My own family was what you'd called "dispersed"—we were all alive, seven of us, I believed we were all alive, but we did not live together in the same house any longer. In fact, the house, an old rented farmhouse twenty miles north of Buffalo, was gone. Burned to the ground.

3   Valentine's Day 1959, the snowstorm began in midafternoon and already by 5 P.M. the power lines were down in Buffalo. Hurriedly we lit kerosene lamps whose wicks smoked and stank as they emitted a begrudging light. We had a flashlight, of course, and candles. In extra layers of clothes we saw our breaths steam as we ate our cold supper on plates like ice. I cleaned up the kitchen as best I could without hot water, for that was always my task, among numerous others, and I said "Goodnight, Aunt Esther" to my aunt who frowned at me seeing someone not me in my place who filled her heart with sisterly sorrow and I said "Goodnight, Uncle Herman" to the man designated as my uncle, who was no blood-kin of mine, a stranger with damp eyes always drifting onto me and a mouth like a smirking scar burn. "Goodnight" they murmured as if resenting the very breath expelled for my sake. *Goodnight don't run on the stairs don't drop the candle and set the house on fire.*

4   Upstairs was a partly finished attic narrow as a tunnel with a habitable space at one end—my "room." The ceiling was covered in strips of peel-

ing insulation and so steep-slanted I could stand up only in the center. The floorboards were splintery and bare except for a small shag rug, a discard of my aunt's, laid down by my bed. The bed was another discard of my aunt's, a sofa of some mud-brown prickly fabric that pierced sheets laid upon it like whiskers sprouting through skin. But this was *a bed of my own* and I had not ever had *a bed of my own* before. Nor had I ever had *a room of my own, a door to shut against others* even if, like the attic door, it could not be locked.

5   By midnight the storm had blown itself out and the alley below had vanished in undulating dunes of snow. Everywhere snow! Glittering like mica in the moonlight! And the moon—a glowing battered-human face in a sky strangely starless, black as a well. The largest snowdrift I'd ever seen, shaped like a right-angled triangle, slanted up from the ground to the roof close outside my window. My aunt and her husband had gone to bed downstairs hours ago and the thought came to me unbidden *I can run away, no one would miss me.*

6   Along Huron Street, which my aunt's house fronted, came a snowplow, red light flashing atop its cab; otherwise there were few vehicles and these were slow-moving with groping headlights, like wounded beasts. Yet even as I watched there came a curiously shaped small vehicle to park at the mouth of the alley; and the driver, a long-legged man in a hooded jacket, climbed out. To my amazement he stomped through the snow into the alley to stand peering up toward my window, his breath steaming. Who? Who was this? *Mr. Lacey, my algebra teacher?*

7   For Valentine's Day that morning I had brought eight homemade valentines to school made of stiff red construction paper edged with paper lace, in envelopes decorated with red-ink hearts; the valentine TO MR. LACEY was my masterpiece, the largest and most ingeniously designed, interlocking hearts fashioned with a ruler and compass to resemble geometrical figures in three dimensions. HAPPY VALEN-TINE'S DAY I had neatly printed in black ink. Of course I had not signed any of the valentines and had secretly slipped them into the lockers of certain girls and boys and Mr. Lacey's onto his desk after class. I had instructed myself not to be disappointed when I received no valentines in return, not a single valentine in return, and I was not disappointed when at the end of the school day I went home without a single one: *I was not.*

8   Mr. Lacey seemed to have recognized me in the window where I stood staring, my outspread fingers on the glass bracketing my white aston-ished face, for he'd begun climbing the enormous snowdrift that lifted to the roof! How assured, how matter-of-fact, as if this were the most nat-ural thing in the world. I was too surprised to be alarmed, or even embar-rassed—my teacher would see me in a cast-off sweater of my brother's that was many sizes too large for me and splotched with oil stains, he would see my shabby little room that wasn't really a room, just part of an unfinished attic. He would know I was the one who'd left the valentine

TO MR. LACEY on his desk in stealth not daring to sign my name. *He would know who I was, how desperate for love.*

9   Once on the roof, which was steep, Mr. Lacey made his way to my window cautiously. The shingles were covered in snow, icy patches beneath. There was a rumor that Mr. Lacey was a skier, and a skater, though his lanky body did not seem the body of an athlete and in class sometimes he seemed distracted in the midst of speaking or inscribing an equation on the blackboard; as if there were thoughts more crucial to him than tenth-grade algebra at Thomas E. Dewey High School which was one of the poorest schools in the city. But now his footing was sure as a mountain goat's, his movements agile and unerring. He crouched outside my window tugging to lift it—*Erin? Make haste!*

10   I was helping to open the window which was locked in ice. It had not been opened for weeks. Already it seemed I'd pulled on my wool slacks and wound around my neck the silver muffler threaded with crimson yarn my mother had given me two or three Christmases ago. I had no coat or jacket in my room and dared not risk going downstairs to the front closet. I was very excited, fumbling, biting my lower lip, and when at last the window lurched upward the freezing air rushed in like a slap in the face. Mr. Lacey's words seemed to reverberate in my ears *Make haste, make haste!—not a moment to waste!* It was his teasing-chiding classroom manner that nonetheless meant business. Without hesitating, he grabbed both my hands—I saw that I was wearing the white angora mittens my grandmother had knitted for me long ago, which I'd believed had been lost in the fire—and hauled me through the window.

11   Mr. Lacey led me to the edge of the roof, to the snowdrift, seeking out his footprints where he knew the snow to be fairly firm, and carefully he pulled me in his wake so that I seemed to be descending a strange kind of staircase. The snow was so fresh-fallen it lifted like powder at the slightest touch or breath, glittering even more fiercely close up, as if the individual snowflakes, of such geometrical beauty and precision, contained minute sparks of flame. *Er-in, Er-in, now your courage must begin* I seemed to hear and suddenly we were on the ground and there was Mr. Lacey's Volkswagen at the mouth of the alley, headlights burning like cat's eyes and tusks of exhaust curling up behind. How many times covertly I'd tracked with my eyes that ugly-funny car shaped like a sardine can, its black chassis speckled with rust, as Mr. Lacey drove into the teachers' parking lot each morning between 8:25 A.M. and 8:35 A.M. How many times I'd turned quickly aside in terror that Mr. Lacey would see *me.* Now I stood confused at the mouth of the alley, for Huron Street and all of the city I could see was so changed, the air so terribly cold like a knifeblade in my lungs; I looked back at the darkened house wondering if my aunt might wake and discover me gone, and what then would happen?—as Mr. Lacey urged *Come, Erin, hurry! She won't even know you're gone* unless he

said *She won't ever know you're gone.* Was it true? Not long ago in algebra class I'd printed in the margin of my textbook

MR.
L.
IS
AL
WA
YS
RI
GH
T!

which I'd showed Linda Bewley across the aisle, one of the popular
tenth-grade girls, a B + student and very pretty and popular, and Linda
frowned trying to decipher the words which were meant to evoke Mr.
Lacey's pole-lean frame, but she never did get it and turned away from
me annoyed.

12   Yet it was so: Julius Lacey was always always right.

13   Suddenly I was in the cramped little car and Mr. Lacey was behind the
wheel driving north on icy Huron Street. *Where are we going?* I didn't dare
ask. When my grades in Mr. Lacey's class were less than 100 percent I was
filled with anxiety that turned my fingers and toes to ice for even if I'd
answered nearly all the questions on a test correctly *how could I know I
could answer the next question? solve the next problem? and the next?*
A nervous passion drove me to comprehend not just the immediate problem but the principle behind it, for behind everything there was an elusive
and tyrannical principle of which Mr. Lacey was the sole custodian; and I
could not know if he liked me or was bemused by me or merely tolerated
me or was in fact disappointed in me as a student who should have been
earning perfect scores at all times. He was twenty-six or -seven years old,
the youngest teacher at the school, whom many students feared and
hated, and a small group of us feared and admired. His severe, angular
face registered frequent dissatisfaction as if to indicate *Well, I'm waiting!
Waiting to be impressed! Give me one good reason to be impressed!*

14   Never had I seen the city streets so deserted. Mr. Lacey drove no more
than twenty miles an hour passing stores whose fronts were obliterated
by snow like waves frozen at their crests and through intersections where
no traffic lights burned to guide us and our only light was the Volkswagen's headlights and the glowering moon large in the sky as a fat navel
orange held at arm's length. We passed Carthage Street that hadn't yet
been plowed—a vast river of snow six feet high. We passed Templeau
Street where a city bus had been abandoned in the intersection, humped
with snow like a forlorn creature of the Great Plains. We passed Sturgeon
Street where broken electrical wires writhed and crackled in the snow
like snakes crazed with pain. We passed Childress Street where a water
main had burst and an arc of water had frozen glistening in a graceful

curve at least fifteen feet high at its crest. At Ontario Avenue Mr. Lacey turned right, the Volkswagen went into a delirious skid, Mr. Lacey put out his arm to keep me from pitching forward—*Erin, take care!* But I was safe. And on we drove.

15   Ontario Avenue, usually so crowded with traffic, was deserted as the surface of the moon. A snowplow had forged a single lane down the center. On all sides were unfamiliar shapes of familiar objects engulfed in snow and ice—parking meters? mailboxes? abandoned cars? Humanoid figures frozen in awkward, surprised postures—hunched in doorways, frozen in midstride on the sidewalk? *Look! Look at the frozen people!* I cried in a raw loud girl's voice that so frequently embarrassed me when Mr. Lacey called upon me unexpectedly in algebra class; but Mr. Lacey shrugged saying *Just snowmen, Erin—don't give them a second glance.* But I couldn't help staring at these statue-figures for I had an uneasy sense of being stared at by them in turn, through chinks in the hard-crusted snow of their heads. And I seemed to hear their faint despairing cries *Help! help us!*—but Mr. Lacey did not slacken his speed.

16   (Yet: who could have made so many "snowmen," so quickly after the storm? Children? Playing so late at night? And where were these children now?)

17   Mysteriously Mr. Lacey said *There are many survivors, Erin. In all epochs, just enough survivors.* I wanted to ask should we pray for them? pressing my hands in the angora mittens against my mouth to keep them from crying, for I knew how hopeless prayer was in such circumstances, God only helps those who don't require His help.

18   Were we headed for the lakefront?—we crossed a swaying bridge high above railroad tracks, and almost immediately after that another sway-ing bridge high above an ice-locked canal. We passed factories shut down by the snowstorm with smokestacks so tall their rims were lost in mist. We were on South Main Street now passing darkened shuttered busi-nesses, warehouses, a slaughterhouse; windowless brick buildings against whose walls snow had been driven as if sandblasted in eerie, almost legible patterns.

These were messages, I was sure!—yet I could not read them.

19   Out of the corner of my eye I watched Mr. Lacey as he drove. We were close together in the cramped car; yet at the same time I seemed to be watching us from a distance. At school there were boys who were fear-ful of Mr. Lacey yet, behind his back, sneered at him muttering what they'd like to do with him, slash his car tires, beat him up, and I felt a thrill of satisfaction *If you could see Mr. Lacey now!* for he was navigating the Volkswagen so capably along the treacherous street, past snowy hulks of vehicles abandoned by the wayside. He'd shoved back the hood of his wool jacket—how handsome he looked! Where by day he often squinted

behind his glasses, by night he seemed fully at ease. His hair was long and quill-like and of the subdued brown hue of a deer's winter coat; his eyes, so far as I could see, had a luminous coppery sheen. I recalled how at the high school Mr. Lacey was regarded with doubt and unease by the other teachers, many of whom were old enough to be his parents; he was considered arrogant because he didn't have an education degree from a state teachers' college, like the others, but a master's degree in math from the University of Buffalo where he was a part-time Ph.D. student. *Maybe I will reap where I haven't had any luck sowing* he'd once remarked to the class, standing chalk in hand at the blackboard which was covered in calculations. And this remark too had passed over our heads.

20   Now Mr. Lacey was saying as if bemused *Here, Erin—the edge. We'll go no farther in this direction.* For we were at the shore of Lake Erie— a frozen lake drifted in snow so far as the eye could see. (Yet I seemed to know how beneath the ice the water was agitated as if boiling, sinuous and black as tar.) Strewn along the beach were massive ice-boulders that glinted coldly in the moonlight. Even by day at this edge of the lake you could see only an edge of the Canadian shore, the farther western shore was lost in distance. I was in terror that Mr. Lacey out of some whim would abandon me here, for never could I have made my way back to my aunt's house in such cold.

21   But already Mr. Lacey was turning the car around, already we were driving inland, a faint tinkling music seemed to draw us, and within minutes we were in a wooded area I knew to be Delaware Park—though I'd never been there before. I had heard my classmates speak of skating parties here and had yearned to be invited to join them as I had yearned to be invited to visit the homes of certain girls, without success. *Hang on! Hang on!* Mr. Lacey said, for the Volkswagen was speeding like a sleigh on curving lanes into the interior of a deep evergreen forest. And suddenly—we were at a large oval skating rink above which strings of starry lights glittered like Christmas bulbs, where dozens, hundreds of elegantly dressed skaters circled the ice as if there had never been any snowstorm, or any snowstorm that mattered to *them.* Clearly these were privileged people, for electric power had been restored for their use and burned brilliantly, wastefully on all sides. *Oh Mr. Lacey I've never seen anything so beautiful* I said, biting my lip to keep from crying. It was a magical, wondrous place—the Delaware Park Skating Rink! Skaters on ice smooth as glass—skating round and round to gay, amplified music like that of a merry-go-round. Many of the skaters were in brightly colored clothes, handsome sweaters, fur hats, fur muffs; beautiful dogs of no breed known to me trotted alongside their masters and mistresses, pink tongues lolling in contentment. There were angel-faced girls in skaters' costumes, snug little pearl-buttoned velvet jackets and flouncy skirts to midthigh, gauzy knit stockings and kidskin boot-skates with blades that flashed like sterling silver—my heart yearned to see such skates for I'd learned to skate on rusted old skates formerly belonging to my older sisters, on a creek

near our farmhouse, in truth I had never really learned to skate, not as these skaters were skating, so without visible effort, strife, or anxiety. Entire families were skating—mothers and fathers hand in hand with small children, and older children, and white-haired elders who must have been grandparents!—and the family dog trotting along with that look of dogs laughing. There were attractive young people in groups, and couples with their arms around each other's waist, and solitary men and boys who swiftly threaded their way through the crowd unerring as undersea creatures perfectly adapted to their element. Never would I have dared join these skaters except Mr. Lacey insisted. Even as I feebly protested *Oh but I can't, Mr. Lacey—I don't know how to skate* he was pulling me to the skate rental where he secured a pair of skates for each of us; and suddenly there I was stumbling and swaying in the presence of real skaters, my ankles weak as water and my face blotched with embarrassment, oh what a spectacle—but Mr. Lacey had closed his fingers firmly around mine and held me upright, refused to allow me to fall. *Do as I do! Of course you can skate! Follow me!* So I had no choice but to follow, like an unwieldy lake barge hauled by a tugboat.

22   How loud the happy tinkling music was out on the ice, far louder than it had seemed on shore, as the lights too were brighter, nearly blinding. *Oh! Oh!* I panted in Mr. Lacey's wake, terrified of slipping and falling; breaking a wrist, an arm, a leg; terrified of falling in the paths of swift skaters whose blades flashed sharp and cruel as butcher knives. Everywhere was a harsh hissing sound of blades slicing the surface of the ice, a sound you couldn't hear on shore. I would be cut to ribbons if I fell! All my effort was required simply to stay out of the skaters' paths as they flew by, with no more awareness of me than if I were a passing shadow; the only skaters who noticed me were children, girls as well as boys, already expert skaters as young as nine or ten who glanced at me with smiles of bemusement, or disdain. *Out! out of our way! you don't belong here on our ice!* But I was stubborn too, I persevered, and after two or three times around the rink I was still upright and able to skate without Mr. Lacey's continuous vigilance, my head high and my arms extended for balance. My heart beat in giddy elation and pride. I was skating! At last! Mr. Lacey dashed off to the center of the ice where more practiced skaters performed, executing rapid circles, figure eights, dancerlike and acrobatic turns, his skate blades flashing, and a number of onlookers applauded, as I applauded, faltering but regaining my balance, skating on. I was not graceful—not by any stretch of the imagination—and I guessed I must have looked a sight, in an old baggy oil-stained sweater and rumpled wool slacks, my kinky-snarly red-brown hair in my eyes—but I wasn't quite so clumsy any longer, my ankles were getting stronger and the strokes of my skate-blades more assured, sweeping. How happy I was! How proud! I was beginning to be warm, almost feverish inside my clothes.

23   Restless as a wayward comet a blinding spotlight moved about the rink singling out skaters, among them Mr. Lacey as he spun at the very

center of the rink, an unlikely, storklike figure to be so graceful on the ice; for some reason then the spotlight abruptly shifted—to me! I was so caught by surprise I nearly tipped, and fell—I heard applause, laughter—saw faces at the edge of the rink grinning at me. Were they teasing, or sincere? Kindly, or cruel? I wanted to believe they were kindly for the rink was such a happy place but I couldn't be sure as I teetered past, arms flailing to keep my balance. I couldn't be certain but I seemed to see some of my high school classmates among the spectators; and some of my teachers; and others, adults, a caseworker from the Erie County family services department, staring at me disapprovingly. The spotlight was tormenting me: rushing at me, then falling away; allowing me to skate desperately onward, then seeking me out again swift and pitiless as a cheetah in pursuit of prey. The harshly tinkling music ended in a burst of static as if a radio had been turned violently up, then off. A sudden vicious wind rushed thin and sharp as a razor across the ice. My hair whipped in the wind, my ears were turning to ice. My fingers in the tight angora mittens were turning to ice, too. Most of the skaters had gone home, I saw to my disappointment, the better-dressed, better-mannered skaters, all the families, and the only dogs that remained were wild-eyed mongrels with bristling hackles and stumpy tails. Mr. Lacey and I skated hastily to a deserted snowswept section of the rink to avoid these dogs, and were pursued by the damned spotlight; here the ice was rippled and striated and difficult to skate on. An arm flashed at the edge of the rink, I saw a jeering white face, and an ice-packed snowball came flying to strike Mr. Lacey between his shoulder blades and shatter in pieces to the ground. Furious, his face reddening, Mr. Lacey whirled in a crouch—*Who did that? Which of you?* He spoke with his classroom authority but he wasn't in his classroom now and the boys only mocked him more insolently. They chanted something that sounded like *Lac-ey! Lac-ey! Ass-y! Assy-Asshole!* Another snowball struck him on the side of the head, sending his glasses flying and skittering along the ice. I shouted for them to *stop! stop!* and a snowball came careening past my head, another struck my arm, hard. Mr. Lacey shook his fist daring to move toward our attackers but this only unleashed a barrage of snowballs; several struck him with such force he was knocked down, a starburst of red at his mouth. Without his glasses Mr. Lacey looked young as a boy himself, dazed and helpless. On my hands and knees I crawled across the ice to retrieve his glasses, thank God there was only a hairline crack on one of the lenses. I was trembling with anger, sobbing. I was sure I recognized some of the boys, boys in my algebra class, but I didn't know their names. I crouched over Mr. Lacey asking was he all right? was he all right? seeing that he was stunned, pressing a handkerchief against his bleeding mouth. It was one of his white cotton handkerchiefs he'd take out of a pocket in class, shake ceremoniously open, and use to polish his glasses. The boys trotted away jeering and laughing. Mr. Lacey and I were alone, the only skaters remaining on the rink. Even the mongrel dogs had departed.

24   It was very cold now. Earlier that day there'd been a warning—temperatures in the Lake Erie—Lake Ontario region would drop as low that night, counting the windchill factor, as − 30 degrees Fahrenheit. The wind stirred snake-skeins of powdery snow as if the blizzard might be returning. Above the rink most of the lightbulbs had burnt out or had been shattered by the rising wind. The fresh-fallen snow that had been so purely white was now trampled and littered; dogs had urinated on it; strewn about were cigarette butts, candy wrappers, lost boots, mittens, a wool knit cap. My pretty handknit muffler lay on the ground stiffened with filth—one of the jeering boys must have taken it from me when I was distracted. I bit my lip to keep from crying, the muffler had been ruined and I refused to pick it up. Subdued, silent, Mr. Lacey and I hunted our boots amid the litter, and left our skates behind in a slovenly mound, and limped back to the Volkswagen that was the only vehicle remaining in the snowswept parking lot. Mr. Lacey swore seeing the front windshield had been cracked like a spider's web, very much as the left lens of his glasses had been cracked. Ironically he said *Now you know, Erin, where the Delaware Park Skating Rink is.*

25   The bright battered-face moon had sunk nearly to the treeline, about to be sucked into blankest night.

26   In the Bison City Diner adjacent to the Greyhound bus station on Eighth Street, Mr. Lacey and I sat across a booth from each other, and Mr. Lacey gave our order to a brassy-haired waitress in a terse mutter—*two coffees, please.* Stern and frowning to discourage the woman from inquiring after his reddened face and swollen, still bleeding mouth. And then he excused himself to use the men's room. My bladder was aching, I had to use the rest room too, but would have been too shy to slip out of the booth if Mr. Lacey hadn't gone first.

27   It was 3:20 A.M. So late! The electricity had been restored in parts of Buffalo, evidently—driving back from the park we saw streetlights burning, traffic lights again operating. Still, most of the streets were deserted; choked with snow. The only other vehicles were snowplows and trucks spewing salt on the streets. Some state maintenance workers were in the Bison Diner, which was a twenty-four-hour diner, seated at the counter, talking and laughing loudly together and flirting with the waitress who knew them. When Mr. Lacey and I came into the brightly lit room, blinking, no doubt somewhat dazed-looking, the men glanced at us curiously but made no remarks. At least, none that we could hear. Mr. Lacey touched my arm and gestured with his head for me to follow him to a booth in the farthest corner of the diner—as if it was the most natural thing in the world, Mr. Lacey and me, sliding into that very booth.

28   In the clouded mirror in the women's room I saw my face strangely flushed, eyes shining like glass. This was a face not exactly known to me; more like my older sister Janice's, yet not Janice's, either. I cupped cold water into my hands and lowered my face to the sink grateful for the

water's coolness for my skin was feverish and prickling. My hair was matted as if someone had used an eggbeater on it and my sweater, my brother's discard, was more soiled than I'd known, unless some of the stains were blood—for maybe I'd gotten Mr. Lacey's blood on me out on the ice. *Er-in Don-egal* I whispered aloud in awe, amazement. In wonder. Yes, in pride! I was fifteen years old.

29   Inspired, I searched through my pockets for my tube of raspberry lipstick, and eagerly dabbed fresh color on my mouth. The effect was instantaneous. *Barbaric!* I heard Mr. Lacey's droll voice for so he'd once alluded to female "makeup" in our class *painting faces like savages with a belief in magic.* But he'd only been joking.

30   I did believe in magic, I guess. I had to believe in something!

31   When I returned to the booth in a glow of self-consciousness there was Mr. Lacey with his face freshly washed too, and his lank hair dampened and combed. His part was on the left side of his head, and wavery. He squinted up at me—his face pinched in a quick frowning smile signaling he'd noticed the lipstick, but certainly wouldn't comment on it. Pushed a menu in my direction—*Order anything you wish, Erin, you must be starving* and I picked up the menu to read it, for in fact I was light-headed with hunger, but the print was blurry as if under water and to my alarm I could not decipher a word. In regret I shook my head no, no thank you. *No, Erin? Nothing?* Mr. Lacey asked, surprised. Elsewhere in the diner a jukebox was playing a sentimental song—"Are You Lonesome Tonight?" At the counter, amid clouds of cigarette smoke, the workmen and the brassy-haired waitress erupted in laughter.

32   It seemed that Mr. Lacey had left his bloody handkerchief in the car and, annoyed and embarrassed, was dabbing at his mouth with a wadded paper towel from the men's room. His upper lip was swollen as if a bee had stung it and one of his front teeth was loose in its socket and still leaked blood. Almost inaudibly he whispered *Damn. Damn. Damn.* His coppery-brown eye through the cracked left lens of his glasses was just perceptibly magnified and seemed to be staring at me with unusual intensity. I shrank before the man's gaze for I feared he blamed me as the source of his humiliation and pain. In truth, I *was* to blame; these things would never have happened to Julius Lacey except for me.

33   Yet when Mr. Lacey spoke it was with surprising kindness. Asking *Are you sure you want nothing to eat, Erin? Nothing, nothing—at all?*

34   I could have devoured a hamburger half raw, and a plate of greasy french fries heaped with ketchup, but there I was shaking my head *no, no thank you Mr. Lacey.*

35   Why?—I was stricken with self-consciousness, embarrassment. To eat in the presence of this man! The intimacy would have been paralyzing, like stripping myself naked before him.

36   Indeed it was awkward enough when the waitress brought us our coffee, which was black, hotly steaming in thick mugs. Once or twice in my life I'd tried to drink coffee, for everyone seemed to drink it, and the taste

was repulsive to me, so bitter! But now I lifted the mug to my lips and sipped timidly at the steaming hot liquid black as motor oil. Seeing that Mr. Lacey disdained to add dairy cream or sugar to his coffee, I did not add any to my own. I was already nervous and almost at once my heart gave odd erratic beats and my pulse quickened.

37   One of my lifetime addictions, to this bitterly black steaming-hot liquid, would begin at this hour, in such innocence.

38   Mr. Lacey was saying with an air of reluctance, finality *In every equation there is always an x-factor, and in every x-factor there is the possibility, if not the probability, of tragic misunderstanding.* Out of his jacket pocket he'd taken, to my horror, a folded sheet of paper—red construction paper!—and was smoothing it out on the tabletop. I stared, I was speechless with chagrin. *You must not offer yourself in such a fashion, not even in secret, anonymously* Mr. Lacey said with a teacher's chiding frown. *The valentine heart is the female genitals, you will be misinterpreted.*

39   There was a roaring in my ears confused with music from the jukebox. The bitter black coffee scalded my throat and began to race along my veins. Words choked me *I'm sorry. I don't know what that is. Don't know what you're speaking of. Leave me alone, I hate you!* But I could not speak, just sat there shrinking to make myself as small as possible in Mr. Lacey's eyes staring with a pretense of blank dumb ignorance at the elaborate geometrical valentine TO MR. LACEY I had made with such hope the other night in the secrecy of my room, knowing I should not commit such an audacious act yet knowing, with an almost unbearable excitement, like one bringing a lighted match to flammable material, that I was going to do it.

40   Resentfully I said *I guess you know about me, my family. I guess there aren't any secrets.*

41   Mr. Lacey said *Yes, Erin. There are no secrets. But it's our prerogative not to speak of them if we choose.* Carefully he was refolding the valentine to return to his pocket, which I interpreted as a gesture of forgiveness. He said *There is nothing to be ashamed of, Erin. In you, or in your family.*

42   Sarcastically I said *There isn't?*

43   Mr. Lacey said *The individuals who are your mother and father came together out of all the universe to produce you. That's how you came into being, there was no other way.*

44   I couldn't speak, I was struck dumb. Wanting to protest, to laugh but could not. Hot tears ran down my cheeks.

45   Mr. Lacey persisted, gravely *And you love them, Erin. Much more than you love me.*

46   Mutely I shook my head *no.*

47   Mr. Lacey said, with his air of completing an algebra problem on the blackboard, in a tone of absolute finality *Yes. And we'll never speak of it again after tonight. In fact, of any of this*—making an airy magician's

gesture that encompassed not just the Bison Diner but the city of Buffalo, the very night—*ever again.*

48 And so it was, we never did speak of it again. Our adventure that night following Valentine's Day 1959, ever again.

49 Next Monday at school, and all the days, and months, to come, Mr. Lacey and I maintained our secret. My heart burned with a knowledge I could not speak! But I was quieter, less nervous in class than I'd ever been; as if, overnight, I'd matured by years. Mr. Lacey behaved exactly, I think, as he'd always behaved toward me; no one could ever have guessed, in any wild flight of imagination, the bond between us. My grades hovered below 100 percent, for Mr. Lacey was surely one to wish to retain the power of giving tests no student could complete to perfection. With a wink he said *Humility goeth in place of a fall, Erin.* And in September when I returned for eleventh grade, Julius Lacey who might have been expected to teach solid geometry to my class was gone: returned to graduate school, we were told. Vanished forever from our lives.

50 All this was far in the future! That night, I could not have foreseen any of it. Nor how, over thirty years later, on the eve of Valentine's Day I would remove from its hiding place at the bottom of a bureau drawer a bloodstained man's handkerchief initialed *JNL,* fine white cotton yellowed with time, and smooth its wrinkles with the edge of my hand, and lift it to my face like Veronica her veil.

51 By the time Mr. Lacey and I left the Bison Diner the light there had become blinding and the jukebox music almost deafening. My head would echo for days *lonely? lonely? lonely?* Mr. Lacey drove us hurriedly south on Huron Street passing close beneath factory smokestacks rimmed at their tops with bluish-orange flame, spewing clouds of gray smoke that, upon impact with the freezing wind off Lake Erie, coalesced into fine gritty particles and fell back to earth like hail. These particles drummed on the roof, windshield, and hood of the Volkswagen, bouncing and ricocheting off, denting the metal. *God damn* Mr. Lacey swore softly *will You never cease!*

52 Abruptly then we were home. At my aunt's shabby woodframe bungalow at 3998 Huron Street, Buffalo, New York, that might have been any one of dozens, hundreds, even thousands of similar woodframe one-and-a-half-story bungalows in working-class neighborhoods of the city. The moon had vanished as if it had never been and the sky was depthless as a black paper cutout, but a streetlamp illuminated the mouth of the snowed-in alley and the great snowdrift in the shape of a right-angled triangle lifting to the roof below my window. *What did I promise, Erin?—no one knows you were ever gone* Mr. Lacey's words seemed to reverberate in my head without his speaking aloud. With relief I saw that the downstairs windows of the house were all darkened but there was a faint flickering light up in my room—the candle still burning, after all these hours. Gripping my hand tightly, Mr. Lacey led me up the snowdrift as up a treacherous stairs, fitting his boots to the footprints he'd originally made, and I

followed suit, desperate not to slip and fall. *Safe at home, safe at home!* Mr. Lacey's words sounded close in my ears, unless it was *Safe alone, safe alone!* I heard. Oh! the window was frozen shut again! so the two of us tugged, tugged, tugged, Mr. Lacey with good-humored patience until finally ice shattered, the window lurched up to a height of perhaps twelve inches. I'd begun to cry, a sorry spectacle, and my eyelashes had frozen within seconds in the bitter cold so Mr. Lacey laughed kissing my left eye, and then my right eye, and the lashes were thawed, and I heard *Goodbye, Erin!* as I climbed back through the window.

Questions for Discussion

1. What kinds of relationships have characterized Erin's home life? How well does she get along with her aunt and her aunt's husband?

2. How does Erin relate to her classmates? Why is she *"desperate for love"?*

3. What do the students and other teachers think of Mr. Lacey? How do they treat him? Why?

4. Erin says of Mr. Lacey, "behind everything there was an elusive and tyrannical principle of which Mr. Lacey was the sole custodian." What does she mean? Why is Erin attracted to Mr. Lacey? What do she and Mr. Lacey have in common?

5. What does Mr. Lacey know about Erin that you would not expect him to know?

6. Did Erin's evening with Mr. Lacey actually happen? Or was it a dream? What details in the story suggest that it might actually have happened? What details suggest it was a dream?

7. What does Erin learn from her evening with Mr. Lacey? How does she mature as a result of her experience?

8. What precisely is Mr. Lacey's role in Erin's life? Explain whether he is good, evil, or both?

"Don't You Know Who I Am?"
The Grotesque in Oates's
"Where Are You Going, Where Have You Been?"[1]

Joyce M. Wegs

Joyce Carol Oates's ability to absorb and then to transmit in her fiction the terror which is often a part of living in America today has been frequently noted and admired. For instance, Walter Sullivan praises her skill by noting that "horror resides in the transformation of what we know best, the intimate and comfortable details of our lives made sud-

[1]Reprinted with permission from *Journal of Narrative Technique* 5 (1975): 66–72.

denly threatening."[2] Although he does not identify it as such, Sullivan's comment aptly describes a classic instance of a grotesque intrusion; a familiar world suddenly appears alien. Oates frequently evokes the grotesque in her fiction, drawing upon both its tranditional or demonic and its contemporary or psychological manifestations.[3] In the prize-winning short story, "Where Are You Going, Where Have You Been?", Oates utilizes the grotesque in many of its forms to achieve a highly skill-ful integration of the multiple levels of the story and, in so doing, to sug-gest a transcendent reality which reaches beyond surface realism to evoke the simultaneous mystery and reality of the contradictions of the human heart. Full of puzzling and perverse longings, the heart persists in mixing lust and love, life and death, good and evil. Oates's teenage protagonist, Connie, discovers that her dream love-god also wears the face of lust, evil and death.

Centering the narrative on the world of popular teenage music and culture, Oates depicts the tawdry world of drive-in restaurants and shopping plazas blaring with music with a careful eye for authentic sur-face detail. However, her use of popular music as a thematic referent is typical also of her frequent illumination of the illusions and grotesquely false values which may arise from excessive devotion to such aspects of popular culture as rock music, movies, and romance magazines. In all of her fiction as in this story, she frequently employs a debased reli-gious imagery to suggest the gods which modern society has substi-tuted for conventional religion. Oates delineates the moral poverty of Connie, her fifteen-year-old protagonist, by imaging a typical evening Connie spends at a drive-in restaurant as a grotesquely parodied reli-gious pilgrimage. Left by her friend's father to stroll at the shopping cen-ter or go to a movie, Connie and her girlfriend immediately cross the highway to the restaurant frequented by older teenagers. A grotesque parody of a church, the building is bottle-shaped and has a grinning boy holding a hamburger aloft on top of it. Unconscious of any ludicrous-ness, Connie and her friend enter it as if going into a "sacred building"[4] which will give them "what haven and blessing they yearned for." (31) It is the music which is "always in the background, like music at a church service" (31) that has invested this "bright-lit, fly-infested" (31) place with such significance. Indeed, throughout the story the music is given an almost mystical character, for it evokes in Connie a mysteri-ous pleasure, a "glow of slow-pulsed joy that seemed to rise mysteri-ously out of the music itself." (33)

[2]Walter Sullivan, "The Artificial Demon: Joyce Carol Oates and the Dimensions of the Real," *The Hollins Critic* 9.4 (Dec., 1972): 2.

[3]Joyce Markert Wegs, "The Grotesque in Some American Novels of the Nineteen-Six-ties: Ken Kesey, Joyce Carol Oates, Sylvia Plath," Diss., University of Illinois, 1973.

[4]Joyce Carol Oates, "Where Are You Going, Where Have You Been?" *The Wheel of Love* (1970; rpt. Greenwich, CT: Fawcett, 1972), 31. All subsequent references to the story appear within parentheses in the text.

Although the story undoubtedly has a moral dimension,[5] Oates does not take a judgmental attitude toward Connie. In fact, much of the terror of the story comes from the recognition that there must be thousands of Connies. By carefully including telltale phrases, Oates demonstrates in an understated fashion why Connies exist. Connie's parents, who seem quite typical, have disqualified themselves as moral guides for her. At first reading, the reader may believe Connie's mother to be concerned about her daughter's habits, views, and friends; but basically their arguments are little more than a "pretense of exasperation, a sense that they [... are] tugging and struggling over something of little value to either of them." (32). Connie herself is uncertain of her mother's motives for constantly picking at her; she alternates between a view that her mother's harping proceeds from jealousy of Connie's good looks now that her own have faded (29) and a feeling that her mother really prefers her over her plain older sister June because she is prettier. (32) In other words, to Connie and her mother, real value lies in beauty. Connie's father plays a small role in her life, but by paralleling repeated phrases, Oates suggests that this is precisely the problem. Because he does not "bother talking much" (30) to his family, he can hardly ask the crucial parental questions, "Where are you going?" or "Where have you been?" The moral indifference of the entire adult society is underscored by Oates's parallel description of the father of Connie's friend, who also "never [... bothers] to ask" what they did when he picks up the pair at the end of one of their evenings out. Similarly, on Sunday morning, "none of them bothered with church," (33) not even that supposed paragon, June.

Since her elders do not bother about her, Connie is left defenseless against the temptations represented by Arnold Friend. A repeated key phrase emphasizes her helplessness. As she walks through the parking lot of the restaurant with Eddie, she can not "help but" (31) look about happily, full of joy in a life characterized by casual pickups and constant music. When she sees Arnold in a nearby car, she looks away, but her instinctive flirtatiousness triumphs and she can not "help but" (31) look back. Later, like Lot's wife leaving Sodom and Gomorrah, she cannot "help but look back" (32) at the plaza and drive-in as her friend's father drives them home. In Connie's case, the consequences of the actions she cannot seem to help are less biblically swift to occur and can not be simply labeled divine retribution.

Since music is Connie's religion, its values are hers also. Oates does not include the lyrics to any popular songs here, for any observer of contemporary America could surely discern the obvious link between Connie's high esteem for romantic love and youthful beauty and the lyrics of scores of hit tunes. The superficiality of Connie's values becomes terrifyingly apparent when Arnold Friend, the external embodiment of the teenage ideal celebrated in popular songs, appears at Connie's home in the country one Sunday afternoon when she is home alone, listening to

[5]See Walter Sullivan, "Where Have All the Flowers Gone?: The Short Story in Search of Itself," *Sewanee Review* 78. 3 (Summer, 1970): 537.]

music and drying her hair. It is no accident that Arnold's clothes, car, speech, and taste in music reflect current teenage chic almost exactly, for they constitute part of a careful disguise intended to reflect Arnold's self-image as an accomplished youthful lover.

Suspense mounts in the story as the reader realizes along with Connie that Arnold is not a teenager and is really thirty or more. Each part of his disguise is gradually revealed to be grotesquely distorted in some way. His shaggy black hair, "crazy as a wig," (34) is evidently really a wig. The mask-like appearance of his face has been created by applying a thick coat of makeup; however, he has carelessly omitted his throat. (41) Even his eyelashes appear to be made-up, but with some tarlike material. In his clothing, his disguise appears more successful, for Connie approves of the way he dresses, as "all of them dressed." (36) in tight jeans, boots, and pullover. When he walks, however, Connie realizes that the runty Arnold, conscious that the ideal teenage dream lover is tall, has stuffed his boots; the result is, however, that he can hardly walk and staggers ludicrously. Attempting to bow, he almost falls. Similarly, the gold jalopy covered with teenage slang phrases seems authentic until Connie notices that one of them is no longer in vogue. Even his speech is not his own, for it recalls lines borrowed from disc jockeys, teenage slang, and lines from popular songs. Arnold's strange companion, Ellie Oscar, is just as grotesque as Arnold. Almost totally absorbed in listening to music and interrupting this activity only to offer threatening assistance to Arnold, Ellie is no youth either; he has the "face of a forty-year-old baby." (39) Although Arnold has worked out his disguise with great care, he soon loses all subtlety in letting Connie know of his evil intentions; he is not simply crazy but a criminal with plans to rape and probably to murder Connie.

However, Arnold is far more than a grotesque portrait of a psychopathic killer masquerading as a teenager; he also has all the traditional sinister traits of that arch-deceiver and source of grotesque terror, the devil. As is usual with Satan, he is in disguise; the distortions in his appearance and behavior suggest not only that his identity is faked but also hint at his real self. Equating Arnold and Satan is not simply a gratuitous connection designed to exploit traditional demonic terror, for the early pages of the story explicitly prepare for this linking by portraying popular music and its values as Connie's perverted version of religion. When Arnold comes up the drive, her first glance makes Connie believe that a teenage boy with his jalopy, the central figure of her religion, has arrived; therefore, she murmurs "Christ, Christ" (34) as she wonders about how her newly-washed hair looks. When the car—a parodied golden chariot?—stops, a horn sounds "as if this were a signal Connie knew." (34) On one level, the horn honks to announce the "second coming" of Arnold, a demonic Day of Judgment. Although Connie never specifically recognizes Arnold as Satan, her first comment to him both hints at his infernal origins and faithfully reproduces teenage idiom: "Who the *hell* do you think you are?" (emphasis mine, 34) When he introduces himself, his name too hints at his identity, for "friend" is uncomfortably close to "fiend"; his initials could well stand for Arch Fiend. The frightened Connie sees Arnold as "only half real"; (39) he "had driven up her driveway all right but had come from nowhere before that and belonged nowhere." (39) Especially supernatural is his mysterious knowledge about her, her family, and her friends. At one point, he even seems to be able to see all the way to the barbecue which Connie's family is attending and to get a clear vision of what all the guests are doing. Typical of his ambiguous roles is his hint that he had something to do with the death of the old woman who lived down the road. It is never clear whether Arnold has killed her, has simply heard of her death, or knows about it in his devil role of having come to take her away to hell. Although Arnold has come to take Connie away, in his traditional role as evil spirit, he may not cross a threshold uninvited; he repeatedly mentions that he is not going to come in after Connie, and he never does. Instead, he lures Connie out to him. Part of his success may be attributed to his black magic in having put his sign on her—X for victim. (37–38) Because the devil is not a mortal being, existing as he does in all ages, it is not surprising that he slips in remembering what slang terms are in vogue. Similarly, his foolish attempt at a bow may result from a mixup in temporal concepts of the ideal lover. In addition, his clumsy bow may be due to the fact that it must be difficult to manipulate boots if one has cloven feet!

Although Oates attempts to explain the existence of Connie, she makes no similar effort to explain the existence of Arnold, for that would constitute an answer to the timeless and insoluble problem of evil in the world. As this story shows, Oates would agree with Pope Paul VI's recent commentary on the "terrible reality" of evil in the world, but she would not, I feel sure, endorse his view of this evil as being literally embodied in a specific being. Pope Paul describes evil as "not merely a lack of something, but an effective agent, a living spiritual being, perverted and perverting. A terrible reality. Mysterious and frightening."[6] Oates's description of her own views on religion is in terms strikingly similar to the language used by Pope Paul. To her, religion is a "kind of psychological manifestation of deep powers, deep imaginative, mysterious powers, which are always with us, and what has in the past been called supernatural. I would prefer simply to call natural. However, though these things are natural, they are still inaccessible and cannot be understood, cannot be controlled."[7] Thus, although Arnold is clearly a symbolic Satan, he also functions on a psychological level.

On this level, Arnold Friend is the incarnation of Connie's unconscious erotic desires and dreams, but in uncontrollable nightmare form. When she first sees Arnold in the drive-in, she instinctively senses his sinister

[6]Andrew M. Greeley, "The Devil, You Say," *The New York Times Magazine*, 4 Feb., 1973, p. 26, quotes an address by Pope Paul on 15 Nov. 1972, as reported in the Vatican newspaper.

[7]Linda Kuehl, "An Interview with Joyce Carol Oates," *Commonweal* 91 (5 Dec. 1969): 308.

attraction, for she cannot "help glancing back" (31) at him. Her "trashy daydreams" (30) are largely filled with blurred recollections of the caresses of the many boys she has dated. That her dreams are a kind of generalized sexual desire—although Connie does not consciously identify them as such—is made evident by Oates's description of Connie's summer dreams: "But all the boys fell back and dissolved into a single face that was not even a face but an idea, a feeling, mixed up with the urgent insistent pounding of the music and the humid night air of July." (32) What is frightening about Arnold is that he voices and makes explicit her own sexual desires; teenage boys more usually project their similar message with "that sleepy dreamy smile that all the boys used to get across ideas they didn't want to put into words." (38) Connie's reaction to his bluntness is one of horror: "People don't talk like that, you're crazy." (40)

Connie's fear drives her into a grotesque separation of mind from body in which her unconscious self takes over and betrays her. Terror-stricken, she cannot even make her weak fingers dial the police; she can only scream into the phone. In the same way that she is Arnold's prisoner, locked inside the house he alternately threatens to knock down or burn down, she is also a prisoner of her own body: "A noisy sorrowful wailing rose all about her and she was locked inside it the way she was locked inside this house." (44) Finally, her conscious mind rejects any connection with her body and its impulses; her heart seems "nothing that was hers" "but just a pounding, living thing inside this body that wasn't really hers either." (45) In a sense, her body with its puzzling desires "decides" to go with Arnold although her rational self is terrified of him: "She watched herself push the door slowly open as if she were back safe somewhere in the other doorway, watching this body and this head of long hair moving out into the sunlight where Arnold Friend waited." (45)

Oates encourages the reader to look for multiple levels in this story and to consider Arnold and Connie at more than face value by her repeated emphasis on the question of identity. The opening of the story introduces the concept to which both Connie and her mother seem to subscribe—being pretty means being someone. In fact, her mother's acid questions as she sees Connie at her favorite activity of mirror-gazing— "Who are you? You think you're so pretty?" (29)—also introduce the converse of this idea, namely, that those who lack physical beauty have no identity. As does almost everything in the story, everything about Connie has "two sides to it." (30) However, Connie's nature, one for at home and one for "anywhere that was not home," (30) is simple in comparison to that of Arnold. Connie's puzzled questions at first query what role Arnold thinks he is playing: "Who the hell do you think you are?" (34) Then she realizes that he sees himself all too literally as the man of her dreams, and she becomes more concerned about knowing his real identity. By the time that Arnold asks, "Don't you know who I am?" (42) Connie realizes that it is no longer a simple question of whether he is a "jerk" (35) or someone worth her attention but of just how crazy he is. By the end she knows him to be a murderer, for she realizes that she will never see her family again. (44) However, only the reader sees Arnold's Satan identity. Connie's gradual realization of Arnold's identity brings with it a recognition of the actual significance of physical beauty: Arnold is indeed someone to be concerned about, even if he is no handsome youth. At the conclusion Connie has lost all identity except that of victim, for Arnold's half-sung sigh about her blue eyes ignores the reality of her brown ones. In Arnold's view, Connie's personal identity is totally unimportant.

Dedicated to contemporary balladeer Bob Dylan, this story in a sense represents Oates's updated prose version of a ballad in which a demon lover carries away his helpless victim. By adding modern psychological insights, she succeeds in revealing the complex nature of the victim of a grotesque intrusion by an alien force; on one level, the victim actually welcomes and invites this demonic visitation. Like Bob Dylan, she grafts onto the ballad tradition a moral commentary which explores but does not solve the problems of the evils of our contemporary society; an analogous Dylan ballad is his "It's a Hard Rain's a Gonna' Fall." Even the title records not only the ritual parental questions but also suggests that there is a moral connection between the two questions: where Connie goes is related to where she has been. Oates does not judge Connie in making this link, however; Connie is clearly not in complete control over where she has been. The forces of her society, her family, and her self combine to make her fate inescapable.

THE PIED PIPER OF TUCSON: HE CRUISED IN A GOLDEN CAR, LOOKING FOR THE ACTION[1]   (1966)

DON MOSER

Hey, c'mon babe, follow me.
I'm the Pied Piper, follow me.
I'm the Pied Piper.
And I'll show you where it's at

—POPULAR SONG, TUCSON, WINTER 1965

At dusk in Tucson, as the stark, yellow-flared mountains begin to blur against the sky, the golden car slowly cruises Speedway. Smoothly it rolls down the long, divided avenue, past the supermarkets, the gas stations and the motels; past the twist joints, the sprawling drive-in restaurants. The car slows for an intersection, stops, then pulls away again. The exhaust mutters against the pavement as the young man driving takes the machine swiftly, expertly through the gears. A car pulls even with him; the teenage girls in the front seat laugh, wave and call his name. The young man glances toward the rearview mirror, turned always so that he can look at his own reflection, and he appraises himself.

[1]*Life*, March 4, 1966.

The face is his own creation: the hair dyed a raven black, the skin darkened to a deep tan with pancake make-up, the lips whitened, the whole effect heightened by a mole he has painted on one cheek. But the deep-set blue eyes are all his own. Beautiful eyes, the girls say.

Approaching the Hi-Ho, the teenagers' nightclub, he backs off on the accelerator, then slowly cruises on past Johnie's Drive-in. There the cars are beginning to orbit and accumulate in the parking lot—neat sharp cars with deep-throated mufflers and Maltese-cross decals on the windows. But it's early yet. Not much going on. The driver shifts up again through the gears, and the golden car slides away along the glitter and gimcrack of Speedway. Smitty keeps looking for the action.

Whether the juries in the two trials decide that Charles Howard Schmid Jr. did or did not brutally murder Alleen Rowe, Gretchen Fritz, and Wendy Fritz has from the beginning seemed of almost secondary importance to the people of Tucson. They are not indifferent. But what disturbs them far beyond the question of Smitty's guilt or innocence are the revelations about Tucson itself that have followed on the disclosure of the crimes. Starting with the bizarre circumstances of the killings and on through the ugly fragments of the plot—which in turn hint at other murders as yet undiscovered, at teenage sex, blackmail, even connections with the *Cosa Nostra*—they have had to view their city in a new and unpleasant light. The fact is that Charles Schmid—who cannot be dismissed as a freak, an aberrant of no consequence—had for years functioned successfully as a member, even a leader of the yeastiest stratum of Tucson's teenage society.

As a high school student Smitty had been, as classmates remember, an outsider—but not that far outside. He was small but he was a fine athlete, and in his last year—1960—he was a state gymnastics champion. His grades were poor, but he was in no trouble to speak of until his senior year, when he was suspended for stealing tools from a welding class.

But Smitty never really left the school. After his suspension he hung around waiting to pick up kids in a succession of sharp cars which he drove fast and well. He haunted all the teenage hangouts along Speedway, including the bowling alleys and the public swimming pool—and he put on spectacular diving exhibitions for girls far younger than he.

At the time of his arrest last November, Charles Schmid was twenty-three years old. He wore face make-up and dyed his hair. He habitually stuffed three or four inches of old rags and tin cans into the bottoms of his high-topped boots to make himself taller than his five-foot-three and stumbled about so awkwardly while walking that some people thought he had wooden feet. He pursed his lips and let his eyelids droop in order to emulate his idol, Elvis Presley. He bragged to girls he knew a hundred ways to make love, that he ran dope, that he was a Hell's Angel. He talked about being a rough customer in a fight (he was, though he was rarely in one), and he always carried in his pocket tiny bottles of salt and pepper, which he said he used to blind his opponents. He liked to use highfalutin language and had a favorite saying, "I can manifest my neurotical emotions, emancipate an epicureal instinct, and elaborate on my heterosexual tendencies."

He occasionally shocked even those who thought they knew him well. A friend says he once saw Smitty tie a string to a tail of his pet cat, swing it around his head and beat it bloody against a wall. Then he turned calmly and asked, "You feel compassion—why?"

Yet even while Smitty tried to create an exalted, heroic image of himself, he had worked on a pitiable one. "He thrived on feeling sorry for himself," recalls a friend, "and making others feel sorry for him." At various times Smitty told intimates that he had leukemia and didn't have long to live. He claimed that he was adopted, that his real name was Angel Rodriguez, that his father was a "bean" (local slang for Mexican, an inferior race in Smitty's view), and that his mother was a famous lawyer who would have nothing to do with him.

He had a nice car. He had plenty of money from his parents, who ran a nursing home, and he was always glad to spend it on anyone who'd listen to him. He had a pad of his own where he threw parties and he had impeccable manners. He was always willing to help a friend and he would send flowers to girls who were ill. He was older and more mature than most of his friends. He knew where the action was, and if he wore make-up—well, at least he was *different*.

Some of the older kids—those who worked, who had something else to do—thought Smitty was a creep. But to the youngsters—to the bored and the lonely, to the dropout and the delinquent, to the young girls with beehive hairdos and tight pants they didn't quite fill out, and to the boys with acne and no jobs—to these people, Smitty was a kind of folk hero. Nutty maybe, but at least more dramatic, more theatrical, more *interesting* than anyone else in their lives; a semi-ludicrous, sexy-eyed pied-piper who, stumbling along in his rag-stuffed boots, led them up and down Speedway.

On the evening of May 31, 1964, Alleen Rowe prepared to go to bed early. She had to be in class by six a.m. and she had an examination the next day. Alleen was a pretty girl of fifteen, a better-than-average student who talked about going to college and becoming an oceanographer. She was also a sensitive child—given to reading romantic novels and taking long walks in the desert at night. Recently she had been going through a period of adolescent melancholia, often talking with her mother, a nurse, about death. She would, she hoped, be some day reincarnated as a cat.

On this evening, dressed in a black bathing suit and thongs, her usual costume around the house, she had watched the Beatles on TV and had tried to teach her mother to dance the Frug. Then she took her bath, washed her hair, and came out to kiss her mother good night. Norma Rowe, an attractive, womanly divorcée, was somehow moved by the girl's clean fragrance and said, "You smell so good—are you wearing perfume?"

"No, Mom," the girl answered, laughing, "it's just me."

A little later Mrs. Rowe looked in on her daughter, found her apparently sleeping peacefully, and then left for her job as a night nurse in a Tucson hospital. She had no premonition of danger, but she had lately been concerned about Alleen's friendship with a neighbor girl named Mary French.

Mary and Alleen had been spending a good deal of time together, smoking and giggling and talking girl talk in the Rowe backyard. Norma Rowe did not approve. She particularly did not approve of Mary French's friends, a tall, gangling boy of nineteen named John Saunders and another named Charles Schmid. She had seen Smitty racing up and down the street in his car and once, when he came to call on Alleen and found her not at home, he had looked at Norma so menacingly with his "pinpoint eyes" that she had been frightened.

Her daughter, on the other hand, seemed to have mixed feelings about Smitty. "He's creepy," she once told her mother, "he just makes me crawl. But he can be nice when he wants to."

At any rate, later that night—according to Mary French's sworn testimony—three friends arrived at Alleen Rowe's house: Smitty, Mary French, and Saunders. Smitty had frequently talked with Mary French about killing the Rowe girl by hitting her over the head with a rock. Mary French tapped on Alleen's window and asked her to come out and drink beer with them. Wearing a shift over her bathing suit, she came willingly enough.

Schmid's two accomplices were strange and pitiable creatures. Each of them was afraid of Smitty, yet each was drawn to him. As a baby, John Saunders had been so afflicted with allergies that scabs encrusted his entire body. To keep him from scratching himself his parents had tied his hands and feet to the crib each night, and when eventually he was cured he was so conditioned that he could not go to sleep without being bound hand and foot.

Later, a scrawny boy with poor eyesight ("Just a skinny little body with a big head on it"), he was taunted and bullied by larger children; in turn he bullied those who were smaller. He also suffered badly from asthma and he had few friends. In high school he was a poor student and constantly in minor trouble.

Mary French, nineteen, was—to put it straight—a frump. Her face, which might have been pretty, seemed somehow lumpy, her body shapeless. She was not dull but she was always a poor student, and she finally had simply stopped going to high school. She was, a friend remembers, "fantastically in love with Smitty. She just sat home and waited while he went out with other girls."

Now, with Smitty at the wheel, the four teen-agers headed for the desert, which begins out Golf Links Road. It is spooky country, dry and empty, the yellow sand clotted with cholla and mesquite and stunted, strangely green palo verde trees, and the great humanoid saguaro that hulk against the sky. Out there at night you can hear the yip and ki-yi of coyotes, the piercing screams of wild creatures—cats, perhaps.

According to Mary French, they got out of the car and walked down into a wash, where they sat on the sand and talked for a while, the four of them. Schmid and Mary then started back to the car. Before they got there, they heard a cry and Schmid turned back toward the wash. Mary went on to the car and sat in it alone. After forty-five minutes, Saunders appeared and said Smitty wanted her to come back down. She refused, and Saunders went away. Five or ten minutes later, Smitty showed up. "He got into the car," says Mary, "and he said, 'We killed her. I love you very much.' He kissed me. He was breathing real hard and seemed excited." Then Schmid got a shovel from the trunk of the car and they returned to the wash. "She was lying on her back and there was blood on her face and head," Mary French testified. Then the three of them dug a shallow grave and put the body in it and covered it up. Afterwards, they wiped Schmid's car clean of Alleen's fingerprints.

More than a year passed. Norma Rowe had reported her daughter missing and the police searched for her—after a fashion. At Mrs. Rowe's insistence they picked up Schmid, but they had no reason to hold him. The police, in fact, assumed that Alleen was just one more of Tucson's runaways.

Norma Rowe, however, had become convinced that Alleen had been killed by Schmid, although she left her kitchen light on every night in case Alleen did come home. She badgered the police and she badgered the sheriff until the authorities began to dismiss her as a crank. She began to imagine a high-level conspiracy against her. She wrote the state attorney general, the FBI, the U.S. Department of Health, Education and Welfare. She even contacted a New Jersey mystic, who said she could see Alleen's body out in the desert under a big tree.

Ultimately Norma Rowe started her own investigation, questioning Alleen's friends, poking around, dictating her findings to a tape recorder; she even tailed Smitty at night, following him in her car, scared stiff that he might spot her.

Schmid, during this time, acquired a little house of his own. There he held frequent parties, where people sat around amid his stacks of *Playboy* magazines, playing Elvis Presley records and drinking beer.

He read Jules Feiffer's novel, *Harry, the Rat with Women,* and said that his ambition was to be like Harry and have a girl commit suicide over him. Once, according to a friend, he went to see a minister, who gave him a Bible and told him to read the first three chapters of John. Instead Schmid tore the pages out and burned them in the street. "Religion is a farce," he announced. He started an upholstery business with some friends, called himself "founder and president," but then failed to put up the money he promised and the venture was short-lived.

He decided he liked blondes best, and took to dyeing the hair of various teenage girls he went around with. He went out and bought two imitation diamonds for about $13 apiece and then engaged himself, on the same day, both to Mary French and to a fifteen-year-old girl named Kathy Morath. His plan, he confided to a friend, was to put each of the girls to work and have them deposit their salaries in a bank account held jointly with him. Mary French did indeed go to work in the convalescent home Smitty's parents operated. When their bank account was fat enough, Smitty withdrew the money and bought a tape recorder.

By this time Smitty also had a girl from a higher social stratum than he usually was involved with. She was Gretchen Fritz, daughter of a prominent Tucson heart surgeon. Gretchen was a pretty, thin, nervous girl of seventeen with a knack for trouble. A teacher described her as "erratic, subversive, a psychopathic liar."

At the horsy private school she attended for a time she was a misfit. She not only didn't care about horses, but she shocked her classmates by telling them they were foolish for going out with boys without getting paid for it. Once she even committed the unpardonable social sin of turning up at a formal dance party accompanied by boys wearing what was described as beatnik dress. She cut classes, she was suspected of stealing and when, in the summer before her senior year, she got into trouble with juvenile authorities for her role in an attempted theft at a liquor store, the headmaster suggested she not return and then recommended she get psychiatric treatment.

Charles Schmid saw Gretchen for the first time at a public swimming pool in the summer of 1964. He met her by the simple expedient of following her home, knocking on the door and, when she answered, saying, "Don't I know you?" They talked for an hour. Thus began a fierce and stormy relationship. A good deal of what authorities know of the development of this relationship comes from the statements of a spindly scarecrow of a young man who wears pipestem trousers and Beatle boots: Richard Bruns. At the time Smitty was becoming involved with Gretchen, Bruns was eighteen years old. He had served two terms in the reformatory at Fort Grant. He had been in and out of trouble all his life, had never fit in anywhere. Yet, although he never went beyond the tenth grade in school and his credibility on many counts is suspect, he is clearly intelligent and even sensitive. He was, for a time, Smitty's closest friend and confidant, and he is today one of the mainstays of the state's case against Smitty. His story:

"He and Gretchen were always fighting," says Bruns. "She didn't want him to drink or go out with the guys or go out with other girls. She wanted him to stay home, call her on the phone, be punctual. First she would get suspicious of him, then he'd get suspicious of her. They were made for each other."

Their mutual jealousy led to sharp and continual arguments. Once she infuriated him by throwing a bottle of shoe polish on his car. Another time she was driving past Smitty's house and saw him there with some other girls. She jumped out of her car and began screaming. Smitty took off into the house, out the back, and climbed a tree in his backyard.

His feelings for her were an odd mixture of hate and adoration. He said he was madly in love with her, but he called her a whore. She would let Smitty in her bedroom window at night. Yet he wrote an anonymous letter to the Tucson Health Department accusing her of having venereal disease and spreading it about town. But Smitty also went to enormous lengths to impress Gretchen, once shooting holes through the windows of his car and telling her that thugs, from whom he was protecting her, had fired at him. So Bruns described the relationship.

On the evening of August 16, 1965, Gretchen Fritz left the house with her little sister Wendy, a friendly, lively thirteen-year-old, to go to a drive-in movie. Neither girl ever came home again. Gretchen's father, like Alleen Rowe's mother, felt sure that Charles Schmid had something to do with his daughters' disappearance, and eventually he hired Bill Heilig, a private detective, to handle the case. One of Heilig's men soon found Gretchen's red compact car parked behind a motel, but the police continued to assume that the girls had joined the ranks of Tucson's runaways.

About a week after Gretchen disappeared, Bruns was at Smitty's home. "We were sitting in the living room," Bruns recalls. "He was sitting on the sofa and I was in the chair by the window and we got on the subject of Gretchen. He said, 'You know I killed her?' I said I didn't, and he said, 'You know where?' I said no. He said, 'I did it here in the living room. First I killed Gretchen, then Wendy was still going *"huh, huh, huh,"* so I [... here Bruns showed how Smitty made a garroting gesture.] Then I took the bodies and put them in the trunk of the car. I put the bodies in the most obvious place I could think of because I just didn't care any more. Then I ditched the car and wiped it clean."

Bruns was not particularly upset by Smitty's story. Months before, Smitty had told him of the murder of Alleen Rowe, and nothing had come of that. So he was not certain Smitty was telling the truth about the Fritz girls. Besides, Bruns detested Gretchen himself. But what happened next, still according to Bruns's story, did shake him up.

One night not long after, a couple of tough-looking characters, wearing sharp suits and smoking cigars, came by with Smitty and picked up Bruns. Smitty said they were Mafia, and that someone had hired them to look for Gretchen. Smitty and Bruns were taken to an apartment where several men were present whom Smitty later claimed to have recognized as local *Cosa Nostra* figures.

They wanted to know what had happened to the girls. They made no threats, but the message, Bruns remembers, came across loud and clear. These were no street-corner punks: these were the real boys. In spite of the intimidating company, Schmid lost none of his insouciance. He said he didn't know where Gretchen was, but if she turned up hurt he wanted these men to help him get whoever was responsible. He added that he thought she might have gone to California.

By the time Smitty and Bruns got back to Smitty's house, they were both a little shaky. Later that night, says Bruns, Smitty did the most unlikely thing imaginable: he called the FBI. First he tried the Tucson office and couldn't raise anyone. Then he called Phoenix and couldn't get an agent there either. Finally he put in a person-to-person call to J. Edgar Hoover in Washington. He didn't get Hoover, of course, but he got someone and told him that the Mafia was harassing him over the disappearance of a girl. The FBI promised to have someone in touch with him soon.

Bruns was scared and said so. It occurred to him now that if Smitty really had killed the Fritz girls and left their bodies in an obvious place, they were in very bad trouble indeed—with the Mafia on one hand and the FBI on the other. "Let's go bury them," Bruns said.

"Smitty stole the keys to his old man's station wagon," says Bruns, "and then we got a flat shovel—the only one we could find. We went to Johnie's and got a hamburger, and then we drove out to the old drinking spot [in the desert]—that's what Smitty meant when he said the most obvious place. It's where we used to drink beer and make out with girls.

"So we parked the car and got the shovel and walked down there, and we couldn't find anything. Then Smitty said, 'Wait, I smell something.' We went in opposite directions looking, and then I heard Smitty say, 'Come here.' I found him kneeling over Gretchen. There was a white rag tied around her legs. Her blouse was pulled up and she was wearing a white bra and Capris.

"Then he said, 'Wendy's up this way.' I sat there for a minute. Then I followed Smitty to where Wendy was. He'd had the decency to cover her—except for one leg, which was sticking up out of the ground.

"We tried to dig with the flat shovel. We each took turns. He'd dig for a while and then I'd dig for a while, but the ground was hard and we couldn't get anywhere with that flat shovel. We dug for twenty minutes and finally Smitty said we'd better do something because it's going to get light. So he grabbed the rag that was around Gretchen's legs and dragged her down in the wash. It made a noise like dragging a hollow shell. It stunk like hell. Then Smitty said wipe off her shoes, there might be fingerprints, so I wiped them off with my handkerchief and threw it away.

"We went back to Wendy. Her leg was sticking up with a shoe on it. He said take off her tennis shoe and throw it over there. I did, I threw it. Then he said, 'Now you're in this as deep as I am.'" By then, the sisters had been missing for about two weeks.

Early next morning Smitty did see the FBI. Nevertheless—here Bruns's story grows even wilder—that same day Smitty left for California, accompanied by a couple of Mafia types, to look for Gretchen Fritz. While there, he was picked up by the San Diego police on a complaint that he was impersonating an FBI officer. He was detained briefly, released and then returned to Tucson.

But now, it seemed to Richard Bruns, Smitty began acting very strangely. He startled Bruns by saying, "I've killed—not three times, but four. Now it's your turn, Richie." He went berserk in his little house, smashing his fist through a wall, slamming doors, then rushing out into the backyard in nothing but his undershorts, when he ran through the night screaming, "God is going to punish me!" He also decided, suddenly, to get married—to a fifteen-year-old girl who was a stranger to most of his friends.

❧

Bruns went to Ohio to stay with his grandmother and to try to get a job. It was hopeless. He couldn't sleep at night, and if he did doze off he had his old nightmare again.

One night he blurted out the whole story to his grandmother in their kitchen. She thought he had had too many beers and didn't believe him. "I hear beer does strange things to a person," she said comfortingly. At her words Bruns exploded, knocked over a chair and shouted, "The one time in my life when I need advice what do I get?" A few minutes later he was on the phone to the Tucson police.

Things happened swiftly. At Bruns's frantic insistence, the police picked up Kathy Morath and put her in protective custody. They went into the desert and discovered—precisely as Bruns had described them—the grisly, skeletal remains of Gretchen and Wendy Fritz. They started the machinery that resulted in the arrest a week later of John Saunders and Mary French. They found Charles Schmid working in the yard of his little house, his face layered with make-up, his nose covered by a patch of adhesive plaster which he had worn for five months, boasting that his nose was broken in a fight, and his boots packed full of old rags and tin cans. He put up no resistance.

John Saunders and Mary French confessed immediately to their roles in the slaying of Alleen Rowe and were quickly sentenced, Mary French to four to five years, Saunders to life. When Smitty goes on trial for this crime, on March 15, they will be principal witnesses against him.

Meanwhile Richie Bruns, the perpetual misfit, waits apprehensively for the end of the Fritz trial, desperately afraid that Schmid will go free. "If he does," Bruns says glumly, "I'll be the first one he'll kill."

As for Charles Schmid, he has adjusted well to his period of waiting. He is polite and agreeable with all, though at the preliminary hearings he glared menacingly at Richie Bruns. Dressed tastefully, tie neatly knotted, hair carefully combed, his face scrubbed clean of make-up, he is a short, compact, darkly handsome young man with a wide, engaging smile and those deepset eyes.

O'CONNOR'S MRS. MAY AND OATES'S CONNIE; AN UNLIKELY PAIR OF RELIGIOUS INITIATES[1]

NANCY BISHOP DESSOMMES

When Joyce Carol Oates was asked in a 1969 interview whether she was like Flannery O'Connor, she responded,

[1]*Studies in Short Fiction* 31.3 (Summer 1994): 430–33, online, Galileo, Academic Search Premier, Galileo 24 January 2002 .

I don't know. I used to think that I was influenced by O'Connor. I don't know that I am really. She is so religious, and her works have to be seen as religious works with this other rather creepy dimension in the background, whereas in my writing there is only the natural world. (Kuehl 307)

A few weeks later, Oates was to publish a collection of stories (eventually titled *The Wheel of Love*) on the theme of love, including the much-debated, often anthologized "Where Are You Going, Where Have You Been?" Perhaps this story stands out from the others in the collection because of its uncharacteristic "other rather creepy dimension in the background." Critics cannot seem to decide whether Connie, the 15-year-old protagonist of the story, has had a dream, seen the devil, or simply been seduced and possibly murdered by a psychotic intruder. But one thing is certain. The story is fraught with religious overtones and nightmarish imagery, and it is doubtful that "only the natural world" is presented. Joyce Carol Oates's respect for Flannery O'Connor's work is well known, and despite Oates's claim to the contrary, "Where Are You Going, Where Have You Been?" is very much like O'Connor's short stories, most notably "Greenleaf." Readers of O'Connor will recognize in Connie the shortcomings of such popular O'Connor figures as Mrs. Turpin, Hulga, and Julian. As in most of O'Connor's stories, the central character is self-centered, complacent, haughty, and essentially, though unwittingly, devoid of true moral conscience. But Connie and her story have the most in common with Mrs. May, the selfish widow of "Greenleaf." Both women are forced, in a moment of self-realization, to recognize the divine presence in the world; they must, if only for an instant, come to terms with moral responsibility and concern for affairs other than those of the self.

The plots of the two stories seem to have little in common; however, both are initiations of a woman who, in response to an intruder—a male sexual figure—is forced to see herself and the world as she never has before. Whereas O'Connor emphasizes the exposition of her story, concentrating on the events that lead up to Mrs. May's being gored by the Greenleafs' bull, Oates sustains the suspense of Connie's meeting with her abductor, suggesting that Arnold Friend's violation of Connie's mind and body, while seductively gradual, is nonetheless as violent as Mrs. May's death.

In Oates's story, Connie has chosen to stay home alone, having declined the offer to accompany her parents and older sister, June, on a family barbecue at her aunt's house. While she is drying her freshly washed hair in the sun, tuned in to a popular teen music station, a stranger, accompanied by a companion, drives into her driveway, claiming he has come to pick her up for a date. Connie has a vague recollection of having seen the stranger peripherally—and having snubbed him—the night before at the local drive-in hamburger joint. As the stranger, who identifies himself as Arnold Friend and his silent companion as Ellie Oscar, continues to pressure Connie into getting into his car, an old jalopy painted gold, Connie gradually realizes to her horror that the visitor is actually much older than he wants to appear. Connie becomes more and more frightened as Arnold Friend makes sexual suggestions and intimations that he is about to seize control of her mind. He has an uncanny knowledge of Connie's family and personal life and suggests that he may have murdered one of Connie's neighbors. After making a veiled threat to hurt Connie's family upon their return, Arnold manages to convince her to come out of the house and join him. She then crosses over into the other world of adulthood; into "the vast sunlit reaches of the land . . . so much land that Connie had never seen before and did not recognize except to know that she was going to it" (Oates 54). What actually happens to Connie from that point is not shown, but to most readers there is little doubt that she will be raped and possibly killed by this gentleman caller who has come to show her what "love" is: "Yes, I'm your lover. You don't know what that is, but you will" (47).

"Greenleaf" is a similar story. Mrs. May, a widow and dairy farmer by necessity, is forced to deal with an intruder on her property, the scrub bull of her tenant family, the Greenleafs. Mrs. May, who struggles to keep her business in order, becomes unhinged at the threatening presence of a Greenleaf bull on her property, one that she feels is sure to breed with her superior dairy cows and "ruin the breeding schedule" (O'Connor 28). After unsuccessful attempts to get Mr. Greenleaf to retrieve the bull, Mrs. May drives him to the pasture and orders him to shoot the animal. During the quarter of an hour or so that Mr. Greenleaf pursues the bull through woods, Mrs. May becomes impatient and blows the horn, apparently exciting the bull, who then emerges from the trees, charges her, and finally "burie[s] his head in her lap, like a wild tormented lover" (52). Mr. Greenleaf arrives, running for the first time in the story, and executes the beast with four shots from the rifle. "She did not hear the shots but she felt the quake in the huge body as it sank, pulling her forward on its head, so that she seemed, when Mr. Greenleaf reached her, to be bent over whispering some last discovery into the animal's ear" (53).

Though on the surface the carefree teenaged Connie and the frustrated middle-aged Mrs. May seem to have little in common, they are strikingly similar in character and share many of the same problems. Both live in an egoistic world psychologically separated from family and spiritually isolated from religion. Typically teenaged, Connie thinks of little beyond maintaining her own good looks, impressing boys, and living for the excitement of the moment. Her greatest challenge in life is to escape parental supervision long enough to sneak across the highway from the mall, where she is supposed to be seeing a movie with a friend, to the forbidden zone: "Sometimes they went across the highway, ducking fast across the busy road, to a drive-in restaurant where older kids hung out" (36). Unlike her dull and obedient sister June, Connie thrives on risk. On her trips across the highway, she is so "breathless with daring" (36) it is no wonder that she dismisses her family as tedious; like most teens, she prefers peer approval to parental and depends on it for her identity: "She had a quick nervous giggling habit of craning her neck to glance into mirrors, or checking other people's faces to make sure her own was all right" (34). Understandably, Connie prefers the hangout to her homelife, which is characterized by antagonism and indifference. Her mother is a source of aggravation, nagging at Connie to "Stop gawking at yourself, who are you? You think you're so pretty?" (34). Her father and June barely exist to Connie. As Joyce M. Wegs points out, "Connie's parents, who seem quite typical, have disqualified themselves as moral guides for her." Wegs continues, "Because [Connie's father] does not 'bother talking much' (30) to his family, he can hardly ask the crucial parental questions, 'Where are you going?' or 'Where have you been?'" (Wegs 88).

Though Connie's self-absorption can be excused as normal, her lack of religious training nonetheless creates a serious deficiency in her ability to be aware of the potential for evil in the world. In Connie's family "none of them bothered with church" (38) and the only reference Connie makes to a deity occurs during her panic over being caught without enough warning to prepare her face and hair for company: "Her heart began to pound and her fingers snatched at her hair, checking it, and she whispered 'Christ. Christ,' wondering how bad she looked" (40). It is clear from Oates's use of imagery that Connie has replaced traditional religion with the false religion of secularism. The drive-in restaurant, steepled with "a revolving figure of a grinning boy who held a hamburger aloft," (36) stands in grotesque tribute to a belief in the superficial world of self-indulgence that "give[s...Connie and her friends] what haven and what blessing they yearned for" (36). It is little wonder that Connie, unprepared for dealing with evil realities of the adult world, succumbs to the pressure of the satanic Arnold Friend. A young woman whose thoughts about sexual love are "of the boy she had been with the night before and about how nice he had been, how sweet it always was . . . sweet, gentle, the way it was in movies and promised in songs" (39) is set up for a fall. As Connie is soon to learn, she only thinks she is in control of the boys, of her love life; a few moments with Arnold Friend, however, and Connie is under his control: "She watched herself push the door slowly open as if she were safe back somewhere in the other doorway, watching this body and this head of long hair moving out into the sunlight where Arnold Friend waited" (54).

Similarly, Mrs. May thinks she is in control of her domain; her family and farm, however, are in decay. Mrs. May is really controlled by Mr. Greenleaf, who takes advantage of her from the first, when he responds to her notice for a farmhand: "I seen your ad and I will come have 2 boys"

(34). As Mr. Greenleaf soon reveals, he has cleverly failed to mention his wife and five daughters, who are apparently part of the package. Soon the farm is populated with three generations of Greenleafs.

Just as Connie cannot look to her parents for protection from the likes of Arnold Friend, Mrs. May cannot depend on her family to help ward off the invasion of the Greenleafs. Her relationship to her sons is at least as antagonistic as Connie's is with her parents. Mrs. May's two older, still unmarried sons—Scofield, an insurance "policy man," and Wesley, an "intellectual"—offer their mother no help on the farm, only ridicule. Aware of her airs of superiority and fear of a Greenleaf takeover, they tease her without mercy: "Scofield would yodel and say, 'Why Mamma, I'm not going to marry until you're dead and gone and then I'm going to marry me some nice fat girl that can take over this place...some nice lady like Mrs. Greenleaf'" (29). Mrs. May's greatest fear is that her farm will degenerate to Greenleaf level, though her family structure is already in the same state as her semi-collapsed farmhouse.

Mrs. May, like Connie, doesn't bother much with religion, but her substitute for faith is her attachment to her good name and the defense of her property. God comes last. In Mrs. May's world God is a cliché: "I thank God for that!" she exclaims in response to Mr. Greenleaf's observation that "all boys ain't alike." But Mr. Greenleaf offers a penetrating and sincere reply: "'I thank gawd for ever thang,' he drawled" (41). Mrs. May tolerates the Greenleaf variety of religion, but she herself has put religion away, compartmentalizing it into its proper place: in a building to serve as a warehouse of nice girls for her boys to meet and a place to contain Jesus' name. "She thought the word, Jesus, should be kept inside the church building like other words inside the bedroom. She was a good Christian woman with a large respect for religion, though she did not, of course, believe any of it was true" (31). David Eggenschwiler, in *The Christian Humanism of Flannery O'Connor*, classifies Mrs. May as a Kierkegaardian Philistine figure: "Mrs. May is one of those characters who exalt intellectuality or common sense and deny their passions, their animality, and the power of the irrational" (52). No one better embodies the power of the irrational than Mrs. Greenleaf, whose rites of healing include rolling in the dirt and swaying on all fours over the news clippings of movie stars' divorces. Mrs. May, who finds Mrs. Greenleaf's behavior abhorrent, considers herself an expert on what Jesus would want; "'Jesus,' she said, drawing herself back, 'would be ashamed of you'" (31). But it is the Greenleaf spirit of surrender to the religious realm of existence that is embodied in the powerful yet humble scrub bull that visits Mrs. May at night "like some patient god come down to woo her" (24). And it is, of course, the bull that is victorious and helps Mrs. May discover, too late, her error.

The most intriguing similarity between the stories is the authors' use of the nightmarish, sexually alarming, male intruder who appears unexpectedly to disturb the comfortable universe the female character has built. Both females are threatened by the grotesque embodiment of spiritual reality and are conquered by that force in a cataclysmic vision at the end of the story. Interestingly, both intruders are anticipated, if not experienced, in a dream. Although the question of whether Arnold Friend is a vision, a "daymare," or a literal abductor has been thoroughly argued, a close reading does reveal that Connie's experience has all the earmarks of a nightmare, one that has been triggered by the shaggy-haired boy in the gold car whom she had seen at the drive-in.[2] Critics who have argued that Arnold Friend is real (and those who have argued the dream theory) have overlooked one detail from the drive-in scene: the car itself, "a convertible jalopy painted gold" (37). Oates makes no mention of the dented bumper, strange slogans, or cartoonish pictures that Connie notices right away when the car is parked in her driveway. The reader would think that such an unusual sight at the local teen hangout would be sure to draw a comment, if not a crowd. But only Connie—not even the group she is walking with—notices the boy who speaks only to her: "Gonna get you, baby" (37). During Connie's imaginary encounter with Friend, the details about the car—especially the sexist comment "DONE BY CRAZY WOMAN DRIVER" written around the smashed fender—take on psychological significance, as does the character of Friend himself.

Connie's vision expresses the anxiety typical of dreams: the search for self-identity, fear of the future, and suppressed sexual desire. Larry Rubin concludes that "the episode with Arnold Friend, then, may be viewed as the vehicle for fulfillment of Connie's deep-rooted desire for ultimate sexual gratification, a fearsome business which, for the uninitiated female, may involve destruction of the person" (59). Greg Johnson sees the dream strictly as feminist allegory: "The story describes the beginning of a young and sexually attractive girl's enslavement within a conventional, male-dominated sexual relationship.[... It] is a cautionary tale, suggesting that young women are 'going' exactly where their mothers and grandmothers have already 'been': into sexual bondage at the hands of a male Friend'" (102–03). Connie cannot help but feel an attraction to this composite of all the boys she has met, the embodiment of all the urges her parents would have her resist. Still, Connie fears that Friend will enter the house where she stands just inside the screen door and take her on his own terms, for she knows instinctively that he is evil. As Joyce Wegs points out, "Although Arnold has come to take Connie away, in his traditional role as evil spirit, he may not cross a threshold uninvited; he repeatedly mentions that he is not going to come in after Connie, and he never does. Instead, he lures

---

[2]Larry Rubin argues convincingly that Connie has fallen asleep in the sun and has had a dream about a composite figure that symbolizes her fear of the adult world. He discusses the references to sleep that frame the Arnold Friend episode and the nightmare quality of her inability to control the situation.

Connie out to him" (90). Connie, like Mrs. May, has not thought much about her own vulnerability and what lies past her immediate concerns of daily living, nor does she expect to meet up with an exaggerated picture of the spiritual dimension of life that she has heretofore not recognized. Just as Arnold Friend appears as a representation of all Connie's desires and fears, the menacing scrub bull that has been stalking Mrs. May has also entered her dreams, wherein its presence suggests the same moral and sexual uncertainties that Connie feels. In the blur between sleep and wake, Mrs. May imagines the bull dominating her space the way Arnold Friend invades Connie's house: "[it] had eaten everything from the beginning of the fence line up to the house and now was eating the house and calmly with the same steady rhythm would continue through the house, eating her and the boys, and then on, eating everything but the Greenleafs" (25). Awakened by the steady chewing sound, she peeks through the blinds and spies the bull "chewing calmly like an uncouth country suitor" (25). Like Arnold Friend, the bull is in no hurry to possess her; he waits like a "patient god" to make his move. He has his territory marked from outside her bedroom window just as Arnold Friend marks Connie with an "X" in the air soon after his arrival. In both stories, with the first appearance of the intruder, the conflict is defined as a struggle for power over the female's body as well as her property. Suzanne Paulson points to Mr. Greenleaf as the real threat to Mrs. May's security— even her sexual security: "Mr. Greenleaf appears to represent male potency: his phallic nature is emphasized in the figure of his sons' bull, which he allows to run loose in Mrs. May's herd—his way of asserting power over his female employer and of establishing his own territory" (40). The bull is an obvious symbol of male sexual aggression, and Mrs. May, who believes that certain "other words [should be kept] inside the bedroom," has likely denied her own sexuality since becoming a widow and assuming the traditional male role of caretaker. It is little wonder that such sexual repression would surface in a dream as an image of fear.

On the spiritual level, the bull is more closely associated with Mrs. Greenleaf, whom Mrs. May describes as "large and loose," yet for all her dirtiness and uncouthness, she is Mrs. May's moral superior. Since Mrs. May is unpracticed at praying for suffering souls and screaming out to Jesus, she feels threatened by these ritual performances she happens upon in the woods, and she attaches to them the same fear she feels toward the bull: "She felt as if some violent unleashed force had broken out of the ground and was charging toward her" (30–31). What Mrs. May senses in this scene is, of course, a foreshadowing of the disaster to come, one that will prove to be her "moment of grace." According to Suzanne Paulson,

> Depicting the worst in human nature is for O'Connor an act of faith, a repetition of God's intention to shock us into "grace." What some readers see

as cynical and distorted views of human life, O'Connor sees as honest representations—however exaggerated and symbolic—of human suffering and sin repressed by the community in order to assuage the guilt of individual members. (86)

Connie's bizarre experience with Arnold Friend could likewise be interpreted as a "cynical and distorted view of human life." But in a more significant reading of the story, Connie's grueling Sunday afternoon appointment with evil symbolizes her coming to terms with the internal and external struggles evident in her life, as well as those of countless young women like her. Like Mrs. May, Connie has been blindsided by a force buried in the mundane that was too obvious for her to recognize. And this force bears the face of evil. David Eggenschwiler speaks of O'Connor's use of the bull as a symbol of evil in "Greenleaf":

> [Mrs. May] even experiences revelation through a demonic form: she becomes aware of God through a symbolic, Dionysian immolation of her self, which is not to say that such immolation is a Christian ideal any more than being pierced by a bull is an ideal form of sexual behavior. Such patterns of reaction also help to explain why Miss O'Connor so often uses satanic instruments to enlighten her characters: she is not only showing that God moves in mysterious ways and brings good out of evil; she is also exploring the psychological and religious view that demonic characters experience God's mercy through demonic structures that oppose or caricature their own forms of idolatry. (64)

The same could be said of Oates and her story. While it is difficult to view Mrs. May or Connie as demonic characters, they are both idolaters of sorts, and both are in need of God's mercy and grace.

At the outcome of each character's ordeal is a moral insight, or revelation, one that elevates the ordinary woman to the state of religious hero. Mrs. May dies getting only a glimpse of the "last discovery" that has come too late for her to act on, but Connie actually becomes a savior to her family. Connie, who has only resented her parents and sister before, cries out for her mother in the end; and in a final act of heroism, surrenders herself to Arnold Friend, who has just reminded her that he plans to harm her family upon their return should she refuse to come out to him. "You don't want them to get hurt" (53), he says, and immediately she stands up to leave with him. She receives her "moment of grace" in classic O'Connor style: by having it violently thrust upon her. Unlike other O'Connor protagonists, she is not hit in the head with a book, forced to watch her mother collapse and die on the sidewalk, or even taken in and mentally raped by a deranged Bible salesman. Instead, like the lonely widow, she endures sexual intimidation by a stranger and is at once destroyed and, ironically, saved by the force that conquers her.

Works Cited

Eggenschwiler, David. *The Christian Humanism of Flannery O'Connor.* Detroit, MI: Wayne State UP, 1972.

Johnson, Greg. *Understanding Joyce Carol Oates.* Columbia: University of South Carolina Press, 1987.

Kuehl, Linda. "An Interview with Joyce Carol Oates." *Commonweal* 91 (1969): 307–10.

Oates. Joyce Carol. "Where Are You Going, Where Have You Been?" In *The Wheel of Love*, 34–54. New York: Vanguard, 1970.

O'Connor, Flannery. "Greenleaf." In *Everything That Rises Must Converge*, 24–53. New York: Farrar, 1965.

Paulson, Suzanne Morrow. *Flannery O'Connor: A Study of the Short Fiction.* Boston: Twayne, 1988.

Rubin, Larry. "Oates's 'Where Are You Going, Where Have You Been?'" *Explicator* 42.4 (1984): 57–59.

Wegs, Joyce M. "'Don't You Know Who I Am?': The Grotesque in Oates's 'Where Are You Going, Where Have You Been?'" *Journal of Narrative Technique* 5 (1975): 66–72. Rpt. in *Critical Essays on Joyce Carol Oates*, ed. Linda W. Wagner, 87–92. Boston: Hall, 1979.

Escape from Reality?

Kimberly Prevett

1 In much of her work, Joyce Carol Oates depicts American life with a violent and mysterious focus. According to her biography in the <u>Encarta Online Encyclopedia</u>,

> Gothic elements, emphasizing the mysterious
> and horrifying aspects of life, also appear
> frequently in Oates's writing. For example,
> violence, often male and sexual, consistently
> plays a prominent role in the lives of her
> characters. ("Oates, J.C.")

2 The short stories "Where Are You Going, Where Have You Been?" and "Valentine" by Joyce Carol Oates both feature as the main character an adolescent girl facing a turning point in her life. In addition to the characterization of Connie in

"Where Are You Going, Where Have You Been?" and Erin in "Valentine," the stories have several other parallels. Although physically living in the same house, Connie is very disconnected from her family; Erin is separated physically from her immediate family and lives with her aunt and uncle. Each girl's desire to escape a less than perfect family leads her to dream-like encounters with an older man who has the power to control her thoughts and actions.

3   According to Dessommes, Connie is a typical teenager who "thinks of little beyond maintaining her own good looks, impressing boys, and living for the excitement of the moment" (1196). Her story occurs during summer vacation; and Connie wears shorts, goes barefoot, and spends time "getting in her mother's way and thinking, dreaming about the boys she met" (Oates, "Where" 1157). Connie struggles to find her identity; "Everything about her had two sides to it, one for home and one for anywhere that was not home" ("Where" 1156).

4   Erin's story takes places during a winter snowstorm, and she bundles herself up in hand-me-down sweaters, wool pants, muffler, and gloves, afraid her teacher will see who she is, "how desperate for love" (Oates, "Valentine" 1170). Erin makes homemade Valentines, sends them anonymously, and convinces herself that she is not disappointed when she receives none. She "Yearned to be invited to visit the homes of certain girls, without success" ("Valentine" 1173). She is obsessed with making good grades and says, "When my grades in Mr. Lacey's class were less than 100 percent I was filled with anxiety that turned my fingers and toes to ice. . ." ("Valentine" 1171).

5   Connie works to separate herself from her family, often escaping by going "across the highway, ducking fast across the

busy road, to a drive-in restaurant where the older kids hung out" ("Where" 1156). According to Wegs, Connie's parents have disqualified themselves as moral guides for her. Her mother picks at her about inconsequential things and her father does not "'bother talking much'" (1155). Wegs also includes Connie's friend's father among the morally indifferent adult society because he "'never [. . . bothers] to ask'" (1155). This lack of a moral compass leaves Connie unprepared to deal with the evil that comes her way.

6   It is not clearly evident what has happened to separate Erin from the other members of her family; however, when the story begins, she is alone with her indifferent Aunt Ester and an uncle, "who was no blood kin of [hers]" ("Valentine" 1168). Oates highlights Erin's sense of isolation when she writes, "'Goodnight' they murmured as if resenting the very breath expelled for my sake" ("Valentine" 1168). She feels that she could run away and no one would miss her. When Erin's teacher says, "<u>Come, Erin, hurry! She won't even know you're gone</u>" Erin thinks he might have said, "<u>She won't ever know you're gone</u>," ("Valentine" 1170).

7   A vaguely familiar stranger, who identifies himself as Arnold Friend, comes to take Connie away. Even though she is the more outgoing and adventuresome of the two girls, she fights against leaving with him. Her early suspicion turns quickly to fear as he makes sexual comments and as she begins to see through his disguise. Arnold threatens to harm her family when he says, ". . . give me you hand and nobody else gets hurt. . .why bring them in this?" ("Where" 1166). With fear for her family as a driving factor, she goes along with him to a fate that is unclear but certainly not positive.

8   Someone she feels she knows well lures Erin from her home. Unlike Connie, Erin goes willingly on a strange dream-like journey with her math teacher, Mr. Lacey. He is the object of her secret affection and the recipient of one of her homemade valentines. She is very embarrassed when he says, "You must not offer yourself in such a fashion, not even in secret. . . .The valentine heart is the female genitals, you will be misinterpreted" ("Valentine" 1178). However, at the end of the evening when she is returned safely to her home, she thinks that he may be saying, "Safe alone, safe alone" ("Valentine" 1249). She does not know at the time that ". . . over thirty years later. . . I would remove from its hiding place. . . a bloodstained man's handkerchief initialed JNL" ("Valentine" 1179).

9   The dream-like effect of Erin's adventure and the implied violent ending of Connie's encounter are consistent with Joyce Carol Oates's view of America as a place of violence where young women are faced with mystery and horror. In "Valentine" and "Where Are You Going? Where Have You Been?" Joyce Carol Oates uses older men who prey upon the minds of the young girls. In their respective realities, they are offered an escape, although it may not be the one they had originally wished for.

[New page]   Works Cited

Dessommes, Nancy Bishop. "O'Connor's Mrs. May and Oates's Connie: An Unlikely Pair of Religious Initiates." Studies in Short Fiction 31.3 (Summer 1994): 433–40. Henderson, Day, and Waller. 1194-1202.

Henderson, Gloria, Bill Day, and Sandra Waller, eds. Literature and Ourselves. 5th ed. New York: Longman, 2006.

Oates, Joyce Carol. "Where Are You Going, Where Have You Been."
The Wheel of Love and Other Stories. N.p.: John Hawkins,
1970. Henderson, Day, and Waller. 1155-67.

---. "Valentine." The Collector of Hearts: New Tales of the
Grotesque. New York: Plume. 1998. 211-27. Henderson, Day,
and Waller. 1168-80.

"Oates, J.C." Microsoft™ Encarta Online Encyclopedia 2001. 6
Feb. 2002 <http://www.encarta.MSN.com>.

Wegs, Joyce M. "'Don't You Know Who I Am?' The Grotesque in
Oates's 'Where Are You Going Where Have You Been?'"
Critical Essays on Joyce Carol Oates. Ed. Linda W. Wagner.
Boston: G. K. Hall & Co., 1979. Henderson, Day, and Waller.
1180-86.

Suggestions for Exploring, Writing, and Persuading

1. In an essay, discuss in detail how you would have responded either to Friend or to Lacey or to both.

2. Rewrite one of the stories so that Connie encounters Mr. Lacey or Erin encounters Arnold Friend.

3. In a researched essay, discuss Oates's use in "Where Are You Going, Where Have You Been?" of Don Moser's article "The Pied Piper of Tucson." How does Oates change the original story? What effects does she create through these clearly deliberate changes?

4. Using Nancy Dessommes's essay as well as other sources, write a detailed essay analyzing Arnold Friend and the Misfit (see Flannery O'Connor's "A Good Man Is Hard to Find" in the Quest unit) as embodiments of evil.

5. Using some of the essays in this casebook, analyze Oates's stories as dreams. As dreams, what do the stories reveal about the hearts and minds of the dreamers?

6. The two stories together might be seen as suggesting the difficulty of distinguishing good from evil. Using the research in this casebook, discuss that difficulty by examining in detail the similarities between Lacey, who appears to be good, and Friend, who appears to be evil.

7. Each story might be read as a journey into self-discovery. Using research in this casebook, write an essay discussing what Connie and Erin learn about themselves.

8. In an argumentative essay, agree, disagree, or modify this statement: Many contemporary situations, such as chat rooms and exposure to sexually explicit movies and television shows, can lead to the victimization of young people.

Imagination and Reality: Suggestions for Exploring, Writing, and Persuading

1. The introduction to this unit claims that because it balances both inner experience and outer experience, both the human imagination and the world it discovers, art raises profound questions about the nature of truth, the essence of reality. Select one or more of the works in this unit and write an essay that illustrates how art can raise questions about truth or reality.

2. In the Freedom and Responsibility unit, Tim O'Brien's narrator in "How to Tell a True War Story" insists that the truth of art does not depend on factual accuracy. Use at least two of the works in this unit to support the claim that art, through imagination, sometimes reveals truth that transcends fact.

3. Select two or more works in this unit to illustrate that imagination can lead to discovery—of self, of others, or of truth.

4. Hold a mock trial for Arnold Friend, charging him with sexual harassment. Then write an essay defending your verdict.

5. Cruz describes the ability of literature and of poems in particular to create or destroy. Using any of the poems in this anthology, write an essay on the power of poetry to (1) create, (2) destroy, (3) communicate, or (4) reveal.

6. Using any three works in this unit, explain the relationship of creator (writer, artist, reader, etc.) to creation.

7. In what ways does a work of art belong to everyone? Explain, using examples from any section of this book.

8. Language, whether in works of literature or in life, is meant to communicate. Using one or more of the works, discuss the problems that arise when communication fails.

9. Select one or more of the works in this unit to discuss emotional involvement in works of art.

10. LeGuin describes symbol and archetype in "The Child and the Shadow." Apply these terms to "The Ones Who Walk Away From Omelas" in the Freedom and Responsibility unit or to a work in this unit.

Imagination and Reality: Writing About Film

1. One of the purposes of art is to provoke our imaginations so that we see the ordinary world in a new way. As an exercise in creating visual

poetry, take an ordinary event from your daily life (getting out of bed, fixing coffee, putting on makeup, playing basketball), and plan a brief screenplay of the event that will freight it with unexpected emotional values—make it seem beautiful, silly, disturbing, or surprising. You will want to write out an outline or draw up a storyboard (a series of cartoonlike drawings) for a sequence of shots and supply a sound track. For your shots, think about what the camera will see (foreground and background), from what angle, and for how long and what movements the camera will make. Then think about how one shot will cut into another and how the image of the first shot will relate to the next. Also consider how you want the action to sound. Do you want to supply inappropriate sounds for actions? Do you want the action to happen in time to specific music?

2. American audiences tend to avoid foreign films because they feel that subtitles interfere with the experience of viewing the movie. In fact, after a few minutes, our minds adjust to reading and watching quite easily, and many foreign films offer us a window into very different cultural dreams. Watch a well-made foreign film and reflect on what it does in terms of event, character, theme, or visual style that an American film wouldn't do. What is new or fresh about the characters, the style of filmmaking, or the construction of the story? Some titles you may find interesting include *City of Lost Children; Red Fireworks, Green Fireworks; Fanny and Alexander; Swept Away; The Horseman on the Roof; Shanghai Triad; Belle Epoque; Eat, Drink, Man, Woman; Yojimbo; Amelie; The Triplets of Belleville; The Man on the Train; Run Lola Run; The Barbarian Invasions;* and *Crouching Tiger, Hidden Dragon.*

3. Some of the most imaginative works of the past sixty-five years have been fantasy and science fiction films. From *The Wizard of Oz* (1939) to the beautiful *Secret of Roan Inish* to *The Lord of the Rings,* fantasy films have intrigued us, entertained us, and puzzled us. Similarly, science fiction films have made comic book characters such as Batman, Spiderman, Catwoman, and the Hulk come back to life or have predicted a wide variety of scenarios for the future. Select one of these films to research and, using the appendix in the back of this text—which uses a fantasy trilogy by J.R.R. Tolkien and a science fiction trilogy—write on one of the following:

   The major theme of the film

   The ways in which this particular fantasy or science fiction film causes us to think about the human condition and the ways to cope with difficult situations

   The battle of good and evil

   The ambiguities we face in trying to decide what is good and what is evil. (You might like also to use LeGuin's "The Child and the Shadow" as a source in this essay.)

The role of the hero

The difficulty of differentiating between reality and appearance or illusion

4. If you prefer to focus on the techniques of film making, select one of the following:

The ways in which the director incorporates special effects to create appropriate illusions or futuristic scenes

The ways the music enhances or detracts from the story

The appropriateness or lack of appropriateness of the actors selected to play the roles

The skill of one actor or actress

5. Finally, you might prefer to study an original text—comic book, short story, or novel—for a film adaptation and evaluate the film maker's interpretation of the work or examine the progression of the story in trilogies or sequels.

Quest

A scene from *Lord of the Rings: The Fellowship of the Ring*. New Line Cinema/Photofest.

Awareness that humanity cannot "live by bread alone" (Matthew 4:4) predates Christ by thousands of years. The theme of the quest, which ultimately reveals humanity in a search for meaning, for a truth beyond the purely physical, is older than written literature. It finds expression in ancient religions and myths, in the Babylonian epic of *Gilgamesh*, and in the great oral epics of Homer, particularly *The Odyssey*. A recurring theme in art, mythology, and religion is the human need and resulting search for a defining direction, order, and meaning. In a sense, the quest, the search for an ultimate truth, might be seen as one defining characteristic of humanity.

The quest for truth begins not in certainty but in doubt, in questioning. In Sophocles's great tragedy, Oedipus insists on asking questions despite dire warnings, proceeding from question to question to a shocking revelation about his own identity. Ozzie, in Philip Roth's "The Conversion of the Jews," is so tormented by his elders' refusal to take seriously his very sincere questions that he ends up casting doubt on all they have believed in. Plato's quest for truth—his philosophy—begins, proceeds, and ends with question after question. The wisdom of Jesus's "Sermon on the Mount" arises out of his questioning of received wisdom, his refusal to accept the status quo. Blake raises without answering the question whether the God who made the lamb could make the tiger.

Anguished questioning torments even writers and characters of profound faith. Faith seems not to end the quest but to begin it anew. Hopkins's "God's Grandeur," though written in praise of God and though ending in a strongly affirmative sestet, nevertheless reveals in its second quatrain grave doubts about our capacity to know God. The woman in Fred Chappell's "An Old Woman Reading the Book of Job" reads Job repeatedly to try to understand "A God who suffers the suffering of man." Flannery O'Connor, a devout Catholic, sees modern men and women as so immersed in the world as to be wholly unaware of their own inadequacy. For O'Connor, only the inexplicable and often violent grace of God can give a person some sense of order and meaning. O'Connor's quest cannot even begin without grace.

The quest for truth may sometimes be quite costly. In Roth's "The Conversion of the Jews," Ozzie's persistent questioning antagonizes both his rabbi and his mother, and Socrates's insistence on questioning received wisdom led to his being condemned to death. Oedipus's fateful quest for truth leads him to blind himself and his wife to hang herself. Because he regards his quest as too costly, Prufrock, the narrator of T. S. Eliot's "The

Love Song of J. Alfred Prufrock," is unable even to ask his most superficial question. We see in him the predicament of many people today, unable to believe in God or any ultimate truth, thoroughly disoriented, searching in spite of themselves for truth and direction in a world that apparently offers neither.

Despite the difficulty of the quest, the search for a truth that transcends the merely physical world continues. Plato's philosopher finds his way out of the cave. Ozzie, in spite of the odds, continues to try to understand. Writers as different as the Old Testament psalmist, William Butler Yeats, and Gerard Manley Hopkins offer us a vision of what we might attain, of a transcendent existence beyond the ravages of pain and age.

As the persistent questioning of Socrates, the endless searching of Alfred, Lord Tennyson's Ulysses, and the eloquent frozen action of John Keats's Grecian urn make clear, often the joy, meaning, and order we seek are in the quest itself. Even one of the most devout of medieval mystics, the monk Brother Lawrence, saw his vocation not as resting in God but as constantly *practicing* God's presence. Like Tennyson's Ulysses, we feel compelled to search: "to strive, to seek, to find, and not to yield."

Writing About Quest

The theme of the quest—whether for knowledge of self, knowledge of the nature of humanity, or knowledge of God—is perhaps the richest source of writing topics. Many works tell of more than one quest, and each genre in this unit offers you a wide variety of subjects. You might select the work that appeals to you most and let that work determine your subject and the type of essay you will write, or you might decide that you would prefer to write about one quest and then select one or more works that illustrate that quest. For example, if you wanted to write about the search for knowledge of self, you might select James Joyce's "Araby," an initiation story. If your professor allows you to use works from other units that include the quest theme, you might write about Katherine Anne Porter's "The Grave," another story about self-discovery. If you prefer to write about poetry, you might write an essay classifying the types of sterility and loneliness portrayed in "The Love Song of J. Alfred Prufrock."

If you choose to write about the quest for the nature of humanity, you will find that it is often inextricably intertwined with the other two types of quests mentioned above. For example, you might write an essay about Tennyson's poem showing how Ulysses, in setting goals for himself, challenges his men to share in his quest. Another essay about the nature of humanity might explain how Hazel in Toni Cade Bambara's "Raymond's

Run," while enjoying the talent that gives her personal satisfaction, learns a new admiration for and understanding of her brother.

The quest for a satisfactory relationship with God permeates great literature, and this unit offers a wide variety of works on this subject. You might, for example, write about the ironic point of view in Arthur C. Clarke's "The Star," which tells of a moral crisis faced by a Jesuit priest, or compare the ways in which Philip Roth and Bernard Malamud create humor in stories about characters who seek to understand the complex role of religion in their lives. The stories in the Flannery O'Connor casebook offer startling accounts of women who are shocked into a recognition of their own nature and their relationship to God. The questions at the end of the casebook suggest a variety of types of essays and subjects. You might, for example, write a character sketch of the Misfit, the grandmother, or Mrs. May. You might write a cause-and-effect essay on the Misfit as a violent agent of change, or you might interpret the symbolism in either of the stories.

For argumentation, you might persuade your audience which of Oedipus's characteristics makes him pursue so diligently the murderer of Laius, the former king of Thebes. You might also take a stab at answering the question posed in Blake's "Tyger" by deciding whether God made both the lamb and the tiger and why. In Cofer's "Latin Women Pray," the women pray that God at least be bilingual. You might write an essay answering the question "why?" Do most members of different races or ethnic groups pray for the same thing? Putting the argumentative edge on most of the works in Quest will make for more insightful essays.

When Quimby Melton was asked to write an essay using the O'Connor casebook, he was already familiar with Flannery O'Connor's fiction, having previously read several of her stories; however, he selected a story he had not read before: "Greenleaf." After reading the story carefully, he thought about the symbolism, themes, and characterization. Then he read the critical essays and constructed his thesis statement based on his interpretation of the story and on his decision about what would make a workable topic. The thesis that he chose allowed him to use his previous knowledge about O'Connor's religious beliefs and about the American South as he discussed the symbols in the story and the ways in which they clarify and vivify the theme. Once he had selected his subject, Quimby wrote the whole essay in one night. His professor suggested a few minor changes, but the essay required little revision. Quimby's essay is included at the end of the O'Connor casebook.

ESSAYS

Plato (c. 429–347 b.c.)

The philosopher and teacher Plato was a high-born Athenian who studied under Socrates and taught Aristotle. Plato founded a school in the grove sacred to the hero Academus and called it the Academy. The Republic, Plato's plan for a utopia, includes the most famous of all allegories, the allegory of the cave, which delineates his philosophical view of reality. Plato customarily wrote in dialogues, often using Socrates as a character. Because of its emphasis on the transcendent, Plato's philosophy influenced many later religions, including Christianity and Islam.

ALLEGORY OF THE CAVE[1]   (FOURTH CENTURY B.C.)

1   And now, I said, let me show in a figure how far our nature is enlightened or unenlightened:—Behold! human beings living in an underground den, which has a mouth open towards the light and reaching all along the den; here they have been from their childhood, and have their legs and necks chained so that they cannot move, and can only see before them, being prevented by the chains from turning round their heads. Above and behind them a fire is blazing at a distance, and between the fire and the prisoners there is a raised way; and you will see, if you look, a low wall built along the way, like the screen which marionette players have in front of them, over which they show the puppets.

2   I see.

3   And do you see, I said, men passing along the wall carrying all sorts of vessels, and statues and figures of animals made of wood and stone and various materials, which appear over the wall? Some of them are talking, others silent.

4   You have shown me a strange image, and they are strange prisoners.

5   Like ourselves, I replied; and they see only their own shadows, or the shadows of one another, which the fire throws on the opposite wall of the cave?

6   True, he said; how could they see anything but the shadows if they were never allowed to move their heads?

7   And of the objects which are being carried in like manner they would only see the shadows?

8   Yes, he said.

9   And if they were able to converse with one another, would they not suppose that they were naming what was actually before them?

[1]From Plato's *The Republic*, translated by Benjamin Jowett.

10   Very true.

11   And suppose further that the prison had an echo which came from the other side, would they not be sure to fancy when one of the passers-by spoke that the voice which they heard came from the passing shadow?

12   No question, he replied.

13   To them, I said, the truth would be literally nothing but the shadows of the images.

14   That is certain.

15   And now look again, and see what will naturally follow if the prisoners are released and disabused of their error. At first, when any of them is liberated and compelled suddenly to stand up and turn his neck round and walk and look towards the light, he will suffer sharp pains; the glare will distress him, and he will be unable to see the realities of which in his former state he had seen the shadows; and then conceive some one saying to him, that what he saw before was an illusion, but that now, when he is approaching nearer to being and his eye is turned towards more real existence, he has a clearer vision,—what will be his reply? And you may further imagine that his instructor is pointing to the objects as they pass and requiring him to name them,—will he not be perplexed? Will he not fancy that the shadows which he formerly saw are truer than the objects which are now shown to him?

16   Far truer.

17   And if he is compelled to look straight at the light, will he not have a pain in his eyes which will make him turn away to take refuge in the objects of vision which he can see, and which he will conceive to be in reality clearer than the things which are now being shown to him?

18   True, he said.

19   And suppose once more, that he is reluctantly dragged up a steep and rugged ascent, and held fast until he is forced into the presence of the sun himself, is he not likely to be pained and irritated? When he approaches the light his eyes will be dazzled, and he will not be able to see anything at all of what are now called realities.

20   Not all in a moment, he said.

21   He will require to grow accustomed to the sight of the upper world. And first he will see the shadows best, next the reflections of men and other objects in the water, and then the objects themselves; then he will gaze upon the light of the moon and the stars and the spangled heaven; and he will see the sky and the stars by night better than the sun or the light of the sun by day?

22   Certainly.

23   Last of all he will be able to see the sun, and not mere reflections of him in the water, but he will see him in his own proper place, and not in another; and he will contemplate him as he is.

24   Certainly.

25   He will then proceed to argue that this is he who gives the season and the years, and is the guardian of all that is in the visible world, and in a

certain way the cause of all things which he and his fellows have been accustomed to behold?

26   Clearly, he said, he would first see the sun and then reason about him.

27   And when he remembered his old habitation, and the wisdom of the den and his fellow-prisoners, do you not suppose that he would felicitate himself on the change, and pity them?

28   Certainly, he would.

29   And if they were in the habit of conferring honours among themselves on those who were quickest to observe the passing shadows and to remark which of them went before, and which followed after, and which were together; and who were therefore best able to draw conclusions as to the future, do you think that he would care for such honours and glories, or envy the possessors of them? Would he not say with Homer,

"Better to be the poor servant of a poor master,"

and to endure anything, rather than think as they do and live after their manner?

30   Yes, he said, I think that he would rather suffer anything than entertain these false notions and live in this miserable manner.

31   Imagine once more, I said, such an one coming suddenly out of the sun to be replaced in his old situation; would he not be certain to have his eyes full of darkness?

32   To be sure, he said.

33   And if there were a contest, and he had to compete in measuring the shadows with the prisoners who had never moved out of the den, while his sight was still weak, and before his eyes had become steady (and the time which would be needed to acquire this new habit of sight might be very considerable), would he not be ridiculous? Men would say of him that up he went and down he came without his eyes; and that it was better not even to think of ascending; and if any one tried to loose another and lead him up to the light, let them only catch the offender, and they would put him to death.

34   No question, he said.

35   This entire allegory, I said, you may now append, dear Glaucon, to the previous argument; the prison-house is the world of sight, the light of the fire is the sun, and you will not misapprehend me if you interpret the journey upwards to be the ascent of the soul into the intellectual world according to my poor belief, which, at your desire, I have expressed— whether rightly or wrongly God knows. But, whether true or false, my opinion is that in the world of knowledge the idea of good appears last of all, and is seen only with an effort; and, when seen, is also inferred to be the universal author of all things beautiful and right, parent of light and of the lord of light in this visible world, and the immediate source of reason and truth in the intellectual; and that this is the power upon which he who would act rationally either in public or private life must have his eye fixed.

36   I agree, he said, as far as I am able to understand you.

37   Moreover, I said, you must not wonder that those who attain to this beatific vision are unwilling to descend to human affairs; for their souls are ever hastening into the upper world where they desire to dwell; which desire of theirs is very natural, if our allegory may be trusted.

38   Yes, very natural.

39   And is there anything surprising in one who passes from divine contemplations to the evil state of man, misbehaving himself in a ridiculous manner; if, while his eyes are blinking and before he has become accustomed to the surrounding darkness, he is compelled to fight in courts of law, or in other places, about the images or the shadows of images of justice, and is endeavouring to meet the conceptions of those who have never yet seen absolute justice?

40   Anything but surprising, he replied.

41   Any one who has common sense will remember that the bewilderments of the eyes are of two kinds, and arise from two causes, either from coming out of the light or from going into the light, which is true of the mind's eye, quite as much as of the bodily eye; and he who remembers this when he sees any one whose vision is perplexed and weak, will not be too ready to laugh; he will first ask whether that soul of man has come out of the brighter life, and is unable to see because unaccustomed to the dark, or having turned from darkness to the day is dazzled by excess of light. And he will count the one happy in his condition and state of being, and he will pity the other; or, if he have a mind to laugh at the soul which comes from below into the light, there will be more reason in this than in the laugh which greets him who returns from above out of the light into the den.

42   That, he said, is a very just distinction.

43   But then, if I am right, certain professors of education must be wrong when they say that they can put a knowledge into the soul which was not there before, like sight into blind eyes.

44   They undoubtedly say this, he replied.

45   Whereas, our argument shows that the power and capacity of learning exists in the soul already; and that just as the eye was unable to turn from darkness to light without the whole body, so too the instrument of knowledge can only by the movement of the whole soul be turned from the world of becoming into that of being, and learn by degrees to endure the sight of being, and of the brightest and best of being, or in other words, of the good.

46   Very true.

47   And must there not be some art which will effect conversion in the easiest and quickest manner; not implanting the faculty of sight, for that exists already, but has been turned in the wrong direction, and is looking away from the truth?

48   Yes, he said, such an art may be presumed.

49   And whereas the other so-called virtues of the soul seem to be akin to bodily qualities, for even when they are not originally innate they can be

implanted later by habit and exercise, the virtue of wisdom more than anything else contains a divine element which always remains, and by this conversion is rendered useful and profitable; or, on the other hand, hurtful and useless. Did you never observe the narrow intelligence flashing from the keen eye of a clever rogue—how eager he is, how clearly his paltry soul sees the way to his end; he is the reverse of blind, but his keen eyesight is forced into the service of evil, and he is mischievous in proportion to his cleverness?

50   Very true, he said.

51   But what if there had been a circumcision of such natures in the days of their youth; and they had been severed from those sensual pleasures, such as eating and drinking, which, like leaden weights, were attached to them at their birth, and which drag them down and turn the vision of their souls upon the things that were below—if, I say, they had been released from these impediments and turned in the opposite direction, the very same faculty in them would have seen the truth as keenly as they see what their eyes are turned to now.

52   Very likely.

53   Yes, I said; and there is another thing which is likely, or rather a necessary inference from what has preceded, that neither the uneducated and uninformed of the truth, nor yet those who never make an end of their education, will be able ministers of State; not the former, because they have no single aim of duty which is the rule of all their actions, private as well as public; nor the latter, because they will not act at all except upon compulsion, fancying that they are already dwelling apart in the Islands of the Blest.

54   Very true, he replied.

55   Then, I said, the business of us who are the founders of the State will be to compel the best minds to attain that knowledge which we have already shown to be the greatest of all—they must continue to ascend until they arrive at the good; but when they have ascended and seen enough we must not allow them to do as they do now.

56   What do you mean?

57   I mean that they remain in the upper world: but this must not be allowed; they must be made to descend again among the prisoners in the den, and partake of their labours and honours, whether they are worth having or not.

58   But is not this unjust? he said; ought we to give them a worse life, when they might have a better?

59   You have again forgotten, my friend, I said, the intention of the legislator, who did not aim at making any one class in the State happy above the rest; the happiness was to be in the whole State, and he held the citizens together by persuasion and necessity, making them benefactors of the State, and therefore benefactors of one another; to this end he created them, not to please themselves, but to be his instruments in binding up the State.

60   True, he said, I had forgotten.

61   Observe, Glaucon, that there will be no injustice in compelling our philosophers to have a care and providence of others; we shall explain to them that in other States, men of their class are not obliged to share in the toils of politics: and this is reasonable, for they grow up at their own sweet will, and the government would rather not have them. Being self-taught, they cannot be expected to show any gratitude for a culture which they have never received. But we have brought you into the world to be rulers of the hive, kings of yourselves and of the other citizens, and have educated you far better and more perfectly than they have been educated, and you are better able to share in the double duty. Wherefore each of you, when his turn comes, must go down to the general underground abode, and get the habit of seeing in the dark. When you have acquired the habit, you will see ten thousand times better than the inhabitants of the den, and you will know what the several images are, and what they represent, because you have seen the beautiful and just and good in their truth. And thus our State which is also yours will be a reality, and not a dream only, and will be administered in a spirit unlike that of other States, in which men fight with one another about shadows only and are distracted in the struggle for power, which in their eyes is a great good. Whereas the truth is that the State in which the rulers are most reluctant to govern is always the best and most quietly governed, and the State in which they are most eager, the worst.

62   Quite true, he replied.

63   And will our pupils, when they hear this, refuse to take their turn at the toils of State, when they are allowed to spend the greater part of their time with one another in the heavenly light?

64   Impossible, he answered; for they are just men, and the commands which we impose upon them are just; there can be no doubt that every one will take office as a stern necessity, and not after the fashion of our present rulers of State.

65   Yes, my friend, I said; and there lies the point. You must contrive for your future rulers another and a better life than that of a ruler, and then you may have a well ordered State; for only in the State which offers this, will they rule who are truly rich, not in silver and gold, but in virtue and wisdom, which are the true blessings of life. Whereas if they go to the administration of public affairs, poor and hungering after their own private advantage, thinking that hence they are to snatch the chief good, order there can never be; for they will be fighting about office, and the civil and domestic broils which thus arise will be the ruin of the rulers themselves and of the whole State.

66   Most true, he replied.

67   And the only life which looks down upon the life of political ambition is that of true philosophy. Do you know of any other?

68   Indeed, I do not, he said.

69   And those who govern ought not to be lovers of the task? For, if they are, there will be rival lovers, and they will fight.

70   No question.

71   Who then are those whom we shall compel to be guardians? Surely they will be the men who are wisest about affairs of State, and by whom the State is best administered, and who at the same time have other honours and another and a better life than that of politics?

72   They are the men, and I will choose them, he replied.

73   And now shall we consider in what way such guardians will be produced, and how they are to be brought from darkness to light,—as some are said to have ascended from the world below to the gods?

74   By all means, he replied.

Questions for Discussion

1. Why does Socrates, the first-person narrator of this dialogue, ask questions rather than make statements?

2. An allegory is a story in which concrete elements signify specific things or ideas other than themselves. Explain the significance of the following elements in Plato's allegory: the cave, the sun, the men in the cave, the one man who escapes, his first reaction to the sun's light, and his subsequent actions and their results.

3. Why, according to Socrates, do those who attain knowledge of "the idea of the good" have difficulty concentrating on ordinary human affairs? Can you cite examples of highly educated people who lack common sense? How does Plato's allegory explain this lack?

4. According to Socrates, how valid is the justice of most societies?

5. What difficulty in finding ideal rulers does Socrates see?

6. What does the allegory of the cave suggest about most human intelligence?

Suggestions for Exploring, Writing, and Persuading

1. Apply Socrates's allegory to contemporary politics. First assess the quality of the United States's political leaders; then explain, based on the cave allegory, the reasons for their quality or lack thereof.

2. Argue for or against the following statement: "The State in which the rulers are most reluctant to govern is always the best and most quietly governed, and the State in which they are most eager, the worst."

William Golding (1911–1993)

British novelist and essayist William Golding is best known for his first novel, Lord of the Flies *(1954). His works, usually allegorical, are enriched with image clusters and symbols and often have unique points of view. The Inheritors (1955), for example, takes place around a symbolic*

waterfall and is seen primarily through the eyes of Nean-
derthals. Golding received the Nobel Prize for Literature in
1983 and was knighted by Queen Elizabeth in 1988.

THINKING AS A HOBBY (1961)

1   While I was still a boy, I came to the conclusion that there were three grades of thinking; and since I was later to claim thinking as my hobby, I came to an even stranger conclusion—namely, that I myself could not think at all.

2   I must have been an unsatisfactory child for grownups to deal with. I remember how incomprehensible they appeared to me at first, but not, of course, how I appeared to them. It was the headmaster of my grammar school who first brought the subject of thinking before me—though neither in the way, nor with the result he intended. He had some statuettes in his study. They stood on a high cupboard behind his desk. One was a lady wearing nothing but a bath towel. She seemed frozen in an eternal panic lest the bath towel slip down any farther; and since she had no arms, she was in an unfortunate position to pull the towel up again. Next to her, crouched the statuette of a leopard, ready to spring down at the top drawer of a filing cabinet labeled A–AH. My innocence interpreted this as the victim's last, despairing cry. Beyond the leopard was a naked, muscular gentleman, who sat, looking down, with his chin on his fist and his elbow on his knee. He seemed utterly miserable.

3   Some time later, I learned about these statuettes. The headmaster had placed them where they would face delinquent children, because they symbolized to him the whole of life. The naked lady was the Venus of Milo. She was Love. She was not worried about the towel. She was just busy being beautiful. The leopard was Nature, and he was being natural. The naked, muscular gentleman was not miserable. He was Rodin's Thinker, an image of pure thought. It is easy to buy small plaster models of what you think life is like.

4   I had better explain that I was a frequent visitor to the headmaster's study, because of the latest thing I had done or left undone. As we now say, I was not integrated. I was, if anything, disintegrated; and I was puzzled. Grownups never made sense. Whenever I found myself in a penal position before the headmaster's desk, with the statuettes glimmering whitely above him, I would sink my head, clasp my hands behind my back and writhe one shoe over the other.

5   The headmaster would look opaquely at me through flashing spectacles.

6   "What are we going to do with you?"

7   Well, what *were* they going to do with me? I would writhe my shoe some more and stare down at the worn rug.

8   "Look up, boy! Can't you look up?"

9   Then I would look up at the cupboard, where the naked lady was frozen in her panic and the muscular gentleman contemplated the hindquarters of the leopard in endless gloom. I had nothing to say to the

headmaster. His spectacles caught the light so that you could see nothing human behind them. There was no possibility of communication.

10 "Don't you ever think at all?"

11 No, I didn't think, wasn't thinking, couldn't think—I was simply waiting in anguish for the interview to stop.

12 "Then you'd better learn—hadn't you?"

13 On one occasion the headmaster leaped to his feet, reached up and plunked Rodin's masterpiece on the desk before me.

14 "That's what a man looks like when he's really thinking."

15 I surveyed the gentleman without interest or comprehension.

16 "Go back to your class."

17 Clearly there was something missing in me. Nature had endowed the rest of the human race with a sixth sense and left me out. This must be so, I mused, on my way back to the class, since whether I had broken a window, or failed to remember Boyle's Law, or been late for school, my teachers produced me one, adult answer: "Why can't you think?"

18 As I saw the case, I had broken the window because I had tried to hit Jack Arney with a cricket ball and missed him; I could not remember Boyle's Law because I had never bothered to learn it; and I was late for school because I preferred looking over the bridge into the river. In fact, I was wicked. Were my teachers, perhaps, so good that they could not understand the depths of my depravity? Were they clear, untormented people who could direct their every action by this mysterious business of thinking? The whole thing was incomprehensible. In my earlier years, I found even the statuette of the Thinker confusing. I did not believe any of my teachers were naked, ever. Like someone born deaf, but bitterly determined to find out about sound, I watched my teachers to find out about thought.

19 There was Mr. Houghton. He was always telling me to think. With a modest satisfaction, he would tell me that he had thought a bit himself. Then why did he spend so much time drinking? Or was there more sense in drinking than there appeared to be? But if not, and if drinking were in fact ruinous to health—and Mr. Houghton was ruined, there was no doubt about that—why was he always talking about the clean life and the virtues of fresh air? He would spread his arms wide with the action of a man who habitually spent his time striding along mountain ridges.

20 "Open air does me good, boys—I know it!"

21 Sometimes, exalted by his own oratory, he would leap from his desk and hustle us outside into a hideous wind.

22 "Now, boys! Deep breaths! Feel it right down inside you—huge draughts of God's good air!"

23 He would stand before us, rejoicing in his perfect health, an open-air man. He would put his hands on his waist and take a tremendous breath. You could hear the wind, trapped in the cavern of his chest and struggling with all the unnatural impediments. His body would reel with shock and his ruined face go white at the unaccustomed visitation. He would stagger back to his desk and collapse there, useless for the rest of the morning.

24   Mr. Houghton was given to high-minded monologues about the good life, sexless and full of duty. Yet in the middle of one of these monologues, if a girl passed the window, tapping along on her neat little feet, he would interrupt his discourse, his neck would turn of itself and he would watch her out of sight. In this instance, he seemed to me ruled not by thought but by an invisible and irresistible spring in his nape.

25   His neck was an object of great interest to me. Normally it bulged a bit over his collar. But Mr. Houghton had fought in the First World War alongside both Americans and French, and had come—by who knows what illogic?—to a settled detestation of both countries. If either country happened to be prominent in current affairs, no argument could make Mr. Houghton think well of it. He would bang the desk, his neck would bulge still further and go red. "You can say what you like," he would cry, "but I've thought about this—and I know what I think!"

26   Mr. Houghton thought with his neck.

27   There was Miss Parsons. She assured us that her dearest wish was our welfare, but I knew even then, with the mysterious clairvoyance of childhood, that what she wanted most was the husband she never got. There was Mr. Hands—and so on.

28   I have dealt at length with my teachers because this was my introduction to the nature of what is commonly called thought. Through them I discovered that thought is often full of unconscious prejudice, ignorance and hypocrisy. It will lecture on disinterested purity while its neck is being remorselessly twisted toward a skirt. Technically, it is about as proficient as most businessmen's golf, as honest as most politicians' intentions, or—to come near my own preoccupation—as coherent as most books that get written. It is what I came to call grade-three thinking, though more properly, it is feeling, rather than thought.

29   True, often there is a kind of innocence in prejudices, but in those days I viewed grade-three thinking with an intolerant contempt and an incautious mockery. I delighted to confront a pious lady who hated the Germans with the proposition that we should love our enemies. She taught me a great truth in dealing with grade-three thinkers; because of her, I no longer dismiss lightly a mental process which for nine-tenths of the population is the nearest they will ever get to thought. They have immense solidarity. We had better respect them, for we are outnumbered and surrounded. A crowd of grade-three thinkers, all shouting the same thing, all warming their hands at the fire of their own prejudices, will not thank you for pointing out the contradictions in their beliefs. Man is a gregarious animal, and enjoys agreement as cows will graze all the same way on the side of a hill.

30   Grade-two thinking is the detection of contradictions. I reached grade two when I trapped the poor, pious lady. Grade-two thinkers do not stampede easily, though often they fall into the other fault and lag behind. Grade-two thinking is a withdrawal, with eyes and ears open. It became my hobby and brought satisfaction and loneliness in either hand. For grade-two thinking destroys without having the power to create. It set

me watching the crowds cheering His Majesty the King and asking myself what all the fuss was about, without giving me anything positive to put in the place of that heady patriotism. But there were compensations. To hear people justify their habit of hunting foxes and tearing them to pieces by claiming that the foxes liked it. To hear our Prime Minister talk about the great benefit we conferred on India by jailing people like Pandit Nehru and Gandhi. To hear American politicians talk about peace in one sentence and refuse to join the League of Nations in the next. Yes, there were moments of delight.

31   But I was growing toward adolescence and had to admit that Mr. Houghton was not the only one with an irresistible spring in his neck. I, too, felt the compulsive hand of nature and began to find that pointing out contradiction could be costly as well as fun. There was Ruth, for example, a serious and attractive girl. I was an atheist at the time. Grade-two thinking is a menace to religion and knocks down sects like skittles. I put myself in a position to be converted by her with an hypocrisy worthy of grade three. She was a Methodist—or at least, her parents were, and Ruth had to follow suit. But, alas, instead of relying on the Holy Spirit to convert me, Ruth was foolish enough to open her pretty mouth in argument. She claimed that the Bible (King James Version) was literally inspired. I countered by saying that the Catholics believed in the literal inspiration of Saint Jerome's *Vulgate*,[1] and the two books were different. Argument flagged.

32   At last she remarked that there were an awful lot of Methodists, and they couldn't be wrong, could they—not all those millions? That was too easy, said I restively (for the nearer you were to Ruth, the nicer she was to be near to) since there were more Roman Catholics than Methodists anyway; and they couldn't be wrong, could they—not all those hundreds of millions? An awful flicker of doubt appeared in her eyes. I slid my arm around her waist and murmured breathlessly that if we were counting heads, the Buddhists were the boys for my money. But Ruth had *really* wanted to do me good, because I was so nice. She fled. The combination of my arm and those countless Buddhists was too much for her.

33   That night her father visited my father and left, red-cheeked and indignant. I was given the third degree to find out what had happened. It was lucky we were both of us only fourteen. I lost Ruth and gained an undeserved reputation as a potential libertine.

34   So grade-two thinking could be dangerous. It was in this knowledge, at the age of fifteen, that I remember making a comment from the heights of grade two, on the limitations of grade three. One evening I found myself alone in the school hall, preparing it for a party. The door of the headmaster's study was open. I went in. The headmaster had ceased to thump Rodin's Thinker down on the desk as an example to the young. Perhaps he had not found any more candidates, but the statuettes were still there, glimmering and gathering dust on top of the cupboard. I stood on a chair and

[1]The Latin Bible as revised in the fourth century A.D. by Jerome and used thereafter as the authoritative text for Roman Catholic ritual.

rearranged them. I stood Venus in her bath towel on the filing cabinet, so that now the top drawer caught its breath in a gasp of sexy excitement. "A-ah!" The portentous Thinker I placed on the edge of the cupboard so that he looked down at the bath towel and waited for it to slip.

35   Grade-two thinking, though it filled life with fun and excitement, did not make for content. To find out the deficiencies of our elders bolsters the young ego but does not make for personal security. I found that grade two was not only the power to point out contradictions. It took the swimmer some distance from the shore and left him there, out of his depth. I decided that Pontius Pilate was a typical grade-two thinker. "What is truth?" he said, a very common grade-two thought, but one that is used always as the end of an argument instead of the beginning. There is still a higher grade of thought which says, "What is truth?" and sets out to find it.

36   But these grade-one thinkers were few and far between. They did not visit my grammar school in the flesh though they were there in books. I aspired to them, partly because I was ambitious and partly because I now saw my hobby as an unsatisfactory thing if it went no further. If you set out to climb a mountain, however high you climb, you have failed if you cannot reach the top.

37   I *did* meet an undeniably grade-one thinker in my first year at Oxford. I was looking over a small bridge in Magdalen Deer Park, and a tiny mustached and hatted figure came and stood by my side. He was a German who had just fled from the Nazis to Oxford as a temporary refuge. His name was Einstein.

38   But Professor Einstein knew no English at that time and I knew only two words of German. I beamed at him, trying wordlessly to convey by my bearing all the affection and respect that the English felt for him. It is possible—and I have to make the admission—that I felt here were two grade-one thinkers standing side by side; yet I doubt if my face conveyed more than a formless awe. I would have given my Greek and Latin and French and a good slice of my English for enough German to communicate. But we were divided; he was as inscrutable as my headmaster. For perhaps five minutes we stood together on the bridge, undeniable grade-one thinker and breathless aspirant. With true greatness, Professor Einstein realized that my contact was better than none. He pointed to a trout wavering in midstream.

39   He spoke: "*Fisch.*"

40   My brain reeled. Here I was, mingling with the great, and yet helpless as the veriest grade-three thinker. Desperately I sought for some sign by which I might convey that I, too, revered pure reason. I nodded vehemently. In a brilliant flash I used up half of my German vocabulary.

41   "*Fisch. Ja Ja.*"

42   For perhaps another five minutes we stood side by side. Then Professor Einstein, his whole figure still conveying good will and amiability, drifted away out of sight.

43   I, too, would be a grade-one thinker. I was irreverent at the best of times. Political and religious systems, social customs, loyalties and traditions,

they all came tumbling down like so many rotten apples off a tree. This was a fine hobby and a sensible substitute for cricket, since you could play it all the year round. I came up in the end with what must always remain the justification for grade-one thinking, its sign, seal and charter. I devised a coherent system for living. It was a moral system, which was wholly logical. Of course, as I readily admitted, conversion of the world to my way of thinking might be difficult, since my system did away with a number of trifles, such as big business, centralized government, armies, marriage. . . .

44   It was Ruth all over again. I had some very good friends who stood by me, and still do. But my acquaintances vanished, taking the girls with them. Young women seemed oddly contented with the world as it was. They valued the meaningless ceremony with a ring. Young men, while willing to concede the chaining sordidness of marriage, were hesitant about abandoning the organizations which they hoped would give them a career. A young man on the first rung of the Royal Navy, while perfectly agreeable to doing away with big business and marriage, got as rednecked as Mr. Houghton when I proposed a world without any battleships in it.

45   Had the game gone too far? Was it a game any longer? In those prewar days, I stood to lose a great deal, for the sake of a hobby.

46   Now you are expecting me to describe how I saw the folly of my ways and came back to the warm nest, where prejudices are so often called loyalties, where pointless actions are hallowed into custom by repetition, where we are content to say we think when all we do is feel.

47   But you would be wrong. I dropped my hobby and turned professional.

48   If I were to go back to the headmaster's study and find the dusty statuettes still there, I would arrange them differently. I would dust Venus and put her aside, for I have come to love her and know her for the fair thing she is. But I would put the Thinker, sunk in his desperate thought, where there were shadows before him—and at his back, I would put the leopard, crouched and ready to spring.

Questions for Discussion

1. Golding uses the three statuettes both symbolically and structurally. Explain what they mean to him as a young boy, as an adolescent, and as an adult.

2. Define the three grades of thinkers according to Golding.

3. Golding implies that most people are grade-three thinkers, dominated by prejudices and unwilling to examine their assumptions. Explain why you do or do not agree with him.

4. Explain the appropriateness of describing grade-three thinkers as cows that "graze all the same way on the side of a hill." Why are grade-three thinkers dangerous? What is dangerous about grade-two thinking? Who are the examples of grade-two and grade-one thinkers?

5. How does Golding's assessment of most human intelligence compare to that of Socrates in the allegory of the cave?

Suggestions for Exploring, Writing, and Persuading

1. In an essay, explain your own classification of thinkers.
2. Discuss how education and experience can change a person's level of thinking.
3. Write an essay using Golding's classification but developing it by using your own acquaintances and experiences as examples.
4. In an essay argue that if Golding's assessment of thinkers is correct; those who live in democracies have much to fear from grade-three thinkers or argue that Golding's belief that a large percent of the population should be classified as grade-three thinkers is or is not correct.

Garrison Keillor (b. 1942)

Garrison Keillor, a storyteller, humorist, and radio personality from rural Minnesota, is best known for A Prairie Home Companion, *his popular radio show broadcast for many years on National Public Radio. The fictional town of Lake Wobegon, Minnesota, originally created on the radio show, is also the setting for several of Keillor's books, including* Lake Wobegon Days *(1985),* Leaving Home: a Collection of Lake Wobegon Stories *(1987), and* Lake Wobegon Boy *(1997). In both the radio show and the books on Lake Wobegon, Keillor, with gentle humor, celebrates the people and customs of rural Minnesota, investing the local and particular with a universal resonance and revealing the wonder of the commonplace. His most recent books include* Me: by Jimmy (Big Boy) Valenta *(1999) and* Love Me *(2000). The following essay comes from Keillor's* Happy to be Here *(1982), a collection of short stories and essays.*

ATTITUDE   (1982)

1   Long ago I passed the point in life when major-league ballplayers begin to be younger than yourself. Now all of them are, except for a few aging trigenarians and a couple of quadros who don't get around on the fastball as well as they used to and who sit out the second games of double-headers. However, despite my age (thirty-nine), I am still active and have a lot of interests. One of them is slow-pitch softball, a game that lets me go through the motions of baseball without getting beaned or having to run too hard. I play on a pretty casual team, one that drinks beer on the bench and substitutes freely. If a player's wife or girlfriend wants to play, we give her a glove and send her out to right field, no questions asked, and if she lets a pop fly drop six feet in front of her, nobody agonizes over it.

2   Except me. This year. For the first time in my life, just as I am entering the dark twilight of my slow-pitch career, I find myself taking the game seriously. It isn't the bonehead play that bothers me especially— the pop fly that drops untouched, the slow roller juggled and the ball then

heaved ten feet over the first baseman's head and into the next diamond, the routine singles that go through outfielders' legs for doubles and triples with gloves flung after them. No, it isn't our stone-glove fielding or pussyfoot base-running or limp-wristed hitting that gives me fits, though these have put us on the short end of some mighty ridiculous scores this summer. It's our attitude.

3   Bottom of the ninth, down 18–3, two outs, a man on first and a woman on third, and our third baseman strikes out. *Strikes out*! In slow-pitch, not even your grandmother strikes out, but this guy does, and after his third strike—a wild swing at a ball that bounces on the plate—he topples over in the dirt and lies flat on his back, laughing. *Laughing*!

4   Same game, earlier. They have the bases loaded. A weak grounder is hit toward our second baseperson. The runners are running. She picks up the ball, and she looks at them. She looks at first, at second, at home. We yell. "Throw it! throw it!," and she throws it, underhand, at the pitcher, who has turned and run to back up the catcher. The ball rolls across the third-baseline and under the bench. Three runs score. The batter, a fatso, chugs into second. The other team hoots and hollers, and what does she do? She shrugs and smiles ("Oh, silly me"); after all, it's only a game. Like the aforementioned strikeout artist, she treats her error as a joke. They have forgiven themselves instantly, which is unforgivable. It is *we* who should forgive them, who can say, "It's all right, it's only a game." They are supposed to throw up their hands and kick the dirt and hang their heads, as if this boner, even if it is their sixteenth of the afternoon—*this* is the one that really and truly breaks their hearts.

5   That attitude sweetens the game for everyone. The sinner feels sweet remorse. The fatso feels some sense of accomplishment; this is no bunch of rumdums forced into an error but a team with some class. We, the sinner's teammates, feel momentary anger at her—dumb! dumb play!—but then, seeing her grief, we sympathize with her in our hearts (any one of us might have made that mistake or one worse), and we yell encouragement, including the shortstop, who, moments before, dropped an easy throw for a force at second. "That's all right! Come on! We got 'em!" we yell. "Shake it off! These turkeys can't hit!" This makes us all feel good, even though the turkeys now lead us by ten runs. We're getting clobbered, but we have a whining attitude.

6   Let me say this about attitude: Each player is responsible for his or her own attitude, and to a considerable degree you can *create* a good attitude by doing certain little things on the field. There are certain little things that ballplayers do in the Bigs, and we ought to be doing them in the Slows.

7   1. When going up to bat, don't step right into the batter's box as if it were an elevator. The box is your turf, your stage. Take possession of it slowly and deliberately, starting with a lot of back-bending, knee-stretching, and torso-revolving in the on-deck circle. Then, approaching the box, stop outside it and tap the dirt off your spikes with your bat. You don't have spikes, you have sneakers, of course, but the significance of the tapping

is the same. Then, upon entering the box, spit on the ground. It's a way of saying, "This here is mine. This is where I get my hits."

8   2. Spit frequently. Spit at all crucial moments. Spit correctly. Spit should be *blown*, not ptuied weakly with the lips, which often results in dribble. Spitting should convey forcefulness of purpose, concentration, pride. Spit down, not in the direction of others. Spit in the glove and on the fingers, especially after making a real knucklehead play; it's a way of saying, "I dropped the ball because my glove was dry."

9   3. At the bat and in the field, pick up dirt. Rub dirt in the fingers (especially after spitting on them). Toss dirt, as if testing the wind for velocity and direction. Smooth the dirt. Be involved with dirt. If no dirt is available (e.g., in the outfield), pluck tufts of grass. Fielders should be grooming their areas constantly between plays, flicking away tiny sticks and bits of gravel.

10   4. Take your time. Tie your laces. Confer with your teammates about possible situations that may arise and conceivable options in dealing with them. Extend the game. Three errors on three consecutive plays can be humiliating if the plays occur within the space of a couple of minutes, but if each error is separated from the next by extensive conferences on the mound, lace-tying, glove adjustments, and arguing close calls (if any), the effect on morale is minimized.

11   5. Talk. Not just an occasional "Let's get a hit now" but continuous rhythmic chatter, a flow of syllables; "Hey babe hey babe c'mon babe good stick now hey babe long tater take him downtown babe . . . hey good eye good eye."

12   Infield chatter is harder to maintain. Since the slow-pitch pitch is required to be a soft underhand lob, infielders hesitate to say, "Smoke him babe hey low heat hey throw it on the black babe chuck it in there back him up babe no hit no hit." Say it anyway.

13   6. One final rule, perhaps the most important of all: When your team is up and has made the third out, the batter and the players who were left on base do not come back to the bench for their gloves. *They remain on the field, and their teammates bring their gloves out to them.* This requires some organization and discipline, but it pays off big in morale. It says, "Although we're getting our pants knocked off, still we must conserve our energy."

14   Imagine that you have bobbled two fly balls in this rout and now you have just tried to stretch a single into a double and have been easily thrown out sliding into second base, where the base runner ahead of you had stopped. It was the third out and a dumb play, and your opponents smirk at you as they run off the field. You are the goat, a lonely and tragic figure sitting in the dirt. You curse yourself, jerking your head sharply forward. You stand up and kick the base. How miserable! How degrading! Your utter shame, though brief, bears silent testimony to the worthiness of your teammates, whom you have let down, and they appreciate it. They call out to you now as they take the field, and as the second baseman runs to his position he says, "Let's get'em now," and tosses you your glove. Lowering your

head, you trot slowly out to right. There you do some deep knee bends. You pick grass. You find a pebble and fling it into foul territory. As the first batter comes to the plate, you check the sun. You get set in your stance, poised to fly. Feet spread, hands on hips, you bend slightly at the waist and spit the expert spit of a veteran ballplayer—a player who has known the agony of defeat but who always bounces back, a player who has lost a stride on the base paths but can still make the big play.

15   This is *ball*, ladies and gentlemen. This is what it's all about.

Questions for Discussion

1. Keillor appears to be less concerned about the quality of his team's hitting and fielding than about such apparently minor details as spitting correctly and knocking dirt from one's cleats. Why? What is his point in focusing on such details?

2. What are these middle-aged men trying to accomplish by playing softball? What do they try to communicate through their elaborate gestures and rituals?

3. Why does the speaker consider it unpardonable for players who make major mistakes to forgive themselves instantly?

4. Clearly the speaker is not serious in his criticism of his teammates' attitudes. What is the serious point he is trying to make?

Suggestions for Exploring, Writing, and Persuading

1. Discuss in detail a particular role you play in which apparently minor details take on exaggerated importance.

2. In an essay argue that a sport or activity that you play, have played, or have watched should change some of the rules. Your essay may be serious or humorous.

Lorian Hemingway (b. 1951)

Brought up in Mississippi, Lorian Hemingway is the granddaughter of Ernest Hemingway. The daughter of an alcoholic mother and a depressed, abusive father, she herself turned to drugs and alcohol in her early adult years. After spending some time in jail and in an alcohol treatment facility, she finally broke free of her addiction in 1988. Her works include Walking into the River, *a novel, and* Walk on Water *(1998), a memoir that was nominated for a National Book Award and from which the selection here is taken. She founded and directs the Lorian Hemingway Short Story Competition to encourage undiscovered young writers. She shares with her grandfather Ernest a passion for fishing and the outdoors.*

FROM WALK ON WATER (1998)

1   I take fish personally, the way I have my life, like a sacrament. This is my body. Eat of it. This is my blood. Drink. I imagine this reverence is what they want of me. The alchemists made an eyewash (collyrium) of fish, believing it would bring omniscience. I've tried to envision the process: cooking the fish, as the alchemists instructed, until it "yellowed," mashing it into a crumbly pulp, mixing it with water, and then filling the eyes with this paste so one might gaze with as much dimension as trout in a clear stream. But as with all things in alchemy, it was the process that mattered, the final result never as important as the ritual preceding it.

2   Knowing fish is a process. I have been acquainting myself for forty years. To know fish you have to have been intimate, the way the alchemists were. One of the first fish I ever caught as a kid was a baby bass netted from a deep Mississippi ravine I lived in in summer. It was my refuge, that ravine, a place of discovery, revealer of miracles, its depth filled with a heavy current of reddish brown water during the spring floods, its red clay bottom dried to a pockmarking of deep holes by mid-July. I was tirelessly curious when I was young, bound inextricably to all natural mysteries behind four walls, nervous and jumpy if made to sit too long indoors, recalcitrant once sprung.

3   I'd watched this particular fish for days, trapped in a pothole in the ravine, swimming in a quick panic from one side to the other, instinctively seeking a tributary from its footwide prison. I empathized, imagined myself locked in my room for days, dizzy and breathless from claustrophobia, frantic enough to pull up the flooring with my bare hands. I understood feeling trapped, my life then nothing more than a crash course in how to escape. Escape meant steering past my mother, who sat limp at the kitchen table, stupid from vodka, or creeping past the time bomb that was my stepfather as he lay snoring, passed out in his recliner. I'd turn the handle quick on the front door and sink into the thick Mississippi heat, feeling, once I'd made it to the ravine, as if I had, by sleight of hand, through sheer caginess, become someone else. My head, which always seemed to buzz with a jumpy current whenever my mother raised a full glass to her lips, was clear.

4   Along the red clay of the ravine lip my bare feet moved with extraordinary balance, and I slid deep into the ravine bed without a sound, a small avalanche of pebbles falling in my wake. I stood then surrounded by wide canyon walls, a young girl ready to trap the very source of summer. I thought often it was the Cherokee in me that let me move like an animal, quiet, steady, aware. My great-grandfather had been a chief. His name was Golden for the strain of burnt-gold hair and green eyes that surfaced every few generations. My mother had the honey-colored hair, the green eyes. And then there was the dark strain. Mine.

5   After a few days the water in the pothole had diminished by half and grew so thick with ravine mud that the fish hung motionless in the ooze, its gills laboring for the oxygen it needed. On my knees I stared into the

hole, goldfish net in hand, thinking it was evil, what I was about to do, snatch a living creature from its habitat and bring it, luckless, into my own. I remember the delicate thin striping on its flanks as I lifted it, unprotesting, from the muck, and how soft and filmy the skin felt as I stroked a finger along its length. I remember, too, how my heart raced as I dropped the fish into the jar, watched him sink quickly and then just as quickly take his first breath in a new world. Within moments he was moving through the jar as manically as he had the pothole days before. I had given resurrection in a pint of water, become God to a fish. Years later I would remember that moment as one of grace.

6   Fish became my fascination and began to appear in dreams, their shadows deep in dark water, cruising, fins breaking the surface from time to time, a teasing swirl of movement as I stood onshore with net or rod or hands poised to strike. In one dream I stood before a pool of monster fish with bare hands greedy, my fingertips singing the way a line does when it's pulled free from the spool. As I leaned forward, a shape would slide deliberately beneath my reach, and I would lunge into water that was dense and thick as oil, only to come up soaked and empty-handed.

7   I don't know now that the dreams had to do with catching fish, but rather with some unconscious, archetypal need. I have consulted Jung on this one for the obvious, loaded symbolism. I have even dreamt, in these later years, of Jung, standing atop the stone fortress of his tower at Bolligen, fly rod in hand, a wooden piscatorial carving dangling from his leader line. He smiles in the dream, proud of himself. He did say that water is the unconscious and that fish are a Christ symbol. I deduce, then, from these two boldly fitting pieces, that I am at times fishing for Jesus, or in some way, in recent dreams, dry-flying for Christ. I like the simplicity of it, the directness. I like that it speaks to Christian and hedonist alike.

8   But during those Mississippi summers that spanned my eighth to thirteenth years I paid little attention to dreams, mesmerized then by a world filled with fish, turtles, frogs, and lizards, anything remotely amphibian. Frogs were a class of fascination all their own, and I would capture them simply to feel the cool, crepey skin of their underbellies and watch the slow blink of their eyes. I progressed quickly from netting bass to catfishing with a bobber and worm, frittering away entire days on the banks of muddy lakes and rivers, certain, always, that the fish lived dead center, in the middle of the lake, assuming the notion that the truly elusive spend their time where we can never hope to reach them. To cast where they hid was my ambition. Eventually I understood that fish went wherever they damned well pleased, unimpressed by my clumsy form hurling hooks into their midst, immune to my need to know them. I had patience, the sort I suspect God has with people like me. It meant nothing to be skunked for days on end. I lived in perpetual hope of seeing that wayward shimmy of the bobber, then the quick dip and tug that signaled I had made contact with aliens. At that time in my life, *this* was my social interaction. I talked to the fish hidden deep in the ponds and streams I visited,

trying to imagine what they saw beneath those mirrored surfaces, and reasoned it was hunger and not stupidity that made them take bait so crudely hitched to an obvious weapon. Compassion surfaced. I pictured scores of starving fish grubbing for worms, only to be duped into death by my slipshod cunning. When I'd haul them to shore I'd cry at what I'd done, at the sight of the hook swallowed to the hilt, at the flat, accusing eyes of the fish, and then I'd club them with a Coke bottle, the heavy green kind with the bottling company's name on the bottom. No one ever said there was another way to do it. In Mississippi, there was the hook, the worm, and the bobber, a holy trinity on a hot day in August—low-maintenance fishing I call it now. My guilt was usually pushed aside by their quick death beneath the bottle, and eating what I had caught seemed to remove the shame considerably.

9   My favorite fishing hole—I look back on it now as Mississippi's version of Mecca—was a place that to this day I am certain only one other knew of, the landowner who'd barbwired it off and posted a huge hand-painted sign along the fence—WARNING: SNAKES—a beacon to me. Yell "snake" and I ran not from, but *to* the source of panic, scooping the creature into my bare hands, trying to remember idly if red bands against yellow meant poisonous, or the other way around.

10   Roaming deep in a pine woods in rural Hinds County one summer afternoon, I came upon the pond, the edges of it rising in volcanic fashion from the otherwise flat land. I was accustomed only to ponds that were slipped like sinkholes into the surrounding pastureland, and as I made my way up the slight incline of earth, hands grasping the barbwire delicately, I beheld, not a rock quarry as I had expected, but instead a perfectly black pool of water, its dimensions no greater than those of an average swimming pool. At first I could not believe the color of the fish who were pushing to the surface, dozens of them, nosing one into another, their bodies opalescent as pearls, and huge, their lengths dissolving into the shadow of the pond. I had never seen albino catfish, had never seen *any* white fish, and thought for a brief, illogical moment that they had been segregated from their darker mates simply because of their color. In Mississippi then, it fit.

11   To have called this pond a fishing hole is misleading. I never actually fished its waters, too mesmerized by the cloudlike shapes that moved without sound through the deep pond, believing, beyond all fishing reason, that to catch them would bring the worst sort of luck. So I watched, alone in the woods with these mutants, some days prodding their lazy bodies with a hickory stick, which they rubbed against curiously, and on others merely counting the number of laps they made around the pond in an afternoon, hypnotized by the rhythm they made tracing one circle upon another.

12   The fish were as truly alien as my starkest imaginings, and I became convinced they were telepathic, reading my thoughts with such ease I had no need to speak to them. I called these journeys "visiting the fish

gods," my treks to that mysterious water that had no business existing in a dry woods, and took into my life the memory of them, as if they were a talisman, granting me privileges and luck in the fishing world others could only dream of.

Questions for Discussion

1. Why was the author as a child attracted to the small ravine near her home?
2. What is the author's attitude toward fish? Why is she so fascinated by fish that they dominate even her dreams and fantasies? Explain her comments about the Jungian archetypes.
3. How does she try to know fish?
4. Why does the author, after catching fish, first cry, then club them with a Coke bottle?
5. What is the author's reason for not trying to catch the albino catfish she finds in the isolated pond surrounded by "barbwire"?

Suggestions for Exploring, Writing, and Persuading

1. Discuss in an essay what being in and around woods and natural bodies of water means to the narrator and why.
2. Examine the Christian symbolism scattered throughout the essay. Next find the Biblical references. Then write an essay giving your suggestions of what Hemingway is implying by her use of these parallels.

FICTION

James Joyce (1882–1941)

One of the most famous, influential, and controversial writers of the twentieth century, James Joyce was born in Dublin in 1882. Joyce excelled at the Irish Catholic schools where he was educated, and his experiences at these schools were a major influence on his later work, especially on his first novel, Portrait of the Artist As a Young Man *(1916). Joyce spent most of his life in Trieste, Rome, and Paris. Both his novels and his short stories are justly ranked as works that, though unique, were major influences on later writers. His collection of stories in* Dubliners, *ending with "The*

Dead," appeared in 1914. The American magazine Little Review *began publication of Joyce's novel* Ulysses *in 1920, but the courts stopped publication when the publishers were convicted of obscenity; it was finally published in 1922.* Finnegan's Wake, *his last novel, was published in 1939, three years before his death.*

ARABY (1914)

1   North Richmond Street, being blind, was a quiet street except at the hour when the Christian Brothers' School set the boys free. An uninhabited house of two stories stood at the blind end, detached from its neighbors in a square ground. The other houses of the street, conscious of decent lives within them, gazed at one another with brown imperturbable faces.

2   The former tenant of our house, a priest, had died in the back drawing room. Air, musty from having been long enclosed, hung in all the rooms, and the waste room behind the kitchen was littered with old useless papers. Among these I found a few paper-covered books, the pages of which were curled and damp: *The Abbot,* by Walter Scott, *The Devout Communicant,* and *The Memoirs of Vidocq.* I liked the last best because its leaves were yellow. The wild garden behind the house contained a central apple tree and a few straggling brushes under one of which I found the late tenant's rusty bicycle pump. He had been a very charitable priest; in his will he had left all his money to institutions and the furniture of his house to his sister.

3   When the short days of winter came dusk fell before we had well eaten our dinners. When we met in the street the houses had grown somber. The space of sky above us was the color of ever-changing violet and towards it the lamps of the street lifted their feeble lanterns. The cold air stung us and we played till our bodies glowed. Our shouts echoed in the silent street. The career of our play brought us through the dark muddy lanes behind the houses where we ran the gauntlet of the rough tribes from the cottages, to the back doors of the dark odorous stables where a coachman smoothed and combed the horse or shook music from the buckled harness. When we returned to the street, light from the kitchen windows had filled the areas. If my uncle was seen turning the corner we hid in the shadow until we had seen him safely housed. Or if Mangan's sister came out on the doorstep to call her brother in to his tea we watched her from our shadow peer up and down the street. We waited to see whether she would remain or go in and, if she remained, we left our shadow and walked up to Mangan's steps resignedly. She was waiting for us, her figure defined by the light from the half-opened door. Her brother always teased her before he obeyed and I stood by the railings looking at her. Her dress swung as she moved her body and the soft rope of her hair tossed from side to side.

4   Every morning I lay on the floor in the front parlor watching her door. The blind was pulled down to within an inch of the sash so that I could

not be seen. When she came out on the doorstep my heart leaped. I ran to the hall, seized my books and followed her. I kept her brown figure always in my eye and, when we came near the point at which our ways diverged, I quickened my pace and passed her. This happened morning after morning. I had never spoken to her, except for a few casual words, and yet her name was like a summons to all my foolish blood.

5   Her image accompanied me even in places the most hostile to romance. On Saturday evenings when my aunt went marketing I had to go to carry some of the parcels. We walked through the flaring streets, jostled by drunken men and bargaining women, amid the curses of laborers, the shrill litanies of shop boys who stood on guard by the barrels of pigs' cheeks, the nasal chanting of street singers, who sang a *come-all-you* about O'Donovan Rossa, or a ballad about the troubles in our native land. These noises converged in a single sensation of life for me: I imagined that I bore my chalice safely through a throng of foes. Her name sprang to my lips at moments in strange prayers and praises which I myself did not understand. My eyes were often full of tears (I could not tell why) and at times a flood from my heart seemed to pour itself out into my bosom. I thought little of the future. I did not know whether I would ever speak to her or not or, if I spoke to her, how I could tell her of my confused adoration. But my body was like a harp and her words and gestures were like fingers running upon the wires.

6   One evening I went into the back drawing room in which the priest had died. It was a dark rainy evening and there was no sound in the house. Through one of the broken panes I heard the rain impinge upon the earth, the fine incessant needles of water playing in the sodden beds. Some distant lamp or lighted window gleamed below me. I was thankful that I could see so little. All my senses seemed to desire to veil themselves and, feeling that I was about to slip from them, I pressed the palms of my hands together until they trembled, murmuring: *"O love! O love!"* many times.

7   At last she spoke to me. When she addressed the first words to me I was so confused that I did not know what to answer. She asked me was I going to *Araby*. I forgot whether I answered yes or no. It would be a splendid bazaar, she said; she would love to go.

8   "And why can't you?" I asked.

9   While she spoke she turned a silver bracelet round and round her wrist. She could not go, she said, because there would be a retreat that week in her convent. Her brother and two other boys were fighting for their caps and I was alone at the railings. She held one of the spikes, bowing her head towards me. The light from the lamp opposite our door caught the white curve of her neck, lit up her hair that rested there and, falling, lit up the hand upon the railing. It fell over one side of her dress and caught the white border of a petticoat, just visible as she stood at ease.

10   "It's well for you," she said.

11   "If I go," I said, "I will bring you something."

12   What innumerable follies laid waste my waking and sleeping thoughts after that evening! I wished to annihilate the tedious intervening days. I chafed against the work of school. At night in my bedroom and by day in the classroom her image came between me and the page I strove to read. The syllables of the word *Araby* were called to me through the silence in which my soul luxuriated and cast an Eastern enchantment over me. I asked for leave to go to the bazaar on Saturday night. My aunt was surprised and hoped it was not some Freemason affair. I answered few questions in class. I watched my master's face pass from amiability to sternness; he hoped I was not beginning to idle. I could not call my wandering thoughts together. I had hardly any patience with the serious work of life which, now that it stood between me and my desire, seemed to me child's play, ugly monotonous child's play.

13   On Saturday morning I reminded my uncle that I wished to go to the bazaar in the evening. He was fussing at the hall stand, looking for the hat brush, and answered me curtly:

14   "Yes, boy, I know."

15   As he was in the hall I could not go into the front parlor and lie at the window. I left the house in bad humor and walked slowly towards the school. The air was pitilessly raw and already my heart misgave me.

16   When I came home to dinner my uncle had not yet been home. Still it was early. I sat staring at the clock for some time and, when its ticking began to irritate me, I left the room. I mounted the staircase and gained the upper part of the house. The high cold empty gloomy rooms liberated me and I went from room to room singing. From the front window I saw my companions playing below in the street. Their cries reached me weakened and indistinct and, leaning my forehead against the cool glass, I looked over at the dark house where she lived. I may have stood there for an hour, seeing nothing but the brown-clad figure cast by my imagination, touched discreetly by the lamplight at the curved neck, at the hand upon the railings and at the border below the dress.

17   When I came downstairs again I found Mrs. Mercer sitting at the fire. She was an old garrulous woman, a pawnbroker's widow, who collected used stamps for some pious purpose. I had to endure the gossip of the tea table. The meal was prolonged beyond an hour and still my uncle did not come. Mrs. Mercer stood up to go; she was sorry she couldn't wait any longer, but it was after eight o'clock and she did not like to be out late, as the night air was bad for her. When she had gone I began to walk up and down the room, clenching my fists. My aunt said:

18   "I'm afraid you may put off your bazaar for this night of Our Lord."

19   At nine o'clock I heard my uncle's latchkey in the hall door. I heard him talking to himself and heard the hall stand rocking when it had received the weight of his overcoat. I could interpret these signs. When he was midway through his dinner I asked him to give me the money to go to the bazaar. He had forgotten.

20   "The people are in bed and after their first sleep now," he said.

21   I did not smile. My aunt said to him energetically:

22   "Can't you give him the money and let him go? You've kept him late enough as it is."

23   My uncle said he was very sorry he had forgotten. He said he believed in the old saying: "All work and no play makes Jack a dull boy." He asked me where I was going and, when I had told him a second time he asked me did I know *The Arab's Farewell to His Steed.* When I left the kitchen he was about to recite the opening lines of the piece to my aunt.

24   I held a florin tightly in my hand as I strode down Buckingham Street towards the station. The sight of the streets thronged with buyers and glaring with gas recalled to me the purpose of my journey. I took my seat in a third-class carriage of a deserted train. After an intolerable delay the train moved out of the station slowly. It crept onward among ruinous houses and over the twinkling river. At Westland Row Station a crowd of people pressed to the carriage doors; but the porters moved them back, saying that it was a special train for the bazaar. I remained alone in the bare carriage. In a few minutes the train drew up beside an improvised wooden platform. I passed out on to the road and saw by the lighted dial of a clock that it was ten minutes to ten. In front of me was a large building which displayed the magical name.

25   I could not find any sixpenny entrance and, fearing that the bazaar would be closed, I passed in quickly through a turnstile, handing a shilling to a weary-looking man. I found myself in a big hall girdled at half its height by a gallery. Nearly all the stalls were closed and the greater part of the hall was in darkness. I recognized a silence like that which pervades a church after a service. I walked into the center of the bazaar timidly. A few people were gathered about the stalls which were still open. Before a curtain, over which the words *Café Chantant* were written in colored lamps, two men were counting money on a salver. I listened to the fall of the coins.

26   Remembering with difficulty why I had come I went over to one of the stalls and examined porcelain vases and flowered tea sets. At the door of the stall a young lady was talking and laughing with two young gentlemen. I remarked their English accents and listened vaguely to their conversation.

27   "O, I never said such a thing!"

28   "O, but you did!"

29   "O, but I didn't!"

30   "Didn't she say that?"

31   "Yes, I heard her."

32   "O, there's a...fib!"

33   Observing me, the young lady came over and asked me did I wish to buy anything. The tone of her voice was not encouraging; she seemed to have spoken to me out of a sense of duty. I looked humbly at the great jars that stood like eastern guards at either side of the dark entrance to the stall and murmured:

34   "No, thank you."

35   The young lady changed the position of one of the vases and went back to the two young men. They began to talk of the same subject. Once or twice the young lady glanced at me over her shoulder.

36   I lingered before her stall, though I knew my stay was useless, to make my interest in her wares seem the more real. Then I turned away slowly and walked down the middle of the bazaar. I allowed the two pennies to fall against the sixpence in my pocket. I heard a voice call from one end of the gallery that the light was out. The upper part of the hall was now completely dark.

37   Gazing up into the darkness I saw myself as a creature driven and derided by vanity; and my eyes burned with anguish and anger.

Questions for Discussion

1. Who is the narrator? What are his feelings toward Mangan's sister?

2. How does the description of the neighborhood set the tone and prepare for the conclusion?

3. What do the many references to the church and religion suggest about the boy's attitude and his sense of mission?

4. What does Araby at first symbolize for the narrator? How does this symbol change?

5. What details at the bazaar reveal the difference between the way the narrator sees Araby and the way those who are holding the bazaar see it?

6. Explain the last sentence of the story. Why does this simple disappointment seem so devastating to the narrator?

Suggestions for Exploring, Writing, and Persuading

1. Write an essay describing one of your experiences in which your expectations were far higher than the reality.

2. Examine the feelings of the narrator for Mangan's sister and write an essay explaining whether his feelings and his subsequent actions are or are not typical of a boy or girl who has become infatuated for the first time.

3. In an essay, analyze the ways in which the narrator changes as the story progresses.

4. How would you explain "Araby" as a quest story? What is the narrator seeking?

5. Write an essay discussing this story as an example of a useful quest.

6. Argue that the narrator is or is not "driven by vanity."

Bernard Malamud (1914–1986)

One of America's foremost writers from the 1950s through the 1980s, Malamud in his fiction treats his fellow Jews as exemplars of all people who find a way to endure with dignity through pain and anguish. As in "Angel Levine," his fiction often reveals the humor in the ordinary and even painful, the miraculous in the mundane. Malamud won a Pulitzer Prize for the novel The Fixer *(1966) and National Book Awards for* The Fixer *and* The Magic Barrel *(1958), the collection of stories from which "Angel Levine" is taken.*

ANGEL LEVINE
(1958)

1   Manischevitz, a tailor, in his fifty-first year suffered many reverses and indignities. Previously a man of comfortable means, he overnight lost all he had, when his establishment caught fire and, after a metal container of cleaning fluid exploded, burned to the ground. Although Manischevitz was insured against fire, damage suits by two customers who had been hurt in the flames deprived him of every penny he had collected. At almost the same time, his son, of much promise, was killed in the war, and his daughter, without so much as a word of warning, married a lout and disappeared with him as off the face of the earth. Thereafter Manischevitz was victimized by excruciating backaches and found himself unable to work even as a presser—the only kind of work available to him—for more than an hour or two daily, because beyond that the pain from standing became maddening. His Fanny, a good wife and mother, who had taken in washing and sewing, began before his eyes to waste away. Suffering shortness of breath, she at last became seriously ill and took to her bed. The doctor, a former customer of Manischevitz, who out of pity treated them, at first had difficulty diagnosing her ailment but later put it down as hardening of the arteries at an advanced stage. He took Manischevitz aside, prescribed complete rest for her, and in whispers gave him to know there was little hope.

2   Throughout his trials Manischevitz had remained somewhat stoic, almost unbelieving that all this had descended upon his head, as if it were happening, let us say, to an acquaintance or some distant relative; it was in sheer quantity of woe incomprehensible. It was also ridiculous, unjust, and because he had always been a religious man, it was in a way an affront to God. Manischevitz believed this in all his suffering. When his burden had grown too crushingly heavy to be borne he prayed in his chair with shut hollow eyes: "My dear God, sweetheart, did I deserve that this should happen to me?" Then recognizing the worthlessness of it, he put aside the complaint and prayed humbly for assistance: "Give Fanny back her health, and to me for myself that I shouldn't feel pain in every step. Help now or tomorrow is too late. This I don't have to tell you." And Manischevitz wept.

3   Manischevitz's flat, which he had moved into after the disastrous fire, was a meager one, furnished with a few sticks of chairs, a table, and bed,

in one of the poorer sections of the city. There were three rooms: a small, poorly-papered living room; an apology for a kitchen, with a wooden ice-box; and the comparatively large bedroom where Fanny lay in a sagging secondhand bed, gasping for breath. The bedroom was the warmest room of the house and it was here, after his outburst to God, that Manischevitz, by the light of two small bulbs overhead, sat reading his Jewish newspaper. He was not truly reading, because his thoughts were everywhere; however the print offered a convenient resting place for his eyes, and a word or two, when he permitted himself to comprehend them, had the momentary effect of helping him forget his troubles. After a short while he discovered, to his surprise, that he was actively scanning the news, searching for an item of great interest to him. Exactly what he thought he would read he couldn't say—until he realized, with some astonishment, that he was expecting to discover something about himself. Manischevitz put his paper down and looked up with the distinct impression that someone had entered the apartment, though he could not remember having heard the sound of the door opening. He looked around: the room was very still, Fanny sleeping, for once, quietly. Half-frightened, he watched her until he was satisfied she wasn't dead; then, still disturbed by the thought of an unannounced visitor, he stumbled into the living room and there had the shock of his life, for at the table sat a Negro reading a newspaper he had folded up to fit into one hand.

4   "What do you want here?" Manischevitz asked in fright.

5   The Negro put down the paper and glanced up with a gentle expression. "Good evening." He seemed not to be sure of himself, as if he had got into the wrong house. He was a large man, bonily built, with a heavy head covered by a hard derby, which he made no attempt to remove. His eyes seemed sad, but his lips, above which he wore a slight mustache, sought to smile; he was not otherwise prepossessing. The cuffs of his sleeves, Manischevitz noted, were frayed to the lining and the dark suit was badly fitted. He had very large feet. Recovering from his fright, Manischevitz guessed he had left the door open and was being visited by a case worker from the Welfare Department—some came at night—for he had recently applied for relief. Therefore he lowered himself into a chair opposite the Negro, trying, before the man's uncertain smile, to feel comfortable. The former tailor sat stiffly but patiently at the table, waiting for the investigator to take out his pad and pencil and begin asking questions; but before long he became convinced the man intended to do nothing of the sort.

6   "Who are you?" Manischevitz at last asked uneasily.

7   "If I may, insofar as one is able to, identify myself, I bear the name of Alexander Levine."

8   In spite of all his troubles Manischevitz felt a smile growing on his lips. "You said Levine?" he politely inquired.

9   The Negro nodded. "That is exactly right."

10   Carrying the jest farther, Manischevitz asked, "You are maybe Jewish?"

11   "All my life I was, willingly."

12   The tailor hesitated. He had heard of black Jews but had never met one. It gave an unusual sensation.

13   Recognizing in afterthought something odd about the tense of Levine's remark, he said doubtfully, "You ain't Jewish anymore?"

14   Levine at this point removed his hat, revealing a very white part in his black hair, but quickly replaced it. He replied, "I have recently been disincarnated into an angel. As such, I offer you my humble assistance, if to offer is within my province and ability—in the best sense." He lowered his eyes in apology. "Which calls for added explanation: I am what I am granted to be, and at present the completion is in the future."

15   "What kind of angel is this?" Manischevitz gravely asked.

16   "A bona fide angel of God, within prescribed limitations," answered Levine, "not to be confused with the members of any particular sect, order, or organization here on earth operating under a similar name."

17   Manischevitz was thoroughly disturbed. He had been expecting something but not this. What sort of mockery was it—provided Levine was an angel—of a faithful servant who had from childhood lived in the synagogues, always concerned with the word of God?

18   To test Levine he asked, "Then where are your wings?"

19   The Negro blushed as well as he was able. Manischevitz understood this from his changed expression. "Under certain circumstances we lose privileges and prerogatives upon returning to earth, no matter for what purpose, or endeavoring to assist whosoever."

20   "So tell me," Manischevitz said triumphantly, "how did you get here?"

21   "I was transmitted."

22   Still troubled, the tailor said, "If you are a Jew, say the blessing for bread."

23   Levine recited it in sonorous Hebrew.

24   Although moved by the familiar words Manischevitz still felt doubt that he was dealing with an angel.

25   "If you are an angel," he demanded somewhat angrily, "give me the proof."

26   Levine wet his lips. "Frankly, I cannot perform either miracles or near miracles, due to the fact that I am in a condition of probation. How long that will persist or even consist, I admit, depends on the outcome."

27   Manischevitz racked his brains for some means of causing Levine positively to reveal his true identity, when the Negro spoke again:

28   "It was given me to understand that both your wife and you require assistance of a salubrious nature?"

29   The tailor could not rid himself of the feeling that he was the butt of a jokester. Is this what a Jewish angel looks like? he asked himself. This I am not convinced.

30   He asked a last question. "So if God sends to me an angel, why a black? Why not a white that there are so many of them?"

31   "It was my turn to go next," Levine explained.

32   Manischevitz could not be persuaded. "I think you are a faker."

33   Levine slowly rose. His eyes showed disappointment and worry. "Mr. Manischevitz," he said tonelessly, "if you should desire me to be of assistance to you any time in the near future, or possibly before, I can be found"—he glanced at his fingernails—"in Harlem."

34   He was by then gone.

35   The next day Manischevitz felt some relief from his backache and was able to work four hours at pressing. The day after, he put in six hours; and the third day four again. Fanny sat up a little and asked for some halvah to suck. But on the fourth day the stabbing, breaking ache afflicted his back, and Fanny again lay supine, breathing with blue-lipped difficulty.

36   Manischevitz was profoundly disappointed at the return of his active pain and suffering. He had hoped for a longer interval of easement, long enough to have some thought other than of himself and his troubles. Day by day, hour by hour, minute after minute, he lived in pain, pain his only memory, questioning the necessity of it, inveighing against it, also, though with affection, against God. Why *so much*, Gottenyu? If He wanted to teach His servant a lesson for some reason, some cause—the nature of His nature—to teach him, say, for reasons of his weakness, his pride, perhaps, during his years of prosperity, his frequent neglect of God—to give him a little lesson, why then any of the tragedies that had happened to him, any *one* would have sufficed to chasten him. But *all together*—the loss of both his children, his means of livelihood, Fanny's health and his—that was too much to ask one frail-boned man to endure. Who, after all, was Manischevitz that he had been given so much to suffer? A tailor. Certainly not a man of talent. Upon him suffering was largely wasted. It went nowhere, into nothing: into more suffering. His pain did not earn him bread, nor fill the cracks in the wall, nor lift, in the middle of the night, the kitchen table; only lay upon him, sleepless, so sharply oppressively that he could many times have cried out yet not heard himself through this thickness of misery.

37   In this mood he gave no thought to Mr. Alexander Levine, but at moments when the pain waivered, slightly diminishing, he sometimes wondered if he had been mistaken to dismiss him. A black Jew and angel to boot—very hard to believe, but suppose he *had* been sent to succor him, and he, Manischevitz, was in his blindness too blind to comprehend? It was this thought that put him on the knife-point of agony.

38   Therefore the tailor, after much self-questioning and continuing doubt, decided he would seek the self-styled angel in Harlem. Of course he had great difficulty, because he had not asked for specific directions, and movement was tedious to him. The subway took him to 116th Street, and from there he wandered in the dark world. It was vast and its lights lit nothing. Everywhere were shadows, often moving. Manischevitz hobbled along with the aid of a cane, and not knowing where to seek in the blackened tenement buildings, looked fruitlessly through store windows. In the stores he saw people and *everybody* was black. It was an amazing thing to observe. When he was too tired, too unhappy to go farther, Manischevitz

stopped in front of a tailor's store. Out of familiarity with the appearance of it, with some sadness he entered. The tailor, an old skinny Negro with a mop of woolly gray hair, was sitting cross-legged on his workbench, sewing a pair of full-dress pants that had a razor slit all the way down the seat.

39   "You'll excuse me, please, gentleman," said Manischevitz, admiring the tailor's deft, thimbled fingerwork, "but you know maybe somebody by the name Alexander Levine?"

40   The tailor, who Manischevitz thought, seemed a little antagonistic to him, scratched his scalp.

41   "Cain't say I ever heared dat name."

42   "Alex-ander Lev-ine," Manischevitz repeated it.

43   The man shook his head. "Cain't say I heared."

44   About to depart, Manischevitz remembered to say: "He is an angel, maybe."

45   "Oh *him*," said the tailor clucking. "He hang out in dat honky tonk down here a ways." He pointed with his skinny finger and returned to the pants.

46   Manischevitz crossed the street against a red light and was almost run down by a taxi. On the block after the next, the sixth store from the corner was a cabaret, and the name in sparkling lights was Bella's. Ashamed to go in, Manischevitz gazed through the neon-lit window, and when the dancing couples had parted and drifted away, he discovered at a table on the side, towards the rear, Levine.

47   He was sitting alone, a cigarette butt hanging from the corner of his mouth, playing solitaire with a dirty pack of cards, and Manischevitz felt a touch of pity for him, for Levine had deteriorated in appearance. His derby was dented and had a gray smudge on the side. His ill-fitting suit was shabbier, as if he had been sleeping in it. His shoes and trouser cuffs were muddy, and his face was covered with an impenetrable stubble the color of licorice. Manischevitz, though deeply disappointed, was about to enter, when a big-breasted Negress in a purple evening gown appeared before Levine's table, and with much laughter through many white teeth, broke into a vigorous shimmy. Levine looked straight at Manischevitz with a haunted expression, but the tailor was too paralyzed to move or acknowledge it. As Bella's gyrations continued, Levine rose, his eyes lit in excitement. She embraced him with vigor, both his hands clasped around her big restless buttocks and they tangoed together across the floor, loudly applauded by the noisy customers. She seemed to have lifted Levine off his feet and his large shoes hung limp as they danced. They slid past the windows where Manischevitz, white-faced, stood staring in. Levine winked slyly and the tailor left for home.

48   Fanny lay at death's door. Through shrunken lips she muttered concerning her childhood, the sorrows of the marriage bed, and loss of her children, yet wept to live. Manischevitz tried not to listen, but even without ears he would have heard. It was not a gift. The doctor panted up the stairs, a broad but bland, unshaven man (it was Sunday) and soon shook his head. A day at most, or two. He left at once, not without pity, to spare

himself Manischevitz's multiplied sorrow; the man who never stopped hurting. He would someday get him into a public home.

49   Manischevitz visited a synagogue and there spoke to God, but God had absented himself. The tailor searched his heart and found no hope. When she died he would live dead. He considered taking his life although he knew he wouldn't. Yet it was something to consider. Considering, you existed. He railed against God—Can you love a rock, a broom, an emptiness? Baring his chest, he smote the naked bones, cursing himself for having believed.

50   Asleep in a chair that afternoon, he dreamed of Levine. He was standing before a faded mirror, preening small decaying opalescent wings. "This means," mumbled Manischevitz, as he broke out of sleep, "that it is possible he could be an angel." Begging a neighbor lady to look in on Fanny and occasionally wet her lips with a few drops of water, he drew on his thin coat, gripped his walking stick, exchanged some pennies for a subway token, and rode to Harlem. He knew this act was the last desperate one of his woe: to go without belief, seeking a black magician to restore his wife to invalidism. Yet if there was no choice, he did at least what was chosen.

51   He hobbled to Bella's but the place had changed hands. It was now, as he breathed, a synagogue in a store. In the front, towards him, were several rows of empty wooden benches. In the rear stood the Ark, its portals of rough wood covered with rainbows of sequins; under it a long table on which lay the sacred scroll unrolled, illuminated by the dim light from a bulb on a chain overhead. Around the table, as if frozen to it and the scroll, which they all touched with their fingers, sat four Negroes wearing skullcaps. Now as they read the Holy Word, Manischevitz could, through the plate glass window, hear the singsong chant of their voices. One of them was old, with a gray beard. One was bubble-eyed. One was humpbacked. The fourth was a boy, no older than thirteen. Their heads moved in rhythmic swaying. Touched by this sight from his childhood and youth, Manischevitz entered and stood silent in the rear.

52   "Neshoma," said bubble eyes, pointing to the word with a stubby finger. "Now what dat mean?"

53   "That's the word that means soul," said the boy. He wore glasses.

54   "Let's git on wid de commentary," said the old man.

55   "Ain't necessary," said the humpback. "Souls is immaterial substance. That's all. The soul is derived in that manner. The immateriality is derived from the substance, and they both, causally an' otherwise, derived from the soul. There can be no higher."

56   "That's the highest."

57   "Over de top."

58   "Wait a minute," said bubble eyes. "I don't see what is dat immaterial substance. How come de one gits hitched up to de odder?" He addressed the humpback.

59   "Ask me something hard. Because it is substanceless immateriality. It couldn't be closer together, like all the parts of the body under one skin—closer."

60   "Hear now," said the old man.

61   "All you done is switched de words."

62   "It's the primum mobile, the substanceless substance from which comes all things that were incepted in the idea—you, me and everything and body else."

63   "Now how did all dat happen? Make it sound simple."

64   "It de speerit," said the old man. "On de face of de water moved de speerit. An' dat was good. It say so in de Book. From de speerit ariz de man."

65   "But now listen here. How come it become substance if it all de time a spirit?"

66   "God alone done dat."

67   "Holy! Holy! Praise His Name."

68   "But has dis spirit got some kind of a shade or color?" asked bubble eyes, deadpan.

69   "Man of course not. A spirit is a spirit."

70   "Then how come we is colored?" he said with a triumphant glare.

71   "Ain't got nothing to do wid dat."

72   "I still like to know."

73   "God put the spirit in all things," answered the boy. "He put it in the green leaves and the yellow flowers. He put it with the gold in the fishes and the blue in the sky. That's how come it came to us."

74   "Amen."

75   "Praise Lawd and utter loud His speechless name."

76   "Blow de bugle till it bust the sky."

77   They fell silent, intent upon the next word. Manischevitz approached them.

78   "You'll excuse me," he said. "I am looking for Alexander Levine. You know him maybe?"

79   "That's the angel," said the boy.

80   "Oh, *him*," snuffed bubble eyes.

81   "You'll find him at Bella's. It's the establishment right across the street," the humpback said.

82   Manischevitz said he was sorry that he could not stay, thanked them, and limped across the street. It was already night. The city was dark and he could barely find his way.

83   But Bella's was bursting with the blues. Through the window Manischevitz recognized the dancing crowd and among them sought Levine. He was sitting loose-lipped at Bella's side table. They were tippling from an almost empty whiskey fifth. Levine had shed his old clothes, wore a shiny new checkered suit, pearl-gray derby, cigar, and big, two-tone button shoes. To the tailor's dismay, a drunken look had settled upon his formerly dignified face. He leaned toward Bella, tickled her ear lobe with his pinky, while whispering words that sent her into gales of raucous laughter. She fondled his knee.

84   Manischevitz, girding himself, pushed open the door and was not welcomed.

85   "This place reserved."

86   "Beat it, pale puss."

87   "Exit, Yankel, Semitic trash."

88   But he moved towards the table where Levine sat, the crowd breaking before him as he hobbled forward.

89   "Mr. Levine," he spoke in a trembly voice. "Is here Manischevitz."

90   Levine glared blearily. "Speak yo' piece, son."

91   Manischevitz shuddered. His back plagued him. Cold tremors tormented his crooked legs. He looked around, everybody was all ears.

92   "You'll excuse me. I would like to talk to you in a private place."

93   "Speak, Ah is a private pusson."

94   Bella laughed piercingly. "Stop it, boy, you killin' me."

95   Manischevitz, no end disturbed, considered fleeing but Levine addressed him:

96   "Kindly state the pu'pose of yo' communication with yo's truly."

97   The tailor wet cracked lips. "You are Jewish. This I am sure."

98   Levine rose, nostrils flaring. "Anythin' else yo' got to say?"

99   Manischevitz's tongue lay like stone.

100   "Speak now or fo'ever hold off."

101   Tears blinded the tailor's eyes. Was ever man so tried? Should he say he believed a half-drunken Negro to be an angel?

102   The silence slowly petrified.

103   Manischevitz was recalling scenes of his youth as a wheel in his mind whirred: believe, do not, yes, no, yes, no. The pointer pointed to yes, to between yes and no, to no, no it was yes. He sighed. It moved but one had still to make a choice.

104   "I think you are an angel from God." He said it in a broken voice, thinking, If you said it it was said. If you believed it you must say it. If you believed, you believed.

105   The hush broke. Everybody talked but the music began and they went on dancing. Bella, grown bored, picked up the cards and dealt herself a hand.

106   Levine burst into tears. "How you have humiliated me."

107   Manischevitz apologized.

108   "Wait'll I freshen up." Levine went to the men's room and returned in his old clothes.

109   No one said goodbye as they left.

110   They rode to the flat via subway. As they walked up the stairs Manischevitz pointed with his cane at his door.

111   "That's all been taken care of," Levine said. "You best go in while I take off."

112   Disappointed that it was so soon over but torn by curiosity, Manischevitz followed the angel up three flights to the roof. When he got there the door was already padlocked.

113   Luckily he could see through a small broken window. He heard an odd noise, as though of a whirring of wings, and when he strained for a wider

view, could have sworn he saw a dark figure borne aloft on a pair of magnificent black wings.

114   A feather drifted down. Manischevitz gasped as it turned white, but it was only snowing.

115   He rushed downstairs. In the flat Fanny wielded a dust mop under the bed and then upon the cobwebs on the wall.

116   "A wonderful thing, Fanny," Manischevitz said. "Believe me, there are Jews everywhere."

Questions for Discussion

1. How does an understanding of the story of Job in the Bible enrich your understanding of Manischevitz's story?

2. Why does Manischevitz not believe that Levine is a Jewish angel? Why do you suppose Malamud chose to portray Levine in a way that is so surprising to Manischevitz?

3. Although "Angel Levine" is a story about a man's intense suffering, it is nevertheless humorous. What details add humor to the story without reducing its pathos?

4. What does the story suggest about the limits or lack of limits of faith?

Suggestions for Exploring, Writing, and Persuading

1. Write a character sketch of either Manischevitz or Levine.

2. Argue in an essay that Manischevitz's actions toward Levine are based on prejudice.

3. Write an essay comparing Manischevitz's experience with that of the grandmother in Flannery O'Connor's "A Good Man Is Hard to Find."

4. Compare Manischevitz's two trips to Harlem and explain the reasons that they have such different results.

5. In an essay, trace and explain the changes in Levine's appearance and speech patterns.

Arthur C. Clarke (b. 1917)

Arthur C. Clarke, a British physicist and mathematician, writes fiction and nonfiction. His works, selling in the millions, have been translated into dozens of languages. A 1945 paper published in Wireless World *helped to set the stage for modern telecommunications. Clarke is, however, probably best known for the screenplay for Stanley Kubrick's 2001: A Space Odyssey, based on Clarke's short story "Sentinel of Eternity." "The Star," published in 1955, won a Hugo award for excellence in science fiction.*

THE STAR (1955)

1   It is three thousand light years to the Vatican. Once, I believed that space could have no power over faith, just as I believed that the heavens declared the glory of God's handiwork. Now I have seen that handiwork, and my faith is sorely troubled. I stare at the crucifix that hangs on the cabin wall above the Mark VI Computer, and for the first time in my life I wonder if it is no more than an empty symbol.

2   I have told no one yet, but the truth cannot be concealed. The facts are there for all to read, recorded on the countless miles of magnetic tape and the thousands of photographs we are carrying back to Earth. Other scientists can interpret them as easily as I can, and I am not one who would condone that tampering with the truth which often gave my order a bad name in the olden days.

3   The crew are already sufficiently depressed: I wonder how they will take this ultimate irony. Few of them have any religious faith, yet they will not relish using this final weapon in their campaign against me—that private, good-natured, but fundamentally serious, war which lasted all the way from Earth. It amused them to have a Jesuit as chief astrophysicist: Dr. Chandler, for instance, could never get over it (why are medical men such notorious atheists?). Sometimes he would meet me on the observation deck, where the lights are always low so that the stars shine with undiminished glory. He would come up to me in the gloom and stand staring out of the great oval port, while the heavens crawled slowly around us as the ship turned end over end with the residual spin we had never bothered to correct.

4   "Well, Father," he would say at last, "it goes on forever and forever, and perhaps *Something* made it. But how you can believe that Something has a special interest in us and our miserable little world—that just beats me." Then the argument would start, while the stars and nebulae would swing around us in silent, endless arcs beyond the flawlessly clear plastic of the observation port.

5   It was, I think, the apparent incongruity of my position that caused most amusement to the crew. In vain I would point to my three papers in the *Astrophysical Journal*, my five in the *Monthly Notices of the Royal Astronomical Society*. I would remind them that my order has long been famous for its scientific works. We may be few now, but ever since the eighteenth century we have made contributions to astronomy and geophysics out of all proportion to our numbers. Will my report on the Phoenix Nebula end our thousand years of history? It will end, I fear, much more than that.

6   I do not know who gave the nebula its name, which seems to me a very bad one. If it contains a prophecy, it is one that cannot be verified for several billion years. Even the word nebula is misleading: this is a far smaller object than those stupendous clouds of mist—the stuff of unborn stars—that are scattered throughout the length of the Milky Way. On the cosmic scale, indeed, the Phoenix Nebula is a tiny thing—a tenuous shell of gas surrounding a single star.

7   Or what is left of a star...

8   The Rubens engraving of Loyola seems to mock me as it hangs there above the spectrophotometer tracings. What would *you*, Father, have made of this knowledge that has come into my keeping, so far from the little world that was all the universe you knew? Would your faith have risen to the challenge, as mine has failed to do?

9   You gaze into the distance, Father, but I have traveled a distance beyond any that you could have imagined when you founded our order a thousand years ago. No other survey ship has been so far from Earth: we are at the very frontiers of the explored universe. We set out to reach the Phoenix Nebula, we succeeded, and we are homeward bound with our burden of knowledge. I wish I could lift that burden from my shoulders, but I call to you in vain across the centuries and the light-years that lie between us.

10   On the book you are holding the words are plain to read. AD MAJOREM DEI GLORIAM, the message runs, but it is a message I can no longer believe. Would you still believe it, if you could see what we have found?

11   We knew, of course, what the Phoenix Nebula was. Every year, in our galaxy alone, more than a hundred stars explode, blazing for a few hours or days with thousands of times their normal brilliance before they sink back into death and obscurity. Such are the ordinary novae—the commonplace disasters of the universe. I have recorded the spectrograms and light curves of dozens since I started working at the Lunar Observatory.

12   But three or four times in every thousand years occurs something beside which even a nova pales into total insignificance.

13   When a star becomes a *supernova*, it may for a little while outshine all the massed suns of the galaxy. The Chinese astronomers watched this happen in A.D. 1054, not knowing what it was they saw. Five centuries later, in 1572, a supernova blazed in Cassiopeia so brilliantly that it was visible in the daylight sky. There have been three more in the thousand years that have passed since then.

14   Our mission was to visit the remnants of such a catastrophe, to reconstruct the events that led up to it, and, if possible, to learn its cause. We came slowly in through the concentric shells of gas that had been blasted out six thousand years before, yet were expanding still. They were immensely hot, radiating even now with a fierce violet light, but were far too tenuous to do us any damage. When the star had exploded, its outer layers had been driven upward with such speed that they had escaped completely from its gravitational field. Now they formed a hollow shell large enough to engulf a thousand solar systems, and at its center burned the tiny, fantastic object which the star had now become—a White Dwarf, smaller than the Earth, yet weighing a million times as much.

15   The glowing gas shells were all around us, banishing the normal night of interstellar space. We were flying into the center of a cosmic bomb that had detonated millennia ago and whose incandescent fragments were still hurling apart. The immense scale of the explosion, and the fact that the

debris already covered a volume of space many billions of miles across, robbed the scene of any visible movement. It would take decades before the unaided eye could detect any motion in these tortured wisps and eddies of gas, yet the sense of turbulent expansion was overwhelming.

16   We had checked our primary drive hours before, and were drifting slowly toward the fierce little star ahead. Once it had been a sun like our own, but it had squandered in a few hours the energy that should have kept it shining for a million years. Now it was a shrunken miser, hoarding its resources as if trying to make amends for its prodigal youth.

17   No one seriously expected to find planets. If there had been any before the explosion, they would have been boiled into puffs of vapor, and their substance lost in the greater wreckage of the star itself. But we made the automatic search, as we always do when approaching an unknown sun, and presently we found a single small world circling the star at an immense distance. It must have been the Pluto of this vanished solar system, orbiting on the frontiers of the night. Too far from the central sun ever to have known life, its remoteness had saved it from the fate of all its lost companions.

18   The passing fires had seared its rocks and burned away the mantle of frozen gas that must have covered it in the days before the disaster. We landed, and we found the Vault.

19   Its builders had made sure that we should. The monolithic marker that stood above the entrance was now a fused stump, but even the first long-range photographs told us that here was the work of intelligence. A little later we detected the continent-wide pattern of radio-activity that had been buried in the rock. Even if the pylon above the Vault had been destroyed, this would have remained, an immovable and all but eternal beacon calling to the stars. Our ship fell toward this gigantic bull's-eye like an arrow into its target.

20   The pylon must have been a mile high when it was built, but now it looked like a candle that had melted down into a puddle of wax. It took us a week to drill through the fused rock, since we did not have the proper tools for a task like this. We were astronomers, not archaeologists, but we could improvise. Our original purpose was forgotten: this lonely monument, reared with such labor at the greatest possible distance from the doomed sun, could have only one meaning. A civilization that knew it was about to die had made its last bid for immortality.

21   It will take us generations to examine all the treasures that were placed in the Vault. They had plenty of time to prepare, for their sun must have given its first warnings many years before the final detonation. Everything that they wished to preserve, all the fruit of their genius, they brought here to this distant world in the days before the end, hoping that some other race would find it and that they would not be utterly forgotten. Would we have done as well, or would we have been too lost in our own misery to give thought to a future we could never see or share?

22   If only they had had a little more time! They could travel freely enough between the planets of their own sun, but they had not yet learned to

cross the interstellar gulfs, and the nearest solar system was a hundred light-years away. Yet even had they possessed the secret of the Transfinite Drive, no more than a few millions could have been saved. Perhaps it was better thus.

23   Even if they had not been so disturbingly human as their sculpture shows, we could not have helped admiring them and grieving for their fate. They left thousands of visual records and the machines for projecting them, together with elaborate pictorial instructions from which it will not be difficult to learn their written language. We have examined many of these records, and brought to life for the first time in six thousand years the warmth and beauty of a civilization that in many ways must have been superior to our own. Perhaps they only showed us the best, and one can hardly blame them. But their words were very lovely, and their cities were built with a grace that matches anything of man's. We have watched them at work and play, and listened to their musical speech sounding across the centuries. One scene is still before my eyes—a group of children on a beach of strange blue sand, playing in the waves as children play on Earth. Curious whiplike trees line the shore, and some very large animal is wading in the shadows yet attracting no attention at all.

24   And sinking into the sea, still warm and friendly and life-giving, is the sun that will soon turn traitor and obliterate all this innocent happiness.

25   Perhaps if we had not been so far from home and so vulnerable to loneliness, we should not have been so deeply moved. Many of us had seen the ruins of ancient civilizations on other worlds, but they had never affected us so profoundly. This tragedy was unique. It is one thing for a race to fail and die, as nations and cultures have done on Earth. But to be destroyed so completely in the full flower of its achievement, leaving no survivors—how could that be reconciled with the mercy of God?

26   My colleagues have asked me that, and I have given what answers I can. Perhaps you could have done better, Father Loyola, but I have found nothing in the *Exercitia Spiritualia* that helps me here. They were not an evil people: I do not know what gods they worshiped, if indeed they worshiped any. But I have looked back at them across the centuries, and have watched while the loveliness they used their last strength to preserve was brought forth again into the light of their shrunken sun. They could have taught us much: why were they destroyed?

27   I know the answers that my colleagues will give when they get back to Earth. They will say that the universe has no purpose and no plan, that since a hundred suns explode every year in our galaxy, at this very moment some race is dying in the depths of space. Whether that race has done good or evil during its lifetime will make no difference in the end: there is no divine justice, for there is no God.

28   Yet, of course, what we have seen proves nothing of the sort. Anyone who argues thus is being swayed by emotion, not logic. God has no need to justify His actions to man. He who built the universe can destroy it

when He chooses. It is arrogance—it is perilously near blasphemy—for us to say what He may or may not do.

29   This I could have accepted, hard though it is to look upon whole worlds and peoples thrown into the furnace. But there comes a point when even the deepest faith must falter, and now, as I look at the calculations lying before me, I know I have reached that point at last.

30   We could not tell, before we reached the nebula, how long ago the explosion took place. Now, from the astronomical evidence and the record in the rocks of that one surviving planet, I have been able to date it very exactly. I know in what year the light of this colossal conflagration reached our Earth. I know how brilliantly the supernova whose corpse now dwindles behind our speeding ship once shone in terrestrial skies. I know how it must have blazed low in the east before sunrise, like a beacon in that oriental dawn.

31   There can be no reasonable doubt: the ancient mystery is solved at last. Yet, oh God, there were so many stars you could have used. What was the need to give these people to the fire, that the symbol of their passing might shine above Bethlehem?

Questions for Discussion

1. What is the point of view in "The Star"? Why is it crucial to the irony of the ending?

2. What are the characteristics of a Jesuit priest? Is this Jesuit priest an exacting scientist? Why does he face a spiritual crisis? Explain his statement at the beginning of the story: "Once, I believed that space could have no power over faith, just as I believed that the heavens declared the glory of God's handiwork. Now I have seen that handiwork, and my faith is sorely troubled."

3. What is the priest's answer to skeptics who argue that "the universe has no purpose and no plan" and that "there is no God"? Is the priest comfortable with his answer?

4. Why is this particular discovery so devastating to his faith?

Suggestions for Exploring, Writing, and Persuading

1. Analyze in an essay how Clark's use of a Jesuit priest as narrator is vital to the irony in the story.

2. Compare the priest's religious dilemma with the quandary faced by Ozzie in Roth's "The Conversion of the Jews."

3. If some event or book such as *The Da Vinci Code* has ever challenged your traditional religious beliefs, write an essay about why and how this event or book challenged these beliefs.

Philip Roth (b. 1933)

Born in Newark, New Jersey, Philip Roth is a contemporary
American novelist, short story writer, and man of letters.
Goodbye, Columbus *(1955), his first book, is a collection of*
short stories including "The Conversion of the Jews." Roth
frequently takes as his subject the urban Jews among whom
he grew up. His novels, often comic, include the hilarious
Portnoy's Complaint *(1969), about a Jewish man afflicted*
with an insatiable sexual desire for gentile women; Letting
Go *(1962);* The Great American Novel *(1973); and the Zuck-*
*erman trilogy—*Zuckerman Bound *(1985),* The Counterlife
(1988), and Deception *(1990);* Sabbath Theater *(1995);*
American Pastoral *(1997), for which he won the Pulitzer*
Prize in 1998; The Human Stain *(2000);* The Dying Animal
(2001); and The Plot Against America *(2004). Among his*
many honors and awards are two National Book Awards
(for Goodbye, Columbus *and* Sabbath Theater*), the National*
Medal of Arts (1998), and the gold medal in fiction from the
American Academy of Arts and Letters.

THE CONVERSION OF THE JEWS (1955)

1   "You're a real one for opening your mouth in the first place," Itzie said.
"What do you open your mouth all the time for?"

2   "I didn't bring it up, Itz, I didn't," Ozzie said.

3   "What do you care about Jesus Christ for anyway?"

4   "I didn't bring up Jesus Christ. He did. I didn't even know what he was
talking about. Jesus is historical, he kept saying. Jesus is historical." Ozzie
mimicked the monumental voice of Rabbi Binder.

5   "Jesus was a person that lived like you and me," Ozzie continued.
"that's what Binder said—"

6   "Yeah?...so what! What do I give two cents whether he lived or not.
And what do you gotta open your mouth!" Itzie Lieberman favored
closed-mouthedness, especially when it came to Ozzie Freedman's questions. Mrs. Freedman had to see Rabbi Binder twice before about Ozzie's
questions and this Wednesday at four-thirty would be the third time. Itzie
preferred to keep *his* mother in the kitchen; he settled for behind-the-
back subtleties such as gestures, faces, snarls and other less delicate
barnyard noises.

7   "He was a real person, Jesus, but he wasn't like God, and we don't
believe he is God." Slowly, Ozzie was explaining Rabbi Binder's position
to Itzie, who had been absent from Hebrew School the previous afternoon.

8   "The Catholics," Itzie said helpfully, "they believe in Jesus Christ, that
he's God." Itzie Lieberman used "the Catholics" in its broadest sense—to
include the Protestants.

9   Ozzie received Itzie's remark with a tiny head bob, as though it were a
footnote, and went on. "His mother was Mary, and his father probably was
Joseph," Ozzie said. "But the New Testament says his real father was God."

10   "His *real* father?"

11   "Yeah," Ozzie said, "that's the big thing, his father's supposed to be God."

12   "Bull."

13   "That's what Rabbi Binder says, that it's impossible—"

14   "Sure it's impossible. That stuff's all bull. To have a baby you gotta get laid," Itzie theologized. "Mary hadda get laid."

15   "That's what Binder says: 'the only way a woman can have a baby is to have intercourse with a man.'"

16   "He said *that*, Ozz?" For a moment it appeared that Itzie had put the theological question aside. "He said that, intercourse?" A little curled smile shaped itself in the lower half of Itzie's face like a pink mustache. "What you guys do, Ozz, you laugh or something?"

17   "I raised my hand."

18   "Yeah? Whatja say?"

19   "That's when I asked the question."

20   Itzie's face lit up. "Whatja ask about—intercourse?"

21   "No, I asked the question about God, how if He could create the heaven and earth in six days, and make all the animals and the fish and the light in six days—the light especially, that's what always gets me, that He could make the light. Making fish and animals, that's pretty good—"

22   "That's damn good." Itzie's appreciation was honest but unimaginative: it was as though God had just pitched a one-hitter.

23   "But making light...I mean when you think about it, it's really something," Ozzie said. "Anyway, I asked Binder if He could make all that in six days, and He could *pick* the six days he wanted right out of nowhere, why couldn't He let a woman have a baby without having intercourse."

24   "You said intercourse, Ozz, to Binder?"

25   "Yeah."

26   "Right in class?"

27   "Yeah."

28   Itzie smacked the side of his head.

29   "I mean, no kidding around," Ozzie said, "that'd really be nothing. After all that other stuff, that'd practically be nothing."

30   Itzie considered a moment. "What'd Binder say?"

31   "He started all over again explaining how Jesus was historical and how he lived like you and me but he wasn't God. So I said I under*stood* that. What I wanted to know was different."

32   What Ozzie wanted to know was always different. The first time he had wanted to know how Rabbi Binder could call the Jews "The Chosen People" if the Declaration of Independence claimed all men to be created equal. Rabbi Binder tried to distinguish for him between political equality and spiritual legitimacy, but what Ozzie wanted to know, he insisted vehemently, was different. That was the first time his mother had to come.

33   Then there was the plane crash. Fifty-eight people had been killed in a plane crash at La Guardia. In studying a casualty list in the newspaper his mother had discovered among the list of those dead eight Jewish

names (his grandmother had nine but she counted Miller as a Jewish name); because of the eight she said the plane crash was "a tragedy." During free-discussion time on Wednesday Ozzie had brought to Rabbi Binder's attention this matter of "some of his relations" always picking out the Jewish names. Rabbi Binder had begun to explain cultural unity and some other things when Ozzie stood up at his seat and said that what he wanted to know was different. Rabbi Binder insisted that he sit down and it was then that Ozzie shouted that he wished all fifty-eight were Jews. That was the second time his mother came.

34   "And he kept explaining about Jesus being historical, and so I kept asking him. No kidding, Itz, he was trying to make me look stupid."

35   "So what he finally do?"

36   "Finally he starts screaming that I was deliberately simple-minded and a wise guy, and that my mother had to come, and this was the last time. And that I'd never get bar-mitzvahed if he could help it. Then, Itz, then he starts talking in that voice like a statue, real slow and deep, and he says that I better think over what I said about the Lord. He told me to go to his office and think it over." Ozzie leaned his body towards Itzie.

37   "Itz, I thought it over for a solid hour, and now I'm convinced God could do it."

38   Ozzie had planned to confess his latest transgression to his mother as soon as she came home from work. But it was a Friday night in November and already dark, and when Mrs. Freedman came through the door she tossed off her coat, kissed Ozzie quickly on the face, and went to the kitchen table to light the three yellow candles, two for the Sabbath and one for Ozzie's father.

39   When his mother lit the candles she would move her two arms slowly towards her, dragging them through the air, as though persuading people whose minds were half made up. And her eyes would get glassy with tears. Even when his father was alive Ozzie remembered that her eyes had gotten glassy, so it didn't have anything to do with his dying. It had something to do with lighting the candles.

40   As she touched the flaming match to the unlit wick of a Sabbath candle, the phone rang, and Ozzie, standing only a foot from it, plucked it off the receiver and held it muffled to his chest. When his mother lit candles Ozzie felt there should be no noise; even breathing, if you could manage it, should be softened. Ozzie pressed the phone to his breast and watched his mother dragging whatever she was dragging, and he felt his own eyes get glassy. His mother was a round, tired, gray-haired penguin of a woman whose gray skin had begun to feel the tug of gravity and the weight of her own history. Even when she was dressed up she didn't look like a chosen person. But when she lit candles she looked like something better; like a woman who knew momentarily that God could do anything.

41   After a few mysterious minutes she was finished. Ozzie hung up the phone and walked to the kitchen table where she was beginning to lay

the two places for the four-course Sabbath meal. He told her that she would have to see Rabbi Binder next Wednesday at four-thirty, and then he told her why. For the first time in their life together she hit Ozzie across the face with her hand.

42   All through the chopped liver and chicken soup part of the dinner Ozzie cried; he didn't have any appetite for the rest.

43   On Wednesday, in the largest of the three basement classrooms of the synagogue, Rabbi Marvin Binder, a tall, handsome, broad-shouldered man of thirty with thick strong-fibered black hair, removed his watch from his pocket and saw that it was four o'clock. At the rear of the room Yakov Blotnik, the seventy-one-year-old custodian, slowly polished the large window, mumbling to himself, unaware that it was four o'clock or six o'clock, Monday or Wednesday. To most of the students Yakov Blotnik's mumbling, along with his brown curly beard, scythe nose, and two heel-trailing black cats, made of him an object of wonder, a foreigner, a relic, towards whom they were alternately fearful and disrespectful. To Ozzie the mumbling had always seemed a monotonous, curious prayer; what made it curious was that old Blotnik had been mumbling so steadily for so many years, Ozzie suspected he had memorized the prayers and forgotten all about God.

44   "It is now free-discussion time," Rabbi Binder said. "Feel free to talk about any Jewish matter at all—religion, family, politics, sports—"

45   There was silence. It was a gusty, clouded November afternoon and it did not seem as though there ever was or could be a thing called baseball. So nobody this week said a word about that hero from the past, Hank Greenberg—which limited free discussion considerably.

46   And the soul-battering Ozzie Freedman had just received from Rabbi Binder had imposed its limitation. When it was Ozzie's turn to read aloud from the Hebrew book the rabbi had asked him petulantly why he didn't read more rapidly. He was showing no progress. Ozzie said he could read faster but that if he did he was sure not to understand what he was reading. Nevertheless, at the rabbi's repeated suggestion Ozzie tried, and showed a great talent, but in the midst of a long passage he stopped short and said he didn't understand a word he was reading, and started in again at a drag-footed pace. Then came the soul-battering.

47   Consequently when free-discussion time rolled around none of the students felt too free. The rabbi's invitation was answered only by the mumbling of feeble old Blotnik.

48   "Isn't there anything at all you would like to discuss?" Rabbi Binder asked again, looking at his watch. "No questions or comments?"

49   There was a small grumble from the third row. The rabbi requested that Ozzie rise and give the rest of the class the advantage of his thought.

50   Ozzie rose. "I forget it now," he said, and sat down in his place.

51   Rabbi Binder advanced a seat towards Ozzie and poised himself on the edge of the desk. It was Itzie's desk and the rabbi's frame only a dagger's-length away from his face snapped him to sitting attention.

52   "Stand up again, Oscar," Rabbi Binder said calmly, "and try to assemble your thoughts."

53   Ozzie stood up. All his classmates turned in their seats and watched as he gave an unconvincing scratch to his forehead.

54   "I can't assemble any," he announced and plunked himself down.

55   "Stand up!" Rabbi Binder advanced from Itzie's desk to the one directly in front of Ozzie; when the rabbinical back was turned Itzie gave it five-fingers off the tip of his nose, causing a small titter in the room. Rabbi Binder was too absorbed in squelching Ozzie's nonsense once and for all to bother with titters. "Stand up, Oscar. What's your question about?"

56   Ozzie pulled a word out of the air. It was the handiest word. "Religion."

57   "Oh, now you remember."

58   "Yes."

59   "What is it?"

60   Trapped, Ozzie blurted the first thing that came to him. "Why can't He make anything He wants to make!"

61   As Rabbi Binder prepared an answer, a final answer, Itzie, ten feet behind him, raised one finger on his left hand, gestured it meaningfully towards the rabbi's back, and brought the house down.

62   Binder twisted quickly to see what had happened and in the midst of the commotion Ozzie shouted into the rabbi's back what he couldn't have shouted to his face. It was a loud, toneless sound that had the timbre of something stored inside for about six days.

63   "You don't know! You don't know anything about God!"

64   The rabbi spun back towards Ozzie. "What?"

65   "You don't know—you don't—"

66   "Apologize, Oscar, apologize!" It was a threat.

67   "You don't—"

68   Rabbi Binder's hand flicked out at Ozzie's cheek. Perhaps it had only been meant to clamp the boy's mouth shut, but Ozzie ducked and the palm caught him squarely on the nose.

69   The blood came in a short, red spurt on to Ozzie's shirt front.

70   The next moment was all confusion. Ozzie screamed, "You bastard, you bastard!" and broke for the classroom door. Rabbi Binder lurched a step backwards, as though his own blood had started flowing violently in the opposite direction, then gave a clumsy lurch forward and bolted out the door after Ozzie. The class followed after the rabbi's huge blue-suited back, and before old Blotnik could turn from his window, the room was empty and everyone was headed full speed up the three flights leading to the roof.

71   If one should compare the light of day to the life of man: sunrise to birth; sunset—the dropping down over the edge—to death; then as Ozzie Freedman wiggled through the trapdoor of the synagogue roof, his feet kicking backwards bronco-style at Rabbi Binder's outstretched arms—at that moment the day was fifty years old. As a rule, fifty or fifty-five reflects accurately the age of late afternoons in November, for it is that

month, during those hours, that one's awareness of light seems no longer a matter of seeing, but of hearing: light begins clicking away. In fact, as Ozzie locked shut the trapdoor in the rabbi's face, the sharp click of the bolt into the lock might momentarily have been mistaken for the sound of the heavier gray that had just throbbed through the sky.

72   With all his weight Ozzie kneeled on the locked door; any instant he was certain that Rabbi Binder's shoulder would fling it open, splintering the wood into shrapnel and catapulting his body into the sky. But the door did not move and below him he heard only the rumble of feet, first loud then dim, like thunder rolling away.

73   A question shot through his brain. "Can this be *me*?" For a thirteen-year-old who had just labeled his religious leader a bastard, twice, it was not an improper question. Louder and louder the question came to him— "Is it me? It is me?"—until he discovered himself no longer kneeling, but racing crazily towards the edge of the roof, his eyes crying, his throat screaming, and his arms flying everywhichway as though not his own.

74   "Is it me? Is it me Me Me Me Me! It has to be me—but is it!"

75   It is the question a thief must ask himself the night he jimmies open his first window, and it is said to be the question with which bridegrooms quiz themselves before the altar.

76   In the few wild seconds it took Ozzie's body to propel him to the edge of the roof, his self-examination began to grow fuzzy. Gazing down at the street, he became confused as to the problem beneath the question: was it, is-it-me-who-called-Binder-a-bastard? or, is-it-me-prancing-around-on-the-roof? However, the scene below settled all, for there is an instant in any action when whether it is you or somebody else is academic. The thief crams the money in his pockets and scoots out the window. The bridegroom signs the hotel register for two. And the boy on the roof finds a streetful of people gaping at him, necks stretched backwards, faces up, as though he were the ceiling of the Hayden Planetarium. Suddenly you know it's you.

77   "Oscar! Oscar Freedman!" A voice rose from the center of the crowd, a voice that, could it have been seen, would have looked like the writing on scroll. "Oscar Freedman, get down from there. Immediately!" Rabbi Binder was pointing one arm stiffly up at him; and at the end of that arm, one finger aimed menacingly. It was the attitude of a dictator, but one— the eyes confessed all—whose personal valet had spit neatly in his face.

78   Ozzie didn't answer. Only for a blink's length did he look towards Rabbi Binder. Instead his eyes began to fit together the world beneath him, to sort out people from places, friends from enemies, participants from spectators. In little jagged starlike clusters his friends stood around Rabbi Binder, who was still pointing. The topmost point on a star compounded not of angels but of five adolescent boys was Itzie. What a world it was, with those stars below, Rabbi Binder below...Ozzie, who a moment earlier hadn't been able to control his own body, started to feel the meaning of the word control: he felt Peace and he felt Power.

79   "Oscar Freedman, I'll give you three to come down."

80   Few dictators give their subjects three to do anything; but, as always, Rabbi Binder only looked dictatorial.

81   "Are you ready, Oscar?"

82   Ozzie nodded his head yes, although he had no intention in the world—the lower one or the celestial one he'd just entered—of coming down even if Rabbi Binder should give him a million.

83   "All right then," said Rabbi Binder. He ran a hand through his black Samson hair as though it were the gesture prescribed for uttering the first digit. Then, with his other hand cutting a circle out of the small piece of sky around him, he spoke. "One!"

84   There was no thunder. On the contrary, at that moment, as though "one" was the cue for which he had been waiting, the world's least thunderous person appeared on the synagogue steps. He did not so much come out the synagogue door as lean out, onto the darkening air. He clutched at the doorknob with one hand and looked up at the roof.

85   "Oy!"

86   Yakov Blotnik's old mind hobbled slowly, as if on crutches, and though he couldn't decide precisely what the boy was doing on the roof, he knew it wasn't good—that is, it wasn't-good-for-the-Jews. For Yakov Blotnik life had fractionated itself simply: things were either good-for-the-Jews or no-good-for-the-Jews.

87   He smacked his free hand to his in-sucked cheek, gently. "Oy, Gut!" And then quickly as he was able, he jacked down his head and surveyed the street. There was Rabbi Binder (like a man at an auction with only three dollars in his pocket, he had just delivered a shakey "Two!"), there were the students, and that was all. So far it-wasn't-so-bad-for-the-Jews. But the boy had to come down immediately, before anybody saw. The problem: how to get the boy off the roof?

88   Anybody who has ever had a cat on the roof knows how to get him down. You call the fire department. Or first you call the operator and you ask her for the fire department. And the next thing there is great jamming of brakes and clanging of bells and shouting of instructions. And then the cat is off the roof. You do the same thing to get a boy off the roof.

89   That is, you do the same thing if you are Yakov Blotnik and you once had a cat on the roof.

90   When the engines, all four of them, arrived, Rabbi Binder had four times given Ozzie the count of three. The big hook-and-ladder swung around the corner and one of the firemen leaped from it, plunging headlong towards the yellow fire hydrant in front of the synagogue. With a huge wrench he began to unscrew the top nozzle. Rabbi Binder raced over to him and pulled at his shoulder.

91   "There's no fire…"

92   The fireman mumbled back over his shoulder and, heatedly, continued working at the nozzle.

93   "But there's no fire, there's no fire…" Binder shouted. When the fireman mumbled again, the rabbi grasped his face with both his hands and pointed it up at the roof.

94   To Ozzie it looked as though Rabbi Binder was trying to tug the fireman's head out of his body, like a cork from a bottle. He had to giggle at
the picture they made: it was a family portrait—rabbi in black skullcap,
fireman in red fire hat, and the little yellow hydrant squatting beside like
a kid brother, bareheaded. From the edge of the roof Ozzie waved at the
portrait, a one-handed, flapping, mocking wave; in doing it his right foot
slipped from under him. Rabbi Binder covered his eyes with his hands.

95   Firemen work fast. Before Ozzie had even regained his balance, a big,
round, yellowed net was being held on the synagogue lawn. The firemen
who held it looked up at Ozzie with stern, feelingless faces.

96   One of the firemen turned his head towards Rabbi Binder. "What, is
the kid nuts or something?"

97   Rabbi Binder unpeeled his hands from his eyes, slowly, painfully, as if
they were tape. Then he checked: nothing on the sidewalk, no dents in
the net.

98   "Is he gonna jump, or what?" the fireman shouted.

99   In a voice not at all like a statue, Rabbi Binder finally answered. "Yes,
Yes, I think so...He's been threatening to..."

100   Threatening to? Why, the reason he was on the roof, Ozzie remembered, was to get away; he hadn't even thought about jumping. He had
just run to get away, and the truth was that he hadn't really headed for
the roof as much as he'd been chased there.

101   "What's his name, the kid?"

102   "Freedman," Rabbi Binder answered. "Oscar Freedman."

103   The fireman looked up at Ozzie. "What is it with you, Oscar? You gonna
jump, or what?"

104   Oscar did not answer. Frankly, the question had just arisen.

105   "Look, Oscar, if you're gonna jump, jump—and if you're not gonna
jump, don't jump. But don't waste our time, willya?"

106   Ozzie looked at the fireman and then at Rabbi Binder. He wanted to
see Rabbi Binder cover his eyes one more time.

107   "I'm going to jump."

108   And then he scampered around the edge of the roof to the corner,
where there was no net below, and he flapped his arms at his sides, swish-
ing the air and smacking his palms to his trousers on the down-beat. He
began screaming like some kind of engine, "Wheeeee...wheeeeee," and
leaning way out over the edge with the upper half of his body. The firemen whipped around to cover the ground with the net. Rabbi Binder
mumbled a few words to Somebody and covered his eyes. Everything
happened quickly, jerkily, as in a silent movie. The crowd, which had
arrived with the fire engines, gave out a long, Fourth-of-July fireworks
oooh-aahhh. In the excitement no one had paid the crowd much heed,
except, of course, Yakov Blotnik, who swung from the door-knob counting heads. "Fier und tsvansik...finf und tsvantsik...Oy, Gut!" It wasn't like
this with the cat.

109   Rabbi Binder peeked through his fingers, checked the sidewalk and
net. Empty. But there was Ozzie racing to the other corner. The firemen

raced with him but were unable to keep up. Whenever Ozzie wanted to he might jump and splatter himself upon the sidewalk, and by the time the firemen scooted to the spot all they could do with their net would be to cover the mess.

110   "Wheeeee...wheeeee..."

111   "Hey, Oscar," the winded fireman yelled, "What the hell is this, a game or something?"

112   "Wheeeee...wheeeee..."

113   "Hey, Oscar—"

114   But he was off now to the other corner, flapping his wings fiercely. Rabbi Binder couldn't take it any longer—the fire engines from nowhere, the screaming suicidal boy, the net. He fell to his knees, exhausted, and with his hands curled together in front of his chest like a little dome, he pleaded, "Oscar, stop it, Oscar. Don't jump, Oscar. Please come down...Please don't jump."

115   And further back in the crowd a single voice, a single young voice, shouted a lone word to the boy on the roof.

116   "Jump!"

117   It was Itzie. Ozzie momentarily stopped flapping.

118   "Go ahead, Ozz—jump!" Itzie broke off his point of the star and coura- geously, with the inspiration not of a wise-guy but of a disciple, stood alone. "Jump, Ozz, jump!"

119   Still on his knees, his hands still curled, Rabbi Binder twisted his body back. He looked at Itzie, then, agonizingly, back to Ozzie.

120   "OSCAR, DON'T JUMP! PLEASE, DON'T JUMP...please please..."

121   "Jump!" This time it wasn't Itzie but another point of the star. By the time Mrs. Freedman arrived to keep her four-thirty appointment with Rabbi Binder, the whole little upside down heaven was shouting and pleading for Ozzie to jump, and Rabbi Binder no longer was pleading with him not to jump, but was crying into the dome of his hands.

122   Understandably Mrs. Freedman couldn't figure out what her son was doing on the roof. So she asked. "Ozzie, my Ozzie, what are you doing? My Ozzie, what is it?"

123   Ozzie stopped wheeeeeing and slowed his arms down to a cruising flap, the kind birds use in soft winds, but he did not answer. He stood against the low, clouded, darkening sky—light clicked down swiftly now, as on a small gear—flapping softly and gazing down at the small bundle of woman who was his mother.

124   "What are you doing, Ozzie?" She turned towards the kneeling Rabbi Binder and rushed so close that only a paper-thickness of dusk lay between her stomach and his shoulders.

125   "What is my baby doing?"

126   Rabbi Binder gaped up at her but he too was mute. All that moved was the dome of his hands; it shook back and forth like a weak pulse.

127   "Rabbi, get him down! He'll kill himself. Get him down, my only baby..."

128   "I can't," Rabbi Binder said, "I can't..." and he turned his handsome head towards the crowd of boys behind him. "It's them. Listen to them."

129   And for the first time Mrs. Freedman saw the crowd of boys, and she heard what they were yelling.

130   "He's doing it for them. He won't listen to me. It's them." Rabbi Binder spoke like one in a trance.

131   "For them?"

132   "Yes."

133   "Why for them?"

134   "They want him to..."

135   Mrs. Freedman raised her two arms upward as though she were conducting the sky. "For them he's doing it!" And then in a gesture older than pyramids, older than prophets and floods, her arms came slapping down to her sides. "A martyr I have. Look!" She tilted her head to the roof, Ozzie was still flapping softly. "My martyr."

136   "Oscar, come down, *please*," Rabbi Binder groaned.

137   In a startlingly even voice Mrs. Freedman called to the boy on the roof. "Ozzie, come down, Ozzie. Don't be a martyr, my baby."

138   As though it were a litany, Rabbi Binder repeated her words. "Don't be a martyr, my baby. Don't be a martyr."

139   "Gawhead, Ozz—*be* a Martin!" It was Itzie. "Be a Martin, be a Martin," and all the voices joined in singing for Martindom, whatever *it* was. "Be a Martin, be a Martin..."

140   Somehow when you're on a roof the darker it gets the less you can hear. All Ozzie knew was that two groups wanted two new things: his friends were spirited and musical about what they wanted; his mother and the rabbi were even-toned, chanting, about what they didn't want. The rabbi's voice was without tears now and so was his mother's.

141   The big net stared up at Ozzie like a sightless eye. The big, clouded sky pushed down. From beneath it looked like a gray corrugated board. Suddenly, looking up into that unsympathetic sky, Ozzie realized all the strangeness of what these people, his friends, were asking: they wanted him to jump, to kill himself; they were singing about it now—it made them happy. And there was an even greater strangeness: Rabbi Binder was on his knees, trembling. If there was a question to be asked now it was not "Is it me?" but rather "Is it us?...Is it us?"

142   Being on the roof, it turned out, was a serious thing. If he jumped would the singing become dancing? Would it? What would jumping stop? Yearningly, Ozzie wished he could rip open the sky, plunge his hands through, and pull out the sun; and on the sun, like a coin, would be stamped JUMP or DON'T JUMP.

143   Ozzie's knees rocked and sagged a little under him as though they were setting him for a dive. His arms tightened, stiffened, froze, from shoulders to fingernails. He felt as if each part of his body were going to vote as to whether he should kill himself or not—and each part as though it were independent of *him*.

144   The light took an unexpected click down and the new darkness, like a gag, hushed the friends singing for this and the mother and rabbi chanting for that.

145   Ozzie stopped counting votes, and in a curiously high voice, like one who wasn't prepared for speech, he spoke.

146   "Mamma?"

147   "Yes, Oscar."

148   "Mamma, get down on your knees, like Rabbi Binder."

149   "Oscar—"

150   "Get down on your knees," he said, "or I'll jump."

151   Ozzie heard a whimper, then a quick rustling, and when he looked down where his mother had stood he saw the top of a head and beneath that a circle of dress. She was kneeling beside Rabbi Binder.

152   He spoke again. "Everybody kneel." There was the sound of everybody kneeling.

153   Ozzie looked around. With one hand he pointed towards the synagogue entrance. "Make *him* kneel."

154   There was a noise, not of kneeling, but of body-and-cloth stretching. Ozzie could hear Rabbi Binder saying in a gruff whisper, "...or he'll *kill* himself," and when next he looked there was Yakov Blotnik off the doorknob and for the first time in his life upon his knees in the Gentile posture of prayer.

155   As for the firemen—it is not as difficult as one might imagine to hold a net taut while you are kneeling.

156   Ozzie looked around again; and then he called to Rabbi Binder.

157   "Rabbi?"

158   "Yes, Oscar."

159   "Rabbi Binder, do you believe in God."

160   "Yes."

161   "Do you believe God can do Anything?" Ozzie leaned his head out into the darkness. "Anything?"

162   "Oscar, I think—"

163   "Tell me you believe God can do Anything."

164   There was a second's hesitation. Then: "God can do Anything."

165   "Tell me you believe God can make a child without intercourse."

166   "He can."

167   "Tell me!"

168   "God," Rabbi Binder admitted, "can make a child without intercourse."

169   "Mamma, you tell me."

170   "God can make a child without intercourse," his mother said.

171   "Make *him* tell me." There was no doubt who *him* was.

172   In a few moments Ozzie heard an old comical voice say something to the increasing darkness about God.

173   Next, Ozzie made everybody say it. And then he made them all say they believed in Jesus Christ—first one at a time, then all together.

174   When the catechizing was through it was the beginning of evening. From the street it sounded as if the boy on the roof might have sighed.

175   "Ozzie?" A woman's voice dared to speak. "You'll come down now?"

176   There was no answer, but the woman waited, and when a voice finally did speak it was thin and crying, and exhausted as that of an old man who has just finished pulling the bells.

177   "Mamma, don't you see—you shouldn't hit me. He shouldn't hit me. You shouldn't hit me about God, Mamma. You should never hit anybody about God—"

178   "Ozzie, please come down now."

179   "Promise me, promise me you'll never hit anybody about God."

180   He had asked only his mother, but for some reason everyone kneeling in the street promised he would never hit anybody about God.

181   Once again there was silence.

182   "I can come down now, Mamma," the boy on the roof finally said. He turned his head both ways as though checking the traffic lights. "Now I can come down..."

183   And he did, right into the center of the yellow net that glowed in the evening's edge like an overgrown halo.

Questions for Discussion

1. How do Itzie's interests contrast with Ozzie's? What do these contrasts suggest about their levels of thinking?

2. Why do adults have difficulty with Ozzie's questions? Is Ozzie, as Rabbi Binder maintains, "deliberately simple-minded"? Are Ozzie's questions intended to be irreverent? Are they valid questions?

3. How effectively does Ozzie's mother handle his questions? How effectively does Rabbi Binder handle them?

4. Why does Ozzie run to the roof? Does he have any serious intention of jumping? Why do Itzie and Ozzie's other friends shout for him to jump?

5. Why does Ozzie make the rabbi, his mother, and all his friends kneel and declare their belief in Jesus Christ? Given their religious beliefs, what does such a declaration mean?

6. Discuss the irony of the title.

Suggestions for Exploring, Writing, and Persuading

1. Attack or defend this statement: Efforts to stifle a child's quest for truth result in rebellion.

2. Write an essay defining the qualities that you think a religious teacher should have.

3. Write a character sketch of Ozzie. Or compare Ozzie and Itzie.

4. Ozzie calls Rabbi Binder a "bastard" twice. Write a character analysis of Rabbi Binder, explaining why Ozzie sees him in this negative way.

5. Ozzie's asking his rabbi, his mother, and his friends to declare their belief in Jesus is an extreme action. In effect, he is requiring them to repudiate their faith. Analyze the causes of Ozzie's extreme action.

6. Write an essay arguing that Ozzie's actions are or are not justified.

Toni Cade Bambara (1939–1995)

Toni Cade adopted the name Bambara from a name she found in a sketchbook in her great grandmother's trunk. This renaming of herself, with an emphasis on personal history, demonstrates her fascination with the myths, music, and history of African Americans. After receiving a bachelor of arts degree in theater art and English from Queens College and studying at Commedia del'Arte in Milan, Italy, Bambara taught at several colleges throughout the Northeast. She settled in Atlanta and taught at Spelman College. Many of her works skillfully portray adolescents coming to grips with their environment and show the politics and cultural activities of the urban community.

RAYMOND'S RUN   (1960)

1   I don't have much work to do around the house like some girls. My mother does that. And I don't have to earn my pocket money by hustling; George runs errands for the big boys and sells Christmas cards. And anything else that's got to get done, my father does. All I have to do in life is mind my brother Raymond, which is enough.

2   Sometimes I slip and say my little brother Raymond. But as any fool can see he's much bigger and he's older too. But a lot of people call him my little brother cause he needs looking after cause he's not quite right. And a lot of smart mouths got lots to say about that too, especially when George was minding him. But now, if anybody has anything to say to Raymond, anything to say about his big head, they have to come by me. And I don't play the dozens or believe in standing around with somebody in my face doing a lot of talking. I much rather just knock you down and take my chances even if I am a little girl with skinny arms and a squeaky voice, which is how I got the name Squeaky. And if things get too rough, I run. And as anybody can tell you, I'm the fastest thing on two feet.

3   There is no track meet that I don't win the first-place medal. I used to win the twenty-yard dash when I was a little kid in kindergarten. Nowadays, it's the fifty-yard dash. And tomorrow I'm subject to run the quarter-meter relay all by myself and come in first, second, and third. The big kids call me Mercury cause I'm the swiftest thing in the neighborhood. Everybody knows that—except two people who know better, my father and me. He can beat me to Amsterdam Avenue with me having a two-fire-hydrant head start and him running with his hands in his pockets and whistling. But that's private information. Cause can you imagine some thirty-five-

year-old man stuffing himself into PAL shorts to race little kids? So as far as everyone's concerned, I'm the fastest and that goes for Gretchen, too, who has put out the tale that she is going to win the first-place medal this year. Ridiculous. In the second place, she's got short legs. In the third place, she's got freckles. In the first place, no one can beat me and that's all there is to it.

4   I'm standing on the corner admiring the weather and about to take a stroll down Broadway so I can practice my breathing exercises, and I've got Raymond walking on the inside close to the buildings, cause he's subject to fits of fantasy and starts thinking he's a circus performer and that the curb is a tightrope strung high in the air. And sometimes after a rain he likes to step down off his tightrope right into the gutter and slosh around getting his shoes and cuffs wet. Then I get hit when I get home. Or sometimes if you don't watch him he'll dash across traffic to the island in the middle of Broadway and give the pigeons a fit. Then I have to go behind him apologizing to all the old people sitting around trying to get some sun and getting all upset with the pigeons fluttering around them, scattering their newspapers and upsetting the wax paper lunches in their laps. So I keep Raymond on the inside of me, and he plays like he's driving a stage-coach which is O.K. by me so long as he doesn't run me over or interrupt my breathing exercises, which I have to do on account of I'm serious about my running, and I don't care who knows it.

5   Now some people like to act like things come easy to them, won't let on that they practice. Not me. I'll high-prance down 34th Street like a rodeo pony to keep my knees strong even if it does get my mother uptight so that she walks ahead like she's not with me, don't know me, is all by herself on a shopping trip, and I am somebody else's crazy child. Now you take Cynthia Procter for instance. She's just the opposite. If there's a test tomorrow, she'll say something like, "Oh, I guess I'll play handball this afternoon and watch television tonight," just to let you know she ain't thinking about the test. Or like last week when she won the spelling bee for the millionth time, "A good thing you got 'receive,' Squeaky, cause I would have got it wrong. I completely forgot about the spelling bee." And she'll clutch the lace on her blouse like it was a narrow escape. Oh, brother. But of course when I pass her house on my early morning trots around the block, she is practicing the scales on the piano over and over and over and over. Then in music class she always lets herself get bumped around so she falls accidently on purpose onto the piano stool and is so surprised to find herself sitting there that she decides just for fun to try out the ole keys. And what do you know—Chopin's waltzes just spring out of her fingertips and she's the most surprised thing in the world. A regular prodigy. I could kill people like that. I stay up all night studying the words for the spelling bee. And you can see me any time of day practicing running. I never walk if I can trot, and shame on Raymond if he can't keep up. But of course he does, cause if he hangs back someone's liable to walk up to him and get smart, or take his allowance from

him, or ask him where he got that great big pumpkin head. People are so stupid sometimes.

6   So I'm strolling down Broadway breathing out and breathing in on counts of seven, which is my lucky number, and here comes Gretchen and her sidekicks: Mary Louise, who used to be a friend of mine when she first moved to Harlem from Baltimore and got beat up by everybody till I took up for her on account of her mother and my mother used to sing in the same choir when they were young girls, but people ain't grateful, so now she hangs out with the new girl Gretchen and talks about me like a dog; and Rosie, who is as fat as I am skinny and has a big mouth where Raymond is concerned and is too stupid to know that there is not a big deal of difference between herself and Raymond and that she can't afford to throw stones. So they are steady coming up Broadway and I see right away that it's going to be one of those Dodge City scenes cause the street ain't that big and they're close to the buildings just as we are. First I think I'll step into the candy store and look over the new comics and let them pass. But that's chicken and I've got a reputation to consider. So then I think I'll just walk straight on through them or even over them if necessary. But as they get to me, they slow down. I'm ready to fight, cause like I said I don't feature a whole lot of chitchat, I much prefer to just knock you down right from the jump and save everybody a lotta precious time.

7   "You signing up for the May Day races?" smiles Mary Louise, only it's not a smile at all. A dumb question like that doesn't deserve an answer. Besides, there's just me and Gretchen standing there really, so no use wasting my breath talking to shadows.

8   "I don't think you're going to win this time," says Rosie, trying to signify with her hands on her hips all salty, completely forgetting that I have whupped her behind many times for less salt than that.

9   "I always win cause I'm the best," I say straight at Gretchen who is, as far as I'm concerned, the only one talking in this ventriloquist-dummy routine. Gretchen smiles, but it's not a smile, and I'm thinking that girls never really smile at each other because they don't know how and don't want to know how and there's probably no one to teach us how, cause grownup girls don't know either. Then they all look at Raymond who has just brought his mule team to a standstill. And they're about to see what trouble they can get into through him.

10   "What grade you in now, Raymond?"

11   "You got anything to say to my brother, you say it to me, Mary Louise Williams of Raggedy Town, Baltimore."

12   "What are you, his mother?" sasses Rosie.

13   "That's right, Fatso. And the next word out of anybody and I'll be *their* mother too." So they just stand there and Gretchen shifts from one leg to the other and so do they. Then Gretchen puts her hands on her hips and is about to say something with her freckle-face self but doesn't. Then she walks around me looking me up and down but keeps walking up Broadway, and her sidekicks follow her. So me and Raymond smile at each

other and he says "Giddyap" to his team and I continue with my breathing exercises, strolling down Broadway toward the ice man on 145th with not a care in the world cause I am Miss Quicksilver herself.

14   I take my time getting to the park on May Day because the track meet is the last thing on the program. The biggest thing on the program is the Maypole dancing, which I can do without, thank you, even if my mother thinks it's a shame I don't take part and act like a girl for a change. You'd think my mother'd be grateful not to have to make me a white organdy dress with a big satin sash and buy me new white baby-doll shoes that can't be taken out of the box till the big day. You'd think she'd be glad her daughter ain't out there prancing around a Maypole getting the new clothes all dirty and sweaty and trying to act like a fairy or a flower or whatever you're supposed to be when you should be trying to be yourself, whatever that is, which is, as far as I am concerned, a poor black girl who really can't afford to buy shoes and a new dress you only wear once a lifetime cause it won't fit next year.

15   I was once a strawberry in a Hansel and Gretel pageant when I was in nursery school and didn't have no better sense than to dance on tiptoe with my arms in a circle over my head doing umbrella steps and being a perfect fool just so my mother and father could come dressed up and clap. You'd think they'd know better than to encourage that kind of nonsense. I am not a strawberry. I do not dance on my toes. I run. That is what I am all about. So I always come late to the May Day program, just in time to get my number pinned on and lay in the grass till they announce the fifty-yard dash.

16   I put Raymond in the little swings, which is a tight squeeze this year and will be impossible next year. Then I look around for Mr. Pearson, who pins the numbers on. I'm really looking for Gretchen if you want to know the truth, but she's not around. The park is jam-packed. Parents in hats and corsages and breast-pocket handkerchiefs peeking up. Kids in white dresses and light blue suits. The parkees unfolding chairs and chasing the rowdy kids from Lenox as if they had no right to be there. The big guys with their caps on backwards, leaning against the fence swirling the basketballs on the tips of their fingers, waiting for all these crazy people to clear out the park so they can play. Most of the kids in my class are carrying bass drums and glockenspiels and flutes. You'd think they'd put in a few bongos or something for real like that.

17   Then here comes Mr. Pearson with his clipboard and his cards and pencils and whistles and safety pins and fifty million other things he's always dropping all over the place with his clumsy self. He sticks out in a crowd because he's on stilts. We used to call him Jack and the Beanstalk to get him mad. But I'm the only one that can outrun him and get away, and I'm too grown for that silliness now.

18   "Well, Squeaky," he says, checking my name off the list and handing me number seven and two pins. And I'm thinking he's got no right to call me Squeaky, if I can't call him Beanstalk.

19   "Hazel Elizabeth Deborah Parker," I correct him and tell him to write it down on his board.

20   "Well, Hazel Elizabeth Deborah Parker, going to give someone else a break this year?" I squint at him real hard to see if he is seriously thinking I should lose the race on purpose just to give someone else a break. "Only six girls running this time," he continues, shaking his head sadly like it's my fault all of New York didn't turn out in sneakers. "That new girl should give you a run for your money." He looks around the park for Gretchen like a periscope in a submarine movie. "Wouldn't it be a nice gesture if you were...to ahhh..."

21   I give him such a look he couldn't finish putting that idea into words. Grownups got a lot of nerve sometimes. I pin number seven to myself and stomp away, I'm so burnt. And I go straight for the track and stretch out on the grass while the band winds up with "Oh, the Monkey Wrapped His Tail Around the Flagpole," which my teacher calls by some other name. The man on the loudspeaker is calling everyone over to the track and I'm on my back looking at the sky, trying to pretend I'm in the country, but I can't because even grass in the city feels hard as sidewalk, and there's just no pretending you are anywhere but in a "concrete jungle" as my grandfather says.

22   The twenty-yard dash takes all of two minutes cause most of the little kids don't know no better than to run off the track or run the wrong way or run smack into the fence and fall down and cry. One little kid, though, has got the good sense to run straight for the white ribbon up ahead so he wins. Then the second-graders line up for the thirty-yard dash and I don't even bother to turn my head to watch cause Raphael Perez always wins. He wins before he even begins by psyching the runners, telling them they're going to trip on their shoelaces and fall on their faces or lose their shorts or something, which he doesn't really have to do since he is very fast, almost as fast as I am. After that is the forty-yard dash which I used to run when I was in first grade. Raymond is hollering from the swings cause he knows I'm about to do my thing cause the man on the loudspeaker has just announced the fifty-yard dash, although he might just as well be giving a recipe for angel food cake cause you can hardly make out what he's saying for the static. I get up and slip off my sweat pants and then I see Gretchen standing at the starting line, kicking her legs out like a pro. Then as I get into place I see that ole Raymond is on the line on the other side of the fence, bending down with his fingers on the ground just like he knew what he was doing. I was going to yell at him but then I didn't. It burns up your energy to holler.

23   Every time, just before I take off in a race, I always feel like I'm in a dream, the kind of dream you have when you're sick with fever and feel all hot and weightless. I dream I'm flying over a sandy beach in the early morning sun, kissing the leaves of the trees as I fly by. And there's always the smell of apples, just like in the country when I was little and used to think I was a choo-choo train, running through the fields of corn

and chugging up the hill to the orchard. And all the time I'm dreaming this, I get lighter and lighter until I'm flying over the beach again, getting blown through the sky like a feather that weighs nothing at all. But once I spread my fingers in the dirt and crouch over the Get on Your Mark, the dream goes and I am solid again and am telling myself, Squeaky you must win, you must win, you are the fastest thing in the world, you can even beat your father up Amsterdam if you really try. And then I feel my weight coming back just behind my knees then down to my feet then into the earth and the pistol shot explodes in my blood and I am off and weightless again, flying past the other runners, my arms pumping up and down and the whole world is quiet except for the crunch as I zoom over the gravel of the track. I glance to my left and there is no one. To the right, a blurred Gretchen, who's got her chin jutting out as if it would win the race all by itself. And on the other side of the fence is Raymond with his arms down to his side and the palms tucked up behind him, running in his very own style, and it's the first time I ever saw that and I almost stop to watch my brother Raymond on his first run. But the white ribbon is bouncing toward me and I tear past it, racing into the distance till my feet with a mind of their own start digging up footfuls of dirt and brake me short. Then all the kids standing on the side pile on me, banging me on the back and slapping my head with their May Day programs, for I have won again and everybody on 151st Street can walk tall for another year.

24   "In first place..." the man on the loudspeaker is clear as a bell now, but then he pauses and the loudspeaker starts to whine. Then static. And I lean down to catch my breath and here comes Gretchen walking back, for she's overshot the finish line too, huffing and puffing with her hands on her hips taking it slow, breathing in steady time like a real pro and I sort of like her a little for the first time. "In first place..." and then three or four voices get all mixed up on the loudspeaker and I dig my sneaker into the grass and stare at Gretchen who's staring back, we both wondering just who did win. I can hear old Beanstalk arguing with the man on the loudspeaker and then a few others running their mouths about what the stopwatches say. Then I hear Raymond yanking at the fence to call me and I wave to shush him, but he keeps rattling the fence like a gorilla in a cage like in them gorilla movies, but then like a dancer or something he starts climbing hand over hand and remembering how he looked running with his arms down to his side and with the wind pulling his mouth back and his teeth showing and all, it occurred to me that Raymond would make a very fine runner. Doesn't he always keep up with me on my trots? And he surely knows how to breathe in counts of seven cause he's always doing it at the dinner table, which drives my brother George up the wall. And I'm smiling to beat the band cause if I've lost this race, or if me and Gretchen tied, or even if I've won, I can always retire as a runner and begin a whole new career as a coach with Raymond as my champion. After all, with a little more study I can beat Cynthia and

her phony self at the spelling bee. And if I bugged my mother, I could get piano lessons and become a star. And I have a big rep as the baddest thing around. And I've got a roomful of ribbons and medals and awards. But what has Raymond got to call his own?

25   So I stand there with my new plans, laughing out loud by this time as Raymond jumps down from the fence and runs over with his teeth showing and his arms down to the side, which no one before him has quite mastered as a running style. And by the time he comes over I'm jumping up and down so glad to see him—my brother Raymond, a great runner in the family tradition. But of course everyone thinks I'm jumping up and down because the men on the loudspeaker have finally gotten themselves together and compared notes and are announcing "In first place—Miss Hazel Elizabeth Deborah Parker." (Dig that.) "In second place—Miss Gretchen P. Lewis." And I look at Gretchen wondering what the "P" stands for. And I smile. Cause she's good, no doubt about it. Maybe she'd like to help me coach Raymond; she obviously is serious about running, as any fool can see. And she nods to congratulate me and then she smiles. And I smile. We stand there with this big smile of respect between us. It's about as real a smile as girls can do for each other, considering we don't practice real smiling every day, you know, cause maybe we too busy being flowers or fairies or strawberries instead of something honest and worthy of respect...you know...like being people.

Questions for Discussion

1. Why is the first person point of view effective here?
2. What is the relationship between Hazel and her brother Raymond? Describe the relationship between Hazel and her father and that between Hazel and her mother.
3. Explain whether Hazel is bragging or just being honest about her area of expertise, running. Why is practicing important to her?
4. What bothers Hazel about Cynthia Procter? Why?
5. Why does Hazel want Mr. Pearson, who pins on the numbers at the race, to call her Hazel Elizabeth Deborah Parker? What is their relationship? Does Pearson really want Hazel to let Gretchen win the race?
6. Describe the dream Hazel has. Why is it important?

Suggestions for Exploring, Writing, and Persuading

1. Looking at Raymond after the race, Hazel has an epiphany or awakening. Hazel asks, "But what has Raymond got to call his own?" Discuss Hazel's new aspirations for Raymond, Gretchen, and herself.

2. At various times Bambara emphasizes a genuine smile or a sarcastic smile or the absence of a smile. Reread the last sentence of the story, and write an essay that discusses "real smiling" and the meaning of that last sentence.

3. Agree, disagree, or modify this statement in an essay: Hazel's awakening is really a selfish act because *she* chooses what life will be like for Raymond and Gretchen.

Isabel Allende (b. 1942)

Born in Lima, Peru, Isabel Allende moved with her family to Chile in 1945. Her uncle, Salvador Allende, was president of Chile until 1973, when he was assassinated. A few years later, Isabel moved to Venezuela with her husband and children. Mixing in her fiction realistic and brutal political observation, a feminist vision, and the imaginative detail of magical realism, Allende is among the most highly regarded of contemporary Latin American novelists. Among her dozen or more books are The House of the Spirits *(1982);* Eva Luna *(1989);* The Stories of Eva Luna *(1990), from which the story below is taken;* Paula *(1994);* Portrait in Sepia *(2000);* My Invented Country *(2003); and* Kingdom of the Golden Dragon *(2003). Though she writes in Spanish, translations of her works have been very popular in the United States.*

AND OF CLAY ARE WE CREATED   1989

1   They discovered the girl's head protruding from the mudpit, eyes wide open, calling soundlessly. She had a First Communion name, Azucena. Lily. In that vast cemetery where the odor of death was already attracting vultures from far away, and where the weeping of orphans and wails of the injured filled the air, the little girl obstinately clinging to life became the symbol of the tragedy. The television cameras transmitted so often the unbearable image of the head budding like a black squash from the clay that there was no one who did not recognize her and know her name. And every time we saw her on the screen, right behind her was Rolf Carlé, who had gone there on assignment, never suspecting that he would find a fragment of his past, lost thirty years before.

2   First a subterranean sob rocked the cotton fields, curling them like waves of foam. Geologists had set up their seismographs weeks before and knew that the mountain had awakened again. For some time they had predicted that the heat of the eruption could detach the eternal ice from the slopes of the volcano, but no one heeded their warnings; they sounded like tales of frightened old women. The towns in the valley went about their daily life, deaf to the moaning of the earth, until that fateful Wednesday night in November when a prolonged roar announced the end

of the world, and walls of snow broke loose, rolling in an avalanche of clay, stones, and water that descended on the villages and buried them beneath unfathomable meters of telluric vomit. As soon as the survivors emerged from the paralysis of that first awful terror, they could see that houses, plazas, churches, white cotton plantations, dark coffee forests, cattle pastures—all had disappeared. Much later, after soldiers and volunteers had arrived to rescue the living and try to assess the magnitude of the cataclysm, it was calculated that beneath the mud lay more than twenty thousand human beings and an indefinite number of animals putrefying in a viscous soup. Forests and rivers had also been swept away, and there was nothing to be seen but an immense desert of mire.

3   When the station called before dawn, Rolf Carlé and I were together. I crawled out of bed, dazed with sleep, and went to prepare coffee while he hurriedly dressed. He stuffed his gear in the green canvas backpack he always carried, and we said goodbye, as we had so many times before. I had no presentiments. I sat in the kitchen, sipping my coffee and planning the long hours without him, sure that he would be back the next day.

4   He was one of the first to reach the scene, because while other reporters were fighting their way to the edges of that morass in jeeps, bicycles, or on foot, each getting there however he could, Rolf Carlé had the advantage of the television helicopter, which flew him over the avalanche. We watched on our screens the footage captured by his assistant's camera, in which he was up to his knees in muck, a microphone in his hand, in the midst of a bedlam of lost children, wounded survivors, corpses, and devastation. The story came to us in his calm voice. For years he had been a familiar figure in newscasts, reporting live at the scene of battles and catastrophes with awesome tenacity. Nothing could stop him, and I was always amazed at his equanimity in the face of danger and suffering; it seemed as if nothing could shake his fortitude or deter his curiosity. Fear seemed never to touch him, although he had confessed to me that he was not a courageous man, far from it. I believe that the lens of the camera had a strange effect on him; it was as if it transported him to a different time from which he could watch events without actually participating in them. When I knew him better, I came to realize that this fictive distance seemed to protect him from his own emotions.

5   Rolf Carlé was in on the story of Azucena from the beginning. He filmed the volunteers who discovered her, and the first persons who tried to reach her; his camera zoomed in on the girl, her dark face, her large desolate eyes, the plastered-down tangle of her hair. The mud was like quicksand around her, and anyone attempting to reach her was in danger of sinking. They threw a rope to her that she made no effort to grasp until they shouted to her to catch it; then she pulled a hand from the mire and tried to move, but immediately sank a little deeper. Rolf threw down his knapsack and the rest of his equipment and waded into the quagmire, commenting for his assistant's microphone that it was cold and that one could begin to smell the stench of corpses.

6   "What's your name?" he asked the girl, and she told him her flower name. "Don't move, Azucena," Rolf Carlé directed, and kept talking to her, without a thought for what he was saying, just to distract her, while slowly he worked his way forward in mud up to his waist. The air around him seemed as murky as the mud.

7   It was impossible to reach her from the approach he was attempting, so he retreated and circled around where there seemed to be firmer footing. When finally he was close enough, he took the rope and tied it beneath her arms, so they could pull her out. He smiled at her with that smile that crinkles his eyes and makes him look like a little boy; he told her that everything was fine, that he was here with her now, that soon they would have her out. He signaled the others to pull, but as soon as the cord tensed, the girl screamed. They tried again, and her shoulders and arms appeared, but they could move her no farther; she was trapped. Someone suggested that her legs might be caught in the collapsed walls of her house, but she said it was not just rubble, that she was also held by the bodies of her brothers and sisters clinging to her legs.

8   "Don't worry, we'll get you out of here," Rolf promised. Despite the quality of the transmission, I could hear his voice break, and I loved him more than ever. Azucena looked at him, but said nothing.

9   During those first hours Rolf Carlé exhausted all the resources of his ingenuity to rescue her. He struggled with poles and ropes, but every tug was an intolerable torture for the imprisoned girl. It occurred to him to use one of the poles as a lever but got no result and had to abandon the idea. He talked a couple of soldiers into working with him for a while, but they had to leave because so many other victims were calling for help. The girl could not move, she barely could breathe, but she did not seem desperate, as if an ancestral resignation allowed her to accept her fate. The reporter, on the other hand, was determined to snatch her from death. Someone brought him a tire, which he placed beneath her arms like a life buoy, and then laid a plank near the hole to hold his weight and allow him to stay closer to her. As it was impossible to remove the rubble blindly, he tried once or twice to dive toward her feet, but emerged frustrated, covered with mud, and spitting gravel. He concluded that he would have to have a pump to drain the water, and radioed a request for one, but received in return a message that there was no available transport and it could not be sent until the next morning.

10   "We can't wait that long!" Rolf Carlé shouted, but in the pandemonium no one stopped to commiserate. Many more hours would go by before he accepted that time had stagnated and reality had been irreparably distorted.

11   A military doctor came to examine the girl, and observed that her heart was functioning well and that if she did not get too cold she could survive the night.

12   "Hang on, Azucena, we'll have the pump tomorrow," Rolf Carlé tried to console her.

13   "Don't leave me alone," she begged.

14   "No, of course I won't leave you."

15   Someone brought him coffee, and he helped the girl drink it, sip by sip. The warm liquid revived her and she began telling him about her small life, about her family and her school, about how things were in that little bit of world before the volcano had erupted. She was thirteen, and she had never been outside her village. Rolf Carlé, buoyed by a premature optimism, was convinced that everything would end well: the pump would arrive, they would drain the water, move the rubble, and Azucena would be transported by helicopter to a hospital where she would recover rapidly and where he could visit her and bring her gifts. He thought, She's already too old for dolls, and I don't know what would please her; maybe a dress. I don't know much about women, he concluded, amused, reflecting that although he had known many women in his lifetime, none had taught him these details. To pass the hours he began to tell Azucena about his travels and adventures as a newshound, and when he exhausted his memory, he called upon imagination, inventing things he thought might entertain her. From time to time she dozed, but he kept talking in the darkness, to assure her that he was still there and to overcome the menace of uncertainty.

16   That was a long night.

❧

17   Many miles away, I watched Rolf Carlé and the girl on a television screen. I could not bear the wait at home, so I went to National Television, where I often spent entire nights with Rolf editing programs. There, I was near his world, and I could at least get a feeling of what he lived through during those three decisive days. I called all the important people in the city, senators, commanders of the armed forces, the North American ambassador, and the president of National Petroleum, begging them for a pump to remove the silt, but obtained only vague promises. I began to ask for urgent help on radio and television, to see if there wasn't *someone* who could help us. Between calls I would run to the newsroom to monitor the satellite transmissions that periodically brought new details of the catastrophe. While reporters selected scenes with most impact for the news report, I searched for footage that featured Azucena's mudpit. The screen reduced the disaster to a single plane and accentuated the tremendous distance that separated me from Rolf Carlé; nonetheless, I was there with him. The child's every suffering hurt me as it did him; I felt his frustration, his impotence. Faced with the impossibility of communicating with him, the fantastic idea came to me that if I tried, I could reach him by force of mind and in that way give him encouragement. I concentrated until I was dizzy—a frenzied and futile activity. At times I would be overcome with compassion and burst out crying; at other times, I was so drained I felt as if I were staring through a telescope at the light of a star dead for a million years.

18   I watched that hell on the first morning broadcast, cadavers of people and animals awash in the current of new rivers formed overnight from the melted snow. Above the mud rose the tops of trees and the bell towers of a church where several people had taken refuge and were patiently awaiting rescue teams. Hundreds of soldiers and volunteers from the Civil Defense were clawing through rubble searching for survivors, while long rows of ragged specters awaited their turn for a cup of hot broth. Radio networks announced that their phones were jammed with calls from families offering shelter to orphaned children. Drinking water was in scarce supply, along with gasoline and food. Doctors, resigned to amputating arms and legs without anesthesia, pled that at least they be sent serum and painkillers and antibiotics; most of the roads, however, were impassable, and worse were the bureaucratic obstacles that stood in the way. To top it all, the clay contaminated by decomposing bodies threatened the living with an outbreak of epidemics.

19   Azucena was shivering inside the tire that held her above the surface. Immobility and tension had greatly weakened her, but she was conscious and could still be heard when a microphone was held out to her. Her tone was humble, as if apologizing for all the fuss. Rolf Carlé had a growth of beard, and dark circles beneath his eyes; he looked near exhaustion. Even from that enormous distance I could sense the quality of his weariness, so different from the fatigue of other adventures. He had completely forgotten the camera; he could not look at the girl through a lens any longer. The pictures we were receiving were not his assistant's but those of other reporters who had appropriated Azucena, bestowing on her the pathetic responsibility of embodying the horror of what had happened in that place. With the first light Rolf tried again to dislodge the obstacles that held the girl in her tomb, but he had only his hands to work with; he did not dare use a tool for fear of injuring her. He fed Azucena a cup of the cornmeal mush and bananas the Army was distributing, but she immediately vomited it up. A doctor stated that she had a fever, but added that there was little he could do: antibiotics were being reserved for cases of gangrene. A priest also passed by and blessed her, hanging a medal of the Virgin around her neck. By evening a gentle, persistent drizzle began to fall.

20   "The sky is weeping," Azucena murmured, and she, too, began to cry.

21   "Don't be afraid," Rolf begged. "You have to keep your strength up and be calm. Everything will be fine. I'm with you, and I'll get you out somehow."

22   Reporters returned to photograph Azucena and ask her the same questions, which she no longer tried to answer. In the meanwhile, more television and movie teams arrived with spools of cable, tapes, film, videos, precision lenses, recorders, sound consoles, lights, reflecting screens, auxiliary motors, cartons of supplies, electricians, sound technicians, and cameramen: Azucena's face was beamed to millions of screens around the world. And all the while Rolf Carlé kept pleading for a pump. The improved technical facilities bore results, and National Television began receiving sharper pictures and clearer sound; the distance seemed suddenly

compressed, and I had the horrible sensation that Azucena and Rolf were by my side, separated from me by impenetrable glass. I was able to follow events hour by hour; I knew everything my love did to wrest the girl from her prison and help her endure her suffering; I overheard fragments of what they said to one another and could guess the rest; I was present when she taught Rolf to pray, and when he distracted her with the stories I had told him in a thousand and one nights beneath the white mosquito netting of our bed.

23   When darkness came on the second day, Rolf tried to sing Azucena to sleep with old Austrian folk songs he had learned from his mother, but she was far beyond sleep. They spent most of the night talking, each in a stupor of exhaustion and hunger, and shaking with cold. That night, imperceptibly, the unyielding floodgates that had contained Rolf Carlé's past for so many years began to open, and the torrent of all that had lain hidden in the deepest and most secret layers of memory poured out, leveling before it the obstacles that had blocked his consciousness for so long. He could not tell it all to Azucena; she perhaps did not know there was a world beyond the sea or time previous to her own; she was not capable of imagining Europe in the years of the war. So he could not tell her of defeat, nor of the afternoon the Russians had led them to the concentration camp to bury prisoners dead from starvation. Why should he describe to her how the naked bodies piled like a mountain of firewood resembled fragile china? How could he tell this dying child about ovens and gallows? Nor did he mention the night that he had seen his mother naked, shod in stiletto-heeled red boots, sobbing with humiliation. There was much he did not tell, but in those hours he relived for the first time all the things his mind had tried to erase. Azucena had surrendered her fear to him and so, without wishing it, had obliged Rolf to confront his own. There, beside that hellhole of mud, it was impossible for Rolf to flee from himself any longer, and the visceral terror he had lived as a boy suddenly invaded him. He reverted to the years when he was the age of Azucena, and younger, and, like her, found himself trapped in a pit without escape, buried in life, his head barely above ground; he saw before his eyes the boots and legs of his father, who had removed his belt and was whipping it in the air with the never-forgotten hiss of a viper coiled to strike. Sorrow flooded through him, intact and precise, as if it had lain always in his mind, waiting. He was once again in the armoire where his father locked him to punish him for imagined misbehavior, there where for eternal hours he had crouched with his eyes closed, not to see the darkness, with his hands over his ears, to shut out the beating of his heart, trembling, huddled like a cornered animal. Wandering in the mist of his memories he found his sister Katharina, a sweet, retarded child who spent her life hiding, with the hope that her father would forget the disgrace of her having been born. With Katharina, Rolf crawled beneath the dining room table, and with her hid there under the long white tablecloth, two children forever embraced, alert to footsteps and voices. Katharina's scent melded with his own sweat, with aromas of cooking,

garlic, soup, freshly baked bread, and the unexpected odor of putrescent clay. His sister's hand in his, her frightened breathing, her silk hair against his cheek, the candid gaze of her eyes. Katharina...Katharina materialized before him, floating on the air like a flag, clothed in the white tablecloth, now a winding sheet, and at last he could weep for her death and for the guilt of having abandoned her. He understood then that all his exploits as a reporter, the feats that had won him such recognition and fame, were merely an attempt to keep his most ancient fears at bay, a stratagem for taking refuge behind a lens to test whether reality was more tolerable from that perspective. He took excessive risks as an exercise of courage, training by day to conquer the monsters that tormented him by night. But he had come face to face with the moment of truth; he could not continue to escape his past. He *was* Azucena; he was buried in the clayey mud; his terror was not the distant emotion of an almost forgotten childhood, it was a claw sunk in his throat. In the flush of his tears he saw his mother, dressed in black and clutching her imitation-crocodile pocketbook to her bosom, just as he had last seen her on the dock when she had come to put him on the boat to South America. She had not come to dry his tears, but to tell him to pick up a shovel: the war was over and now they must bury the dead.

24   "Don't cry. I don't hurt anymore. I'm fine," Azucena said when dawn came.

25   "I'm not crying for you," Rolf Carlé smiled. "I'm crying for myself. I hurt all over."

26   The third day in the valley of the cataclysm began with a pale light filtering through storm clouds. The President of the Republic visited the area in his tailored safari jacket to confirm that this was the worst catastrophe of the century; the country was in mourning; sister nations had offered aid; he had ordered a state of siege; the Armed Forces would be merciless, anyone caught stealing or committing other offenses would be shot on sight. He added that it was impossible to remove all the corpses or count the thousands who had disappeared; the entire valley would be declared holy ground, and bishops would come to celebrate a solemn mass for the souls of the victims. He went to the Army field tents to offer relief in the form of vague promises to crowds of the rescued, then to the improvised hospital to offer a word of encouragement to doctors and nurses worn down from so many hours of tribulations. Then he asked to be taken to see Azucena, the little girl the whole world had seen. He waved to her with a limp statesman's hand, and microphones recorded his emotional voice and paternal tone as he told her that her courage had served as an example to the nation. Rolf Carlé interrupted to ask for a pump, and the President assured him that he personally would attend to the matter. I caught a glimpse of Rolf for a few seconds kneeling beside the mudpit. On the evening news broadcast, he was still in the same position; and I, glued to the screen like a fortune-teller to her

crystal ball, could tell that something fundamental had changed in him. I knew somehow that during the night his defenses had crumbled and he had given in to grief; finally he was vulnerable. The girl had touched a part of him that he himself had no access to, a part he had never shared with me. Rolf had wanted to console her, but it was Azucena who had given him consolation.

27   I recognized the precise moment at which Rolf gave up the fight and surrendered to the torture of watching the girl die. I was with them, three days and two nights, spying on them from the other side of life. I was there when she told him that in all her thirteen years no boy had ever loved her and that it was a pity to leave this world without knowing love. Rolf assured her that he loved her more than he could ever love anyone, more than he loved his mother, more than his sister, more than all the women who had slept in his arms, more than he loved me, his life companion, who would have given anything to be trapped in that well in her place, who would have exchanged her life for Azucena's, and I watched as he leaned down to kiss her poor forehead, consumed by a sweet, sad emotion he could not name. I felt how in that instant both were saved from despair, how they were freed from the clay, how they rose above the vultures and helicopters, how together they flew above the vast swamp of corruption and laments. How, finally, they were able to accept death. Rolf Carlé prayed in silence that she would die quickly, because such pain cannot be borne.

28   By then I had obtained a pump and was in touch with a general who had agreed to ship it the next morning on a military cargo plane. But on the night of that third day, beneath the unblinking focus of quartz lamps and the lens of a hundred cameras, Azucena gave up, her eyes locked with those of the friend who had sustained her to the end. Rolf Carlé removed the life buoy, closed her eyelids, held her to his chest for a few moments and then let her go. She sank slowly, a flower in the mud.

29   You are back with me, but you are not the same man. I often accompany you to the station and we watch the videos of Azucena again; you study them intently, looking for something you could have done to save her, something you did not think of in time. Or maybe you study them to see yourself as if in a mirror, naked. Your cameras lie forgotten in a closet; you do not write or sing; you sit long hours before the window, staring at the mountains. Beside you, I wait for you to complete the voyage into yourself, for the old wounds to heal. I know that when you return from your nightmares, we shall again walk hand in hand, as before.

Questions for Discussion

1. Who is the narrator of the story? What is she like? How does her perspective on the events enrich the story? What does she mean when she says, " . . . I felt as if I were staring through a telescope at the light of a star dead for a million years"?

2. What happened to produce the tragic deaths in this story? How do you know?

3. Why do the media, in the midst of such widespread tragedy, focus so much attention on one little girl? Why can they get all of their elaborate equipment to the site when no one seems to be able to bring the needed pump? How and why does she become "the symbol of the tragedy"?

4. The narrator says that Rolf Carlé was "buoyed by a premature optimism." What does she mean? Why is he optimistic when there appears to be no hope?

5. Explain the narrator's comment that Rolf Carlé "accepted that time had stagnated and reality had been irreparably distorted."

6. Why do the politicians provide "only vague promises," not real help and certainly not the pump needed to help save Azucena?

7. Why and how does his experience with Azucena enable Rolf to remember long-forgotten and repressed suffering from his past? What experiences does he recall? Who is Katharina and what role does she play in Rolf's memories? How does his past help explain his heroic effort to save Azucena?

8. What does the narrator mean by "He was Azucena; he was buried in the clayey mud"? How had he "[taken] refuge behind a lens to test whether reality was more tolerable from that perspective"?

9. Just before Azucena died, the narrator says, "I felt how in that instant both were saved from despair, how they were freed from the clay. . . ." What does she mean by this and in what ways can it be true?

Suggestions for Exploring, Writing, and Persuading

1. The narrator says that she felt as if she were "spying on them from the other side of life." In an essay argue that we, as television viewers, are spying on the lives of others or that we are merely staying informed. Use examples of specific news stories to support your points.

2. How can a rigid focus on immediate fact obscure truth? Write an essay explaining this supposition using examples from newspaper accounts or personal experience.

3. The beginning of the story says that Rolf Carlé went on this assignment "never suspecting that he would find a fragment of his past, lost thirty years before." How had Rolf tried to distort and repress the reality of his own past through his experience as a reporter? In what ways is this a story of an accidental quest?

4. Write an essay illustrating how Allende uses vivid images and metaphors to help readers visualize and empathize with the characters.

POETRY

Psalm 8, traditionally attributed to David, is one of the 150 poems that make up the book of Psalms in the Old Testament. The translations here are from the King James version. Often described as a lyrical echo of the first book of Genesis, this psalm celebrates God's creations.

PSALM 8   <small>(ELEVENTH–TENTH CENTURY B.C.)</small>

To the chief Musician upon Gittith, A Psalm of David.

1 O Lord our Lord, how excellent *is* thy name in all the earth! who hast set thy glory above the heavens.
2 Out of the mouth of babes and sucklings hast thou ordained strength because of thine enemies, that thou mightest still the enemy and the avenger.
3 When I consider thy heavens, the work of thy fingers, the moon and the stars, which thou hast ordained;
4 What is man, that thou art mindful of him? and the son of man, that thou visitest him?
5 For thou hast made him a little lower than the angels, and hast crowned him with glory and honour.
6 Thou madest him to have dominion over the works of thy hands; thou hast put all *things* under his feet:
7 All sheep and oxen, yea, and the beasts of the field;
8 The fowl of the air, and the fish of the sea, *and whatsoever* passeth through the paths of the seas.
9 O Lord our Lord, how excellent *is* thy name in all the earth!

Questions for Discussion

1. In what order does the psalmist perceive the wonders of God?

2. What prompts the psalmist's questions? What is the tone in the psalm?

3. What vision of humanity and its purpose does the psalmist present? What is man's responsibility to God? How well has humanity fulfilled that purpose? What does man return to God for His gifts.

While Psalm 8 offers praise to God, Psalm 13 reveals some of the human fears of the psalmist and the faith that comforts him and encourages him still to sing.

PSALM 13

For the leader. A psalm of David.

1 How long, LORD? Will you utterly forget me? How long will you hide your face from me?

2 How long must I carry sorrow in my soul, grief in my heart day
after day? How long will my enemy triumph over me?
3 Look upon me, answer me, LORD, my God! Give light to my
eyes lest I sleep in death,
4 Lest my enemy say, "I have prevailed," lest my foes rejoice at
my downfall.
5 I trust in your faithfulness. Grant my heart joy in your help,
That I may sing of the LORD, "How good our God has been
to me!"

Questions for Discussion

1. In contrast to Psalm 8, here the psalmist begins by expressing distress.
   What does he ask of God?

2. How does the tone of the psalm change in verses 4 and 5? How would
   you explain the difference in tone?

Suggestion for Exploring, Writing, and Persuading

1. Write an essay comparing the tone of the two psalms. How do these
   changes reflect changes in the psalmist? What are your interpretations
   of the reasons for the changes in the psalmist's moods?

John Donne (1572–1631)

*A brief biography of John Donne appears in the Men and
Women Unit.*

HOLY SONNET 14   (CA. 1610)

Batter my heart, three person'd God; for, you
As yet but knocke, breathe, shine, and seeke to mend;
That I may rise, and stand, o'erthrow mee, and bend
Your force, to breake, blowe, burn and make me new.
5   I, like an usurpt towne, to another due,
Labour to admit You, but Oh, to no end;
Reason Your viceroy in mee, mee should defend
But is captiv'd, and proves weake or untrue,
Yet dearely I love You, and would be lov'd faine,
10 But am betroth'd unto Your enemie,
Divorce mee, untie, or breake that knot againe,
Take mee to You, imprison mee, for I
Except You enthrall mee, never shall be free,
Nor ever chaste, except You ravish mee.

Questions for Discussion

1. What does the strong verb "batter" suggest? What is the speaker asking God to do in this anguished and unorthodox prayer? Why?

2. The first four lines of the sonnet are dominated by strong action verbs. What is the effect of these verbs? What is the effect of the alliterative *b*s in these lines?

3. Explain the extended simile developed in the second quatrain.

4. Explain the paradoxes in the last two lines.

Suggestion for Exploring, Writing, and Persuading

1. In an analysis, show how imagery, sound, diction, and syntax develop the tone of Donne's "Holy Sonnet 14."

John Milton (1608–1674)

John Milton, educated at Cambridge and a master of Greek, Latin, Italian, and Hebrew, isolated himself after gradua-tion from college to read the great books. After writing sev-eral controversial pamphlets, including Areopagitica *(1644), an argument for freedom of the press, he served as foreign secretary under Oliver Cromwell, Puritan Lord Protector of England from 1653 to 1658. Milton's* Paradise Lost *(1667), based on the Genesis account of humanity's fall, is regarded as the greatest epic poem written in English. Both* Paradise Lost *and* Paradise Regained *(1671) were written during Mil-ton's last years, when he was blind and embittered.*

SONNET 16   (1655)

When I consider how my light is spent,
   Ere half my days, in this dark world and wide,
   And that one talent which is death to hide,
   Lodged with me useless, though my soul more bent
5   To serve therewith my Maker, and present
   My true account, lest he returning chide,
   Doth God exact day-labour, light denied,
   I fondly ask; but Patience to prevent
That murmur, soon replies, "God doth not need
10   Either man's work or his own gifts, who best
   Bear his mild yoke, they serve him best. His state
Is kingly. Thousands at his bidding speed
   And post o'er land and ocean without rest:
   They also serve who only stand and wait."

Questions for Discussion

1. To what does Milton refer when he speaks of "that one talent which is death to hide / Lodged with me useless . . . "? What effect has this loss had on his attitude?

2. Milton asks, "Doth God exact day-labour, light denied?" What does he imply?

3. Patience says that man is not going to be judged on his "work" or "gifts." On what is man going to be judged?

4. Explain the last line of the poem.

Suggestions for Exploring, Writing, and Persuading

1. Milton speaks of presenting the "true account" of his life and actions to God. If you had to present the true account of yourself to God or to someone else in authority, what would it be? Why?

2. In an essay, discuss whether you agree with the last line of Milton's poem.

William Blake (1757–1827)

A brief biography of William Blake appears in the Freedom and Responsibility Unit.

THE TYGER   (1794)

Tyger! Tyger! burning bright
In the forests of the night,
What immortal hand or eye
Could frame thy fearful symmetry?

5   In what distant deeps or skies
Burnt the fire of thine eyes?
On what wings dare he aspire?
What the hand, dare seize the fire?

And what shoulder, & what art,
10 Could twist the sinews of thy heart?
And when thy heart began to beat,
What dread hand? & what dread feet?

What the hammer? what the chain?
In what furnace was thy brain?
15 What the anvil? what dread grasp
Dare its deadly terrors clasp?

When the stars threw down their spears,
And water'd heaven with their tears,
Did he smile his work to see?
20 Did he who made the Lamb make thee?

Tyger! Tyger! burning bright
In the forests of the night,
What immortal hand or eye
Dare frame thy fearful symmetry?

Questions for Discussion

1. What qualities of the tiger are suggested by the phrase "fearful symmetry"?
2. What is Blake alluding to in the lines "When the stars threw down their spears / And water'd heaven with their tears"?
3. Can the question "Did he who made the Lamb make thee?" be answered? If so, how? If not, why not?
4. What does the tiger symbolize?

Suggestion for Exploring, Writing, and Persuading

1. In an essay, analyze "The Tyger" as representing a question that has always bothered thoughtful people.

William Wordsworth (1770–1850)

A brief biography of William Wordsworth appears in the
Freedom and Responsibility Unit.

MY HEART LEAPS UP   (1807)

My heart leaps up when I behold
   A Rainbow in the sky:
So was it when my life began;
So is it now I am a Man;
5 So be it when I shall grow old,
   Or let me die!
The Child is Father of the Man;
And I could wish my days to be
Bound each to each by natural piety.

Questions for Discussion

1. What very familiar figure of speech does the poet use in the first line? What does it suggest about his feeling for nature? Why would he rather die than lose the capacity for this feeling?
2. What does the paradox "The Child is Father of the Man" mean?
3. What does the speaker mean by "natural piety"?

Suggestions for Exploring, Writing, and Persuading

1. In an essay, explain what things in life make your "heart leap up."
2. Write an essay in which you attempt to prove that one's enjoyment of life is increased by preservation of a childlike sense of wonder at the beauty of nature.

Alfred, Lord Tennyson (1809–1892)

Tennyson succeeded Wordsworth as English Poet Laureate. Tennyson's early poems were not acclaimed; however, after the death of a friend caused him to write an extended elegy, In Memoriam *(1853), and Queen Victoria named him a Lord, Tennyson became one of the most popular poets of his day. Among his works are* Maud, and Other Poems *(1855) and* Idylls of the King *(1859), an extended poem about King Arthur.*

ULYSSES (1833)

It little profits that an idle king,
By this still hearth, among these barren crags,
Match'd with an aged wife, I mete and dole
Unequal laws unto a savage race,
5   That hoard, and sleep, and feed, and know not me.
I cannot rest from travel: I will drink
Life to the lees: all times I have enjoy'd
Greatly, have suffer'd greatly, both with those
That loved me, and alone; on shore, and when
10   Thro' scudding drifts the rainy Hyades
Vext the dim sea: I am become a name;
For always roaming with a hungry heart
Much have I seen and known; cities of men
And manners, climates, councils, governments,
15   Myself not least, but honour'd of them all;
And drunk delight of battle with my peers,
Far on the ringing plains of windy Troy.
I am a part of all that I have met;
Yet all experience is an arch wherethro'
20   Gleams that untravell'd world, whose margin fades
For ever and for ever when I move.
How dull it is to pause, to make an end,
To rust unburnish'd, not to shine in use!
As tho' to breathe were life. Life piled on life
25   Were all too little, and of one to me
Little remains: but every hour is saved
From that eternal silence, something more,
A bringer of new things; and vile it were
For some three suns to store and hoard myself,
30   And this gray spirit yearning in desire
To follow knowledge like a sinking star,
Beyond the utmost bound of human thought.
    This is my son, mine own Telemachus,
To whom I leave the sceptre and the isle—
35   Well-loved of me, discerning to fulfil

This labour, by slow prudence to make mild
A rugged people, and thro' soft degrees
Subdue them to the useful and the good.
Most blameless is he, centred in the sphere
40   Of common duties, decent not to fail
In offices of tenderness, and pay
Meet adoration to my household gods
When I am gone. He works his work, I mine.
        There lies the port; the vessel puffs her sail:
45   There gloom the dark broad seas. My mariners,
Souls that have toil'd, and wrought, and thought with me—
That ever with a frolic welcome took
The thunder and the sunshine, and opposed
Free hearts, free foreheads—you and I are old;
50   Old age hath yet his honour and his toil;
Death closes all: but something ere the end,
Some work of noble note, may yet be done,
Not unbecoming men that strove with Gods.
The lights begin to twinkle from the rocks:
55   The long day wanes: the slow moon climbs: the deep
Moans round with many voices. Come, my friends,
'Tis not too late to seek a newer world.
Push off, and sitting well in order smite
The sounding furrows; for my purpose holds
60   To sail beyond the sunset, and the baths
Of all the western stars, until I die.
It may be that the gulfs will wash us down:
It may be we shall touch the Happy Isles,
And see the great Achilles, whom we knew.
65   Tho' much is taken, much abides; and tho'
We are not now that strength which in old days
Moved earth and heaven, that which we are, we are;
One equal temper of heroic hearts,
Made weak by time and fate, but strong in will
70   To strive, to seek, to find, and not to yield.

Questions for Discussion

1. Who is Ulysses' audience in this dramatic monologue? What is he trying to persuade them to do?
2. Why does Ulysses say that he "will drink / Life to the lees"? Why does he still crave the "untravel'd world"?
3. Ulysses says he has "enjoyed greatly" and "suffered greatly." Why is the word *greatly* important?
4. Why is Telemachus Ulysses's ideal heir?
5. Explain Ulysses's claim, "I am a part of all that I have met."

Suggestions for Exploring, Writing, and Persuading

1. Write an essay about someone who has the same characteristics and the same yearnings as Ulysses.

2. "Do Not Go Gentle into That Good Night" by Dylan Thomas has a similar message. Compare the poems' themes.

3. Are you a Ulysses or a Telemachus? Discuss.

4. In an essay, describe Ulysses's quest. What does he want for the rest of his life? What does he not want?

5. Write an essay in which you try to convince your audience "To strive, to seek, to find, and not to yield," in other words, to live every minute of life fully.

Gerard Manley Hopkins (1844–1889)

Born into a High Anglican family in England, Gerard Manley Hopkins in 1866 converted to Catholicism. Two years later, he entered the Jesuit order and in 1877 was ordained a Jesuit priest. His sometimes anguished poems, which were not published until 1918, reveal a man of strong faith sometimes racked by doubts about the adequacy of his devotion and service. Hopkins developed an experimental metrical system he called sprung rhythm, basing his lines on the number of accents rather than the number of syllables.

GOD'S GRANDEUR (1877)

The world is charged with the grandeur of God.
　　It will flame out, like shining from shook foil;
　　It gathers to a greatness, like the ooze of oil
Crushed. Why do men then now not reck his rod?
5　Generations have trod, have trod, have trod;
　　And all is seared with trade; bleared, smeared with toil;
　　And wears man's smudge and shares man's smell: the soil
Is bare now, nor can foot feel, being shod.
And for all this, nature is never spent:
10　　There lives the dearest freshness deep down things;
And though the last lights off the black West went
　　Oh, morning, at the brown brink eastward, springs—
Because the Holy Ghost over the bent
World broods with warm breast and with ah! bright wings.

Questions for Discussion

1. What is the effect of the word *charged* in the first line?

2. What images does Hopkins use to characterize the grandeur of God? Where does this grandeur appear?

3. What effect does the repetition in line 5 have?

4. What is Hopkins's answer to the question in line 4? Compare his answer to Wordsworth's lament in "The World Is Too Much with Us."

5. Explain the final image?

Suggestion for Exploring, Writing, and Persuading

1. Hopkins's poem celebrates the grandeur and freshness of God's creation, sensitizing readers to even the apparently dull and ordinary. Write an essay on the way Hopkins's sense of divine imminence is imaged in the poem.

William Butler Yeats (1865–1939)

A brief biography of William Butler Yeats appears in the Family Unit.

SAILING TO BYZANTIUM   (1927)

I

That is no country for old men. The young
In one another's arms, birds in the trees
—Those dying generations—at their song,
The salmon-falls, the mackerel-crowded seas,
5   Fish, flesh, or fowl, commend all summer long
Whatever is begotten, born, and dies.
Caught in that sensual music all neglect
Monuments of unageing intellect.

II

An aged man is but a paltry thing,
10   A tattered coat upon a stick, unless
Soul clap its hands and sing, and louder sing
For every tatter in its mortal dress,
Nor is there singing school but studying
Monuments of its own magnificence;
15   And therefore I have sailed the seas and come
To the holy city of Byzantium.

III

O sages standing in God's holy fire
As in the gold mosaic of a wall,
Come from the holy fire, perne in a gyre,

20 And be the singing-masters of my soul.
Consume my heart away; sick with desire
And fastened to a dying animal
It knows not what it is; and gather me
Into the artifice of eternity.

IV

25 Once out of nature I shall never take
My bodily form from any natural thing,
But such a form as Grecian goldsmiths make
Of hammered gold and gold enamelling
To keep a drowsy Emperor awake;
30 Or set upon a golden bough to sing
To lords and ladies of Byzantium
Of what is past, or passing, or to come.

Questions for Discussion

1. What place is the speaker describing in the first stanza? Why is it "no country for old men"? What images define this world?
2. What does the "artifice of eternity" suggest about Yeats's conception of life after death?
3. Why would Yeats want to be resurrected as a golden bird?
4. At the beginning of the poem Yeats refers to "[w]hatever is begotten, born, and dies." At the end he imagines himself a golden bird singing of "what is past, or passing, or to come." How do these three-part phrases define the difference between the speaker in his original country and the speaker in Byzantium?

Suggestions for Exploring, Writing, and Persuading

1. In an essay examine the symbolism of the bird. For example, does the bird symbolize a means of transcending the physical world?
2. Yeats says in *A Vision* that Byzantium represented for him a culture so unified in its religious, cultural, and practical life that an artist spoke for and was heard by the whole people. Read Book V, section IV of *A Vision*, research Byzantium, and write a paper on why Byzantium meant so much to Yeats that he would prefer to spend eternity there.

T. S. Eliot (1888–1965)

Eliot, born an American and the grandson of a Unitarian minister, changed his nationality and his religion, becoming a British citizen and a devout Anglican. Eliot's early poems, like "The Love Song of J. Alfred Prufrock" and "The Hollow Men," expressed the disenchantment and disillusionment of many people in the early twentieth century. The Waste Land *(1922) is considered by many critics to be the ultimate expression of the modern condition. Eliot's conversion to the Anglican faith, however, changed his outlook completely; and his later works such as "Ash Wednesday" and* Four Quartets *(1934–1944) depict human beings' search for a sustaining faith. An ardent admirer of Dante, Eliot learned medieval Italian in order to read* The Divine Comedy *in its original form. The quotation with which Eliot begins "The Love Song of J. Alfred Prufrock" is a statement of Guido da Montefeltro, a sinner in Dante's* Inferno, *who says that he would not tell Dante his story if he thought that there was any chance that Dante would return to earth to repeat it.*

THE LOVE SONG OF J. ALFRED PRUFROCK   (1917)

S' io credessi che mia risposta fosse
A persona che mai tornasse al mondo,
Questa fiamma staria senza piú scosse.
Ma perciocchè giammai di questo fondo
Non tornò vivo alcun, s' i' odo il vero,
Senza tema d'infamia ti rispondo.

Let us go then, you and I,
When the evening is spread out against the sky
Like a patient etherized upon a table;
Let us go, through certain half-deserted streets,
5   The muttering retreats
Of restless nights in one-night cheap hotels
And sawdust restaurants with oyster-shells:
Streets that follow like a tedious argument
Of insidious intent
10   To lead you to an overwhelming question...

Oh, do not ask, "What is it?"
Let us go and make our visit.

In the room the women come and go
Talking of Michelangelo.
15   The yellow fog that rubs its back upon the window panes,
The yellow smoke that rubs its muzzle on the window panes,
Licked its tongue into the corners of the evening,
Lingered upon the pools that stand in drains,
Let fall upon its back the soot that falls from chimneys,
20   Slipped by the terrace, made a sudden leap,
And seeing that it was a soft October night,
Curled once about the house, and fell asleep.

And indeed there will be time
For the yellow smoke that slides along the street,
25 Rubbing its back upon the window panes;
There will be time, there will be time
To prepare a face to meet the faces that you meet;
There will be time to murder and create,
And time for all the works and days of hands
30 That lift and drop a question on your plate:
Time for you and time for me,
And time yet for a hundred indecisions,
And for a hundred visions and revisions,
Before the taking of a toast and tea.

35 In the room the women come and go
Talking of Michelangelo.

And indeed there will be time
To wonder, "Do I dare?" and, "Do I dare?"—
Time to turn back and descend the stair,
40 With a bald spot in the middle of my hair—
(They will say: "How his hair is growing thin!")
My morning coat, my collar mounting firmly to the chin,
My necktie rich and modest, but asserted by a simple pin—
(They will say: "But how his arms and legs are thin!")
45 Do I dare
Disturb the universe?
In a minute there is time
For decisions and revisions which a minute will reverse.

For I have known them all already, known them all:
50 Have known the evenings, mornings, afternoons,
I have measured out my life with coffee spoons;
I know the voices dying with a dying fall
Beneath the music from a farther room.
       So how should I presume?

55 And I have known the eyes already, known them all—
The eyes that fix you in a formulated phrase.
And when I am formulated, sprawling on a pin,
When I am pinned and wriggling on the wall,
Then how should I begin
60 To spit out all the butt-ends of my days and ways?
       And how should I presume?

And I have known the arms already, known them all—
Arms that are braceleted and white and bare
(But in the lamplight, downed with light brown hair!)
65   Is it perfume from a dress
       That makes me so digress?

Arms that lie along a table, or wrap about a shawl.
    And should I then presume?
        And how should I begin?

70   Shall I say, I have gone at dusk through narrow streets,
And watched the smoke that rises from the pipes
Of lonely men in shirtsleeves, leaning out of windows?...
I should have been a pair of ragged claws
Scuttling across the floors of silent seas.

75   And the afternoon, the evening, sleeps so peacefully!
Smoothed by long fingers,
Asleep...tired...or it malingers,
Stretched on the floor, here beside you and me.
Should I, after tea and cakes and ices,

80   Have the strength to force the moment to its crisis?
But though I have wept and fasted, wept and prayed,
Though I have seen my head (grown slightly bald) brought
        in upon a platter,
I am no prophet—and here's no great matter;
I have seen the moment of my greatness flicker,

85   And I have seen the eternal Footman hold my coat, and snicker,
        And in short, I was afraid.

    And would it have been worth it, after all,
After the cups, the marmalade, the tea,
Among the porcelain, among some talk of you and me,

90   Would it have been worth while
To have bitten off the matter with a smile,
To have squeezed the universe into a ball
To roll it toward some overwhelming question,
To say: "I am Lazarus, come from the dead,

95   Come back to tell you all, I shall tell you all"—
If one, settling a pillow by her head,
        Should say: "That is not what I meant at all;
            That is not it, at all."

    And would it have been worth it, after all,

100   Would it have been worth while,
After the sunsets and the dooryards and the sprinkled streets,
After the novels, after the teacups, after the skirts that trail
        along the floor—
And this, and so much more?—
It is impossible to say just what I mean!

105   But as if a magic lantern threw the nerves in patterns on a screen:
Would it have been worth while
If one, settling a pillow or throwing off a shawl,
And turning toward the window, should say: "That is not it at all,
        That is not what I meant, at all."

110   No! I am not Prince Hamlet, nor was meant to be;
       Am an attendant lord, one that will do
       To swell a progress, start a scene or two,
       Advise the prince: withal, an easy tool,
       Deferential, glad to be of use,
115   Politic, cautious, and meticulous;
       Full of high sentence, but a bit obtuse;
       At times, indeed, almost ridiculous—
       Almost, at times, the Fool.

       I grow old...I grow old...
120   I shall wear the bottoms of my trousers rolled.

          Shall I part my hair behind? Do I dare to eat a peach?
       I shall wear white flannel trousers, and walk upon the beach.
       I have heard the mermaids singing, each to each.
       I do not think that they will sing to me.

125   I have seen them riding seaward on the waves,
       Combing the white hair of the waves blown back
       When the wind blows the water white and black.
       We have lingered in the chambers of the sea
       By seagirls wreathed with seaweed red and brown,
130   Till human voices wake us, and we drown.

Questions for Discussion

1. What does Eliot suggest about Prufrock by beginning the poem with a quotation from Dante's *Inferno?*

2. Explain the effect of the description in the opening ten lines. What does this description tell you about Prufrock's world?

3. Why must Prufrock "prepare a face to meet the faces that you meet"? How is this similar to the Beatles' song about Eleanor Rigby's "wearing the face / that she keeps in a jar by the door"?

4. Explain the following line: "I have measured out my life with coffee spoons."

5. Why does Prufrock say that he "should have been a pair of ragged claws / Scuttling across the floors of silent seas"? Why might he have been more fulfilled as a crab?

6. Explain the pathos of Prufrock's saying, "I have heard the mermaids singing, each to each. / I do not think that they will sing to me." How is his opinion of himself affected by his having "heard the mermaids" sing? Why does he refer to mermaids here?

7. From what do "human voices wake us," and why, then, do "we drown"?

8. What is Prufrock afraid to ask? Why is he afraid to ask it?

Suggestions for Exploring, Writing, and Persuading

1. Write an essay arguing that J. Alfred Prufrock is the perfect example of the indecisiveness and insecurity of many people in the modern world.

2. In his poem, Eliot alludes to Andrew Marvell's "To His Coy Mistress," thereby inviting comparison between Marvell's speaker and Prufrock. Write an essay in which you contrast these two speakers.

3. Compare Prufrock to someone contemporary and convince your readers that this person is a modern Prufrock.

Langston Hughes (1902–1967)

A brief biography of Langston Hughes appears in the Family unit

HARLEM   (1951)

What happens to a dream deferred?

    Does it dry up
    like a raisin in the sun?
    Or fester like a sore—
5   And then run?
    Does it stink like rotten meat?
    Or crust and sugar over—
    like a syrupy sweet?

    Maybe it just sags
10   like a heavy load.

    Or does it explode?

Questions for Discussion

1. What does Hughes mean by "a dream deferred"? Why would a dream be deferred?

2. Hughes uses several strong verbs in describing what could happen to a "dream deferred": the dream could "dry up," "fester," "run," "stink," "crust and sugar over," "sag," or "explode." What is your response to these verbs?

3. Why does Hughes never identify the kind of dream he has in mind?

Suggestions for Exploring, Writing, and Persuading

1. If you, or a friend or relative, have had an unfulfilled or postponed dream, describe the experience and its results.

2. Research the race riots in the United States in the 1950s and 1960s. Then write an essay in which you argue whether one of these riots could have happened because of a dream deferred that exploded.

N. Scott Momaday (b. 1934)

N. Scott Momaday, a Kiowa, studied at the University of New Mexico and received his doctorate from Stanford University in 1963. His first novel, House Made of Dawn *(1968), won a Pulitzer Prize and brought him accolades for bringing prestige to Native American writers.* The Way to Rainy Mountain *(1969) describes the oral histories and migration stories of his ancestors as imagined by his grandmother. His second novel,* The Ancient Child *(1989), is a story about a spiritual journey.*

CARRIERS OF THE DREAM WHEEL   (1992)

This is the Wheel of Dreams
Which is carried on their voices,
By means of which their voices turn
And center upon being.
5   It encircles the First World,
This powerful wheel.
They shape their songs upon the wheel
And spin the names of the earth and sky,
The aboriginal names.
10   They are old men, or men
Who are old in their voices,
And they carry the wheel among the camps,
Saying: Come, come,
Let us tell the old stories,
15   Let us sing the sacred songs.

Questions for Discussion

1. Explain what Momaday means when he says that the "Wheel of dreams" is "carried on their voices."

2. In Kiowa cosmology, the wheel suggests the continuing cycle of oral tales and songs. What are all of the uses of the wheel? Why are these uses and dreams important to the Kiowa?

3. Explain the imagery of the wheel.

Suggestions for Exploring, Writing, and Persuading

1. In an essay explain why the telling of old stories is important to your family or culture.

2. In an argumentative essay, compare the ideas concerning dreams with those of Hughes in the preceding poem, persuading your audience that Momaday's poem is or is not a prelude to Hughes's poem.

Fred Chappell (b. 1936)

Fred Chappell spent his childhood in the Appalachian Mountains of Canton, North Carolina, where he learned to shape his poems in many forms and to tell a story with humor and a serious moral thread. A graduate of Duke University, Chappell has taught at the University of North Carolina at Greensboro for many years. His books of poetry include The World Between the Eyes *(1971),* Source *(1985), and* Spring Garden *(1995). His ten novels include* I Am One of You Forever *(1985),* Brighten the Corner Where You Are *(1989),* Look Back All the Green Valley *(1999), and* Family Gathering *(2000). In addition to the Bollingen Prize in Poetry, Chappell has won the Ingersoll Foundation's T. S. Eliot Prize.*

AN OLD MOUNTAIN WOMAN
READING THE BOOK OF JOB (1989)

The veiny wrist, the knobby finger joints,
The scar-creased palm, the thumb she lifts to wet
And lift the corner of the memoried page,
Turning once more through Job's bewilderment:
5   What histories are written into her hand...

Aforetime she was as a tabret, but now
They change the night to day, the light is short,
The world delivered to ungodly shadow.
The darkness of her hand darkens the page.
10   She straightens her bifocals in which the words,
Reflected, jitter, then come to rest like moths.
It is November. The woodstove shifts its log
And grumbles. The night is longer than her fire.

She moves her lips to read but does not speak.
15   What is there to answer to the terrible words,
To these sharp final words that engrave the fate
Of an old man hammered to bronze. She sees the man
As if he stood before her, thrown by the storm
Of time to be her husband, her dead husband.
20   She knows the man as man, his house and fields
Up Jarvis Creek going down in sawbriar,
The doctor bills chewing the farm like locusts.
Bleak Job scourged ceaseless in the starless night,
Her husband whom lean ravishment made holy:
25   The whirlwind-savage hand of God forecloses
The mortgage; the fields are auctioned clod by clod,
The skies are auctioned cloud by pallid cloud.

The Book of Job draws all its shadow over
Her thumbed-limp Bible. Saint Paul does not escape,
30   Jesus Himself does not shine clear of Job,
The darkness of that blindly punished lament.
Shall any teach God knowledge?—But if He knows,
And still permits...

　　　There is a weeping madness
35   In thoughts she tries so tiredly to push away.
Her trust lies down in dirt like a fractured tower.
Everything shall be restored, the Book
Tells her. But why should it be taken away?
Or given at the start? Her husband Charles,
40   The man she knows as Job, mild unto death,
She doubts shall be restored. The Book of Job
Distills to salt in the tear that seals her eye.

Let her then go out on Ember Mountain,
And cry out in his stead and say those words
45   She shall imagine for him, picturing
Herself there in the dark, in pitiless wind,
Raising her old fist to dare the lightning
And gates of wrath, herself alone in wind,
Saying the words that God's wind lacerates.
50   Let it be her stricken, blasted, shriveled
Like a candlewick and not the man
Her husband, whom the Lord like a hunting lion
Has carried off, her Job who suffered silence
As he went down never to rise again.

55   That silence does not yield. Her vision tears;
She never shall curse God, she never shall
Climb Ember Mountain again, nor ever weep.
But now she feels a throb in this old house
In which she sits alone, nursing her fire,
60   Her fear. A tremor as of someone walking
Another room, the kitchen or cold bedroom.
Someone unfamiliar is walking there,
Someone no kin to her, maybe no friend,
Who comes to bring her tidings the dead have risen
65   And all the wholeness of the earth restored.
She holds her breath; the phantom goes away.

She shuts the book of Job. She will not suffer
A God Who suffers the suffering of man,
Who sends the fatherless their broken arms,
70   Who sends away the widows empty of faith.
Tonight's no night for the heartless bedside prayer.

Questions for Discussion

1. To whom does "they" refer in the second stanza?
2. Why does the woman choose Job to read? How does she apply the story of Job to her life?
3. What does Chappell mean when he says, "She knows the man as man, his house and fields"?
4. Explain the line: *"Shall any teach God knowledge?"*
5. Explain why the woman wants to push away her thoughts. What is her "trust" and why does it lie in "dirt"? Explain what her questions mean.
6. Would it have helped the old woman to go out on Ember Mountain to shout the words her husband did not? Defend your answer.
7. Explain the last line of the poem in terms of tomorrow night.
8. What is the woman's quest?

Suggestions for Exploring, Writing, and Persuading

1. Write about an experience in which you questioned God's role in something that happened. How did you resolve your questioning?
2. Chappell writes, "She shuts the book of Job. She will not suffer / A God Who suffers the suffering of man,..." Write a persuasive essay in which you agree or disagree with the speaker's position.

Joseph Brodsky (1940–1996)

Joseph Brodsky was a native of Leningrad but moved to the United States in 1972, when he was exiled by the Soviet Union. Known primarily as a poet, he also wrote plays and essays. Brodsky received the Nobel Prize for Literature in 1987; as a tribute to his works, he was appointed Poet Laureate of the United States in 1992.

DECEMBER 24, 1971   (1972)

FOR V.S.

TRANSLATED BY ALAN MYERS WITH THE AUTHOR

When it's Christmas we're all of us magi.
At the grocers' all slipping and pushing.
Where a tin of halvah, coffee-flavored,
is the cause of a human assault-wave
by a crowd heavy-laden with parcels:
each one his own king, his own camel.

Nylon bags, carrier bags, paper cones,
caps and neckties all twisted up sideways.
Reek of vodka and resin and cod,

5

10 orange mandarins, cinnamon, apples.
Floods of faces, no sign of a pathway
toward Bethlehem, shut off by blizzard.

And the bearers of moderate gifts
leap on buses and jam all the doorways,
15 disappear into courtyards that gape,
though they know that there's nothing inside there:
not a beast, not a crib, nor yet her,
round whose head gleams a nimbus of gold.

Emptiness. But the mere thought of that
20 brings forth lights as if out of nowhere.
Herod reigns but the stronger he is,
the more sure, the more certain the wonder.
In the constancy of this relation
is the basic mechanics of Christmas.

25 That's what they celebrate everywhere,
for its coming push tables together.
No demand for a star for a while,
but a sort of good will touched with grace
can be seen in all men from afar,
30 and the shepherds have kindled their fires.

Snow is falling: not smoking but sounding
chimney pots on the roof, every face like a stain.
Herod drinks. Every wife hides her child.
He who comes is a mystery: features
35 are not known beforehand, men's hearts may
not be quick to distinguish the stranger.

But when drafts through the doorway disperse
the thick mist of the hours of darkness
and a shape in a shawl stands revealed,
40 both a newborn and Spirit that's Holy
in your self you discover; you stare
skyward, and it's right there:
                                        a star.

Questions for Discussion

1. Who are the "magi" referred to in the first line? What does Brodsky mean by "When it's Christmas we're all of us magi"?

2. How do the people in the first two stanzas differ from the magi of the Christmas story in Matthew 2?

3. What does the author mean by "Floods of faces, no sign of a pathway / toward Bethlehem, shut off by blizzard"?

4. Explain why Brodsky says that December 24 is "Emptiness."

5. Whom does Brodsky refer to in the lines "her, / round whose head gleams a nimbus of gold"?

6. Who was Herod? What does Brodsky mean by "Herod reigns but the stronger he is, / the more sure, the more certain the wonder"? What does Herod symbolize in this context?

7. What or whom does the speaker encounter in the last stanza? Does the last stanza contradict or enhance the message of the other six?

Suggestions for Exploring, Writing, and Persuading

1. Explain the third line of the fifth stanza—"No demand for a star for a while"—in relation to the last three lines: "you stare / skyward, and it's right there: / a star."

2. Write an essay about what you seek just before Christmas, on Christmas Day, or during an annual event celebrated by your family or in your culture.

3. After discussing the commercialism of the Christmas season, Brodsky says that you, the shopper/observer, feel "both a newborn and Spirit that's Holy / in your self you discover." Write an essay arguing whether this spirit is or is not potentially within every person.

Judith Ortiz Cofer (b. 1952)

A brief biography of Judith Ortiz Cofer appears in the Men and Women Unit.

LATIN WOMEN PRAY   (1987)

Latin women pray
In incense sweet churches
They pray in Spanish to an Anglo God
With a Jewish heritage.
5 And this Great White Father
Imperturbable in his marble pedestal
Looks down upon his brown daughters
Votive candles shining like lust
In his all seeing eyes
10 Unmoved by their persistent prayers.

Yet year after year
Before his image they kneel
Margarita Josefina Maria and Isabel
All fervently hoping
15 That if not omnipotent
At least he be bilingual

Questions for Discussion

1. What is the significance of the "Latin" in the title and in the poem's first line? What associations do you have with "Latin"?

2. Besides sending a sensory message, what is the symbolic significance of "incense" in line 2? What does incense do? What is it associated with?

3. Why is it ironic, in line 3, that the women "pray in Spanish to an Anglo God"? What is Cofer's purpose and the cumulative effect of referring to God as an Anglo, Jewish "Great White Father"? How is this description related to the line "Looks down upon his brown daughters"?

4. Why is God "Imperturbable" and "in his marble pedestal"? What does the pedestal made of marble mean to the Latin women? How does this line relate to "Unmoved by their [Latin women's] persistent prayers"?

5. In line 8, why do the "Votive candles [shine] like lust / In his all seeing eyes"? What are votive candles and why are they compared to lust? What is usually meant by lust? Who is doing the lusting and why?

6. Why do the Latin women wonder if God is not "omnipotent"? What has probably been their experience in the past?

7. What is the Latin women's hope? Why is this hope important to the women? Does the humor distract from the seriousness of their hope?

Suggestions for Exploring, Writing, and Persuading

1. Using specific examples from the poem, in an essay, examine the assumptions of these women about the race, language, sex, and the power of God.

2. Write an essay that argues that all believers in religion tend or do not tend to envision God in their own image.

DRAMA

Sophocles (496?–406 B.C.)

Sophocles, the second of the three great Greek tragedians, wrote at least 120 plays, and his tragedies won first place at the festival of Dionysus twenty-four times. Sophocles's long life spanned the time in history when the culture of Athens was at its peak. Born to a wealthy Athenian family, Sophocles was honored as a producer of tragedies and as a citizen. He was selected for the highest elective office as one of the ten generals of Athens and was awarded priesthoods for his religious piety. Three of the seven extant plays of Sophocles, Oedipus the King, Oedipus at Colonus, *and* Antigone, *tell the story of the royal family of Thebes. Aristotle gave* Oedipus Rex *the highest praise of any extant Greek tragedy, and it is often described as the best example of dramatic irony in literature.*

ANCIENT GREEK DRAMA

Ancient Greek drama was performed in huge outdoor amphitheaters that seated as many as 20,000 spectators on great semicircular stone benches that climbed the slope of a hill. At the bottom center was the skene building, which served both as a dressing room for the actors and as the scenery, most often as the front of a palace or temple. In front of the skene was a circular acting space, the orchestra.

Because of the massive size of such amphitheaters, where many spectators would have been hundreds of feet from the stage, ancient Greek drama emphasizes large, clearly visible, and stylized effects. Actors declaimed their lines through the amplifying mouthpieces of masks and apparently later, in tragedies, wore elevated shoes to enhance their stature. Probably, because of the size of the theaters and the masks, ancient Greek drama relied on bold and dramatic movements rather than on subtle gestures, facial expressions, and asides.

Deriving from the worship of the god Dionysus, Athenian drama was a community celebration. Audiences apparently were quite volatile and deeply involved in the drama. Because almost the only subjects accepted for performance were the Greek myths, the audience already knew the stories behind each play; therefore, Greek drama provided the perfect vehicle for dramatic irony, a form of irony made possible by the audience's knowledge of events and relationships of which the characters were often ignorant. In dramatic irony, the character's words have a double meaning unknown to the character but known to the audience or to other characters. Apparently, too, the audience had extraordinary attention spans; on each of the last three days of the Dionysian festival, they would sit through five plays—three tragedies, one satyr play, and one comedy.

OEDIPUS REX   (FIFTH CENTURY B.C.)

ENGLISH VERSION BY DUDLEY FITTS AND ROBERT FITZGERALD

Persons Represented

OEDIPUS

A PRIEST

CREON

TEIRESIAS

IOCASTE [JOCASTA]

MESSENGER

SHEPHERD OF LAÏOS

SECOND MESSENGER

CHORUS OF THEBAN ELDERS

THE SCENE—*Before the palace of* OEDIPUS, *King of Thebes. A central door and two lateral doors open onto a platform which runs the length of the façade. On the platform, right and left, are altars; and three steps lead down into the* "ORCHESTRA," *or chorus-ground. At the beginning of the action these steps are crowded by suppliants who have brought branches and chaplets of olive leaves and who lie in various attitudes of despair.* OEDIPUS *enters.*

PROLOGUE

OEDIPUS: My children, generations of the living
    In the line of Kadmos, nursed at his ancient hearth:
    Why have you strewn yourselves before these altars
    In supplication, with your boughs and garlands?
    The breath of incense rises from the city
    With a sound of prayer and lamentation.
    Children,
    I would not have you speak through messengers,
    And therefore I have come myself to hear you—
10   I, Oedipus, who bear the famous name.

    (*To a* PRIEST.)

    You, there, since you are eldest in the company,
    Speak for them all, tell me what preys upon you,
    Whether you come in dread, or crave some blessing:
    Tell me, and never doubt that I will help you
    In every way I can; I should be heartless
    Were I not moved to find you suppliant here.
PRIEST: Great Oedipus, O powerful King of Thebes!
    You see how all the ages of our people
20   Cling to your altar steps: here are boys
    Who can barely stand alone, and here are priests
    By weight of age, as I am a priest of God,
    And young men chosen from those yet unmarried;
    As for the others, all that multitude,
    They wait with olive chaplets in the squares,
    At the two shrines of Pallas, and where Apollo
    Speaks in the glowing embers.
    Your own eyes
    Must tell you: Thebes is tossed on a murdering sea
30   And can not lift her head from the death surge.
    A rust consumes the buds and fruits of the earth;
    The herds are sick; children die unborn,
    And labor is vain. The god of plague and pyre
    Raids like detestable lightning through the city,
    And all the house of Kadmos is laid waste,

All emptied, and all darkened; Death alone
Battens upon the misery of Thebes.
You are not one of the immortal gods, we know;
Yet we have come to you to make our prayer
40   As to the man surest in mortal ways
And wisest in the ways of God. You saved us
From the Sphinx, that flinty singer, and the tribute
We paid to her so long; yet you were never
Better informed than we, nor could we teach you:
It was some god breathed in you to set us free.
Therefore, O mighty King, we turn to you:
Find us our safety, find us a remedy,
Whether by counsel of the gods or men.
A king of wisdom tested in the past
50   Can act in a time of troubles, and act well.
Noblest of men, restore
Life to your city! Think how all men call you
Liberator for your triumph long ago;
Ah, when your years of kingship are remembered,
Let them not say *We rose, but later fell*—
Keep the State from going down in the storm!
Once, years ago, with happy augury,
You brought us fortune; be the same again!
No man questions your power to rule the land:
60   But rule over men, not over a dead city!
Ships are only hulls, citadels are nothing,
When no life moves in the empty passageways.
OEDIPUS: Poor children! You may be sure I know
All that you longed for in your coming here.
I know that you are deathly sick; and yet,
Sick as you are, not one is as sick as I.
Each of you suffers in himself alone
His anguish, not another's; but my spirit
Groans for the city, for myself, for you.
70   I was not sleeping, you are not waking me.
No, I have been in tears for a long while
And in my restless thought walked many ways.
In all my search, I found one helpful course,
And that I have taken: I have sent Creon,
Son of Menoikeus, brother of the Queen,
To Delphi, Apollo's place of revelation,
To learn there, if he can,
What act or pledge of mine may save the city.
I have counted the days, and now, this very day,
80   I am troubled, for he has overstayed his time.

What is he doing? He has been gone too long.
Yet whenever he comes back, I should do ill
To scant whatever duty God reveals.
PRIEST: It is a timely promise. At this instant
They tell me Creon is here.
OEDIPUS: O Lord Apollo!
May his news be fair as his face is radiant!
PRIEST: It could not be otherwise: he is crowned with bay,
The chaplet is thick with berries.
90 OEDIPUS: We shall soon know;
He is near enough to hear us now.

(*Enter* CREON.)

O Prince:Brother: son of Menoikeus:
What answer do you bring us from the god?
CREON: A strong one. I can tell you, great afflictions
Will turn out well, if they are taken well.
OEDIPUS: What was the oracle? These vague words
Leave me still hanging between hope and fear.
100 CREON: Is it your pleasure to hear me with all these
Gathered around us? I am prepared to speak,
But should we not go in?
OEDIPUS: Let them all hear it.
It is for them I suffer, more than for myself.
CREON: Then I will tell you what I heard at Delphi.
In plain words
The god commands us to expel from the land of Thebes
An old defilement we are sheltering.
It is a deathly thing, beyond cure;
We must not let it feed upon us longer.
OEDIPUS: What defilement? How shall we rid ourselves of it?
110 CREON: By exile or death, blood for blood. It was
Murder that brought the plague-wind on the city.
OEDIPUS: Murder of whom? Surely the god has named him?
CREON: My lord: long ago Laïos was our king,
Before you came to govern us.
OEDIPUS: I know;
I learned of him from others; I never saw him.
CREON: He was murdered; and Apollo commands us now
To take revenge upon whoever killed him.
OEDIPUS: Upon whom? Where are they? Where shall we find a clue
120 To solve that crime, after so many years?
CREON: Here in this land, he said.
If we make enquiry,
We may touch things that otherwise escape us.

OEDIPUS: Tell me: Was Laïos murdered in his house,
  Or in the fields, or in some foreign country?
CREON: He said he planned to make a pilgrimage.
  He did not come home again.
OEDIPUS: And was there no one,
  No witness, no companion, to tell what happened?
130 CREON: They were all killed but one, and he got away
  So frightened that he could remember one thing only.
OEDIPUS: What was that one thing? One may be the key
  To everything, if we resolve to use it.
CREON: He said that a band of highwaymen attacked them,
  Outnumbered them, and overwhelmed the King.
OEDIPUS: Strange, that a highwayman should be so daring—
  Unless some faction here bribed him to do it.
CREON: We thought of that. But after Laïos' death
  New troubles arose and we had no avenger.
140 OEDIPUS: What troubles could prevent your hunting down the killers?
CREON: The riddling Sphinx's song
  Made us deaf to all mysteries but her own.
OEDIPUS: Then once more I must bring what is dark to light.
  It is most fitting that Apollo shows,
  As you do, this compunction for the dead.
  You shall see how I stand by you, as I should,
  To avenge the city and the city's god,
  And not as though it were for some distant friend,
  But for my own sake, to be rid of evil.
150 Whoever killed King Laïos might—who knows?—
  Decide at any moment to kill me as well.
  By avenging the murdered king I protect myself.
  Come, then, my children: leave the altar steps,
  Lift up your olive boughs!
  One of you go
  And summon the people of Kadmos to gather here.
  I will do all that I can; you may tell them that.

  (*Exit a* page.)

  So, with the help of God,
  We shall be saved—or else indeed we are lost.
160 PRIEST: Let us rise, children. It was for this we came,
  And now the King has promised it himself.
  Phoibos has sent us an oracle; may he descend
  Himself to save us and drive out the plague..

  (*Exeunt* OEDIPUS *and* CREON *into the palace by the central door. The*
  priest *and the* suppliants *disperse R and L. After a short pause the*
  chorus *enters the orchestra.*)

PARODOS

CHORUS: What is God singing in his profound

(STROPHE 1)

Delphi of gold and shadow?
What oracle for Thebes, the sunwhipped city?
Fear unjoints me, the roots of my heart tremble.
Now I remember, O Healer, your power, and wonder:
Will you send doom like a sudden cloud. or weave it
170   Like nightfall of the past?
Speak, speak to us, issue of holy sound:
Dearest to our expectancy: be tender!
Let me pray to Athené, the immortal daughter of Zeus,

(ANTISTROPHE 1)

And to Artemis her sister
Who keeps her famous throne in the market ring,
And to Apollo, bowman at the far butts of heaven—
O gods, descend! Like three streams leap against
The fires of our grief, the fires of darkness;
Be swift to bring us rest!
180   As in the old time from the brilliant house
Of air you stepped to save us, come again!

(STROPHE 2)

Now our afflictions have no end,
Now all our stricken host lies down
And no man fights off death with his mind;
The noble plowland bears no grain,
And groaning mothers can not bear—
See, how our lives like birds take wing,
Like sparks that fly when a fire soars,
To the shore of the god of evening.

(ANTISTROPHE 2)

190   The plague burns on, it is pitiless,
Though pallid children laden with death
Lie unwept in the stony ways,
And old gray women by every path
Flock to the strand about the altars
There to strike their breasts and cry
Worship of Phoibos in wailing prayers:
Be kind, God's golden child!

(STROPHE 3)

There are no swords in this attack by fire,
No shields, but we are ringed with cries.
200   Send the besieger plunging from our homes
Into the vast sea-room of the Atlantic
Or into the waves that foam eastward of Thrace—
For the day ravages what the night spares—
Destroy our enemy, lord of the thunder!
Let him be riven by lightning from heaven!

(ANTISTROPHE 3)

Phoibos Apollo, stretch the sun's bowstring,
That golden cord, until it sing for us,
Flashing arrows in heaven!
Artemis, Huntress,
210   Race with flaring lights upon our mountains!
O scarlet god, O golden-banded brow,
O Theban Bacchos in a storm of Maenads,

(*Enter* OEDIPUS, C.)

Whirl upon Death, that all the Undying hate!
Come with blinding torches, come in joy!

SCENE I

OEDIPUS: Is this your prayer? It may be answered. Come,
Listen to me, act as the crisis demands,
And you shall have relief from all these evils.
220   Until now I was a stranger to this tale,
As I had been a stranger to the crime.
Could I track down the murderer without a clue?
But now, friends,
As one who became a citizen after the murder,
I make this proclamation to all Thebans:
If any man knows by whose hand Laïos, son of Labdakos,
Met his death, I direct that man to tell me everything,
No matter what he fears for having so long withheld it.
Let it stand as promised that no further trouble
Will come to him, but he may leave the land in safety.
Moreover: If anyone knows the murderer to be foreign,
Let him not keep silent: he shall have his reward from me.
However, if he does conceal it; if any man
230   Fearing for his friend or for himself disobeys this edict,
Hear what I propose to do:
I solemnly forbid the people of this country,
Where power and throne are mine, ever to receive that man
Or speak to him, no matter who he is, or let him
Join in sacrifice, lustration, or in prayer.
I decree that he be driven from every house,

Being, as he is, corruption itself to us: the Delphic
240   Voice of Zeus has pronounced this revelation.
Thus I associate myself with the oracle
And take the side of the murdered king.
As for the criminal, I pray to God—
Whether it be a lurking thief, or one of a number—
I pray that that man's life be consumed in evil and wretchedness.
And as for me, this curse applies no less
If it should turn out that the culprit is my guest here,
Sharing my hearth.
You have heard the penalty.
250   I lay it on you now to attend to this
For my sake, for Apollo's, for the sick
Sterile city that heaven has abandoned.
Suppose the oracle had given you no command:
Should this defilement go uncleansed for ever?
You should have found the murderer: your king,
A noble king, had been destroyed!
Now I,
Having the power that he held before me,
Having his bed, begetting children there
260   Upon his wife, as he would have, had he lived—
Their son would have been my children's brother,
If Laïos had had luck in fatherhood!
(But surely ill luck rushed upon his reign)—
I say I take the son's part, just as though
I were his son, to press the fight for him
And see it won! I'll find the hand that brought
Death to Labdakos' and Polydoros' child,
Heir of Kadmos' and Agenor's line.
And as for those who fail me,
270   Many the gods deny them the fruit of the earth,
Fruit of the womb, and may they rot utterly!
Let them be wretched as we are wretched, and worse!
For you, for loyal Thebans, and for all
Who find my actions right, I pray the favor
Of justice, and of all the immortal gods.
CHORAGOS: Since I am under oath, my lord, I swear
I did not do the murder, I can not name
The murderer. Might not the oracle
That has ordained the search tell where to find him?
280   OEDIPUS: An honest question. But no man in the world
Can make the gods do more than the gods will.
CHORAGOS: There is one last expedient—
OEDIPUS: Tell me what it is.
Though it seem slight, you must not hold it back.
CHORAGOS: A lord clairvoyant to the lord Apollo,

As we all know, is the skilled Teiresias.
One might learn much about this from him, Oedipus.
OEDIPUS: I am not wasting time:
    Creon spoke of this, and I have sent for him—
290   Twice, in fact; it is strange that he is not here.
CHORAGOS: The other matter—that old report—seems useless.
OEDIPUS: Tell me. I am interested in all reports.
CHORAGOS: The King was said to have been killed by highwaymen.
OEDIPUS: I know. But we have no witnesses to that.
CHORAGOS: If the killer can feel a particle of dread,
    Your curse will bring him out of hiding!
OEDIPUS: No.
    The man who dared that act will fear no curse.

(Enter the blind seer TEIRESIAS, *led by a* PAGE.)

CHORAGOS: But there is one man who may detect the criminal.
300   This is Teiresias, this is the holy prophet
    In whom, alone of all men, truth was born.
OEDIPUS: Teiresias: seer: student of mysteries,
    Of all that's taught and all that no man tells,
    Secrets of Heaven and secrets of the earth:
    Blind though you are, you know the city lies
    Sick with plague; and from this plague, my lord,
    We find that you alone can guard or save us.
    Possibly you did not hear the messengers?
    Apollo, when we sent to him,
310   Sent us back word that this great pestilence
    Would lift, but only if we established clearly
    The identity of those who murdered Laïos.
    They must be killed or exiled.
    Can you use
    Birdflight or any art of divination
    To purify yourself, and Thebes, and me
    From this contagion? We are in your hands.
    There is no fairer duty
    Than that of helping others in distress.
320 TEIRESIAS: How dreadful knowledge of the truth can be
    When there's no help in truth! I knew this well,
    But made myself forget. I should not have come.
OEDIPUS: What is troubling you? Why are your eyes so cold?
TEIRESIAS: Let me go home. Bear your own fate, and I'll
    Bear mine. It is better so: trust what I say.
OEDIPUS: What you say is ungracious and unhelpful
    To your native country. Do not refuse to speak.
TEIRESIAS: When it comes to speech, your own is neither temperate
    Nor opportune. I wish to be more prudent.

330 OEDIPUS: In God's name, we all beg you—
TEIRESIAS: You are all ignorant.
No; I will never tell you what I know.
Now it is my misery; then, it would be yours.
OEDIPUS: What! You do know something, and will not tell us?
You would betray us all and wreck the State?
TEIRESIAS: I do not intend to torture myself, or you.
Why persist in asking? You will not persuade me.
OEDIPUS: What a wicked old man you are! You'd try a stone's
Patience! Out with it! Have you no feeling at all?
340 TEIRESIAS: You call me unfeeling. If you could only see
The nature of your own feelings ...
OEDIPUS: Why,
Who would not feel as I do? Who could endure
Your arrogance toward the city?
TEIRESIAS: What does it matter!
Whether I speak or not, it is bound to come.
OEDIPUS: Then, if "it" is bound to come, you are bound to tell me.
TEIRESIAS: No, I will not go on. Rage as you please.
OEDIPUS: Rage? Why not!
350 And I'll tell you what I think:
You planned it, you had it done, you all but
Killed him with your own hands: if you had eyes,
I'd say the crime was yours, and yours alone.
TEIRESIAS: So? I charge you, then,
Abide by the proclamation you have made:
From this day forth
Never speak again to these men or to me;
You yourself are the pollution of this country.
OEDIPUS: You dare say that! Can you possibly think you have
360 Some way of going free, after such insolence?
TEIRESIAS: I have gone free. It is the truth sustains me.
OEDIPUS: Who taught you shamelessness? It was not your craft.
TEIRESIAS: You did. You made me speak. I did not want to.
OEDIPUS: Speak what? Let me hear it again more clearly.
TEIRESIAS: Was it not clear before? Are you tempting me?
OEDIPUS: I did not understand it. Say it again.
TEIRESIAS: I say that you are the murderer whom you seek.
OEDIPUS: Now twice you have spat out infamy. You'll pay for it!
TEIRESIAS: Would you care for more? Do you wish to be really angry?
370 OEDIPUS: Say what you will. Whatever you say is worthless.
TEIRESIAS: I say you live in hideous shame with those
Most dear to you. You can not see the evil.
OEDIPUS: It seems you can go on mouthing like this for ever.
TEIRESIAS: I can, if there is power in truth.
OEDIPUS: There is:

But not for you, not for you,
You sightless, witless, senseless, mad old man!
TEIRESIAS: You are the madman. There is no one here
Who will not curse you soon, as you curse me.
380 OEDIPUS: You child of endless night! You can not hurt me
Or any other man who sees the sun.
TEIRESIAS: True: it is not from me your fate will come.
That lies within Apollo's competence.
As it is his concern.
OEDIPUS: Tell me.
Are you speaking for Creon, or for yourself?
TEIRESIAS: Creon is no threat. You weave your own doom.
OEDIPUS: Wealth, power, craft of statesmanship!
Kingly position, everywhere admired!
390 What savage envy is stored up against these,
If Creon, whom I trusted, Creon my friend,
For this great office which the city once
Put in my hands unsought—if for this power
Creon desires in secret to destroy me!
He has bought this decrepit fortune-teller, this
Collector of dirty pennies, this prophet fraud—
Why, he is no more clairvoyant than I am!
Tell us.
Has your mystic mummery ever approached the truth?
400 When that hellcat the Sphinx was performing here,
What help were you to these people?
Her magic was not for the first man who came along:
It demanded a real exorcist. Your birds—
What good were they? or the gods, for the matter of that?
But I came by,
Oedipus, the simple man, who knows nothing—
I thought it out for myself, no birds helped me!
And this is the man you think you can destroy,
That you may be close to Creon when he's king!
410 Well, you and your friend Creon, it seems to me,
Will suffer most. If you were not an old man,
You would have paid already for your plot.
CHORAGOS: We can not see that his words or yours
Have been spoken except in anger, Oedipus,
And of anger we have no need. How can God's will
Be accomplished best? That is what most concerns us.
TEIRESIAS: You are a king. But where argument's concerned
I am your man, as much a king as you.
I am not your servant, but Apollo's.
420 I have no need of Creon to speak for me.
Listen to me. You mock my blindness, do you?
But I say that you, with both your eyes, are blind:

You can not see the wretchedness of your life,
Nor in whose house you live, no, nor with whom.
Who are your father and mother? Can you tell me?
You do not even know the blind wrongs
That you have done them, on earth and in the world below.
But the double lash of your parents' curse will whip you
Out of this land some day, with only night
430   Upon your precious eyes.
Your cries then—where will they not be heard?
What fastness of Kithairon will not echo them?
And that bridal-descant of yours—you'll know it then,
The song they sang when you came here to Thebes
And found your misguided berthing.
All this, and more, that you can not guess at now,
Will bring you to yourself among your children.
Be angry, then. Curse Creon. Curse my words.
I tell you, no man that walks upon the earth
440   Shall be rooted out more horribly than you.
OEDIPUS: Am I to bear this from him?—Damnation
    Take you! Out of this place! Out of my sight!
TEIRESIAS: I would not have come at all if you had not asked me.
OEDIPUS: Could I have told that you'd talk nonsense, that
    You'd come here to make a fool of yourself, and of me?
TEIRESIAS: A fool? Your parents thought me sane enough.
OEDIPUS: My parents again!—Wait: who were my parents?
TEIRESIAS: This day will give you a father, and break your heart.
OEDIPUS: Your infantile riddles! Your damned abracadabra!
450 TEIRESIAS: You were a great man once at solving riddles.
OEDIPUS: Mock me with that if you like; you will find it true.
TEIRESIAS: It was true enough. It brought about your ruin.
OEDIPUS: But if it saved this town?
TEIRESIAS: (to the PAGE) Boy, give me your hand.
OEDIPUS: Yes, boy; lead him away.
    —While you are here
  We can do nothing. Go; leave us in peace.
TEIRESIAS: I will go when I have said what I have to say.
  How can you hurt me? And I tell you again:
460   The man you have been looking for all this time,
The damned man, the murderer of Laïos,
That man is in Thebes. To your mind he is foreign-born,
But it will soon be shown that he is a Theban,
A revelation that will fail to please.
A blind man,
Who has his eyes now; a penniless man, who is rich now;
And he will go tapping the strange earth with his staff
To the children with whom he lives now he will be
Brother and father—the very same; to her

470 Who bore him, son and husband—the very same
Who came to his father's bed, wet with his father's blood.
Enough. Go think that over.
If later you find error in what I have said,
You may say that I have no skill in prophecy.

(*Exit* TEIRESIAS, *led by his* page. OEDIPUS *goes into the palace.*)

ODE I

CHORUS: The Delphic stone of prophecies

(STROPHE 1)

Remembers ancient regicide
And a still bloody hand.
That killer's hour of flight has come.
He must be stronger than riderless
480 Coursers of untiring wind,
For the son of Zeus armed with his father's thunder
Leaps in lightning after him;
And the Furies follow him, the sad Furies.
Holy Parnassos' peak of snow

(ANTISTROPHE 1)

Flashes and blinds that secret man,
That all shall hunt him down:
Though he may roam the forest shade
Like a bull wild from pasture
To rage through glooms of stone.
490 Doom comes down on him; flight will not avail him;
For the world's heart calls him desolate,
And the immortal Furies follow, for ever follow.
But now a wilder thing is heard

(STROPHE 2)

From the old man skilled at hearing Fate in the wingbeat of a bird.
Bewildered as a blown bird, my soul hovers and can not find
Foothold in this debate, or any reason or rest of mind.
But no man ever brought—none can bring
Proof of strife between Thebes' royal house,
Labdakos' line, and the son of Polybos;
500 And never until now has any man brought word
Of Laïos' dark death staining Oedipus the King.
Divine Zeus and Apollo hold

(ANTISTROPHE 2)

Perfect intelligence alone of all tales ever told;
And well though this diviner works, he works in his own night;

No man can judge that rough unknown or trust in second sight,
For wisdom changes hands among the wise.
Shall I believe my great lord criminal
At a raging word that a blind old man let fall?
I saw him, when the carrion woman faced him of old,
510   Prove his heroic mind! These evil words are lies.

SCENE II

CREON: Men of Thebes:
    I am told that heavy accusations
    Have been brought against me by King Oedipus.
    I am not the kind of man to bear this tamely.
    If in these present difficulties
    He holds me accountable for any harm to him
    Through anything I have said or done—why, then,
    I do not value life in this dishonor.
    It is not as though this rumor touched upon
520   Some private indiscretion. The matter is grave.
    The fact is that I am being called disloyal
    To the State, to my fellow citizens, to my friends.
CHORAGOS: He may have spoken in anger, not from his mind.
CREON: But did you not hear him say I was the one
    Who seduced the old prophet into lying?
CHORAGOS: The thing was said; I do not know how seriously.
CREON: But you were watching him! Were his eyes steady?
    Did he look like a man in his right mind?
CHORAGOS: I do not know.
530   I can not judge the behavior of great men.
    But here is the King himself.
        (enter OEDIPUS.)
OEDIPUS: So you dared come back.
    Why? How brazen of you to come to my house,
    You murderer!
    Do you think I do not know
    That you plotted to kill me, plotted to steal my throne?
    Tell me, in God's name: am I coward, a fool,
    That you should dream you could accomplish this?
540   A fool who could not see your slippery game?
    A coward, not to fight back when I saw it?
    You are the fool, Creon, are you not? hoping
    Without support or friends to get a throne?
    Thrones may be won or bought: you could do neither.
CREON: Now listen to me. You have talked; let me talk, too.
    You can not judge unless you know the facts.
OEDIPUS: You speak well: there is one fact; but I find it hard
    To learn from the deadliest enemy I have.

CREON: That above all I must dispute with you.

550   OEDIPUS: That above all I will not hear you deny.

CREON: If you think there is anything good in being stubborn
    Against all reason, then I say you are wrong.

OEDIPUS: If you think a man can sin against his own kind
    And not be punished for it, I say you are mad.

CREON: I agree. But tell me: what have I done to you?

OEDIPUS: You advised me to send for that wizard, did you not?

CREON: I did. I should do it again.

OEDIPUS: Very well. Now tell me:
    How long has it been since Laïos—

560   CREON: What of Laïos?

OEDIPUS: Since he vanished in that onset by the road?

CREON: It was long ago, a long time.

OEDIPUS: And this prophet,
    Was he practicing here then?

CREON: He was; and with honor, as now.

OEDIPUS: Did he speak of me at that time?

CREON: He never did;
    At least, not when I was present.

OEDIPUS: But...the enquiry?

570   I suppose you held one?

CREON: We did, but we learned nothing.

OEDIPUS: Why did the prophet not speak against me then?

CREON: I do not know; and I am the kind of man
    Who holds his tongue when he has no facts to go on.

OEDIPUS: There's one fact that you know, and you could tell it.

CREON: What fact is that? If I know it, you shall have it.

OEDIPUS: If he were not involved with you, he could not say
    That it was I who murdered Laïos.

CREON: If he says that, you are the one that knows it!—

580   But now it is my turn to question you.

OEDIPUS: Put your questions. I am no murderer.

CREON: First, then: You married my sister?

OEDIPUS: I married your sister.

CREON: And you rule the kingdom equally with her?

OEDIPUS: Everything that she wants she has from me.

CREON: And I am the third, equal to both of you?

OEDIPUS: That is why I call you a bad friend.

CREON: No. Reason it out, as I have done.
    Think of this first: Would any sane man prefer

590   Power, with all a king's anxieties,
    To that same power and the grace of sleep?
    Certainly not I.
    I have never longed for the king's power—only his rights.
    Would any wise man differ from me in this?

As matters stand, I have my way in everything
With your consent, and no responsibilities.
If I were king. I should be a slave to policy.
How could I desire a scepter more
Than what is now mine—untroubled influence?
600 No, I have not gone mad; I need no honors,
Except those with the perquisites I have now.
I am welcome everywhere; every man salutes me,
And those who want your favor seek my ear,
Since I know how to manage what they ask.
Should I exchange this ease for that anxiety?
Besides, no sober mind is treasonable.
I hate anarchy
And never would deal with any man who likes it.
Test what I have said. Go to the priestess
610 At Delphi, ask if I quoted her correctly.
And as for this other thing: if I am found
Guilty of treason with Teiresias,
Then sentence me to death! You have my word
It is a sentence I should cast my vote for—
But not without evidence!
You do wrong
When you take good men for bad, bad men for good.
A true friend thrown aside—why, life itself
Is not more precious!
620 In time you will know this well:
For time, and time alone, will show the just man,
Though scoundrels are discovered in a day.
CHORAGOS: This is well said, and a prudent man would ponder it.
Judgments too quickly formed are dangerous.
OEDIPUS: But is he not quick in his duplicity?
And shall I not be quick to parry him?
Would you have me stand still, hold my peace, and let
This man win everything, through my inaction?
CREON: And you want—what is it, then? To banish me?
630 OEDIPUS: No, not exile. It is your death I want,
So that all the world may see what treason means.
CREON: You will persist, then? You will not believe me?
OEDIPUS: How can I believe you?
CREON: Then you are a fool.
OEDIPUS: To save myself?
CREON: In justice, think of me.
OEDIPUS: You are evil incarnate.
CREON: But suppose that you are wrong?
OEDIPUS: Still I must rule.
640 CREON: But not if you rule badly.

OEDIPUS: O city, city!

CREON: It is my city, too!

CHORAGOS: Now, my lords, be still. I see the Queen,
Iocaste, coming from her palace chambers;
And it is time she came, for the sake of you both.
This dreadful quarrel can be resolved through her.

(*enter* IOCASTE.)

IOCASTE: Poor foolish men, what wicked din is this?
With Thebes sick to death, is it not shameful
That you should rake some private quarrel up?

(*to* OEDIPUS:)

650   Come into the house.
—And you, Creon, go now:
Let us have no more of this tumult over nothing.

CREON: Nothing? No, sister: what your husband plans for me
Is one of two great evils: exile or death.

OEDIPUS: He is right.
Why, woman I have caught him squarely
Plotting against my life.

CREON: No! Let me die
Accurst if ever I have wished you harm!

660   IOCASTE: Ah, believe it, Oedipus!
In the name of the gods, respect this oath of his
For my sake, for the sake of these people here!

(STROPHE 1)

CHORAGOS: Open your mind to her, my lord. Be ruled by her, I beg you!

OEDIPUS: What would you have me do?

CHORAGOS: Respect Creon's word. He has never spoken like a fool,
And now he has sworn an oath.

OEDIPUS: You know what you ask?

CHORAGOS: I do.

670   OEDIPUS: Speak on, then.

CHORAGOS: A friend so sworn should not be baited so,
In blind malice, and without final proof.

OEDIPUS: You are aware, I hope, that what you say
Means death for me, or exile at the least.

CHORAGOS: No, I swear by Helios, first in Heaven!

(STROPHE 2)

May I die friendless and accurst,
The worst of deaths, if ever I meant that!
It is the withering fields
That hurt my sick heart:

Must we bear all these ills,
680   And now your bad blood as well?
OEDIPUS: Then let him go. And let me die, if I must,
    Or be driven by him in shame from the land of Thebes.
    It is your unhappiness, and not his talk,
    That touches me.
    As for him—
    Wherever he goes, hatred will follow him.
CREON: Ugly in yielding, as you were ugly in rage!
    Natures like yours chiefly torment themselves.
OEDIPUS: Can you not go? Can you not leave me?
690   CREON: I can.
    You do not know me; but the city knows me,
    And in its eyes, I am just, if not in yours.

    (*Exit* CREON.)

    (ANTISTROPHE 1)

CHORAGOS: Lady Iocaste, did you not ask the King to go to his chambers?
IOCASTE: First tell me what has happened.
CHORAGOS: There was suspicion without evidence, yet it rankled
    As even false charges will.
IOCASTE: On both sides?
CHORAGOS: On both.
700   IOCASTE: But what was said?
CHORAGOS: Oh let it rest, let it be done with!
    Have we not suffered enough?
OEDIPUS: You see to what your decency has brought you:
    You have made difficulties where my heart saw none.
CHORAGOS: Oedipus, it is not once only I have told you—

    (ANTISTROPHE 2)

    You must know I should count myself unwise
    To the point of madness, should I now forsake you—
    You, under whose hand,
    In the storm of another time,
710   Our dear land sailed out free.
    But now stand fast at the helm!
IOCASTE: In God's name, Oedipus, inform your wife as well:
    Why are you so set in this hard anger?
OEDIPUS: I will tell you, for none of these men deserves
    My confidence as you do. It is Creon's work,
    His treachery, his plotting against me.
IOCASTE: Go on, if you can make this clear to me.
OEDIPUS: He charges me with the murder of Laïos.
IOCASTE: Has he some knowledge? Or does he speak from hearsay?

720 OEDIPUS: He would not commit himself to such a charge,
        But he has brought in that damnable soothsayer
        To tell his story.
    IOCASTE: Set your mind at rest.
        If it is a question of soothsayers, I tell you
        That you will find no man whose craft gives knowledge
        Of the unknowable.
        Here is my proof:
        An oracle was reported to Laïos once
        (I will not say from Phoibos himself, but from
730   His appointed ministers, at any rate)
        That his doom would be death at the hands of his own son—
        His son, born of his flesh and of mine!
        Now, you remember the story: Laïos was killed
        By marauding strangers where three highways meet.
        But his child had not been three days in this world
        Before the King had pierced the baby's ankles
        And left him to die on a lonely mountainside.
        Thus, Apollo never caused that child
        To kill his father, and it was not Laïos' fate
740   To die at the hands of his son, as he had feared.
        This is what prophets and prophecies are worth!
        Have no dread of them.
        It is God himself
        Who can show us what he wills, in his own way.
    OEDIPUS: How strange a shadowy memory crossed my mind,
        Just now while you were speaking; it chilled my heart.
    IOCASTE: What do you mean? What memory do you speak of?
    OEDIPUS: If I understand you, Laïos was killed
        At a place where three roads meet.
750 IOCASTE: So it was said;
        We have no later story.
    OEDIPUS: Where did it happen?
    IOCASTE: Phokis, it is called: at a place where the Theban Way
        Divides into the roads toward Delphi and Daulia.
    OEDIPUS: When?
    IOCASTE: We had the news not long before you came
        And proved the right to your succession here.
    OEDIPUS: Ah, what net has God been weaving for me?
760 IOCASTE: Oedipus! Why does this trouble you?
    OEDIPUS: Do not ask me yet.
        First, tell me how Laïos looked, and tell me
        How old he was.
    IOCASTE: He was tall, his hair just touched
        With white; his form was not unlike your own.
    OEDIPUS: I think that I myself may be accurst

By my own ignorant edict.

IOCASTE: You speak strangely.

It makes me tremble to look at you, my King.

OEDIPUS: I am not sure that the blind man can not see.

770   But I should know better if you were to tell me—

IOCASTE: Anything—though I dread to hear you ask it.

OEDIPUS: Was the King lightly escorted, or did he ride

With a large company, as a ruler should?

IOCASTE: There were five men with him in all: one was a herald,

And a single chariot, which he was driving.

OEDIPUS: Alas, that makes it plain enough!

But who—

Who told you how it happened?

IOCASTE: A household servant,

780   The only one to escape.

OEDIPUS: And is he still

A servant of ours?

IOCASTE: No; for when he came back at last

And found you enthroned in the place of the dead king,

He came to me, touched my hand with his, and begged

That I would send him away to the frontier district

Where only the shepherds go—

As far away from the city as I could send him.

I granted his prayer; for although the man was a slave,

790   He had earned more than this favor at my hands.

OEDIPUS: Can he be called back quickly?

IOCASTE: Easily.

But why?

OEDIPUS: I have taken too much upon myself

Without enquiry; therefore I wish to consult him.

IOCASTE: Then he shall come.

But am I not one also

To whom you might confide these fears of yours?

OEDIPUS: That is your right; it will not be denied you,

800   Now least of all; for I have reached a pitch

Of wild foreboding. Is there anyone

To whom I should sooner speak?

Polybos of Corinth is my father.

My mother is a Dorian: Meropê.

I grew up chief among the men of Corinth

Until a strange thing happened—

Not worth my passion, it may be, but strange.

At a feast, a drunken man maundering in his cups

Cries out that I am not my father's son!

810   I contained myself that night, though I felt anger

And a sinking heart. The next day I visited

My father and mother, and questioned them. They stormed,
Calling it all the slanderous rant of a fool;
And this relieved me. Yet the suspicion
Remained always aching in my mind;
I knew there was talk; I could not rest;
And finally, saying nothing to my parents,
I went to the shrine at Delphi.
The god dismissed my question without reply;
820   He spoke of other things.
                Some were clear,
Full of wretchedness, dreadful, unbearable:
As, that I should lie with my own mother, breed
Children from whom all men would turn their eyes;
And that I should be my father's murderer.
I heard all this, and fled. And from that day
Corinth to me was only in the stars
Descending in that quarter of the sky,
As I wandered farther and farther on my way
830   To a land where I should never see the evil
Sung by the oracle. And I came to this country
Where, so you say, King Laïos was killed.
I will tell you all that happened there, my lady.
There were three highways
Coming together at a place I passed;
And there a herald came towards me, and a chariot
Drawn by horses, with a man such as you describe
Seated in it. The groom leading the horses
Forced me off the road at his lord's command;
840   But as this charioteer lurched over towards me
I struck him in my rage. The old man saw me
And brought his double goad down upon my head
As I came abreast.
                He was paid back, and more!
Swinging my club in this right hand I knocked him
Out of his car, and he rolled on the ground.
I killed him.
        I killed them all.
                Now if that stranger and Laïos were—kin,
850   Where is a man more miserable than I?
More hated by the gods? Citizen and alien alike
Must never shelter me or speak to me—
I must be shunned by all.
                And I myself
Pronounced this malediction upon myself!
Think of it: I have touched you with these hands,
These hands that killed your husband. What defilement!
Am I all evil, then? It must be so,

860   Since I must flee from Thebes, yet never again
       See my own countrymen, my own country,
       For fear of joining my mother in marriage
       And killing Polybos, my father.
       Ah,
       If I was created so, born to this fate,
       Who could deny the savagery of God?
       O holy majesty of heavenly powers!
       May I never see that day! Never!
       Rather let me vanish from the race of men
       Than know the abomination destined me!

870   CHORAGOS: We too, my lord, have felt dismay at this.
       But there is hope: you have yet to hear the shepherd.

       OEDIPUS: Indeed, I fear no other hope is left me.

       IOCASTE: What do you hope from him when he comes?

       OEDIPUS: This much:
       If his account of the murder tallies with yours,
       Then I am cleared.

       IOCASTE: What was it that I said
       Of such importance?

       OEDIPUS: Why, "marauders," you said,
880   Killed the King, according to this man's story.
       If he maintains that still, if there were several,
       Clearly the guilt is not mine: I was alone.
       But if he says one man, singlehanded, did it,
       Then the evidence all points to me.

       IOCASTE: You may be sure that he said there were several;
       And can he call back that story now? He can not.
       The whole city heard it as plainly as I.
       But suppose he alters some detail of it:
       He can not ever show that Laïos' death
890   Fulfilled the oracle: for Apollo said
       My child was doomed to kill him; and my child—Poor
       baby!—it was my child that died first.
       No. From now on, where oracles are concerned,
       I would not waste a second thought on any.

       OEDIPUS: You may be right.
       But come: let someone go
       For the shepherd at once. This matter must be settled.

       IOCASTE: I will send for him.
       I would not wish to cross you in anything,
900   And surely not in this.—Let us go in.

       (*Exeunt into the palace.*)

ODE II

CHORUS: Let me be reverent in the ways of right,

(STROPHE 1)

Lowly the paths I journey on;
Let all my words and actions keep
The laws of the pure universe
From highest Heaven handed down.
For Heaven is their bright nurse,
Those generations of the realms of light;
Ah, never of mortal kind were they begot,
Nor are they slaves of memory, lost in sleep;
910　Their Father is greater than Time, and ages not.
The tyrant is a child of Pride

(ANTISTROPHE 1)

Who drinks from his great sickening cup
Recklessness and vanity,
Until from his high crest headlong
He plummets to the dust of hope.
That strong man is not strong.
But let no fair ambition be denied;
May God protect the wrestler for the State
In government, in comely policy,
920　Who will fear God, and on His ordinance wait.
Haughtiness and the high hand of disdain

(STROPHE 2)

Tempt and outrage God's holy law;
And any mortal who dares hold
No immortal Power in awe
Will be caught up in a net of pain:
The price for which his levity is sold.
Let each man take due earnings, then,
And keep his hands from holy things,
And from blasphemy stand apart—
930　Else the crackling blast of heaven
Blows on his head, and on his desperate heart;
Though fools will honor impious men,
In their cities no tragic poet sings.
Shall we lose faith in Delphi's obscurities,

(ANTISTROPHE 2)

We who have heard the world's core
Discredited, and the sacred wood
Of Zeus at Elis praised no more?
The deeds and the strange prophecies
Must make a pattern yet to be understood.
940　Zeus, if indeed you are lord of all,

Throned in light over night and day,
Mirror this in your endless mind:
Our masters call the oracle
Words on the wind, and the Delphic vision blind!
Their hearts no longer know Apollo,
And reverence for the gods has died away.

SCENE III

(*Enter* IOCASTE.)

IOCASTE: Princes of Thebes, it has occurred to me
   To visit the altars of the gods, bearing
   These branches as a suppliant, and this incense.
950   Our King is not himself: his noble soul
   Is overwrought with fantasies of dread,
   Else he would consider
   The new prophecies in the light of the old.
   He will listen to any voice that speaks disaster,
   And my advice goes for nothing.

(*She approaches the altar*, R.)

To you, then, Apollo,
   Lycean lord, since you are nearest, I turn in prayer.
   Receive these offerings, and grant us deliverance
   From defilement. Our hearts are heavy with fear
960   When we see our leader distracted, as helpless sailors
   Are terrified by the confusion of their helmsman.

(*Enter* MESSENGER.)

MESSENGER: Friends, no doubt you can direct me:
   Where shall I find the house of Oedipus,
   Or, better still, where is the King himself?
CHORAGOS: It is this very place, stranger, he is inside.
   This is his wife and mother of his children.
MESSENGER: I wish her happiness in a happy house,
   Blest in all the fulfillment of her marriage.
IOCASTE: I wish as much for you: your courtesy
970   Deserves a like good fortune. But now, tell me:
   Why have you come? What have you to say to us?
MESSENGER: Good news, my lady, for your house and your husband.
IOCASTE: What news? Who sent you here?
MESSENGER: I am from Corinth.
   The news I bring ought to mean joy for you,
   Though it may be you will find some grief in it.
IOCASTE: What is it? How can it touch us in both ways?
MESSENGER: The word is that the people of the Isthmus

Intend to call Oedipus to be their king.

980 IOCASTE: But old King Polybos—is he not reigning still?

MESSENGER:

No. Death holds him in his sepulchre.

IOCASTE: What are you saying? Polybos is dead?

MESSENGER: If I am not telling the truth, may I die myself.

IOCASTE: (*to a* MAIDSERVANT:) Go in, go quickly; tell this to your master.

O riddlers of God's will, where are you now!

This was the man whom Oedipus, long ago,

Feared so, fled so, in dread of destroying him—

But it was another fate by which he died.

(*Enter* OEDIPUS, C.)

990 OEDIPUS: Dearest Iocaste, why have you sent for me?

IOCASTE: Listen to what this man says, and then tell me

What has become of the solemn prophecies.

OEDIPUS: Who is this man? What is his news for me?

IOCASTE: He has come from Corinth to announce your father's death!

OEDIPUS: Is it true, stranger? Tell me in your own words.

MESSENGER: I can not say it more clearly: the King is dead.

OEDIPUS: Was it by treason? Or by an attack of illness?

MESSENGER: A little thing brings old men to their rest.

OEDIPUS: It was sickness, then?

1000 MESSENGER: Yes, and his many years.

OEDIPUS: Ah!

Why should a man respect the Pythian hearth, or

Give heed to the birds that jangle above his head?

They prophesied that I should kill Polybos,

Kill my own father, but he is dead and buried,

And I am here—I never touched him, never,

Unless he died of grief for my departure,

And thus, in a sense, through me. No. Polybos

Has packed the oracles off with him underground.

1010 They are empty words.

IOCASTE: Had I not told you so?

OEDIPUS: You had; it was my faint heart that betrayed me.

IOCASTE: From now on never think of those things again.

OEDIPUS: And yet—must I not fear my mother's bed?

IOCASTE: Why should anyone in this world be afraid,

Since Fate rules us and nothing can be foreseen?

A man should live only for the present day.

Have no more fear of sleeping with your mother:

How many men, in dreams, have lain with their mothers!

1020 No reasonable man is troubled by such things.

OEDIPUS: That is true; only—

If only my mother were not still alive!

But she is alive. I can not help my dread.

IOCASTE: Yet this news of your father's death is wonderful.

OEDIPUS: Wonderful. But I fear the living woman.

MESSENGER: Tell me, who is this woman that you fear?

OEDIPUS: It is Meropê, man; the wife of King Polybos.

MESSENGER: Meropê? Why should you be afraid of her?

OEDIPUS: An oracle of the gods, a dreadful saying.

1030   MESSENGER: Can you tell me about it or are you sworn to silence?

OEDIPUS: I can tell you, and I will.

    Apollo said through his prophet that I was the man

    Who should marry his own mother, shed his father's blood

    With his own hands. And so, for all these years

    I have kept clear of Corinth, and no harm has come—

    Though it would have been sweet to see my parents again.

MESSENGER: And is this the fear that drove you out of Corinth?

OEDIPUS: Would you have me kill my father?

MESSENGER: As for that

1040   You must be reassured by the news I gave you.

OEDIPUS: If you could reassure me, I would reward you.

MESSENGER: I had that in mind, I will confess: I thought

    I could count on you when you returned to Corinth.

OEDIPUS: No: I will never go near my parents again.

MESSENGER: Ah, son, you still do not know what you are doing—

OEDIPUS: What do you mean? In the name of God tell me!

MESSENGER: —If these are your reasons for not going home.

OEDIPUS: I tell you, I fear the oracle may come true.

MESSENGER: And guilt may come upon you through your parents?

1050   OEDIPUS: That is the dread that is always in my heart.

MESSENGER: Can you not see that all your fears are groundless?

OEDIPUS: How can you say that? They are my parents, surely?

MESSENGER: Polybos was not your father.

OEDIPUS: Not my father?

MESSENGER: No more your father than the man speaking to you.

OEDIPUS: But you are nothing to me!

MESSENGER: Neither was he.

OEDIPUS: Then why did he call me son?

MESSENGER: I will tell you:

1060   Long ago he had you from my hands, as a gift.

OEDIPUS: Then how could he love me so, if I was not his?

MESSENGER: He had no children, and his heart turned to you.

OEDIPUS: What of you? Did you buy me? Did you find me by chance?

MESSENGER: I came upon you in the crooked pass of Kithairon.

OEDIPUS: And what were you doing there?

MESSENGER: Tending my flocks.

OEDIPUS: A wandering shepherd?

MESSENGER: But your savior, son, that day.

OEDIPUS: From what did you save me?

1070 MESSENGER: Your ankles should tell you that.

OEDIPUS: Ah, stranger, why do you speak of that childhood pain?

MESSENGER: I cut the bonds that tied your ankles together.

OEDIPUS: I have had the mark as long as I can remember.

MESSENGER: That was why you were given the name you bear.

OEDIPUS: God! Was it my father or my mother who did it?
Tell me!

MESSENGER: I do not know. The man who gave you to me
Can tell you better than I.

OEDIPUS: It was not you that found me, but another?

1080 MESSENGER: It was another shepherd gave you to me.

OEDIPUS: Who was he? Can you tell me who he was?

MESSENGER: I think he was said to be one of Laïos' people.

OEDIPUS: You mean the Laïos who was king here years ago?

MESSENGER: Yes; King Laïos; and the man was one of his herdsmen.

OEDIPUS: Is he still alive? Can I see him?

MESSENGER: These men here
Know best about such things.

OEDIPUS: Does anyone here
Know this shepherd that he is talking about?

1090 Have you seen him in the fields, or in the town?
If you have, tell me. It is time things were made plain.

CHORAGOS: I think the man he means is that same shepherd
You have already asked to see. Iocaste perhaps
Could tell you something.

OEDIPUS: Do you know anything
About him, Lady? Is he the man we have summoned?
Is that the man this shepherd means?

IOCASTE: Why think of him?
Forget this herdsman. Forget it all.

1100 This talk is a waste of time.

OEDIPUS: How can you say that,

IOCASTE: For God's love, let us have no more questioning!
Is your life nothing to you?
My own is pain enough for me to bear.

OEDIPUS: You need not worry. Suppose my mother a slave,
And born of slaves: no baseness can touch you.

IOCASTE: Listen to me, I beg you: do not do this thing!

OEDIPUS: I will not listen; the truth must be made known.

IOCASTE: Everything that I say is for your own good!

1110 OEDIPUS: My own good
Snaps my patience, then; I want none of it.

IOCASTE: You are fatally wrong! May you never learn who you are!

OEDIPUS: Go, one of you, and bring the shepherd here.
Let us leave this woman to brag of her royal name.

IOCASTE: Ah, miserable!
> That is the only word I have for you now.
> That is the only word I can ever have.

(*Exit into the palace.*)

CHORAGOS: Why has she left us, Oedipus? Why has she gone
> In such a passion of sorrow? I fear this silence:
1120
> Something dreadful may come of it.
OEDIPUS: Let it come!
> However base my birth, I must know about it.
> The Queen, like a woman, is perhaps ashamed
> To think of my low origin. But I
> Am a child of Luck; I can not be dishonored.
> Luck is my mother; the passing months, my brothers,
> Have seen me rich and poor.
> If this is so,
> How could I wish that I were someone else?
1130
> How could I not be glad to know my birth?

ODE III

(STROPHE)

CHORUS: If ever the coming time were known
> To my heart's pondering,
> Kithairon, now by Heaven I see the torches
> At the festival of the next full moon,
> And see the dance, and hear the choir sing
> A grace to your gentle shade:
> Mountain where Oedipus was found,
> O mountain guard of a noble race!
> May the god who heals us lend his aid,
1140
> And let that glory come to pass
> For our king's cradling-ground.

(ANTISTROPHE)

> Of the nymphs that flower beyond the years,
> Who bore you, royal child,
> To Pan of the hills or the timberline Apollo,
> Cold in delight where the upland clears,
> Or Hermês for whom Kyllenê's heights are piled?
> Or flushed as evening cloud,
> Great Dionysos, roamer of mountains,
> He—was it he who found you there,
1150
> And caught you up in his own proud
> Arms from the sweet god-ravisher
> Who laughed by the Muses' fountains?

SCENE IV

OEDIPUS: Sirs: though I do not know the man,
    I think I see him coming, this shepherd we want:
    He is old, like our friend here, and the men
    Bringing him seem to be servants of my house.
    But you can tell, if you have ever seen him.

(*Enter* SHEPHERD *escorted by servants.*)

CHORAGOS: I know him, he was Laïos' man. You can trust him.
OEDIPUS: Tell me first, you from Corinth: is this the shepherd
1160   We were discussing?
MESSENGER: This is the very man.
OEDIPUS: (*to* SHEPHERD) Come here. No, look at me. You must answer
    Everything I ask. —You belonged to Laïos?
SHEPHERD: Yes: born his slave, brought up in his house.
OEDIPUS: Tell me: what kind of work did you do for him?
SHEPHERD: I was a shepherd of his, most of my life.
OEDIPUS: Where mainly did you go for pasturage?
SHEPHERD: Sometimes Kithairon, sometimes the hills near-by.
OEDIPUS: Do you remember ever seeing this man out there?
1170 SHEPHERD: What would he be doing there? This man?
OEDIPUS: This man standing here. Have you ever seen him before?
SHEPHERD: No. At least, not to my recollection.
MESSENGER: And that is not strange, my lord. But I'll refresh
    His memory: he must remember when we two
    Spent three whole seasons together, March to September,
    On Kithairon or thereabouts. He had two flocks;
    I had one. Each autumn I'd drive mine home
    And he would go back with his to Laïos' sheepfold.—
    Is this not true, just as I have described it?
1180 SHEPHERD: True, yes; but it was all so long ago.
MESSENGER: Well, then: do you remember, back in those days,
    That you gave me a baby boy to bring up as my own?
SHEPHERD: What if I did? What are you trying to say?
MESSENGER: King Oedipus was once that little child.
SHEPHERD: Damn you, hold your tongue!
OEDIPUS: No more of that!
    It is your tongue needs watching, not this man's.
SHEPHERD: My King, my Master, what is it I have done wrong?
OEDIPUS: You have not answered his question about the boy.
1190 SHEPHERD: He does not know...He is only making trouble...
OEDIPUS: Come, speak plainly, or it will go hard with you.
SHEPHERD: In God's name, do not torture an old man!
OEDIPUS: Come here, one of you; bind his arms behind him.
SHEPHERD: Unhappy king! What more do you wish to learn?
OEDIPUS: Did you give this man the child he speaks of?
SHEPHERD: I did.

And I would to God I had died that very day.

OEDIPUS: You will die now unless you speak the truth.

SHEPHERD: Yet if I speak the truth, I am worse than dead.

1200 OEDIPUS: Very well; since you insist upon delaying—

SHEPHERD: No! I have told you already that I gave him the boy.

OEDIPUS: Where did you get him? From your house? From somewhere else?

SHEPHERD: Not from mine, no. A man gave him to me.

OEDIPUS: Is that man here? Do you know whose slave he was?

SHEPHERD: For God's love, my King, do not ask me any more!

OEDIPUS: You are a dead man if I have to ask you again.

SHEPHERD: Then...Then the child was from the palace of Laïos.

OEDIPUS: A slave child? or a child of his own line?

1210 SHEPHERD: Ah, I am on the brink of dreadful speech!

OEDIPUS: And I of dreadful hearing. Yet I must hear.

SHEPHERD: If you must be told, then...

They said it was Laïos' child;

But it is your wife who can tell you about that.

OEDIPUS: My wife!—Did she give it to you?

SHEPHERD: My lord, she did.

OEDIPUS: Do you know why?

SHEPHERD: I was told to get rid of it.

OEDIPUS: An unspeakable mother!

1220 SHEPHERD: There had been prophecies ...

OEDIPUS: Tell me.

SHEPHERD: It was said that the boy would kill his own father.

OEDIPUS: Then why did you give him over to this old man?

SHEPHERD: I pitied the baby, my King,

And I thought that this man would take him far away

To his own country.

He saved him—but for what a fate!

For if you are what this man says you are,

No man living is more wretched than Oedipus.

1230 OEDIPUS: Ah God!

It was true!

All the prophecies!

—Now,

O Light, may I look on you for the last time!

I, Oedipus,

Oedipus, damned in his birth, in his marriage damned,

Damned in the blood he shed with his own hand!

(*He rushes into the palace.*)

ODE IV

CHORUS: Alas for the seed of men.

(STROPHE 1)

What measure shall I give these generations
1240   That breathe on the void and are void
And exist and do not exist?
Who bears more weight of joy
Than mass of sunlight shifting in images,
Or who shall make his thought stay on
That down time drifts away?
Your splendor is all fallen.
O naked brow of wrath and tears,
O change of Oedipus!
I who saw your days call no man blest—
1250   Your great days like ghósts góne.
That mind was a strong bow.

(ANTISTROPHE 1)

Deep, how deep you drew it then, hard archer,
At a dim fearful range,
And brought dear glory down!
You overcame the stranger—
The virgin with her hooking lion claws—
And though death sang, stood like a tower
To make pale Thebes take heart.
Fortress against our sorrow!
1260   True king, giver of laws,
Majestic Oedipus!
No prince in Thebes had ever such renown,
No prince won such grace of power.
And now of all men ever known

(STROPHE 2)

Most pitiful is this man's story:
His fortunes are most changed, his state
Fallen to a low slave's
Ground under bitter fate.
O Oedipus, most royal one!
1270   The great door that expelled you to the light
Gave at night—ah, gave night to your glory:
As to the father, to the fathering son.
All understood too late.
How could that queen whom Laïos won,
The garden that he harrowed at his height,
Be silent when that act was done?
But all eyes fail before time's eye,

(ANTISTROPHE 2)

All actions come to justice there.
Though never willed, though far down the deep past,

1280   Your bed, your dread sirings,
        Are brought to book at last.
        Child by Laïos doomed to die,
        Then doomed to lose that fortunate little death,
        Would God you never took breath in this air
        That with my wailing lips I take to cry:
        For I weep the world's outcast.
        I was blind, and now I can tell why:
        Asleep, for you had given ease of breath
        To Thebes, while the false years went by.

EXODOS

(Enter, from the palace, SECOND MESSENGER.)

1290   SECOND MESSENGER: Elders of Thebes, most honored in this land,
        What horrors are yours to see and hear, what weight
        Of sorrow to be endured, if, true to your birth,
        You venerate the line of Labdakos!
        I think neither Istros nor Phasis, those great rivers,
        Could purify this place of the corruption
        It shelters now, or soon must bring to light—
        Evil not done unconsciously, but willed.
        The greatest griefs are those we cause ourselves.
        CHORAGOS: Surely, friend, we have grief enough already;
1300   What new sorrow do you mean?
        SECOND MESSENGER: The Queen is dead.
        CHORAGOS: Iocaste? Dead? But at whose hand?
        SECOND MESSENGER: Her own.
        The full horror of what happened you can not know,
        For you did not see it; but I, who did, will tell you
        As clearly as I can how she met her death.
        When she had left us,
        In passionate silence, passing through the court,
        She ran to her apartment in the house,
1310   Her hair clutched by the fingers of both hands.
        She closed the doors behind her; then, by that bed
        Where long ago the fatal son was conceived—
        That son who should bring about his father's death—
        We hear her call upon Laïos, dead so many years,
        And heard her wail for the double fruit of her marriage,
        A husband by her husband, children by her child.
        Exactly how she died I do not know:
        For Oedipus burst in moaning and would not let us
        Keep vigil to the end: it was by him
1320   As he stormed about the room that our eyes were caught.
        From one to another of us he went, begging a sword,

Cursing the wife who was not his wife, the mother
Whose womb had carried his own children and himself.
I do not know: it was none of us aided him,
But surely one of the gods was in control!
For with a dreadful cry
He hurled his weight, as though wrenched out of himself,
At the twin doors: the bolts gave, and he rushed in.
And there we saw her hanging, her body swaying
1330   From the cruel cord she had noosed about her neck.
A great sob broke from him, heartbreaking to hear,
As he loosed the rope and lowered her to the ground.
I would blot out from my mind what happened next!
For the King ripped from her gown the golden brooches
That were her ornament, and raised them, and plunged them down
Straight into his own eyeballs, crying, "No more,
No more shall you look on the misery about me,
The horrors of my own doing! Too long you have known
The faces of those whom I should never have seen,
1340   Too long been blind to those for whom I was searching!
From this hour, go in darkness!;" And as he spoke,
He struck at his eyes—not once, but many times;
And the blood spattered his beard,
Bursting from his ruined sockets like red hail.
So from the unhappiness of two this evil has sprung,
A curse on the man and woman alike. The old
Happiness of the house of Labdakos
Was happiness enough: where is it today?
It is all wailing and ruin, disgrace, death—all
1350   The misery of mankind that has a name—
And it is wholly and for ever theirs.

CHORAGOS: Is he in agony still? Is there no rest for him?

SECOND MESSENGER: He is calling for someone to lead him to the gates
So that all the children of Kadmos may look upon
His father's murderer, his mother's—no,
I can not say it!
And then he will leave Thebes,
Self-exiled, in order that the curse
Which he himself pronounced may depart from the house.
1360   He is weak, and there is none to lead him,
So terrible is his suffering.
But you will see:
Look, the doors are opening; in a moment
You will see a thing that would crush a heart of stone.

(*The central door is opened;* OEDIPUS, *blinded, is led in.*)

CHORAGOS: Dreadful indeed for men to see.
    Never have my own eyes

Looked on a sight so full of fear.
Oedipus!
What madness came upon you, what daemon
1370   Leaped on your life with heavier
Punishment than a mortal man can bear?
No: I can not even
Look at you, poor ruined one.
And I would speak, question, ponder,
If I were able. No.
You make me shudder.

OEDIPUS: God. God.
Is there a sorrow greater?
Where shall I find harbor in this world?
1380   My voice is hurled far on a dark wind.
What has God done to me?

CHORAGOS:
Too terrible to think of, or to see.

OEDIPUS: O cloud of night,

(STROPHE 1)

Never to be turned away: night coming on,
I can not tell how: night like a shroud!
My fair winds brought me here.
O God. Again
The pain of the spikes where I had sight,
1390   The flooding pain
Of memory, never to be gouged out.

CHORAGOS: This is not strange.
You suffer it all twice over, remorse in pain,
Pain in remorse.

(ANTISTROPHE 1)

OEDIPUS: Ah dear friend
Are you faithful even yet, you alone?
Are you still standing near me, will you stay here,
Patient, to care for the blind?
The blind man!
1400   Yet even blind I know who it is attends me,
By the voice's tone—
Though my new darkness hide the comforter.

CHORAGOS: Oh fearful act!
What god was it drove you to rake black
Night across your eyes?

(STROPHE 2)

OEDIPUS: Apollo. Apollo. Dear
Children, the god was Apollo.

He brought my sick, sick fate upon me.
But the blinding hand was my own!
1410   How could I bear to see
When all my sight was horror everywhere?
CHORAGOS: Everywhere; that is true.
OEDIPUS: And now what is left?
    Images? Love? A greeting even,
    Sweet to the senses? Is there anything?
    Ah, no, friends: lead me away.
    Lead me away from Thebes.
    Lead the great wreck
    And hell of Oedipus, whom the gods hate.
1420   CHORAGOS: Your fate is clear, you are not blind to that.
    Would God you had never found it out!

(ANTISTROPHE 2)

OEDIPUS: Death take the man who unbound
    My feet on that hillside
    And delivered me from death to life! What life?
    If only I had died,
    This weight of monstrous doom
    Could not have dragged me and my darlings down.
CHORAGOS: I would have wished the same.
OEDIPUS: Oh never to have come here
1430   With my father's blood upon me! Never
    To have been the man they call his mother's husband!
    Oh accurst! Oh child of evil,
    To have entered that wretched bed—
    The selfsame one!
    More primal than sin itself, this fell to me.
CHORAGOS: I do not know how I can answer you.
    You were better dead than alive and blind.
OEDIPUS: Do not counsel me any more. This punishment
    That I have laid upon myself is just.
1440   If I had eyes,
    I do not know how I could bear the sight
    Of my father, when I came to the house of Death,
    Or my mother: for I have sinned against them both
    So vilely that I could not make my peace
    By strangling my own life.
    Or do you think my children,
    Born as they were born, would be sweet to my eyes?
    Ah never, never! Nor this town with its high walls,
    Nor the holy images of the gods.
1450   For I,
    Thrice miserable!—Oedipus, noblest of all the line

Of Kadmos, have condemned myself to enjoy
These things no more, by my own malediction
Expelling that man whom the gods declared
To be a defilement in the house of Laïos.
After exposing the rankness of my own guilt,
How could I look men frankly in the eyes?
No, I swear it,
If I could have stifled my hearing at its source,
1460   I would have done it and made all this body
A tight cell of misery, blank to light and sound:
So I should have been safe in a dark agony
Beyond all recollection.
Ah Kithairon!
Why did you shelter me? When I was cast upon you,
Why did I not die? Then I should never
Have shown the world my execrable birth.
Ah Polybos! Corinth, city that I believed
The ancient seat of my ancestors: how fair
1470   I seemed, your child! And all the while this evil
Was cancerous within me!
For I am sick
In my daily life, sick in my origin.
O three roads, dark ravine, woodland and way
Where three roads met: you, drinking my father's blood,
My own blood, spilled by my own hand: can you remember
The unspeakable things I did there, and the things
I went on from there to do?
O marriage, marriage!
1480   The act that engendered me, and again the act
Performed by the son in the same bed—
Ah, the net
Of incest, mingling fathers, brothers, sons,
With brides, wives, mothers: the last evil
That can be known by men: no tongue can say
How evil!
No. For the love of God, conceal me
Somewhere far from Thebes; or kill me; or hurl me
Into the sea, away from men's eyes for ever.
1490   Come, lead me. You need not fear to touch me.
Of all men, I alone can bear this guilt.

(*Enter* CREON.)

CHORAGOS: We are not the ones to decide; but Creon here
    May fitly judge of what you ask. He only
    Is left to protect the city in your place.
OEDIPUS: Alas, how can I speak to him? What right have I

To beg his courtesy whom I have deeply wronged?

CREON: I have not come to mock you, Oedipus,
 Or to reproach you, either.

 (*To* ATTENDANTS:)—You, standing there:

1500 If you have lost all respect for man's dignity,
 At least respect the flame of Lord Helios:
 Do not allow this pollution to show itself
 Openly here, an affront to the earth
 And Heaven's rain and the light of day. No, take him
 Into the house as quickly as you can.
 For it is proper
 That only the close kindred see his grief.

OEDIPUS: I pray you in God's name, since your courtesy
 Ignores my dark expectation, visiting
1510 With mercy this man of all men most execrable:
 Give me what I ask—for your good, not for mine.

CREON: And what is it that you would have me do?

OEDIPUS: Drive me out of this country as quickly as may be
 To a place where no human voice can ever greet me.

CREON: I should have done that before now—only,
 God's will had not been wholly revealed to me.

OEDIPUS: But his command is plain: the parricide
 Must be destroyed. I am that evil man.

CREON: That is the sense of it, yes; but as things are,
1520 We had best discover clearly what is to be done.

OEDIPUS: You would learn more about a man like me?

CREON: You are ready now to listen to the god.

OEDIPUS: I will listen. But it is to you
 That I must turn for help. I beg you, hear me.
 The woman in there—
 Give her whatever funeral you think proper:
 She is your sister.
 —But let me go, Creon!
 Let me purge my father's Thebes of the pollution
1530 Of my living here, and go out to the wild hills,
 To Kithairon, that has won such fame with me,
 The tomb my mother and father appointed for me,
 And let me die there, as they willed I should.
 And yet I know
 Death will not ever come to me through sickness
 Or in any natural way: I have been preserved
 For some unthinkable fate. But let that be.
 As for my sons, you need not care for them.
 They are men, they will find some way to live.
1540 But my poor daughters, who have shared my table,
 Who never before have been parted from their father—

Take care of them. Creon; do this for me.
And will you let me touch them with my hands
A last time, and let us weep together?
Be kind, my lord,
Great prince, be kind! Could I but touch them,
They would be mine again, as when I had my eyes.

(*Enter* ANTIGONE *and* ISMENE, *attended.*)

Ah, God!
Is it my dearest children I hear weeping?
1550   Has Creon pitied me and sent my daughters?
CREON: Yes, Oedipus: I knew that they were dear to you
    In the old days, and know you must love them still.
OEDIPUS: May God bless you for this—and be a friendlier
    Guardian to you than he has been to me!
    Children, where are you?
    Come quickly to my hands: they are your brother's—
    Hands that have brought your father's once clear eyes
    To this way of seeing—
    Ah dearest ones,
1560   I had neither sight nor knowledge then, your father
    By the woman who was the source of his own life!
    And I weep for you—having no strength to see you—,
    I weep for you when I think of the bitterness
    That men will visit upon you all your lives.
    What homes, what festivals can you attend
    Without being forced to depart again in tears?
    And when you come to marriageable age,
    Where is the man, my daughters, who would dare
    Risk the bane that lies on all my children?
1570   Is there any evil wanting? Your father killed
    His father; sowed the womb of her who bore him;
    Engendered you at the fount of his own existence!
    That is what they will say of you.
    Then, whom
    Can you ever marry? There are no bridegrooms for you,
    And your lives must wither away in sterile dreaming.
    O Creon, son of Menoikeus!
    You are the only father my daughters have,
    Since we, their parents, are both of us gone for ever.
1580   They are your own blood: you will not let them
    Fall into beggary and loneliness;
    You will keep them from the miseries that are mine!
    Take pity on them; see, they are only children,
    Friendless except for you. Promise me this,
    Great Prince, and give me your hand in token of it.

(CREON *clasps his right hand.*)

Children:
I could say much, if you could understand me,
But as it is, I have only this prayer for you:
Live where you can, be as happy as you can—
1590   Happier, please God, than God has made your father!
CREON: Enough. You have wept enough. Now go within.
OEDIPUS: I must; but it is hard.
CREON: Time eases all things.
OEDIPUS: But you must promise—
CREON: Say what you desire.
OEDIPUS: Send me from Thebes!
CREON: God grant that I may!
OEDIPUS: But since God hates me ...
CREON: No, he will grant your wish
1600   OEDIPUS: You promise?
CREON: I can not speak beyond my knowledge.
OEDIPUS: Then lead me in.
CREON: Come now, and leave your children.
OEDIPUS: No! Do not take them from me!
CREON: Think no longer
    That you are in command here, but rather think
    How, when you were, you served your own destruction.

(*Exeunt into the house all but the* CHORUS; *the* CHORAGOS *chants directly to the audience*:)

CHORAGOS: Men of Thebes: look upon Oedipus.
    This is the king who solved the famous riddle
1610   And towered up, most powerful of men.
    No mortal eyes but looked on him with envy,
    Yet in the end ruin swept over him.
    Let every man in mankind's frailty
    Consider his last day; and let none
    Presume on his good fortune until he find
    Life, at his death, a memory without pain.

Questions for Discussion

1. How would you describe the relationship between Oedipus and the people of Thebes as the play begins? What kind of ruler does Oedipus appear to be?

2. What does Oedipus think of himself? What qualities dominate his character? Explain whether he does or does not have a tragic flaw.

3. What is the condition of Thebes as the play begins? Look up the myth of the fisher king and explain how it applies to this condition.

4. What role does the chorus play? How does its attitude change?

5. Why does Oedipus act so unreasonably toward Teiresias and Creon?

6. Explain why Oedipus insists on hearing what he must know will be horrifying news.

7. At the end, how does Oedipus maintain his position as savior and father to his people? What kind of father does he appear to be to his daughters? Discuss whether he retains nobility and dignity in his fall.

Suggestions for Exploring, Writing, and Persuading

1. Discuss in detail the changing attitudes of the chorus in the play. Why is the accusation against Oedipus so terrifying to them? What dilemma does the accusation pose for them?

2. Contrast Iocaste's skepticism with Oedipus's insistence on knowing the truth. Explain whether he is persuaded by her skepticism.

3. Discuss the degree to which Oedipus is triumphant at the end of the play.

4. In an essay, analyze Sophocles's use of image clusters of light and dark and/or of sight and blindness.

5. Discuss in detail in an essay the complex familial and communal relationships in Sophocles's play. What light do these relationships shed on the changing nature of American families?

6. Both Creon and Teiresias act as dramatic foils to Oedipus: they emphasize characteristics of Oedipus through marked contrast. In an essay show how one of these characters is an effective dramatic foil.

Casebook
on Flannery O'Connor
WRITING ABOUT FAITH

The final casebook in this text combines several quests seen in other works in this unit: the quest for God, the quest for knowledge of one-self, and the quest for ways in which to understand one's relationships with others. Though Flannery O'Connor writes from the point of view of a woman who grew up in the South and of a devout Catholic, the questions her very unusual characters seek to answer are universal. O'Connor's comments in her essay "The Fiction Writer and His Country" will help you to gain insight into her own views about writing, and the essays by literary scholars will help you as you write your own essays about the stories.

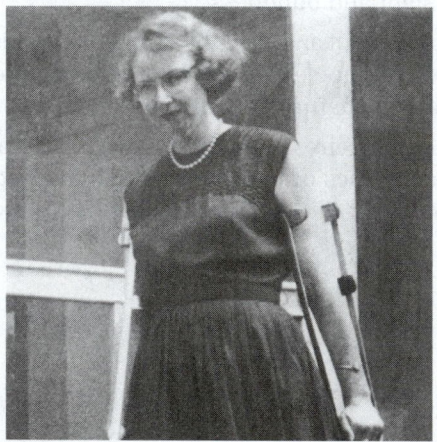

Flannery O'Connor (1925–1964)

Flannery O'Connor was a devout Catholic who, in the short time that she lived, wrote two novels and many short stories that vividly portray the incompleteness of human beings without God. Except for her graduate study at the University of Iowa, O'Connor spent most of her life in Milledgeville, Georgia, where she observed the people and the land that would become the basis for most of her works. Because her characters are far from ordinary and because their fates are often disastrous, O'Connor is frequently described as a Southern Gothic writer. Her characters range from unbelievers, like Mrs. May in "Greenleaf" and the grandmother

*in "A Good Man Is Hard to Find" who, in spite of their
superficiality and self-centeredness, believe themselves to be
good Christians, to committed if unorthodox Christians,
like Mrs. Greenleaf. O'Connor's stories tell of events that
cause arrogant and imperceptive people to see more clearly
into reality and to begin their quest for truth.*

A GOOD MAN IS HARD TO FIND   (1953)

1   The grandmother didn't want to go to Florida. She wanted to visit
some of her connections in east Tennessee and she was seizing at every
chance to change Bailey's mind. Bailey was the son she lived with, her
only boy. He was sitting on the edge of his chair at the table, bent over
the orange sports section of the *Journal.* "Now look here, Bailey," she
said, "see here, read this," and she stood with one hand on her thin hip
and the other rattling the newspaper at his bald head. "Here this fellow
that calls himself The Misfit is aloose from the Federal Pen and headed
toward Florida and you read here what it says he did to these people. Just
you read it. I wouldn't take my children in any direction with a criminal
like that aloose in it. I couldn't answer to my conscience if I did."

2   Bailey didn't look up from his reading so she wheeled around then and
faced the children's mother, a young woman in slacks, whose face was
as broad and innocent as a cabbage and was tied around with a green
headkerchief that had two points on the top like rabbit's ears. She was
sitting on the sofa, feeding the baby his apricots out of a jar. "The children have been to Florida before," the old lady said. "You all ought to take
them somewhere else for a change so they would see different parts of
the world and be broad. They never have been to east Tennessee."

3   The children's mother didn't seem to hear her but the eight-year-old
boy, John Wesley, a stocky child with glasses, said, "If you don't want to
go to Florida, why dontcha stay at home?" He and the little girl, June Star,
were reading the funny papers on the floor.

4   "She wouldn't stay at home to be queen for a day," June Star said without raising her yellow head.

5   "Yes and what would you do if this fellow, The Misfit, caught you?" the
grandmother said.

6   "I'd smack his face," John Wesley said.

7   "She wouldn't stay at home for a million bucks," June Star said "Afraid
she'd miss something. She has to go everywhere we go."

8   "All right, Miss," the grandmother said. "Just remember that the next
time you want me to curl your hair."

9   June Star said her hair was naturally curly.

10   The next morning the grandmother was the first one in the car, ready to
go. She had her big black valise that looked like the head of a hippopotamus in one corner, and underneath it she was hiding a basket with Pity
Sing, the cat, in it. She didn't intend for the cat to be left alone in the house
for three days because he would miss her too much and she was afraid he

might brush against one of the gas burners and accidentally asphyxiate himself. Her son, Bailey, didn't like to arrive at a motel with a cat.

11   She sat in the middle of the back seat with John Wesley and June Star on either side of her. Bailey and the children's mother and the baby sat in front and they left Atlanta at eight forty-five with the mileage on the car at 55890. The grandmother wrote this down because she thought it would be interesting to say how many miles they had been when they got back. It took them twenty minutes to reach the outskirts of the city.

12   The old lady settled herself comfortably, removing her white cotton gloves and putting them up with her purse on the shelf in front of the back window. The children's mother still had on slacks and still had her hair tied up in a green kerchief, but the grandmother had on a navy blue straw sailor hat with a bunch of white violets on the brim and a navy blue dress with a small white dot in the print. Her collars and cuffs were white organdy trimmed with lace and at her neckline she had pinned a purple spray of cloth violets containing a sachet. In case of an accident, anyone seeing her dead on the highway would know at once that she was a lady.

13   She said she thought it was going to be a good day for driving, neither too hot nor too cold, and she cautioned Bailey that the speed limit was fifty-five miles an hour and that the patrolmen hid themselves behind bill-boards and small clumps of trees and sped out after you before you had a chance to slow down. She pointed out interesting details of the scenery: Stone Mountain; the blue granite that in some places came up to both sides of the highway; the brilliant red clay banks slightly streaked with purple; and the various crops that made rows of green lacework on the ground. The trees were full of silver-white sunlight and the meanest of them sparkled. The children were reading comic magazines and their mother had gone back to sleep.

14   "Let's go through Georgia fast so we won't have to look at it much," John Wesley said.

15   "If I were a little boy," said the grandmother, "I wouldn't talk about my native state that way. Tennessee has the mountains and Georgia has the hills."

16   "Tennessee is just a hillbilly dumping ground," John Wesley said, "and Georgia is a lousy state too."

17   "You said it," June Star said.

18   "In my time," said the grandmother, folding her thin veined fingers, "children were more respectful of their native states and their parents and everything else. People did right then. Oh look at the cute little pick-aninny!" she said and pointed to a Negro child standing in the door of a shack. "Wouldn't that make a picture, now?" she asked and they all turned and looked at the little Negro out of the back window. He waved.

19   "He didn't have any britches on," June Star said.

20   "He probably didn't have any," the grandmother explained. "Little nig-gers in the country don't have things like we do. If I could paint, I'd paint that picture," she said.

21   The children exchanged comic books.

22   The grandmother offered to hold the baby and the children's mother passed him over the front seat to her. She set him on her knee and bounced him and told him about the things they were passing. She rolled her eyes and screwed up her mouth and stuck her leathery thin face into his smooth bland one. Occasionally he gave her a faraway smile. They passed a large cotton field with five or six graves fenced in the middle of it, like a small island. "Look at the graveyard!" the grandmother said, pointing it out. "That was the old family burying ground. That belonged to the plantation."

23   "Where's the plantation?" John Wesley asked.

24   "Gone With the Wind," said the grandmother. "Ha. Ha."

25   When the children finished all the comic books they had brought, they opened the lunch and ate it. The grandmother ate a peanut butter sandwich and an olive and would not let the children throw the box and the paper napkins out the window. When there was nothing else to do they played a game by choosing a cloud and making the other two guess what shape it suggested. John Wesley took one the shape of a cow and June Star guessed a cow and John Wesley said, no, an automobile, and June Star said he didn't play fair, and they began to slap each other over the grandmother.

26   The grandmother said she would tell them a story if they would keep quiet. When she told a story, she rolled her eyes and waved her head and was very dramatic. She said once when she was a maiden lady she had been courted by a Mr. Edgar Atkins Teagarden from Jasper, Georgia. She said he was a very good-looking man and a gentleman and that he brought her a watermelon every Saturday afternoon with his initials cut in it, E. A. T. Well, one Saturday, she said, Mr. Teagarden brought the watermelon and there was nobody at home and he left it on the front porch and returned in his buggy to Jasper, but she never got the watermelon, she said, because a nigger boy ate it when he saw the initials, E. A. T.! This story tickled John Wesley's funny bone and he giggled and giggled but June Star didn't think it was any good. She said she wouldn't marry a man that just brought her a watermelon on Saturday. The grandmother said she would have done well to marry Mr. Teagarden because he was a gentlemen and had bought Coca-Cola stock when it first came out and that he had died only a few years ago, a very wealthy man.

27   They stopped at The Tower for barbecued sandwiches. The Tower was a part stucco and part wood filling station and dance hall set in a clearing outside of Timothy. A fat man named Red Sammy Butts ran it and there were signs stuck here and there on the building and for miles up and down the highway saying, TRY RED SAMMY'S FAMOUS BARBECUE. NONE LIKE FAMOUS RED SAMMY'S! RED SAM! THE FAT BOY WITH THE HAPPY LAUGH. A VETERAN! RED SAMMY'S YOUR MAN!

28   Red Sammy was lying on the bare ground outside The Tower with his head under a truck while a gray monkey about a foot high, chained to a small chinaberry tree, chattered nearby. The monkey sprang back into the tree and got on the highest limb as soon as he saw the children jump out of the car and run toward him.

29   Inside, The Tower was a long dark room with a counter at one end and tables at the other and dancing space in the middle. They all sat down at a board table next to the nickelodeon and Red Sam's wife, a tall burnt-brown woman with hair and eyes lighter than her skin, came and took their order. The children's mother put a dime in the machine and played "The Tennessee Waltz," and the grandmother said that tune always made her want to dance. She asked Bailey if he would like to dance but he only glared at her. He didn't have a naturally sunny disposition like she did and trips made him nervous. The grandmother's brown eyes were very bright. She swayed her head from side to side and pretended she was dancing in her chair. June Star said play something she could tap to so the children's mother put in another dime and played a fast number and June Star stepped out onto the dance floor and did her tap routine.

30   "Ain't she cute?" Red Sam's wife said, leaning over the counter. "Would you like to come be my little girl?"

31   "No I certainly wouldn't," June Star said. "I wouldn't live in a broken-down place like this for a million bucks!" and she ran back to the table.

32   "Ain't she cute?" the woman repeated, stretching her mouth politely.

33   "Aren't you ashamed?" hissed the grandmother.

34   Red Sam came in and told his wife to quit lounging on the counter and hurry up with these people's order. His khaki trousers reached just to his hip bones and his stomach hung over them like a sack of meal swaying under his shirt. He came over and sat down at a table nearby and let out a combination sigh and yodel. "You can't win," he said. "You can't win," and he wiped his sweating red face off with a gray handkerchief. "These days you don't know who to trust," he said. "Ain't that the truth?"

35   "People are certainly not nice like they used to be," said the grandmother.

36   "Two fellers come in here last week," Red Sammy said, "driving a Chrysler. It was a old beat-up car but it was a good one and these boys looked all right to me. Said they worked at the mill and you know I let them fellers charge the gas they bought? Now why did I do that?"

37   "Because you're a good man!" the grandmother said at once.

38   "Yes'm, I suppose so," Red Sam said as if he were struck with this answer.

39   His wife brought the orders, carrying the five plates all at once without a tray, two in each hand and one balanced on her arm. "It isn't a soul in this green world of God's that you can trust," she said. "And I don't count nobody out of that, not nobody," she repeated, looking at Red Sammy.

40   "Did you read about that criminal, The Misfit, that's escaped?" asked the grandmother.

41   "I wouldn't be a bit surprised if he didn't attack this place right here," said the woman. "If he hears about it being here, I wouldn't be none surprised to see him. If he hears it's two cent in the cash register, I wouldn't be a tall surprised if he..."

42   "That'll do," Red Sam said. "Go bring these people their Co'-Colas," and the woman went off to get the rest of the order.

43   "A good man is hard to find," Red Sammy said. "Everything is getting terrible. I remember the day you could go off and leave your screen door unlatched. Not no more."

44   He and the grandmother discussed better times. The old lady said that in her opinion Europe was entirely to blame for the way things were now. She said the way Europe acted you would think we were made of money and Red Sam said it was no use talking about it, she was exactly right. The children ran outside into the white sunlight and looked at the monkey in the lacy chinaberry tree. He was busy catching fleas on himself and biting each one carefully between his teeth as if it were a delicacy.

45   They drove off again into the hot afternoon. The grandmother took cat naps and woke up every five minutes with her own snoring. Outside of Toombsboro she woke up and recalled an old plantation that she had visited in this neighborhood once when she was a young lady. She said the house had six white columns across the front and that there was an avenue of oaks leading up to it and two little wooden trellis arbors on either side in front where you sat down with your suitor after a stroll in the garden. She recalled exactly which road to turn off to get to it. She knew that Bailey would not be willing to lose any time looking at an old house, but the more she talked about it, the more she wanted to see it once again and find out if the little twin arbors were still standing. "There was a secret panel in this house," she said craftily, not telling the truth but wishing that she were, "and the story went that all the family silver was hidden in it when Sherman came through but it was never found..."

46   "Hey!" John Wesley said. "Let's go see it! We'll find it! We'll poke all the woodwork and find it! Who lives there? Where do you turn off at? Hey, Pop, can't we turn off there?"

47   "We never have seen a house with a secret panel!" June Star shrieked. "Let's go to the house with the secret panel! Hey Pop, can't we go see the house with the secret panel!"

48   "It's not far from here, I know," the grandmother said. "It wouldn't take over twenty minutes."

49   Bailey was looking straight ahead. His jaw was as rigid as a horseshoe. "No," he said.

50   The children began to yell and scream that they wanted to see the house with the secret panel. John Wesley kicked the back of the front seat and June Star hung over her mother's shoulder and whined desperately into her ear that they never had any fun even on their vacation, that they could never do what THEY wanted to do. The baby began to scream and John Wesley kicked the back of the seat so hard that his father could feel the blows in his kidney.

51   "All right!" he shouted and drew the car to a stop at the side of the road. "Will you all shut up? Will you all just shut up for one second? If you don't shut up, we won't go anywhere."

52   "It would be very educational for them," the grandmother murmured.

53   "All right," Bailey said, "but get this: this is the only time we're going to stop for anything like this. This is the one and only time."

54   "The dirt road that you have to turn down is about a mile back," the grandmother directed. "I marked it when we passed."

55   "A dirt road," Bailey groaned.

56   After they had turned around and were headed toward the dirt road, the grandmother recalled other points about the house, the beautiful glass over the front doorway and the candle-lamp in the hall. John Wesley said that the secret panel was probably in the fireplace.

57   "You can't go inside this house," Bailey said. "You don't know who lives there."

58   "While you all talk to the people in front, I'll run around behind and get in a window," John Wesley suggested.

59   "We'll all stay in the car," his mother said.

60   They turned onto the dirt road and the car raced roughly along in a swirl of pink dust. The grandmother recalled the times when there were no paved roads and thirty miles was a day's journey. The dirt road was hilly and there were sudden washes in it and sharp curves on dangerous embankments. All at once they would be on a hill, looking down over the blue tops of trees for miles around, then the next minute, they would be in a red depression with the dust-coated trees looking down on them.

61   "This place had better turn up in a minute," Bailey said, "or I'm going to turn around."

62   The road looked as if no one had traveled on it for months.

63   "It's not much farther," the grandmother said and just as she said it, a horrible thought came to her. The thought was so embarrassing that she turned red in the face and her eyes dilated and her feet jumped up, upsetting her valise in the corner. The instant the valise moved, the newspaper top she had over the basket under it rose with a snarl and Pity Sing, the cat, sprang onto Bailey's shoulder.

64   The children were thrown to the floor and their mother, catching the baby, was thrown out the door onto the ground; the old lady was thrown into the front seat. The car turned over once and landed right-side-up in a gulch off the side of the road. Bailey remained in the driver's seat with the cat—gray-striped with a broad white face and an orange nose—clinging to his neck like a caterpillar.

65   As soon as the children saw they could move their arms and legs, they scrambled out of the car, shouting, "We've had an ACCIDENT!" The grandmother was curled up under the dashboard, hoping she was injured so that Bailey's wrath would not come down on her all at once. The horrible thought she had had before the accident was that the house she had remembered so vividly was not in Georgia but in Tennessee.

66   Bailey removed the cat from his neck with both hands and flung it out the window against the side of a pine tree. Then he got out of the car and started looking for the children's mother. She was sitting against the side

of the red gutted ditch, holding the screaming baby, but she only had a cut down her face and a broken shoulder. "We've had an ACCIDENT!" the children screamed in a frenzy of delight.

67   "But nobody's killed," June Star said with disappointment as the grandmother limped out of the car, her hat still pinned to her head but the broken front brim standing up at a jaunty angle and the violet spray hanging off the side. They all sat down in the ditch, except the children, to recover from the shock. They were all shaking.

68   "Maybe a car will come along," said the children's mother hoarsely.

69   "I believe I have injured an organ," said the grandmother, pressing her side, but no one answered her. Bailey's teeth were clattering. He had on a yellow sport shirt with bright blue parrots designed in it and his face was as yellow as the shirt. The grandmother decided that she would not mention that the house was in Tennessee.

70   The road was about ten feet above and they could see only the tops of the trees on the other side of it. Behind the ditch they were sitting in there were more woods, tall and dark and deep. In a few minutes they saw a car some distance away on top of a hill, coming slowly as if the occupants were watching them. The grandmother stood up and waved both her arms dramatically to attract their attention. The car continued to come on slowly, disappeared around a bend and appeared again, moving even slower, on top of the hill they had gone over. It was a big black battered hearse-like automobile. There were three men in it.

71   It came to a stop just over them and for some minutes, the driver looked down with a steady expressionless gaze to where they were sitting, and didn't speak. Then he turned his head and muttered something to the other two and they got out. One was a fat boy in black trousers and a red sweat shirt with a silver stallion embossed on the front of it. He moved around on the right side of them and stood staring, his mouth partly open in a kind of loose grin. The other had on khaki pants and a blue striped coat and a gray hat pulled down very low, hiding most of his face. He came around slowly on the left side. Neither spoke.

72   The driver got out of the car and stood by the side of it, looking down at them. He was an older man than the other two. His hair was just beginning to gray and he wore silver-rimmed spectacles that gave him a scholarly look. He had a long creased face and didn't have on any shirt or undershirt. He had on blue jeans that were too tight for him and was holding a black hat and a gun. The two boys also had guns.

73   "We've had an ACCIDENT!" the children screamed.

74   The grandmother had the peculiar feeling that the bespectacled man was someone she knew. His face was as familiar to her as if she had known him all her life but she could not recall who he was. He moved away from the car and began to come down the embankment, placing his feet carefully so that he wouldn't slip. He had on tan and white shoes and no socks, and his ankles were red and thin. "Good afternoon," he said. "I see you all had you a little spill."

75   "We turned over twice!" said the grandmother.

76   "Oncet," he corrected. "We seen it happen. Try their car and see will it run, Hiram," he said quietly to the boy with the gray hat.

77   "What you got that gun for?" John Wesley asked. "Whatcha gonna do with that gun?"

78   "Lady," the man said to the children's mother, "would you mind calling them children to sit down by you? Children make me nervous. I want all you all to sit down right together there where you're at."

79   "What are you telling US what to do for?" June Star asked.

80   Behind them the line of woods gaped like a dark open mouth. "Come here," said their mother.

81   "Look here now," Bailey began suddenly, "we're in a predicament! We're in..."

82   The grandmother shrieked. She scrambled to her feet and stood staring. "You're The Misfit!" she said. "I recognized you at once!"

83   "Yes'm," the man said, smiling slightly as if he were pleased in spite of himself to be known, "but it would have been better for all of you, lady, if you hadn't of reckernized me."

84   Bailey turned his head sharply and said something to his mother that shocked even the children. The old lady began to cry and The Misfit reddened.

85   "Lady," he said, "don't you get upset. Sometimes a man says things he don't mean. I don't reckon he meant to talk to you thataway."

86   "You wouldn't shoot a lady, would you?" the grandmother said and removed a clean handkerchief from her cuff and began to slap at her eyes with it.

87   The Misfit pointed the toe of his shoe into the ground and made a little hole and then covered it up again. "I would hate to have to," he said.

88   "Listen," the grandmother almost screamed, "I know you're a good man. You don't look a bit like you have common blood. I know you must come from nice people!"

89   "Yes ma'am," he said, "finest people in the world." When he smiled he showed a row of strong white teeth. "God never made a finer woman than my mother and my daddy's heart was pure gold," he said. The boy with the red sweat shirt had come around behind them and was standing with his gun at his hip. The Misfit squatted down on the ground. "Watch them children, Bobby Lee," he said. "You know they make me nervous." He looked at the six of them huddled together in front of him and he seemed to be embarrassed as if he couldn't think of anything to say. "Ain't a cloud in the sky," he remarked, looking up at it. "Don't see no sun but don't see no cloud neither."

90   "Yes, it's a beautiful day," said the grandmother. "Listen," she said, "you shouldn't call yourself The Misfit because I know you're a good man at heart. I can just look at you and tell."

91   "Hush!" Bailey yelled. "Hush! Everybody shut up and let me handle this!" He was squatting in the position of a runner about to sprint forward but he didn't move.

92   "I pre-chate that, lady," the Misfit said and drew a little circle in the ground with the butt of his gun.

93   "It'll take a half a hour to fix this here car," Hiram called, looking over the raised hood of it.

94   "Well, first you and Bobby Lee get him and that little boy to step over yonder with you," The Misfit said, pointing to Bailey and John Wesley. "The boys want to ast you something," he said to Bailey. "Would you mind stepping back in them woods there with them?"

95   "Listen," Bailey began, "we're in a terrible predicament! Nobody realizes what this is," and his voice cracked. His eyes were as blue and intense as the parrots in his shirt and he remained perfectly still.

96   The grandmother reached up to adjust her hat brim as if she were going to the woods with him but it came off in her hand. She stood staring at it and after a second she let it fall on the ground. Hiram pulled Bailey up by the arm as if he were assisting an old man. John Wesley caught hold of his father's hand and Bobby Lee followed. They went off toward the woods and just as they reached the dark edge, Bailey turned and supporting himself against a gray naked pine trunk, he shouted, "I'll be back in a minute, Mamma, wait on me!"

97   "Come back this instant!" his mother shrilled but they all disappeared into the woods.

98   "Bailey Boy!" the grandmother called in a tragic voice but she found she was looking at The Misfit squatting on the ground in front of her. "I just know you're a good man," she said desperately. "You're not a bit common!"

99   "Nome, I ain't a good man," The Misfit said after a second as if he had considered her statement carefully, "but I ain't the worst in the world neither. My daddy said I was a different breed of dog from my brothers and sisters. 'You know,' Daddy said, 'it's some that can live their whole life out without asking about it and it's others has to know why it is, and this boy is one of the latters. He's going to be into everything!'" He put on his black hat and looked up suddenly and then away deep into the woods as if he were embarrassed again. "I'm sorry I don't have on a shirt before you ladies," he said, hunching his shoulders slightly. "We buried our clothes that we had on when we escaped and we're just making do until we can get better. We borrowed these from some folks we met," he explained.

100   "That's perfectly all right," the grandmother said. "Maybe Bailey has an extra shirt in his suitcase."

101   "I'll look and see terrectly," The Misfit said.

102   "Where are they taking him?" the children's mother screamed.

103   "Daddy was a card himself," The Misfit said. "You couldn't put anything over on him. He never got in trouble with the Authorities though. Just had the knack of handling them."

104   "You could be honest too if you'd only try," said the grandmother. "Think how wonderful it would be to settle down and live a comfortable life and not have to think about somebody chasing you all the time."

105   The Misfit kept scratching in the ground with the butt of his gun as if he were thinking about it. "Yes'm, somebody is always after you," he murmured.

106   The grandmother noticed how thin his shoulder blades were just behind his hat because she was standing up looking down on him. "Do you ever pray?" she asked.

107   He shook his head. All she saw was the black hat wiggle between his shoulder blades. "Nome," he said.

108   There was a pistol shot from the woods, followed closely by another. Then silence. The old lady's head jerked around. She could hear the wind move through the tree tops like a long satisfied insuck of breath. "Bailey Boy!" she called.

109   "I was a gospel singer for a while," The Misfit said. "I been most everything. Been in the arm service, both land and sea, at home and abroad, been twict married, been an undertaker, been with the railroads, plowed Mother Earth, been in a tornado, seen a man burnt alive oncet," and he looked up at the children's mother and the little girl who were sitting close together, their faces white and their eyes glassy; "I even seen a woman flogged," he said.

110   "Pray, pray," the grandmother began, "pray, pray..."

111   "I never was a bad boy that I remember of," The Misfit said in an almost dreamy voice, "But somewheres along the line I done something wrong and got sent to the penitentiary. I was buried alive," and he looked up and held her attention to him by a steady stare.

112   "That's when you should have started to pray," she said. "What did you do to get sent up to the penitentiary that first time?"

113   "Turn to the right, it was a wall," The Misfit said, looking up again at the cloudless sky. "Turn to the left, it was a wall. Look up it was a ceiling, look down it was a floor. I forget what I done, lady. I set there and set there, trying to remember what it was I done and I ain't recalled it to this day. Oncet in a while, I would think it was coming to me, but it never come."

114   "Maybe they put you in by mistake," the old lady said vaguely.

115   "Nome," he said. "It wasn't no mistake. They had the papers on me."

116   "You must have stolen something," she said.

117   The Misfit sneered slightly. "Nobody had nothing I wanted," he said. "It was a head-doctor at the penitentiary said what I had done was kill my daddy but I known that for a lie. My daddy died in nineteen ought nineteen of the epidemic flu and I never had a thing to do with it. He was buried in the Mount Hopewell Baptist churchyard and you can go there and see for yourself."

118   "If you would pray," the old lady said, "Jesus would help you."

119   "That's right," The Misfit said.

120   "Well then, why don't you pray?" she asked trembling with delight suddenly.

121   "I don't want no hep," he said. "I'm doing all right by myself."

122   Bobby Lee and Hiram came ambling back from the woods. Bobby Lee was dragging a yellow shirt with bright blue parrots in it.

123   "Thow me that shirt, Bobby Lee," The Misfit said. The shirt came flying at him and landed on his shoulder and he put it on. The grandmother
couldn't name what the shirt reminded her of. "No, lady," The Misfit said
while he was buttoning it up, "I found out the crime don't matter. You can
do one thing or you can do another, kill a man or take a tire off his car,
because sooner or later you're going to forget what it was you done and
just be punished for it."

124   The children's mother had begun to make heaving noises as if she
couldn't get her breath. "Lady," he asked, "would you and that little girl
like to step off yonder with Bobby Lee and Hiram and join your husband?"

125   "Yes, thank you," the mother said faintly. Her left arm dangled helplessly and she was holding the baby, who had gone to sleep, in the other.
"Hep that lady up, Hiram," The Misfit said as she struggled to climb out
of the ditch, "and Bobby Lee, you hold onto that little girl's hand."

126   "I don't want to hold hands with him," June Star said. "He reminds me
of a pig."

127   The fat boy blushed and laughed and caught her by the arm and pulled
her off into the woods after Hiram and her mother.

128   Alone with The Misfit, the grandmother found that she had lost her
voice. There was not a cloud in the sky nor any sun. There was nothing
around her but woods. She wanted to tell him that he must pray. She
opened and closed her mouth several times before anything came out.
Finally she found herself saying, "Jesus, Jesus," meaning, Jesus will help
you, but the way she was saying it, it sounded as if she might be cursing.

129   "Yes'm," The Misfit said as if he agreed. "Jesus thown everything off
balance. It was the same case with Him as with me except He hadn't committed any crime and they could prove I had committed one because they
had the papers on me. Of course," he said, "they never shown me my
papers. That's why I sign myself now. I said long ago, you get you a signature and sign everything you do and keep a copy of it. Then you'll know
what you done and you can hold up the crime to the punishment and see
do they match and in the end you'll have something to prove you ain't
been treated right. I call myself The Misfit," he said, "because I can't make
what all I done wrong fit what all I gone through in punishment."

130   There was a piercing scream from the woods, followed closely by a
pistol report. "Does it seem right to you, lady, that one is punished a heap
and another ain't punished at all?"

131   "Jesus!" the old lady cried. "You've got good blood! I know you wouldn't
shoot a lady! I know you come from nice people! Pray! Jesus, you ought
not to shoot a lady. I'll give you all the money I've got!"

132   "Lady," The Misfit said, looking beyond her far into the woods, "there
never was a body that give the undertaker a tip."

133   There were two more pistol reports and the grandmother raised her
head like a parched old turkey hen crying for water and called "Bailey
Boy, Bailey Boy!" as if her heart would break.

134   "Jesus was the only One that ever raised the dead," The Misfit contin-ued, "and He shouldn't have done it. He thown everything off balance. If He did what He said, then it's nothing for you to do but thow away every-thing and follow Him, and if He didn't, then it's nothing for you to do but enjoy the few minutes you got left the best way you can—by killing some-body or burning down his house or doing some other meanness to him. No pleasure but meanness," he said and his voice had become almost a snarl.

135   "Maybe He didn't raise the dead," the old lady mumbled, not knowing what she was saying and feeling so dizzy that she sank down in the ditch with her legs twisted under her.

136   "I wasn't there so I can't say He didn't," The Misfit said. "I wisht I had of been there," he said, hitting the ground with his fist. "It ain't right I wasn't there because if I had of been there I would of known. Listen lady," he said in a high voice, "if I had of been there I would of known and I wouldn't be like I am now." His voice seemed about to crack and the grandmother's head cleared for an instant. She saw the man's face twisted close to her own as if he were going to cry and she murmured, "Why you're one of my babies. You're one of my own children!" she reached out and touched him on the shoulder. The Misfit sprang back as if a snake had bitten him and shot her three times through the chest. Then he put his gun down on the ground and took off his glasses and began to clean them.

137   Hiram and Bobby Lee returned from the woods and stood over the ditch, looking down at the grandmother who half sat and half lay in a pud-dle of blood with her legs crossed under her like a child's and her face smiling up at the cloudless sky.

138   Without his glasses, The Misfit's eyes were red-rimmed and pale and defenseless-looking. "Take her off and thow her where you thown the others," he said picking up the cat that was rubbing itself against his leg.

139   "She was a talker, wasn't she?" Bobby Lee said, sliding down the ditch with a yodel.

140   "She would of been a good woman," The Misfit said, "if it had been somebody there to shoot her every minute of her life."

141   "Some fun!" Bobby Lee said.

142   "Shut up, Bobby Lee," The Misfit said. "It's no real pleasure in life."

Questions for Discussion

1. How is the end of the story foreshadowed in the events that precede it?

2. What is the purpose of the incident at Red Sammy's? What do this inci-dent and the story about Mr. Teagarden reveal about the grandmother?

3. Explain the significance of O'Connor's choice of a title. What is her point? Why does the grandmother tell Red Sammy and the Misfit that they are good men? On what does the grandmother base her moral judgments of people? How would you describe a "good man"? Does anyone in the story fit that description?

4. Discuss whether the grandmother is to blame for what happens to the family.

5. Discuss the symbolism of the hearse, the woods, and the sky without a sun.

6. Why does the Misfit call himself by that name? What is your definition of a Misfit? What characteristics make the Misfit a misfit? What does he resent about Jesus? He says, "If He did what He said, then it's nothing for you to do but thow away everything and follow Him." How does the Misfit's assessment of Christianity here accord with Jesus's gospel?

7. Why does the grandmother say to the Misfit, "Why you're one of my babies. You're one of my own children"? Why does he kill her when she touches him?

8. Explain the Misfit's statement that the grandmother "would of been a good woman...if it had been somebody there to shoot her every minute of her life." Explain why you do or do not agree with him.

GREENLEAF   (1956)

1   Mrs. May's bedroom window was low and faced on the east and the bull, silvered in the moonlight, stood under it, his head raised as if he listened—like some patient god come down to woo her—for a stir inside the room. The window was dark and the sound of her breathing too light to be carried outside. Clouds crossing the moon blackened him and in the dark he began to tear at the hedge. Presently they passed and he appeared again in the same spot, chewing steadily, with a hedge-wreath that he had ripped loose for himself caught in the tips of his horns. When the moon drifted into retirement again, there was nothing to mark his place but the sound of steady chewing. Then abruptly a pink glow filled the window. Bars of light slid across him as the venetian blind was slit. He took a step backward and lowered his head as if to show the wreath across his horns.

2   For almost a minute there was no sound from inside, then as he raised his crowned head again, a woman's voice, guttural as if addressed to a dog, said, "Get away from here, Sir!" and in a second muttered, "Some nigger's scrub bull."

3   The animal pawed the ground and Mrs. May, standing bent forward behind the blind, closed it quickly lest the light make him charge into the shrubbery. For a second she waited, still bent forward, her nightgown hanging loosely from her narrow shoulders. Green rubber curlers sprouted neatly over her forehead and her face beneath them was smooth as concrete with an egg-white paste that drew the wrinkles out while she slept.

4   She had been conscious in her sleep of a steady rhythmic chewing as if something were eating one wall of the house. She had been aware that whatever it was had been eating as long as she had had the place and had eaten everything from the beginning of her fence line up to the house and

now was eating the house and calmly with the same steady rhythm would continue through the house, eating her and the boys, and then on, eating everything but the Greenleafs, on and on, eating everything until nothing was left but the Greenleafs on a little island all their own in the middle of what had been her place. When the munching reached her elbow, she jumped up and found herself, fully awake, standing in the middle of her room. She identified the sound at once: a cow was tearing at the shrubbery under her window. Mr. Greenleaf had left the lane gate open and she didn't doubt that the entire herd was on her lawn. She turned on the dim pink table lamp and then went to the window and slit the blind. The bull, gaunt and long-legged, was standing about four feet from her, chewing calmly like an uncouth country suitor.

5   For fifteen years, she thought as she squinted at him fiercely, she had been having shiftless people's hogs root up her oats, their mules wallow on her lawn, their scrub bulls breed her cows. If this one was not put up now, he would be over the fence, ruining her herd before morning—and Mr. Greenleaf was soundly sleeping a half mile down the road in the tenant house. There was no way to get him unless she dressed and got in her car and rode down there and woke him up. He would come but his expression, his whole figure, his every pause, would say: "Hit looks to me like one or both of them boys would not make their maw ride out in the middle of the night thisaway. If hit was my boys, they would have got thet bull up theirself."

6   The bull lowered his head and shook it and the wreath slipped down to the base of his horns where it looked like a menacing prickly crown. She had closed the blind then; in a few seconds she heard him move off heavily.

7   Mr. Greenleaf would say, "If hit was my boys they would never have allowed their maw to go after hired help in the middle of the night. They would have did it theirself."

8   Weighing it, she decided not to bother Mr. Greenleaf. She returned to bed thinking that if the Greenleaf boys had risen in the world it was because she had given their father employment when no one else would have him. She had had Mr. Greenleaf fifteen years but no one else would have had him five minutes. Just the way he approached an object was enough to tell anybody with eyes what kind of a worker he was. He walked with a high-shouldered creep and he never appeared to come directly forward. He walked on the perimeter of some invisible circle and if you wanted to look him in the face, you had to move and get in front of him. She had not fired him because she had always doubted she could do better. He was too shiftless to go out and look for another job; he didn't have the initiative to steal, and after she had told him three or four times to do a thing, he did it; but he never told her about a sick cow until it was too late to call the veterinarian and if her barn had caught on fire, he would have called his wife to see the flames before he began to put them out. And of the wife, she didn't even like to think. Beside the wife, Mr. Greenleaf was an aristocrat.

9   "If it had been my boys," he would have said, "they would have cut off their right arm before they would have allowed their maw to..."

10   "If your boys had any pride, Mr. Greenleaf," she would like to say to him some day, "there are many things that they would not *allow* their mother to do."

11   The next morning as soon as Mr. Greenleaf came to the back door, she told him there was a stray bull on the place and that she wanted him penned up at once.

12   "Done already been here three days," he said, addressing his right foot which he held forward, turned slightly as if he were trying to look at the sole. He was standing at the bottom of the three back steps while she leaned out the kitchen door, a small woman with pale near-sighted eyes and grey hair that rose on top like the crest of some disturbed bird.

13   "Three days!" she said in the restrained screech that had become habitual with her.

14   Mr. Greenleaf, looking into the distance over the near pasture, removed a package of cigarets from his shirt pocket and let one fall into his hand. He put the package back and stood for a while looking at the cigaret. "I put him in the bull pen but he torn out of there," he said presently. "I didn't see him none after that." He bent over the cigaret and lit it and then turned his head briefly in her direction. The upper part of his face sloped gradually into the lower which was long and narrow, shaped like a rough chalice. He had deep-set fox-colored eyes shadowed under a grey felt hat that he wore slanted forward following the line of his nose. His build was insignificant.

15   "Mr. Greenleaf," she said, "get that bull up this morning before you do anything else. You know he'll ruin the breeding schedule. Get him up and keep him up and the next time there's a stray bull on this place, tell me at once. Do you understand?"

16   "Where you want him put at?" Mr. Greenleaf asked.

17   "I don't care where you put him," she said. "You are supposed to have some sense. Put him where he can't get out. Whose bull is he?"

18   For a moment Mr. Greenleaf seemed to hesitate between silence and speech. He studied the air to the left of him. "He must be somebody's bull," he said after a while.

19   "Yes, he must!" she said and shut the door with a precise little slam.

20   She went into the dining room where the two boys were eating breakfast and sat down on the edge of her chair at the head of the table. She never ate breakfast but she sat with them to see that they had what they wanted. "Honestly!" she said, and began to tell about the bull, aping Mr. Greenleaf saying, "It must be *somebody's* bull."

21   Wesley continued to read the newspaper folded beside his plate but Scofield interrupted his eating from time to time to look at her and laugh. The two boys never had the same reaction to anything. They were as different, she said, as night and day. The only thing they did have in common

was that neither of them cared what happened on the place. Scofield was a business type and Wesley was an intellectual.

22   Wesley, the younger child, had had rheumatic fever when he was seven and Mrs. May thought that this was what had caused him to be an intellectual. Scofield, who had never had a day's sickness in his life, was an insurance salesman. She would not have minded his selling insurance if he had sold a nicer kind but he sold the kind that only Negroes buy. He was what Negroes call a "policy man." He said there was more money in nigger-insurance than any other kind, and before company, he was very loud about it. He would shout, "Mamma don't like to hear me say it but I'm the best nigger-insurance salesman in this county!"

23   Scofield was thirty-six and he had a broad pleasant smiling face but he was not married. "Yes," Mrs. May would say, "and if you sold decent insurance, some *nice* girl would be willing to marry you. What nice girl wants to marry a nigger-insurance man? You'll wake up some day and it'll be too late."

24   And at this Scofield would yodel and say, "Why Mamma, I'm not going to marry until you're dead and gone and then I'm going to marry me some nice fat farm girl that can take over this place!" And once he had added, "—some nice lady like Mrs. Greenleaf." When he had said this, Mrs. May had risen from her chair, her back stiff as a rake handle, and had gone to her room. There she had sat down on the edge of her bed for some time with her small face drawn. Finally she had whispered, "I work and slave, I struggle and sweat to keep this place for them and soon as I'm dead, they'll marry trash and bring it in here and ruin everything. They'll marry trash and ruin everything I've done," and she had made up her mind at that moment to change her will. The next day she had gone to her lawyer and had had the property entailed so that if they married, they could not leave it to their wives.

25   The idea that one of them might marry a woman even remotely like Mrs. Greenleaf was enough to make her ill. She had put up with Mr. Greenleaf for fifteen years, but the only way she had endured his wife had been by keeping entirely out of her sight. Mrs. Greenleaf was large and loose. The yard around her house looked like a dump and her five girls were always filthy; even the youngest one dipped snuff. Instead of making a garden or washing their clothes, her preoccupation was what she called "prayer healing."

26   Every day she cut all the morbid stories out of the newspaper—the accounts of women who had been raped and criminals who had escaped and children who had been burned and of train wrecks and plane crashes and the divorces of movie stars. She took these to the woods and dug a hole and buried them and then she fell on the ground over them and mumbled and groaned for an hour or so, moving her huge arms back and forth under her and out again and finally just lying down flat and, Mrs. May suspected, going to sleep in the dirt.

27   She had not found out about this until the Greenleafs had been with her a few months. One morning she had been out to inspect a field that

she had wanted planted in rye but that had come up in clover because Mr. Greenleaf had used the wrong seeds in the grain drill. She was returning through a wooded path that separated two pastures, muttering to herself and hitting the ground methodically with a long stick she carried in case she saw a snake. "Mr. Greenleaf," she was saying in a low voice, "I cannot afford to pay for your mistakes. I am a poor woman and this place is all I have. I have two boys to educate. I cannot . . ."

28   Out of nowhere a guttural agonized voice groaned, "Jesus! Jesus!" In a second it came again with a terrible urgency. "Jesus! Jesus!"

29   Mrs. May stopped still, one hand lifted to her throat. The sound was so piercing that she felt as if some violent unleashed force had broken out of the ground and was charging toward her. Her second thought was more reasonable: somebody had been hurt on the place and would sue her for everything she had. She had no insurance. She rushed forward and turning a bend in the path, she saw Mrs. Greenleaf sprawled on her hands and knees off the side of the road, her head down.

30   "Mrs. Greenleaf!" she shrilled, "what's happened?"

31   Mrs. Greenleaf raised her head. Her face was a patchwork of dirt and tears and her small eyes, the color of two field peas, were red-rimmed and swollen, but her expression was as composed as a bulldog's. She swayed back and forth on her hands and knees and groaned. "Jesus, Jesus."

32   Mrs. May winced. She thought the word, Jesus, should be kept inside the church building like other words inside the bedroom. She was a good Christian woman with a large respect for religion, though she did not, of course, believe any of it was true. "What is the matter with you?" she asked sharply.

33   "You broken my healing," Mrs. Greenleaf said, waving her aside. "I can't talk to you until I finish."

34   Mrs. May stood, bent forward, her mouth open and her stick raised off the ground as if she were not sure what she wanted to strike with it.

35   "Oh Jesus, stab me in the heart!" Mrs. Greenleaf shrieked. "Jesus, stab me in the heart!" and she fell back flat in the dirt, a huge human mound, her legs and arms spread out as if she were trying to wrap them around the earth.

36   Mrs. May felt as furious and helpless as if she had been insulted by a child. "Jesus," she said, drawing herself back, "would be *ashamed* of you. He would tell you to get up from there this instant and go wash your children's clothes!" and she had turned and walked off as fast as she could.

37   Whenever she thought of how the Greenleaf boys had advanced in the world, she had only to think of Mrs. Greenleaf sprawled obscenely on the ground, and say to herself, "Well, no matter how far they *go*, they *came* from that."

38   She would like to have been able to put in her will that when she died, Wesley and Scofield were not to continue to employ Mr. Greenleaf. She was capable of handling Mr. Greenleaf; they were not. Mr. Greenleaf had pointed out to her once that her boys didn't know hay from silage. She

had pointed out to him that they had other talents, that Scofield was a successful business man and Wesley a successful intellectual. Mr. Greenleaf did not comment, but he never lost an opportunity of letting her see, by his expression or some simple gesture, that he held the two of them in infinite contempt. As scrub-human as the Greenleafs were, he never hesitated to let her know that in any like circumstance in which his own boys might have been involved, they—O. T. and E. T. Greenleaf—would have acted to better advantage.

39   The Greenleaf boys were two or three years younger than the May boys. They were twins and you never knew when you spoke to one of them whether you were speaking to O. T. or E. T., and they never had the politeness to enlighten you. They were long-legged and raw-boned and red-skinned, with bright grasping fox-colored eyes like their father's. Mr. Greenleaf's pride in them began with the fact that they were twins. He acted, Mrs. May said, as if this were something smart they had thought of themselves. They were energetic and hard-working and she would admit to anyone that they had come a long way—and that the Second World War was responsible for it.

40   They had both joined the service and, disguised in their uniforms, they could not be told from other people's children. You could tell, of course, when they opened their mouths but they did that seldom. The smartest thing they had done was to get sent overseas and there to marry French wives. They hadn't married French trash either. They had married nice girls who naturally couldn't tell that they murdered the king's English or that the Greenleafs were who they were.

41   Wesley's heart condition had not permitted him to serve his country but Scofield had been in the army for two years. He had not cared for it and at the end of his military service, he was only a Private First Class. The Greenleaf boys were both some kind of sergeants, and Mr. Greenleaf, in those days, had never lost an opportunity of referring to them by their rank. They had both managed to get wounded and now they both had pensions. Further, as soon as they were released from the army, they took advantage of all the benefits and went to the school of agriculture at the university—the taxpayers meanwhile supporting their French wives. The two of them were living now about two miles down the highway on a piece of land that the government had helped them to buy and in a brick duplex bungalow that the government had helped to build and pay for. If the war had made anyone, Mrs. May said, it had made the Greenleaf boys. They each had three little children apiece, who spoke Greenleaf English and French, and who, on account of their mothers' background, would be sent to the convent school and brought up with manners. "And in twenty years," Mrs. May asked Scofield and Wesley, "do you know what those people will be?

42   "*Society,*" she said blackly.

43   She had spent fifteen years coping with Mr. Greenleaf and, by now, handling him had become second nature with her. His disposition on any

particular day was as much a factor in what she could and couldn't do as the weather was, and she had learned to read his face the way real country people read the sunrise and sunset.

44   She was a country woman only by persuasion. The late Mr. May, a business man, had bought the place when land was down, and when he died it was all he had to leave her. The boys had not been happy to move to the country to a broken-down farm, but there was nothing else for her to do. She had the timber on the place cut and with the proceeds had set herself up in the dairy business after Mr. Greenleaf had answered her ad. "i seen yor add and i will come have 2 boys," was all his letter said, but he arrived the next day in a pieced-together truck, his wife and five daughters sitting on the floor in back, himself and the two boys in the cab.

45   Over the years they had been on her place, Mr. and Mrs. Greenleaf had aged hardly at all. They had no worries, no responsibilities. They lived like the lilies of the field, off the fat that she struggled to put into the land. When she was dead and gone from overwork and worry, the Greenleafs, healthy and thriving, would be just ready to begin draining Scofield and Wesley.

46   Wesley said the reason Mrs. Greenleaf had not aged was because she released all her emotions in prayer healing. "You ought to start praying, Sweetheart," he had said in the voice that, poor boy, he could not help making deliberately nasty.

47   Scofield only exasperated her beyond endurance but Wesley caused her real anxiety. He was thin and nervous and bald and being an intellectual was a terrible strain on his disposition. She doubted if he would marry until she died but she was certain that then the wrong woman would get him. Nice girls didn't like Scofield but Wesley didn't like nice girls. He didn't like anything. He drove twenty miles every day to the university where he taught and twenty miles back every night, but he said he hated the twenty-mile drive and he hated the second-rate university and he hated the morons who attended it. He hated the country and he hated the life he lived; he hated living with his mother and his idiot brother and he hated hearing about the damn dairy and the damn help and the damn broken machinery. But in spite of all he said, he never made any move to leave. He talked about Paris and Rome but he never went even to Atlanta.

48   "You'd go to those places and you'd get sick," Mrs. May would say. "Who in Paris is going to see that you get a salt-free diet? And do you think if you married one of those odd numbers you take out that *she* would cook a salt-free diet for you? No indeed, she would not!" When she took this line, Wesley would turn himself roughly around in his chair and ignore her. Once when she had kept it up too long, he had snarled, "Well, why don't you do something practical, Woman? Why don't you pray for me like Mrs. Greenleaf would?"

49   "I don't like to hear you boys make jokes about religion," she had said. "If you would go to church, you would meet some nice girls."

50   But it was impossible to tell them anything. When she looked at the two of them now, sitting on either side of the table, neither one caring the

least if a stray bull ruined her herd—which was their herd, their future—when she looked at the two of them, one hunched over a paper and the other teetering back in his chair, grinning at her like an idiot, she wanted to jump up and beat her fist on the table and shout, "You'll find out one of these days, you'll find out what *Reality* is when it's too late!"

51   "Mamma," Scofield said, "don't you get excited now but I'll tell you whose bull that is." He was looking at her wickedly. He let his chair drop forward and he got up. Then with his shoulders bent and his hands held up to cover his head, he tiptoed to the door. He backed into the hall and pulled the door almost to so that it hid all of him but his face. "You want to know, Sugarpie?" he asked.

52   Mrs. May sat looking at him coldly.

53   "That's O. T. and E. T.'s bull," he said. "I collected from their nigger yesterday and he told me they were missing it," and he showed her an exaggerated expanse of teeth and disappeared silently.

54   Wesley looked up and laughed.

55   Mrs. May turned her head forward again, her expression unaltered. "I am the only *adult* on this place," she said. She leaned across the table and pulled the paper from the side of his plate. "Do you see how it's going to be when I die and you boys have to handle him?" she began. "Do you see why he didn't know whose bull that was? Because it was theirs. Do you see what I have to put up with? Do you see that if I hadn't kept my foot on his neck all these years, you boys might be milking cows every morning at four o'clock?"

56   Wesley pulled the paper back toward his plate and staring at her full in the face, he murmured, "I wouldn't milk a cow to save your soul from hell."

57   "I know you wouldn't," she said in a brittle voice. She sat back and began rapidly turning her knife over at the side of her plate. "O. T. and E. T. are fine boys," she said. "They ought to have been my sons." The thought of this was so horrible that her vision of Wesley was blurred at once by a wall of tears. All she saw was his dark shape, rising quickly from the table. "And you two," she cried, "you two should have belonged to that woman!"

58   He was heading for the door.

59   "When I die," she said in a thin voice, "I don't know what's going to become of you."

60   "You're always yapping about when-you-die," he growled as he rushed out, "but you look pretty healthy to me."

61   For some time she sat where she was, looking straight ahead through the window across the room into a scene of indistinct greys and greens. She stretched her face and her neck muscles and drew in a long breath but the scene in front of her flowed together anyway into a watery grey mass. "They needn't think I'm going to die any time soon," she muttered, and some more defiant voice in her added: I'll die when I get good and ready.

62   She wiped her eyes with the table napkin and got up and went to the window and gazed at the scene in front of her. The cows were grazing on

two pale green pastures across the road and behind them, fencing them in, was a black wall of trees with a sharp sawtooth edge that held off the indifferent sky. The pastures were enough to calm her. When she looked out any window in her house, she saw the reflection of her own character. Her city friends said she was the most remarkable woman they knew, to go, practically penniless and with no experience, out to a rundown farm and make a success of it. "Everything is against you," she would say, "the weather is against you and the dirt is against you and the help is against you. They're all in league against you. There's nothing for it but an iron hand!"

63   "Look at Mamma's iron hand!" Scofield would yell and grab her arm and hold it up so that her delicate blue-veined little hand would dangle from her wrist like the head of a broken lily. The company always laughed.

64   The sun, moving over the black and white grazing cows, was just a little brighter than the rest of the sky. Looking down, she saw a darker shape that might have been its shadow cast at an angle, moving among them. She uttered a sharp cry and turned and marched out of the house.

65   Mr. Greenleaf was in the trench silo, filling a wheelbarrow. She stood on the edge and looked down at him. "I told you to get up that bull. Now he's in with the milk herd."

66   "You can't do two thangs at oncet," Mr. Greenleaf remarked.

67   "I told you to do that first."

68   He wheeled the barrow out of the open end of the trench toward the barn and she followed close behind him. "And you needn't think, Mr. Greenleaf," she said, "that I don't know exactly whose bull that is or why you haven't been in any hurry to notify me he was here. I might as well feed O. T. and E. T.'s bull as long as I'm going to have him here ruining my herd."

69   Mr. Greenleaf paused with the wheelbarrow and looked behind him. "Is that them boys' bull?" he asked in an incredulous tone.

70   She did not say a word. She merely looked away with her mouth taut.

71   "They told me their bull was out but I never known that was him," he said.

72   "I want that bull put up now," she said, "and I'm going to drive over to O. T. and E. T.'s and tell them they'll have to come get him today. I ought to charge for the time he's been here—then it wouldn't happen again."

73   "They didn't pay but seventy-five dollars for him," Mr. Greenleaf offered.

74   "I wouldn't have had him as a gift," she said.

75   "They was just going to beef him," Mr. Greenleaf went on, "but he got loose and run his head into their pickup truck. He don't like cars and trucks. They had a time getting his horn out the fender and when they finally got him loose, he took off and they was too tired to run after him—but I never known that was him there."

76   "It wouldn't have paid you to know, Mr. Greenleaf," she said. "But you know now. Get a horse and get him."

77   In a half hour, from her front window she saw the bull, squirrel-colored, with jutting hips and long light horns, ambling down the dirt road that ran in front of the house. Mr. Greenleaf was behind him on the horse. "That's a Greenleaf bull if I ever saw one," she muttered. She went out on the porch and called, "Put him where he can't get out."

78   "He likes to bust loose," Mr. Greenleaf said, looking with approval at the bull's rump. "This gentleman is a sport."

79   "If those boys don't come for him, he's going to be a dead sport," she said. "I'm just warning you."

80   He heard her but he didn't answer.

81   "That's the awfullest looking bull I ever saw," she called but he was too far down the road to hear.

82   It was mid-morning when she turned into O. T. and E. T.'s driveway. The house, a new red-brick, low-to-the-ground building that looked like a warehouse with windows, was on top of a treeless hill. The sun was beating down directly on the white roof of it. It was the kind of house that everybody built now and nothing marked it as belonging to the Greenleafs except three dogs, part hound and part spitz, that rushed out from behind it as soon as she stopped her car. She reminded herself that you could always tell the class of people by the class of dog, and honked her horn. While she sat waiting for someone to come, she continued to study the house. All the windows were down and she wondered if the government could have air-conditioned the thing. No one came and she honked again. Presently a door opened and several children appeared in it and stood looking at her, making no move to come forward. She recognized this as a true Greenleaf trait—they could hang in a door, looking at you for hours.

83   "Can't one of you children come here?" she called.

84   After a minute they all began to move forward, slowly. They had on overalls and were barefooted but they were not as dirty as she might have expected. There were two or three that looked distinctly like Greenleafs; the others not so much so. The smallest child was a girl with untidy black hair. They stopped about six feet from the automobile and stood looking at her.

85   "You're mighty pretty," Mrs. May said, addressing herself to the smallest girl.

86   There was no answer. They appeared to share one dispassionate expression between them.

87   "Where's your Mamma?" she asked.

88   There was no answer to this for some time. Then one of them said something in French. Mrs. May did not speak French.

89   "Where's your daddy?" she asked.

90   After a while, one of the boys said, "He ain't hyar neither."

91   "Ahhhh," Mrs. May said as if something had been proven. "Where's the colored man?"

92   She waited and decided no one was going to answer. "The cat has six little tongues," she said. "How would you like to come home with me and

let me teach you how to talk?" She laughed and her laugh died on the silent air. She felt as if she were on trial for her life, facing a jury of Greenleafs. "I'll go down and see if I can find the colored man," she said.

93   "You can go if you want to," one of the boys said.

94   "Well, thank you," she murmured and drove off.

95   The barn was down the lane from the house. She had not seen it before but Mr. Greenleaf had described it in detail for it had been built according to the latest specifications. It was a milking parlor arrangement where the cows are milked from below. The milk ran in pipes from the machines to the milk house and was never carried in no bucket, Mr. Greenleaf said, by no human hand. "When you gonter get you one?" he had asked.

96   "Mr. Greenleaf," she had said, "I have to do for myself. I am not assisted hand and foot by the government. It would cost me $20,000 to install a milking parlor. I barely make ends meet as it is."

97   "My boys done it," Mr. Greenleaf had murmured, and then—"but all boys ain't alike."

98   "No indeed!" she had said. "I thank God for that!"

99   "I thank Gawd for ever-thang," Mr. Greenleaf had drawled.

100   You might as well, she had thought in the fierce silence that followed; you've never done anything for yourself.

101   She stopped by the side of the barn and honked but no one appeared. For several minutes she sat in the car, observing the various machines parked around, wondering how many of them were paid for. They had a forage harvester and a rotary hay baler. She had those too. She decided that since no one was here, she would get out and have a look at the milking parlor and see if they kept it clean.

102   She opened the milking room door and stuck her head in and for the first second she felt as if she were going to lose her breath. The spotless white concrete room was filled with sunlight that came from a row of windows head-high along both walls. The metal stanchions gleamed ferociously and she had to squint to be able to look at all. She drew her head out of the room quickly and closed the door and leaned against it, frowning. The light outside was not so bright but she was conscious that the sun was directly on top of her head, like a silver bullet ready to drop into her brain.

103   A Negro carrying a yellow calf-feed bucket appeared from around the corner of the machine shed and came toward her. He was a light yellow boy dressed in the cast-off army clothes of the Greenleaf twins. He stopped at a respectable distance and set the bucket on the ground.

104   "Where's Mr. O. T. and Mr. E. T.?" she asked.

105   "Mist O. T. he in town, Mist E. T. he off yonder in the field," the Negro said, pointing first to the left and then to the right as if he were naming the position of two planets.

106   "Can you remember a message?" she asked, looking as if she thought this doubtful.

107   "I'll remember it if I don't forget it," he said with a touch of sullenness.

108   "Well, I'll write it down then," she said. She got in her car and took a stub of pencil from her pocket book and began to write on the back of an empty envelope. The Negro came and stood at the window. "I'm Mrs. May," she said as she wrote. "Their bull is on my place and I want him off *today*. You can tell them I'm furious about it."

109   "That bull lef here Sareday," the Negro said, "and none of us ain't seen him since. We ain't knowed where he was."

110   "Well, you know now," she said, "and you can tell Mr. O. T. and Mr. E. T. that if they don't come get him today, I'm going to have their daddy shoot him the first thing in the morning. I can't have that bull ruining my herd." She handed him the note.

111   "If I knows Mist O. T. and Mist E. T.," he said, taking it, "they goin to say you go ahead on and shoot him. He done busted up one of our trucks already and we be glad to see the last of him."

112   She pulled her head back and gave him a look from slightly bleared eyes. "Do they expect me to take my time and my worker to shoot their bull?" she asked. "They don't want him so they just let him loose and expect somebody else to kill him? He's eating my oats and ruining my herd and I'm expected to shoot him too?"

113   "I speck you is," he said softly. "He done busted up..."

114   She gave him a very sharp look and said, "Well, I'm not surprised. That's just the way some people are," and after a second she asked, "Which is boss, Mr. O. T. or Mr. E. T.?" She had always suspected that they fought between themselves secretly.

115   "They never quarls," the boy said. "They like one man in two skins."

116   "Hmp. I expect you just never heard them quarrel."

117   "Nor nobody else heard them neither," he said, looking away as if this insolence were addressed to some one else.

118   "Well," she said, "I haven't put up with their father for fifteen years not to know a few things about Greenleafs."

119   The Negro looked at her suddenly with a gleam of recognition. "Is you my policy man's mother?" he asked.

120   "I don't know who your policy man is," she said sharply. "You give them that note and tell them if they don't come for that bull today, they'll be making their father shoot it tomorrow," and she drove off.

121   She stayed at home all afternoon waiting for the Greenleaf twins to come for the bull. They did not come. I might as well be working for them, she thought furiously. They are simply going to use me to the limit. At the supper table, she went over it again for the boys' benefit because she wanted them to see exactly what O. T. and E. T. would do. "They don't want that bull," she said, "—pass the butter—so they simply turn him loose and let somebody else worry about getting rid of him for them. How do you like that? I'm the victim. I've always been the victim."

122   "Pass the butter to the victim," Wesley said. He was in a worse humor than usual because he had had a flat tire on the way home from the university.

123   Scofield handed her the butter and said, "Why Mamma, ain't you ashamed to shoot an old bull that ain't done nothing but give you a little scrub strain in your herd? I declare," he said, "with the Mamma I got it's a wonder I turned out to be such a nice boy!"

124   "You ain't her boy, Son," Wesley said.

125   She eased back in her chair, her fingertips on the edge of the table.

126   "All I know is," Scofield said, "I done mighty well to be as nice as I am seeing what I come from."

127   When they teased her they spoke Greenleaf English but Wesley made his own particular tone come through it like a knife edge. "Well lemme tell you one thang, Brother," he said, leaning over the table, "that if you had half a mind you would already know."

128   "What's that, Brother?" Scofield asked, his broad face grinning into the thin constricted one across from him.

129   "That is," Wesley said, "that neither you nor me is her boy...," but he stopped abruptly as she gave a kind of hoarse wheeze like an old horse lashed unexpectedly. She reared up and ran from the room.

130   "Oh, for God's sake," Wesley growled. "What did you start her off for?"

131   "I never started her off," Scofield said. "You started her off."

132   "Hah."

133   "She's not as young as she used to be and she can't take it."

134   "She can only give it out," Wesley said. "I'm the one that takes it."

135   His brother's pleasant face had changed so that an ugly family resemblance showed between them. "Nobody feels sorry for a lousy bastard like you," he said and grabbed across the table for the other's shirtfront.

136   From her room she heard a crash of dishes and she rushed back through the kitchen into the dining room. The hall door was open and Scofield was going out of it. Wesley was lying like a large bug on his back with the edge of the over-turned table cutting him across the middle and broken dishes scattered on top of him. She pulled the table off him and caught his arm to help him rise but he scrambled up and pushed her off with a furious charge of energy and flung himself out of the door after his brother.

137   She would have collapsed but a knock on the back door stiffened her and she swung around. Across the kitchen and back porch, she could see Mr. Greenleaf peering eagerly through the screenwire. All her resources returned in full strength as if she had only needed to be challenged by the devil himself to regain them. "I heard a thump," he called, "and I thought the plastering might have fell on you."

138   If he had been wanted someone would have had to go on a horse to find him. She crossed the kitchen and the porch and stood inside the screen and said, "No, nothing happened but the table turned over. One of the legs was weak," and without pausing, "the boys didn't come for the bull so tomorrow you'll have to shoot him."

139   The sky was crossed with thin red and purple bars and behind them the sun was moving down slowly as if it were descending a ladder. Mr.

Greenleaf squatted down on the step, his back to her, the top of his hat on a level with her feet. "Tomorrow I'll drive him home for you," he said.

140   "Oh no, Mr. Greenleaf," she said in a mocking voice, "you drive him home tomorrow and next week he'll be back here. I know better than that." Then in a mournful tone, she said, "I'm surprised at O. T. and E. T. to treat me this way. I thought they'd have more gratitude. Those boys spent some mighty happy days on this place, didn't they, Mr. Greenleaf?"

141   Mr. Greenleaf didn't say anything.

142   "I think they did," she said. "I think they did. But they've forgotten all the nice little things I did for them now. If I recall, they wore my boys' old clothes and played with my boys' old toys and hunted with my boys' old guns. They swam in my pond and shot my birds and fished in my stream and I never forgot their birthday and Christmas seemed to roll around very often if I remember it right. And do they think of any of those things now?" she asked. "NOOOOO," she said.

143   For a few seconds she looked at the disappearing sun and Mr. Greenleaf examined the palms of his hands. Presently as if it had just occurred to her, she asked, "Do you know the real reason they didn't come for that bull?"

144   "Naw I don't," Mr. Greenleaf said in a surly voice.

145   "They didn't come because I'm a woman," she said. "You can get away with anything when you're dealing with a woman. If there were a man running this place..."

146   Quick as a snake striking Mr. Greenleaf said, "You got two boys. They know you got two men on the place."

147   The sun had disappeared behind the tree line. She looked down at the dark crafty face, upturned now, and at the wary eyes, bright under the shadow of the hatbrim. She waited long enough for him to see that she was hurt and then she said, "Some people learn gratitude too late, Mr. Greenleaf, and some never learn it at all," and she turned and left him sitting on the steps.

148   Half the night in her sleep she heard a sound as if some large stone were grinding a hole on the outside wall of her brain. She was walking on the inside, over a succession of beautiful rolling hills, planting her stick in front of each step. She became aware after a time that the noise was the sun trying to burn through the tree line and she stopped to watch, safe in the knowledge that it couldn't, that it had to sink the way it always did outside of her property. When she first stopped it was a swollen red ball, but as she stood watching it began to narrow and pale until it looked like a bullet. Then suddenly it burst through the tree line and raced down the hill toward her. She woke up with her hand over her mouth and the same noise, diminished but distinct, in her ear. It was the bull munching under her window. Mr. Greenleaf had let him out.

149   She got up and made her way to the window in the dark and looked out through the slit blind, but the bull had moved away from the hedge and at first she didn't see him. Then she saw a heavy form some distance away, paused as if observing her. This is the last night I am going to put

up with this, she said, and watched until the iron shadow moved away in the darkness.

150   The next morning she waited until exactly eleven o'clock. Then she got in her car and drove to the barn. Mr. Greenleaf was cleaning milk cans. He had seven of them standing up outside the milk room to get the sun. She had been telling him to do this for two weeks. "All right, Mr. Greenleaf," she said, "go get your gun. We're going to shoot that bull."

151   "I thought you wanted theseyer cans . . ."

152   "Go get your gun, Mr. Greenleaf," she said. Her voice and face were expressionless.

153   "That gentleman torn out of there last night," he murmured in a tone of regret and bent again to the can he had his arm in.

154   "Go get your gun, Mr. Greenleaf," she said in the same triumphant toneless voice. "The bull is in the pasture with the dry cows. I saw him from my upstairs window. I'm going to drive you up to the field and you can run him into the empty pasture and shoot him there."

155   He detached himself from the can slowly. "Ain't nobody ever ast me to shoot my boys' own bull!" he said in a high rasping voice. He removed a rag from his back pocket and began to wipe his hands violently, then his nose.

156   She turned as if she had not heard this and said, "I'll wait for you in the car. Go get your gun."

157   She sat in the car and watched him stalk off toward the harness room where he kept a gun. After he had entered the room, there was a crash as if he had kicked something out of his way. Presently he emerged again with the gun, circled behind the car, opened the door violently and threw himself onto the seat beside her. He held the gun between his knees and looked straight ahead. He'd like to shoot me instead of the bull, she thought, and turned her face away so that he could not see her smile.

158   The morning was dry and clear. She drove through the woods for a quarter of a mile and then out into the open where there were fields on either side of the narrow road. The exhilaration of carrying her point had sharpened her senses. Birds were screaming everywhere, the grass was almost too bright to look at, the sky was an even piercing blue. "Spring is here!" she said gaily. Mr. Greenleaf lifted one muscle somewhere near his mouth as if he found this the most asinine remark ever made. When she stopped at the second pasture gate, he flung himself out of the car door and slammed it behind him. Then he opened the gate and she drove through. He closed it and flung himself back in, silently, and she drove around the rim of the pasture until she spotted the bull, almost in the center of it, grazing peacefully among the cows.

159   "The gentleman is waiting on you," she said and gave Mr. Greenleaf's furious profile a sly look. "Run him into that next pasture and when you get him in, I'll drive in behind you and shut the gate myself."

160   He flung himself out again, this time deliberately leaving the car door open so that she had to lean across the seat and close it. She sat smiling

as she watched him make his way across the pasture toward the opposite gate. He seemed to throw himself forward at each step and then pull back as if he were calling on some power to witness that he was being forced. "Well," she said aloud as if he were still in the car, "it's your own boys who are making you do this, Mr. Greenleaf." O. T. and E. T. were probably splitting their sides laughing at him now. She could hear their identical nasal voices saying, "Made Daddy shoot our bull for us. Daddy don't know no better than to think that's a fine bull he's shooting. Gonna kill Daddy to shoot that bull!"

161   "If those boys cared a thing about you, Mr. Greenleaf," she said, "they would have come for that bull. I'm surprised at them."

162   He was circling around to open the gate first. The bull, dark among the spotted cows, had not moved. He kept his head down, eating constantly. Mr. Greenleaf opened the gate and then began circling back to approach him from the rear. When he was about ten feet behind him, he flapped his arms at his sides. The bull lifted his head indolently and then lowered it again and continued to eat. Mr. Greenleaf stooped again and picked up something and threw it at him with a vicious swing. She decided it was a sharp rock for the bull leapt and then began to gallop until he disappeared over the rim of the hill. Mr. Greenleaf followed at his leisure.

163   "You needn't think you're going to lose him!" she cried and started the car straight across the pasture. She had to drive slowly over the terraces and when she reached the gate, Mr. Greenleaf and the bull were nowhere in sight. This pasture was smaller than the last, a green arena, encircled almost entirely by woods. She got out and closed the gate and stood looking for some sign of Mr. Greenleaf but he had disappeared completely. She knew at once that his plan was to lose the bull in the woods. Eventually, she would see him emerge somewhere from the circle of trees and come limping toward her and when he finally reached her, he would say, "If you can find that gentleman in them woods, you're better than me."

164   She was going to say, "Mr. Greenleaf, if I have to walk into those woods with you and stay all afternoon, we are going to find that bull and shoot him. You are going to shoot him if I have to pull the trigger for you." When he saw she meant business he would return and shoot the bull quickly himself.

165   She got back into the car and drove to the center of the pasture where he would not have so far to walk to reach her when he came out of the woods. At this moment she could picture him sitting on a stump, marking lines in the ground with a stick. She decided she would wait exactly ten minutes by her watch. Then she would begin to honk. She got out of the car and walked around a little and then sat down on the front bumper to wait and rest. She was very tired and she lay her head back against the hood and closed her eyes. She did not understand why she should be so tired when it was only mid-morning. Through her closed eyes, she could feel the sun, red-hot overhead. She opened her eyes slightly but the white light forced her to close them again.

166   For some time she lay back against the hood, wondering drowsily why she was so tired. With her eyes closed, she didn't think of time as divided

into days and nights but into past and future. She decided she was tired because she had been working continuously for fifteen years. She decided she had every right to be tired, and to rest for a few minutes before she began working again. Before any kind of judgement seat, she would be able to say: I've worked, I have not wallowed. At this very instant while she was recalling a life-time of work, Mr. Greenleaf was loitering in the woods and Mrs. Greenleaf was probably flat on the ground, asleep over her holeful of clippings. The woman had got worse over the years and Mrs. May believed that now she was actually demented. "I'm afraid your wife has let religion warp her," she said once tactfully to Mr. Greenleaf. "Everything in moderation, you know."

167   "She cured a man once that half his gut was eat out with worms," Mr. Greenleaf said, and she had turned away, half-sickened. Poor souls, she thought now, so simple. For a few seconds she dozed.

168   When she sat up and looked at her watch, more than ten minutes had passed. She had not heard any shot. A new thought occurred to her: suppose Mr. Greenleaf had aroused the bull chunking stones at him and the animal had turned on him and run him up against a tree and gored him? The irony of it deepened: O. T. and E. T. would then get a shyster lawyer and sue her. It would be the fitting end to her fifteen years with the Greenleafs. She thought of it almost with pleasure as if she had hit on the perfect ending for a story she was telling her friends. Then she dropped it, for Mr. Greenleaf had a gun with him and she had no insurance.

169   She decided to honk. She got up and reached inside the car window and gave three sustained honks and two or three shorter ones to let him know she was getting impatient. Then she went back and sat down on the bumper again.

170   In a few minutes something emerged from the tree line, a black heavy shadow that tossed its head several times and then bounded forward. After a second she saw it was the bull. He was crossing the pasture toward her at a slow gallop, a gay almost rocking gait as if he were overjoyed to find her again. She looked beyond him to see if Mr. Greenleaf was coming out of the woods too but he was not. "Here he is, Mr. Greenleaf!" she called and looked on the other side of the pasture to see if he could be coming out there but he was not in sight. She looked back and saw that the bull, his head lowered, was racing toward her. She remained perfectly still, not in fright, but in a freezing unbelief. She stared at the violent black streak bounding toward her as if she had no sense of distance, as if she could not decide at once what his intention was, and the bull had buried his head in her lap, like a wild tormented lover, before her expression changed. One of his horns sank until it pierced her heart and the other curved around her side and held her in an unbreakable grip. She continued to stare straight ahead but the entire scene in front of her had changed—the tree line was a dark wound in a world that was nothing but sky—and she had the look of a person whose sight has been suddenly restored but who finds the light unbearable.

171   Mr. Greenleaf was running toward her from the side with his gun raised and she saw him coming though she was not looking in his direc-

tion. She saw him approaching on the outside of some invisible circle, the tree line gaping behind him and nothing under his feet. He shot the bull four times through the eye. She did not hear the shots but she felt the quake in the huge body as it sank, pulling her forward on its head, so that she seemed, when Mr. Greenleaf reached her, to be bent over whispering some last discovery into the animal's ear.

Questions for Discussion

1. What does Mrs. May's comment about Mr. Greenleaf that "he didn't have the initiative to steal" reveal about her?

2. Who does Mrs. May feel is responsible for any success the Greenleaf boys have had? Why?

3. Why does Mrs. May get so angry and frustrated at Mr. Greenleaf? Why does she dislike Mrs. Greenleaf so intensely?

4. What does Mrs. May mean when she refers to the Greenleafs as "scrub-humans"?

5. In the confrontations between Mrs. May and Mr. Greenleaf, who wins? How?

6. Describe the relationship between Mrs. May and her sons. Why do they not appreciate her financial support and advice?

7. Mrs. May says to Mrs. Greenleaf: "Jesus...would be ashamed of you. He would tell you to get up from there this instant and go wash your children's clothes!" How do you suppose Jesus would have responded to Mrs. Greenleaf? To Mrs. May? On what do you base your answer?

8. How does Mrs. Greenleaf's prayer to Jesus as she lies on the ground foreshadow the end of the story?

9. The narrator says of Mrs. May, "She felt as if she were on trial for her life, facing a jury of Greenleafs." How does this observation define Mrs. May's relationship to the Greenleafs?

10. Mrs. May says of religion, "Everything in moderation." Would O'Connor agree? Do you agree?

11. When the bull gores Mrs. May, the narrator says, "she had the look of a person whose sight has been suddenly restored but who finds the light unbearable." Explain this passage.

THE FICTION WRITER AND HIS COUNTRY   (1957)

1   . . . I am no disbeliever in spiritual purpose and no vague believer. I see from the standpoint of Christian orthodoxy. This means that for me the meaning of life is centered in our Redemption by Christ and what I see in the world I see in its relation to that. I don't think that this is a position that can be taken halfway or one that is particularly easy in these times to make transparent in fiction.

2   Some may blame preoccupation with the grotesque on the fact that here we have a Southern writer and that this is just the type of imagination that Southern life fosters. I have written several stories which did not seem to me to have any grotesque characters in them at all, but which have immediately been labeled grotesque by non-Southern readers. I find it hard to believe that what is observable behavior in one section can be entirely without parallel in another. At least, of late, Southern writers have had the opportunity of pointing out that none of us invented Elvis Presley and that that youth is himself probably less an occasion for concern than his popularity, which is not restricted to the Southern part of the country. The problem may well become one of finding something that is *not* grotesque and of deciding what standards we would use in looking.

3   My own feeling is that writers who see by the light of their Christian faith will have, in these times, the sharpest eyes for the grotesque, for the perverse, and for the unacceptable. In some cases, these writers may be unconsciously infected with the Manichean spirit of the times and suffer the much-discussed disjunction between sensibility and belief, but I think that more often the reason for this attention to the perverse is the difference between their beliefs and the beliefs of their audience. Redemption is meaningless unless there is cause for it in the actual life we live, and for the last few centuries there has been operating in our culture the secular belief that there is no such cause.

4   The novelist with Christian concerns will find in modern life distortions which are repugnant to him, and his problem will be to make these appear as distortions to an audience which is used to seeing them as natural; and he may well be forced to take ever more violent means to get his vision across to this hostile audience. When you can assume that your audience holds the same beliefs you do, you can relax a little and use more normal means of talking to it; when you have to assume that it does not, then you have to make your vision apparent by shock—to the hard of hearing you shout, and for the almost-blind you draw large and startling figures.

5   Unless we are willing to accept our artists as they are, the answer to the question, "Who speaks for America today?" will have to be: the advertising agencies. They are entirely capable of showing us our unparalleled prosperity and our almost classless society, and no one has ever accused them of not being affirmative. Where the artist is still trusted, he will not be looked to for assurance. Those who believe that art proceeds from a healthy, and not from a diseased, faculty of the mind will take what he shows them as a revelation, not of what we ought to be but of what we are at a given time and under given circumstances; that is, as a limited revelation but revelation nevertheless.

6   When we talk about the writer's country we are liable to forget that no matter what particular country it is, it is inside as well as outside him. Art requires a delicate adjustment of the outer and inner worlds in such a way that, without changing their nature, they can be seen

through each other. To know oneself is to know one's region. It is also to know the world, and it is also, paradoxically, a form of exile from that world. The writer's value is lost, both to himself and to his country, as soon as he ceases to see that country as a part of himself, and to know oneself is, above all, to know what one lacks. It is to measure oneself against Truth, and not the other way around. The first product of self-knowledge is humility, and this is not a virtue conspicuous in any national character.

7   St. Cyril of Jerusalem, in instructing catechumens, wrote: "The dragon sits by the side of the road, watching those who pass. Beware lest he devour you. We go to the Father of Souls, but it is necessary to pass by the dragon." No matter what form the dragon may take, it is of this mysterious passage past him, or into his jaws, that stories of any depth will always be concerned to tell, and this being the case, it requires considerable courage at any time, in any country, not to turn away from the storyteller.

Questions for Discussion

1. List and explain O'Connor's statements about the grotesque.
2. According to O'Connor, what is the duty of the Christian novelist?
3. Explain O'Connor's metaphor of the dragon and the passage.

THE SEARCH FOR REDEMPTION: FLANNERY O'CONNOR'S FICTION[1]

FREDERICK J. HOFFMAN

The first impression one has of Flannery O'Connor's work is of its extraordinary lucidity; given, that is, what she expects to communicate, she does communicate it with most remarkable clarity and ease. Of course, one needs to know just what it is; she is concerned with the problem of how a writer, "by indirections, finds directions out." She has a reputation for obscurity, for not giving the expected turn to the reader, for not rewarding him for his having taken the trouble to read her.

The best statement she has given of her purpose and method is a talk she gave at the College of Saint Teresa (Winona, Minnesota) in the fall of 1960. Responding to a critic's suggestion that she is probably not a "Catholic novelist" because she doesn't write on "Catholic subjects," she said:

> The Catholic novelist in the South is forced to follow the spirit into strange places and to recognize it in many forms not totally congenial to him. But the fact that the South is the Bible Belt increases rather than decreases his sympathy for what he sees. His interest will in all likelihood go immedi-

[1]From *The Added Dimension: The Art and Mind of Flannery O'Connor*, ed. Melvin J. Friedman and Lewis A. Lawson (New York: Fordham University Press, 1977), 32–48.

ately to those aspects of Southern life where the religious feeling is most intense and where its outward forms are farthest from the Catholic.[2]

Her major subjects are the struggle for redemption, the search for Jesus, and the meaning of "prophecy": all of these in an intensely evangelical Protestant South, where the need for Christ is expressed without shyness and where "prophecy" is intimately related to the ways in which men are daily challenged to define themselves.[3] The literary problem raised by this peculiarity of "place" (though it may be located elsewhere as well, as a "need for ceremony," or a desperate desire to "ritualize" life) is neatly described by Miss O'Connor: she must, she says, define in unnaturally emphatic terms what would not otherwise be accepted, or what might be misunderstood. The sentiment (or some emotional reaction) will get in the way. "There is something in us," she said, in the same talk, "as storytellers and as listeners to stories, that demands the redemptive act, that demands that what falls at least be offered the chance to be restored."[4] But the rituals of any church are not comprehended by a large enough majority of readers; therefore,

> When I write a novel in which the central action is a baptism, I know that for the larger percentage of my readers, baptism is a meaningless rite: therefore I have to imbue this action with an awe and terror which will suggest its awful mystery.[5]

Miss O'Connor writes about intensely religious acts and dilemmas in a time when people are much divided on the question of what actually determines a "religious act." Definitions are not easy, and, frequently, what is being done with the utmost seriousness seems terribly naive, or simple-minded, to the reader. She must, therefore, force the statement of it into a pattern of "grotesque" action, which reminds one somewhat of Franz Kafka,[6] at least in its violation of normal expectations.

---

[2]Flannery O'Connor, "The Role of the Catholic Novelist," *Greyfriar* [Siena Studies in Literature] 7 (1964): 8.

[3]See Sister M. Bernetta Quinn, "View from a Rock: The Fiction of Flannery O'Connor and J. F. Powers," *Critique* 2 (Fall 1958): 19–27: "The center of all Catholic fiction is the Redemption. However mean or miserable or degraded human life may seem to the natural gaze, it must never be forgotten that God considered it valuable enough to send His only Son that He might reclaim it" (21). See *A Handbook of Christian Theology* (New York: Meridian Books, 1958), 296: "Thus the God who ransoms, redeems, and delivers Israel out of her bondage is the God who, in Christ, pays the price which restores sinful mankind to freedom and new life. In this act of redemption two interrelated theological emphases are dominant: God's *love* by which He takes the initiative, and man's sin which occasions the situation from which God redeems him."

[4]"The Role of the Catholic Novelist," pp. 10–11.

[5]Ibid., p. 11.

[6]See Melvin J. Friedman, in *Recent American Fiction*, ed. Joseph J. Waldmeir (Boston: Houghton Mifflin, 1963), 241. Friedman also cites Nathanael West, as does John Hawkes, "Flannery O'Connor's Devil," *Sewanee Review* 70 (Summer 1962): 396. Hawkes mentions an interesting conjunction of influences on himself: "it was Melville's granddaughter [Eleanor Melville Metcalf], a lady I was privileged to know in Cambridge, Massachusetts, who first urged me to read the fiction of Flannery O'Connor, and—further—[...] this experience occurred just at the time I had discovered the short novels of Nathanael West."

We have the phenomenon of a Catholic writer describing a Protestant, an evangelical, world, to a group of readers who need to be forced or shocked and/or amused into accepting the validity of religious states. The spirit of evil abounds, and the premonition of disaster is almost invariably confirmed. Partly, this is because the scene is itself grotesquely exaggerated (though eminently plausible at the same time); partly it is because Christian sensibilities have been, not so much blunted as rendered bland and over-simple. The contrast of the fumbling grandmother and The Misfit, in Miss O'Connor's most famous story, "A Good Man Is Hard to Find," is a case in point. The grandmother is fully aware of the expected terror, but she cannot react "violently" to it. She must therefore use commonplaces to meet a most uncommon situation:

> "If you would pray," the old lady said, "Jesus would help you."
> "That's right," The Misfit said.
> "Well then, why don't you pray?" she asked trembling with delight suddenly.
> "I don't want no hep," he said. "I'm doing all right by myself."

Another truth about Miss O'Connor's fiction is its preoccupation with the Christ figure, a use of Him that is scarcely equalled by her contemporaries. The Misfit offers an apparently strange but actually a not uncommon observation:

> "Jesus was the only One that ever raised the dead, . . . and He shouldn't have done it. He thown everything off balance. If He did what He said, then it's nothing for you to do but thow away everything and follow Him, and if He didn't, then it's nothing for you to do but enjoy the few minutes you got left the best you can—by killing somebody or burning down his house or doing some other meanness to him. No pleasure but meanness," he said and his voice became almost a snarl.

One of Paul Tillich's most effective statements has to do with the relationship of man to Jesus Christ, in volume two of his most impressive *Systematic Theology*. "Jesus Christ," he says, "combines the individual name with the title, 'the Christ,'" and "Jesus as the Christ is both a historical fact and a subject of believing reception."[7] Perhaps more important, and in line with his attempt to review theology in existentialist terms, Tillich says, "Son of God becomes the title of the one in whom the essential unity of God and man has appeared under the conditions of existence. The essentially universal becomes existentially unique."[8]

---

[7]*Systematic Theology* (Chicago: University of Chicago Press, 1951), vol. 2, 98. It is interesting that many of Miss O'Connor's characters want to "see a sign": that is, they want Christ's divinity manifested directly. The Misfit is such a one; Hazel Motes of *Wise Blood* struggles against a Christian mission on the grounds that Christ as God has never revealed Himself; Mr. Head and his grandson have a remarkable experience of illumination when they see the plaster statue of a Negro (in "The Artificial Nigger"); and the young Tarwater of *The Violent Bear It Away* has a "voice" (variously called "stranger," "friend," and "mentor") who tries to deny Jesus because there has been no "sign" of Him.
[8]Ibid, p. 110.

As all of us know, the crucifixion was historically a defeat for the messianic cause, whose followers wanted Jesus literally to triumph over the Romans and to restore the Jews to power. But it was also, and most importantly, the source of grace; or, as Tillich puts it, "'Christ' became an individual with supernatural powers who, through a voluntary sacrifice, made it possible for God to save those who believe in him."[9] It is this latter figure whom Miss O'Connor's heroes spend so much energy and time denying; many of them also are on the way to accepting Him.

In almost all of Miss O'Connor's fiction, the central crisis involves a confrontation with Jesus, "the Christ." In the manner of Southern Protestantism, these encounters are quite colloquial and intimate. The "Jesus" on the lips of her characters is someone who hovers very near; with Him, her personalities frequently carry on a personal dialogue. The belief, or the disbelief, in Him is almost immediate. He is "Jesus" made almost entirely human and often limited in theological function. Man often "takes over" from Him, or threatens to do so. The so-called "grotesques" of Flannery O'Connor's fiction are most frequently individual souls, imbued with religious sentiments of various kinds, functioning in the role of the surrogate Christ or challenging Him to prove Himself. Not only for literary strategy, but also because such manifestations *are* surreal, Miss O'Connor makes these acts weird demonstrations of human conduct: "irrational" in the sense of their taking issue with a rational view of events. . . .

The figure of Jesus haunts almost all of her characters. They are, half the time, violently opposed to Him (or, in His image, opposed to some elder who has tried to force His necessity upon them), because they cannot see beyond themselves to a transcendent existence. Hazel Motes and Tarwater are both haunted by the rank and stinking corporeality of their elders, whom they have seen dead and—in dream or in reality—been obliged to bury.

These experiences serve to make them resist the compunctions of grace and turn away from the prospects of redemption. But the alternative is singularly uninviting. Hazel Motes has no success preaching the new church "without Christ," and Tarwater finds his uncle either pathetic or farcical. They react violently at the turn of their journeys: Motes blinds himself in a mixture of the desire for penitence and the will to prove his courage; Tarwater has recourse both to water and fire, from mixed motives of defiance and fear.

This clarity of vision comes in part from Miss O'Connor's having herself had a satisfactory explanation of these religious drives, and therefore being in a position to portray the violent acts of those who possess the drives but are unable to define goals or direct energies toward them. The grotesqueries of her fiction are in effect a consequence of her seeing what she calls "the Manichean spirit of the times," in which the religious metaphors retain their power but cannot be precisely delineated by persons driven by the necessities they see in them. Violence, in this setting,

---

[9]Ibid, p. 111.

assumes a religious meaning; it is, in effect, the sparks caused by the clash of religious desire and disbelief.

> The novelist with Christian concerns will find in modern life distortions which are repugnant to him, and his problem will be to make these appear as distortions to an audience which is used to seeing them as natural; and he may well be forced to take ever more violent means to get his vision across to his hostile audience.[10]

The matter becomes extremely delicate, in the light of her other observations: for example, that "Art requires a delicate adjustment of the outer and inner worlds in such a way that, without changing their nature, they can be seen through each other."[11] This remark suggests that the religious metaphors are, above all, psychological realities; that these are dramatized in the desperate struggles her characters have, at one time against but finally in the mood of accepting the Christian demands and rewards. When Miss O'Connor makes the following summary of her vision, therefore, she is simply defining the ultimate goals of her characters, whether they have been represented or not in the act of achieving them.

> I see from the standpoint of Christian orthodoxy. This means that for me the meaning of life is centered in our Redemption by Christ and that what I see in the world I see in its relation to that. I don't think that this is a position that can be taken halfway or one that is particularly easy in these times to make transparent in fiction.[12]

[10]"The Fiction Writer and His Country," in *The Living Novel, A Symposium*, ed. Granville Hicks (New York: Macmillan, 1957), 162–63.
[11]Ibid, p. 163.
[12]Ibid, p. 162.

VIOLENCE AND THE GROTESQUE[1]

GILBERT H. MULLER

Miss O'Connor's technical strategy in the application of violence is to show precisely how the destructive impulse brings the horror of man's grotesque state home to him. Because this kind of violence is religiously motivated, it differs considerably from those gratuitous forms of violence in fiction which are used to exploit current tastes. The violence in Miss O'Connor's fiction is real, yet it has a metaphysical dimension arising from man's loss of theological identity. If in terms of effect this violence partakes of exaggeration, sensationalism, and shock, it nevertheless raises problems which treat the moral and religious order of the universe. The author was quick to distinguish violence in the pure grotesque from its presence in other adulterated forms. She objected to the attempts of some critics to place her within the School of Southern Degeneracy, and

[1]From *Nightmares and Visions: Flannery O'Connor and the Catholic Grotesque* (Athens: University of Georgia Press, 1972), 72–98.

she asserted that every time she was associated with this gothic beast she "felt like Br'er Rabbit stuck on the tarbaby."[2] She was emphatic in denying that she utilized violence as a gothic contrivance, remarking that gothicism was a degeneracy which was rarely recognized as such. Fictional assessment of violence in ethical and theological terms is one quality which sets the grotesque apart from a gothic aesthetic, since the violence implicit in gothic fiction has little moral foundation: it exists to satisfy itself and does not serve as a meaningful vision. Conversely, when violence appears in the grotesque, as in the hecatomb which frames "A Good Man is Hard to Find," it is used to suggest the lack of any framework of order in the universe; it reinforces the grotesque by working *against* the ideals of social and moral order to create an alienated perspective. . . .

Acts of violence in Miss O'Connor's fiction illuminate a world of continual spiritual warfare. The Misfit in "A Good Man Is Hard to Find" kills people not because he enjoys murder, but because like Meursault in *L'Etranger* he is powerless to control his impulses when faced with the indifference of the universe. His act of violence is not totally irrational because its manifestation points toward the spiritual disorder of the world. The Misfit therefore is not presented merely as a pathological murderer, but as a crazed latter-day anchorite, wielding a gun instead of a gnarled club. Still he is without grace, and he complicates the grotesque situation of the Bailey family as well as of himself by ignoring the cardinal commandment—"Thou shalt not kill." Slaughter is a part of the natural process, and modern war demonstrates that it is a part of the human process as well. Yet from a Catholic perspective the injunction placed upon man not to kill is a radical one—and one which must be obeyed. In human and theological terms to kill is to lapse into evil.

Ultimately violence in Flannery O'Connor's fiction forces the reader to confront the problem of evil and to seek alternatives to it. Because Miss O'Connor uses violence to shock her characters (and readers), it becomes the most singular expression of sin within her grotesque landscape. Time and again in her stories violence intrudes suddenly upon the familiar and seemingly secure world and turns the landscape into a secular hell. Thus the slow pastoral seduction planned by Hulga in "Good Country People" is disrupted by Manley Pointer's outrages against her body and spirit. Similarly Julian's world in "Everything That Rises Must Converge" suddenly becomes chaotic when violence ruins what previously had been an innocuous, albeit distasteful, bus trip. Obviously violence of this type occupies a crucial position in making the world seem strange, terrifying, and deprived of grace. As Frederick J. Hoffman remarks in what is perhaps the finest book on violence in contemporary literature, "Surprise is an indispensable element of the fact of violence in modern life. A carefully plotted pattern of expected events has always been needed to sustain a customary existence. A sudden break in the rou-

[2]"Some Aspects of the Grotesque in Southern Fiction," in *Mystery and Manners*, ed. Sally Fitzgerald and Robert Fitzgerald (New York: Farrar, Strauss & Giroux, 1969), 38.

tine challenges the fullest energy of man's power of adjustment. Suddenness is a quality of violence. It is a sign of force breaking through the design established to contain it."[3] . . .

The violent figure frequently becomes an extension of the world that he inhabits. His spiritual desolation is reflected in the very landscape through which he moves, for in this landscape images of violence and disorder prevail. Flannery O'Connor pays strict attention to scene, to landscape in disarray, because by being a reflection of the interior self of the character, it assumes a complicity, despite its supposedly inanimate nature, in the bizarre disjunctiveness of the universe. The potentially violent and hostile landscape is a mark of Miss O'Connor's fiction and serves as a vivid image of a worldly Inferno. And of course with the author, a violent landscape is almost by extension a grotesque landscape. In other words the reductive power of violence unleashes essentially grotesque currents of feeling. In "A Good Man Is Hard to Find," for instance, the deranged mind of the Misfit, and the secular impulses of a family preordained to destruction, find an objective correlative in images of a distorted and inimical wasteland. The twisted setting in the story mirrors spiritual and moral decay, and the peaceful rhythms usually associated with a family trip are continually undercut by the images of destruction which are juxtaposed against it. Cotton fields with small islands of graves, the dirt road with "sudden washes in it and sharp curves on dangerous embankments," the line of woods which gapes "like a dark open mouth" create a landscape which is menacing and alien. Even the diner the family stops at for lunch is a precarious structure, lacking any solidarity or harmony, and is presided over by a sadistic monkey that bites fleas between its teeth with delight. Here, and in other stories such as "A Circle in the Fire" (1954) and "A View of the Woods" (1957), the environment impinges upon characters and is potentially violent: physical description consistently works in opposition to people's desire for harmony and order, and it also affords a premonition of disaster.

Flannery O'Connor's technique of description is terse and severe, tending always toward the impressionistic, in which landscape is distilled into primary images that render a picture of a violent physical world. Miss O'Connor, a watercolorist of considerable talent, concentrates upon line and color to evoke locale swiftly; considering the premium she placed upon the stark outlines of her fiction, any profusion of description would work against her overall narrative intentions, and thus she relied upon the synthetic method of drawing objects in the physical world together to achieve a concentrated effect. Whether describing the countryside or the metropolis, the author is carefully selective and austere, building up a pattern of imagery and frequently counterpointing these images in order to create a charged atmosphere and to make a thematic statement.

[3]*The Mortal No: Death and the Modern Imagination* (Princeton, N.J.: Princeton University Press, 1964), 292.

The landscapes depicted in Flannery O'Connor's fiction seem to intensify man's propensity for physical, psychological, and spiritual violence. In a world deprived of meaning, in a world which is ruthless and cruel, the only consolation which her characters have is an ability to exploit others through violence. Arson, rape, mutilation, suicide, and murder are some of the extremes of violent behavior that appear in O'Connor's fiction, and what is curious about these manifestations is that characters such as Rufus, Shiftlet, and the Bible salesman actually take pleasure in wanton acts of destruction. This pleasure in violence, a phenomenon which preoccupies many behavioral scientists and such philosophers as Karl Jaspers, deprives men of being, although the malefactors believe mistakenly that it serves to define their lives. As such, violence becomes a manifestation of the demonic, understood in the medieval sense of the word, as a force which obliterates identity and damns human beings. Even the Misfit, with his debased logic, comprehends a world without meaning, and in such a world, where it is impossible to attach one's loyalties to any overriding ethical or theological position, the only pleasure and consolation for the lack of meaning must come from amoral acts of violence. Unlike the Hemingway protagonist, who attempts to channel violence into such acceptable institutions as war, hunting, and the bullfight, the characters in O'Connor's fiction rarely seek social justification for their destructive acts. If any justification is required, it exists in the universe itself, in a fallen and grotesque world where a perverse Creator forces man to attest to his damnation every moment of his life.

At the root of violence in Miss O'Connor's fiction lies this concept of the depraved and potentially lethal world, in which the destiny of man is seemingly imposed upon him by a vaguely apprehended source. W. M. Frohock in *The Novel of Violence in America* cogently explains the dilemma facing the violent protagonist: "The hero finds himself in a predicament such that the only possible exit is through infliction of harm on some other human. In the infliction of harm he also finds the way to his own destruction. But still he accepts the way of violence because life, as he sees it, is like that: violence is man's fate." Life—in the existential sense of the word—is like that, even at the most mundane level. . . .

The entire strategy of violence in Flannery O'Connor's stories of the grotesque is to reveal how complicity in destruction carries men away from God, away from that center of mystery she was constantly trying to define and which Catholics term grace. This is why violent death is the one act of paramount importance in O'Connor's fiction: it serves to define evil in society. The feud violence that exists in "Greenleaf," for example, is clearly delineated not only in terms of class hatreds but also in terms of good and evil. The pervasive aura of violence in this story reveals the corruption of the will and the need of grace. This kind of violence is a form of spiritual punishment, and in "Revelation," "The Lame Shall Enter First," and many other of her tales it is admonitory. Mrs. May obviously disdains the low origins and primitive ways of the Greenleafs as well as their newly acquired success. With their fox-colored eyes and dark crafty faces, they seem to be cast in the mold of Faulkner's tenacious Snopes clan. Yet the Greenleafs, as their name implies, are in basic harmony with nature. More importantly Mrs. Greenleaf embraces a variety of worship which is reminiscent of early mystery religions based on vegetation and on earth. Her mortification and ecstasy, which are appalling to Mrs. May, are ways of experiencing the spiritual through nature; moreover, Mrs. Greenleaf thinks in terms of a primitive salvation for mankind. Mrs. May's failure to understand the rituals that Mrs. Greenleaf enacts before her eyes signifies the modern failure to integrate religious mystery with culture. It also explains why Mrs. May's destiny of necessity must be violent, because hers is the fate of the individual who is estranged from the basic forces of the community and from grace.

Another indication of evil in "Greenleaf" is the alienation that exists among the members of the May family. Estrangement within the family is of course one of the most common forms of sublimated violence and overt feuding in Flannery O'Connor's fiction. In "Greenleaf" Mrs. May's two sons loathe their mother and hate each other as well. Wesley, the younger of the brothers, bears spiritual kinship to Hulga, Asbury, and other effete intellectuals who are encountered frequently in Miss O'Connor's stories. He is sickly, sardonic, ill-natured, and rude—a vacuous academician consumed by a brutal sense of determinism. Scofield is much coarser than his brother; patterned after Jason Compson, he displays a marked degeneracy in his manners. Both brothers are perversely preoccupied with their mother's death, and this act suggests how individuals can consciously choose to perform or to wish acts of evil. . . .

The ultimate battle is against evil—and against the devil incarnated in concrete forms—in the figure of a Bible salesman, an old man with a peppermint cane, or a friendly figure in a panama hat. In this situation violence becomes a mark of faith. As the noted historian Jacques Ellul has written, "The whole meaning of the violence of love is contained in Paul's word that evil is to be overcome with good (Romans 12:17–21). This is a generalization of the Sermon on the Mount. And it is important for us to understand that this sermon shows what the violence of love is. Paul says, 'Do not let yourself be overcome by evil.' This then is the fight— and not only spiritual, for Paul and the whole Bible are very realistic and see that evil is constantly incarnated."[4]

The violence of love is synonymous with faith, and only this sort of violence is effectual in face of the grotesque. Characters like Thomas in

[4]*Violence: Reflections from a Christian Perspective* (New York: Seabury, 1969), 172–73. I am indebted to Mr. Ellul for his concept of love as a spiritual force and also for his cogent explanation of the incarnation of spiritual forms. The latter, of course, is standard Catholic doctrine. Miss O'Connor, for instance, in referring to Christ rather than the devil, states, "Christ didn't redeem us by a direct intellectual act, but became incarnate in human form, and he speaks to us now through the mediation of a visible Church. All this may seem a long way from the subject of fiction, but it is not, for the main concern of the fiction writer is with mystery as it is incarnated in human life" (*Mystery and Manners*, 176).

"The Comforts of Home" and Hulga in "Good Country People" fail to recognize the true battle. But others accept it reluctantly, undergo violence and suffering, and rage successfully against the absurd. All O'Connor's protagonists are denied basic needs. A few perceive the grotesque nature of the world; they demand recognition of their own worthiness in this world, sense the futility and frustration arising from this need, and consequently embrace what seemingly is the most lucid course of action—violence. In short, whether we are speaking of the Misfit or of Francis Marion Tarwater, this kind of antagonist revolts against an unsatisfactory state of affairs. He indulges in violence because he wants to see if faith can survive. Flannery O'Connor considers all her characters—and the society they compose—as ruled by this harsh geometry of religion. Against the potential framework of religious order she sets violence and disorder, and then she tries to resolve the ambiguity by forcing her characters into those varieties of extreme situation which test the limits of the grotesque.

The extreme situation reveals the paradoxical nature of violence in O'Connor's fiction. Young Bevel's drowning in "The River," for instance, permits him a unique salvation, as does the drowning of Bishop in *The Violent Bear It Away*. Guizac's crucifixion in "The Displaced Person" is also his sacrifice for a depraved culture. The Misfit's murders reveal the horror of a world without Christ. The flagellation of O. E. Parker, the physical assaults of Manley Pointer, the depravities of Rufus Johnson are all examples of violence operating from the shifting and highly ambiguous perspective, for we see in these stories that the infliction of pain and suffering leads to purification and self-knowledge, either for the victimizer or the victim, or for that curious figure, like the Misfit and Shiftlet, Tarwater and Hazel Motes, who is both victim and victimizer, who initiates violence only to discover that it rebounds upon him. . . .

Revelation of the true kingdom—or, as Miss O'Connor called it, the true country—is a primary concern in her fiction, and it is for this reason that she utilized motifs of violence to get at the incongruous nature of reality and to reveal the vitality of the grotesque as technique and vision. In a paragraph that has become a classic statement on the value of the grotesque, one can see how the concept of violence fits into Flannery O'Connor's vision:

> The novelist with Christian concerns will find in modern life distortions which are repugnant to him, and his problem will be to make these appear as distortions to an audience which is used to seeing them as natural; and he may well be forced to take ever more violent means to get his vision across to this hostile audience. When you assume that your audience holds the same beliefs you do, you can relax a little and use more normal ways of talking to it; when you have to assume that it does not, then you have to make your vision apparent by shock—to the hard of hearing you shout, and for the almost-blind you draw large and startling figures.[5]

[5]*Mystery and Manners*, pp. 33–34.

The world of the grotesque, whether we are talking about O'Connor and Faulkner, Thomas Pynchon and James Purdy, or Vladimir Nabokov and Jorge Borges, is a world of distortions—in character and landscape and also in spirit. Demonic and violent acts therefore are a means whereby we can fix the precise limits of meaning in this alien and mysterious world. At the same time violence becomes a source of hope whereby man can transcend his grotesque condition. As Miss O'Connor has written in reference to "A Good Man Is Hard to Find":

> We hear many complaints about the prevalence of violence in modern fiction, and it is always assumed that this violence is a bad thing and meant to be an end in itself. With the serious writer, violence is never an end in itself. It is the extreme situation that best reveals what we are essentially, and I believe these are times when writers are most interested in what we are essentially, than in the tenor of our daily lives. Violence is a force which can be used for good or evil, and among the things taken by it is the kingdom of heaven. But regardless of what can be taken by it, the man in the violent situation reveals those qualities least dispensable in his personality, those qualities which are all he will have to take into eternity with him; and since the characters in this story are all on the verge of eternity, it is appropriate to think of what they take with them.[6]

In the broadest sense, to reflect on the grotesque is to reflect upon violence: essentially the modern condition reveals that violence creates a perilous balance between the horrifying and the ludicrous. Flannery O'Connor knew that the grotesque, by descending into the claustral world of violence, of the incongruous and irrational, contains within itself the germ whereby a transcendent order can be discovered: in an ambiguous world you look for absolutes, and when you face the unknown you invariably recognize spiritual mystery. Violence speaks to us about our experience of such a world by revealing the human need for something beyond a purely secular vision.

[6]Ibid., pp. 113–14.

Understanding Flannery O'Connor: Greenleaf[1]
Margaret Earley Whitt

"Greenleaf" is the earliest story of the collection [*Everything That Rises Must Converge*] and her first top-award recipient for the O. Henry. It was published first in the summer 1956 issue of the *Kenyon Review*, appearing a year after the publication of *A Good Man Is Hard to Find*. The story was also included in *The Best American Short Stories of 1957*. "Greenleaf" joins three earlier stories in featuring a lone woman who seeks to protect her farm property and to control the people who live on it. Mrs. May has hired some "good country people" to assist in working the land,

[1]From *Understanding Flannery O'Connor* (Columbia: University of South Carolina Press, 1995), 121–26.

whose irritating ways irk the stubborn landowner. "Greenleaf" is O'Connor's last story that features a hard-working farm-owning woman who has problems of control with both the hired help and her children. As a transition story, it is the first of four stories that O'Connor writes about a single mother struggling with an adult still-at-home son.

All of the single threads of the story line—Mrs. May's struggling dynamics with her sons, their constant comparisons to the more successful Greenleaf boys, the striking contrast of Mrs. May's and Mrs. Greenleaf's responses to religion—converge in the momentary dilemma of this story: the scrub bull that has come to court Mrs. May and to invade her property and her herd of cows. This bull has connections with the myth in which Zeus disguises himself as a white bull and carries off Europa to Crete,[2] as well as biblical connections to the holy hunt of the unicorn, where the courting animal becomes a symbolic Christ figure that pierces Mrs. May through the heart with a deeper understanding of Christian reality.[3] Before the bull and Mrs. May have a final and fatal meeting, O'Connor makes clear the limited perspective with which Mrs. May views the world.

Mrs. May, "a small woman with pale near-sighted eyes and grey hair that [rises] on top like the crest of some disturbed bird" (503), has sole responsibility for the success of her farm. Her two adult sons—thirty-six-year-old Scofield, the "nigger-insurance salesman" (504), and Wesley, the younger intellectual—have one thing in common: "neither of them care[s] what happen[s] on the place" (504). Both sons verbally abuse their mother at every opportunity. Scofield suggests that she can easily be replaced by some "nice fat farm girl" wife that he will choose upon her death (505). Wesley, who causes her "real anxiety" (509), "wouldn't milk a cow to save [her] soul from hell" (510). As a final blow in this daily barrage, he also strips his mother of parenthood; to Scofield, he taunts: "Neither you nor me is her boy" (517). Mrs. May, on the other hand, remains foremost a Southern mother. She feels a duty to her sons and takes whatever treatment they offer. Although she does not eat breakfast with them, she sits "with them to see that they [have] what they wanted" (504). She makes sure that Wesley maintains his salt-free diet. Mrs. May's downfall, however, is that she constantly reminds her sons how great her own sacrifice has been, and she stands at the ready with plenty of good advice about how they could improve their lives. For example, if Scofield would sell "decent insurance, some *nice* girl would be willing to marry [him]. What nice girl wants to marry a nigger-insurance man?" (505). Mrs. May does not hear her racist comments. Her simplistic worldview extends to every aspect of her life and beyond: "I'll die when I get good and ready" (511).

[2]See John C. Shields, "Flannery O'Connor's 'Greenleaf' and the Myth of Europa and the Bull," *Studies in Short Fiction* 18 (1981): 421–31. Shields presents a detailed study of how the myth's portrayal of the union of sky and earth informs a reading of this story.

[3]See Kristen Meek, "Flannery O'Connor's 'Greenleaf' and the Holy Hunt for the Unicorn," *Flannery O'Connor Bulletin* 19 (1990): 30–37. Meek's essay makes a biblical connection with the events of the story.

Mrs. May's relationship with her sons is complicated by the success of her hired people's twin sons, a few years younger than her own. Mr. Greenleaf, her employee for fifteen years, is always quick to point out what his sons would do by comparison. Because of the rigid class structure that so permeated the South of O'Connor's day, the upper-class land-owning Mrs. May has to endure the comeuppance from a lower class that refuses to adhere to old rules: "As scrub-human as the Greenleafs were, [Mr. Greenleaf] never hesitated to let her know that in any like circumstance in which his own boys might have been involved—O. T. and E. T. Greenleaf—would have acted to better advantage" (507). Mrs. May is prepared to credit anything outside and beyond the boys with their elevated place in the world: the war that sent them to Europe, where they could "disguise" themselves in uniform (507), court and marry French women who do not realize they are "murder[ing] the king's English" (508), and "manage" to get wounded and receive a pension (508). She takes credit as well for her contribution to their rise and wants to hold it over them when she discovers that the scrub bull on her property belongs to O. T. and E. T. She reminds Mr. Greenleaf, with a repetition of the first person possessive pronoun, that his boys "wore my boys' old clothes and played with my boys' old toys and hunted with my boys' old guns"; further, for Mrs. May, those twins had access to "my pond . . . , my birds . . . , my stream" (518). Mrs. May is without subtlety or nuance; her only deficiency is that she is a woman: "You can get away with anything when you're dealing with a woman. If there were a man running this place" (519). She tolerates her own sons' fighting: "Nobody feels sorry for a lousy bastard like you" (517), shouts one to the other before the dishes crash, the table is overturned, and the boys are grabbing each other's shirtfronts. Because her own boys fight, Mrs. May is sure the Greenleafs do, but according to their hired help, "they never quarls. [...] They like one man in two skins" (516). Mrs. May and her sons are denied the superiority she feels is the privilege of her class.

Mrs. May carries her superficial thinking into matters of religion as well. She has reduced religion to attending church, a "proper" place for her boys to "meet some nice girls" (510). Mrs. Greenleaf, by contrast, takes religion to the "preoccupation" of "prayer healing" (505). By clipping appropriate stories from the paper—rape, burned children, escaped criminals, train wrecks, plane crashes, and movie star divorces—burying them in the ground, and praying over them, she is in direct communication with the healing power of her Jesus: "Oh Jesus, stab me in the heart!" (506). Mrs. May is shocked at her first encounter with Mrs. Greenleaf's ritual, for her Jesus is a practical man. She knows that Jesus would be "*ashamed*" of Mrs. Greenleaf and tell her to "get up from there this instant and go wash [her] children's clothes!" (507). Mrs. Greenleaf, with her backwoods fundamentalist perspective, values the mystery of Jesus as deity, accepting his power to right the wrongs of the day. Mrs. May understands the language of the Christian religion where it fits in society, and how she might work it to her advantage, but "she [does] not, of course, believe any of it [is] true" (506).

Into the melee of these relationships comes the bull, an "uncouth country suitor" (502). The May boys have the advantage over their mother as Scofield knows it is the Greenleaf boys' bull. The Greenleaf boys have no intention of reclaiming the bull and are willing to let Mrs. May assume the responsibility of having their father kill it. As O'Connor closes in on the activity of the killing scene, she advances the bull to symbol. From the opening scene with his Christlike hedge wreath "caught in the tips of his horns" (501), his presumptuous invasion of her property, until the end when he picks up the pace of his wooing, no longer the "patient god" (501), the bull, as an image of Christ, crosses at a "slow gallop" and then, suddenly, is "racing toward her" (523). Until this point in the story, Mrs. May has set her own schedule and controlled her world, but now the bull changes everything. Mrs. May moves from "freezing unbelief" (523), not just her response to the bull's charge but her response to religion's role in her life, to "the look of a person whose sight has been suddenly restored but who finds the light unbearable" (523). O'Connor uses repetition of language and image to draw the parallel between Mrs. May's response to the earlier scene of Mrs. Greenleaf in her prayer healing and the charging bull. With Mrs. Greenleaf, Mrs. May stops still: "The sound was so piercing that she felt as if some violent unleashed force had broken out of the ground and was charging toward her" (506). Facing the bull, Mrs. May remains perfectly still: "She stared at the violent black streak bounding toward her as if she had no sense of distance" until his horn "sank until it pierced her heart" (523). Mrs. Greenleaf's figurative chant for Jesus to stab her in the heart takes on a literal action as the bull stabs Mrs. May through her heart. O'Connor has set up the scene of the "last discovery" of Mrs. May, as she whispers "into the animal's ear" (524), to be the beginning of understanding her own limitations. O'Connor suggests that Mrs. May reaches the Teilhardian Omega Point of God in the "unbearable" light.

Works Cited

Meek, Kristen. "Flannery O'Connor's 'Greenleaf' and the Holy Hunt of the Unicorn." *Flannery O'Connor Bulletin* 19 (1990): 30–37.

Shields, John C. "Flannery O'Connor's 'Greenleaf' and the Myth of Europa and the Bull." *Studies in Short Fiction* 18 (1981): 421–31.

Greenleaf's Destructive Bull and Paean to the

Common Man

Quimby Melton IV

1   Beyond a field of common travail lies a structure of human

social interaction which divides worker and owner. Though both

work the field, though both love and bleed in the common field, one owns and one does not. Taken with the linguistic, financial, familial-historic, and general physical appearances that divide human society, this owner versus worker relationship seems quite unjust. The relationship between the owner/worker and his quasi-serf employee is nowhere better seen than in the rural, post-reconstruction American South. This "rigid class structure that so [permeates] the South of O'Connor's day" (Whitt 1388) serves as a perfect canvas for the story "Greenleaf," which exists as a song of praise for the worker and the injustice he and his family face from the higher social strata: a stratification upon which O'Connor seemingly frowns throughout the story as she lauds the common man. O'Connor is not content, however, simply to frown upon this injustice; rather, through the use of the bull as both symbolic and manifest character of Greenleaf, she destroys those who would denounce the common man.

2   O'Connor uses the Greenleafs as her embodiment of the common man, i.e., the common laborer. She fixes the social standing of her characters early in the story as Mrs. May is awakened by a bull, crowned by a wreath of greenery, chewing on a bush directly outside her bedroom window. She immediately curses her worker, Mr. Greenleaf, for "[leaving] the lane gate open" (O'Connor 1358) as if all problems on her farm are Mr. Greenleaf's fault. However, directly before this curse, O'Connor has defended the Greenleafs by establishing their safety in the strange dream Mrs. May is having. In this apocalyptic dream, the bull is eating Mrs. May's entire surroundings. Her whole world, as it is in this dream, is in danger of being consumed by this bull. "[E]verything from the beginning of [Mrs. May's] fence line up to the house" has been eaten by the bull; and now, "with

the same steady rhythm" (1357-58), the bull is threatening the house, Mrs. May, and her two sons. The bull, a continued symbol of destruction throughout the story, threatens to destroy Mrs. May's world much like the Apocalyptic Dragoons of the Christian faith: a faith "she [does] not, of course, believe. . .[is] true" (1361). The Greenleafs, symbols of the simple faithful as well as of the common worker, will be safe from the apocalyptic bull's destruction "on a little island all their own in the middle of what [was Mrs. May's] place" (1358). By placing the bull as a symbol of apocalyptic destruction, O'Connor establishes the saved and the damned: the "salt-of-the-earth" (Matthew 5:13) Greenleafs will be saved while the hypocritical and judgmental Mays will be consumed.

3   O'Connor also praises the simple faith of the common laborer. The Greenleafs will be saved from the apocalypse because their earthly religion is a living, active one built on the pillars of prayer, practice, and faith. Mrs. Greenleaf buries the evil she sees in the daily paper not to overlook the negativity but to give to God of the problems of the world. Like Donne's cry, "Batter my heart, three person'd God," Mrs Greenleaf cries to God to "stab [her] in the heart" (1361) as she prays over the buried newspaper clippings. Mr. Greenleaf also shows his religious faith when he softly mentions to Mrs. May, "I thank Gawd for ever-thang" (1367). The Greenleafs are not ashamed of their faith and do not believe, as Mrs. May does, that Jesus, "should be kept inside the church building" (1361). Mrs. May respects religion but is "shocked at. . .Mrs. Greenleaf's ritual...and understands...where [the Christian religion] fits in society and how she might work it to her advantage" (Whitt 1368); but she does not understand the

spiritual fervor of the Greenleafs. Even O. T. and E. T. Greenleaf's children will be "sent to a convent school and brought up with manners" (1362) by the religious faithful. Ironically, through hard work, sacrifice, and the final honing of religious education, the common worker Greenleafs will have achieved in two generations the status of "society," which Mrs. May has lost in one.

4   O'Connor praises the unity of the Greenleafs and uses the symbols of unity versus disunity to further separate the class of worker and owner/worker. The Greenleafs are unified as a family unit. They have peace not strife; Mrs. May notices that "over the years [the Greenleafs] had been on her place, [they] had aged hardly at all." The Greenleafs have "no worries, no responsibilities" and live "like the lilies of the field" (1363). The Greenleaf boys, O. T. and E. T., are "fine boys" (1364), according to Mrs. May; according to O. T. and E. T.'s hired hand, they never quarrel as if they are "one man in two skins" (1362). Unity pervades the Greenleafs in religion, brotherhood, and peace. The May boys, however, are "as different...as night and day" (1359) and there is constant strife in the May family. The boys fight with their mother and are dissatisfied with life; as a culmination of the strife, Scofield and Wesley physically assault one another at the dinner table. Through the great corpus of evidence O'Connor supplies, it is obvious that the unity and simple wants and needs as well as faith of the Greenleafs afford their happiness. O'Connor praises them for this by showing the alternative to their happiness through the form of the Mays and their disunity and resulting strife.

5   Between the families, there is also strife, not unity. Mrs. May does not like the Greenleafs, and Mr. Greenleaf is quite sardonic in his unspoken way towards his boss. The bull as destroyer furthers the separation of the families. Because of the bull, Mrs. May judges and dislikes the Greenleafs even more, and Mr. Greenleaf further despises his boss. The bull sweeps in and destroys the already fragile relationship that exists between owner/worker and worker, thus pushing reconciliation further from their grasp. The bull also creates the final destruction as he destroys the person and life of Mrs. May. Mrs. May, by the end of the story, has created for herself a grand inferiority to the Greenleafs. She feels she is neither appreciated for her work nor any longer in control of her farm. By commanding the destruction of the bull, Mrs. May feels that she will reassert her authority and destroy the bull before he both symbolically and literally destroys her. Ultimately, the bull is reasserted as destroyer and true authority, for he takes the life of Mrs. May and teaches her the truth of life and religion. The bull is enrobed in a Christ-like persona as he stabs Mrs. May's heart in a final revelation of Mrs. Greenleaf's prayer. She who supposed she would "die when [she got] good and ready" (1364) is taught a lesson on the fragility of life by a pesky, charging bull with an aversion to automobiles. The light she sees is radiant because of the religious and mortal lessons Mrs. May has learned about truth and the mutability of life.

6   In the final moments of life, Mrs. May realizes the truth and inherent goodness of the Greenleaf way of life. She forgets her petty worries and injuries and, for an instant, is human. In the moment of death, she is neither rich nor poor, neither

simple nor educated. Mrs. May transcends the temporal aspects of life and is shown the truth of life: all are human and equally susceptible to death and resurrection. Ultimately both bull and Mrs. May are destroyed by the common man in the form of Mr. Greenleaf in a final cry of victory and praise for the worker over the oppressive elite. Victory, at the end of "Greenleaf," belongs to the Greenleafs: O'Connor's final affirmation of the superiority of the common man.

[New page]   Works Cited

Henderson, Gloria Mason, Bill Day, and Sandra Stevenson Waller, eds. <u>Literature and Ourselves</u>, 5th ed. New York: Longman, 2006.

O'Connor, Flannery. "Greenleaf." In <u>The Complete Stories</u>. New York: The Noonday Press, 1998. 311–34. Henderson, Day, and Waller. 1357–74.

Whitt, Margaret Earley. <u>Understanding Flannery O'Connor</u>. Columbia: University of South Carolina Press, 1995. 121–26. Henderson, Day, and Waller. 1386–89.

Suggestions for Exploring, Writing, and Persuading

1. In a documented essay, argue that the grandmother is responsible for the deaths of her family members in "A Good Man Is Hard to Find."
2. Using one or more of the critical essays in the casebook, discuss some of the things that the bull, appearing at the beginning and the ending of "Greenleaf," might symbolize.
3. Write an essay comparing Mrs. May's sons with E.T. and O.T.
4. What are the standards Mrs. May uses to classify people?
5. In a character analysis, illustrate how Mrs. May's jealousy, rage, self-pity, and obsession with control define her character. Use one or more of the secondary sources in the casebook.
6. In an essay discuss the symbolism of the names in the O'Connor stories.

7. Using the critical essays and at least two characters from the O'Connor stories, discuss what the characters substitute for a belief in God.

8. Compare Mrs. May to the grandmother. Using the secondary sources in this casebook, show how Flannery O'Connor might regard them.

9. O'Connor is especially skillful at using irony to portray the problems faced by people who lack a sincere belief in God. Using the critical essays in this casebook and O'Connor's essay, discuss her use of irony in "A Good Man Is Hard to Find" and/or "Greenleaf."

10. Each of the protagonists in the O'Connor stories reaches a point where she realizes her personal inadequacy and helplessness. O'Connor might say that each experiences divine grace. After reading O'Connor's stories and the critical essays in this casebook, write a researched paper analyzing the nature of divine grace as manifested in O'Connor's fiction.

11. O'Connor has a good eye for the humorously grotesque, seemingly irrelevant details that realistically characterize people. Carefully examine her use of such detail in the stories, and explain how her grotesque descriptions of people express her religious vision. Use the critical essays in the casebook.

12. Examine O'Connor's use of vivid descriptive detail and its often ironic implications in one or both of the stories. Then write an essay analyzing or classifying this aspect of her style.

13. The Misfit's father said of him, "'It's some that can live their whole life without asking about it, and it's others has to know why it is, and this boy is one of the latters.'" Compare this Misfit to one or more other questioning misfits such as Mrs. May or Ozzie Freedman.

14. Argue that the Misfit is the only character in "A Good Man is Hard to Find" who has truly thought about the meaning of life.

15. The Misfit and the bull are violent agents of change in O'Connor's protagonists' lives. With the help of the critical sources in the casebook, discuss what each appears to represent in O'Connor's Christian vision.

16. What attitudes toward Christianity do the characters exemplify? Which of the characters are most clearly followers of Christ?

Quest: Suggestions for Writing

1. Several characters in this section think they have all the answers they need about the meaning and purpose of their lives. In an essay, show how these characters are made to see that they, like others, are pilgrims or seekers, that their lives must be a continual quest for meaning.

2. Taking into consideration that the goals of the quest can be defined in a number of ways, choose two selections from this unit and show how they define two different aspects of the quest.

3. Using at least two of the works in this unit, discuss one quest or several quests that seem to be universal.

4. The individual's search for his or her own identity is a major theme in literature. Using two stories and/or the play from this section, write a documented essay on this theme.

5. Write an essay on one of the following topics: quests of the modern individual, religion and the quest, my quest, or my search for identity.

Quest: Writing About Film

1. Action-adventure movies are among the most popular for today's audiences. In these movies, often a single character overcomes unbelievable odds to accomplish a task or quest. Compare the characters and events in a popular action-adventure movie to the characters and events in one of the short stories in this unit. How do they differ in their portrayals of quest?

2. *The Lord of the Rings* is a marvelous film about a mythical quest. The heroes of the film—Frodo, Gandalf, and Strider—are based on ancient models, and they differ from contemporary heroes like Neo, Trinity, and Morpheus in *The Matrix* trilogy, although both sets of characters face foes of superhuman capabilities. Compare characters from *The Lord of the Rings* with the heroes of a quest film in a modern setting. Consider their emotional ranges, their abilities, the characters' independence or dependence, and their understanding of themselves. If you have read *The Lord of the Rings*, compare one of the characters as portrayed in the books with the same character in the film.

3. Many films—old and new—have used the quest theme. From older classic films such as *Citizen Kane* to more recent ones like *Under the Tuscan Sun, Hidalgo, Tomb Raider, Cold Mountain, X-Men II, Kill Bill (Vol. 2), Finding Nemo, Sea Biscuit, Finding Neverland, Million Dollar Baby*, and *Spiderman II*, films portray the struggles of individuals in search of a variety of goals such as their own identity, wealth, power, sense of belonging, happiness, justice, or even home. Select one film in which the main character has embarked upon a quest and write an essay detailing the goals of the character and the steps by which he or she attempts to reach that goal.

4. Other films depict the quest as a group endeavor, for example, films like the two trilogies discussed in the appendix on film: *The Matrix* trilogy and *The Lord of the Rings* trilogy. Many movies such as *Saving*

Private Ryan, Miracle, El Dorado, and *Pirates of the Caribbean* also portray group quests. Select one of the movies that portrays a group quest and analyze (1) the ways in which the characters do or do not cooperate in the search for their goals, (2) the success or lack of success that the group achieves and the reasons for success or failure, or (3) the worthiness or unworthiness of the goals of the quest.

Appendix A

CRITICAL APPROACHES TO LITERATURE

In the twentieth century, literary theorists have developed a variety of approaches to literature that are more narrowly defined than the three general approaches described in our introduction—text-oriented, author-oriented, and reader-oriented approaches. These critical approaches to literature often overlap and frequently have more than one name. Some of the most important are formalism (or New Criticism), biographical criticism, historical criticism, sociological criticism, psychological criticism, archetypal (or mythic) criticism, gender criticism, deconstructionist criticism, and cultural studies criticism.

Formalism

Formalism, or **New Criticism,** describes the work of literature as the sum of its parts. Formalism developed in part as a reaction to what its proponents saw as an excessive emphasis on autobiographical, historical, and sociological criticism. Formalists reject analysis of a work of literature that is based on whether or not the author achieved his or her goals, labeling this form of analysis the "intentional fallacy" because it is based on what is unknowable and irrelevant. Similarly, they reject reader-response criticism as irrelevant and overly subjective, labeling it the "affective fallacy." Instead, formalism focuses on a close reading, or **explication,** of the literary work itself.

Formalism also emphasizes an examination of the words and patterns within the work, especially as they are used as images and symbols. Formalists often examine the ways in which irony and paradox are used to develop theme. For example, a formalist approach might consider the ways in which the words, images, symbols, paradoxes, and irony effectively create the tone in Edwin Arlington Robinson's "Richard Cory" or might examine Flannery O'Connor's use of dialogue between the Misfit and the grandmother in "A Good Man Is Hard to Find" to reveal the shallowness of the grandmother's definition of goodness and the emptiness of both characters' lives without divine grace. Furthermore, formalism recognizes the differences in genres and may examine whether a work fulfills the expectations for its genre.

Biographical Criticism

Other critics examine influences outside the literary works in order to analyze and interpret the works. **Biographical criticism** focuses on how the author's life has influenced the work. Biographical critics believe that a reader who is familiar with details about the author's family, education, career, or religion may know which clues to look for in interpreting a work or may have added insight into the meaning of that work. For example, knowing that Ursula K. Le Guin's father was an anthropologist may aid the reader in understanding the moral implications of the worlds she creates in her novels and in "The Ones Who Walk Away from Omelas." Similarly, knowing about the differences between Alice Walker's background and her mother's life may help the reader to understand how members of the same family can have such differing lifestyles and views of heritage in "Everyday Use."

Historical Criticism

Historical criticism reminds readers that authors are influenced by the cultural milieus in which they live and that their works reflect these milieus. Historical critics contend that the reader who knows details about the specific time, place, and events depicted in a work can read it with greater understanding. For example, a historical critic might examine the history of share-cropping in the post–Civil War South in order to elucidate meaning in Arna Bontemps's "A Summer Tragedy." Historical critics also examine the ways in which interpretations may have changed over the life of the work.

Sociological Criticism

Sociological criticism begins by examining the cultures and beliefs of the time during which a work of literature was created. Believing that art imitates life, sociological critics point out that both the artist and the work of art are directly influenced by the artist's values, belief systems, roles, mores, and demographics. Sociological critics may consider the way in which the work reflects its society. For example, these critics might compare the drug culture as it existed within the musical community in Harlem during the 1930s and 1940s with James Baldwin's description in "Sonny's Blues" or might compare the concept of a "fit mother" in the second half of the twentieth century in the United States with Madison Smartt Bell's portrayal of the mother in "Customs of the Country"—a story that suggests a sociological approach even in its title. Because sociological critics believe that an author's knowledge of and concern for his or her audience invariably affect that author's work, they also assess information about that audience.

One sociological approach, **Marxist criticism,** takes an exclusively political point of view in interpreting literature. Marxist critics believe that every work of literature, whether intentionally or unintentionally, promotes or espouses a political ideology. Thus, a Marxist critic might examine Arna Bontemps's "A Summer Tragedy" to demonstrate the unfortunate consequences of the capitalist exploitation of labor. For the Marxist critic, the ideal work of art will make readers aware of the class struggle so as to encourage them to side with the proletariat.

Psychological Criticism

Psychological criticism is based mainly on the theories of Freud and his followers. Freud himself began the psychological examination into the nature of creativity, describing it as an escape into fantasy that can provide insights for both the author and the reader. Freud's theory that a work of literature is an expression of the author's unconscious desires is the basis for much psychological criticism; a good example is the critical discussion of Charlotte Perkins Gilman's portrayal of a mental breakdown in "The Yellow Wallpaper."

Another psychological approach suggested by Freud's work focuses on using psychoanalytic techniques to interpret fictional characters. For example, a critic interpreting Shakespeare's tragedy *Othello* might use Freud's concept of the id, ego, and superego to explain Iago's vengeful and destructive actions. A psychological critic might study the reasons for the interactions between the migrant workers in Eric Skipper's "The Runt."

Archetypal Criticism

Another approach, which grew partially out of psychological theory, is **archetypal,** or **mythic, criticism.** In his theory of the "collective unconscious," Swiss psychologist Carl Jung asserted that all humans unconsciously share in the total experience of the human race. Jung also suggested that this collective unconscious reveals itself in the form of "archetypes," universal symbols or images that occur repeatedly in creative human history. These recurring archetypes often take the form of opposites, such as light and dark or heaven and hell. An example of the light–dark dichotomy is found in the imagery in James Baldwin's "Sonny's Blues." A few archetypal figures include the hero; the villain; the woman as earth mother, platonic ideal, or temptress; and the scapegoat, of which Ursula K. Le Guin's "The Ones Who Walk Away from Omelas" presents an excellent example.

Jung's theory of archetypes reinforces Sir James George Frazer's earlier work, published in *The Golden Bough*, the first anthropological study of myth and ritual. Through his studies, Frazer found that cultures with no common history and no physical contact have similar mythic explanations for their experiences and for the natural phenomena that puzzle them. For example, almost all cultures believe in a destruction myth, the most frequent describing the destruction of humanity by flood. The death–rebirth myth, which follows the cycle of the seasons and the life cycle, is the most universal of archetypes. Other archetypal motifs include the quest, the initiation, and the journey. The final thematic section of *Literature and Ourselves* includes examples of the quest. The Jesuit priest in Arthur C. Clarke's "The Star" seeks to reconcile his religious faith with his newly acquired scientific knowledge, and Ozzie in Philip Roth's "The Conversion of the Jews" searches for intelligent answers to his religious questions. The initiation rite is illustrated by Miranda's growing awareness of her femininity and her mortality in Katherine Anne Porter's "The Grave." Because the archetypal or mythic approach examines recurring universal figures and motifs, it offers an effective way to compare literature over the centuries.

Gender Criticism

Gender criticism explores the effects of gender roles, attitudes, and dynamics on writers, works, and audiences. Feminist critics in particular believe that literature previously has been written primarily by men for men, and they see one of the roles of their criticism as including women writers and the "woman's point of view." These critics have also focused attention on previously neglected works by women authors, including Zora Neale Hurston and Charlotte Perkins Gilman. Virginia Woolf pointed out difficulties faced by women writers who had not been allowed to reach their creative potential; her essay "Professions for Women" tells of the Victorian woman's struggles with the "Angel in the House." Feminist critics also attempt to expose hidden sexual biases in literary works and to help readers identify and question stereotypes of women. Feminist criticism of Emily Dickinson has revealed previously overlooked meanings in many of the poems. Almost all of the works in the Men and Women thematic unit could be subjects of gender criticism. For example, Kate Chopin's story describes a situation faced by a woman who lives in a world dominated by men, and the poems of Edna St. Vincent Millay and Janice Mirikitani illustrate some of the new freedoms of women.

Gender criticism has not, however, been exclusively feminist criticism. In response to feminist criticism, other critics have begun to examine the impact of male authorship, the masculine point of view, and male stereotypes on literature. David Osborne in "Beyond the Cult of Fatherhood" examines the expanding roles of modern men. Gender criticism can shed new light on older works or influence new authors.

Deconstructionist Criticism

Like the formalists, the **deconstructionists** begin with a close reading of the text; however, the deconstructionists believe that textual explication is not enough. These critics believe that accurate readings of a work entail a distrust of both the language and the author. Such a reading may result in a discovery that the work has no organic unity and indeed no distinct boundaries. The deconstructionist critic views the work and the author with great skepticism and unravels the text in order to uncover hidden truths that even the author may not be aware of. For example, a deconstructionist critic might contend that the attitudes of other characters toward Othello reveal a racism beyond that directly stated in Shakespeare's play and perhaps beyond anything that Shakespeare himself had imagined. Deconstructionists attempt to expose the inability of the text to achieve closure or to reveal "objective" truth. In other words, deconstructionists claim that the work cannot validate itself.

Cultural Studies Criticism

Cultural studies applies the methods of literary criticism to previously overlooked or undervalued areas of our common everyday culture. Cultural studies "reads," or critically analyzes, more than just literary texts; cultural studies critics examine both textual and nontextual subjects from beyond the scope of the literary canon. Semiotics (the science of signs) allows cultural critics to "read" common objects as texts in order to investigate the underlying meanings and assumptions that guide our day-to-day existence. For example, wearing blue jeans to the mall is now considered acceptable, whereas wearing blue jeans to church might be seen as disrespectful. Blue jeans still convey some of the rebel reputation they possessed during the 1950s, when blue-jean-wearing teenagers were often viewed as juvenile delinquents. The negative connotations have faded sufficiently so that blue jeans are common casual wear, yet enough of the old interpretation remains that few would find them acceptable in more formal situations. The people frowning at the teenagers wearing blue jeans in church are, in a way, performing a semiotic analysis of their clothing and reading them as disrespectful. Cultural studies critics are interested in how the underlying meanings of common objects and practices are created and conveyed. From fast food to fashion trends, from punk rock to hip-hop, from television commercials to romance novels, cultural studies calls into question the dividing lines between "high" and "low" art and literature while investigating the assumptions that shape our attitudes and behaviors.

When applied to literary texts, cultural studies analysis seeks to clarify the contexts in which any literary work is composed and understood. A critic analyzing Joyce Carol Oates's "Where Are You Going, Where Have You Been?" from a cultural studies perspective might investigate aspects of 1960s youth culture in the story such as rock'n'roll, fashion, and teen slang in order to gain a deeper perspective of the character of Connie. A critic might utilize lyrics from rock songs of the time to illustrate the nature of the "glow of slow pulsed joy" that Connie feels when she listens to the music. Many popular songs of the period resonate with sexual double entendres, and Connie herself is beginning to explore a newfound sexuality as part of her defiance of parental authority. Further, a cultural studies critic might interpret Arnold Friend, with his promise of sexual violence coupled with an awkward use of teen slang and mock-worship of rock'n'roll, as a representation of Connie's own insecurities and fears regarding her disavowal of her family's values and behaviors. In sum, a cultural studies critic is willing to go outside the boundaries of the text in order to explore the contexts in which a literary work is conveyed or portrayed.

Appendix B

WRITING ABOUT FILM: *THE MATRIX* AND *THE LORD OF THE RINGS* AS CASE STUDIES

PATRICK MCCORD

Film and Literature: a Guide for Thinking and Writing

This section is designed to teach you how to think critically about film, how to apply some of the terms you know from literature to film, and how to use the conventions of writing critically about film and film adaptations. We will rely on Andy and Larry Wachowski's film *The Matrix* (1999), J. R. R. Tolkien's novel *The Fellowship of the Ring*, and Peter Jackson's 2001 adaptation, *Lord of the Rings: Fellowship of the Ring* for examples and models.

Difference in Story-telling Media

Both movies and literature are media for communicating stories. This textbook is largely dedicated to methods for analyzing and writing about the way written texts—literature—affect us, but it's important to think about audiovisual texts like movies, television, and video games analytically, too. In fact, many of the skills you learn for thinking about literature are directly transferable to film, TV, and video.

Consider the differences between stories in literature and those on film: when you read, you don't really make a movie in your head. As the authors of this book have observed earlier, the meaning of words is suggested by sound, imagery, tone, implication, and association. These mental stimulations work in complex ways to create an impression in the reader's mind—a story or a poem. But audiovisual narratives don't use abstract words to create impressions; they act directly on our perceptions, telling us stories with photography, digital imaging, and sound recording. So instead of imagining a story based on reading—our interpretation of word-symbols—we actually see and hear the real-appearing characters as images and sounds that look very much like our life experiences.

This appendix will help you to think and write more clearly about films, television, and video. In critical thinking about audiovisual narratives (movies, television, video), we can use most of the same formal methods we use to write about literature: character, setting, plot, theme, and, although it's trickier, point of view. However, because film is narrated in photographic and sound images and not in words, we need to use different vocabulary and analytic devices for discussing the sound and light information a film presents.

Consider the Differences

The following passage is from the beginning of J. R. R. Tolkein's fantasy-adventure, *The Fellowship of the Ring*. It occurs while Frodo, the main character, is talking to Gandalf, a great Wizard, deciding to take charge of a magical Ring on which the fate of his world, Middle Earth, may hang:

> He did not tell Gandalf, but as he was speaking, a great desire to fol-
> low Bilbo flamed up in his heart—to follow Bilbo, and even perhaps
> to find him again. It was so strong that it overcame his fear: he could
> almost have run out of there and then down the road without his hat,
> as Bilbo had done on a similar morning long ago. (61)

The words tell us what Frodo is thinking and feeling as he talks, and, although it's a very short paragraph, it tells us a great deal about Frodo's character traits and helps set up the story-to-come. By telling us what he is thinking, this paragraph shows us that Frodo is receptive to ideas; he is impulsive; he has great courage in his heart and loves Bilbo; he feels a connection to the past, and he desires a sense of mission. This passage also foreshadows Frodo's journey, which will take up the next 1,000 pages of text, and suggests the direction that he must go to grow and change in the course of the narrative-to-come. As a character, he seems young, and this may very well be a story in which he grows up as he learns from his mistakes, masters his impulses, and plans with more thought. By the end of his journeys he will have metaphorically learned "to take his hat when leaving the house." Notice that these are all impressions of Frodo's *thinking* created by the words of text, which a movie could not show us.

Yet movies show us characters just as rich in traits and just as complex in emotions. However, because they can show us only character surfaces with photography and sound recording, we often overlook the ways movies create deep stories. The task of art generally is to create new feelings in us by revealing depths and complications in life that we normally don't notice. Films can touch our deeper feelings in subtle ways; and the art of movie-making is in the techniques of filming, editing, scripting, acting, and designing visual and sound effects. Before outlining these techniques, however, let's look at the main differences between the way we experience the story written and the story shown on screen and the way those differences affect us.

Exercise:

Break the class into groups of three or four. Half the groups should write a brief passage from a short story as it would appear in film (without using voiceover): you can use dialogue, camera position, music, or any other filmic technique to make your points. The other half should take a short scene from a commercial or film and write from an interior character voice what is going on. Try to convert all the information on the screen to character thoughts or feelings.

Interior Writing/Exterior Filming—Five Main Differences

The key difference between written and filmed stories is that the experience of a written story is interior while a movie is an exterior event. When we read, we create a story in our imaginations, and because words have shades of different meanings to different readers, every reader will imagine a slightly different story. Also, in many written texts, we are able to directly access the thoughts, beliefs, and feelings of characters. In both these ways, literature is "interior." Movies, however (unless they use voiceover), show us the way things look or sound, so movies are essentially exterior experiences.

Now let's look at these fundamental contrasts in more detail.

There are **five main differences** between audiovisual and literary narratives. If you pause to think about film and literature, most of these differences are obvious, but because we often *don't* think about how media create images and ideas, we need to bring them to mind.

1. Literary narratives are written in *words* that are, for the most part, *abstract* or *arbitrary* signs that convey *only* symbolic meaning. The English word "dog" refers to certain furry, four-legged canines; the French word "*chien*" means essentially the same thing. Both words stimulate our brains to think about dogs, but there is no direct connection from word to brain except that it is the symbol we learned to associate with dogs. Films, on the other hand, are recorded or constructed *sound and light images* taken from the real world. A dog on film refers to very specific dog qualities. Benji is a small terrier-mix; Scooby-Doo is a Great Dane.

2. Literary narratives are organized using only *the single information track of language*. Because words are powerful signs that can suggest complex associations, the single track of writing can stimulate us to imagine whole story-worlds (the fictional world of the narrative). In contrast, audiovisual narratives use photography and sound recording to organize five information *tracks—dialogue, situation,* and *music sound tracks, picture track,* and *written track*. Although our minds tend to unify our experience of the separate tracks just as we unify our sense-perceptions in real life, to perform analysis, we need to break down the different tracks the same way we would break down a poem into rhythm, imagery, symbol, and music.

3. Reading stories or poems requires effort and concentration. The story takes place entirely in your imagination; you make associations between words to create characters, settings, and actions in your mind. On the other hand, films are self-propelled; they unspool before us with the ease of dreaming. And because we enter their story-worlds using the same perceptual abilities we use in daily life, everyone gets the

same perceptual story information; however, not everyone will pay the same kind of attention to the images nor will each of us make the same associative meanings out of the image and sound symbols.

4. Written stories are ancient forms of communication going back to the invention of the alphabet, while film is comparatively modern. Written stories can seem timeless, but movies age rapidly. Indeed, the latest methods of film production make even films as recent as the 1990s look a bit dated, but a good translation of Homer's *Iliad* can still feel quite fresh in our imaginations.

5. Literature is generally the language of a single writer, perhaps working with a few friends and editors, so sometimes we pay special attention to the author; however, in order to record the sounds and images of a film, vast teams of artisans are organized by a director and production team; usually hundreds but sometimes thousands of people work on a single film. Directors are considered the "authors" (*auteurs*) of films, but they usually don't write the screenplay and are really more like generals organizing a military campaign than like lonely scribblers in a world of thought.

Exercise:
Divide the class into groups.

Group 1—Problem: How do images carry symbolic value? This group selects a TV show that most of the class will know and outlines ways that the actors and events on the show symbolize issues in American culture today (hint: *The Simpsons* symbolizes various kinds of normal American family problems and relationships).

Group 2—Problem: How can we recognize all the tracks in audiovisual narrative? This group takes a television commercial that has characters speaking and music and looks to find out how many tracks of meaning are possible to recognize.

Group 3—Problem: How can we pay the same attention to a film as to a poem? This group takes a short clip from a famous film like *Citizen Kane* and treats each shot as a basic carrier of meaning. How does each shot have special significance? Rewrite each shot as a line of poetry (use special language, metaphor, rhyme, etc).

Group 4—Problem: How do film images and word images affect our sense of time and place? This group agrees on a film from the 1980s, like *Ferris Bueller's Day Off* or *The Breakfast Club*, and catalogues all the ways that it seems dated by today's standards. Then find a passage from a recent translation of *The Iliad* that seems especially vivid.

Group 5—Problem: Who works on film? This group looks at a sequence from a blockbuster to find each element (lights, costumes, make-up, casting, and so forth) and lists all the designers and assistants it took to get to make that sequence. Then imagine who is on the other side of the camera from the actors and what they are doing during the shots.

What Do Differences Mean?
Differences between film and literature affect the way we think about the possible meanings and effects of the two media. As you have learned from

this book, meanings are not always easy to understand and are seldom simply on the surface of a story. Here are some of the problems embedded in the difference between literary and audiovisual narratives.

Literary narratives come to us as "important." Because literary narratives *already* make us think abstractly as we translate word-symbols to imaginary images, we might think that literature is naturally the more abstract and connotative medium. Because of its symbolic delivery system and the effort it takes to read, literature seems to *require* a certain amount of analytic interpretation. Moreover, because of the use of a single track of words, we may think the author is speaking directly to us as we read. Finally, because literature requires concentration and is often associated with "old" stuff, young people can get impatient with translating words into imaginary worlds when it's so easy to simply switch on the TV or go to the cinema to see a prefabricated story-world.

In contrast, because movies are easy and fun to watch, we can think that they're "just entertainment" and that they don't affect our understanding of the world. Because everyone gets the same information at the same pace in a movie, we may think that the meanings are "obvious" and that there's really nothing to analyze or interpret. Finally, because films seem so contemporary and are often consciously constructed to make money, it's easy to dismiss them as "Hollywood eye-candy."

If you have had any of these considerations, reflect on the following: like movies, much of "great literature" was popular and was often profitable "entertainment" when it was written. Even today, millions of "literary" novels are sold every year, and because the books are popular, many are made into movies. Although the words of a story and images of a movie are perceived by different parts of the brain, *when we analyze stories—whether cinematic or literary—we mobilize the same parts of the brain;* so, when it comes to understanding why we have thoughts and feelings about literature and movies, we work with similar mental tools. Yes, words may *seem* more challenging to decipher or interpret, but if you learn to concentrate as if you were reading while you are watching a movie, you'll discover you can "read" the connotative implications of the film images in much the same way as you can read a printed page. In fact, this appendix is designed to help you "read" in this way. Finally, just as every word in a short story or novel was carefully chosen by a writer, every image in a film was carefully created by teams of artists and their assistants. Movies have a distinct design in which all the details of costume, setting, acting, and camera work have been carefully planned or selected by the director, a designer, or an editor. Movies are not "natural" or accidental creations; they are fabulously complicated works of art. The best "reading" of a film will account for as many details and nuances of the images and sounds as possible.

A final point: we think of ourselves, of our lives, in narrative terms—you are the main character in *The Story of [Your Name]'s Life.* It is a fascinating and epic tale with many events, settings, and characters seen from your first-person point of view (as well as from a third-person point of view when you recall the past or imagine the future). But stop to consider how you learned to think this way. The way we conceptualize our lives as stories is learned from and determined by other stories—models—by which we gauge ourselves, learn appropriate behavior, and derive our values. Therefore, it is important to be conscious of the potential meanings of our "entertainments," whether literary or cinematic, because these stories can profoundly affect our lives. In fact, sometimes the analytic or interpretive methods we use in analyzing these narratives can be useful in considering our own behaviors as we make decisions about what we want and who we are.

Tools for Interpreting Film

When we *interpret* a written story, we focus on the single information track of the writing: What do the words mean? How are they organized? What do they sound like? What images do they conjure? How do they work as an artistic system of meaning?

We need to be able to *perform similar focused operations* with the many tracks of film and to look at cinematic images with the same attention you pay to words in a poem. If you know how to organize cinematic images into bits of information in the same way you organize your reading of a poem into verses, images, and rhymes, you can quickly learn to see the art of filmmaking.

Recall that there are five information tracks in a movie. Your skill as an critical thinker about movies begins when you train yourself to simply separate each track in the back of your mind as you spectate—actively watch—a film:

a. The *photography track* shows the characters and events (this track may also include special visual effects or computer-generated images). Because we are visual beings, this is the most dominant track, and most movies make perfect sense if you carefully observe only the photographic track. All camera movement is part of the photography track.

b. The dialogue track is the characters speaking the words of the screenplay. We usually judge good and bad acting primarily by how sincere or spontaneous actors appear speaking words someone else has written for them.

c. The *situation soundtrack* is any incidental noise that occurs during the action such as a door closing, a car crash, or a pistol shot (these sounds are usually manufactured in a special acoustic design studio). Sometimes, the sound of a band or a radio that we can see on the photography track will start on the situation soundtrack but then will merge with the music soundtrack.

d. The *music soundtrack* is any music that accompanies the images of action. This can be scored—written for orchestra—or be mixed from pop music, but the soundtrack is usually added to assist the audience in feeling a more intense emotional response to the action on screen. Love scenes are accompanied by soft, sweet music while action scenes are underscored by a driving beat.

e. Sometimes, on the photography track, *written words are shown* either in the story-world—like newspaper headlines or traffic signs—or, as in the case of early silent movies, titles or cards appeared between shots to explain the film. In any case, both the dialogue track and the written track require us to amplify the images of the film language using interpretive skills.

The art of moviemaking is the special way that information on all five tracks is carefully designed to influence our feelings and our unconscious thoughts as we watch the film. All production teams include special designers for camera, film editing, light, sound, music, setting, costumes, and properties as well as acting and dialogue coaches, location scouts, and computer and graphic artists to make sure that the movie has a maximum impact on our senses, thoughts, and emotions. Once you've learned to separate the five information tracks of a movie, you can start to pay attention to what the camera does, how the film stock is then edited (cut and spliced together), and how design details—the *mise en scène*—supplied by lights, sets, props, costumes, and actors create meaning.

Exercise:
Divide the class into groups to play a game of addition. Each group will perform each exercise, then pass it to a new group so that everyone is adding to another group's ideas all the time.

First, each group will write a short exchange of dialogue between two or more characters in which the characters express strong desires to do or get something. (Dialogue soundtrack). Write only the words of dialogue with no further explanation.

Pass this to the next group. This group will supply a situation soundtrack (remember, no picture exists, so characters may be doing strange things in strange settings, which noises will reveal).

Pass this on. The next group will supply the music sound track; you may include instructions as to what emotional tone the music is emphasizing or possibly what new note the sound adds to the scene as written so far. Any music is possible, depending on the effect you want it to have, pop to classic rock to jazz or classical. You may wish just to describe a certain kind of scored music ("Trumpets blare to a racing beat; suddenly a clarinet screams as the other sounds fall away…silence.").

Finally, a group will break the script into shots and then write out directions for camera—angles, framing, movement—and write descriptions of the characters.

Read your concoctions to each other.

Camera
Although we use lots of terms to describe camera work and editing, you probably already know many of them. With a little practice, you'll notice a basic logic to the way image systems work, and you'll be able to coordinate these terms with the kinds of interpretation you did with literary texts. If you try to memorize terms in *italics*, you'll be able to focus better on what the camera, the editors, the actors, and the designers are doing. The technical terms will be followed by analysis of Andy and Larry Wachowski's 1999 science-fiction blockbuster, *The Matrix*, so you can see how to write critically.

Shot, Sequence, Scene—Plot and Narrative Purpose
Just as the *word* is the basic element of written language, the *shot* is the basic cinematic element. A shot is just what the camera sees in one "look" or one continuous film exposure; a movie is a series of shots that our brains link logically together. Shots can be quite brief, or they can last a long time, but each shot is created to supply definite *narrative information*. Each shot has a specific story-telling purpose and is a building block in the complete story.

A shot's duration, camera angle or movement, lighting, kind of film, and acting and design elements are all part of its narrative information. When you examine a shot, notice how all the details of the visual and audio tracks work together to create an image-message; then consider how that shot relates to the movie as a whole. Shots are linked together by *cuts* (so called because the film stock is cut with scissors or a razor and spliced together by editors to make the final version of the movie out of hundreds or thousands of shots).

In *The Matrix* (Andy and Larry Wachowski, 1999), the first shot of Neo (Keanu Reeves) shows him lying face down by his computer screen. On the screen we notice newspaper articles about Morpheus. This shot then cuts to another angle on Neo and, as we watch, the screen writes out, "Wake up, Neo…" and in the next shot, he does. Denotatively, the shots simply show us that Neo has fallen asleep at his computer and that it might have a mind of its own; connotatively, however, this first shot sequence sets up the movie's main themes. It foreshadows the basic conflict of the film—man versus computer—and it also suggests that Neo is "asleep" to the workings of the Matrix and that in the course of the movie he will have an "awakening."

Just as words are organized into larger structures like sentences, paragraphs, and scenes or chapters, shots are organized into *sequences* and *scenes*. When you write about film, you will want to refer to specific shots, sequences, or scenes to focus your reader's attention.

A *scene*—as it is in drama—is an event that occurs continuously at one physical location; scenes usually have one or two sequences. A *sequence* is a series of linked shots that show one continuous action or a continuous conversation: there are two general kinds of sequences, *action sequences* and *dialogue sequences*;

We see two sequences of shots in the first scene at Neo's apartment. The first sequence shows him waking up by his computer—an *action sequence* using camera and situation sound tracks to focus on activity and the appearance of words on the computer screen. This symbolizes Neo's overall character development in the film: he will "wake up" to his true nature as The One. The next sequence shows his conversation at the door when he decides—like Alice—to follow the white rabbit. This is a *dialogue sequence* in which camera and editing help us to focus on the words of the dialogue track, which turn out to be important foreshadowing: "Hallelujah. You're my savior, man. My own personal Jesus Christ!"

Usually, a single scene is divided into shots and the shots may be organized into just one or two sequences at one location, but sometimes a sequence will range over several scenic locations. One kind is a *chase sequence*; another kind is a *montage sequence*, in which a series of emotionally connected scenes that suggest a changing relationship are linked with a continuous musical background.

The first *action sequence* in *The Matrix* follows Trinity from her cell phone conversation in the Heart o' the City Hotel through her fight with the cops. However, this sequence is *cross-cut* with another sequence that shows the arrival of the Agents in the street below and their progress through the building. Eventually, both sequences come together in the thrilling chase scene over the rooftops until Trinity escapes from the Agents at the phone booth.

Exercise:
To really see what the camera is doing, turn the sound off as you watch some scenes from a movie (try to select a character-focused movie, maybe *Training Day* or *Almost Famous*). After watching a modern film, watch a black and white classic without sound. *Citizen Kane, To Kill a Mockingbird,* or *The Magnificent Ambersons* are good choices. If you have time, you could compare these viewings to a silent film like Charlie Chaplin's 1922 hit, *The Gold Rush.*

The plot of a narrative is all the information the movie directly shows us in the order in which we see it (a flashback may provide information that occurred before the first scene but is revealed later in the plot). Movie plots are divided into scenes (or sometimes sequences) the same way scenes are divided into shots. Just as each shot is a story building block, so each scene has been planned for specific purposes. Each scene in a movie will serve one or two of the following purposes:

1. Introduction of setting and characters
2. Explanation of state of affairs
3. Initiating event that changes in the state of affairs
4. Emotional response or statement of a goal by the main character (protagonist) in reaction to initiating event
5. Complicating actions or barrier to goal, opposition by antagonist character
6. Conflict and outcome
7. Reactions to outcome

In a feature-length film, depending on the complexity of a plot, you will see that these chains of events repeat themselves in and out of sequence throughout a story; although we'll tend to see more of 1, 2, and 3 in the early going when we need to get *exposition*, or background information, and more of 4, 5, 6, and 7 as we come to know our characters' desires and the conflicts they cause as the movie builds toward a *crisis* or final conflict.

When beginning your analysis of a film, try to see what the purpose of a scene is and recognize how the various artistic choices assist that purpose.

You can see how Trinity's and Neo's first scenes at the hotel and the apartment are *introducing* us to their characters. When they meet, their scene at the club explains a *state of affairs*, and Neo's scene with his boss at the office continues to explain his state of affairs as well as to show us Neo's traits. However, the delivery of the cell phone is an *initiating event* that changes the state of affairs and gives Neo a chance to make choices. Similarly, at the end of the film, when the Agents capture Morpheus, this scene also acts as an initiating event that causes Neo and Trinity to *respond* by deciding to rescue him. Their shootout in the lobby begins a series of *complicating actions* leading to the martial arts *conflict* between Neo and Agent Smith. Now, interestingly, the *outcome* of that conflict is that Neo dies; however, Trinity's emotional response then initiates a new change of affairs that sets up Neo's final conflict in which he sees the Matrix and defeats Agent Smith.

Exercise:
Break into groups. Each group should select a setting from around the school, then decide on a genre like sci-fi or horror to explore. Now invent

two characters who are appropriate both for the genre and the setting—a protagonist, who has a strong goal, and an antagonist, who will oppose that goal. You may also decide on allies for either character. Briefly outline in steps 1–7 a full narrative cycle. The stronger the characters' motivations, the more interesting your plot will be.

Framing

Once you notice shots, sequences, scenes, and events, you need to look for the way the camera frames images to create emphasis or stimulate emotional response. As a general rule, a shot will focus on just a character or two to bear important plot information. The camera will center the important information within a T-shaped area in the middle 40 percent of the frame. Almost all the time we spend watching a movie, we are concentrating on this area called the T-bar; however, you will want to move your attention around the frame because even small details outside the T-bar often are designed to underscore themes.

Shots frame the action in roughly three distances:

Close-up is usually used to show a face that nearly fills the frame, with the background out of focus. Close-ups create a sense of intimacy or intensity. Sometimes close-ups frame an object or gesture to focus us on a particular possibility, action, or motif.

Medium shot is a shot of a character or characters from the knees or waist up in a specific setting. Medium shots generally show how characters relate to each other or to a specific context.

Long shot shows the whole character usually doing something, and it emphasizes the character's activity (running, riding a horse, fighting).

We usually also describe a shot by the number of characters in the frame.

In the scenes in which Neo meets the other members of Morpheus's team, the camera frames these meetings to suggest emotional terms in the relationships. When Neo meets Morpheus the first time, a long shot of Morpheus jump-cuts to a medium close-up, which then zooms in to a full close-up; we see him both as imposing and as someone we will be intimate with in a very short time. The camera movement brings us—like Neo—quickly close to him. This shot sequence is followed by a medium two-shot of Neo and Trinity as they calmly walk into a medium three-shot with Morpheus. The balanced framing is telling us that these three characters belong together.

In addition, we occasionally see three other framing distances that create specific effects.

Extreme close-ups occur when a facial or body part or a particular object completely fills the frame. They give a sense of extreme intimacy or urgency, like the extreme close-up of the ringing phone just before Trinity sprints to the phone booth to be taken out of the Matrix.

Extreme long shots show a small character or characters in a dramatic physical setting; they tend to emphasize the character's relationship to the larger physical surroundings. We see Neo flying in extreme long shots.

Panoramic shots show vast landscapes and may or may not include characters, but they emphasize the power and/or beauty of the physical setting.

Exercise:

Use strips of masking tape to outline a T-shape to the screen of a video monitor. The top cross of the T should be just above 1/4 of the way down from the top and extend to just below halfway; the edges of the cross should reach across the center 3/4 of the screen; the shaft of the T should take up about 1/3 of the center of the screen and extend to just below 3/4 of the screen (from the top). Now, watch several sequences from different classic black and white films (which don't cut as fast as modern films). Identify what kind of shot you are watching; then decide what important narrative information the cinematographer has put in the T.

Angles

Usually, the camera is situated to make the viewer feel at the same eye level as characters in the frame; this brings us in on the action so that we are not even aware that the camera is there: the action is *framed* so that we feel like an invisible person on the scene. However, when the camera is *angled* for a shot, the change in framing can have an effect on how we feel.

Angle up: The camera is looking up at a character so that the character seems above us; therefore, we may respect or fear the character.

Angle down: Looking down on a character can imply pity, disdain, or vulnerability.

A *ceiling shot* or *shot from above* is from a very high point above the characters and is often used to suggest that characters believe they are alone, are in an intimate circumstance, or are vulnerable to attack.

One of the first shots of Neo is a ceiling shot that shows him asleep and surrounded by electronic clutter; it suggests his loneliness and reliance on gadgets for companionship and entertainment.

A *point-of-view shot* shows us what a character would see. Instead of being an invisible presence on the scene, the camera photographs from the position of the character's eyes (and usually ears). Point-of-view shots are used to get us aligned with a particular character and thereby make us feel closer to her/him emotionally; they are sometimes used for humor.

When Neo opens the door on his friends, we see them from his point of view and then see him from theirs. The friends, shown in a group, are well dressed and fashionably late; they appear social and hip. Neo, from their point of view, is peering out from a chained slit and seems isolated and suspicious.

Camera Movement

Within a particular shot, the camera may move in order to create an effect or render an emotional quality.

Some camera moves are very similar to the way we move our heads on our necks; these moves tend to intensify the sense that the camera is involved in the scene. When the camera swivels horizontally to follow action, it is *panning;* when the camera swivels vertically, to look up or look down, it is *tilting up or down.* When the camera sees the normal horizontal line on a diagonal in the frame, the way you would if you cocked your head to one side, this is a *Dutch angle* and often is used to suggest something is wrong.

When the camera itself is moving to follow action, it is *tracking, trucking,* or *dollying,* depending on whether it is mounted on tracks, a truck, or a dolly. When the camera seems to float above ground level, it is usually a *crane shot,* but it may also be a *helicopter shot* if the camera point of view actually flies.

When a camera is moving in the action—usually following a character—and it seems to bounce or move the way a person bounces when she walks, this is a *hand-held shot*. If it moves at character-level but makes twists and turns without bouncing, it is probably a *Steadicam shot*. Steadicam is the registered trademark for a camera harness that a specially trained cameraperson wears to take the bounce out of long, hand-held takes. As you learn to notice camera movement, you'll recognize that when making an analytic statement, you will want to link up the camera-work with a specific purpose that makes artistic sense.

Movement can also be suggested by working with the camera lens. A *zoom in* causes the image in frame to grow larger, while in a *zoom out* the image shrinks.

The first time we see Morpheus, the camera *angles up* on him in a *medium close-up*, making him seem imposing and possibly dangerous. In addition, the lens slowly zooms in on him while we hear a thunderclap on the sound track; this camera work and sound design make him seem impressive and powerful.

When a shot changes the focus of the lens from one part of the frame to another, it is *racking focus*.

In the scene when the cops bust Trinity in the hotel, we see a shot that focuses first on a close-up of a cop's handcuffs in the left *foreground*, then racks focus to a medium shot of Trinity defenseless in the right *background*, hands on her head and apparently defenseless. The effect of the rack focus, however, seems to emphasize and energize Trinity, and it leads into the fight sequence.

Exercise:
Watch the first shot from Orson Welles's *Touch of Evil*. It's a very long take (the shot lasts five minutes). Such long takes are called *sequence shots* because they change framing in the same way a sequence would but they don't cut. Identify all the different angles and camera movements in this shot.

Editing
Editing is done after the film has been shot. By joining the various shots together to make narrative sense, an editor makes many artistic choices that create emphasis or cause emotional reactions. Editors have various ways to join film, and an editor should have a good reason for every cut made.

Ways of Joining Shots
Straight cuts—when one shot is joined directly to the next—are the most common method for linking shots.

Jump cuts break a continuous action into a series of shots. Using straight cuts, the editor removes some of the frames from an action shot or a zoom. Jump cuts can create a jittery mood or convey a sense of tension or threat. Many of the fight scenes in *The Matrix* employ jump cuts as well as *slow motion*.

Fade in occurs when the screen starts black and then lightens to reveal the shot image; a *fade out* goes from the shot to black. Fades are usually at the beginning or end of a scene, and they stretch out time in a way that feels contemplative.

A *lap dissolve* fades out of one shot as the next image fades in. Dissolves are also used to begin or end scenes, and they tend to emphasize the relationship between the two situations or to show the passage of time.

The Matrix begins with a computer-screen sequence that is a clever series of fades, zooms, and dissolves creating the impression that the viewer is being taken inside the computer screen (much as Alice went through the looking glass).

A *wipe* is used to join sequences and occurs when the image from the next shot seems to wipe the image of the previous shot off the screen. (While there aren't any wipes in *The Matrix*, *Home Improvement* is a television show that often used creative wipes.)

Matching and Other Editing Choices

The shots that make up a sequence have been carefully planned. Editors cut together—sequence—the shots after shooting so that we won't consciously notice the individual shots but will experience the film's story with the seamless continuity of a dream. This method of editing to create story flow has been perfected in Hollywood and is called *continuity editing*. Just as a poet will choose to arrange words to create effects, an editor chooses to join shots that can create specific tensions or relationships between shots.

The most basic technique in continuity editing is *matching shots* to create a seamless feeling of flowing action, conversation, or emotion. *Match cuts* will take a specific element in the visual or sound track and will join shots to fit that element.

Eyeline matches are used in almost every cut to give a continuous feeling of viewer-to-character relationship. In an eyeline match, eyes appear in exactly the same place in the frame regardless of close-up, medium, or long shot. In most films, eyes are in the top of the T-bar, 1/3 of the frame from the top, which is the "natural" framing of a face in close up or the way we frame a friend's face when conversing over dinner. In fact, we naturally look for the face first in our field of vision, and finding a character's eyeline in the same place in every shot disguises cutting so that the viewer feels a consistent relationship to characters.

Action matches match the way that characters' movements, like running, driving, or fighting, logically flow from shot to shot. Trinity is always running from left to right when pursued by the agents. Morpheus and Neo seem always to be facing each other when they are sparring.

An editor must also decide *when to cut*. In action sequences, a certain part of the action needs emphasis, so if a door closes or a character throws a punch, chances are it signals a cut. You can watch Morpheus and Neo punching and kicking for the way the cutting emphasizes the impact of the blows. *Action cutting* puts our attention on motions or activities; action cutting will follow an activity from shot to shot.

Dialogue cutting creates different emphasis, not on the flow of action, but on the meaning of words. Using a technique called *shot/reverse shot*, the editor cuts from speaker to speaker, pretty much as we would shift our visual focus while watching a play. But unlike the theatre, the scene is shot twice: once with the camera positioned just behind the shoulder of one character, then from the *reverse position* behind the other character; then the two shots are cut together with straight cuts. Shot/reverse shot style includes the viewer in the conversation as an intimate eavesdropper watching the speaker, cutting to the silent person only if we need a *reaction shot* to tell us how that character is feeling.

In *cross-cutting* one sequence is straight cut into another that is happening at the same time (see above: the Agents' arrival is cross-cut with Trinity fighting the cops). Cross-cutting preserves the continuous flow of time while allowing us to see two different sequences that might affect each other.

A *cutaway* is a dissolve. A shot of a character in close up dissolves to another scene to suggest what the character is thinking.

Each shot has a *duration* in which it needs to present its information. A shot that is very quick is a *short take*. A shot that goes on and on is a *long take* (or a *sequence shot*). Editors use shot durations much as drummers use a beat to create a feeling of *pace*. Sequences are paced to create emotional effects or *tones*, and dialogue scenes that convey plans or thoughts tend to have longer takes and, therefore, a slower pace than action scenes. Because pace is rhythmic, it is often emphasized with the music track.

In the scene when Neo and Trinity meet at the club, their sequence is paced slowly with cuts on dialogue to give it a romantic tone as we focus on their body language. When, at the end of the movie, they have the shootout, the cutting is rapid, creating a tone of anxiety that adds to a sense of danger and conflict.

Try to pick up when editors don't use continuity editing. If two characters exchange dialogue in two-shot instead of shot/reverse shot, the editor may want the viewers to see something special about the way the characters are relating to each other or to notice something about the setting. If a shot seems to be going on too long, the editor may want viewers to look for subtle information in faces or setting.

Mise en Scène: The Design Within the Frame

When we look at camera work and editing, we are observing how the action is being delivered to our eyes; however, the richest vein of meaning in a film is what is in the frame. The details of what the camera sees and how these details work with the script to create profound impressions of meaning are usually the focus of our attention. *Mise en scène* (French for "staging an action," pronounced "meez en sehn") is the technical term for the way design elements are organized in a particular frame. Why French? Because French critics were the first to regard movies as an art form, and their work is historically the basis for discussing film art. *Mise en scène* includes the same design elements that we would notice in the theatre: acting, lighting, setting, costume, and properties (portable items like guns, handbags, laptop computers, and rolling pins).

In order to give you a better understanding of the complexities of creating *mise en scène*, we will look at the preproduction as well as the production phases of movie-making.

Exercise:

Look at some paintings of groups of people by Caravaggio, Rembrandt, and Norman Rockwell. Notice how the framing focuses your attention; many of these paintings are organized by the T-bar. Look closely at the facial expressions: what is each person feeling? What does his or her body language convey? Now, consider where the light is coming from and how the shadows affect the emotional feeling of the picture. Who has power in the painting and why? Note every object in the frame; the painter has put everything in the frame for a reason: can you think of a reason that each object underscores the theme of the painting

The Preproduction Phase of Movie-making

Because of the intense fight choreography in *The Matrix*, the main characters all had to be in excellent condition with excellent fighting skills. During three months of *preproduction*, Keanu Reeves, Laurence Fishburne, Carrie-Anne Moss, and Hugo Weaving all practiced martial arts for several hours a day.

Preproduction is the time of tactical planning before shooting when the director and the designers devise the "look" of the film. Before shooting, all the elements that will appear in frame must be anticipated and prepared: sets and costumes must be colored properly; car crashes and explosions must be safely staged; supplies, medical personnel, food, and money must be available; and costumes and sets must be constructed so that props, lights, and microphones can be placed properly. Most important, however, is that the director plan every element of the film so that the tiny specifics of design work together to make a consistent artistic statement that will be reflected in the film's *mise en scène*.

By noticing the details of *mise en scène*, we begin to notice how every detail of a film is chosen for thematic effect. Indeed, most directors plan their shooting by making *storyboards* in the preproduction phase, often before the actors are hired. Storyboards are drawings of every shot arranged in comic book fashion to plot out camera work, continuity, possible edits, and various design elements. Once the director has "the boards," he or she meets with the film's designers to make sure that all the elements will work together to match an overall "vision" of the story-world and to ensure that all the necessary materials and purchases will be made on time for the shooting schedule.

Because actors are the most foregrounded aspect of any film, directors want their characters to look a certain way: and more importantly, they want to be confident that the actor has excellent on-camera skills; as a result, the longest process in preproduction is usually casting. Actors are often selected for their star power, but even a star must be believable as a particular kind of character. In addition to the stars, however, many films have hundreds of other actors, of which dozens may have significant speaking roles. We may think that people are just who they are, but in fact, people—their appearances and personalities—carry symbolic information, and the arts of acting and of directing actors is knowing how to mold an actor into a character/symbol.

Keanu Reeves may be a nice-looking young man, but his image on film doesn't have neutral significance; he has appeared as other characters in other movies that audiences will know, and in American culture, he is an ideal of male beauty, aka, a *sex symbol*. His image also has many possible symbolic associations: He is lithe and is in good physical condition, possibly an athlete; he is a white-skinned American male and, therefore, culturally knowledgeable about white American male behaviors; the Wachowskis considered all of these traits and connotations when they chose Reeves to play Neo.

Because nothing is random or accidental in a film, when making a critical analysis, consider how an actor's gestures, emotions, costumes, and props have all been designed to create a specific impression of who that character is, what he or she wants or needs, and what strengths or weaknesses he or she may have.

Reeves is a good cast for Neo, not only because he is handsome and athletic but also because as a person with a reading disability, he can seem "not too bright," as the Oracle (Gloria Foster) says. These traits give him a childlike quality that is good for an innocent savior figure who is "reborn" twice during the film. Casting Morpheus as a complicated black man (Laurence Fishburne) and completing the central trinity with a tough, smart woman (Carrie-Anne Moss) creates a multicultural, postfeminist power base for the film. Add to this African American Dozer (Anthony Rae Parker); Tank (Marcus Chong), who is African/Asian/Hispanic American; South Asian American Apoch (Julian Arahanga); and Switch (Belinda McClory), who is a pale blonde and possibly lesbian, and you have a range of types that generally imply a cross-section of American culture and have connotations of democratic pluralism compared to Agents, who are all very similar.

The Production Phase

Once the film begins principal photography, it is *in production*. Production is focused on the photography and sound recording of the scenes as scripted. We have discussed most of the ways the camera can suggest meaning; however, a *director of photography* will pay special attention to *lighting* during production. Lighting is another aspect of the *mise en scène* that is easy to think of as just "natural," yet lighting can create mood and atmosphere—the lighting can make a character seem beautiful or diseased or indecisive, or when working with other design aspects, it can help create contrasting worlds.

In *The Matrix*, lighting is one of the ways the world of the Matrix is made to appear different from the real earth. When characters are aboard *The Nebuchadnezzar*—in the real world—they are dressed in tattered clothing, they eat gruel, and they are lit to appear bluish and cool. However, when characters are in the Matrix, the lighting is yellow and warm, although with a noticeable greenish glow. This gives the story-world within the Matrix an artificial feeling, a feeling which is amplified by other obviously artificial details of *mise en scène*: the guerillas now wear designer fashions, they carry designer firearms and designer cell phones, and, when Cypher sells out, he is dining on steaks and fine wine. These *mise en scène* elements, heightened by the lighting design, draw our attention to the contrast between the world of the Matrix and reality; and, in the process, they emphasize themes of values: what is important in life, materialistic illusions or honest realities? Do we want to make our own choices and relationships, or do we want them to be plotted for us by media and advertising interests?

What to Look For in Design Elements

You should examine each shot as you examined the paintings earlier; look hard for details and systems; remind yourself of the aspects of *mise en scène*—acting, lighting, sets, costumes, props, and framing—then ask yourself three key questions to help your analysis:

1. **How do details in the frame *help* or *focus* the script meanings?**
   Neo keeps his contraband software in a hollowed-out book, a prop, which we see is titled *Simulacra and Simulations*, by Jean Baudrillard, an actual book. This detail is there to make us think about reality versus virtual-reality. Baudrillard wrote that simulacra are

media-created experiences we mistake for "real." The use of the book serves to underscore the thematic problem of identifying reality, and it suggests not only that Neo is surrounded by computers and technology but also that he has thought about what it all means and about technology's effects on people. (Keanu Reeves read this very difficult book in preparation for this role.)

2. **How do the elements *change* over the course of the film?**
When we first meet Neo, he is a mess; he lives in a sloppy apartment, seems indecisive and confused, wears geeky clothing, works in a sterile office at a job he hates, and doesn't even have a girlfriend. By the end of the film, he is a martial arts master decked out in leather clothing with a similarly attired mate, and he seems to be the master of a complex and visually interesting world. This dramatic change—which is central to the movie's thematic meanings—is created, to a large degree, by acting and design elements.

3. **How can various design or script elements be *linked to form a system* or systems of meaning?**
In the scene when his friends arrive to buy his contraband software, we notice that Neo's apartment number is 101. This numeral is not an accident; it signals several associative networks of meaning central to the film's main themes. It refers to the basic binary code used in computer programming and sets up the theme of Human versus Computer. In addition, it connects Neo with the number 1, suggesting to us that he will, eventually, be "the one" who—like the biblical Jesus—saves humanity. Even his name, "Neo," is an anagram of "one." Moreover, "neo" is Latin for "new," suggesting that Neo is the new man, "the one" to save humankind from machine domination. This theme is picked up by the dialogue with his friends in the same scene. When Neo hands Choi (Marc Gray) the contraband software, Choi exclaims, "Hallelujah. You're my savior, man. My own personal Jesus Christ!" This scene subtly foreshadows the ending in which Neo dies but is then resurrected via Trinity's kiss, after which he goes on to vanquish the smoothly satanic Agent Smith.

Writing

When writing about film, you will need knowledge of these elements to make an *exact point—a thesis statement*—about the movie you're analyzing. The illustrations supplied above about *The Matrix* might be used in essays with the following theses:

1. *The Matrix* is a high-tech religious story in which Neo appears, very much like Jesus, to save mankind from evil illusions.
2. On the surface, *The Matrix* is a science-fiction action movie; but on a deeper level, it is an inquiry into values: as the world becomes increasingly computer- and media-dependent, what is real and what is valuable—worth fighting for?
3. Neo's adventures in *The Matrix* are much like Alices's in Lewis Carroll's famous books, *Alice's Adventures in Wonderland* and *Through the Looking Glass*; both Neo and Alice start out unformed and childish, yet by various strange and challenging experiences, they come to a deeper understanding of themselves and the world.

Correct Style for Writing About Film

When writing your essay, the first time you mention a film, name the director and give the year of release in parentheses after the title; thereafter, when you want to make a claim about the film, attribute your claim to the film itself, *not* to the director's intention (unless you have talked to the director about what he or she intended). Always refer to the characters by their character names (*not* the actors' names) and, after the first mention of each character, give the actor's name in parentheses (you may take notes during the credits or find most cast lists on the Internet; a handy site is http://us.imdb.com, the Internet Movie Database).

Example:

```
Andy and Larry Wachowski's film The Matrix

(1999) depicts Neo (Keanu Reeves) as a Sci-Fi

Jesus-the-Son figure in a cyberworld trinity with

a God-the-Father figure, Morpheus (Laurence Fish-

burne), and a Holy Spirit figure—who else?—Trin-

ity (Carrie-Anne Moss).
```

On your Works Cited page, the following is the correct MLA style for citing a movie.

```
                    Works Cited

The Fellowship of the Ring. Dir. Peter Jackson. Perf.

    Elijah Wood, Ian McKellen, Viggo Mortenson, Sean

    Astin, Ian Holm, Liv Tyler, and Christopher Lee.

    New Line, 2001.

The Matrix. Dir. Andy and Larry Wachowski. Perf. Keanu

    Reeves, Laurence Fishburne, Carrie-Anne Moss, Joe

    Pantoliano, and Hugo Weaving. Warner Brothers,

    1999.
```

Case Study in Film and Adaptation—
The Lord of the Rings: The Fellowship of the Ring

Have you ever heard someone put down a film by declaring, "I read the book, and it was sooo much better than the movie"? Hmmm. Has anyone *ever* liked the movie as much as the book? When a film is based on a classic or popular book, we call it an *adaptation*: the film is adapting the elements of character, setting, and plot from written literature to the screen.

There are two ways to think about such films. The first way is to consider the film as a lesser form and to claim that, as such, it should slavishly attempt to provide accurate illustrations of the book's characters, settings, events, and imagery. This is certainly the viewpoint we usually hear in book-to-movie discussions—and it seems that the book is always superior. But, as we have already discussed, the reading experience is really nothing like the film experience. So this facile comparison is based on an illogical assumption: that both experiences should somehow be "the same."

Think logically about this connection: because words mean slightly different things to different readers, every reader's imagination creates a slightly different idea from a written text. The "cat" I imagine is not the same kitty that you imagine. Also, a book takes many hours of personal concentration to read while a movie unspools before our eyes in an effortless hundred minutes or so. No matter how good a movie is, it can't include in ninety minutes the same information conveyed by eight or more hours of reading. Adaptations inevitably change the plot, leave out scenes or characters, or add details in order for the shorter version to make sense. If you go to the film expecting your experience of the book, you're going to be disappointed.

On the other hand, what if you went to the film expecting a fresh experience? If film and literature are different yet *equally important* narrative forms, and if the film simply *can't* slavishly illustrate the book, you might see the film adaptation as another version of similar events, characters, and settings. As *another version*, it has a different kind of artistic vision and integrity and has its own thematic drives and meanings. This critical approach can free you from rigid expectations or illustrative needs; instead, you can enjoy the inevitable differences between the narratives. Indeed, some of the fun of reading and watching comes from noticing possible differences and considering what purposes they serve; after all, the film makers are narrative artists in their own right, and they have made their design choices for a reason.

In fact, the literary text and the film text are in a kind of conversation with each other. By considering significant similarities and differences, we can detect deeper meanings in both texts. These comparisons can be fun to write about.

A Writing Process

The following process was created to explore the differences between J. R. R. Tolkien's *The Fellowship of the Ring* and Peter Jackson's *The Lord of the Rings: The Fellowship of the Ring* (2001). This process was geared to *focus the writer's ideas first* and then to engage in research to amplify those interests. You can use or adapt this process to generate your own ideas or essays.

Probably the most important aspect of this kind of work is to *make notes and write out ideas* at each step.

Step One: Review the basic texts without prejudice, keeping an eye out for important literary or cinematic moments. Begin by reading Tolkien's 1954 fantasy adventure *The Fellowship of the Ring*—which is a novel but is really just the first part of the very long trilogy, *The Lord of the Rings*. Here is an example of reading notes:

Style and Tone: As a writer, Tolkien seems most interested in moving his story along, not exploring the potential of words and sentences to present complex feelings or ideas. The tone is simple and direct, in a third-person omniscient point of view.

Plot: The story is an *epic quest*, many events over a long period of time requiring many choices by several main characters. Reminiscent of *The*

Odyssey or *Jason and the Argonauts*, it might also be a disguised *coming-of-age tale*.

Setting: Emphasis is on mythological places and inhabitants. The story-world is very much like the story-worlds in Middle English literature ("Middle Earth" seems to be very much like medieval England when they spoke Middle-English). The pleasures of the book are as much in visiting its imaginary geography—lots of description and every terrain has character-like traits—as in following the adventure.

Character: The books appeal to young readers because the Hobbits seem like boys: they are small, emotional, given to mischief, needing adult—human or Wizard—guidance, and vulnerable, but like the best of boys, courageous, loyal, and possessed of a simple understanding of right and wrong. These characters live in a world uncomplicated by sex, and the women characters all seem like mothers. In fact, all the other ethnicities of the Fellowship—Elves, Humans, and Dwarves—seem like grown-ups compared to the Hobbits.

Influences from other texts: *The Fellowship of the Ring* was written by an English teacher for students of English Literature: the tale refers to or imitates classics from literature including Norse epics like *Beowulf* or even Wagner's *Ring* cycle of operas (same interest in swords with names and rings). As in Old English epics, women act like wise warrior-wives but don't take action. Also, Tom Bombadil seems like the *Gawain* poet's Green Knight: an immortal fertility god mated to an ethereal goddess, Goldberry. There are similarities to Arthurian legends as well: Gandalf seems very Merlin-like; the Fellowship is like the Knights of the Round Table—formed for a good cause but dissolved by treachery and moral flaws; Aragorn's Sword of Elendil is reminiscent of Excalibur. The mythical lands, names, and references to Elves, Trolls, and Dwarves seem to refer to Celtic folklore. Songs and poetry are injected into the story as they are in oral tradition epics, to heighten emotional moments or develop character.

Themes: The book's world shows that characters have a destiny that they must discover and follow. It shows the seductiveness and corrupting power of gold. The Fellowship versus Sauron clearly represents Good versus Evil, but Evil has no motive or ideology other than to dominate the world and people it with demons—possibly a nod to Milton's Satan building Pandemonium. In that regard, it sounds a bit like a child's view of Nazism or possibly Cold War Communism. Gandalf seems to have knowledge of good (essentially "trust in your nature and don't be seduced by the Ring"). Frodo seems like a naive Messiah character—maybe the personification of moral goodness—flawed but knowing right from wrong.

Step Two: View Peter Jackson's *Lord of the Rings: The Fellowship of the Ring*, adapted for the screen by Frances Walsh, Philippa Boyens, and Peter Jackson (2001), and watch for similarities and differences between it and Tolkien's book; here are some examples:

Similarities—
Style and Tone: The camera is usually in a continuity or "invisible" style, telling the story, as Tolkien does, simply and directly, without drawing attention to the fact that we're watching a movie with a clever director. When Jackson moves the camera or cuts, he does it to amplify a specific feeling that connects us to the characters' experiences, and he often uses

God-like, third-person-omniscient camera angles with helicopter or panorama shooting.

Plot: The film seems to take its major inspiration from the book. It uses voiceover that sounds like Tolkien's words to fill in exposition, and most of the quotable lines are directly taken from the book. It is recognizably the same quest plot with the climactic event in the middle being the formation of the Fellowship and tragic conclusion in which Boromir is corrupted by the Ring and the Fellowship is broken.

Setting: The photography and *mise en scène* make Middle Earth more dynamic and vast than the book. But having read the book, many details in the film stand out, including the creation of fantastic but believable "worlds" within Middle Earth: The Shire, Mordor, Rivendale, Mirkwood, etc.

Characters: Physical characteristics of the various ethnicities of Middle Earth include tall, beautiful elves; short, hairy Hobbits; short, stocky dwarves; and hideous but powerful Orcs.

Themes: The good versus evil theme begins to take more definite shape in the movie— different ethnicities of the Fellowship seem "normal" while all the evil demon armies are mass-produced grotesques. The imagery and the point of view of the storytelling suggest a democratic, pluralistic theme of good versus totalitarian evil. The Fellowship, operating democratically, suggests that the group, even if not unanimous, is stronger/wiser/more courageous than the individual.

Frodo finds his true self by resisting evil.

The film also makes a connection between gold and power over others in the Ring and shows how the ring seductively corrupts, preying on a character's moral weakness.

Differences—

Settings: The film is able to show a vastness in the scenery and in the numbers, while sometimes the book feels a bit claustrophobic, as if written from a Hobbit's point of view.

Design details seem to be influenced by a compromise between nineteenth-century decorative arts, the Pre-Raphaelites, and Art Nouveau, as well as by Tolkienesque Elvish script and Ancient British Celtic design motifs.

Plot: Much of the book is concerned with the history of Middle Earth, usually told as stories-within-the-story that go back and forth in time. The film has a prologue with voiceover and develops its plot in a more linear fashion.

The subplot between Saruman and Gandalf is cross-cut into major parts of the film, but in the book it's just a few pages long.

The film adds an entire new love plot between a new character, Arwen, and Aragorn.

Characters: Costumes seemed similar in many details but not as magical as in the book—no Elvish camouflage capes, no explanation of the precious metal mithril. Hobbits seem younger and goofier. In the book, Bilbo is in his fifties—however boyishly he acts—but in the film, the four Hobbits of the Fellowship seem in their early twenties at the oldest.

Strider seems to take a more pronounced role in the center of the plot, and the scale of the film seems more human than Hobbit. The Hobbits are small in the camera-view of their world but seem "normal" sized in the book. There is no Tom Bombadil, so an entire section of the plot is gone.

Some of the Elvish characters are different genders: Glorfindal, the hero Elf in the book, is transformed to Arwen (Liv Tyler), a babe-heroine. The conflict between Elves and Dwarves has been smoothed over in the film.

Themes: The film seems to set up Frodo as a *coming-of-age character* more than the book does: he looks as if he's in late adolescence; he's made a part of Pippin and Merry's pranks, is unworldly and seemingly very youthful in outlook. The film is taking the boyish feel of the book's Hobbits and making the Hobbit characters into actual boys.

Romantic love between a man and a woman is a motivating theme, and the women are very attractive characters. Arwen is willing to give up her immortality for love of Aragorn.

Finally, the Fellowship is in tune with nature, especially the pastoral world of The Shire, while evil is like a giant corporation gone mad, mass-producing fighting machine-like Orc while destroying the ecology.

<u>Step Three</u>: You now have enough information to write several *comparison-contrast* essays. For students using this book, this is the best essay to attempt. A good essayist could select a point of strong similarity or difference and use details from the book and the movie to illustrate a thesis. Possible ideas for theses include the following:

- Both book and film are stories of Ultimate Evil pitted against a fumbling Good, but they show slightly different versions of good and evil. What does the book suggest is the nature of good or the nature of evil? Both texts seem to imply that democracy is good while totalitarianism is evil, but they use different images and events to show the two systems. In a totalitarian system—personified by Saruman and his Orcs and Trolls—power is the ultimate goal of the state—the strong rule and exploit the weak, and they use surveillance to locate and control "enemies of the state." In contrast, The Fellowship is formed by and works like a democracy—the powerful protect the weak; various groups cooperate and pool resources; understanding is achieved through dialogue and compromise; and people are not regimented or kept under surveillance.
- Both book and film are stories in which Frodo starts out naive and steadily learns that he is stronger and more resourceful than he at first suspected. However, the book is a tale of a hero whom Fate favors, while the film is more a traditional coming-of-age story in which the main character "grows up" in the course of making both poor and wise choices.
- The stories contrast each other in that the film seems to be much more ecologically oriented in depicting evil as corporate (mass production, strip mining, draining the earth of resources) and good as pastoral (farming, respectful of nature, enjoying natural foods).

<u>Step Four: Research Possibilities</u>—Research papers can be fun to write because they amplify or expand our own ideas. Research papers, however, are usually long-term assignments which include finding information in the library and online. ***Research can't be done in one sitting the night before your paper is due*** and is best done over the course of two or more weeks. Here are several possible research strategies and examples of how to begin to question and where to research.

Research on Symptomatic Meaning

Cultural critics believe that when commercial stories like novels or movies become popular, they are expressing a current concern of the culture at-large in the guise of a narrative. By finding connections between the details of a novel or a movie's plot or story-world and connecting them to the events and the details of a real-world issue, we can better understand the cultural values that are being played out. The film or novel is a *symptom* of greater social concerns.

The Fellowship of the Ring was written during and just after the Second World War. If you briefly research the values of the Nazi Party compared to Anglo-American democratic ideals, you can easily see that the book—despite Tolkien's protestations—has pro-democratic and anti-fascist themes that connect it to its period of creation. However, it was revived and was arguably even *more* popular, in the 1960s at the same time that the hippies revolted against the Vietnam War and against the consumer conformity of Cold War morality. Then, in 2001, Jackson's version (released just after September 11, 2001) proved one of the most popular movies of all time. What are the connections to make the book so appealing to 1960s counterculturalists and the film to millennial audiences?

Research: 1) Review the history of WWII, particularly ideology and imagery of democracy in contrast to Nazism. 2) Review ideology and imagery of the "Youth Movement" of the late 1960s and early 1970s. How do hippies resemble Hobbits? 3) Review the imagery and ideology of the autumn of 2001. Find ways that specific details in the book and film resemble details from the historical period. What lesson does the book or the film teach us about "good," and how is it relevant to the historical period?

Research on Influence

Although the two texts are similar in some general ways, the two creative artists, Tolkien and the Jackson team, seem to be responding to different influences. Tolkien is obviously writing from a grounding in English literature, in particular Old and Middle English lore. Jackson is more of a *Dungeons and Dragons* kind of fantasy guy with visual ideas that come out of nineteenth-century modern design amplified by computer graphics.

1. Take one important *influence* for each text and compare how this influence affected the telling of the stories. You might show how the book echoes ideas in some of the stories from *Morte D'Arthur* by Sir Thomas Malory, and then you could show how the film images or tunnels and unforeseen problems are like a game of *Dungeons and Dragons*.
2. Another paper might argue that the book and film depict women's roles very differently. The book is faithful to the Anglo-Saxon tradition of *Beowulf*, while the film, in changing the roles of women, is closer to contemporary films like *Braveheart*, in which women and romantic love are key motivators.

Research on Reception

A *reception study* looks at the way the critics, the box office, and various awards committees receive a text. If critics hate a movie and the box office is wonderful, or if the box office is dismal but the film wins four Oscars, a reception critic has interesting questions to answer.

Reception studies usually focus on how critics and audiences responded to the text when it was first published or released. More than checking to see if the critics liked or hated the book or movie, a reception study is interested in comparing *why* the critics felt the way they did. By looking for patterns in the rhetoric of their arguments, a reception study can detect trends in cultural or critical thinking.

There are several possible ways to platform the thesis for your reception study, but for *LOTR: The Fellowship of the Ring*, because the film is an adaptation of a very popular and—for the 1960s generation—very influential book, it would be fun to see how critics responded to the film *as* an adaptation. Would all critics look to see if the film "accurately illustrated" the book? If so, would their responses be prejudiced by this assumption? Would there be any difference between American and British responses (the British critics would be more familiar with Tolkien's influences)? Would the initial critical response reflect the outstanding box office the film generated or would it pinpoint the trends in Oscars over the *LOTR* cycle? Why?

Check Internet sites and the library for press reviews, and be sure to consult the more thoughtful critical venues: *The New Yorker, The New York Times, The New York Review of Books, The New Republic, The Nation, Slate, Salon.com, Time*, and *Newsweek*.

Research to Write a Critical Commentary

This research involves finding everything that is written about the film in the popular and the academic presses. Writing a full-fledged critical commentary is labor-intensive and is usually reserved for senior seminar and graduate students because it is so difficult for undergraduates to find and carefully read academic criticism. To begin a critical commentary, review *all the academic writing* on a particular work. For a film, this means reviewing academic journals like *Screen, Mosaic*, and *The Film and Literature Quarterly Review*. This usually requires getting the assistance of a reference librarian for a thorough search of many databases and possibly for inter-library loan of materials. After you have taken notes on every critical article you can find, you then might write a long paper that summarizes your findings and gives reasons why you find one trend in criticism better than another. The most difficult strategy is to find a point about which *no one has yet written* (like comparing the role of women as suggested in "Research on Influences" above), and to write a long and very thorough essay that incorporates existing criticism to support your interpretation.

Under the Tuscan Sun

Stephanie Minter

Audrey Wells's film <u>Under the Tuscan Sun</u> (2003) portrays the life of Frances Mayes (Diane Lane), a 35-year-old divorcee, through water, a necessity of life. Frances matures throughout the film from a scared, childlike woman into a full-grown, vibrant woman. Although the film is extremely different from Frances Mayes's biographical novel, several aspects were also brought into the comedic and romantic film such as the beautiful scenery, the magnificent Signor Martini, and even the exquisite culinary masterpieces. A connotative aspect of water is often biblical in the sense that water is used for baptismal purposes to cleanse and give new life. Three specific instances where water is present symbolize Frances's rebirth from a childlike woman gradually into a more mature woman through her own various trials and tribulations, a sort of self-discovery. Water is used to symbolize the steps necessary to moving on throughout the film. These steps, however, take time.

Frances experiences a lot of grief after she divorces her cheating husband, Tom. She, like her ex-husband, expresses her childish ways in various forms. Tom shows his immaturity through reliving his teenage fantasies by committing adultery with a significantly younger female. Frances expresses her lack of mature development through a simple act involving water. In the final scene in her San Franciscan home, a long shot depicts Frances's maturity level as she picks up a small blue vase from the table, empties the contents (flowers), and pours the water all over the hardwood floors in the foyer as she conspicuously looks around and across the

ceilings. Frances's act of intentionally dumping
the water shows her immature actions despite her
actual age. This behavior shows that, as in
life, people must grow from specific events to
fully recover and resume a "normal" lifestyle
again. Upon the entrance into the Bramasole
estate in Cortona, Italy, Frances walks into an
antique faucet that protrudes from the wall.
This specific faucet symbolically portrays
Frances's life in that when she first appears in
Bramasole, she is slightly harmed and taken
aback by the faucet (much as her husband's
infidelity took her by surprise). The framing of
the faucet centers it before Lane's character
(Frances) even enters the villa. As Frances
appears from stage left, she brushes against the
spigot with her left shoulder. Her attention is
drawn to this faucet, this outlet of a long
repressed force; it is as though the faucet is a
burden in dire need of being released and
lifted. Water and lack thereof represent one of
the many steps Frances must take in the stages
of her recovery.

Through her upcoming challenges in the
film, Frances encounters many varied ups and
downs in Italy. In a humorous scene while in
Rome, she introduces herself to a handsome
Italian named Marcello (Raoul Bora), who then
takes her to his family's hometown in Positano.
This lovely town is one of the country's most
beautiful peninsular cities. Frances is

surrounded by breathtaking oceanic views, only
one of the many "painting-like landscape[s]" the
film captures, throughout her brief, but most
eventful, weekend getaway (Toscano, para. 2).
The panoramic framing of the natural landscape
expands the viewer's perception of the
remarkable beauty of the peninsula. The water is
so abundant and changing, yet ever powerful.
Frances and Marcello's lust-filled weekend
proves to be just the medicine necessary to mend
a broken heart; unfortunately, the treatment
proves also to be temporary as she will soon
after be filled with hurt again. Throughout this
time, the faucet in her Tuscan home begins
gradually to drip, symbolically showing
Frances's personal improvement in moving on with
her life and her gradual emergence as a new and
stronger woman. The dripping faucet is a sound
element to the featured film. Whether the sound
is "direct" or "postdubbed" (recorded then or
added later), Frances first notices the nuisance
of a noise while she is in her library. This is
a dramatic change from the fact that, when she
first moved into the rundown villa, the faucet
showed no sign of working just as Frances showed
no sign of being able to move on from her
divorce. After this vast and exciting incident
(in the eyes of a remodeling homeowner), there
is a final step to be taken in order for Frances
to be like the woman she once was and to be
fully recovered.

The final scenes of <u>Under the Tuscan Sun</u> are filled with love, joy, and happiness; yet, Frances still feels lonely and, in essence, unhappy in the romance department of her life. In one of the scenes of the reception after the wedding celebration of Chiara (Giulia Steigerwalt) and Pawel (Pawel Szajda) a new character is introduced: Ed (David Sutcliffe). Ed enters the mid-life fairy tale while Frances, lying in her lawn chair, is absorbing all the realities and celebrations she is experiencing and has experienced. As he picks a ladybug off Frances's arm, he introduces himself as a fellow writer who, long before, received a poor review from Frances that motivated him to try again. Ed fatefully finds himself at the little Tuscan villa and takes on the role, eventually, of Frances's well-needed and desired male companion and soul mate. The scenes lapse into celebration in the Tuscan household at Christmastime where, surrounding the table, there are all of the people who were necessary in the full development of Frances's final character: Chiara, Pawel, Patti (Sandra Oh), Alexandra, and most importantly, Ed. The scenes finally fade into the most symbolic finale—the faucet pouring water all over the tiled floors. The shot begins with the framing focusing on the splattering water on the floors, slowly pans over to Frances's bare feet and the joyous sounds of Frances giggling as the cold water floods over and around her feet. The final shot centers the faucet as its main focal point in a sort of medium shot. The concept that this antique, almost 300 year-old faucet is now flooding the tiled entryway captures the excitement and the changes in Frances's life. Just as the faucet needed time to exert the raging force it had held back for years, Frances's timely progression into a woman who is now capable of being, once again, romantically involved with another man is measured through the changes of this faucet.

Despite the mediocre reviews received, <u>Under the Tuscan Sun</u> thematically and visually evokes a great number of viewers' arousals and connections with the cultural compilations and with the artistic composition. Director Audrey Wells symbolically uses water, a sign of cleansing and new birth, to illustrate Frances's growth from the shattered, naive woman she was before into a new and improved woman. A "[s]impler but no less memorable image . . ., a water faucet on the wall," acts as a growth chart, emotionally and spiritually, for Frances's rebirth (Putman, para. 4). Through time and various stages, she becomes vibrant, alive, and outgoing once again just as the faucet in her Bramasole villa becomes again a source of life-giving water. Frances finds sadness, hurt, and happiness through her interactions with water in her San Franciscan

home, in her sexual encounters at the beaches of
Positano, and in her glorious celebration of the
once unpromising, antique faucet which, through
the times, the hopes, and the adventures
surrounding it, becomes functional. <u>Under the
Tuscan Sun</u> is a classic tale of Cinderella with
a twist in which the damsel in distress rescues
herself, thus, recreating a self-discovery
through water.

[New page]   Works Cited

Corrigan, Timothy. <u>A Short Guide to Writing
     About Film</u>. 5th ed. New York: Pearson
     Longman, 2004. 70.

Putman, Dustin. Rev. of <u>Under the Tuscan Sun</u>
     (2003). 14 May 2004. http://www.URL

Toscano, Tony. Rev. of <u>Under the Tuscan Sun</u>
     (2003). 14 May 2004. http://
     www.rottentomatoes.com/click/
     movie-1125789/
     reviews.php?critic=columns&sortby=default&
     page=2&rid=1201299.

<u>Under the Tuscan Sun</u>. Dir. Audrey Wells. Perf.
     Diane Lang, Sandra Oh, Lindsay Duncan,
     Vincent Riotta. 2003. Videocassette/DVD.
     Touchstone Pictures, 2004.

<u>Under the Tuscan Sun</u>. <u>Internet Movie Database</u>.
     May 2004. 14 May 2004. http://us.imdb.com/
     title/tt0328589.

Appendix C

DOCUMENTING A RESEARCH PAPER: MLA STYLE SHEET

When assigned a research paper, ask your instructor what documentation system you should use in your paper. Several excellent style sheets are available, some designed for particular disciplines. Two of the most often used for papers in the humanities are *The MLA [Modern Language Association] Handbook for Writers of Research Papers* and *The Chicago Manual of Style.* In this text, the *MLA Handbook* will be the basis for documentation in the sample essays. The MLA form is briefly summarized in this section. You might want to consult the *MLA Handbook* for further information and examples.

Documentation of Quotations, Paraphrases, and Summaries

Unless the information is common knowledge, you *must* document any information borrowed from other sources, whether quoted, paraphrased, or summarized. **Paraphrasing** is retelling the original material *in your own words;* if your paraphrase includes any of the original wording, those words must be put in quotation marks. In paraphrasing, be careful not to alter the author's tone or meaning. A paraphrase differs from a summary primarily in length: a paraphrase is about the same length as the original source, but a summary is a concise overview. Because paraphrases and summaries are based on ideas that are not your own, you must document them even though you are not quoting the author directly. Failure to do so is **plagiarism,** the academic equivalent of stealing. Any material quoted must be put in quotation marks and documented. Use quotations judiciously, and avoid back-to-back quotations. Most teachers prefer that no more than one-fifth of your paper be in quotation marks. To prevent your paper from becoming a string of quotations, you should develop the technique of blending paraphrase with short quotations.

Parenthetical Citations

The MLA style sheet uses parenthetical in-text citations containing information that will lead your readers to the correct alphabetical entry on the Works Cited page and give them the specific page, paragraph, or screen for your reference. Electronic sources are documented in a variety of ways. If the electronic source has page numbers, you can document the page number. If it has paragraph or screen numbers, use them instead of page numbers. If the source has none of these, you may identify it by author or title alone, depending on how the source is alphabetized on the Works Cited page. Note that some professors may require that you print the electronic sources and number the paragraphs yourself.

You should always introduce your quotations, making sure that they connect with your sentences grammatically. One method of introducing quotations is simply to mention the speaker or writer:

```
Prufrock repeats, "In the room the women come

and go / Talking of Michelangelo" (Eliot 35-36).
```

You may also use a whole sentence followed by a colon to introduce a quotation:

```
Walker's narrator realizes that her younger

daughter is uncomfortable about Dee's visit: "Mag-

gie will be nervous until after her sister goes: she

will stand hopelessly in corners, homely and ashamed

of the burn scars down her arms and legs, eying her

sister with a mixture of envy and awe" (136).
```

If the material quoted is already in quotation marks, put a single quotation inside the double quotation marks:

```
Upset and angry, Ozzie (1334) tells Rabbi

Binder, "'You don't know anything about God!'"
```

As these examples show, the *MLA Handbook* requires parenthetical citation immediately following a quotation, paraphrase, or summary. The citations correspond to titles listed on the Works Cited page at the end of the paper. After a paraphrase, the documentation precedes any appropriate punctuation. After quotations, the parenthetical documentation follows quotation marks and precedes terminal punctuation. If the final punctuation is a question mark or an exclamation point, the parenthetical documentation should be included earlier in the sentence:

```
The grandmother (O'Connor 367) asks, "'You

wouldn't shoot a lady, would you?'"
```

Your parenthetical citation must give the reader (1) enough information to locate the complete bibliographical information on the Works Cited page and (2) the exact page or line where the cited material appears in the source. If the Works Cited page lists only one source by an author and the author's name has not already been mentioned in the sentence, your citation will consist of the author's last name and the page number. If the author's name has been given in the sentence, you need give only the page number. Notice that no comma appears before the page number. In paraphrases, an effective technique is to introduce the borrowed material with the author's name and to add the page number at the end of the borrowed material. This method lets the reader know exactly where the paraphrase begins. The following examples illustrate correct documentation where a paraphrase or quotation is introduced with the author's name:

> In Gilman's "The Yellow Wallpaper," the narrator implies that, although her husband loves her, he wants to tell her exactly what to do (253).
>
> Didion says, "Marriage is the classic betrayal" (167).

If the Works Cited page includes two or more works by the same author, your parenthetical citation must include a title. Long titles may be shortened. In the following examples, the full title is "A Good Man Is Hard to Find."

> O'Connor describes the Misfit: "He was an older man than the other two. His hair was just beginning to gray and he wore silver-rimmed spectacles that gave him a scholarly look" ("A Good Man" 146).
>
> The grandmother says, "'If you would pray, . . . Jesus would help you'" (O'Connor, "A Good Man" 150).

If you want to use information that is already quoted, you should first try to find the original source. If you cannot find the original, however, you may use the material by giving credit to both sources, as in the following example:

> James Russell Lowell decided to omit Thoreau's last sentence in <u>The Maine Woods</u>, which says, "It [the pine tree] is as immortal as I am, and perchance will go to as high a heaven, there to tower above me still" (qtd. in Matthews 251).

The complete bibliographical material on the Works Cited page would be listed under Matthews, not under Thoreau.

If your source has two or three authors, all last names are listed in the parenthetical citation; if there are more than three authors, the first author is listed followed by "et al.," meaning "and others."

```
According to the article, "The group has a
suspicious history" (McGee et al. 29).
```

If the source has no author, use its title. Thus, the citation should be as follows: ("Wife Is Not Convicted of Murder" 20).

If the work referred to has more than one volume, the volume number must be included: (Graves 1: 256).

If several works provide the same information that is being paraphrased, the documentation should give credit to all: (Graves 1: 256; Campbell 112; Hamilton 29). If more than three authors give the same information and it is not considered general knowledge, content notes are effective (see below).

Long Quotations and Poetry

If your quotation is long, more than four lines, you must indent it on the left. The indentation indicates that the information is quoted. Therefore, quotation marks are not needed unless the material quoted was already in quotation marks, as in the second example below. Note that in an indented quotation final punctuation precedes the parenthetical citation.

```
Capote's narrator says,

This is our last Christmas together.

Life separates us. Those who Know Best decide

that I belong in a military school. . . . I

have a new home too. But it doesn't count.

Home is where my friend is, and there I never

go. (48-49)

Ozzie tells his friend Itzie about the rabbi's

extreme reaction:

"Finally, he starts screaming that I was

deliberately simple-minded and a wise guy, and

that my mother had to come, and this was the

last time. And that I'd never get bar-mitzva-

hed if he could help it." (Roth 456)
```

Quotation marks are necessary here because the passage is quoted in the source.

When you are quoting poetry, if you cite one or two lines, include the quotation in the text, using a slash to show where the line ended:

> In "A Prayer for My Daughter," Yeats wishes,
>
> "And may her bridegroom bring her to a house /
>
> Where all's accustomed" (74–75).

If you quote more than two lines of poetry, indent the quotation and set the lines as the poet does:

> Yeats prays that his daughter will have beauty
>
> but know how to value it:
>
>> May she be granted beauty and yet not
>>
>> Beauty to make a stranger's eye dis-
>>
>> traught,
>>
>> Or hers before a looking glass. (17–19)

Notice that citations to poetry list line rather than page numbers.

You must reproduce quotations *exactly* unless you indicate that changes have been made. Changes may be indicated by using ellipses or brackets.

If you omit something from a quotation, let the reader know by using ellipses (three spaced dots). If you omit a whole sentence, use four dots (three ellipses and a period). If you omit a line or more of poetry, include an entire line of spaced dots. Most teachers prefer that if you quote only a few words and make them a grammatical part of your sentence, you omit the ellipses.

> Greiner describes Frost's "An Old Man's Win-
>
> ter Night" as "nothing if not a poem of despair,
>
> and . . . a companion piece . . . to T. S. Eliot's
>
> equally fine 'Gerontion'" (231).
>
> Frost, in his poem "Out, Out—," personifies
>
> the saw, saying,
>
>> . . . At the word, the saw,
>>
>> As if to prove saws knew what supper
>
> meant,
>
>> Leaped out at the boy's hand, [. . .]
>>
>> . . . .
>>
>> Neither refused the meeting. (13–17)

```
     Gerber believes that Frost's "Home Burial" is
```
```
"modern in theme" (229).
```

Brackets are used to add information inside a quotation for clarification or grammatical correctness or to indicate that the original material contains an error:

```
     When Kugelmass visits Persky the Great, Per-
```
```
sky "[removes] some old silk handkerchiefs that
```
```
were lying on [the cabinet's] top" (Allen 341).
```

The Latin word *sic* is used to indicate an error in a quotation:

```
     The reporter accused the senator of "having
```
```
forgotten his principals [sic]" (Johnson A1).
```

Works Cited Page

On the Works Cited page, list alphabetically *all* sources for your paper.

Books

Basic citations for books include the following information if it is available or applicable: author, title, editor, edition, place, publisher, publication date, and volume. Examples of some book citations follow:

Book with One Author

```
Keillor, Garrison. Happy to Be Here: Stories and Comic
```
```
     Pieces. New York: Atheneum, 1982.
```

Two or More Works by the Same Author

```
O'Connor, Flannery. The Violent Bear It Away. New
```
```
     York: Farrar, Straus & Cudahy, 1960.
```
```
-----.Wise Blood. 2nd ed. New York: Farrar, Straus &
```
```
     Cudahy, 1962.
```

Work with Two Authors or Editors

```
Andrew, Malcolm, and Ronald Waldron, eds. The Poems of
```
```
     the Pearl Manuscript: Pearl, Cleanness, Patience,
```
```
     Sir Gawain and the Green Knight. Berkeley: U of
```
```
     California P, 1979.
```

Work with More Than Three Authors or Editors

Abrams, M. H., et al., eds. <u>The Norton Anthology of</u>
<u>English Literature</u>. New York, W. W. Norton, 1968.

Work with Both Author and Editor

Webster, John. <u>The White Devil</u>. Ed. John Russell
Brown. Oxford: Manchester UP, 1968.

Work with a Translator

Mann, Thomas. <u>The Magic Mountain</u>. Trans. H. T. Lowe-
Porter. New York: Knopf, 1953.

An Introduction or Preface

Woollcott, Alexander. Introduction. <u>The Complete</u>
<u>Works of Lewis Carroll</u>. New York: Modern
Library, n.d.

Notice the use of n.d. when the book does not include a publication date. Similarly, n.p. means no place or no publisher is given in the book.

Article or Story Printed as a Part of a Book

Money, Mary Alice. "The Undemonization of Supporting
Characters in <u>Buffy</u>." <u>Fighting the Forces: What's</u>
<u>at Stake in Buffy the Vampire Slayer</u>. Ed. Rhonda
V. Wilcox and David Lavery. Lanham, MD: Rowman and
Littlefield, 2002. 98-107.

Poem, Story, or Article Reprinted in a Book

Kenny, Maurice. "Wild Strawberry." <u>Dancing Back Strong</u>
<u>the Nation</u>. Fredonia, NY: White Pine Press, 1981.
Rpt. in <u>Harper's Anthology of 20th Century Native</u>
<u>American Poetry</u>. Ed. Duane Niatum. New York:
Harper and Row, 1988. 37-38.

Notice that when a work is published or reprinted as a part of a book, as illustrated in the two entries above, specific pages are given.

Work of Several Volumes

Bullough, Geoffrey, ed. <u>Narrative and Dramatic Sources</u>

    <u>of Shakespeare</u>. 8 vols. London: Routledge and

    Kegan Paul, 1966-1975.

One Volume of a Multiple Volume Set

Bullough, Geoffrey, ed. <u>The Comedies: 1597-1603</u>. Lon-

    don: Routledge and Kegan Paul, 1968. Vol. 3 of

    <u>Narrative and Dramatic Sources of Shakespeare</u>. 8

    vols. 1966-1975.

Periodicals

Basic citations for periodicals include the following information: author, article title, periodical name, series number or name, volume number (for a scholarly journal), publication date, and page numbers.

Article in a Scholarly Journal

Licala, Elizabeth. "Charles Clough's Dreampix." <u>Art in</u>

    <u>America</u> 80 (July 1992): 94-97.

Article from a Monthly Magazine

Barrett, Michael J. "The Case for More School Days."

    <u>Atlantic Monthly</u> Nov. 1990: 78, 80-81.

Article in a Weekly Magazine

McCallister, J. F. O. "The Other Player." <u>Time</u> 10 Aug.

    1992: 30.

Article from a Journal Found on Microfilm

Marston, Jane. "Epistemology and the Solipsistic Con-

    sciousness in Flannery O'Connor's 'Greenleaf.'"

    Microfilm. <u>Studies in Short Fiction</u> 21 (Fall

    1984): 375-82.

Newspaper Article

Mydans, Seth. "In an Assault on Tradition, More Schools

    Last All Year." <u>New York Times</u> 18 Aug. 1991: A1, A22.

CD-ROM

If you are documenting material that you found in full text form on a CD-ROM, use an entry like the following, taken from the Government Reporter section of SIRS, on your works cited page.

```
Grant, Agnes, and LaVina Gillespie. "Using Literature

    by American Indians and Alaska Natives in Sec-

    ondary Schools." ERIC Digest Sept. 1992: n.p. SIRS

    Government Reporter. CD-ROM. Social Issues

    Resources Series. May 1996.
```

Electronic Sources

A wealth of material is also available on the Internet, from indexes to full text articles, accessible through the World Wide Web. In addition to the materials available through search engines, you may be able to access materials from other libraries such as the Library of Congress or the British Library, from any branch of the federal government, or from current news sources such as CNN. To document sources that have previously been published but that you found through a web source, first follow the directions for documenting the book or article. Then add the following information, when it is available or pertinent:

1. Name of the author or editor, if available
2. Title of work: in quotation marks if an article, a poem, or a short story; underlined if a book
3. Publication information if previously published, arranged as it would be if it were not on the Internet
4. Name of the database or professional site
5. Version number, if given
6. Date of the posting of the electronic publication
7. Name of the sponsor of the webpage (university or institution, for example)
8. Date on which the material was found during research
9. Electronic address of the source in angle brackets

Scholarly Database

```
Martinez, Z. Nelly. "Isabel Allende's Fictional World:

    Roads to Freedom." Latin American Literary Review

    30.60 (July-Dec. 2002): 51ff. Research Library.

    GALILEO. ProQuest. Hightower Lib., Gordon College.

    24 Jul. 2004. http://proquest.umi.com Path: Isabel

    Allende.
```

Short Work Within a Scholarly Project

Heaney, Seamus. "Bogland." <u>Seamus Heaney</u>. Ed. Paul Jones.
    April 1997. University of North Carolina. 29 June 1998
    http://sunsite.unc.edu/ipa/heaney/bogland.html.

Personal or Professional Site

Atwood, Margaret. "Spotty-Handed Villainesses." O. W.
    Toad, Ltd., 1994. 12 April 1998 http://www.io.org-
    toadaly/vlness.htm.

Nunes, Mark. <u>Online Theory</u>. 29 June 1998
    http://www.dc. peachnet.edu/~mnunes/theory.html.

Book

Austen, Jane. <u>Pride and Prejudice</u>. cit 1813. Ed. R. W.
    Chapman. 23 Aug. 1998. Wiretap
    ftp://wiretap.area.com/Library/ Classic/pride.ja.

Article in a Scholarly Journal

Churchill, Mary Faggan. "Alice Walker and Zora Neale
    Hurston: The Common Bond." <u>MELUS</u> 22.3 (Fall 1997).
    29 June 1998 callisto.gsu.edu:4000/
    QUERY:fel+1:Chkscreen+11:bad+html/.

Bilger, Audrey. "Goblin Laughter: Violent Comedy and
    the Condition of Women in Fanney Burney and Jane
    Austen." <u>Women's Studies</u> 24.4 (1995): n.pag. 14
    Feb. 1998 http://www.cognito.com/0003/arti-
    cles/00016736/16736229.htm.

Online Posting

Blackmon, Samantha. "Human Element." Online posting. 4
    May 2003. Computers & Writing Online. 3 Feb. 2005
    http://www.cw-online.org/lists/cw-online/
    archives.May 2003.

Synchronous Communication

Thorne. Online discussion of "Literature and Ourselves
   Greeting." 2 Feb 2005. Nouspace. 3 Feb. 2005
   http://nouspace.net:7000/5956.

Home Page for a Course

Koch, Jr., Robert T. English 1102. Spring 2005. 1 Feb.
   2005 http://www.gdn.edu/faculty/rkoch/teach.htm-
   pdf/e1102sHsp05.pdf.

Unsigned Article in a Newspaper or on a Newswire

"Pathfinder Mission Reshaped Knowledge About Mars."
   CNNinteractive 29 June 1998. 4 May 2005
   http://cnn.com. TECH/space/9806/29/
   pathfinder.whatwelearned/.

Article in a Magazine

VanBiema, David. "In Search of Moses." Time 14 Dec.
   1998. 16 Dec. 1998. http://cgi.pathfinder.com/
   time/magazine/1998/ dom/981214/cover1.htm.

E-mail (Electronic mail)

Sample, Maxine. "Re: African Writers." E-mail to Sandra Waller. 1 July 2004.

Other Sources

There are many other sources of information, including computer software,
television and radio programs, recordings, performances, works of art, letters, interviews, and films. Consult the *MLA Handbook* for complete details.
Representative samples are shown here:

Personal Interview

Montgomery, Michael. Personal interview. 25 June 2004.

Film

Bram Stoker's Dracula. Dir. Francis Ford Coppola.
   Columbia, 1992.

Videotape

<u>Barnburning</u>. Dir. Peter Werner. Prod. Calvin Scaggs.

   American Short Story Series. Videocassette. Mon-

   terey Home Video. 1980.

Works from One Book

If you are using several works from one book—for example, if you are writing
a documented essay using one of the casebooks in this textbook—you have a
choice of two forms for the Works Cited page. You may give the complete information about the textbook in each entry, or you may include one complete
entry for the textbook and list only the editor or editors and page numbers at
the end of each additional entry. The first form would look like this:

Works Cited

Melton, Quimby, IV. "Greenleaf's Destructive Bull and

   Paean to the Common Man." <u>Literature and</u>

   <u>Ourselves</u>. 5th ed. Ed. Gloria Mason Henderson,

   Bill Day, and Sandra Stevenson Waller. New York:

   Longman, 2006. 1382-94.

Muller, Gilbert H. "Violence and the Grotesque."

   <u>Nightmares and Visions: Flannery O'Conner and the</u>

   <u>Catholic Grotesque</u>. Athens: U of Georgia P., 1972.

   Rpt. in <u>Literature and Ourselves</u>. 5th ed. Ed. Glo-

   ria Mason Henderson, Bill Day, and Sandra Steven-

   son Waller. New York: Longman, 2006. 1380-86.

O'Connor, Flannery. "Greenleaf." <u>The Complete Stories</u>.

   New York: Noonday Press, 1998. 311-34. Rpt. in

   <u>Literature and Ourselves</u>. 5th ed. Ed. Gloria Mason

   Henderson, Bill Day, and Sandra Stevenson Waller.

   New York: Longman, 2006. 1357-74.

The same Works Cited page using the second form would look like this:

Works Cited

Henderson, Gloria Mason, Bill Day, and Sandra Steven-

   son Waller, eds. <u>Literature and Ourselves</u>. 5th ed.

   New York: Longman, 2006.

Melton, Quimby, IV. "Greenleaf's Destructive Bull and
     Paean to the Common Man." Henderson, Day, and
     Waller. 1382-94.

Muller, Gilbert H. "Violence and the Grotesque."
     Nightmares and Visions: Flannery O'Conner and the
     Catholic Grotesque. Athens: U of Georgia P., 1972.
     Henderson, Day, and Waller. 1380-86.

O'Connor, Flannery. "Greenleaf." The Complete Stories.
     New York: Noonday Press, 1998. 311-34. Henderson,
     Day, and Waller. 1357-74.

Content Notes

You may use content notes to add information that you would like the reader to know but that would interfere with the flow or organization of your paper. Content notes do not, as a rule, give documentation, but if you are citing so many sources that listing them in the text would be awkward, you could list them in content notes instead. Also, if the content note itself includes a quotation, give the citation and list the source in the Works Cited page. Include the notes on a separate page before the Works Cited page. Indicate notes in the text with consecutive numbers one-half space above the line, like this: [1] On the Content Notes page, indent the first line of each note and precede it with a raised number corresponding to the number in the text.

Some examples of content notes follow:

Acknowledgments

[1]The author would like to thank Maxine Sample for lending her essential materials on Alice Walker.

Comparison

[2]Cf. Carlos Baker's comment on Hemingway's return (121–22).

Note: Baker must be listed on the Works Cited page. (The abbreviation "cf." means "compare.")

[3]Similar opinions are expressed by Marcus (123–27), Johnston (14–19), and Wilcox (211–21).

Exceptions to Prevailing Point of View

[4]Wilson disagrees with this interpretation (198–203).

Johna Childers

Dr. Henderson

English 1102

20 May 2005

Symbolism in "Sonny's Blues"

James Baldwin, the author of Sonny's blues,

"viewed himself as an American writer, not a

'Negro-American' writer" (Kaplan, par. 1), yet he

"almost always wrote about race relations and about

being black in America" (Kaplan, par. 2). Because

he grew up in Harlem, Baldwin understood the

struggles of the black American, and he was able to

effectively portray the black American's story in

his works of fiction. James Baldwin's "Sonny's

Blues" is a short story rich in symbolism. A story

about a family living in the ghetto of Harlem, it

describes many of the hardships of that life.

Sonny and his brother, the narrator, are two very

different individuals struggling to find their

identities in a culture that seeks to dictate their

future from birth. Throughout the story, Baldwin

uses various methods to portray a deeper meaning of

the story. Specifically, Baldwin uses the symbols

of light and darkness and music.

Light and darkness, two opposite symbols, are

ironically seen together throughout the story.

Where light is present, many times darkness is

revealed. According to Donald C. Murray's essay

"Complicated and Simple," "Images of light and

darkness are used by Baldwin to illustrate man's

painful quest for identity" (224). Murray goes on

to say that "Light can represent the harsh glare of reality" (224).

This concept is evident throughout the story; for example, at the beginning of the story, light and darkness are used as symbols when the narrator is riding the subway to work. It is there, in the darkness of the subway car that the narrator learns of Sonny's trouble. He reads in the newspaper that Sonny has been arrested for possession of drugs. Baldwin writes that the narrator "stared at [the newspaper] in the swinging light of the subway car" (101). It is in the subway car, "trapped in the darkness which roared outside" that the lights reveal the reality of Sonny's fate (Baldwin 101).

Another instance where light is used to reveal reality occurs when the narrator recalls his childhood days. He remembers that the children would sit in the living room on Sunday afternoon and listen to their parents talk about the old days. As the children sit in the comfort of the room, they feel safe. Baldwin uses the symbolism of the dark room to portray the safety of the womb. The narrator recalls that "you can see the darkness growing against the windowpane . . . , but it's real quiet in the room" (Baldwin 108). As time goes on, the old folk's faces begin to resemble the growing darkness outside, and "the darkness in the faces frightens the child obscurely" (Baldwin 109). The darkness shown in the faces of the adults represents a darkness inside them that the children cannot yet know. It is the pain and struggles that

they have endured and that their children will
endure after them. Eventually, "someone will get
up and turn on the light," and "when the light
fills the room, the child is filled with darkness"
(Baldwin 109). The light reminds the child of his
reality, the potential disaster of his life. Even
when the children go into the streets "for light
and air," they find themselves "encircled" by it
(Baldwin 107). When the lights are turned on, the
children know that they have just moved "a little
closer to that darkness outside" (Baldwin 109).

Another example of the symbolism of light and
darkness can be found in the story within the
story. On the night that Sonny's uncle was killed,
"there was a moon . . . , it was bright like day"
(Baldwin 110). This tragic event occurred not in
the darkness, but rather in the light of the moon.
Immediately before he is run over by a drunk
driver, Sonny's uncle "stepped from behind the tree
. . . into the moonlight" (Baldwin 110). The full,
bright moon shed light on the harsh reality of this
tragic murder. Sonny's father later comments to
his wife that "he never in his life seen anything
as dark as that road after the lights of that car
had gone away" (Baldwin 110). The light that has
revealed the tragedy of death leaves the victim and
the witness in total darkness.

Music is the most prominent symbol in the
story "Sonny's Blues." Music permeates Harlem's
culture, from the schoolyards and the street
revivals to the nightclubs. Baldwin introduces

music very early in the story by painting a picture
of a young boy whistling a tune. This young boy's
tune is "at once very complicated and very simple .
. . [;] it sounded very cool and moving through all
that harsh, bright air, only just holding its own
through all those other sounds" (Baldwin 102). The
tune this boy is whistling is symbolic of both
Sonny's and the narrator's lives in Harlem and
their quest to find themselves. Although Sonny and
his brother seem to be very complex individuals,
they are also straightforward in their desires,
simply seeking love, acceptance, and individuality.
Many times the characters appear to be hanging by a
thread, barely "holding [their] own through all
those other sounds" (Baldwin 102).

   Robert Frost describes poetry as "a momentary
stay against confusion." This statement could also
be applied to music in "Sonny's Blues." For many
of the people of Harlem, music is a way to cope
with the disaster of everyday life. According to
Williams, "Music is the medium through which the
musician achieves enough understanding and strength
to deal with the past and present hurt" (147).
This can be extended to not only the musician who
makes the music, but also to the individual who
listens. The street revivals are a picture of
music playing this vital role. While the sisters
sing "The Old Ship of Zion," the passersby stop to
listen. Baldwin points out that no one believes
what the sisters are singing, but the crowd listens
anyway. As the sisters sing, for a brief moment

"faces underwent a change . . . ; the music seemed
to soothe a poison out of them" (Baldwin 118).
Although it is only for a brief moment in time, the
music of the street meeting calms and distracts the
desperate individuals who stop to listen. They
know that when the music stops, they will have to
move on. But for them, the music is a "momentary
stay against confusion."

For Sonny, music gives a sense of control that
he feels he has nowhere else in his life. After
observing the sisters singing in one of the street
revivals, Sonny comments "her voice reminded me for
a minute of what heroin feels like sometimes. . . .
It makes you feel—in control" (Baldwin 119). In a
society where many things are reeling out of
control, individuals cling to the one thing that
makes them feel safe. For Sonny it is initially
drugs but later becomes his music.

Although communication is a major theme that
runs throughout the story, often using windows as a
symbol, it is most beautifully conveyed in the last
scene. Sonny's music begins as a combination of
pain, self-defeat, and disaster; however, it
becomes his story, the means by which he is finally
able to communicate his struggles to his brother
and by which his brother examines for the first
time his own pain.

The musician must first communicate his passion
and thoughts with the instrument. The narrator says
that he "had never before thought of how awful the

relationship must be between the musician and his
instrument" (Baldwin 123). The musician must put
into the instrument what he cannot put into words.
The musician must also find a way to communicate
through his music to the audience. For Sonny, this
is initially a struggle. He "started one way, got
scared, stopped" (Baldwin 124). But suddenly,
"Sonny began to play" (Baldwin 124). He begins to
communicate to his brother all his struggles and
hardships. But why does Sonny go to such great
lengths to play the blues? Because "While the tale
we tell of how we suffer . . . is never new, it
always must be heard" (Baldwin 124). As Sonny
plays, the narrator truly begins to hear the music.
He says, "I seemed to hear with what burning he had
made [the music] his, with what burning we had yet
to make it ours" (Baldwin 124-25). Finally, the
narrator is able to truly relate to Sonny through
Sonny's music. For the first time, he truly
listens, and he hears. The narrator sends a drink
to Sonny, a Scotch and milk, which the barmaid sets
on the piano. Sonny takes a sip, and then begins to
play again; and as he begins to play, the narrator
notices that "[the drink] glowed and shook above my
brother's head like the very cup of trembling"
(Baldwin 124). This Scotch and milk which the
narrator offers to his brother is a final symbol of
the light and the music merging together. For
Sonny, music is reality. For the narrator, he
finally accepts Sonny and his blues. Everyone knows

that the music cannot provide a solution for the
struggles and hardships of life, but "it's the only
light we've got in all this darkness" (Baldwin 124).

[New page]   Works Cited

Baldwin, James. "Sonny's Blues." <u>Going to Meet the
    Man</u>. N.p.: Doubleday, 1957. Henderson, Day,
    and Waller. 101-25.

Henderson, Gloria Mason, Bill Day, and Sandra
    Stevenson Waller, eds. <u>Literature and
    Ourselves</u>. 5th ed. New York: Longman, 2006.

Kaplan, Roger. "Though His Oeuvre Is Uneven,
    Baldwin Wrote True and Well." Rev. of <u>James
    Baldwin: Collected Essays</u>, ed. Toni Morrison
    and <u>James Baldwin: Early Novels and Stories</u>,
    ed. Toni Morrison. <u>Insight on the News</u> 14.15
    (1998): 36. 21 May 2004 <http://
    proquest.umi.com/pqdweb?index=20&did=
    000000028636951$SrchMode=1&sid=1....>

Murray, Donald C. "James Baldwin's 'Sonny's Blues':
    Complicated and Simple." <u>Studies in Short
    Fiction</u>. 1977: 355-57.

Williams, Sherley Anne. "The Black Musician: The
    Black Hero as Light Bearer." <u>Give Birth to
    Brightness</u>. New York: Dial Press, 1972. 145-
    66. Rpt. In <u>James Baldwin: A Collection of
    Critical Essays</u>. Ed. Kinnamon. Englewood
    Cliffs, N.J.: Prentice-Hall, 1974. 147-54.

Glossary

Allegory A work in which concrete elements such as characters, objects, or incidents represent abstract qualities. This form of writing is often used to teach religious principles or ethical behavior or to espouse political agendas. Allegories were very popular in the Middle Ages. The play *Everyman* and Dante's *Divine Comedy* are examples. A more modern allegory is George Orwell's *Animal Farm*.

Alliteration Repetition at close intervals of consonant sounds in phrases or lines of poetry: for example, "bend / Your force to breake, blow, burn, and make me new."

Allusion An indirect reference to literature, a historical event, a famous person or character, or a work of art.

Anagnorisis In tragedy, the point at which a character reaches recognition, discovery, or self-awareness; the change from ignorance to knowledge.

Analogy Comparison of things otherwise thought to be dissimilar; point-by-point comparison.

Analysis Examination of a subject by separating it or breaking it down into parts.

Anaphora Rhetorical device that repeats a word, phrase, or clause at the beginning of consecutive sentences. For an example, see Elizabeth Barrett Browning's Sonnet 43, lines 7–9.

Antagonist An opposing force or character; that element which opposes or clashes with the main character or protagonist.

Apostrophe An address to a real or fictional person or thing.

Archetypal or **mythic criticism** Criticism that focuses on universal figures, symbols, images, and motifs; similar mythic explanations and experiences used to compare literature of different eras.

Archetype A prototype (situation, character, or action) or model from which all others or similar types are patterned; anything that appears repeatedly in literature, such as a legend, quest, or situation.

Aside A dramatic device in which a character delivers a short speech or remark to the audience. This remark usually reveals the speaker's emotions or thoughts; the assumption is that no one except the audience can hear the remark.

Assonance Repetition at close intervals of similar vowel sounds in phrases or in lines of poetry; for example, "I love thee to the depth, and breadth and height / My soul can reach, when feeling...."

Beat movement A movement that climaxed in 1956 in San Francisco and New York City and whose members, disgusted by the crass commercialism of society, dropped out, invented their own vocabulary, and experimented with illegal drugs. Beat movement members included writers such as Jack Kerouac, Lawrence Ferlinghetti, Allen Ginsberg, and Norman Mailer.

Biographical criticism Criticism that focuses on the way in which the author's family life, education, religion, career, and/or nationality influence the work; analyzing beyond the work itself for evidence of personal influences.

Blank verse Unrhymed poetry in iambic pentameter (ten syllables with the stress on every second syllable).

Blocking Grouping and arranging action and characters on stage.

Caesura A natural, strong pause within a line of poetry.

Character A person in a work; the personality traits or qualities of that person.

Characterization Development and presentation of the personality of a character, usually through actions, speech, reputation, appearance, and the author's attitude toward this person.

Claim A thesis statement; a debatable proposal; a judgment about what must, should, or needs to be done; a controversial statement in an argument; a statement that has a counterclaim.

Classification Organization according to a methodical division into groups or clusters; the system of grouping or arranging.

Cliché Expression, idea, or saying that loses its effectiveness through overuse; a platitude; a trite remark.

Climax The moment of greatest excitement, interest, or tension before the resolution of a play or narrative; a turning point.

Comedy A literary work, usually a play, that ends happily and that often includes humor and laughter.

Complication A plot stage in which a conflict appears; a part of the rising action of the narrative.

Concession An acknowledgment that the opposition in an argument has a good or strong point.

Conflict The opposition between protagonist and antagonist in a play or narrative; the opposition between the protagonist and another force, either within him- or herself or without, e.g., between the person and the environment, the person and society, or the person and the cosmic.

Connotation Suggestive, implied, or emotional meaning of a word or phrase.

Consonance Repetition of consonant sounds in a line of verse either at the beginning of or within the words.

Counterclaim An argumentative statement made by those who oppose your thesis or claim; some argumentative essays include at least one counterclaim showing respect for the opposition.

Couplet A pair of consecutive rhymed lines in verse. A closed couplet has two self-contained, rhymed lines that express a complete thought. An open couplet contains two rhymed lines that do not form a complete thought. A heroic couplet consists of a closed couplet in iambic pentameter.

Crisis A turning point or crucial moment in literature when the protagonist has to make a decision or resolve friction; crisis and climax may arrive at the same time or at entirely different times.

Cultural studies criticism Criticism that examines both textual and nontextual subjects beyond the scope of the usual literary canon.

Deconstructionist criticism Contention that the author and the text cannot be trusted to reveal objective reality; criticism that insists that the work must be completely unraveled through close reading of the text to reveal hidden meanings, or the lack thereof, beyond what the author intended or what the work implies.

Deductive reasoning The use of widely accepted general principles to demonstrate the truth of a more specific statement; reasoning from known facts or general principles, going from general to specifics.

Denotation The dictionary, literal, or exact meaning of a word.

Denouement A French term meaning resolution or settlement of loose ends; the untangling of the plot.

Dialect Speech or speech patterns of a particular region, occupational or social group, or culture. Dialect is usually perceived as deviating from "standard" speech.

Dialogue Conversation between at least two characters.

Diction An author's choice and arrangement of words and phrases.

Dramatic foil In drama, a character who sets off or intensifies the qualities of another character through a marked contrast.

Dramatic irony Marked difference in knowledge between the audience and a character in the play. The audience understands the meaning of certain words or events that the character does not understand. The most famous example of dramatic irony appears in Sophocles's *Oedipus the King*.

Dramatic monologue Poem spoken by one person but addressed to one or more listeners, revealing the speaker's character.

Dynamic Term used to refer to a character who undergoes a change in personality or behavior by the end of the literary work.

Elegy Lyric poem meditating on or celebrating a death.

Enjambment The running on of one line of poetry to the next line without end punctuation.

Epic A long narrative poem written in a dignified style on a majestic theme, relating the exploits of a national hero.

Epigram A short, witty poem or saying that makes a satirical point.

Epiphany In literature, a sudden manifestation or revelation of meaning; an instinctive perception of reality.

Epistolary Suitable to letters; poetry or fiction composed as a series of letters.

Evidence In argumentation the facts, statistics, observations, first-hand accounts, or expert opinions; in literary argumentation, the passages from the primary source, the text itself, and/or the secondary source(s), other sources or opinions, that support the warrant and help to prove the claim.

Exposition The beginning or opening of a play or a story; the introduction of characters, conflicts, and other information important to the reader.

Fable A short narrative that usually teaches a moral; a short story that has an uplifting message. Fables often use animals to make a point.

Fiction An imaginative narrative such as a short story or novel.

Figure of speech Language not taken literally; image conveyed through nonliteral language, such as with a metaphor or simile.

Film *See* definitions and explanations in Appendix B.

First-person point of view Narration using *I* or *we*. *See* unreliable narrator.

Flashback A break in the chronological presentation of a story to return to the past or to an earlier episode.

Flat character A character who is not fully developed; the character is often one-dimensional.

Foil A character who, through sharply defined opposing traits, emphasizes the characteristics of another; a foil is usually a minor character.

Foot In poetry, a unit of stressed and unstressed syllables or heavy and light stresses. The metrical patterns include the following: *Anapest:* two unstressed syllables followed by one stressed syllable. *Dactyl:* a stressed syllable followed by two unstressed syllables. *Iamb:* an unstressed syllable followed by a stressed syllable. *Trochee:* a stressed syllable followed by an unstressed syllable. *Spondee:* two stressed syllables.

Foreshadowing Hints or clues that help to predict a later event.

Formalism or **new criticism** Criticism that repudiates reader response, author's intention, or biographical analysis. Formalism focuses on a close reading of the work with emphasis on how the parts work to create the whole: irony, paradox, theme, images, and symbols.

Gender criticism Literary analysis based on the differences between female and male perspectives in writing and reading literature; this criticism considers gender biases and stereotypes in literary works.

Genre Literary type or kind of literature; the four most general kinds are fiction, drama, poetry, and nonfiction. Genres can be further subdivided, such as nonfiction into the essay or the autobiography, and fiction into the novel or the short story.

Gothic A literary style using a mysterious environment and mood to set the stage for terror and mystery.

Grotesque A bizarre, distorted, or incongruous approach to a subject, often including violence.

Hamartia The Greek term for the hero's flaw in character or for an error in judgment leading to the hero's downfall.

Historical criticism Criticism that studies the influences of the author's cultural milieu on the work or examines the ways in which interpretations may have changed over the history of the work.

Hyperbole Figurative language that uses exaggeration for effect: for example, "It's raining cats and dogs."

Image A mental or visual impression that employs an appeal to one of the five senses.

Imagists Poets and other artists belonging to a movement that rebelled against Romanticism in the early 1900s. These artists focused on free verse (unrhymed verse without a metrical pattern) and imagery.

Inductive reasoning The use of specific observations or evidence to arrive at a general conclusion; most often used in argumentation.

Initiation story A narrative in which a character undergoes some ordeal that leads to maturity.

Irony Contradiction; discrepancy or contrast between what is implied and what is real. Verbal irony is the use of words to impart double or opposite meanings. Situational irony relates to an event that turns out contrary to what is expected. *See* also dramatic irony.

Lyric A short poem expressing the emotions of the writer or singer. In the past, a lyric was usually accompanied by the lyre, a musical instrument.

Marxist criticism *See* sociological criticism.

Metaphor Figure of speech that uses an implied comparison between two distinctly different things; one term is defined in relationship to another term: for example, life is a cabaret.

Metaphysical poets A group of seventeenth-century English poets (especially John Donne and Robert Herrick) whose works are characterized by incredible and subtle imagery.

Meter The rhythm or beat of verse; a measured pattern of stressed and unstressed syllables. *See also* foot.

Metonymy Figurative language that uses a closely associated attribute to represent the thing itself. For example, the White House often symbolizes the president of the United States.

Minimalism The use of as few words as possible to convey meaning accurately; in art, as few strokes as possible; the bare minimum.

Monologue A long speech by a person or character to the audience, to a character not present, or to him- or herself.

Motivation The reason a character behaves, talks, or becomes what he or she is; the driving force or forces behind a character's actions.

Mystery A narrative whose plot involves the solution of a puzzle or crime and usually creates suspense.

Mythic criticism *See* archetypal criticism.

Narration A story, fictional or nonfictional; the process of telling a story.

Narrator The teller of a story or novel.

New criticism *See* formalism.

Nonfiction novel A novel that deals with real rather than fictional characters or situations.

Novel A long fictional prose work with a complex plot.

Objective point of view The simple reporting of observable events, similar to unbiased newspaper reporting.

Octave An eight-line stanza or the first eight lines of a sonnet.

Ode A long lyrical poem addressing or exalting a person or object using a distinguished style and elaborate format.

Omniscient point of view Literally all-knowing point of view whereby the author can recall the thoughts and actions of all characters and can be in several places at one time.

Onomatopoeia The use of words that sound like the actions they name; for example, *splash* or *buzz*.

Oxymoron A figure of speech that joins two words with contradictory meaning; for example, a heavy lightness or a thunderous silence.

Parable A short story that illustrates a moral or religious lesson.

Paradox A seemingly contradictory or unbelievable statement that, upon reflection, reveals a truth.

Paraphrase Restatement in the writer's or speaker's own words.

Parody A satirical or humorous imitation of another work; a literary work that imitates the style of another work; ridiculing something through imitation.

Personification Figurative language giving an inanimate object, animal, or abstraction human characteristics; for example, the jungle swallowed him.

Plot The sequence of events in a narrative. Elements of plot include conflict, complication, climax, and resolution.

Poem An arrangement of written or spoken words in lines with or without rhyme or meter and typically using figurative language.

Point of view The perspective from which a story is narrated.

Premise An assertion serving as the basis for an argument.

Primary source The text (essay, short story or novel, poem or play) that the writer is concentrating on, writing about, or discussing.

Props, properties Furniture or other movable articles in a play. Props do not include costumes, curtains, or background.

Protagonist The main or central character in fiction or drama.

Psychological criticism Based mainly on the theories of Freud, psychological criticism asserts that a literary work is an expression of the author's unconscious yearnings and that psychoanalytic techniques can be used to interpret fictional characters.

Pun Rhetorical device humorously using a word or words with different meanings but with similar sounds; sometimes referred to as a play on words.

Quatrain A four-line stanza of poetry.

Quintet A five-line stanza of poetry.

Resolution *See* denouement.

Rhetorical question A question that does not require an answer; a question that is asked for effect or to make a point.

Rhyme In poetry, the repetition of sounds at the ends of lines or within lines.

Rhythm Pattern of stressed and unstressed sounds in poetry.

Round character A character who is fully developed; a multidimensional character.

Satire A literary work that ridicules some aspect of society or some human folly or vice.

Satirist A person who writes satires.

Secondary source Anything that is written about a text that is under study or concentration; in argumentation, a source that is not a firsthand witness; secondary sources must be cited or documented.

Sestet A six-line stanza or the last six lines of a Petrarchan sonnet, which rhyme *cde*, *cde*.

Set The scenery and properties on the stage.

Setting The time, place, and physical and cultural environment of a story, play, or poem.

Simile Figure of speech that compares two distinctly different things using the words *as* or *like*.

Sociological criticism Criticism that considers the way in which a work reflects society's values, roles, beliefs, mores, and demographics or the way in which a critic can assess information about the audience that the author is writing for. One type of sociological approach is Marxist criticism, which maintains that works of literature are politically motivated, whether intentionally or unintentionally, and makes the reader aware of class struggle through literature.

Soliloquy A stylistic technique in which a character voices thoughts aloud to the audience.

Sonnet A fourteen-line poem in iambic pentameter.

Speaker The person who speaks in a poem.

Sprung rhythm A highly irregular metrical pattern developed by English poet Gerard Manley Hopkins. A metrical foot may consist either of a single stressed syllable or of a stressed syllable followed by one or more unstressed syllables; for example, "Oh, morning at the brown brink eastward springs—"

Stage directions Instructions given by the playwright to the stage manager, director, actors, and all others involved in the production of a play.

Static A term used to refer to a stereotypical, simplified character who fails to grow or change in personality or behavior by the end of the work.

Stereotype A fixed or traditional conception of a person, group, or idea held by a number of people without allowing for individuality.

Style The manner in which the author expresses himself or herself. Style includes imagery, symbolism, diction, and sentence structure—the language the author uses.

Symbol An object, person, or action that suggests something else, usually a feeling or abstract quality.

Symbolism The use of symbols in a literary work.

Synaesthesia Concurrent responses to senses; blending of two or more senses, as in "green-black smear of smell" or "a sweet cold silver noise."

Synecdoche A figure of speech in which the whole stands for a part (e.g., army for a soldier) or a part stands for the whole (e.g., wheels for a car).

Syntax Sentence structure and word order; planned arrangement of words to show relationships.

Terza rima A stanza form utilizing three-line units (tercets) with interlocking rhymes; *aba, bcb, cdc, ded*, and so forth.

Theater of the absurd Drama movement of the mid-twentieth century that used absurd, inconsistent, often meaningless situations and conversations expressing existentialism or isolation.

Theme Major idea, moral precept, or abstract principle underlying a work; the main idea expressed in a work of literature.

Thesis The central idea of an essay, usually expressed in one sentence in the introduction and then developed in the body paragraphs.

Third-person limited Narration of a story in the third person strictly limited to the thoughts and perceptions of a single character.

Tone The attitude of author, speaker, and/or narrator toward the subject or situation of a literary work; for example, ironic, nonchalant, humorous, melancholy, objective, or sarcastic.

Tragedy A play (or other work) showing the protagonist in an internal or external struggle that eventually leads to his downfall or ruin; a work in which the protagonist goes from happiness to misery.

Tragic hero or **heroine** Protagonist in a tragedy who, according to Aristotle, must be basically good but flawed, must be aristocratic, must be believable, and must behave consistently. Modern tragic heroes and heroines do not always fit Aristotle's definition; in particular, they are often working-class people.

Unreliable narrator The teller of a story whose narration is biased or limited.

Villanelle A nineteen-line poem made up of five tercets and one quatrain and rhyming *aba, aba, aba, aba, aba, abaa*. The first line is repeated in lines 6, 12, and 18; the third line is repeated in lines 9, 15, and 19.

Warrant In argumentation, the reasons for the writer's position, stated so that the warrant may be supported with facts or evidence.

Acknowledgments

FAMILY

Essays

"On Going Home," from *Slouching Towards Bethlehem* by Joan Didion. Copyright © 1966, 1968, renewed 1996 by Joan Didion. Reprinted by permission of Farrar, Straus and Giroux, LLC.

"Jewish Christmas," from *And the Bridge is Love* by Faye Moskowitz. Copyright © 1991 by Faye Moskowitz. Reprinted by permission of Beacon Press, Boston.

"Bramare: (Archaic) To Yearn For," from *Under the Tuscan Sun,* © 1996 by Frances Mayes. Used with permission of Chronicle Books LLC, San Francisco. Visit ChronicleBooks.com.

"Native Genius," from Janisse Ray, *Ecology of a Cracker Childhood* (Minneapolis: Milkweed Editions, 1999). Copyright © 1999 by Janisse Ray. Reprinted with permission from Milkweed Editions.

Fiction

"A Domestic Dilemma," from *The Ballad of the Sad Café and Collected Short Stories* by Carson McCullers. Copyright © 1936, 1941, 1942, 1950, 1951, © 1955 by Carson McCullers, renewed 1979 by Floria V. Lasky. Reprinted by permission of Houghton Mifflin Company. All rights reserved.

"Sonny's Blues," © 1957 by James Baldwin was originally published in *Partisan Review.* Copyright renewed. Collected in *Going to Meet the Man,* published by Vintage Books. Reprinted by arrangement with the James Baldwin Estate.

"A Christmas Memory," from *A Christmas Memory* by Truman Capote, copyright © 1956 by Truman Capote. Used by permission of Random House, Inc.

"Everyday Use," from *In Love & Trouble: Stories of Black Women,* copyright © 1973 by Alice Walker, reprinted by permission of Harcourt, Inc.

"Because My Father Always Said He Was the Only Indian Who Saw Jimi Hendrix Play *The Star Spangled Banner,*" from *The Lone Ranger and Tonto Fistfight in Heaven* by Sherman Alexie. Copyright © 1993 by Sherman Alexie. Used by permission of Grove/Atlantic, Inc.

Poetry

"A Prayer for My Daughter," reprinted with the permission of Scribner, an imprint of Simon & Schuster Adult Publishing Group, from *The Collected Works of W.B. Yeats, Volume 1: The Poems, Revised,* edited by Richard Finneran. Copyright © 1924 by The Macmillan Company; copyright renewed © 1952 by Bertha Georgie Yeats.

"Mother to Son," from *The Collected Poems of Langston Hughes* by Langston Hughes, copyright © 1994 by The Estate of Langston Hughes. Used by permission of Alfred A. Knopf, a division of Random House, Inc.

"My Papa's Waltz," copyright 1942 by Hearst Magazine, Inc., from *The Collected Poems of Theodore Roethke* by Theodore Roethke. Used by permission of Doubleday, a division of Random House, Inc.

Drama

Casebook on August Wilson

MEN AND WOMEN

Essays

Fiction

Women by Ernest Hemingway. Copyright © 1927 by Charles Scribner's Sons. Copyright © renewed 1955 by Ernest Hemingway. All rights reserved.

Excerpt from *Mama Day* by Gloria Naylor. Copyright © 1988 by Gloria Naylor. Reprinted by permission of Houghton Mifflin Company. All rights reserved.

"A Temporary Matter," from *The Interpreter of Maladies* by Jhumpa Lahiri. Copyright © 1999 by Jhumpa Lahiri. Reprinted by permission of Houghton Mifflin Company. All rights reserved.

Poetry

"To Helen," by Edgar Allen Poe from *The Poems of Edgar Allen Poe* by Floyd Stovall, ed. Copyright © 1965 University of Virginia Press. Reprinted by permission of the University of Virginia Press.

199, 339, reprinted by permission of the publishers and the Trustees of Amherst College from *The Poems of Emily Dickinson*, Thomas H. Johnson, ed., Cambridge, Mass.: The Belknap Press of Harvard University Press, Copyright © 1951, 1955, 1979 by the President and Fellows of Harvard College.

"The Death of the Hired Man," "Home Burial," "Design," "Once by the Pacific," from *The Poetry of Robert Frost* edited by Edward Connery Lathem. Copyright 1936, 1956, 1958 by Robert Frost, © 1964, 1967 by Lesley Frost Ballantine, copyright 1928, 1969 by Henry Holt and Company. Reprinted by permission of Henry Holt and Company, LLC.

"Helen," by HD (Hilda Doolittle), from *Collected Poems*, 1912–1944, copyright © 1982 by The Estate of Hilda Doolittle. Reprinted by permission of New Directions Publishing Corp.

"Myth," from *The Collected Poems of Muriel Rukeyser* by Muriel Rukeyser. Copyright © 1982 by Muriel Rukeyser. Reprinted by permission of International Creative Management, Inc.

"Chess," by Rosario Castellanos, page 94 from *A Rosario Castellanos Reader* as translated by Maureen Ahern, edited by Maureen Ahern, translated by Maureen Ahern and others, Copyright © 1988. By permission of Maureen Ahern, fondo de Cultura Economica, and the University of Texas Press.

"The Judgment of Paris," © 1988 by W.S. Merwin. Reprinted with permission of The Wylie Agency, Inc.

"Phenomenal Woman," copyright © 1978 by Maya Angelou, from *And Still I Rise* by Maya Angelou. Used by permission of Random House, Inc.

"Incompatibilities," from *Collected Poems* by Ted Hughes. Copyright © 2003 by Ted Hughes. Reprinted by permission of Farrar, Straus and Giroux, LLC. Reprinted by permission of Faber and Faber Ltd.

"Barbie Doll," from *Circles On The Water* by Marge Piercy, copyright © 1982 by Marge Piercy. Used by permission of Alfred A. Knopf, a division of Random House, Inc.

"Breaking Tradition," from *Shedding Silence*, copyright © 1987 by Janice Mirikitani. Reprinted by permission of Celestial Arts, P.O. Box 7123, Berkeley, CA 94707.

"Anniversary," from *The Latin Deli: Prose & Poetry* by Judith Ortiz Cofer. Copyright 1993 by Judith Ortiz Cofer. Reprinted by permission of the University of Georgia Press.

"Courtship," from *Beulah and Thomas* (Carnegie-Mellon University Press, Pittsburgh). Copyright © 1986 by Rita Dove. Reprinted by permission of the author.

"Courtship, Diligence," from *Beulah and Thomas* (Carnegie-Mellon University Press, Pittsburgh). Copyright © 1986 by Rita Dove. Reprinted by permission of the author.

"Daddy: Sylvia Plath's Debt to Anne Sexton," by Heather Cam, in *American Literature*, volume 59, no. 3, pp. 429–432. Copyright 1987, Duke University Press. All rights reserved.

"Colossal Influences on Sylvia Plath" by Thomas Dilworth, appeared in the June 2003 issue of *English Language Notes*, Volume 40, issue 4. Copyright 2003 by English Language Notes. Reprinted by permission of *English Language Notes*.

FEAR AND LOSS

Essays

"Terrorism: The Problem of Definition Revisited," by H.H.A. Cooper, *The American Behavioral Scientist*, Volume 44, Issue 6; Pages 181–194, copyright © 2001 by Sage Publications. Reprinted by Permission of Sage Publications, Inc.

"Yom Kippur: The Day Without Forgiveness," from *Legends of Our Time* by Elie Wiesel. Copyright © 1968 by Elie Wiesel. Reprinted by permission of Georges Borchardt, Inc., for the author.

"Loss," from *Beyond Belief* by V.S. Naipaul. Copyright © 1998 by V.S. Naipaul. Reprinted by permission of Gillon Aitken Associates Limited and Random House, Inc.

"Coyote v. Acme," from *Coyote v. Acme* by Ian Frazier. Copyright © 1996 by Ian Frazier. Reprinted by permission of Farrar, Straus, and Giroux, LLC.

Fiction

"The Grave," from *The Leaning Tower and other Stories*, copyright 1944 and renewed 1972 by Katherine Anne Porter, reprinted by permission of Harcourt, Inc.

"A Rose for Emily," copyright 1930 and renewed 1958 by William Faulkner, from *Collected Stories of William Faulkner* by William Faulkner. Used by permission of Random House, Inc.

"A Summer Tragedy," from *The Old South and Other Stories* by Arna Bontemps. Copyright © 1933 by Arna Bontemps, renewed © 1961. Reprinted by permission of Harold Ober Associates Incorporated.

"Dead Men's Path," from *Girls At War and Other Stories* by Chinua Achebe, copyright © 1972, 1973 by Chinua Achebe. Used by permission of Harold Ober Associates Incorporated and Doubleday, a division of Random House, Inc.

"The Management of Grief," from *The Middleman and Other Stories* by Bharati Mukherjee. Copyright © Bharati Mukherjee, 1988. Reprinted by permission of Penguin Group (Canada) and Grove/Atlantic, Inc.

"Customs of the Country," © 1988, by Madison Bell, from the collection titled *Barking Man and Other Stories* (Ticknor and Fields, 1990). Used by permission of the author. First published in Harper's Magazine.

"The Runt," by Eric Skipper from the *Roanoke Review*, Volume XXVI, Number 2, Winter 2001. Reprinted by permission.

Poetry

"The Death of the Hired Man," "Home Burial," from *The Poetry of Robert Frost* edited by Edward Connery Lathem. Copyright 1936, 1956, 1958 by Robert Frost, © 1964, 1967 by Lesley Frost Ballantine, copyright 1928, 1969 by Henry Holt and Company. Reprinted by permission of Henry Holt and Company, LLC.

"If We Must Die," from *Selected Poems of Claude McKay* (Harcourt Brace, 1981), by Claude McKay. Reprinted by permission of Archives of Claude McKay, Carl Cowl, Administrator.

"Amy Tan: A Critical Companion," pages 19–31 and 113–121 from *Amy Tan: A Critical Companion* by E.D. Huntley. Copyright © 1998 by Greenwood Publishing Group. Reprinted by permission of Greenwood Publishing Group.

"Chinese American Women, Language, and Moving Subjectivity," by Victoria Chen from *Modern Critical Views, Amy Tan*, edited by Harold Bloom.

The Salon Interview: Amy Tan, The Spirit Within. This article first appeared in Salon.com, at http://www.salon.com. An online version remains in the Salon archives. Reprinted with permission.

FREEDOM AND RESPONSIBILITY

Essays

"The Slave Who Dared to Feel Like a Man," reprinted by permission of the publisher from "The Slave Who Dared to Feel like a Man" in *Incidents In The Life of A Slave Girl, Written by Herself*, by Harriet A. Jacobs, with an introduction by Jean Fagen Yellin, pp. 17–26, Cambridge, Mass.: Harvard University Press, Copyright © 1987, 2000 by the President and Fellows of Harvard College.

"Letter from Birmingham City Jail," reprinted by arrangement with the Estate of Martin Luther King Jr., c/o Writers House as agent for the proprietor New York, NY. Copyright 1963 Martin Luther King Jr., copyright renewed 1991 Coretta Scott King.

"The Trial," from *Open Letters: Selected Writings 1965–1990* by Vaclav Havel, translated by Paul Wilson, copyright © 1991 by A.G. Brian. Preface/translation copyright © 1985, 1988, 1991 by Paul Wilson. Used by permission of Alfred A. Knopf, a division of Random House, Inc.

Fiction

"Harrison Bergeron," from *Welcome To The Monkey House* by Kurt Vonnegut, Jr, copyright © 1961 by Kurt Vonnegut Jr. Used by permission of Dell Publishing, a division of Random House, Inc.

"Minority Report," reprinted by permission of the author and the author's agents, Scovil Chichak Galen Literary Agency, Inc.

"The Ones Who Walk Away from Omelas," from *The Wind's Twelve Quarters* by Ursula K. LeGuin. Copyright © 1973 by Ursula K. LeGuin; first appeared in *New Dimensions 3*. Reprinted by permission of the author and the author's agent, Virginia Kidd.

"A&P," from *Pigeon Feathers And Other Stories* by John Updike, copyright © 1962 and renewed 1990 by John Updike. Used by permission of Alfred A. Knopf, a division of Random House, Inc.

Poetry

"I, Too," from *The Collected Poems of Langston Hughes* by Langston Hughes, copyright © 1994 by The Estate of Langston Hughes. Used by permission of Alfred A. Knopf, a division of Random House, Inc.

"The Unknown Citizen", copyright 1940 & renewed 1968 by W.H. Auden, "Musee des Beaux Arts", copyright 1940 & renewed 1968 by W.H. Auden, from *Collected Poems* by W.H. Auden. Used by permission of Random House, Inc.

"The Conscientious Objector," © 1978 Estate of Karl Shapiro c/o Wieser & Elwell, Inc., New York.

"The Woman at the Washington Zoo," from *The Complete Poems* by Randall Jarrell. Copyright © 1969, renewed 1997 by Mary von S. Jarrell. Reprinted by permission of Farrar, Straus and Giroux, LLC.

Drama

Casebook on Tim O'Brien

IMAGINATION AND REALITY
Essays

1975 by Ursula K. Le Guin. Reprinted by permission of the author and the author's agent, Virginia Kidd.

"My One Conversation with Collin Walcott," from *River Teeth: Stories and Writings* by David James Duncan, copyright © 1995 by David James Duncan. Used by permission of Doubleday, a division of Random House, Inc.

Fiction

"A Fable," from Mark Twain, *Fables of Man*, edited by John Tuckey. Copyright © 1972 by Mark Twain Company. Reprinted by permission of The Regents of the University of California.

"There Will Come Soft Rains," by Ray Bradbury from *Collier's National Weekly Magazine*. Copyright © 1950 by the Crowell-Collier Publishing Company, renewed 1977 by Ray Bradbury. Reprinted by permission of Don Congdon Associates, Inc.

"The Kugelmass Episode," copyright © 1977 by Woody Allen, from *Side Effects* by Woody Allen. Used by permission of Random House, Inc.

"Naked Woman Playing Chopin: A Fargo Romance," © 1998 by Louise Erdrich. Reprinted with permission of The Wylie Agency, Inc.

Poetry

"Ars Poetica," from *Collected Poems, 1917–1982* by Archibald MacLeish. Copyright © 1985 by The Estate of Archibald MacLeish. Reprinted by permission of Houghton Mifflin Company. All rights reserved.

"Yet Do I Marvel," reprinted by permission of GRM ASSOCIATES, INC., Agents for the Estate of Ida M. Cullen. From the book *Color* by Countee Cullen. Copyright © 1925 by Harper & Brothers; copyright renewed 1953 by Ida M. Cullen.

"Musée des Beaux Arts", copyright 1940 & renewed 1968 by W.H. Auden, from *Collected Poems* by W.H. Auden. Used by permission of Random House, Inc.

"Constantly Risking Absurdity," by Lawrence Ferlinghetti, from *A Coney Island of the Mind*, copyright © 1958 by Lawrence Ferlinghetti. Reprinted by permission of New Directions Publishing Corp.

"The Art of Response," from *Our Dead Behind Us* by Audre Lorde. Copyright © 1986 by Audre Lorde. Used by permission of W. W. Norton & Company, Inc.

"Digging," from *Opened Ground: Selected Poems 1966–1996* by Seamus Heaney. Reprinted by permission of Farrar, Straus and Giroux, LLC, and Faber and Faber Ltd.

"Poem," from *The Apple that Astonished Paris* by Billy Collins. Copyright 1988 by Billy Collins. Reprinted by permission of The University of Arkansas Press.

"today is a day of great joy," by Victor Hernández Cruz from *Rhythm, Content & Flavor*. Reprinted by permission of Arte Publico Press–University of Houston.

"The Vietnam Wall," by Alberto Ríos from *Currents from the Dancing River: Contemporary Latino Fiction, Nonfiction, and Poetry*. Published originally in *The Lime Orchard Woman*. Copyright © 1988 by Alberto Ríos. Reprinted by permission of the author.

Drama

"The Real Inspector Hound," from *The Real Inspector Hound and Other Plays* by Tom Stoppard. Copyright © 1968 by Tom Stoppard. Used by permission of Grove/Atlantic Inc.

Casebook on Joyce Carol Oates

"Where Are You Going, Where Have You Been?" copyright © 1970 by *Ontario Review*. Reprinted by permission of John Hawkins & Associates, Inc.

QUEST

Essays

Fiction

Poetry

Drama

Casebook on Flannery O'Connor

Photo Credits

Index

Key Terms Index

Italic numbers refer to the Glossary, pages 1453–1459.